The Law and Practice Relating to Charities

The Law and Practice Relating to Charities

Hubert Picarda

BCL, MA (Oxon), of the Inner Temple
and Lincoln's Inn, Barrister,
Profumo Scholar

With a Foreword by
The Rt. Hon. Lord Wilberforce CMG OBE
A Lord of Appeal in Ordinary
Fellow of All Souls College, Oxford

London
Butterworths
1977

England Butterworth & Co. (Publishers) Ltd.
London   88 Kingsway WC2B 6AB

Australia Butterworths Pty, Ltd.
Sydney   586 Pacific Highway, Chatswood, NSW 2067
Also at Melbourne, Brisbane, Adelaide and Perth

Canada Butterworth & Co. (Canada) Ltd.
Toronto   2265 Midland Avenue, Scarborough M1P 4S1

New Zealand Butterworths of New Zealand Ltd.
Wellington   26/28 Waring Taylor Street 1

South Africa Butterworth & Co. (South Africa) (Pty) Ltd.
Durban   152/154 Gale Street

USA Butterworth & Co. (Publishers) Inc.
Boston   19 Cummings Park, Woburn, Mass. 01801

ISBN: 0 406 64276 1

Foreword

I am glad to give a welcome to this new book on the Law of Charities. Although the classic works on the subject, remarkably well, retain their usefulness, continuous development in the substance and in the procedure of the law makes it necessary from time to time to rearrange the material, to generalise it in a different way, and to extract new principles. This Mr. Picarda has done. The generous reference to and use of Commonwealth and American material is of especial interest and value from two points of view. First because it demonstrates the continuing vitality across the frontiers, of the method of legal reasoning by which this branch of the law, mainly judge-made, has developed. Secondly because it may persuade some who would have us believe that the legal conception of "charity" is outdated, and should be replaced by some state administered service, that other nations, with varying social philosophies, have found and continue to find use and benefit in charitable trusts.

Apart from this, charity as a branch of the law touches life at many points and the law of it contains much elegant and distinguished thinking. This book should give a fresh stimulus to the study of it.

RICHARD WILBERFORCE

HOUSE OF LORDS,
MARCH 1977.

Preface

This book is intended to present, at a time when the law of charities is being subjected to considerable discussion, a comprehensive and up-to-date statement of the law and practice relating to charities. To some the very word "charity" is anathema. But I share the sentiment of the original advertisement to Duke's *Law of Charitable Uses* (1676) that the subject of charities is the "best subject". I cannot, alas, claim, as Henry Twyford claimed for Duke's book, that "here is more for charitable uses than ever yet came together in print, or could have been hoped for". All the same I have covered much ground, some of it little trodden.

The subject is deeply rooted in history. The reader will therefore perhaps excuse the occasional excursion into the history of a particular point. Certainly it is hard to find a section of our law where so many old cases are still relevant. On the other hand, the administration of charities and their fiscal privileges focus attention on many recent cases statutes and taxes. The definition of charity is a continuing and topical problem; and the application of the *cy-près* doctrine continues to generate argument. The law is both ancient and modern.

My main concern has been to set out the law and practice in England and Wales. But, following many modern precedents, I have referred to numerous Commonwealth authorities and some American ones too. In so doing I have had two purposes in mind: first to show the universality of many of the legal principles; secondly to indicate how other jurisdictions have solved points not covered by English authority. Reasons of space and the demands of a practitioner's life have prevented any exhaustive citation of Commonwealth authority, or any analysis of the Commonwealth statutes bearing on the subject. But I hope the book may still be of use to Commonwealth lawyers. It is for that reason that the position of charity appeals prior to 1960 is discussed at some length.

The citation of periodical literature and the bibliography are designed to help those who wish to pursue particular points further. There is, however, no discussion of what, if any, reforms might be desirable. Reasons of space again forbade such discussion. This is a big book already. Moreover the Goodman Report on Charity Law and Voluntary Organisations did not appear until my manuscript was with the printers. Nevertheless I was able, at page-proof stage, to make some references to the Goodman Report in footnotes.

Dr. J. C. Brady's *Religion and the Law of Charities in Ireland* and the new study entitled *The Comparative Law of Trusts in the Commonwealth and the Irish Republic* by Professors Keeton and Sheridan were also published at a point of time when only footnote references could be made to those works.

The arrangement of material has sometimes been a ticklish problem. For example, the expression "exempt charity" raises it head in many sections. It therefore seemed to me that that expression (and cognate statutory definitions and concepts) should appear at the beginning of the book, just as definition clauses are placed at the beginning of conveyancing documents. The resultant turgidity in the first few pages will, I hope, be redeemed by what follows.

In covering the important subject of lotteries—of great concern to many charities—I optimistically assumed that by publication date the Lotteries and Amusements Act 1976 would have been brought into operation. Under the Lotteries Act 1975 (Commencement No. 2) Order 1977 the relevant date is 1st May 1977.

While writing this book I have trespassed on the good nature and benevolence (I will not say charity!) of many friends.

In particular, Mr. Leonard Hoffmann Q.C., of the Chancery Bar and formerly fellow of University College Oxford, kindly read and commented on Part I of this book. Professor Gareth Jones, Fellow of Trinity College Cambridge and Downing Professor of the Laws of England, read and criticised the same portion of the book and discussed other topics of charity law with me, invariably advancing my education in the subject. Mr. J. D. Davies, Fellow of St. Catherine's College Oxford, sacrificed much of his valuable time at the start of the academic year at Oxford to read and make detailed comments on the whole of Parts II and III of the book. He too was kind enough to discuss particular points with me. My debt to the learning of all these gentlemen is very considerable. But none of my intellectual creditors can be blamed for any errors or heresies which there may be. These must be laid at my door. The process of authorship is a continuing one; and up to the last minute I was making additions, necessarily without reference to my benevolent censors.

The librarians and staff of the libraries of the Inns of Court, of the Bodleian Library at Oxford and the Witwatersrand Bar Library in Johannesburg have all been of the greatest help. During my visit to the University of California at Berkeley I received much hospitality, and friendly guidance in relation to the American law of charities from Edward C. Halbach Jr. now Professor of Law at that University.

Those on the editorial staff at Butterworths and at the printers who had the unenviable task of putting order into the chaos of my handwritten manuscript deserve separate tribute; and I acknowledge with gratitude the patience of those members of the editorial team whom I plagued with additions and queries. I am also grateful to the publishers for preparing the Table of Cases, Appendices and Index, and to the Charity Commissioners for permission to reprint extracts from their annual reports and leaflets.

Lastly, I must underline the indispensable role played by my wife Ann. She encouraged me to finish what might otherwise have shared the fate of Mr. Casaubon's work. It was her prodding and forbearing which enables me to echo, with poetic licence, the introductory words of Martial's well known poem,

> "Ohe iam satis est, ohe libelle,
> iam pervenimus usque ad umbilicos."

The text states the law as at 1st March 1977.

HUBERT PICARDA

10 OLD SQUARE
LINCOLN'S INN
LONDON WC2
14TH APRIL 1977

Contents

PART III
SCHEMES

Chapter 24 219
The *cy-près* principle

Chapter 25 225
Basic principles of the *cy-près* application

Chapter 26 249
Gifts to charitable institutions

Chapter 27 264
Surplus capital

PART VI
COURT PROCEEDINGS

PART VII
TAXATION AND RATING

Table of Cases

In the following Table references are given to the English and Empire Digest where a digest of the case may be found.

Both the Middle Temple Library and the Bodleian Library at Oxford house large collections of American Law Reports. The latter library and the Inner Temple Library contain most of the Law Reports from the Commonwealth. American and Commonwealth cases referred to in this Table can be traced at the above libraries.

A

PAGE

PAGE

G

N

PAGE

Table of Statutes

References in this Table to "*Statutes*" are to Halsbury's Statutes of England (Third Edition) showing the volume and page at which the annotated text of the Act will be found. Page references printed in bold type indicate where the Act is set out in part or in full.

Bibliography

Books

Bogert, G. G. *Cases on the Law of Trusts* (1958) 3rd Edn. *Law of Trusts and Trustees* (1935) (with supplement)

Bourchier-Chilcott, T. *Administration of Charities* (1912)

Boyle, W. R. *A Practical Treatise on the Law of Charities* (1837)

Brady, J. C. *Religion and the Law of Charities in Ireland* (1976)

Cooray, L. J. M. *Reception in Ceylon of the English Trust* (1971)

Cracknell, D. G. *Law Relating to Charities* (1973)

Crowther, C. E. *Religious Trusts* (1954)

Daniell, E. R. *Chancery Practice* (1914) 8th Edn.

Delany, V. T. H. *Law Relating to Charities in Ireland* (1962) Revised Edn.

Duke, G. *Law of Charitable Uses* (1676) ed. R. W. Bridgman (1805)

Finlason, W. F. *History of the Laws of Mortmain* (1853)

Fisch, E. L. *The Cy-près Doctrine in the United States* (1950)

Fisch, E. L., Freed, D. J. and Schachter, E.R. *Charities and Charitable Foundations* (1974)

Garrow, J. M. E. *Law of Trusts and Trustees* (NZ) (1972) 4th Edn.

Gray, J. C. *The Rule against Perpetuities* (1942) 4th Edn.

Hamilton, F. A. P. *Law Relating to Charities in Ireland* (1881)

Herne, J. *Law of Charitable Uses* (1663)

Highmore, A. *History of Mortmain and Statutes concerning Charitable Uses* (1809) 2nd Edn.

Hill, C. P. *A Guide For Charity Trustees* (1974) 2nd Edn.

Holdsworth, W. S. *A History of English Law*, 16 vols. (1966 reprint)

Honoré, A. M. *The South African Law of Trusts* (1976) 2nd Edn.

Jacobs, K. S. *Law of Trusts in New South Wales* (1971) 3rd Edn.

Jarman, T. *Treatise on Wills* (1951) 8th Edn.

Jones, G. H. *History of the Law of Charity 1532-1827* (1969)

Jordan, W. K. *Philanthropy in England 1480-1660* (1959) *The Charities of London 1480-1660* (1960) *The Charities of Rural England 1480-1660* (1961)

Keeton, G. W. *Modern Developments in the Law of Trusts* (1971)

Keeton, G. W. and Sheridan, L. A. *The Modern Law of Charities* (1971) 2nd Edn. with Supplement (1975)

Keeton, G. W. and Sheridan, L. A. *Comparative Law of Trusts in the Commonwealth and Irish Republic* (1976)

Kutner, L. *Legal Aspects of Charitable Trusts and Foundations* (1970) Chicago

Maurice, S. G. *The Charities Act 1960* (1962)

Mitcheson, R. E. *Charitable Trusts* (1887)

Mitcheson, R. E. *Opinion on the Visitation of Charities* (1887) (Privately printed; available at the Bodleian Library, Oxford)

Moore, E. J. *Law of Charities in Ireland* (1906)

Morris J. H. C. and Leach W. B. *The Rule Against Perpetuities* (1962) 2nd Edn. and Supplement (1964)

Nathan, Lord *The Charities Act 1960* (1962)

Nightingale, B. *Charities* (1973)

Owen, D. *English Philanthropy 1660-1960* (1964)

Owen, Sir H. *Education Acts Manual* (1936) 23rd Edn.

Scott, A. W. *The Law of Trusts* (1967) 3rd Edn.

Seton, Sir H. W. *Judgments and Orders* (1912) 7th Edn.

Shelford, L. *Law of Mortmain* (1836)

Sheridan, L. A. and Delany, V. T. H. *The Cy-près Doctrine* (1959) with supplement (1961)

Squibb, G. D. *Founders' Kin* (1972)
Theobald, Sir H. S. *Wills* (1971) 13th
Edn.
Tudor, O. *Law of Charities* (1967) 6th
Edn.; (1906) 4th Edn.
Tyssen, A. D. *Law of Charitable Bequests*
(1921) 2nd Edn.
Waters, D. W. M. *Law of Trusts in
Canada* (1974)
Williams, W. J. *Law Relating to Wills*
(1974) 4th Edn. with supplement (1977)
Wylie, J. C. W. *Irish Land Law* (1975)

Government Publications

Report of the Committee on the Law and
Practice relating to Charitable Trusts
(1952) Cmd. 8710.
Charity Committee Report (1956) N.I.
Cmd. 396.
Tenth Report from the Expenditure
Committee (1974–75): Charity
Commissioners and their Accountability
    Volume I   Report
    Volume II Minutes of Evidence and
             Appendices

Part I

What is a Charity?

Chapter 1

The Law of Charities and the Legal Meaning of Charity

Law of charities

GENERAL

The law relating to charities comprises a very substantial body of case law upon which have been overlaid various statutory provisions relating largely to matters of administration. The main statute in England and Wales[1] is the Charities Act 1960. The administration of charities is covered by statutes in both parts of Ireland[2] and in New Zealand.[3] Canada has advanced less far along the road of statutory intervention: only in Ontario is there legislation specifically concerning charities, and the four statutes concerned cover only restricted areas.[4]

Many administrative matters relating to charities are now in practice dealt with by the Charity Commissioners for England and Wales, a body originally set up by the Charitable Trusts Act 1853 and now functioning pursuant to the provisions of the Charities Act 1960. The Charity Commissioners apply the law established by decisions in the courts as well as exercising various supervisory powers presently reposed in them by the Charities Act 1960. Statements of the practice of the Charity Commissioners are to be found in the Annual Reports of the Charity Commissioners for England and Wales.[5]

It is convenient before turning to consider the question of what constitutes a charity to define two expressions which occur in the Charities Act 1960, namely "charity" and "exempt charity". These definitions it should be stressed are definitions for the purposes of the Act. A brief introductory word about excepted charities is also desirable.

---

1 The other principal statutes are Charitable Trusts (Validation) Act 1954 and Recreational Charities Act 1958.
2 Northern Ireland: Charities Act (Northern Ireland) 1964 following Newark, Charity Committee Report (N.I.) (Cmd. 396, 1958); Republic: Charities Act 1961 and Charities Act 1973.
3 New Zealand Charitable Trusts Act 1957.
4 Mortmain and Charitable Uses Act (RSO 1970, c. 280; amended 1972, c. 85); Charitable Gifts Act (RSO 1970, c. 61; amended 1971, c. 50, s. 15); Charitable Institutions Act (RSO 1970, c. 62; amended 1971, c. 50, s. 16; 1972, c. 61; 1973, c. 24); Charities Accounting Act (RSO 1970, c. 63). On these Acts see Waters, *Law of Trusts in Canada* (1974) 537–547.
5 The reports are published as House of Commons Parliamentary Papers. As to the Charity Commissioners' duty to make annual reports, see C.A. 1960, s. 1 (5).

Terminology

STATUTORY DEFINITION OF CHARITY

For the purposes of the Charities Act 1960 "charity" means "any institution, corporate or not, which is established for charitable purposes and is subject to the control of the High Court in the exercise of the court's jurisdiction with respect to charities".[1] Institution includes any trust or undertaking; and charitable purposes means purposes which are exclusively charitable according to the law of England and Wales.[2] Accordingly the question of whether purposes are or are not charitable is determined by reference to the principles established by the courts prior to 1960 and developed in the courts since that date.

EXEMPT CHARITY

Certain charities termed "exempt charities" which come within the definition of "charity" for the purposes of the Charities Act 1960 are nevertheless exempt from many provisions of that Act. These charities are listed in the Second Schedule to the Charities Act 1960 and, for the most part, comprise institutions which were previously exempt from the jurisdiction of the Charity Commissioners. The basis for exempting them from the supervision of the Charity Commissioners is that they are sufficiently supervised and protected by other statutory provisions.

Exempt charities for the purposes of the Charities Act 1960 comprise the following categories:

(a) Any institution which, if that Act had not been passed, would be exempted from the powers and jurisdiction under the Charitable Trusts Acts 1853 to 1939 of the Commissioners (apart from any power of the Commissioners to apply those Acts in whole or in part to charities otherwise exempt) by the terms of any enactment not contained in those Acts, other than section 9 of the Places of Worship Registration Act 1855.[3] Institutions so exempted are the universities of Birmingham, Liverpool, Manchester, Leeds, Sheffield, Bristol, Reading, Nottingham, Southampton, Hull, Exeter and Leicester;[4] the Imperial War Museum[5] and the National Maritime Museum;[6] also the Representative Body of the Welsh Church[7] and any property vested in or administered by it,[8] the Central Board of Finance of the Church of England[9] in respect of the adminis-

---

1 CA 1960, s. 45 (1). Certain ecclesiastical property is excluded by s. 45 (2).

2 CA 1960, s. 46.

3 See CA 1960, Sch. 2, para. (a). The Places of Worship Registration Act 1855, s. 9 is amended by CA 1960, s. 48; Sch. 6.

4 See the following Acts respectively: Birmingham University Act 1900, s. 14; Liverpool University Act 1903, s. 14; Victoria University of Manchester Act 1904, s. 11; University of Leeds Act 1904, s. 12; University of Sheffield Act 1905, s. 11; University of Bristol Act 1909, s. 12; University of Reading Act 1926, s. 10; University of Nottingham Act 1949, s. 10; University of Southampton Act 1953, s. 10; University of Hull Act 1955, s. 11; University of Exeter Act 1957, s. 10; University of Leicester Act 1958, s. 10.

5 Imperial War Museum Act 1920, s. 5.

6 National Maritime Museum Act 1934, s. 7.

7 See the Welsh Church Act 1914, s. 13.

8 Welsh Church (Temporalities) Act 1919, s. 7 (1).

9 Or any body substituted for that board in pursuance of para. 17 of the scheme scheduled to the Church Funds Investment Measure 1958: see s. 8 of the 1958 Measure.

tration of an investment fund or a deposit fund constituted in pursuance of the scheme brought into effect by the Church Funds.[1]

(*b*) The universities of Oxford, Cambridge, London and Durham, the colleges and halls in the universities of Oxford, Cambridge and Durham and the colleges of Winchester and Eton.[2] All the institutions mentioned in this paragraph were exempted under previous legislation also.[3]

(*c*) Any university, university college, or institution connected with a university college, which Her Majesty declares by Order in Council to be an exempt charity for the purposes of the Charities Act 1960. The Nathan Committee was not in favour of granting automatic exemption to university bodies which might come into existence in the future but on the other hand considered that such bodies should not be put to the trouble and expense of a private Act of Parliament: the procedure of an Order in Council obviates that trouble and expense.

Since the passing of the Charities Act 1960 five Orders in Council have been made pursuant to paragraph (c) of the Second Schedule.[4] They cover various universities and university colleges and various institutions connected with the University of London, the University of Wales and the University of Manchester. The *universities* which are exempt charities by virtue of Orders in Council are: Keele, Sussex, Wales, East Anglia, Essex, Kent, Lancaster, Warwick, York, Surrey, Aston in Birmingham, Bradford, the Loughborough University of Technology, the Bath University of Technology, the City University, Brunel, Salford and the Open University. The *university colleges* which are exempt are the University College of Wales, Aberystwyth, the University College of North Wales, the University College of South Wales and Monmouthshire, the University College of Swansea and St. David's College, Lampeter. The institutions connected with London University which are exempt fall into three categories: general, medical and post-graduate medical. In the first category are numbered: Bedford College, Birkbeck College, Imperial College of Science and Technology, the London School of Economics and Political Science, Queen Elizabeth College, Queen Mary College, the Royal Holloway College, the Royal Veterinary College, the School of Oriental and African Studies, the School of Pharmacy University of London, Westfield College, the College of St. Gregory and St. Martin at Wye, the Chelsea College of Science and Technology. The *medical schools* connected with the University of London and exempted by Order are: Charing Cross Hospital Medical School, Guy's Hospital Medical School, King's College Hospital Medical School, the London Hospital Medical College, the Middlesex Hospital Medical School, the Royal Dental Hospital of London School of Dental Surgery, the Royal Free Hospital School of Medicine, the Medical College of St. Bartholomew's Hospital in the City of London, St. George's Medical Hospital School, St. Mary's Hospital Medical School, St. Thomas' Hospital Medical School, University College

---

1 Church Funds Investment Measure 1958, s. 5.

2 CA 1960, Sch. 2, para. (b). This provision is deemed to include the University of Newcastle: Universities of Durham and Newcastle upon Tyne Act 1963, s. 18.

3 Eton and Winchester had been exempted under Charitable Trusts Amendment Act 1855, s. 49; the other institutions were exempted by Charitable Trusts Act 1853, s. 62. The Nathan Committee proposed that all existing university bodies should be exempted under the Act: see Nathan Report, paras. 404–407. But only those with close connections with the University Grants Committee are so exempted.

4 Exempt Charities Orders 1962, No. 1343; 1965, No. 1715; 1966, No. 1460; 1967, No. 821; 1969, No. 1496.

Hospital Medical School, Westminster Medical School. The *post-graduate* medical institutions which are exempt comprise the London School of Hygiene and Tropical Medicine and the Institutes forming the British Post-graduate Medical Federation. These are: Post-graduate Medical School of London, the Institute of Cancer Research, Royal Cancer Hospital, the Institute of Cardiology, the Institute of Child Health, the Institute of Dental Surgery, the Institute of Dermatology, the Institute of Diseases of the Chest, the Institute of Laryngology and Otology, Institute of Neurology (Queens Square), the Institute of Obstetrics and Gynaecology, the Institute of Ophthalmology, the Institute of Orthopaedics, the Institute of Psychiatry and the Institute of Urology. The Welsh National School of Medicine which is connected with the University of Wales has been exempted by Order in Council: likewise the University of Manchester Institute of Science and Technology.

(*d*) The British Museum. The exemption includes the British Museum (Natural History).[1] The British Museum was specifically exempted by section 62 of the Charitable Trusts Act 1853.

(*e*) Any institution which is administered by or on behalf of an institution included in the foregoing heads (*a*) to (*d*) and which is established for the general purposes of, or for any special purpose of, or in connection with, such institution. For this purpose, as elsewhere, "institution" includes "trust"[2] so that this paragraph exempts the special endowments and trust funds of any charity exempted under the foregoing paragraphs in addition to the corporate property of such a charity.

(*f*) The Church Commissioners and any institution administered by them.[3] The exemption does not of course extend to other funds of the Church of England which are administered by diocesan boards of finance, parochial church councils or other bodies.

(*g*) Any registered society within the meaning of the Industrial and Provident Societies Act 1893, and any registered society or branch within the meaning of the Friendly Societies Act 1896. These societies are charitable only if under their rules poverty is an essential qualification for the receipt of relief. They are sufficiently controlled by the special legislation relating to them and it is for this reason that they are exempted from the supervision of the Charity Commissioners.

(*h*) The Board of Governors of the Museum of London[4].

(*i*) The British Library Board.[5]

EXCEPTED CHARITIES

The distinction between exempt charities and excepted charities must be underlined. The former mentioned, as we have seen, in the Second Schedule to the Charities Act 1960 are exempt from all the supervisory powers of the Charity Commissioners. Excepted charities are those which are excepted from certain of the obligations imposed by the Act but are in other respects subject to those powers. The three obligations from which a charity may be excepted are the

---

1 British Museum Act 1963, s. 8 (4); Sch. 2.
2 CA 1960, s. 46.
3 For the ambit of the previous exemption enjoyed by Queen Anne's Bounty under Charitable Trusts Act 1853, s. 62: see Nathan Report (Cmd. 8710) paras. 424–431.
4 CA 1960, Sch. 2, para. (h) added by Museum of London Act 1965, s. 11.
5 CA 1960, Sch. 2, para. (i) added by British Library Act 1972, s. 4 (2).

obligation to register,[1] the obligation to transmit yearly statements of account[2] and the obligation to obtain the sanction of the Commissioners for any dealing with land.[3]

Charities may be excepted from one or more of these obligations either by order of the Charity Commissioners or by excepting regulations made by the Home Secretary. The regulations are made by statutory instrument which is subject to annulment in pursuance of a resolution of either House of Parliament.[4] Exception may be permanent or temporary and it may be subject to conditions.[5] The terms of the relevant order or regulations must be carefully analysed in order to identify the precise ambit of any exception. The extent of the exceptions made from the three obligations referred to is discussed later in relation to each obligation.[6]

Legal meaning of charity[7]

INTRODUCTION

The word charity in its widest sense denotes all the good affections men ought to bear towards each other; in its most restricted and common sense relief of the poor.[8] But lawyers and the courts do not employ the word in either of these senses. The legal meaning of the word differs from the popular meaning, and it has been said on the highest authority that charity in the legal sense is a word of art of precise and technical meaning.[9] And yet, paradoxically, no satisfactory and precise definition of charity in its legal sense has ever been found. The dictum of Viscount SIMONDS in *I.R.Comrs.* v. *Baddeley*[10] is still true:

"no comprehensive definition of legal charity has been given either by the legislature or in judicial utterance".

Attempts to crystallise the basic concept of charity have invariably failed. Nobody (in this country at any rate) has ever got further than Lord CAMDEN L.C.'s definition in *Jones* v. *Williams*[11] in which he said:

"Definition of charity; a gift to a general public use which extends to the poor as well as the rich."

---

1 CA 1960, s. 4 (4) (b).
2 CA 1960, s. 8 (1).
3 CA 1960, s. 29 (4).
4 CA 1960, s. 43.
5 CA 1960, s. 45 (6).
6 See chapter 42 (registration); chapter 36 (accounts); chapter 37 (dealings).
7 See J. W. Brunyate (1945) 61 L.Q.R. 268; and see G. Cross (1956) 72 L.Q.R. 187; Keeton, "The Charity Muddle" (1949) 2 Current Legal Problems 86. On the history of charities, see Keeton and Sheridan, *Modern Law of Charities* (2nd edn.) 1–21; and Jordan, *Philanthropy in England* (1959); Scott, *Trusts* (3rd edn.) para. 348.2; Gareth Jones, *History of the Law of Charities (1532–1827)* (1969).
8 *Morice* v. *Bishop of Durham* (1805), 9 Ves. 399, at 405; *on appeal*, 10 Ves. 522.
9 *National Anti-Vivisection Society* v. *I.R.Comrs.*, [1948] A.C. 31, at 41, H.L. *per* Lord WRIGHT.
10 [1955] A.C. 572; [1955] 1 All E.R. 525.
11 (1767), Amb. 651; see also *I.R.Comrs.* v. *Educational Grants Association, Ltd.*, [1967] Ch. 993, at 1011, *per* HARMAN, L.J.

Such a "definition" does not, of course, carry matters very far. And such other definitions as have been attempted amount to no more than a classification of those purposes which have been held to be charitable.

> "Charity, in a legal sense, is rather a matter of description than of definition."[1]

Most definitions of the descriptive or classifying kind do not even, on the face of them, purport to be exhaustive. An exception, however, is the definition of GRAY J. in an American case:[2]

> "A charity, in the legal sense, may be more fully *defined* as a gift, to be applied consistently with existing laws, for the benefit of an indefinite number of persons, either by bringing their minds or hearts under the influence of education or religion, by relieving their bodies from disease, suffering or constraint, by assisting them to establish themselves in life, or by erecting or maintaining public buildings or works or otherwise lessening the burdens of government."

Yet this definition is not broad enough. It includes objects which are unquestionably charitable. but these are not the only objects which are held to be charitable. It omits, for example, animal charities and trusts for the protection of human life or property.[3]

PREAMBLE TO THE STATUTE OF ELIZABETH I

Any discussion of the various attempts at classifying charitable purposes must, inevitably, hark back to the Charitable Uses Act 1601, often also referred to as the Statute of Elizabeth I.[4] This Act was not passed for the purpose of giving a definition of "charity" but was directed to providing for the reformation of abuses in the application of property devoted to charitable uses. But, by a singular construction, it was held to authorise certain gifts to charity which otherwise would have been void. And it contained in the preamble a list of charities so varied and comprehensive that it became the practice of the Court to refer to it as a sort of index or chart.[5] At the same time it was never forgotten that the "objects there enumerated" as Lord CRANWORTH L.C. observes,[6] "are not to be taken as the only objects of charity but are given as instances".

The purposes set out in the preamble are, in modernised English, as follows:

> "The relief of aged, impotent and poor people; the maintenance of sick and maimed soldiers and mariners, schools of learning, free schools and scholars in universities; the repair of bridges, ports, havens, causeways, churches, sea-banks and highways; the education and preferment of

---

1 *Per* WAYNE J. in *Perin* v. *Carey*, 24 How. 465, at 494 (1860).
2 *Jackson* v. *Phillips*, 14 Allen 539, at 556 (1867) (U.S.) (emphasis added).
3 See the discussion of these two categories in chapters 10 and 12 respectively, *infra*.
4 43 Eliz. 1, c. 4.
5 *Income Tax Special Purposes Comrs.* v. *Pemsel*, [1891] A.C. 531, at 581, *per* Lord MACNAGHTEN. The examples are guideposts for the courts in the differing circumstances of a developing civilisation and economy: *Incorporated Council of Law Reporting for England and Wales* v. *A.-G.* [1972] Ch. 73, at 87, *per* RUSSELL L.J.
6 *London University* v. *Yarrow* (1857), 1 De G. & J. 72, at 79.

orphans; the relief, stock or maintenance of houses of correction; the marriages of poor maids, the supportation, aid and help of young tradesmen, handicraftsmen and persons decayed; the relief or redemption of prisoners or captives; and the aid or ease of any poor inhabitants concerning payment of fifteens, setting out of soldiers and other taxes."

Several writers,[1] have drawn attention to the fact that the fourteenth-century poem *The Vision of Piers Plowman* strikingly anticipated the language of the definition contained in the preamble to the Statute of Elizabeth I. In the poem Truth advises anxious and rich merchants to obtain remission of sins and a happy death by devoting their wealth to charitable purposes in the following way:

> And therewith repair hospitals
> help sick people
> mend bad roads
> build up bridges that had broken down
> help maidens to marry or to make them nuns
> find food for prisoners and poor people
> put scholars to school or to some other craft,
> help religious orders and
> ameliorate rents or taxes.

This enumeration of charitable objects is, indeed, so close to that contained in the preamble that it is difficult to believe that the draftsman of the Act did not draw on it.[2]

However that may be, the practice of referring to the preamble for guidance[3] had, by the beginning of the nineteenth century, become a rule of law[4]. Yet it was not only the objects enumerated in the preamble which in law ranked as charitable, but also all other purposes "which by analogies are deemed within its spirit and intendment".[5] In other words, the objects named in the preamble were regarded as instances and not the only objects of charity. On the other hand, objects which were neither enumerated in the preamble nor within its spirit and intendment were not charitable, no matter how beneficial to the public they might be.[6]

The Charitable Uses Act 1601 was repealed by the Mortmain and Charitable Uses Act 1888[7] but section 13 (2) of the latter Act, after reciting that in divers enactments and documents reference was made to charities within the meaning, purview, and interpretation of the statute, provided that references to such charities should be construed as references to charities within the meaning, purview, and interpretation of the preamble to the statute. The effect of section 13 (2) has in the past been misinterpreted. It did not save the preamble from

---

1 (1894–95) 8 Harvard Law Review 69; and see Jordan, *Philanthropy in England 1480–1660* (1959) 112; Keeton and Sheridan, *Modern Law of Charities* (2nd edn.) 4.
2 (1894–95) 8 Harvard Law Review 69, at 70; *cf.* Keeton and Sheridan, *op. cit.*, at 4.
3 See *A.-G.* v. *Ruper* (1722), 2 P. Wms. 125, at 126, *per* Sir Joseph Jekyll M.R.; *A.-G.* v. *Whorwood* (1750), 1 Ves. Sen. 534, Lord Hardwicke L.C.
4 *Morice* v. *Bishop of Durham* (1804), 9 Ves. 399 (Sir William Grant M.R.); on appeal (1805), 10 Ves. 522 (Lord Eldon L.C.) is the watershed.
5 *Morice* v. *Bishop of Durham* (1804), 9 Ves. 399, at 405.
6 *Gilmour* v. *Coats*, [1949] A.C. 426, at 442–443, *per* Lord Simonds L.C.; *National Anti-Vivisection Society* v. *I.R.Comrs.*, [1948] A.C. 31, at 41, *per* Lord Wright.
7 51 & 52 Vict., c. 42.

repeal: it merely preserved the preamble for the limited purpose of making references in other documents intelligible. And it is questionable whether it was even necessary so to provide. The preamble never had the force of an enactment. The position was that the practice of the courts was to refer to the preamble as a guide and gradually this practice became an inflexible rule of law. It is difficult to see how the repeal of the Charitable Uses Act 1601 and its preamble could affect the principle formulated by the courts that a charity must be within the spirit and intendment of the Act of 1601. The Mortmain and Charitable Uses Act 1888 has now itself been repealed by section 38 of the Charities Act 1960. It is nevertheless provided in section 38 (4) that any reference in any enactment or document to a charity within the meaning, purview and interpretation of the Charitable Uses Act 1601 or its preamble shall be construed as a reference to a charity within the meaning which the word bears as a legal term according to the law of England and Wales. The purport of this subsection is not as clear as it should be. For example, need the reference in the relevant enactment or document to a charity expressly specify that the charity was within the meaning, purview and interpretation of the Act of 1601, or would a reference to charity *simpliciter* impliedly attract the operation of the subsection? The better view[1] is that the subsection means:

> "Any reference in any enactment or document to a charity which before the passing of this Act would have been held to come within the meaning, purview and interpretation of the Charitable Uses Act 1601, or to the preamble to it, shall hereafter be construed as a reference to a charity within the meaning which the word bears as a legal term according to the law of England and Wales ..."

It was at one time suggested[2] that the legal meaning of charity is now to be ascertained solely from the reported cases from which all references to, and all reasoning based on the existence of, the preamble should be expunged. But it is now well established that the court will satisfy itself that an alleged charitable purpose is within the spirit and intendment of the preamble.[3]

THE EQUITY OF THE STATUTE OF ELIZABETH I

Even at the time of its passing the list of objects enumerated in the preamble to the Statute of Elizabeth I was not exhaustive. And from the start the courts have discussed whether a particular purpose is or is not within the equity of the statute or its spirit and intendment. The Court of Appeal in *Re Strakosch*[4] held that in order to be charitable a purpose need not be in any way *eiusdem generis* with the purposes recited in the preamble but need only be charitable in the same sense. RUSSELL L.J. in *Incorporated Council of Law Reporting for England and Wales* v. *A.-G.*[5] went somewhat further:[6]

> "The Courts, in consistently saying that not all 'objects of general public

---

1 See Professor O. R. Marshall on the Charities Act 1960 in (1961), 24 M.L.R. 444, at 445.

2 *Ibid.*, at 446.

3 *Scottish Burial Reform and Cremation Society* v. *Glasgow Corporation*, [1968] A.C. 138, H.L.; *Incorporated Council of Law Reporting for England and Wales* v. *A.-G.*, [1971] Ch. 626; affd., [1972] Ch. 73.

4 [1949] Ch. 537, at 538.

5 [1972] Ch. 73.   6 [1972] Ch. 73, at 87–88.

utility' are necessarily charitable in law, are in substance accepting that if a purpose is shown to be so beneficial or of such utility it is *prima facie* charitable in law, but have left open a line of retreat based on the equity of the Statute in case they are faced with a purpose (e.g. a political purpose) which could not have been within the contemplation of the Statute.'

CLASSIFICATIONS OF CHARITABLE OBJECTS

Romilly's classification

The first classification of charitable objects attempted by a lawyer after the Charitable Uses Act 1601 was made by Sir Samuel Romilly (then Mr. Romilly) when arguing in *Morice* v. *Bishop of Durham*.[1] He itemised as heads of charity: first, relief of the indigent, second advancement of learning, third the advancement of religion, fourth "which is the most difficult"[2] the advancement of objects of general public utility.

Pemsel's case

Lord MacNaghten in *Income Tax Special Purposes Comrs.* v. *Pemsel*[3] produced a similar classification, with very slight variations.

"Charity," he said,[4] "in its legal sense comprises four principal divisions: trusts for the relief of poverty; trusts for the advancement of education; trusts for the advancement of religion; and trusts for other purposes beneficial to the community not falling under any of the preceding heads." There is no material difference between the first and third heads enumerated in this classification and the first and third heads of Sir Samuel Romilly's classification. The substitution of education for learning is, however, more precise. And "purposes beneficial to the community" seems to be a more satisfactory umbrella class than "objects of general public utility"[5] and is not merely a paraphrase of it.[6] It should, however, be noted that Sir Samuel Romilly did not mean that *all* objects of general public utility were charitable[7] and Lord MacNaghten did not mean that *all* purposes beneficial to the community not falling under any of his preceding three heads of charity were charitable.[8]

Suggested classification[9]

The law of charities has progressed considerably since Lord MacNaghten put forward his classification of charitable purposes. It is still not possible to give an

---

1 (1805), 10 Ves. 522.
2 It has been called "a wilderness": see Bentwich (1933) 149 L.Q.R. 520.
3 [1891] A.C. 531.
4 *Ibid.*, at 583.
5 See *I.R.Comrs.* v. *Baddeley*, [1955] A.C. 572, at 608, *per* Lord Reid.
6 On this very nice point see *Tudor on Charities* (6th edn.) 70–71.
7 See *Re Macduff*, [1896] 2 Ch. 451, at 466, *per* Lindley L.J.
8 See *A.-G.* v. *National Provincial and Union Bank of England*, [1924] A.C. 262, at 265, *per* Lord Cave L.C.
9 For other classifications see Scott, *Trusts* (3rd edn.); Sheridan (1957), *Malayan Law Journal*, lxxvi, "Nature of Charity"; Goodman Report (1976) 123–125.

exhaustive list of charitable objects, so that any attempted classification will include a sweeping-up head to cover miscellaneous objects which have been held to be charitable. But, nevertheless, a new classification seems to be called for and the following classification of charitable objects is suggested as appropriate:

> relief of poverty
> advancement of education
> advancement of religion
> promotion of health
> provision of recreational facilities
> municipal betterment and relief of the tax and rating burden
> gifts for the benefit of a locality
> certain patriotic purposes
> protection of life and property
> social rehabilitation
> protection of animals
> other miscellaneous objects that are beneficial to the community

This classification is adopted in the present work it being axiomatic that, relief of poverty apart, such purposes are *only* charitable in so far as they are of a public nature.

One writer suggests that "a trust is charitable if a Chancery judge thinks that accords with contemporary social ideas and policy on public good".[1] As an *ex post facto* rationalisation of judicial attitudes this statement may have some validity. But, in the search for a definition of charity, the statement offers little help. Again it is an overstatement to say (as one member of Parliament observed in a debate on the Recreational Charities Act 1958) that the journey from the Statute of Elizabeth I to modern times is "a maze of caprice, fantasy and historical humbug".[2] The aberrations are relatively few.

"CHARITY" ACCORDING TO THE LAW OF OTHER JURISDICTIONS

Where English authority is scant, practising lawyers and judges have shown a growing inclination to refer to authorities from other common law jurisdictions.[3] It is for this purpose that some Scots, Irish, Commonwealth and American cases are cited in this work. Public policy and social needs vary from country to country, and this factor must inevitably dilute the persuasive strength of authorities from other jurisdictions. But a short survey of the legal concept of charity in other systems is appropriate, so that the persuasiveness of any decision outside England can be viewed in a proper perspective.

Scots law[4]

The expressions "charity" and "charitable" have not acquired a technical meaning in the *general* law of Scotland. But for the purposes of construing

---

1 See [1968] New Law Journal Annual Charities Review 42, at 46 (Alec Samuels).
2 H.C. debates, 11 February 1958, Vol. 582, col. 332; but see *Re Tetley*, [1923] 1 Ch. 258, at 266–267; *Re Howley*, [1940] I.R. 109, at 114.
3 See the extra-curial statement of Lord DENNING M.R. in the Foreword to *Annual Survey of Commonwealth Law*.
4 See T. B. Smith, *Scotland, The Development of its Laws and Constitution* (1962) 585–590.

income tax legislation applicable to the whole United Kingdom "charity" is (and must be) given the same meaning in Scotland as it bears in England.

(i) General law

The basic distinction taken in Scots law is between private and public trusts.[1] And in very many cases there is no need to decide whether a particular public trust is charitable or not. This is partly because the court exercises its *cy-près* jurisdiction if the trust is one in which a section of the public has an interest and partly because the general attitude of Scots law towards perpetuities is benevolent and this makes it unnecessary for a public trust to claim it is charitable to secure relaxation of the rules against perpetuities.

In the late nineteenth century charity was construed rather narrowly in Scotland so as to cover only the relief of poverty.[2] But historically this view was inaccurate:[3] "charity" and "charitable" in Scotland had a much wider meaning than eleemosynary purposes and could include certain religious[4] and educational purposes,[5] the relief of suffering and even bridge building[6] and harbour repairs:[7] they embraced all objects which a well-disposed person might promote from motives of philanthropy.[8]

The development of the general law as to "charities" in Scotland and England has progressed since 1891 in the direction of a widening divergence and the crucial test whether the Attorney-General is competent to intervene has no counterpart in Scots law and practice.[9] In *Chichester Diocesan Fund and Board of Finance Incorporated* v. *Simpson*[10] Lord PORTER drew attention to the fact that the Statute of Elizabeth I never applied to Scotland and that charities, speaking generally, are not controlled by the Scots courts[11] and he concluded that no satisfactory guidance could be obtained from the decision, in the Scottish courts in a case where the validity of a gift in an English will depends on its charitable nature.[12]

(ii) Income tax law

It has been laid down in the House of Lords[13] that for the purposes of construing income tax legislation applicable to the whole United Kingdom the English law

---

1 See McLaren, *Wills and Succession*, Vol. II, 917, approved *Anderson's Trustees* v. *Scott* 1914 S.C. 942.

2 *Baird's Trustees* v. *Lord Advocate* 1888 15 R. (Ct. of Sess.) 682; *Blair* v. *Duncan*, [1902] A.C. 37, H.L.; *Grimond or Macintyre* v. *Grimond*, [1905] A.C. 124, H.L.; *Reid's Trustees* v. *Cattanach's Trustees* 1929 SC. 727, at 731, *per* Lord MACKAY.

3 See *Income Tax Special Purposes Comrs.* v. *Pemsel*, [1891] A.C. 531, at 558–563, *per* Lord WATSON.

4 *Ibid.*, at 559; *Allan's Executors* v. *Allan* 1908 S.C. 807.

5 *Ibid.*, at 556; *Ferguson* v. *Marjoribanks* (1853), 15 Dunl. (Ct. of Sess.) 637 (school); *Aberdeen University* v. *Irvine* (1868), L.R. 1 Sc. & Div. 289, H.L. (bursaries or scholarships); *Andrews* v. *M'Guffog* (1886), 11 App. Cas. 313, H.L. (school); *Chalmers Trustees* v. *Turiff Parish School Board* 1917 S.C. 676 (educational scheme for poor); *M'Lean* v. *Henderson's Trustees* 1880 7 R. (Ct. of Sess.) 601 (for the advancement and diffusion of the science of phrenology and the practical application thereof).

6 *Income Tax Special Purposes Comrs.* v. *Pemsel*, [1891] A.C. 531, at 559.

7 *Lord Saltoun* v. *Lady Pitsligo* 1700 Mor. Dict. 9948.

8 *Income Tax Special Purposes Comrs.* v. *Pemsel*, [1891] A.C. 531, at 558.

9 *I.R.Comrs.* v. *Glasgow (City) Police Athletic Association* 1952 S.C. 102 (Ct. of Sess.) at 118, *per* Lord COOPER Lord President.

10 [1944] A.C. 341.   11 *Ibid.*, at 366–367   12 *Ibid.*, at 367.

13 *I.R.Comrs.* v. *Glasgow (City) Police Athletic Association*, [1953] A.C. 380; [1953] 1 All E.R. 747.

of charity has to be regarded as part of the law of Scotland. The inconvenience of this principle has been much criticised by Scots lawyers.[1]

Irish law[2]

In Ireland the governing statute on the law of charities was not the Statute of Elizabeth but a statute passed in the reign of Charles I. This Irish statute[3] was eventually held to be exactly analogous to its English counterpart and to fulfil in Ireland all the functions which the latter Act was deemed to perform in England. Sir Edward SUGDEN L.C. said in *Incorporated Society* v. *Richards*,[4] "The statute of Charles seems, therefore, an almost exact pattern of the statute of Elizabeth, and I have but little doubt that its framers had the latter Act before them at the time they were preparing it."[5] But, on analysis, it becomes clear that the term charity does not have precisely the same meaning in Ireland as it has in England. Admittedly, PALLES C.B. in *A.-G.* v. *Delaney*[6] said, "We may deem a charitable purpose in Ireland to be identical with that which—excluding any difference arising from the law of superstitious uses—would be a charitable purpose in England under the Act 43 Eliz., c. 4."[7] And the well-known classification of legally charitable purposes made by Lord MACNAGHTEN in *Income Tax Special Purposes Comrs.* v. *Pemsel*[8] has been habitually followed in Ireland in cases coming before the courts there. Nevertheless there are a number of instances where Irish judges have adopted an independent attitude towards charitable trusts; and, not surprisingly, this has tended to be in the field of religious charities.[9] Now that the Republic of Ireland is completely independent the possibility of further divergences has increased and it can no longer be assumed that the word "charity" will necessarily bear the same meaning in Ireland as in this country. That is not, of course, to say that Irish decisions are of no assistance in the English courts or *vice versa*: it merely means that a *caveat* should be put on their usefulness.

Law in the Commonwealth[10]

The only generalisation possible about the law of charities in the Commonwealth is that it has broadly followed the lines of authorities in the English courts. Thus, in India English law and practice on charities is followed so far as possible.[11] In Malaya the law as to what purposes are charitable is based on the

---

1 See T. B. Smith, *op. cit.*
2 See generally V. T. H. Delany, *Law relating to Charities in Ireland* (1962); F. A. P. Hamilton, *Law relating to Charities in Ireland* (1881); Moore, *Law of Charities in Ireland* (1906); J. C. Brady, *Religion and the Law of Charities in Ireland.*
3 Stat. 10 Car. 1 Sess. 2 Cap. 1.
4 (1841), 1 Dr. & War. 258.
5 *Ibid.*, at 320.
6 (1876), I.R. 10 Ch. 104.
7 *Ibid.*, at 125.
8 [1891] A.C. 531.
9 See 65–74, *infra.*
10 See generally *A.S.C.L.* [1965–   ]; 8 (1) *English and Empire Digest* (Reissue) 230–482 and the relevant supplements; and Sir Kenneth Roberts-Wray, *Commonwealth and Colonial Law* (1966) Chapter 11; Keeton and Sheridan, *Comparative Law of Trusts* (1976).
11 *Shivramdas* v. *Nerurkar*, [1937] I.L.R. Bomb. 843.

same principles as in England[1] and the *Pemsel* classification has been adopted. In Canada in Manitoba[2] and Ontario[3] where the Statute of Elizabeth I was never in force the courts will still refer to the preamble to that Act as interpreted by innumerable decisions. Countries with different religious systems provide interesting illustrations of the law of religious trusts and superstitious uses.[4]

In Sri Lanka for example while a public benefit is required in the case of educational trusts and trusts under the fourth head of *Pemsel's* case the requirement of public benefit in religious trusts is virtually non-existent.[5] This is partly because of the ritualistic nature of the local religions and partly because in the nineteenth century the only means of administering the property of a religious institution was by treating it as a charitable trust. To this must be added the failure in many local cases to cite English authorities on public benefit.[6] The Trusts Ordinance 1918, section 99 in defining charity adopts the *Pemsel* classification but includes under the third head "the maintenance of religious rites and practices" and under the fourth head "purposes beneficial or of interest to mankind". It has therefore been suggested that in Sri Lanka an animal trust would *not* be charitable whereas a trust to promote sport would be charitable.[7]

South Africa

The English law of trusts has only been partially received in South Africa[8] and it is therefore necessary to treat South African cases on the law of charities with caution. For the purposes of determining whether a particular project is charitable the South African courts do not refer to the preamble of the Statute of Elizabeth I. While trusts for the relief of poverty,[9] the advancement of education[10] and the advancement of religion[11] are all accounted *ad pias causas* or charitable, there is some doubt as to whether all trusts for the public benefit are charitable,[12] South African courts have followed the English Law in requiring an element of public benefit in the case of religious trusts: they require proof of a direct or indirect tendency to the instruction or edification of the public.[13] Public benefit in charitable trusts generally is construed to include a benefit to a section of the public.[14]

1 Per MAXWELL C.J. in *Choa Choon Neoh* v. *Spottiswoode* (1869), 1 Ky. 216 (Straits Settlement); Keeton and Sheridan, *Comparative Law of Trusts* (1976) 307–313.
2 *Re Oldfield Estate No. 2*, [1949] 2 D.L.R. 175; *Re Angell Estate* (1955), 63 Man. R. 331.
3 *Re Angell Estate, supra*; and see Waters, *Law of Trusts in Canada* (1974).
4 See L. A. Sheridan (1957) *Malayan Law Journal*, lxxvi; L. A. Sheridan, *The British Commonwealth*, Vol. 9, *Malaya and Singapore and the Borneo Territories*, 355–357; Mukherjea, *Hindu Law of Religious and Charitable Trusts* (3rd edn., 1970).
5 Cooray, *Reception in Ceylon of the English Trust* (1971) 168.
6 But see *Fernando* v. *Sivasubramaniam* (1959), 61 N.L.R. 241 where *Gilmour* v. *Coates*, [1949] A.C. 426 was discussed but misunderstood.
7 Cooray, *op. cit.*, 170.
8 See Honoré, *The South African Law of Trusts* (2nd edn.) 10–14.
9 *Ex parte Rattray* 1963 (1) S.A. 556 (home for destitute children).
10 *Marks* v. *Estate Gluckman*, [1946] A.D. 289.   11 *Ex parte Hart* 1947 (4) S.A. 464.
12 *Marks* v. *Estate Gluckman*, [1946] A.D. 289 at 301, *cf. Standard Bank of South Africa, Ltd.* v. *Betts Brown* 1958 (3) S.A. 713; and see Honoré, *op. cit.*, 119.
13 *Ex parte Hart* 1947 (4) S.A. 464 following *Cocks* v. *Manners* (1871), L.R. 12 Eq. 574.
14 *Ex parte Hart* 1947 (4) S.A. 464 at 479; *Re Estate Denton*, 1951 (4) S.A. 582; *Ex parte Marriott N.O.* 1960 (1) S.A. 814.

American law

In the Restatement of Trusts it is pointed out that a purpose is charitable if its accomplishment is of such social interest to the community as to justify permitting property to be devoted to the purpose in perpetuity.[1] Courts in the United States have frequently had recourse to the Charitable Uses Act 1601 as showing the kind of purpose which is charitable. Some judges and writers thought that the law of charities had its origin in the statute of 1601 and that charitable trusts could not be upheld in a state which had rejected that statute. This historically inaccurate view was exploded by the decision of the Supreme Court of the United States in *Vidal* v. *Girards Executors*.[2] In the result the American concept of a charity is fairly close to the English one. The chief divergences are on the questions of trusts to promote changes in the law and of public benefit. The notion that a trust for a purpose otherwise charitable is not charitable if the accomplishment of its purposes involves a change in existing laws has in the United States been pretty thoroughly rejected. Trusts for the promotion of health, isolated as a separate head of charity by the Restatement of Trusts,[3] are not robbed of their charitable status if the benefits are confined to the employees of a particular railway company or industrial organisation.[4] And a trust for the relief of poverty or the advancement of education or the promotion of health is charitable although the beneficiaries are limited to the members or relations of members of a Masonic Lodge or other fraternal organisation.[5] The Restatement also classifies as a separate head "governmental and municipal purposes". Professor Hanbury thinks that this opens the door more widely than we should admit[6] but the examples given correspond fairly closely to the examples given in this work of "municipal betterment and the relief of the rate and tax burden".

PUBLIC BENEFIT[7]

General

Before discussing in detail the various heads of charity it is convenient to consider the general rule (to which there is only one exception) that a purpose is not charitable unless it is directed to the public benefit. "This is sometimes stated in the proposition that it must benefit the community or a section of the community. Negatively it is said that a trust is not charitable if it confers only

---

1 Restatement of Trusts (2d) Vol. 2, s. 368; and see generally Scott, *Trusts* (3rd edn. para. 368; Luis Kutner, *Some Aspects of Charitable Trusts and Foundations* (1970).

2 2 How. 127 (U.S.) (1844).

3 See *Restatement of Trusts* (2d) Vol. 2, para. 372.

4 *Union Pacific Rail. Co.* v. *Artist* 60 Fed. 365 (1894); *Illinois Central Railroad Co.* v. *Buchanan* 126 Ky. 288 (1907).

5 Scott, *Trusts* (3rd edn.) para. 375.2.

6 See 2 University of Toronto Law Journal 68.

7 S. Maurice (1951) 15 Conv. N.S. 328; G. H. L. Fridman (1953) 31 Can. Bar. Rev. 537; P. S. Atiyah (1958) 21 M.L.R. 138.

private benefits."[1] The court in determining whether particular named purposes are charitable has always applied this overriding test. But the difficulty lies in determining what is sufficient to satisfy the test.

It is as well to remember that the requirement of public benefit has two aspects. There must be a *benefit* and it must be a *public* benefit. In *Gilmour* v. *Coats*,[2] for example, it was held that the purposes of a community of cloistered and contemplative nuns were not legally charitable because the benefit to mankind of intercessory prayer and of the example of pious lives was too vague and incapable of proof. The benefit itself was in question.

In other cases there is a discernible benefit, but not to the public, merely to private individuals. A trust for the protection of private investors confers merely private benefits:[3] so do trusts for the education of relations or the descendants of named persons,[4] or of the children of employees of a particular employer.[5] For the same reason the provision of a convalescent home for members of a trade union and their wives is not charitable.[6]

Many mutual benefit schemes where there is no means test fail to achieve charitable status. For example in *Re Hobourn Aero Components, Ltd.'s Air-Raid Distress Fund*[7] a contributory fund for the relief of air raid distress among the contributors who were employees of a particular company was held to be private and therefore not charitable. Lord GREENE M.R. commented thus:[8]

> "the point to my mind, which really puts this case beyond reasonable doubt is the fact that a number of employees of this company, activated by motives of self-help, agreed to a deduction from their wages to constitute a fund to be applied for their own benefit without any question of poverty coming into it. Such an arrangement seems to me to stamp the whole transaction as one having a personal character, money put up by a number of people, not for the general benefit, but for their own individual benefit".

A mutual benefit society[9] such as a friendly society[10] or a trade union[11] is not a charitable organisation, although of course such a society may hold particular property on trust for a stated charitable purpose.[12] Gifts to societies for promoting the interests of the memebers of a particular profession are gifts which do

---

1 *Oppenheim* v. *Tobacco Securities Trust Co., Ltd.*, [1951] A.C. 297, at 305, *per* Lord SIMONDS.

2 [1949] A.C. 426, H.L.; see also *Cocks* v. *Manners* (1871), L.R. 12 Eq. 574.

3 *Foreign Bondholders Corporation* v. *I.R.Comrs.*, [1944] K.B. 403, CA. So too a pig marketing board: *Pig Marketing Board (Northern Ireland)* v. *I.R.Comrs.*, [1945] N.I. 155.

4 *Re Compton*, [1945] Ch. 123, C.A.

5 *Oppenheim* v. *Tobacco Securities Trust Co., Ltd.*, [1951] A.C. 297, H.L.

6 *Re Mead's Trust Deed*, [1961] 1 W.L.R. 1244.

7 [1946] Ch. 194, C.A.

8 *Ibid.*, at 200.

9 *Carne* v. *Long* (1860) 2 De G.F. & J. 75; *Re Dutton* (1878) 4 Ex.D. 54; *Linen and Woollen Drapers' Institution* v. *I.R.Comrs.* (1887), 4 T.L.R. 345; *Re Hobourn Aero Components, Ltd.'s Air-Raid Distress Fund*, [1946] Ch. 194, C.A.; *Lord Nuffield* v. *I.R.Comrs.* (1946), 175 L.T. 465; *I.R.Comrs.* v. *Royal Naval and Royal Marine Officers' Association* (1955), 36 T.C. 187; *Waterson* v. *Hendon Borough Council*, [1959] 1 W.L.R. 985; *cf. Perpetual Trustee Co., Ltd.* v. *Ferguson* (1951), 51 S.R. (N.S.W.) 256.

10 *Re Clark's Trust* (1875), 1 Ch.D. 497; *Cunnack* v. *Edwards*, [1896] 2 Ch. 679, C.A.; *Braithwaite* v. *A.-G.*, [1909] 1 Ch. 510.

11 *Re Amos*, [1891] 3 Ch. 159; *Re Mead's Trust Deed*, [1961] 1 W.L.R. 1244.

12 *Pease* v. *Pattinson* (1886), 32 Ch.D. 154 (where the headnote wrongly states that a friendly society is a charity).

not promote a public benefit but rather a private benefit.[1] So too a body formed to register and regulate the members of a profession is not charitable.[2]

On the other hand a gift may be for the public benefit in the eyes of the law even though by its very nature only a limited number of persons are likely to avail themselves, or are, perhaps, even capable of availing themselves of its benefits. There is, as Viscount SIMONDS pointed out in *I.R.Comrs.* v. *Baddeley*,[3] a distinction

> "between a form of relief extended to the whole community yet, by its very nature, advantageous only to the few, and a form of relief accorded to a selected few out of a larger number equally willing and able to take advantage of it".[4]

The former type may still be for the public benefit, even though confined to the inhabitants of a particular area, but the latter type is not for the public benefit. Even then, Viscount SIMONDS' dictum requires amplification. In a sense, any limitation of benefits to a section of the community results in a relief being accorded to a selected few out of a larger number equally willing and able to take. It all depends on what is meant by "few". Lord WRENBURY delivering the judgment of the Privy Council in *Verge* v. *Somerville*[5] said that to be a charity a trust must be for the benefit of the community or of an *appreciably important class* of the community.[6] The inhabitants of a parish or town, or any particular class of such inhabitants might, he continued, be the object of such a gift, but private individuals or a fluctuating body of private individuals cannot. It has, however, been established that a trust cannot qualify as a charity within the fourth class in *Pemsel*'s case (i.e. as being of general public utility) if the bene-ficiaries are a class of persons not only confined to a particular area but selected from within it by reference to a particular creed.[7]

One comes then to the problem: What is an appreciably important class of the community? BUCKLEY L.J., as long ago as 1915, observed that in his view the salient point to be considered in ascertaining whether a charity is public or private is to see whether the class is one which extends to a substantial body of the public.[8]

Likewise Lord SIMONDS discussing the meaning of the phrase "section of the community" in *Oppenheim* v. *Tobacco Securities Trust Co., Ltd.*[9] said that the words conveniently indicated (1) that the *possible* beneficiaries must not be numerically negligible and (2) that the quality which distinguishes them from

---

1 R. v. *Income Tax Special Comrs., Ex parte Headmasters' Conference* (1925), 41 T.L.R. 651, D.C. (headmasters); *Geologists' Association* v. *I.R.Comrs.* (1928), 14 T.C. 271, C.A. geo-logists); *Midland Counties Institution of Engineers* v. *I.R.Comrs.* (1928), 14 T.C. 285, C.A.; *Honourable Company of Master Mariners* v. *I.R.Comrs.* (1932), 17 T.C. 298; *Chartered Insurance Institute* v. *London Corporation*, [1957] 1 W.L.R. 867, D.C.

2 *Miley* v. *A.-G. for Northern Ireland*, [1918] 1 I.R. 455, C.A. (Royal College of Surgeons in Ireland); *General Medical Council* v. *I.R.Comrs.* (1928), 97 L.J.K.B. 578, C.A.; *General Nursing Council for Scotland* v. *I.R.Comrs.* 1929 S.C. 664; *General Nursing Council for England and Wales* v. *St. Marylebone Corporation*, [1959] A.C. 540, H.L.; and see Samuels "Fiscal Relief for Professional Bodies as Charities" (1963), 27 Conv. N.S. 469.

3 [1955] A.C. 572.

4 *Ibid.*, at 592.

5 [1924] A.C. 496.

6 *Ibid.*, at 499.

7 *I.R.Comrs.* v. *Baddeley*, [1955] A.C. 572.

8 *Shaw* v. *Halifax Corporation*, [1915] 2 K.B. 170, C.A., at 182.

9 [1951] A.C. 297.

other members of the community so that they form by themselves a section of it, must be a quality which does not depend on their relationship to a particular individual or particular individuals.[1] A group of persons may be numerous but if the nexus between them is their personal relationship to a single *propositus* or to several *propositi*, they are neither the community nor a section of the community for charitable purposes.[1] (This test has been referred to as the *Compton*[2] test.) Counsel[3] for the appellants in the *Oppenheim* case pointed to some of the anomalies that might flow from this principle. Those following a profession or calling—clergymen, lawyers, colliers, tobacco workers and so on—are a section of the public. Applying the test of relationship to a single *propositus*, one reaches strange results where, as in the case of railwaymen, those who follow a particular calling are all employed by one employer. Would a trust for the education of railwaymen be charitable but a trust for the education of men employed on the railways by the Transport Board not be charitable? And what of service of the Crown, whether in the civil service or the armed forces?[4] Is there a difference between soldiers and soldiers of the King? Lord SIMONDS[5] stated that he was not impressed by this sort of argument and would consider on its merits any case where the description of the occupation would enable one to know the name of the employer. But the points taken by counsel for the appellants in the *Oppenheim* case are (it is submitted) valid criticisms of the *Compton* test as a universal solvent and they caused one of the learned law lords to dissent. Lord MACDERMOTT[6] agreed with the result arrived at in the *Compton* case itself and did not doubt that the *Compton* test might often prove of value and lead to a correct determination of the question, but he was unable to regard it as a criterion of general applicability and conclusiveness. Used in that way he considered the *Compton* test to be a very arbitrary and artificial rule. Moreover the test necessarily made the quantum of public benefit a consideration of little moment. He also considered that the educational value and scope of the work actually to be done must have a bearing on the question of public benefit.[7] Finally he suggested that the *Compton* test was likely to unsettle the law.[8] He put the case of a trust for the provision of university education for boys coming from a particular school and commented[9]

"The common quality binding the members of that class seems to reside in the fact that their parents or guardians all contracted for their schooling within the same establishment or body. That the school in such a case may itself be a charitable foundation seems altogether beside the point and quite insufficient to hold the *Compton* test at bay if it is well founded in law."

In fact Lord SIMONDS expressly classified a trust of that kind as charitable:[10] the *Compton* test does not affect a trust for the benefit of an existing institution.

---

1 *Ibid.*, at 306.
2 *Re Compton*, [1945] Ch. 123.
3 PENNYCUICK K.C. (as he then was).
4 An educational trust for the children of Crown servants is altruistic and should be upheld: (1951) 67 L.Q.R. 164 (A.L.G.).
5 [1951] A.C. 297, at 307.
6 *Ibid.*, at 317.
7 *Ibid.*, at 318.
8 *Ibid.*
9 *Ibid.*, at 319.
10 *Ibid.*, at 306.

Furthermore in the example put there is an absence of self-interest which is not so when the trust is designed to make the conditions of service with one employer better than that with a competitor.[1]

The Nathan Committee on Charitable Trusts adverted to the practical difficulties canvassed by Lord MACDERMOTT but concluded that it would be a mistake to alter the law by providing that the element of public benefit should not be excluded by reason only of the nexus of common employment.[2] Accordingly it was not surprising that the Charities Act 1960 left the law unchanged.

In *Dingle* v. *Turner*[3] Lord CROSS OF CHELSEA in referring to the *Oppenheim*[4] case pointed out that although in that case the majority evidently agreed with the view that the *Compton*[5] rule was of universal application outside the field of poverty it would no doubt be open to the House of Lords without overruling *Oppenheim* to hold that the scope of the rule was more limited. The question did not arise in *Dingle* v. *Turner* but Lord CROSS indicated that his inclination would be to draw a distinction between the practical merits of the *Compton* rule and the reasoning by which Lord GREENE M.R. sought to justify it. That reasoning, based on the distinction between personal and impersonal relationships was in his view not very satisfactory and he felt the force of the criticism to which Lord MACDERMOTT subjected it in his dissenting speech in *Oppenheim*. The phrase a "section of the public" was, he said, a vague phrase which might mean different things to different people. In the law of charity judges have sought to elucidate its meaning by contrasting it with a "fluctuating body of individuals". But he found the antithesis of little help because there was no true contrast: the same aggregate of persons might well be describable both as a section of the public and as a fluctuating body of private individuals.[6]

Whether the beneficiaries constitute a section of the public

> "is a question of degree and cannot be by itself decisive of the question whether the trust is a charity. Much must depend upon the purpose of the trust."[7]

The other law lords who included Lord MACDERMOTT agreed with what Lord CROSS had to say about the phrase "section of the public". In the light of these remarks the Charity Commissioners have canvassed the possibility that if another and entirely altruistic educational trust were to come before the House of Lords, the personal link of common employment which proved fatal in the *Oppenheim* case might well be found not by itself to jeopardise charitable status if the size of the company was sufficiently large.[8] This may, however, be an over-simplification. For Lord CROSS OF CHELSEA and Lord SIMON a trust for the education of the children of employees, however numerous, is a company and not a public purpose, which the courts and taxpayers should not subsidise.[9]

---

1 See (1951) 67 L.Q.R. 164 (A.L.G.).
2 [1952] Cmd. 8710, paras. 135 and 136.
3 [1972] A.C. 601.
4 *Oppenheim* v. *Tobacco Securities Trust Co., Ltd.*, [1951] A.C. 297.
5 *Re Compton*, [1945] Ch. 123, C.A.
6 [1972] A.C. 601, at 623 where Lord CROSS itemises the ratepayers of the Royal Borough of Kensington and Chelsea.
7 [1972] A.C. 601, at 624.
8 [1971] Ch. Com. Rep. 9, para. 21. Lord MACDERMOTT would still hold it to be charitable as would probably Viscount DILHORNE and Lord HODSON.
9 [1972] A.C. 601, at 625.

In deciding whether or not an element of public benefit is present in the case of an alleged charitable trust it is an open question whether the courts should have regard to the fiscal privileges accorded to charities. In *Dingle* v. *Turner*[1] Lord CROSS, with whose speech Lord SIMON concurred, thought that the courts should take those fiscal privileges into account, but the other three law lords expressed their doubts on this point. Certainly there is no case in which the fiscal implications of a determination in favour of charity have been expressly considered. But Lord CROSS thought that the decisions in *Compton*[2] and *Oppenheim*[3] "were pretty obviously influenced by the consideration that if such trusts as were there in question were held valid they would enjoy an undeserved fiscal immunity":[4] a trust for the education of the children of employees of a company represents a "fringe benefit" for the employees which ought not to be purchased at the expense of the taxpayer. There was not the same danger of abuse in the case of trusts for the relief of poverty among employees and Lord CROSS considered that the privileged position of such trusts in the law of charities might be justified on the practical ground that such a tax-free trust does not constitute a very attractive "fringe benefit". For the same sort of reason a trust to promote religion among employees of a company might, he thought, perhaps safely be held to be charitable provided it was clear that the benefits were to be purely spiritual, though purposes under Lord MACNAGHTEN's fourth head if confined to a class of employees would clearly be open to the same sort of objection as educational trusts so confined.[5]

Variations in the standard of public benefit

The necessary quantum of public benefit may well vary from charity to charity. This emerges from the speech of Lord SIMONDS in *Gilmour* v. *Coats*[6] in which he dealt with an argument that, just as the endowment of a scholarship open to public competition was a charity, so also was a gift to enable any man or woman to enter a fuller religious life a charity. After observing that the law of charity had been built up not logically but empirically Lord SIMONDS continued:[7]

> "It would not, therefore, be surprising to find that, while in every category of legal charity some element of public benefit must be present, the court had adopted the same measure in regard to different categories, but had accepted one standard in regard to those gifts which are alleged to be for the advancement of education and another for those which are alleged to be for the advancement of religion, and it may be yet another in regard to the relief of poverty."

Lord SOMERVELL OF HARROW made a similar point in *I.R.Comrs.* v. *Baddeley*[8] when he declared himself unable to accept the principle

> "that a section of the public sufficient to support a valid trust in one category must as a matter of law, be sufficient to support a trust in any other category. . . . There might well be a valid trust for the promotion of

---

1 [1972] A.C. 601, H.L.   2 [1945] Ch. 123.
3 [1951] A.C. 297.   4 [1972] A.C. 601, at 624–625.
5 [1972] A.C. 601, at 625.   6 [1949] A.C. 426, H.L.
7 [1949] A.C. 426, at 449.   8 [1955] A.C. 572.

religion benefiting a very small class. It would not follow at all that a recreation ground for the exclusive use of the same class would be a valid charity, though it is clear . . . that a recreation ground for the public is a charitable purpose."[1]

Again, the courts' notion of public benefit may vary with the passing of time. In *Re Foveaux*[2] the Court of Appeal upheld an anti-vivisection trust, but in *National Anti-Vivisection Society* v. *I.R.Comrs.*[3] the House of Lords denied that the anti-vivisection cause was charitable. Two of the learned law lords commented on the changing standards of public benefit. Lord WRIGHT said[4] that:

"Where a society has a religious object it may fail to satisfy the test [of public benefit] if it is unlawful, and the test may vary from generation to generation as the law successively grows more tolerant . . . It cannot be for the public benefit to favour trusts for objects contrary to the law. Again eleemosynary trusts may, as economic ideas and conditions and ideas of social service change, cease to be regarded as being for the benefit of the community, and trusts for the advancement of learning or education may fail to secure a place as charities, if it is seen that the learning or education is not of public value."

Lord SIMONDS for his part said[5] that:

"if, today, a testator made a bequest for the relief of the poor, and required that it should be carried out in one way only, and the court was satisfied by evidence that that way was injurious to the community, I should say that it was not a charitable gift, though three hundred years ago the court might, upon different evidence, or in the absence of any evidence, have come to a different conclusion."

Charity overseas and the public benefit

It by no means follows that the public to be benefited under the doctrine of public benefit must be the United Kingdom public. Certainly there are a number of authorities holding that a trust for the benefit of a foreign public may be charitable. For example in *Re Geck*[6] it was held that a trust for the poor in a certain German town was a valid charity, while in *Re Robinson*[7] a trust for the relief of German soldiers disabled in the First World War was held by MAUGHAM J. to be valid. And the advancement of religion abroad by missionaries has long been considered charitable.[8] That a trust for the benefit of a foreign public, or of a section of such a public is valid, is implicit also in other decisions.[9]

---

1 *Ibid.*, at 615.
2 [1895] 2 Ch. 501, C.A.
3 [1948] A.C. 31, H.L.
4 *Ibid.*, at 42.
5 *Ibid.*, at 69.
6 (1893), 69 L.T. 819; see also *Re British Red Cross Balkan Fund*, [1914] 2 Ch. 419.
7 [1931] 3 Ch. 122.
8 See *Re Redish* (1909) 26 T.L.R. 42 and the other cases discussed under Trusts for missionary and cognate purposes at 63–64 *infra*.
9 *A.-G.* v. *Sturge* (1854), 19 Beav. 597; *Lyons Corporation* v. *East India Co.* (1836) 1 Moo. P.C.C. 175, at 295.

But in *Camille and Henry Dreyfus Foundation Inc.* v. *I.R.Comrs.*[1] Lord EVER-SHED M.R. indicated that there might by some limits to charity abroad with this observation:[2]

> "It may be that on very broad and general grounds, relief of poverty and distress in any part of the world, or the advancement of the Christian[3] religion in any part of the world, would be regarded as being for the benefit of the community in the United Kingdom. I see, however, formidable difficulties, where the objects of the trust were, say, the setting out of soldiers or the repair of bridges or causeways in a foreign country. To such cases the argument of public policy (meaning United Kingdom public policy) might be the answer.

A similar view is taken by the Charity Commissioners.[4] They entertain no doubt that the advancement of religion, the advancement of education and the relief of poverty are charitable purposes in whatever part of the world they are carried out. In the case of poverty however (which is to be interpreted as including the relief of poor refugees or victims of a disaster) the Commissioners think that it must actually exist in observable cases and not merely be inferred from statistics. Moreover the measures designed to relieve it, e.g. irrigation, must have a reasonably direct result. If, however, the measures are directed merely to improving the general economy or standard of living of an overseas community they would not in the Commissioners' eyes be charitable subject to what is said below about public works within the British Commonwealth. Charities within the fourth head of the classification in the *Pemsel* case, i.e. for other purposes beneficial to the community will, according to the Commissioners, only be charitable if of benefit to the community of the United Kingdom. Such benefit, they say

> "need not be material or direct but must not be too remote. Charities with general humanitarian objects (e.g. cancer research) can benefit the community of the United Kingdom even if carried on in foreign countries. But where the purposes are the local provision of public works or development projects such as roads and irrigation these will generally be charitable only if... they are a reasonably direct means to the end of relieving existing poverty in observable cases; but they appear not to be charitable if the purpose is the general economic improvement of another country."

They also suggest that a benefit to the United Kingdom community might arise from charitable purposes for the general benefit of a British Commonwealth country which is in close association with the United Kingdom.[5]

There are certainly cases in the books upholding trusts for the advancement of education abroad.[6] However in an Australian case a bequest to establish musical

---

1 [1954] Ch. 672.
2 *Ibid.*, at 684.
3 *Semble* that a gift by an English testator to promote a non-Christian religion abroad would be non-charitable. A fund for the purpose of encouraging idolatry would not be for the benefit of the native inhabitants of Dacca: see *Mitford* v. *Reynolds* (1842), 1 Ph. 185, at 193, *per* Lord LYNDHURST L.C.
4 [1963] Ch. Com. Rep. para. 72; criticised by D. M. Evans (1965), 29 Conv. N.S. 123.
5 *Cf. Mitford* v. *Reynolds* (1842), 1 Ph. 185 (where the country was India).
6 *A.-G.* v. *Sturge* (1854), 19 Beav. 597 (school in Genoa); *Whicker* v. *Hume* (1858), 7 H.L.C. 124 (in every part of the world); *President of United States* v. *Drummond* (1838), cited

prizes for the composition of orchestral works and song cycles in Austria was initially held invalid.[1] The judge said:[2]

> "It is necessary in the particular context of foreign charitable purposes to consider the nature of the gift and the relationship between this State and the foreign jurisdiction. . . . Anything which is a need in this State and which is recognised as involving a community obligation will involve the same need and the same community obligation towards the foreign jurisdiction. . . . The provision of hospitals[3] or the assistance of those who are in some need, even though it be not a financial need, are all obligations which go beyond the bounds of any particular country, but the encouragement of musical competitions or the encouragement of the fine arts in a particular country seems to me to be very much a matter internal to the country itself. I do not think that it is sufficient that it may result in an overflow of cultural endeavour."

This approach, which has much to commend it, has not yet been adopted by the courts in England. In *Re Shaw's Will Trusts*[4] a trust for (in effect) the promotion of culture in Ireland was held by the English court to be valid; and there is American authority to the same effect.[5]

Examples are also to be found of valid charitable trusts for purposes abroad not being for the relief of poverty or distress or for the advancement of education or religion or for the promotion of health. Thus a trust for charitable objects in Cephalonia has been upheld.[6] A trust for the prevention of cruelty to animals abroad has also been held charitable,[7] as has a gift to the Government of Bengal to be applied to charitable beneficial and public works at and in the city of Dacca in Bengal for the exclusive benefit of the native inhabitants in such manner as they and the Government might regard as most conducive to that end.[8] In Canada a trust for the upkeep of a municipal cemetery in France was held good.[9] In *Re Jacobs*[10] a gift "for the purpose of planting a grove of trees in Israel to perpetuate my name on the eternal soil of the Holy Land" was held to be a valid charitable gift being a gift for re-afforestation which is charitable;[11] the report of the decision does not, however, indicate whether the question of public benefit was argued and having regard to what was said by Lord EVERSHED M.R. in the *Camille and Henry Dreyfus Foundation Inc.* v. *I.R.Comrs.* it is open to doubt whether the gift ought to have been sealed with charitable exemption.

---

in *Whicker* v. *Hume, supra,* at 155 (increase of knowledge among men); *Re Marrs' Will Trusts,* [1936] Ch. 671 (school in Scotland); *Re Masoud* [1961] O.R. 583 (Can.) (education of schoolchildren in Mount Lebanon, Syria).

1 *Re Lowin,* [1965] N.S.W.R. 1624; revsd. [1967] 2 N.S.W.R. 140.

2 [1965] N.S.W.R. 1624, at 1627, *per* JACOB J. His conclusion (but not approach) was held wrong.

3 See *Kytherian Association of Queensland* v. *Sklavos,* [1959] A.L.R. 5; *Re Burnham* (1958), 17 D.L.R. (2d) 298 (Can.) (poor sick and afflicted in Montenegro, Macedonia and Armenia).

4 [1952] Ch. 163.

5 *Martin* v. *Haycock* 140 N.J.Eq. 450 (1947) (U.S.) (for library in Irish town).

6 *Re Vagliano,* [1905] W.N. 179. In *re Dreyfuss* 276 N.Y. Supp. 438 (1934) (U.S.) a bequest to city officials of a German city for charitable purposes was upheld.

7 *Armstrong* v. *Reeves,* (1890), 25 L.R. Ir. 325; *Re Jackson* (1910), *Times,* 11th June.

8 *Mitford* v. *Reynolds* (1842), 1 Ph. 185.

9 *Re Oldfield Estate (No. 2),* [1949] 2 D.L.R. 175 (Manitoba).

10 (1970), 114 Sol. Jo. 515; see also *Re Storr* (1970) 91 WN (NSW) 704 but *cf. Jewish National Fund Inc.* v. *Royal Trust Co. and Richter,* [1965] S.C.R. 784.

11 On the principle of *I.R.Comrs.* v. *Yorkshire Agricultural Society,* [1928] 1 K.B. 611.

Exception to rule requiring public benefit

In one category of charitable trusts the element of public benefit does not appear to be required. This is where there is a trust to relieve the poverty of a very limited class of beneficiaries, not being named or designated individuals. For example, the courts have upheld trusts for the benefit of poor relations,[1] poverty-stricken employees and ex-employees (or their families) of a company,[2] and members of a club who have fallen on evil days.[3] Public benefit is wholly absent from such trusts, unless one accepts that the relief of poverty is of so altruistic a character that the public benefit may be necessarily inferred.[4]

MOTIVE OF DONOR

It is quite clear that the motive of the donor or testator is immaterial in determining whether a gift is charitable.[5] The test is objective not subjective. Whether funds are dedicated to a charitable use depends, therefore, not on the source from which the funds are derived, but on the purpose to which they are to be applied. Thus a gift to provide a parish church with stained glass windows is a good charitable gift notwithstanding that the motive of the donor is not to beautify the church but to perpetuate the memory of the donor and his relatives.[6] Many educational gifts also have a dual role: to advance education and, incidentally, to commemorate the donor or some relation of the donor.[7]

CONTROL BY THE COURT

One of the tests, and a crucial test, whether a trust is charitable, lies in the competence of the court to control and reform it and for the Attorney-General, on behalf of the Sovereign who, as *parens patriae*, is the guardian of charity, to intervene and inform the court if the trustees fall short of their duty.[8] As such intervention is made *pro bono publico*[9] this may be regarded as a facet of the test of public benefit.

MAKING A PROFIT

An undertaking conducted for private profit is not charitable.[10] This is true although the purposes are such that, if it were not conducted for private profit,

---

1 See 32–35, *infra.*
2 *Gibson v. South American Stores, Ltd.,* [1950] Ch. 177; *Dingle v. Turner,* [1972] A.C. 601, H.L.
3 *Re Young's Will Trusts,* [1955] 1 W.L.R. 1269.
4 See *Re Scarisbrick,* [1951] Ch. 622, at 639, *per* EVERSHED M.R.
5 *Hoare v. Osborne* (1866), L.R. 1 Eq. 385, at 587.
6 *Re King,* [1923] 1 Ch. 243.
7 So fellowships, scholarships, exhibitions and prizes frequently bear the names of the founder or a relation of the founder, see Squibb, *Founders' Kin* (1972).
8 *National Anti-Vivisection Society v. I.R.Comrs.,* [1948] A.C. 31, at 62, *per* Lord SIMONDS.
9 *Ibid.,* at 65.
10 *Re Smith's Will Trusts,* [1962] 1 W.L.R. 763, C.A.

it would be charitable, as for example an educational institution or a hospital or a home owned and conducted for the financial benefit of the owner.

Nevertheless charities can make charges for their services without losing their charitable status,[1] even if the charges produce a profit. There are numerous cases in the books illustrating this principle in relation to educational institutions[2] and hospitals[3] and homes.[4] But it also applies to recreational facilities, such as a public recreation ground or a municipal covered swimming pool.[5] And no doubt other cases may occur where the participants in the charity may be required to contribute some small charge or fee without imperilling the status of the charity. The question is not whether the institution may receive a profit, but what disposition is to be made of the profit, if any, received. Where the profits are to enure to the benefit of individuals, the institution is not charitable; but if the profits, if any, are to be applied wholly for charitable purposes the institution is charitable.

HOSPITALITY OR ENTERTAINMENT

A trust whose dominant purpose, or one of whose dominant purposes, is hospitality or entertainment is not charitable. Thus a bequest for establishing what was, in effect, a hotel for the entertainment of distinguished visitors from far-flung countries was held not to be charitable.[6] But if the object of the trust is otherwise charitable the fact that it will afford incidental entertainment or pleasure to the public will not render it non-charitable.[7]

A bequest by a member of a livery company upon trust (*inter alia*) to give a livery dinner on each anniversary of his birthday is not a good charitable gift.[8] But a trust to apply the income of a fund in the payment of the expenses of dinners consumed by members of a charitable religious society,[9] or of the trustees of a charitable trust attending meetings, has been held to be charitable as increasing the usefulness of the society or promoting the efficient management of the trust.[10]

One case which does not fit easily into the framework of the principles just stated is *A.-G.* v. *Barham*[11] which in fact concerned the application of increased rents among a number of charities. Sir Charles PEPYS M.R. did not in that case question the validity of one of the charities founded by an ancient trust in a will executed in 1612. Out of the yearly rent of a property in Southwark the trustees were directed to pay 30 shillings to provide dinner every St. Thomas's Day before Christmas Day for the householders and married people of the town of

---

1 *Scottish Burial Reform and Cremation Society, Ltd.* v. *Glasgow Corporation*, [1968] A.C 138, H.L.; *Incorporated Council of Law Reporting for England and Wales* v. *A.-G.*, [1972] Ch. 73, C.A.
2 *Brighton College* v. *Marriott*, [1926] A.C. 192, H.L.; *The Abbey, Malvern Wells, Ltd.* v. *Minister of Local Government and Planning*, [1951] Ch. 728.
3 *Re Resch's Will Trusts*, [1969] 1 A.C. 514, P.C.
4 *Re Estlin* (1903), 72 L.J.Ch. 687; *Re Clarke*, [1923] 2 Ch. 407; *Re Chaplin*, [1933] Ch. 115.
5 *Northern Ireland Valuation Comr.* v. *Lurgan Borough Council*, [1968] N.I. 104, C.A.
6 *Re Corelli*, [1943] Ch. 332.
7 *Royal Choral Society* v. *I.R.Comrs.*, [1943] 2 All E.R. 101.
8 *Re Barnett* (1908), 24 T.L.R. 788.
9 *Re Charlesworth* (1910), 101 L.T. 908 (quarterly meetings).
10 *Re Coxen*, [1948] Ch. 747 (annual meeting).
11 (1835), 4 L.J.Ch. 128. The case was cited in argument in *Re Charlesworth, supra.*

Bootle in Lancashire and 30 shillings for a supper on the same day for all the youth and young people of the same town. Unless the trust was one for the relief of poverty it is hard to see how it could be charitable; classification of the gift as being for the advancement of religion would be too far fetched. Support for this proposition is to be found in *Re Geere's Will Trusts (No. 1)*[1] where the testator by his will had bequeathed £1000 to the vicar and churchwardens of a church "to expend the income . . . in the purchase of seasonable food and drink to be distributed by them upon Christmas Eve in every year in the said church among twenty men or women to be communicating members of the said church . . . each recipient being informed that such food and drink is the gift of [the testator]". HARMAN J. held that there was no express intention in the terms of the bequest of benefit to the deserving poor, and he would not infer it. The element of poverty was absent and so the bequest failed, there being no charitable trust.

---

1 [1954] C.L.Y. 402; and see (1954), *The Times*, 20th March.

Chapter 2

Relief of Poverty

General

As has been pointed out, charity in its most restricted and common sense means relief of the poor. And in a sense the relief of poverty lies at the very heart of the law of charities. Many of the charitable trusts created prior to the Charitable Uses Act 1601 and mentioned in the Calendars of Chancery and the 37 volumes of the Reports of the Commissioners of Charities (1818–37) were trusts for the relief of poverty. The relief of the poor is expressly mentioned in the preamble to the Charitable Uses Act 1601 but the theme of relieving poverty runs through many of the other purposes enumerated in the preamble; as, for example: education and preferment of orphans, marriages of *poor* maids, aid of young tradesmen, handicraftsmen and persons decayed, and aid of poor inhabitants concerning taxes.

Definition of poverty

Numerous cases have established that poverty is a relative term. It is not confined to destitution. There are degrees of poverty less acute than abject poverty or destitution, but poverty nevertheless.[1] The term poverty is in fact as Lord EVERSHED M.R. once observed:[2]

> "of wide and somewhat indefinite import; it may not unfairly be paraphrased for present purposes as meaning persons who have to 'go short' in the ordinary acceptation of that term, due regard being had to their status in life and so forth".

Thus in the latter decades of the nineteenth century gifts for incapacitated actors not having an income of more than £50[3] or to aid persons in receipt of less than £120 a year were upheld as charitable.[4] Homes for decayed or distressed gentlefolk[5] and hostels for working men[6] or young girls[7] fulfil a charitable

---

1 *Per* EVE J. in *Re Gardom*, [1914] 1 Ch. 662.
2 *Re Coulthurst*, [1951] Ch. 661, at 666.
3 *Spiller v. Maude* (1881), 32 Ch.D. 158 n.
4 *Re Lacy*, [1899] 2 Ch. 149; *Re de Carteret*, [1933] 1 Ch. 103.
5 *A.-G. v. Power* (1809), 1 Ball. & B. 145; *Re Estlin* (1903), 72 L.J.Ch. 687; *Trustees of the Mary Clark Home v. Anderson*, [1904] 2 K.B. 645; *Re Gardom, supra*; *Shaw v. Halifax Corporation*, [1915] 2 K.B. 170; *Re Clarke*, [1923] 2 Ch. 407; *Re Campbell*, [1930] N.Z.L.R. 713; *Re Harvey*, [1941] 3 All E.R. 284; *Re Young*, [1951] Ch. 344; *cf. Re Norgate* (1944), *Times*,

purpose even though the inmates are required to make some contribution to the expense of maintaining the home. Similarly a trust to assist poor emigrants is valid even though it is envisaged that such emigrants will pay part of their passage.[1] A trust to advance loans to help educated women and girls to become self-supporting is also good.[2] The word "needy" has come to be synonymous with "poor".[3] The word "deserving" on the other hand does not necessarily connote poverty so that, whatever else it is, a trust to provide dowries for deserving Jewish girls is not for the relief of poverty.[4] The context may, however, show that the word does connote poverty. A trust for "necessitous *and* deserving" persons was upheld in *Gibson* v. *South American Stores (Gath and Chaves) Ltd.*[5] but that is inconclusive since it could be said that the word "deserving" adds to, and is not synonymous with, necessitous. In *Re Coulthurst*[6] the beneficiaries were to be those chosen by the bank as being "by reason of his, her or their financial circumstances . . . the most deserving of such assistance"; here the word "deserving" plainly meant a person needing help. A more difficult case was *Re Bethel*[7] where a trust for "needy *or* deserving" members of a club was in issue. The Ontario High Court held that while the word "needy" related to poverty, "deserving" did not and the gift failed. On appeal it was held, by a majority, that the word "deserving" indicated poverty: in other words the words used were synonymous and the linking "or" was, in effect, exegetic or explanatory.

Persons "in genuine need of financial assistance" are not necessarily poor or "needy".[8] A direction to trustees to consider persons "in special need" should be construed as an instruction to satisfy the special needs of a selected beneficiary by alleviating poverty.[9]

Relief of poverty implicit in gift

Sometimes the intention to relieve poverty is not expressed in the gift but may be inferred from its very nature. It is not absolutely necessary to find poverty expressed in so many words, but the court will look at the whole gift, and, if it comes to the conclusion that the relief of poverty was meant, will give effect to

---

21st July; 88 Sol. Jo. 267 n. (rest home for vegetarians, teetotallers, pacifists, and conscientious objectors).

6 *Guinness Trust (London Fund)* v. *West Ham Borough Council*, [1959] 1 W.L.R. 233. But the working classes are not necessarily poor: *Re Sanders' Will Trusts*, [1954] Ch. 265.

7 *Rolls* v. *Miller* (1884), 27 Ch.D. 71; *Re Strong*, [1956] N.Z.L.R. 275; *Re Pearse*, [1955] 1 D.L.R. 801 (sick or overworked young governesses).

1 *Barclay* v. *Maskelyne* (1858), 32 L.T. O.S. 205; *Re Rosenblum* (1924), 131 L.T. 21; *Re Tree*, [1945] Ch. 325. But a trust to encourage emigration *simpliciter* was held to be noncharitable in *Re Sidney*, [1908] 1 Ch. 488. See also *Re Wallace*, [1908] V.L.R. 636 (Aus.).

2 *Re Central Employment Bureau*, [1942] 1 All E.R. 232.

3 *Re Payne* (1954), 11 W.W.R. 424 (B.C.) (needy Imperial Veterans); *Re Angell Estate* (1955), 16 W.W.R. 342; *Re Wedge* (1968), 63 W.W.R. 397 (B.C.C.A.) (needy displaced persons).

4 *Re Cohen* (1919), 36 T.L.R. 16.

5 [1950] Ch. 177, C.A.

6 [1951] Ch. 661, C.A.

7 (1971), 17 D.L.R. (3d) 652 *sub. nom. Jones* v. *Executive Officers of T. Eaton Co., Ltd.* (1973), 35 D.L.R. (3d) 97, at 104–105 (Can. Supr. Ct.).

8 *Re Gillespie*, [1965] V.R. 402.

9 *Re Cohen*, [1973] 1 W.L.R. 415.

it although the word poverty is not to be found in it.[1] The collocation of the
words "widows" and "orphaned children" gives rise to the inference of poverty,
whether they be widows and orphans of a particular parish[2] or of deceased
officers or ex-officers of a bank.[3] Again in *Thompson* v. *Corby*[4] a gift to *aged*
widows and spinsters of a parish was held necessarily to imply that it was for
poor widows and spinsters. The same inference arose from a gift to "the widows
and children of seamen belonging to the town of Liverpool".[5] Poverty has also
been discerned in a gift for the benefit of respectable single women of good
character above the age of 60, the limit of £10 a year each indicating that
straitened circumstances were a prerequisite.[6] In *Re Gosling*[7] a gift to form a
"superannuation" fund "for the purpose of pensioning off old and worn out
clerks" of a particular firm was held charitable. Doubt has been cast on the
correctness of the decision by one textbook[8] which suggests that the clerks were
not a sufficient section of the public. The doubt was probably unjustified even
at the time it was raised. Trusts for poor employees or poor ex-employees had
been thrice blessed in the Court of Appeal:[9] the decision of the House of Lords
in *Dingle* v. *Turner*[10] has now put the matter beyond doubt.

Many of the cases in which poverty was inferred were cases where the gifts
could be justified on a disjunctive reading of the preamble to the Statute of
Elizabeth: they were gifts for the relief of the aged or the "impotent".

A further possibility is that an intention to relieve poverty can be inferred
from surrounding circumstances of which the testator is aware. Thus in *Re
Bingham*[11] it could be inferred from the circumstances and the context of the
will of the testatrix that the latter was aware that no home of the character
envisaged by her existed, so that a gift to a home "caring for aged women"
envisaged (*inter alia*) the relief of poverty among aged women.

Methods of relieving poverty

There are many methods of relieving poverty: some are direct, some indirect.

DIRECT RELIEF

The most obvious way of relieving poverty is to give sums of money to the
poor. In modern times the word "dole" is principally associated with "being
on the dole" that is, drawing unemployment benefit. But the word "dole" in
the context of charitable activity means a distribution. In former times dole

---

1 *Re Lucas*, [1922] Ch. 52, at 58, *per* RUSSELL J.
2 *A.-G.* v. *Comber* (1824), 2 Sim. & St. 93.
3 *Re Coulthurst*, [1951] Ch. 661, C.A.
4 (1860), 27 Beav. 649.
5 *Powell* v. *A.-G.* (1817), 3 Mer. 48.
6 *Re Dudgeon* (1896), 74 L.T. 613; see also *Re Lucas*, [1922] Ch. 52.
7 (1900), 48 W.R. 300.
8 *Tudor on Charities* (6th edn.) 10.
9 *Re Sir Robert Laidlaw* (1935), unreported but see [1950] Ch. 177, at 195; *Gibson* v.
South American Stores (Gath and Chaves) Ltd., [1950] Ch. 177; *Re Coulthurst*, [1951] Ch. 661.
10 [1972] A.C. 601.
11 [1951] N.Z.L.R. 491.

charities were very common[1] and some still survive to this day.[2] Distributions of food, fuel and articles of clothing were unlikely to be abused. But money doles often had a most unfortunate effect and were frequently criticised.[3] A representative comment was that of Sir GEORGE JESSEL M.R. in *Re Campden Charities:*[4]

"There is no doubt that it tends to demoralise the poor and benefit no one. Like our present ideas on the subject, and our present experience which [has been gathered as the result of very careful inquiries by various committees and commissions on the state of the poor in England, we know that the extension of doles is simply the extension of mischief."

Rather more constructive methods of direct relief are to be found in gifts for apprenticing poor children;[5] for providing allotments or buying land to be let to the poor at a low rent;[6] for providing flats to be let to aged persons of small means at economic rents;[7] for providing clothes for the poor[8] and for providing interest-free loans to poor and deserving inhabitants of a particular parish.[9] Similarly the establishment, maintenance and support of institutions or funds for the relief of various forms of poverty or distress are charitable; for example, soup kitchens,[10] hospitals, infirmaries or dispensaries,[11] nursing homes or societies[12] for persons of moderate means,[13] almshouses,[14] orphan and other asylums, convalescent homes,[15] homes of rest,[16] orphanages for children of particular classes of persons (such as railway servants,[17] policemen[18] or clergymen)[19], institutions for the support of decayed actors and actresses[20] or the distressed widows or medical men,[21] and homes for ladies in reduced circumstances[22] or working girls[23] all relieve poverty and are therefore charitable.

---

1 See Owen, *English Philanthropy, passim.*
2 Nightingale, *Charities* (1973) 10–13.
3 Kenny, *Endowed Charities* (1880) 40–52; Hobhouse, *The Dead Hand* (1880) 195–215.
4 (1881), 18 Ch.D. 310, at 327.
5 *A.-G. v. Minshull* (1798), 4 Ves. 11; *A.-G. v. Earl of Winchelsea* (1791), 3 Bro. C.C. 373; *A.-G. v. Wansay* (1808), 15 Ves. 231.
6 *Crafton v. Frith* (1851), 4 De G.M. & G. 237.
7 *Re Cottam's Will Trusts,* [1955] 1 W.L.R. 1299.
8 *Fatimah v. Logan* (1871), 1 Ky. 255 (Malaya–Penang).
9 *Re Monk,* [1927] 2 Ch. 197.
10 *Biscoe v. Jackson* (1887), 35 Ch.D. 460.
11 *Pelham v. Anderson* (1764), 2 Eden 296; *A.-G. v. Gascoigne* (1833), 2 My. & K. 647; *Biscoe v. Jackson, supra* (cottage hospital); *Re Cox* (1877), 7 Ch.D. 204.
12 *Re Clarke,* [1923] 2 Ch. 407; *cf. I.R.Comrs. v. Peebleshire Nursing Association* 1927 S.C. 215.
13 *Mayor of London's case* (1639), cited in Duke, ed. Bridgman 300; *Re Whiteley,* [1910] 1 Ch. 600; and see *Chamberlayne v. Brockett* (1872), 8 Ch. App. 206.
14 *Harbin v. Masterman* (1871), L.R. 12 Eq. 559; *Harbin v. Masterman,* [1894] 2 Ch. 184, C.A. affd. *sub. nom. Wharton v. Masterman,* [1895] A.C. 186, H.L.
15 *Re De Rosaz* (1889), 5 T.L.R. 606; *Henshaw v. Atkinson* (1818), 3 Madd. 306 (blind asylum).
16 *I.R.Comrs. v. (Trustees) Roberts Marine Mansions* (1927), 43 T.L.R. 270, C.A. (seaside home at reduced charges for members of drapery and allied trades requiring rest and change of air for their health's sake).
17 *Hall v. Derby Sanitary Authority* (1885), 16 Q.B.D. 163.
18 *Re Douglas* (1887), 35 Ch.D. 472.
19 *Re Clergy Society* (1856), 2 K. & J. 615.
20 *Re Lacy,* [1899] 2 Ch. 149; *Spiller v Maude* (1881), 32 Ch.D. 158, n.
21 *I.R.Comrs. v. Society for Relief of Widows and Orphans of Medical Men* (1926), 136 L.T. 60.
22 See cases cited in note 5 at 29, *supra.*　　　23 See cases cited in note 6 at 29, *supra.*

INDIRECT RELIEF

There are some cases where the relief of poverty is at one remove; the relief is indirect. Examples of indirect relief are the provision of accommodation for relatives who come from a distance to visit patients critically ill in hospital,[1] the provision of a home of rest for nurses at a particular hospital[2] or extra comforts for nurses at Christmas[3] or for patients in paying beds at hospitals.[4] Gifts to the sick and poor funds of a parish church[5] or to religious communities having for their object the relief of the sick and poor[6] effect an indirect relief of poverty: likewise gifts to friendly societies under whose rules relief may only be given to members who are poor[7] or gifts to those endeavouring to uplift the needy.[8] A gift tending to promote the efficient administration of a trust for the relief of poverty is itself charitable.[9]

It should be noted that relief of poverty is charitable where it is given by way of bounty and not by way of bargain[10] even though the beneficiaries contribute to the cost of the benefits they get.[11]

Public benefit

In the case of gifts for the relief of poverty the requirement of public benefit is not essential or is at least greatly modified.

Donors frequently specify that the relief shall be confined to a fairly limited group of beneficiaries. Sometimes the relief is confined to relatives of the donor —"the poor relations" cases: sometimes it is confined to some other limited group. The poor relations cases will be first discussed, and then the other cases.

GIFTS FOR POOR RELATIONS

Former law

The question of charities for poor relations was for a long time in a state of great uncertainty. This stemmed principally from a distinction (which was ultimately rejected by the Court of Appeal[12]) between perpetual trusts for the benefit of poor relations, and bequests for *distribution* immediately or within

---

1 *Re Dean's Will Trusts*, [1950] 1 All E.R. 882.
2 *Re White's Will Trusts*, [1951] 1 All E.R. 528.
3 *Re Bernstein's Will Trusts* (1971), 115 Sol. Jo. 808.
4 *Re Adams*, [1968] Ch. 80.
5 *Re Garrard*, [1907] 1 Ch. 382.
6 *Cocks* v. *Manners* (1871), L.R. 12 Eq. 574; *Re Delany*, [1902] 2 Ch. 642.
7 *Re Buck*, [1896] 2 Ch. 727.
8 *Re Orr* (1917), 40 D.L.R. 567 (Can.).
9 *Re Coxen* [1948] Ch. 747; *Re Charlesworth* (1910), 101 L.T. 908; *cf. Re Barnett* [(1908), 24 T.L.R. 788. This principle would appear to apply to all charitable purposes.
10 *I.R.Comrs.* v. *Society for Relief of Widows and Orphans of Medical Men* (1926), 136 L.T. 60, at 65.
11 *Re Estlin* (1903), 72 L.J.Ch. 687; *Re Clarke*, [1923] 2 Ch. 407; *Re Chaplin*, [1933] Ch. 115; *.I.R.Comrs.* v. *Peeblesshire Nursing Association*, 1927 S.C. 215, *per* Lord SANDS.
12 *Re Scarisbrick*, [1951] Ch. 622.

the perpetuity period among poor relations. However, before classifying the earlier cases it is worth pointing out that a gift to named relatives can never be charitable. Such a gift may perhaps be made from charitable motives but it is in essence a gift to individuals and not to purposes.[1]

Perpetual trusts

A gift for the perpetual benefit of the poor relations of the testator or any other person is a good charitable gift,[2] but the persons entitled to share in it must be actually (and not just relatively) poor. "No court has ever held that a man who had £10,000 a year was an object of charity within the purview of the Statute of Elizabeth" though no doubt such a person "might be the 'poorest' of a dozen persons each of whom had more than £10,000 a year".[3]

Bequests for immediate distribution or distribution within the perpetuity period

The earlier cases disclose a conflict of authority on the charitable nature of these bequests. One line of authorities held that such gifts were not charitable but might be saved from invalidity on the ground of uncertainty by being confined to the testator's next of kin.[4] In several of these cases the court reached this solution to escape the application of the Mortmain Acts. But, in the other line of cases it was held that a gift for immediate distribution among the testator's poor relations was charitable.[5]

The decision in re Scarisbrick

Most of the earlier cases were discussed and analysed by the Court of Appeal in *Re Scarisbrick*. In that case a testatrix left her residuary estate on trust for such relatives of her son and daughters as in the opinion of the survivor of them should be in needy circumstances. ROXBURGH J. held that on the authorities the recipients were beneficiaries under a family trust and did not constitute a particular section of the poor so that the gift was not charitable.[6] On appeal,[7] however, his decision was reversed. JENKINS L.J., after referring to the general rule that an aggregate of persons ascertained by some personal tie (e.g. of blood or contract) does not

---

1 *Liley* v. *Hey* (1842), 1 Hare 580.
2 *Isaac* v. *Defriez* (1753), Amb. 595; *White* v. *White* (1802), 7 Ves. 423; *A.-G.* v. *Price* (1810), 17 Ves. 371; *Bernal* v. *Bernal* (1838), 3 My. & Cr. 559; *Browne* v. *Whalley*, [1866] W.N. 386; *Gillam* v. *Taylor* (1873), L.R. 16 Eq. 581; *A.-G.* v. *Northumberland* (1877), 7 Ch.D. 745. In the first two cases it was not altogether clear whether the gift was in perpetuity or for immediate distribution.
3 *A.-G.* v. *Northumberland* (1877), 7 Ch.D. 745, at 752, *per* JESSEL M.R. disapproving WICKENS V.C. in *Gillam* v. *Taylor* (1873), L.R. 16 Eq. 581: "How the Vice-Chancellor came to make such a singular mistake, supposing he is correctly reported, I cannot tell; because there was nobody on the bench or off it who was more familiar with charity cases than he was."
4 *Carr* v. *Bedford* (1678), 2 Rep. Ch. 146; *Griffiths* v. *Jones* (1686), Freem. 96; *Goodinge* v. *Goodinge* (1749), 1 Ves. Sen. 231; *Edge* v. *Salisbury* (1749), Amb. 70; *Widmore* v. *Woodruffe* (1766), Amb. 636. In *Brunsden* v. *Woolredge* (1765), Amb. 507 it was far from clear whether there was to be an immediate distribution of the whole fund or the creation of an endowment.
5 *A.-G.* v. *Buckland* (1741) cited in Amb. 71; 2 Atk. 328; *White* v. *White* (1802), 7 Ves. 423 as explained in *Re Scarisbrick*, [1951] Ch. 622, at 641; *Mahon* v. *Savage* (1803), 1 Sch. & Lef. 111 (Lord REDESDALE).
6 [1950] Ch. 226.
7 [1951] Ch. 622.

D

amount to the public or a section of the public, said that there was an exception to the general rule in that trusts or gifts for the relief of poverty had been held to be charitable even though they were limited in their application to some aggregate of persons who were not a section of the public. This exception, he continued:[1]

> "cannot be accounted for by reference to any principle, but is established by a series of authorities of long standing, and must at the present date be accepted as valid, at all events as far as this Court is concerned (see *Re Compton*[2]) though doubtless open to review in the House of Lords (as appears from the observations of Lords Simonds and Morton of Henryton in *Oppenheim* v. *Tobacco Securities Trust Co., Ltd.*[3])."

Faced with the contention that a gift for the benefit of poor relations only qualified as charitable if it was perpetual in character, JENKINS L.J. observed that there was no sufficient ground in the authorities for such a view and held[4] that a gift for immediate distribution among poor relations, kindred and so forth is charitable, except in cases where the intention of the donor, derived from the construction of the documents, is to confine the benefit to statutory next of kin. Outside this limit, the court confirmed, no line could be drawn, and objects ought not therefore to be treated as less extensive where the gift is for immediate distribution than where a perpetual trust is intended.

The decision in Dingle v. Turner

The anomalous nature of the poor relations cases was much commented on. As HARMAN L.J. said in *I.R.Comrs.* v. *Educational Grants Association, Ltd.*[5] they "stick out like a sore thumb". Their fate in the House of Lords was naturally the subject of speculation. There had been at least one decision of the supreme tribunal overruling a relatively long standing decision in this field.[6] But the overruled case in question was a decision at first instance and stood on its own. It is true that the House of Lords has power to overrule even a long established *course of decisions* of the courts, but in general the House will only exercise this power in plain cases where serious inconvenience or injustice would result from perpetuating an erroneous rule of law.[7] Moreover Lord SIMONDS observed in *Oppenheim* v. *Tobacco Securities Trust, Ltd.*[8] that it would be very unwise "to cast any doubt upon decisions of respectable antiquity in order to introduce a greater harmony into the law of charity as a whole". Ancient decisions should not be lightly disturbed when men have accepted them and regulated their dispositions in reliance upon them.[9] This approach was adopted by the House of Lords when it was called upon to review the poor relations cases in *Dingle* v. *Turner*.[10] The testator directed the application of the income of a particular fund

---

1 *Ibid.*, 649–650.
2 [1945] Ch. 123.
3 [1951] A.C. 297.
4 [1951] Ch. 622, at 657, citing *Tudor on Charities* (5th edn.) 27.
5 [1967] Ch. 993, at 1011; and see Goodman Report (1976) 17–18.
6 *National Anti-Vivisection Society* v. *I.R.Comrs.*, [1948] A.C. 31 overruling *Re Foveaux*, [1895] 2 Ch. 501.
7 *Admiralty Comrs.* v. *Valverda*, [1938] A.C. 173, at 194, *per* Lord WRIGHT.
8 [1951] A.C. 297, at 308–309.
9 *Bourne* v. *Keane*, [1919] A.C. 815, at 860.
10 [1972] A.C. 601.

in paying pensions to poor employees of a family company. The case therefore concerned poor employees and not poor relations but Lord CROSS reviewed the poor relations cases as well as the cases on poor employees.

GIFTS FOR OTHER LIMITED CLASSES

In trusts for the relief of poverty the fact that the relief is to be confined to employees of a particular limited company or industrial organisation does not invalidate the trust. Thus in *Re Gosling*[1] a gift to form a fund for the purpose of pensioning off the old and worn out clerks of a firm was held to be a good charitable bequest while in *Gibson* v. *South American Stores, Ltd.*[2] a trust for the relief of poverty amongst the employees and ex-employees of a company and their families has held to be a charity by the Court of Appeal.

In *Re Young's Will Trusts*[3] a testator by his will gave the residue of his estate to the trustees of the benevolent fund of the Savage Club on trust to use the same for the assistance of members of that club who might fall on evil days. DANCKWERTS J. upheld the gift on the ground that there was no distinction between a gift for the relief of poverty of employees of a limited company and a similar gift in favour of members of a club. This argument also applies where the necessitous beneficiaries are members of a trade union or other similar body.[4] A trust for needy or deserving Toronto members of a club has also been upheld as being for the relief of poverty.[5]

A trust for the relief of poverty may be valid even though the persons to be benefited are limited to those of a particular sex or condition, such as widows,[6] spinsters,[7] or working men,[8] or to persons of a particular age group such as "the aged",[9] or "young women".[10] The benefits may also be validly limited to persons answering a particular description such as poor emigrants,[11] poor struggling youths of merit,[12] poor pious persons[13] or debtors.[14] Even indigent bachelors and widowers "who have shown sympathy with science" are good objects of charity.[15]

---

1 (1900), 48 W.R. 300; and see *Re Rayner* (1920), 122 L.T. 577 where one of the gifts was to relieve incapacitated employees of a company. The latter case was criticised on other grounds; see *Re Compton*, [1945] Ch. 123, 134. And see *Dingle* v. *Turner, supra*.

2 [1950] Ch. 177; and see *Re Coulthurst*, [1951] Ch. 661 (trust to apply income for widows and orphans of deceased bank officials).

3 [1955] 1 W.L.R. 1269.

4 *Spiller* v. *Maude* (1881), 32 Ch.D. 158 n.; *Re Lacy*, [1899] 2 Ch. 149 (Royal General Theatrical Association); *Pease* v. *Pattinson* (1886), 32 Ch.D. 154 (Miners Permanent Relief Fund Friendly Society); *Re Buck*, [1896] 2 Ch. 727 (Commercial Travellers Society); *Re Mead's Trust Deed*, [1961] 1 W.L.R. 1244 ("NATSOPA": but all bar one of trusts non-charitable because no poverty restriction).

5 *Re Bethel* (1971), 17 D.L.R. (3d) 652.

6 *Re Coulthurst*, [1951] Ch. 661, C.A.

7 *Re Dudgeon* (1896), 74 L.T. 613.

8 *Guinness Trust (London Fund)* v. *West Ham Borough Council*, [1959] 1 W.L.R. 233.

9 *Re Dudgeon, supra*.

10 See cases cited in note 7, at 29 *supra*.

11 See cases cited in note 1, at 29 *supra*.

12 *Milne's Executors* v. *Aberdeen University Court* (1905), 7 F. (Ct. of Sess.) 642.

13 *Nash* v. *Morley* (1842), 5 Beav. 177.

14 *A.-G.* v. *Painter-Stainers' Co.* (1788) 2 Cox Eq. Cas. 51; *A.-G.* v. *Ironmongers Co.* (1834), 2 My. & K. 576.

15 *Weir* v. *Crum-Brown*, [1908] A.C. 162, H.L.

Likewise the inmates of a work-house[1] or a hospital[2] may be the objects of a valid trust for the relief of poverty.

The permutations of limited groups are virtually endless: the victims of a particular disaster,[3] the members of a particular regiment,[4] the poor of a particular religion[5] or religious denomination.[6] Indeed in America a trust was upheld although limited to worthy, deserving, poor, white, American, Protestant, Democratic widows and orphans residing in the town of Bridgeport.[7]

Lord HARDWICKE L.C. in *A.-G.* v. *Pearce*[8] said that a gift for poor house-keepers was charitable and there is a respectable line of authorities confirming the charitable nature of trusts for needy persons in a trade, profession or calling. Thus a trust to relieve the poverty of old decayed tradesmen,[9] domestic servants,[10] soldiers[11] or seamen[12] is charitable. In *Moggridge* v. *Thackwell*[13] a trust for the relief of poor clergymen was held valid and in *Spiller* v. *Maude*[14] a trust for the aid of poor actors was upheld. A similar result would undoubtedly attend a trust for the relief of poor barristers, doctors or other professional men.[15]

Again a gift for the relief of the poor in a city[16] or town[17] is certainly charitable. But what if the geographical limitation is more restricted? It has been held that the poor of a village of less than 400 inhabitants are proper objects of charity,[18] likewise the poor of a particular parish.[19] In *Bristow* v. *Bristow*[20] a trust for the poor on a particular estate was upheld and though the decision is criticised by Professor Scott,[21] on the ground that the class to be benefited was too narrow, it

---

1 *A.-G.* v. *Vint* (1850), 3 De G. & Sm. 704.
2 *Reading Corporation* v. *Lane* (1601), Duke, *The Law of Charitable Uses*, ed. Bridgman 361.
3 *Pease* v. *Pattinson* (1886), 32 Ch.D. 154; *Re Hartley Colliery Accident Relief Fund* (1908), 102 L.T. 165 n.; *Cross* v. *Lloyd-Greame* (1909), 102 L.T. 163 (only six victims).
4 *Re Donald*, [1909] 2 Ch. 410. A fortiori ex-servicemen generally; *Downing* v. *Taxation Comr.* (1971), 125 C.L.R. 185; and see *Re Gillespie*, [1965] V.R. 402; *Re Payne Estate* (1954), 11 W.W.R. 424 and *Re Booth*, [1954] N.Z.L.R. 1114.
5 *De Costa* v. *De Paz* (1754), 2 Swan. 487 n.; *Re Haendler* (1931), Times, 4th July (Jews); *A.-G.* v. *Mathieson*, [1907] 2 Ch. 383, C.A. (Mildmay Mission to the Jews).
6 *A.-G.* v. *Wansay* (1808), 15 Ves. 231 (Presbyterians); *Income Tax Special Purposes Comrs.* v. *Pemsel*, [1891] A.C. 531 (Moravians); *A.-G.* v. *Shore* (1843), 11 Sim. 592; *Shore* v. *Wilson* (1842), 9 Cl. & Fin. 355 (Unitarians); *A.-G.* v. *Lawes* (1849), 8 Hare. 32 (Irvingites); *Dawson* v. *Small* (1874), L.R. 18 Eq. 114 (Methodists).
7 *Beardsley* v. *Selectmen of Bridgeport* 53 Conn. 489 (1885) (U.S.).
8 (1740), 2 Atk. 87.
9 *Re White's Trusts* (1886), 33 Ch.D. 449; *A.-G.* v. *Painter-Stainers' Co.* (1788) 2 Cox Eq. Cas 51.
10 *Loscombe* v. *Wintringham* (1850), 13 Beav. 87; *Manorama Dassi* v. *Kali Charan Banerjee* (1904), I.L.R. 31 Calc. 616 (testator's poor servants) (HARINGTON J.).
11 *Re Donald*, [1909] 2 Ch. 410; *Re Robinson*, [1931] 2 Ch. 122.
12 *Powell* v. *A.-G.* (1817), 3 Mer. 48.
13 (1792), 1 Ves. 464.
14 (1881), 32 Ch.D. 158 n.; and see *Thompson* v. *Thompson* (1844), 1 Coll. 381 (unsuccessful literary men).
15 *Re Denison* (1974), 42 D.L.R. (3d) 652 (impoverished or indigent members of the Law Society of Upper Canada, their wives, widows and children).
16 *A.-G.* v. *Exeter Corporation* (1827), 2 Russ. 362; *Re Lousada* (1887), 82 L-T. Jo. 358.
17 *Russell* v. *Kellett* (1855), 3 Sm. & G. 264; *Re Lucas*, [1922] 2 Ch. 52; *Powell* v. *A.-G.* (1817), 3 Mer. 48.
18 *Re Monk*, [1927] 2 Ch. 197.
19 *Woodford* v. *Parkhurst* (1639), Duke 70 (378); *A.-G.* v. *Matthews* (1677), 2 Lev. 167; *A.-G.* v. *Comber* (1824), 2 Sim. & Str. 93; *Re Roadley*, [1930] 1 Ch. 524.
20 (1842), 5 Beav. 289.
21 *Trusts* (3rd edn.) para. 369.5.

is submitted that it is unobjectionable. There is, after all, the nexus of common employment in the case of the tenantry on a particular estate so that such a trust should be upheld on the principle of *Gibson* v. *South American Stores, Ltd.*[1] Admittedly in Ireland charitable status was refused to a trust for the benefit of the children of the settlor's tenants[2] but this was because there was nothing to indicate that the gift was for the children of *poor* persons. Nevertheless there is a decision of CHITTY J. which appears to be inconsistent with *Bristow* v. *Bristow*. In *Hoare* v. *Hoare*[3] a trust for keeping in order four existing almshouses for poor labourers on the estate of the settlor was held to be void. The *ratio decidendi* of this case was that the other gifts in the will indicated that the testator's intention was really to benefit the estate and not to do charity. Since it has been settled that the motive of the settlor is irrelevant it is submitted that *Hoare* v. *Hoare* cannot be considered a reliable authority on this point.

Another writer asserts that a gift for the poor of a particular street would not be charitable, again because the class of beneficiaries would be too narrow.[4] Yet the authority cited for this proposition does not support it,[5] and the proposition itself is on principle difficult to accept. If the poor of a village with less than 400 inhabitants or the poor of a small parish or presbytery are not too narrow a class, it seems illogical to draw the line so as to exclude the poor of other small geographical areas. Moreover since a trust for the relief of poverty among members of a club who have fallen on evil times is good, the same is surely true of a trust for the poor in a particular street.

---

1 [1950] Ch. 177, *cf. Manorama Dassi* v. *Banerjee* (1904), I.L.R. 31 Calc. 616 (poor relations, dependants and *servants* of the testator).

2 *Browne* v. *King* (1885), 17 L.R. Ir. 488; and see *A.-G. for Northern Ireland* v. *Forde*, [1932] N.I. 1, C.A.

3 (1886), 56 L.T. 147; *Re Tunno*, [1886] W.N. 154 (CHITTY J.) may be a similar case but the report is inadequate.

4 See P. S. Atiyah (1958), 21 M.L.R. 138, at 145.

5 Lord SIMONDS in *I.R.Comrs.* v. *Baddeley*, [1955] A.C. 572, at 591, was in fact discussing the fourth head in *Pemsel's* case (and not relief of poverty) when he gave his example of the inhabitants of a particular street. See also *Rogers* v. *Thomas* (1837), 2 Keen. 8 (gift to inhabitants of a street with no poverty restriction: not charitable) with which it is very difficult to reconcile *Re Christchurch Inclosure Act* (1888), 38 Ch.D. 520. The latter case has been doubted by J.W. Brunyate in 61 L.Q.R. 268, at 276 and 282.

Chapter 3

The Advancement of Education

The preamble to the Statute of Elizabeth recognises the charitable nature of education. There is reference there to "the maintenance of schools ... and scholars in universities" and to "the education and preferment of orphans". Gifts for the advancement of education expressed in the most general terms have been upheld in the courts. Thus a gift "for the increase of knowledge among men" is charitable:[1] so too is a gift "for the benefit, advancement and propagation of education and learning in every part of the world".[2] A gift "for educational purposes" is *prima facie* valid: in the absence of a context subverting it, a gift for educational purposes will be read as being a gift for such educational purposes as are charitable.[3] Such a construction is not only consistent with common sense, which should treat as synonymous "the purposes of education" and "educational purposes", but also follows the sound maxim "ut res magis valeat quam pereat". In the case of testamentary gifts there is a further argument: a testator should not be presumed to have intended to enact a solemn farce.[4] The court should lean against intestacy and in favour of charity.

Definition of education

It is convenient to start with a dictionary definition. The primary meaning, in modern parlance, of the word "education" is "the systematic instruction, schooling or training given to the young (and by extension to adults) in preparation for the work of life".[5] In the context of the law of charities, that is an adequate working definition. But it is apparent from the decided cases that there is considerable room for argument about what is required to equip a person for the work of life. In many cases the educational tendency or value of a particular gift will be obvious. Most people, for example, would agree on the educational value of studying a foreign language,[6] law,[7] natural history,[8] archaeology,[9]

---

1 *United States of America (President)* v. *Drummond* (1838), cited in 7 H.L.C. 124.

2 *Whicker* v. *Hume* (1858), 7 H.L.C. 124.

3 *Re Ward*, [1941] Ch. 308, at 317–318.

4 *Re Harrison* (1885), 30 Ch.D. 390.   5 Shorter Oxford Dictionary.

6 *A.-G.* v. *Flood* (1816), Hayes. & Jo. App. xxi, at xxxviii (Irish language); *Brownjohn* v. *Gale*, [1869] W.N. 133; *Re Mariette*, [1915] 2 Ch. 284 (Classics); *Re Koettgen's Will Trusts*, [1954] Ch. 252; *Re Schulz's Estate*, [1961] S.A.S.R. 377 (German studies at Adelaide University).

7 *Smith* v. *Kerr*, [1902] 1 Ch. 774, C.A.; *Re Mason*, [1971] N.Z.L.R. 714.

8 *Re Mellody*, [1918] 1 Ch. 228 (annual field day for children as an aid to nature study); *Re Benham*, [1939] S.A.S.R. 450.

9 *Yates* v. *University College London* (1873), 8 Ch. App. 454; (1875), L.R. 7 H.L. 438; *Re British School of Egyptian Archaeology*, [1954] 1 W.L.R. 546 (Egyptology).

economics,[1] geology,[2] or shorthand typewriting and book-keeping.[3] Again mechanical sciences and engineering,[4] theology,[5] religious instruction,[6] medicine[7] and technical education[8] are obviously charitable objects. On the other hand, certain objects are too frivolous to rank as educational. The compilation of lists of Derby winners,[9] the study of racing or football "form", the study and preservation of steam engines,[10] the provision of facilities for model engineering without any instruction,[11] a library of thrillers, a public exhibition of junk:[12] none of these is a charitable object. They also are clear cases.

Other cases provide more difficulty. As Lord CRANWORTH remarked, in another context:[13]

> "There is no possibility of mistaking midnight for noon; but at what precise moment twilight becomes darkness is hard to determine."

The point at which education shades into hobby is a difficult one to gauge, and in this twilight world the search for principle is like looking for a needle in a haystack.

In any event, the alleged educational purposes must not be improper. A school for prostitutes or pickpockets would obviously fail to qualify as charitable.[14] So too a public library if found to be devoted entirely to works of pornography or of a corrupting nature would not be charitable.[15]

Another limit is that it is not enough that the object should be educational in the sort of loose sense in which all experience may be said to be educative.[16]

Perhaps the nearest that one can get to a statement of principle that is not completely tautologous is to say that a gift will be of educational value if it has the effect of (1) training the mind or, (2) raising the artistic taste of the country or (3) improving the sum of communicable knowledge in an area which education may cover. Many of the cases which "go to the verge of the law" are concerned with the first question: does the gift have the effect of training the mind? Gifts in favour of those at school and university are singled out for special preference in this respect. They will be discussed first. Then it is convenient to deal with gifts to promote culture and the fine arts, which raise the artistic taste of the country. Lastly the extent to which gifts for research are valid must be considered.

---

1 *Re Berridge* (1890), 63 L.T. 470, C.A.; *Re Cobbett* (1921), 17 Tas.L.R. 139 (political economy).
2 *Re Spencer* (1928), 34 O.W.N. 29 (scholarship fund at Manitoba University for research)
3 *Re Koettgen's Will Trusts*, [1954] Ch. 252.
4 *Institution of Civil Engineers v. I.R.Comrs.*, [1932] 1 K.B. 149; *Salvation Army (Victoria) Property Trust v. Fern Tree Gully Corporation* (1952), 85 C.L.R. 159 (aviation).
5 *Re Regan* (1957), 8 D.L.R. (2d) 541.
6 *A.-G. v. Stepney* (1804), 10 Ves. 22.
7 *In the Estate of Schulz* [1961] S.A.S.R. 377 (medical research at University of Hamburg); *Royal College of Surgeons of England v. National Provincial Bank, Ltd.*, [1952] A.C. 631 (surgery); and see *M'Lean v. Henderson's Trustees* (1880), 7 R. (Ct. of Sess.) 601 (phrenology).
8 *Royal North Shore Hospital of Sydney v. A.-G. for New South Wales* (1938), 60 C.L.R. 396.
9 Brunyate (1945), 61 L.Q.R. 268, at 273.
10 [1965] Ch. Com. Rep. 30 (Norfolk Steam Engine Club).
11 *Whitchurch (Cardiff) and District Model Engineering Society*, [1967] Ch. Com. Rep. 48 App. D.8.
12 *Re Pinion*, [1965] Ch. 85.
13 *Boyse v. Rossborough* (1857), 6 H.L.Cas. 22, at 45.
14 *Re Pinion*, [1965] Ch. 85, at 105, *per* HARMAN L.J.; *Re Macduff*, [1896] 2 Ch. 451, at 464.
15 [1965] Ch. 85, at 106, *per* HARMAN L.J.
16 *I.R.Comrs. v. Baddeley*, [1955] A.C. 572, *per* Lord SIMONDS, at 585.

CONTENT OF EDUCATION AT SCHOOLS AND UNIVERSITIES

Where school children are the intended beneficiaries of a gift the courts have usually shewn themselves willing to stretch the concept of education to very benevolent limits. Judges have tended to echo the attitude and sentiments of EVE J. in *Re De Noailles*:[1]

> "Here again I think one must have regard to the main object of education. I know that there are a large number of purists who tell you that the only object of education is to get information, but that is a class of person who I think might be asked what is the use of information unless you turn it to some practical use. The mere stuffing of information into a boy or girl may make them very priggish, but it does not make them of much use in life unless they know how to apply that information for the purpose of becoming useful citizens."[2]

It is hardly surprising that EVE J. himself accepted the argument that organised games are part and parcel of a public school education: *mens sana in corpore sano* was a truism of the public school system. In *Re Mariette*[3] he upheld various gifts to Aldenham School: one gift, endowing a book prize for Classics, clearly promoted academic endeavour[4] but there were other gifts which the learned judge upheld to be used in building Eton fives courts and squash courts and in providing athletic prizes. This decision was followed by HARMAN J. in *Re Geere's Will Trusts (No. 2)*[5] where it was held a bequest of £10,000 to Marlborough College for the provision of "a proper swimming bath and hot water baths" was a valid charitable gift. Likewise the fostering of rugby at a university has been held to be a charitable purpose.[6]

A trust to provide a suitable playground for children in a city is also charitable.[7] In *Re Mellody*[8] EVE J. went a step further than his decision in *Re Mariette*[9] and upheld a trust to provide an annual treat or field day for school children. Such a field day might well, the judge said, be made the occasion for pointing out those objects of the countryside and nature which they had learnt about at school, and the possibility of being included in the list of those elected to participate would be an incentive to regular attendance and hard work at school.[10] One writer has commented that *Re Mariette* and *Re Mellody* "go to the verge of the law".[11] But today they seem less surprising. The decision in *Re*

---

1 (1916), 85 L.J. Ch. 807.

2 A not dissimilar theory of education was propounded by Mr. Wackford Squeers (see Charles Dickens, *Nicholas Nickleby*, Chapter 8) "We go upon the practical mode of teaching Nickleby; the regular education system. C-l-e-a-n, clean, verb active, to make bright, to scour. W-i-n, win, d-e-r, der, winder, a casement. When the boy knows this out of book [*sic*] he goes and does it."

3 [1915] 2 Ch. 284.

4 As does a cash prize: *Re Weaver*, [1963] V.R. 256.

5 [1954] C.L.Y. 388; see also (1954), *Times*, May 19. The gift was applied *cy-près* since the school already had a sufficient swimming pool and baths.

6 *Kearins* v. *Kearins* (1957), S.R. (N.S.W.) 286 (Sydney University).

7 *Re Chesters* (1934), cited in *I.R.Comrs.* v. *Baddeley*, [1955] A.C. 572.

8 [1918] 1 Ch. 228.

9 [1915] 2 Ch. 284.

10 [1918] 1 Ch. 228, at 230–231.

11 *Tyssen on Charitable Bequests* (3rd edn.) 117.

Mellody was followed in *Re Ward's Estate*[1] where a trust to provide an annual outing for the children of members of an ex-servicemen's club was upheld. The virtues of first-hand experience were also stressed by FARWELL J. in holding the Zoological Society to be a charity:[2]

> "A ride on an elephant may be educational. At any rate it brings the reality of the elephant and its uses to the child's mind and in that broad sense is charitable."[3]

A bequest falling on the other side of the line, going beyond the verge of the law, is to be found in *Re Ward's Estate*[4] where a testator left a gift to provide on every Bank Holiday a pennyworth of sweets each for all boys and girls below the age of 14 resident within a certain parish. RUSSELL J. held this to be a non-charitable object because the benefits were not confined to children who had attended school.

In *Re Dupree's Deed Trusts*[5] a trust to promote annual chess tournaments among boys unders 21 of a city was held to be charitable. Evidence was in fact given by a local education officer who said that the playing of chess was of considerable educational value. VAISEY J. confessed that the case was a little near the line and continued:[6]

> "One feels perhaps that one is on a rather slippery slope. If chess, why not draughts? if draughts, why not bezique? and so on, through to bridge,[7] whist and by another route stamp-collecting and the acquisition of birds' eggs. When these particular pursuits come up for consideration in connection with the problem whether or no there is in existence a charitable trust, the problem will have to be faced and dealt with. I say nothing about that. Nor do I say that if this trust had been without a geographical limitation, if it had been for the promotion of chess-playing *in vacuo* or at large, it might not well be that the area of what is regarded as charitable would have been overstepped."

The suggestion that a non-charitable gift can be invested with a charitable nature if it is localised is now discredited.[8] On the other hand, it is reasonable to assume from the doubts expressed about chess-playing *in vacuo* that the gift in *Re Dupree's Deed Trusts* would not have been held charitable had it not been confined to youths under 21.[9] The hobbies of an adult may widen the minds of school children and in that broad sense fulfil an educational purpose. Stamp-collecting may bring the reality of geography and history to the child's mind: the acquisition of birds' eggs may stimulate his or her enthusiasm for natural history. But these activities can hardly be said to train the minds of adults.

---

1 (1937), 81 Sol. Jo. 397.
2 *Re Lopes*, [1931] 2 Ch. 130.
3 [1931] 2 Ch. 130, at 136.
4 (1937), 81 Sol. Jo. 397.
5 [1945] Ch. 16.
6 *Ibid.*, at 20–21.
7 It is possible that bridge would be held to be educational in schools: see 61 L.Q.R. 12.
8 *Baddeley* v. *I.R.Comrs.*, [1953] Ch. 504, at 527, *per* JENKINS L.J. explaining *Goodman* v. *Saltash* (1882), 7 App. Cas. 633; and see also *Re Gwyon*, [1930] 1 Ch. 255 which was not cited to VAISEY J.
9 *Cf. Re Mariette*, [1915] 2 Ch. 284.

The Boy Scout Movement is clearly charitable. The instruction of boys of all classes in the principles of discipline, loyalty and good citizenship is obviously "training in preparation for the work of life", and so educational. The Boy Scouts Association (to give the Movement its proper name) was incorporated by royal charter in 1912 and was always treated as a charity: its status as such was confirmed judicially by CLAUSON J. in *Re Alexander*[1] and VAISEY J. in *Re Webber*.[2] At the other end of the scale the Charity Commissioners accept that receiving and caring for children between the ages of three and five years in a day nursery is charitable.[3]

A case in which the Court of Appeal showed itself rather less than benevolent was *Re Cole*.[4] There charitable status was denied to a gift to apply income to the general benefit and general welfare of children in a delinquents' home. The trust failed on the majority view because it was not limited to charitable purposes. Lord EVERSHED dissented on the grounds that the words "general benefit" and "general welfare" postulated the application of the gift towards the welfare and benefit of the children taken as a whole. It is true that under the terms of the gift the income might have been used to amuse and interest the children by providing amenities such as television or gramophones, but such amenities could be said to play a proper and even necessary part in the rehabilitation of such children, just as they do in hospitals.[5] In one report of the judgment of EVE J. in *Re Mariette*[6] the learned judge pointed out[7] that the education of boys and young men between the ages of ten and nineteen:

> "involves periods of relaxation and leisure, and no-one with experience of youth will deny that unless these periods are usefully occupied the truth of the old saying that there is a certain individual always ready to find mischief for idle hands will soon be demonstrated".

This argument applies *a fortiori* in the case of delinquent children. If Eton fives are a necessary part of an Aldenham schoolboy's education one might be forgiven for thinking that the decision in *Re Cole* is unduly harsh. Though it has been followed in a more recent case,[8] it was with reluctance; and it has been much criticised.[9]

CULTURE AND THE FINE ARTS

The content of education is not confined merely to those subjects usually taught in schools or other educational institutions: it includes some subjects

---

1 (1932), *Times*, 30th June (gift for providing holiday camps for the boy scouts of Clapham and Brixton).
2 [1954] 1 W.L.R. 1500; *cf. Re Lipinski's Will Trusts*, [1976] Ch. 235, at 242.
3 [1966] Ch. Com. Rep. 30.
4 [1958] Ch. 877.
5 See *Re Adams*, [1968] Ch. 80.
6 (1915), 113 L.T. 920.
7 *Ibid.*, at 923. This oblique reference to Satan does not appear in [1915] 2 Ch. 284.
8 *Re Sahal's Will Trusts*, [1958] 1 W.L.R. 1243.
9 See 74 L.Q.R. 481; 75 L.Q.R. 22.

more naturally classifiable under the head of "culture". Thus trusts to establish or maintain public libraries,[1] museums,[2] zoos[3] and botanical gardens[4] are valid, and in one case a trust to maintain certain picturesque Elizabethan cottages was upheld.[5]

Doubts were formerly entertained whether trusts to encourage the fine arts were charitable. Lord COZENS-HARDY M.R., for example, denied the charitable nature of a gift to encourage artistic pursuits or assist needy students in art.[6] In *Re Allsop*[7] the Nottingham Sacred Harmonic Society successfully contended that it was not a charity in order to avoid the application of the Mortmain Acts. CHITTY J. found as a fact that the expressed objects of the society were not merely to promote public music as an art but also to provide amusement for its members. In the light of these two cases one textbook[8] stated that the fine arts are probably not regarded as objects of charity. This view was, however, hardly warranted by the two cases cited;[9] and it was difficult to reconcile with the decision in *Re Shakespeare Memorial Trust*[10] where a gift to provide a national theatre to perform Shakespeare's plays and revive classical drama was upheld. At any rate the Court of Appeal in *Royal Choral Society* v. *I.R.Comrs.*[11] stigmatised the textbook statement as "inadequate and misleading" and held that the Royal Choral Society should be exempt from income tax as an educational charity. There were in fact only ten members of the Royal Choral Society and they were not performers. MACNAGHTEN J. at first instance implied that the incidental amusement of the members might have vitiated the society's status[12] but Lord GREENE M.R.[13] and DU PARCQ L.J.[14] both pointed out that the element of pleasure in teaching and participating in choral music is not the purpose of those processes but a by-product.

Two later cases have established that gifts to promote the training of singers

---

1 *Abbott* v. *Fraser* (1874) L.R. 6 P.C. 96. *Aliter* if the library is private: *Carne* v. *Long* (1860), 2 De G.F. & J. 75; *Re Russell Institution*, [1898] 2 Ch. 72; *Re Jones*, [1898] 2 Ch. 83; *Re Pitt-Rivers*, [1902] 1 Ch. 403, C.A.

2 *Re Holburne* (1885), 53 L.T. 212; *Re Spence*, [1938] Ch. 96; *British Museum* v. *White* (1826), 2 Sim. & St. 594; *Re Allsop* (1884), 1 T.L.R. 4. Likewise picture galleries: *Gwynn* v. *Cardon* cited in (1805), 10 Ves. 522, at 533; *Abbott* v. *Fraser* (1874), L.R. 6 P.C. 96; *Re Shaw's Will Trusts*, [1952] Ch. 163.

3 *Re Lopes*, [1931] 2 Ch. 130; *North of England Zoological Society* v. *Chester Rural District Council*, [1959] 1 W.L.R. 773.

4 *Townley* v. *Bedwell* (1801), 6 Ves. 194 discussed in *Jarman on Wills* (8th edn.) 228; *Harrison* v. *Southampton Corporation* (1854), 2 Sm. & G. 387.

5 *Re Cranstoun*, [1932] 1 Ch. 537.

6 *Re Ogden* (1909), 25 T.L.R. 382.

7 (1884), 1 T.L.R. 4.

8 *Tudor on Charities* (5th edn.) 39. The error was corrected in the 6th edn.

9 The report of *Re Ogden, supra*, is unsatisfactory; see *per* Lord GREENE M.R. in *Royal Choral Society* v. *I.R.Comrs.* [1943] 2 All E.R. 101, at 107 and *per* DANCKWERTS J. in *Crystal Palace Trustees* v. *Minister of Town and Country Planning*, [1951] Ch. 132, at 140. The decision in *Re Allsop, supra*, really turned on the finding of fact that amusement was an expressed object of the society.

10 [1923] 2 Ch. 398.

11 [1943] 2 All E.R. 101.

12 [1942] 2 All E.R. 610. This prompted one learned writer to comment that the distinction between this case and *Re Allsop, supra*, was that apparently the members of the *Royal Choral Society* were not amused while the members of the Nottingham Society were: see 59 L.Q.R. 113.

13 [1943] 2 All E.R. 101, 104.

14 *Ibid.*, at 109.

of serious music[1] and better organists[2] or to foster the appreciation of the works of a noted composer[3] are valid.

In *Re Shaw's Will Trusts*[4] VAISEY J. in construing the will of Bernard Shaw's wife, upheld a gift expressed to be for the purpose of bringing masterpieces of fine art within the reach of the people of Ireland and of teaching them various social graces. The charitable nature of the latter part of the gift seems a little far fetched and indeed Lord SOMERVELL OF HARROW in *I.R.Comrs.* v. *Baddeley*[5] observed that "training in social behaviour ... in manners is plainly not a charity". Although it has been said that "manners makyth man" the decision in *Re Shaw's Will Trusts* as to the latter part of the gift seems wrong.

On the other hand in *Re Hales*,[6] which was decided not long after the *Royal Choral Society*[7] case but before *Re Levien*,[8] a gift to provide prizes for annual competitions to encourage local industries in North Staffordshire such as engravers, painters, throwers, designers and artists and such meritable achievements as singing and pianoforte and violin playing was held not to be a valid charitable bequest for educational purposes. No reason was given for the decision in the short report which is available but it appears to have been argued that a mere trust to encourage music or the arts was not charitable. Now it is perfectly true that a gift "to encourage artistic pursuits" has been held to be invalid[9] and would probably still be held so. As Lord GREENE M.R. said,[10] such a gift could be applied

> "in merely providing for one or two individuals paints and paint brushes, or a grand piano on which the beneficiaries could play in their drawing room".

But encouragement by means of *competitions* can only have the effect of raising musical or artistic standards generally and both these objects have been held charitable. In the light of more recent cases it is probable that the decision in *Re Hales* would not be followed: it was certainly criticised at the time,[11] before lapsing into obscurity.[12]

Sometimes, of course, it is plain from the context that the settlor is using the word "artistic" in a particularly wide sense which includes objects which are neither educational nor charitable. Thus in *Associated Artists, Ltd.* v. *I.R.Comrs.*[13] UPJOHN J. held that a non-profit making theatrical association whose objects were *inter alia* to present classical artistic cultural and educational dramatic works was not a charity. Having construed the words disjunctively the learned judge found that in the particular context before him it was impossible to define what was meant by an *artistic* dramatic work: the term was too vague.[14]

---

1 *Re Levien*, [1955] 3 All E.R. 35. *Semble* the music must be "serious".
2 *Ibid.*
3 *Re Delius' Will Trusts*, [1957] Ch. 299. ROXBURGH J., at 306, implies that the position would be different if the music were by some inadequate composer.
4 [1952] Ch. 163.
5 [1955] A.C. 572, at 616.
6 (1944), *Times*, 9th November.
7 [1943] 2 All E.R. 101.
8 [1955] 3 All E.R. 35.
9 *Re Ogden*, *supra*.
10 *Royal Choral Society* v. *I.R.Comrs.*, *supra*, at 107.
11 See 9 Conv. (N.S.) 85.
12 It is nowhere else noted.
13 [1956] 1 W.L.R. 752.
14 *Ibid.*, at 758.

RESEARCH

It has been said that in order for a gift to rank as charitable under the head of education an element of teaching should be present. Thus HARMAN J. in *Re Shaw*[1] was of the opinion that

> "if the object be merely the increase of knowledge that is not in itself a charitable object unless it be combined with teaching or education".

Other cases indicate that teaching in this sense is more akin to imparting knowledge than to formal class-room instruction. But HARMAN J.'s dictum, which is based on earlier dicta,[2] might suggest that academic research without any element of teaching is not for the advancement of education.

In *Re Shaw* itself the dramatist George Bernard Shaw left the residue of his estate upon trust for a period of 21 years to ascertain how much time and expense could be saved by the substitution of a new alphabet for the present English alphabet. This gift was held not to be charitable. One of the two grounds of the decision appears to be that the trust was not educational because it merely added to the sum of knowledge without propagating it.[3]

In the later case of *Re Hopkins Will Trusts*[4] WILBERFORCE J. upheld a trust for research into the evidence in favour of Bacon's authorship of the plays ascribed to Shakespeare. He discussed the extent to which a gift for research could be considered educational and concluded that the words *combined with teaching or education* "though well-explaining what Harman J. had in mind when he rejected the gift in *Re Shaw* are not easy to interpret in relation to other facts". While accepting that research of a private character for the benefit of members of a society would not normally be educational or charitable WILBERFORCE J. thought that academic research would be. To be charitable, he said,[5] "research must either be of educational value to the researcher or must be so directed as to lead to something which will pass into the store of educational material or so as to improve the sum of communicable knowledge in an area which education may cover—education in this last context extending to the formation of literary taste and appreciation".

A very similar approach had in fact been adopted by the High Court of Australia some fifty years previously. In *Taylor* v. *Taylor*[6] a gift to the advancement of scientific research generally was upheld as charitable. GRIFFITH C.J. thought that the term "the advancement of scientific research generally" imported the disclosure of the results of the research to the public[7] but he expressed doubts on the validity of the distinction between the acquisition and the diffusion of knowledge. "I confess my inability", he said, "to apprehend how the stock of available knowledge can be increased without diffusion of the

---

1 [1957] 1 W.L.R. 729.

2 *Whicker* v. *Hume* (1858), 7 H.L.Cas 124 at 154 (Lord CHELMSFORD L.C.) and 166 (Lord WENSLEYDALE); *Re Macduff*, [1896] 2 Ch. 451, at 472 (RIGBY L.J.).

3 The other *ratio* was that the court could not say that the gift promoted a public benefit when the purpose of the research was to prove that very fact.

4 [1965] Ch. 669.

5 *Ibid.*, at 680.

6 (1910), 10 C.L.R. 218.

7 The court was unanimous on this point.

addition to the existing stock. Knowledge confined to the bosom of the discoverer is not to my mind 'available' in any rational sense of the term."[1] He did not however have to pronounce upon the correctness of the various dicta cited from *Whicker* v. *Hume*[2] because he grounded his decision on the point of construction. ISAACS J. on the other hand would have followed *Whicker* v. *Hume* if he had thought that scientific research and mere learning were the same.[3]

The test propounded by WILBERFORCE J. is clearly right. According to that test the trust in *Re Shaw*[4] would perhaps still have failed to qualify as charitable on the basis that research into a new alphabet would not be of educational value to the researcher, and would not be so directed as to lead to something which would pass into the store of educational material, or to improve the sum of communicable knowledge in an area which education may cover. On the other hand by the same test, trusts for scientific or historical research are clearly charitable. Certainly in America trusts for scientific[5] and historical[6] research have been held to be charitable and it is inconceivable that an English court would decide otherwise.[7] Medical[8] and veterinary[9] research have been held to be charitable; and in South Africa the encouragement of inventors has been held to be capable of qualifying as a charitable purpose.[10] The Charity Commissioners too have itemised examples of research charities which they have registered. Some are medical research charities such as the Heart Valve Research Fund and the Brain Research Trust, others are concerned with scientific and technological research. The Borrow Dental Milk Foundation carries out research into the fluoridation of milk for human consumption: The International Hydrofoil Society was formed to advance the study of and research into the science, technology and safety of hydrofoils.[11]

Educational value

With many gifts the purpose is so obviously of educational value to the community that to call evidence on the matter would be absurd. But there are, as we have seen, border-line cases and it then falls to the court to ascertain by evidence whether the gift has any educational tendency. The leading case on this point is *Re Pinion*.[12] The testator gave his studio, paintings, old furniture, silver and other objects to his trustees to offer to the National Trust. He left his residuary estate as an endowment to maintain the collection as a museum should

---

1 (1910), 10 C.L.R. 218, at 224.

2 (1858), 7 H.L.Cas. 124.

3 *Ibid.*, at 235.

4 [1957] 1 W.L.R. 729.

5 *Matter of Frasch* 245 N.Y. 174 (1927) (U.S.) (agricultural chemistry); *People ex rel. Hellyer* v. *Morton* 373 Ill. 72 (1940) (U.S.) (practical scientific research in horticulture and arboriculture); *Taysum* v. *El Paso National Bank* 256 S.W. (2d) 172 (1953) (U.S.) (electricity).

6 *Molly Varnum Chapter, D.A.R.* v. *City of Lowell* 204 Mass. 487, at 492 (1910) (U.S.).

7 See *Re Compton*, [1945] Ch. 123, at 127, *per* Lord GREENE M.R. (*semble* historical or scientific research charitable).

8 *Re Travis*, [1947] N.Z.L.R. 382 (cancer research); *In the Estate of Schulz*, [1961] S.A.S.R. 377 (medical research at University of Hamburg).

9 *London University* v. *Yarrow* (1857), 1 De G. & J. 72.

10 *Standard Bank of SA, Ltd.* v. *Betts Brown* 1958 (3) SA 713 (N).

11 [1971] Ch. Com. Rep. 29 (para. 98).

12 [1965] Ch. 85, C.A. An identical decision in the U.S.A. was *Medical Society of South Carolina* v. *South Carolina National Bank* 197 S.C. 96 (1941) (U.S.).

the National Trust decline the gift (which it did). Expert witnesses were agreed that the collection was of a low quality and they were also of the opinion that the collection had no educational value. WILBERFORCE, J. rejected the argument that the court should not inquire into the educational merits of the collection but reached the conclusion that the evidence did not establish with sufficient certainty that no recognisable benefit enured to the public. The Court of Appeal unanimously reversed his decision on the later point[1] but agreed with the learned judge on the need to hear expert evidence when the utility of such a gift was brought into question. In most of the previous authorities such a need had not been expressly recognised because the educational value of the gifts in question was usually accepted by all parties.[2] Thus in *Royal Choral Society* v. *I.R.Comrs.*[3] there was no dispute about the high standard of the Society's work, while in *Re Delius*[4] it was unanimously agreed that no question could arise as to the adequacy of Delius as a composer.

The principle in *Re Pinion* is not, of course, confined to art museums. A trust to publish writings which are of no literary historical or other educational value whatever would not be upheld as charitable since *ex hypothesi* the gift would be of no *benefit* to the public. That was the ground of decision in the Australian case of *Re Elmore*[5] where it was held that the testator's manuscripts were of no literary merit or educational value: the judge followed *Re Pinion*.[6] A biographical work may lack literary critical or biographical merit but still be educational because it stimulates interest by reason of its demerits.[7] And provided a gift is for the advancement of literature or beneficial to the literary development of the country the fact that it promotes other objects too does not matter.[8]

Sometimes a general charitable intent is discoverable in the framework of a testator's gift. Thus in one case an American court applied *cy-près* a fund given to publish writings which were clearly irrational, finding within the will an intention to benefit mankind by scientific and philosophic researches.[9]

Another American case of interest concerned a gift by a testatrix to edit, print and publish at a reasonable cost the diaries of her ancestor, an early lawyer and banker in Indianapolis. The gift failed even though the diaries, which covered a period of 50 years, were written by a man of literary ability and contained unique material relating to the early history of the city. The court was unable to discover an intent to establish a public trust since no beneficiary was disclosed and the purpose was as consistent with private gain as with charity. Moreover, it was held, there was no obligation to devote the diaries to educational purposes.[10] The reasoning is difficult to follow. The failure to express an

---

1 HARMAN L.J. observing (at 107) "I can conceive of no useful object to be served in foisting upon the public this mass of junk. It has neither public utility nor educative value." For a case where a collection of minor works of art worth £12,000 were held to be of no educative value: see *Sutherland's Trustees* v. *Verschoyle* 1968 S.L.T. 3 (following and extending *Re Pinion*).

2 But see *Re Hummeltenberg*, discussed at 48 *infra*.

3 [1943] 2 All E.R. 101.

4 [1957] Ch. 299.

5 [1968] V.R. 390.

6 [1965] Ch. 85.

7 *Re Hamilton-Grey* (1938), 38 S.R. (N.S.W.) 262 (works about the poet Henry Kendall).

8 *Re Litchfield*, [1961] A.L.R. 750.

9 *Wilber* v. *Astbury Park National Bank and Trust Co.* 142 N.J. Eq. 99 (1948) affd. *sub. nom.* *Wilber* v. *Owens* 2 N.J. 167 (1949); see also 63 Harv. L.R. 348.

10 *Emmert* v. *Union Trust Co. of Indianapolis* 86 N.E. 2d 450 (1949).

intent to establish a public trust is irrelevant, if the trust is in fact one to enable the public to read the diaries: the public is the beneficiary. Nor in the absence of an expressed intention should it have been assumed that a commercial venture was intended. An educational benefit to the public was discernible and so the case should have been decided the other way.

If the court finds that writings have an educational tendency so that it is for the public benefit to publish them, the fact that incidentally the owner of the copyright will benefit will not subvert the gift.[1]

As with literature so with music: the promotion of music in a public way may be challenged on the grounds that no *benefit* will accrue to the public. It has been said that a trust to promote the work of some inadequate composer would fail.[2] A trust to promote the appreciation of folk music or folk dancing might be charitable, even though they are not fine arts.[3] But ballroom dancing would fall on the other side of the line.[4] Ballet, of course. is capable of being a charitable object.[5]

The case of *Re Hummeltenberg*[6] provides another example of a gift whose beneficial quality was denied. The testator left money on trust to establish a college for the training of spiritualist mediums. It was contended that the gift was charitable either as being for the advancement of education or as being otherwise beneficial to the public. No evidence was adduced in support of the alleged beneficial nature of the gift and the gift was therefore held to be void.

The founding of schools, colleges and universities and the maintenance of existing ones are the two most obvious methods of advancing education. In this connection it is worth mentioning that the Statute of Elizabeth refers to schools of learning without any reference to poverty. Consequently (it has been held) all schools of learning are to be considered charities and it makes no difference that the school is one for the sons of gentlemen[7] or for the children of railway workers[8] or for the poorest of the poor.[9] Nor is it relevant that the school charges fees provided it is not a profit-making venture.[10] All the same, the school must be a school of learning. A school of dancing or fencing is not included "because they are matters of delicacy not of necessity".[11] However a school of art qualifies[12] and so probably does a ballet school,[13] provided of course that they are not mere profit-making ventures.

The term "college" covers a variety of institutions of learning: colleges within the ancient universities,[14] public schools incorporated in connection with a

---

1 *Re Newsom* 1971 N. No. 423. 14th March, 1973, unreported; see further at 75 *infra*.

2 *Re Delius' Will Trusts*, [1957] Ch. 299.

3 *O'Sullivan* v. *English Folk Dance and Song Society*, [1955] 1 W.L.R. 907.

4 *Linlithgow Town Council Entertainments Committee* v. *I.R.Comrs.* 1953 S.L.T. 287.

5 *Cf. O'Sullivan* v. *English Folk Dance and Song Society*, *supra*.

6 [1923] 1 Ch. 237.

7 *A.-G.* v. *Earl of Lonsdale* (1827), 1 Sim. 105, at 109; *Brighton College* v. *Marriott*, [1926] A.C. 192, H.L. (school for sons of noblemen and gentlemen).

8 *Hall* v. *Derby Sanitary Authority* (1885), 16 Q.B.D. 163 (an orphanage).

9 *Re Hedgman* (1878), 8 Ch.D. 156.

10 *The Abbey, Malvern Wells, Ltd.* v. *Ministry of Local Government and Planning*, [1951] Ch. 728; *cf. Re Girls, Public Day School Trust, Ltd.*, [1951] Ch. 400 (not charitable).

11 Sir Francis Moore, Expositions upon the Statute of Elizabeth contained in Duke ed. Bridgman, 128.

12 *Re Allsop* (1884), 1 T.L.R. 4.

13 See *O'Sullivan* v. *English Folk Dance and Song Society*, *supra*.

14 *Plate* v. *St. John's College* (1638), Duke ed. Bridgman 379; *Christ's College, Cambridge, Case* (1757), 1 Wm. Bl. 90.

university,[1] the Royal College of Surgeons,[2] a teachers' training college,[3] a Roman Catholic college[4] and a university college.[5] All of these institutions, if they are not profit-making ventures, are charitable. On the other hand the support of a staff training college for employees of a limited company who attended compulsorily is not charitable.[6] Universities themselves constitute institutions for the advancement of learning[7] as did the ancient Inns of Chancery.[8]

The activities of schools and universities can, of course, be furthered by the endowment of professorial chairs, fellowships and lectureships,[9] scholarships[10] and prizes[11] and educational bursaries.[12] In the case of scholarships it is accepted that the eligible candidates may be confined to a particular university[13] or school.[14] Where the prize is a cash prize the mere fact that it can be used for any purpose does not deprive the endowment of its charitable nature: the prize is the spur to academic achievement.[15]

Gifts to establish new departments or faculties in a college are also charitable[16] as are gifts to learned societies[17] and institutions for the advancement of science[18] such as the Royal Society and the Royal Geographical Society,[19] the Royal Literary Society,[20] the Royal College of Surgeons[21] and the Zoological Society.[22]

---

1 E.g. Winchester College.

2 *Royal College of Surgeons of England* v. *National Provincial Bank, Ltd.,* [1952] A.C. 631.

3 *Re Wright,* [1951] Tas. S.R. 13.

4 *Walsh* v. *Gladstone* (1843), 1 Ph. 290.

5 *R.* v. *Income Tax Special Commissioners, Ex parte University College of North Wales* (1909), 78 L.J.K.B. 576, C.A.

6 *Re Leverhulme,* [1943] 2 All E.R. 143.

7 See *Aberdeen University* v. *Irvine* (1868), L.R. 1 Sc. & Div. 289, H.L.; *Wilson* v. *Toronto General Trusts Corpn. and Saskatchewan University Board of Governors,* [1954] 3 D.L.R. 136.

8 *Smith* v. *Kerr,* [1902] 1 Ch. 774, at 778, C.A. As to the Inns of Chancery see Sir Robert Megarry, *Inns Ancient and Modern* (Selden Society 1972) 27–48.

9 Professorships: *Yates* v. *University College London* (1875), W.R. 7 H.L. 438 (archaeology); *Re Buckland* (1887), 22 L.J.N.C. 7 (economic fish culture); fellowship: *Jesus College Case* (1615) Duke ed. Bridgman 363; lectureship: *A.-G.* v. *Cambridge Margaret and Regius Professors* (1682), 1 Vern. 55.

10 *Re Levitt* (1885), 1 T.L.R. 578; *University College of North Wales* v. *Taylor,* [1908] P. 140, C.A.; *Re Williams* (1908), 24 T.L.R. 716; *Re Spencer* (1928), 34 O.W.N. 29 (research in geology at Manitoba University); *Re Gott,* [1944] Ch. 193 (post-graduate scholarship at Leeds University); *Re Welton,* [1950] 2 D.L.R. 280; *Wilson* v. *Toronto General Trusts Corporation,* [1954] 3 D.L.R. 136; *Re Johnson* (1961), 30 D.L.R. (2d) 474.

11 *Thompson* v. *Thompson* (1844), 1 Coll., 381, at 398; *Farrer* v. *St. Catharine's College, Cambridge* (1873), L.R. 16 Eq. 19; *Re Mariette,* [1915] 2 Ch. 284 (prize for classics); *Chesterman* v. *Federal Comr. of Taxation,* [1926] A.C. 128, P.C.

12 *Re Evans,* [1957] S.R.Q. 345; *Re Mackenzie,* [1962] 2 All E.R. 890.

13 *Re Welton,* [1950] 2 D.L.R. 280.

14 *Re Loggie* (1934), 8 M.P.R. 298. There are numerous closed awards at Oxford and Cambridge.

15 *Re Weaver,* [1963] V.R. 257.

16 *Davenport* v. *Davenport Foundation* 222 P (2d) 11 (1950) (department of philosophy and religion).

17 *British Museum Trustees* v. *White* (1826), 2 Sim. & St. 594; *President of the United States* v. *Drummond* (1838), cited in 7 H.L.Cas, at 155 (Smithsonian Institution).

18 As to "science": see *Weir* v. *Crum-Brown,* [1908] A.C. 162, at 167–169, H.L.

19 *Beaumont* v. *Oliveira* (1869), 4 Ch. App. 309; *Royal Society of London and Thompson* (1881), 17 Ch.D. 407.

20 *Thomas* v. *Howell* (1874), L.R. 18 Eq. 198.

21 *Royal College of Surgeons of England* v. *National Provincial Bank, Ltd.,* [1952] A.C. 631, H.L.

22 *Re Lopes,* [1931] 2 Ch. 130; followed in *North of England Zoological Society* v. *Chester Rural District Council,* [1959] 1 W.L.R. 773, C.A.

Similarly the Royal College of Nursing, the British School of Egyptian Archaeology and the Institution of Civil Engineers are charitable.[1] The Charity
Commissioners have allowed the Huguenot Society, a society which exists for
the purposes of interchange and publication of knowledge about Huguenots, to
be registered as a charity.[2]

The provision of residences for teachers is not a charitable purpose[3] unless,
perhaps, they are required to live there for the better performance of their
duties.[4] A home for teachers in need of rest[5] and a gift for "aiding young
governesses who may be sick or overworked"[6] may be charitable on the ground
that they are conducive to the advancement of education.

A gift to a college library is charitable because a good representative library
tends to the promotion of education.[7] On the other hand a library for the benefit
of subscribers is not charitable.[8] Some of the purposes for which a local Law
Society Library is used may be charitable. Such was the case in *Re Mason*[9] where
it was held that a fund set up to advance legal learning in Auckland could be
used for the purchase of less usual reports, journals and books useful to the
researcher and the learned but not for the purchase of basic law books. The law
library for which the purchases were canvassed had the character of a professional library providing services for its members and its maintenance was thus
not a charitable object.[10] On the other hand the publication of law reports on
a non-profit-making basis was held in *Incorporated Council of Law Reporting for
England and Wales v. A.-G.*[11] to be charitable not only under the fourth head of
Lord MACNAGHTEN's classification in *Income Tax Special Purposes Comrs.* v.
Pemsel[12] but also, on the majority view, as for the advancement of education.
RUSSELL L.J. was the member of the Court of Appeal who dissented on the
latter point. He considered that the purposes of the Council were not purely
educational although they clearly fell under the fourth head of the *Pemsel*
classification. The earlier decision of the High Court of Australia in *Incorporated
Council of Law Reporting for the State of Queensland* v. *Federal Taxation Commissioner*[13] concerning the Queensland Council of Law Reporting[14] in which it
was held that the Council was not a "public educational institution" was not
cited to the English Court of Appeal. This was hardly surprising since the

---

1 See *Royal College of Nursing* v. *St. Marylebone Borough Council*, [1959] 1 W.L.R. 1077;
Re British School of Egyptian Archaeology, [1954] 1 W.L.R. 546 ("school" was in fact a
learned society); *Institution of Civil Engineers* v. *I.R.Comrs.*, [1932] 1 K.B. 149.

2 *The Huguenot Society of London*, [1965] Ch. Com. Rep. 29 (App. C.).

3 *Heron* v. *Monaghen* (1888), 22 L.R. Ir. 532; *Northern Ireland Valuation Comr.* v. *Fermanagh
Protestant Board of Education*, [1969] 1 W.L.R. 1708, H.L.; *Poor Clares of the Immaculate
Conception* v. *Valuation Comr.*, [1971] N.I. 174.

4 *Valuation Comr.* v. *Newry Christian Brothers*, [1971] N.I. 114.

5 *Re Estlin* (1903), 72 L.J.Ch. 687.

6 *Re Pearse*, [1955] 1 D.L.R. 801.

7 *A.-G.* v. *Marchant* (1866), L.R. 3 Eq. 424, at 430 (Trinity College, Oxford); and see
Re Good, [1905] 2 Ch. 60 (regimental library charitable).

8 *Carne* v. *Long* (1860), 2 De G.F. & J. 75.

9 [1971] N.Z.L.R. 714. For comment on the case see [1972] A.S.C.L. 252-253 (J. D.
Davies).

10 See *Society of Writers to Her Majesty's Signet* v. *I.R.Comrs.* (1886), 2 T.C. 257; *Ex parte
St. John Law Society* (1891), 30 N.B.R. 501.

11 [1972] Ch. 73.

12 [1891] A.C. 531.

13 (1924), 34 C.L.R. 580.

14 The Queensland Council had the same principal object.

Australian case was not noted in any of the source books on the law of charities. The later decision of the High Court of Australia in *Incorporated Council of Law Reporting of the State for Queensland* v. *Federal Taxation Comr.*[1] held that the Council did not have purely educational purposes but was charitable under the fourth head in *Pemsel's* case. BARWICK C.J. said:[2]

> "However much a student may and should profit by reading the law reports, the purpose of their production cannot, in my opinion, be held to be educational. Further, in my opinion, their function for the judiciary is informative rather than educational."

Public benefit

An educational trust will only qualify as charitable if it promotes a *public* benefit. The element of benefit has been discussed already. But it is necessary that the benefit should be available to a sufficiently important section of the community. The following limited classes of persons have been treated as constituting a sufficiently important section of the community and gifts for their education have been held valid: the daughters of missionaries,[3] children of railway workers,[4] persons professing particular religious doctrines[5] and women and girls who are not self-supporting.[6] But if the nexus between the beneficiaries is their personal relationship to a single *propositus* or to several *propositi* the trust will not be charitable. To start at the bottom of the scale, a trust established by a father for the education of his son is not a charity. The public element is not supplied by the fact that from that son's education all may benefit.[7] In *Re Compton*[8] a trust to provide scholarships to advance the education of lawful descendants of three named persons was held invalid. Likewise in *Oppenheim* v. *Tobacco Securities Trust Co., Ltd.*[9] a trust to advance the education of children of employees or former employees of the British American Tobacco Co., Ltd. was classified as non-charitable because again the nexus between the beneficiaries was their personal relationship to a single *propositus*, namely the British American Tobacco Co., Ltd.

There are, however, two special cases which merit further discussion.

The first is what the Privy Council has called "the ancient English institution of educational provision for 'Founders Kin' in certain schools and colleges."[10] A trust for the education of the donor's descendants and kinsmen at a school or college is not by nature charitable.[11] But where a school or college is endowed

---

1 (1971), 45 A.L.J.R. 552.
2 (1971) 45 A.L.J.R. 552, at 554.
3 *German* v. *Chapman* (1877), 7 Ch.D. 271.
4 *Hall* v. *Derby Sanitary Authority* (1885), 16 Q.B.D. 163.
5 *Income Tax Special Purposes Commissioners* v. *Pemsel*, [1891] A.C. 531.
6 *Re Central Employment Bureau for Women and Students' Careers Association (Incorporated)*, [1942] 1 All E.R. 232.
7 See *Oppenheim* v. *Tobacco Securities Trust Co., Ltd.* [1951] A.C. 297, at 306, *per* Lord SIMONDS.
8 [1945] Ch. 123.
9 [1951] A.C. 297; but see at 18–21 *supra*; and see *Re Leverhulme*, [1943] 2 All E.R. 143.
10 *Caffoor (Trustees of Abdul Gaffoor Trust)* v. *Income Tax Comr. Colombo*, [1961] A.C. 584, at 602; [1961] 2 All E.R. 436, at 444 P.C. See also Squibb, *Founders' Kin* (1972).
11 *Re Compton*, [1945] Ch. 123 explaining *A.-G.* v. *Sidney Sussex College* (1869), 4 Ch. App. 722; *Re Lavelle*, [1914] 1 I.R. 194.

with money and directed in the question of scholarships or fellowships to give preference to the founder's kin the gift is still charitable. An example of such a gift is to be found in *Spencer* v. *All Souls College*[1] of which Lord GREENE M.R. in *Re Compton* said[2] that the primary object of the founder

> "was to endow a college for the advancement of learning: the preference to his own kin was merely a method of giving effect to this intention".

The validity of such dispositions has never been questioned from remote ages and was not questioned in *Spencer*'s case. Indeed, at least one attempt to wriggle out of a founder's kin provision was frustrated by the Court of Chancery in *Re Christ's Hospital*.[3] In 1724 Thomas Guy the founder of Guy's Hospital made a gift to Christ's Hospital and charged the funds of Guy's Hospital with payment of £400 a year to Christ's Hospital upon condition that Guy's Hospital should have liberty to put into Christ's Hospital every year four poor children, with a preference to founder's kin. From 1724 until 1889 the annual payment was made and every year four children of Guy's family were appointed to Christ's Hospital by Guy's Hospital. In 1830, apparently, Christ's Hospital finding that the charge of maintaining and teaching Guy's children exceeded the value of the annuity, tried to renounce it, but was compelled to continue it by a decree of the Court of Chancery. More recently the Privy Council commented[4] that educational provisions for founder's kin

> "were commonly accepted as validly instituted, though there seems to be virtually no direct authority as to the principle on which they rested and they should probably be regarded as belonging more to history than to doctrine".

Most founder's *fellowships* at Oxford and Cambridge were abolished by the Oxford University Act 1854 and the Cambridge University Act 1856 respectively.

The other case is *Re Koettgen's Will Trusts*[5] in which it was held that where the primary object of an educational trust is of a public nature, an *imperative* direction that in selecting beneficiaries the trustees should give preference to the employees of a particular company and members of their families would not invalidate the trust. The preference was only to be operated in respect of 75% of the trust income. UPJOHN J. held that it was at the stage when the primary class of eligible persons was ascertained that the question of the public nature of the trust arises and falls to be decided. Counsel for the residuary legatee had argued that the trust was one "primarily for the benefit of the employees . . . and their families and that it was only if there were insufficient employees or members of their families that the public would come in as beneficiaries under the trust". But the learned judge rejected this argument though conceding that there was much force in it. He identified the primary class as consisting of persons without sufficient means to obtain commercial education at their own expense. The class of beneficiaries was not "confined" to the preferred class and UPJOHN J. was also plainly affected by the point that it was uncertain in any future year how much of the 75% would actually be used for the preferred class.

---

1 (1762), Wilm. 163.
2 [1945] Ch. 123, at 132.
3 (1889), 15 App. Cas. 172, at 186.
4 *Caffoor* (*Trustees of Abdul Gaffoor Trust*) v. *Income Tax Comr. Colombo, supra.*
5 [1954] Ch. 252.

The case of *Re Koettgen's Will Trusts* has been much criticised.[1]

In *Caffoor (Trustees of Abdul Gaffoor Trust)* v. *Income Tax Comr. Colombo*[2] the facts were more extreme. Under a trust established by a grantor by deed the *whole* of the trust income was to be treated as if appropriated for the "education, instruction or training . . . of deserving youths of the Islamic Faith in such professions, vocations, occupations, industries, arts or crafts, trades, employments, subjects, lines or any other departments of learning or human activity whatsoever" as a board set up under the deed might decide. Under the provisions of the deed, so long as there were male descendants in either the male or female line of the grantor or any of his brothers or sisters for whose education the board were prepared to provide or reserve money on the ground that they qualified as youths of the Islamic Faith, no other youth of that faith could obtain any benefit under the trust purpose. As Lord RADCLIFFE observed:[3]

> "the only fair way to describe this trust is as a family trust under which the income is made available to provide for the education or training of relatives of the *propositus* in this case the grantor himself, provided only that they are young, deserving and of the required Faith".

In effect an absolute priority to the benefit of the trust income was conferred on the grantor's own family. After summarising the construction which UPJOHN J. had put upon the relevant wording in *Re Koettgen's Will Trusts*[4] LORD RADCLIFFE said:[5]

> "It is not necessary for their Lordships to say whether they would have put the same construction on the will there in question as the judge did, or whether they regard the distinction which he made as ultimately maintainable. The decision edges very near to being inconsistent with *Oppenheim's* case, but it is sufficient to say that the construction of the gift which was there adopted does not tally with the construction which their Lordships are bound to place upon the trust which is now before them."

---

1 See *Theobald on Wills* (13th edn.) 376, para. 1066; *Tudor on Charities* (6th edn.) 27–28; and see also *I.R.Comrs.* v. *Educational Grants Association, Ltd.*, [1967] Ch. 123, at 143, *per* PENNYCUICK J.; [1967] Ch. 993, at 1010, *per* Lord DENNING M.R.

2 [1961] A.C. 584, P.C.

3 [1961] A.C. 584, at 603.

4 [1954] Ch. 252.

5 [1961] A.C. 584, at 604.

Chapter 4

The Advancement of Religion[1]

General

The advancement of religion is also a charitable purpose. True, it was not mentioned in the preamble to the Statute of Elizabeth, the nearest approach to it being "the repair of churches". But as has been said[2] the purpose of the preamble was to illustrate charitable purposes rather than to draw up an exhaustive definition of charity. Sir Francis Moore, a member of the Parliament which enacted The Statute of 1601,[3] explained that the omission of religious purposes was intentional and was done[4]

> "lest the gifts intended to be employed upon purposes grounded upon charity, might, in change of times (contrary to the minds of the givers) be confiscated into the King's Treasury. For religion being variable according to the pleasure of succeeding princes, that which at one time is held for orthodox, may at another be accounted superstitious, and then such lands are confiscated."

Certainly this view accords with the turbulent background of Tudor and Elizabethan times[5] but, be that as it may, it was not long before the advancement of the established religion was conceded to be within the equity of the Act. In 1639 it was held that a trust to maintain a preaching minister was charitable.[6] But it was only gradually that trusts for the advancement of religious faith outside the Established Church were upheld. Indeed until the Toleration Act 1688 various penal laws ensured that only gifts to the Established Church would be upheld. Thus, gifts for the support of students for the Roman Catholic priesthood[7] or Roman Catholic priests[8] or non-conformist ministers[9] were

---

1 Crowther, *Religious Trusts* (1954); Brady, *Religion and the Law of Charities in Ireland* (1976).

2 At 8 *ante.*

3 But not it seems its draftsman: Gareth Jones, *History of the Law of Charity 1532–1827*, 232–234.

4 See Moore, "Readings upon the Statute 43 Elizabeth" in Duke, *Law of Charitable Uses* (1676) 131, 132; also printed in Boyle, *A Practical Treatise on the Law of Charities* (1837) Appendix.

5 It has been suggested that religion was deliberately omitted because it was not *Ejusdem generis* with the other objects: see 62 L.Q.R. (1946) 234 (F. H. Newark). But this is unconvincing: See Gareth Jones, *op cit.*, 32–33.

6 *Pember v. Inhabitants of Kington* (1639), Toth 34. The report is unsatisfactory: there is a fuller report in the Entry Books: see Gareth Jones, *op. cit.*, 34–35.

7 *Croft v. Evetts* (1606), Moore K.B. 784.

8 *Gates v. Jones* (1690), cited, in 7 Ves. 495; 2 Vern. 266 and [1893] 2 Ch. 49 n.

9 *A.-G. v. Baxter* (1684), 1 Vern. 248.

held invalid though the funds directed to such purposes were often (para-doxically) applied to the purposes of the Established Church. Protestant dis-senters were relieved of some of their disabilities by the Toleration Act so that the gift to non-conformist ministers held invalid in *A.-G.* v. *Baxter*[1] in 1684 were upheld on appeal four years later.[2] Roman Catholics, Jews and Unitarians were, however, expressly excluded from the Act's provisions, and for a long period of time gifts for the education of children in the Roman Catholic faith[3] or for instructing the people in the Jewish religion[4] were held invalid though again they were applied to the purposes of the Established Church.

The legal emancipation of Unitarians, Roman Catholics and Jews was piecemeal. Three Acts spaced over the first half of the nineteenth century re-moved the relevant disabilities[5] and as a result trusts for the promotion of the religious purposes of Unitarians[6] and for the promotion of Roman Catholicism[7] and the Jewish faith[8] were held to be valid.

The position has now been reached that the court makes no distinction between one religion and another or one sect and another unless the tenets of a particular sect inculcate doctrines adverse to the very foundation of all religion and sub-versive of all morality.[9] As between different religions the law stands neutral, but it assumes that any religion is at least likely to be better than none.[10] In one sense the high-water mark of tolerance was washed by the case of *Thornton* v. *Howe*[11] where it was held that a trust for the publication of the works of Joanna Southcott was valid. This remarkable woman claimed that she was pregnant by the Holy Ghost and would give birth to a second Messiah and at her death left a box which her followers believe will be a panacea of all the world's ills if opened in the presence of twenty-four bishops. Sir JOHN ROMILLY M.R. said[12] that a religious trust would be charitable if

> "the tendency were not immoral and although this court might consider the opinions sought to be propagated foolish or even devoid of foundation".

The proposition that all religions regardless of merit are charitable could open the door (as it has done in the United States) to all sorts of bizarre religions, enjoying unmerited fiscal privileges. In this country certain sects have been

---

1 *A.-G.* v. *Baxter* (1684), 1 Vern. 248.

2 *Sub. nom. A.-G.* v. *Hughes* (1689), 2 Vern. 105. The reasons for the reversal are not reported. *Semble* the gift was not charitable: *Thomas* v. *Howell* (1874), L.R. 18 Eq. 198, at 208–209.

3 *Cary* v. *Abbott* (1802), 7 Ves. 490; *A.-G.* v. *Power* (1809), 1 Ball & B. 145. A trust to promote the doctrine of the supremacy of the Pope was also held void: *De Themmines* v. *de Bonneval* (1828) 5 Russ. 288.

4 *Da Costa* v. *De Paz* (1754) 2 Swan. 487 n. *Isaac* v. *Gompertz* (1786), cited in 7 Ves. 61 (synagogue); but *cf. Straus* v. *Goldsmid* (1837), 8 Sim. 614.

5 Unitarian Relief Act 1813; Roman Catholic Charities Act 1832; Religious Disabilities Act 1846 (Jews). Both the last mentioned Acts were held to be retrospective in their opera-tion: see *Bradshaw* v. *Tasker* (1834), 2 Myl. & K. 221 and *Re Michel's Trust* (1860), 28 Beav. 39.

6 *Shore* v. *Wilson* (1842), 9 Cl. & F. 355; *Shrewsbury* v. *Hornby* (1846), 5 Hare 406.

7 *Bradshaw* v. *Tasker*, *supra*.

8 *Straus* v. *Goldsmid* (1837), 8 Sim. 614; *Re Braham* (1892), 36 Sol. Jo. 712 (synagogue reader).

9 *Thornton* v. *Howe* (1862), 31 Beav. 14.

10 *Gilmour* v. *Coats*, [1949] A.C. 426, 457–458, *per* Lord REID; *Neville Estates Ltd.* v. *Madden*, [1962] Ch. 832, at 853.

11 (1862), 31 Beav. 14.

12 *Ibid.*, at 19. But see the discussion at 75–76, *infra*.

held not to be religious institutions. Thus the "Church" of the Agapemonites[1] was held not to be a religious institution[2] and it would appear that Scientology is not a religion.[3]

In *Re Hummeltenberg*[4] it was held that a trust to establish a college to train suitable persons as spiritualist mediums was not a charitable trust. It was not, however, contended that the trust was for the promotion of religion: the case was only argued on the footing that the trust either was educational or was beneficial to the community. Some jurisdictions have upheld trusts to promote spiritualism as being for the advancement of religion. In *Jones* v. *Watford*[5] a trust to purchase and make available books on the philosophy of spiritualism was held to be a valid religious trust. If one accepts the tolerant criteria of Sir JOHN ROMILLY in *Thornton* v. *Howe*, the decision in *Jones* v. *Watford* seems unexceptionable. On the other hand in a South African case[6] it was held that a gift "to the spiritualistic society which may conduct the common service" on the death of the testator was not charitable. The judge held that the possibility that persons in the next world might send back warnings or exhortations based on their own experiences of the consequences of their earthly life did not show such a direct or indirect tendency on the part of spiritualism to the instruction or edification of the public[7] as would make its promotion charitable.[8] In the United States one court upheld the will of Mary Baker Eddy who left the greater part of her fortune to the Mother Church for the repair of the church building and "for the purpose of more effectually promoting and extending the religion of Christian Science as taught by me,"[9] and another court upheld a trust for the Christian Science Monitor.[10]

There is no direct authority in this country on whether non-Christian religions (other than the Jewish faith) are valid objects of a trust. Christianity is not part of the law of England and there are sizeable communities of Hindus and Moslems here. Certainly regulations made under the Charities Act 1960 assume that a trust for the advancement of a non-Christian religion is good.[11] But an atheist society can hardly be a charitable object. In *Bowman* v. *Secular Society Ltd.*[12] where the point was not directly in issue Lord PARKER seems to be suggesting that a trust for a society with "humanist" objects would not be charitable:

> "The abolition of religious tests, the disestablishment of the Church, the secularisation of education, the alteration of the law touching religion

---

1 See *Nottidge* v. *Prince* (1860), 2 Giff. 246. The history of the Agapemonites is conveniently and amusingly set out in *Encyclopaedia Britannica*, (11th Edn.) (1911).

2 *Re Fysh* (1957), *Times*, 1st July.

3 *R.* v. *Registrar General, Ex Parte Segerdal*, [1970] Q.B. 697 at 707, *per* Lord DENNING M.R. The case was concerned with the question whether the chapel of the "Church" of Scientology was a place of worship within the Places of Worship Registration Act 1855.

4 [1923] 1 Ch. 237.

5 62 N.J. Eq. 339 (1901); 64 N.J. Eq. 785 (1902) (U.S.) see also *Lockwood's Estate* 344 Pa. 293 (1942) (U.S.) (outright gift to an incorporated spiritualist college: valid).

6 *Ex parte Hart* 1947 (4) S.A. 464 (W).

7 This test derives from *Cocks* v. *Manners* (1871), L.R. 12 Eq. 574.

8 *Ex parte Hart*, 1947 (4) S.A. 464, at 479 (W). *Chase* v. *Dickey*, 99 N.E. 410 (1912).

9 *Glover* v. *Baker*, 83 Atl. 916 (1912).

10 *Chase* v. *Dickey*, 99 N.E. 410 (1912).

11 See S.I. 1962 No. 1421; S.I. 1963 No. 2074. Whether a polytheistic religion is a permissible object of charity in England is an open question.

12 [1917] A.C. 406.

or marriage, or the observation of the Sabbath are purely political objects. Equity has always refused to recognise such objects as charitable."

There is, moreover, an Australian decision which bears out Lord PARKER'S dictum. In *Re Jones*[1] it was held that a bequest to the "Incorporated Body of Freethinkers of Australia", a society which advocated the doctrine "that science provides for life and that materialism can be relied upon in all phases of society", was void; and there is Canadian authority[2] to the same effect. One writer[3] suggests that a trust to promote atheism, although not a trust for the advancement of religion can nevertheless be upheld as a trust for the advancement of education. But if the courts accept that any religion is likely to be better than none, it is difficult to see what educational benefit to the community would accrue from such a trust. It is adverse to the very foundation of all religion. It is submitted that a trust to promote atheism or "humanism" cannot be accounted beneficial to the community under the fourth head in *Pemsel's* case for the same reason. At the very most such a trust is a political trust and should accordingly fail to rank as charitable.[4]

Methods of advancing religion

Religion may be advanced or promoted in a variety of ways.

Lord HANWORTH M.R. in *Keren Kayemeth Le Jisroel Ltd.* v. *I.R.Comrs.*[5] defined the promotion of religion as:[6]

"the promotion of spiritual teaching in a wide sense, and the maintenance of the doctrines on which it rests, and the observances that serve to promote and manifest it—not merely a foundation or cause to which it can be related".

In a rating case[7] DONOVAN J. made a similar point:[8]

"To advance religion means to promote it, to spread its message ever wider among mankind; to take some positive steps to sustain and increase religious belief; and these things are done in a variety of ways which may be comprehensively described as pastoral and missionary."

Freemasonry does not have as its main objects the advancement of religion. There is no religious instruction, no programme for the persuasion of unbelievers, no religious supervision to see that its members remain active and constant in the various religions they may profess, no holding of religious services, no pastoral or missionary work of any kind. The same is true of Theosophy.[9]

---

1 [1907] S.A.L.R. 190.
2 *Kinsey* v. *Kinsey* (1894), 26 O.R. 99.
3 See Scott, *Trusts* (3rd edn.) para. 377; Goodman Report (1976) 23 para. 53.
4 *Cf. Re Stenson's Will Trusts*, [1970] Ch. 16 at 20–21.
5 [1931] 2 K.B. 465.
6 *Ibid.*, at 477.
7 *United Grand Lodge of Ancient Free and Accepted Masons of England* v. *Holborn Borough Council*, [1957] 1 W.L.R. 1080.
8 *Ibid.*, at 1090.
9 *Berry* v. *St. Marylebone Corporation*, [1958] Ch. 406.

Religion may even be advanced indirectly. So in *Re Charlesworth*[1] a bequest to officers of a society of clergymen of a fund to be held on trust to pay the expenses of an annual dinner at the meeting of members was upheld. Eve J. held that the society advanced religion and that the provision made for dinners would further the usefulness of the society by increasing attendances at meetings. The provision of prizes at a Baptist Sunday School affords another example of the indirect advancement of religion.[2] Sport, too, can be ancillary to religious charities as well as to educational trusts, just as social purposes can be ancillary to religious purposes. During the present century a considerable change has been discernible in the methods employed to advance Christianity among young people. The emphasis now appears to be rather less on dogma and more on the Christian's duty to his neighbour and his need to prepare himself to take his place in the world. And this change, perhaps more obvious in some quarters than in others, has been accompanied by a fuller realisation that the energies and enthusiasms of the young in physical and mental spheres cannot be neglected or ignored by those who would minister to their spiritual requirements.[3]

It is proposed to discuss in this section (A) trusts expressed to be for religious purposes, (B) trusts for the maintenance and promotion of public worship and (C) trusts to spread religion. To some extent these categories overlap but the classification is convenient.

A TRUSTS FOR RELIGIOUS PURPOSES GENERALLY

In two decisions of the Court of Appeal[4] it has been held that a trust "for religious purposes" (without more) is charitable. Nevertheless at least one leading text-book[5] suggests that the point is still open in view of later House of Lords cases which say that a gift for religious purposes is not charitable unless there is an element of public benefit. In *Gilmour* v. *Coats*[6] as appears from observations of Lord SIMONDS[7] and Lord REID[8] it was *conceded* by the parties that not all religious purposes are charitable purposes.

It is one thing, however, to concede that not all religious purposes are charitable and quite another to say that a trust "for religious purposes" is therefore not charitable. The proper approach, it is submitted, was the one taken by CLAUSON J. in upholding a gift "for the furtherance of religious purposes of Roman Catholics in the British Empire":[9]

> "It must be taken to be settled law, at all events in this Court . . . that in the absence of a context enabling the court to place some more extended meaning on the words 'religious purposes' the phrase must be taken to mean 'purposes conducive to the advancement of religion' ".

---

1 (1910), 26 T.L.R. 214.

2 *Re Strickland's Will Trusts*, [1936] 3 All E.R. 1027.

3 *City of Belfast Y.M.C.A.* v. *Northern Ireland Valuation Comr.* [1969] N.I. 3, C.A.

4 *Re White*, [1893] 2 Ch. 41, C.A.; *Wilkinson* v. *Lindgren* (1870), 5 Ch. App. 570, C.A. The earlier cases were *Baker* v. *Sutton* (1836), 1 Keen. 224; *Townsend* v. *Carus* (1844), 3 Hare 257.

5 *Theobald on Wills* (13th edn.) 378. The suggestion emanates from the previous learned editor Dr. J. H. C. Morris, but it is clear that Theobald himself would have shared his editor's view: see his preface to the 7th edition.

6 [1949] A.C. 426, H.L.

7 At 449.

8 At 454.   9 *Re Ward*, [1941] Ch. 308.

In other words a gift to "religious purposes" means *prima facie* to such religious purposes as are charitable".[1]

B TRUSTS FOR THE MAINTENANCE AND PROMOTION OF PUBLIC WORSHIP

There are three main ways in which public worship is stimulated. These are (1) the building and repair of churches, chapels and so on, (2) the orderly administration of divine service and (3) the support of the clergy.

Building and repair of churches

The repair of churches is one of the charitable objects listed in the preamble to the Statute of Elizabeth and therefore, as one author remarks, trusts for the preservation of church fabric possess the most indisputable claim to charitable status.[2] Even before the Statute a gift for the repair and ornamentation of a church was held to be valid.[3] So the completion of Westminster Cathedral was held plainly to be a charitable purpose.[4]

Since the greater includes the less, a gift for the repair of a particular *part*[5] of the church is obviously on the same footing as a trust for the general maintenance of the church; and so is a gift to pay for additions to the fabric.[6] A trust for the maintenance of a churchyard is also charitable.[7] NORTH J. in considering such a trust remarked[8]

"I do not see any difference between a gift to keep in repair what is called 'God's House' and a gift to keep in repair the churchyard round it, which is often called 'God's Acre'".

He also commented[9] that the repair of a parish churchyard was clearly for the benefit of the inhabitants of the parish. Similarly the maintenance of a cemetery[10] or a burial ground for a particular sect[11] is also a charitable purpose.

Nor does the law draw a distinction between the upkeep of churches and the upkeep of synagogues,[12] dissenting chapels[13] or other buildings used for religious

---

1 *Re Morton's Estate*, [1941] 1 W.W.R. 310 (Can.).
2 See Crowther, *Religious Trusts* (1954), at 106.
3 *Hart* v. *Brewer* (1595), Cro. Eliz. 449.
4 *Re Van Wart* (1911), *Times*, 17th Feb.
5 *A.-G.* v. *Day*, [1900] 1 Ch. 31 (gallery); *Hoare* v. *Osborne* (1866) L.R. 1 Eq. 585 (chancel); *Re Manser*, [1905] 1 Ch. 68 (furniture).
6 *Re Hendry* (1887), 56 L.T. 908 (new church clock); *Re King*, [1923] 1 Ch. 243 (stained glass window); *Re Barker* (1909), 25 T.L.R. 753 (monument).
7 *Re Vaughan* (1886), 33 Ch.D. 187.
8 *Ibid.*, at 192.
9 *Ibid.*, at 191.
10 *A.-G.* v. *Blizard* (1855), 21 Beav. 233.
11 *Re Manser*, [1905] 1 Ch. 68, at 74: "I think that one naturally connects the burial of the dead with religion."
12 *Isaac* v. *Gompertz* (1786), cited in 7 Ves. 61.
13 *A.-G.* v. *Cock* (1751), 2 Ves. Sen. 273 (Baptist); *Re Wall* (1889), 42 Ch.D. 510 (unitarian); *Re Brown*, [1898] 1 I.R. 423 (Plymouth Brethren); *Re Williams* (1910), 26 T.L.R. 307 (Congregational); *Re Ramsay* (1911), *Times*, 17th Feb. (Roman Catholic: Westminster Cathedral).

purposes such as a parsonage[1] or a religious college or seminary.[2] But in *Re Porter*[3] a trust for the maintenance of a masonic "temple" was held not to be charitable because such a building is not a temple in the strict sense of the word, but is devoted to masonic purposes generally and these include social and business activities. The difficulty inherent in the last mentioned decision is to know exactly where one should draw the line. A church hall is used for parish purposes not all of which are in themselves charitable.[4] It might therefore be argued that a trust to maintain or repair a church hall is not charitable. In *Neville Estates, Ltd.* v. *Madden*[5] however, a trust for the purposes of a synagogue was not robbed of its charitable nature because one clause of the trust deed purported to authorise the Catford Synagogue to establish, *inter alia*, halls for religious and social purposes. CROSS J. pointed out that the chief purposes of a synagogue are the holding of religious services and the giving of religious instruction to the younger members of the congregation. But he continued:[6]

> "Just as today church activity overflows from the church itself to the parochial hall, with its whist drives, dances and bazaars so many synagogues today organise social activities among the members."

These social activities were, in CROSS J.'s view, merely ancillary to the strictly religious activities: the case was therefore different from *I.R.Comrs.* v. *Baddeley*[7] where the religious flavour of Methodism was swamped by the predominantly social aspect of the trust. In short, the distinction is probably one of degree.[8]

The orderly administration of divine service

In his commentary on the Statute of Elizabeth Sir Francis Moore stated[9] that in construing the words "repairs of churches" one includes under the term church

> "all convenient ornaments and concurrents convenient for the decent and orderly administration of Divine Service (as for the finding of a pulpit or a sermon bell) . . . for reparations of churches are but preparations for the administration of Divine Service".

Music is clearly a fitting concurrent of Divine Service. Thus a gift to provide a stipend for the organist in a church[10] or for the upkeep of an organ[11] is charitable.

---

1 *A.-G.* v. *Bishop of Chester* (1785), 1 Br.C.C. 44.
2 *Walsh* v. *Gladstone* (1843), 1 Ph. 290; *Wallis* v. *Solicitor General for New Zealand*, [1903] A.C. 173.
3 [1925] Ch. 746.
4 See *Farley* v. *Westminster Bank, Ltd.*, [1939] A.C. 430; *Re Stratton*, [1931] 1 Ch. 197.
5 [1962] Ch. 832.
6 *Ibid.*, at 851. This dictum seems to be based on some observations of Professor Newark in 62 L.Q.R. 234, at 244.
7 [1955] A.C. 572.
8 See also *Northern Ireland Valuation Comr.* v. *Trustees of Fisherwick Presbyterian Church*, [1927] N.I. 76 (a rating case) in which, again, the *main* user of the Church hall was for denominational activities.
9 See Duke, *Law of Charitable Uses* (ed. Bridgman) 124.
10 *A.-G.* v. *Oakaver* (1736), cited in 1 Ves. Sen. 536.
11 *Adnam* v. *Cole* (1843), 6 Beav. 353; *Carbery* v. *Cox* (1852), 3 I.Ch.R. 231, n.

In the *Re Royce*[1] SIMONDS J. upheld a legacy "for the benefit of the choir" on the ground that the advancement and improvement of musical services in a church is a charitable object. An annual peal of bells to commemorate the restoration of the monarchy has been held to connote "a notion of worship",[2] but the same does not apply to an annual payment to bell ringers in consideration of their ringing the bells on the anniversary of the testator's death.[3]

The ornamentation of a church was considered to be a charitable object both before the Statute of Elizabeth[4] and by Sir Francis Moore, who instanced sermon bells and pulpits.[5] In *Hoare* v. *Osborne*[6] KINDERSLEY V.C. conceded that a gift for church ornaments was within the equity of the Statute and cited as an example mural tablets. So too in *Re Eighmie*[7] a gift for (*inter alia*) the maintenance of decorations in a parish church was held to be charitable.

The support of the clergy

Despite the contrary opinion of Sir Francis Moore,[8] gifts for the benefit or support of the clergy were soon admitted to be within the intendment of the Act.[9] Thus the establishment of a bishopric[10] and the provision of clergy or preachers[11] have both been held charitable objects, even though conditions may be attached.[12] Gifts for the increase of clergy stipends generally[13] or to increase the stipend of the incumbent of a specified church[14] or his curate[15] are also charitable. But the gift must in the last two cases be for the office-holder for the time being, and not restricted to the individual filling the office at the time.[16] These

---

1 [1940] Ch. 514. Lord Hardwicke had reached a contrary conclusion in *A.-G.* v. *Oakaver* (1736), cited in 1 Ves. Sen. 536; *A.-G.* v. *Whorwood* (1750), 1 Ves. Sen. 534 on the ground that the choir as such was not recognised as part of the established institution in a *parish* church; but he cited no authority for this proposition. See also *Turner* v. *Ogden* (1787), 1 Cox Eq. Cas. 316; *Re Hendry* (1887), 56 L.T. 908.

2 *Re Pardoe*, [1906] 2 Ch. 184.

3 *Re Archer* (1919), *Times*, 13th Dec. PETERSON J. said that this was an attempt by a testator to commemorate his own memory and was therefore not charitable.

4 *Hart* v. *Brewer* (1595), Cro. Eliz. 449.

5 Duke ed. Bridgman, *Law of Charitable Uses* (1805) 124.

6 (1866), L.R. 1 Eq. 585.

7 [1935] Ch. 524; and see *Re Greene*, [1914] 1 I.R. 305 (decoration of a Roman Catholic Church). As to what is meant by the ornaments of a church, see *Re Palatine Estate Charity* (1888), 39 Ch.D. 54.

8 See at 54 *supra*.

9 *Pember* v. *Inhabitants of Kington* (1639), Toth 34.

10 *A.-G.* v. *Bishop of Chester* (1785), 1 Br. C.C. 444.

11 *Dundee Magistrates* v. *Dundee Presbytery* (1861), 4 Macq. 228, H.L. *Pennington* v. *Buckley* (1848), 6 Hare 451, at 453; *Penstred* v. *Payer* (1639), Duke ed. Bridgman 381; *Grieves* v. *Case* (1792), 4 Bro. C.C. 67. Cf. *Re Braham* (1892), 36 S.J. 712 (reader and lecturer for Hebrew congregation).

12 *A.-G.* v. *Molland* (1832), 1 You. 563 (preaching certain doctrines); *Durour* v. *Motteux* (1749), 1 Ves. Sen. 320; *Re Parker's Charity* (1863), 32 Beav. 654 (preaching a sermon in commemoration of the testator); *Re Randell* (1888), 38 Ch.D. 213 (permitting free sittings); and see *Re Robinson*, [1897] 1 Ch. 85; *Re Hussey's Charities* (1861), 30 L.J. Ch. 491; *Re Corcoran*, [1913] 1 I.R. 1; *Re Macnamara* (1911), 104 L.T. 771.

13 *A.-G.* v. *Brereton* (1752), 2 Ves. Sen. 425.

14 *Durour* v. *Motteux, supra*.

15 *Re Baron Burton's Charity*, [1938] 3 All E.R. 90; *Pennington* v. *Buckley* (1848), 6 Hare 453.

16 *Doe d. Phillips* v. *Aldridge* (1791), 4 Term Rep. 264.

principles apply equally to gifts for the benefit of non-conformist[1] or Roman Catholic clergy.[2]

A gift for masses has been held to be good because *inter alia* the honoraria received by the priest for the celebration of the masses form part of his income. The gift is for the benefit or support of the clergy.[3]

The privilege of charity is not confined solely to the direct support of the clergy: if the gift helps even indirectly to support the clergy that may be enough. This was emphasised in *Re Forster*[4] where a gift for the relief of sick and aged Roman Catholic priests in the Clifton diocese was upheld. In his judgment BENNETT J. commented:[5]

> "Such a fund, I think, tends to make the ministry more efficient, by making it easy for the sick and old to retire and give place to the young and healthy."

A similar conclusion was reached upon a gift for retired missionaries on the ground that potential missionaries would be encouraged by the security offered at the end of their active service.[6] Again, in *Re James*[7] a rest home for, among others, the members of a religious community and the clergy of a diocese was held to be a charitable purpose both on the broader ground that a home of rest is *prima facie* a charitable object, and also on the narrower ground that the home was for the benefit of persons carrying on charitable work, namely the advancement of religion.[8] A gift of cottages for retired aged missionaries is also charitable.[9] In *Re Macgregor*[10] it was held that a provision for the subsistence of clergymen retired by reason of old age was charitable. Likewise in the same case a fund for the maintenance of a retired bishop and subsequently his widow, a fund to provide a car for a bishop, and a fund to aid the expenses of a bishop attending the Lambeth conference were all charitable.

C TRUSTS TO SPREAD RELIGION

Introduction

The spread of religion or of Christianity generally is a charitable purpose.[11] There are numerous examples in the books of gifts using general words indicating a religious purpose.[12] In this category are gifts for the service of God,[13] for

---

1 *A.-G.* v. *Cock* (1751), 2 Ves. Sen. 273.

2 *A.-G.* v. *Stewart* (1872), L.R. 14 Eq. 17.

3 *Re Caus*, [1934] 1 Ch. 162. This case and gifts for masses in general are discussed at 65–68, *infra*.

4 [1939] Ch. 22. The gift was not for the relief of poverty.

5 *Ibid.*, at 25.

6 *Re Mylne*, [1941] Ch. 204. *Cf. Baptist Union of Ireland (Northern) Corporation, Ltd.* v. *I.R.Comrs.*, [1945] N.I. 99 (subscribing ministers, their widows and orphans: charities).

7 [1932] 2 Ch. 25.

8 *Ibid.*, per FARWELL J., at 32.

9 *Re White's Will Trusts*, [1955] Ch. 188.

10 (1932), 32 S.R. N.S.W. 483, at 497.

11 *A.-G.* v. *Stepney* (1804), 10 Ves. 22; *Re Macduff*, [1896] 2 Ch. 451, at 471–472, C.A.

12 *A.-G.* v. *London Corporation* (1790), 1 Ves. 243; *Re Hood*, [1931] 1 Ch. 240 (spreading Christian principles and minimising drink traffic).

13 *Re Darling*, [1896] 1 Ch. 50; see also *Powerscourt* v. *Powerscourt* (1824), 1 Mol. 616 (Ir.).

the worship of God,[1] and for the spread of the Gospel.[2] In all such cases there is a presumption that the gift is intended to be applied for the purposes of the Established Church. But this presumption is easily rebutted. Thus in *Re Barker's Will*[3] *Trusts* JENKINS J. upheld a gift "for God's work" but directed that the fund should be applied for Baptist religious purposes, that clearly being the intention of the testator.

Trusts to spread the tenets of a particular sect are similarly charitable.[4] On the other hand the establishment of a Catholic newspaper has in Australia been held to be a non-charitable purpose.[5]

Trusts for missionary and cognate purposes

Trusts to promote the work of home and foreign missions are charitable if couched in sufficiently unambiguous language. A trust for spreading Christianity among infidels was upheld in 1790.[6] In the heyday of the British Empire there was very considerable missionary activity, and numerous societies carrying on such work were recognised as charitable, for example the Society for Promoting Christian Knowledge,[7] the Society for the Propagation of the Gospel in Foreign Parts,[8] the Church Missionary Society[9] and the Sunday School Association.[10] A bequest for the maintenance and advancement of the missionary establishments of the Moravian church among heathen nations of the world was also upheld.[11] Other examples of charitable gifts for missionary purposes are: a gift to the Protestant Alliance (an association formed to defend the doctrines of the Reformation);[12] a gift to editors of a missionary periodical for the furtherance of missions in Africa;[13] and a gift to the editors of a missionary periodical to be applied by them "for such objects as they may think fit".[14]

The expression "missionary purposes" on its own is ambiguous: it may comprise objects which are not charitable. Thus in the Irish case of *Scott* v. *Brownrigg*[15] it was held that a trust for "missionary purposes" was void because there was no obligation to apply the gift to strictly charitable purposes. But the context[16] or surrounding circumstances[17] may indicate that the donor used the expression in the more restricted popular sense of Christian missionary work. If the nominated trustee is someone who has been engaged for many years in

---

1 *A.-G.v. Pearson* (1817), 3 Mer. 353, at 409.
2 *Re Lea* (1887), 34 Ch.D. 528
3 [1948] W.N. 155.
4 See 55–56, *supra*.
5 *Re Lawlor* (1934), 51 C.L.R. 1.
6 *A.-G.* v. *City of London* (1790), 1 Ves. 243.
7 *Re Clergy Society* (1856), 2 K. & J. 615.
8 *Re Maguire* (1870), L.R. 9 Eq. 632.
9 *Ibid.*
10 *R.* v. *Special Comrs. of Income Tax*, [1911] 2 K.B. 434.
11 *Income Tax Special Purposes Comrs.* v. *Pemsel* [1891] A.C. 531.
12 *Re Delmar Charitable Trust*, [1897] 2 Ch. 163.
13 *Re Redish* (1909), 26 T.L.R. 42.
14 *Re Norman*, [1947] Ch. 349.
15 (1881), 9 L.R. Ir. 246. Cf. *Re Rees*, [1920] 2 Ch. 59.
16 *Dunne* v. *Duignan*, [1908] 1 I.R. 228 (foreign missions); *Re Hall* (1915), 31 T.L.R. 396 (City Mission cause in London); *Jackson* v. *A.-G.*, [1917] 1 I.R. 332 (Presbyterian missions).
17 See the cases cited in the footnotes following.

the work of Christian missions[1] or if the testator had helped a particular missionary body[2] or Christian missionary work generally[3] during his lifetime the ambiguity may be resolved in favour of charity.

Public benefit

In *Verge* v. *Somerville*[4] LordWRENBURY stated[5] that:

> "To ascertain whether a gift constitutes a valid charitable trust . . . a first enquiry must be made whether it is public—whether it is for the benefit of the community or an appreciably important class of the community."

Some 20 years later in 1945 Lord GREENE M.R. in *Re Compton*[6] approved the textbook statement that "it may be laid down as a universal rule that the law recognises no purpose as charitable unless it is of a public character". Only the anomalous "poor relations" trusts were held to be excepted.

The application of this "universal" rule to religious trusts was queried in a learned article[7] by Professor Newark in 1946. But the House of Lords in *Gilmour* v. *Coats*[8] confirmed that religious trusts are required to negotiate the test of public benefit. This was not always so. Before the Reformation, when only one religion enjoyed legal recognition, gifts for religious purposes were accepted as charitable because of their piety, and without further consideration of the question of public benefit. As Lord REID observed:[9]

> "It was natural that the law should accept the beliefs of that religion without question and act on them."

But once a diversity of religious beliefs arose and became lawful the judges could find no basis for drawing a distinction in the matter of charity between the Established Church and other churches. Perhaps the natural corollary to this position, in which all religions were equal in the eyes of the law, was the same kind of objective test as was applied to other heads of charity.

The test of public benefit was not always expressly invoked but the vast majority of cases before *Gilmour* v. *Coats*[10] recognised the necessity of public benefit in religious gifts. For example in *Hoare* v. *Hoare*[11] a gift to provide for Church of England services in a *private* chapel was held not to be charitable because no benefit to the public could accrue from such a gift. The chapel was "simply a private chapel in a gentleman's house".[12] So too the promotion of individual prayer cannot be charitable because its purpose is "a mere improvement of the individual".[13]

---

1 *Re Kenny* (1907), 97 L.T. 130; *Re Moon's Will Trusts*, [1948] 1 All E.R. 300.
2 *Re Rees*, [1920] 2 Ch. 59 and see *Re Redish* (1910), 26 T.L.R. 42.
3 *Re Moon's Will Trusts*, [1948] 1 All E.R. 300.
4 [1924] A.C. 496.
5 *Ibid.*, at 499.
6 [1945] Ch. 123.
7 (1946), 62 L.Q.R. 234; see also Brady (1974), 25 N.I.L.Q. 174.
8 [1949] A.C. 426.
9 *Ibid.*, at 457.
10 [1949] A.C. 476.
11 (1886), 56 L.T. 147.
12 *Ibid.*, at 150; followed in *Iyenda* v. *Ajike* (1948), 19 Nig. L.R. 11 (private mosque).
13 *Re Joy* (1888), 60 L.T. 175.

The problem of public benefit has loomed largest where property has been given to endow masses, religious orders or tombstones. But it can arise in other cases too. Worship in church is not the only religious observance likely to impel testators to beneficence and any endowment to promote a particular religious observance must pass the test of public benefit.

GIFTS FOR THE CELEBRATION OF MASSES[1]

Legal validity

The attitude of the English courts to gifts for the celebration of masses was for several hundred years conditioned by the interpretation put on the Statute of Chantries of 1547.[2] This Act, which did not apply in Ireland,[3] made retrospective provisions to deal with existing endowments for the maintenance of masses for the repose of souls of deceased persons: the endowments were appropriated by the Crown and diverted to the founding of schools. Duke in his treatise on Charitable Uses,[4] written after the Reformation, said that the intention of the Statute was to condemn gifts for masses as superstitious uses. For a long time, of course, the mass was an illegal service[5] so that it was unnecessary in fact to appeal to the doctrine of superstitious uses. But, after various statutes had removed the principal disabilities on Roman Catholics, it was assumed that a gift for masses was void as superstitious.[6] Ultimately in 1919 the question fell to be determined by the House of Lords. In *Bourne* v. *Keane*,[7] the case in point, the House of Lords decided by a majority that such gifts were valid and that the earlier cases were wrong, having proceeded on the assumption that there was a prohibition in the Statute of Chantries which did not, in fact, exist.

Charitable nature

The case of *Bourne* v. *Keane* was only concerned with the legal validity of bequests for masses: it did not consider whether they were charitable. However 15 years later LUXMOORE J. in *Re Caus*[8] held that they were. Gifts for the saying of masses were, he held, for the advancement of religion (i) because they

---

1 Curran (1931), 7 Notre Dame Law. 42; Curran, 5 De Paul Law Rev. 246; Brady, *Religion and the Law of Charities in Ireland* (1976), 66–119.

2 (1547), 1 Edw. 6, c. 14.

3 Where in consequence the legality of bequests for masses was admitted almost a century before it was in England: see *Charitable Donations and Bequests Comrs.* v. *Walsh* (1823), 7 I.Eq.R. 34 n., *per* Lord MANNERS C.; and see *Read* v. *Hodgens* (1844), 7 I.Eq.R. 34 (BLACKBURNE M.R. upheld bequest for "masses for my soul's sake").

4 1st edn. (1676), 106.

5 By virtue of the Acts of Uniformity 1548 and 1558.

6 *West* v. *Shuttleworth* (1835), 2 My. & K. 684; *A.-G.* v. *Fishmongers' Company* (1841), 2 Beav. 151, at 171; *Heath* v. *Chapman* (1854), 2 Drew 417; *Re Michel's Trusts* (1860), 28 Beav. 39; *Re Blundell's Trusts* (1861), 30 Beav. 360; *Re Fleetwood* (1880), 15 Ch.D. 594; *Re Elliott*, [1891] W.N. 9.

7 [1919] A.C. 815; see also Hogg (1920), 36 L.Q.R. 53; Bourchier-Chilcott (1920), 36 L.Q.R. 152.

8 [1934] 1 Ch. 162 not following *Heath* v. *Chapman* (1854), 2 Drew 417.

E

enable a ritual act to be performed which is the central act of the religion of a large proportion of Christian people and (ii) because they assist in the endowment of priests whose duty it is to perform the act. In reading this conclusion LUXMOORE J. was much influenced by the decision of PALLES C.B. in the Irish case of *O'Hanlon* v. *Logue*.[1] In *Gilmour* v. *Coats*, however, the Court of Appeal[2] doubted the correctness of LUXMOORE J.'s reasoning and in the same case the House of Lords expressly reserved its right to comment on the soundness of LUXMOORE J.'s decision and of the Irish cases. It therefore becomes relevant to consider the basis of the Irish decisions and the attitude of one or two other jurisdictions before hazarding a guess at the position the House of Lords will finally take on gifts for the celebration of masses.

The attitude of the Irish courts has not always been entirely consistent, although the position today is settled enough. In *A.-G.* v. *Delaney*[3] which came before the Court of Exchequer in 1876 a gift for masses was held not to be charitable on the ground that there was no element of public benefit in the gift in question. PALLES C.B. observed that if the will had expressly required the masses to be said in *public* then the gift would probably have been charitable, but despite the Chief Baron's dictum gifts for masses to be celebrated in public continued to be treated as non-charitable.[4] However in 1897 the tide turned and gifts for public masses were at last admitted to the privilege of charity.[5] There, for a time, the matter rested,[6] but in 1906 in *O'Hanlon* v. *Logue*[7] the Irish Court of Appeal abandoned the distinction between public and private masses, holding both to be charitable objects. PALLES C.B. had an opportunity to reconsider the opinion which he had expressed in *A.-G.* v. *Delaney* and concluded that it could no longer stand. Gifts for the celebration of masses were, he said, charitable (1) because of their piety; (2) because they were devoted to the support and maintenance of the clergymen, the celebrants. The Chief Baron took the view that the court was entitled to accept the teaching of the Catholic Church regarding the mass as sufficient to establish the necessary element of public benefit, and the other members of the court concurred in this view. Later Irish cases[8] have subtracted nothing from the principle enunciated in the Irish Court of Appeal. In one case where there was a bequest to a Roman Catholic priest for masses and that priest had been an attesting witness to the will, this fact was held not to invalidate the bequest under the Wills Act, for he did not take beneficially though he might himself benefit incidentally in a material sense.[9]

---

1 [1906] 1 I.R. 247.

2 *Re Coats' Trusts*, [1948] Ch. 340.

3 (1876), Ir.R. 10 C.L. 104 followed in *Beresford* v. *Jervis* (1877), 11 I.L.T.R. 128; *McCourt* v. *Burnett* (1877), 11 I.L.T.R. 130; *Raftery* v. *Coleman* cited in Hamilton Law Relating to Charities in Ireland (2nd edn.) 1881, 77.

4 *Kehoe* v. *Wilson* (1880), 7 L.R. Ir. 10 (CHATTERTON V.C.); *Morrow* v. *McConville* (1883), 11 L.R. Ir. 236; *Dorrian* v. *Gilmore* (1884), 15 L.R. Ir. 69; *Phelan* v. *Slattery* (1887), 19 L.R. Ir. 177; *Perry* v. *Tuomey* (1888), L.R. 21 Ir. 480 (PORTER M.R.).

5 *A.-G.* v. *Hall*, [1896] 2 I.R. 291; [1897] 2 I.R. 426.

6 *McMullen* v. *McVeigh* (1900), 1 N.I.J.R. 176; *Healy* v. *A.-G.*, [1902] 1 I.R. 342 where CHATTERTON V.-C. resiled from his view in *Kehoe* v. *Wilson, supra*; *Buchanan* v. *Brady* (1902), 36 I.L.T.R. 146; *Richardson* v. *Murphy*, [1903] I.R. 227, 234; *Kavanagh* v. *Kelly* (1903), 37 I.L.T.R. 71; *Fanning* v. *Fricker* (1904), 38 I.L.T.R. 235.

7 [1906] 1 I.R. 247. Bequests for masses in the Chief Baron's own will specified that they should be celebrated in public, but only because he did not trust the people across the water: V. T. H. Delany, *Christopher Palles*, 171–172.

8 *Re Gibbons*, [1917] 1 I.R. 448; *Re Ryan* (1926), 60 I.L.T. 57; *Re Howley*, [1940] I.R. 109.

9 *Kelly* v. *Walsh*, [1948] I.R. 388; and see Charities Act 1961, s. 45 (Eire).

In Australia the question whether masses for the dead are charitable came before a court in Victoria in *Re Pursell*[1] and an affirmative answer was given. The same result was reached in New South Wales[2] and Queensland[3] and the High Court of Australia.[4] In New Zealand a trust for masses to be said on behalf of the testatrix was upheld as charitable, the judge saying:[5]

> "As the Roman Catholic faith is a lawful religion and its trusts are lawful trusts, a bequest to the Church or to a particular priest of that Church for masses for the dead is therefore . . . an effective charitable use, the priest receiving the gift for and on account of and for the benefit of the church."

The position in Canada is somewhat uncertain. In *Re Hallisy*[6] the Ontario Court of Appeal held that a bequest of the annual income of a trust fund for the saying of masses in perpetuity was valid as a charitable trust outside the scope of the rule against perpetuities. The court purported to follow *Bourne* v. *Keane*[7] which had not, in fact, even considered the question of the *charitable* nature of a trust for masses for the dead. On that score the reasoning in *Re Hallisy*, although it was followed in Nova Scotia in *Re Samson*,[8] is suspect but the conclusion was probably right.

The great weight of authority in the United States favours the charitable nature of a trust for masses.[9] Professor Scott[10] comments that these cases seem clearly sound because the benefits of a trust for masses are not confined to the particular soul commemorated but extend to the other members of the church and to all the world, according to the doctrines of the Roman Catholic Church. Yet if *Re Caus*[11] is to be supported in the House of Lords, it is thought that it will not be on the ground that the court is entitled to accept the teaching of the Catholic Church regarding the mass as sufficient to establish the necessary element of public benefit. Gifts for masses would seem to be charitable because they are for the endowment of priests whose function and duty it is to advance the teaching of the Roman Catholic Church.[12] The annexation of a condition to the gift, namely that the priest shall say masses to commemorate the testator or a relative of his, does not sabotage the charitable nature of the endowment. In *Re Parker's Charity*[13] a gift of residue to be applied in augmentation of the vicarage was subject to a condition that the vicar should preach an annual sermon in commemoration of the testator. Sir JOHN ROMILLY M.R. had no hesitation in upholding the gift as charitable although he did not consider a

---

1 (1895), 21 V.L.R. 249.
2 *Re Harnett* (1907), 7 S.R. N.S.W. 463; *Re Keenan* (1913), 30 W.N. (N.S.W.) 214.
3 *Re Byrne's Will*, [1938] Q.S.R. 346.
4 *Nelan* v. *Downes* (1917), 23 C.L.R. 546. See also *Public Trustee* v. *Smith* (1944), 44 S.R. N.S.W. 348; *Thomson* v. *Whittard* (1925), 28 S.R. N.S.W. 430.
5 *Carrigan* v. *Redwood* (1910), 30 N.Z.L.R. 244.
6 [1932] 4 D.L.R. 516 overruling *Re Zeagman* (1916), 37 O.L.R. 536.
7 [1919] A.C. 815, H.L.
8 (1967), 59 D.L.R. (2d) 132.
9 See Scott, *Trusts* (3rd edn.) para. 371.5 and cases there cited.
10 *Ibid.*
11 [1934] 1 Ch. 162.
12 See *Re Coat's Trusts*, [1948] Ch. 340, at 365, *per* EVERSHED L.J.; *Lindsay's Executor* v. *Forsyth* 1940 S.C. 568; *cf. Hoare* v. *Hoare* (1886), 56 L.T. 147 where the endowed priest was to act as a *private* chaplain.
13 (1863), 32 Beav. 654.

commemorative sermon to be a charitable object.[1] This case was not cited in
Re Caus[2] notwithstanding that it supports LUXMOORE J.'s decision.

Where the masses are to be said in public there will be a further justification in
upholding a gift for masses: the maintenance of religious services tending
directly or indirectly towards the instruction or edification of the public is a
good, charitable purpose.[3]

GIFTS FOR RELIGIOUS COMMUNITIES[4]

Introduction

Pious testators sometimes wish to benefit a religious community, as for example
a monastic order or a convent. According to the tenets of the testator's religion
such a gift may be considered as for the advancement of religion on the ground
that it is for a pious use. However the courts apply their own objective test and
must be satisfied that the gift promotes a public benefit.

A proper appreciation of the case-law on this topic can only be made in an
historical context.

Law prior to 1926

Until 1926, when the Roman Catholic Relief Act[5] was placed on the Statute
book, *male* religious orders of the Roman Catholic Church were illegal.[6] In
consequence any gift to a male religious order was tainted with illegality and
was deemed to be void in law. This taint disappeared with the removal of the
remaining statutory restrictions on monastic orders and it became relevant to
determine whether such gifts could be charitable.

Even before 1926 it had already been decided in *Re Smith*[7] that of a gift for
"the Society . . . known as the Franciscan Friars of Clevedon . . . absolutely"
could be construed as an absolute immediate gift to the individual friars com-
posing the Society at the testator's death.

Moreover the statutory restrictions on religious orders did not apply to
female religious communities.[8] But, although a gift to a community of nuns
associated for legally charitable works such as teaching or nursing was held to
be charitable,[9] a bequest to a convent for the use and benefit of the community
was held not to be charitable.[10] The constructional escape adopted by the court

---

1 *Sed quaere.* This would depend on the content of the commemorative sermon. A "Reith
Lecture" is not devoted to a eulogy of Lord Reith and there is only a brief foreword com-
memorating the founder of the Hamlyn Trust in the published Hamlyn Lectures.

2 [1934] 1 Ch. 162.

3 See *per* Lord HANWORTH M.R. in *Re Barclay*, [1929] 2 Ch. 173 at 190; *Re Delany*,
[1902] 2 Ch. 642 (FARWELL J.).

4 See Delany, *Law Relating to Charities in Ireland* (Revised edn.) 63–78.

5 16 & 17 Geo. 5 c. 55, s. 1.

6 See Roman Catholic Relief Act 1829 (10 Geo. 4 c. 7) ss. 28 and 29.

7 [1914] 1 Ch. 937.

8 Roman Catholic Relief Act 1829, s. 37.

9 *Cocks* v. *Manners* (1871), L.R. 12 Eq. 574; and see *Mahony* v. *Duggan* (1883), 11 L.R. Ir.
260.

10 *Morrow* v. *Mc'Conville* (1883), 11 L.R. Ir. 236.

in *Re Smith*[1] could not avail where the words of the gift made it plain that the bequest was not for immediate distribution but was intended to be for the perpetual benefit of the order. In other words a gift in favour of a religious order of women which has not assigned in some sufficient way to a charitable purpose and was on its proper construction a gift to the order as a continuing body would fail.[2]

The attitude of the courts was very well illustrated by the decision of Sir JOHN WICKENS V.C. in *Cocks* v. *Manners*,[3] a case which merits some examination. In that case a testatrix had directed that her property, real and personal, should be sold and that the proceeds, after the payment of certain legacies, should be distributed in equal shares between certain specified religious institutions. The first of these was "to the Sisters of Charity of St Paul, at Selley Oak, payable to the Superior thereof for the time being". The Vice-Chancellor held that the bequest was valid. He said:[4]

> "The community of Sisters at Selley Oak is, in point of law, a voluntary association for the purpose of teaching the ignorant and nursing the sick. I cannot distinguish it in this respect from any of the numerous voluntary associations established in London . . . in which zealous persons unite for the purpose of performing charitable functions, taking out of funds of the association so much as is necessary for their own wants and extending their operations as their means permit."

The second bequest in *Cocks* v. *Manners* was to the Dominican Convent at Carisbrook, payable to the Superior for the time being. The convent in question was a "contemplative order" in which the sisters were associated for retirement and devotion and not for external works of charity. Dealing with the argument that religious purposes were charitable the Vice-Chancellor pointed out[5] that:

> "that can only be true as to religious services tending directly or indirectly towards the instruction or edification of the public; an annuity to an individual so long as he spent his time in retirement and constant devotion would not be charitable; nor would a gift to ten persons, so long as they lived together in retirement and performed acts of devotion, be charitable".

Accordingly the gift could not be upheld as charitable, although it could be supported as a good non-charitable gift to the nuns.

Modern law

Today both monastic and conventual orders are legal. However the principles laid down in *Cocks* v. *Manners*[6] are still law, having been approved by the House

---

1 *Supra.*
2 *Stewart* v. *Green* (1871), I.R. 5 Eq. 470. *cf. Re Wilkinson's Trusts* (1887), 19 L.R. Ir. 531, at 533; *Bradshaw* v. *Jackman* (1887), 21 L.R. Ir. 12; *Re Delany's Estate* (1881), 9 L.R. Ir. 226, at 236.
3 (1871), L.R. 12 Eq. 574.
4 *Ibid.*, at 584.
5 *Ibid.*, at 585; see further *Re Delany*, [1902] 2 Ch. 642. For varying Irish approaches see *Charitable Donations and Bequests Comrs.* v. *McCartan*, [1917] 1 I.R. 388; *Munster and Leinster Bank* v. *A.-G.*, [1940] I.R. 19; *Re Howley*, [1940] I.R. 109; *Maguire* v. *A.-G.*, [1943] I.R. 238.
6 (1871), L.R. 12 Eq. 574.

of Lords in *Gilmour* v. *Coats*.[1] In *Gilmour* v. *Coats* the income of a trust fund was
to be applied to the purposes of a Carmelite convent if those purposes were
charitable. The convent comprised an assosiation of strictly cloistered and
purely contemplative nuns who devoted themselves entirely to worship,
prayers and meditation and engaged in no activities for the benefit of anyone
outside their own association. It was held that these purposes were not charitable—there was no public benefit. Counsel for the prioress of the convent sought
to argue that there was a sufficient element of public benefit (1) because the
teaching of the Roman Catholic Church is that intercessory prayers bring
spiritual benefit to mankind (2) because the example of the pious lives led by the
nuns is a source of great edification to other Catholics and (3) because the
community was open to any Roman Catholic woman having the necessary
vocation. The House of Lords rejected each of these three contentions. The
court (it was held) could only act on *proof* of public benefit and not on belief;
and the value of intercessory prayers was manifestly incapable of proof. The
benefit to be derived by others from the example of pious lives was something
too vague and intangible to satisfy the test of public benefit. As to the argument
that the convent was open to any Roman Catholic woman with a vocation,
that was immaterial once the law was disabled from recognising any public
benefit resulting from the existence of the community. In the words of Lord
SIMONDS:[2]

> "it would be irrational to the point of absurdity, on the one hand, to deny
> to a community of contemplative nuns the character of a charitable
> institution, but, on the other, to accept as a charitable trust a gift which had
> no other object than to enable it to be maintained in perpetuity by recruit-
> ment from the outside world".

It is interesting to note that in Ireland where the saying of masses has been
definitely established as a charitable object there is some uncertainty as to the
nature of gifts to support an order of contemplative nuns. GAVAN DUFFY J.
commented in *Re Howley*[3] that "the assumption that the Irish public finds no
edification in cloistered lives devoted to purely spiritual ends postulates a close
assimilation of the Irish outlook to the English, not obviously warranted by the
traditions and *mores* of the Irish people". This was a mere dictum but the same
judge returned to do battle on this point in a later case in which it was directly
raised. In *Maguire* v. *A.-G.*[4] the validity of a gift to found a convent for the
perpetual adoration of the Blessed Sacrament was in issue. Adoration of the
Blessed Sacrament is "a form of devotion . . . whereby arrangements are made,
necessarily by a community, for an unbroken succession of persons to be present
in *private* prayer and contemplation before the Blessed Sacrament exposed to
the view of the worshippers". In the course of a long and outspoken judgment
GAVAN DUFFY J. said[5] that "it is a shock to one's sense of propriety, and a grave
discredit to the law that there should in this Catholic country be any doubt
about the validity of such a bequest". The basis of his decision was that "the
common law knew the Mass. The common law knew the adoration of the
Blessed Sacrament. Therefore I know them judicially. The doctrine known to

---

1 [1949] A.C. 426.
2 *Ibid.*, at 449.
3 [1940] I.R. 109, at 113; and see Brady, *op. cit.*, 88–94.
4 [1943] I.R. 238; see also *Bank of Ireland Trustee Co., Ltd.* v. *A.-G.*, [1957] I.R. 257.
5 [1943] I.R. 238, at 244.

the common law is the doctrine of the Catholic church." And he reasoned that just as the mass was charitable at common law (being a gift to God), so too the provision of a convent carrying on this activity is also "a gift directly intended to perpetuate the worship of God" and is therefore charitable. *Cocks* v. *Manners*[1] was merely a statement of public policy in England in 1871 and bore no relation to Ireland.

The decision in *Maguire* v. *A.-G.*[2] is binding, in the Republic at least, until the Supreme Court overrules it. But it is, of course, of no authority in the United Kingdom. Unless the House of Lords re-considers its decision in *Gilmour* v. *Coats*[3] (as it is now entitled to do[4]) *Maguire* v. *A.-G.* must remain as an interesting illustration of a different (and some might say preferable) approach to such gifts.

In *Re Warre's Will Trust*[5] another type of religious activity was denied a charitable label. HARMAN J. in that case held, relying on *Cocks* v. *Manners*[6] and *Gilmour* v. *Coats*,[7] that an Anglican retreat house was not a charity and GOFF J. has expressly approved that decision.[8] Nevertheless the decision is unsatisfactory.[9] HARMAN J. reached the conclusion that a gift for a diocesan retreat house was not charitable because he defined the term "retreat" as retirement from the activities of the world for a space of time for religious contemplation and the cleansing of the soul. Such activity or inactivity, though highly beneficial for the person who undertakes it, is not, on the well-known authorities which he cited, a charitable activity. Many retreats are, however, specially conducted and these are usually accompanied by devotional addresses and religious services. Since the individual retreatants return after their short stay to the outside world to pursue their mundane lives, it is difficult to see why the necessary public element is lacking. A diocesan retreat house is open to any member of the Church of England and in that sense "opens out to reach the public".[10] There is surely a material difference between a closed religious community consisting of private individuals working out their own salvation in private and a retreat house to which members of the public resort for only a very limited period of time and possibly only once. The crucial test is whether the community "opens out to reach the public". In *Re Banfield*[11] GOFF J. decided that the Pilsdon community did. Despite GOFF J.'s endorsement of HARMAN J.'s decision it is submitted that a retreat house does the same.

GIFTS FOR TOMBS OR MONUMENTS

Despite an early diversity of views on the topic it is now settled that, as a general rule, a gift for the erection or maintenance of a particular tomb in a churchyard

---

1 (1871), L.R. 12 Eq. 574.
2 [1943] I.R. 238; *cf. Re Keogh*, [1945] I.R. 13; Charities Act 1961, s. 45 (2).
3 [1949] A.C. 426.
4 See [1966] 1 W.L.R. 1234 discussed in Walker & Walker, *The English Legal System* (4th edn.) 128–130.
5 [1953] 1 W.L.R. 725.
6 *Supra.*
7 *Supra.*
8 *Re Banfield*, [1968] 1 W.L.R. 846.
9 See also the criticism in *Tudor on Charities* (6th edn.) 63–64 and of LUSH J. in *Association of Franciscan Order of Friars Minor* v. *City of Kew*, [1967] V.R. 732.
10 See *Re Banfield*, [1968] 1 W.L.R. 846, at 852.
11 [1968] 1 W.L.R. 846.

is not charitable.[1] The motive behind such gifts is usually the self-gratification of the settlor or testator, but motive is, of course, irrelevant. The real reason for holding such gifts to be non-charitable[2] is that normally they lack any public benefit. As Andrew Marvell observes:[3] "The grave's a fine and *private* place."

It is another matter if the tomb is part of the fabric of the church or chapel itself: a gift to maintain such a tomb is considered to be charitable.[4] Thus in *Re Barker*[5] the maintenance of a memorial tablet in the crypt of St. Paul's Cathedral was held to be a charitable object. A gift for the perpetual repair of a monument in a church may be upheld although it is not part of the fabric: for it is an ornament.

The distinction is also made between a gift to keep in repair an *individual* vault or tomb in a churchyard and a gift to maintain a *whole* churchyard or burial ground. The latter is charitable,[6] the former is not[7]. It seems, moreover, that a trust for the maintenance and upkeep of the tombs of a class of persons constituting a section of the public is also charitable.[8] Accordingly it is possible to argue that a trust for the repair and maintenance of part or parts of a churchyard or other burial ground is charitable.

It is thought, however, that a gift by a testator to erect or maintain a tomb or monument of some illustrious man (other than the testator) would be valid. There is scanty and inconclusive authority[9] in this country on the subject, but the Charity Commissioners have treated the Wellington Monument in Somerset and the Cobden Obelisk at Midhurst as charitable objects. In America, on the other hand, it is recognised that a trust for a monument in honour of some illustrious man is charitable.[10] The question how prominent the deceased must have been and how great his services to his country or state or local community is one of degree. But if such a gift is valid it would seem to be so either on educational grounds, or on the grounds that it is somehow beneficial to the community under the fourth head of *Pemsel's* case. Professor Bogert, for example, says that trusts to construct monuments to citizens of high character

---

1 See, for example, *Masters* v. *Masters* (1718), 1 P. Wms. 421, at 423 n. 1; *Durour* v. *Motteux* (1749), 1 Ves. Sen. 320; *Gravenor* v. *Hallum* (1767), Amb. 643; *Doe d. Thompson* v. *Pitcher* (1815), 3 M. & S. 407, at 410 (Lord ELLENBOROUGH C.J.); and contrast *Doe d. Thompson* v. *Pitcher* (1815), 6 Taunt. 359, 369–370 (GIBBS C.J.); *Mellick* v. *Asylum President and Guardians* (1821), Jac. 180.

2 If limited to the perpetuity period the trust may still be valid; see Underhill, *Law of Trusts and Trustees* (12th edn.) 117–118.

3 To His Coy Mistress, line 31 (emphasis added).

4 *Hoare* v. *Osborne* (1866), L.R. 1 Eq. 585; *Re Rigley's Trusts* (1866), 36 L.J. Ch. 147.

5 (1909), 25 T.L.R. 753.

6 *Re Vaughan* (1886), 33 Ch.D. 187; *Re Douglas*, [1905] 1 Ch. 279; *Re Eighmie*, [1935] Ch. 524. A gift of land for a cemetery is charitable: *A.-G.* v. *Blizard* (1855), 21 Beav. 233.

7 *Rickard* v. *Robson* (1862), 31 Beav. 244; *Lloyd* v. *Lloyd* (1852), 2 Sim. N.S. 255. The distinction seems illogical: see *Re Quinn* (1954), 88 I.L.T. 161; and consider *Re Vaughan* (1886), 33 Ch.D. 187, at 192 reproduced on 59, *supra*.

8 *Re Manser*, [1905] 1 Ch. 68, at 73 (Quakers). *Re Pardoe*, [1907] 2 Ch. 184 (almshouse pensioners).

9 *Re Jones* (1898), 79 L.T. 154 (trust for a monument of the philosopher John Locke held non-charitable); and see *M'Caig's Trustees* v. *Kirk Session of United Free Church of Lismore* 1915 S.C. 426.

10 *Gilmer's Legatees* v. *Gilmer's Executors*, 42 Ala. 9 (U.S.) (1868) (monument of General Stonewall Jackson: charitable); *Owens* v. *Owens' Executor*, 236 Ky 118 (U.S.) (1930) (Washington, Lincoln, Jefferson and Jackson).

and achievement are charitable in that they encourage patriotism and the emulation of desirable qualities.[1]

A trust to maintain a memorial or monument which is an acknowledged work of art would, presumably, qualify as charitable on the grounds of its educational character.[2] In certain circumstances it may be enough if the memorial is of a useful character. Thus in *Murray* v. *Thomas*[3] it was held to be a charitable object to promote for the benefit of two villages some useful war memorial, preferably of the type of a village hall. But a gift to a parish council for the purpose of providing some useful memorial of the testator was held in *Re Endacott*[4] not to be charitable. The decision in *Murray* v. *Thomas* was not cited to the Court of Appeal in *Re Endacott* and the distinction between the two cases is very fine.

ORGANISED RELIGIOUS PLIGRIMAGES

The courts in this country have not yet had an opportunity to consider the validity of a trust to promote organised religious pilgrimages. Although the Roman Catholic Church encourages pilgrimages and recognises them as a public manifestation of religion, the question of public benefit is one that must be resolved by the court.

Not surprisingly, this question has been mooted in Ireland. In *Re Mac-Carthy*,[5] *deceased* the testatrix bequeathed the sum of £600 to the Archbishop of Dublin on trust to apply the annual income existing therefrom "in defraying wholly or partially the travelling expenses and maintenance of two or more invalid persons taking part in organised Religious Pilgrimages to the Grotto of Our Lady at Lourdes, such invalid persons to be chosen for the benefit of such income to be in equal numbers each year from the areas now represented by the Catholic Parishes of Dun Laoghaire and Glasthule." Evidence was given to the effect that *organised* religious pilgrimages were only permitted with the sanction and approval of the ecclesiastical authorities and were either organised by such ecclesiastical authorities or religious organisations approved of by them.[6] An affidavit from the Secretary of the Dublin Diocesan Pilgrimage to Lourdes set out the Catholic teaching concerning pilgrimages and stressed that Lourdes was the most frequented place of pilgrimage in the Catholic world. It also pointed out that care was always taken to ensure that such pilgrimages maintained their religious character and that various religious exercises were also performed by the pilgrims at Lourdes. BUDD J. in upholding the bequest as a valid charitable gift said:[7]

"Apart from what is stated in the affidavit, I think a pilgrimage has always been regarded as a religious act. It is something done in the public

1 See Bogert, *Cases on the Law of Trusts* (3rd edn.) 247; and see *Owens* v. *Owens' Executor*, *supra*.
2 But see *M'Caig* v. *Glasgow University* 1907, S.C. 231 (trust to erect monuments of testator and his family and artistic trusts with young and rising artists: not charitable). A trust for keeping in repair a portrait has been held non-charitable: *Re Gassiot* (1901), 70 L.J. Ch. 242.
3 [1937] 4 All E.R. 545.
4 [1960] Ch. 232, C.A.
5 [1958] I.R. 311.
6 *Ibid.*, at 316.
7 *Ibid.*, at 316–317.

eye and is, therefore, a matter of public benefit and edification. Furthermore I have had pointed out to me the definition of a pilgrimage in the
Oxford Dictionary:—'A journey (usually of considerable duration) made
to some sacred place as an act of religious devotion.' This gift is to aid one
or two of the sick people of the two parishes mentioned to take part in
these organised religious pilgrimages, and having regard to the nature of
these pilgrimages, it is clearly a gift for the advancement of religion."

Even allowing for the tenderness with which Irish judges treat Roman Catholic
religious purposes, the decision seems reasonable in principle. The decisive consideration is the nature of the pilgrimage. A pilgrimage organised by religious
authorities and done in the public eye does not confer merely private benefits:
there is an element of corporate devotional edification. But a lone pilgrimage
by an individual will be an act of private devotion. There must therefore be
some evidence that the pilgrimages which the testator had in mind are not
merely acts of private devotion. So, in a Malayan case[1] where the court was
asked to consider the nature of a gift "for pilgrimages to Mecca" HYNDMAN-
JONES C.J. said[2]

> "There being no evidence nor indeed any suggestion that these pilgrim-
> ages do anything more than merely solace the pilgrim, and possibly his
> family, I am of the opinion that this purpose is not charitable."

The gift, it will be noticed, was expressed in the broadest terms. There was no
reference to organised pilgrimages and the gift was not to a religious officeholder as trustee. There was no evidence or suggestion of public benefit, as
indeed HYNDMAN-JONES C.J. stressed. The absence of all these things is the
distinguishing feature of the Malayan case: it is reconcilable in principle with
Re MacCarthy.

RELIGIOUS WRITINGS

The cases about religious writings proceed on the footing that the court will
not assess the rationality of religious writings: so long as the writings are not
immoral or irreligious a gift to publish and circulate them is charitable. In
Thornton v. *Howe*[3] the writings of Joanna Southcott were read by Sir JOHN
ROMILLY M.R. for the purpose of seeing whether they contained anything
which, in his opinion, was likely to corrupt the morals of her followers or make
her readers irreligious. He found much that was very foolish and considered
that her works were in a great measure incoherent and confused but they were
"written obviously with a view to extend the influence of Christianity".

The decision in *Thornton* v. *Howe* has been described as a high water mark
of toleration.[4] In fact the decision that the gift was charitable enabled the gift
to be struck down under the Mortmain Act of 1736[5] because it was a gift out of
land. Had that been any pure personalty the gift would have been *pro tanto*
valid. But the decision was a decision in favour of the heiress-at-law. The

---

1 *Re Hadjee Esmail bin Kassim* (1911), 12 S.S.L.R. 74 (Singapore).
2 *Ibid.*, at 80.
3 (1862), 31 Beav. 14.
4 See Hanbury, *Modern Equity* (9th edn.) 262.
5 See Jones, *History of the Law of Charity 1532–1827* (1969), 115–117.

toleration was therefore a kiss of death so far as the object of the testatrix was concerned.

In *Re Newsom*[1] there was a trust to produce a new edition of a book entitled *Verdict on Jesus*. The theological merit of the book was put in issue by an affidavit sworn by the Professor of Moral and Social Theology at King's College London but this was countered by academic evidence to the contrary effect. In the result it was accepted by all parties that the trust was for the advancement of religion and therefore charitable, and PLOWMAN J. approved a scheme brought in by the trustees of the will.

In *Re Watson*[2] it was held by PLOWMAN J. that the will of the testatrix created a trust for the publication and distribution of the religious works of Mr. H. G. Hobbs. The question in issue was, then, whether or not such a trust was charitable. The author whose writings were in question was a builder by trade who retired so as to devote himself more fully to religious activities particularly writing in which he was extremely prolific. The writings were mostly in the form of short commentaries on the Scriptures and were "fundamentalist and Pauline (and hence millennialist and pacifist) in inspiration, with considerable Calvinistic elements."[3] An affidavit sworn by the Professor of Moral and Social Theology already mentioned was filed on behalf of the Attorney-General. The affidavit said that the pamphlets undoubtedly displayed a religious tendency but that their intrinsic worth was nil and they were unlikely to extend the knowledge of the Christian religion through they might confirm in their religious opinions the members of the "in-group" in which they were produced. Counsel for the next of kin submitted that *Thornton* v. *Howe* was inconsistent with the approach of the House of Lords in *National Anti-Vivisection Society* v. *I.R. Comrs.*[4] and *Gilmour* v. *Coats*[5] where it had been said that whether or not there is sufficient public benefit is a matter for the court to decide on evidence, irrespective of the opinion of the donor. On a proper analysis of the evidence there was, he submitted, no sufficient element of public benefit. PLOWMAN J. rejected this attack on *Thornton* v. *Howe* which he held to be on all fours with the case before him. After reviewing a number of cases in which *Thornton* v. *Howe* was treated a good law[6] the learned judge put forward the following propositions: first the court does not prefer one religion to another or one sect to another; second, where the purposes in question are of a religious nature the court assumes a public benefit unless the contrary appears; and third, the *only* way of disproving a public benefit is to show that the doctrines inculcated are "adverse to the very foundations of all religion and that they are subversive of all morality".[7]

It is to be observed that the learned judge in *Re Watson* did not discuss the case of *Gilmour* v. *Coats* although it is mentioned in his judgment. The difficulty in reconciling his decision with *Gilmour* v. *Coats* is considerable. The religious

1 *Re Newsom* 1971 N. No. 423 (1973), 14th March, unreported.
2 [1973] 1 W.L.R. 1472.
3 [1973] 1 W.L.R. 1472, at 1476.
4 [1948] A.C. 31.
5 [1949] A.C. 426.
6 See *Bowman* v. *Secular Society, Ltd.*, [1917] A.C. 406, at 442; *Re Price*, [1943] Ch. 422, at 432–433; *Re Pinion*, [1965] Ch. 85, at 95 and 105. For Canadian and Australian approval, see *Re Orr* (1917), 40 D.L.R. 567; *Re Knight*, [1937] O.R. 462, at 465; *Congregational Union of New South Wales* v. *Thistlethwaite*, [1952] 87 C.L.R. 375.
7 [1973] 1 W.L.R. 1472, at 1482–1483.

activities of Carmelite nuns are not adverse to the very foundations of all religion nor are they subversive of all morality, so that if the approach adopted to public benefit in *Re Watson* is correct, *Gilmour* v. *Coats* should have been decided the other way. In fact, although Lord SIMONDS in *Gilmour* v. *Coats* seems to have been saying that in religious trusts public benefit had to be *proved*, the case "has little to say on how the court should set about discharging this task and as to the nature of the material on which it should reach a conclusion".[1] It is of little help to read that the question of the necessary element of public benefit is "a question of fact to be answered ... by means of evidence cognisable by the court" if no guidance is to be found on what evidence is cognisable.[2] If the evidence of Cardinal Griffin that the practice of the religious life by Carmelites is a source of great edification to Catholics and innumerable others is to be rejected, why should the opinion of a Professor of Moral and Social Theology ordained by the Church of England carry any weight on the question whether non-conformists would be edified or confirmed in their faith?

One pertinent distinction between the decisions in *Re Watson* and *Gilmour* v. *Coats* is that the former concerned a trust to propagate religion while the latter case was to benefit an essentially introverted community. The pamphlets would be distributed among the public: the edification said to flow from the example of a pious life and intercessory prayer in *Gilmour* v. *Coats* was held to be too intangible to be recognised by the court.

The case of *Re Watson* highlights rather than solves the problem of public benefit in religious trusts. It is surely legitimate to ask[3] whether a sufficiently substantial number of people will be benefited by a particular religious trust. Such an approach has certainly been canvassed in the context of educational charities, and would serve to exclude some obviously eccentric trusts in the religious field. In the second place benefit ought not to be assumed in the case of religious writings of a foolish or incoherent nature. Thirdly, if suitably qualified persons of the religion or sect concerned consider the writings to be of no intrinsic or other value then a mere religious tendency should not be justification for publishing the works under the aegis of charity; but when opinions differ, the court should lean in favour of charity.

Superstitious uses[4]

A superstitious use may be defined generally to be one which has for its object the propagation of the rites of a religion not tolerated by the law. This definition, by the nineteenth-century author, Boyle, is in the words of Lord BIRKENHEAD "not exhaustive, but will serve as a working definition". Many uses formerly accounted superstitious are no longer so. This is partly because various relieving Acts, which have been referred to, have produced a state of affairs where almost all religions are tolerated by the law.[5] But it is also because

---

1 *Valuation Comr.* v. *Trustees, Newry Christian Brothers*, [1971] N.I. 114, at 128, *per* Lord MACDERMOTT L.C.J.

2 *Belfast City Young Men's Christian Association* v. *Valuation Comrs.*, [1969] N.I. 3, at 30, *per* McVEIGH L.J.

3 See J. Hackney (1973), A.S.C.L. 464, at 469; cf. Goodman Report (1976) 24 para. 54.

4 See generally T. Bourchier-Chilcott, "Superstitious Uses" (1929), 36 L.Q.R. 152; Keeton, *Modern Law of Charities* (1962), Chapter 3; Crowther, *Religious Trusts*, Chapter 4.

5 *Boyle on Charities*, 242.

of the decision of the House of Lords in *Bourne* v. *Keane*,[1] which established that gifts for masses for the souls of the dead had ceased to be impressed with the stamp of superstitious uses when the Roman Catholic Relief Act 1829 became law. Lord BIRKENHEAD L.C., whose speech in *Bourne* v. *Keane* contains a comprehensive summary of the history of superstitious uses, canvassed as possible examples of superstitious uses: gifts in connection with relics, gifts for the sustenance of miracle workers and gifts for the veneration of saints.[2] Lord WRENBURY also stated that in his opinion the Roman Catholic Charities Act 1860 recognised and affirmed that there were tenets of the Roman Catholic religion which were superstitious.[3] Historically it is true that the law of superstitious uses came into being to safeguard the doctrine of the established church. It may be doubted whether in the ecumenical mood of these times particular rites of the Roman Catholic faith would be stigmatised as superstitious. If anything is held void for superstition in future it is likely to be on the broader grounds of public policy and not on narrow doctrinal grounds.[4]

---

1 [1919] A.C. 815. The decision has been criticised on technical grounds: see Keeton, *op. cit.*, at 53–55 (omitted from Keeton and Sheridan).

2 *Ibid.*, at 855–856; and see *A.-G.* v. *Vivian* (1826), 1 Russ. 226.

3 *Ibid.*, at 925.

4 It has been fancifully suggested that on the logic of *Thornton* v. *Howe* (1862), 31 Beav. 14 a trust for an altar for Baal or a grove for Diana would be charitable: see F. H. Newark (1946), 62 L.Q.R., at 244. But a trust for pagan religions would probably fail either as a superstitious use or alternatively as not for the public benefit: see Keeton, *Modern Law of Charities*, 58; *Mitford* v. *Reynolds* (1842), 1 Ph. 185.

Chapter 5

The Promotion of Health[1]

Introduction

A trust for the promotion of health is charitable. The Charitable Uses Act 1601 recognised as charitable trusts for the maintenance of sick and maimed soldiers and mariners and trusts for the relief of the aged or impotent. The promotion of maternal welfare[2] the furtherance of psychological healing[3] and indeed faith healing[4] are all charitable objects. Such a trust may well also all within one of the first three heads of *Pemsel*'s case. Thus gifts to furnish nurses to attend the poor are for the relief of poverty,[5] as are gifts for the maintenance of patients from a particular parish[6] or to enable persons of moderate means to have surgical operations or medical treatment on the payment of some moderate contribution.[7] Again, a trust for medical research is valid as being for the advancement of education as well as being beneficial to the community,[8] and faith healing promotes both religion and health.[9]

But even where the promotion of health cannot be subsumed under the heads of relief of poverty or advancement of education or religion, a trust for such an object will inevitably fall within the fourth residual category. So, in *Re Hillier*[10] VAISEY J. held that a trust for the sick and wounded was clearly within the fourth heading of "charity" laid down in *Pemsel*'s case being a provision for a purpose beneficial to the community.

It should be noted that organisations which are engaged in fringe medicine or which promote and practice unorthodox methods of healing may have to submit evidence to show that their methods are efficacious if they wish to be registered as charities.[11]

---

1 Several writers have already isolated this as a separate head of Charity: see Scott, *Trusts* (3rd edn.), para. 372; Sheridan (1957), *Malayan Law Journal* lxxvi, at lxxxviii; Hanbury, *Modern Equity* (8th edn.) 205 (last edition edited by Professor Hanbury).
2 *McGregor v. Stamp Duties Comr.*, [1942] N.Z.L.R. 164.
3 *Re Osmund*, [1944] Ch. 206.
4 *Re Kerin* (1966), *Times*, 24th May. On appeal the order was set aside by consent.
5 *Re Webster*, [1912] 1 Ch. 106.
6 *Re Roadley*, [1930] 1 Ch. 524.
7 *Re Clarke*, [1923] 2 Ch. 407.
8 *McGregor v. Stamp Duties Comr.*, [1942] N.Z.L.R. 164 (gynaecology); *Re Travis*, [1947] N.Z.L.R. 382 (cancer and tuberculosis).
9 *Re Kerin, supra.*
10 [1944] 1 All E.R. 480.
11 See *New Age Healing Trust*, [1975] Ch. Com. Rep. 22, paras. 68–69; and for the Commissioners' declared policy see [1975] Ch. Com. Rep. 22, para. 70.

Relief of the aged

The very first charitable purpose set out in the Act of Elizabeth I was the relief of the aged, impotent and poor people.[1] There are several statements in the books to the effect that these words should be read disjunctively,[2] so that the relief of aged people who are not also poor comes within them.[3] Thus in *Re Glyn's Will Trusts*[4] DANCKWERTS J. said that aged people need not be also poor to be subjects of charity. But this proposition gives rise to difficulties to which no final quietus has yet been given. In a recent case in New South Wales[5] STREET C.J. said that the trend of authority in England marks a developing acceptance of the proposition that a trust for aged persons is itself charitable. But the thin line of authorities, all at first instance, alleged to constitute the trend is not conclusive: one at least of the authorities did not raise the issue[6] and another[7] has been explained away by a later judge.[8]

There has been some rather academic discussion as to whether a trust to support aged peers or aged inhabitants of Mayfair would be charitable.[9] Presumably there are some peers who are both aged and indigent but a gift to support aged peers would probably fail for lack of public benefit. A trust for the relief of aged inhabitants of Mayfair could not, it is thought, automatically fail. The key to the problem lies surely in the words "relief of the aged". It is implicit in these words that the aged persons in question are in need of relief. Financial assistance would only be charitable in so far as it is given to persons who are both elderly and poor. But research in the field of gerontology would be a charitable object though it would benefit rich and poor alike. The trustees of a trust for the relief of the aged would have to consider carefully the particular needs of the aged persons in question.[10]

There is clear authority for the proposition that erecting and fitting a home for the aged is a charitable object. The cases which establish this proposition clearly assume, even where the gift does not expressly so provide,[11] that the inmates shall be persons in need of the relevant accommodation.[12] Where it is plain that the inmates are to be persons who will pay in full (other than for the

---

1 See at 8, *ante*.
2 *Re Glyn's Will Trusts*, [1950] 2 All E.R. 1150 n.; *Re Bradbury*, [1950] 2 All E.R. 1150 n.; *Re Robinson*, [1951] Ch. 198.
3 *Re Glyn's Will Trusts*, [1950] 2 All E.R. 1150 n.; *Re Bradbury*, *supra*; *Re Robinson*, *supra*.
4 [1950] 2 All E.R. 1150 n.
5 *Hilder v. Church of England Deaconers' Institution, Sydney, Ltd.*, [1973] 1 N.S.W.L.R. 506, at 512 not following: *N.S.W. Nursing Service and Welfare Association for Christian Scientists v. Willoughby Municipal Council* (1968), 88 W.N. (Pt. 1) (N.S.W.) 75; *Church of England Property Trust, Diocese of Canberra and Goulburn v. Imlay Shire Council*, [1971] 2 N.S.W.L.R. 216; but *cf. Trustees of Church Property for the Diocese of Newcastle v. Lake Macquarie Shire Council* (1973), 26 L.G.R.A. 408.
6 *Re Lewis*, [1955] Ch. 104.
7 *Re Glyn's Will Trust*, [1950] 2 All E.R. 1150.
8 *Re Sanders' Will Trusts*, [1954] Ch. 265.
9 See (1951), 67 L.Q.R. 164 (R.E.M.); (1955), 71 L.Q.R. 16 (R.E.M.); (1958), 21 M.L.R. 138, at 140 (P. S. Atiyah).
10 See (1945), 61 L.Q.R. 268, at 272 (John Brunyate).
11 As in *Re Neal* (1966), 110 Sol. Jo. 549; *Re Forgan* (1961), 29 D.L.R. (2d) 585.
12 *Re Bradbury*, [1950] 2 All E.R. 1150 n. (*maintenance* of an aged person or persons in a nursing home); *Re McFee* (1929), 37 O.W.N. 266; *Re Bingham*, [1951] N.Z.L.R. 491; *Re Pearse*, [1955] 1 D.L.R. 801; *In the Will of Clarke*, [1957] V.L.R. 171.

capital cost of the building) the gift will fail.[1] The provision of extra comforts for inmates presupposes that the inmates would not otherwise get those comforts and so is charitable.[2] A home may be for the *relief* of the aged even if there is no nursing element in the facilities available.[3]

Relief of the disabled

The preamble to the Statute of Elizabeth I mentions relief of the "impotent". The word impotent in this context is used in its wide and archaic sense of physically weak, disabled or helpless. Under this heading gifts for the blind or for disabled or wounded members of the forces are clearly charitable.

As in the case of gifts for the relief of the aged one does not imply a poverty restriction: the words "the aged, impotent and poor people" in the preamble must, it appears, be read disjunctively.[4] It has therefore been suggested that a trust for impotent millionaires might be charitable,[5] but the suggestion is undoubtedly misconceived. A gift may be charitable even though it benefits the rich as well as the poor,[6] but gifts for the *exclusive* benefit of rich are not charitable.[7] Thus a trust to establish a home of rest for millionaires would fail.[8] On the other hand although the relief of (for example) blindness or some other disability must be regarded as charitable whether the person relieved is rich or poor, some methods of relief applicable to the poor do not in the case of the rich achieve their genuine charitable object. By giving money to a rich man who is blind one does nothing to relieve his blindness, since, unlike a *poor* blind man, he can already purchase such means as exist for relieving the disability. Yet by curing blindness, by translating books into braille by inventing new aids and so forth the blindness of a rich man may be relieved.[9]

Prevention of alcoholism and drug addiction

The reduction of intemperance obviously benefits those who have fallen or may fall under the curse of drink but it is also beneficial to society at large.

Alcoholism and drug addiction are both social evils causing crime[10] and domestic unhappiness. The curing of alcoholics and drug addicts obviously

---

1 *Re Clark House* (1972), 5 N.B.R. (2d) 431.

2 *Martin v. Pelan* (1954), 13 W.W.R. 154; *cf. Re Mitchell*, [1963] N.Z.L.R. 934 ("creature comforts"). The latter case was probably wrongly decided.

3 *Re St. Anne's Tower Corporation of Toronto and City of Toronto* (1973), 41 D.L.R. (3d) 481; on appeal (1974), 51 D.L.R. (3d) 374; and see [1974] A.S.C.L. 510–511; [1975] A.S.C.L. 446.

4 *Re Fraser* (1883), 22 Ch.D. 827; *Barber v. Chudley* (1922), 128 L.T. 766; *Re Lewis*, [1955] Ch. 104. Sometimes the requirement of poverty is imported: *Re Elliott* (1910), 102 L.T. 528.

5 See P. S. Atiyah (1958), 21 M.L.R. 138, 140.

6 *Jones v. Williams* (1767), Amb. 651; *Verge v. Somerville*, [1924] A.C. 496; *Keren Kayemeth le Jisroef, Ltd. v. I.R.Comrs.*, [1931] 2 K.B. 465, at 492, C.A.; affd., [1932] A.C. 650.

7 *A.-G. v. Duke of Northumberland* (1877), 7 Ch.D. 745, at 752, *per* Sir GEORGE JESSEL M.R.; *Re Macduff*, [1896] 2 Ch. 451, at 471, C.A.

8 *Re White's Will Trusts*, [1951] 1 All E.R. 528, at 530, *per* HARMAN J.

9 See John Brunyate (1945), 61 L.Q.R. 268, at 272.

10 *I.R.Comrs. v. Temperance Council of Christian Churches of England and Wales* (1926), 136 L.T. 27; *I.R.Comrs. v. Falkirk Temperance Café Trust* 1927 S.C. 261 (subsidy to unlicensed hotel charitable).

falls within relief of the impotent. But prevention is better than a cure,[1] and the courts have taken the view that a trust to promote temperance by propaganda is charitable,[2] as is the study of the causes and cures of intemperance. It is otherwise if the trust is to promote temperance by advocating reform of the licensing laws.[3] A law reform trust is not charitable, because it is in essence political. Propaganda designed to combat drug taking and drug addiction would likewise be a charitable object if no legislation were called for.

In the United States, on the other hand, there are numerous authorities upholding trusts for the promotion of temperance in the use of intoxicating liquors. The American cases do not draw any distinctions as to the methods employed by the trust or institution in question to promote temperance. Whether the trust advocates changes in the law, for example "prohibition",[4] or promotes temperance by educational methods as by the use of pamphlets or lectures or by a study of the causes and cures of intemperance,[5] the trust is charitable.

In Ireland a gift to promote temperance amongst the poor and labouring classes has predictably been held to be charitable.[6]

Hospitals

Before the National Health Service Act 1946 a voluntary hospital whose funds were applied exclusively to the relief of the sick was a charity, but a private nursing home, health farm or sanatorium run for profit was not. Gifts to endow or maintain voluntary hospitals were accordingly charitable.[7] Nursing homes for persons of moderate means could also be the object of a charitable gift, the words "moderate means" implying the necessity for some contribution from the bounty of the testator before the recipient would be able to procure the surgical operation or medical treatment of which the recipient might stand in need.[8] Even a seaside convalescent home offering additional facilities to persons in need of rest and change of air for the benefit of their health could be charitable, provided no profit was made.[9] Dispensaries supported by voluntary contributions were equally charitable institutions. But a testator who left property to be divided among voluntary *hospitals* was held not to have indicated an intention to benefit voluntary dispensaries.[10] The word hospital *prima facie* indicates a place in which in-patients are received for continuous treatment and excludes

---

1 The protection of life and property is charitable.

2 *Re Hood*, [1931] 1 Ch. 240, C.A.

3 *I.R.Comrs.* v. *Temperance Council of Christian Churches of England and Wales* (1926), 136 L.T. 27, *cf. Farewell* v. *Farewell* (1892), 22 O.R. 573.

4 *Buell* v. *Gardner*, 83 Misc. 513 (1914) (U.S.); and see the Canadian case of *Farewell* v. *Farewell* (1892), 22 O.R. 573.

5 *Haines* v. *Allen*, 78 Ind. 100 (1881) (U.S.).

6 *Clancy* v. *Valuation Comrs.*, [1911] 2 I.R. 173.

7 *Pelham* v. *Anderson* (1764), 2 Eden 296; *A.-G.* v. *Gascoigne* (1833), 2 My. & K. 647; *A.-G.* v. *Kell* (1840) 2 Beav. 575; *Wharton* v. *Masterman*, [1895] A.C. 186, H.L.; *Re Cox* (1877), 7 Ch.D. 204; *Re Garrard*, [1907] 1 Ch. 382; *Re Weir Hospital*, [1910] 2 Ch. 124, C.A.; *Re Welsh Hospital (Netley) Fund*, [1921] 1 Ch. 655; *Re Roadley*, [1930] 1 Ch. 524.

8 *Re Clarke*, [1923] 2 Ch. 407.

9 *I.R.Comrs.* v. *Roberts Marine Mansions (Trustees)* (1927), 11 T.C. 425, C.A. (seaside home at reduced charges for members of drapery and allied trades).

10 *Re Ford*, [1945] 1 All E.R. 288.

places to which only out-patients resort for the purpose of occasional medical or surgery aid. More recently in *Re Smith's Will Trusts*[1] the Court of Appeal held that a testator who made his will in 1931 would not use the word hospital to describe a private nursing home or sanatorium. In those days "when people spoke . . . of giving money to a 'hospital' or 'hospitals' they meant, as of course, voluntary hospitals which were helped by collections and gifts of money from people of goodwill".

In 1948 the National Health Service Act 1946 came into operation. It destroyed the autonomy of the voluntary hospitals and the management of them was vested in bodies responsible for a number of hospitals. It was held shortly after the Act of 1946 came into operation that the individual hospitals continued to exist as separate charities, in the sense that separate charitable work was continued to be carried on in each of them after the Act just as it had been carried on before it, and that if testators made gifts to the individual hospitals effect could be given to these gifts.[2] Gifts to nationalised hospitals are discussed elsewhere in this book.

The endowment of hospital beds is also a well established form of charity. As appears from the judgment of SWINFEN EADY J. in *A.-G.* v. *Belgrave Hospital*[3] it was common even in his day for voluntary hospitals to describe a donor as having endowed a bed and to commemorate his beneficence by some visible memorial like a plaque in the hospital if he gave the hospital a substantial sum of money. Such a gift was construed as a gift of a capital sum to be invested and the income to be applied for the general purposes of the hospital. The capital could not be expended in the ordinary way to pay the expenditure of a hospital.[4] More recently the Court of Appeal in *Re Adams*[5] considered what was meant by a trust for endowing beds for paying patients. "Endowing beds for paying patients" was (it was held) a phrase of a most elastic character.[6] It included expenditure in the provision of an increased number of beds available for paying patients but was also well able to embrace investment of funds and application of income in improving the services and therefore the treatment accorded to paying patients. DANCKWERTS L.J.[7] accepted that it would be perfectly proper to apply income to any of the following improvements: (a) the provision of better beds, bedding, furniture, crockery, cutlery, floor coverings, curtains and other furnishing, and the better maintenance of all such things; (b) the more frequent redecoration of the accommodation; (c) the sound-proofing of rooms; (d) the provision of telephones and television sets for the use of the patients; (e) the provision of better food and a wider choice of food; (f) the provision for patients (who are not required to remain in bed) of a day or sitting room and also a dining room.

The Charity Commissioners, too, have indicated that in their view provision of, or payment for various items, services or facilities will charitably assist the services provided by the State.[8]

Items that could be provided either outright or on loan, preferably the latter

---

1 [1962] 2 All E.R. 563; [1962] 1 W.L.R. 763.
2 *Re Ginger*, [1951] Ch. 458.
3 [1910] 1 Ch. 73.
4 *Ibid.*; and see also *Re Ginger*, [1951] Ch. 458.
5 [1968] Ch. 80.
6 *Ibid.*, at 94, *per* RUSSELL L.J.
7 *Ibid.*, at 93.
8 [1966] Ch. Com. Rep., 32–33.

in the case of expensive apparatus, include bedding, clothing, food (including special food), fuel, heating appliances, medical or other aids, nursing requisites or comforts, television or wireless sets or licences, washing machines (suitable for soiled clothing and bed linen).

Services that could be provided include bathing, escort services, exchange of library books, foot care, gardening, hair washing, shaving, help in the home, house decorating and repairs, laundering, meals on wheels, nursing aid, outings and entertainment, physiotherapy in the home, reading, shopping, sitting in, tape recording for the housebound, travelling companions.

Facilities that could be provided include arrangements for a period of rest or change of air or to secure the benefits of any convalescent home or other institution or organisation or to provide temporary relief for those having the care of the sick or handicapped person: help for close relatives to visit or care for patients: transport facilities.

Rest homes

A rest home for those needing it is a charitable object. This has been established in a series of cases. In *Re White's Will Trusts*[1] a gift to establish a home of rest for nurses of the Sheffield Royal Infirmary was upheld since it provided a means of restoring the efficiency of the nurses in the performance of their duties. The Sheffield Royal Infirmary was undoubtedly a charitable institution and the proposed home of rest would, it was held, increase its efficiency to the benefit of the community. A rest home for the members of a religious community, for the clergy of a diocese and for such persons as the Mother Superior of the Community should nominate has been held to be a charitable purpose;[2] likewise a rest home for lady teachers, such an object being *inter alia* conducive to the spread of education.[3] In the last three cases cited the intended beneficiaries themselves carried out charitable work. And yet it would be wrong to assume that a rest home can only be charitable if it is confined to people carrying out charitable work. It must, however, be clear that such a home is intended for people who are truly in need of a home of rest.[4] The donor himself may put this matter beyond doubt as in *Re Chaplin*,[5] where the rest home was to be for "persons in need of rest by reason of the stress and strain caused or partly caused by the conditions in which they ordinarily live and/or work". In the absence of any such express indication by the donor the words "home of rest" are *prima facie* understood as meaning something in the nature of a hospital.[6] Where the intended beneficiaries of the rest home are carrying out charitable work the *prima facie* meaning of the words is unlikely to be upset. But where the intended beneficiaries of the rest home are chosen for whimsical or capricious reasons the rest home may be no more than a guest house. Moreover it is more than likely that it will also fail as a charity because the element of public benefit

---

1 [1951] 1 All E.R. 528.
2 *Re James*, [1932] 2 Ch. 25. It was held to be implicit in the gift that the nominees must be in need of a home of rest: at 33.
3 *Re Estlin* (1903), 72 L.J. Ch. 687 (KEKEWICH J.).
4 *Re James*, [1932] 2 Ch. 25, at 31, *per* FARWELL J.; and see *Re Estlin, supra*, at 689, *per* KEKEWICH J.
5 [1933] Ch. 115; see also *Re Pearse*, [1955] 1 D.L.R. 801.
6 *Re James, supra*.

will be lacking. Thus a trust to establish a rest home for millionaires would fail.[1] Another example of a rest home which lacked the necessary public benefit is to be found in *Re Norgate*[2] where an eccentric testator left property to be used to establish a rest home for vegetarians, teetotallers, pacifists and conscientious objectors. Although "each of the occupants would have some subject matter of conversation namely the curious views held by each member of the other three classes" a gift to such an object cannot be charitable. Cranks are not a sufficient section of the public, so that a trust for the benefit of cranks will not be a trust for the public benefit.

In another case a gift to Oxford University of a house of rest for artists was held not valid, on the grounds that the dominant purpose was the preservation of the house as a memorial.[3]

Family planning centres

The suggestion has been made that a trust to promote family planning is charitable, at any rate if contraceptive advice and assistance are provided at a centre by properly qualified medical people and if psychologists are available either on the premises or on a reference system. In that case (it is argued) the trust would be for the promotion of medical and psychological well-being.[4] This seems sensible and indeed the Charity Commissioners have recognised that "to preserve and protect the good health both mental and physical of parents, young people and children and to prevent the poverty, hardship and distress caused by unwanted conception" is a charitable object.[5]

There is no authority in this country directly in point. But the matter has been raised in United States courts. In *Slee* v. *I.R.Comrs.*[6] it was held by LEARNED HAND J. that a particular institution was not exclusively charitable. The objects of the institution were to collect and disseminate lawful information about the consequences of uncontrolled procreation, to maintain a medical clinic for the giving of advice to married women as to birth control if in the judgment of the physicians such advice was necessary for the protection of their health and also to enlist the support of legislators and others to effect the lawful repeal and amendment of statutes dealing with the prevention of conception. It was this last object which deprived the institution of an exclusively charitable nature because agitation for a change in the law is not charitable.

On the other hand in *Faulkner* v. *Internal Revenue Comrs.*[7] a gift to the Birth Control League of Massachusetts was upheld as charitable. The League had decided to abandon its political and legislative objects prior to the date of the gift.

In Alberta organisations to support unmarried mothers are charitable.[8]

---

1 *Per* HARMAN J. in *Re White's Will Trusts*, [1951] 1 All E.R. 528, at 530.
2 (1944), *Times*, 21st July.
3 (1962), *Times*, 25th January.
4 Alec Samuels (1968), *New Law Journal Annual Charities Review*, 42.
5 *The Family Planning Association*, [1969] Ch. Com. Rep. 11, para. 25.
6 42 F (2d) 184 (1930) (U.S.).
7 112 Fed (2d) 987 (1940).
8 *Re Andrae* (1967), 61 W.W.R. 182.

Chapter 6

Recreational Facilities

General

A distinction has been drawn between gifts to promote sport (or "mere" sport as it is sometimes called) and gifts to provide recreational facilities. While sport is not treated as a charitable object (except in one or two special cases) the latter may be a charitable object if the provisions of the Recreational Charities Act 1958 are satisfied. It is convenient to deal first with sport. In dealing with trusts to provide recreational facilities, the position before the 1958 Act will be considered in order that the ambit of the 1958 Act can be properly appreciated.

Sport

A gift for the encouragement of a mere sport or game, it has been held, is not charitable. The leading authority is *Re Nottage*[1] where the Court of Appeal held that a gift to encourage the sport of yacht-racing was not charitable. LINDLEY L.J. observed:[2]

> "Now I should say that every healthy sport is good for the nation—cricket, football, fencing, yachting or any other healthy exercise or recreation; but if it had been the idea of lawyers that a gift for the encouragement of such exercises is therefore charitable, we should have heard of it before now."

Similarly the promition of angling[3] or fox-hunting[4] and the assistance of riding establishments[5] are not charitable objects. An exception however is made where the gift is to encourage sport in a school[6] or a regiment[7] or if the game has educational value.[8] So, in *Re Mariette*[9] the testator bequeathed £1000 to the governing body of Aldenham School to build Eton fives courts or squash rackets courts and £100 to the headmaster to use the interest to provide an athletics prize. EVE J. upheld both gifts on the ground that sport was a necessary

---

1 *Ibid.*, at 655. 2 [1895] 2 Ch. 649.
3 *Re Clifford*, [1912] 1 Ch. 29.
4 *Re Thompson*, [1934] Ch. 342; *Peterborough Royal Foxhound Show Society v. I.R.Comrs.*, [1936] 2 K.B. 497.
5 *The Riding Establishments Advisory Association, Ltd.*, [1965] Ch. Com. Rep. 30, App. C. 16.
6 Or in a university: *Kearins v. Kearins*, [1957] S.R. N.S.W. 286 (rugby at Sydney University).
7 *Re Gray*, [1925] Ch. 362. 8 *Re Dupree's Deed Trusts*, [1945] Ch. 16.
9 [1915] 2 Ch. 284; and see *Re Geere's Will Trusts (No. 2)*, [1954] C.L.Y. 388.

part of the education of boys and young men between the ages of ten and nineteen.

ROMER J. in a later case[1] remarked that:

> "One might equally well say that no person can be trained to be an efficient and useful soldier unless as much attention is given to the development of his body as is given to the development of his mind."

and accordingly upheld a gift to promote shooting, fishing, cricket, football and polo in the Carabiniers. On the other hand in *Re Patten*[2] he took a stricter view of a gift to provide for the teaching and coaching of young cricketers who might become cricket professionals. The youths concerned were from the working and lower middle classes and mainly aged between seventeen and twenty-one. It was not possible to argue that this was a trust for the advancement of education but it was contended that the trust was one for the "supportation, aid and help of young tradesmen or handicrafts men" within the meaning of the Statute of Elizabeth. This contention was rejected by the learned judge who said that it was reasonably clear that the object of the fund was the encouragement of the game of cricket and nothing else. The trust was not charitable.

Again in *I.R.Comrs.* v. *City of Glasgow Police Athletic Association*[3] the House of Lords held that the athletic association of the City of Glasgow Police was not "established for charitable purposes only" within section 30 of the Finance Act 1921. The Special Commissioners had found on the evidence before them that among the purposes of the association were the encouragement of recruiting, the improvement of the efficiency of the force and the public advantage. But their lordships, with the exception of Lord OAKSEY, considered that the non-charitable purpose of providing recreation to the members was not merely incidental to the public charitable purpose. The private benefits to members were seen to be essential. As Lord NORMAND aptly put it:[4]

> "The recreation of the members is an end in itself, and without its attainment the public purpose would never come into view. . . . The private advantage of members is a purpose for which the association is established, and it therefore cannot be said that this is an association established for a public charitable purpose only."

Recreational facilities prior to 1958

The legislative impliedly recognised the charitable nature of public recreation grounds over 100 years ago. The Public Recreations Grounds Act 1859,[5] now

---

1 *Re Gray*, [1925] 2 Ch. 362, at 1. But this case was doubted in *I.R.Comrs.* v. *City of Glasgow Police Athletic Association*, [1953] A.C. 380, at 391 (Lord NORMAND) and 401 (Lord MORTON OF HENRYTON).
2 [1929] 2 Ch. 276.
3 [1953] A.C. 380.
4 *Ibid.*, at 396.
5 22 Vict. c. 27.

repealed, by section 7 permitted a bequest of money of a limited amount for the purpose and upkeep of public recreation grounds; a bequest which, but for that enabling Act would have been void under the Mortmain Act. Moreover by section 5 of the game Act, the Charity Commissioners were given a power to settle a scheme for the appointment of managers and directors of lands granted for the purposes of the Act where none were named or there was a failure of such persons. Nor, by reason of section 6, could any bye-laws restricting the public use or enjoyment of the grounds be valid unless sanctioned with the approbation of the Charity Commissioners.

Clearer legislative recognition of the charitable nature of public recreation grounds was to be found in the Mortmain and Charitable Act uses 1888,[1] section 6 which provided that Part II of the Act which related to assurances to charitable uses should not apply to an assurance of a limited amount of land for the purposes of a park garden or other land dedicated or to be dedicated to the recreation of the public. This enactment, to use the words of CLAUSON J. in *Re Hadden:*[2]

"Seems ... necessarily to involve that in the view of the legislature dedication of land to the recreation of the public is dedication to a charitable use".

In Ireland, certainly, it was held in *Shillington* v. *Portadown Urban District Council*[3] that the purpose of providing the means of healthy recreaton for the inhabitants of a particular town was a charitable purpose. And in *Re Hadden* the Irish case was approved and applied where there was no limitation to a defined area. *Re Hadden* was itself followed in two unreported cases. In *Re Foakes*[4] in 1933 LUXMOORE J. held that a bequest of certain fields and a barn (together with a sum for their upkeep) for use as a recreation ground was a valid charitable gift, and in *Re Chesters*[5] in 1934 BENNETT J., held that a bequest of money to provide public recreation or playgrounds for the children was a valid charitable gift. In *Re Morgan*[6] HARMAN J. upheld as charitable a gift for a public recreation ground for amateur activities for the benefit of a particular parish.

The decision of the House of Lords in *I.R.Comrs.* v. *Baddeley*[7] threw the law on this topic into a state of uncertainty. The short issue in that case was whether a conveyance of land to trustees should be stamped at a reduced rate under section 13 of the Stamp Act 1891, on the ground that the trusts upon which it was held were exclusively charitable. The objects of the trusts were "the moral, social and physical well-being of persons resident in West Ham and Leyton who for the time being were or were likely to become members of the Methodist Church and who were of insufficient means otherwise to enjoy the advantages provided". Attainment of these objects was to be secured by "the provision of

---

1 51 & 52 Vict. c. 42.
2 [1932] 1 Ch. 133, at 141–142.
3 [1911] 1 I.R. 247.
4 (1933), 21st Feb., unreported but cited in *I.R.Comrs.* v. *Baddeley,* [1955] A.C. 572, at 596. *Semble* the facilities may be indoor, see at 92–93, *infra.*
5 (1934), 25th July, unreported but cited in *I.R.Comrs.* v. *Baddeley,* [1955] A.C. 572, at 596.
6 [1955] 1 W.L.R. 738.
7 [1955] A.C. 572.

facilities for moral, social and physical training and recreation and by promoting and encouraging all forms of such activities". The House of Lords by a majority of four (Lords SIMONDS, PORTER, TUCKER and SOMERVELL) to one (Lord REID) held that the objects were not exclusively charitable. Their *ratio decidendi* was that the trusts were not for the relief of poverty[1] or for the advancement of education[1] or religion[2] and that they did not fall under the fourth head of charity (other purposes beneficial to the community) because the beneficiaries were a class of persons not only confined to a particular area but selected from within it by reference to a particular creed[3] and also because social well-being was not a purpose within the spirit and intendment of the preamble to the Statute of Elizabeth I: the concept was too vague.[4]

Recreational Charities Act 1958[5]

The Recreational Charities Act 1958[6] provides in section 1 (1) that:

> "it shall be and be deemed always to have been charitable to provide, or assist in the provision of facilities for recreation or other leisure time occupation, if the facilities are provided in the interests of social welfare".

Before proceeding to elaborate on the meaning of "the interests of social welfare' the Act makes a special provision that nothing in section 1 (1) shall be taken to derogate from the principle that a trust or institution to be charitable must be for the public benefit. In other words in order to be charitable such a trust or institution must be (1) for the public benefit and (2) provided in the interest of social welfare.

So far as public benefit is concerned, the words of Lord SOMERVELL OF HARROW in *I.R.Comrs.* v. *Baddeley* should be noted. The necessary quantum of public benefit may be less in the case of a religious trust than in the case of a recreational trust.[7] A different degree of public benefit is requisite according to the class in which the charity is said to fall.[8] A trust cannot qualify as a charity within the fourth class in *Pemsel*'s case if the beneficiaries are a class of persons not only confined to a particular area but selected from within it by reference to a particular creed.[9] Whether the same result will ensue whenever there is a class within a class is an open question.[10] A conveyance of land to be used as a recreation ground for the benefit of employees of a company is clearly not a charitable object.[11]

---

1 *Ibid.*, at 585.
2 This point was not argued at any stage: see *Neville Estates, Ltd.* v. *Madden*, [1962] Ch. 832, at 852, *per* CROSS J.
3 [1955] A.C. 572, at 591.
4 *Ibid.*, at 586, *per* Viscount SIMONDS, at 613, *per* Lord TUCKER.
5 See Leolin Price (1958), 21 M.L.R. 534; S. G. Maurice, *Recreational Charities* (1959), 23 Conv. (N.S.) 15.
6 6 & 7 Eliz. 2, c. 17.
7 See the dictum cited on 21, *ante*.
8 [1955] A.C. 572, at 590, *per* Viscount SIMONDS.
9 *Ibid.*, at 592, *per* Viscount SIMONDS.
10 *Ibid.*, at 591, *per* Viscount SIMONDS.
11 *Wernher's Charitable Trust* v. *I.R.Comrs.*, [1937] 2 All E.R. 488.

The requirement that the facilities be provided in the interest of social welfare[1] will not, according to section 1 (2) of the Act, be satisfied unless—

(a) the facilities are provided with the object of improving the conditions of life[2] for the persons for whom the facilities are primarily intended; and

(b) that either

    (i) those persons have need of such facilities as aforesaid by reason of their youth, age, infirmity or disablement, poverty or social and economic circumstances; or

    (ii) the facilities are to be available to the members or the female members of the public at large.[3]

"Youth" and "age" for the purposes of section 1 (2) (b) (i) of the 1958 Act have not been defined. The Commissioners have registered as charitable a day nursery "for the purpose of receiving and caring for children between the ages of three and five years" in a certain district as being a recreational facility within the meaning of the 1958 Act as well as for the advancement of education.[4] They also take the view that youth includes university students so that a trust to provide facilities to enable and encourage pupils at schools and universities to play cricket or other games or sports is registrable under the 1958 Act.[5]

The provision of recreational facilities for blind and partially sighted persons over the age of sixteen was treated by the Commissioners as clearly within the Act: the facilities were provided in the interests of social welfare for persons who needed such facilities by reason of their special disablement. The payment of a small annual subscription was disregarded: the association was open to all persons over sixteen suffering from the particular disability.[6]

The special reference to women in section 1 (2) (b) (ii) was intended to cover women's institutes. It is odd that facilities provided for men and women or for women only should be able to satisfy the statutory test, whereas facilities for men only are necessarily unable to do so. A club which is simply a club for men will therefore not be registered[7] unless the trusts are such that they can be validated under the Charitable Trusts Validation Act 1954[8] or applied *cy-près* under section 13 (1) (e) (ii) of the Charities Act 1960.[9] No satisfactory explanation of this anomaly was given in Parliament. It may even be that certain women's clubs of a character very different from women's institutes may be

---

1 See generally D. W. M. Waters (1959), 23 Conv. (N.S.) 365.

2 See *Northern Ireland Housing Trust* v. *Valuation Comr.*, [1970] N.I. 208 (Community centre improves the conditions of life of the occupants of a housing estate).

3 A community centre for workers living on a housing estate is not for the benefit of members of the public: *Northern Ireland Housing Trust* v. *Valuation Comr.*, [1970] N.I. 208.

4 *Brockham Day Nursery*, [1966] Ch. Com. Rep. 30 (App. A).

5 *Kent Cricket Youth Trust*, [1973] Ch. Com. Rep. 27. The trust is also valid on the principle of *Re Mariette*, [1915] 2 Ch. 284.

6 *Manchester and District Social Club of the Blind*, [1965] Ch. Com. Rep. 27 (App. C).

7 *Wollerton Working Men's Club, Salop*, [1965] Ch. Com. Rep. 30, *cf. Fowey Working Men's Institute*, [1965] Ch. Com. Rep. 31 (no restriction to men only).

8 *Station Street Institute, Ipswich*, [1965] Ch. Com. Rep. 27 (trust for the spiritual and temporal benefit of youths and men of Ipswich).

9 *Whitchurch Working Men's Club, Salop*, [1965] Ch. Com. Rep. 29 (Institution 100 years old for extensive use of working classes, charitable when founded).

able to claim, or even to alter their constitution to claim, charitable status under the 1958 Act.[1]

The application of these provisions is illustrated by the decision in *Wynn* v. *Skegness Urban District Council*[2] In that case UNGOED-THOMAS J. held that to provide north Derbyshire miners or the miners and their wives and families (and in each case in need of a change of air) with the facilities of a holiday centre improves their conditions of life. In addition such persons have need of the facilities of a holiday centre by reason of their "social and economic circumstances".

Some instances of recreational and other leisure time facilities within the meaning of section 1 (1) are specified in section 1 (3) but the latter subsection is not an exhaustive statement of such facilities. Subject to the requirements of social welfare being satisfied, section 1 (1) applies in particular to the provision of facilities at village halls, community centres and women's institutes and to the provision and maintenance of grounds and buildings to be used for purposes of recreation or leisure time occupation, and extends to the provision of facilities for those purposes by the organising of any activity.

---

1 See Hansard H.L. Vol. 207, col. 242.
2 [1967] 1 W.L.R. 52.

Chapter 7

Municipal Betterment and the Relief of the Tax and Rating Burden

Many benefactions made during the Tudor and Stuart periods were concerned with what may conveniently be called municipal betterment.[1] Private generosity supplied what government did not in respect of buildings, works, services or facilities. The preamble to the Statute of Elizabeth I includes as charitable purposes: the repair of bridges, ports, havens, causeways, churches, sea-banks and highways.

Public works and services

There are many examples in the books of public works and services which would otherwise be supplied at the expense of the taxpayer but which are valid objects of charitable gifts or trusts. Some of them are precisely within the language of the preamble of the Statute of Elizabeth I, others are charitable by analogy. Thus the courts have upheld trusts for repairing highways,[2] building bridges[3] and protecting the sea coast against encroachment.[4] In A.-G. v. Shrewsbury Corporation[5] the repair, improvement and fortification of the town's bridges, gates, towers and walls was held to be a charitable purpose. Non-profit-making canals and navigable waterways open to public navigation are capable of being charitable objects on the analogy of the maintenance of highways.

The income of charities for the maintenance of highway bridges and similar works (of which there are some 300 registered) is now in most cases paid to the local authority and applied by the latter towards the discharge of its statutory responsibility. Action to make cy-près schemes for these charities can be taken only if the trustees are willing to apply for a scheme. The Commissioners, who favour relating these ancient charities more closely to present day needs, have stated that in making schemes for such charities they would consider the appropriate cy-près provision for the new application of their resources to be a fairly general one, namely, for charitable purposes for the benefit of the local inhabitants. This would enable the money to be used for such diverse purposes as encouraging the arts or cultural activities, improving amenities, assisting other local charities or financing new local projects.[6]

---

1 See Jordan, *Philanthropy in England*, 46–47.
2 *A.-G. v. Harrow School Governors* (1754), 2 Ves. Sen. 551; *A.-G. v. Day*, [1900] 1 Ch. 31.
3 *Forbes v. Forbes* (1854), 18 Beav. 552.
4 *A.-G. v. Brown* (1818), 1 Swan. 265; *Wilson v. Barnes* (1886), 38 Ch.D. 507.
5 (1843), 6 Beav. 220.   6 [1968] Ch. Com. Rep. 16–17, paras. 67–72.

A trust to put up lamp posts or for paving or lighting or cleaning streets or providing homes for policemen is charitable.[1]

Gifts for the purpose of supplying a town with water[2] or a district fire brigade[3] or a lifeboat service[4] or municipal markets[5] or a cemetery[6] or crematorium[7] are all charitable.

A gift for the improvement of a city is a good charitable gift.[8] A trust of the whole of the capital and income of a testator's residuary estate for the beautification and advancement of a township is to be construed as a trust for the general purpose of advancing the township by means which beautify it, and is accordingly charitable.[9] Likewise a trust for the beautification of a city street and paths is a good charitable trust.[10]

The provision of a court-house is a charitable object.[11]

Public Amenities

The provision of a library,[12] museum,[13] gallery,[14] public hall[15] or reading room[16] is charitable as constituting a public amenity quite apart from any educational advantages produced by such buildings. Again the provision of a botanical garden[17] or an observatory[18] is charitable. The provision of public recreation grounds[19] and public parks has been upheld as a charitable object in cases in

---

1 *A.-G.* v. *Brown* (1818), 1 Swan. 265; *A.-G.* v. *Heelis* (1824), 2 Sim. & St. 67; *A.-G.* v. *Eastlake* (1853), 11 Hare 205; *Gort (Viscount)* v. *A.-G.* (1817), 6 Dow. 136, H.L.

2 *Jones* v. *Williams* (1767), Amb. 651; *A.-G.* v. *Heelis* (1824), 2 Sim. & St. 67.

3 *Re Wokingham Fire Brigade Trusts*, [1951] Ch. 373; *Solicitor-General* v. *Wanganui Corporation*, [1919] N.Z.L.R. 763, C.A.

4 *Johnston* v. *Swann* (1818), 3 Madd. 457.

5 *Re Smith*, [1967] V.R. 341.

6 *A.-G.* v. *Blizard* (1855), 21 Beav. 233.

7 *Scottish Burial Reform and Cremation Society, Ltd.* v. *Glasgow Corporation*, [1968] A.C. 138, H.L.

8 *Howse* v. *Chapman* (1799), 4 Ves. 542 (Bath); *Re Bones*, [1930] V.L.R. 346 (Ballarat).

9 *Schellenberger* v. *Trustees Executors and Agency Co., Ltd.* (1953), 86 C.L.R. 454 (township of Bunyip).

10 *Re Knowles*, [1938] 3 D.L.R. 178. But not if the trust is principally to enure to the benefit of the inhabitants of the street; see *Longton Avenue Residents Association, Ltd.*, [1967] Ch. Com. Rep. 47 (App. D5).

11 Duke, *Law of Charitable Uses* (1676) 109; ed. Bridgman, 136.

12 *Harrison* v. *Southampton Corporation* (1854), 2 Sm. & G. 387; *Abbott* v. *Fraser* (1874), L.R. 6 P.C. 96; *Re Scowcroft*, [1898] 2 Ch. at 642.

13 *British Museum Trustees* v. *White* (1826), 2 Sim. & St. 594; *Re Allsop* (1884), 1 T.L.R. 4; *Re Holburne* (1885), 53 L.T. 212.

14 *Tarver* v. *Weaver*, 130 So. 209 (1930) (U.S.).

15 *Re Spence*, [1938] Ch. 96 (public hall); *Monds* v. *Stackhouse* (1948), 77 C.L.R. 232 (hall for its citizens for entertainments and meetings of educational value); *Re Vernon Estate*, [1948] 2 W.W.R. 46 (a strictly non-sectarian community hall); *Re Cumming*, [1951] N.Z.L.R. 498.

16 *Re Scowcroft*, [1898] 2 Ch. 638.

17 *Townley* v. *Bedwell* (1801), 6 Ves. 194; *Harrison* v. *Southampton Corporation* (1854), 2 Sm. & G. 387.

18 *Harrison* v. *Southampton Corporation* (1854), 2 Sm. & G. 387.

19 The cases are discussed at 86–87 *supra*. Whether recreational facilities must be open air as Lord MacDermott L.C.J. suggests in *Northern Ireland Valuation Comr.* v. *Lurgan Corporation*, [1968] N.I. 104, at 125 is questionable. A gift for a public gymnasium is charitable: *Re Hadden*, [1932] 1 Ch. 133. So is a gift for squash courts and Eton fives courts: *Re Mariette*,

virtually all jurisdictions. Parks in towns are of course more frequent and the provision,[1] maintenance and beautification[2] of such parks improve a municipality, and are treated as charitable purposes. In *Re Mair*[3] the testator donated land "upon trust in memory of my father . . . as a public park to be named as the 'Stephen Mair Memorial Park'—such park to be for the use of the public generally for picnic parties, and to provide facilities for the comfort and amusement of picnickers in the said park, and in particular to provide spaces for picnic parties and for the playing of football, cricket, baseball and other games, provided that such spaces be used purely for the amusement of the public and not for organised competitions between outside bodies". Since the devise had as its object the healthy outdoor recreation of the public it was held to be a valid charitable gift, being a gift for the public benefit and falling within the spirit and intendment of the preamble to the Statute of Elizabeth. Similarly a gift for the maintenance of a National Park or area of outstanding natural beauty is also charitable. In *Re Bruce*[4] the New Zealand Court of Appeal held that a gift for the purpose of afforestation on the making of domains or national parks in New Zealand was a good charitable gift. A gift for the beautification of a lake and its foreshore for its development as a beauty spot and tourist resort has been upheld on the same grounds[5] and land held in trust for the improvement and protection of a river is held upon trust for charitable purposes.[6]

In England the National Trust is undoubtedly a charitable institution. The National Trust for Places of Historic Interest or National Beauty to give it its full name was incorporated "for the purpose of promoting the permanent preservation for the benefit of the nation of lands and tenements (including buildings) of beauty or historic interest and as regards lands for the preservation (so far as practicable) of their natural aspect, features, and animal and plant life". In *Re Verrall*[7] ASTBURY J. held that these were plainly charitable purposes. It does not follow that merely because the National Trust is constituted a trustee for a particular purpose, the trust so constituted is charitable.[8]

A gift to preserve Elizabethan cottages has been held charitable[9] and also a

---

[1915] 2 Ch. 284. Provided the facilities are for *healthy* recreation (see *Shillington* v. *Portadown Urban District Council*, [1911] 1 I.R. 247) whether they are indoor or outdoor is surely irrelevant, *cf. Linlithgow Town Council Entertainments Committee* v. *I.R.Comrs.* 1953 S.L.T. 287 (indoor *entertainment* like dancing not charitable). Despite the remarks of Lord MacDermott L.C.J. in *Northern Ireland Valuation Comr.* v. *Lurgan Corporation, supra*, at 122 a skating rink though not a bowling alley might pass muster.

1 *Re Hadden*, [1932] 1 Ch. 133; *Re Gemmill*, [1946] 2 D.L.R. 716; *Re Lushington*, [1964] N.Z.L.R. 161; *Re Smith*, [1967] V.R. 770. There are many cases in the United States: see Scott, *Trusts* (3rd edn.) para. 373, n. 1.

2 *Grant* v. *Stamp Duties Comr.*, [1943] N.Z.L.R. 113 (Peter Pan statue to commemorate husband of testatrix).

3 [1964] V.R. 529.

4 [1918] N.Z.L.R. 16.

5 *Re Spehr*, [1965] V.R. 770.

6 *Kaikoura County* v. *Boyd*, [1949] N.Z.L.R. 233.

7 [1916] 1 Ch. 100; and see the decision of the Charity Commissioners in *The Upper Teesdale Defence Fund*, [1969] Ch. Com. Rep. 10–11, paras. 23–24 (preservation of flora and fauna of Upper Teesdale).

8 *Re Spensley's Will Trusts*, [1954] Ch. 233, C.A. (house for use of Australian High Commissioner); *cf. Re Courtauld-Thomson Trusts* (1954), *Times*, 1st Dec., VAISEY J.

9 *Re Cranstoun*, [1932] 1 Ch. 537.

gift to provide prizes for best-kept cottages and gardens.[1] The Charity Commissioners registered as charitable an association whose main object was preserving and promoting crafts and craftsmanship for the benefit of the public,
notwithstanding that incidental benefits accrued to the craftsmen.[2] They have
also conceded charitable status to a trust for the preservation of one or more
examples of a type of sailing ship.[3]

Relief of the tax and rating burden

Many of the purposes already discussed in this Chapter are purposes which if not
supported by individual donations would have to be supported by the raising
of tax or levying of rates. Other examples are to be found in the next two
Chapters.

---

1 *Re Pleasants* (1923), 39 T.L.R. 675.
2 *Clerkenwell Green Association for Craftsmen*, [1973] Ch. Com. Rep. 24–26, paras. 71–75.
3 *The Humber Keel Trust*, [1965] Ch. Com. Rep. 28 (App. C) 14.

Chapter 8

Gifts for the Benefit of a Locality

Gifts in general terms for the benefit of a country or of a district, not indicating a specific purpose, are charitable, apparently on the principle that they are impliedly for purposes recognised by the law as charitable.[1] Gifts of this kind which have been upheld include gifts for the benefit of a county[2], a borough or a town,[3] a ward,[4] and a parish.[5] Even a gift "unto my country England to and for —— own use and benefit absolutely" has been upheld.[6]

Trusts in general terms for the inhabitants or a class of the inhabitants of particular localities have also been upheld as charitable. There are numerous examples in the books. A trust for the benefit of inhabitants of a town[7] or of a borough[8] or of a village[9] or a parish[10] is valid. Even the free inhabitants of certain tenements in a borough[11] or cottages in a manor[12] or the freemen of a borough[13] are valid objects of this kind of charitable trust. These cases are anomalous,[14] and attempts to reconcile them with the principle that a non-charitable purpose will not be rendered charitable by localising the benefits[15] are surely doomed to failure.[16]

While the principle will not be extended it will be applied in similar cases.[17]

---

1 *Williams' Trustees* v. *I.R.Comrs.*, [1947] A.C. 447, at 459, *per* Lord SIMONDS.
2 *A.-G.* v. *Lonsdale (Earl)* (1827), 1 Sim. 105.
3 *Wrexham Corporation* v. *Lamplin* (1873), 21 W.R. 768; *A.-G.* v. *Dartmouth Corporation* (1883), 48 L.T. 933; *Re Baynes*, [1944] 2 All E.R. 597.
4 *Baylis* v. *A.-G.* (1741), 2 Atk. 239.
5 *West* v. *Knight* (1669), 1 Cas. in Ch. 134; *Dolan* v. *Macdermot* (1868), 3 Ch. App. 676; *A.-G.* v. *Hotham (Lord)* (1823), Turn. & R. 209; *A.-G.* v. *Lonsdale (Earl)* (1827), 1 Sim. 105; *A.-G.* v. *Webster* (1875), L.R. 20 Eq. 483; *Re St. Bride's Fleet Street* (1877), 35 Ch.D. 147 n.; *Re St. Botolph Without Bishopsgate* (1887), 35 Ch.D. 142; *Re St. Alphage London Wall* (1888), 59 L.T. 614; *Re St. Stephen Coleman Street* (1888), 39 Ch.D. 492; *Re St. Nicholas Acons* (1889), 60 L.T. 532; *Re Norton's Will Trust*, [1948] 2 All E.R. 842.
6 *Re Smith*, [1932] 1 Ch. 153.
7 *A.-G.* v. *Carlisle Corporation* (1828), 2 Sim. 437; *Mitford* v. *Reynolds* (1842), 1 Ph. 185; *A.-G.* v. *Cashel Corporation* (1843), 3 Dr. & War. 294; *A.-G.* v. *Galway Corporation* (1829), 1 Mol. 95.
8 *Re Norwich Town Charity* (1888), 40 Ch.D. 298, C.A.; and see *Stanley* v. *Norwich Corporation* (1887), 3 T.L.R. 506.
9 *Wright* v. *Hobert* (1723), 9 Mod. Rep. 64.   10 *Re Mann*, [1903] 1 Ch. 232.
11 *Goodman* v. *Saltash Corporation* (1882), 7 App. Cas. 633.
12 *A.-G.* v. *Meyrick*, [1893] A.C. 1; *Re Christchurch Inclosure Act* (1888), 38 Ch.D. 520; *Wilson* v. *Barnes* (1888), 38 Ch.D. 507, C.A.
13 *Re Norwich Town Charity* (1888), 40 Ch.D. 298, C.A.
14 *Williams' Trustees* v. *I.R.Comrs.*, [1947] A.C. 447, 459–460.
15 *Houston* v. *Burns*, [1918] A.C. 337; *Re Gwyon*, [1930] 1 Ch. 255; *Williams' Trustees* v. *I.R.Comrs.*, [1947] A.C. 447; *Re Sanders' Will Trusts*, [1954] Ch. 265.
16 For a subtle attempt see *Tudor on Charities* (6th edn.) 104–110.
17 *Re Fishermen of Newbiggin-by-the-Sea* (1957), *Times*, 15th Nov.

Chapter 9

Certain Patriotic Purposes

Introduction

In *A.-G.* v. *National Provincial and Union Bank*[1] the House of Lords held that a trust "for patriotic purposes" was void. Patriotic purposes, it was pointed out, are not *necessarily* charitable. Nevertheless, some purposes which could aptly be described as patriotic are charitable.

The defence of the realm

Trusts to promote the security of the nation are charitable. Thus a bequest in furtherance of the protection of the country from hostile aircraft[2] or a gift for the provision of a voluntary fire brigade[3] is charitable. A trust for the benefit of a volunteer corps is also good[4] and so is a trust for training boys as officers in the Royal Navy or the Mercantile Marine.[5]

The efficiency of the armed forces is at the root of the nation's security.[6] Consequently trusts which increase the expertise, physical fitness and morale of the forces are valid.[7] A fund formed in time of war to send "Christmas presents from the whole nation to every sailor afloat and every soldier at the front" was clearly charitable.[8] In *Re Gray*[9] a gift for the promotion of shooting, fishing, cricket and polo in a regiment was upheld. In *Re Stephens*[10] the court went even further and approved a trust to promote rifle shooting among the people on the ground that it would tend to make them more efficient if called upon to serve in the army. By that token it is arguable that a trust to promote yacht-racing should be valid because it might tend to make people more

1 [1924] A.C. 262.
2 *Re Driffill*, [1950] Ch. 92; [1949] 2 All E.R. 933.
3 *Re Wokingham Fire Brigade Trusts*, [1951] Ch. 373; [1951] 1 All E.R. 454.
4 *Re Stratheden*, [1894] 3 Ch. 265.
5 *Re Corbyn*, [1941] Ch. 400.
6 *Re Good*, [1905] 2 Ch. 60 (gift to maintain a library and plate in an officers' mess); see also *Re Donald*, [1909] 2 Ch. 410 (for an officers' mess).
7 *Re Barker* (1909), 25 T.L.R. 753 (prize for cadets).
8 *Re Princess Mary's Fund*, unreported [1921] 1 Ch. 655, at 656, 657, 661, 662, a decision of PETERSON J.
9 [1925] Ch. 362. The actual decisions in this case and in *Re Good*, *supra*, were doubted by two of the Law Lords in *I.R.Comrs.* v. *City of Glasgow Police Athletic Association*, [1953] A.C. 380, at 391 and 401.
10 (1892), 8 T.L.R. 792.

efficient if called upon to serve in the navy but in *Re Nottage*[1] such a trust was in fact held not to be charitable. The difference between the two cases is perhaps one of degree.

The Charity Commissioners have accepted that the mixing together of serving officers and former officers helps to keep service traditions alive and to improve *esprit de corps* thus improving the efficiency of the services.[2] Fostering the spirit of the army by keeping alive and in the public eye by means of public parades and so forth the spirit and attitude of the volunteers of 1914 is a charitable object.[3] But the promotion of reunions, social functions and similar events for the benefit of members of an ex-servicemen's association is not charitable.[4]

Gifts to the National Revenue

Yet another purpose with claims to be described as patriotic is the aid of the National Revenue. The preamble to the Statute of Elizabeth mentions "the payment of fifteenths . . . and other taxes" and the relief of the National Debt is a patriotic purpose which is also charitable. In the historic case of *Thellusson* v. *Woodford*,[5] the ultimate gift over was to the Crown to be applied in reducing the national debt. Some ten years later Lord ELDON L.C. in *Newland* v. *A.-G.*[6] upheld as charitable a bequest of stock "to His Majesty's Government in exoneration of the National Debt" and directed that the stock should be transferred to such person as the King under his sign-manual should appoint. The case is very briefly reported and the *ratio decidendi* is not stated but it is perhaps fair to suppose that the gift was considered charitable as being for the relief of taxes. At any rate it was assumed in *Nightingale* v. *Goulburn*[7] to have been decided on that ground. In the latter case the testator made a bequest to the Chancellor of the Exchequer "to be by him appropriated to the benefit and advantage of my beloved country Great Britain". The House of Lords upheld the decision of the Vice-Chancellor[8] that the bequest was charitable. From the judgment delivered by Lord COTTENHAM L.C. it is apparent that he considered a gift "for the benefit of my country Great Britain" to be no different from a gift for the benefit of the inhabitants of a parish, town or city but he also seems from his citation of *Newland* v. *A.-G.*[9] to have come to the conclusion that the gift was one in relief of taxes.

A rather more difficult case is *Re Smith*[10] decided by the Court of Appeal in 1931. The testator bequeathed his residuary estate "unto my country England for —— own use and benefit absolutely". Although there is no Chancellor of the Exchequer for England, counsel for the Attorney-General argued on appeal that the gift was in aid of the National Exchequer and could only be applied in relief of taxes. Alternatively he argued that the gift was, on the authority of

---

1 [1895] 2 Ch. 649.
2 *R.A.F.C. Co., Ltd. and Royal Air Force Club*, [1967] Ch. Com. Rep. 45 (App. D I A).
3 *Old Contemptibles Association*, [1964] Ch. Com. Rep. 60 (App. E I A 11).
4 *Great Yarmouth Far East Prisoners of War Association*, [1966] Ch. Com. Rep. 32 (App. A II 2).
5 (1799), 4 Ves. 227.
6 (1809), 3 Mer. 684; see also *Ashton* v. *Lord Langdale* (1851), 4 De G. & M. 402.
7 (1848), 2 Ph. 594.
8 (1847), 5 Hare 484.
9 (1809), 3 Mer. 684.
10 [1932] 1 Ch. 153.

F

Nightingale v. *Goulbourn*,[1] tantamount to a gift for the benefit of inhabitants of a particular locality and was therefore clearly charitable. The Court of Appeal unanimously upheld the gift on the second of these two grounds. However both LAWRENCE and ROMER L.J.J. discounted[2] the suggestion made in an earlier case[3] that in *Nightingale* v. *Goulbourn* the decision of the Vice-Chancellor and, in the House of Lords, of Lord COTTENHAM L.C. was affected by the restriction of the gift to the Chancellor of the Exchequer. This, it is submitted, is difficult to accept. There appear to have been two *rationes decidendi* of *Nightingale* v. *Goulbourn* and the first, that the gift was in relief of taxes, was clearly affected by the nomination of the Chancellor of the Exchequer.

Whether a gift to a foreign government would be charitable is perhaps more doubtful. Such a gift has been upheld in Canada, the gift being one to the government and legislature of Vermont.[4] But in the United Kingdom such a gift might fail as not disclosing a sufficient public benefit.[5]

The encouragement of patriotism

In America trusts to stimulate or inculcate patriotism have been upheld.[6] As one judge remarked:[7]

> "The fostering of love of country and of respect for our civic institutions . . . tends to raise the standard and improve the quality of citizenship, and not only relieves the burdens of government but advances the public good."

Courts across the Atlantic have therefore experienced little difficulty in approving a trust for the purchase and display of the flag,[8] a trust for the celebration of Memorial Day,[9] and a trust to construct monuments to citizens of high character and achievement.[10]

In this country the courts have not yet pronounced on trusts "to stimulate patriotism" but it is submitted that such trusts would be upheld. In the much criticised case of *Re Pardoe*[11] one of the gifts was a trust to ring a peal of bells on the anniversary of the restoration of the monarchy. KEKEWICH J. by a very benevolent, though possibly justified,[12] view of the nature of trusts for the

---

1 (1848), 2 Ch. 594.   2 See *Re Smith*, [1932] 1 Ch. 153, at 172–173 and 174–175.
3 *Per* YOUNGER L.J. in *Re Tetley*, [1923] 1 Ch. 258, at 275.
4 *Parkhurst* v. *Roy* (1882), 7 O.A.R. 614.
5 See *Camille and Henry Dreyfus Foundation Inc.* v. *I.R.Comrs.*, [1956] A.C. 39.
6 *Thorp* v. *Lund*, 227 Mass. 474 (1917) (U.S.). And see generally Scott, *Trusts* (3rd edn.), para. 374.3.
7 *Molly Varnum Chapter D.A.R.* v. *Lowell* (1910) 204 Mass. 487, at 494.
8 *Sargent* v. *Cornish*, 54 N.H. 18 (1873) (U.S.).
9 *Re De Long*, 250 N.Y. Supp. 504 (1931).
10 *Owens* v. *Owens' Executors*, 236 Ky. 118 (1930).
11 [1906] 2 Ch. 184. The case is criticised by Brunyate (1945), 61 L.Q.R. 268, 274; Hanbury, *Modern Equity* (9th edn.) 263; Crowther, *Religious Trusts*, 11.
12 See *Turner* v. *Ogden* (1787), 1 Cox Eq. Cas. 316 (keeping a church's chimes in tune is charitable).
The American Restatement on Trusts (2d) para. 374, states that trusts to celebrate or commemorate by appropriate ceremonies important historical events are charitable.
Reeve v. *A.-G.* (1843), 3 Hare 191 (the charity point was not argued); *Loscombe* v. *Wintringham* (1850), 13 Beav. 87. The latter case may well be considered obsolete: see Hanbury, *Modern Equity* (4th edn.) 219.
Re Webber, [1954] 1 W.L.R. 1500.

advancement of religion upheld the gift. It does not appear to have been argued that the trust was charitable because it stimulated patriotism but it is possible that the decision could be justified only on this ground. If a trust to encourage good servants can properly be regarded as charitable, a trust to encourage good citizens (who are servants of the state) should also be valid. Certainly the Boy Scouts Association, whose purposes include the instruction of boys in the principles of discipline, loyalty and good citizenship is considered to be a charity.

Chapter 10

Protection of Human Life and Property

It will be remembered that one of the purposes recited in the preamble to the Charitable Uses Act 1601 was the repair of sea-banks. It is not surprising, therefore, that it has been held that a Parliamentary grant of duty on coal imported into a town in aid of the pecuniary inability of the inhabitants to protect themselves against the ravages of the sea is a charitable use;[1] so too, it has been held, is a trust for the benefit of copyhold tenants for the repair of the sea-dykes within the manor.[2] Since the encroachment of the sea threatens both life and property, it is clear that the protection of human life and property is within the equity of the Statute. Certainly the courts have held that the protection of human life is a charitable purpose within the spirit and intendment of the Statute, though not, in fact, on any expressed analogy with the repair of sea-banks. Thus gifts for providing lifeboats,[3] for the Royal National Life-boat Institution[4] and the Royal Humane Society for Saving Life,[5] have all been upheld as charitable.

In *Re Wokingham Fire Brigade Trusts*[6] DANCKWERTS J. held that a voluntary non-profit-making fire brigade which had been formed at a public meeting to meet a public need of fighting fires in the district was holding its assets and funds subject to charitable trusts and he commented thus:[7]

> "The brigade was not formed for the benefit of the members, but for the benefit of the public, and its purpose was to prevent damage and loss of life in that community. It seems to me that the provision of a public fire brigade of this kind is as much a public charitable purpose as the provision of a lifeboat, which has been held in a number of cases to be a public charitable purpose."

A trust for the promotion of road safety,[8] or for the prevention of accidents (whether upon the roads or elsewhere) would obviously be valid as being directed to the prevention of damage and loss of life. The provision of lifeguards on beaches is likewise charitable.[9] And there is copious authority that trusts for

---

1 *A.-G.* v. *Brown* (1818), 1 Swan. 265.
2 *Wilson* v. *Barnes* (1886), 38 Ch.D. 507, C.A.
3 *Johnston* v. *Swann* (1818), 3 Madd. 457.
4 *Thomas* v. *Howell* (1874), L.R. 18 Eq. 198; *Re Richardson* (1887), 56 L.J. Ch. 784; *Re David* (1889), 43 Ch.D. 27, C.A.
5 *Beaumont* v. *Oliveira* (1869), 4 Ch. App. 309.
6 [1951] Ch. 373.
7 *Ibid.*, at 377.
8 See *The League of Highway Safety and Safe Drivers, Ltd.,* [1965] Ch. Com. Rep. 27.
9 *Richardson* v. *Mullery*, 200 Mass. 247 (1908) (U.S.) (lifesaving station).

the defence of the realm (which are, of course, ultimately directed at protecting the lives and properties of the Queen's subjects) are valid.[1] The preservation of public order is similarly for the protection of lives and property and is a charitable object.[2]

1 See at 96, *supra.*
2 *I.R.Comrs.* v. *City of Glasgow Police Athletic Association,* [1953] A.C. 380.

Chapter 11

Social Rehabilitation

Even before the Charitable Uses Act 1601 there were, as Professor Jordan has shown,[1] a considerable number of gifts for social rehabilitation. Under this head we may include not only gifts for the re-establishment in civilian life of members of the armed forces[2] but also trusts to assist discharged prisoners to make good[3] or trusts to reclaim prostitutes.[4] The rehabilitation of alcoholics and drug addicts must also rank as charitable under this title. Gifts for the relief of refugees[5] or of the victims of some disaster[6] are classifiable under the same rubric. But it is important to note that a disaster fund will not be charitable in nature unless the help is given only to those in need. An unsuitably worded appeal or an inappropriately drafted trust deed may deprive a particular fund of charitable status. One danger is that, if the purposes of the fund are not worded satisfactorily, persons within the beneficial class may be entitled as of right to claim a proportionate share of the capital and income, thus probably preventing the fund from being recognised as a charity. The Charity Commissioners therefore suggest that those responsible for drawing up appeals and trust deeds should use words to show that no person will receive assistance unless he is in need. Statements to the effect that no account need be taken of means should be avoided, since they would, for instance, allow a widow to receive money even if she were rich and in no real need.[7] The Commissioners have also stated[8] that it is most desirable to provide that if there is an ultimate surplus after all needs have been met the fund shall go to some charitable purpose reasonably analogous to the original purpose. An example of a provision for the destination of a surplus that was held to be too vague is to be found in *Re Gillingham Bus Disaster Fund*[9] where the appeal stated that the fund was to be devoted, among other things, to defraying the funeral expenses, caring for the boys who might be disabled and then to such worthy cause or causes in memory of the boys who lost their lives as the mayors might determine.

Other examples of charitable gifts for resettlement or rehabilitation are: loan funds (free of interest) for those who are temporarily distressed, especially

---

1 See Jordan, *Philanthropy in England*, at 368 and 370.
2 *Verge v. Somerville*, [1924] A.C. 496.
3 See Scott, *Trusts* (3rd edn.) para. 374.12.
4 *Mahony v. Duggan* (1880), 11 L.R. Ir. 260 (upheld as a *religious* charity).
5 *Re Morison* (1967), *Times*, 8th July.
6 *Re North Devon and West Somerset Relief Fund Trusts*, [1953] 1 W.L.R. 1260; *Re Hobourn Aero Components, Ltd.'s Air Raid Distress Fund*, [1946] Ch. 194.
7 See [1965] Ch. Com. Rep. 17–19; [1966] Ch. Com. Rep. 5–8.
8 [1965] Ch. Com. Rep. 19.
9 [1959] Ch. 62.

craftsmen and small tradesmen; apprenticeship schemes; marriage subsidies for poor girls; and gifts for orphanages or homes established by local authorities pursuant to section 15 of the Children Act 1948. All of these can, no doubt, be looked on as being for the relief of poverty but gifts for orphanages and local authority homes are not necessarily for the exclusive benefit of the poor. Lord EVERSHED M.R. in one case,[1] generalising from some of the purposes set out in the preamble, said that:

> "the care and upbringing of children, who for any reason have not got the advantage or opportunity of being looked after and brought up by competent persons, or who could, for these or other reasons, properly be regarded as defenceless or 'deprived' are matters which *prima facie* qualify as charitable purposes".

It may be doubted whether this statement or any of the decided cases justify the assertion that gifts or trusts for the care, upbringing and establishment in life of children and young persons generally is charitable.[2] A gift or trust for the care, upbringing and establishment in life of children and young persons would appear to be charitable only if the children or young persons in question are defenceless, underprivileged or otherwise necessitous. Nor is it altogether clear that the principle is confined to children or young persons. Professor Scott[3] isolates "trusts for persons of limited opportunities" and observes that the community has an interest in the promotion of the happiness and well-being of the underprivileged. Most of the cases which he cites deal with trusts for the benefit of young men or young women. But in *Gibson* v. *Frye Institute*,[4] to which he refers, a trust to erect a building to include a library and dance hall for the free use of working men and women of a city and their families was held to be charitable. This rather liberal decision, which goes further than any English case or the Recreational Charities Act 1958, would probably have been differently decided in England where the courts have taken a rather restrictive view of trusts for working class people. For example in *Re Sanders' Will Trusts*[5] HARMAN J. denied validity to a gift to provide dwelling-houses for the working classes (with a preference for dockworkers) in a particular area because the expression "working class" does not necessarily connote poverty. In *Re Drummond*[6] EVE J. would not uphold a bequest of shares to be held on trust for the purpose of contributing to the holiday expenses of workpeople employed in one of the departments of a company. The workpeople in question were paid an average of 15 shillings a week (in 1913) and yet the judge felt that he could not judicially hold that a large body of workpeople working at what did indeed seem to him to be a very small wage should properly be regarded as being in such a condition of poverty as to be poor people within the statute. He also held that the class of beneficiaries was too narrow. There were, however, 500 possible beneficiaries and had he treated the trust as being for the relief of poverty and not for a general public purpose the mere narrowness of the class would not have been an obstacle.

---

1 *Re Cole*, [1958] Ch. 877, at 892. The judgment was a dissenting one but the other members of court seem not to have disagreed with this statement of principle.
2 See *Tudor on Charities* (6th edn.) 94.
3 Scott, *Trusts* (3rd edn.) para. 374.11.
4 137 Tenn. 452 (1916).
5 [1954] Ch. 265.
6 [1914] 2 Ch. 90.

Neither a gift for a "community project"[1] nor a gift to a boys club[2] can be charitable as such unless confined in some way, as for example to the under-privileged. In a case on appeal from Guyana the Privy Council held that an organisation founded to provide advice for the community on domestic, health etc. matters was not charitable.[3] In the Guyana Court of Appeal STOBY C. in his dissenting judgment pointed out[4] "today accurate information and skilled advice may be more important than money". In this connection it is interesting to note that in Fiji the Governor in Council can declare to be charitable "the furtherance of thrift and the improvement of standards of living by education and advice in matters of self-help".[5] The Charity Commissioners have regis-tered a law centre which provided legal advice as charitable.[6]

---

1 *Re Jacques* (1967), 63 D.L.R. (2d) 673.
2 *Re Kiwam's Club*, [1967] 2 O.R. 223.
3 *D'Augiar v. Guyana I.R.Comrs.* (1970), 49 A.T.C. 33, P.C.
4 (1967), 10 W.L.R. 209, at 216; and see [1969] A.S.C.L. 419 (J. D. Davies).
5 LN No. 92 Royal Gazette Supplement 1967, 293.
6 See [1974] Ch. Com. Rep. 20–21, paras. 67–72 (Camden Community Law Centre).

Chapter 12

The Protection of Animals

A trust to prevent cruelty to animals or suffering by animals is at present considered charitable. Elizabethan England was not over-concerned with suffering in the animal kingdom, and that perhaps explains the absence of the relief of animals in the famous preamble. A society in which cock-fighting and bear-baiting flourished would be unlikely to rate the prevention of cruelty to animals as sufficiently important. Indeed, it was not until the nineteenth century that public agitation secured legislation to prevent cruelty to animals. Today, however, the purpose of relieving animal suffering is certainly recognised as one in which the community has an interest, and millions of pounds are devoted to animal charities. Whether such purposes should be recognised as charitable and should therefore enjoy the fiscal privileges attaching to a charity is another matter.

In Ireland the ground on which gifts to prevent cruelty to animals are upheld has been stated to be the simple and obvious ground of the welfare of the animals themselves,[1] but in this country such trusts are considered charitable because they promote morality and check man's innate tendency to cruelty and are thus of benefit to humanity.[2]

The earliest case in which a gift for the benefit of animals was upheld as charitable was *University of London* v. *Yarrow*[3] where a trust to found an institution for studying and curing the diseases of animals useful to man was held to be good. Not long afterwards a gift to the Society for the Prevention of Cruelty to Animals was upheld as charitable,[4] and subsequently various gifts to establish or maintain homes for lost dogs[5] or cats[6] or even homeless animals[7] have been recognised as charitable the last mentioned gift being taken to refer to *domestic* animals.

Other examples of animal charities are trusts to establish humane slaughter-houses,[8] trusts to promote periodicals[9] or lectures[10] dedicated to propaganda

---

1 *Armstrong* v. *Reeves* (1890), 15 L.R. Ir. 325.
2 *Re Wedgwood*, [1915] 1 Ch. 113; *Re Moss*, [1949] 1 All E.R. 495.
3 (1857), 1 De G. & J. 72.
4 *Tatham* v. *Drummond* (1864), 4 De G. J. & Sm, 484; see also *Armstrong* v. *Reeves* (1890), 25 L.R. Ir. 325. In Pennsylvania a court has taken judicial notice of the meaning of "S.P.C.A.": *Siemens Estate*, 346 Pa. 610 (1943) (U.S.).
5 *Re Douglas* (1887), 35 Ch.D. 472, C.A.; *Adamson* v. *Melbourne*, [1929] A.C. 142, at 148, P.C.
6 *Swifte* v. *Colam* (1909), unreported, *per* MEREDITH M.R., cited in Delany, *Law of Charities in Ireland* (Revised 1962) 82; *Swifte* v. *A.-G. for Ireland*, [1912] 1 I.R. 133; *Re Moss, supra*.
7 *A.-G. for South Australia* v. *Bray*, [1964] A.L.R. 955 (High Court of Australia).
8 *Tatham* v. *Drummond, supra*; *Re Wedgwood*, [1915] 1 Ch. 113, at 116; *Re Winton* (1953), *Times*, 31st Jan.; *Re Gemmill*, [1946] 2 D.L.R. 716.
9 *Marsh* v. *Means* (1857), 3 Jur. N.S. 790.
10 *Re Cranston*, [1898] 1 I.R. 431, at 143, *per* Lord ASHBOURNE C.

against cruelty to animals and even (oddly enough) trusts to promote vegetarianism.[1]

The last mentioned purpose is of dubious public benefit if one applies an objective test: in *Re Cranston* the subjective test was applied by the two judges who formed the majority.[2] A legacy to trustees on trust to promote therewith prosecutions for cruelty to animals is a valid charitable gift which cannot be defeated on the grounds of champerty.[3] Thus, in an Irish case,[4] A. bequeathed money to be invested as a fund to reward policemen for reporting to the proper authorities and helping to bring to justice cases of cruelty to animals and this was held to be a good charitable gift.

Trusts for the prevention of cruelty to animals abroad are charitable[5] and a trust to promote the abolition of bull-fighting in Spain might therefore be upheld.

In *Re Foveaux*[6] a trust for the suppression of vivisection was held to be a valid charitable trust, but some 50 years later the House of Lords in *National Anti-Vivisection Society* v. *I.R.Comrs.*[7] took a contrary view and overruled the earlier case. Their Lordships concluded on the evidence before them that the purpose of the Society was such as to hinder medical research, and that it could not therefore be beneficial to the community.[8] They also took the view that as one of the express objects of the Society was the repeal of a statute permitting vivisection, thus changing the existing law, the purpose was political and therefore not charitable.[9] A trust or organisation to promote the abolition of fox hunting by legislation would presumably be non-charitable for the same reason.

Again, the courts will not uphold trusts for the benefit of animals which are of a quixotic character. There is no benefit to the community in a trust to support mad dogs[10] or to suppress cruelty to animals by means of united prayer.[11] In these matters the court's decision must be dictated by reason and common sense. The argument that a hospital for hedgehogs is too irrational and absurd an object to be charitable[12] is undoubtedly right. But perhaps the paradigm of all such gifts was that of the testatrix in *Re Grove-Grady*.[13] There, the testatrix

---

1 *Re Cranston*, [1898] 1 I.R. 431; *Re Slatter* (1905), 21 T.L.R. 295.

2 *Re Cranston*, [1898] 1 I.R. 431, *per* Lord ASHBOURNE C., at 444–445; *per* FITZGIBBON L.J., at 446–447. For one judicial view of vegetarians: see *Re Norgate* (1944), *Times*, 21st July.

3 *Re Vallance* (1876), cited in 2 *Seton's Judgments* (7th edn.) 1304.

4 *Re Herrick* (1918), 52 I.L.T. 213. The inconsistent case of *Re Hollywood* (1917), 52 I.L.T. 51 would probably not be followed: its distinguishing feature was that officers of the R.S.P.C.A. were excluded and this negatived a paramount charitable intent.

5 *Armstrong* v. *Reeves* (1890), 25 L.R. Ir. 325; *Re Jackson* (1910), *Times*, 11th June; *Re Inman*, [1965] V.R. 238 (legislation not dominant purpose).

6 [1895] 2 Ch. 501.

7 [1948] A.C. 31.

8 The American Restatement takes a more benevolent view and concedes charitable status both to trusts for the promotion of vivisection and to trusts for its abolition.

9 *Cf. Animal Defence and Anti-Vivisection Society* v. *I.R.Comrs.* (1950), 66 (Pt. I) T.L.R. 1112; 32 T.C. 55 where abolition by legislation was not one of the expressed objects of the appellant society and the society was held nevertheless to be non-charitable.

10 *Re Wedgwood, supra*, at 121.

11 *Re Joy* (1888), 60 L.T. 175.

12 *Thellusson* v. *Woodford* (1799), 4 Ves. 227, at 299.

13 [1929] 1 Ch. 557, C.A.; compromised on appeal *sub nom. A.-G.* v. *Plowden*, [1931] W.N. 89, H.L.; see also *Re Glyn's Will Trusts* (1953), *Times*, 28th March (sanctuary for birds and wild flowers: non-charitable).

left money to establish and maintain an institution to be run by anti-vivisection-ists and opponents of blood-sports who were to set up a natural sanctuary or reserve for "animals birds or other creatures not human". In denying the chari-table nature of the gift Lord HANWORTH M.R. pointed out that under the trust the struggle for existence was to be given free play:

> "The one characteristic of the refuge is that it is free from the molesta-tion of man, while all the fauna within it are to be free to molest and harry one another".

Accordingly it was impossible to discover any benefit to the community in the gift.

It is a moot point whether a trust to feed birds is charitable. In an old case it was said in argument that the court would not enforce an indifferent use such as to feed sparrows in perpetuity.[1] But in an Irish case[2] CHATTERTON V.C. seems to have thought that a trust to feed birds was charitable, and in the United States drinking fountains for horses,[3] dogs and birds[4] have been held to be charitable objects. In *Re Vernon*[5] a trust to erect a drinking fountain with a trough for the use of horses, cattle and dogs was upheld as charitable. All these animals, of course, are considered useful to man. Birds, other than carrier pigeons, are not, and a trust to feed ordinary common birds ought not to qualify as a charitable trust. English courts should follow the decision in *Royal Society for the Prevention of Cruelty to Animals v. Benevolent Society of New South Wales*[6] where a trust to feed, water and to keep free from molestation birds visiting a half-acre side in suburban Sydney was held by the High Court of Australia not to be charitable. A suburban householder cannot convert his house into a public charity by keeping a basin full of water on the window ledge with some breadcrumbs.[7] The whole idea of appropriating money to such a purpose is too quirkish.[8] A trust to apply income in improving the breeding and racing of Homer pigeons is not charitable in the legal sense.[9]

---

1 *A.-G.* v. *Whorwood* (1750), 1 Ves. Sen. 534, at 536.
2 *Armstrong* v. *Reeves* (1890), 25 L.R. Ir. 325.
3 *Re Estate of Graves*, 242 Ill. 23 (1909) (U.S.) (horses).
4 *Estate of Coleman*, 167 Cal. 212 (1914) (U.S.).
5 (1957), *Times*, 27th June.
6 (1960), 102 C.L.R. 629.
7 *Ibid.*, at 648–649, per WINDEYER J.
8 *Ibid.*, at 647, per MENZIES J.
9 *Royal National Agricultural and Industrial Association* v. *Chester* (1974), 48 A.L.J.R. 304 (High Court).

Chapter 13

Other Miscellaneous Purposes Beneficial to the Community

No list of charitable purposes can be exhaustive and it is perhaps inevitable that any classification of purposes will leave a rag bag of individual charitable gifts with no easily discernible common thread.

Some of the individual cases now seem out of date. When the domestic labour force was a considerable element in the community, it was perhaps natural that a trust to encourage good domestic servants should be upheld. Whether the fiscal privileges that now appertain to charities should be conferred on such a trust in these days is another matter, and it is probable that cases like *Reeve* v. *A.-G.*[1] and *Loscombe* v. *Wintringham*[2] would not nowadays be followed. A gift to give training in domestic science on the other hand would undoubtedly be upheld as an educational purpose.

Since there is now ample authority for the proposition that a gift for the promotion of art for the public benefit is for the advancement of education there is little to be served by grouping such gifts under an independent head of their own.[3] Occasionally, of course, a gift for the promotion of art may equally well be classified under the head of municipal betterment.[4]

The promotion of industry and commerce for the public benefit has been upheld as charitable[5] in a case which turned on the true construction of the wording of the Crystal Palace Act 1914. On reading the Act in question it emerges that the trustees constituted by the Act are, to a large extent, representative trustees, representing the public authorities who contributed to the moneys required for the acquisition of the site of Crystal Palace, which was to be administered by the trustees as a concern which would not distribute any profits. In the title and preamble and throughout the Act the note which is stressed is the provision of benefits to the public. DANCKWERTS J. held that it followed that the promotion of industry and commerce mentioned in the Act must be promotion for the benefit of the public and not in furtherance of the interests of the individuals engaging in trade, industry or commerce.

If horticulture and agriculture are to be treated as included in the term "industry" there are certainly other examples of gifts to promote industry being upheld. In *Re Pleasants*[6] a gift whose result would be to improve horticulture (as well as good housewifery) was upheld. The promotion of agriculture generally (as opposed to the furtherance of the interests of the persons engaged

---

1 (1843), 3 Hare 191.
2 (1850), 13 Beav.87.
3 See at 43, *supra*.
4 See at 92, *supra*.
5 *Crystal Palace Trustees* v. *Minister of Town and Country Planning*, [1951] Ch. 132.
6 (1923), 39 T.L.R. 675.

in it) was held to be charitable in *I.R.Comrs.* v. *Yorkshire Agricultural Society*[1] where the society in question had as its object the general improvement of agriculture. It is of course otherwise if the association in question is directed to furthering the interests of the association members as one of its main objects.[2] And it may be doubted whether the promotion of agriculture in another country with no overspilling benefit to the United Kingdom community is charitable.[3]

A transatlantic example of a gift to promote industry and commerce for the *public* benefit is to be found in a case where the court upheld a trust for an award to a citizen who should by his application to its manufacturing and commercial interests produce the best results for the prosperity of the city.[4]

The Supreme Court of India has likewise stated that the promotion of economic prosperity is for the public good,[5] even though it is shared by those in industry, but it was unwilling to hold that a registered trade union which was potentially able to distribute its profits among its members and which also pursued objects of a purely union nature was charitable even though it promoted the sugar industry. The non-charitable benefits to the members were not merely incidental.

It has been suggested that one can isolate a further head of charity consisting of "trusts for certain purposes which are not religious but tend to promote the moral or spiritual welfare[6] of the community or a sufficiently important section of the community".[7] But this far from compendious head is fashioned from meagre materials. No general principle should be deduced from animal charities[8] which are an anomaly.[9] Trusts for the promotion of temperance are more surely justified as charities by reference to the promotion of health than by reference to some vague concept of moral improvement. Once these two groups of charities are put aside one is left with *Re Scowcroft*[10] and *Re Price*.[11] Neither of these two cases warrant the erection of a structure of general principle. The first was almost certainly wrongly decided; and *Re Price* is hardly more satisfactory as an authority. The gift in *Re Price* was to an unincorporated association called the Anthroposophical Society of Great Britain and was impressed with the direction that it should be used for carrying on the teachings of Dr. Rudolph Steiner. COHEN J. held that the Society was at liberty to spend capital as well as income in carrying out the trusts of the bequest and

---

1 [1928] 1 K.B. 611.
2 *National House-Builders Registration Council*, [1969] Ch. Com. Rep. 10, para. 22 (not charitable); *Hadaway* v. *Hadaway*, [1955] 1 W.L.R. 16, P.C. (grant of loans at low rate of interest to planters and agriculturalists); *cf. Council of Industrial Design*, [1973] Ch. Com. Rep. 23, paras. 68–70.
3 The Charity Commissioners obviously had this doubt prior to *Re Jacobs* (1970), 114 Sol. Jo. 515: see *Farm Buildings Centre, Ltd.*, [1965] Ch. Com. Rep. 27 (App. C6).
4 *Powell Estate* (1950), 71 D. & C. 51. But the standards of supervisory management are too vague: *The Institute of Supervisory Management*, [1967] Ch. Com. Rep. 46–47 (App. D).
5 *Income Tax Comr.* v. *Indian Sugar Mills Association* A.I.R. 1975, S.C. 506 following *C.I.T.* v. *Andhra Chamber of Commerce* A.I.R. 1965, S.C. 1281.
6 A trust to elevate the community spiritually has been upheld in Canada: see *Re Orr* (1917), 40 O.L.R. 567.
7 See *Tudor on Charities* (6th edn.) 117.
8 Otherwise a trust for philanthropic purposes should be valid which is not so.
9 It is difficult to see how animal charities are within the siprit and intendment of the preamble to the Statute of Elizabeth I.
10 [1898] 2 Ch. 638.
11 [1943] Ch. 422.

that accordingly no perpetuity was created and the bequest was valid. In view of COHEN J.'s conclusion on this issue everything which he proceeded to say on the subject of charity was, strictly, *obiter*. But since the question of charity was fully argued before him and fully considered by him his judgment on this issue too merits analysis. The learned judge on hearing evidence that the teachings of Dr. Rudolph Steiner were directed to the mental or moral improvement of man and were not *contra bonos mores* decided that they *might* result in such mental or moral improvement and upheld the gift under Lord MACNAGHTEN's fourth head of charity. It is submitted that the gift was either charitable as being for the advancement of education or was not charitable at all. Mental improvement is synonymous with education: moral improvement it is submitted is too vague a concept to be an object of charity.[1]

---

1 But see *Re Wright* (1923), 56 N.S.R. 364 (training in higher ideals); *cf. Cameron* v. *Church of Christ Scientist* (1918) 57 S.C.R. 298, at 304 (uplifting of humanity).

Chapter 14

Politics

A trust for political purposes is not charitable.[1] The rule is easy to state but not to apply, and the cases disclose inconsistencies.

It is now established that a trust to support a particular party or its doctrines is not charitable. The first case in which this was clearly laid down was *Re Jones*[2] where a gift of land "to the Primrose League of the Conservative cause to be used as a habitation in connection with the league or in a manner which will benefit the cause" was held to be void. The Primrose League was a political organisation whose manual stressed that it was "most essential that the political character of the Primrose League should be conspicuously maintained". A trust for the purpose of providing education in the principles of a political party for the furtherance of that party is also not charitable. In *Bonar Law Memorial Trust* v. *I.R.Comrs.*[3] the objects of the trust were: (i) to honour the memory of Mr. Bonar Law; (ii) to preserve a great and historical building (namely Ashridge House in Hertfordshire) from destruction; and (iii) to cause the building and surrounding grounds to be used for the purposes of an educational centre or college for educating persons in economics, in political and social science, in political history with special reference to the development of the British constitution and the growth and expansion of the British Empire, and in such other subjects as the governing body might deem desirable. The specific subjects mentioned are recognised academic disciplines;[4] but FINLAY J. thought that the discretion conferred on the governing body would enable the governing body to arrange lectures which were really nothing but propaganda of the Conservative Party. Such lectures would be both within the wide wording "such other subjects as the governing body may from time to time deem desirable" and an effectuation of the first mentioned purpose which was to honour the memory of a leading Conservative politician.

The question whether "the promotion of Liberal principles in politics" was a charitable object was never canvassed in *Re Ogden*[5] because the case turned on the identification of beneficiaries: there was no purpose trust in issue. However it is now clear that such an object could not be charitable. It is true that in the old case of *Russell* v. *Jackson*[6] a secret trust for the purpose of establishing a school for the education of children in the doctrines of Socialism was not

---

1 See Sheridan, "Charity versus Politics" (1973), 2A.-A.L.R. 47.
2 (1929), 45 T.L.R. 259.
3 (1933), 7 T.C. 508.
4 See *Re Berridge* (1890), 63 L.T. 470, C.A. (economic science); *Re The Trusts of the Arthur MacDougall Fund*, [1957] 1 W.L.R. 81 (political or economic science).
5 [1933], Ch. 678.
6 (1852), 10 Hare 204.

held invalid. Sir George TURNER V.C. there held that the trust was either illegal or charitable, and directed an inquiry into the nature of the doctrines of Socialism referred to by the testator, to establish whether there were any doctrines of Socialism other than the doctrines of Socialism propounded by Robert Owen,[1] what those doctrines were and whether they were illegal. The evidence about the terms of the secret trust which the court discovered in *Russell* v. *Jackson* was unsatisfactory: there was an uncertainty whether the testator wished to further Socialist doctrines generally or Socialist doctrines as propounded by Robert Owen. The affairs of a company for establishing a school on the principles of Robert Owen had been the subject of a suit in Chancery without any objection as to its legality.[2]

The decision in *Russell* v. *Jackson* has been treated as authority for the proposition that the spread of particular doctrines that are not subversive of morality or otherwise pernicious may be charitable.[3] It was referred to by counsel for the Attorney-General in his argument in *Re Scowcroft*[4] as supporting the proposition that the furtherance of Conservative principles was a good charitable object; but STIRLING J. did not mention the case in his judgment and did not decide that the furtherance of Conservative principles was or was not charitable.[5] On the issue of charity *Russell* v. *Jackson* would now be decided differently: Socialism is clearly identified as a political creed and not as some kind of philosophy. A trust to advance adult education on the lines of the Labour Party's memorandum "A Note on Education in the Labour Party" was held by VAISEY J. in *Re Hopkinson*[6] to be a trust for the attainment of political objects and not charitable. The memorandum in question was concerned, *inter alia*, to further the ends of Socialism and to encourage the solution of contemporary problems by the application of Socialist principles.[7] In the light of this decision it is hardly surprising that in *Re Bushnell*[8] a trust "for the advancement and propagation of the teaching of socialised medicine" in accordance with certain defined conditions was identified as a predominantly political trust: the testator never for a moment desired the education of the public so that they could choose for themselves, he was trying to promote political theories.

In Canada a trust for the purpose of promoting and propagating the doctrines and teachings of Socialism was held not to be charitable.[9] Legacies to the Socialist-Labour Party which is an unincorporated association have been denied charitable status in several American cases.[10] Courts in the United States have also classified as not charitable a corporation organised for the purpose of promoting the interests of the Socialist party and of workers' organisations by

---

1 The doctrines as propounded by Robert Owen were "to establish a new system, called the rational system of society, derived solely from nature and experience and ultimately to terminate all existing religions, governments, laws and institutions" (at 215).

2 *Jones* v. *Morgan* (1846), 10 Jur. 238.

3 See 5 *Halsbury's Laws of England* (4th edn.) para. 543.

4 [1898] 2 Ch. 638, at 640.

5 *Ibid.*, at 641.

6 [1949] 1 All E.R. 346.

7 See [1949] 1 All E.R., at 349–350. The title of the memorandum is also significant: "Education *in* the Labour Party".

8 [1975] 1 All E.R. 721.

9 *Re Loney*, [1953] 4 D.L.R. 539 (Manitoba).

10 *Re Andrejevich*, 57 N.Y.S. 2d 86 (1945); *Re Grossman*, 75 N.Y.S. 2d 335 (1947); *Liapis Estate*, 8 D. & C. 303 (Pa. 1954); *Re Estate of Carlson*, 9 Cal. App. 3d 479 (1970).

education of the young and by lectures,[1] and an institution organised to create a centre of education and a bureau of information for Republican women in a particular state.[2]

In Australia a gift to the Communist Party of Australia for its sole use and benefit was held to be void because the purposes designated were not in the legal sense charitable.[3]

Before leaving the topic of party political propaganda the status of *Re Scowcroft*[4] should be considered. In that case the vicar of a parish devised to his successors a building known as the Conservative Club and Village Reading Room to be maintained "for the furtherance of Conservative principles and religious and mental improvement and to be kept free from all intoxicants and dancing". The devise was upheld. STIRLING J. construed the gift as one by virtue of which Conservative principles could only be promoted in so far as they were consistent with religious and mental improvement. In effect then he construed the gift as one for the furtherance of religious and mental improvement. The case has been much criticised[5] and is of doubtful authority even though it has been followed in the Court of Appeal[6] and in the Privy Council.[7] It is possible to justify the decision as one which merely shows "that a certain degree of mingling or association with a political object is by no means fatal to a primary object that is clearly charitable in law".[8]

Peace and international understanding

Another group of cases which can aptly be described as promoting political purposes concerns trusts to promote peace and international understanding.

There is in fact authority in this country for the proposition that peace is a charitable object. The case in point is invariably cited for its relevance to the doctrine of *cy-près* and has therefore been neglected by the textbooks. In *Re Harwood*[9] one of the gifts in question was a gift to the Peace Society of Belfast: there was hearsay evidence before the court suggesting that there might have been such a society in Belfast prior to the First World War. FARWELL J. thought that the testatrix had a desire to benefit any society which was formed for the purpose of promoting peace and was connected with Belfast. He held that although there was no society in existence answering the description in the will the gift was a good charitable gift and should be applied *cy-près*. A similar gift to the non-existent Dublin Peace Society was also applied *cy-près*. It is submitted that the promotion of peace is a political purpose and therefore not charitable. Its political nature is apparent when in relation to a particular area of conflict

---

1 *Workmen's Circle Educational Center* v. *Assessors of Springfield*, 51 N.E. 2d 313 (1943).
2 *Deichelmann Estate*, 21 D. & C. 2d 659 (Pa. 1959).
3 *Bacon* v. *Pianta*, [1966] A.L.R. 1044.
4 [1898] 2 Ch. 638.
5 See *Bonar Law Memorial Trust* v. *I.R.Comrs.* (1933), 49 T.L.R. 220; and see, also, Scott, *Trusts* (3rd edn.) para. 374.6; Crowther, *Religious Trusts* (1954), 108; Keeton and Sheridan, *Modern Law of Charities* (2nd edn.) 36; Hanbury and Maudsley, *Modern Equity* (10th edn.) 396. But not *Tudor on Charities* (6th edn.) 33.
6 *Re Hood*, [1931] 1 Ch. 240.
7 *Tribune Press* v. *Punjab Tax Comr.*, [1939] 3 All E.R. 469.
8 *Re Bushnell*, [1975] 1 All E.R. 721, at 729, *per* GOULDING J.
9 [1936] Ch. 285.

one asks the question: peace on what terms? That question cannot be answered without making a political decision.

The Charity Commissioners will not admit to the Register organisations for the promotion of international friendship or understanding.[1] The promotion of a closer and more sympathetic understanding between the English and Swedish peoples was held by ROWLATT J. in *Anglo-Swedish Society* v. *I.R.Comrs.*[2] not to be charitable because it "was a trust to promote an attitude of mind, a view of one nation by another". In the light of that decision it is hardly surprising that the counsel appearing in *Buxton* v. *Public Trustee*[3] agreed that a trust "to promote and aid the improvement of international relations and intercourse" by various stated methods was not charitable. In the United States such trusts have been admitted to charitable status.[4] Thus a trust to foster and encourage the spirit of international understanding and co-operation, and to promote the enlightenment of individuals by broadcasting radio and television programmes of a cultural educational artistic or spiritual nature has been upheld.[5] Again in the United States it has been held that a legacy to the World Peace Foundation, a body campaigning by educational means against war, was charitable.[6]

Changes in the existing law

A very difficult question which has given rise to much discussion[7] is whether a body whose object is to change the existing law can be charitable. The difficulty results from an inconsistency of approach in the decided cases. Some jurisdictions go further than the English Courts in admitting to the privilege of charity organisations which seek changes in the law.

At one end of the spectrum the principle is clear. A trust, *the* main object of which is the reform of a particular law is political and not charitable. Thus in *Bowman* v. *Secular Society, Ltd.*[8] Lord PARKER OF WADDINGTON said that:

"The abolition of religious tests, the disestablishment of the Church, the secularisation of education, the alteration of the law touching religion or marriage or the observation of the Sabbath are purely political objects. Equity has always refused to recognise such objects as charitable."

Although this observation was strictly *obiter* there can be no doubt that it accurately states the law.

But what if the trust has *several* main objects, one of which is a change in the existing law? In *National Anti-Vivisection Society* v. *I.R.Comrs.*[9] the appellant society was held not to be charitable on two grounds: first because vivisection

---

1 [1963] Ch. Com. Rep. 14, para. 39 following *Buxton* v. *Public Trustee* (1962), 41 T.C. 235.
2 (1931), 47 T.L.R. 295.
3 (1962), 41 T.C. 235 (PLOWMAN J.).
4 12 A.L.R. 2d 882.
5 *Assessors of Boston* v. *World Wide Broadcasting Foundation*, 317 Mass. 598 (1945); 59 N.E. 2d 188; and see *Re Harmon*, 80 N.Y.S. (2d) 903 (1948).
6 *Parkhurst* v. *Burrill*, 117 N.E. 39 (1917) (Supreme Judicial Court of Massachusetts).
7 See principally Sheridan, "Charity versus Politics" (1973) 2 A.-A.L.R. 47, at 50–62; Benedict Nightingale, *Charities* (1973) 45–67; Scott, *Trusts* (3rd edn.) Vol. IV, para. 374.4; "Validity of charitable trust to promote change in laws" 22 A.L.R. 3d 886–896 (1968).
8 [1917] A.C. 406, at 442.
9 [1948] A.C. 31.

was for the public benefit so that the abolition of vivisection could not be so; and secondly because one of the main objects was political. The objects of the society included the repeal of the Cruelty to Animals Act 1876 and the substitution of a new enactment prohibiting vivisection altogether. Lord WRIGHT and Lord SIMONDS both considered that the society was not charitable because one of the main objects was in essence political: the society could not claim to be exclusively charitable and accordingly was not a charity. Viscount SIMON associated himself with this conclusion. Lord NORMAND thought it clear that the society was a political association and not a charity but reached that conclusion by asking himself whether the general purposes of the society were in the main political or in the main charitable. He considered that if legislation was merely *ancillary* to the attainment of what is *ex hypothesi* a good charitable object the position would be different. Lord PORTER dissented from the conclusion that the society was not charitable. In his view an object was only political if it necessitated a change in the law: if the desired purpose could be achieved by persuasion and not by a change in the law, then it was not political.

Later decisions denying charitable status to the anti-vivisectionist cause have usually done so both on the ground that the cause is not charitable and on the ground that the political object of a change in the law has been expressed in the will or constitutional document in question.[1] In *Animal Defence and Anti-Vivisection Society* v. *I.R.Comrs.*,[2] however, the objects of the society in question did not specifically refer to changing the law, but included general opposition to vivisection. DANCKWERTS J. could have decided the case simply on the ground that opposition to vivisection was not for the public benefit and so not charitable. But he chose to base his decision on the additional ground that the society had a political object since its activities "must necessarily in the end involve an attack on the Cruelty to Animals Act 1876 and the promotion of the support of legislation for repealing that Act and for suppressing vivisection altogether".

Other causes necessarily or expressly involving changes in the law have been classified as political. Thus in England,[3] New Zealand[4] and Tasmania[5] it has been held that the promotion of temperance by legislation is not charitable. But in Canada[6] and the United States[7] there are decisions to the opposite effect. Some of these transatlantic decisions may be attributed to the sympathy which the judges had for the cause of prohibition:[8] others concern organisations which were also dedicated to fighting the white slave traffic and the narcotic drugs traffic.[9]

The advocacy of tax reform, such as for example the adoption of the single tax proposed by Henry George, is not charitable.[10] But the mere exposition of

---

1 *Re Inman*, [1965] V.R. 238; *Re Jenkins' Will Trusts*, [1966] Ch. 249.

2 (1950), 66 (Part 2) T.L.R. 1091.

3 *I.R.Comrs.* v. *Temperance Council of Christian Churches of England and Wales* (1926), 136 L.T. 27.

4 *Knowles* v. *Stamp Duties Comr.*, [1945] N.Z.L.R. 522.

5 *Re Cripps*, [1941] Tas.S.R. 19.

6 *Farewell* v. *Farewell* (1892), 22 O.R. 573.

7 *Collier* v. *Lindley* 203 Cal. 641 (1928); *Girard Trust Co.* v. *I.R.Comrs.* (1941), 138 A.L.R. 448; *International Reform Federation* v. *District Unemployment Compensation Board*, 131 Fed. 2d 337 (1942).

8 *Farewell* v. *Farewell* (1892) 22 O.R. 573, at 579, *per* BOYD C. ("not only legitimate but praiseworthy").

9 *Collier* v. *Lindley supra* (alcohol or narcotics).

10 *Re Knight*, [1937] 2 D.L.R. 285.

the principles of the tax (as opposed to the promotion of legislation to secure its adoption) has been held to be charitable in the United States.[1]

Again, a body dedicated to the reform of the law relating to birth control was in America held political and therefore not charitable.[2]

A trust for advancing civil rights by the promotion of legislation is plainly political. In England such a trust could not be upheld as charitable. In the United States however there are conflicting authorities. The most conservative approach has been adopted in Massachusetts where in two cases trusts to promote the cause of women's rights have been interpreted as being directed to the securing of legislative reform, and so have been held non-charitable.[3] In other states the courts have treated trusts for securing equal rights under the law for women as being trusts having the primary purpose of removing discrimination, with legislation as *one* of the means to that end, and have held such trusts charitable.[4] The predicament of other minorities has excited sympathy and trusts "to promote, aid and protect citizens of the United States of African descent, in the enjoyment of their civil rights"[5] and to promote legislation to secure justice for the American Indian have been upheld.[6] The earliest case of this kind was *Jackson* v. *Phillips*[7] where a gift to be used to "create a public sentiment that will put an end to negro slavery in this country" was upheld. Neither legislation nor political action was specified as a means of achieving the end, which GRAY J. found to be within the spirit and intendment of the preamble to the Statute of Elizabeth I, being analogous to the relief or redemption of prisoners or captives. On the other hand in *Marshall* v. *Comr. of Internal Revenue*[8] a trust to safeguard existing civil liberties and to advance them by promoting legislation was held not to be charitable.

The Charity Commissioners have refused to register an organisation whose main objects were to expose the failures and dangers of such practices as vaccination and inoculation, to resist the imposition of vaccination or any kind of inoculation by means of any form of legislative compulsion and to secure the abolition of any regulation requiring vaccination or inoculation. Such objects were in their view political and therefore not charitable.[9]

Just because a trust to *promote* a change in the law is not charitable, it is not to be assumed that a trust to *oppose* a change in the law is charitable. Indeed in *Re Hopkinson*[10] VAISEY J., after quoting Lord PARKER OF WADDINGTON's proposition that promoting a change in the law is not charitable because the court has no means of judging whether a proposed change in the law will or will not be for the public benefit, said:[11]

---

1 *Leubuscher* v. *I.R.Comr.*, 54 F. 2d 998 (1932); and see *George* v. *Braddock*, 45 N.J. Eq. 757 (1889).

2 *Slee* v. *I.R.Comr.*, 72 A.L.R. 400 (1930); *cf. Faulkner* v. *I.R.Comr.*, 112 F. 2d 987 (1940), noted in 41 Col. L. Rev. 335 (political and legislative objects abandoned before gift made).

3 *Jackson* v. *Phillips*, 96 Mass. 539 (1867); *Bowditch* v. *A.-G.*, 28 A.L.R. 713 (1922).

4 *Garrison* v. *Little*, 75 Ill. App. 402 (1898); *Registrar of Wills for Baltimore City* v. *Cook*, 22 A.L.R. 3d 872 (Maryland) (1966); *cf. Vanderbilt* v. *Comr. of Internal Revenue*, 93 F. 2d 360 (1937) (gifts to National Women's Party not charitable).

5 *Re Lewis' Estate*, 25 A. 878 (1893).

6 *Collier* v. *Lindley*, 266 Pac. 526 (1928).

7 96 Mass. 539 (1867).   8 147 F. 2d (1945).

9 *National Anti-Vaccination League*, [1967] Ch. Com. Rep. 47 (App. D6).

10 [1949] 1 All E.R. 346.

11 [1949] 1 All E.R. 346, at 350; and see *National Anti-Vaccination League*, [1967] Ch. Com. Rep. 47 (App. D6).

"I venture to add as a corollary to that statement that it would be equally true to apply it to the advocating or promoting of the maintenance of the present law, because the court would have no means in that case of judging whether the absence of a change in the law would or would not be for the public benefit."

What the learned judge was discussing here was proposing or approving a particular change in the law.

A distinction must be drawn between opposing a change in the law and seeking to have the law enforced. The former is an example of bringing pressure to bear on the legislature, which is political. But adherence to the law is the duty of every citizen and is not political.

There are several cases in the books where a trust to aid the enforcement of some particular law has been upheld. Thus a trust to promote prosecutions for cruelty to animals or to reward policemen for doing their duty in such cases is charitable.[1]

The reasons for holding that a trust to reform the law have been variously stated. Lord WRIGHT said that "the law could not stultify itself by holding that it was for the public benefit that the law itself should be changed".[2] But recently the judiciary has not been so reticent in suggesting that the law may be in need of reform. Hardly more satisfactory is the explanation that the courts' reluctance to uphold "law-reform" trusts is because the courts do not have satisfactory criteria by which to judge whether a particular reform is for the public benefit.[3] Perhaps the most convincing reason for denying charitable status to such trusts was put by Lord SIMONDS in the *National Anti-Vivisection Society* case when he asked[4] whether

"it is for a moment to be supposed that it is the function of the Attorney-General on behalf of the Crown to intervene and demand that a trust shall be established and administered by the court, the object of which is to alter the law in a manner highly prejudicial, as he and His Majesty's Government may think, to the welfare of the state".

It may also be that advocating or promoting changes in, or the maintenance of, existing laws is a minor aspect of an organisation's objects and merely ancillary to a more charitable purpose.[5] Where that is the case the organisation may still be charitable and may be registered as such.[6]

---

1 See *Re Vallance* (1876), 2 *Seton's Judgments* (7th edn.) 1304; *Re Herrick* (1918), 52 I.L.T. 213.

2 He was citing with approval Tyssen, *Law of Charitable Bequests* (1921, 2nd edn.).

3 *Per* Lord PARKER OF WADDINGTON in *Bowman* v. *Secular Society, Ltd.,* [1917] A.C. 406, at 442.

4 [1948] A.C. 31, at 62–63.

5 See *Incorporated Council of Law Reporting for England and Wales,* [1972] Ch. 73, at 84c: "purposes merely ancillary to a main charitable purpose, which if taken by themselves would not be charitable will not vitiate the claim of an institution to be established for purposes that are exclusively charitable".

6 *The Commonwealth Magistrates Association,* [1975] Ch. Com. Rep. 20–21, paras. 63–64 (trust to preserve independence of judiciary in Commonwealth).

Promotion of good race relations

It has been seen that a trust to promote understanding between *nations* is not charitable.[1] That prompts the question whether a trust to promote better relations between various races and creeds within the domestic community is a good charitable purpose, or is rather a political purpose.

Of particular relevance in this connection is the decision of the Court of Appeal in *Re Strakosch*.[2] There a trust for the purpose of strengthening the bonds of unity between the Union of South Africa and the United Kingdom and of conducing to the appeasement of racial feeling between the Dutch and English speaking sections of the South African community was held non-charitable on the ground that the purpose was a political one. In the course of argument counsel for one set of next of kin was asked by the Master of the Rolls whether he considered that the narrower object of appeasement was not charitable. He assented saying that the appeasement of racial ill feeling might be attempted in many ways inherently in a political field: it was not (he said) as if the testator had directed its accomplishment by education. An affidavit had been filed by Field Marshal Smuts who expressed the strong opinion that "the proper method for the appeasement of racial feeling is education in its widest sense—students' education, journalistic training, interchange of young men and women between Britain and South Africa and between young South Africans of different racial origins". Lord GREENE M.R. who delivered the judgment of the court commented:[3]

> "It is unfortunate if those methods were in the testator's mind that he did not seek to constitute a trust which might well have been valid as an educational trust notwithstanding that the education has the ultimate aims as set out in the will."

The court, however, found it impossible to construe the trust as one confined to educational purposes. These might be the best methods, but they were certainly not the only methods. "The problem of appeasing racial feeling within the community is a political problem, perhaps primarily political. One method conducive to its solution might well be to support a political party or a newspaper which had such appeasement most at heart." It was also easy, Lord GREENE suggested, to think of arrangements for mutual hospitality conducive to the appeasement of racial feeling but not charitable.

This emphasis on means rather than ends is puzzling. It is one thing if a trust specifies that the end is to be pursued by non-charitable means, for example by promoting changes in the law. But if the end is in fact charitable and there is no specific indication that particular means should be used one should not assume that the trustees will use those means. If the means adopted promote other objects then arguably the trustees will be in breach of trust.

On the other hand *Re Strakosch*[4] is clear authority for the proposition that a trust to appease racial feeling within the community is a political purpose and therefore not charitable. Nevertheless the Charity Commissioners have registered as charities the Institute for Race Relations, various branches of the

---

1 See *Anglo-Swedish Society* v. *I.R.Comrs.* (1931), 47 T.L.R., 295 discussed at 114, *supra*.
2 [1949] Ch. 529.
3 [1949] Ch. 529, at 538.
4 [1949] Ch. 529.

Community Relations Commission, The Joost de Blank Trust and the Keighley Community Relations Council. These bodies all have carefully worded trusts which are expressed to be for the advancement of education and for the provision of facilities within the meaning of the Recreational Charities Act 1958.[1]

Policy of the charity commissioners

The Charity Commissioners have on several occasions drawn attention to the difficulties into which registered or would-be charitable organisations will run if they seek to carry out propagandist activities. The content of their Annual Report in 1969 which sets out their view on this point is so important that it is reproduced as an appendix.[2]

---

1 See Nightingale, *Charities* (1973), 52–54.
2 See Appendix 3, *infra*.

Part II

Creation of Charitable Trusts

Chapter 15

Settlors and the Property Settled

What may be settled

Any property real or personal may be given to charity, assuming that there is no bar on its transferability. It is clear that incorporated hereditaments such as rent charges and advowsons may be the subject matter of a charitable gift. Thus in *A.-G.* v. *West*[1] a variable rent charge which varied according to the annual price of corn was held for charity. Formerly it was supposed that an advowson in gross could not be limited to a charitable use[2] but no such suggestion is to be found in any of the modern cases.[3] More recently it has been stated that an easement such as a right of way or passage cannot be granted to a charitable use.[4] The suggestion originated in an early nineteenth century work but is hardly justified.[5] An easement may be granted to trustees for sale[6] and that is no good reason why a grant should not be made to charity trustees. There must be many cases where charities are in fact entitled to easements.

Commonable rights also might be the subject matter of a charitable trust although in two cases which the Charity Commissioners have considered there was no evidence of charitable trusts.[7]

Who may be a settlor

The courts of equity have not laid down any special rules as to the capacity to create a trust. If an owner of property has the capacity to make an effective conveyance or transfer of it, he has the requisite capacity to create a trust to bind the property. Personal and corporate incapacity will be dealt with in turn.

---

1 (1858), 27 L.J. Ch. 789.

2 Duke, ed. Bridgman, *Law of Charitable Uses* (1805), 137.

3 *A.-G.* v. *Ward* (1829), 7 L.J. O.S. Ch. 114; *A.-G.* v. *Archbishop of York* (1853), 17 Beav. 495; *A.-G.* v. *St. John's Hospital, Bedford* (1864), 10 Jur. N.S. 897; *Re St. Stephen, Coleman Street* (1888), 39 Ch.D. 492; *Hunter* v. *A.-G.*, [1899] A.C. 309 at 322, H.L.; *Re Church Patronage Trust*, [1904] 2 Ch. 643, C.A.

4 *Tudor on Charities* (6th ed.) 127.

5 Duke, ed. Bridgman, *op. cit.* 137.

6 See 7 *Encyclopaedia of Forms and Precedents* (4th edn.) 761.

7 *Conservators of Coity Wallia Commons*, [1966] Ch. Com. Rep. 32; *The rights of commoners or allotment owners in the Great Forest of Brecknock*, [1967] Ch. Com. Rep. 46.

PERSONAL INCAPACITY

An infant or minor[1] cannot hold a legal estate in land[2] and so cannot settle it. In relation to other property the position mirrors the general rule in contract. Accordingly an *inter vivos* settlement by a minor in favour of charity is voidable in the sense that it will bind him after he comes of age unless he repudiates it on or shortly after coming of age.[3] A minor cannot make a valid will[4] unless he is a soldier[5] being in actual military service or a mariner or seaman being at sea.[6] Only in the latter exceptional cases can there be any question of the minor being able to make a valid charitable bequest.

The court has always recognised that a wealthy person has a moral obligation to make charitable donations. Accordingly a beneficiary under a settlement may indeed in many cases be recognisably entitled to regard himself as under a moral obligation to make donations towards charity. Once the beneficiary recognises this obligation, then it seems that the trustees may properly regard it as improving his material situation to discharge the obligation out of the trust fund.[7]

A voluntary conveyance by a person suffering from mental disorder, even though no receiver is acting[8] is absolutely void.[9] This is so whether or not the conveyance was during a lucid interval. The same applies *a fortiori* where a receiver has been appointed since upon the making of the order appointing the receiver the property of the patient passes out of his control.[10] But a will made by such a person during a lucid interval will be valid.[11]

Under the provisions of the Mental Health Act 1959 jurisdiction is given to the judges of the High Court nominated for this purpose by the Lord Chancellor to direct the settlement or gift of property of the patient[12] provided the patient is of full age.[13] The jurisdiction of the court to make an *inter vivos* settlement on behalf of a patient has been complemented by a power, exercisable by the court, to direct the execution for the patient of a will making any provision, whether by way of disposing of property or exercising a power or otherwise which could be executed by the patient if he were not mentally disordered.[14] This power is not exercisable unless the judge has reason to believe that the patient is not of testamentary capacity and, in any event, is not exercisable at any time when the patient is an infant.[15]

---

1 I.e. since 31st December 1969 someone under the age of 18: Family Law Reform Act 1969, ss. 1 and 2.

2 LPA 1925, s. 1 (6).

3 *Edwards* v. *Carter*, [1893] A.C. 360, H.L.

4 Wills Act 1837, s. 7 as amended by Family Law Reform Act 1969, s. 3.

5 Soldier includes a member of the Royal Air Force: Wills (Soldiers and Sailors) Act 1918, s. 5 (2).

6 Wills Act 1837, s. 11 as amended by the Wills (Soldiers and Sailors) Act 1918. A member of the Royal Naval and Marine forces who is in a position equivalent to actual military service may also make a will, though under age.

7 *Re Clore's Settlement Trust*, [1966] 1 W.L.R. 955.

8 See Mental Health Act 1959, s. 105.

9 *Elliott* v. *Ince* (1857), 7 De G.M. & G. 475; *Manning* v. *Gill* (1872), L.R. 13 Eq. 485.

10 *Re Marshall*, [1920] 1 Ch. 284.

11 *In the Estate of Walker* (1912), 28 T.L.R. 466.

12 Mental Health Act 1959, ss. 102 and 103 (1).

13 *Ibid.*, s. 103 (3).

14 *Ibid.*, s. 103 (1) and (3), as amended by Administration of Justice Act 1969, ss. 17 and 18.

15 *Ibid.*, s. 103 (3), as amended.

No settlement or will can be authorised unless it can be shown to be necessary or expedient for any one or more of the purposes set out in section 102 of the Mental Health Act 1959.[1] These include "making provision for other persons *or purposes* for whom or which the patient might be expected to provide if he were not mentally disordered". A gift for *purposes* for which the patient might be expected to provide can also be authorised.

In one case of a settlement, the court directed the property to be held on trust for the patient for life with a remainder over to masonic charities because the patient has benefited under a will whose testator expected that the patient would devote the bequest to such objects.[2] Charitable benefits contained in an earlier will may provide a guide to what the patient might be expected to provide.[3]

CORPORATE INCAPACITY

A corporation, created by or under a statute or otherwise for a particular purpose, has no capacity beyond the object for which it is established. Its ability to make a charitable gift by settlement or otherwise is circumscribed by its constitution. "Being the mere creature of law, it possesses only those properties which the charter of its foundation confers upon it, either expressly or incidental to its very existence. These are such as are supposed best calculated to effect the object for which it was created."[4] If the company is expressly authorised to give its property away, its charitable gifts will not be *ultra vires*.[5] But even in the absence of an express authorisation the courts have, on occasions, been able to discover an implied authorisation. This is on the basis that money can only be spent for purposes that are reasonably incidental to the carrying on of the company's business.[6] Thus Eve J. in *Re Lee, Behrens & Co.*[7] posed three pertinent questions in relation to grants involving an expenditure of the company's money namely: (i) is the transaction reasonably incidental to the carrying on of the company's business? (ii) is it a *bona fide* transaction? and (iii) is it done for the benefit and to promote the prosperity of the company? A charitable donation from the funds of a commercial company may well be good for its business.[8] That assumption underlies a provision[9] in the Companies Act 1967 that such donations be disclosed in the directors' report if the total amount given exceeds £50. In a case[10] decided in New Jersey the supreme court of that state held that "modern conditions require that corporations acknowledge and discharge social as well as private responsibilities as members of the communities

---

1 *Ibid.*, s. 103 (1) (d).
2 *Re T.C.W.* 1941 No. 1675 cited in Heywood and Massey, *Court of Protection Practice* (9th edn.) 192.
3 *Cf. Re H.M.F.*, [1976] Ch. 33; [1975] 3 W.L.R. 395.
4 *Dartmouth College Trustees* v. *Woodward*, 4 Wheat 518, at 6421 (1819), *per* Marshall C.J.
5 E.g. a guarantee company founded to administer a charity.
6 *Hutton* v. *West Cork Rail Co.* (1883), 23 Ch.D. 654, C.A.; *Evans* v. *Brunner Mond & Co.*, [1921] 1 Ch. 359.
7 [1932] 2 Ch. 46, at 51.
8 *Evans* v. *Brunner Mond & Co.*, [1921] 1 Ch. 359.
9 Companies Act 1967, s. 19.
10 *A. P. Smith Manufacturing Co.* v. *Barlow*, 98A 2d 581 at 586 (1953), (gift to Princeton University); noted in 67 Harvard Law Review 343; see Note "Power of a business corporation to donate to a charitable or similar institution" 39 A.L.R. 2d 1192 (1955).

within which they operate. Within this broad concept there is no difficulty in sustaining as incidental to that proper object and in aid of the public welfare the power of corporations to contribute corporate funds within reasonable limits in support of academic institutions." In *Evans* v. *Brunner Mond & Co.*[1] one of the clauses of the memorandum of the defendant company enabled the company to do "all such business and things as may be incidental or conducive to the attainment of the above objects or any of them". The previously enumerated objects included the primary object of carrying on business as chemical manufacturers.[2] At an extraordinary general meeting the company passed a resolution authorising the directors "to distribute to such universities or other scientific institutions in the United Kingdom as they may select for the furtherance of scientific education and research the sum of £100,000 out of invested surplus reserve account". The plaintiff shareholder claimed that the resolution was *ultra vires*. The chairman and directors filed evidence to the effect that they wished to encourage science at the universities and in the scientific schools of the country so as to have a larger reservoir of trained experts upon which to draw for the company's research work. All the affidavits, which were uncontradicted, favoured the proposed expenditure. EVE J. held that the expenditure was *intra vires* as being conducive to and indeed necessary to the continued progress of the company's business. But if the company is about to go out of business, a charitable donation is liable to be attacked, because it is not reasonably incidental to the carrying on of the company's business.[3]

The foregoing principles apply equally to statutory corporations and municipal corporations as well as to companies registered under the Companies Acts. But a corporation created by royal charter has *prima facie* the same power of disposition as a natural person.[4]

Enabling powers of gift

A tenant for life under the Settled Land Act 1925 is given certain somewhat cramped powers to grant lands for public and charitable purposes. Provided it is for the development, improvement or general benefit of the settled land or any part of it a tenant for life may make a gratuitous grant in fee simple of any part of the settled land, with or without any easement, right or privilege out or in relation to the settled land or any part thereof for all or any one or more of certain specified purposes.[5] The purposes specified are:

(i) For the site, or the extension of any existing site, of a place of religious worship, residence for a minister of religion, school house, town hall, market house, public library, public baths, museum, hospital infirmary or other public building, literary or scientific institution, drill hall, working men's club, parish room, reading room or village institute, with or without in any case any yard, garden, or other ground to be held with any such building: or

(ii) For the construction, enlargement, or improvement of any railway, canal, road (public or private), dock, sea-wall, embankment, drain, watercourse or reservoir; or

---

1 [1921] 1 Ch. 359.
2 The company is now Imperial Chemical Industries Limited.
3 *Parke* v. *Daily News*, [1962] Ch. 927.
4 See *Sutton Hospital Case* (1612), 10 Co. Rep. 1a, 23a, at 30b.
5 SLA 1925, s. 55.

(iii) For any other public or[1] charitable purpose in connection with the settled land, or any part thereof, or tending to the benefit of the persons residing, or for whom dwellings may be erected, on the settled land or any part thereof.

Not more than one acre may in any particular case be considered for any purpose under the first and third heads, nor more than five acres for any purpose mentioned under the third head unless the full consideration be paid or reserved in respect of the excess. The one acre allowed for a purpose under the third head is not enough for a cricket or football field, recreation ground or rifle range, so that a grant for such purposes would require express authorisation in the settlement for some larger area to be granted.

A lease or grant to the National Trust is deemed to be for the general benefit of the settled land and for a charitable purpose in connection with the settled land and the limit is extended to five acres instead of one for the purposes of the section.[2]

The above mentioned power to grant land for public and charitable purposes is conferred on persons having the powers of a tenant for life as well as on the tenant for life. Trustees for sale also have the same enabling power[3] as do personal representatives acting in the course of administration or during a minority or during the subsistence of a life interest or until the period of distribution arrives.[4]

The Universities of Oxford, Cambridge and Durham and the colleges and halls within those universities together with Eton and Winchester have a power, mirroring that of the tenant for life, to grant land for certain public and charitable purposes[5] and a similar power is conferred upon the Crown Estate Commissioners with the consent of Her Majesty under the royal sign manual.[6] As has been seen the power is hedged about with restrictions.

Particular classes of donor have also been empowered to give limited areas of land for special charitable purposes. Thus a grant of land for the purposes of School Sites Act 1841 may be made by any life tenant, a lord of a manor in respect of common land,[7] a beneficiary under a trust,[8] the guardian of a minor[8] and "any corporation, ecclesiastical or lay, whether sole or aggregate, and . . . any officers, justices of the peace, trustees, or commissioners holding land for public, ecclesiastical, parochial, charitable or other purposes or objects".[9] A grant involving parochial property requires the seal of the Secretary of State for Social Services.[10] In the case of a grant by any officers, trustees or commissioners, other than parochial trustees, it is sufficient if a majority or quorum authorised

---

1 It has been doubted that "or" is here used disjunctively: see *Lewin on Trusts* (16th edn.) 527.

2 National Trust Act 1937, s. 6.

3 LPA 1925, s. 28 (1).

4 AEA 1925, s. 39 (1) (i) and (iii).

5 Universities and College Estates Act 1925, s. 15, reproducing *mutatis mutandis* SLA 1925, s. 55 discussed, *supra*.

6 Crown Estate Act 1961, s. 4.

7 School Sites Act 1841, s. 2.

8 *Ibid.*, s. 5.

9 *Ibid.*, s. 6. An ecclesiastical corporation sole below the dignity of a bishop requires the written consent of the bishop of the diocese to which the corporation is subject: *ibid.*

10 *Ibid.* By a chain of legislative provisions the Secretary of State has succeeded to the function of the poor law commissioners: Local Government Board Act 1871, s. 2; Ministry of Health Act 1919, ss. 3 (1) (a), 5 and Sch. 1 (Repealed); Secretary of State for Social Services Order 1968, S.I. 1968 No. 1699.

to act of such officers, trustees or commissioners assembled at a meeting duly convened assents to the grant and executes the deed even though they do not constitute a majority of the actual body of such officers, trustees or commissioners.[1] The purposes for which in such cases a grant of up to one acre of land may be made are: for the site of a school for the education of poor persons, or for the residence of the schoolmaster or schoolmistress, or otherwise for the purposes of the education of such poor persons in religious and useful knowledge.[2]

The powers for granting land to an extent not exceeding one acre as a site for a school conferred on limited owners by the School Sites Acts 1841 and 1849 extend to the grant of land for the enlargement of churchyards or burial places.[3] Similar provisions have been enacted to assist gifts for the promotion of science, literature and the fine arts.[4] Accordingly gifts of land of up to an acre for institutions established for those purposes and for adult instruction, the diffusion of useful knowledge, the foundation of libraries and reading rooms for general use open to the public,[5] of public museums and galleries of paintings and other works of art, collections of natural history, mechanical and philosophical inventions, instruments, or designs may be made by the same class of limited owners mentioned in the School Sites Acts 1841 and 1849. Gifts of land up to an acre in size are likewise[6] facilitated for the site of a church, chapel, meeting house or other place of worship,[7] or for the residence of a minister officiating in a place of worship within one mile of the site or for a burial place,[8] but no part of a demesne or pleasure ground attached to a mansion house may be so conveyed.[9]

Repeal of the law of mortmain

Brief mention should be made of the statutory restrictions known as the law of mortmain and now fortunately swept away.

Statutes preventing corporations from holding land without a licence from the Crown go back in time to Magna Carta. Their purpose was to prevent the accumulation of land in the dead hand ("mortmain") of artificial persons who never died, and in particular of the monasteries. If land were permitted to remain in mortmain the Crown would be deprived of its feudal revenues, the most important of which were payable on the death of the tenant for life.

After the Reformation gifts to charitable uses became more common in place of gifts to religious corporations, and parallel provisions prohibiting gifts and sales to charities except under certain conditions were enacted by the Mortmain Act 1735 also referred to as the Charitable Uses Act 1735.[10]

---

1 School Sites Act 1841, s. 6.
2 *Ibid.*, s. 2.
3 Consecration of Churchyards Act 1867, s. 4; Charities Act 1960, s. 48 (2), Sch. 7, Part II.
4 Literary and Scientific Institutions Act 1854.
5 The Act is not confined to institutions of a public or charitable nature but includes private institutions: *Re Russell Institution*, [1898] 2 Ch. 72.
6 The class of persons so empowered is the same as under the School Sites Act 1841.
7 Of any denomination.
8 Places of Worship Sites Act 1873, s. 1.
9 *Ibid.*
10 9 George 2 c. 36. The Act is discussed in Jones, *History of the Law of Charity 1532–1827* (1969), 109–119 and in Holdsworth, *A History of English Law*, Vol. XI, 590–593.

The old law of mortmain and the Act of 1736 were repealed and substantially re-enacted by the Mortmain and Charitable Uses Act 1888. As regards charities one of the main provisions of the last-mentioned Act, requiring every assurance of land to charity to be enrolled in the Central Office of the Supreme Court within six months of its execution, was repealed and replaced by a provision in the 1925 legislation which substituted an obligation to have the assurance recorded with the Charity Commissioners.[1]

The position before 29th July 1960, the date of the passing of the Charities Act 1960, was that assurances *inter vivos* of land, or of personal estate to be laid out in the purchase of land, in favour of charity were, with various exceptions, subject to certain restrictions. Such assurances had to take effect in possession and they might be made subject to certain reservations only; if not for valuable consideration, they had to be made not less than a certain period before the death of the donor; and they had to comply with certain provisions as to form and recording. If an assurance did not comply with these restrictions it was void.

Immediately prior to the passing of the Charities Act 1960 land might be assured by will to charity, but unless the devisee was authorised to retain the land by an order of the court or the Charity Commissioners the land had to be sold within one year after the testator's death or such longer period as might be duly authorised.

The law of mortmain also forbade the assurance of land to charitable and other corporations except by royal licence or statutory authority. Any land so assured was forfeit to the Crown.

The law of mortmain was repealed by the Charities Act 1960.[2] The repeal, which affects not merely charities, necessitated various consequential provisions.

No right or title to any property may be defeated or impugned, and no assurance or disposition of property may be treated as void or voidable, by virtue of any of the enactments relating to mortmain, if on 29th July 1960 the possession was in accordance with that right or title or with that assurance or disposition, and no step has been taken to assert a claim by virtue of any such enactment.[3] But this provision does not validate any assurance or disposition so as to defeat a right or title acquired by adverse possession before 29th July 1960.[4]

As regards the wills of persons dying before 29th July 1960, the repeal of the Mortmain and Charitable Uses Act 1891 put an end to any requirement to sell land then unsold, but it does not enable effect to be given to a direction to lay out personal estate in land without an order under that Act, nor does it affect the power to make such an order.[5]

---

1 SLA 1925, s. 29 (4). Assurances of land for educational purposes were subsequently required to be recorded with the Minister of Education: Education Act 1944, s. 87 (2).
2 CA 1960, s. 38 (1).
3 *Ibid.*, s. 38 (2).
4 *Ibid.*, s. 38 (2), proviso.
5 *Ibid.*, s. 38 (3).

G

Chapter 16

Formalities

Introduction

A charitable trust of personalty is enforceable without any evidence in writing of the terms of the trust.[1] But where money is subscribed or contributed for a charitable purpose in response to an appeal before any trust deed has been drawn up,[2] it is the responsibility of those who receive the money to execute a trust deed declaring precise trusts.[3] A charitable trust of land must as a general rule either be constituted by will or manifested and proved by some writing signed by a person able to declare such a trust, if it is to be enforceable.[4]

Prior to the Statute of Frauds in 1676, a trust of land as well as of personalty could be effectively created *inter vivos* without a written instrument. However, the Statute of Frauds (whose avowed purpose was to prevent false claims)[5] provided that "all declarations or creations of trusts or confidences of any lands, tenements or hereditaments shall be manifested and proved by some writing signed by the party who is by law enabled to declare such trust, or by his last will in writing, or else they shall be utterly void and of no effect."[6] An exception to this provision was where "a trust or confidence shall or may arise or result by the implication or construction of law". In so far as the Statute dealt with testamentary trusts, it has been superseded by the provisions of the Wills Act 1837;[7] and in so far as the Statute dealt with *inter vivos* trusts, it has been superseded by the Law of Property Act 1925, section 53, which uses somewhat different language.

According to section 53 (1) (b) of the Law of Property Act 1925:

> "A declaration of trust respecting any land or any interest therein must be manifested and proved by some writing signed by some person who is able to declare such trust or by his will."

It is important to analyse just what in fact constitutes a sufficient "writing" for the purposes of the provision, and what consequences ensue where there is no

---

1 *Lyell* v. *Kennedy* (1889), 14 App. Cas. 437, at 457.
2 *A.-G.* v. *Kell* (1840), 2 Beav. 575; *Re Welsh Hospital (Netley) Fund*, [1921] 1 Ch. 655; *Re North Devon and West Somerset Relief Fund Trusts*, [1953] 1 W.L.R. 1260.
3 *A.-G.* v. *Mathieson*, [1907] 2 Ch. 383; and for the practice relating to disaster appeals, see at 102, *supra*.
4 LPA 1925, s. 53 (1) (b).
5 See preamble to 29 Car. 2, c. 3.
6 Statute of Frauds 1676, s. 7.
7 7 Will. 4 & 1 Vict. c. 26.

writing. This leads naturally to the question whether, as in the case of contracts for the sale of land, acts of part performance can be a substitute for writing.

Writing

An express trust of land is constituted either by a settlor declaring himself to be trustee of the relevant property or by a settlor conveying the property to trustees. In either case it is necessary to decide when and by whom the writing or memorandum should be signed.

DECLARATION OF TRUST

Where the owner of an interest in land declares himself trustee of it for some charitable purpose, then obviously he (and he alone) is the proper party to sign the memorandum. If, as is usually the case, he signs the memorandum at the time when he declares himself trustee no problem arises. But what is the position if he signs some time before or after the declaration itself? The law has not been fully worked out in this country so that it is sensible to turn to the United States for guidance.

There it has been held that it is sufficient that the settlor signs a memorandum *prior to* the creation of the trust, if the writing is made with reference to the declaration of trust or if the settlor subsequently adopts it at the time of the declaration of trust, or even later.[1] Conversely, a prior memorandum is not sufficient if not made with reference to the declaration and not subsequently adopted.

A *subsequent* memorandum, that is to say a memorandum made some time after the declaration of trust, is clearly sufficient, because all that is required is that the trust should be manifested and proved by some writing: there is no requirement that the trust should be created in writing.[2] Only if the settlor has already transferred the interest to another is a subsequent memorandum by the settlor insufficient. The nature of the subsequent memorandum is immaterial provided that it is signed and complete: it may be a letter under hand,[3] an affidavit,[4] a recital in a bond[5] or deed.[6]

TRANSFER TO TRUSTEES

The signature of the settlor alone to an instrument which conveys or transfers land to trustees and recites the trust is a sufficient memorandum of the trust.

---

1 *Brackenbury* v. *Hodgkin*, 116 Me. 399 (1917); *Compo* v. *Jackson Iron Co.*, 49 Mich. 39 (1882).

2 *Ambrose* v. *Ambrose* (1716), 1 P. Wms. 321; *Bellamy* v. *Burrow* (1735), Cas. temp. Talb. 97.

3 *Forster* v. *Hale* (1798), 3 Ves. 696; *Morton* v. *Tewart* (1842), 2 Y. & C. Ch. Cas. 67.

4 *Hampton* v. *Spencer* (1693), 2 Vern. 287 (answer in Chancery); *Cottington* v. *Fletcher* (1740), 2 Atk. 155. But a pleading will not do, because it is not usually signed by the settlor or trustee but by an agent; and the words "or by his agent thereunto lawfully authorised in wrting" do not appear in s. 53 (1) (b).

5 *Moorecroft* v. *Dowding* (1725), 2 P. Wms. 314.

6 *Deg* v. *Deg* (1727), 2 P. Wms. 412.

But the intention to create a trust does not, strictly, have to be referred to in the instrument of transfer. A contemporaneous memorandum stating that the transfer is in trust will do, for at any time before the transfer is completed the transferor can declare a trust.[1] Indeed a prior memorandum is a sufficient memorandum, provided it is made with reference to the transfer in trust or is adopted by the settlor at the time of the transfer.[2] However, a memorandum signed by the settlor after the transfer does not satisfy the statutory requirements, because once his interest is transferred a settlor can no longer declare a trust of it.[3]

CONTENTS OF THE "WRITING"

When the court is called upon to establish or act upon a trust of land, it must not only be manifested and proved by writing signed by the person enabled by law to declare the trust that there is a trust, but it must also be manifested and proved by such writing what the trust is.[4] The trust will not, in other words, be executed if the precise nature of the trust cannot be ascertained. The writing, therefore, must show with reasonable precision the trust property and a clear charitable intention. Whether it would need to define the precise *objects* is perhaps a moot point. In relation to private trusts the rule is that the writing must contain all the terms of the trust.[5] But time and again the courts have refused to allow any charitable trust to fail for a defect of form.[6]

A memorandum evidencing the creation of a trust of an interest in land may consist of several documents,[7] and the same principles which govern the linking of several documents in order to constitute a memorandum of a contract for the sale of land presumably apply. It must appear from the face of the documents that they are connected; and if this does appear, then it matters not that only one of the documents is signed in accordance with section 53 (1) (b) of the 1925 Act.[8] Just how clear the connection between two documents is required to be is illustrated by the case of *Kronheim* v. *Johnson*[9] where the court held that there was no sufficient memorandum. The absolute beneficial owner of land vested in a trustee wrote a letter to the mother of her infant grandson. The letter was signed with the writer's initials. Enclosed in the same envelope, but on a separate piece of paper, was another document in the handwriting of the same person, and headed "Supplement". This document was not signed in any way. It commenced: "I had quite omitted to tell you" but it contained no other reference to the letter, and the letter in no way referred to it. It was alleged that the "supplement" contained a declaration of trust in favour of the infant. Nevertheless FRY J. held that the supplement could not be connected with the letter and thus the alleged memorandum was insufficient.

---

1 *Patterson* v. *McClenathan*, 296 Ill. 475 (1921).
2 *Childers* v. *Childers* (1857), 1 De G. & J. 482.
3 *Clark* v. *Watson*, 141 Mass. 248 (1886).
4 *Smith* v. *Matthews* (1861), 3 De G.F. & J. 139.
5 *Ibid.*
6 See Gareth Jones, *History of the Law of Charity 1532–1827* (1969), 60–65 and 135–138.
7 *Oliver* v. *Hunting* (1890), 44 Ch.D. 205.
8 See Scott, *Trusts* (3rd edn.), para. 48.
9 (1877), 7 Ch.D. 60.

Effect of absence of writing

It seems that just as with contracts for the sale of land the absence of writing goes only to enforceability and not to validity. The trustee cannot be compelled to perform the trust nor can any person succeeding to his interest.

Part performance

Equity has long recognised that a plaintiff may sue on an oral *contract* for the sale of land in spite of any lack of writing, provided the plaintiff has acted in part performance of the contract or in reliance on the contract. Part performance is accepted as a substitute for writing.

The doctrine that part performance is sufficient to make an oral *trust* of land enforceable, in spite of statutory provisions requiring writing, is well settled in the United States,[1] though surprisingly the point has never been decided in this county.[2] Arguably the draftsman of the 1925 legislation would appear to have thought that the doctrine *did* apply to declarations of trust because the oft-overlooked section 55 of the Law of Property Act 1925 provides that:

"Nothing in the last two foregoing sections shall . . . affect the operation of the law relating to part performance.

Equally it could be said that section 55 (d) is neutral since it is not expressly directed to section 53 (1) (b). In *Smith* v. *Matthews*[3] the doctrine of part performance was attempted to be brought in to bolster up an inadequate memorandum. It is significant that TURNER L.J. did not reject the doctrine as inapplicable *per se*: the particular act relied upon was merely insufficient.

THE ACT OF THE BENEFICIARY

In the case of *private* trusts there are numerous decisions in the United States where the court has held that an act of part performance by the beneficiary was such as to take the trust out of the operation of the Statute of Frauds. Even then, there is no unanimity as to what constitutes a sufficient act of part performance. Thus, where there is an absolute deed of transfer and the grantor alleges an oral agreement by the transferee to hold the land on trust for the grantor, some courts hold that the retention of possession or the continued exercise of dominion over the land by the grantor is sufficient part performance of the alleged trust.[4]

---

1 Scott, *Trusts* (3rd edn.) para. 50 cites cases from 13 states including seven cases from New York alone. See particularly *McKinley* v. *Hessen*, 202 N.Y. 24 (1911) (Bogert, *Cases on the Law of Trusts* (3rd edn., 1958) 328).

2 On a procedure summons under R.S.C. Order 14 CROSS J. (to whom the American cases were cited) accepted the proposition as self-evident, and gave the defendant, who alleged part performance of an oral trust for religious purposes, unconditional leave to defend: *Lomanex Productions, Ltd.* v. *Henrich Feldman and others*, 1965 L. No. 1230 heard on 29th July 1965. The case was compromised by a Tomlin Order before PLOWMAN J. on 10th May 1967.

3 (1861), 3 De G.F. & J. 139.

4 *Gallagher* v. *Northrup*, 215 Ill. 563 (1905); *Gray* v. *Beard*, 66 Ore. 59 (1913).

Other courts hold that the retention of possession or the performance of acts of dominion over the land, such as the collection of rents or the payment of taxes by the grantor-beneficiary is not enough;[1] only if the grantor has, in addition to retaining possession of the land, made substantial improvements to it or so changed his position that it would be inequitable to shut him out from recovering the land, do they hold there to be a sufficient act of part performance.[2] Equally, where a landowner orally declares himself trustee of his land for another, or transfers it to another upon an oral trust for a third person, the oral trust is enforceable if the beneficiary, in reliance on the declaration of trust, enters into possession of the land and makes valuable improvements thereon.[3] In one American case it was held that if the beneficiary has entered into possession, but has not made any valuable improvements or otherwise so changed his position that it would be inequitable to shut him out from enforcing the trust, there is no sufficient act of part performance.[4]

In the context of *charitable* trusts the beneficiary is of course the public, or a substantial section of the public. Expenditure on charity land by members of the public in reliance on an oral declaration of trust is presumably a sufficient act of part performance, if the land is being used for the declared charitable purposes.

THE ACT OF THE TRUSTEES

There has been a difference of opinion in the United States courts whether part performance by an oral trustee renders the trust enforceable. Some courts hold that it does not;[5] others that it does.[6]

Secret trusts for charity

The doctrine of secret trusts[7] applies to charitable trusts as to private trusts.

Thus where a testator devises or bequeaths property to a person without any reference in the will to any intended trust, but the devisee or legatee agreed with the testator either before or after the execution of the will that he would hold the property for certain charitable purposes, he will not be permitted to keep the property for himself, but will be compelled to hold it upon a constructive trust for the intended purposes.[8] In this case, of course, the trust is *fully secret*: not a hint of it appears on the face of the will.

On the other hand where on the face of the will it is clear that a legatee or devisee is to hold the property given to him on trust but the terms of the trust

---

1 *Woolley v. Stewart*, 222 N.Y. 347 (1918); *Hazleton v. Lewis*, 267 Mass. 533 (1929).

2 *Goff v. Goff*, 98 Kan. 201 (1916); *ibid.*, 700.

3 *Canda v. Totten*, 157 N.Y. 281 (1898) (declaration of trust); *Harman v. Fisher*, 90 Neb. 688 (1912) (transfer to trustee).

4 See *Cooley v. Lobdell*, 153 N.Y. 596 (1897).

5 *Willard v. Sturkie*, 213 Ala. 609 (1925); *Pearson v. Pearson*, 125 Ind. 341 (1890).

6 *Rushton v. Isom*, 204 Ark. 804 (1942); *Van Auken v. Tyréll*, 130 Conn. 289 (1943); *Neilly v. Hennessey*, 208 Iowa 1338 (1928); *Poe v. Poe*, 208 Okl. 406 (1951).

7 See *Lewin on Trusts* (16th edn.), 35 *et seq.*; Keeton and Sheridan, *The Law of Trusts* (1974, 10th edn.).

8 *O'Brien v. Tyssen* (1884), 28 Ch.D. 372; *Re Wedgwood*, [1915] 1 Ch. 113.

are not set out, there may be a *half-secret* trust. The will may make it clear that the half-secret trust is a charitable one,[1] but equally it might leave the trust unclarified. There is some doubt whether communication of the relevant trusts made after the execution of the will is effective in the case of a half-secret trust:[2] it is undoubtedly effective in the case of a fully-secret trust.[3]

Where the terms of the oral agreement cannot be discovered, as happened in *Re Huxtable*,[4] the general charitable intent will be effectuated. In that case there was a bequest of £4000 to A "for the charitable purposes agreed between us". The legatee's evidence of the agreement contradicted the will. A scheme was directed.

The operation of the doctrine in the field of charities is no different from its operation in the field of private trusts. Thus the testator's intention must be communicated to the donee and accepted by him;[5] and once the existence of a secret charitable trust is admitted evidence to prove its terms is admissible.[6] However, where there is no communication in a testator's lifetime of his intention to create a secret trust for charity,[7] or where no secret trust is proved,[8] the donee takes absolutely, unless it appears that he is a trustee and takes upon a resulting trust.[9]

In *Re Maddock*[10] which concerned a fully-secret trust evidenced by a written memorandum there is a moot dictum of COZENS-HARDY L.J. which is sometimes reproduced as though it were trite law.[11] After classifying a secret trust as "a personal obligation binding the individual devisee or legatee", the learned Lord Justice continued:[12]

> "If he renounces and disclaims, or dies in the lifetime of the testator the persons claiming under the memorandum can take nothing . . .

This statement seems to proceed on the assumption that the secret trust only arises when the property in question vests in someone under the will. Putting it another way: "If the owner of property makes a gift of it on the faith of a promise by the donee that he will deal with the property in a particular way, an obligation so to deal with it is placed on the donee and can be enforced in [the] courts *if the donee becomes entitled*."[13] The assumed consequence is that if the property does not vest in the named person no trust arises.

There is at the very least an argument that in the case of a half-secret trust the

---

1 *Re Huxtable*, [1902] 2 Ch. 793, C.A.; and see *Re Williams*, [1933] Ch. 244 where there was probably an express trust.

2 See *Re Keen*, [1937] Ch. 236, C.A. and the discussion in Hanbury and Maudsley, *Modern Equity* (10th edn.), 210–211.

3 *Re Gardner*, [1920] 2 Ch. 523.

4 [1902] 2 Ch. 793.

5 *Re Huxtable*, [1902] 2 Ch. 793, C.A.; *Moss* v. *Cooper* (1861), 1 John. & H. 352.

6 *Edwards* v. *Pike* (1759), 1 Eden 267.

7 *Juniper* v. *Batchellor* (1868), 19 L.T. 200; *Carter* v. *Green* (1857), 3 K. & J. 591; *Littledale* v. *Bickersteth* (1876), 24 W.R. 507.

8 *Re Downing's Residuary Estate* (1888), 60 L.T. 140; *Baldwin* v. *Baldwin* (*No.* 1) (1856), 22 Beav. 413.

9 *Ommanney* v. *Butcher* (1823), Turn. & R. 260.

10 [1902] 2 Ch. 220, C.A.

11 See 5 Halsbury's Laws of England (4th edn.), para. 567.

12 [1902] 2 Ch. 220, at 231.

13 *Re Gardner* (No. 2), [1923] 2 Ch. 230, at 232, *per* ROMER J. (italics supplied).

death of the trustee during the testator's lifetime or his disclaimer on the testator's death would not sabotage the trust. On the face of the will there is a trust and equity will not allow a trust to fail for want of a trustee.[1] Accordingly (the argument runs) the property could be vested in the personal representatives on the secret trust.

Moreover, even in the case of a fully-secret trust there is at least one judicial suggestion that disclaimer by the legatee will not subvert the secret trust. Lord BUCKMASTER in *Blackwell* v. *Blackwell*[2] said:

> "In the case where no trusts are mentioned the legatee might defeat the whole purpose by renouncing the legacy and the breach of trust would not in that case inure to his own benefit, but I entertain no doubt that the court having once admitted the evidence of the trust, would interfere to present its defeat."

This dictum leaves unanswered the question of when the trust arises. On an analogy with mutual wills the answer should be the date of the death of the testator.[3] Lord WARRINGTON in *Blackwell* v. *Blackwell*[4] impliedly recognised this when he said:

> "It has long been settled that if a gift be made to a person in terms absolutely but in fact upon a trust communicated to the legatee and accepted by him, the legatee would be bound to give effect to the trust, on the principle that the gift may be presumed to have been made on the faith of his acceptance of the trust, and a refusal after the death of the testator to give effect to its would be a fraud on the part of the legatee."

Although there is one old case[5] upholding a fully-secret trust despite the death of the secret trustee during the testator's lifetime, such a trust would probably be held to fail because of the failure of the legacy upon which it was to operate.[6]

Difficult problems may also arise from the revocation of the acceptance of a secret trust before the testator's death.[7]

There were at any rate two circumstances in which the courts would not uphold secret trusts. Prior to the repeal of the mortmain laws the court would not enforce a secret trust designed to evade the mortmain restrictions.[8] Equally in the days when papist purposes were unlawful the courts would not enforce secret trusts for those purposes.[9]

Presumption of charitable trust from usage

A charitable trust whether of land or of personality may be evidenced by long usage alone. So where the origin of a charity is obscure or where the instrument

---

1 *Mallótt* v. *Wilson*, [1903] 2 Ch. 494.
2 [1929] A.C. 318, at 328.
3 See *Re Hagger*, [1930] 2 Ch. 190.
4 [1929] A.C. 318, at 341.
5 *Earl of Inchiquin* v. *French* (1745), 1 Cox 1.
6 *Re Maddock*, [1902] 2 Ch. 220, C.A.
7 See Nathan and Marshall, *Cases and Commentary on the Law of Trusts* (6th edn.), 414–415.
8 *Boston* v. *Statham* (1760), 1 Eden 508; *Edwards* v. *Pike* (1759), 1 Eden 267; *Stickland* v. *Aldridge* (1804), 9 Ves. 516.
9 *Croft* v. *Evetts* (1605), Moo. K.B. 784; and see Gareth Jones, *History of the Law of Charity 1532–1827* (1969), 82.

of endowment is lost, usage constitutes presumptive evidence of charitable trusts.[1] In order to give such usage a legal origin and render it valid, the court will presume whatever may be necessary:[2] a lost grant,[3] enrolment of a lost grant,[4] a conveyance to charitable trustees,[5] any necessary consent[6] or dispensation.[7] Even an Act of Parliament may be presumed.[8]

On the other hand where a deed of foundation is produced and is clear, usage cannot upset what is declared in the deed. Usage cannot sanction a breach of trust.[9]

A charitable trust may be presumed from such circumstances as the receipt for a long period of a rentcharge by a charity,[10] or the letting of certain rights of pasturage by a parish vestry[11] or the exercise by the free inhabitants of a borough of a right of oyster fishing.[12] The trustees' accounts showing the application of the income of a fund for a long period may determine the charitable purposes on which the fund is held.[13] Where property has been held from time immemorial for the use and repairs of what originally was the only church in a parish, the moneys are not applicable for the purposes of a new church in the same parish.[14]

Conformity with the law of the land

Charities must conform with the law of the land. This rule has many applications.

In some transatlantic jurisdictions charities enjoy a total or partial immunity from liability in tort[15] but in England there is no such immunity: charities are as vulnerable as other bodies to claims in tort. This was established as long ago as 1866 by the decision of the House of Lords in *Mersey Docks and Harbour Board*

---

1 *A.-G. v. St. Cross Hospital* (1853), 17 Beav. 435, at 464; *A.-G. v. Ewelme Hospital* (1853), 17 Beav. 366; *A.-G. v. Gould* (1860), 28 Beav. 485, at 501.
2 *A.-G. v. Moor* (1855), 20 Beav. 119 (compliance with mortmain laws); *A.-G. v. Middleton* (1751), 2 Ves. Sen. 327 (repeal of statutes governing a school), *cf. A.-G. v. Scott* (1750), 1 Ves. Sen. 413; *Hull v. Horner* (1774), 1 Cowp. 102.
3 *Goodman v. Saltash Corporation* (1882), 7 App. Cas. 633, H.L., at 640, 644.
4 *Haigh v. West*, [1893] 2 Q.B. 19, C.A., at 26.
5 *Re St. Nicholas Acons* (1889), 60 L.T. 532; *A.-G. v. Dalton* (1851), 13 Beav. 141, *cf. A.-G. v. Stephens* (1854), 1 K. & J. 724.
6 *Re Parker's Charity* (1863), 32 Beav. 654; *A.-G. v. Drapers' Co.* (1843), 6 Beav. 382.
7 *Case of Queen's College* (1821), Jac. 1.
8 *A.-G. v. Ewelme Hospital, supra; A.-G. v. Mercers' Co., Re St. Paul's School* (1870), 18 W.R. 448, at 449.
9 *A.-G. v. St. Cross Hospital, supra; A.-G. v. Gould, supra; A.-G. v. Mayor of Rochester* (1854), 5 De G.M. & G. 797, 822; and see *Edinburgh Corporation v. Lord Advocate* (1879), 4 App. Cas. 823, H.L.
10 *A.-G. v. West* (1858), 27 L.J. Ch. 789; and see *Stanley v. Norwich Corporation* (1887), 3 T.L.R. 506 (where certain rents had been paid to freemen of a city for a long period).
11 *Haigh v. West*, [1893] 2 Q.B. 19, C.A., at 26; and see *A.-G. v. Cashel Corporation* (1842), 3 Dr. & War. 294.
12 *Goodman v. Saltash Corporation* (1882), 7 App. Cas. 633, H.L.; and *cf. Lord Fitzhardinge v. Purcell*, [1908] 2 Ch. 139, at 165.
13 *Re St. Bride's, Fleet Street (Church or Parish Estate)* (1877), 35 Ch.D. 147 n.; affd., [1877] W.N. 149, C.A.
14 *Re Church Estate Charity, Wandsworth* (1871), 6 Ch. App. 296.
15 See Scott, *Trusts* (3rd edn.), para. 402; Kutner, *Legal Aspects of Charitable Trusts and Foundations*, 8–12.

Trustees v. *Gibbs*.[1] Accordingly charities are vicariously liable for the negligence of their servants within the scope of their employment and may be liable under the Occupiers Liability Act 1957 to persons injured on charity premises. A charity or charitable institution must not be established in such a manner or place as to constitute a nuisance whether to neighbours[2] or to the public.[3] This principle will yield to statutory authority provided the statute is so directory and specific as to take away from the neighbours or the public the right which they would otherwise have to complain of the nuisance.[4] In default of any sufficient statutory authority the nuisance may, of course, be restrained by injunction. This is illustrated by the various cases which have arisen with regard to small-pox hospitals.[5]

Charities must also observe any relevant restrictive covenants binding the land which they occupy. Two covenants in particular, which are frequently combined, have proved to be stumbling blocks to charitable institutions, namely a covenant not to use a house otherwise than as a private dwelling-house and not to carry on any trade or business on the premises. In *German* v. *Chapman*[6] a purchaser had covenanted that "no house or other building to be erected or built upon the land shall be used or occupied otherwise than as and for a private residence only, and not for any purpose of trade". The erection of a building to be used for the education and lodging of 100 girls in connection with a charitable institution for the daughters of missionaries supported by voluntary contributions was held by the Court of Appeal to be a breach of the covenant. The contention that the effect of the two branches of the sentence taken together was to do away with the force and meaning of the first branch was rejected. There were two obligations and it was impossible to say that in the ordinary use of the English language the using of a place for a large institution was using it as "a private residence only". A covenant not to use a house otherwise than as a private dwelling-house is infringed by the user of the house as a children's hospital for surgical tuberculosis.[7]

In relation to a covenant not to carry on any trade or business it is to be noted that while the word "trade" imports buying and selling,[8] "business" is a word of wider import.[9] A hospital, the patients of which make small payments according to their means is a business,[10] and those who run it are pursuing an "occupation" or "calling."[11] It was held by the Court of Appeal in *Rolls* v.

---

1 (1866), L.R. 1 H.L. 93.   2 *Bendelow* v. *Wortley Union Guardians* (1887), 57 L. J. Ch. 762.
3 *A.-G.* v. *Nottingham Corporation*, [1904] 1 Ch. 673 where both public and private nuisance were alleged and on the facts that was no nuisance.
4 *Metropolitan Asylum District* v. *Hill* (1881), 6 App. Cas. 193, H.L.; *Dunne* v. *North Western Gas Board*, [1964] 2 Q.B. 806, C.A.
5 *Baines* v. *Baker* (1752), Amb. 158; *Metropolitan Asylum District* v. *Hill* (1881), 6 App. Cas. 193, H.L.; *Fleet* v. *Metropolitan Asylums Board* (1886), 2 T.L.R. 361, C.A.; *Matthews* v. *Sheffield Corporation* (1887), 31 Sol. Jo. 773; *Bendelow* v. *Wortley Union Guardians* (1887), 57 L.J. Ch. 762; *A.-G.* v. *Manchester Corporation*, [1893] 2 Ch. 87; *A.-G.* v. *Nottingham Corporation*, [1904] 1 Ch. 673.
6 (1877), 7 Ch.D. 271, C.A.
7 *Frost* v. *King Edward VII Welsh etc., Association*, [1918] 2 Ch. 180; compromised on appeal, 35 T.L.R. 138, C.A.
8 *Westripp* v. *Baldock* (1938), 159 L.T. 65.
9 *Rolls* v. *Miller* (1884), 27 Ch.D. 71, C.A., at 85–86.
10 *Bramwell* v. *Lacy* (1879), 10 Ch.D. 691. A hospital may constitute an "annoyance" or "grievance" to neighbours: *Tod-Heatly* v. *Benham* (1888), 40 Ch.D. 80, C.A.
11 *Portman* v. *Home Hospital Association* (1879), 27 Ch.D. 81, n. (covenant preventing user in the exercise or carrying on of any art trade, or business, occupation or calling whatsoever).

Miller[1] that a charitable institution called a "Home for Working Girls" where the inmates were provided with board and lodging, whether any payment was taken or not, was a business, and therefore came within the restrictions of a covenant against carrying on "any trade or business of any description whatsoever". Carrying on a school as a charity and not for profit is nevertheless a business and so within a covenant against business user.[2]

---

1 (1884), 27 Ch.D. 71.
2 *Doe* d. *Bish* v. *Keeling* (1813, 1 M. & S. 95 (private school-master); *Barnard Castle Urban District Council* v. *Wilson*, [1901] 2 Ch. 813, at 817, affd. on this point but revd. on other grounds, [1902] 2 Ch. 746, at 755, 758, C.A. (charity school).

Chapter 17

Necessary Contents of Declaration of Trust

Introduction

"To constitute a valid trust" Sir WILLIAM GRANT M.R. once said,[1] "undoubtedly three circumstances must concur: sufficient words to raise it; a definite subject and a certain or ascertained object". These three circumstances are usually referred to as the three certainties[2]—certainty of words, certainty of subject, and certainty of object. Charitable trusts, no less than private trusts, must disclose certainty of words and certainty of subject matter. But it is sometimes said that they constitute an exception to the rule that the *objects* of a trust must be certain if the trust is to be valid. The exception (if such it is) is an exception in a very special sense, for the settlor must manifest a definite intention to devote the whole or some ascertainable part of the trust fund exclusively to charity. Subject to this, he may be as vague as he pleases: the recipient of his bounty, and the means by which it is to be dispensed, need not be specified. There is, to put it another way, a substituted criterion of validity, namely, certainty of an exclusively charitable intention.

Certainty of words

Technical words are not required to create a trust: a trust obligation may be inferred from the nature and manner of the gift considered as a whole. The question in each case is whether, on the true construction of the words used, the settlor or testator has manifested an intention to create a trust. The words employed must be so couched that, taken as a whole, they could be deemed to be imperative.[3]

A direction that a fund shall be applied by or be at the disposal of a person for the charitable purpose intended may be as effectual as the use of the word trust.[4] But an expression of wish[5] or desire[6] will not set up a trust unless the context[7] indicates that those words were used in an imperative sense. And

---

1 See *Cruwys* v. *Colman* (1804), 9 Ves. 319. To the same effect are: *Wright* v. *Atkyns* (1823), Turn. & R. 143, at 157, *per* Lord ELDON L.C.; *Knight* v. *Knight* (1840), 3 Beav. 148, at 172, *per* Lord LANGDALE (often cited as the *fons et origo* of the three certainties).
2 See Glanville Williams (1940), 4 M.L.R. 20.
3 See *Knight* v. *Knight* (1840), 3 Beav. 148, at 173, *per* Lord LANGDALE.
4 *Salusbury* v. *Denton* (1857), 3 K. & J. 529.
5 *Wheeler* v. *Smith* (1860), 1 Giff. 300.
6 *McCulloch* v. *McCulloch* (1863), 1 New. Rep. 535.
7 *Re Burley*, [1910] 1 Ch. 215; *Re Cammell* (1925), 69 Sol. Jo. 345.

precatory or recommendatory words have frequently been held to create trusts where the intention of the testator has been considered imperative.[1]

Sometimes the effect of the words used is not to create a trust but to subject the enjoyment of property to a condition or to subject the property itself to a charge. It is relevant therefore to distinguish the cases of "trust", "condition" and "charge".

A trust is created where the whole of the property is devoted to purposes which exclude all beneficial interest of the donee, though the words used are primarily words of condition, as where the gift is expressed to be "for this intent and purpose and upon this condition"[2] or "to this intent and upon this condition."[3] As Lord CAIRNS said in the first of the two cases just cited:[4]

> "If I give an estate to A upon condition that he shall apply the rents for the benefit of B, that is a trust to all intents and purposes."

Again where property is given *upon condition* that a fixed and definite sum, which does not exhaust the entire income shall be applied in a specified charitable way, for example for providing a school house and staff, a trust is constituted.[5] Thus in *Re Richardson*[6] a legacy was left to a charitable institution upon condition that it maintained two lifeboats; there was a gift over in case the institution failed to construct the lifeboats and CHITTY J. construed the gift as a trust.

On the other hand, a gift may on its true construction be a gift imposing a personal obligation on the donee to make certain payments or do certain acts for the benefit of charity without giving the charity any right against the subject matter of the gift.[7] Thus in *Jack* v. *Burnett*[8] there was a gift of land to the principal and professors of a college for the maintenance of three bursars subject to a condition, the penalty for the breach of which was forfeiture, that the college should admit to the bursarships the presentees of the donor and his family. It was held that this was a grant upon *condition* and not a mere trust and that the principal and professors were entitled to appropriate to themselves any surplus after fulfilling the condition.

The relevant gift in *A.-G.* v. *Cordwainers' Co.*[9] was also held to be a gift upon a condition. Under a will made in 1547 the Cordwainers' Company was devisee of three properties, subject only to the payment of certain fixed and limited sums which the testator had directed to be paid. By 1833 the rental of the properties had increased some thirty-fold. Sir JOHN LEACH M.R. held that the

---

1 *Pilkington* v. *Boughey* (1841), 12 Sim. 114; *Kirkbank* v. *Hudson* (1819), 7 Price 212; and see *A.-G.* v. *Davies* (1802), 9 Ves. 535, at 546.

2 *A.-G.* v. *Master, Wardens, etc. of the Wax Chandlers' Co.* (1873), L.R. 6 H.L. 1.

3 *Merchant Taylors' Co.* v. *A.-G.* (1871), 6 Ch. App. 512.

4 (1873), L.R. 6 H.L. 1, at 21, cited with approval by Lord SELBORNE L.C. in *Goodman* v. *Saltash Corporation* (1882), 7 App. Cas. 633, at 642, H.L.; and see *Wright* v. *Wilkin* (1862), 2 B. & S. 259 ("upon express condition").

5 *A.-G.* v. *Grocers' Co.* (1843), 6 Beav. 526.

6 *Re Richardson* (1887), 56 L.J. Ch. 784.

7 *A.-G.* v. *Master, Warden, etc. of the Wax Chandlers' Co.* (1873), L.R. 6 H.L. 1, at 19, where Lord Cairns was dealing with a devise of land subject to a condition.

8 (1846), 12 Cl. & Fin. 812, H.L.

9 (1833), 3 My. & K. 534; and see *A.-G.* v. *Fishmongers' Co.* (1841), 5 Myl. & Cr. 11; *A.-G.* v. *Trinity College, Cambridge* (1856), 24 Beav. 383.

company had a right to apply the surplus rents to its own use. The imposition of a penalty for non-performance of the condition implied a benefit, if the condition were performed, and was inconsistent with any other intention than that the testator meant to give a beneficial interest to the company upon the terms of complying with the directions contained in his will.[1]

A distinction must also be drawn between a *charge* and a trust in favour of charity.[2] Whether a charge or a trust is created is again a question of construing the relevant instrument. If the intention is to impose a duty upon the transferee to deal with the property for the benefit of the charity and to give the charity a beneficial interest in the property a trust is created; if the intention is to give the beneficial interest to the transferee and to give a security interest to the charity a charge is created. The language used is not decisive. Where property is given to a donee subject to,[3] or in trust to make,[4] specified charitable payments which do not exhaust the whole estate the donee takes the property impressed with a charge to secure the payments. The charity or charities in whose favour the charge operates will have an equitable right by virtue of the charge[5] but it is not this right of a beneficiary under a trust. The donee is obliged to make the payment if the donee receives the property: and the obligation has been described as fiduciary.[6] Subject to the specific appropriations the donee will be entitled to any surplus[7] unless the donor has manifested a paramount intention to devote the whole of the property to charity.[8]

Certainty of subject matter

The subject matter of a trust may refer to the property which is the subject of the trust or the beneficial interest. The former is the more commonly understood meaning. But in either case certainty is required: the property to be held on trust must be certain[9] and the beneficial interests must be certain.

A charitable purpose or charitable institution may be one of several "beneficiaries" under a trust and in so far as there is any uncertainty as to the quantum of various beneficial interests the trust will fail: but apparent uncertainties are sometimes cured by apportionment. It is convenient to discuss in turn: (1) Gifts of uncertain amounts and (2) Apportionment.

---

1 (1833), 3 My. & K. 534, at 543.

2 See *Charitable Donations and Bequests Comrs.* v. *Wybrants* (1845), 2 Jo. & Lat. 182 at 198.

3 *Southmolton Corporation* v. *A.-G.* (1854), 5 H.L. Cas. 1; *A.-G.* v. *Dean and Canons of Windsor* (1860), 8 H.L. Cas. 369.

4 *Beverley Corporation* v. *A.-G.* (1857), 6 H.L. Cas. 310 ("in and with this trust and confidence in them reposed").

5 *Parker* v. *Judkin*, [1931] 1 Ch. 475 (non-charitable).

6 *Charitable Donations and Bequests Comrs.* v. *Wybrants* (1845), 2 Jo. & Lat. 182, at 198. at 198.

7 *A.-G.* v. *Bristol Corporation* (1820), 2 Jac. & W. 294; *A.-G.* v. *Grocers' Co.* (1843), 6 Beav. 526; *A.-G.* v. *Skinners' Co.* (1827), 2 Russ. 407. In *Re Stanford*, [1924] 1 Ch. 73 there was held to be a resulting trust, but the decision is unsatisfactory: see 264, *infra*.

8 *A.-G.* v. *Bristol Corporation* (1820), 2 Jac. & W. 294.

9 *Palmer* v. *Simmonds* (1854), 2 Drew. 221 (bulk of my residuary estate: uncertain).

GIFTS OF UNCERTAIN AMOUNTS

If the amount of a charitable gift is not ascertainable the gift is bad.[1] The most obvious case is where in a will the amount of the gift is left in blank.[2] Thus in *Ewen* v. *Bannerman*[3] there was a direction that a fund should accumulate till it amounted to   for building a hospital for   boys. Yet if the amount, though not specified, is nevertheless ascertainable the gift is good. For example, in *Magistrates of Dundee* v. *Morris*[4] the testator directed that a hospital (by which he meant a school) for 100 boys should be established in Dundee without stating what amount should be applied to this object. The House of Lords held, reversing the decision of the Court of Session, that the subject matter of the gift was ascertainable: the gift was of whatever sum should be necessary. Nor is there uncertainty where there is a gift of a sum "not exceeding" a named figure: for this is construed as a gift of the named sum.[5]

On the other hand, if part of a fund is directed to be applied for charitable purposes, but the actual amount or the proportion to be so applied is not stated in the relevant instrument and no guidance is given as to how the amount or proportion is to be ascertained, the attempted charitable trust fails for uncertainty.[6]

GIFTS OF UNCERTAIN PROPORTIONS

When a testator gives funds to be applied partly for objects which are not charitable[7] or fail[8] and neither part of the gift is residuary upon the other, the court will, in the absence of any specified apportionment in the will itself, make its own apportionment. Thus in *Salusbury* v. *Denton*[9] the testator left a moiety of a sum of personalty "to be at the disposal by her will of my dear wife therewith to apply a part of the fund for the foundation of a charity school or such other charitable endowment for the benefit of the poor at Offley as she may prefer and under such regulations as she may prescribe herself and the remainder of the said money to be at her disposal among my relatives in such proportions as she may be pleased to direct". The trust to found the school was bad, but the trust for the endowment of half the fund was held good and half the fund was applied for this purpose under a scheme. The other half went to the testator's next of kin. But the position is different if the testator gives a *power* to named persons to distribute part of his estate. In *Down* v. *Worrall*[10] the testator had directed the trustees to settle the unappointed part of his residuary estate at their

---

1 *Peek* v. *Peek* (1869), 17 W.R. 1059.
2 *Hartshorne* v. *Nicholson* (1858), 26 Beav. 58.
3 (1830), 2 Dow. & Cl. 74.
4 (1858), 3 Macq. 134, especially at 159.
5 *Thompson* v. *Thompson* (1844), 1 Coll. 381, at 395; *Gough* v. *Bult* (1848), 16 Sim. 45.
6 *Chapman* v. *Brown* (1801), 6 Ves. 404; *Re Porter*, [1925] Ch. 746.
7 *Adnam* v. *Cole* (1843), 6 Beav. 353; *Hoare* v. *Osborne* (1866), L.R. 1 Eq. 585; *Re Rigley's Trusts* (1866), 36 L.J. Ch. 147; *Re Vaughan* (1886), 33 Ch.D. 187 *cf*. *Fowler* v. *Fowler* (1864), 33 Beav. 616 where the whole gift failed.
8 *Salusbury* v. *Denton* (1857), 3 K. & J. 529; *cf*. *Down* v. *Worrall* (1833), 1 My. & K. 561.
9 (1857), 3 K. & J. 529.
10 (1833), 1 My. & K. 561.

discretion either for pious and charitable purposes or otherwise for the benefit of the testator's sister and her children. Sir JOHN LEACH M.R. said:[1]

> "Where a disposition is made in favour of charity and the trust fails, the Court will interfere and execute the trust: but here no disposition is made in favour of charity as to the appointed part. The trustees had a personal discretion as to the application of the fund; and as they have died without exercising the discretion, this part of the property is undisposed of by the testator and belongs to the next of kin."

An inquiry as to the amounts which would be required for the respective objects may be directed[2] although in simple cases the amount sufficient for the non-charitable purpose may be ascertained by affidavit.[3] But if such an inquiry is impracticable, the court will divide the fund into equal shares, on the basis that equality is equity, the share applicable to non-charitable purposes falling into residue.[4] Equal division was decreed in two cases where the objects of the gift were poor relations and charitable purposes in unascertained proportions.[5] Likewise the principle was applied to a case where there was a gift partly for educational purposes and partly for the purchase of land to be let out to the poor at a low rent, the second gift being invalid under the mortmain laws.[6] Equal division has also been directed where a fund was given partly for the repair of a tomb and partly for charitable purposes[7] but in other cases of this kind the fund has been apportioned.[8] It matters not whether the non-charitable purpose is definite or indefinite. It is true, of course, that where such purposes are indefinite it is impossible to say how much is required for those purposes since the purposes cannot be ascertained.[9] But that is a reason for equal division and not for invalidating the whole gift.

Invalidation is, as will be seen, the usual consequence when there is a gift to "charitable or benevolent purposes".[10] But that sort of case is distinguishable from the equal apportionment cases just discussed. The distinction was well pointed by PAGE-WOOD V.-C. in *Salusbury* v. *Denton*" itself:

> "It is one thing to direct a trustee to give *a part* of a fund to one set of objects, and the *remainder* to another, and it is a distinct thing to direct him to give 'either' to one set of objects 'or' to another . . . This is a case of the former description. Here the trustee was bound to give a part to each."

The crucial point is that the fund should not be wholly applicable to objects which are not charitable. Once this is plain the court can consider apportionment.

---

1 (1833), 1 My. & K. 561, at 563–564.

2 See the first three cases cited in footnote at 143, *supra*; and see, at first instance, *Re Gardom*, [1914] 1 Ch. 662.

3 *Re Vaughan* (1886), 33 Ch.D. 187, at 194.

4 *Re Rigley's Trusts* (1866), 36 L.J. Ch. 147.

5 *Doyley* v. *A.-G.* (1735), 4 Vin. Abr. 485, at 486 (deserving relations and charitable purposes); *Salusbury* v. *Denton* (1857), 3 K. & J. 529.

6 *Crafton* v. *Frith* (1851), 4 De G. & Sm. 237.

7 *Hoare* v. *Osborne* (1866), L.R. 1 Eq. 585; *Re Birkett* (1878), 9 Ch.D. 576.

8 *Adnam* v. *Cole* (1843), 6 Beav. 353; *Re Rigley's Trusts* (1866), 36 L.J. Ch. 147; *Re Vaughan* (1886), 33 Ch.D. 187.

9 *Re Clarke*, [1923] 2 Ch. 407, at 418, *per* ROMER J.

10 See 149, *infra*. Statutory validation is possible in a decreasing number of cases: see 157, *infra*.

11 (1857), 3 K. & J. 529, at 539. The italics appear in the judgment.

Division into equal parts may in some cases be absurd, and where that is so the court will try to find the means to quantify the appropriate parts. In *Re Coxen*[1] JENKINS J. stressed that where the amount applicable to the non-charitable purpose cannot be quantified, the whole gift fails for uncertainty. The case concerned a trust for the benefit of orthopaedic hospitals with provisons in favour of the aldermen who were to be the trustees. It was argued that the provisions were invalid. JENKINS J. however held that they were charitable and valid as promoting the better administration of the charity.[2] Even assuming that they were invalid the learned judge considered that "the court would find means to quantify the income applicable to the invalid trusts rather than divert from purposes admittedly charitable (say) eleven twelfths of the income of a fund because a part of such income incapable of exact quantification but incapable on any reasonable estimate of exceeding (say) one twelfth is directed to be held on invalid trusts".[3] He pointed out that there were two exceptions to the general rule.

The first exception is of a more general and indeed important character, although it was mentioned by JENKINS J. as the second of the two exceptions. The effect of the exception is that where as a matter of construction the gift to charity is a gift of the entire fund of income, subject to the payments out of the fund required to give effect to the non-charitable purpose, the amount set free by the failure of the non-charitable gift is caught by and passed under the charitable gift.[4] In *Re Coxen*[5] itself the sum which the testator had left to the charitable trustees amounted to £200,000 and was held in trust to apply annually a sum not exceeding £100 to provide a dinner for the six trustees and to pay each of them a guinea at each meeting and to apply the balance for the benefit of orthopaedic hospitals. In the event the disputed provisions for the trustees were upheld as valid. But JENKINS J. said that even if the provisions were invalid the whole of the property should be devoted to the charitable purpose, since the testator clearly intended to devote the whole income to the charitable purpose, although subjecting part of it to trusts designed to further that purpose by particular means to which effect could not legally be given.[6] The exception is perhaps too narrowly stated: it is not restricted to cases where the purpose which fails is non-charitable. This is demonstrated by the Irish case of *Kelly* v. *A.-G.*[7] where a testator donated land in trust to apply the income to erect a chapel and thereafter to pay one half to the parish priest for masses and to divide the other half among the poor annually. The initial purpose was impossible because the bishop of the diocese would not consent to the erection of a chapel for which there was in fact no need. Although argument was addressed to the court inviting a *cy-près* application of the property, O'CONNOR M.R. held that the gift for masses and the gift to the poor should be accelerated. The meaning of the gift was that the whole property was to be devoted to the final purpose subject to whatever might be required for the first named purpose.

The second exception, which is of a more limited kind, is to be found in what are commonly known as the "Tomb cases", that is to say, cases in which there

---

1 [1948] Ch. 747.
2 See at 26, *supra*.
3 [1948] Ch. 747, at 753.
4 [1948] Ch. 747, at 752.
5 [1948] Ch. 747.
6 [1948] Ch. 747, at 754.
7 [1917] 1 I.R. 183.

is a primary trust to apply the income of a fund in perpetuity in the repair of a tomb not in a church, followed by a charitable trust extending only to the balance or residue of such income. The established rule in cases of this particular class is to ignore the invalid trust for the repair of the tomb and treat the whole income as devoted to the charitable purpose.[1] This principle applies whether the gift to charity relates to the residue[2] surplus[3] balance[4] or remainder[5] of the fund. In cases of this kind the tomb repairing obligation is apparently treated as a moral one and not legally binding.[6] Such cases will not, it seems, be regarded as precedents for cases not involving trusts for the maintenance of tombs.[7]

If, however, a fund is bequeathed primarily for a void object and the surplus is given for a charitable purpose, and the amount required for the first purpose can be ascertained, an apportionment is necessary, unless it is manifest that no surplus can exist[8] and an inquiry may be directed to ascertain the amount needed to fulfil the primary void object.[9]

Where there is a gift of a fund to be applied in the first place to a particular purpose with a gift over of the surplus to charity, then if the prior gift cannot be carried out because it is unlawful[10] and it is also so indefinite that the amount required for it cannot be reasonably ascertained, the gift fails entirely.[11] The ground for such failure is that if the purpose were lawful and the entire fund might have been applied to it there is no ascertainable residue for the charitable purpose. The same result ensues if the testator, though estimating the cost of carrying out the first purpose, gives his executors a discretion to exceed that amount.[12] But where the amount necessary to satisfy the first purpose can be reasonably ascertained, the gift of the surplus to charity will be valid.[13]

Where trustees are given a discretionary power to divide a fund among specified charitable objects and they fail to exercise their discretion the fund will be divided equally between the named objects[14] unless a contrary intention appears in the will.[15]

---

1 *Re Coxen*, [1948] Ch. 747, at 752; see *Fisk* v. *A.-G.* (1867), 4 Eq. 521; *Hunter* v. *Bullock* (1872), 14 Eq. 45; *Dawson* v. *Small* (1874), 18 Eq. 114; *Re Williams* (1877), 5 Ch.D. 735; *Re Birkett* (1878), 9 Ch.D. 576; *Re Vaughan* (1886), 33 Ch.D. 187; *Re Rogerson*, [1901] 1 Ch. 715.

2 *Fisk* v. *A.-G.* (1867), 4 Eq. 521; *Re Vaughan* (1886), 33 Ch.D. 187.

3 *Hoare* v. *Osborne* (1866), L.R. 1 Eq. 585; *Dawson* v. *Small* (1874), L.R. 18 Eq. 114; *Re Williams* (1877), 5 Ch.D. 735.

4 *Hunter* v. *Bullock* (1872), L.R. 14 Eq. 45.

5 *Re Birkett* (1878), 9 Ch.D. 576.

6 See per COHEN J. in *Re Dalziel*, [1943] Ch. 277.

7 *Re Porter*, [1925] Ch. 746, at 751. For earlier criticism of the tomb cases see *Re Birkett* (1878), 9 Ch.D. 576.

8 *Cramp* v. *Playfoot* (1858), 4 K. & J. 479; and see *Re Rogerson*, [1901] 1 Ch. 715.

9 *Chapman* v. *Brown* (1801), 6 Ves. 404, at 410; *Mitford* v. *Reynolds* (1842), 1 Ph. 185, at 199; see also *Dundee Magistrates* v. *Morris* (1858), 3 Macq. 134, H.L.

10 E.g. under the old mortmain laws (now repealed).

11 *Chapman* v. *Brown* (1801), 6 Ves. 404, explained in *Re Birkett* (1878), 9 Ch.D. 576, at 579, per JESSEL M.R.; *Cherry* v. *Mott* (1836), 1 My. & Cr. 123, at 134; *Cramp* v. *Playfoot* (1858), 4 K. & J. 479; *Peek* v. *Peek* (1869), 17 W.R. 1059; *Kirkmann* v. *Lewis* (1869), 38 L.J. Ch. 570; *Re Taylor* (1888), 58 L.T. 538; *Re Porter*, [1925] Ch. 746; *Re Dalziel*, [1943] Ch 277.

12 *Limbrey* v. *Gurr* (1819), 6 Madd. 151.

13 *Dundee Magistrates* v. *Morris* (1858), 3 Macq. 134, H.L.; *Mitford* v. *Reynolds* (1842), 1 Ph. 185; and see *A.-G.* v. *Parsons* (1803), 8 Ves. 186, at 192; *Re Coxen*, [1948] Ch. 747, at 752.

14 *Re Hall's Charity* (1851), 14 Beav. 115.

15 *Re Macduff*, [1896] 2 Ch. 451, at 465, 470, C.A.

Certainty of an exclusively charitable intention

POSITION APART FROM STATUTE

Certainty of objects is not required in a charitable trust, but there must be a certainty of an exclusively charitable intention. Putting it another way, if a gift or trust is to be upheld as charitable, the application of the funds to charitable purposes must be obligatory.[1] The validity of a trust depends in the last resort upon the power of the court to administer it and execute it.[2] Provided a trust is limited in terms to charitable purposes the fact that those purposes are not defined does not matter. The court can always execute the charitable intent of the donor by means of a scheme.[3] But the charitable intent must be unalloyed. It must be clear on the face of the gift that the trustees are bound to apply the funds to charitable purposes, and that they are not at liberty to apply the funds to non-charitable purposes. The process of ascertaining this intention in the case of a will is well established: one "must take the whole will together and see what, as a fair result, is the meaning of the testator". But there must be some indication of charity or else the uncertain gift will fail. Purposes which are not defined or indicated will not be presumed charitable,[4] except where a general intention to give to a charity is to be gathered from the will taken as a whole, in which case a general lack of definition as to the particular object does not invalidate the gift.[5] In *Buckle* v. *Bristow*[6] a testator gave the residue of his property to his executors upon trust for such purposes as he should by deed or codicil direct and in default of such direction "in such way and manner and for such purposes as they or the majority of them may in their judgment and discretion agree upon". It was held that the residue was held in trust but that the objects were too uncertain and the trust therefore void: no charitable intent was discoverable. On the other hand a recital of a charitable intention does not make charitable a trust for objects which are not charitable,[7] though such a recital may have effect where the objects are ambiguous.[8]

Difficulties arise where the testator has made provisions which go beyond the limits of an exclusively charitable application of the property in question. The cases may be divided into two main categories. The first category is where the donor designates as the object of his bounty a purpose of such wide and indefinite import that it includes both charitable and non-charitable objects. The second is where there is a gift to charitable or other purposes in the alternative.

Indefinite purpose not limited to charity

A trust for purposes which are not limited to (but are broad enough to include) charity fails altogether. Nor does it matter that the trustees have in fact exercised

---

1 *Morice* v. *Bishop of Durham* (1805), 10 Ves. 522.
2 *Re White*, [1893] 2 Ch. 41, C.A.
3 *Hunter* v. *A.-G.*, [1899] A.C. 309, at 320, H.L., *per* Lord DAVEY.
4 *Buckle* v. *Bristow* (1864), 5 New Rep. 7.
5 *Re Willis*, [1921] 1 Ch. 44, C.A.
6 (1864), 5 New Rep. 7.
7 *Re Sanders' Will Trusts*, [1954] Ch. 265.
8 *A.-G.* v. *Jesus College, Oxford* (1861), 29 Beav. 163, at 168.

their discretion by applying the fund for a charitable purpose if they were not obliged by the terms of the gift to do so. As HALL V.C. observed in *Re Jarman*:[1]

"The court is not to wait and see whether the executors will appoint to charitable objects or not, but to look at the will as at the date of the death of the testator, and at once say whether the gift is definite or indefinite, and if the latter that it is inoperative".

Thus, in the leading case of *Morice* v. *Bishop of Durham*[2] a testatrix left the residue of her estate to the Bishop of Durham upon trust "to dispose of the ultimate residue to such objects of benevolence and liberality as the Bishop of Durham in his own discretion shall most approve of". The court held the gift to be void for uncertainty: some "objects of benevolence and liberality" *might* be charitable, but others were not. The bishop was, therefore, held to be a trustee on a resulting trust for the testatrix even though he had expressed his willingness to carry out the purposes of the testatrix. This decision was followed in a long line of cases.

A gift simply to "benevolent purposes" is objectionable:[3] a benevolent purpose may be (but is not necessarily) charitable. The same is true of gifts to philanthropic purposes,[4] utilitarian purposes,[5] emigration,[6] patriotic,[7] and public[8] purposes: they all go further than legal charity. Likewise gifts for encouraging undertakings of general utility,[9] for hospitality,[10] for such societies as should be in the opinion of the trustees "most in need of help",[11] and for such purposes, civil or religious as a class of persons should appoint,[12] are too wide.

Pious purposes are not (it has been held) necessarily charitable;[13] nor is a gift for missionary purposes[14] or for parish work.[15] Again a gift to the Pope to be used "in the carrying out of his sacred office" has also been held to be void.[16]

A gift to such objects as trustees should think most deserving is void[17] as is a gift to be disposed of to such persons and in such manner and form as my trustees shall think proper.[18]

---

1 (1878), 8 Ch.D. 584, at 587.
2 (1805), 10 Ves. 522.
3 *James* v. *Allen* (1817), 3 Mer. 17 (such benevolent purposes as trustees may agree on); *Re Barnett* (1908), 24 T.L.R. 788 (general benevolent objects or purposes of livery company); *Lawrence* v. *Lawrence* (1913), 42 N.B.R. 260.
4 *Re Macduff*, [1896] 2 Ch. 451; *Re Eades*, [1920] 2 Ch. 353. Yet a trust to promote kindness to animals (rather than to men) is charitable: see *supra*, at 105–107.
5 *Re Woodgate* (1886), 2 T.L.R. 674.
6 *Re Sidney*, [1908] 1 Ch. 488.
7 *A.-G.* v. *National Provincial Bank*, [1924] A.C. 262.
8 *Re Da Costa*, [1912] 1 Ch. 337; *Vezey* v. *Jamson* (1822), 1 Sim. & St. 69; *Blair* v. *Duncan*, [1902] A.C. 37; *Houston* v. *Burns*, [1918] A.C. 337; and see *Re Davis*, [1923] 1 Ch. 225 (public institutions in Wales).
9 *Kendall* v. *Granger* (1842), 5 Beav. 300; *Langham* v. *Peterson* (1903), 87 L.T. 749.
10 *Re Hewitt* (1883), 53 L.J. Ch. 132 (hospitality or charity); *A.-G.* v. *Whorwood* (1750), 1 Ves. Sen. 534.
11 *Re Freeman*, [1908] 1 Ch. 720.
12 *Re Friends Free School*, [1909] 2 Ch. 675.
13 *Heath* v. *Chapman* (1854), 2 Drew 417; and see *A.-G.* v. *Herrick* (1772), Amb. 712.
14 *Scott* v. *Brownrigg* (1881), 9 L.R. Ir. 246; and see *Adam's Trustees* v. *Adam* (1908), 16 S.L.T. 144.
15 *Farley* v. *Westminster Bank, Ltd.*, [1939] A.C. 430, H.L.
16 *Re Moore*, [1919] 1 I.R. 316.
17 *Harris* v. *Du Pasquier* (1872), 26 L.T. 689.
18 *Gibbs* v. *Rumsey* (1813), 2 Ves. & B. 294.

The permutations are endless, and the Commonwealth bears witness to some other possibilities. In *Re Young*[1] a gift to "any needful and worthy institution or institutions, or any needy and worthy individual or individuals" was held not to be for exclusively charitable purposes. The word "worthy" goes beyond the boundaries of charity[2] so that a gift to an executor "to aid and help any worthy cause or causes as he shall think fit" does not create a valid charitable trust.[3] Equally a gift "to J.B. to be disposed of for worthy causes as he considers fit" in certain provinces is too vague and uncertain.[4] "Good and benevolent Christian objects" and "good and worthy objects" are not charitable[5] because a good or worthy cause is not necessarily charitable. Public purposes of a religious or useful nature are again not exclusively charitable.[6]

Gift to charitable or other objects in the alternative

Where upon the true construction of a particular gift trustees have a power to apply a fund either to charitable purposes or, alternatively, to indefinite purposes which are not charitable, the gift in question will be void for uncertainty, unless it is saved by the Charitable Trusts (Validation) Act 1954.

There is a voluminous case law on this topic, and it is convenient to classify the authorities according to whether they are examples of true alternative purposes and the purposes are to be construed disjunctively, or whether the purposes are cumulative and to be construed conjunctively. Then we must examine the very restricted saving provisions of the Charitable Trusts (Validation) Act 1954 which only save gifts contained in certain instruments.

DISJUNCTIVE ALTERNATIVES: THE WORD "OR"

No part of a gift need be applied to charity if the terms of the gift, on their true construction, permit the trustees to apply the trust fund to charity or, alternatively, to some other non-charitable purpose. Thus gifts for "charitable or public",[7] or for "charitable or other",[8] or for "public benevolent or charitable" purposes in connection with a particular parish,[9] or for "charitable, religious or other societies, institutions, persons or objects in connection with the Roman Catholic faith"[10] or for "charitable or benevolent"[11] purposes or for "charitable

---

1 (1907), 9 O.W.R. 566.
2 Cf. *Re Wykes*, [1961] Ch. 229.
3 *Planta* v. *Greenshields*, [1931] 2 D.L.R. 189 (Br. Columbia Ct.).
4 *Re Aydt Estate* (1965), 55 W.W.R. 315.
5 *Brewster* v. *Foreign Mission Board of the Baptist Convention of Maritime Provinces* (1900), 2 N.B. Eq. 172.
6 *Nelson Diocesan Trust Board* v. *A.-G.*, [1924] G.L.R. 259.
7 *Vezey* v. *Jamson* (1822), 1 Sim. & St. 69; *Re Davis*, [1923] 1 Ch. 225; *Blair* v. *Duncan*, [1902] A.C. 37, H.L.; and see *Langham* v. *Peterson* (1903), 87 L.T. 744 (charity or works of public utility).
8 *Ellis* v. *Selby* (1836), 1 My. & Cr. 286; *Re Chapman*, [1922] 2 Ch. 479, C.A.
9 *Houston* v. *Burns*, [1918] A.C. 337.
10 *Re Davidson*, [1909] 1 Ch. 567.
11 *Re Jarman's Estate* (1878), 8 Ch.D. 584; *Re Riland's Estate*, [1881] W.N. 173.

uses or emigration uses"[1] or for "charitable or philanthropic purposes"[2] have all been held invalid on the ground of uncertainty. In all these cases, it will be noted, the alternative non-charitable use is expressly stated. And the word "or" is in each case construed disjunctively. That does not mean that in other contexts the word "or" may not have a different meaning. The primary meaning of "or" is disjunctive, but there is a secondary meaning which may perhaps be called exegetical or explanatory. So used the word is equivalent to "alias" or "otherwise called", the dictionary examples of this use being generally topographical as "Papua or New Guinea". However this use of the word "or" is only possible if the words or phrases which it joins connote the same thing and are interchangeable one with the other.[3] And there are in fact several cases where the word "or" has been construed not as introducing an alternative but conjunctively or as introducing words which are synonymous or *ejusdem generis*. Thus gifts for "religious or charitable purposes"[4] for "charitable or religious purposes"[5] or for "any charitable or religious purpose he may please"[6] have all been upheld on the footing that in each case "religious" was to be construed as charitably religious.[7] It may be that a gift for charitable or *beneficent* purposes would be so construed.[8]

In *Re Bennett*[9] the court was able to escape from the harsh restrictiveness of the word "or". The words used in that case were "charity or *other* public objects in the parish of Faringdon", and Eve J. held that the addition of the word "other" entitled him to apply the *ejusdem generis* rule of construction and dispensed him from the necessity of reading the two things disjunctively: accordingly the gift was upheld.

CONJUNCTIVE CONSTRUCTION: THE WORD "AND"

Lord DAVEY in *Blair* v. *Duncan*[10] said that if the words for consideration in that case had been "charitable *and* public" effect might be given to them by construing them to mean charitable purposes of a public character. Gifts to "charitable and deserving objects"[11] and "charitable and benevolent"[12] objects and "charitable and pious uses"[13] and "charitable and philanthropic purposes"[14] have

---

1 *Re Sidney*, [1908] 1 Ch. 488.

2 *Re Macduff*, [1896] 2 Ch. 451 (bequest "for some one or more purposes, charitable, philanthropic or —— held bad not because of the blank but because there may be philanthropic purposes that are not charitable"); *Re Poole* (1931), 40 O.W.N. 558 (for some religious or philanthropic causes).

3 *Chichester Diocesan Fund and Board of Finance (Inc.)* v. *Simpson*, [1944] A.C. 341, at 369, *per* Lord SIMONDS.

4 *Rickerby* v. *Nicholson*, [1912] 1 I.R. 343; *McPhee's Trustees* v. *McPhee*, 1912 S.C. 75.

5 *Re Salter*, [1911] 1 I.R. 289.

6 *Re Sinclair's Trust* (1884), 13 L.R. Ir. 150. But the gift continued "whether public or private" which seems objectionable.

7 See also *Re Morton Estate*, [1941] 1 W.W.R. 310 (to a missionary society for the support of a woman missionary for religious and/or charitable work). *Cf. Tede* v. *Federal Comr. of Taxation* (1940), 63 C.L.R. 201 (charitable or religious causes or institutions: void).

8 See *per* VAISEY J. (extra-curially) in *Nathan Report* (1952), Cmd. 8710, 129, para. 520.

9 [1920] 1 Ch. 305.

10 [1902] A.C. 37.

11 *Re Sutton* (1885), 28 Ch.D. 464.

12 *Re Best*, [1904] 2 Ch. 354; *Caldwell* v. *Caldwell* (1921), 91 L.J.P.C. 95.

13 *A.-G.* v. *Herrick* (1772), Amb. 712.

14 *Re Huyck* (1905), 10 O.L.R. 480.

been upheld on similar principles. In such cases the gifts are held good on the ground that any object to be benefited must possess both characteristics. This reasoning also underlay the decision in *Re Lloyd*[1] that a gift for "religious and benevolent societies or objects, chiefly the former" is good. The learned editors of *Tudor*[2] find the reasoning in *Re Lloyd* less easy to follow, the words "chiefly the former" seeming to their view to indicate a disjunctive use of the word "and". But perhaps the words "chiefly the former" referred to the words "societies" as opposed to objects.

Certainly there is no special magic in the word "and" any more than in the word "or". *Prima facie* the word "and" causes words to be read conjunctively, but "and" may be used disjunctively. Thus in *Williams* v. *Kershaw*[3] a gift to three purposes "benevolent, charitable, and religious", without any conjunction, copulative or disjunctive between the first two adjectives failed being construed by Sir CHARLES PEPYS M.R.[4] disjunctively; and his decision was endorsed (though distinguished) by PEARSON J. in *Re Sutton*.[5] Had the gift in *Williams* v. *Kershaw* been to benevolent *and* charitable *and* religious purposes Sir CHARLES PEPYS M.R. might conceivably have come to a different conclusion.

Moreover, as SARGANT J. observed in *Re Eades:*[6]

"the greater the number of qualifications or characteristics enumerated, the more probable . . . is a construction which regards them as multiplying the kinds or classes of objects within the area of selection, rather than as multiplying the number of qualifications to be complied with, and so diminishing the objects within the area of selection".

The terms of the gift in *Re Eades* were "to such religious charitable and philanthropic objects" as three named persons might select. SARGANT J. refused to uphold the gift commenting that:

"the ordinary careful student of English language and literature would . . . almost certainly come to the conclusion that the three epithets here are epithets creating conjunctive or cumulative classes of objects, not epithets creating conjunctive or cumulative qualifications for each object".[7]

A disjunctive construction has also been applied to a gift for "charitable needful and necessary purposes"[8] to a gift for "such patriotic purposes or objects and such charitable institution or institutions or charitable object or objects in the British Empire" as trustees should select.[9] Again in the Scottish case of *Edgar, etc.* v. *Cassells*[10] the words "benevolent charitable and religious institutions in G" were construed disjunctively, although such a construction did not render the gift void by Scottish law.

---

1 (1893), 10 T.L.R. 66.
2 *Tudor on Charities* (6th edn.) 145, where the case is in fact referred to as *Re Lloyd-Greame*.
3 (1835), L.J. Ch. 84; *Re Metcalfe*, [1947] 1 D.L.R. 567 (religious charitable and benevolent purposes).
4 Later Lord Cottenham. *Tudor on Charities* (6th edn.) incorrectly states that it was Lord Langdale who decided the case.
5 (1885), 28 Ch.D. 464 (charitable and benevolent institutions in Birmingham and in the Midland Counties: valid).
6 [1920] 2 Ch. 353, at 357.
7 [1920] 2 Ch. 353, at 357.
8 *A.-G.* v. *Dartmouth Corporation* (1883), 48 L.T. 933.
9 *A.-G.* v. *National Provincial and Union Bank of England*, [1924] A.C. 262.
10 1922 S.C. 395.

In *Baker* v. *Sutton*[1] the relevant gift was for such religious and charitable institutions and purposes within the Kingdom of England as in the opinion of the major part of the trustees should be deemed fit and proper and Lord LANGDALE M.R. upheld the gift. Not all religious institutions are necessarily charitable[2] so that if the word "and" in this instance is read disjunctively the gift could only be upheld by construing the word "religious" as meaning "religious in the charitable sense".[3] That construction is an obvious one where the only other objects stated are overtly or *prima facie* charitable. Thus in *Re McClellan's Will*[4] WHITE J. upheld a gift "for the benefit advantage assistance or the founding of . . . charitable, religious, educational or sanitary institutions". A gift for founding or assisting charitable, religious or educational institutions would presumably rank as charitable because each of the adjectives points to a *prima facie* charitable purpose. By the addition of the word "sanitary" the testator was held to have intended the promotion of health. With this decision may be contrasted the case of *Brewer* v. *McCauley*[5] where the Supreme Court of Canada struck down a gift "for charitable, religious educational or philanthropic purposes". The last mentioned purpose has been held to go beyond the limits of charity and could not even in the context be read restrictively. A similar fate overtook a trust "for such charitable religious philanthropic educational or scientific institution or institutions" as the trustee should select.[6]

Incidental non-charitable activities and benefits

In determining whether a company or a trust is exclusively charitable a frequently recurring problem is what has been called "the incidental question".[7] The problem is how far a corporation or trustees may be authorised to carry on activities or produce benefits which viewed on their own are not charitable, without sabotaging the claim of the corporation or trust to be treated as charitable. In some cases the court has classified the activities or benefits as mostly subsidiary or incidental (and so innocuous) to the charitable object or objects in question. In other cases the authorisation of the activities or benefits has been held fatal. The crucial distinction is between ends, means and consequences. If the activities or benefits are *ends* in themselves and are not charitable there is no charity. But if they are merely the *means* of carrying out the charitable purpose or the *consequences* of carrying out that charitable purpose the overriding charitable purpose is not subverted.

ENDS

If the non-charitable activity or benefit is an end in itself, in other words an independent object, the trust or corporation authorised to pursue that end is

---

1 (1836), 1 Keen 224.

2 See *Gilmour* v. *Coats*, [1948] Ch. 340.

3 See *Re White*, [1893] 2 Ch. 41; *Wilkinson* v. *Lindgren* (1870), L.R. 5 Ch. App. 570 discussed at 58, *supra*.

4 (1919), 46 N.B.R. 161.

5 [1955] 1 D.L.R. 415.

6 *Re White*, [1933] S.A.S.R. 129; and see *A.-G. for New South Wales* v. *Adams* (1908), 7 C.L.R. 100 (charitable benevolent or philanthropic institutions).

7 See M. C. Cullity, "Charities—The Incidental Question" (1967), 6 Melbourne University Law Review 35–52.

not exclusively charitable. The leading example of such a case is *Oxford Group* v. *I.R.Comrs.*[1] The Oxford Group was incorporated with *inter alia* the following objects:

> "3 (A) The advancement of the Christian religion, and, in particular, by the means and in accordance with the principles of the Oxford Group Movement . . .
> (B) The maintenance, support, development and assistance of the Oxford Group Movement in every way . . .
> (C) The exercise of all or any of the following powers . . .
>
> > 9. To establish and support or aid in the establishment and support of any charitable or benevolent associations or institutions, and to subscribe or guarantee money for charitable or benevolent purposes in any way connected with the purposes of the association or calculated to further its objects.
> >
> > 10. To do all such things as are incidental, or the association may think conducive to the attainment of the above objects or any of them."

The primary object set out in clause 3 (A) was clearly charitable.[2] But the secondary object set out in clause 3 (B) extended far beyond purely religious activities, and permitted the company to engage in secular activities and authorised the expenditure of its funds on matters which were not charitable. COHEN L.J. echoed an observation of TUCKER L.J.[3] that while a religious body may, without losing its religious character, engage in a number of subsidiary activities which are not purely religious, a trust which permits the expenditure of income on such subsidiary activities is not a good charitable trust.[4] Finally COHEN L.J. (with whom TUCKER L.J. agreed) held that the objects set out in clause 3 (C), paragraphs (9) and (10) of the memorandum were not merely ancillary to the main objects expressed in sub-clauses (A) and (B) but themselves conferred powers on the company which were so wide that they could not be regarded as charitable.[5] An institution could be connected with the advancement of religion without being itself an institution for the advancement of religion, hence paragraph (9) was too wide. Moreover, there was a dictum of high authority suggesting that an object *conducive* to the attainment of a main charitable object is not necessarily charitable;[6] and the wording of paragraph (10) was even looser because it only required that the object should be thought by the association to be conducive to the main object.[7] It is to be noted, however, that in *Tennant Plays, Ltd.* v. *I.R.Comrs.*[8] the final part of the objects clause was in the following terms:

> "(S) To do all such other things as are incidental or conducive to the attainment of the above objects or any of them."

---

1 [1949] 2 All E.R. 537, C.A.; see also *Ellis* v. *I.R.Comrs.* (1949), 31 T.C. 178.
2 This was conceded by the Crown: [1949] 2 All E.R. 537, at 539E.
3 [1949] 2 All E.R. 537, at 540.
4 *Ibid.*, at 543.   5 *Ibid.*, at 544–547.
6 See *Dunne* v. *Byrne*, [1912] A.C. 407, at 410. Lord MACNAGHTEN analysing "conducive to the good of religion".
7 See on this point, *Keren Kayemeth Le Jisroel, Ltd.* v. *I.R.Comrs.*, [1931] 2 K.B. 465, at 482, *per* LAWRENCE L.J.; *Dunne* v. *Byrne*, [1912] A.C. 407 ("as the Archbishop may judge most conducive to the good of religion").
8 [1948] 1 All E.R. 506.

and that provision was held to be unobjectionable.[1] There, of course, the matter was *not* expressed to be one for the discretion of the directors;[2] and it may be that a court could be persuaded that the authorisation of activities *conducive* to a main object is not necessarily fatal to the charitable status of a trust or company. A court would be more likely to come to that conclusion where there is no possibility of inferring that the directors or trustee have any discretion in the matter[3] and where the enabling provision is placed in a clause suitably segregated from the objects and purposes of the trust or company.[4]

Another case in which an independent non-charitable purpose appeared in the objects clause of a memorandum was *Tennant Plays, Ltd.* v. *I.R.Comrs*.[5] where the performance of theatrical and musical works for philanthropic or charitable purposes was held to be a separate object and clearly non-charitable.

MEANS

Where an authorised activity is in fact a means to an end (and not an end in itself), the fact that it is not on its own a charitable activity is irrelevant provided the end is charitable. Some activities are obviously incidental means to an end. A hospital needs doctors and nursing staff; a school needs teachers. Indeed many charitable endeavours require money to be expended on staff or equipment. Authority to employ and remunerate staff, or to spend money on equipment or to incur any other necessary expenses[6] does not detract from the main purpose in hand.

In other cases the activity is not so obviously a means to an end. In *Re Hood*[7] a testator directed his residuary trust estate and the income thereof to be applied in spreading specified Christian principles and in aiding all active steps to minimise and extinguish the drink traffic. Lord HANWORTH M.R.[8] did not think that two *separate* spheres of activity were indicated. The overriding intention apparent from various recitals as well as from the operative part was to advance Christian principles, with a particular method by which that advancement—namely by extinguishing the drink traffic. In *Congregational Union of New South Wales* v. *Thistlethwayte*[9] the High Court of Australia also reached a very benevolent decision in favour of charity. The fundamental purpose of the Congregational Union was the advancement of religion but at least two of its subsidiary objects were non-charitable namely "united action for the creation, maintenance and improvement of our educational religious and philanthropic agencies" and "the presentation of civil and religious liberty". All five judges agreed that the Congregational Union was a charity. They held

---

1 *Ibid.*, at 512.

2 *Cf. Dunne* v. *Byrne, supra; Oxford Group* v. *I.R.Comrs, supra.*

3 Oddly, such a discretion was inferred in *Ellis* v. *I.R.Comrs.* (1949), 31 T.C. 178, at 192 (for the use in such manner for the promotion and aiding of the work of the Roman Catholic Church as the Trustees with the consent of the Bishop may prescribe).

4 As in *Crystal Palace Trustees* v. *Minister of Town and Country Planning*, [1951] Ch. 132.

5 [1948] 1 All E.R. 506.

6 *Re Newsom* 1971 N. No. 423 (1973), 14th March, unreported, discussed at 75 (royalty to author).

7 [1931] 1 Ch. 240.

8 *Ibid.*, at 248–249.

9 (1952–53), 87 C.L.R. 375.

that the subsidiary objects could only be validly carried on in furtherance of the primary charitable object:[1]

> "The fundamental purpose of the Union is the advancement of religion. It can create, maintain and impose educational, religious and philanthropic agencies only to the extent to which such agencies are conducive to the achievement of this purpose. The same may be said, *mutatis mutandis*, of the other object, the preservation of civil and religious liberty. The object is to preserve civil liberty so that Congregationalists may worship according to their religious beliefs."

At least two other cases involving *testamentary* gifts for the furtherance of religion have been upheld in this country even though such furtherance has been linked with non-charitable objects.[2] In *Re Scowcroft*[3] the furtherance of religious and mental improvement was held to be the essential portion of the gift and the furtherance of Conservative principles a subsidiary part. In *Re Charlesworth*[4] a trust to apply the income of a fund in payment of the expenses of the dinners consumed by members of a charitable religious society was upheld by EVE J.: the main purpose was the furtherance of religion. On the other hand in cases where the contest has been between the taxpayer and the Revenue the argument that the activity in issue was only a means to an end has tended to be rejected. Thus in *I.R.Comrs.* v. *Temperance*[5] *Council* the gift was not for the promotion of temperance generally, but was for the promotion of temperance *mainly* by political means: the means were themselves an object. So too in *National Anti-Vivisection Society* v. *I.R.Comrs.*[6] the appellant society was not a society for the prevention of cruelty to animals generally but for the prevention of cruelty to animals by political means. The means were the ends.

The cases discussed so far involve the *means* (or methods) by which funds are applied to a charitable end (or object). These cases must be distinguished from those in which the means of advancing charity involve the methods of raising funds to be applied to charity.

The point is well put in a rating case concerning rating relief available to organisations which, *inter alia*, were not "established or conducted for profit". In *National Deposit Friendly Society Trustees* v. *Skegness Urban District Council*[7] Lord DENNING said:

> "Many charitable bodies, such as colleges and religious foundations, have large funds which they invest at interest in stocks and shares, or purchase land which they let at a profit. Yet they are not established or conducted for profit. The reason is because their objects are to advance education or religion, as the case may be. The investing of funds is not one of their objects properly so called, but only a means of achieving these objects."

---

1 *Ibid.*, at 442.
2 For other cases of religious trusts combining religion and non-charitable activities: see *Neville Estates, Ltd.* v. *Madden*, [1962] Ch. 832 (communal hall); *Belfast City Young Men's Christian Association Trustees* v. *Northern Ireland Valuation Comr.*, [1969] N.I. 3 C.A. (sporting facilities).
3 [1898] 2 Ch. 638.
4 (1910), 101 L.T. 908.
5 (1926), 10 T.C. 748.
6 [1948] A.C. 31, at 78, *per* Lord NORMAND.
7 [1959] A.C. 293, at 319.

But the receipt of income from investments or land held by a charity is only one of the sources of income for a charity. Thus a charitable trust will still be charitable despite an express authority for the trustees to carry on a business, provided the profits have to be applied to charity.[1] Thus in *Incorporated Council of Law Reporting for England and Wales* v. *A.-G.*[2] it was held by the Court of Appeal that the publication of law reports was for the advancement of education or alternatively charitable under the fourth head in *Pemsel's* case. The fact that in publishing the law reports the council was carrying on a business did not prevent its purposes from being charitable since the profits, if any, could not be distributed to the members of the council but could only be applied in the further pursuit of the council's objects. But if the commercial enterprise is in itself an end rather than a means the trust will not be valid. A substantial non-charitable activity which has no connection with the charitable purposes of the body in question will give rise to an inference that the activity is not just a means of raising money for charity, but is an independent object.[3] Again, it may well be that the charitable character of a main object will not be destroyed because the ancillary powers, which are incidental to it, are, some of them, in themselves, not charitable.[4] But when the question is whether the primary object is itself charitable, it is legitimate, in reaching a conclusion upon that head, to consider the effect of the incidental powers, and it may well be that the incidental powers are such as to indicate or give some indication that the primary object is not itself charitable.[5]

CONSEQUENCES

If non-charitable activities or benefits do not represent a collateral or independent purpose, but are incidental to and *consequent* upon the way in which the charitable purpose of the body in question is carried on the body is charitable. In many cases the private benefits accruing as a consequence of advancing the main purpose could equally well be classified as a necessary part of the means of achieving the main purpose. The employees who benefit as a consequence of helping to advance the charitable cause represent the means to its advancement. But consequence and means are not necessarily synonymous. This is conveniently demonstrated by some of the cases relating to professional bodies which advance charitable purposes. Thus Cliffords Inn[6] and the Institution of Civil Engineers[7] were held to be established for charitable purposes only, notwithstanding that in the course of promoting the charitable purposes the members of each institution benefited. *In Geologists' Association* v. *I.R.Comrs.*[8] GREER L.J. formulated the following test:[9]

---

1 *Brighton College* v. *Marriott*, [1926] A.C. 192, H.L.; *Incorporated Council of Law Reporting or England and Wales* v. *A.-G.*, [1972] Ch. 73, at 86, 90, C.A.

2 [1972] Ch. 73; and see *Coman* v. *Governors of the Rotunda Hospital, Dublin*, [1921] 1 A.C. 1; *R.* v. *Income Tax Special Comrs., ex parte Shaftesbury Homes*, [1923] 1 K.B. 393.

3 *Tennant Plays, Ltd.* v. *I.R.Comrs.*, [1948] 1 All E.R. 506, at 510, *per* COHEN L.J. (charity running a public house).

4 *Keren Kayemeth Le Jisroel, Ltd.* v. *I.R.Comrs.*, [1932] A.C. 650, at 658, *per* Lord TOMLIN.

5 *Keren Kayemeth Le Jisroel, Ltd.* v. *I.R.Comrs.*, [1932] A.C. 650.

6 *Smith* v. *Kerr*, [1902] 1 Ch. 774.

7 *Institution of Civil Engineers* v. *I.R.Comrs.*, [1932] 1 K.B. 149.

8 (1928), 14 T.C. 271.

9 *Ibid.*, at 283.

"If you come to the conclusion, as you may in many cases, that one of the ways in which the public objects of an association can be served is by giving special advantages to the members of the association, then the association does not cease to be an association with a charitable object because incidentally and in order to carry out the charitable object it is both necessary and desirable to confer special benefits on the members."

The process of construction is not always easy. The status of the Royal College of Surgeons is in point. In 1899 the Court of Appeal had held that the college was set up to promote not only the science of surgery but also the interests of surgeons: it could not therefore claim exemption under the Customs and Inland Revenue Act 1885 from the duty imposed by that Act for all its property and income but only for that which was legally appropriated so as to create a legal obligation to apply it to the promotion of the science of surgery.[1] In 1951 the Court of Appeal felt bound by its earlier decision to hold that the college was not a charity.[2] But the House of Lords in *Royal College of Surgeons of England* v. *National Provincial Bank, Ltd.*[3] reversed that decision. The main object set out in the charter of the college was "the due promotion and encouragement of the study and practice" of the art and science of surgery. The professional protection of the members of the college provided for in its bye-laws did not affect the charitable status of the college. In the words of Lord MORTON OF HENRYTON:[4]

"the promotion of the interests of practising surgeons is 'an incidental, though an important and perhaps a necessary, consequence' of the work of the college in carrying out its main object, the promotion and encouragement of the study and practice of the art and science of surgery".

In the last resort the matter is one of degree. It is a question of fact whether there is so much personal benefit, intellectual or professional, to the members of the society or body in question as to be incapable of being disregarded.[5] In any event if the main object of an institution is to provide protection and advantage to those practising a particular profession the institution cannot be a charity even though the effectuation of the main object has as a consequence the benefiting of the community.[6] Here the boot is on the other foot: private advantage is the main object. The charitable benefit is merely incidental.

Statutory validation

From the foregoing discussion it is plain that in many cases the charitable intentions of testators have been frustrated. In some Commonwealth jurisdictions legislation has been introduced to rectify this situation.[7] England too has

---

1 *Re Royal College of Surgeons of England*, [1899] 1 Q.B. 871.
2 *Re Bland-Sutton's Will Trusts*, [1951] Ch. 485. 3 [1952] A.C. 631.
4 [1952] A.C. 631, at 659; and see *Royal College of Nursing* v. *St. Marylebone Borough Council*, [1959] 1 W.L.R. 1077 C.A.
5 *Midland Counties Institution of Engineers* v. *I.R.Comrs.* (1928), 14 T.C. 285, at 293, C.A., per ROWLATT J.
6 *General Nursing Council for England and Wales* v. *St. Marylebone Borough Council*, [1959] A.C. 540; *Geologists' Association* v. *I.R.Comrs.* (1928), 14 T.C. 271; *Chartered Insurance Institute* v. *London Corporation*, [1957] 1 W.L.R. 867.
7 For a discussion of the Commonwealth legislation, see M. C. Cullity (1967), 16 I.C.L.Q. 464–490; and see L. A. Sheridan (1966), 17 N.I.L.Q. 235–255.

enacted salvage legislation, but the relevant statute, the Charitable Trusts (Validation) Act 1954 is a sorry creature. Both its draftsmanship and its restricted and retrospective operation have been criticised.

So far as its draftsmanship is concerned HARMAN L.J. commented in one case that it had been his misfortune on a previous occasion to have had to wrestle with the terms of the Act, and he confessed to having been floored by them on both occasions.[1] In the same case he described the Act as so difficult to construe that in his view one could only go along step by step, giving each word the best meaning one could.[2] Lord EVERSHED M.R. similarly "found very considerable difficulty in following the language of the Act and still more in comprehending its true purpose and effect."[3] Other judges, taking a more liberal view of the scope of the Act, have found less difficulty in interpreting it, and have described provisions which troubled their brethren as "clear"[4] or "clear and unambiguous".[5]

RETROSPECTIVE OPERATION

It is of vital importance to note that the 1954 Act is entirely retrospective. Only imperfect trust provisions contained in an instrument taking effect before 16th December 1952 are affected by the Act. All other imperfect trust provisions are governed by the principles developed by the general law. As CROSS J. observed in *Re Harpur's Will Trusts:*[6]

> "The Act leaves the law untouched for the future but, for some reason which I do not pretend to understand, validates retrospectively a limited number of dispositions which had already failed. I do not know on what principle these particular dispositions were selected for favourable treatment and so I see no reason for construing this Act liberally".

In fact, the reasons given by the Nathan Committee for not recommending *prospective* salvage legislation were that it would be a dangerous precedent to enact an exemption from the principle that every person must be presumed to know the law; and that it would have serious repercussions on the doctrine of certainty in testamentary dispositions.

DISPOSITIONS AND COVENANTS TO WHICH ACT APPLIES

Section 2 (1) of the 1954 Act provides that the Act applies to any disposition of property to be held or applied for objects declared by an imperfect trust provision, and to any covenant to make such a disposition, where apart from the Act the disposition or covenant is invalid under the law of England and Wales, but would be valid if the objects were exclusively charitable.[7] The wording of this provision also has occasioned difficulties of interpretation.

---

1 *Re Harpur's Will Trusts*, [1962] Ch. 78, C.A., at 95.
2 *Ibid.*, at 96.
3 *Ibid.*, at 87.
4 *Per* ORMEROD L.J. dissenting in *Re Gillingham Bus Disaster Fund*, [1959] Ch. 62, at 80.
5 *Per* BUCKLEY J. in *Re Wykes' Will Trusts*, [1961] Ch. 229, at 242.
6 [1961] Ch. 38, at 48; affd. [1962] Ch. 78.
7 The Act binds the Crown: CTVA 1954, s. 6.

Certainly it would seem that property may be "disposed" of otherwise than by the instrument which contained the imperfect trust provision and that any *act* whereby property is provided for the purpose of being held or applied for charitable purposes is a "disposition" of that property. Thus the property donated by the contributors in *Re Gillingham Bus Disaster*[1] in response to an appeal was "disposed of".

IMPERFECT TRUST PROVISION

The term "imperfect trust provision"[2] is defined in section 1 (1) of the 1954 Act as:

> "any provision declaring the objects for which property is to be held or applied, and so describing those objects that, consistently with the terms of the provision, the property could be used exclusively for charitable purposes, but could nevertheless be used for purposes which are not charitable".

The ambit of this definition is best explored by reference to the cases which have arisen both here and in the Commonwealth, even though in the case of the latter the statutory provisions that applied are differently worded.

Trusts for objects specified separately

There is no doubt that the Act applies to and is effective to rescue trusts expressed to be for charitable or non-charitable purposes in the alternative. Thus a trust for "charitable or benevolent purposes" is an imperfect trust provision. But where the testator or settlor provides that the property shall be divided between each of such purposes the Act does not authorise the application of all the property to charity.[3] This is because section 1 (1) requires that "consistently with the terms of the provision the property could be used exclusively for charitable purposes".

Trusts for objects not specified separately

A difficult question which has provoked much judicial controversy is whether the Act was intended to save trusts for purposes described in a compendious expression which is apt to include both charitable and non-charitable purposes. For example, would a trust simply for "benevolent purposes" or "worthy objects" be within the terms of section 1 (1)? Some judges have taken a wide view of the statutory provision, others a restrictive view.

In *Re Gillingham Bus Disaster*[4] at first instance HARMAN J. took a restrictive view

---

1 [1959] Ch. 62.
2 In the following pages use has been made of material in an article by M. C. Cullity in (1967), 16 I.C.L.Q. 464–490.
3 See *Vernon v. I.R.Comrs.*, [1956] 1 W.L.R. 1169. In Victoria, providing the proportions are *unspecified*, the relevant statute saves such a gift: *Re Spehr*, [1965] V.R. 770.
4 [1958] Ch. 300; affd., [1959] Ch. 62.

of the application of the Act as an alternative ground for holding that there was a resulting trust to the donors. In his view the Act[1]

> "was, as the long title shows, intended to cure dispositions whereby part of the trust fund is devoted to charitable purposes and part to purposes not charitable, or not wholly charitable, so long as the whole of the money could be devoted to charity by excluding words which were too wide or too vague".

It could not, therefore, be applied to curb the vagueness of a gift to "worthy objects". Lord Evershed M.R. in the Court of Appeal expressly refrained from deciding this point,[2] as did Romer L.J.[3] though both appear to have sympathised with the view of Harman J., at any rate as regards a formula so vague and wide as "for such purposes as the trustees think fit".

A wide view was propounded by Ormerod L.J., in *Re Gillingham Bus Disaster*[4] who expressed the opinion, in a dissenting judgment, that section 1 (1) was clear and unambiguous and permitted the validation of a trust provision in favour of "such worthy cause or causes as the trustees should determine". The majority of the Court of Appeal decided the case on different grounds so that his opinion on the point was strictly *obiter*. But the issue was squarely raised in the case of *Re Wykes*[5] where a fund was given to the board of directors of a company "to be used at their discretion as a benevolent or welfare fund or for welfare purposes for the past, present and future employees of the company". Buckley J. held that since the whole of the fund bequeathed could, consistently with the terms of the bequest, be applied for a charitable purpose, notwithstanding that it could also be used exclusively for non-charitable purposes the bequest was an imperfect trust provision within the meaning of section 1 (1) of the Act. It has been suggested that this *ratio decidendi* is so wide as to admit to the category of imperfect trust provisions a bequest "for such objects as my trustees think fit".[6] But Buckley J. was at pains to point out that the "charitable or benevolent" kind of trust was not the only form of defective quasi-charitable trust that the Act was intended to validate; and all the examples which he discussed were trusts within the ambit of whose objects some charitable object could be found. Putting it another way they were all trusts having some flavour of charity about them.[7] Nowhere did he say that, if the property could within the terms of the will be used exclusively for charitable purposes, that was sufficient whether or not there was any express or implied mention of charity.

The last case deserving mention under this head is *Re Saxone Shoe Co., Ltd.'s Trust Deed*[8] where Cross J. had to consider a clause providing that the fund and the income thereof should be applied at the discretion of the trustees for various

---

1 [1958] Ch. 300, at 306. Reference to the title of the Act would be inadmissible if the Act was clear and unambiguous (as Ormerod L.J. said it was).
2 [1959] Ch. 62, at 75.
3 [1959] Ch. 62, at 77.
4 [1959] Ch. 52.
5 [1961] Ch. 229.
6 See M. C. Cullity (1967), 16 I.C.L.Q. 464, at 482.
7 The expression is that of Cross J. in *Re Saxone Shoe Co., Ltd.'s Trust Deed*, [1962] 1 W.L.R. 943, at 957–958; and see the overlooked analysis in *Leahy* v. *A.-G. for New South Wales*, [1959] A.C. 457, at 474–476, on comparable legislation.
8 [1962] 1 W.L.R. 943.

specified purposes including the provision of pensions to present or former employees, the maintenance or education of their dependants and "any other purpose whatsoever which the [trustees] shall in their discretion consider to be for the benefit of the employees or dependants". Counsel for the Attorney-General argued that the trust had been validated by being turned into a trust for the relief of poverty among such members of the class of beneficiaries as may from time to time be poor persons. CROSS J. proceeded on the footing that the case of *Re Wykes*[1] was correctly decided. This meant that he was prepared to assume as BUCKLEY J. did in that case that a trust "for welfare purposes" was validated by the Act. But he drew a distinction between a trust "for welfare purposes" for the benefit of a class which is not a section of the public and a trust to pay or apply a fund for the benefit of such members of such a class as the trustees think fit. The distinction he acknowledged was very fine and "would not be appreciated by a lay man".[2] He concluded that the trust provision with which he was concerned was in effect a private discretionary trust and not a rust for "quasi-charitable" purposes. In such phrases as "welfare purposes"

> "there is at least some flavour of charity which may justify [one] in saying that the testator was seeking to benefit the public through the relief of a limited class".

But in the case of the clause in issue all that it really said was that the trustees were to apply the capital and income for the benefit of the class in question *in any way* they thought fit, though certain modes of application were suggested. There was no sufficient flavour of charity. On the other hand in *Re McCullough*[3] LOWRY J. rejected the argument that "in order to save the gift, there must be in the will some indication of a charitable intention" but in the event held the relevant statutory provision[4] inapplicable, because the testator had died before it came into force.

Trusts for persons and bodies corporate or unincorporate

Only one case[5] in this country has raised the question whether the section applies only to trusts for purposes or whether it can be applied to trusts which give the trustees a power of selection amongst persons and charitable institutions or purposes. Suppose for example a testator directed his trustees to divide his residuary estate in their discretion "amongst other persons than my said near relatives and/or charitable institutions or organisations,"[6] or take a trust "for such charitable institutions or other public bodies in such shares as my trustee shall declare".[7] Apart from rescuing legislation both these gifts would fail. In Australia and New Zealand the relevant salvage provisions are formulated only in terms of *purposes* but the antipodean courts have construed the provisions

---

1 [1961] Ch. 229.
2 [1962] 1 W.L.R. 943, at 958.
3 [1966] N.I. 73, at 81. *Cf. Re Ashton*, [1955] N.Z.L.R. 192, N.Z.C.A.
4 Charities Act (Northern Ireland) 1964, s. 24, based on CTVA 1954, s. 1 (1).
5 *Re Harpur's Will Trusts*, [1961] Ch. 38 (CROSS J.); affd., [1962] Ch. 78, C.A.
6 *Re Griffiths*, [1926] V.L.R. 212.
7 *Re Thureau*, [1948] 2 A.L.R. 487.

liberally to save gifts for charitable or non-charitable institutions[1] and trusts for charitable objects or unascertainable persons. Section 1 (1) of the Charitable Trusts (Validation) Act 1954 would appear on the face of it more amenable to a liberal construction than the Australian and New Zealand statutes because it defines an imperfect trust provision as a provision declaring the *objects* for which property was to be held those "objects" being so described that the property could be used "exclusively for charitable or non-charitable purposes". The contrast between the word "objects" and "purposes" suggests that the Act is not confined to purpose trusts. Yet in *Re Harpur's Will Trusts*[2] it was held that the Act was so confined.

Trusts for one entire purpose

In *Roman Catholic Archbishop of Melbourne* v. *Lawlor*[3] there was a bequest to the Archbishop "to establish a Catholic daily newspaper". The Supreme Court of Victoria held this gift to be non-charitable and invalid.[4] On appeal to the High Court of Australia that decision was affirmed because the appellate court was equally divided: three judges holding the gift to be charitable the other three agreeing with the court below. Only the last mentioned members of the High Court considered whether the gift could be saved by the relevant salvage provision.[5] Rich J. was "quite unable to see . . . how any definite and ascertainable charitable purpose can be isolated and segregated out of the description Catholic daily newspaper. It is one entire description of one entire purpose. To confine the publication to purposes of religion which are charitable is to change the whole character of the newspaper intended by the testator."[6] "Such a newspaper", said Dixon J. "is necessarily different in character and its establishment is another purpose, not part of the same purpose."[7] Likewise Starke J. said the relevant section could not "be applied to a gift directing the application of the fund for a single purpose—e.g. establishing a Catholic daily newspaper—the charitable and non-charitable elements of which cannot be disentangled separated or delimited".[8] Plowman J. in *Buxton* v. *Public Trustee*[9] reached a like conclusion under the 1954 Act, which applies only where the property which is the subject matter of the trust can be applied exclusively for charitable purposes. The trust in question was a trust "to promote and aid the improvement of international relations and intercourse" by various methods including educational methods. The particular language of the trust deed did not "so describe the objects of the trust that the income from the endowment could be used exclusively for charitable purposes". The objects of the trust had nothing at all to do with charity.[10]

---

1 *Re Thureau, supra*; *Re Ingram*, [1951] V.L.R. 424.
2 [1961] Ch. 38; affd., [1962] Ch. 78, C.A.
3 (1934), 51 C.L.R. 1.
4 [1934] V.L.R. 231.
5 Property Law Act 1928, s. 131.
6 (1934), 51 C.L.R. 1, at 23–24.
7 *Ibid.*, at 37.
8 (1934), 51 C.L.R. 1, at 26.
9 (1962), 41 T.C. 235.
10 *Ibid.*, at 238–240.

Trusts for unascertainable persons not constituting a section of the public

As has been seen, trusts for ostensibly charitable purposes are deprived of charitable status if the class of possible beneficiaries is too restricted.[1] In most cases such trusts are beyond redemption. But where the testator has expressly provided for the relief of poverty as well as for payments for other non-charitable purposes the trust may be saved and confined to the relief of poverty. That this is not only the case in Australia[2] but also in this country is shown by the decision of CROSS J. in *Re Mead's Trust Deed*[3] which validated a trust for providing a convalescent home for trade union members and home for aged members of the union and their wives by treating it as capable of being limited to the relief of poverty.

In that case the first issue was whether a trust to provide a convalescent home for members of a trade union and a home for aged poor retired members of the union and their wives was charitable. Because the convalescent home was not restricted to poor members of the union it was held that the trust was not charitable. Members of a trade union were not a sufficient section of the public for the purpose of the law relating to charities. However the learned judge accepted the argument of the Attorney-General that the trust set up in 1920 could be validated by confining the access to the convalescent home to *poor* members of the trade union. The decision is astonishing. It resulted in a restriction almost certainly contrary to the intentions of those who provided most of the money for the building and maintenance of the convalescent home and drastically cut down the number of members of the society who could qualify for "convalescent benefit".

Instruments whose imperfect trust provisions are saved

As has been said,[4] only imperfect trust provisions contained in an instrument taking effect before 16th December 1952 are affected by the Act.[5] For this purpose section 1 (3) of the Act provides that:

> "A document inviting gifts of property to be held or applied for objects declared by the document shall be treated for the purposes of this section as an instrument taking effect when it is first issued."

Lord EVERSHED M.R. in *Re Gillingham Bus Disaster*[6] said that a published appeal for contributions for some public cause, though not amounting to a "disposition" of any property, might well be an "instrument" on the basis that it was a document inviting a gift of property within section 1 (3) of the Act. He was considering an appeal contained in a letter to a newspaper but the same principle must apply to an advertisement in a newspaper.

---

1 See 18–21, *supra*.
2 *Re Gillespie*, [1965] V.R. 402.
3 [1961] 1 W.L.R. 1244.
4 See 158, *supra*.
5 CTVA 1954, s. 1 (2); the date is that of the publication of the Nathan Report.
6 [1959] Ch. 62.

Savings for adverse claims

The Act contains a saving for adverse claims by persons who, apart from the Act, would have had a right to recover property on the ground of the invalidity of the disposition, provided that the disposition *either* was contained in an instrument which took effect after 16th December 1946, *or*, though contained in an instrument which took effect before that date, was, until after that date, subject to a prior interest for which the whole of the property (or the income arising from it) was held or applied.[1]

There is, however, a time limit on the enforcement of such claims. Any such claim had to be made before 30th July 1955, or where the right of the claimant first accrued to him or to some person through whom he claims after 30th July 1954, within one year from the date of such accrual.[2] There are two exceptions to this time limit. First, time will not run where the right (before or after its accrual) (*a*) has been concealed by the fraud of some person administering the imperfect trust provision or his agent or (*b*) has been acknowledged by some such person or his agent by means of a written acknowledgment given to the person having the right (or his agent) and signed by the person making it, or by means of a payment or transfer of property in respect of the right.[3] Secondly, the right is not to be deemed to accrue to anyone so long as he is under a disability, or has a future interest only, or so long as the invalid disposition is subject to another disposition made by the same person, and the whole of the property or the income arising from it is held or applied for the purposes of that other disposition.[4]

Subsections (2) to (4) of section 31 of the Limitation Act 1939 (which define the circumstances in which, for the purposes of that Act, a person is to be deemed to be under a disability or to claim through another person) apply to the provisions of subsection (3) of section 3 of the 1954 Act.[5]

Once the period of time prescribed for any person to bring proceedings to recover any property has expired without his having recovered the property or begun proceedings to do so, not just his right of action but also his title to the property is extinguished.[6] And the Act does not extend the time for bringing any proceedings beyond the period of limitation prescribed by any other enactment.[7]

The persons administering an imperfect trust provision and any trustee for them or for the persons on whose behalf they administered the provision are entitled as against a person whose right to the property is saved by subsection (1) of section 3 to deal with the property as if that subsection had not been passed, unless they have express notice of a claim by him to enforce his right.[8] Once trustees have express notice of a claim they can no longer deal safely with the property: if they do deal with it the prejudiced claimant may be entitled to damages or other relief.[9]

---

1 CTVA 1954, s. 3 (1).
2 *Ibid.*, s. 3 (2).
3 *Ibid.*, s. 3 (2).
4 *Ibid.*, s. 3 (3); and see *Re Chitty's Will Trusts*, [1970] Ch. 254; *Re Thomas's Will Trusts*, [1969] 3 All E.R. 1492 (right accrued at date of life tenant's death).
5 *Ibid.*, s. 3 (4).
6 *Ibid.*, s. 3 (2).   7 *Ibid.*
8 CTVA 1954, s. 3 (1).   9 *Ibid.*, s. 3 (5).

A covenant entered into before 30th July 1954[1] is not enforceable by virtue of the Act unless confirmed by the covenanter after that date. But a disposition made in accordance with such a covenant is treated for the purposes of the Act as confirming the covenant and any previous disposition made in accordance with it.[2]

Pending proceedings, past decisions and tax payments

Section 4 of the 1954 Act which makes provisions as to proceedings pending at the time the Act was passed and as to past decisions and payments, is now only of historical interest. No commentary on those provisions is offered.[3]

---

1 The date of the commencement of the Act.
2 CTVA 1954, s. 3 (6).
3 The provisions of section 4 are set out in Appendix 1.

Chapter 18

Construction

General principle: benignant construction

There is a well-established maxim that the court leans in favour of charity when construing charitable gifts. Charity is always favoured by equity.[1]

In the words of Lord LOREBURN "there is no better rule than that a benignant construction will be placed upon charitable bequests".[2] Thus where a gift is capable of two constructions, one which would make it void and the other which would render it effectual, the latter must be adopted.[3] It is better to effectuate than to destroy the intention.[4] Accordingly if a testator declares his intention to give the whole of his estate to charity but specifically appropriates part only, the general intention in favour of charity prevails, and the proportion not appropriated by him will be appropriated by the court to charity.[5]

The court is in some cases prepared to infer from very tenuous indications that a testator means to give the whole of his estate to charity.[6] Where, however, it is plain that the testator was aware that the specific charitable payments directed by him do not exhaust the property given to the trustees, no such inference will be drawn.[7] And a charitable intention is not inferred from the fact that the trustees are a charitable society and are given a wide discretion.[8] Nor will the most unequivocal protestation of a general charitable intention serve to validate a gift to a purpose which is *not* charitable.[9]

The court must not on the other hand strain the will to gain money for the charity.[10] For in doing so it will cheat the residuary legatees or next of kin. One judge once put this very forcefully when he said that he liked charity well enough but that "I will not steal leather to make poor men's shoes."[11] And there is one very glaring example of the court not adopting a benignant construction, namely where there is a gift to charitable or other objects in the alternative.[12]

---

1 *Re Watt*, [1932] 2 Ch. 243 n., at 246, *per* Lord HANWORTH M.R.
2 *Weir* v. *Crum-Brown*, [1908] A.C. 162, at 167.
3 *Bruce* v. *Presbytery of Deer* (1867), L.R. 1 H.L. Sc. 96, at 97.
4 *Re Lloyd* (1893), 10 T.L.R. 66.
5 *Beverley Corporation* v. *A.-G.* (1857), 6 H.L.C. 310, at 316, *per* Lord CRANWORTH L.C.
6 *A.-G.* v. *Skinners' Co.* (1827), 2 Russ. 407.
7 *Beverley Corporation* v. *A.-G.* (1857), 6 H.L. Cas. 310, at 320; *A.-G.* v. *Dean and Canons of Windsor* (1860), 8 H.L. Cas. 369.
8 *Re Freeman*, [1908] 1 Ch. 720. 9 *Re Sanders' Will Trusts*, [1954] Ch. 265.
10 *Dolan* v. *Macdermot* (1868), 3 Ch. App. 676, *per* Lord CAIRNS L.C.
11 *A.-G.* v. *Sutton* (1721), 1 P. Wms. 754, at 765–766, *per* Lord HARCOURT quoting in part a dictum of TWISDEN J. in an unreported case.
12 See at 149, *supra*.

Extrinsic evidence

Extrinsic evidence, in the discussion which follows, means any evidence other than the document the contents of which are under consideration.[1] Such evidence may, in general, be received whenever a knowledge of extrinsic facts can be made ancillary to the right interpretation of the will or written instrument in question.[2]

However, extrinsic evidence is not admissible to rebut plain words. Thus in *A.-G.* v. *Clapham*[3] where a Methodist chapel was conveyed to trustees by a deed which gave them a power after the death of John Wesley to appoint ministers, it was held that extrinsic evidence was not admissible to show that such a power was inconsistent with the intention of the founders and would, after the death of John Wesley, clash with the general system of Methodism. Similarly the accurate use of a name in a will creates a strong presumption against any rival who is not the possessor of the name mentioned in the will. It is a very strong presumption and one which cannot be overcome except in exceptional circumstances.[4] Nor can evidence be given to prove that a gift of a sum was intended to be a gift of the income of it only.[5]

Ambiguity

Extrinsic evidence is not admissible for the purpose of interpreting a *patent* ambiguity. So, if the amount of a legacy is left blank in a will it cannot be ascertained from parole evidence.[6]

On the other hand, evidence other than of intention is admissible to cure a *latent* ambiguity. As Lord LYNDHURST observed in *Shore* v. *Wilson:*[7]

> "If . . . the terms which are made use of are obscure, doubtful, or equivocal, either in themselves or in the application of them, it then becomes the duty of the court to ascertain by evidence, as well as it is able, what was the intent of the founder of the charity, in what sense the particular expressions were used."

In that case the interpretation of a gift to "poor and godly preachers of Christ's holy gospel" was in issue, and COLERIDGE J. heard evidence of the existence of a religious sect (of which the settlor was a member) by whom that and other expressions in the deed were used and of the manner in which they were used. In *Drummond* v. *A.-G.*[8] extrinsic evidence was admitted to show that Unitarians were not intended to have the benefit of a gift to "Protestant Dissenters".

---

1 *Cross on Evidence* (4th edn.) 532.
2 See *Wigram on Wills* (3rd edn.) 14.
3 (1855), 4 De G.M. & G. 591.
4 See *per* Lord LOREBURN in *National Society for Prevention of Cruelty to Children* v. *Scottish National Society for Prevention of Cruelty to Children*, [1915] A.C. 207, at 212.
5 *Re Huxtable*, [1902] 2 Ch. 793.
6 *Baylis* v. *A.-G.* (1741), 2 Atk. 239.
7 (1842), 9 Cl. & F. 355, at 390.
8 (1849), 2 H.L. Cas. 837.

Misdescription

Where a legacy has been bequeathed to a specified charitable institution the first step is to identify the institution. For if it exists, well and good; but if it does not, a *cy-près* problem arises.[1] In most cases executors should be able to identify a named institution by reference to the registers kept by the Charity Commissioners.[2] It is usually only where a testator has named or described incompletely the institution intended to benefit that a point of construction may arise for the court. But the fact that an existing institution is accurately described does not preclude all possibility of there being an ambiguity.[3] There is no absolute rule that a person, whether juridical or natural, answering the description in the will must have the gift whatever other considerations arise.[4]

The Charity Commissioners have drawn attention to the important functions of the Attorney-General in relation to the possible solution of a problem of misdescription in a will. Before deciding either to pay over a gift bequeathed to a misdescribed charity to an existing charity which the executors believe to be the institution intended by the testator, or to divide a gift between two or more charities each of which might justifiably claim to be the intended beneficiary and each of which consent, it is advisable that the executors should communicate with the Treasury Solicitor (who acts for the Attorney-General in relation to charities) in order to seek the Attorney-General's views. It may be that the Attorney-General can give his consent to the proposed course of action or he may be able to suggest some other course which will avoid the expense to the estate of an application to the court.[5]

If there is no existing charity which could justifiably claim to be the intended beneficiary of a gift to a misdescribed charity the Treasury Solicitor may be able to advise the executors as to how to arrange for the disposal of the gift by means of a direction under the Royal Sign Manual, in appropriate cases, without the necessity of an application to the court.[6]

Application to the Treasury Solicitor is made direct to the offices of the Treasury Solicitor.[7]

A trivial error in the description of a charitable legatee does not matter, provided the intention of the testator is clear.[8] Examples of immaterial misdescriptions are where a vicar is described as a rector,[9] or a suffragan bishop is described as a bishop,[10] or where a society has changed its name but not its objects.[11] And where an institution is accurately described, a direction as to the

---

1 See 250–254.
2 As to such registers see chapter 42, *post*.
3 *National Society for Prevention of Cruelty to Children* v. *Scottish National Society for Prevention of Cruelty to Children*, [1925] A.C. 207, H.L., at 212, 214.
4 *Re Meyers*, [1951] Ch. 534; and see *Re Satterthwaite's Will Trusts*, [1966] 1 W.L.R. (gift to "London Animal Hospital", a business carried on by an individual held to be a gift for purposes).
5 [1964] Ch. Com. Rep. 34, para. 65.
6 *Ibid.*, para. 66.
7 *Ibid.*, 35, para. 66.
8 *Makeown* v. *Ardagh* (1876), I.R. 10 Eq. 445; *Re Pritt* (1916), 85 L.J. Ch. 166.
9 *Hopkinson* v. *Ellis* (1842), 5 Beav. 34.
10 *Re Smith* (1934), 51 T.L.R. 108.
11 *Re Kilvert's Trusts* (1871), 7 Ch. App. 170, at 174. Or where an archdeaconry is described as a diocese: *ibid.*

utilisation of the money which does not fit the circumstances of the case is immaterial.[1]

The context of the will is also important. It may show that the description of a charity is precise and not loose.[2] Or the will may show that the testator did not intend to benefit institutes of a particular character.[3]

Where there is an ambiguity but the testator has described the institution which he intends to benefit as being in a particular locality, the legacy will, *prima facie*,[4] go to an institution situated in the locality named, even though the name used is more like that of an institution in another locality.[5] In other words the locality is usually the governing term in the testator's description. Thus in *Re Lycett*[6] the "King's Cross Hospital" was construed to mean the Great Northern Hospital, King's Cross, in preference to the King's Cross Hospital at Dundee, and in *Bradshaw* v. *Thompson*[7] the "Westminster Hospital Charing Cross" was construed to mean the Charing Cross Hospital rather than the Westminster Hospital or the Royal Westminster Ophthalmic Hospital Charing Cross. There was no Westminster Hospital at Charing Cross and the general hospital was preferred to the ophthalmic hospital because elsewhere in his will when the testator meant institutions for particular complaints to benefit he said so specifically. Again a testamentary gift to "the Chelsea Hospital" has been held to be intended for the Royal Hospital Chelsea and not to any other hospital merely having "Chelsea" as part of its name.[8]

On the other hand, a legacy to the hospitals of London was held not to be limited to hospitals within the City of London:[9] London had to be construed in a popular sense.[10]

A gift to "all and every the hospitals" without further description was in *Masters* v. *Masters*[11] confined to hospitals in the locality in which the testatrix resided. There is a presumption that "hospital" means a general hospital[12] and what before The National Health Service Act 1946 used to be called a "voluntary hospital".[13]

Sometimes, of course, the will does not provide all the answers. In such cases if a description in the will applies equally to more than one institution, extrinsic evidence is admissible to resolve the latent ambiguity and to determine which institution the testator had in mind.[14] Evidence may thus be adduced to show

---

1 *Smith* v. *Ruger* (1859), 5 Jur. N.S. 905 (direction to complete non-existent almshouses).

2 *Bradshaw* v. *Thompson* (1843), 1 Y. & C. Ch. Cas. 295; *Re Alchin's Trusts* (1872), L.R. 14 Eq. 230; and see *Wallace* v. *A.-G.* (1864), 33 Beav. 384, at 392; *British Home and Hospital for Incurables* v. *Royal Hospital for Incurables* (1904), 90 L.T. 601.

3 *Lechmere* v. *Curtler* (1855), 24 L.J. Ch. 647; *Re Davies' Trusts* (1872), 21 W.R. 154.

4 See *Re Morgan* (1909), 25 T.L.R. 303 (specific address displaced by accurate nomination of secretary); and see *British Home and Hospital for Incurables* v. *Royal Hospital for Incurables* (1904), 90 L.T. 601, C.A.

5 *Wilson* v. *Squire* (1842), 1 Y. & C. Ch. Cas. 654.   6 (1897), 13 T.L.R. 373.

7 (1843), 2 Y. & C. Ch. Cas. 295.   8 *Re De Jong* (1929), 46 T.L.R. 70.

9 *Wallace* v. *A.-G.* (1864), 33 Beav. 384; and see *Ditcham* v. *Chivis* (1828), 4 Bing. 706; *Beckford* v. *Crutwell* (1832), 5 C. & P. 242.

10 London in the popular sense probably means Inner London and not Greater London.

11 (1718), 1 P. Wms. 421, at 425 (one a mile outside excluded).

12 *Re Alchin's Trusts* (1872), L.R. 14 Eq. 230; *Bradshaw* v. *Thompson* (1843), 2 Y. & C. Ch. Cas. 295.

13 *Re Smith*, [1962] 1 W.L.R. 763.

14 *Middleton* v. *Clitherow* (1798), 3 Ves. 734; *Wilson* v. *Squire* (1842), 1 Y. & C. Ch. Cas. 654, at 656; *Re Briscoe's Trusts* (1872), 26 L.T. 149; *Re Fearn's Will* (1879), 27 W.R. 392; *Re Raven*, [1915] 1 Ch. 673, at 681; *Re King* (1918), 53 I.L.T. 60.

that one of the institutions which claimed the legacy did not exist when the testator resided in the locality.[1] Proof that the testator was interested in[2] or had subscribed[3] to a particular charity is also receivable. And evidence that he had declared that he would leave a legacy to a particular institution may be admitted.[4] In one case the entries in a contributions book kept by a testatrix were examined by the court.[5]

Inevitably there are cases where it is quite impossible to determine which of several charities the testator had in mind. In such cases the court by *cy-près* application, divides the fund between the claimants[6] in equal shares[7] or otherwise[8].

Evidence of contemporaneous matter

Evidence may be given of the circumstances attending the execution of the trust document[9] or of contemporaneous documents and usage. Evidence of usage is discussed separately.[10]

Naturally the contemporaneous acts of the *donor* are of particular importance for the purpose of construing a deed of gift executed by him.[11] Evidence is also admissible of the early application or distribution of the fund,[12] and of the construction placed on doubtful questions which arose in the early administration of the trust.[13]

The contemporaneous acts of the *donee* are, however, of little value for the purpose of placing a construction upon any instrument of gift executed by a donor; they only show the intention and the view with which the donee accepted the gift.[14] It is otherwise where the trusts are accepted conditionally or subject to certain qualifications, which the court may collect from contemporaneous transactions as evidenced by documents or usage.[15]

---

1 *King's College Hospital* v. *Wheildon* (1854), 18 Beav. 30.

2 *Gibson* v. *Coleman* (1868), 18 L.T. 236.

3 *Bunting* v. *Marriott* (1854), 19 Beav. 163; *Re Kilvert's Trusts* (1871), 7 Ch. App. 170, at 173; *Makeown* v. *Ardagh* (1876), I.R. 10 Eq. 445; *Re Fearn's Will* (1879), 27 W.R. 372; *Re Bradley* (1887), 3 T.L.R. 668; *Re Howard* (1899), 43 Sol. Jo. 380.

4 *A.-G.* v. *Hudson* (1720), 1 P. Wms. 674.

5 *British Home and Hospital for Incurables* v. *Royal Hospital for Incurables* (1904), 90 L.T. 601, C.A.

6 *Simon* v. *Barber* (1829), cited in 3 Hare 195 n.; *Gibson* v. *Coleman* (1868), 18 L.T. 236; *Re Alchin's Trusts* (1872), L.R. 14 Eq. 230; *Re Barnard* (1890), 7 T.L.R. 73; and see *Waller* v. *Childs* (1765), Amb. 524.

7 *Bennett* v. *Hayter* (1839), 2 Beav. 81 (equal division between two claimants of "gifts to the Jews' poor Mile End").

8 *Bunting* v. *Marriott* (1854), 19 Beav. 163 (whole fund given by consent to one of two claimants); *Bennett* v. *Hayter, supra*.

9 *Shore* v. *Wilson* (1842), 9 Cl. & Fin. 355; *Drummond* v. *A.-G.* (1849), 2 H.L. Cas. 837, at 857; *University of Aberdeen* v. *Irvine* (1868), L.R. 1 Sc. & Div. 289, H.L.

10 See 171–172, *infra*.

11 *A.-G.* v. *Trinity College, Cambridge* (1856), 24 Beav. 383, at 399; *A.-G.* v. *Windsor (Dean and Canons)* (1860), 8 H.L. Cas. 369, at 402; *A.-G.* v. *Dartmouth Corporation* (1883), 48 L.T. 933.

12 *Shore* v. *Wilson* (1842), 9 Cl. & Fin. 355, H.L., at 569; *A.-G.* v. *Brazen Nose College* (1834), 2 Cl. & Fin. 295, H.L. (donor a trustee).

13 *A.-G.* v. *Caius College* (1837), 2 Keen, 150.

14 *A.-G.* v. *Trinity College, Cambridge* (1856), 24 Beav. 383.

15 *A.-G.* v. *Master of Catherine Hall* (1820), Jac. 381, at 391–392; *A.-G.* v. *Draper's Co.* (1843), 6 Beav. 382, at 386; and see *A.-G.* v. *Caius College* (1838), 2 Keen 150, at 163.

Evidence of usage

There is a general rule of construction that "if the words of an instrument be ambiguous we may call in the acts done under it as a clue to the intention of the parties",[1] in particular, of acts done shortly after the date of the instrument. This principle is expressed in the maxim *contemporanea expositio est fortissima in lege*.[2] But evidence of the acts done cannot be admitted to contradict the clear meaning of an instrument.[3]

The principle of construction by contemporaneous usage is primarily applicable to *ancient* documents, and most of the statements of principle are concerned with ancient documents. For example Sir EDWARD SUGDEN L.C. in *A.-G.* v. *Drummond*[4] said:

> "One of the most settled rules of law for the construction of ambiguities in *ancient* instruments is, that you may resort to contemporaneous usage to ascertain the meaning of the deed; tell me what you have done under *such* a deed, and I will tell you what that deed means."

And Lord HARDWICKE in *A.-G.* v. *Parker*[5] said that "in the construction of *ancient* grants and deeds, there is no better way of construing them than by usage". In the past there have been suggestions that the principle may also be invoked for the purpose of explaining ambiguities, both latent and patent, in *modern* instruments. In the much cited case of *Watcham* v. *A.-G. of the East Africa Protectorate*[6] the Judicial Committee held that, in cases of ambiguity, evidence of usage can be given to show the sense in which the parties used the language employed in construing a modern as well as an ancient instrument. And the dictum of TINDAL C.J. quoted above[7] referred in fact to what was at the time a modern instrument. Nearly all the dicta which seem to exclude evidence of usage in the case of modern instruments are referring to cases where there is attempted to use the conduct of the parties to contradict the clear meaning of the document.[8] Be that as it may, the House of Lords has now held that evidence of user under a deed is not admissible as an aid to construction in the case of a modern deed, except perhaps where the instrument concerned is an instrument of title to land.[9] It has since been held that usage is a permissible guide to the construction of a description of property assured in a modern instrument.[10]

The sort of doubt on construction of the instrument which prompts a

---

1 *Doe d. Pearson* v. *Ries* (1832), 8 Bing. 178, at 181, *per* TINDAL C.J.

2 2 Co. Inst. 136.

3 *Chad* v. *Tilsed* (1821), 2 Brod. & Bing. 403, at 406, *per* DALLAS C.J.; *North Eastern Rail. Co.* v. *Lord Hastings*, [1900] A.C. 260, H.L., at 263, 270.

4 (1842), 1 Dr. & War. 162.

5 (1747), 3 Atk. 576, at 577.

6 [1919] A.C. 533, P.C.

7 See note 1, *supra*.

8 *Monro* v. *Taylor* (1848), 8 Hare 51, at 56, *per* WIGRAM V.C. (affd. (1852), 3 Mac. & G. 713); *Bruner* v. *Moore*, [1904] 1 Ch. 305; *Belton* v. *Bass, Ratcliffe and Gretton, Ltd.*, [1922] 2 Ch. 449; *North Eastern Rail. Co.* v. *Lord Hastings*, [1900] A.C. 260, H.L., at 263, *per* Lord HALSBURY L.C.

9 *Schuler A.-G.* v. *Wickman Machine Tool Sales, Ltd.*, [1974] A.C. 235, at 252 and 261, H.L.

10 *St. Edmundsbury and Ipswich Diocesan Board of Finance* v. *Clark (No. 2)*, [1973] 1 W.L.R. 1 572 (MEGARRY J.); see also *Neilson* v. *Poole* (1969), 20 P. & C.R. 909.

reference to usage may occur because of the use of general words[1] or because, in consequence of lapse of time, the words may have changed their meaning[2] or on account of some other uncertainty or ambiguity.[3]

Evidence of usage is not restricted to direct evidence of contemporaneous usage, which it is often impossible to get. Modern usage, if there is nothing to suggest a recent origin, raises a presumption that the usage was the same immediately after the date of the instrument, and so evidence of modern usage is admissible to explain an ancient deed.[4]

The application of the foregoing general principles of construction to charitable trusts is straightforward. The true construction of ancient trust deeds may be solved by evidence of long usage and acquiescence. Indeed, where the instrument of foundation may be construed in two ways the court will lean in favour of the construction supported by usage[5] rather than assume that a long series of breaches of trust has been committed.[6] On the other hand, usage cannot be held to justify a clear breach of trust[7] or to vary a trust which is unambiguous.[8]

Religious trusts

There is a cardinal principle in the law of charities that the intentions of the founder must be carried into effect so far as they are capable of being so, and so far as they are not contrary to law or morality.[9] Accordingly, if the founder of a charity has directed that only persons conforming to particular religious doctrines shall be recipients of his bounty, his wishes must be followed[10] unless the trusts are varied by some competent authority.[11] But, in the absence of such an express direction, there is a presumption in the case of eleemosynary and educational charities against the intention of the founder being that the recipients shall be confined to persons holding a particular form of religious belief.[12] In the case of an eleemosynary charity this presumption is so strong that nothing

---

1 *Chad* v. *Tilsed* (1821), 2 Brod. & Bing. 403, at 406; *Weld* v. *Hornby* (1806), 7 East 195, at 599; *Lord Waterpark* v. *Fennell* (1859), 7 H.L. Cas. 650, at 680.

2 See *Lord Hastings* v. *North Eastern Rail. Co.*, [1899] 1 Ch. 656, C.A., at 663, *per* LINDLEY M.R., affd., [1900] A.C. 260, H.L.

3 *Ibid.*, at 661, *per* VAUGHAN WILLIAMS L.J.

4 *Hastings Corporation* v. *Ivall* (1874), L.R. 19 Eq. 558, at 581; *Earl De La Warr* v. *Miles* (1881), 17 Ch.D. 535, C.A., at 573.

5 *A.-G.* v. *Bristol Corporation* (1820), 2 Jac. & W. 294, at 321; *A.-G.* v. *Smythies* (1833), 2 Russ. & M. 717, at 749; and see *A.-G.* v. *Rochester Corporation* (1854), 5 De G.M. & G. 797, at 822.

6 *A.-G.* v. *Sidney Sussex College* (1869), 4 Ch. App. 722, at 732; *Bruce* v. *Deer Presbytery* (1867), L.R. 1 Sc. & Div. 96, H.L.

7 *A.-G.* v. *Bristol Corporation, supra*; *Drummond* v. *A.-G. for Ireland* (1849), 2 H.L. Cas. 837, at 861; *A.-G.* v. *Rochester Corporation, supra*; *A.-G.* v. *St. John's Hospital, Bedford* (1865), 2 De G.J. & Sm. 621; *Re Swansea Free Grammar School*, [1894] A.C. 252.

8 *A.-G.* v. *Calvert* (1857), 23 Beav. 248, at 263.

9 *Ibid.*, at 255.

10 *A.-G.* v. *Calvert* (1857), 23 Beav. 248, at 255, *per* ROMILLY M.R.; *Re Malling Abbey Trusts, Beaumont* v. *Dale* (1915), 31 T.L.R. 397, C.A. (Church of England); *Craigdallie* v. *Aikman* (1820), 2 Bli. 529, H.L. (Scottish seceders); *A.-G.* v. *Pearson* (1817), 3 Mer. 353, at 410; *Milligan* v. *Mitchell* (1837), 3 My. & Cr. 72 (Scottish dissenters).

11 The court or The Charity Commissioners.

12 *A.-G.* v. *Calvert* (1857), 23 Beav. 248, at 256–258; *A.-G.* v. *Clifton* (1863), 32 Beav. 596; and see *Re St. Leonard, Shoreditch, Parochial Schools* (1884), 10 App. Cas. 304.

short of an expression of unequivocal import will do; and evidence of the tenets and opinions of the founder is not admissible as evidence of his intention.[1]

In many cases a charity is established for purely religious purposes either generally or for the purpose of religious instruction. Here two presumptions arise. The first is that the founder or founders intended a particular form of religion to be promoted. The second is that the form intended was that professed by the founder or founders.[2]

Ascertainment of founder's intentions

The intention of the founder is a question of fact[3] not always easily ascertained.[4]

Of course, if the founder's intentions are expressed *cadit quaestio*.[5] But where there is no expressed intention[6] or the language is ambiguous,[7] and in those cases only, extrinsic evidence is admissible. In this connection the court may consider the known opinions of the founder.[8] Reference may also be made to contemporaneous Acts of Parliament to see in what sense the words were used when the deeds were executed,[9] to contemporaneous deeds relating to the same chapel[10] to a contemporaneous declaration of trust[11] or even to the ecclesiastical history of the period.[12] Where the trust is for the benefit of an existing congregation the character of the congregation may be made the subject of an inquiry.[13]

The meaning of the founder of the trust may be explained by evidence as to the character of the congregation for whose benefit the gift was made.[14]

Many denominations of dissenters, in order to secure uniformity in the trusts of their chapels, schools, and other property, use model deeds which are in fact carefully prepared deeds relating to particular chapels, schools etc., by reference to which the trusts of other chapels etc. can be declared. Denominations which use such model deeds are the Methodist Church,[15] and the Baptists and the Congregationalists.[16] Certain other denominations, for example the Calvinistic

---

1 *A.-G.* v. *Calvert, supra; A.-G.* v. *St. John's Hospital, Bath* (1876), 2 Ch.D. 554. For an eleemosynary charity for dissenters, see *Shore* v. *Wilson* (1842), 9 Cl. & Fin. 355.

2 *A.-G.* v. *Calvert* (1857), 23 Beav. 248, at 255–256; *A.-G.* v. *Pearson* (1817), 3 Mer. 353, at 410; *Craigdallie* v. *Aikman* (1812), 1 Dow. 1; and see *Dill* v. *Watson* (1836), 2 Jones Ex. R. 48.

3 *Shore* v. *Wilson* (1842), 9 Cl. & Fin. 355, at 390, H.L., *per* Lord LYNDHURST.

4 *Foley* v. *Wontner* (1820), 2 Jac. & W. 245.

5 See *supra*.

6 *A.-G.* v. *Murdoch* (1849), 7 Hare 445; affd. (1852), 1 De G.M. & G. 86.

7 *A.-G.* v. *Calvert* (1857), 23 Beav. 248, at 263; *A.-G.* v. *Gould* (1860), 28 Beav. 485.

8 *A.-G.* v. *Calvert* (1857), 23 Beav. 248, at 256; *Shore* v. *Wilson* (1842), 9 Cl. & Fin. 355; *Free Church of Scotland* (General Assembly) v. *Overtoun* (Lord), [1904] A.C. 515, at 613.

9 *Drummond* v. *A.-G. for Ireland* (1849), 2 H.L. Cas. 857, at 863; *Shore* v. *Wilson* (1842), 9 Cl. & Fin. 355, H.L., at 413.

10 *A.-G.* v. *Anderson* (1888), 57 L.J. Ch. 543.

11 *A.-G.* v. *Clapham* (1855), 4 De G.M. & G. 591, at 626; *A.-G.* v. *Mathieson*, [1907] 2 Ch. 383, at 394.

12 *A.-G.* v. *Bunce* (1868), L.R. 6 Eq. 563, at 571–572.

13 *A.-G.* v. *Murdoch* (1849), 7 Hare, 445; affd. (1852), 1 De G.M. & G. 86; and see *Dill* v. *Watson* (1836), 2 Jo. Ex. Ir. 48.

14 *A.-G.* v. *Molland* (1832), 1 You. 562 (teaching "the Gospel of Christ under the name of orthodoxy" explained).

15 See the Methodist Church Union Act 1929.

16 See the Baptist and Congregational Trusts Act 1951.

Methodist Church,[1] the Presbyterian Church in England and the Free Church of England "provide" forms of deeds which it is generally expedient to use.[2]

Form of religious worship intended

Sometimes the courts experience difficulty in establishing the form of religious worship intended by the founders of a religious charity. In particular, the task of executing trusts of dissenting chapels has been found to be one of the greatest difficulty[3] and Lord ELDON said long ago that it was the duty of the founders of such trusts to declare their intentions clearly.[4] But though desirable it is not essential that the terms of the trust should be in writing,[5] because it is always open to the court to ascertain what form of religious worship was intended from the established usage of the congregation.[6]

The constant difficulties which arose in determining which of several dissenting sects was intended to have the benefit of a charity, and whether, in the execution of the trusts, the founders' principles had been departed from, led to statutory intervention. The Nonconformist Chapels Act 1844[7] contained a provision that where in the deed of foundation of a nonconformist place of worship there was no express statement as to the particular doctrines for which it was to be used, 25 years' usage was to be conclusive evidence of the founders' principles.[8]

Where any minister's house, school, or fund is given or created by any deed, will, or other instrument which declares in express terms or by reference the particular religious doctrines or opinions for the promotion of which the same are intended, then they must be applied to promoting the doctrines or opinions so specified, any usage of the congregation to the contrary notwithstanding.[9] A gift of a meeting house "for Protestant Dissenters of the Presbyterian or Independent denomination to worship in as the same is now used" was held in one case to be sufficiently express to take the case out of the ambit of the 1844 Act.[10] But in another case the term Presbyterian on its own was held to be too imprecise to denote any particular doctrine or mode of worship.[11] Again in *A.-G.* v. *Hutton*[12] a gift to a named dissenting congregation "for the service and worship of God in that way" was not sufficiently express to fall outside the 1844 Act nor was a trust to instruct a congregation and their successors for ever "in the true principles of the Christian religion".[13] Where the direction is clear it is immaterial that it was contained in a deed void under the Charitable Uses Act 1735:[14] the case fell outside the 1844 Act.[15]

---

1 See the Calvinistic Methodist or Presbyterian Church of Wales Act 1933.

2 As to such forms, see 8 Encyclopaedia of Forms and Precedents (4th edn.) 61–68.

3 *A.-G.* v. *Pearson* (1817), 3 Mer. 353, at 397; *Foley* v. *Wontner* (1820), 2 J. & W. 245.

4 *A.-G.* v. *Pearson* (1817), 3 Mer. 353, at 410.

5 See 131, *supra*.

6 *A.-G.* v. *Pearson* (1817), 3 Mer. 353, at 400; *A.-G.* v. *Murdoch* (1849), 7 Hare 445; affd. (1852), 1 De G.M. & G. 86; *Drummond* v. *A.-G. for Ireland* (1849), 2. H.L. Cas. 837.

7 (7 & 8 Vict. c. 45).   8 Section 2.

9 Nonconformists Chapels Act 1844, s. 2, proviso.

10 *A.-G.* v. *Anderson* (1888), 57 L.J. Ch. 543.

11 *A.-G.* v. *Bunce* (1868), L.R. 6 Eq. 563.

12 (1844), 7 I. Eq. 612; (1844), Dr. 480.   13 *Ibid.*

14 9 Geo. 2 c. 36, s. 3 (replaced by the Mortmain and Charitable Uses Act 1888, which was in turn repealed by the Charities Act 1960, s. 48, Sched. 7, Pt. II).

15 *A.-G.* v. *Ward* (1848), 6 Hare 477, at 483.

These cases are now largely of historical interest because the 1844 Act was repealed as obsolete by the Charities Act 1960 with a gaining for charities taking effect before the commencement of the Act.

In the case of Roman Catholic charities the trusts, in the absence of written documents, are to be ascertained from the usage during the last period of 20 years during which there has been a consistent usage.[1]

Gifts for benefit of a church

The decided cases illustrate various ways in which charitable donors seek to benefit a particular church and these cases raise interesting questions of construction.

Sometimes a fund is given for the "reparation" of a church. In a proper case such a fund may be applied in erecting new buildings[2] or even in paying the salaries of persons who look after the fabric or ornaments of the building as for example the sexton, the verger and the organ-tuner (though not the organist or bell-ringer[3]). In A.-G. v. Parr[4] the income of a fund directed to be used by the churchwardens of a parish "about the parish church" was held to be applicable to general expenditure about the church as a whole including repairs to the chancel. Elsewhere it has been held that the words "reparations, ornaments[5] and other necessary occasions" of a parish church are sufficiently wide to cover the erection of a spire.[6]

Where there is a gift for the endowment of a church, this means that the income only of the fund is to be applied for the benefit of the incumbent,[7] and this principle surely applies to the endowment of a Roman Catholic church or Nonconformist chapel.

In one old case a gift to a particular parish church was construed as a gift to the parson and parishioners and their successors for ever.[8] Nowadays such a gift is treated as a gift intended to be devoted to purposes in the parish connected with church services and the fund in question will be administered by the parochial church council.[9]

Whether a gift to a vicar or other religious officeholder is for the benefit of the office or a personal legacy to the officeholder at the date of the gift is a matter of construction. Gifts of this kind are discussed elsewhere in this work.[10]

Gifts for institutions

Where gifts are made to existing charitable institutions, or to the governors or treasurer of such an institution, generally,[11] or for promoting certain definite

---

1 Roman Catholic Charities Act 1860 (23 & 24 Vict. c. 134), s. 5.
2 Re Palatine Estate Charity (1888), 39 Ch.D. 54; and see also A.-G. v. Wax Chandlers' Co. (1873), L.R. 6 H.L. 1; Re Booth's Charities (1866), 14 W.R. 161.
3 Re Palatine Estate Charity, supra.   4 [1920] 1 Ch. 339.
5 As to "ornaments", see Cripps, Law relating to the Church and Clergy (8th edn.) 225–238.
6 Re Palatine Estate Charity, supra.
7 Re Robinson, [1892] 1 Ch. 95, at 100; on appeal, [1897] 1 Ch. 85, C.A.
8 Cheeseman v. Partridge (1739), 1 Atk. 436.   9 Re Gare, [1952] Ch. 80.
10 See at 181–188.
11 Green v. Rutherforth (1750), 1 Ves. Sen. 462, at 472 (gift to a college); Re White, [1893] 2 Ch. 41, C.A., at 52.

objects which are in fact the objects of such institutions,[1] the gifts are applicable by the trustees, governors, or other officials for the general purposes of the institution.

A gift to an existing institution for a purpose which is in fact within the objects of the institution is *prima facie* a gift for the performance of that purpose by the institution in the course of its own activities. So a gift of a fund to a city company to be employed in apprenticing young men should *prima facie* be applicable for apprenticing them in the craft to which the corporate body belonged.[2]

Gifts for the poor

The circumstances when gifts to the poor are charitable have already been discussed. There are, however, cases where difficulty is experienced in identifying the *class* of poor intended to benefit under a charitable gift. This applies particularly where there is a gift for the poor giving preference to poor relations or a discretion to distribute to poor relations.[3] If necessary an inquiry may be directed as to who are poor relations.[4]

A charity for the poor generally is not to be applied in such a way as directly to benefit the rich, as by relieving persons entitled to relief from public funds. This principle was established in cases deciding that persons receiving poor law relief were not proper objects of charity[5] but is equally applicable to persons receiving supplementary benefits which has replaced poor law relief.[6] But the principle does not apply where the intention is clear that the gift is to be applied in such a way.[7]

Participants in charity benefits

Problems have often arisen as to who are entitled to participate in a gift for the benefit of persons falling within a particular description. Two classes of participants commonly designated are (1) parishioners and inhabitants of a specified parish or locality and (2) descendants, relations or kin of the founder.

PARISHIONERS AND INHABITANTS

In common parlance a parishioner is one of the inhabitants or community of a parish.[8] But neither "parishioner" nor "inhabitant" has a fixed legal meaning:

---

1 *Incorporated Society* v. *Richards* (1841), 1 Dr. & War. 258, at 294, 332.
2 *A.-G.* v. *Sidney Sussex College* (1869), 4 Ch. App. 722, at 730.
3 *Waldo* v. *Caley* (1809), 16 Ves. 206.
4 *A.-G.* v. *Price* (1810), 17 Ves. 371; *A.-G.* v. *Sidney Sussex, Cambridge* (1865), 34 Beav. 654.
5 See *A.-G.* v. *Leage* (1881), reported in *Tudor on Charities* (4th edn.) 1041; *A.-G.* v. *Bovill* (1840), 1 Ph. 762; *Deptford Churchwardens* v. *Sketchley* (1847), 8 Q.B. 394, at 405; *A.-G.* v. *Wilkinson* (1839), 1 Beav. 370; *A.-G.* v. *Exeter Corporation* (1827), 3 Russ. 395.
6 See National Assistance Act 1948, s. 1; Ministry of Social Security Act 1966, ss. 4, 39 (3), Sch. 8.
7 *A.-G.* v. *Blizard* (1855), 21 Beav. 233; *Re Richmond Parish Charity Lands* (1965), 11 R.R.C. 89, reversed on appeal on some points (1965), 11 R.R.C. 283, C.A.
8 See *Shorter Oxford English Dictionary*.

each is construed according to the subject matter in question,[1] the meaning varying according to the circumstances under which it is applied.[2]

The most quoted definition of the term parishioner is that of Lord HARD-WICKE in *A.-G. v. Parker*[3]:

"Parishioner is a very large word and takes in, not only inhabitants of the parish, but persons who are occupiers of lands that pay the several rates and duties, tho' they are not [resident][4] nor do contribute to the ornaments of the church."

In other words the term includes all persons who occupy land and pay rates in the parish, wherever they reside.[5] A casual sojourner, however, is not a parishioner.[6]

In *Etherington v. Wilson*[7] there was a charity scheme sanctioned by the court by which a parish was empowered to elect children for Christ's Hospital and it was provided that no child should be eligible unless born in the parish or unless his parents or one of them should be or should have been parishioners or a parishioner of the parish. The father of the defendant took a house temporarily, for which he paid rent and rates before the election for the purpose of obtaining a qualification for his son. The Court of Appeal held that the word parishioner should be taken in its ordinary sense of a person occupying premises liable to be rated in the parish and upheld the boy's qualification for election and his election.

In reference to church privileges the term parishioner also includes persons lodging in the parish;[8] and the tenant of a house in an ecclesiastical parish who pays rates but does not reside in it can maintain a suit for a faculty in respect of the church.[9]

The word "inhabitants" is even wider in ambit than "parishioners".[10] It "takes in housekeepers, though not rated to the poor, also persons who are not housekeepers, as for instance such as who have gained a settlement[11] and by that means have become inhabitants".[12] An inhabitant of a place, speaking generally, is one who has his permanent home there[13] or who dwells there[14] but the word

---

1 *A.-G. v. Forster* (1804), 10 Ves. 335.

2 *R. v. Mashiter* (1837), 6 Ad. & El. 153.

3 (1747), 3 Atk. 576, at 577.

4 He used the word "resiant".

5 *Jeffrey's Case* (1589), 5 Co. 66b; *Drury v. Harrison* (1794), 3 Phillim. 515 n., at 517 n.; *A.-G. v. Parker* (1747), 3 Atk. 576; *A.-G. v. Forster* (1804), 10 Ves. 335, at 339, 343; *Veley v. Burder* (1841), 12 Ad. & El. 265, Ex. Ch., at 301.

6 See Steer's *Parish Law* (6th edn.), 12, citing *Holledge's Case* (1622), 2 Roll. Rep. 238 (market day stall-holder not an inhabitant rateable to poor rate).

7 (1875) 1 Ch.D. 160 reversing the decision of MALINS V.C. in (1875) L.R. 20 Eq. 606.

8 *St. Swithin's Parish Case* (1695), Holt K.B. 139.

9 *Kensit v. Rector of St. Ethelburga, Bishopsgate Within*, [1900] P. 80; *Davey v. Hinde*, [1901] P. 95.

10 See *A.-G. v. Parker* (1747), 3 Atk. 576, at 577.

11 I.e. have established their right to relief from the poor rates by legal residence.

12 Per Lord HARDWICKE in *A.-G. v. Parker*, supra.

13 *R. v. Mitchell* (1809), 10 East 511. *Semble* the inhabitants of houses illegally erected on common land and liable to demolition at any moment are not inhabitants of a parish: per JESSEL M.R. in *Chilton v. Corporation of London* (1878), 7 Ch.D. 735. A casual sojourner is not an inhabitant: see Steer's *Parish Law* (6th edn.) p. 12.

14 Servants and lodgers except if some burden is to be put on the property: *R. v. North Curry* (1825), 4 B. & C. 953.

has no definite legal meaning its signification varying according to the subject matter[1] or the context[2] or sometimes according to usage.[3]

Thus we find in the case of charitable gifts for the poor inhabitants of a place that only persons not in receipt of rating or parochial relief may participate in the charity.[4]

The expression "inhabitants and parishioners" means "inhabitants who are also parishioners."[5] In *A.-G.* v. *Rutter*[6] the right of voting at the election of a person was vested in "the inhabitants and parishioners" of a particular parish and this was held to mean persons paying church and poor rates.

Evidence of usage is admissible to determine the sense in which the word "inhabitant" or the word "parishioner" are used either alone or together.[7] Uniform usage is conclusive[8] but varied usage is not.[9] Usage may show that "inhabitants and parishioners" entitled to vote at the election of a person are confined to ratepayers:[10] or it may show that a wider class has participated and is entitled.[11]

In those cases where the words "inhabitant" or "parishioner" or "inhabitants and parishioners" are confined to ratepayers the question arises whether the rates must in fact have been paid. Some cases seem to require actual payment as a condition precedent to qualification:[12] elsewhere the court treats liability to rating as enough.[13] Here again, usage may be the determining factor.[14]

DESCENDANTS, RELATIONS OR KINDRED

It has been seen that except in the case of relief of poverty[15] and special cases of educational endowment for the founder's kin[16] a trust confined to persons related to a particular individual cannot be charitable. Thus a trust purporting to confer educational benefits for the "lawful descendants" of three named persons was classified in *Re Compton*[17] as not charitable. And a similar fate overtook an educational trust primarily for the male descendants along either the male or female line of the grantor or any of his brothers or sisters.[18] But a trust for poor

---

1 *A.-G.* v. *Forster* (1804), 10 Ves. 335.

2 *R.* v. *Mashiter* (1837), 6 Ad. & El. 153, at 165, *per* LITTLEDALE J.; *R.* v. *Dane* (1837), 6 Ad. & El. 374.

3 See *infra*.

4 *A.-G.* v. *Clarke* (1762), Amb. 422.

5 *Fearon* v. *Webb* (1802), 14 Ves. 13 (where the words "chiefest" and "discreetest" were also construed).

6 (1778), 2 Russ. 101 n.; and see *Carter* v. *Cropley* (1856), 8 De G.M. & G. 1680; *A.-G.* v. *Dalton* (1851), 13 Beav. 141; *Faulkner* v. *Elge* (1825), 4 B. & C. 449.

7 *R.* v. *Mashiter* (1837), 6 Ad. & El. 165.

8 *A.-G.* v. *Forster* (1804), 10 Ves. 335.

9 *Edenborough* v. *Archbishop of Canterbury* (1826), 2 Russ. 93.

10 *A.-G.* v. *Newcombe* (1807), 14 Ves. 1.

11 *A.-G.* v. *Parker* (1747), 3 Atk. 577.

12 *Edenborough* v. *Archbishop of Canterbury* (1826), 2 Russ. 110, at 111, *per* Lord ELDON; and see *A.-G.* v. *Forster* (1804), 10 Ves. 335.

13 *Etherington* v. *Wilson* (1875), 1 Ch.D. 160, especially at 168, *per* MELLISH L.J.

14 *A.-G.* v. *Newcombe* (1807), 14 Ves. 1.

15 See at 32–35, *supra*.

16 See at 51–52, *supra*.

17 [1945] Ch. 123.

18 *Caffoor* (*Trustees of Abdul Gaffoor Trust*) v. *Income Tax Comr. Colombo*, [1961] A.C. 584, P.C.

relations described as such or for poor descendants or poor kinsmen is a good charity. It is clearly important to establish who fall within the differing descriptions.

Descendants

"Descendants" has been described as a perfectly unambiguous word which no laymen or lawyer would use to designate children only.[1] In the words of JAMES L.J. in *Ralph* v. *Carrick*:[2]

> "Descendants means children and their children and their children to any degree and it is difficult to conceive any context by which the word 'descendants' could be limited to mean children only."

BRETT L.J. in the same case considered that in ordinary parlance the *prima facie* meaning of "descendants" is all descendants of any degree and not only children.[3] Despite the strong words of JAMES L.J. just cited cases can be found in which the context caused the court to restrict the meaning to children[4] or to children and grandchildren.[5] Equally in the past the context or circumstances have led the court to construe descendants so as to include cousins[6] or collateral descendants.[7] But today it must be very questionable whether descendants could be so construed. PENNYCUICK V.-C. in *Re Thurlow*[8] found it impossible to say that either in the ordinary use of the English language or in legal language the word "descendants" was apt to include collateral relations.

The problem did not arise in *Gillam* v. *Taylor*[9] where the intended objects of charitable benefit were "such of the lineal descendants of Richard Wilson . . . as they may severally need". The testator had directed that trustees should hold the residue of his real and personal estate for investment in Government securities and pay the interest from time to time to such lineal descendants. It was argued that the gift could not be charitable because it contained no reference to "poor" descendants but Sir JOHN WICKENS V.-C. held that need connoted a poverty restriction.[10]

If an idiosyncratic trust for the benefit of poor *male* descendants were set up it would presumably be construed so as to cover male descendants descended through females.[11]

---

1 *Ralph* v. *Carrick* (1879), 11 Ch.D. 873, at 883, *per* JAMES L.J.

2 (1879), 11 Ch.D. 873, at 883.

3 (1879), 11 Ch.D. 873, at 885.

4 *Smith* v. *Pepper* (1859), 27 Beav. 86 (in proportions under the Statute) not cited in *Ralph* v. *Carrick, supra*; *Williamson* v. *Moore* (1862), 8 Jur. N.S. 875 (my nephews and nieces being descendants of my brothers and sisters).

5 *Legard* v. *Haworth* (1800), 1 East. 120.

6 *Craik* v. *Lamb* (1844), 1 Coll. 489 (relationship to me by lineal descent, testator having no wife or issue).

7 *Best* v. *Stonehewer* (1864), 34 Beav. 66; on appeal (1865), 2 De G.J. & S. 537.

8 [1972] Ch. 379, at 383.

9 (1873), L.R. 16 Eq. 581.

10 His dicta on *Isaac* v. *Defriez* (1754), Amb. 595 were criticised by JESSEL M.R. in *A.-G.* v. *Duke of Northumberland* (1877), 7 Ch.D. 745. On the construction of "needy", "in need", see 29, *supra*.

11 *Re Drake's Will Trusts*, [1971] Ch. 179 C.A., overruling *Bernal* v. *Bernal* (1838), 3 My. & Cr. 559 (male descendants in want).

Where there is a preference to be given to descendants of the founder of an educational endowment the word is interpreted as meaning lineal descendants.

Relations

Gifts for the benefit of poor relations have already been discussed.[1] It will be remembered that in former times a distinction was drawn between perpetual trusts for the benefit of poor relations and trusts for distribution immediately or within the perpetuity period among poor relations. This distinction no longer applies. Not only are perpetual trusts for the benefit of poor relations charitable[2] but so too are gifts for poor relations intended for immediate distribution.[3]

The word "relation" is vague, and in order to prevent gifts to relations of a person from being void for uncertainty, the courts adopted a rule of construction that *prima facie* the word relations in a bequest means next of kin according to the Statutes of Distribution.[4] Yet if the gift is to *poor* relations and is construed as charitable, then since charitable gifts do not fail for uncertainty there is no need to construe the word "relations" restrictively. However the rule is established and so inevitably the question arises in each case: do the words "poor relations" mean "such of the statutory next of kin as are poor" or "such of the kindred of every degree as are poor"? There is even a third possibility namely that the word poor is used as a term of endearment: but such cases must be rare and do not call for particular comment.[5]

Where it is clear on the face of the trust document that the trust is to be a continuing or perpetual trust for "poor relations" that term can hardly be restricted to poor next of kin; and indeed so the courts reason.

The conflict of authorities on the charitable nature of bequests for immediate distribution of funds among poor relations (or distribution within the perpetuity period) has already been noted. Because some judges treated the gifts as not being charitable, those gifts could only be saved (as they were) by being construed as gifts to the next of kin. That was not a necessary construction where the court found the gift to be charitable. But once it was held, as it was held in *Re Scarisbrick*,[6] that a gift for immediate distribution among poor relations is *prima facie* charitable, only clear evidence of an intention to confine the benefit to statutory next of kin will displace that *prima facie* position.

Kinsmen or kindred

The words kinsman and kinswoman are used by some people[7] instead of "relation". And trusts for the benefit of poor kinsmen and kinswomen of the

---

1 See 32–35, *supra*.

2 *White v. White* (1802), 7 Ves. 423 (trust for apprenticing poor relations); *Isaac v. Defriez* (1754), Amb. 595 (poorest relations).

3 *Re Scarisbrick*, [1951] Ch. 622, C.A.

4 *Edge v. Salisbury* (1749), Amb. 70, [1558–1774] All E.R. Rep. 628; and see *Carr v. Bedford* (1678), 2 Rep. Ch. 146.

5 *Anon.* (1716), 1 P. Wms. 327; but see on this case *Sugden on Powers* (8th edn.), 654–655.

6 [1951] Ch. 622.

7 See Nancy Mitford, *Noblesse Oblige* (1956) 75. The Shorter Oxford English Dictionary (3rd edn.) classifies the word as literary. For obvious reasons it is used throughout Squibb, *Founders' Kin* (1972).

testator are treated like trusts for the benefit of poor relations. In *A.-G.* v. *Price* a trust of a fund to be distributed for ever among the testator's poor kinsmen and kinswomen and their issue dwelling in the county of Brecon was upheld as charitable.

There are numerous educational endowments still on foot with a preference for the kindred or kinsmen of the founder.[1] In such cases in the absence of any evidence of the founder's intentions[2] it is not sound construction to limit consanguinity to any degree. As WILMOT J. concluded in *Spencer* v. *All Souls College*[3] "no boundary line could ever be drawn to ... consanguinity, but by the hand of time, which sooner or later levels all distinctions of families, and obliterates every other memorial of Human Greatness".

Gifts to officeholders

Sometimes a testator will designate as the object of a particular bequest the holder of an office the duties of which are charitable.[4] A question then arises as to how the gift should be construed. Cases of this kind (which usually concern *religious* officeholders) abound, and they contain hair-splitting subtleties and refinements which even lawyers disdain.[5] But the cases can be subdivided into five recognisable categories.

PERSONAL GIFT

The testator may by the terms of his will have made it clear that the gift was a personal one. Thus in *Donnellan* v. *O'Neill*[6] there was a devise to Cardinal Cullen, and in case of his death, to the Roman Catholic Archbishop and his heirs etc. "absolutely for his and their own use and benefit" and the court had no difficulty in deducing that a personal gift was intended because the concluding words of the gift made this clear. Likewise in *Doe d. Phillips* v. *Aldridge*[7] a devise to the Rev. A. A. "late of Amesbury but now preacher at the meeting-house in Lyndhurst" for life was held a gift to him for his own benefit. KINDERSLEY V.C. in *Thornber* v. *Wilson*[8] observed that while a gift to a minister *as such* is a charitable bequest, a gift to "the person *now* minister" would have been different; for the testator might be unacquainted with his name, and so only be capable of describing him by his office.

---

1 See Squibb, *Founders' Kin* (1972), 127–167.
2 Francis Harrison a benefactor of Sedbergh School gave preference to kindred within five degrees: Squibb, *op. cit.*, 58 and 163.
3 (1762), Wilm. 163, at 169 and 176.
4 See Delany, "Gifts *Virtute Officii* to Donees of a Charitable Character" (1960), 24 Conveyancer N.S. 306.
5 See Hanbury and Maudsley, *Modern Equity* (10th edn.) 247 where the distinctions are said to "bring no credit to our jurisprudence".
6 (1870), I.R. 5 Eq. 525.
7 (1791), 4 Term. Rep. 264.
8 (1858), 4 Drew. 350, at 351.

GIFT TO OFFICEHOLDER SIMPLICITER

A gift to a person occupying an office of a charitable nature for the time being, or a gift to an officer "and his successors" without more, takes effect as a valid charitable gift for the purposes of the office in question.

Thus a gift to the minister belonging to the meeting house or chapel at a particular place is a gift to charity.[1] In *Re Braham*[2] a gift of income of residue directed to be paid in equal shares to the lecturer and reader of the Liverpool old Hebrew congregation was held a good charitable and not a beneficial trust. In *Re Ingleby*[3] where the term "resident priest" was construed, a bequest of the yearly sum of £20 on trust for "the resident priest for the time being of the Roman Catholic chapel in Lawkland" was held payable to a priest who kept a house at Lawkland, but usually lived at a mission six miles away.

A gift to the officiating minister at a particular place *and to his successors for ever* is even more clearly a perpetual trust for charity.[4] In *Re Delany*[5] there were gifts to named members of a religious community "*or*[6] their successors". It was unsuccessfully argued that the words "*or* their successors" were inserted, not to indicate the persons who might hold office at the time the gift took effect, but to prevent lapse. FARWELL J. commented that the primary meaning of the word "successors" is persons in succession and continued:[7]

> "The persons named were known to the testator to be holders of offices in the association, and the only succession to which he can refer is the succession to those offices."

On the other hand in *Robb and Reid* v. *Bishop Dorrian*[8] where there was a devise of land "to the Right Rev. P. Dorrian, Roman Catholic Bishop of Down and Connor, and his successor in said bishoprick" the judges differed as to whether this gave the defendant a life estate, or the fee, for his own use or was intended as a perpetual endowment of the bishoprick; but they held on other grounds that the plaintiffs had no right to the land in any case.

GIFT TO OFFICEHOLDER CONFERRING ON HIM COMPLETE DISCRETION

A gift to an officeholder of a charitable nature followed by super-added words which merely confer on him a complete discretion or impose on him some specific limitation within the scope of his office, is a valid charitable gift.

The leading case is *Re Garrard*[9] where there was a gift for the vicar and church

---

1 *A.-G.* v. *Cock* (1751), 2 Ves. Sen. 273; *Thornber* v. *Wilson* (1858), 4 Drew. 350; *A.-G.* v. *Sparks* (1753), Amb. 201; and see *In the Estate of Pesca* (1930), 74 Sol. Jo. 59; and *Re Van Wart* (1911), *Times*, 17th Feb.

2 (1892), 36 Sol. Jo. 712.

3 (1890), 34 Sol. Jo. 676.

4 *Thornber* v. *Wilson* (1855), 3 Drew. 245; *Anon.* (1680), 2 Vent. 349; *Gibson* v. *Representative Church Body* (1881), 9 L.R. Ir. 1; *A.-G.* v. *Molland* (1832), You. 562.

5 [1902] 2 Ch. 642.

6 Not "*and their successors*", as *Tudor on Charities* (6th edn.) 52 wrongly asserts.

7 [1902] 2 Ch. 642, at 646.

8 (1875), I.R. 9 C.L. 483; affd. (1877), I.R. 11 C.L. 293.

9 [1907] 1 Ch. 382.

wardens for the time being of a named parish "to be applied by them in such manner as they shall in their sole discretion think fit". JOYCE J. held that the bequest was a good charitable gift since the words used merely directed that "the particular mode of application within the charitable purposes of the legacy is to be settled by those individuals, or rather that there is power given by them to do it . . ."[1]. The decision in *Re Garrard* has been followed in a number of later cases. For example, a gift to a clergyman "for his work in the parish" was held in *Re Simson*[2] to be a valid gift *virtute officii* for charity. In *Re Norman*[3] a gift by a testatrix of the residue of her moneys to the editors of the missionary periodical "Echoes of Service" to be applied by them or him (*sic*) for such objects as they might think fit was upheld by VALSEY J. as a gift to the trustees of a charitable organisation who were obliged to apply it for such of the charitable purposes of the organisation as they thought fit. Likewise a gift to a Roman Catholic archbishop for the time being "to be used by him for such purposes as he shall in his absolute discretion think fit" is a gift to charity.[4] So, too, is a gift to a bishop "for such purposes in the diocese as he wishes"[5] or a gift to the vicar and churchwardens of a named parish "for any purposes they might think proper to apply it".[6]

Again, a gift to be applied by a bishop in his discretion for such charitable purposes as he should think fit[7] or direct[8] is valid in accordance with the principle of *Re Garrard*, as is a gift to the Archbishop of Westminster on trust that he should forthwith "in his absolute discretion devote the same to the furtherance of educational or charitable or religious purposes for Roman Catholics in the British Empire in such manner in all respects as he may think fit."[9]

In *Re Rumball*[10] the testator left his residuary estate "to the bishop for the time being of the diocese of the Windward Islands to be used by him as he thinks fit in his diocese". The Court of Appeal unanimously upheld the decision of DANCKWERTS J. at first instance that this gift constituted a valid charitable trust. The question before the court was whether the words "to be used by him as he thinks fit in his diocese" were merely super-added words conferring wide powers of disposition, or were words imposing trusts which according to their terms were not, exclusively or necessarily, of a charitable nature. In other words had the testator left the purposes of the gift to be implied from the charitable character of the bishop's office, and merely added a provision to the effect that the bishop was to have full discretion in the application of the fund for these purposes, or had he defined the trusts on which the property was to be held in terms capable of including objects which were not charitable? The Court

---

1 *Ibid.*, at 384.
2 [1946] Ch. 299. The cure of souls in the particular parish is the *work* or function of the vicar and such work is charitable; see *per* ROMER J., at 301.
3 [1947] Ch. 349.
4 *Re Flinn*, [1948] Ch. 241.
5 *Halpin* v. *Hannon* (1948), 82 I. L.T. 74 (BLACK J. dissenting); *cf. Re Beddy*, unreported, [1956] Ch. 105, at 120 ("to use for such purposes in the diocese as he may choose": void). The latter case was not expressly endorsed by the Court of Appeal in *Re Rumball* and seems wrong.
6 *Re Hurley* (1900), 17 T.L.R. 115; *cf. Cunningham* v. *Talbot*, [1932] 3 D.L.R. 665; *Re Green*, [1942] V.L.R. 210.
7 *Copinger* v. *Crehane* (1877), 1 I.R. Eq. 429.
8 *Blount* v. *Viditz*, [1895] 1 I.R. 42.
9 *Re Ward*, [1941] Ch. 308.
10 [1956] Ch. 105, C.A.

of Appeal concluded that the question should be answered in the former sense. A gift to the bishop for the time being, without more, would have been charitable. The addition of the words "to be used by him as he thinks fit" merely directed the bishop that he was to settle the particular mode of application within the charitable purposes of the legacy (that is to say, ecclesiastical purposes in his diocese); and the words "in his diocese" were no more than an expression of that which would have been implied in any event.[1] In the result the super-added words added nothing. It seems likely that other words of *restriction* would be treated in the same way as words of territorial restriction[2] e.g. restrictions as to time or quantum or[3] excluding some specified charitable purpose.

GIFT TO OFFICEHOLDER WHERE SUPER-ADDED WORDS ARE RESTRICTIVE

In some cases the words used by a testator mark out the objects of the gift as clearly confined within the orbit of the officeholder's charitable functions. The gift remains charitable.

In *Re Bain*[4] the testatrix made a residuary bequest to the vicar of a particular parish "for such objects connected with the Church as he shall think fit". EVE J. held that "objects connected with the Church" were so wide and vague that they might fall far outside any religious purposes; and he held that the gift failed. All the members of the Court of Appeal considered that "the Church" meant the particular parish church in question.[5] The majority of the court in order to save the gift[6] construed the words "objects connected with the Church" in a narrow sense as meaning "for the fabric of the church and for the services which are conducted therein". But RUSSELL L.J. dissenting "with diffidence" was of the opinion that the natural meaning of the words used by the testatrix was that she wished the fund to be applied to some or all of the various objects run by or under the aegis of the particular parish church; and he saw no reason to depart from the natural meaning of the words.[7]

The decision in *Re Bain* was followed by JENKINS J. in *Re Eastes*[8] where the testatrix bequeathed her residuary estate on trust to pay the income to the vicar and churchwardens of a named church to be used by them "for any purposes in connexion with the said church which they may select, it being my wish that they shall especially bear in mind the requirements of the children in the said parish of" the named church, and further directed that they should not use any portion of the moneys in connection with overseas missions. The learned judge rejected the argument that the words "connected with" or "in connexion with" necessarily have an enlarging effect. This argument was based on *Re Davies*[9] where the relevant words were "for work connected with the Roman

---

1 [1956] Ch. 105, C.A., at 124, *per* JENKINS L.J.

2 See 71 L.Q.R. 466 (R.E.M.).

3 EVERSHED M.R. expressly dealt with this in *Re Rumball*, [1956] Ch. 105, at 118.

4 [1930] 1 Ch. 224, C.A.

5 *Ibid.*, at 232, 234, 235. If they had construed "the Church" to mean the Church of England the case would have been like *Re Davies* (1932), 49 T.L.R. 5.

6 "If we were to give a loose interpretation to the words . . . we should be violating the rule which requires us to make an effort to give an effective interpretation to the testatrix's words": *per* Lord HANWORTH M.R., at 232.

7 [1930] 1 Ch. 224, C.A. at 236.

8 [1948] Ch. 257.

9 (1932), 49 T.L.R. 5.

Catholic Church in the Archdiocese of Cardiff". But that case is distinguishable from *Re Bain*, as JENKINS J. was at pains to show. In the result the words "for any purpose in connexion with the said church" were virtually indistinguishable from the words used in *Re Bain* and JENKINS J. found nothing else in the super-added words (whose effect he held to be merely precatory) to cause him to place some different construction on the primary trust from the construction placed on the primary trust in *Re Bain*. It is worth noting that in Australia it has been held that the "purposes" of a particular church are not synonymous with the activities of that church.[1] Moreover an Australian court has also held that the expression "Church purposes", whether used generically or in connection with a particular sacred edifice administered by a minister of the Christian religion, denotes religious and *prima facie* charitable purposes.[2]

A gift to the General of the Salvation Army "for corps purposes" has been upheld as a valid charitable gift.[3]

GIFT TO OFFICEHOLDER WHERE SUPER-ADDED WORDS HAVE ENLARGING EFFECT

Unless he is very circumspect a testator who puts a gloss on his gift to an officeholder runs the risk of defeating his own purpose. For if the language used by him is wide enough to include purposes which would not be charitable in law, then notwithstanding the charitable character of his trustee, the gift will fail: the court will not, in such a case, look to the character of the trustee in order to cut down those purposes.

Thus, in *Re Davidson*,[4] a gift to the Archbishop of Westminster for the time being "to be divided amongst such bodies as he shall in his absolute discretion think fit" was held to be void. FARWELL L.J. refused to accept the argument that inasmuch as the gift was to a Roman Catholic Archbishop of a particular archdiocese for the time being the gift was a gift to a religious office and was therefore *prima facie* charitable. His ground for doing so was that the gift was not to the Archbishop for the time being for the *religious* purposes of his archdiocese,[5] but was for what was actually specified immediately afterwards. The argument that the Archbishop could, in fact, apply the gift to *ecclesiastical* purposes alone was irrelevant. The question is not whether the trustee may not apply it upon purposes strictly charitable, but whether he is bound so to apply it.[6]

The case of *Dunne* v. *Byrne*[7] provided a similar result. There a residuary bequest by a testator, who was a Roman Catholic priest, "to the Roman Catholic Archbishop of Brisbane and his successors to be used wholly or in part as such Archbishop may judge most conducive to the good of religion in his diocese" was held by the Privy Council to be void. Lord MACNAGHTEN, who delivered the judgment of the Privy Council, pointed out that it would be in the discretion of the Archbishop to apply the fund to other than charitable objects,

---

1 *Re Moroney, Maguire* v. *Reilly* (1939), 39 S.R. N.S.W. 249.
2 *Ibid.*
3 *Re Lawler* (1914), 31 T.L.R. 102.
4 [1909] 1 Ch. 567.
5 *Ibid.*, at 572.
6 See *Morice* v. *Bishop of Durham* (1805), 10 Ves. 522.
7 [1912] A.C. 407, P.C.

to purposes which he might think conducive to the good of religion whether in law charitable or not; and he gave as an example a trust for the benefit of a closed order,[1] which a devout Roman Catholic would no doubt consider conducive to the good of religion but which is certainly not charitable.[2]

There are several other cases where enlarging words have invalidated the gift to the officeholder. In *Re Stratton*[3] a bequest of money to the vicar of a parish for the time being on trust to distribute the same "among such parochial institutions or purposes as he shall select" failed because, it was held, "parochial institutions or purposes" might include objects which were not charitable. So, too, a gift to a vicar "for his benevolent work" failed,[4] as did a gift to the Archbishop of Wales for the time being to be applied "in his discretion in any manner as he might think best for helping to carry on the work of the Church in Wales".[5] Again a gift "for work connected with the Roman Catholic Church in the said Archdiocese"[6] and a gift to the Pope "to use and apply at his sole and absolute discretion in the carrying out of the sacred office"[7] have both been held void for uncertainty, the latter on the ground that the Pope had functions which were not charitable.

In *Farley* v. *Westminster Bank*[8] it was held that bequests to the vicars and churchwardens of two parishes "for parish work" were not charitable. The words "parish work" (it was held) would in their ordinary sense include objects which were not charitable. Lord ATKIN expressly approved[9] what had been said in the court below by Sir WILFRED GREENE M.R.[10] who considered that the words "parish work" covered "any activity in the parish, any work in the parish which trustees of that character may be expected to perform, whether that work be strictly a religious purpose or strictly a charitable purpose, or whether it be a work considered to be conducive to the good of religion, or considered to be benevolent or generally useful to the inhabitants of the parish or the congregation of the church". The words could not be cut down or limited, either by construing them in isolation, or by reference to the character of the trustees.[11]

One case cited in vain to the House of Lords in *Farley's* case was the Australian case of *Re Macgregor*[12] where the cases on the subject were elaborately reviewed. The bequests in the Australian case were to the Anglican Bishop for the time being of the Diocese of Grafton and Armidale "for diocesan purposes" and for "diocesan purposes generally". LONG INNES J. upheld the bequests on the ground that strictly every diocesan purpose proper was a religious purpose and therefore a charitable purpose in the legal sense. In the light of *Farley's* case this decision is probably now bad law. Significantly the principles laid down in *Dunne* v.

---

1 [1914] A.C. 407, at 410–411.

2 See *Cocks* v. *Manners* (1871), L.R. 12 Eq. 574; *Gilmour* v. *Coats*, [1949] A.C. 426.

3 [1931] 1 Ch. 197; *Aliter* if the gift is for *"church* purposes" in the parish: *Re Moroney* (1939), 39 S.R.N.S.W. 483.

4 *Re Simson*, [1946] Ch. 299.

5 *Re Jackson*, [1930] 2 Ch. 389.

6 *Re Davis* (1932), 49 T.L.R. 5.

7 *Re Moore*, [1919] 1 I.R. 316.

8 [1939] A.C. 430.

9 [1939] A.C. 430, at 435.

10 *Re Ashton*, [1938] Ch. 482, at 495–496.

11 [1938] Ch. 482, at 496.

12 (1932), 32 S.R. N.S.W. 483, at 498 following *Re Van Wart* (1911), *Times*, 17th Feb. to Archbishop for parochial purposes of his diocese.

Byrne[1] and *Farley* v. *Westminster Bank, Ltd.*[2] were applied in *Queensland Trustees, Ltd.* v. *Halse*[3] where the residuary gift was "to the Archbishop for the time being of the Corporation of the Synod of the Diocese of Brisbane to apply the income thereof as he shall in his sole and uncontrolled discretion think fit for the benefit of the said Diocese". The kernel of the judgment of the majority in the Supreme Court of Queensland is contained in the following words of MACROSSAN C.J.:[4]

> "I am unable to see how it is reasonably possible to give a narrower meaning to the phrase 'for the benefit of the diocese' than to the phrase 'most conducive to the good of religion in the diocese' so as to be able to hold that a bequest for the former purpose would be valid even though a bequest for the latter purpose must fail as the Privy Council held that it must. Surely any thing that can properly be described as being 'most conducive to the good of religion in a diocese' could not be excluded from the category of things for the benefit of the diocese."

Equally what is "most conducive to the good of religion in the diocese" must surely be a *diocesan* purpose.[5]

In *Re McCauley*[6] a testator had devised land to a bishop in trust for "the use of the Catholic Diocese of London Ontario". As STREET J. observed not all diocesan objects are charitable and so the gift was not to a charitable use. "A devise to a bishop in trust simply for his diocese is not a devise to a 'charitable use'.... A devise direct to the diocese would certainly not be a devise to a charitable use, and a devise to the Bishop in trust for the diocese does not help the matter."

A more liberal attitude is perhaps discernible in some of the more recent cases in Canada. In *Roman Catholic Archiepiscopal Corporation of Winnipeg* v. *Ryan*[7] there was a bequest to the appellant corporation "for the benefit of the Church of the Immaculate Conception . . . or otherwise as [the corporation] shall see fit". At first instance the gift was construed as a gift upon trust and the words "or otherwise" were held to take the gift outside the ambit of charity, because the corporation was given a discretion by those words to use the gift for other than charitable purposes. On appeal the appellants argued for the first time that the gift was an absolute gift to the corporation. This contention was upheld but one member of the appellate court O'HALLORAN J.A. added that even if the gift was a gift on trust, it was charitable because "it was clearly for the advancement and propagation of religion".[8] Another example of benignant construction is to be found in *Blais* v. *Touchet*[9] where the testator, himself a priest, left his estate to "Mgr Léo Blais, évêque de Prince Albert pour ses œuvres, mais pour les œuvres qui aideraient la cause des Canadiens Français dans son diocèse." The passage of the case through the courts illustrates the vagaries of the law in this field. At first instance, the bequest was held to be charitable. The Saskatchewan Court of Appeal held that it was not. Both the trial judge and the Court

---

1 [1912] A.C. 407.
2 [1939] A.C. 430.
3 [1949] St.R.Qd. 270.
4 [1949] St.R.Qd., 270, at 276.
5 See *Dunne* v. *Byrne*, [1912] A.C. 407.
6 (1892), 28 O.R. 610.
7 (1957), 12 D.L.R. 2d 23.
8 (1957), 12 D.L.R. 2d 23, at 25.
9 [1963] S.C.R. 358.

of Appeal were of the opinion that the bishop did not take beneficially, but as trustee, and that by virtue of his office the gift was limited to his charities or works arising from his religious responsibilities as the bishop. The trial judge held that by saying "mais pour ses œuvres qui aideraient les Canadians Français" the testator was merely confining the charities within a certain field and that these were words of limitation in no way affecting the gift as a charity. The Court of Appeal, on the other hand, held that these words enlarged the field of application of the gift and no longer made it imperative to apply it to purposes strictly charitable. The case then went on appeal to the Supreme Court of Canada, and the appeal was allowed. The Supreme Court held that "this particular gift to the bishop was charitable by virtue of his office and the testator did not step outside the charitable field in imposing the limitation to work among French Canadians".[1]

Mention should also be made of *Re Whitehead*[2] where a bequest to a bishop "to be applied by him for such general or special purposes in connection with" a named cathedral church "as he in his absolute and uncontrolled discretion may think fit" was held to be charitable. Such a bequest may (it seems) be applied in paying the stipend of an honorary canon having a stall in the cathedral, even though his main work lies outside the parish in which the cathedral is situate, or of a canon missioner with duties inside the cathedral though liable to be employed in the diocese outside the parish, but may not be applied in paying the stipend of a canon missioner with general diocesan duties and having only an honorary stall in the cathedral.

---

1 [1963] S.C.R. 358, at 361, *per* JUDSON J.
2 (1908), *Times*, 14th Oct.

Chapter 19

Variation, Alteration or Revocation of Charitable Trusts

Variation

Once a charity has been founded and its trusts have been declared those trusts cannot be revoked varied or added to by the founder[1] or founders[2] unless a valid power of appointment or revocation was reserved at the time the trusts were declared. Thus in *Re Holloway's Trusts*[3] the deed poll founding the Royal Holloway College contained an express power for a majority of three quarters of the governors to revoke or alter the rules and regulations governing the college and that power enabled the relevant majority to change a rule which barred the appointment of a woman governor. Sometimes a scheme will contain a power to modify the provisions of the scheme.[4] Indeed one convenient method of forestalling applications to the Commissioners for amendment of a scheme in respect of some relatively administrative matter is for the scheme to provide that the trustees shall have power to make byelaws and to amend the same for the administrative convenience of the charity.

The rule which prohibits any variation or addition to trusts binds the trustee as well as the founder or founders. In *Baldry* v. *Feintuck*[5] the officers of a university students' union were seeking to apply union funds to objects charitable and non-charitable outside the objects of the union which was charitable. It was held that they could be restrained by injunction from so doing.

In default of any enabling provision in the trust instrument or scheme governing the charity alterations of its trusts can only be effected by the court or the Charity Commissioners in the exercise of the jurisdiction to make *cy-près* schemes.[6] In rare cases an alteration may be made under the Variation of Trusts Act 1958. Such a case was *Re Roberts' Settlement Trusts*[7] where the court approved on behalf of the settlor's spectral spouses[8] an arrangement excluding the settlor and any wife of his from benefit under a charitable trust.

---

1 *Re Hartshill Endowment* (1861), 30 Beav. 130.
2 *A.-G.* v. *Kell* (1840), 2 Beav. 575; *A.-G.* v. *Bovill* (1840), 1 Ph. 762 (a body of subscribers).
3 (1909), 26 T.L.R. 62; and see *Re Harrison* (1915), 85 L.J. Ch. 77.
4 *Re Jewish Orphanage Endowment Trusts*, [1960] 1 W.L.R. 344.
5 [1972] 1 W.L.R. 552.
6 CA 1960, s. 18.
7 (1959), *Times*, 27th Feb.
8 As to these creatures, see *Re Steed's Will Trusts*, [1960] Ch. 407, at 420.

Power to revoke charitable trusts

If the trustees of a charitable trust are given a power to revoke the trusts and to declare new non-charitable trusts the mere existence of this unexercised power does not make the original trusts non-charitable.[1] There has, apparently, been no decision on the validity of such a power except in relation to the rule against perpetuities.[2] In *Re Sir Robert Peel's School at Tamworth*[3] a testator had given a fund to trustees to apply the income in supporting a school which he had founded but had reserved a power of revocation to the person for the time being entitled to his devised estates. The tenant for life had become the sole trustee and was refusing to render accounts to the Charity Commissioners on the basis that the trusts were not for exclusively charitable purposes in view of the power of revocation. The leading judgment of PAGE WOOD L.J. assumed that the power was valid and held that a charity is no less a charity because its endowment is not perpetual but subject to revocation. In *Gibson* v. *South American Stores (Gath and Chaves), Ltd.*[4] the reasoning of PAGE WOOD L.J. was accepted; here again the validity of the power was not in issue: the court was merely concerned with the effect of its presence on the status of the trust.

In one case concerning a trust constituted *inter vivos* the trustees' power of revocation was *not* limited to the perpetuity period and permitted new non-charitable trusts to be declared: the power was held to be void *ab initio*.[5]

---

1 *Gibson* v. *South American Stores (Gath and Chaves), Ltd.*, [1950] Ch. 177, C.A. But it may mean that for tax purposes the trust is not established for charitable purposes only: *George Drexler Ofrex Foundation Trustees* v. *I.R.Comrs.*, [1966] Ch. 675; *cf. I.R.Comrs.* v. *Yorkshire Agricultural Society*, [1928] 1 K.B. 611.

2 *Re Watson's Settlement Trusts*, [1959] 1 W.L.R. 732.

3 (1868), 3 Ch. App. 543.

4 [1950] Ch. 177, C.A.

5 *Re Watson's Settlement Trusts*, [1959] 1 W.L.R. 732.

Chapter 20

Delegation of Power to Determine Objects or Nominate Beneficiaries

The general rule is clear that a testator making his will must declare his wishes, and not leave it in wide and uncertain terms to someone else to make a will for him. Special treatment is, however, meted out to a gift for charitable purposes, and in that case the courts have recognised that it is open to a testator who declares a charitable purpose to leave it to his trustees to select the charities for whose benefit his fund is to be applied.[1] This special treatment is only available "so long as charitable and no other objects may benefit".[2] The exception from the general principle that the testator has to decide in his will the specific destination of his property is allowed because of the special favour which the English law shows to charities.[3]

There are many examples of cases where a delegated power to determine the particular charitable object to be benefited has been accepted as valid. Thus a trust for such charitable institutions as trustees consider worthy,[4] or for such charitable purposes and bequests to such of my relations as my trustees may think proper,[5] or for such charitable purposes as they shall see fit[6] or for such charitable institutions and schemes as my trustees shall in their absolute discretion select[7] is valid. Likewise a gift among such protestant charitable institutions as my trustees may deem proper and advisable[8] or to be invested in war charities at trustees' discretion to be selected by trustees is good.[9] Equally a trust for such charitable purpose as "Archbishop" should direct[10] is valid. Again a bequest to such charitable objects of a definite class as the trustees select is valid and not void for uncertainty.[11]

Whether the trustees are to appoint capital or income to the selected object

---

1 *A.-G.* v. *National Provincial and Union Bank of England*, [1924] A.C. 262, at 264, *per* Lord CAVE L.C.

2 *Chichester Diocesan Fund and Board of Finance (Incorporated)* v. *Simpson*, [1944] A.C. 341, at 371, *per* Lord SIMONDS.

3 *Ibid.*, at 348, *per* VISCOUNT SIMON L.C.

4 *In the Will of Nilen*, [1908] V.L.R. 332.

5 *Re Green*, [1942] V.L.R. 210.

6 *Re Cohn*, [1952] 3 D.L.R. 833; *Copinger* v. *Crehane* (1877), I.R. 11 Eq. 429; and see *Doe d. Vancott* v. *Read* (1847), 3 U.C.R. 244.

7 *Cunningham* v. *Talbot*, [1932] 3 D.L.R. 665; *Re Cunningham's Estate* (1932), 45 B.C.R. 543; and see *Re Gilliland*, [1956] 10 D.L.R (2d) 769.

8 *Manning* v. *Robinson* (1898), 29 O.R. 483.

9 *Re Hammond* (1921), 68 D.L.R. 599.

10 *Blount* v. *Viditz*, [1895] 1 I.R. 42.

11 See *Re Garrard*, [1907] 1 Ch. 382; *Re Bennett*, [1920] 1 Ch. 305; *Re Bain*, [1930] 1 Ch. 224, C.A.; *Re Norman*, [1947] Ch. 349; *Re Flinn*, [1948] Ch. 241; *Re Eastes*, [1948] Ch. 257.

is a question of construction.[1] The question arose in *Re Beesty's Will Trusts*[2] where the testatrix left a bequest in the following terms:

> "The net revenue of my estate I give to my brother and sister for their lives and at their deaths to go to charities which they may have selected during their lives. Having given largely to charities and to help win the Great War which was very costly to myself I am not leaving money directly to charities."

WILBERFORCE J. thought that he was entitled to have regard to the fact that money was not given directly to the charities, but that instead the brother and sister were enabled to make dispositions in favour of charities. Having regard to the incomplete language used, the will could be read as conferring a power on the brother and sister to make a disposition of the *capital* to charity. The testatrix did not in terms make a gift of income in favour of the charities and such an intention should not be imputed unless one finds some indication that an endowment or trust fund shall be set up.

The court will modify an appointment which is clearly not in conformity with the testator's wishes. In *A.-G.* v. *Buller*[3] there was a bequest for the relief of the poor in such parishes and in such manner as the trustees should think fit, but so that the parish of St. Nicholas in Rochester should be one of those benefited. A small part of the income had been devoted[4] to the only named parish the rest of it had been applied to purposes in a parish in Devon. The court varied the application of income by splitting it between the two parishes in equal shares and would have enlarged the list of participating parishes had it been practicable. On the other hand, where the trustees are given the widest possible discretion within certain limits in the choice of objects, they need not exercise their discretion in accordance with the known views of the testator.[5]

If the person to whom the power of determination is delegated does not exercise it, the gift does not fail on that account. Hence a gift does not fail because a trustee neglects to appoint[6] or an executor renounces[7] or because his appointment is revoked[8] or because the person given the power to nominate the beneficiary does in the lifetime of the testator.[9] The gift is likewise still valid even though the name of the intended nominator has been left blank[10] or the trustees or nominator have refused to act,[11] or have died without exercising the discretion.[12]

---

1 Likewise the question whether the discretion extends to the *whole* gift: see *Re Hall's Charity* (1851), 14 Beav. 115.

2 [1966] Ch. 223.

3 (1822), Jac. 407.

4 Under a scheme.

5 *Re Squire's Trusts* (1901), 17 T.L.R. 724 ("sole uncontrolled discretion"). The history of the bequest is discussed in Squibb, *Founders' Kin* (1972), 133–134.

6 *Re Douglas* (1887), 35 Ch.D. 472.

7 *A.-G.* v. *Fletcher* (1835), 5 L.J. Ch. 75. Subsequently appointed trustees cannot exercise the power: *Hibbard* v. *Lamb* (1756), Amb. 309.

8 *White* v. *White* (1778), 1 Bro. C.C. 12; *Moggridge* v. *Thackwell* (1803), 7 Ves. 36, at 78.

9 *Moggridge* v. *Thackwell, supra*; *Re Willis*, [1921] 1 Ch. 44. *Aliter* if the personality of the trustee is crucial: see the cases cited at 280–281, *infra*.

10 *Baylis* v. *A.-G.* (1741), 2 Atk. 239; *contra: Angus's Executrix* v. *Batchan's Trustees* 1949 S.C. 335.

11 *Doyley* v. *A.-G.* (1735), 2 Eq. Cas. Abr. 194.

12 *A.-G.* v. *Bucknall* (1742), 2 Atk. 328.

The right to nominate who shall be a beneficiary of the charity (known as "patronage") is a more particular power of selection. Like visitation it belongs naturally to the founder of the charity and his heirs[1] or nominees.[2] Unlike visitation it is not limited to corporations. Thus the founder of an almshouse and his heirs have the right of nominating the alms people but may forfeit it by a corrupt or improper nomination of persons who are not fit objects of the charity or by making no nominations at all after notice of the vacancy.[3]

The right of nomination is capable of being alienated either expressly or by implication.

In *A.-G. v. Brentwood School*[4] a grammar school was founded and endowed under letters patent which prescribed that the school should be completely in the patronage and disposition of the founder and his heirs and that the schoolmasters and guardians should be nominated by them forever. Accordingly held that the right of patronage might be lawfully alienated. The testator in *A.-G. v. Boucherét*[5] bequeathed a sum to a trustee upon trust to lay it out in lands for the endowment of a school and appointed that the trustee and his heirs "should be feoffees in trust and patrons and protectors of the said school for the electing a fit and sufficient schoolmaster". Sir JOHN ROMILLY M.R. held that the right of patronage was quite as much within the power of alienation as it was in *A.-G. v. Brentwood School*:[6] in both cases there was a trust to be performed namely the appointment of a fit and proper schoolmaster.

The right of nomination may also pass by implication. In *A.-G. v. Dean and Canons of Christ Church*[7] property was devised to the defendants in trust to constitute and support a grammar school at Portsmouth, to appoint a master and usher, and pay them a salary. The trustees were given the power to direct the management of the school. The power to nominate free scholars was held to be implicit in the other powers. Lord ELDON L.C. posed the rhetorical question:[8] "Is it not part of the management to nominate and send to the school the persons who are to be educated?"

Where the right of nomination is vested in subscribers to a charity who vote in proportion to the amount of their subscriptions, bargains between individual voters as to the way each shall vote, where the only consideration for the bargain is the vote of the other party are not against public policy and are therefore enforceable.[9]

When trustees have to select charitable objects they must comply with the directions laid down in the instrument of foundation.[10] Accordingly if the beneficiaries are required to possess certain qualifications, for example, to be parishioners of a certain parish,[11] or to have been pupils at a particular school for a period of years immediately before election,[12] the persons exercising the power

---

1 Descent to the heir has been abolished: the effect on patronage is unclear.
2 *A.-G. v. Leigh* (1721), 3 P. Wms. 145 n.; *Green v. Rutherforth* (1750), 1 Ves. Sen. 462; *Philips v. Bury* (1694), 2 Term Rep. 346, at 352–353.
3 *A.-G. v. Leigh* (1721), 3 P. Wms. 145 n.
4 (1832), 3 B. & Ad. 59.
5 (1858), 25 Beav. 116.
6 (1832), 2 B. & Ad. 59.
7 (1822), Jac. 474; and see *A.-G. v. Scott* (1750), 1 Ves. Sen. 413.
8 (1822), Jac. 474, at 486.
9 *Bolton v. Madden* (1873), L.R. 9 Q.B. 55.
10 For the consequences of non-compliance, see 194, *infra*.
11 *Etherington v. Wilson* (1875), 1 Ch.D. 160, C.A.
12 *Re Storie's University Gift* (1860), 3 L.T. 638.

of nomination must see that the beneficiaries are properly qualified. In *Re Nettle's Charity*[1] the scheme of management at a grammar school provided for a scholarship tenable at Oxford or Cambridge and open to any child of any resident inhabitant of Guildford "preference being given *ceteris paribus* to the son of a freeman of the town of Guildford". There was a competitive examination and it was held that the preference could only be exercised where the difference in performance between two candidates was very slight. If one candidate plainly had the advantage over the other (as was the case) there was no room for the preference of the son of a freeman.

The motive prompting the acquisition of a qualification is usually irrelevant. In *Etherington* v. *Wilson*[2] it was in effect held at first instance[3] that a man is not entitled to be considered qualified for a benefit if he expressly and avowedly obtains the qualification for that purpose and that purpose alone. This proposition was firmly rejected as wrong by the Court of Appeal. JAMES L.J. said:[4]

> "A man has a right to give himself, if he can, a qualification. If he does so, then he is qualified, and there is no equity to deprive a man of that qualification which the law entitles him to get."

Of course the scheme in question may make special provisions to prevent a man from benefiting where the qualification was obtained *ad hoc*: that is another matter. Equally if a person conforms with the rules of a charity requiring certain religious observances, the trustees are not entitled to examine him as to his sincerity[5].

Where a nomination does not comply with the directions of the instrument of foundation it may be set aside,[6] unless it was made in good faith in the mistaken construction of the scheme.[7] In *Re Storie's University Gift*[8] the election of a pupil from Shrewsbury School to an exhibition tenable at Oxford or Cambridge was impeached because although at one time the pupil had been at Wakefield School for three years he had been at Shrewsbury School for the five years preceding his election. The gift, it was held, required a successful candidate to have been at Wakefield School for the three years immediately preceding election. But the exhibitioner in question had proceeded to University and some 11 months had elapsed between his election and the presentation of the petition. The Court of Appeal in Chancery which reversed the decision of Sir JOHN ROMILLY M.R.[9] was affected by this delay and by the injustice that would result to an innocent party in displacing the successful candidate as well as by the fact that the learned Master of the Rolls had reached a different conclusion on the construction of the scheme. The governors had made an honest mistake and the court in its discretion would not disturb it.[10] TURNER L.J. also rejected the contention that the court could in the circumstances substitute another candi-

---

1 (1872), L.R. 14 Eq. 434.
2 (1875), 1 Ch.D. 160, C.A.
3 (1875), L.R. 20 Eq. 606 (MALINS V.-C.).
4 (1875), 1 Ch.D. 160, at 166.
5 *A.-G.* v. *Calvert* (1857), 23 Beav. 248.
6 *Re Nettle's Charity* (1872), L.R. 14 Eq. 434.
7 *Re Storie's University Gift* (1860), 3 L.T. 638.
8 (1860), 3 L.T. 638.
9 (1860), 2 L.T. 559; and see *A.-G.* v. *Rigby* (1732), 3 P. Wms. 145 (payments made by wrong persons allowed to stand with no order for an account).
10 Following *A.-G.* v. *Hartley* (1820), 2 Jac. & W. 353.

date: under the scheme the election rested with the governors, and the court could not elect for them.[1]

A person claiming to be a proper object of a charity and wishing to apply to the court to set aside the election of a particular person must first obtain the authorisation of the Charity Commissioners, unless the charity in question is an exempt charity.[2]

---

1 (1860), 3 L.T. 638, at 641–642.
2 CA 1960, s. 28 (2); and see *Rooke* v. *Dawson*, [1895] 1 Ch. 480. As to exempt charities, see 4–6, *supra*.

Chapter 21

Surplus Income

Testators or donors do not always expressly provide that the *whole* income of a fund or estate is to go to charity. They sometimes provide that a specific sum or specific sums shall be paid out of income to one or more charitable objects. A question then arises as to whether the intention was to devote the whole income (from time to time) to charity or just the aggregate of the specified sums.

The problem of surplus income is conventionally discussed in connection with the *cy-près* doctrine.[1] This is no doubt because judges such as Lord THURLOW[2] and Sir RICHARD ARDEN M.R.[3] treated cases of surplus income as applications of that doctrine. But it is questionable whether all the surplus income cases are properly classified as examples of the application of *cy-près*. Except in the limited sense that "the court reserves to itself the disposition of such a surplus with the view of taking care, that it shall be applied under the control of the court *as nearly as possible* to the uses and purposes to which the testator meant his property to be subservient."[4] The classic operation of the *cy-près* doctrine is where there is a *failure* of the charitable object in question: sometimes the failure is initial, sometimes it is supervening. But in many surplus income cases there is no failure or impossibility. All that the court is faced with is a question of construction: should the surplus go to a *subsisting* charitable purpose (or subsisting charitable purposes) designated by the testator in his will? The approach to be adopted in answering this question was, according to Lord CAMPBELL in *A.-G. v. Windsor (Dean & Canons)*,[5] that one:

> "must look at the instruments to be construed and see whether, taking them altogether, we discover an intention on the part of the donors that the [income] should be divided in certain proportions and given to the different objects of the bounty of the donors in those proportions, or whether the intention manifested is that specified sums should be permanently paid to particular objects of the bounty of the donors, and that they should be entitled to nothing more than the payment of these specified sums, without abatement and without argumentation".

The variety of situations giving rise to problems of surplus income is attested by the volume of case law. Such problems do not arise in practice very often

---

1 See *Tudor on Charities* (6th edn.). As to the *cy-près* doctrine, see Chapters 24 and 25, *post*.
2 *A.-G. v. Painters-Stainers Co.* (1788), 2 Cox Eq. Cas. 51.
3 *A.-G. v. Earl of Winchelsea* (1791), 3 Bro. C.C. 373. See *A.-G. v. Minshull* (1798), 4 Ves. 11.
4 See *per* Lord ELDON L.J. in *A.-G. v. Coopers Co.* (1812), 19 Ves. 187, at 189.
5 (1860), 8 H.L. Cas. 369, at 393.

nowadays no doubt because testamentary gifts of income in favour of charity are not favoured. The only recent case on the subject is *Re Lepton's Charity*[1] where the provisions of section 13 of the Charities Act 1960 were invoked.

The cases can conveniently be divided into the following categories: (1) when the whole property is given and there is a surplus when the gift takes effect, (2) where there is an express gift of the surplus, (3) where there is no express gift of any surplus and the income is not exhausted (initial surplus); and (4) where there is no express gift of any surplus and the income is exhausted at the date of the gift ("subsequent surplus").

Whole property given

The first situation to be considered is the one where a testator has purported to deal with the whole income from a particular property but at the date of his death it emerges that there is an immediate surplus. This may happen because specific sums are directed to go to particular objects with the balance to go to another object, and the income exceeds the needs of the residual object. Thus in *A.-G.* v. *Earl of Winchelsea*[2] a will directed specific sums to be paid out of income to particular charities and the residue (if any) to be expended in apprenticing three children. The amount available for the latter purpose was more than sufficient. Sir RICHARD ARDEN M.R. held that the next of kin were not entitled to the surplus which should be applied to the charitable purposes mentioned in the will and he directed a scheme to be brought in. On a true construction of the will the testator had intended to devote the whole income to charity and had been merely mistaken as to the quantum available. The testator in *Arnold* v. *A.-G.*[3] had made his intention equally clear. Having expressed his determination to settle certain lands for charitable uses he devised an estate to trustee to pay annuities amounting in all to £120 per annum. He left £2 out of his personal estate to his heir at law. The estate produced £240 per annum at the date of his death: the surplus went to the charities. Another example is to be found in *A.-G.* v. *Minshull*[4] where the testator directed the income of certain property to be used for apprenticing children with a restriction of £10 for each child. At the date of the will this was considered a suitable amount and it was thought that there would be a sufficient number of objects to exhaust the whole provision. The available surplus was therefore used to increase the amount of the apprentice fees. In both *A.-G.* v. *Minshull* and *A.-G.* v. *Earl of Winchelsea* Sir RICHARD ARDEN M.R. referred to *A.-G.* v. *Bishop of Oxford*[5] and expressed the view that the doctrine of *cy-près* had hitherto been pushed to extravagant lengths. References to *cy-près* in the context of surplus income cases influenced the subsequent law in causing judges to investigate the nice question whether a testator had a general or a specific charitable intention.

The testator may make it clear on the face of his will that he knew that the value of his estate was or might be more than the amount of specific appropriations. Where he does so, and he has expressed no intention of devoting the whole

---

1 [1972] Ch. 276. The charity concerned went back to 1716.
2 (1791), 3 Bro. C.C. 373.
3 (1698), Show. Parl. Cas. 22 H.L.
4 (1798), 4 Ves. 11.
5 (1786), cited in 4 Ves. 418, at 431–432.

to charity the surplus does not go to charity, but either goes beneficially to the trustees[1] or results to the testator and those claiming under him.

Express gift of surplus

Where particular sums, not exhausting the entire income, are given to specified charities and the remainder to other charitable purposes, a question of construction may arise whether any increase of income is divisible *pro rata* among the specified and other objects or purposes[2] or whether the whole increase goes to the objects entitled to the remainder of the income.[3]

If there is an express gift of the surplus income to the donee who is charged with the payments, this may be construed in two ways: (1) as a gift of the residue whatever it may amount to, in which case the donee is entitled to any increased income,[4] or (2) as a gift of an aliquot portion of the whole, in which case the donee shares rateably with the other donees in any increase.[5] Which construction is adopted is decided on a construction of the instrument of foundation as a whole.[6] Such words as "overplus", "surplus" or "residue" do not necessarily indicate that the gift is residuary.[7] No difficulty arises, of course, where the instrument expressly directs the surplus income[8] or any subsequent increase[9] to be applied for charitable or other purposes or for the benefit of the donees.[10] But an express gift of surplus will be disregarded where the intention of the donor would be defeated by giving effect to it. Thus in *Re Ashton's Charity*[11] where surplus income was, according to the will of the founder, to be distributed among six almswomen, application of the increase *pro rata* would have made the almswomen not almswomen at all, but persons of wealth and position: the money was therefore devoted to endowing a school.[12]

---

1 *A.-G.* v. *Skinners' Co.* (1827), 2 Russ. 407, at 443; *A.-G.* v. *Skinners' Co.* (1833), 5 Sim. 596; and see *Re Jordeyn's Charity* (1833), 1 My. & K. 416; *A.-G.* v. *Trinity College, Cambridge* (1856), 24 Beav. 383; *cf. Re Stanford*, [1924] 1 Ch. 73; *Re Waite*, [1964] N.Z.L.R. 1034.

2 *A.-G.* v. *Caius College* (1837), 2 Keen 150. See *A.-G.* v. *Coopers' Co.* (1812), 19 Ves. 187; *A.-G.* v. *Solly* (1835), 5 L.J. Ch. 5.

3 *Re Avenon's Charity* (1912), 56 Sol. Jo. 241; for other consideration, [1913] 2 Ch. 261; *Re Lepton's Will Trusts*, [1972] Ch. 276.

4 *Southmolton Corporation* v. *A.-G.* (1854), 5 H.L. Cas. 1; *Beverley Corporation* v. *A.-G.* (1857), 6 H.L. Cas. 310, at 326; *Re Rowe* (1914), 30 T.L.R. 528.

5 *A.-G.* v. *Drapers' Co.* (1841), 4 Beav. 67; *A.-G.* v. *Jesus College, Oxford* (1861), 29 Beav. 163.

6 *A.-G.* v. *Windsor (Dean and Canons)* (1860), 8 H.L. Cas. 369, at 405–406, *per* Lord CAMPBELL.

7 *Beverley Corporation* v. *A.-G.* (1857), 6 H.L. Cas. 310; *Southmolton Corporation* v. *A.-G.* (1854), 5 H.L. Cas. 1, at 25–26; see also as to the expression "or thereabouts", *A.-G.* v. *Trinity College, Cambridge* (1856), 24 Beav. 383, at 392–394; *cf. A.-G.* v. *Smythies* (1833), 2 Russ. & M. 717.

8 *Re Jordeyn's Charity* (1833), 1 My. & K. 416; *Southmolton Corporation* v. *A.-G.* (1854), 5 H.L. Cas. 1, at 5.

9 *Charitable Donations and Bequests Comrs.* v. *Baroness De Clifford* (1841), 1 Dr. & War. 245.

10 *A.-G.* v. *Gascoigne* (1833), 2 My. & K. 647 (where the executors took beneficially); *A.-G.* v. *Skinners' Co.* (1827), 2 Russ. 407; *A.-G.* v. *Drapers' Co.* (1841), 4 Beav. 67.

11 (1859), 27 Beav. 115.

12 See also *Re Sekforde's Charity* (1861), 4 L.T. 321.

No express gift of surplus

The majority of surplus income cases decided by the courts have been cases where no express gift of the surplus has been made. These cases may be subdivided into those cases where the income was not in fact exhausted at the date of the gift (initial surplus) and those where it was exhausted and the surplus occurred later ("subsequent surplus").

INITIAL SURPLUS

Where there is an initial surplus of income and no express gift of such surplus, but there is a clear intention, express or implied, to attach a charitable trust to the whole property, then however deficient may be the appropriation of the whole income, the surplus will be applicable to charity, for the general intention will prevail.[1]

The donees will not be entitled to the increase unless they are themselves a charity,[2] or there are other circumstances from which a contrary intention can be collected.[3] If, however, there is no general intention to devote the whole to charity, the surplus income belongs to the parties who are charged with making the payments and not the charities,[4] notwithstanding that such specific payments, by lapse of time or otherwise, have become insufficient to satisfy the purposes for which they were originally made;[5] this is because the absence of any disposition of the surplus is an indication of an intention to benefit the donee.[6]

This rule has been frequently applied in the case of gifts to corporations, such as colleges,[7] city companies,[8] or municipal corporations,[9] or a dean and canons,[10] subject to or charged with specific charitable payments which do not exhaust the income; but the principle is not confined to gifts to such bodies.[11]

---

1 *Southmolton Corporation* v. *A.-G.* (1854), 5 H.L. Cas 1; *Beverley Corporation* v. *A.-G* (1857), 6 H.L. Cas. 310; *A.-G.* v. *Dean and Canons of Windsor* (1860), 8 H.L. Cas. 369; cf. *Re Waite*, [1964] N.Z.L.R. 1034 criticised in [1965] A.S.C.L. 335–337 (J. D. Davies).

2 *A.-G.* v. *Trinity College, Cambridge* (1856), 24 Beav. 383, at 389.

3 *A.-G.* v. *Drapers' Co.* (1840), 2 Beav. 508.

4 *A.-G.* v. *Bristol Corporation* (1820), 2 Jac. & W. 294, at 307; *Merchant Taylors' Co.* v. *A.-G.* (1871), 6 Ch. App. 512, at 519.

5 *A.-G.* v. *Gascoigne* (1833) 2 My. & K. 647; *Charitable Donations and Bequests Comrs.* v. *Baroness De Clifford* (1841) 1 Dr. & War. 245.

6 *A.-G.* v. *Trinity College, Cambridge* (1856), 24 Beav. 383, at 392.

7 *A.-G.* v. *Catherine Hall, Cambridge* (1820), Jac. 381; *A.-G.* v. *Brazen Nose College* (1834), 2 Cl. & Fin. 295, H.L.; *Jack* v. *Burnett* (1846), 12 Cl. & Fin. 812, H.L.; *A.-G.* v. *Trinity College, Cambridge* (1856), 24 Beav. 383; *A.-G.* v. *Sidney Sussex College* (1869), 4 Ch. App. 722; *Re Lavelle*, [1914] 1 I.R. 194.

8 *A.-G.* v. *Cordwainers Co.* (1833), 3 My. & K. 534; *A.-G.* v. *Fishmongers Co.* (1841), 5 My. & Co. 11; *A.-G.* v. *Grocers' Co.* (1843), 6 Beav. 526; *A.-G.* v. *Wax Chandlers Co.* (1873), L.R. 6 H.L. 1, at 9, 19.

9 *A.-G.* v. *Bristol Corporation* (1820), 2 Jac. & W. 294; *Southmolton Corporation* v. *A.-G.* (1854), 5 H.L. Cas. 1, at 34; *Beverley Corporation* v. *A.-G.* (1857), 6 H.L. Cas. 310.

10 *A.-G.* v. *Dean and Canons of Windsor* (1860), 8 H.L. Cas. 369.

11 *Merchant Taylors' Co.* v. *A.-G.* (1871), 6 Ch. App. 512, at 519.

SUBSEQUENT SURPLUS

If there is no express gift of the surplus income but the specific payments exhaust the income at the time of the gift, any subsequent increase[1] in the income is applicable to similar purposes and *prima facie* in similar proportions. This was established in the *Thetford School Case*[2] where land of the then value of £35 per annum was devised for the maintenance of a preacher, a schoolmaster and certain poor persons, specific sums totalling £35 in all being given to each. The land had increased in value and it was held by the judges that the whole of the increased rents went to the charitable purposes. The decision accords with what must have been the actual intention of the donor in dedicating the rents to his particular charities in named amounts:

> "It appears by his distribution of the profits that he intended the whole should be employed in works of piety and charity . . . if the land had decreased in value, the preacher, schoolmaster etc. and poor people should lose; so when the lands increase in value, *pari ratione* they shall gain."[3]

The *Thetford School Case* has been followed in many later cases[4] but its *ratio decidendi* has often been misunderstood. Essentially the doctrine of *cy-près* has nothing to do with cases of this kind,[5] except perhaps in a very limited sense.[6] As is so often the case Lord ELDON L.C. puts the principle of the *Thetford School Case* and the other old cases on this topic into perspective:[7]

> "As far as I have read these ancient cases they state it to depend upon the intention of the donor, and that one way of finding out the intention is, to inquire whether the whole of the annual value of the property was, at the time of foundation of the charity, distributed among the objects of the charity. If it was, they say that that circumstance is evidence of the donor's intention to give the whole of the increased value to the same objects."

Nevertheless there are numerous instances of judges treating the *Thetford School Case* (and the rule of construction adopted in it) as an example, if not the *fons et origo*, of the *cy-près* doctrine.[8]

---

1 *Southmolton Corporation* v. *A.-G.* (1854), 5 H.L. Cas. 1, at 32.

2 (1609), 8 Co. Rep. 130b. The case is discussed in Gareth Jones, *History of the Law of Charity 1532–1827* (1969) 92–93 and 154.

3 (1609), 8 Co Rep. 131a.

4 *A.-G.* v. *Johnson* (1753), Amb. 190; *A.-G.* v. *Painters-Stainers' Co.* (1788), 2 Cox Eq. Cas. 51; *A.-G.* v. *Minshull* (1798), 4 Ves. 11; *A.-G.* v. *Smythies* (1833) 2 Russ. & M. 717; *A.-G.* v. *St. John's College, Cambridge* (1834), Coop. temp. Brough 394.

5 See *A.-G.* v. *Marchant* (1866), L.R. 3 Eq. 424 where KINDERSLEY V.C. made no reference to *cy-près* after it had been argued (at 428) that *cy-près* was irrelevant.

6 See 220 *infra*.

7 *A.-G.* v. *Mayor of Bristol* (1820), 2 Jac. & W. 294, at 308, and see *A.-G.* v. *Skinners' Co.* (1827), 2 Russ. 407, at 437.

8 *A.-G.* v. *Painters-Stainers' Co.* (1788) 2 Cox Eq. 51; *A.-G.* v. *Earl of Winchelsea* (1791), 3 Bro. C.C. 373; *A.-G.* v. *Minshull* (1798), 4 Ves. 11.

WHETHER DONEES TAKE SURPLUS AND INCREASE

The donees are entitled to the surplus where it has been charged with the expense of repairs,[1] or where they have bound themselves by penalties or covenanted to pay fixed sums to charity whether the income of the property is sufficient or not.[2] But donees will not take beneficially where there has been long usage to the contrary,[3] or where by the instrument of foundation they are given power to regulate the charity.[4]

In the case of a gift to a particular body for the benefit of the body with a provision that certain members or officials are to receive specific annual sums, the body is entitled to the bulk of the property with the full increase and the particular members or officers are entitled only to the sums specifically given them.[5] For example in *A.-G.* v. *Smythies*[6] there was a gift to a corporation consisting of a master and almsmen with a direction that the almsmen should receive fixed stipends and it was held that the almsmen were not entitled to share rateably with the master in the increased income.

---

1 *A.-G.* v. *Skinners' Co.* (1827), 2 Russ. 407; *A.-G.* v. *Coopers Co.* (1840), 3 Beav. 29.

2 *Jack* v. *Burnett* (1846), 12 Cl. & Fin. 812, H.L., at 828; and see *A.-G.* v. *Merchant Venturers' Society* (1842), 5 Beav. 338.

3 *A.-G.* v. *Mercers' Co., Re St Paul's School* (1870), 18 W.R. 448.

4 *Ibid.*

5 *Southmolton Corporation* v. *A.-G.* (1854), 5 H.L. Cas. 1, at 32–33; and see *A.-G.* v. *Bristol Corporation* (1820), 2 Jac. & W. 294, at 317.

6 (1833), 2 Russ. & M. 717

Chapter 22

Conditional and Determinable Interests

A charitable gift may be made subject to a condition *precedent*. The testator may provide, for example, that the gift shall take effect only if the income of his estate amounts to a certain sum[1] or if the capital value of his estate is sufficient for the intended object.[2] Gifts to hospitals have often been made subject to conditions precedent relating to nationalisation.[3]

Sometimes the condition precedent is not expressed but is to be implied. Thus in *Re London University Medical Sciences Institute Fund*[4] the testator had bequeathed a legacy of £25,000 to "The Institute of Medical Sciences Fund, University of London". The fund had been started by voluntary contributions during the testator's lifetime with the object of carrying out a proposed scheme for the establishment of an Institute of Medical Sciences and the testator himself had contributed largely to the fund. The legacy was held to have been given subject to an implied condition precedent that the particular purpose for which it was given should be practicable. The implied condition precedent is sometimes found to be that the property in question was handed out contingently on other property being given.[5] But such a construction raises, at least at common law, a perpetuity problem, since the contingency might not occur within the perpetuity period.

Where after a gift has come into effect it is capable of being defeated by the operation of a condition, the condition is a condition *subsequent*.[6] If the condition infringes the rule against perpetuities or involves a breach of trust or is void for uncertainty the charity takes the gift discharged from the condition. Accordingly a gift over linked with the objectionable condition subsequent fails with it.[7]

A gift may be made to charity of an interest which is not absolute but limited. The interest may be limited to last only during the continuance of a particular state of affairs, or to be determinable upon the happening of some event which is contingent and which may never occur. The distinction between a *determinable* interest and an interest defensible by condition subsequent is not always easy to see. The essential distinction is that the determining event in the case of the former sets the limit for the interest first granted: the interest "bears

---

1 *Thomas* v. *Howell* (1874), L.R. 18 Eq. 198.
2 *Cherry* v. *Mott* (1836), 1 My. & Cr. 123.
3 *Re Frere*, [1951] Ch. 27; *Re Buzzacott*, [1953] Ch. 28; *Connell's Trustees* v. *Milngavie District Nursing Association* 1953 S.C. 230; *Re Lowry's Will Trusts*, [1967] Ch. 368.
4 [1909] 2 Ch. 1.
5 *McCormick* v. *Queen's University of Belfast*, [1958] N.I. 1.
6 There are many such conditions relating to fears of nationalisation, see at 259, *infra*.
7 *Re Tyler* [1891] 3 Ch. 252, C.A.; *Re Dalziel*, [1943] Ch. 277.

the seed of its own destruction and is said to determine automatically."[1] A conditional interest is complete but with an independent clause added which may operate to defeat it. Certain words like "while" "during" "so long as" or "until" are identified with determinable interests. On the other hand words which form a separate clause of defeasance "but if" "provided that" "on condition that" operate as a condition subsequent. But it is not just a matter of particular phrases: one should look at the instruments as a whole.

A good example of a determinable interest is to be found in *A.-G.* v. *Pyle*[2] where freehold land was devised to a charity school with a direction that the rents should be applied for the benefit of the school "so long as it shall continue to be endowed with charity". Likewise a gift of income for certain schools so long as they should be conducted in accordance with a particular trust deed confers a limited interest only.[3] Land is, indeed, frequently given to trustees for so long as the land shall be used in a particular way, as for a school[4] or a church[5] maintaining a particular belief[6] or a courthouse.[7] In *A.-G.* v. *Molland*[8] there was a gift for the benefit of the minister of a particular church so long as particular doctrines was preached and it was held that the minister for the time being was entitled so long as such doctrines were preached. The same applies if the minister is to benefit so long as he conducts the services in a particular way[9] or permits the sittings to be occupied free of pew rents.[10] Where there is a gift to a particular purpose "and for no other purpose whatsoever"[11] the interest given to charity is not limited or automatically determinable. On principle the presence of a gift over after such a gift ought not to affect the situation, but in *Re Cooper's Conveyance Trusts*[12] where there was a gift of land "to trustees their heirs and assigned for ever in trust nevertheless for the purposes of the Orphan Girls' Home at Kendal . . . and upon or for no other trust or purpose whatsoever" the presence of a gift over persuaded UPJOHN J. that the gift was only for a limited time. The decision has been criticised.[13]

A gift to trustees to pay the income from the gift to a cemetery company "during such period as they shall continue to maintain and keep" two specified graves in good order and condition is another example of a determinable interest.[14] But the determinable interest becomes an absolute one once it becomes established that the determining event must occur, if at all, outside the perpetuity period.[15]

---

1 See J. D. Davies (1961), 25 Conv. N.S. 56, at 64.

2 (1738), 1 Atk. 435; *Re McKellar*, [1972] 3 O.R. 16.

3 *Re Blunt's Trusts*, [1904] 2 Ch. 767.

4 *Re Tilbury West Public School Board and Hastie*, [1966] 55 D.L.R. 2d 407 (Ontario) (as long as the land shall be used and needed for school purposes and no longer).

5 *First Reformed Dutch Church* v. *Croswell*, 206 N.Y. Supp. 132, (1924); *Yarborough* v. *Yarborough*, 269 S.W. 36, (1924) (Tennessee).

6 *Brown* v. *Independent Baptist Church*, 91 N.E. 2d 922, (1950) noted in 64 Harvard Law Rev. 864.

7 *Wood* v. *County of Cheshire*, 32 N.H. 421, (1855) (New Hampshire).

8 (1832), 1 You. 562.   9 *Re Hartshill Endowment* (1861), 30 Beav. 130.

10 *Re Randell* (1888), 38 Ch.D. 213.

11 *A.-G.* v. *Earl of Craven* (1856), 21 Beav. 392.

12 [1956] 1 W.L.R. 1096; see the discussion at 209, *infra*.

13 See (1961), 25 Conv. N.S. 56, at 72.

14 *Re Chardon*, [1928] Ch. 464. The will and the court's order are more fully set out in *Tudor on Charities* (5th edn.) 701; See also *Re Chambers' Will Trusts*, [1950] Ch. 267; *cf. Re Wightwick's Will Trusts*, [1950] Ch. 260.

15 Perpetuities and Accumulation Act 1964, ss. 12 (1) and 3.

If the gift to charity within the perpetuity period is not to take effect until a particular event occurs, a resulting trust exists in favour of the donor and his heirs until the charity arises:[1] the interest given is a limited interest because it is limited not to take effect until the posited event happens.[2]

---

1 *A.-G.* v. *Earl of Craven* (1856), 21 Beav. 392, at 400, *per* Sir JOHN ROMILLY M.R. (*obiter*).

2 See *Yates* v. *University College London* (1875), L.R. 7 H.L. 438 (where gift was on its true construction complete); *Re Roberts* (1881), 19 Ch.D. 520, C.A. (charities took after life interest).

Chapter 23

Perpetuities and Accumulations

Rule against perpetuities

The topic of perpetuities[1] is bedevilled by ambiguous terminology. Discussion of the subject in relation to charities must, therefore, be preceded by an attempt to define terms. The main difficulty and confusion arise because the word "perpetuity" is used in two different senses. It is used to signify (1) an interest which may *vest* at too remote a date and (2) a trust which *lasts* too long. A similar ambiguity permeates judicial references to the Rule against Perpetuities.

For the purpose of the present discussion, references to the Rule against Perpetuities are, save where the contrary appears, to the rule which at common law invalidates interests which *vest* too remotely. The analogous rule directed against the undue duration of trusts (which, as we shall see, some judges also refer to as the Rule against Perpetuities) is in the chapter referred to by the author as the Rule against Perpetual Duration.

The Rule against Perpetuities has been qualified by statute in the United Kingdom and in some Commonwealth jurisdictions.[2]

There are several statements in the books, some by judges of the highest repute, that charitable gifts are not subject to the Rule against Perpetuities. "No charitable trust", said Lord SELBORNE in *Goodman* v. *Mayor of Saltash*,[3] "can be void on the ground of perpetuity." Lord MACNAGHTEN in *Pemsel*'s case said that charitable trusts were "not obnoxious to the Rule against Perpetuities".[4] Lord HALDANE was even more explicit: "The Rule against Perpetuities does not apply to charities".[5]

These statements are imprecise in so far as they suggest that charitable gifts cannot be void for remoteness of vesting. But in so far as these statements are saying that a charitable trust, unlike any other trust, may be of perpetual duration, they are quite accurate. If, using the author's terminology, one substitutes the words "the Rule against Perpetual Duration" for "the Rule against Perpetuities" the statements of Lords SELBORNE, MACNAGHTEN and HALDANE cease to have an appearance of inaccuracy.

In fact with one exception the Rule against Perpetuities (properly so called)

---

1 See Morris and Leach, *The Rule against Perpetuities* (2nd edn.); Gray, *The Rule against Perpetuities* (4th edn.)
2 See 207–208, 211, 213, *infra*; Keeton and Sheridan, *Comparative Law of Trusts* (1976).
3 (1882), 7 App. Cas. 633, at 642.
4 [1891] A.C. 531, at 580–581.
5 *A.-G.* v. *National Provincial Bank*, [1924] A.C. 262.

applies to gifts in favour of charities. Its application to charities can be conveniently illustrated by reference to four different situations: (*a*) gift to charity upon a remote condition precedent, (*b*) gift over from non-charity to charity, (*c*) gift over from charity to non-charity, (*d*) gift over from charity to charity. Except in relation to the last situation the rule applies in each case. In the discussion relating to each of these situations it is necessary to analyse the position both at common law and under the Perpetuities and Accumulations Act 1964[1] which governs instruments coming into operation after 16th July 1964.

GIFT TO CHARITY UPON A REMOTE CONDITION PRECEDENT

Common law

At common law if the initial vesting of a gift in favour of charity is contingent. Upon an event which might not happen within the perpetuity period the gift fails. Lord SELBORNE L.C. summarised the position thus:[2]

> "If the gift in trust for charity is itself conditional upon a future and uncertain event, it is subject to the same rules and principles as any other estate depending for its coming into existence upon a condition precedent. If the condition is never fulfilled, the estate never arises, if it is so remote and indefinite as to transgress the limits of time prescribed by the rules of law against perpetuities, the gift fails *ab initio*."

In accordance with this principle, a gift to retain a fund until a candidate for the priesthood came forward from a certain church was held in *Re Mander*[3] to be too remote and so failed *ab initio*. Also held void for remoteness were gifts to charity where the vesting was postponed until "the appointment of the next lieutenant-colonel"[4] or "the death of the last of my dogs"[5] or "the practice of vivisection is abolished".[6] If a primary trust for a corporate legatee enables that legatee to renounce the benefit of the gift at any time, any gift over for charitable purposes will be void for remoteness at common law.[7]

Irish[8] and Australian courts have followed the English decisions. In *Re Will of Nilen*,[9] a testator had directed that a certain allotment should be held until such time as the extension of the Alexandra Road Railway should have been definitely settled, and that it should then be sold and the proceeds divided as in the will

---

1 See J. H. C. Morris and H. W. R. Wade "Perpetuities Reform at Last" (1964), 80 L.Q.R. 486.

2 *Chamberlayne* v. *Brockett* (1872), 8 Ch. App. 206, at 211.

3 [1950] Ch. 547.

4 *Re Lord Stratheden and Campbell*, [1894] 3 Ch. 265. An interest to become effective only on the happening of a future event may likewise be void at common law: *Worthing Corporation* v. *Heather*, [1906] 2 Ch. 532, at 538 (option given to charity).

5 *Re Kelly*, [1932] I.R. 255.

6 *Re Wightwick's Will Trusts*, [1950] Ch. 260.

7 *Re Spensley's Will Trusts* [1954] Ch. 233, C.A. (where a primary trust was held not to be charitable).

8 *Kingham* v. *Kingham*, [1897] 1 I.R. 170; *Re Gordon* (1901), 35 I.L.T. 25, *Re Hawe* (1959) 93 I.L.T. 175.

9 [1908] V.L.R. 332; and see *Muir* v. *Archdall* (1919), 19 S.R.N.S.W. 10 (gift to St. Andrew's Cathedral Chapter when they should build and window).

directed. It was held that even if the division was for charitable purposes the gift was void for remoteness. A gift in trust for charity, limited to take effect after prior gifts themselves void for remoteness is also invalid.[1] So too if a gift in trust for charity is itself conditional upon a future and uncertain event, it is subject in Australia to the same rules and principles as any other estate depending for its coming into existence upon a condition precedent.[2] A gift contingent upon a fund sufficient for the named charitable purpose being subscribed is also perpetuitous.[3]

Statute

The Perpetuities and Accumulations Act 1964, which affects instruments coming into effect after 16th July 1964,[4] now enables testators or settlor to choose as the initial period within which a gift to charity shall vest a period of up to 80 years.[5] Such period must be specified in that behalf in the instrument.[5] It should be stressed that such a period is an alternative to the conventional life or lives on being plus 21 years. The Act also provides for a wait and-see period: if the gift vests within that period it is saved, and until it is clear that it will in fact vest outside the period it is treated as valid.[6] Accordingly a gift such as that in *Re Mander*[7] will no longer be treated as void *ab initio* but will await the outcome of the wait-and-see period.

Gift over from non-charity to charity

COMMON LAW

The rule against perpetuities applies equally when the limitation to charity is by way of a gift over following a gift in favour of private individuals[8] or non-charitable purposes.

In an old Irish case[9] there was an immediate gift to charity together with a further provision that surplus rents should go to members of certain families who should for the time being be lords or ladies of a particular manor, and in case they failed to satisfy certain conditions or became extinct, then to charity. Sir EDWARD SUGDEN L.C. held that the gift over was void. The operation of the rule was however considered in *Re Johnson's Trusts*[10] where a fund of personality was directed to be held on trust to pay the income to such person

---

1 *Re Bullen* (1915), 17 W.A.L.R. 73; *Re Zahell* (1931), Q.S.R. 1.
2 *Re Finkelstein*, [1926] V.L.R. 240 (conditional upon directions for accumulation void for remoteness).
3 *Re Dyer*, [1935] V.L.R. 273 (metropolitan permanent orchestra).
4 Perpetuities and Accumulations Act 1964, s. 1.
5 *Ibid.*, s. 1. The gift should therefore state that the period selected is the perpetuity period for the purposes of the will or settlement.
6 *Ibid.*, s. 3.
7 [1950] Ch. 547.
8 *Re Bowen*, [1893] 2 Ch. 491, at 494, *per* STIRLING J.
9 *Charitable Donations and Bequest Comrs.* v. *Baroness De Clifford* (1841), 1 Dr. & War. 245.
10 (1866), L.R. 2 Eq. 716.

or persons as for the time being should be entitled to certain freeholds which the testator had settled. The will further provided that if the issue of the persons named should fail, there should be a gift over to Magdalen College, Oxford. Since this latter limitation could take effect outside the perpetuity period it was held void.

Where the primary gift is to a non-charitable purpose and there is a gift over to a charity the primary gift will in most cases fail (either because it does not fall into the class of anomalous and exceptional cases[1] where purpose trusts are upheld, or because it is not confined to the perpetuity period although being a permissible purpose trust. The primary gift in *Re Wightwick's Will Trusts*[2] was objectionable on both grounds: it was a gift to further the purposes of the anti-vivisection cause and was not confined to the perpetuity period. The gift over to charity was expressed to take effect when vivisection should be abolished by law "in the United Kingdom of Great Britain and Ireland on the continent of Europe and elsewhere". Such total abolition was a contingent and uncertain event which could occur outside the perpetuity period so that the gift over was too remote. In another case the gift over to charity was expressed to take effect if the trustee for the primary trust should renounce the bequest "at any future date": because such renunciation could take place outside the perpetuity period the gift over failed.[3]

The initial non-charitable purpose trust in the Irish case of *Re Macnamara's Estate*[4] was to apply income for the maintenance of a rest and holiday home for Protestant men. The testatrix had devised her house Glenseskin to the Young Men's Christian Association in Cork, expressing the desire that it should be used as a rest and holiday home for Protestant men; and that gift was held to be an absolute gift to the Association. But the testatrix had gone on to provide that "in the event of it being impracticable to use Glenseskin as such holiday home . . . the income from [the] said property shall be applied for the general benefit of" the Association in Cork. Even if, as was apparent, the primary trust was factually impracticable the gift over was too remote and could not operate because it was dependent on a void gift.

If a gift over to charity is preceded by successive limitations to individuals and the last such limitation infringes the rule against perpetuities the gift over if contingent (rather than vested with enjoyment deferred) will itself be invalid.[5]

STATUTE

Where there is a gift over following upon a non-charitable initial gift the fate of the gift over under the 1964 Act will depend on (1) the nature of the initial gift and (2) the wait-and-see rule. If the initial gift is to a non-charitable purpose the gift over can only be valid if the purpose falls within one of the anomalous exceptions to the rule invalidating non-charitable purpose trusts,[6] and in the events vests within the relevant perpetuity period. Where the initial gift

---

1 See *Re Astor's Settlement Trusts*, [1952] Ch. 534. The cases comprise trusts for the up-keep of tombs and individual animals and to promote hunting.
2 [1950] Ch. 260.
3 *Re Spensley's Will Trusts*, [1952] Ch. 233 (primary trust non-charitable).
4 [1943] I.R. 372.
5 *Re Metcalfe*, [1947] 1 D.L.R. 567 (Ont.); *cf. Re Hart*, [1951] 2 D.L.R. 30 (N.S.).
6 O.e. gifts to maintain individual animals or graves or to promote hunting.

is to an individual the potentially perpetuitous gift over to charity will fail only when it becomes established that the vesting must occur, if at all, after the end of the perpetuity period.[1]

Gift over from charity to non-charity

COMMON LAW

A gift over from a charity to individuals or to non-charitable purposes is similarly subject to the rule against perpetuities. While the rule applies to a gift over on a condition subsequent, it does not, at common law,[2] apply to determinable interests. The distinction between an interest defeasible upon a condition subsequent and a determinable interest has already been made.[3]

Condition subsequent

The application of the rule to a gift over upon a condition subsequent is well illustrated by the case of *Re Bowen*.[4] The testator bequeathed two sums of money on trust to establish schools in certain parishes and to continue the same *forever* thereafter. He declared that if at any time thereafter the Government should establish a general system of education the trusts of the legacies should cease and determine and the money go to his residuary legatees. This was a case where (the court held) the testator had made an immediate disposition in favour of charity in perpetuity, followed by a gift over of a future interest to arise upon an event which would not necessarily occur within perpetuity limits. Accordingly under the common law rules then applicable the gift over failed. In *Re Davies*[5] there was a gift to the vicar of C. and his successors with a gift over to the superannuation fund of the Cardiganshire Constabulary if the vicar and his successors should at any time fail to comply with directions as to the care of certain graves and tombstones in the churchyard at C. The testator had not sufficiently described the police "pension fund"; but even if he had done so the fund was not wholly charitable. Accordingly, the gift over on failure to repair the graves was void for remoteness. The initial gift to the vicar and his successors became a permanent endowment, free from the condition as to repairing the graves.

Where on its true construction the initial gift to charity is subject to a condition subsequent (and is not a determinable interest) the failure of the gift over leaves the initial interest as an absolute interest: there is no resulting trust. Although in a sense the provision of a gift over in the event of a defeasance anticipates the termination of the initial gift, the initial gift is still treated as absolute. Nor is this result dependent, as some appear to think, on the presence of words like "for ever" or their equivalent in the initial gift. Those words

---

1 Perpetuities and Accumulations Act 1964, s. 3.
2 Under perpetuities legislation the position is different.
3 See 202, *supra*.
4 [1893] 2 Ch. 491 (italics supplied).
5 [1915] 1 Ch. 543.

appeared, it is true, in the initial gift in *Re Bowen*[1]; and in *Re Peel's Release*[2] also the initial gift of land was to be appropriated for the education of poor children "for ever thereafter", with a gift over into residue in certain events. But there are several cases where the initial gift was not expressed to be "for ever" but the court has nevertheless treated the gift as absolute because the gift over into reversion[3] or into residue[4] or to other persons[5] or purposes[6] was void for remoteness.

Determinable interest

By the use of appropriate conveyancing language it is possible under the common law rule to evade the rule against perpetuities, and enable funds held for charitable purposes to devolve upon individuals outside the perpetuity period. If the first interest was dressed up as a *determinable* interest, the possibility of reverter or in the case of personalty the analogous resulting trust consequent upon the termination of the determinable interest was immune from the perpetuity rule. In other words on the termination of the charitable trust there was a reverter or resulting trust for the donor or his personal representatives and this took effect. So where a freehold estate was devised on trust for a charity school so long as it should continue endowed, the trust only operated during the specified period and, when the school ceased to be endowed, the gift reverted to the heir at law.[7] Where the gift was of personalty it would fall into residue.[8] The mere fact that the testator expressly provides that the property after the cesser of the determinable interest shall fall into residue makes no difference. Such a direction means that the property goes as the law independently of that direction would give it: it is mere surplusage. In *Re Randell*[9] a testatrix left £14,000 on trust to pay the income to the successive incumbents of a church "so long as the ... incumbents shall permit all the sittings in the said church to be occupied free of pew rents". There was a direction that the money should fall into residue if pew rents were claimed. NORTH J. upheld the validity of the direction: the trust was one conferring the equivalent of a determinable interest which would end automatically if a claim were made whereupon the property would be held upon resulting trust for those entitled to residue and the direction did no more than express what the law implied. The decision in *Re Randell*[10] was approved and followed by BUCKLEY J. in *Re Blunt's Trusts*[11]

---

1 [1893] 2 Ch. 491.
2 [1921] 2 Ch. 218.
3 *Re Hollis' Hospital Trustees and Hague's Contract*, [1899] 2 Ch. 540 (reversion to right heirs of T); *Fitzmaurice* v. *Monck School Trustees*, [1950] 1 D.L.R. 239 (reverter to grantor); and see *Re Baillie* (1907), 7 S.R.N.S.W. 265 (gift over to next of kin).
4 *Re Hardy*, [1933] N.I. 150; *Re Engels*, [1943] 1 All E.R. 506; *Re Maclachlan* (1900), 28 V.L.R. 548.
5 *Re Bland-Sutton's Will Trusts*, [1951] Ch. 485, C.A. (non-charitable institution) reversed on other grounds in H.L. *sub nom Royal College of Surgeons* v. *National Provincial Bank*, [1952] A.C. 631; and see *Re Talbot*, [1933] Ch. 895 (where MAUGHAM J. treated the initial gift as disclosing no general charitable intent). For criticism of the reasoning in *Re Talbot*, see J. D. Davies (1961) 25 Conv. N.S. 56, at 71–72.
6 *Re Da Costa*, [1912] 1 Ch. 337; *Re Davies*, [1915] 1 Ch. 543.
7 *A.-G.* v. *Pyle* (1738), 1 Atk. 435.
8 *Ibid.*
9 (1888), 38 Ch.D. 213.   10 (1888), 38 Ch.D. 213.
11 [1904] 2 Ch. 767; *cf. Re Talbot*, [1933] Ch. 895.

and by the Court of Appeal in *Gibson* v. *South American Stores* (*Gath and Chaves*), *Ltd.*[1]

STATUTE

Under the rules introduced by the Perpetuities and Accumulations Act 1964 possibilities of reverter and analogous interests in personalty are as much subject to the Rule against Perpetuities as rights of entry for condition broken.[2] Thus the resulting trust in *Re Randell* would now be subject to the Rule against Perpetuities and a wait-and-see period would apply. The effect of that would be that if during the perpetuity period pew rents should be claimed the resulting trust would come into operation; but if no such claim should be made within the period the initial gift would become absolute. The relevant wait-and-see period for a limitation such as that in *Re Randell* would now be 21 years in the case of a will[3] or the life of the donor in the case of a deed of gift.[4] But in all cases it will not necessarily be 21 years: the relevant period will be identified by reference to section 3 of the Perpetuities and Accumulations Act 1964 unless there has been an express selection of an 80 year period in the will or deed in question. A provision for reverter such as that contained in *Re Peel's Release*[5] would not be invalid *ab initio*: it would only become so after the expiry of a wait-and-see period consisting of the life of the donor plus 21 years.[6]

Gift over from charity to charity

COMMON LAW

A gift over from one charitable purpose to another upon the happening of an event which may happen beyond the period of the Rule against Perpetuities is valid. Nor does it matter whether the same or new trustees are, upon the happening of the event, to hold the property for the same or other charitable purposes. The leading case is *Christ's Hospital* v. *Grainger*[7] where a bequest was made to the Corporation of Reading in trust for the poor with a provision that if the Corporation should for one year neglect to observe the directions of the will the property should be transferred to the Corporation of London in trust for a school. Over two centuries after the death of the testator the event occurred, and it was held that the gift over was valid. Lord COTTENHAM justified his decision in the following way:[8]

> "It was then argued that it was void, as contrary to the rules against perpetuities. These rules are to prevent, in the cases in which they apply, property from being inalienable beyond certain periods. Is this effect

---

1 [1950] Ch. 177, C.A.
2 See Perpetuities and Accumulations Act 1964, s. 12.
3 *Ibid.*, s. 3 (4) (b).
4 *Ibid.*, s. 3 (5) (b) (ii).
5 [1921] 2 Ch. 218.
6 Perpetuities and Accumulations Act 1964, s. 3 (5).
7 (1848), 16 Sim. 83; affd. (1849), 1 Mac. & G. 460.
8 (1849), 1 Mac. & G. 460, at 464.

produced, and are these rules invaded by the transfer, in a certain event, of property from one charity to another? If the Corporation of Reading might hold the property for certain charities in Reading, why may not the Corporation of London hold it for the charity of Christ's Hospital in London? The property is neither more nor less alienable on that account."

Both the leading textbooks on the Rule against Perpetuities[1] criticise this reasoning on the ground that it confuses perpetuity in the sense of inalienability with perpetuity in the sense of remoteness. And there is justice in the comment that on Lord COTTENHAM's reasoning a gift over from a charity to an individual upon a remote event ought to be valid "because on the happening of the event the property would once more be in the stream of commerce and freely alienable".[2] However that is not in fact the case: as we have seen, such a gift over is void. The House of Lords followed the decision in *Royal College of Surgeons* v. *National Provincial Bank*[3] although only Lord MORTON[4] seems to have agreed with Lord COTTENHAM's reasoning, Lord TUCKER[5] and Lord COHEN[6] rationalising the exception by reference to "the leaning of the court in favour of charity". Since the Rule against Perpetuities is directed against remoteness of vesting, a simpler rationalisation of the exception is surely that where the so-called gift over is from one charity to another, the property is throughout *vested in charity*. No question of remoteness of vesting in charity can arise. "There is no more perpetuity created in giving to two charities in that form than by giving to one."[7] Moreover, if it is permissible for the court in the exercise of its *cy-près* jurisdiction to divert funds from one charitable purpose to another, there is at least an argument that a testator should be able, in effect, to make his own *cy-près* direction. The question is one of policy upon which there are different opinions.[8]

The exception established by *Christ's Hospital* v. *Grainger* has been applied in India[9] and Ontario.[10] In *Re Mountain*[11] the testator left a sum of money in trust to supply an income for a Bishop of Cornwall, of if such a Bishop was not elected within 25 years after the testator's death, the money was to go to a university for the endowment of a Professorship of Natural Science. BOYD C. held that there was an immediate primary gift to charity though particular application might be delayed for 25 years and might never take place. The gift over, being for a charitable purpose, did not offend against the rule concerning perpetuities. An immediate primary gift to charity was also discovered in *Re Short*[12] where the annual income from a sum was to be applied for the oldest and poorest inhabitants of a particular place for 90 years, with payment to

---

1 Gray, *The Rule against Perpetuities* (4th edn.) 573–574; Morris and Leach, *The Rule against Perpetuities* (2nd edn.) 192.

2 Morris and Leach, *op. cit.*, 192.

3 [1952] A.C. 631.

4 *Ibid.*, at 650.

5 *Ibid.*, at 663.

6 *Ibid.*, at 667.

7 Per SHADWELL V.-C. in *Christ's Hospital* v. *Grainger* (1848), 16 Sim. 83, at 100.

8 See Morris and Leach, *Rule against Perpetuities* (2nd edn.) 193; J. D. Davies (1961), 25 Conv. N.S. 56, at 62–63.

9 *Administrator-General of Bengal* v. *Hughes* (1912), I.L.R. 40 Calc. 192.

10 *Re Mountain* (1912), 26 O.L.R. 163 (C.A.)

11 (1912), 26 O.L.R. 163.

12 (1914), 7 O.W.N. 525.

commence on the death of the testator's widow. After 90 years the capital was to be paid to the Methodist Missionary Society. Here again there was no infringement of the rule against perpetuities: throughout the capital and income was vested in charity.

It has been held that a gift over from charity to charity is valid even though the remote event upon which the gift over is to take effect has no connection with the administration of the charitable trust itself. For example in *Re Tyler*[1] a testator bequeathed money to the trustees of a missionary society with a request that his vault should be kept in repair and directed that should this request not be complied with, there should be a gift over to a particular school. The Court of Appeal held that the condition imposed by the request was valid and the gift over was good. In this way a settlor is enabled to do indirectly what he cannot do directly. This seems wrong in principle. If it is against public policy to permit the settlor to create a trust for the perpetual maintenance of a vault or tomb, it should equally be against public policy to permit him through the creation of a charitable trust indirectly to secure this result. Professor Gray suggested[2] that by use of the *Re Tyler* device it might be possible for a settlor to endow a school on condition that if on the 1st of January every year the school failed to pay a certain amount to the donor's heirs the endowment fund should go over to another charity. Perpetual endowment of the settlor's family would thus be secured. However no decided case goes this far. The only authorities in which indirect provision has been made for the accomplishment in perpetuity of a non-charitable purpose have been cases involving the perpetual maintenance of a vault or tomb or other modest memorial.[3] So far at any rate as the United Kingdom is concerned, *Re Tyler* is virtually on its own.[4] But although it has been much criticised[5] and doubted,[6] Lord MORTON in *Royal College of Surgeons* v. *National Provincial Bank* mentioned *Re Tyler* without disapproval and it has been approved in Canada.[7] Since many wills must have been drafted in reliance upon it, the chances of it being overruled have now receded. All the same, the likelihood is that the principle of *Re Tyler* will be confined to "tombstone" or analogous conditions and will not be extended to the sort of case mooted by Gray.[8] In the United States it has been held that if the condition on which a gift over from charity to charity is to take effect is contrary to public policy, it is invalid: accordingly the original charitable trust will not terminate and the gift over will not take effect.[9]

STATUTE

The principle in *Christ's Hospital* v. *Grainger*[10] does not appear to have been affected by the provisions of the Perpetuities and Accumulations Act 1964.

---

1 [1891] 3 Ch. 252, C.A.

2 Gray, *The Rule against Perpetuities* (4th edn.) 576, para. 603.4.

3 See *Re Lopes*, [1931] 2 Ch. 130 (portrait).

4 See also *Re Lopes*, [1931] 2 Ch. 130 and *Re Martin*, [1952] W.N. 339.

5 Gray, *The Rule against Perpetuities* (4th edn.) 576.

6 *Per* DIXON C.J. in *Royal Society for the Prevention of Cruelty to Animals of N.S.W.* v. *Benevolent Society of N.S.W.* (1960), 102 C.L.R. 629, 641.

7 *Re Harding* (1904), 4 O.W.R. 316.

8 The fact that no such distinction has yet been made is, it is submitted, irrelevant; *cf.* Morris and Leach, *op. cit.*, 194.

9 *Re Sterne*, 263 N.Y. Supp. 304 (1933).   10 (1849), 1 Mac. & G. 460.

The modification to the common law rule introduced by the 1964 Act only applies where the disposition, apart from the statute, might not become vested until too remote a time.[1] No change is made, nor is any change necessary, where there is a gift over from one charity to another: such a disposition would not vest at *too* remote a time.

Accumulations

RULE AGAINST ACCUMULATIONS

The rule against accumulations is designed to prevent trust income from being tied up or accumulated for an unreasonable length of time. Its purpose thus resembles the rule against inalienability.

The rule at *common law* was that a direction to accumulate income would be invalid if it involved an accumulation beyond the perpetuity period.[2] As a result of the leading English case of *Thellusson* v. *Woodford*[3] legislation was introduced in England to restrict further the power to direct accumulations of income.[4]

The legislation introduced in England was initially contained in the Accumulations Act 1800 (usually called the Thellusson Act).[5] But that Act was repealed by and re-enacted in section 164 of the Law of Property Act 1925 which has in turn been amplified by the Perpetuities and Accumulations Act 1964.[6] There are now six permissible alternative periods of accumulation. These are:

(a) The life of the grantor or settlor.

(b) A term of 21 years from the death of the grantor, settlor or testator.

(c) The duration of the minority or respective minorities of any person or persons living or *en ventre sa mere* at the death of the grantor, settlor or testator.

(d) The duration of the minority or respective minorities only of any person or persons who under the limitations of the instrument directing the accumulation would for the time being, if of full age, be entitled to the income directed to be accumulated.

(e) A term of 21 years from the date of the making of the disposition.[7]

(f) The duration of the minority or respective minorities of any person or persons in being at that date.[8]

Accumulations of income for the benefit of charity must be confined within whichever period is selected or seemingly selected by the donor.[9] In the case of *private* trusts the statutory provisions specify[10] what is to happen to excessive

---

1 Perpetuities and Accumulations Act 1964, s. 3 (1).
2 *Harrison* v. *Harrison* (1787), cited 4 Ves. 338.
3 (1799), 4 Ves. 227; affd. (1805), 11 Ves, 112.
4 See Keeton, *Modern Developments in the Law of Trusts* (1971) 215–275.
5 Its official title is derived from the Short Titles Act 1896.
6 Perpetuities and Accumulations Act 1964, s. 13.
7 *Ibid.*, s. 13 (1) (a).
8 *Ibid.*, s. 13 (1) (b).
9 The accumulation may be directed impliedly: see *Re Rochford's Settlement Trusts*, [1965] Ch. 111.
10 LPA 1925, s. 164 (1).

accumulations. But if the income of a charitable fund is directed to be accumulated for an excessive period a scheme *may* be settled by the court for the application of the surplus. Whether a scheme is possible depends on finding a general charitable intent:[1] an invalid accumulation for a specific charitable purpose would follow the general rule if no general charitable interest can be discovered.

TERMINATING AN ACCUMULATION

By a well-known rule of equity known as the rule in *Saunders* v. *Vautier*[2] if a settlor or testator has given a beneficiary a vested interest in property but postpones payment until some future time and in the meantime either expressly or by implication directs an accumulation, the beneficiary can, on attaining majority and being otherwise legally capable, call for his interest and thereby stop the accumulation. The rule only operates if it is clear that the beneficiary is solely and absolutely entitled. It does not operate where the beneficiary's interest is contingent.

After some uncertainty on the point[3] it was held in *Wharton* v. *Masterman*[4] that the rule in *Saunders* v. *Vautier* applied in the case of charities. Accordingly, if an accumulation is directed, and the capital and accumulations are given absolutely to a particular charity (whether corporate or unincorporate) the charity has the same right as an individual would have in the same circumstances to stop the accumulations and call for the immediate payment of the gift. The trust amounts to a directory provision of a kind which the trustees ought *prima facie* to bear in mind and carry out.[5]

The principle in *Saunders* v. *Vautier*[6] does not, however, apply where on the true construction of the gift there is no right to call for the *corpus* of the fund, as for example where there is an indefinite gift of the income of a fund to a charity for its general purposes.[7] In *Re Jefferies*[8] an unsuccessful attempt was made to extend the rule in *Saunders* v. *Vautier* to a case of a future gift to charitable legatees to be ascertained *in futuro*. A testator left property to trustees on trust out of the income to pay an annuity to M for life and after M's death to hold the proceeds and the balance of the income accumulated during M's life and the interest on trust to divide the same amongst such hospitals in the county of London and in such properties as they should think proper. Counsel for the Attorney-General arguing for charity submitted (1) that immediately the testator died there was a vested gift to charity, postponed as to the time of payment, (2) that the Attorney-General could stop the accumulations; and

---

1 *Martin* v. *Maugham* (1844), 14 Sim. 230; *Re Monk*, [1927] 2 Ch. 197; *Re Bradwell*, [1952] Ch. 575; *Re Burns* (1960), 25 D.L.R. (2d) 427; *Jewish Home for Aged of British Columbia* v. *Toronto General Trusts Corporation*, [1961] S.C.R. 465.

2 (1841), 4 Beav. 115; affd. Cr. & Ph. 240.

3 *Harbin* v. *Masterman* (1871), L.R. 12 Eq. 559, *per* WICKENS V.-C.; affd. in the C.A.: [1894] 2 Ch. 184.

4 [1895] A.C. 186, H.L.; *Re Travis* [1900] 2 Ch. 541; *Re Blake*, [1937] Ch. 325, affd. *sub. nom. Berry* v. *Green*, [1938] A.C. 575.

5 *Re Knapp, Spreckley* v. *A.-G.*, [1929] 1 Ch. 341, at 344, *per* MAUGHAM J.

6 (1841), 4 Beav. 115.

7 *Re Levy*, [1960] Ch. 346, C.A. A similar result had already been obtained in Canada: *Halifax School for the Blind* v. *Chipman*, [1937] 3 D.L.R. 9.

8 [1936] 2 All E.R. 626, criticised in 54 L.Q.R. 25 and see also Delany, *Law Relating to Charities in Ireland*, 132–134.

(3) that the question whether the accumulation provision could be carried out was merely a question of how to administer the trust property. CLAUSON J. rejected this approach saying that *Wharton* v. *Masterman*[1] did not apply to a future gift to legatees to be ascertained *in futuro*. He accordingly held that 21 years after the testator's death the accumulations were stopped by the Act and the surplus income went to those entitled on intestacy. It was perhaps regrettable that the case of *Martin* v. *Maugham*[2] was not cited to CLAUSON J. because in that case SHADWELL V.C. disregarded an attempted illegal accumulation[3] and applied the property *cy-près* observing:

> "If a testator has expressed his intention that his personal estate shall be, in substance, applied for charitable purposes, the particular mode which he may have pointed at for effecting those purposes has nothing to do with the question whether the devotion for charitable purposes shall take place or not."

Where the charitable legatee is already ascertained the gift to charity after an excessive accumulation may be valid.[4]

---

1 [1895] A.C. 186, H.L.
2 (1844), 14 Sim. 230.
3 Interest was to be accumulated and added to capital until £600 per annum was reached: the income was then to be split among various schools according to a specified plan.
4 *Re Hart*, [1972] S.A.S.R. 147.

Part III

Schemes

Chapter 24

The "Cy-près" Principle

Definition and rationale

The doctrine of *cy-près*[1] is one of cardinal importance in the law of charities both in this country and in other jurisdictions which have received the trust concept.

There have been many attempts to define the doctrine, mostly by way of description of its application. Subject to the substitution of "paramount intention" for "more general intention" and "paramount charitable intention" for "general charitable intention",[2] the most satisfactory modern formulation is a transatlantic one:[3]

"If property is given in trust to be applied to a particular charitable purpose, and it is or becomes impossible or impracticable or illegal to carry out the particular purpose, and if the settlor manifested a more general intention to devote the property to charitable purposes, the trust will not fail but the court will direct the application of the property to some charitable purpose which falls within the general charitable intention of the settlor."

The substituted charitable purpose will be as near as possible to the one originally specified.

Earlier judicial formulations[4] in this country have referred to the failure of a particular *mode* and the substitution of a new mode to carry out the charitable intention of the settlor. But the formulation cited above follows the tendency of modern writers[5] who suggest that the ambit of the doctrine should be confined to the situations where a particular charitable *purpose* cannot be carried out, leaving other situations to be covered by other principles. Where, for example, difficulty arises because no trustee has been named the court can rely on the familiar rule of equity that equity will not allow a trust to fail for want

---

1 Sheridan and Delany, *The Cy-près Doctrine* (1959) and supplement (1961). The cases since 1961 are surveyed by Professor Sheridan in (1968) 6 Alberta Law Review 16 and (1972) 1 A.-A. L.R. 101.

2 See *Re Lysaght*, [1966] Ch. 191 discussed at 232, and 244, *infra*.

3 Restatement of Trusts (2d) s. 399.

4 See *Moggridge* v. *Thackwell* (1802), 7 Ves. 36, at 69, *per* Lord ELDON, L.C.; affd. (1807), 13 Ves. 416 H.L.; *Mills* v. *Farmer* (1815), 1 Mer. 55; *A.-G.* v. *Bristol Corporation* (1820), 2 Jac. & W. 294, at 308; *Chamberlayne* v. *Brockett* (1872), 8 Ch. App. 206.

5 Fisch, *The Cy-près Doctrine in the United States* (1950) 177–178; and see Gareth Jones, *History of the Law of Charity 1532–1827* (1969) 73.

of a trustee.[1] Again, where there is some failure of machinery the court has power under its general jurisdiction over the administration of trusts to remedy the failure.[2] Much confusion has resulted from the use (or misuse) of the term *cy-près* in situations where there is no question of carrying out the intention of the donor "as nearly as possible". Nowhere is this confusion more apparent than in the cases relating to surplus income. The question whether the donor intended the surplus to go to the very charitable objects which he had designated is not a question of *cy-près* at all.[3]

By limiting the application of the *cy-près* doctrine to cases where there is a failure of a particular charitable *purpose* such confusion is averted and precision is obtained.

The rationale was originally a religious one as WILMOT C.J. in *A.-G.* v. *Lady Downing*[4] observed:

> "The donation was considered as proceeding from a general principle of piety in the testator. Charity was an expiation of sin, to be rewarded in another state; and therefore if political reasons negatived the particular charity given, [the] courts thought the merits of charity ought not to be lost to the testator, nor to the public, and that they were carrying on his general pious intention".

The secular justification of the doctrine is that it is directed to "keeping in existence a gift to charity so that it may continue as a public benefit from generation to generation".[5] In resorting to the principle of *cy-près* the courts were guided by a supposed discovery of intention on the part of the donor to devote the subject of his gift at all events to charity and to deprive his representatives of every claim to the property.[6] "Charity is always favoured by equity,"[7] and this supposed discovery of intention is yet another example of that tendency.

Summary of the application of the doctrine

Considerable changes were effected in the law relating to the *cy-près* doctrine by the Charities Act 1960. Prior to that Act it was only where a charitable gift had become impossible or impracticable to perform that the doctrine could be invoked. Putting it another way, the only "*cy-près* occasion" was impossibility or impracticability. Moreover it was also required that in a case of *initial* impossibility or impracticability a paramount or general intention on the part of the donor to benefit charity should be shown. The Charities Act 1960 has now modified both these requirements. *Cy-près* may now operate on certain other occasions. And, in some cases, statute now presumes a paramount intention of charity.

Today, in order that *cy-près* application may be ordered there must be (1) a designated charitable object (2) a *cy-près* occasion and (3) in the case of

---

1 *Ellison* v. *Ellison* (1802), 6 Ves. 656, *per* Lord ELDON L.C.
2 See e.g. *A.-G.* v. *Lady Downing* (1767), Wilm. 1 at 22, *per* WILMOT C.J.
3 Gareth Jones, *History of the Law of Charity 1532–1827* (1969) at 156.
4 (1769), Amb. 571.
5 Nathan Report (1952), Cmd. 8710, para. 71.
6 See W. R. Boyle, *A Practical Treatise on the Law of Charities* (1837) 148.
7 *Re Watt*, [1932] 2 Ch. 243, n. at 246, *per* Lord HANWORTH M.R.

initial impossibility (but in no other case) a paramount or general charitable intent. However, before turning to deal in more detail with the basic principles underlying the operation of the *cy-près* doctrine, its origins and history will first be discussed, including the statutory modifications introduced prior to the Charities Act 1960.

Origins and history

In a modern treatise on the law of charities as a whole, an extended discussion of the origins and history of the *cy-près* doctrine would be wasteful.[1] Nevertheless, a brief summary of the evolution of the doctrine may be helpful to a proper understanding of the decided cases, and more particularly the older ones.

The principle of *cy-près* application can be traced back to Roman times.[2] Wills were originally the province of the Ecclesiastical courts, and while many civil law rules of construction were received into the Ecclesiastical courts, canon law too probably played a part in the development of the *cy-près* doctrine.

Statements are to found in textbooks[3] and in cases[4] to the effect that when *cy-près* was first introduced into equity it was construed in a very liberal manner. One example of a generous interpretation of the "impossibility" of trust provisions that is a condition of *cy-près* is to be found in the decision of Sir FRANCIS BACON L.K. in *Emmanuel College Cambridge* v. *English*.[5] But judicial references to the fact that the *cy-près* doctrine had been "pushed to a most extravagant length"[6] or "wildly and extravagantly acted upon"[7] were prompted by a disapproval of the way in which earlier judges had deprived the heir of surplus income in favour of charity, rather than of a liberal interpretation of the word "impossible".

Statutory modifications of the *cy-près* doctrine prior to 1960

The reorganisation of the law of charities in the mid-nineteenth century was closely linked in its origins with the cause (espoused in particular by Lord Brougham) of bringing education to the masses. The question of variation in educational trusts to meet the altered circumstances of the day, and new views of education was, as Mitcheson pointed out,[8] dealt with in the older cases with extraordinary strictness. Thus no schemes could be sanctioned which introduced into a grammar school instituted for the teaching of Greek and Latin

---

1 For the history of the doctrine: see Sheridan and Delany, *The Cy-près Doctrine* (1959) 5–28; Gareth Jones, *History of the Law of Charities 1532–1827* (1969); Willard, "Illustrations of the Origin of Cy-près" (1894) 8 Harvard L.R. 69; Gray, "The History and Development in England of the Cy-près Principle in Charities" (1953) Boston University L.R. 30 *et seq.*

2 H. F. Jolowicz, *Roman Foundations of Modern Law* (1957) 138–139; and see D. 31.2. 16 (Modestinus).

3 E.g. Delany, *Law of Charities in Ireland* (Rev. ed.) 142.

4 *A.-G.* v. *Whitchurch* (1796), 3 Ves. 141, at 144, *per* ARDEN M.R.

5 (1617), Cas. temp. Bac. 27, at 28 discussed in Gareth Jones, *op. cit.*, 74–75.

6 *A.-G.* v. *Minshull* (1798), 4 Ves. 11, at 14, *per* ARDEN M.R.

7 *A.-G.* v. *Whitchurch, supra* at 144, *per* ARDEN M.R.

8 *Charitable Trusts* (1887), 87.

any of the more modern branches of learning such as mathematics, natural science or modern languages.[1] It is hardly surprising therefore that this cramping effect of the *cy-près* doctrine was subjected to statutory attack.

The first breach in the doctrine was relatively insignificant.

The Grammar Schools Act 1840 (sometimes called Sir Eardley Wilmot's Act)[2] enabled courts of equity, by means of schemes, to reform grammar schools (*i.e.* endowed schools originally founded for the teaching of Latin and Greek) by extending the scope of their education to subjects other than classical languages and making other reforms such as enlarging the class of scholars who might be admitted to the school, or uniting schools. This Act did not, however, affect any of the public schools subsequently subjected to the Public Schools Act 1868 except Shrewsbury. The Grammar Schools Act 1840 has been repealed.[3]

An attempt was made in the Bill introduced in 1853 (which was to become the Charitable Trusts Act 1853) to give the Charity Commission power either on proper application or on its own initiation to alter trust purposes over a very much wider field. But the attempt was abortive and the projected clause[4] still-born.

Next, the Public Schools Act 1868[5] gave new flexibility to the foundations within its purview.[6] The existing governing bodies of the seven schools concerned were given power to alter their constitutions, which they did.[7] The new governing bodies were empowered to make statutes on a wide-ranging number of matters[8] and to consolidate and amend the then existing statutes and regulations,[9] and to repeal or alter any new statutes made pursuant to the Act.[10] Repeals or alterations of the new statutes must be laid before the Privy Council and any trustees, person or body corporate directly affected thereby can petition Her Majesty in Council to withhold her approval from the whole or any part of such statute.[11]

The most substantial breach, however, in the *cy-près* doctrine was effected by the Endowed Schools Act 1869, the first of a series of Acts (now all repealed[12]) affecting educational endowments. Under that Act power was given (subject to ultimate control by the Privy Council or its Judicial Committee) to an independent commission set up for a term of years to reorganise educational trusts subject thereto "in such manner as may render [them] most conducive to the advancement of education of boys and girls or either of them"; to alter and add to existing educational trusts, to make new trusts or to consolidate or divide them—all without the necessity for an application from trustees. Thus the purposes of a trust of sufficient antiquity could be changed before they had become impracticable of execution. A limited power was also given to the Charity Commissioners to transfer doles to educational purposes.

---

1 *A.-G.* v. *Whiteley* (1805), 11 Ves. 241 (Leeds Grammar School); *A.-G.* v. *Dean and Canons of Christ Church* (1822), Jac. 484; *Re Highgate School* (1838), 2 Jur. 774.

2 See Owen, *English Philanthropy 1660–1960* (1964) 249.

3 CA 1960, s. 39 and Sch. 5.

4 The terms of clause XXV are conveniently set out in the Natham Report (1952), Cmnd. 8710, 23.

5 31 and 32 Vict. c. 118.

6 Eton, Winchester, Westminster, Charterhouse, Rugby, Harrow and Shrewsbury.

7 P.S.A. 1868, s. 5.

8 *Ibid.*, s. 6.

9 *Ibid.*, s. 7.   10 *Ibid.*, s. 11.

11 *Ibid.*, ss. 9 and 10.   12 See Education Act 1973, s. 2.

Another very limited qualification of the *cy-près* doctrine was to be found in the Prison Charities Act 1882[1] which conferred a power on the Charity Commissioners to make a scheme respecting prison charities on the application of any Secretary of State if they would have had power to do so on the application of the trustees or other persons acting in the administration of the charity. This Act was repealed by the Charities Act 1960.[2]

More important was the City of London Parochial Charities Act 1883. The resident population of the City declined with startling rapidity during the nineteenth century with the result that for "the connoisseur of obsolete charities the mid-Victorian City of London offered an incomparable museum and for the charity reformer an irresistible challenge".[3] The movement for reform of the City charities without regard to parochial limits and the founder's wishes was initiated by Thomas Hare, one of the Charity Commissioners' inspectors in his 1860 report, to which in 1863 the Charity Commissioners added their support.[4] Other critics in and outside Parliament called for action and finally a Royal Commission sat under the chairmanship of the Duke of Northumberland. When it reported on 12th March 1880 its proposals encountered bitter opposition as did two bills introduced by James Bryce with drafting assistance from Sir Arthur Hobhouse, a well known protagonist of *cy-près* reform.[5] The Act which finally emerged in 1883 constituted a body known as "The Trustees of the London Parochial Charities". The general effect of the Act was to give the Charity Commissioners) with two additional Commissioners) power to frame schemes under which, except in the five largest City parishes, the endowment of parochial trusts in the City (other than property held on ecclesiastical trusts) could be applied throughout metropolitan London to such causes as education, libraries and museums, open spaces, recreation and drill grounds, provident institutions, convalescent hospitals, and, in general, for the improvement of "the physical, social and moral condition of the poorer inhabitants of the metropolis '.[6] The five large parishes[7] continued to handle their own charities, though in conformity with schemes to be made by the Charity Commissioners. Endowments held on ecclesiastical trusts could be pooled so as to serve the whole metropolis though in other respects the objects of the trusts could not be changed. The Act was repealed.

Mention must finally be made of three minor pieces of legislation which made further, though very limited, inroads into the *cy-près* doctrine. The first was the Charitable Trusts Act 1914[8]—a private Member's Bill introduced by Lord Parmoor—which dealt with trusts whose benefits were confined to a borough or part of a borough. It empowered the Court and the Commissioners to extend the scope of such trusts to adjacent boroughs and, in the case of "dole trusts", to apply the funds "for the relief of distress or sickness or for improving ... the physical, social or moral condition of the poor in the area extended".[9]

---

1 See Mitcheson, *op. cit.*, 359–360.
2 See CA 1960, Sch. 7, Pt. 1.
3 Owen, *op. cit.*, 276 *et seq.*
4 See Mitcheson, *op. cit.*, 330–331.
5 See A. Hobhouse, *The Dead Hand.*
6 CLPCA 1883, s. 14.
7 St. Andrews, Holborn; St. Botolph, Aldgate; St. Botolph, Bishopsgate; St. Bride's, Fleet Street; St. Giles, Cripplegate: see CLPCA 1883, Sch. 1.
8 4 & 5 Geo. 5 c. 56.
9 CTA 1914, s. 1 (repealed).

Next, when various voluntary hospitals began to run into financial difficulties the Commissioners were empowered by the Voluntary Hospitals (Paying Patients) Act 1936[1] to make schemes permitting the governing bodies to admit paying patients despite the terms of the original trust deed. Then in 1939 the Commissioners were empowered by a short Act to make schemes for the sale of fuel allotments or for their use for any purpose specified in the scheme.[2]

---

1 Voluntary Hospitals (Paying Patients) Act 1936, s. 2 (repealed).
2 The Charities (Fuel Allotments) Act 1939.

Chapter 25

Basic Principles of "Cy-près" Application

There must be charity

In the law of wills there was a rule of construction known as the *cy-près* doctrine by which limitations of real estate in themselves void as infringing the rule in *Whitby* v. *Mitchell* were saved.[1] The doctrine of *cy-près* discussed in this work is, however, a doctrine whose rules are applicable only to charitable dispositions. Accordingly the first prerequisite of the *cy-près* doctrine as applied in the law of charities is that the purpose or institution to which a disposition has been made is a charity. Recent reminders of this fundamental principle are to be found in overseas jurisdictions,[2] as well as in England[3] and Scotland.[4]

There must be a *cy-près* occasion

The next prerequisite of a *cy-près* application is that some situation should arise which the law recognises as being one in which the *cy-près* doctrine can operate. The term "*cy-près* occasion" is used in this book to describe such a situation. Courts of equity recognised only two *cy-près* occasions, namely (1) cases where the charitable purpose in question had become impossible to perform and (2) cases where it had become impracticable to carry out the charitable purpose. Inexpediency was not enough: nor was partial impossibility.

Statute, in the form of the Charities Act 1960, has added to the number of *cy-près* occasions which can arise in England and Wales, while confirming the *cy-près* occasions recognised and developed by the courts of equity.

In jurisdictions where there has been no legislative extension of the *cy-près* doctrine the courts will only apply funds *cy-près* if there is impossibility or impracticability. Moreover the Charities Act 1960 confirms in statutory form the equitable doctrine of *cy-près*. Hence it is convenient to discuss the "equitable" *cy-près* occasions first.

EQUITABLE *CY-PRÈS* OCCASIONS: IMPOSSIBILITY OR IMPRACTICABILITY

Apart from statute, the *cy-près* principle can only be invoked if it can be clearly established that the mode of application specified by the donor cannot be

---

1 See *Theobald on Wills* (13th edn.) para. 1474; and see Sheridan and Delany, *The Cy-près Doctrine* 11–15.
2 Rhode Island: *Edwards* v. *De Simone* 252 A. 2d 327, (1969); India: *Mudaliar* v. *Mudaliar* A.I.R. 1970 S.C. 1839.   3 *Re Jenkins's Will Trusts*, [1966] Ch. 249.
4 *MacTavish's Trustees* v. *St. Columba High Church* 1967 S.L.T. Notes 50.

carried into practical effect. But the principle does not apply to cases in which—there being neither failure of objects nor obsolescence of method—the changing circumstances of society have made the duties of the trustees and managers of the foundation much more arduous and discouraging in their results.[1] The point was well put by Sir JOHN ROMILLY M.R. in *Philpott* v. *St. George's Hospital*:[2]

> "If the testator has, by his will, pointed out clearly what he intends to be done, and his directions are not contrary to the law, this Court is bound to carry that intention into effect, and has no right, and is not at liberty to speculate upon whether it would have been more expedient or beneficial for the community that a different mode of application of the funds in charity should have occurred to the mind of the testator, or that he should have directed some different scheme for carrying his charitable intentions into effect. Accordingly instances of charities of the most useless description have come before the Court, but which it has considered itself bound to carry into effect."

The court thus had no power to vary charitable trusts where the original foundation was capable of taking effect, even in a manner which it might surmise that the founder himself would have contemplated had he been able to foresee the changes wrought by time.[3]

In countries where there is no enlarging statutory definition of *cy-près* occasions, the strict requirement of impossibility or impracticability continues to apply.[4] Here again inexpediency is not enough.[5] Nor will partial impossibility amount to a *cy-près* occasion.[6] Thus in *Edinburgh Corporation* v. *Cranston's Trustees*[7] there was a gift for 12 poor persons fulfilling certain conditions, but only two such persons could be found: the gift remained operative and no occasion for *cy-près* arose.

The intended purpose need not be *immediately* practicable.[8] If it is impossible to carry out the purpose in question at the relevant date, there must be an inquiry whether there is any reasonable prospect that it will become practicable at some future date.[9] In this context the relevant date is the date on which the gift first vests in interest in charity whether in possession[10] or in reversion or re-

---

1 *Trustees of the Domestic Training School etc. Glasgow*, 1923 S.C. 892.
2 (1859), 27 Beav. 107, at 111.
3 *A.-G.* v. *Sherborne Grammar School Governors* (1854), 18 Beav. 256, at 280.
4 *Re Sugrabai Mohamedai Alibhai Karirujee Charitable Trust*, [1960] E.A. 521 (Tanganyika); *City of Worcester* v. *Directors of the Worcester Free Public Library*, 211 N.E. 2d 356 (1965) (Massachusetts); *Destitute of Bennington County* v. *Henry W. Putman Memorial Hospital*, 215 A. 2d 134 (1965) (Vermont); *Re Barry's Estate*, 139 N.W. 2d 72 (1966) (Wisconsin); *Re MacAuley* (1971) 18 D.L.R. 3d 726 (Prince Edward Island).
5 *Philpott* v. *St. George's Hospital* (1859), 27 Beav. 107, at 111–112.
6 *Ex parte Estate Hofmeyr*, 1962 (3) S.A. 314 (South Africa).
7 1960 S.C. 244.
8 See *A.-G.* v. *Bishop of Chester* (1785), 1 Bro. C.C. 44; *Re Villiers-Wilkes* (1895) 11 T.L.R. 250; *Chamberlayne* v. *Brockett* (1872), 8 Ch. App. 206; *Biscoé* v. *Jackson* (1887), 35 Ch.D. 460, C.A.; *Sinnett* v. *Herbert* (1872), 7 Ch. App. 232; *A.-G.* v. *Lady Downing* (1769), Wilm. 1; *A.-G.* v. *Bowyer* (1798), 3 Ves. 714, at 728; *Re Swain* [1905] 1 Ch. 669, C.A.
9 See *Re White's Will Trusts*, [1955] Ch. 188, at 193; *Re Tacon*, [1958] Ch. 447; *A.-G. for South Australia* v. *Bray* (1964), 111 C.L.R. 402.
10 *Re Slevin*, [1891] 2 Ch. 236, C.A.: *Re Geikie* (1911), 27 T.L.R. 484.

mainder.[1] If there is a reversionary gift and it is defeasible, the possibility that it may be divested is to be ignored;[2] the question must be decided by reference to the value of the whole fund at the relevant date, not the value at that date of the reversionary interest.[3] Only if the answer to the inquiry is in the negative will there be a true case of initial impossibility or impracticability.[4] The burden of proving that a given purpose is impossible or impracticable is on the person who alleges that a gift has failed by reason thereof.[5]

There are very many examples in the books of impossibilities occasioning failure of charitable objects. Some classification is possible and indeed convenient, although in the examples which follow no attempt has been made to distinguish between cases of initial impossibility and cases of subsequent or supervening impossibility. Such a distinction will in due course be drawn.

Insufficient funds

Where the amount or value of a gift is so small that the donor's intentions cannot be accomplished even to a limited extent, there is a plain case of impossibility. Insufficiency of funds has frustrated many a specified charitable gift, but does not necessarily lead to lapse. Gifts of money to provide stipends for curates[6] or a cottage hospital[7] or a home for aged seamen[8] or feeble minded children[9] or a public hall[10] have all been applied *cy-près* because of inadequacy of funds. In *Re Beck*[11] there was a legacy to the Royal National Life-boat Institution of £3000 to defray the cost of building two lifeboats; the sum was not enough and fell into residue and went to the same institution. Where a fund is subscribed for several objects and is insufficient to effectuate all of them the court may by scheme direct that the money be applied to the primary object.[12] Sometimes, however, the court has discovered an intent that the gift shall only be applied to a particular charitable purpose if sufficient funds are raised and if the object fails for lack of funds from other sources the gift lapses.[13] Again it may appear that there was no general charitable intention behind the inadequate gift, as where a testator left a completely inadequate sum for the restoration of a ruined abbey.[14] Or the charitable intention may be subordinate to a dominant non-charitable intention. That was the conclusion reached by GAVAN DUFFY J. in *Re ffrench*[15] where the testatrix devised Monivea Castle "to the Irish Nation as a home for aged and indigent teachers". The gift was

1 *Re Soley* (1900), 17 T.L.R. 118; *Re Moon's Will Trusts*, [1948] 1 All E.R. 300; *Re Wright*, [1954] Ch. 347.
2 *Re Tacon*, [1958] Ch. 447.
3 *Ibid.*, Ch. 447.
4 *A.-G. for South Australia v. Bray* (1964), 111 C.L.R. 402 (High Court of Australia).
5 *Re Tacon*, [1958] Ch. 447, at 454.
6 *Re Burton's Charity*, [1938] 3 All E.R. 90.
7 *Re Whittaker*, [1951] 2 T.L.R. 955.
8 *Hay v. Murdoch*, [1952] W.N. 145.
9 *Ex parte Bloemfontein Child Welfare Society*, [1938] O.P.D. 34.
10 *Parker v. Moseley*, [1965] V.R. 580.
11 (1926), 42 T.L.R. 244.
12 *Rodwell v. A.-G.* (1886), 2 T.L.R. 712 (Anglican church in Paris).
13 *Re University of London Medical Sciences Institute Fund*, [1909] 2 Ch. 1, C.A.
14 *Re O'Meara's Will Trusts* (1939), 73 I.L.T. 22.
15 (1939) Reported as a footnote to *Re McGwire*, [1941] I.R. 33, at 49.

impracticable for lack of funds and the Attorney-General applied for a *cy-près* scheme. It was held that the paramount intention of the donor was the perpetuation of the castle and that the charity was a subordinate object. The gift therefore failed and could not be applied *cy-près*.

No available or suitable site

Certain charities can only function if they have premises from which to operate. Insufficiency of funds may make it impossible to acquire or develop a site. Many cases where no site is available are cases where, no doubt, a site might have been available at a price. But the absence of an available property makes the specified purpose impossible and a *cy-près* question then arises. A cognate situation arises where a site is available but it is unsuitable. Here too, the root cause of the unsuitability may be lack of money; but it may be a lack of foresight on the part of the testator who has failed to appreciate the unsuitability of the premises devised by him.

Where the premises upon which the charity is to operate have been compulsorily acquired[1] or sold during the course of administration[2] there is a clear case of failure and the intention of the donor comes into question.

In *Re White's Trusts*[3] the testator bequeathed a small legacy of £1000 consols to a City livery company upon trust, as soon as conveniently might be, and when a proper site could be obtained to erect almshouses for the benefit of defined classes of poor persons. He obviously realised that his gift might well be too small, since he declared that he had made the bequest in the hope that some other person, actuated by the same charitable feelings, would thereafter sufficiently endow the almshouses. In fact, after his death, the company could not find a suitable site, and there was no reasonable prospect of doing so. Moreover the company had no income available for the endowment and maintenance of the almshouses. BACON V.-C. held that the gift could not be applied *cy-près* but fell into residue like a lapsed legacy. He was unable to discover any general charitable intention in the gift.

On the other hand the court was able to discover a general charitable intention in *Biscoe* v. *Jackson*.[4] The testator in that case directed his trustees to set apart a sum of money out of such part of his personal estate as might by law be applied for charitable purposes, and to apply it in the establishment of a soup kitchen and cottage hospital for the parish of Shoreditch, in such manner as not to violate the Mortmain Acts. No land already in mortmain could be obtained within the parish. The will contained other legacies for the relief of poverty in Shoreditch and the Court of Appeal concluded that the object of the gift in question was to establish a charity for the benefit of the poor, with a particular mode of doing it. LINDLEY L.J. was influenced by the absence of any particular direction as to where the kitchen and hospital were to be or as to whether they were to be in the parish or out of the parish.[5] Yet there was a similar lack of particularity in that respect in *Re White's Trusts*.[6] In other respects

---

1 *Pedrotti* v. *Marin County, Cal.*, 152 F 2d 829 (C.A. 9th, 1946) (ranch taken on eminent domain).
2 *Re Trenhaile* (1911), 20 O.W.R. 610; *Re Evans Estate* [1947] 2 W.W.R. 639.
3 (1886), 33 Ch.D. 449.
4 (1887), 35 Ch.D. 460, C.A.
5 (1887), 35 Ch.D., at 470, C.A.   6 (1886), 33 Ch.D. 449.

the wishes of the testator had been spelt out with considerable particularity, and the actual decision seems very much on the border-line.[1] The words used in the instrument of gift may of course make it clear that there is an overriding charitable intent: in such a case the intention will not be defeated merely because the mode of executing that intent is made dependent on future uncertain events.[2]

Where land is devised as a site for a particular charitable purpose it may happen that the land is (or becomes) *unsuitable* for the purpose. The trust as constituted is impossible or at any rate impracticable. If the land is unsuitable at the date of the testator's death the gift will fail, unless the court can discover a general charitable intent, in which case a *cy-près* scheme will be directed. A good example of such unsuitability occurred in *A.-G. for New South Wales* v. *Perpetual Trustees Co., Ltd.*[3] where a testatrix left her homestead known as "Milly Milly" to a trustee to be held "for the training farm for orphan lads being Australians". To use the property as a training farm was found to be impracticable: it was too small, the plant was too old and the income produced was insufficient to meet the running expenses. But the High Court of Australia applied the property *cy-près* because there was a paramount charitable intention.[4] In other cases a paramount charitable intention has been lacking because the testator or donor had a very particular scheme in mind: here there will be a resulting trust.[5] If the land is used for the designated purpose but subsequently becomes unsuitable for that purpose the court will, without considering whether there is or is not a general charitable intention make a *cy-près* order.[6] The terms of such an order will either sanction removal to another site[7] or direct the use of the site (or the proceeds of sale thereof) for some other purpose. Where the terms of the trust provide that the trust is to continue only so long as the land is used as a site for the charity, or that the trust is to determine if the land ceases to be used for this purpose the express limitation or condition subsequent is subject to the rule against perpetuities;[8] accordingly where the site does become unsuitable a *cy-près* application will still be possible.

Gift illegal or against public policy

A gift for an object which is charitable but illegal, or for an object which is charitable by means which are illegal or against public policy, is impossible.

It may seem paradoxical that an object can be simultaneously charitable and illegal. But that was at one time the position with regard to gifts to promote any

---

1 See *Re Wilson*, [1913] 1 Ch. 314, at 322, *per* PARKER J.

2 *Chamberlayne* v. *Brockett* (1872) 8 Ch. App. 206.

3 (1940), 63 C.L.R. 209. Again the property may be in an inconvenient situation: *Re Dutch Reformed Church Wynberg* (1896) 13 S.C. 5 (no congregation in vicinity); *Ex parte Trustees of Boys Mission School, Simonstown* (1902), 11 S.C. 305.

4 See also *Re Wiseman's Trusts*, [1915] V.L.R. 439 (unimproved bushland given as a site for a children's home); *Re McGwire*, [1941] I.R. 33 (house unsuitable for use as sanatorium); *Hay* v. *Murdoch* [1952] W.N. 145, H.L. (Scot.)

5 *Re Gwilym*, [1952] V.L.R. 282; *Re Barry*,]1971] V.R. 395.

6 *Wallis* v. *Solicitor General for New Zealand*, [1903] A.C. 173.

7 *A.-G. for New South Wales* v. *Perpetual Trustee Co., Ltd.* (1940), 63 C.L.R. 209; and see many American cases cited in Scott, *Trusts* (3rd edn.) para. 399.2, n. 28.

8 *Re Cooper's Conveyance Trusts*, [1956] 1 W.L.R. 1096.

religion other than that of the established church;[1] and, as we have seen, this position was only gradually changed.[2] In such cases, the courts would find a general charitable intention to advance religion, and apply the trust funds *cy-près* for the benefit of the established church,[3] a truly remarkable feat of intellectual acrobatics. Even after the abandonment of this approach, certain religious practices were condoned as superstitious[4] but since these practices were not considered charitable, there could be no possibility of *cy-près*.

If from the context of a gift the general charitable intention of the donor is plain, but the prescribed manner of carrying out that intention is illegal, or against public policy, the court will execute the gift *cy-près*. Thus in *A.-G.* v. *Vint*[5] there was a gift by will to provide poor inmates of a workhouse aged over 60 with porter. Under the Poor Law Amendment Act 1834 and regulations thereunder, alcohol could only be brought into workhouses under medical supervision. KNIGHT BRUCE V.-C. did not discuss the question of a general charitable intent but merely said that care should be taken that the law be obeyed, adding that: "If fermented liquors should be prohibited the fund may be applied in some manner so as to give the poor old people in the [workhouse] tea, sugar and the like. The benefit of this good-natured bequest ought not to fail."[6] Again, where there is a general charitable intention, the fact that there is a trust to accumulate income beyond the legal period allowed by section 164 of the Law of Property Act 1925 (as now amended) will not defeat that intention: the income will be applied *cy-près*.[7]

The gift will fail altogether if the general intention is, in fact, illegal or contrary to public policy. A trust is illegal if its performance involves criminal conduct or tends to encourage such conduct. So, in one old case a bequest to trustees "to make seats for poor people to beg in by the highways" was held invalid because such begging was a criminal offence.[8] The trust disclosed no general intention to relieve poverty: it was a trust to encourage begging. Again, notwithstanding the mention in the Statute of Elizabeth I of the "relief or redemption of prisoners or captives" as a charitable purpose, a bequest to purchase the release of persons committed to prison for non-payment of fines under the game laws could have only one effect: to encourage further offences; such a bequest therefore fails.[9] It is contrary to public policy to promote a purpose which will involve the violation of the law of another country[10] or which might tend to promote a revolution in a friendly country.[11] A gift to "further the development of the Irish Republic" was held by a New York court

---

1 See for example *A.-G.* v. *Baxter* (1684), 1 Vern. 248.

2 See at 55, *supra*.

3 *Da Costa* v. *De Paz* (1754), 2 Swan 487, n.; *Cary* v. *Abbot* (1802), Ves. 490.

4 E.g. masses.

5 (1850), 3 De. G. & Sm. 704.

6 *Ibid.*, at 705.

7 *Martin* v. *Margham* (1844), 14 Sim. 230; *Re Bradwell*, [1952] Ch. 575; *cf. Re Lushington*, [1963] N.Z.L.R. 313; [1964] N.Z.L.R. 161, N.Z.C.A. (no general charitable intention).

8 *Anon*, Duke 133.

9 *Thrupp* v. *Collett* (1858), 26 Beav. 125.

10 *A.-G.* v. *Guise* (1692), 2 Vern. 266 (*cy-près* application ordered because of general charitable intention).

11 *Habershon* v. *Vardon* (1851), 4 De. G. & Sm. 467 (trust to restore Jews to Jerusalem, then under Turkish rule). A similar trust was upheld in 1924 when Palestine was no longer under Turkish rule: *Re Rosenblum* (1924), 131 L.T. 21.

in 1925 to be against public policy as having a tendency to embroil the United States with a friendly power.[1]

Impracticable condition

If a gift to a charitable purpose is subject to a condition which makes it impracticable to carry out the gift the condition in effect occasions a failure of the gift.[2] It then becomes necessary to see whether the condition is subsidiary to the main intention of the donor or is an essential part of the donor's scheme.

In *Re Robinson*[3] P. O. LAWRENCE J. had to deal with a fund bequeathed many years earlier for the endowment of a church of an evangelical nature. Conditions were attached to the gift including what was called an "abiding" condition that a black gown should be worn in the pulpit unless this should become illegal. Evidence was adduced that the use of the black gown in the pulpit was practically unknown in the other related churches, and that its use was calculated to alienate the congregation and to defeat the main objects of the testatrix, namely the teaching of and practice of evangelical doctrine and services. The judge accepted that the dominant charitable purpose of the testatrix as expressed in her will was to endow an evangelical church. Insistence upon the subsidiary condition relating to the black gown would sabotage the main purpose. Accordingly, since compliance with the condition would be impractacable the trust was modified by dispensing with it.

On similar principles a condition restricting a hostel to members of the British Empire of European origin was dispensed with because it had come to be in conflict with the main purpose of the relevant trusts, which was that of promoting community of citizenship, culture and tradition among all members of the British Commonwealth of Nations.[4]

In *Re Lysaght*[5] the dominant declared purpose of the testamentary gift in issue was to found medical studentships within the gift of the Royal College of Surgeons. However the testatrix imposed a condition that students who were of the Jewish or Roman Catholic faith should not be eligible. The college was not prepared to accept the gift with such a discriminatory provision but was prepared to accept the gift with that provision omitted. BUCKLEY L. held that the impracticability of giving effect to what he found to be an inessential part of the intentions of the testatrix should not be allowed to defeat her paramount general intent. Her paramount intention (he held) was confined to establishing a charitable trust of which the college should be trustees and was conditional upon the college being willing and able to accept that office:[6]

"it was the particular wish of the testatrix that the college should be the trustee of this fund because of its peculiar aptitude for the office and that it

---

1 *Re Killen*, 124 Misc. 720, 209 N.Y. Supp. 206 (1925).
2 See *Re Wilson*, [1913] 1 Ch. 314; *Re Mitchell's Will Trusts* (1966), 110 Sol. Jo. 291.
3 *Re Robinson*, [1923] 2 Ch. 332; and see also *Re Richardson's Will* (1887), 58 L.T. 45, *cf.* *Re Macdonald* (1971), 18 D.L.R. (3d) 52.
4 *Re Dominion Students' Hall Trust*, [1947] Ch. 183. For the relevant statutory provisions now affecting discriminatory trusts, see 571, *infra*. The American experience is set out in Kutner, *Legal Aspects of Charitable Trusts and Foundations* (1970) 101–112.
5 [1966] Ch. 191.   6 [1966] Ch. 191, at 205.

was to the college and to no-one else that she meant to confide these discretionary powers."

This finding was crucial to the decision. Accordingly he ordered by way a scheme that the trusts should be carried out without the discriminating provision.

In this context there is what has aptly been called a "time honoured distinction between essential and accidental characteristics".[1] In some cases the condition is a fundamental part of the gift: if it is impossible to carry out such a condition the gift fails but *cy-près* is not possible.[2]

Charity deprived of objects

A charitable gift is impossible to carry out if there is no need for it. There are numerous cases in the books of gifts designed to remedy a non-existent evil or to carry out an object which has already been achieved.

Thus a charity may be deprived of its objects by the abolition of a particular form of punishment[3] or evil such as slavery[4] or the dying out of a particular disease.[5] Alternatively the particular class of person intended to benefit from the charity may have disappeared, so that a trust for Huguenot *refugees* in London,[6] or to advance Christianity among the infidels of Virginia,[7] or to to hold services in the Gaelic language in London[8] is unable to operate in any sensible way. A particular congregation may change its tenets[9] or disperse,[10] and when this happens a gift for the benefit of that congregation is robbed of effect. The same is true when there is a lack of applicants[11] or persons entitled to benefit under the trusts. Gifts which postulate the continuance of a particular state of affairs give rise to a *cy-près* question when that state of affairs comes to an end.[12] There are, for example, several cases where the underlying assumption behind the gift was that certain public services would continue to be available on a voluntary basis only.[13]

---

1 *A.-G. for New South Wales* v. *Perpetual Trustee Co., Ltd.* (1940), 63 C.L.R. 209, at 226.
2 See *Re Welstead* (1858), 25 Beav. 612; *Re Wilson*, [1913] 1 Ch. 314; *Re Mitchell's Will Trusts* (1966), 110 Sol. Jo. 291.
3 *A.-G.* v. *Hankey* (1867), L.R. 16 Eq. 140, n. (imprisonment for debt abolished: funds applied to help discharged prisoners); and see *Re Prison Charities* (1873) L.R. 16 Eq. 129.
4 *A.-G.* v. *Gibson* (1835), 2 Beav. 317, n. (in the colonies); *A.-G.* v. *Ironmongers Co.* (1834), 2 My. & K. 576; (1840)2 Beav. 313 (in Turkey and Barbary); *Jackson* v. *Phillips* 14 Allen. 539 (1867) (in the U.S.A.). Malins V.C. in 1867 considered that black people in the U.S.A. had achieved equal civil rights: *New* v. *Bonaker* (1867), L.R. 4 Eq. 655.
5 *A.-G.* v. *Hicks* (1809), 3 Bro. C.C. 166 n.; Highmore, *Law of Mortmain* (2nd edn.) 336 (leprosy); *A.-G.* v. *Earl of Craven* (1856), 21 Beav. 392 (plague funds applied to hospital).
6 *A.-G.* v. *Daugars* (1864), 33 Beav. 621 (funds applied to French Protestants in London).
7 *A.-G.* v. *London Corporation* (1790), 3 Bro. C.C. 171.
8 *A.-G.* v. *Stewart* (1872), L.R. 14 Eq. 17; but see *Rodwell* v. *A.-G.* (1886), 2 T.L.R. 712.
9 *A.-G.* v. *Bunce* (1868), L.R. 6 Eq. 563.
10 *Andersons Trustees* v. *Scott* 1914 S.C. 942.
11 *Philipps* v. *A.-G.*, [1932] W.N. 100; and see *Aberdeen Servants Benevolent Fund* 1914 S.C. 8; *Re Borland* 1908 S.C. 852; *A.-G.* v. *Forde*, [1932] N.I. 1.
12 *Ex parte Magniac* 1942 E.D.L. 160 (drought); *Ex parte Trustees of Transvaal Volunteers Sustentation Fund* 1914 W.L.D. 105.
13 *Re Mackenzie*, [1962] 1 W.L.R. 880 (education); and see *Re Leitch*, [1965] V.R. 204; *Re Hillier*, [1954] 1 W.L.R. 700, C.A. (hospital building); *Re Wokingham Fire Brigade Trusts* [1951] Ch. 373 (local fire brigade); see also *Richmond Corporation* v. *Morell* (1965), 11 R.R.C. 283, C.A. (gift in aid of the poor rate).

OTHER *CY-PRÈS* OCCASIONS ADDED BY CHARITIES ACT 1960

As has already been said, the Charities Act 1960 relaxed the rule that the only *cy-près* occasion was impossibility or impracticability in executing the trusts. Section 13 set out the circumstances in which charitable funds may be applied *cy-près* and these are very much wider than under the old law. But it still remains true that the purposes of a charity cannot be altered merely because the court thinks that some other application of the available funds would be more beneficial to the community.

Some of the circumstances set out in section 13 allowed of a *cy-près* application under the old law. Thus *cy-près* was available even before the Act "where the original purposes, in whole or in part, (i) have been as far as may be fulfilled, or (ii) cannot be carried out, or not according to the directions given and to the spirit of the gift".[1] Again *cy-près* was also available "where the original purposes provide a use for part only of the property available by virtue of the gift".[2]

Conventionally section 13 has been treated as engrafting on to the principles relating to initial failure and subsequent failure further *cy-près* occasions which fall short of being occasions of *subsequent* impossibility or impracticability. But the wording may be wide enough to allow the argument that the law relating to *initial* impossibility or impracticability has been qualified. In the case of a will the original purposes may have been conceived many years before the death of the testator.[3] By the time the trust takes effect it is possible that the original purposes "cannot be carried out . . . according to the directions given and to the spirit of the gift"[4] or that they have "ceased . . . to provide a suitable and effective method of using the property available by virtue of the gift regard being had to the spirit of the gift."[5] Is *cy-près* available immediately the trust comes into being? If it is not available, the trustees would merely need to wait for a token period and then apply to the court, which would, to say the least, be an odd result. Yet if the statutory provisions go as far as to allow *cy-près* at the initial stage to cover the idiosyncrasies of cases like *Re Robinson*,[6] they have given to the courts a very ample and as yet unappreciated power.

One expression which occurs several times in section 13 is "the spirit of the gift". This has been held to mean "the basic intention underlying the gift, that intention being ascertainable from the terms of the relevant instrument and in the light of the admissible evidence".[7]

The additional statutory *cy-près* situations may be split into three categories.

Conjunction of funds

The circumstances in which the original purposes of a charitable gift can be altered to allow the property given or part of it to be applied *cy-près* include the case:

"Where the property available by virtue of the gift and other property applicable for similar purposes can be more effectively used in conjunction,

---

1 CA 1960, s. 13 (1) (a).   2 *Ibid.*, s. 13 (1) (b).

3 Or a life tenant under an *inter vivos* trust may live for many years before the trusts in remainder for charity take effect.

4 CA 1960, s. 13 (1) (a) (ii).   5 *Ibid.*, s. 13 (1) (e) (iii).

6 [1923] 2 Ch. 332.   7 *Re Lepton's Charity*, [1972] Ch. 276, at 285.

and to that end can suitably, regard being had to the spirit of the gift, be made applicable to common purposes."[1]

The Nathan Committee considered that there was a strong presumption in favour of uniting all non-ecclesiastical charities in the same parish, and often in two or more parishes.[2] And such a merger may be recommended by a local authority following a review under section 11 of the 1960 Act. The provision quoted above authorises the making of a scheme for merger in such a case. As a means of reducing the costs of administering several small charities in the same area the provision is plainly useful, although its application is not confined to cases of this sort. Such a scheme is not, strictly, a *cy-près* scheme; and, indeed, it was never necessary to show that the original purposes of a charity had become impossible to carry out in order to justify consolidating it with other charities.

Extension of area or class

A further set of circumstances in which the original purposes of a charitable gift can be altered to allow the property given or part of it to be applied *cy-près* is specified in section 13 (1) (d) of the Charities Act 1960, which covers the case:

> "Where the original purposes were laid down by reference to an area which was then but has since ceased to be a unit for some other purpose, or by reference to a class of persons or to an area which has for any reason since ceased to be suitable, regard being had to the spirit of the gift, or to be practical in administering the gift."

In so far as this provision relates to *areas* three cases are covered. The first is the case of an area which originally was but has since ceased to be a unit for some other purpose. Clearly, this will be the case where the area is difficult to identify because of changes in the boundaries of local government areas. But the jurisdiction to apply property *cy-près* arises wherever there is a change of boundaries, regardless of any difficulty in identification, although one would expect the court in its discretion to refuse to order a scheme where the change has not really caused any inconvenience or difficulty to the trustees. The second case is of an area which has for any reason since ceased to be suitable, regard being had to the spirit of the gift. Under the old law a *cy-près* application would only have been possible if restriction of the charity to the designated area would have made the accomplishment of charity impossible or impractical. For *impossibility* and *impracticability* is substituted *unsuitability*, regard being had to the spirit of the gift. Thirdly, one has the case of an area which has for any reason since ceased to be practical in administering the gift. This probably reproduces the old law under which the court had already allowed impracticability as a substitute for impossibility.

In its application to a *class of persons* the provisions of section 13 (1) (d) makes *cy-près* application available if the class has for any reason since ceased to be suitable, regard being had to the spirit of the gift. This breaks new ground

---

1 CA 1960, s. 13 (1) (c).
2 See Nathan Report (1952), Cmnd. 8710 para. 596.

unsuitability being substituted for impossibility or impracticability. *Cy-près* application is also available if the class has for any reason since ceased to be practical in administering the gift. This probably reproduces the old law.

Where property is held for charitable purposes which are laid down by reference to one of certain types of area, a scheme may be made in exercise of the court's jurisdiction over charities so as to enlarge the area to another specified area.[1] The types of existing area together with the permissible areas of enlargement are as follows:[2]

EXISTING AREA	PERMISSIBLE ENLARGEMENT
1 Greater London:	1 Any area comprising Greater London;
2 Any area in Greater London and not in, or partly in, the City of London:	2 (i) Any area in Greater London, and not in, or partly in, the City of London; (ii) the area of Greater London exclusive of the City of London; (iii) any area comprising the area of Greater London exclusive of the City of London; (iv) any area partly in Greater London and partly in any adjacent parish or parishes (civil or ecclesiastical) and not in the City of London;
3 A district:	3 Any area comprising the district;
4 Any area in a district:	4 (i) Any area in the district; (ii) the district; (iii) any area comprising the district; (iv) any area partly in the district and partly in any adjacent district;
5 A parish (civil or ecclesiastical) or two or more parishes or an area in a parish or partly in each of two or more parishes:	5 Any area not extending beyond the parish or parishes comprising or adjacent to the existing area.

The power to enlarge the permissible area of a charity is without prejudice to the court's powers to make true *cy-près* schemes in similar places.[3]

Adequate alternative provision

The Charities Act 1960 also authorises a *cy-près* application:

> "Where the original purposes, in whole or in part, have, since they were laid down, been adequately provided for by other means."[4]

Under the old law this was a situation not covered by the *cy-près* doctrine; and so, for example, in *A.-G.* v. *Day*[5] NORTH J. held that a trust to maintain a road did not become impossible when the local authority was clothed with liability to maintain it. There are, indeed, numerous cases where benefits which were originally provided by a charity have become the statutory responsibility

---

1 CA 1960, s. 13 (4).
2 *Ibid.*, Sch. 3; London Government Act 1963, s. 81 (9) (c); Local Government Act 1972, s. 210 (9) (f).
3 CA 1960, s. 13 (4).
4 *Ibid.*, s. 13 (1) (e) (i).
5 [1900] 1 Ch. 31.

of a public or local authority: the advancement of those purposes under a trust in effect does little more than relieve the rates or the national exchequer. In such cases, the court now has jurisdiction to make a scheme for a more useful application of the trust's funds.

Under this provision the Commissioners have made schemes for a number of charities established for the repair of roads and bridges, substituting for those purposes other general purposes for the benefit of local inhabitants which could include, for instance, the promotion of the arts, the provision of seats and shelters, the preservation of old buildings or the improvement of local amenities.[1] Indeed the Commissioners consider it appropriate for them to make schemes under this provision wherever the objects to which a charity's benefits were originally directed have become the statutory responsibility of the central or local government authorities.[2]

No longer charitable

Cy-près application is now authorised where the original purposes, in whole or in part, have, since they were laid down, ceased, as being useless or harmful to the community or for other reasons, to be in law charitable.[3] Prior to 1960 such a case, if it existed, must have been very rare indeed: certainly there is no reported case in which the court has held that a trust which was once a valid charitable trust has since ceased in law to be so. The case of *National Anti-Vivisection Society* v. *I.R.Comrs.*[4] is not in point, for the actual decision there was that anti-vivisection societies were not charitable and never had been so; the earlier case of *Re Foveaux*,[5] where such societies had been held to be charitable, was overruled as wrongly decided. No question, therefore, of a *cy-près* application could have arisen, even prior to 1960: *cy-près* could only have operated if the purpose was originally charitable but had become impossible to perform as a charitable trust because of some change in the law. The decision in *National Anti-Vivisection Society* v. *I.R.Comrs.*,[4] was that anti-vivisection never had been a charitable purpose.

The possibility of an institution or purpose originally charitable ceasing to be so is, since the passing of the 1960 Act, more likely. This is because an institution (which includes any trust or undertaking[6]) registered by the Charity Commissioners is conclusively presumed to be a charity while it is on the register, for all purposes other than rectification of the register.[7] Accordingly, if a charity is removed from the register on the ground that its purposes are not in law charitable, it seems that the trustees will be entitled, indeed bound, to apply for a *cy-près* scheme, for the original purposes are conclusively presumed to have been charitable while it was on the register, and have since ceased in law to be charitable.[8]

---

1 [1970] Ch. Com. Rep. 16, para. 43.
2 [1968] Ch. Com. Rep. 17, para. 68.
3 CA 1960, s. 13 (1) (e) (ii).
4 [1948] A.C. 31.
5 [1895] 2 Ch. 501.
6 CA 1960, s. 46.
7 CA 1960, s. 5 (1).
8 The conclusive presumption is for all purposes other than rectification of the register and so applies for the purposes of CA 1960, s. 13.

Ineffectiveness

Cy-près application is available where the original purposes,[1] in whole or in part, have since they were laid down "ceased in any other way to provide a suitable and effective method of using the property available by virtue of the gift, regard being had to the spirit of the gift".[2] It is not enough to show only that some other application of the property of the charity would be more effective or more suitable than the original one chosen by the donor; it must be shown that the mode of application chosen by the donor has ceased to be suitable or effective.

The Charity Commissioners believe that it is an application of the *cy-près* principle to remove a limitation on the amount of any grant which may be given to relieve need, hardship or distress and that it is generally desirable to do this.[3] Presumably this is an application of the principle set out in section 13 (1) (e) (iii) of the 1960 Act.

Requirement of paramount charitable intent

It has already been noted[4] that in the case of an initial failure or impossibility of the charitable purpose the *cy-près* doctrine can only operate where there is a paramount charitable intent.[5] In cases of supervening impossibility a paramount charitable intent is irrelevant:[6] *cy-près* application will in such cases follow, provided there is no alternative and valid[7] disposition directed to take effect in the event of supervening impossibility. The basis of *cy-près* application in the case of supervening failure is the effective dedication of the fund to charity. Accordingly it is convenient to discuss in turn (1) the relevance of paramount charitable intent in the case of initial failure (2) its irrelevance in the case of supervening failure and then (3) the doctrine (if one may so call it) of effective dedication to charity.

INITIAL FAILURE

The principle that where there is a paramount charitable intent an initially impossible gift will be applied *cy-près* is well established in this country.[8] Conversely the absence of such an intent is fatal to *cy-près* application.[9]

---

1 The original purposes of a gift refer to the gift as a whole and not to parts of a gift separately: *Re Lepton's Charity*, [1972] Ch. 276.

2 CA 1960, s. 13 (1) (e) (iii).

3 [1968] Ch. Com. Rep. 7, para. 18.

4 See 220–221, *supra*.

5 *Re Richardson's Will* (1887), 58 L.T. 45; *Biscoe v. Jackson* (1887), 35 Ch.D. 460, C.A.; *Re Reed* (1893), 10 T.L.R. 87; *Re Robinson*, [1923] 2 Ch. 332; *Re Beck* (1926), 42 T.L.R. 244; *Re Whittaker*, [1951] 2 T.L.R. 955; *Re Bradwell*, [1952] Ch. 575; *Re Hillier's Trusts*, [1954] 1 W.L.R. 700, C.A.

6 *Re Wright*, [1954] Ch. 347, C.A. discussed at 239, *infra*. This applies to other supervening *cy-près* occasions under the Charities Act 1960.

7 I.e. non-perpetuitous.

8 *Biscoe v. Jackson* (1887), 35 Ch.D. 460, C.A.; *Re Wilson*, [1913] 1 Ch. 314, at 320–321; *Re Lysaght*, [1966] Ch. 191.

9 *Re Wilson*, [1913] 1 Ch. 314.

These principles are accepted in Ireland,[1] Australia,[2] Canada,[3] New Zealand[4] and South Africa.[5] And they are also accepted in numerous states in the United States.[6]

SUPERVENING FAILURE

The irrelevance of paramount or general charitable intent in the context of supervening impossibility has not always been recognised. In several cases in England the court has appeared to consider that a general charitable intent was necessary for cy-près application even in cases of supervening impossibility and has proceeded to discover such an intent.[7] As regards Scotland the House of Lords has insisted on a general charitable intent as a prerequisite to cy-près application in all cases.[8] In the Irish case of Re Templemoyle Agricultural School[9] which concerned the destination of the property of a school that ceased to exist CHATTERTON V.-C. felt it necessary to discover a general charitable intent. Australian[10] and Canadian[11] courts have also, on occasions, searched unnecessarily for such an intent, and found it. These statements in the Irish and other Commonwealth courts[12] are not statements of the preponderant view. Both in the Republic of Ireland and in Northern Ireland it has been held that absence of a general charitable intent is not fatal where there is supervening impossibility; and this has applied both to cases where the purposes have ceased to exist after the gift has taken effect[13] and to cases of surplus.[14] There are numerous authorities in Australia which do not insist on general charitable intent where

---

1 *Daly v. A.-G.* (1860), 11 I.Ch.R. 41; *Re Motherwell's Estate*, [1910] 1 I.R. 249; *Re McGwire*, [1941] I.R. 33.

2 *A.-G. for New South Wales v. Perpetual Trustee Co., Ltd.* (1940), 63 C.L.R. 209; *Re Mulcahy*, [1969] V.R. 545; *Re Tyrie*, [1970] V.R. 264.

3 *St. Andrews-Wesley Church Congregation v. Toronto General Trust Corporation* [1948] 4 D.L.R. 241 (Sup. Ct); *Jewish Home for the Aged of British Columbia v. Toronto General Trusts Corporation*, [1961] S.C.R. 465.

4 *Wallis v. Solicitor-General for New Zealand*, [1903] A.C. 173; *Re Joseph's Will Trusts* (1907), 26 N.Z.L.R. 504; *Re Macklin*, [1931] G.L.R. 152.

5 *Re Denton's Estate*, [1951] 4 S.A. 582; *Ex parte Estate Impey*, [1963] 1 S.A. 740.

6 *Rogers v. A.-G.*, 196 N.E. 2d 855 (1964) (Massachusetts); *Cinnaminson Corporation v. First Camden National Bank and Trust Co.*, 238 A2d 70 (1968) (New Jersey); *Re MacDowell* 112 N.E. 177 (1916) (New York); *Good Samaritan Hospital and Medical Center v. United States National Bank of Oregon* 425 P2d 541 (1967).

7 *Re Cunningham*, [1914] 1 Ch. 427; *Re Welsh Hospital (Netley) Fund*, [1921] 1 Ch. 655; *Re Edwin Riley Charities* (1930), 70 L.J. 409; *Re North Devon and West Somerset Relief Fund Trusts*, [1953] 1 W.L.R. 1260.

8 *Hay v. Murdoch*, [1952] W.N. 145.

9 (1869) I.R. 4 Eq. 295; and see *A.-G. v. Davis* (1870), 18 W.R. 1132.

10 *Lewis v. Benson*, [1944] V.L.R. 106; *Re Ethel Pedley Memorial Travelling Scholarship Trust* (1949), 49 S.R. N.S.W. 329; *Re Peacock's Charities*, [1956] Tas. S.R. 142; *Parker v. Moseley* [1965] V.R. 580.

11 *A.-G. v. Bullock*, R.E.D. 249 (1877) (Nova Scotia); *Re Fallis Estate*, [1948] 1 D.L.R. 27 (Saskatchewan).

12 For the Malayan decisions: see Sheridan and Delany, *op. cit.*, 96–97 and see also *Tia Kien Luing v. Tye Poh Sun* (1960), 27 M.L.J. 78 (Penang).

13 *Munster and Leinster Bank, Ltd. v. A.-G.* (1957), 91 I.L.T. 34; cf. *Re Hardy*, [1933] N.I. 150.

14 *Re Trusts of Rectory of St. John in the City of Cork* (1869) I.R. 3 Eq. 335; *A.-G. v. Forde*, [1932] N.I. 1; *Re Royal Kilmainham Hospital*, [1966] I.R. 451.

supervening impossibility occurs.[1] The orthodox view is well put by ADAM J. in *Beggs* v. *Kirkpatrick*:[2]

> "where the fund may be considered to have once vested in charity, or been effectively dedicated to charity, that is strong authority for the view that the court has jurisdiction to direct an application *cy-près* of funds belonging to that charity and that it is irrelevant to consider whether donations to it had been made originally for a specific purpose only, or with some more general charitable intention."

Even before the decision of the Court of Appeal in *Re Wright*[3] there were authorities in England[4] and Ireland[5] in which the court had directed a *cy-près* application where there had been a supervening failure without inquiring into general charitable intent or whether the gift was out and out. For example in *Re Hardy*[6] the trust constituted by the will of the testatrix was for a specific charitable purpose, namely to carry on a school erected by her during her lifetime. The trusts were fully carried out until by the operation of a new Act of Parliament it was closed permanently. MEGAW J. expressly found that there was no general charitable intent and made no mention of the gift being out and out.

EFFECTIVE DEDICATION TO CHARITY

In *Re Wright*[7] a testatrix who died in 1933 directed the trustees of her will to hold her residuary estate, subject to a prior life interest, upon trust to found and maintain a convalescent home for impecunious gentlewomen. The charitable purpose was practicable in 1933 but it was contended that practicability should be tested as at the date of the death of the tenant for life. ROMER L.J., with whom DENNING L.J. agreed,[8] held that the crucial date was that of the death of the testatrix, saying:[9]

> "Once money is effectually dedicated to charity, whether in pursuance of a general or a particular charitable intent, the testator's next of kin or residuancy legatees are for ever excluded and no question of subsequent lapse, or anything analogous to lapse, between the date of the testator's death and the time when the money becomes available for actual application to the testator's purpose can affect the matter so far as they are concerned."

---

1 *Hixon* v. *Campbell* (1924), 24 S.R. (N.S.W.) 505; *Re Swaine*, [1939] S.A.S.R. 25; *Williams* v. *A.-G.* (1948), 48 S.R.N.S.W. 505; *Re Wright*, [1951] Tas.S.R. 13; *Re Woollnough*, [1953] Tas.S.R. 25; *A.-G. for South Australia* v. *Bray* (1964), 111 C.L.R. 402; *Re Dutton*, [1968] S.A.S.R. 295. For New Zealand: see *Solicitor General* v. *Wanganui Corporation* [1919] N.Z.L.R. 63.
2 [1961] V.R. 764, at 767.
3 [1954] Ch. 347, C.A.
4 *A.-G.* v. *Glyn* (1841), 12 Sim. 84; *A.-G.* v. *Bushby* (1857), 24 Beav. 299; *A.-G.* v. *Edalji* (1907), 97 L.T. 292; *Re Colonial Bishoprics Fund 1841*, [1935] Ch. 148; *Re Whittaker* [1951] 2 T.L.R. 955.
5 *Re Shillelagh Parochial School* (1900), 1 N.I.J.R. 20; *Re Hardy*, [1933] N.I. 150.
6 [1933] N.I. 150.
7 [1954] Ch. 347, C.A.
8 [1954] Ch. 347, at 364. There was no other member of the court.
9 *Ibid.*, at 362–363.

This conclusion followed, in his view, upon the reasoning in *Re Slevin*.[1] In this respect the "charity" is assimilated to an ordinary individual legatee.[2] The principle formulated by ROMER L.J. in *Re Wright* was echoed by JENKINS L.J. in *Re Ulverston etc.*[3] when he said that "once the charity for which the fund was raised had been effectively brought into action the fund was to be regarded as permanently devoted to charity to the exclusion of any resulting trust". And it was accepted by BUCKLEY J. in *Re Lysaght*.[4] The principle may therefore be taken to be established. For the purposes of the principle there is no distinction between a gift to a charitable institution existing at the death of a testator and a gift to trustees to apply income for certain charitable purposes in existence at the death of a testator and to which the income could be applied.[5] In each case the property which vests effectively in charity does not fall into residue if subsequently the institution closes or the purposes become impracticable.

A question remains as to the applicability of the doctrine of effective dedication to gifts *inter vivos*. It is evident that HARMAN J. in *Re British School of Egyptian Archaeology*[6] was troubled by this point. The society in that case received subscription from various subscribers and on the winding up of the society the question was whether any subscriber was entitled to have any money back. HARMAN J. having posed the question said:[7]

> "The well known case of *Re Slevin* was concerned with a gift by will; it indicated that if money once be given by will to a charity, it matters not that the charity comes to an end shortly after the death of the testator and before the bequest is given effect to by the executors; it showed that once the testator is dead, his money is devoted to charity subject, of course to the rights of creditors; and that it makes no difference if the charity is thereafter dissolved."

He continued:[8]

> "That principle, of course, is not easy to apply to subscriptions and gifts *inter vivos*."

In consequence he justified his decision that there was no resulting trust by reference to two cases[9] "where it was decided that the money had been given out and out and could not be paid back".[10] It is noteworthy that HARMAN J. did not indicate precisely what the difficulties were in applying the principle to *inter vivos* gifts. Logically there appears to be no good reason for excluding *inter vivos* gifts from the ambit of *Re Wright*.[11] If a donor has failed to express an intention that his gift is one of a limited interest, the devotion of that gift to charitable purposes should exclude him from any further interest in the money,

---

1 [1891] 2 Ch. 236.
2 *Re Tacon*, [1958] Ch. 447, C.A., at 453.
3 *Re Ulverston and District New Hospital Building Trusts*, [1956] Ch. 622, at 636.
4 [1966] Ch. 191, at 208.
5 *Re Geikie* (1911), 27 T.L.R. 484, at 485.
6 [1954] 1 W.L.R. 546.
7 [1954] 1 W.L.R. 546, at 552.
8 [1954] 1 W.L.R. 546, at 552.
9 *Re Welsh Hospital (Netley) Fund*, [1921] 1 Ch. 655; *Re North Devon and West Somerset Relief Fund Trusts*, [1953] 1 W.L.R. 1260.
10 [1954] 1 W.L.R. 546, at 553.
11 [1954] Ch. 347, C.A.

just as the effectual devotion of a testamentary gift excludes the interests of next of kin or residuary legatees. Were the law otherwise it might be necessary in the case of the supervening failure of a trust set up *inter vivos* a century ago for a particular purpose to trace those persons entitled under the resulting trust. But there is no suggestion of this in those decided cases where a general charitable intent was lacking, and the failure was supervening.

Mention has already been made of the exception to the general rule that *cy-près* is available on supervening failure of a charitable gift.[1] The exception is where there is an expression of a contrary intention in the gift. The possibility of such an exception in the case of testamentary gifts was envisaged by KAY L.J. in *Re Slevin*[2] when he said:

> "it is possible that a will might be so framed as that a subsequent failure of the object of the charitable gift might occasion a resulting trust for the benefit of the testator's estate".

But he confessed: "We have not been referred to any such case, nor have we found any".[3] Several cases subsequent to *Re Slevin* illustrate the exception. However the earliest case precedes *Re Slevin*. The testatrix in *Re Randell*[4] bequeathed money on trust to pay the annual proceeds to the successive incumbents of a church "*so long as* they should permit all sittings in the said church to be occupied free of all claims for pew rents". There was an express provision that the money should fall into residue should the pew rents be claimed. NORTH J. held (1) that the limitation was one which would terminate automatically on pew rents being claimed, and (2) that when the interest determined there would be a resulting trust for those entitled to the residue, regardless of the express provision to that effect: the express provision said what the law in any case implied. The same was true of the limitation and provision for what was to happen on termination in *Re Blunt's Trusts*.[5] There the testatrix directed an annuity to be paid to the treasurer of certain schools so long as those schools were carried on under the conditions contained in a particular trust deed and provided that on the termination of the limited interest the fund should fall into residuary estate. BUCKLEY J. followed *Re Randell*,[6] and upheld the gift into residue. These cases should be contrasted with *Re Bowen*[7] and *Re Peel's Release*[8] in both of which the initial gift to charity was absolute with a clause of defeasance. In the former case a testator had bequeathed money to trustees to establish certain schools in certain parishes "and to continue the same for ever thereafter". This provision was followed by a declaration that "if at any time hereafter the Government of this kingdom shall establish a general system of education, the trusts . . . shall cease and determine and I bequeath the said sums in the same manner as I have bequeathed the residue of my personal estate". STIRLING J. held that the gift over was void as infringing the rule against perpetuities. The original absolute gift remained. In *Re Peel's Release*[9] the original beneficial gift was again in express terms made perpetual. The donor conveyed

---

1 See 237, *supra*.
2 [1891] 2 Ch. 236, at 239.
3 *Ibid.*
4 (1888), 38 Ch.D. 213.
5 [1904] 2 Ch. 767.
6 (1888), 38 Ch.D. 213.
7 [1893] 2 Ch. 491.
8 [1921] 2 Ch. 218.
9 *Ibid.*

an acre of land to trustees upon trust to permit the same to be "for ever there-after" used as and for a place for the instruction of seventy poor children, but the deed went on to provide that if in the future certain conditions could not be complied with the trustees should hold the land in trust for the donor his heirs and assigns. SARGANT J. found that the event contemplated by the clause of reverter had arisen; but he held that the clause was void as a perpetuity and the original gift being expressed to be perpetual, there could be no reverter or resulting trust to the donors, heirs or personal representatives: accordingly a *cy-près* scheme was appropriate.

In *Re Cooper's Conveyance Trusts*[1] there was a void gift over following an initial gift to "trustees their heirs and assigns for ever in trust nevertheless for the purposes of the Orphan Girls' Home at Kendal . . . and upon or for no other trust or purpose whatsoever". UPJOHN J. appears to have deduced the deter-minability of the initial gift from the mere existence of the gift over,[2] and held that the limited time and purpose having come to an end the money was held upon a resulting trust for the estate of the donor. The propriety of deducing determinability from the mere existence of a void gift over has been criticised.[3] Had the initial gift in *Re Cooper's Conveyance Trusts* stood on its own it would not have been determinable[4] and there is authority which suggests that the mere presence of a void gift over does not of itself connote determinability in the initial gift.[5] The decision in *Re Cooper's Conveyance Trusts*[6] has been justified as a matter of construction of the relevant conveyance.[7] But it is submitted that it is inconsistent with *Re Peel's Release*[8] and introduces an unwelcome extension to the concept of determinable interests. It has been followed in Australia[9] but it is to be hoped that it will not be given further support. Effec-tive dedication to charity should only be capable of being undone in the clearest cases. Nothing short of an express provision should suffice; and such a provision must take effect subject to the operation of section 12 (1) of the Perpetuities and Accumulations Act 1964. This provides that where a possibility of reverter or resulting trust is held void for remoteness, the prior gift becomes absolute.

A further example of a contrary intention militating against *cy-près* applica-tion after dedication, is where property is handed over contingently on other property being given: if such other property is not given there will be a result-ing trust.[10]

The court has power to direct a scheme regulating the trusts of an initial gift to charity notwithstanding that the effect of such a scheme might be to defeat a gift over. DANCKWERTS J. so held in *Re Hanbey's Will Trusts*[11] where, however, he refused to exercise the power and the gift over took effect.

---

1 [1956] 1 W.L.R. 1096.

2 Following *Re Talbot*, [1933] Ch. 895 and *Gibson v. South American Stores (Gath & Chaves), Ltd.*, [1950] Ch. 177.

3 See (1961), 25 Conv. N.S. 56, at 70–74; see also Hanbury, *Modern Equity* (9th edn.) 285, and [1967] A.S.C.L. 376, at 402–403 (J. D. Davies).

4 See *A.-G. v. Earl of Craven* (1856), 21 Beav. 392; *Re Cooper's Conveyance Trusts*, [1956] 1 W.L.R. 1096, at 1103.

5 See *Re Engels*, [1943] 1 All E.R. 506.　　　　6 [1956] 1 W.L.R. 1096.

7 *Tudor on Charities* (6th edn.) 281.　　　　8 [1921] 2 Ch. 218.

9 *Re Smith*, [1967] V.R. 341 (where there was no question of *cy-près*).

10 *McCormick v. Queen's University of Belfast*, [1958] N.I. 1; and see *Taylor v. Danby* (1896), 2 A.L.R. 133 (where there had been no dedication).

11 [1956] Ch. 364; discussed in (1956), 19 M.L.R. 405–408; see also (1961) 25 Conv.N.S. 56, at 75–76.

WHEN INITIAL FAILURE IS ASCERTAINED

Whether a gift is initially impossible is, with one exception, determined by reference to the facts existing at the time when the gift was made.

Thus, where in a will a charitable gift is expressed to take place immediately on the testator's death and at that date it is clear that the purpose cannot be carried out no problem arises: there is an *initial* failure or impossibility which can bring *cy-près* into play.[1] If the gift is possible at the date of death but is impossible by the time the deceased's assets come to be administered the case is one of *supervening* or *subsequent* impossibility.[2]

But suppose a testator postpones a gift to some charitable purpose to an immediate life interest, what then? Here, it has been held, the charitable gift vests immediately but does not actually take effect until the happening of the future event.[3] Taking the facts at the testator's death one must ask "whether at the date of the death ... it was practicable to carry out the intentions of the [testator] into effect or whether at the said date there was any reasonable prospect that it would be practicable to do so at some future time".[4] If there be no such reasonable prospect the gift will lapse. In this connection regard must be had to the prospective worth of the property bequeathed at the time of the death of the life tenant and not merely to the value at the testator's death of the reversionary interest.[5]

Where a future charitable gift is vested but not yet in possession the court should ignore the possibility of it not taking effect by reason of a clause of defeasance: what must be determined is the possibility of the gift if it does take effect.[6] The position where the remainder to charity is contingent is as yet undecided.[7]

In the case of funds raised by charity appeals the courts define initial impossibility in an exceptional way. The purpose of such a fund is said to be initially impossible (or to fail *ab initio*) if the project fails before there has been any effective application of funds.

DEFINITION OF PARAMOUNT CHARITABLE INTENTION

In the discussion which follows the terms "paramount charitable intention" and "general charitable intention" are used interchangeably: they mean the same thing, but although the latter expression has been used more frequently in the books, the author has a preference for the former expression. The adjective "general" in this context is somewhat obscure in meaning,[8] while the adjective "paramount" conveys perhaps a better idea of what is required by way of

---

1 Or the gift lapses. This principle applies whether the gift is to an institution or to a purpose: *Re Wright*, [1954] Ch. 347, C.A.

2 *Re Slevin*, [1891] 2 Ch. 236, C.A.

3 *Re Moon's Will Trusts*, [1948] 1 All E.R. 300; *Re Wright*, [1954] Ch. 347, C.A.

4 *Re White's Will Trusts*, [1955] Ch. 188.

5 *Re Tacon*, [1958] Ch. 447, C.A.

6 *Ibid.*

7 *Ibid.*, at 454, *per* EVERSHED M.R.

8 The expression was popularised by Sir RICHARD ARDEN M.R. See Jones, *History of the Law of Charities 1532–1827* (1969) 144.

charitable intention to save an initially impossible gift.[1] It avoids the notion that the requisite intention must be unqualified in any way or confined only to some general head of charity.

The classic statement of the law on this topic is to be found in the judgment of PARKER J. in *Re Wilson*[2] where the learned judge divided the cases into two categories.[3]

"First of all," he said, "we have a class of cases where, in form, the gift is given for a particular charitable purpose, but it is possible, taking the will as a whole, to say that, notwithstanding the form of the gift, the paramount intention, according to the true construction of the will, is to give property in the first instance for a general charitable purpose rather than a particular charitable purpose, and to graft on to the general gift a direction as to the desires or intentions of the testator as to the manner in which the general gift is to be carried into effect. In that case, though it is impossible to carry out the precise directions, on ordinary principles the gift for the general charitable purposes will remain and be perfectly good, and the court, by virtue of its administrative jurisdiction, can direct a scheme as to how it is to be carried out. In fact, the will will be read as though the particular direction had not been in the will at all, but as though there had been simply a general direction as to the application of the fund for the general charitable purpose in question."

"Then there is the second class of cases, where, on the true construction of the will, no such paramount general intention can be inferred, and where the gift, being in turn a particular gift—a gift for a particular purpose—and it being impossible to carry out that particular purpose, the whole gift is held to fail."

"It does not mean merely an intention to give to charity generally, without reference to a specified object; but it means an intention the substance of which is charitable, whether generally and without any specified object, in which case the Crown will prescribe the mode of effectuating it, or for an object more or less accurately specified, but with a mode of benefiting that object superadded, which cannot be lawfully or at all carried into execution, in which case the court will carry out the substantial intention."

In *A.-G. for New South Wales* v. *Perpetual Trustee Co., Ltd.*[4] DIXON and EVATT J.J. said in their joint judgment that "general intention of charity means only an intention which, while not going beyond the bounds of the legal conception of charity, is more general than a bare intention that [any] impracticable direction be carried into execution as an indispensable part of the trust declared".

The most recent attempt to define "general charitable intention" is that of BUCKLEY J. in *Re Lysaght*:[5]

> "A general charitable intention ... may be said to be a paramount intention on the part of a donor to effect some charitable purpose which the court can find a method of putting into operation, notwithstanding that it is impracticable to give effect to some direction by the donor which is not an essential part of his true intention not, that is to say, part of his paramount intention".

---

1 *Re Lysaght*, [1966] Ch. 191; and see *Re Taylor* (1888), 58 L.T. 538, at 543.
2 [1913] 1 Ch. 314.
3 [1913] 1 Ch. 314, at 320–331.
4 (1940), 63 C.L.R. 209.
5 [1966] Ch. 191, at 202.

The earliest formulation of general charitable intention in the terms of para-mount charitable intention is to be found in the judgment of KAY J. in *Re Taylor*.[1] The line between general and particular charitable intent (he said) was a very clear one, although it was (and is) sometimes difficult to say on which side of the line a particular case comes. The line was thus defined by KAY J.[2]:

> "if upon the whole scope and intent of the will you discern the paramount object of the testator was to benefit not a particular institution, but to effect a particular form of charity independently of any special institution or mode, then, although he may have indicated the mode in which he desires that to be carried out, you are to regard the primary paramount intention chiefly, and if the particular mode for any reason fails, the court, if it sees a sufficient expression of a general intention of charity, will . . . execute that *cy-près*, that is, carry out the general paramount intention indicated without which his intention itself cannot be effectuated."

Whether a gift evinces a paramount charitable intention is a question of construction for the court, and the answer depends on the construction of the particular instrument in question,[3] if indeed the donor has not in terms expressed such an intention.[4] The process has been compared to "something approaching more nearly to divination or intuition than to interpretation in the accustomed sense"[5] but this is perhaps over-stating the case.

The terms of the gift may so clearly define the particular object of the gift as to render the testator's intention incapable of execution otherwise than in the mode specified in the will. The mode is then of the substance, and if it can-not be pursued the legacy will fail altogether.[6] It may be clear that the testator had only one particular purpose in mind, such as to build almshouses[7] or a hospital[8] or to found a school[9] at a particular place.

On the other hand there are cases where the plurality of charitable gifts expresses a clear general charitable intention.[10] But there are nice distinctions. In *Re Satterthwaite's Will Trusts*[11] the testatrix told an official at her bank in London that she hated all human beings and would leave all her money to animals and she asked him to obtain a list of animal charities. He made a list from the London classified telephone directory. At a later stage she produced a list of additional organisations probably culled from the current ordinary telephone directory. She left her residuary estate among nine organisations all of whose names appeared to show that they were indeed concerned with animal welfare. One was unidentifiable, one was a society which had long been

---

1 (1888), 58 L.T. 538.

2 *Ibid.*, at 542.

3 *Re Wilson* [1913] 1 Ch. 314, at 320.

4 See *Ex parte Transvaal Volunteers' Sustentation Funds, (Trustees)* [1914] W.L.D. 105; *Phillips* v. *Roberts*, [1975], 2 N.S.W.L.R. 207 discussed at 307, *infra*.

5 *Executor Trustee and Agency Co. of South Australia, Ltd.* v. *Warbey*, [1973] S.A.S.R. 336, at 345.

6 *Re Randell* (1888), 38 Ch.D. 213.

7 *Re White's Trusts* (1886), 33 Ch.D. 449; and see *Re Packe*, [1918] 1 Ch. 437 (retreat for clergy and wives).

8 *Re Ulverston and District New Hospital Building Trusts*, [1956] Ch. 622; and see *Re Hillier's Trusts*, [1954] 1 W.L.R. 700; *Re Pochin*, [1948] Ch. 182, n.

9 *Re Wilson*, [1913] 1 Ch. 314.

10 *Re Templemoyle Agricultural School* (1869), I.R. 4 Eq. 295.

11 [1966] 1 W.L.R. 277.

considered (but was not) a charity, six were charities and the last, the London
Animal Hospital, was the registered business name of a veterinary surgeon and
latterly also two of his employees. The Court of Appeal held that the gift to
the last named "beneficiary" was in its true construction a gift for purposes
and that the individual who had run the business could not take beneficially. A
general charitable intent was also discovered, so that the share could be applied
cy-près. The fact that one of the other institutions was not charitable (a fact
unknown to the testatrix) was treated as irrelevant: the society in question
existed to save animals from suffering and a general intention could be discerned in all the other gifts in favour of charity through the medium of kindness to animals. This case is to be contrasted with *Re Jenkins's Will Trusts*[1]
decided a few days later but in which *Re Satterthwaite's Will Trusts*[2] was not
cited although the same counsel had appeared for the Attorney-General in both
cases. The testatrix in the later case left her estate to seven bodies concerned
with animal welfare. One of the seven bodies was an anti-vivisection society and
thus was not charitable. Although the society was incorporated the gift to it
was to be held upon overtly political (and so non-charitable) trusts. The argument employed by counsel for the Attorney-General was that the testatrix
had shown an overriding intention to protect animals from cruelty which is a
charitable purpose, and he prayed in aid the charitable nature of the other gifts
to save the non-charitable gift.[3] BUCKLEY J. refused to accept the argument
saying:[4]

> "the principle of nostitur a sociis does not in my judgment entitle one to
> overlook self-evident facts. If you meet seven men with black hair and one
> with red hair you are not entitled to say that here are eight men with black
> hair. In finding one gift for a non-charitable purpose among a number of
> gifts for charitable purposes, the court cannot infer that the testator or
> testatrix meant the non-charitable gift to take effect as a charitable gift
> when in its terms it is not charitable, even though the non-charitable gift
> may have a close relation to the purposes for which the charitable gifts are
> made."

The distinction between the two cases is in the purposes behind the gift in
question. In *Re Satterthwaite's Will Trusts*[5] there was held to be a gift for an
unexpressed charitable purpose: in *Re Jenkins's Will Trusts*[6] there was a gift for
an expressed non-charitable purpose.

Supervening possibility is not a *cy-près* occasion

As yet no-one in England has seen fit to argue that an established *cy-près* application of funds should subsequently be defeated by the supervening *possibility* of
the testator's original plans. Should this happen the court could well take a leaf
from the book in which the New Jersey case of *Cinnaminson Corporation* v.
First Camden National Bank and Trust Co.[7] is reported. In that case, which came

---

1 [1966] Ch. 249.
2 [1966] 1 W.L.R. 277.
3 [1966] Ch. 249 at 253.
4 [1966] Ch. 249 at 256.
5 [1966] 1 W.L.R. 277.
6 [1966] Ch. 249.   7 238 A. 2d 701 (1968).

before the Supreme Court of New Jersey Chancery Division, the court refused to re-open a *cy-près* scheme, which had been made on the footing that a purpose was no longer practicable, when it subsequently became so. The recipient under a *cy-près* order should not be a conditional recipient and there must be some finality to an order of the court of this kind. The judge said that to rule otherwise would be to open challenge to application of the doctrine *ad infinitum*:[1]

> "The judgment of the court would never be finalised, nor could the recipient of funds awarded under the doctrine justifiably rely thereon. The entire doctrine of *cy-près* was developed out of recognition of the social benefit to be derived from devoting of property to charitable purposes, the policy being to preserve charitable trusts whenever possible ... This court cannot believe that it was intended that the recipient of this social benefit under *cy-près* would be deemed to be a conditional recipient, the condition being that the original intent of the testator not become feasible at some later time. If this were so, the social benefit to be derived by the substituted charity would be plainly limited, for never could the recipient make full use of these funds with the possibility of their loss looming in the future. Indeed, planning and operations for the present necessarily depend largely upon foreseeable financial certainty and stability which, if plaintiffs' viewpoint prevails, would be lacking."

This reasoning is plainly correct and ought to be followed in England.

The out-and-out gift theory

Some commentators assume that an intention to part with all interest in the property concerned is a sufficient foundation for the exercise of the *cy-près* jurisdiction.[2] The argument is that "the absence of a general charitable intent is not fatal"[3] if there is "no expectation by the donor that he or his successors will ever get the property back".[4] The proposition is hard to sustain in the face of the authorities. In the case of an initially impossible gift there is an abundance of authority, ancient[5] and modern[6], to the effect that the absence of a general charitable intent is conclusive bar to a *cy-près* application. Two decisions of the Court of Appeal which have been cited[7] in support of the proposition that an out-and-out gift is in itself a sufficient basis for a *cy-près* order do not in fact go so far as to do that. The decision in *Re Hillier's Trusts*[8] is not one from which

---

1 *Ibid.*, at 708–709.
2 See Sheridan and Delany, *The Cy-près Doctrine* (1959) 37; Keeton and Sheridan, *Modern Law of Charities* (2nd edn.) 157. The view was first propounded in (1954) 32 Can. Bar. Rev. 599 (Sheridan).
3 Sheridan and Delany, *op. cit.*, 33.
4 *Ibid.*, at 37.
5 *A.-G.* v. *Whitchurch* (1796), 3 Ves. 141; *Corbyn* v. *French* (1799), 4 Ves. 418, at 431–433; *Cherry* v. *Mott* (1836), 1 My. & Cr. 123; *Re White's Trusts* (1886), 33 Ch.D. 449; *Re Taylor* (1888), 58 L.T. 538.
6 *Re University of London Medical Sciences Institute Fund*, [1909] 2 Ch. 1; *Re Wilson*, [1913] 1 Ch. 314; *Re Packe*, [1918] 1 Ch. 437; *Re Ulverston and District New Hospital Building Trusts*, [1956] Ch. 622.
7 See Sheridan and Delany *op. cit.*, 80–85.
8 [1954] 1 W.L.R. 700, C.A.

it is safe to draw general propositions: Lord EVERSHED M.R. discovered a
general charitable intent, while ROMER L.J. (who dissented) considered that there
should be a resulting trust in favour of known donors even though counsel
had conceded that the unknown donors had given out-and-out, and only
DENNING L.J. seems to have considered that "out-and-out" was the basis for an
order directing *cy-près* application. In *Re Ulverston and District New Hospital
Building Trusts*[1] JENKINS L.J. who delivered the leading judgment did not say
that the intention to make a gift out-and-out was the decisive factor: the basis
of his decision was that since no general charitable intention was shown on the
part of known donors, the donations by them *therefore* fell to be repaid to
them.

In the case of subsequent or supervening impossibility it is said that "there
is overwhelming authority that an out-and-out gift is applied *cy-près* . . . without any question of general charitable intent".[2] But it by no means follows that
an out-and-out gift is a prerequisite. Certainly a *cy-près* application may be
ordered even where there is no general charitable intent; but in the case of
subsequent impossibility a *cy-près* application is possible even though the gift
was not an out-and-out gift, as for example where there is a perpetuitous gift
over from charity into residue.[3]

---

1 [1956] Ch. 622.

2 Sheridan and Delany, *op. cit.*, 102. The main authorities cited in the text are *Re Peel's
Release*, [1921] 2 Ch. 218; *Re British School of Egyptian Archaeology*, [1954] 1 W.L.R. 546.

3 See the discussion at 209, *supra*; and see, for further detailed criticisms of the out-and-
out theory: (1960), 76 L.Q.R. 601 (J. D. Davies); [1960] C.L.J. 104, at 106–108 (S. J. Bailey).

Chapter 26

Gifts to Charitable Institutions

The question of the failure of a disposition also arises where it is made to an institution which has never existed or had ceased to exist when the disposition was made or has subsequently ceased to exist.[1] Such cases are almost invariably concerned with gifts by will.

The first step is to determine the primary object of the testator's bounty. Is it the institution itself, or the purposes promoted by the institution? Once that question is answered, one must consider whether the institution itself is still in existence, or, if the gift is a purpose gift, whether the purpose is practicable. If a particular institution was intended to benefit and has ceased to exist the gift lapses. But if the primary object of the testator was to help the work carried on by the institution, the demise or non-existence of the institution does not matter. Provided the purpose can still be carried out the court will, according to the circumstances, either apply the gift *cy-près*, on the basis of an alleged general charitable intent,[2] or identify the charity in some other organisation.

All this is deceptively simple to state. But the point of construction—institution or purpose—is far from simple. In the first place a charitable body, whether or not it is incorporated, does not exist for its own benefit. Its very nature is dependent upon the purposes which it promotes. This is true not only of an unincorporated body which must necessarily hold its property on trust for purposes but also of an incorporated charity. The latter may indeed receive and hold property without the interposition of a trust. But the institution is there to promote charitable purposes. Accordingly it is not hard to infer *some* element of purpose gift in almost any gift to a charitable body. Secondly, the courts in this regard, as in so many others, have leaned in favour of charity. In consequence, as WILBERFORCE J. observed in *Re Roberts*:[3] "the position is that the courts have gone very far in the decided cases to resist the conclusion that a legacy to a charitable institution lapses, and a number of very refined arguments have been found acceptable with a view to avoiding that conclusion".

A gift to an institution which has ceased to exist in the testator's lifetime, whether before[4] or after[5] the date of the will, lapses unless a general intention can be shown.

---

1 See J. B. E. Hutton, "The Lapse of Charitable Bequests" (1969) 32 M.L.R. 283; R. B. M. Cotterrell, "Gifts to Charitable Institutions" (1972) 36 Conv. N.S. 198; J. Martin, "The Construction of Charitable Gifts" (1974) 38 Conv. N.S. 187.

2 See e.g. *Re Songest*, [1956] 1 W.L.R. 897, C.A. (equal division between two organisations).

3 [1963] 1 W.L.R. 406, at 412.　　　　　4 *Re Ovey* (1885), 29 Ch.D. 560.

5 *Re Rymer*, [1895] 1 Ch. 19; *Re Joy* (1888), 60 L.T. 175, *Makeown v. Ardagh* (1876), I.R. 10 Eq. 445.

There appear to be three arguments available against lapse. First, despite appearances, the specified institution may still be in existence. Secondly, it may be argued that the gift in question is on its true construction a gift for a purpose and not for the institution. Thirdly, the gift may be saved by the existence of a general charitable intent. The second and third arguments are often combined: they are certainly not mutually exclusive.

In this context there appears to be a distinction between incorporated and unincorporated bodies. A bequest to a corporate body takes effect simply as a gift to that body beneficially, unless there are circumstances which show that the recipient is to take the gift as a trustee. The reverse presumption applies in the case of an unincorporated association. A gift to an unincorporated association established for charitable purposes is a gift upon trust for those purposes, unless the context makes it clear that the continued existence of the association is of the essence of the gift.[1]

In one case the conclusion that the gift is a purpose gift is almost, if not absolutely, inescapable. That is where the gift is not to some named unincorporated body but to a home or hospital, in other words something having a physical existence.[2] Other cases are not so straightforward, and examples are to be found of gifts which on their true construction have been held to be for purposes and of gifts held to be gifts to the institution.

Sometimes, of course, the context of the bequest may make it clear that the continued existence of the institution was fundamental to the gift, as where superadded words make it plain that only the particular institution is to benefit.[3]

Fictitious institutions

A gift is sometimes made to an institution which is named but which has never existed. This is an example of *initial* impossibility. The court in such cases looks at the instrument of gift as a whole to see whether it is possible to gather from the context of the gift (1) that the institution would be charitable if it existed and (2) that there is a paramount charitable intent.

The name or description of the institution will normally enable one to deduce whether the institution if it existed would be charitable. Thus gifts to "a society instituted for the increase and encouragement of good servants"[4] to the "Church Building Fund for Native Churches in India"[5] to the "Home for the Homeless 27 Red Lion Square"[6] to the "Mission Coast Homes for Destitute Children"[7] to "Lord Milner's Homes for Mentally Disabled Soldiers"[8] and to "the Protestant Church Bible Society"[9], were obviously gifts to institutions which would have been charitable had they existed.

---

1 See the discussion at 262, *infra*.
2 *Re Finger's Will Trusts*, [1972] Ch. 286, at 296 explaining *Re Roberts*, [1963] 1 W.L.R. 406 and the hospital cases.
3 *Langford* v. *Gowland* (1862), 3 Giff. 617 ("for the benefit of that institute"); and see *Re Stemson's Will Trusts*, [1970] Ch. 16 discussed at 262, *infra*.
4 *Loscombe* v. *Wintringham* (1850), 13 Beav. 87.
5 *Re Hyde's Trusts* (1873), 22 W.R. 69.
6 *Re Davis*, [1902] 1 Ch. 876.
7 *Re Thompson* (1908), *Times*, 16th Nov.
8 *Re Gordon* (1936), 80 Sol. Jo. 288.
9 *Re Parkes* (1909), 25 T.L.R. 523.

In *Re Songest*[1] there was a gift of residue to be held upon trust for the Disabled Soldiers, Sailors and Airmen's Association absolutely. There never had been an association of that name. Two well-known societies whose purpose was the care of disabled ex-servicemen contended that the testatrix meant one of them to the exclusion of the other; but there was no relevant evidence to help in the determination of this question. Accordingly the Court of Appeal, by way of *cy-près* scheme, directed an equal division between the two institutions on the footing that testatrix's intention was to benefit disabled ex-servicemen.

There are many examples in the books. The English cases include several reported in somewhat inaccessible reports,[2] as well as some which appear in the official law reports.[3] In the Irish case of *Daly* v. *A.-G.*[4] a gift of £1000 for the use of the Protestant *school* attached to the Episcopal Chapel in Upper Baggot Street Dublin was applied *cy-près* because neither of the Episcopal Chapels in the street concerned had a school attached. The Irish courts have also directed *cy-près* application where it was impossible to identify "the Home Mission of the Gospel of Christ in Ireland",[5] "the Director of the African Mission"[6] and "The Seaman's Institute Sir John Rogerson's Quay Dublin".[7]

In Canada too there are plentiful examples of gifts to non-existent institutions with names which clearly show that the testator wished to promote a particular charitable activity such as: "the Home for Fallen Girls",[8] "the Institute for the Blind in New Brunswick",[9] "the Protestant Home for Crippled Children Toronto Ontario",[10] "the Home for Sick and Crippled Children" and "the Home for Poor and Feeble Women",[11] and "the Humane Society for Animals".[12] Similar examples are to be found in New Zealand where a gift to the Society for Prevention of Cruelty to Animals in New Zealand was divided between several local societies for the prevention of cruelty to animals,[13] and in South Africa.[14]

It is particularly easy to infer a general charitable intent where a donor has given property to an institution which has never existed. If the donor has not even bothered to check whether the institution which he has designated exists,

---

1 [1956] 1 W.L.R. 897, C.A.

2 *Re Leader* (1905), 49 Sol. Jo. 551 ("Church of England Protestant Association": divided among three claimants); *Re Hill* (1909), 53 Sol. Jo. 228 (£5000 to Jewish Maternity Institution to endow a memorial ward); *Re Cranmer* (1928) *Times*, 17th Nov. (to the Home Missions of the Church of England); *Re Hurst* (1935), 79 Sol. Jo. 252 (King Edward VII Royal Hospital London).

3 *Re Harwood*, [1936] Ch. 285 (gifts to various "Peace Societies"); *Re Preston's Estate*, [1951] Ch. 878 ("the Widows' and Orphans' Fund of the Royal Merchant Navy").

4 [1860], 11 I.Ch.R. 41. An asylum for female penitents was attached to one of the chapels.

5 *Re Geary's Trusts* (1890), L.R. 25. Ir. 171 (gift applied to Church of Ireland Home Mission).

6 *Re Mulcahy*, [1931] I.R. 239.

7 *Re Julian*, [1950] I.R. 57.

8 *Re Gilroy*, [1937] 3 D.L.R. 351.

9 *Hanson* v. *Torrence*, [1938] 4 D.L.R. 470.

10 *Re Hogle*, [1939] 4 D.L.R. 817; and see also *Re Clapper* (1910), 17 O.W.R. 57 (The Methodist Children's Orphans Home Kingston.)

11 *Re Rice*, [1944] 1 D.L.R. 62.

12 *Re Johnston*, [1968] 1 O.R. 483.

13 *Re Buckley*, [1928] N.Z.L.R. 148.

14 *Ex parte Robinson*, [1953] 2 S.A. 430; *Ex parte Blum*, [1964] 2 S.A. 643.

that is a clear indication that he is more concerned with the assumed purpose of such an institution than with its identity.[1] An apposite example is to be found in *Re Murray*[2] where a testatrix left her Australian residuary estate on trust "to pay the balance to the English Cancer Appeal Fund". There was no such organisation. The court took judicial notice of the fact that for many years before the date of the will cancer constituted a major health problem in the community and that although there had been much research into the disease there had been little progress in controlling it. Having regard to such considerations and to the language of the will the dominant intention of the will (it was held) was to ensure that the estate was made available for research into the causes, treatment and control of cancer. The failure sufficiently to identify the organisation did not destroy the gift and the court had jurisdiction to settle a scheme to fill the gaps apparent in the expression of the precise intentions of the testatrix.

In *Re Constable*[3] a testatrix left the residue of her estate to "The Methodist Homes for the Aged at Cheltenham". The Methodist Church in Victoria (of which the testatrix was a member) ran homes for the aged but did not have one at Cheltenhan. But a Home for the Aged did exist in Cheltenham having no connection with the Methodists. PAPE J. held that the case was not one of misdescription but of a charitable gift to a body which had never existed. He accordingly divided the gift equally between the Methodist Church and the Cheltenham Home and Hospital for the Aged on the footing that the intention of the testatrix was to relieve the aged. In *Re Daniels*[4] a gift to the Spastic Children's Home at Frankston was one of three gifts of residue; the other two gifts were to identifiable charities but there was no entity corporate or otherwise known as the Spastic Children's Home at Frankston. The court had little difficulty in finding that the will disclosed a general charitable intention of disposing of the residuary estate and accordingly directed a *cy-près* scheme.

A gift to an institution which has never existed should not be considered in isolation but in the whole context of the will.[5]

The court will in this class of cases—where there is a gift to a charity which has never existed at all—lean in favour of a general charitable purpose, and will accept even a small indication of the testator's intention as sufficient to show that a purpose, and not a person is intended.[6] The gift in question in *Re Davis*[6] was to the Home for the Homeless: it came in a list of gifts to charitable institutions and the testatrix has specifically provided that her gifts were not to fail for misdescription although there was a residuary gift to charity. On the other hand in *Re Goldschmidt*[7] HARMAN J. considered that the residuary gift to charity negatived a general charitable intent in the primary gift.

Of course the context may show that the testator wanted to benefit a particular organisation of whose existence he was firmly convinced, and not the purpose. Where that is so a paramount charitable intent will be negatived. In

---

1 *Ex parte Blum*, [1964] 2 S.A. 643.

2 [1964–5] N.S.W.R. 121 (HARDIE J.); *Re Conroy* (1973), 35 D.L.R. (3rd) 752 (gift to "The Cancer Fund of British Columbia" applied *cy-prés*).

3 [1971] V.R. 742. For earlier Australian cases: see *Re Carmichael*, [1936] St. R. Qd. 196; *Re Bertling*, [1956] St. R. Qd. 379; *Re Kerr*, [1957] Q.S.R. 292.

4 [1970] V.R. 72.

5 *Re Clergy Society* (1856) 2 K. & J. 615 (gift to "the Clergy Society"); *Re Knox*, [1937] Ch. 109 ("Newcastle-upon-Tyne Nursing Home").

6 *Re Davis*, [1902] 1 Ch. 876, at 884.   7 [1957] 1 W.L.R. 524.

Re Tharp[1] there was a gift to the Tangier Society for the Prevention of Cruelty to Animals. There was no such institution and BENNETT J. held that the gift lapsed for want of a general charitable intent. On appeal the decision was reversed and it was held that the named institution was a misdescription of an existing one. Illustrations of an intention to benefit a specific organisation and not a purpose are to be found in Ireland.[2]

If there is nothing to show that the objects of the fictitious institution would have been charitable the gift will fail.[3]

A direct legacy to a charitable institution which had never existed was held by VAISEY J. in *Re Bennett*[4] to be applicable in accordance with the directions of the Sovereign under the sign manual, the learned judge being satisfied of the existence of a paramount charitable intention. VAISEY J. referred to several earlier cases[5] which conflicted with the principle laid down by Lord ELDON in *Moggridge* v. *Thackwell*[6] and dismissed them as out of line and step with *Moggridge* v. *Thackwell*: the court, he held, had no jurisdiction in the absence of a trust. Yet if the presence of a trust removes the case from the jurisdiction of the Crown and brings it into the jurisdiction of the court it is difficult to see how any testamentary gift is applicable under the Royal Prerogative, since all the property of the deceased devolves upon his personal representatives *upon trust*. This point was not argued in *Re Bennett* and perhaps if the attention of VAISEY J. had been directed to it he might not have held the gift to be applicable under the Royal Prerogative.

Inchoate institutions

There are various types of inchoate institutions of a charitable nature which testators are minded to benefit. Sometimes the institution is one which has been mooted but which has never, so to speak, left the drawing board. In *Re Loomis's Estate*[7] it was held that a gift to an institution whose establishment had been proposed at the time the will was made and discussed afterwards but which had never in fact been set up was void because one particular institution *and no other* was intended. On the other hand in *Richardson* v. *Mullery*[8] a gift was made to the life-saving station to be built and established at X: the court discovered a general charitable intent and the gift was applied *cy-près* in pensions to life-savers.

In other cases the testator has in mind the establishment of an institution that is his own brain child.[9] There is no question here of a fictitious institution. The object of bounty is a purpose; and the question will be whether that purpose is possible and if not whether the testator had a specific or a paramount charitable intent.

1 [1942] 2 All E.R. 358; reversed on appeal [1943] 1 All E.R. 257, C.A.
2 *Re Mulcahy*, [1931] I.R. 239; *Re Buckley*, [1942] Ir. Jur. Rep. 43.
3 *MacTavish's Trustees* v. *St. Columba High Church* 1957 S.L.T. 50.
4 [1960] Ch. 18.
5 *Re Clergy Society* (1856), 2 K. & J. 615; *Bennett* v. *Hayter* (1839), 2 Beav. 81; *Re Maguire* (1870), L.R. 9 Eq. 632.
6 [1960] Ch. 18, at 24.
7 451 P. 2d, 195 (1969) (Kansas S.C.).
8 86 N.E. 319 (1908).
9 *Re Mann*, [1903] 1 Ch. 232 ("the Mann Institute"); *Morton* v. *A.-G.* (1911), 11 S.R. (N.S.W.) 473.

Expired institutions

Sometimes a donor will have in mind an institution which has in fact existed, but which has come to an end by the time his gift takes effect. Usually this problem arises in connection with a will: the institution shuts down between the time when the will is executed and the date of the testator's death. But a settlor *inter vivos* might well be unaware that the object of his bounty has closed down. In either case, unless a paramount charitable intent is discoverable, the property cannot be applied *cy-près*. In the absence of such an intent "when a gift is made by will to a charity which has expired, it is as much a lapse as a gift to an individual who has expired".[1] The doctrine of lapse, of course, has no application to an *inter vivos* trust; but in the event of a beneficiary predeceasing (or expiring before) the constitution of such a trust, the trustees will hold the property on a resulting trust for the settlor, where no general charitable intent is found. On the other hand, if such an intent is discoverable the gift will be applicable *cy-près*.[2] Such is the law not only in this country but also in Ireland,[3] Australia[4] and Canada.[5] In one of the Australian cases a society which was misdescribed in the testator's will ceased to exist before his death: in the absence of a paramount charitable intent the gift lapsed.[6] A similar case of misdescription combined with extinction occurred in South Africa and again the gift lapsed.[7]

Reverting to the English experience, it is important to note that *Clark* v. *Taylor*[8] is badly reported. The case was *not* one of supervening impossibility: the institution had in fact come to an end in the testator's lifetime. If it was not a case of lapse it was wrongly decided and should therefore be disregarded.[9] Where there is a gift to a particular institution in a particular locality and the institution has come to an end before the gift can take effect the gift will lapse. Thus a gift "to the rector for the time being of St Thomas' Seminary for the education of priests in the diocese of Westminster for the purposes of such seminary lapsed because the seminary had ceased to exist in the testator's lifetime.[10] In *Re Goldney*[11] a testatrix by her will gave her books to "St Luke's Home for Children near Reading" and left her residuary estate to be divided between that institution and Cancer Research Work. Before the death of the testatrix the children's home was sold and the proceeds of sale were transferred to a

---

1 *Fisk* v. *A.-G.* (1867), L.R. 4 Eq. 521, at 528, *per* PAGE-WOOD V.-C.

2 *Marsh* v. *A.-G.* (1860), 2 John & H. 61; *Clark* v. *Taylor* (1853), 1 Drew 642, at 644; *Re Bradfield* (1892), 8 T.L.R. 696; *Re Hutchinson's Will Trusts*, [1953] Ch. 387; *Re Morison* (1967), *Times*, 8th July.

3 *Makeown* v. *Ardagh* (1876), I.R. 10 Eq. 445.

4 *In the Will of Haines* (1892), 18 V.L.R. 553 (lapse); *Re Jones*, [1907] S A.L.R. 190; *Re Mills* [1934] V.L.R. 158; *Re Weiss*, [1934] V.L.R. 269; *Re Carmichael*, [1936] St.R.Qd. 196; *Re Cripps*, [1941] Tas. S.R. 19; *Re Smith*, [1954] S.A.S.R. 151; *Re Quesnel*, [1959] S.A.S.R. 106 (lapse).

5 *Re Ogilvy*, [1953] 1 D.L.R. 44; *Re Fisher*, [1959] O.W.N. 46; *Re Allendorf*, [1963] 38 D.L.R. (2d) 459.

6 *Re Guidi*, [1948] S.A.S.R. 207.

7 *Ex parte Estate Cauvin*, [1954] 2 S.A. 144 (Cape Province).

8 (1853), 1 Drew 642.

9 *See Re Slevin*, [1891] 2 Ch. 236, cf. 243, *per* KAY L.J.

10 *Re Rymer*, [1895] 1 Ch. 19, C.A.

11 (1946), 115 L.J. Ch. 337.

children's hospital in another town. It was held by ROXBURGH J. that the gifts in favour of the children's home lapsed because the home had altogether come to an end. The fact that the testatrix wished the books and the money applied for the purposes of the home, which she knew to be engaged in work for sick children, did not entitle the court to hold that the gifts were for the carrying on of a particular work and were not for a particular institution. Although the tide had flowed strongly in favour of charities in that class of case, the question was, in the last resort, one of construction and, however strong the tide might be, the court ought not to hold that there had been no lapse where, as in the instant case, there was a gift to a particular institution and that institution had come to an end.

Changed institutions

Debate frequently centres on the issue whether an institution has in fact ceased to exist or has merely changed in some immaterial way. An institution may still exist even though a large part of its activity has ceased. Thus in *Re Waring*[1] a charity school which was the object of a testamentary gift and had been an elementary school and a Sunday school ceased to be anything but a Sunday school. KEKEWICH J. held that there was no lapse of the gift and that the school was entitled to the legacy.

In *Re Slatter's Will Trusts*[2] the point at issue was one of identification rather than of *cy-près* application. The testatrix had left her residue on trust "for the Malahide Red Cross Hospital ... absolutely, the receipt of the treasurer for the time being of the said hospital to be a sufficient discharge to my trustees". The hospital had been opened and carried on as part of the activities of a Red Cross society. The hospital became redundant and was closed down three weeks after the date of the will and its buildings and land were sold the proceeds being received by the division of the Red Cross society which had supervised its activities. PLOWMAN J. held that on the true construction of the will the gift was not a gift to the society, and he relied, in this connection, on the provision that the receipt of the treasurer of the *hospital* would be a sufficient discharge. Even assuming that the gift was one for particular charitable purposes (namely the work carried on at the hospital) to that the gift would not necessarily lapse on the hospital ceasing to exist the gift was nevertheless held to have lapsed. The learned judge reached this conclusion because on the closing down of the hospital its work was not transferred elsewhere because the need for it had gone, and because the hospital had no funds dedicated to its general work through which it could sustain its existence. An unendowed charity was in *Re Withall*[3] said to cease to exist when the work ceased for lack of necessary funds. This principle according to PLOWMAN J.:[4]

> "must be applicable equally in a case where the hospital closes down because the need for it has gone and where it closes down for lack of funds".

---

1 [1907] 1 Ch. 166; see also *Re Buck*, [1896] 2 Ch. 727 and *Re Roberts* (1957), *Times*, 23rd May.
2 [1964] Ch. 512; see also *Re Bradfield* (1892), 36 Sol. Jo. 646.
3 [1932] 2 Ch. 236.
4 [1964] Ch. 512, at 527.

Once one finds that there are no funds dedicated to the work which was carried on before the institution closed down, then it seems that the institution must cease to exist in such a way as to cause a lapse in the absence of any paramount charitable intention.[1]

An institution still exists though its future is precarious[2] but not if it is merely nugatory. What has been discussed so far is change of an immaterial kind.[3] But what if between the making of a will and the death of the testator a charitable institution ceases to exist as a separate and independent entity? Institutions, unlike individuals, can experience metamorphosis. They can be amalgamated or absorbed into other institutions; or their functions may be divided between two institutions; or they may be reorganised in some other way. Such constitutional changes may be effected under a scheme made by the Charity Commissioners or the court or under some statute or under the charity's own constitution. Or the change may have been effected informally.

A series of decisions[4] starting with *Re Faraker*[5] has established that so long as there are funds held in trust for the purposes of a charity the charity continues in existence and is not disqualified from taking a gift by any alteration in its constitution name or objects made in accordance with law, or even by amalgamation with another charity. The crucial point seems to be that there is a fund in existence perpetually dedicated to charity. As long as the charity has endowments it exists.

In *Re Roberts*[6] a testatrix left a share of her residuary estate to the Sheffield Boys Working Home. This charitable institution was founded in 1881, apparently without a trust instrument, but in 1889 acquired new premises by a conveyance imposing a trust for the benefit of orphan or destitute boys and containing a provision that the governors of the home, if they considered it ought to be discontinued, might authorise the trustees to sell the premises or otherwise dispose of them and pay the proceeds for the benefit of charitable institutions or poor inhabitants in Sheffield. In 1945 all the property of the institution was sold and £1000 of the proceeds was given to a named hostel for boys while the balance was transferred to the Sheffield Town Trust with a request that the income be used for the benefit of boys organisations in the city. It was argued on behalf of the Sheffield Town Trust that the testatrix made the gift on the trust and powers of the 1889 conveyance including the exercised power to give the funds to the Sheffield Town Trust. WILBERFORCE J. decided that this power really involved the termination of the institution, and that it would be an unjustifiable extension to apply the principle[7] that a gift to a charity can take effect despite an alteration or even an amalgamation of its objects to such a case.

He went on to hold that the bequest was a gift for the *purposes* of the home and was not so exclusively tied up with a particular home physically located on the premises used by the home or to enable one to say that when the trusts of the physical home ceased to exist, the charity ended. Since the machinery of the home no longer existed a scheme was directed.

---

1 For critical comment on this case, see (1964) 28 Conv. N.S. 313–315 (J. T. Farrand).
2 *Re Roberts*, [1963] 1 W.L.R. 406.
3 *Re Meyers*, [1951] Ch. 534.
4 *Re Lucas*, [1948] Ch. 424, C.A.; *Re Bagshaw*, [1954] 1 W.L.R. 238; *Re Roberts* [1963]
1 W.L.R. 406; *Re Slatter's Will Trusts*, [1964] Ch. 512.
5 [1912] 2 Ch. 488, C.A.   6 [1963] 1 W.L.R. 406.
7 See *Re Bagshaw* [1954] 1 W.L.R. 238; *Re Faraker* [1912] 2 Ch. 488.

CHANGES EFFECTED UNDER A SCHEME

So long as there are funds held in trust for the purposes of a charity the charity continues in existence and is not destroyed by an alteration in its constitution or objects made in accordance with law, as for example by a scheme[1] under the Charities Act 1960. The objects of an established charity may be changed either by the court in exercise of its jurisdiction over charities or by schemes formed by the Charity Commissioners to whom Parliament has entrusted that particular duty.[2] Neither the Charity Commissioners nor the court could take an existing charity and *destroy* it; they are obliged to administer it.[3] But this does not necessarily apply to a case where the trustees of the charity are given express powers to terminate the charity.[4] The leading case about changes effected by a scheme and their impact on a charitable institution as a donee is *Re Faraker*.[5]

The case of *Re Faraker*[5] has occasioned much discussion.[6] The testatrix who died in 1911 gave by her will a legacy of £200 "to Mrs Bailey's Charity, Rotherhithe". There was at Rotherhithe a charity known as Hannah Bayly's Charity founded in 1756 by a Mrs. Bayly for the benefit of poor widows resident in and parishioners of St. Mary's Rotherhithe. In 1905 the Charity Commissioners sealed a scheme in the matter of Hannah Bayly's Charity and thirteen other charities in Rotherhithe, whereby the endowments of all those charities were consolidated, trustees were appointed and trusts declared for the benefit of the poor of Rotherhithe. There was no mention of widows in the scheme. But at the date of the sealing of the scheme 27 widows were receiving pensions of £5 a year from Hannah Bayly's Charity, and these pensions were continued under the scheme and increased to £15 a year; there were 16 of these pensioned widows in 1912 and the amount given to widows under the scheme was more than the total income of Hannah Bayly's fund. NEVILLE J. held that the effect of this was that the gift had lapsed because the constitution of Hannah Bayly's Charity had been so altered that it could no longer be treated as being in existence. The Court of Appeal reversed NEVILLE J.'s decision, accepting the argument that an endowed charity is indestructible either by the court or the Charity Commissioners. The decision in *Re Faraker*[7] could have been grounded on the principle that although there had been a change in the management of the charity, the charitable purpose of benefiting poor widows in Rotherhithe was still being carried on, with the result that the gift did not lapse.[8] The case was not, however, expressly put in that way.[9] In fact, the

---

1 *Re Lucas*, [1948] Ch. 424, at 426, *per* Lord GREENE M.R. citing *Re Faraker*, [1912] 2 Ch. 488.

2 *Re Faraker*, [1912] 2 Ch. 488, at 493, *per* COZENS-HARDY M.R.

3 *Ibid.*, at 495, *per* FARWELL L.J.

4 *Re Roberts*, [1963] 1 W.L.R. 406, at 416, *per* WILBERFORCE J.

5 [1912] 2 Ch. 488.

6 Sheridan and Delany, *The Cy-près Doctrine* (1959) 110–111; Keeton and Sheridan, *The Modern Law of Charities* (2nd edn.) 143; J. B. E. Hutton (1969) 32 M.L.R. 283; R. B. M. Cotterrell (1972) 36 Conv. N.S. 198.

7 [1912] 2 Ch. 488.

8 *Cf. Re Watt*, [1932] 2 Ch. 243, n.

9 The continuing substantial benefit to widows under the scheme was referred to. For a summary of the various interpretations see Cotterrell, *loc. cit.*, 200.

L

Court of Appeal did not expressly state what construction they gave to the bequest. In *Re Lucas*[1] ROXBURGH J., at first instance, said that the essence of the decision in *Re Faraker* was that once a fund has been subjected to charitable trusts, its identity cannot be destroyed by any alteration lawfully made in those trusts by the court or the Charity Commissioners and that any subsequent augmentation of that fund would take effect and be held upon the trusts so altered. He construed the bequest in *Re Lucas*[2] as being for the upkeep of a particular crippled children's home in a particular place. But the Court of Appeal construed the bequest as an addition to the funds of the home and negatived any lapse.

It is well established, therefore, that a charity founded as a perpetual charity does not come to an end, even though its objects and its name may be altered according to due process of law. In *Re Faraker*[3] and *Re Lucas*[4] the objects and name of the charity concerned had been altered by a scheme established either by the court or by the Charity Commissioners. In *Re Bagshaw*,[5] however, the alteration had not been effected by means of any scheme made by an outside body such as the Charity Commissioners or the court, but the objects and the name had been altered in a perfectly legal manner through the machinery provided in the trust deed created by the founders of the charity itself. It was held that the charity remained the same charity: there was no lapse.

CHANGES EFFECTED UNDER SOME STATUTE

So long as there are funds held in trust for the purposes of a charity, the charity still exists and will not be destroyed by any change in its constitution or objects effected under some statute. Accordingly a legacy to such a charity does not lapse. Most of the cases illustrating this principle concern hospitals nationalised and reorganised under the National Health Service Act 1946. But the principle has also been applied in connection with the reorganisation of the auxiliary forces of the Crown and is one of some importance to public schools and other independent schools soliciting charitable donations.

In *Re Morgan's Will Trusts*[6] a testatrix directed her trustees in a will made in 1944 to hold part of her residuary estate "for the benefit of the Liskeard Cottage Hospital" (by which she meant the Passmore Edwards Cottage Hospital at Liskeard). She died in 1948. ROXBURGH J. held that although before the death of the testatrix the hospital was vested by the National Health Service Act 1946 in the local hospital management committee, the gift in the will was for the *purposes* which in 1944 were carried on in that hospital and were still carried on there. The gift was accordingly valid and the fund was ordered to be paid over to the hospital management committee controlling (*inter alia*) the cottage hospital in question. Similarly, in *Re Glass*[7] the testator who died on 21st January 1949 by his will dated 21st July 1948 provided a legacy "to the King

---

1 [1948] Ch. 175, at 181; see also *Re Hutchinson's Will Trusts*, [1953] Ch. 387, at 393, *per* UPJOHN J.
2 [1948] Ch. 424.
3 [1912] 2 Ch. 488.
4 [1948] Ch. 424.
5 [1954] 1 W.L.R. 238.
6 [1950] Ch. 637.
7 [1950] Ch. 643, n.

Edward VII Memorial Hospital, Ealing". VAISEY J. said that it was not possible to distinguish the effect of the words used in the will of the testator and that of the words used in relation to the bequest in *Re Morgan's Will Trusts*.[1] Accordingly he held that the legacy to the hospital should be paid to the local management committee.

The provisions of the 1946 Act did not cause the lapse of a gift in trust for a hospital which became nationalised before the testator's death,[2] or a bequest given to such a hospital for endowment purposes or given to a hospital which became nationalised before the gift was paid over.[3]

It is another matter if the testator has foreseen the possibility of legislation and provided for it.[4] Where there was a gift of a share of residue to a teaching hospital which was still in existence at the testator's death, there was no lapse because the institution had not ceased to exist under the National Health Service Act 1946;[5] but where there was a proviso that if any of the funds had come under government control the gift was to go over to other institutions the gift to the teaching hospital did not take effect.[6]

A gift to any three hospitals in a county most in need of assistance was good although the hospitals had been taken over under the 1946 Act.[7]

In *Re Hayes' Will Trusts*[8] trustees were given a discretion to divert the gift if impracticable or inequitable in consequence of amalgamation; it was held, however, that the effect of the hospital vesting in the Minister under the 1946 Act was not such an amalgamation. Such an amalgamation is effected when two institutions are together named as a teaching hospital but not where one institution becomes part of a group.[9]

A gift for a general and ordinary purpose of a charitable organisation which previously existed notwithstanding it was for a particular purpose (a building fund) and not for the general purposes of the charity, did not fail because the charity being a hospital had been brought under the 1946 Act.[10]

In one case it was held that where trustees had a power to divert property to other charitable purposes this power could not be exercised if on the appointed day the premises were being used as a hospital and passed into public ownership.[11]

Where a gift stated that if at any time any of the said charities had ceased to exist as an independent charity, the gift so far as it was given to hospitals subject to the 1946 Act failed.[12] Such a gift was a contingent gift and not a vested interest subject to divesting.[13]

---

1 [1950] Ch. 675.
2 *Re Hutchinson's Will Trusts*, [1953] Ch. 387.
3 *Re Frere*, [1951] Ch. 27.
4 *Re Buzzacott*, [1953] Ch. 28.
5 *Re Kellner's Will Trusts*, [1950] Ch. 46. See, also, *Re Gartside*, [1949] 2 All E.R. 546 (where, however, the estate had been fully administered).
6 *Re Buzzacott*, [1953] Ch. 28.
7 *Re Perreyman*, [1953] 1 All E.R. 223.
8 [1953] 2 All E.R. 1242.
9 *Re Bawden's Settlement*, [1953] 2 All E.R. 1235.
10 *Re Little*, [1953] 2 All E.R. 852.
11 *Minister of Health v. Fox*, [1950] Ch. 369; *Re Marjoribanks' Trust Deed*, [1952] Ch. 181.
12 *Re Lowry's Will Trusts*, [1967] Ch. 638.
13 *Ibid.*

CHANGES EFFECTED UNDER CONSTITUTION

Some trust deeds authorise the trustees to effect constitutional changes in the charity, so as for example to alter its name or objects. Where in accordance with such a power the trustees have made constitutional changes in the charity a gift in a will executed before (but taking effect after) the changes will be payable to the altered charity.[1]

CHANGES EFFECTED INFORMALLY

Changes in the constitution of charities are sometimes effected informally. Strictly, such changes can only be made if authorised by the trust deeds of the charities concerned. But in practice informal changes are made with scant regard to the relevant trust deeds. Where there has been an unauthorised informal division[2] or amalgamation[3] of charities, a gift by name to the original body will go to the revised body or bodies, so long as it is possible to construe the gift as being for the general work of the original charity generally and in augmentation of that charity's funds.

In *Re Joy*[4] a testator gave two legacies to two institutions with similar objects.[5] Between the date of the will and the date of the testator's death the institutions informally amalgamated. It was held that the united institution was entitled to both legacies. This principle applies *a fortiori* where there is evidence that the testator has subscribed to the combined charity.[6]

An instructive case is *Re Watt*[7] which the Court of Appeal found to be "a matter of some difficulty".[8] Four years before he died the testator (a cleric) made a will leaving a fraction of his residuary estate to the Southwark Diocesan Society. At the date of the testator's death there was no society of that name. But in the year preceding the testator's death a society called the "South London Church Fund and Southwark Diocesan Board of Finance" was incorporated for the purpose of taking over *inter alia* the assets of the "Southwark Diocesan and South London Church Fund" upon the existing trusts and for continuing the work of the latter society. Moreover, there was evidence that the Southwark Diocesan and South London Church Fund often adopted the short title Southwark Diocesan Fund when giving receipts for subscriptions. However, against that it was said that when the fund was transferred to the new body the agreement made contained a provision that the former society should cease to function, but that the new body should represent it for the receipt of gifts. A legatee (it was argued) was incapable of providing against

---

1 *Re Bagshaw*, [1954] 1 W.L.R. 238.
2 *Re Souter* (1907), *Times*, 24th Jan.; *Re Wilson* (1909), 25 T.L.R. 465.
3 *Re Pritt* (1915), 113 L.T. 136; *Re Withall*, [1932] 2 Ch. 236; *Re Hutchinson's Will Trusts*, [1953] Ch. 387; *Re Dawson's Will Trusts*, [1957] 1 W.L.R. 391.
4 (1888), 60 L.T. 175 (CHITTY J.).
5 Viz. anti-vivisection which in 1888 was mistakenly believed to be a charitable purpose; See *Re Foveaux*, [1895] 2 Ch. 501 (CHITTY J.) which was overruled in *National Anti-Vivisection Society* v. *I.R.Comrs.*, [1948] A.C. 31. But the principle of *Re Joy* is unimpaired.
6 *Re Pritt* (1915), 113 L.T. 136.
7 [1932] 2 Ch. 243, n.
8 At 246, n., *per* Lord HANWORTH M.R.

lapse by agreeing with another that that other should stand in his place and take the legacy which the legatee was incapable of taking; and the legatee in *Re Watt* had ceased to be clothed with the necessary legal status to be able to take the legacy.[1] This argument succeeded before CLAUSON J. but failed in the Court of Appeal where it was held that the testator intended to benefit a *purpose* and not a particular legatee. This intention was evidenced by the fact that many years before the testator had subscribed to a society called "the "Rochester Diocesan Society" which had for its object the promotion of church work in South London and other parts of the diocese. Then, when the diocese of Rochester was divided into the diocese of Rochester and the diocese of Southwark, the "Rochester Diocesan Society" changed its name to the "Southwark Diocesan and South London Church Fund" and the testator continued to subscribe to the fund in its new guise.[2] In addition, of course, he was himself a clergyman who had lived in South London. Lord HANWORTH M.R. was clearly affected by these considerations when he said that:[3]

> "the testator has substantially designated under the words he has used the body that still carries on the work in which he was interested years ago, work carried on in a district in which he lived and which is now in charge of and being administered by this more modern body".

The legatee in *Re Withall*[4] was the "Margate Cottage Hospital" whose trustees had after the date of the will (but before the testatrix's death) closed the hospital, transferring its assets to a new hospital—the Margate and District General Hospital. The testatrix had been an annual subscriber to the Margate Cottage Hospital for several years, including the year of her death, and she had contributed to the fund for the new building which became the Margate and District General Hospital. Two months or so before the testatrix's death the latter hospital took over the work, medical and nursing staff and the patients of the Margate Cottage Hospital, but was not a free hospital in the same sense as the old hospital and admitted patients from a more exclusive district. CLAUSON J. held that the testatrix intended that her residue should be added to the funds dedicated to the purposes of the Margate Cottage Hospital and observed:[5]

> "The proceeds are to be paid to the Margate Cottage Hospital. That does not mean, as has been picturesquely said, the bricks and mortar; that means that they are to be paid to the persons administering the trusts to which the funds of the Margate Cottage Hospital are dedicated, as an accretion to those funds, to be used for those purposes."

But the learned judge refused to deal with the purely academic question as to the sense (if any) in which the new hospital could be said to retain the identity of the old hospital. His decision was that there was no lapse and that the testatrix's residue was to be applied for the purposes of the Margate Cottage Hospital; and since there was a scheme in existence which had been settled and approved by the Charity Commissioners, though not finally made binding, which would in due course govern the application of the funds of the Margate Cottage Hospital that was the end of the matter.

---

1 *Ibid.*, 245, n., relying on *Re Rymer*, [1895] 1 Ch. 19.
2 *Ibid.*, at 243, n.–244 n.
3 *Ibid.*, at 246, n.
4 [1932] 2 Ch. 236.
5 At 242.

In *Re Goldney*[1] the testatrix left certain gifts to "St Luke's Home for Children near Reading." Between the date of her will and her death the institution, which was incorporated as a company, was dissolved all its assets having been realised and transferred to an institution pursuing similar purposes. ROX-BURGH J. held that the gifts were on their true construction gifts to a particular institution in a particular locality and not for the purpose of carrying on a particular charitable work. Accordingly the *cy-près* doctrine did not apply and the gift lapsed.

In *Re Hutchinson's Will Trusts*[2] the hospital named in the will was closed down by the trustees, with the approval of the Minister of Health, in anticipation of the passing of the National Health Service Act 1946 and no scheme had been made. UPJOHN J. upheld the claim of the hospital management committee to the legacy. He commented that in order |for the committee to give a good receipt for the gift the court of the Commissioners might have to approve a scheme.[3]

In cases where some constitutional change has taken place informally a scheme is either necessary or desirable even though in most of the cases referred to no scheme was in fact required. A scheme was certainly thought to be necessary by WILBERFORCE J. in *Re Roberts*[4] and there was certain support for that in two cases apparently cited to him.[5]

DUE DISSOLUTION OF INSTITUTION

There are several important cases dealing with the effect of particular gifts to institutions which have been duly dissolved. In *Re Stemson's Will Trusts*[6] there was a testamentary gift of residuary estate "unto the Rationalist Endowment Fund Ltd. absolutely". Superadded to the gift were words requesting the said association to found a hostel but without imposing any trust upon it. The association was dissolved not long before the testator died and pursuant to its memorandum requiring transfer of its assets on dissolutions to some institution having similar objects the association transferred its assets to another company, which was registered as a charity with charitable objects although none for the relief of poverty corresponding to those of the dissolved association. PLOW-MAN J. declined to find any general charitable intention in the gift: the wording of the relevant clause in the will showed that the testator was particularly relying on the particular association to carry out his wishes. It was argued that the principle in *Re Faraker*[7] was applicable when the donee charity was liable to dissolution under its own constitution so as to prevent a lapse.[8] But PLOWMAN J. concluded that where funds come to the hands of a charitable organisation which is founded, not as a perpetual charity but as one liable to termination, and its constitution provides for the disposal of its funds in that event, then if the organisation ceases to exist and its funds are disposed of, the charity or

---

1 (1946), 115 L.J. Ch. 337.
2 [1953] Ch. 387.
3 *Ibid.*, at 394.
4 [1963] 1 W.L.R. 406.
5 *Re Wedgwood*, [1914] 2 Ch. 245; *Re Dawson's Will Trusts*, [1957] 1 W.L.R. 391.
6 [1970] Ch. 16.
7 [1912] 2 Ch. 488, C.A.
8 *Cf. Re Servers of the Blind League*, [1960] 1 W.L.R. 564.

charitable trust itself ceases to exist and there is nothing to prevent the operation of the doctrine of lapse. The necessary continuity between the dissolved corporation and its successor is lacking. An express provision for transfer does not constitute continuity in the case of a charitable corporation. There may be greater scope for manœuvre in the case of a charitable trust for construing a power to transfer as not occasioning a complete termination, a point to which the draftsman should be alert.

The distinction between an unincorporated association and an incorporated one in this regard appears from the decision of GOFF J. in *Re Finger's Will Trusts*.[1] A gift to an unincorporated charity by name without more must take effect as a gift for a charitable purpose.[2] The survival of the named charity in such a case is not crucial unless there is something positive to show that the continued existence of the donee was essential to the gift. In the case of a corporation however the position is different, as there has to be something positive in the will to create a purpose trust at all. In the case before him GOFF J. held that a gift to the Radium Commission was a trust for the work of the commission which was still being carried on, and, there being nothing in the context of the will showing that the continued existence of the commission was essential to the gift, effect could be given to it by means of a scheme. The gift to the incorporated charity, however, failed despite the fact that the work was still being carried on, for there was no sufficient context to fasten a purpose trust on the corporation which had been voluntarily wound up. However since the will showed a general charitable intention the share did not lapse but could be applied *cy-près*. GOFF J. was obviously unhappy with the distinction which he considered authority compelled him to make: had the matter been *res integra* he would have decided otherwise. Certainly drawing such a distinction produces anomalous results.[3]

INSTITUTIONS CEASING TO EXIST BETWEEN DATE OF GIFT AND PAYMENT OVER

Where an institution ceases after a gift takes effect but before actual payment over there will be a *cy-près* application of the gift: the case is one of supervening failure and no paramount charitable intent need be shown. In *Re Slevin*[4] a testator bequeathed "the pecuniary legacies following" one of which was a legacy of £200 to a particular orphanage which closed between the date of his death and the payment over of the legacy. The Court of Appeal held that the gift fell to be administered by the Crown[5] who would apply it according to custom for some analogous purpose of charity.[5] *Cy-près* was also ordered where a school which was entitled in remainder under a will closed during the subsistence of the life interest[6] and has been ordered in Australia where between the testator's death and the availability of the estate for distribution some three years later the institution was being wound up and its activities were no longer necessary.[7]

---

1 [1972] Ch. 286.   2 *Re Vernon's Will Trusts* (1962), reported [1970] Ch. 300, n.
3 [1972] Ch. 286, at 294. For further comment, see [1972] A.S.C.L. 248, at 260–261 (J. D. Davies).
4 [1891] 2 Ch. 236.   5 *Cf. Re Soley, infra.*
6 *Re Soley* (1900), 17 T.L.R. 118. *Cy-près* application was by the *court* not by the Crown.
7 *Williams* v. *A.-G.* (1948), 48 S.R. N.S.W. 505.

Chapter 27

Surplus Capital

The cases concerning the application of surplus capital[1] can be conveniently classified into those cases where the gift in question was made in response to a charity appeal with no instrument of gift and those cases where the gift in question was made under some instrument in writing.

Surplus where no instrument of gift

Where money is collected from the public in response to a charity appeal a surplus may arise without there ever having been an instrument of gift. This topic is discussed elsewhere.[2]

Surplus where there is an instrument of gift

In *Re King*[3] a residue worth £1094 was bequeathed for the installation of one memorial stained-glass window. The cost of a stained-glass window of the best possible character could not exceed £800 according to an estimate provided. The trustees therefore applied to the court for directions as to the application of the surplus. ROMER J. held that the gift was charitable and ordered *cy-près* application (in fact for a second window) despite the absence of a general charitable intention, such intention being (he held) irrelevant.

In *Re Stanford*[4] the testator left £5000 on trust for the completion and publication of his etymological dictionary. After publication a surplus remained in the hands of the trustee. EVE J. held that the surplus was held on a resulting trust because no general charitable intent was discoverable. He did not refer to *Re King* although that case had been cited in argument. Had he done so he would, of course, have had to deal with ROMER J.'s statement that general charitable intent was irrelevant. On the other hand in *Re Monk*,[5] four years

---

1 See W. H. D. Winder, "The Cy-près Application of Surplus Charitable Funds" (1941) 5 Conv. N.S. 198.

2 See 267, *infra*.

3 [1923] 1 Ch. 243.

4 [1924] 1 Ch. 73. The *ratio decidendi* is criticised in *Tudor on Charities* (6th edn.) 287 because it does not fit in with the editors' out-and-out gift theory of *cy-près* application. Since the case was one of supervening failure a better objection is that it is inconsistent with *Re Wright*, [1954] Ch. 347.

5 [1927] 2 Ch. 197.

later, *Re King*[1] was not even cited to the Court of Appeal. The testator in *Re Monk* had given his residuary property to provide a coal fund and a loan fund for poor and deserving inhabitants of his native village. The residue (about £20,000 in value) far exceeded what was needed for these objects. Argument centred on whether or not there was a general charitable intent and the Court of Appeal held that there was a general charitable intent—relief of the deserving poor of the village—and therefore that the surplus should be applied *cy-près*.

Not until the decision in *Re Robertson*[2] was the distinction between *Re King* and *Re Stanford* considered. A testatrix left her residue "to be used towards the restoration or maintenance of" a named church. BENNETT J. held that she intended that the residue should be used either for the restoration or maintenance of the church, or for both purposes, and that there being a general charitable intention any surplus had to be applied *cy-près*. The distinction between *Re King*[3] and *Re Stanford*[4] was (he held) that in the former case there was, while in the latter case there was not, a general charitable intent.[5]

A general charitable intent was also discovered in *Re Royce*[6] where the testator had left a legacy and a large share of residue to the vicar and churchwardens of a church at Oakham "for the benefit of the choir." SIMONDS J. was able to find a general charitable intention in the will and directed a *cy-près* scheme for the application of what was surplus to the choir's needs. Several factors seem to have helped him to find a general charitable intention. First, he relied on the residuary nature of the gift.[7] Secondly, he relied on the provision for the payment of the legacy to the vicar and churchwardens: "In more than one case it has been held that a gift out-and-out to a vicar and churchwardens or to any body of trustees is an indication that the testator intended the whole of the fund to be employed, if not in a particular mode, then according to a general intent".[8] Thirdly he found that the gift was one of several gifts, all charitable, to which the testator had devoted his residuary estate and he said that that was "a factor which has more than once been taken into account in determining whether or not there is a general charitable intent".[9] Fourthly, he said that "a gift simply for the musical services in a church is not charitable unless there is an underlying charitable intention"[10] and held that the real underlying intention of the testator in *Re Royce* was the advancement of religion through musical services.[11]

The latest pronouncement in this area of the law is even less satisfactory. In *Re Raine*[12] a testatrix had directed that the whole of her residuary estate should be sold and the proceeds used "for the continuation of the seating" of a named church. After provision for the requisite seating a surplus of about £2000

---

1 [1923] 1 Ch. 243.

2 [1930] 2 Ch. 71. 3 [1923] 1 Ch. 243.

4 [1924] 1 Ch. 73. 5 [1930] 2 Ch. 71, at 74.

6 [1940] Ch. 514.

7 *Ibid.*, at 521. That on its own would not be enough. See *A.-G.* v. *Painters-Stainers Co.* (1788), 2 Cox Eq. Cas. 51, at 59, *per* Lord THURLOW L.C. But KEKEWICH J. wrongly held otherwise in *Re Douglas*, [1905] 1 Ch. 279. 8 [1940] Ch. 514 at 521.

9 *Ibid.*, at 522. But FARWELL J., somewhat surprisingly, refused to deduce a general charitable intention from this fact in *Re Harwood* [1936] Ch. 285.

10 *Ibid.*, at 521–522. *Sed quaere.* Musical services do in fact advance religion and the intention behind the form of this gift is surely irrelevant: see *Re King*, [1923] 1 Ch. 243.

11 This conception of general charitable intent was criticised by W. H. D. Winder in (1941), 5 Conv. N.S. 198, at 209–210; but see now *Re Lysaght*, [1966] Ch. 191.

12 [1956] Ch. 417.

remained. VAISEY J. held that this surplus should be applied *cy-près* for the benefit of the church in question. He distinguished two distinct forms of general charitable intention, the one "in the wider and vaguer significance of that expression" and the other being "a general and comprehensive intention" that a residuary gift is "to be devoted to a charitable purpose"; and while he could not find a general charitable intention in the former sense he found one in the latter sense. It is to be noted that the learned judge also stated that the application of the doctrine probably differs very much according to whether it is applied to residue or a share of residue. In the former case "the overriding intention of a charitable disposition should still prevail".[1]

The repeated, but by no means unanimous, insistence on discovering a general charitable intent in these cases of surplus has been criticised. Thus one writer[2] comments that the result of *Re Monk*[3] "has been to introduce an additional element of artificiality into these cases". Yet the artificiality is inevitable because as often as not, the law is imputing an intention to a donor who probably never applied his mind to the question of how any surplus should devolve. And is it really inapposite to discuss general charitable intent in cases where what is in issue is surely initial impossibility as to part of the gift? Initial impossibility, it will be remembered, is to be determined at the time the gift takes effect;[4] and in all of these cases an inquiry at that stage has either revealed or would have revealed that the donor had provided too much for the purpose in hand: his gift was *pro tanto* impossible. For reasons which have already been put forward[5] it is submitted that the out-and-out gift theory does not provide a satisfactory basis for *cy-près* application in cases of "initial surplus" any more than other cases. The doctrine of effective dedication to charity laid down in *Re Wright*[6] is one applicable only where there is a *supervening* impossibility. In all cases where a gift turns out to have been excessive the proper course is to determine whether this could have been discovered at the date of the gift. If it could, then the case is one of initial impossibility *pro tanto* and an inquiry into general charitable intent is appropriate. In *Re King*,[7] as has been seen, a general charitable intent was said to be absent, but in any event irrelevant. The case turned on the effective dedication of the fund to charity. Yet a paramount intention to beautify the church could no doubt have been spelled out of the gift if the case had been treated as one of a failure *pro tanto*. Certainly in the majority of cases where *cy-près* application has been ordered a general charitable intent is discoverable,[8] even though the court has held that no such intention is present.[9] The cases of *Re Robertson*,[10] *Re Royce*,[11] and *Re Raine*[12] are borderline cases. In each the court leant in favour of charity. But the court might with equal justification have discovered only a *particular* charitable intent. The leaning in favour of charities was a policy decision.

---

1 *Ibid.*, at 423.
2 Keeton and Sheridan, *Modern Law of Charities* (3rd edn.) 160.
3 [1927] 2 Ch. 197. General charitable intent was in fact discussed in the earlier case of *Re Stanford*, [1924] 1 Ch. 73.
4 See 243, *supra*.   5 See 247, *supra*.
6 [1954] Ch. 347, C.A. discussed at 239, *supra*.
7 [1923] 1 Ch. 243.
8 *Re Monk*, [1927] 2 Ch. 197; *Re Robertson*, [1930] 2 Ch. 71; *Re Royce*, [1940] Ch. 514. The case of *Re Douglas*, [1905] 1 Ch. 279 is unsound: see 265, *supra* (footnote 7).
9 *Re Raine*, [1956] Ch. 417.
10 [1930] 2 Ch. 71.
11 [1940] Ch. 514.   12 [1956] Ch. 417.

Chapter 28

Charity Appeals

Charities frequently raise money by conducting "appeals". Such appeals are made on the wireless and television, by advertisements on hoardings or in newspapers and magazines, by letters in the correspondence columns of news-papers, by circulars and, informally by street collectors. Normally all goes well; but what happens if the charitable purpose which is the subject of the appeal fails?[1] The answer to this question depends upon when the failure occurred. The purpose may fail at the outset because insufficient funds are raised;[2] or the purpose may by fulfilled and a surplus may remain.[3]

The case of a failure for lack of funds is often classified as an "initial" failure in contrast to the supervening failure where a surplus remains. But the term is perhaps imprecise. Where money is subscribed over a period of time it is only at the end of the period that it becomes clear that the purpose is impracticable. It is arguable that such a case is one of *supervening* failure, because it could not have been said at the moment of each gift that there was no reasonable prospect that the purposes would at some future time be practicable.[4] Nevertheless the description "initial" failure is used in such cases, although sometimes the gift is treated as a gift upon a condition precedent that the purpose will be practicable,[5] which gives rise at common law to a perpetuity problem.[6]

In the discussion which follows a distinction is drawn between initial and supervening failure. The case law on initial failure has produced some knotty problems many of which have been solved by the statutory presumption intro-duced by the Charities Act 1960. However in order to point the relevance of the statutory provision concerned it is necessary to investigate the earlier cases which have, of course, a continuing relevance in jurisdictions where no statu-tory gloss has been added. In relation to initial failure the position of (1) identifi-able donors (2) unidentifiable donors and (3) mixed funds of identifiable and unidentifiable donations will be discussed in turn.

---

1 See Thompson, "'Public' Charitable Trusts Which Fail" (1971) 36 Saskatchewan Law Review 110.
2 *Re Ulverston and District New Hospital Building Trusts*, [1956] Ch. 622, C.A.; *Re Hillier*, [1954] 1 W.L.R. 700, C.A.
3 *Re Hartley Colliery Accident Relief Fund* (1908), 102 L.T. 165 n.; *Re Welsh Hospital (Netley) Fund*, [1921] 1 Ch. 655; *Re North Devon and West Somerset Relief Fund Trusts*, [1953] 1 W.L.R. 1260.
4 This test is derived from the form of the inquiry in *Re White's Will Trusts*, [1955] Ch. 188.
5 *McCormick* v. *Queen's University of Belfast*, [1958] N.I. 1.
6 See 207, *supra*.

Initial failure

IDENTIFIABLE DONORS

Where there is an initial failure of the purpose for which funds were subscribed and *all* the subscribers are traceable the trustees will, *prima facie*, hold the money on a resulting trust for those subscribers. But the presumption of a resulting trust is rebutted if the court is able to deduce, either from the language of the appeal or the circumstances in which the money was given, that the particular mode of application mentioned in the appeal was ancillary to the advancement of a wider (and charitable) purpose. In such a case the court imputes a general charitable intent to the donors and the fund will be applied *cy-près*.[1]

The language of the appeal in *Re Ulverston and New Hospital Building Trusts*[2] was such that the learned Vice-Chancellor in the Lancaster Palatine Court was satisfied that the donors had had only a specific charitable intent and that the trust failed *ab initio*: a resulting trust therefore arose by implication of law and all *named*[3] donors were entitled to be repaid such proportion of the fund remaining as the total of their subscriptions to the fund bore to the total funds collected. The Court of Appeal confirmed his decision.

When the Charities Act 1960 came into force a *cy-près* application became possible if the identifiable donors to a specific charitable purpose which failed *ab initio* gave a written disclaimer or could not be traced after such advertisements or inquiries as were reasonable. Named donors may also be deprived of their right to return of the property and a *cy-près* application of funds may be ordered where the case falls within the provisions of section 14 (3) of the Charities Act 1960.

UNIDENTIFIABLE DONORS

Prior to the Charities Act 1960 the fate of anonymous donations to an initially impossible charitable purpose was a matter in respect of which the cases gave no satisfactory guidance. In *Re Hillier's Trusts*[4] the Court of Appeal had to decide what should be done with a fund which had been subscribed partly by covenantors and partly by anonymous donors through concerts, church collections, whist drives and so forth. There was an initial failure because at all material times the building of a new voluntary hospital at Slough (the object of the appeal) was impossible: first because of the 1939–1945 war and then because of the National Health Service Act 1946. The Court of Appeal, ROMER L.J. dissenting, held that the whole fund should be applied *cy-près*. EVERSHED M.R. concluded that the named donors had a general charitable intention. In reaching that conclusion the learned Master of the Rolls was affected by the view that

---

1 See *Re Hillier's Trusts*, [1954] 1 W.L.R. 700 as explained in *Re Ulverston and New Hospital Building Trusts*, [1956] Ch. 622.

2 [1956] Ch. 622, following *Re University of London Medical Sciences Institute Fund*, [1909] 2 Ch. 1.

3 *Semble* there were no unidentifiable donors.

4 [1954] 1 W.L.R. 700, C.A.

where the circumstances affecting the presumed intention of a donor are, at best equivocal, "it is a relevant and admissible fact in determining his true intention that when he contributed to the fund he must be taken to have known that his contributions would be mingled with thousands of others, substantial numbers of whom were contributing in circumstances which negatived any right or expectation on their part to any return of their money in any circumstances".[1] This is in effect *cy-près* by infection. DENNING L.J. went further. In discussing the proper destination for money collected in church, on flag days and so on for a specified charity which failed *ab initio* he said that the same rule applied as in the case of a surplus[2]:

> "The money has been given out and out. No one of those who gave it ever intended that it should be returned. If any one of them had been asked what was to happen to the money if the named purpose became impossible of fulfilment, he would have said 'If that should happen I will expect you to use it for some other good cause,[3] but I will not expect it back.' The law gives him credit for the best of intentions and presumes that he would have wished it so."

EVERSHED M.R. likewise treated anonymous donations as given with the intention of making an out-and-out gift and equated such presumed intention with a general charitable intent.[4] However in *Re Ulverston and District New Hospital Building Trusts*[5] JENKINS L.J. in his leading judgment found serious difficulty in the inference that, because anonymous donors have given their money out-and-out, therefore a general charitable intent must be imputed to them, however exclusive and specific the avowed purpose of the fund might be; and he thought it at least arguable that such anonymous subscribers intended to contribute only to a specific charity, without forming any intention as to the disposal of the money if the specific intention could not be carried out. If the anonymous subscriber could prove conclusively that he had in fact contributed some specified amount to the fund there should be a resulting trust in his favour;[6] if not, the money would be *bona vacantia*, and on waiver of the Crown's claim (in accordance with the usual practice) would be applied *cy-près*.[7] Lord EVERSHED M.R. took the opportunity of explaining his dicta in *Re Hillier's Trusts*[8] concerning what has been called *cy-près* by infection. The court, he said, should only resort to such inferences if it was in doubt as to the intention of named subscribers.[9] He also drew attention to the material fact that in the *Hillier* case no named donor had demanded the return of his gift which was "in marked contrast to the circumstances" of the *Ulverston* case itself.[10] The distinction is a crucial one.

---

1 *Ibid.*, at 712.
2 [1954] 1 W.L.R. 700, at 715.
3 DENNING L.J. should perhaps have said "some other *charitable* cause", because a good cause is not necessarily charitable; see *Re Wood*, [1949] Ch. 498. But he was echoing the language of the man in the street.
4 [1954] 1 W.L.R. 700, at 711.
5 [1956] Ch. 622, C.A.
6 *Ibid.*, at 633.
7 *Ibid.*, at 634.
8 [1954] 1 W.L.R. 700.
9 [1956] Ch. 623, at 642.
10 *Ibid.*, at 643.

For if there is a demand it must be very strong evidence in favour of a resulting trust. Where there is no demand the position is less clear.[1]

In two of the three Canadian cases concerning charity appeals there was an initial impossibility or impracticability in implementing the purpose of the relevant appeal. In *Re Young Women's Christian Association Extension Campaign Fund*[2] public subscriptions were solicited for the purpose of providing increased accommodation for the Young Women's Christian Association in a particular area. Before any part of the fund had been applied to that end the increased accommodation became unnecessary, and the Association wished to use the funds raised to pay off its operating deficit. It was held that the division of the fund to the payment of operating costs would not be within the principle under which the court exercised a general purpose *cy-près*. The particularisation of the object of the appeal seems to have weighed with the court, but the decision was not that there was no general charitable intent, only that the general charitable intent was very limited in scope and would not permit the proposed application. In other words the case supports the proposition that so far as the intitial impracticability of a charity appeal is concerned a general charitable intention is a prerequisite of *cy-près* application. In *Halifax School for the Blind* v. *A.-G.*[3] an appeal was launched to raise money to build a home for blind children and in particular those blinded by a particular explosion. Contributions came in from children all over Canada but they were mostly small and the fund fell far short of what was required. Moreover it was discovered that only 11 children had been blinded by the explosion that prompted the appeal. The judge followed the decision of P. O. LAWRENCE J. *Re Welsh Hospital (Netley) Fund*[4] in discovering an intention on the part of the donors to make an absolute gift in favour of a charitable object. Presumably he was following the reasoning of P. O. LAWRENCE J.[5] that an out-and-out gift intention demonstrates a general charitable intent, although he did not actually say that that was what he was doing.

It is not quite clear whether the impracticability which was the handle of a *cy-près* application in *Re Ethel Pedley Memorial Travelling Scholarship Trust*[6] was initial or supervening, but it looks as if it was the former. Three trust funds were set up by public subscription: one was to send female students of singing and the violin to England to continue their studies: the other two were to send female students of the piano to England for the same purpose. The combined annual income of all three trusts was £207 and it was plainly impracticable to run each trust separately. The court therefore consolidated the trusts in one scheme and invoked the *cy-près* doctrine for that purpose. There was, however, a failure from the inception in the case of *Beggs* v. *Kirkpatrick*[7] where money was subscribed for the erection of a new hospital. It was held that subject to one qualification the gifts could not be applied *cy-près* unless there was a general charitable intent in the gifts. However "a gift made solely for a particular pur-

---

1 Contrast what was said by JENKINS L.J. in [1956] Ch. 623, at 641, with the view of DENNING L.J. in *Re Hillier's Trust*, [1954] 1 W.L.R. 700, at 715.
2 [1934] 3 W.W.R. 49.
3 [1935] 2 D.L.R. 347.
4 [1921] 1 Ch. 655.
5 The reasoning of P. O. LAWRENCE J. on this point has been criticised: see Sheridan and Delany, *The Cy-près Doctrine* (1959) 123–124.
6 (1949), 49 S.R.N.S.W. 329.
7 [1961] V.R. 764, especially at 767–770.

pose, although it has failed *ab initio*, will be administered *cy-près* if the gift was an out-and-out gift—the donor having abandoned all interest in it—and the Attorney-General has waived the claim of *bona vacantia* and by bringing in a scheme or otherwise has consented to its application for some other charitable purpose".[1]

The question of what intention ought to be imputed to anonymous donors to a charity which fails has now been rendered academic in England by the provisions of section 14 of the Charities Act 1960. This section has rescued for charity substantial sums of money which might otherwise have lain dormant in court because the donors were untraceable. Such funds can now be put to use by means of a *cy-près* scheme if after reasonable advertisements and inquiries the donors cannot be identified or found for in that event the donors will be deemed to have had a general charitable intention.[2]

In certain cases no advertisement or inquiry is needed. One such case is where the property in question consists of the proceeds of cash collections made by means of collecting boxes or by other means not adapted for distinguishing one gift from another.[3] Another case is where the property consists of the proceeds of any lottery, competition, entertainment, sale or similar money raising activity; but allowance must be made for any property given to provide prizes or articles for sale or otherwise to enable the activity to be undertaken.[4] In both these cases there is a conclusive presumption that the donors are un-identifiable and had a general charitable intention. In any other case where it appears to the court that it would be unreasonable, having regard to the amounts likely to be returned to the donors, to incur expense with a view to returning the property, or that it would be unreasonable, having regard to the nature, circumstances and amount of the gifts and to the lapses of time since they were made, for the donor to expect the property to be returned the court may dispense with any advertisements or inquiries and direct that the property shall be treated as belonging to donors who cannot be found.[5] The property will then be applicable *cy-près*.[6] It should be noted that such a direction cannot be given by the Commissioners, but only by the court.

The question what advertisements and inquiries are reasonable is left open by the section; and there is no provision corresponding to that in section 27 of the Trustee Act 1925 which entitles trustees or personal representatives to distribute trust property not less than two months after making certain prescribed advertisements.[7] If the trustees took and followed the advice of the Charity Commissioners on what inquiries and advertisements to make they would be protected.[8] Otherwise they would probably be held to have made reasonable advertisements if they complied with section 27 (1) of the Trustee Act 1925 and advertised in the London Gazette and in a newspaper circulating in the area in which the funds were collected, stating their intention to apply for a *cy-près* scheme after the expiration of two months. In *Re Henry Wood National*

---

1 *Ibid.*, at 767, *per* ADAM J.
2 CA 1960, s. 14 (1).
3 *Ibid.*, s. 14 (2) (a).
4 *Ibid.*, s. 14 (2) (b).
5 *Ibid.*, s. 14 (3).
6 *Ibid.*, s. 14 (1).
7 This was apparently intentional: see H. of C. Official Report of Standing Committee A (30th June 1960) col. 360 (Solicitor General); but see Nathan, *The Charities Act 1960*, 81.
8 CA 1960, s. 24.

Memorial Trusts[1] STAMP J. held that the following notices would constitute reasonable advertisements and inquiries for identifying and finding donors who have not disclaimed viz. notices inviting a donor who does not wish to give such a written disclaimer to notify his name and address in writing to the designated agents of the trustees, so as to be received by them before a specified date not less than two months after publication or posting of the notice, such a notice to be inserted in two issues of each of the following newspapers, namely, *The Times*, *The Daily Telegraph* and *The Scotsman*, and to be sent by ordinary post to the address, as recorded in the books and papers of the trustees, of every donor who made any such gift and has such a recorded address (not being an address of a formation or unit of Her Majesty's Forces) but who has not already given such a written disclaimer.

Where a *cy-près* scheme is made under these provisions[2] a donor who cannot be identified or found[3] is nevertheless able to make a claim to recover any part of his gift that has been applied *cy-près* at any time within 12 months after the date of the scheme except in a case to which subsections (2) or (3) apply. Where there is a possibility of such claims being made, the scheme must specify the total amount of the property affected by it and the sum which the donor may recover is a sum equal to the part of the specified amount given by him, less any expenses properly incurred by the charity trustees after that date in connection with claims relating to his gift. The scheme may include directions as to the provision to be made for meeting any such claim.[4]

Illustrations of the way in which the Charity Commissioners apply section 14 of the 1960 Act are to be found in the Annual Reports of the Commissioners.[5]

MIXED FUNDS OF IDENTIFIABLE AND UNIDENTIFIABLE DONATIONS

In the *Ulverston*[6] case the Court of Appeal unanimously[7] held that there was no reason why the imputation of a general charitable intention to anonymous contributors (if rightly made) should by itself afford any ground for imputing a general charitable intention to subscribers to the same fund who give their names. But on the other hand they held that it is not the case that contemporaneous anonymous donations must always be irrelevant in determining the intention, general or particular, of named subscribers.[8] The inclusion of anonymous contributions is a factor which may be taken into account for the purpose of resolving in favour of charity any doubt (raised by the equivocal language of an appeal) as to the intention of named contributors. The court will have regard to the realities of the situation and take account of the fact that named sub-

---

1 [1967] 1 All E.R. 238, n., at 239.
2 CA 1960, s. 14.
3 A disclaiming donor is deemed to have parted with the entirety of his interest.
4 CA 1960, s. 14 (4).
5 *Mile End Memorial Hall Fund Colchester*, [1965] Ch. Com. Rep. 8; *Stewartby United Church Building Fund*, [1969] Ch. Com. Rep. 20; *Bedford Church Hall Fund, Hartsthorn St. Peter Derbyshire*, [1971] Ch. Com. Rep. 22.
6 [1956] Ch. 622.
7 See *per* JENKINS L.J. at 640–641. HODSON L.J. (at 641) merely agreed *in toto* with the judgment of JENKINS L.J. as did Lord EVERSHED M.R. (641–642) who also added a gloss on his earlier judgment in *Re Hillier's Trust*, [1954] 1 W.L.R. 700.
8 [1956] Ch. 622, at 640.

scribers are or are not asking for the return of their money.[1] Thus in the *Hillier*[2] case Lord EVERSHED M.R. was to some extent influenced by the circumstances (in marked contrast to the circumstances of the *Ulverston* case) that despite extensive advertisement no single contributor had come forward who was ready to contend that he had contributed to a single and specific object which had failed, and so was entitled to return of his money.[3] ROMER L.J. who dissented in the *Hillier* case was less impressed by this factor:[4]

> "for it needs some moral courage to ask for the return of money already subscribed, and still more to play the role of Shylock (for some people might so regard it) in litigation which is of considerable local interest".

Now that there is a statutory presumption that anonymous donors have a general charitable intention, identifiable donors who contribute to a mixed fund will be infected by the general charitable intention attributed to the anonymous donors, unless at the time of the gift a specific charitable intent is expressed by such identifiable donors.

Supervening failure

The section which follows discusses the case of a charity appeal where the purpose has been achieved and there is a surplus. In such a case the court has sometimes imputed to both named and anonymous subscribers a general charitable intent as to that surplus which has then been applied *cy-près*.[5] There is only one case[6] of such an appeal where a resulting trust has been allowed and that case was an aberration.[7] It is submitted however that the court does not even need to consider the question of a general charitable intent in these surplus cases. General charitable intent is irrelevant to cases of supervening impossibility.[8] Moreover it is submitted that an out-and-out gift intent is not a positive vital requirement, although it has been relied on in two decided cases.[9] *Cy-près* application should be ordered on the simple footing that once the charity for which the fund is raised has been effectively brought into action, the fund is to be regarded as permanently devoted to charity to the exclusion of any resulting trust.[10]

The Commonwealth cases on the supervening failure of charity appeals are not entirely satisfactory in the reasoning which they have adopted.

---

1 [1956] Ch. 622, at 643; and see 269, *supra*.

2 [1954] 1 W.L.R. 700.

3 *Ibid.*, at 719–720.

4 *Ibid.*, at 719–720.

5 See *Re Hartley Colliery Accident Relief Fund* (1908), 102 L.T. 165, n.; *Re Welsh Hospital (Netley) Fund*, [1921] 1 Ch. 655; *Re North Devon and West Somerset Relief Fund Trusts*, [1953] 1 W.L.R. 1260 (where WYNN-PARRY J. discovered a general charitable intent).

6 *Re British Red Cross Balkan Fund*, [1914] 2 Ch. 419.

7 The Attorney-General should have been a defendant and in his absence a resulting trust was wrongly admitted: see [1921] 1 Ch. 655, at 662; *cf. Re Stanford*, [1924] 1 Ch. 73 (where a surplus fell into residue) which also seems incorrect: see 264, *supra*.

8 See 238–239, *supra*.

9 *Re Wokingham Fire Brigade Trusts*, [1951] Ch. 373; *Re British School of Egyptian Archaeology*, [1954] 1 W.L.R. 546.

10 *Per* JENKINS L.J. in *Re Ulverston and District New Hospital Building Trusts*, [1956] Ch. 622, at 636, citing SARGANT L.J. in *Re Monk*, [1927] 2 Ch. 197, at 211; and see the discussion at 239, *supra*.

The earliest Australian case[1] on a charity appeal concerned a fund raised by subscription for the relief of the distress caused by the Maori rebellion in New Zealand. The amount raised was found to be in excess of the requirements and a surplus remained in the hands of the treasurers of the fund which was applied *cy-près*. The case of *Lewis* v. *Benson*[2] was also one of supervening impossibility: a fund was raised for charitable purposes which ultimately became impossible of fulfilment. A general charitable intent was deduced from the out-and-out character of the gift. But general charitable intent, as has been seen, is irrelevant in such cases: the fund had been effectively devoted to charity so as to exclude any resulting trust.

In the Canadian case of *Re Northern Ontario Fire Relief Trusts*[3] a fund had been raised for the relief of sufferers from a disastrous forest fire. A surplus remained after this purpose had been achieved, and was applied *cy-près*. The case turned only on the terms of the *cy-près* order. General charitable intent was not mentioned, but was of course irrelevant: the case was one of supervening failure. Equally, it is submitted, any intention on the part of the donors to give out-and-out was irrelevant. The *cy-près* application was justified because the fund was effectively dedicated to charity.

Given that in the case of a supervening failure there can never be a resulting trust, section 14 of the Charities Act 1960 does not appear to affect the law set out above. Charitable purposes only "fail" within the meaning of section 14 where any difficulty in applying property to those purposes makes that property or the part not applicable *cy-près* available to be returned to the donors.[4]

---

1 *A.-G.* v. *Lorimer* (1866), 3 W.W. & A.B. (E.) 82.
2 [1944] V.L.R. 106, especially at 110.
3 (1913), 11 D.L.R. 15.
4 CA 1960, s. 14 (5).

Chapter 29

Schemes other than "Cy-près" Schemes

Mode of executing charitable gift undefined

In some cases where a donor's directions are indefinite, ambiguous or insufficient the court has power to order a scheme to carry the donor's charitable intention into effect. This power is closely analogous to the power of the court to make a cy-près order. Indeed some judges and text-books[1] treat such schemes as applications of the cy-près doctrine. But there is, in such cases, no question of choosing an object as near as possible to that designated by the donor: the scheme effectuates the donor's intention by spelling out the details. For that reason although discussed in connection with the cy-près principle such schemes are here not referred to as cy-près schemes.

Where the mode of executing a charitable gift is not defined by the donor it is, of course, impossible to select an object cy-près to that which has failed:[2] for, ex hypothesi, there is no such mode. The law therefore provides a mode[3] and the gift will be applied to charitable objects to be nominated by the Crown the court[4] or the Commissioners[5] as the case may be.

A seminal case in this area was *Moggridge* v. *Thackwell*.[6] In that case a testatrix gave the residue of her personal estate to a particular legatee "desiring him to dispose of the same in such charities as he shall see fit, recommending clergymen who have large families and good characters". The legatee predeceased the testatrix by some nine years and the latter had never made any alteration to her will. The first hearing of the case[7] was before Lord THURLOW who held that the gift to the legatee having been for the purpose of creating a charity the legatee was merely a trustee, and the trust would not fail for the want of a trustee. A scheme was directed to be settled in Chambers, but subsequently the case was ordered to be reheard.[8] On the rehearing Lord ELDON L.C. upheld the decision of Lord THURLOW, after an elaborate review of all the earlier cases.

It appears from later observations in *Mills* v. *Farmer*[9] that Lord ELDON reached the conclusion which he did in *Moggridge* v. *Thackwell* much against

---

1 E.g. Boyle, *Law of Charities* (1837) 48; Sheridan and Delany, *The Cy-près Doctrine* (1959) 53–73.
2 *Barclay* v. *Maskelyne* (1858), 4 Jur. N.S. 1294, at 1297.
3 See *Mills* v. *Farmer* (1815), 1 Mer. 55, at 99.
4 *White* v. *White* (1778), 1 Bro. C.C. 12; *Mills* v. *Farmer* (1815), 1 Mer. 55, at 96.
5 CA 1960, s. 18.
6 (1802), 7 Ves. 36; affd. (1807), 13 Ves. 416; [1803–1813] All E.R. Rep. 754.
7 (1792), 1 Ves. 464.
8 By Lord ROSSLYN L.C.: see (1802), 7 Ves. 36.
9 (1815), 1 Mer. 55, at 99; [1814–1823] All E.R. Rep. 53, at 58.

his inclination, and entirely by the force of precedents. In *Mills* v. *Farmer* a testator after providing in his will for the payment of his debts and certain legacies, directed that the residue of his estate be applied for "promoting the gospel in foreign parts and in England, for bringing up ministers in different seminaries and other charitable purposes as I do intend to name hereafter after all my worldly property is disposed of to the best advantage". Just over a year later he wrote a letter which was proved as a codicil to the will; but the letter contained no reference to any charitable purposes. Sir WILLIAM GRANT M.R. held the gift void for uncertainty. It was impossible, he considered, to say what proportion should go to which purpose; and the reference to a further specification of particulars never afterwards made was also, he thought, void for uncertainty. Lord ELDON L.C. reheard the case and held that upon the true construction of the will the testator had effectually devoted the whole of his residue to charity. Uncertainty in the mode of fulfilling that intention would not defeat it any more than an impossibility in the mode. Accordingly he directed a scheme to be brought in by the executors.

There are of course numerous examples in the books of gifts to charity in wide and very general terms. Thus the courts have provided more precise directions for carrying out the charitable intentions behind gifts for charity generally[1] or for general purposes of an undeniably charitable character as for the poor[2] or the blind[3] or incurables[4] or for educational[5] or religious[6] purposes or purposes synonymous therewith. In the last mentioned category are gifts for or towards Christian work[7] or the work of the Lord[8] or to further the cause of our Lord Jesus Christ[9] or for foreign missions.[10] So too a direction to divide residue between heart diseases and cancer research[11] evinces a general charitable intention that should be effectuated by scheme. But some gifts are too vague, as for example a gift to help in any good work[12] or for a community project[13] or for friends relations and labourers in the Lord's work.[14] The elevation of man is another benevolent object which usually fails for uncertainty. Thus a gift to uplift humanity will fail.[15] But a gift to elevate the community *spiritually*[16] will be upheld and effectuated by a scheme. In *Re Wright*[17] the court was able to discover a general charitable intention in a gift of this nature. A

---

1 *Clifford* v. *Francis* (1679), Freem. Ch. 330; *A.-G.* v. *Herrick* (1772), Amb. 712; *Legge* v. *Asgill* (1818), Turn & R. 265 n.; *Kane* v. *Cosgrave* (1833), I.R. 10 Eq. 211; *Re Cronin* (1910), 15 O.W.R. 819 ("some charitable object").
2 See the cases cited at 28–31, *supra*.
3 *Re Bond*, [1929] V.L.R. 333.
4 *Public Trustee* v. *Denton*, [1917] N.Z.L.R. 263.
5 *Whicker* v. *Hume* (1858), 7 H.L.C. 124; *United States of America* v. *Drummond* (1838), cited in 7 H.L.Cas., at 155; *Re Macduff*, [1896] 2 Ch. 451.
6 *Re White*, [1893] 2 Ch. 41.
7 *Brown* v. *Whitty* (1901), 11 Q.L.J. 133.
8 *Re Brooks Estate* (1969), 3 D.L.R. (3d) 700.
9 *Phelps* v. *Lord* (1894), 25 O.R. 259.
10 *Re Long* (1930), 37 O.W.N. 351.
11 *Ballingal's Judicial Factor* v. *Hamilton* 1973 S.L.T. 236; discussed in [1974] A.S.C.L. 514–515 (J. Hackney).
12 *Re Ashton*, [1955] N.Z.L.R. 192.
13 *Re Jacques* (1967), 63 D.L.R. (2d) 673 (B.C.).
14 *Re Wilson* (1899), 30 O.R. 353.
15 *Cameron* v. *Church of Christ Scientist* (1919), 43 D.L.R. 668.
16 *Re Orr* (1917), 40 O.L.R. 567.
17 (1923), 56 N.S.R. 364, C.A.

testator had bequeathed a named sum "in order to provide for a higher form of amusement than is at present placed before the people, and for a building to be erected for the purpose of bringing the people together to uplift and train them to higher ideals, such building to be also used for meetings lectures and to provide clean amusement in order to check the lure and bad influence of the streets". There followed a gift of a named sum from the residue "to be applied in carrying on the work before mentioned". It appeared that the work to which the testator had referred elsewhere in the will was the work of the Women's Council and the suppression of evils which the testator had endeavoured to put down. A general charitable intent was expressly found to be present by CHISHOLM J.[1] and leave was given to the Attorney-General to apply if and when he thought fit for the approval of a scheme.

Sometimes there is a little more particularity in the expressed charitable intention but the mode of executing that intention is not defined.[2] In these cases too the law provides the requisite mode that is lacking.

The case of *Mills* v. *Farmer*[3] which has been referred to earlier is authority for the proposition that where a testator gives property to such charitable uses as he shall name and names none a mode will be supplied to effect his charitable intent; for the mere omission to make the particular nomination is not, by itself,[4] sufficient to revoke the charitable intention originally expressed.[5] The most recent example[6] of a failure by a testator to nominate the charities intended to benefit is *Re Leslie*,[7] a Canadian case. The testator in his will stated that he would "designate by codicil to what charities" the capital of the trust fund should go on his wife's death, but he failed to make any codicil. GREEVE J. held that the will showed a general charitable intention and that the court ought to supply a mode for effecting it. "The court" he said[8] "will make the selection which the testator intended to have made himself, because that is only a mode of carrying out the bequest".

In *A.-G.* v. *Syderfen*[9] the testator gave £1000 to be applied to such charitable uses as he had in writing already directed. No such direction could be found but a scheme was directed to give effect to the obvious charitable intent of the testator. Similarly where the name of the charity legatee is left blank, the gift will be subjected to a scheme.[10] But it is otherwise where the amount of the gift is left blank: no scheme is possible because the subject matter is uncertain.[11]

A benevolent decision was reached by the court in the old Irish case of *Charitable Donations Comrs.* v. *Sullivan*[12] where a testatrix bequeathed certain

---

1 *Ibid.*, at 371. RUSSELL J. and MCKENZIE J. did not mention the point.
2 *A.-G.* v. *Hickman* (1732), 2 Eq. Cas. Abr. 193; *White* v. *White* (1778), 1 Bro.C.C. 12; *A.-G.* v. *Gladstone* (1842), 13 Sim. 7.
3 (1815), 1 Mer. 55.
4 *Wheeler* v. *Sheer* (1730), Mos. 288, at 301.
5 *Mills* v. *Farmer* (1815), 1 Mer. 55, at 103; and see *Stackpoole* v. *Stackpoole* (1843), 6 I.Eq.R. 260.
6 For other examples see *Cook* v. *Duckenfield* (1743), 2 Atk. 562; *A.-G.* v. *Fletcher* (1835), 5 L.J.Ch. 75; *Pocock* v. *A.-G.* (1876), 3 Ch.D. 342; *Re Pyne*, [1903] 1 Ch. 83.
7 [1940] O.W.N. 345.
8 *Ibid.*, at 347. 9 (1683), 1 Vern. 224.
10 *Pieschel* v. *Paris* (1825), 2 Sim. & St. 384.
11 *Hartshorne* v. *Nicholson* (1858), 26 Beav. 58; *Ewen* v. *Bannerman* (1830), 2 Dow. & Cl. 74.
12 (1841), 1 Dr. & War. 501; and see *Re Watters* (1928), 62 I.L.T. 61 ("charitable purposes and objects known to my executors": conversations admitted); *A.-G.* v. *Madden* (1843), 2 Con. & Law. 519; *Re Buckley*, [1942] Ir. Jur. Rep. 43.

stocks to trustees to be applied by them to charitable purposes "according to my instructions, deposited with" one of the trustees. The word "deposited" arguably indicated that *written* instructions had been given to the trustee. But the trustee stated that he had been given *oral* instructions which left the disposal of the stocks to his judgment within the sphere of charity. The bequest was held to be charitable and a scheme was directed.

In cases falling under this head particular regard is paid to any indications casting light on the donor's intention.[1] His intention may be gleaned from his religious opinions,[2] his interest in a particular locality,[3] precatory directions in the will in favour of a certain class[4] or even wishes expressed in an unattested codicil.[5] The existence of other charitable gifts in the same instrument may be relevant.[6] Thus in *Re Satterthwaite's Will Trusts*[7] the testatrix left a share of her residuary estate to the London Animal Hospital. An individual had carried on business under that title at one time but had ceased to do so at the date of the will: this fact prevented him from taking beneficially. But since the other residuary legatees were concerned with animal welfare the Court of Appeal was able to discover a general charitable intent namely to promote kindness to animals and the residuary share in question was applied *cy-près*.[8] All the same the maxim *noscitur a sociis* does not enable one to overlook self-evident facts.[9] A gift to a non-charitable purpose even if closely related to a gift for a charitable purpose is[10] not converted into a charitable gift just because it is rubbing shoulders with charitable gifts in the same part of the will.[11]

Where no indication can be gathered as to the particular intention of the donor, regard is had to his general intention; and if his general intention is confined to a particular form of charity the scheme evolved must keep within those confines.[12] In *Philpott* v. *St. George's Hospital*[13] a charity was founded for *almshouses* for poor men and women reduced by sickness, misfortune or infirmity and it was held that this did not authorise the court in settling a scheme to sanction the building of a *hospital* or infirmary with accommodation for the almspeople. But if no particular charitable purpose is indicated, and if the general charitable intention is subject to no restrictions express or implied, the discretion of the court in the application of the fund in what seems the most expedient manner is unlimited.[14] Accordingly, gifts for charity generally may be applied for the benefit of hospitals[15] schools[16] or other charitable objects.[17]

---

1 *Cook* v. *Duckenfield* (1743), 2 Atk. 562; *Ironmongers' Co.* v. *A.-G.* (1844), 10 Cl. & Fin. 908, at 922, 924–929.

2 *Re Ashton's Charity* (1859), 27 Beav. 115.

3 *Re Mann*, [1903] 1 Ch. 232.

4 *Moggridge* v. *Thackwell* (1803), 7 Ves. 36 ("clergymen who have large families and good characters").

5 *A.-G.* v. *Madden* (1843), 2 Con. & Law. 519.

6 See *Mills* v. *Farmer* (1815) 1 Mer. 55, at 103 and 722, *per* Lord Eldon; *Ironmongers' Co.* v. *A.-G.* (1844), 10 Cl. & Fin. 908, H.L.; *Lyons Corporation* v. *Advocate-General of Bengal* (1876), 1 App. Cas. 91, at 114, P.C.; *Pieschel* v. *Paris* (1825), 2 Sim. & St. 384.

7 [1966] 1 W.L.R. 277.

8 Even though one residuary legatee was non-charitable.

9 *Re Jenkins's Will Trusts*, [1966] Ch. 249, at 256.

10 *Ibid*.

11 *Ibid*.

12 *A.-G.* v. *Peacock* (1676), Cas. *temp* Finch, 245 (poverty); and see *Re Hill* (1909), 53 Sol. Jo. 228.

13 (1859), 27 Beav. 107.

[Footnotes 14–17 on facing page

Failure of machinery for ascertaining objects

A scheme will also be directed where the machinery for ascertaining the intended objects of a charitable trust breaks down. The case where objects are intended to be, but are not, named by the donor has already been mentioned.[1] A similar result ensues where the nomination of a particular object is entrusted to an executor whose appointment is revoked,[2] or who renounces,[3] or to a trustee who neglects or refuses to appoint[4] or to a person who dies in the testator's lifetime,[5] or before appointing.[6] The same principles apply where a fund is to be divided among a particular class at the discretion of persons who fail to make the division.[7]

Failure of trust machinery

Two situations call for discussion under this head. The first is where the donor has failed to provide the machinery to carry his charitable purpose into effect. The second is where he has provided a machinery but it has broken down.

NO TRUST MACHINERY PROVIDED

Provided it is clear that the donor intended to establish a *continuing* charitable trust, the execution of which is committed to trustees (other than an existing charitable institution engaged in that particular charitable purpose or an officer or officers of such an institution[8]) a scheme will generally be directed if the donor has not prescribed all the details of administration, even though such details are expressly confined to the discretion of the trustees.[9] In a simple case a scheme may not be necessary[10] for example where the donor has authorised an immediate distribution[11] or a distribution at intervals for a limited period[12]

---

14 *Philpott* v. *St. George's Hospital* (1859), 27 Beav. 107, at 112; *Re Ashton's Charity* (1859), 27 Beav. 115.

15 *Legge* v. *Asgill* (1818), 3 Hare 194, n.; affd. Turn. & R. 265, n.

16 *A.-G.* v. *Syderfen* (1683), 1 Vern. 224. See also *Pieschel* v. *Paris* (1825), 2 Sim. & St. 384.

17 *Re Dickason* (1837), 3 Hare 195, n.

1 See at 277, *supra*.

2 *White* v. *White* (1778), 1 Bro.C.C. 12.

3 *A.-G.* v. *Fletcher* (1835), 5 L.J.Ch. 75. Trustees subsequently appointed cannot, in the absence of an expressed intention in the will, make the selection: *Hibbard* v. *Lamb* (1756), Amb. 309.

4 See *A.-G.* v. *Boultbee* (1796), 3 Ves. 220.

5 *Moggridge* v. *Thackwell* (1802), 7 Ves. 36.

6 *White* v. *White* (1778), 1 Bro.C.C. 12.

7 *A.-G.* v. *Gladstone* (1842), 13 Sim. 7; and see *A.G.* v. *Wansay* (1808), 15 Ves. 231; *Pease* v. *Pattinson* (1886) 32, Ch.D. 154.

8 See 253–284, *infra*.

9 *Wellbeloved* v. *Jones* (1822), 1 Sim. & St. 40; *Sons of the Clergy Corporation* v. *Mose* (1839) 9 Sim. 610; *A.-G.* v. *Stepney* (1804), 10 Ves. 22, *Re Mann*, [1903] 1 Ch. 232; *Re Webster*, [1912] 1 Ch. 106.

10 *Nash* v. *Morley* (1842) 5, Beav. 177, at 185.

11 *Re Barnett* (1860), 29 L.J. Ch. 871.

12 *Waldo* v. *Caley* (1809), 16 Ves. 206; *Powerscourt* v. *Powerscourt* (1824), 1 Moll. 616, *Horde* v. *Earl of Suffolk* (1833), 2 My. & K. 59.

and the trustees are in existence and accept the trust. The principle is that, wherever a permanent charitable trust was intended, the court will not part with a fund under its control without seeing that a proper trust is established.[1]

TRUST MACHINERY BREAKS DOWN

Equity does not normally permit a trust to fail for want of a trustee.[2] This maxim applies to charitable trusts as well as to private trusts.[3] Accordingly a charitable trust will not ordinarily fail because of a failure of trustees. It is otherwise if the donor makes it clear that the trust is not to operate unless the designated trustee accepts the trust and continues to act as a trustee.[4]

A failure of trustees may occur in a number of different ways.

Death is one example. In *A.-G.* v. *Hickman*[5] there was a gift of residue for the use of non-conformist clergymen. The trustees to whom the disposal and appointment of the charity was given both died in the testator's lifetime. Lord KING L.C. held that the substance of the charity remained despite the death of the trustees before the testator and directed a scheme. In *Moggridge* v. *Thackwell*[6] the testatrix left all the rest of her personal estate to J.B. desiring him to dispose of the same in such charities as he should think fit, recommending poor clergymen with large families and good characters. The trustee had died some nine years before the testatrix. The court directed a scheme to be settled. Likewise a scheme will be ordered where there is a gift to the president of an institution *by name* for the benefit of that institution and he or she dies before the testator.[7] The same principle applies where a trustee to whom a choice is delegated dies before exercising his discretion, but after the death of the testator,[8] and selection by the particular trustee is not an essential part of the scheme of the testator.

Where the designated trustee or trustees decline or disclaim the trust the same test is applicable namely: is the discretion of the particular trustee of the essence of the gift? Usually it is not. Thus in *Barclay* v. *Maskelyne*[9] the Colonial Secretary declined to act in the trusts of a charity for the existence of emigrants where the selection of objects was a matter for the trustee: a scheme was directed. Whether the trustee in question is an individual as in *Barclay* v. *Maskelyne*[10] or a college[11] or some other charitable institution[12] the principle is

---

1 *Wellbeloved* v. *Jones* (1822), 1 Sim. & St. 40.
2 *Ellison* v. *Ellison* (1802), 6 Ves. 656.
3 *A.-G.* v. *Lady Downing* (1766), Ambl. 550; *Moggridge* v. *Thackwell* (1792), 3 Bro. C.C. 517.
4 *Reeve* v. *A.-G.* (1843), 3 Hare 191, at 197; *Re Wilson-Barkworth* (1933), 50 T.L.R. 82; *Re Lawton*, [1936] 3 All E.R. 378.
5 (1732), 3 Eq. Cas. Abr. 193, at 14; *A.-G.* v. *Gladstone* (1842), 13 Sim. 7.
6 (1803), 7 Ves. 36.
7 *Walsh* v. *Gladstone* (1843), 1 Ph. 290 (President of college); *In the Goods of M'Auliffe*, [1895] P. 290 (Head of convent): *In the Goods of Lalor* (1901), 85 L.T. 643 (Bishop of Roman Catholic diocese).
8 *Re Childs*, [1917] V.L.R. 112.
9 (1859), 4 Jur. N.S. 1294; see also *Re Burley*, [1910] 1 Ch. 215 when precatory words were construed as imperative.
10 (1859), 4 Jur. N.S. 1294.
11 *A.-G.* v. *Andrew* (1798), 3 Ves. 633.
12 *Denyer* v. *Druce* (1829), Taml. 32 (Christ's Hospital).

the same. In *Reeve* v. *A.-G.*[1] there were two charitable bequests, one to the "Society for Bettering the Condition of the Poor" and one to the "Society for the Encouragement of Female Servants". Both societies renounced the respective trusts attached to the bequests. Sir JAMES WIGRAM V.-C. said that he found no ground, either in the language of the will or in the circumstances of the case for supposing that the discretion of the particular societies named in the will was of the essence of the gifts. Of course, in most cases trustees are chosen because of their particular fitness to carry out the donor's purpose. But that does not make their disclaimer fatal to the gift. As has been said in a case relating to a private trust,[2] if the trust is to fail by reason of the failure of the nominated trustees "the testator's reliance on the individuals to the exclusion of the holders of the office for the time being must be expressed in clear and apt language".[3]

On a parity of reasoning, a charitable trust will not fail by reason of the incapacity of a trustee. The court will come to the rescue with a scheme. So a gift of realty or personalty to a corporation will not fail by reason of some legal incapacity on the part of the corporation. A gift to the Public Trustee exclusively for charitable purposes does not fail just because he is precluded by the Public Trustee Act 1906[4] from accepting such a trust.[5] Charitable gifts have been subjected to schemes where the designated trustees were churchwardens[6] or local authorities[7] and unable to hold the particular property on trust for the particular designated purpose. The court can also remedy the situation where there is no person able to give a good receipt for the gift.[8]

The negligence or default of a trustee is not sufficient to prevent a charitable intention from prevailing,[9] whether there is or is not a gift over,[10] unless the donor expressly makes the gift over depend upon the conduct of the trustee.[11] It has been said to be practically impossible to discover what is the dividing line between the two types of case.[12] Likewise a charitable gift does not fail owing to the neglect of the persons charged with the duty of dividing it among specified charities.[13] In such circumstances the specified charities take equally.[14]

---

1 (1843), 3 Hare 191; and see *Dillon* v. *Reilly* (1873), I.R. 10 Eq. 152 (Sisters of Charity).
2 *Re Smith*, [1904] Ch. 139.
3 *Ibid.*, at 144, *per* FARWELL J.
4 Section 2 (5).
5 *Re Hampton* (1918), 88 L.J.Ch. 103.
6 *Gravenor* v. *Hallum* (1767), Amb. 643; *Tufnell* v. *Constable* (1838), 7 Ad. & El. 798. They cannot in their quasi-corporate capacity hold *realty* on trust, but can hold personalty on trust for *Church* purposes.
7 *Re Woolnough's Will Trusts* (1959), *Times*, 22nd Oct; *Re Armitage*, [1972] Ch. 438.
8 *Re Meyers*, [1951] Ch. 534.
9 *A.-G.* v. *Boultbee* (1794), 2 Ves. 380, at 389–390; affd. (1796), 3 Ves. 220; *A.-G.* v. *Davis* (1870), 18 W.R. 1132 (Ireland).
10 *Re Parish of Upton Warren* (1833), 1 My & K. 410; and see *A.-G.* v. *Leigh* (1721), 3 P. Wms. 145, n.
11 *Christ's Hospital* v. *Grainger* (1849), 1 Mac. & G. 460, at 463.
12 *Re Hanbey's Will Trusts*, [1956] Ch. 264, at 274, *per* DANCKWERTS J.
13 *Doyley* v. *A.-G.* (1735), 4 Vin. Abr. 485; *A.-G.* v. *Lady Downing* (1767), Wilm. 1 at 24.
14 *Salusbury* v. *Denton* (1857), 3 K. & J. 529.

Chapter 30

Direction of Schemes

Introduction

When it becomes necessary to define or delimit the objects of a charity or to regulate the mode of its administration the method used is the scheme. The court has an inherent jurisdiction to direct a scheme in respect of any charitable trust. Legislation in England and Wales,[1] Northern Ireland,[2] the Republic of Ireland[3] has provided that a control authority shall also have a scheme making power. This power is exercised in England and Wales by the Charity Commissioners, in Northern Ireland by the Department of Finance[4] and in the Republic of Ireland by the Commissioners of Charitable Donations and Bequests for Ireland.

The Crown under the royal prerogative has power to apply gifts made to charity generally without the interposition of any trust to specific charitable purposes. Such application is under the sign manual and is an exercise of the royal prerogative.[5]

General principles

WHERE A SCHEME IS REQUIRED

Wherever a *cy-près* application is desired a scheme is needed. But it is as well to recall the observation of MAUGHAM J. in *Re Robinson*[6] that a scheme directed by the court in relation to gifts for charitable purposes is not necessarily or, indeed, generally a scheme for the application of the fund *cy-près*. A charitable gift does not fail merely because there is an uncertainty as to the mode of carrying out the gift. As the learned judge pointed out:

> "In numerous cases of gifts for charitable purposes it is necessary to fill up a number of details in regard to which the testator or the donor has not described his wishes in clear terms. In such cases the gift does not fail, but the court fills up the details of the donor's charitable intention by means of a scheme: there is no question of selecting objects *cy-près*, because the objects to be benefited are the very objects pointed out by the testator,

1 CA 1960, ss. 18–20; and see also s. 22 (common investment schemes).
2 Charities Act (N.I.) 1964, ss. 10–13.
3 Charities Act 1961, ss. 29–30.
4 Formerly Ministry of Finance.
5 See 418, *infra*.
6 [1931] 2 Ch. 122, at 128.

but the court is doing no more than completing the trusts to carry out objects which ... have been indicated in sufficiently clear terms by the testator."

A scheme may be used to give effect to the donor's intention, for example by dealing not only with the details of administration but also with the substance of the trust and by defining it.[1] So long as the purpose is charitable, uncertainty as to the *particular* charitable purpose intended is immaterial: the scheme will cure the uncertainty.[2] A scheme will be selected where the trusts declared are ambiguous or insufficient as well as where no particular objects are defined.[3] Thus in the Irish case of *Re Julian*,[4] where extrinsic evidence of intention was rightly excluded, by KINGSMILL MOORE J. it was impossible to say which specific charity the testatrix had in mind and a scheme was directed.

A scheme is also appropriate where there has been a failure in the trust machinery either because no machinery has been provided by the founder, or because the machinery has broken down as where the trustees are dead or refuse to act.[5]

An increase or diminution in the revenue of the charity may call for a scheme.[6] That remedy will likewise be appropriate where though the income has grown its purchasing power has not.[7] The extension of the permissible range of investments has in the past been dealt with by way of scheme: such extension if carefully framed and judiciously exercised can correct some of the ill effects of monetary inflation.[8] Apart from these specific examples the court has jurisdiction where for any reason it is thought expedient to regulate the administration of the charity.[9]

WHERE NO SCHEME REQUIRED

In some cases it is well established that no scheme is required. Thus a scheme is dispensed with in the case of a legacy for the benefit of an established institution, whether incorporated[10] or unincorporated,[11] or to its president,[12] trustees,

---

1 *Re Gott*, [1944] Ch. 193.

2 *Ibid.*, at 197.

3 *A.-G.* v. *Clarke* (1762), Amb. 422; *Re White*, [1893] 2 Ch. 41, C.A.; *Re Gardner's Will Trusts*, [1936] 3 All E.R. 938 (half secret trust of "Edward Gardner Charity"); see *Re Mason's Orphanage and London and North-Western Rail Co.*, [1896] 1 Ch. 54, at 57–58; on appeal, [1896] 1 Ch. 596, C.A.

4 *Re Julian*, [1950] I.R. 57; and see *Re Mulcahy's Will*, [1931] I.R. 239.

5 See 280, *supra.*

6 *Re Campden Charities* (1880), 18 Ch.D. 310.

7 *Re Burton's Charity*, [1938] 3 All E.R. 90 (income insufficient for three curates: scheme allowed two).

8 *Re Royal Society's Charitable Trusts*, [1956] Ch. 87; *Re Shipwrecked Fishermen and Mariners' Royal Benevolent Society*, [1959] Ch. 220; *Re Royal Naval and Royal Marine Children's Homes*, [1959] 1 W.L.R. 755; *Re University of London Charitable Trusts*, [1964] Ch. 282.

9 *A.-G.* v. *St. Olave's, Southwark, Grammar School* (1837), Coop Pr. Cas. 267; *A.-G.* v. *Dedham School* (1857), 23 Beav. 350; *Re Forbes* (1910) 27 T.L.R. 27.

10 *Emery* v. *Hill* (1826), 1 Russ. 112; *Society for the Propagation of the Gospel* v. *A.-G.* (1826), 3 Russ. 142; *A.-G.* v. *Christ's Hospital* (1831), 1 Russ. & M. 626; *Re Richardson* (1887), 56 L.J.Ch. 784.

11 *In the Goods of M'Auliffe*, [1895] P. 290 (convent).

12 *Walsh* v. *Gladstone* (1843), 1 Ph. 290 (president of Roman Catholic college).

treasurer or other officers[1] as part of the general funds of the institution, or upon similar trusts to those upon which the general funds are held.[2] If in the case of an unincorporated association no particular trustee or officer is singled out by the donor to receive the gift for the benefit of the association, the court will select a suitable person within the association to receive the gift. In *Walsh* v. *Gladstone*,[3] for example, payment was directed without any scheme to the president of a Roman Catholic college. A similar course was taken in the case of *In the Goods of M'Auliffe*,[4] where there was a legacy to C to be disposed of as she should think fit at her discretion for the benefit of a certain convent; the court, having been satisfied as to the permanence of the institution and the fitness of its head, directed payment to the mother superior of the convent. Where there is a gift to an institution for its general purposes but special conditions are attached to the gift payment can still be made to the institution or its proper officer without any scheme being directed. In *A.-G.* v. *Christ's Hospital*[5] a bequest to Christ's Hospital on condition of having certain rights of nomination to the hospital was dealt with on this simple basis. Similarly in *Re Richardson*[6] where there was a bequest to the Royal National Life-boat Institution on condition that certain lifeboats should be maintained no scheme was considered necessary.

A gift to an individual carrying on a charitable activity for the purposes of that activity may also be paid to that individual without a scheme.[7] Likewise, unless the Attorney-General objects, a gift for the purposes of an unincorporated association which has ceased to exist may be paid without a formal scheme to the only other institution carrying out that work.[8]

Trusts to be executed abroad

GENERAL PRINCIPLE

The general rule is that the court will not direct a scheme in respect of a charitable trust which is intended to be executed out of the jurisdiction. The earliest authority on this point is *Edinburgh Corporation* v. *Aubery*[9] where there was a gift of property to be applied for poor labourers in Edinburgh. Lord HARDWICKE L.C. would not order a scheme on the ground that the fund belonged to the jurisdiction of the courts in Scotland. He did however direct that the fund should be transferred to such persons as the plaintiffs should appoint, to be applied to the trusts of the will. Lord ELDON L.C. voiced a similar view in *A.-G.* v. *Lepine*:[10]

> "where a charity is to be administered in Scotland, this court does not take into its own hands the administration."

---

1 *Wellbeloved* v. *Jones* (1822), 1 Sim. & St. 40, at 43; *Emery* v. *Hill* (1826), 1 Russ. 112.
2 See *Minet* v. *Vulliamy* (1819), cited in 1 Russ. 113, n., *Carter* v. *Green* (1857), 3 K. & J. 591; *cf. Sons of the Clergy Corporation* v. *Mose* (1839), 9 Sim. 610.
3 (1843), 1 Ph. 290.
4 [1895] P. 290.
5 (1830), 1 Russ. & M. 626.   6 (1887), 56 L.J.Ch. 784.
7 *Re Rees*, [1920] 2 Ch. 59.   8 *Re Finger's Will Trusts*, [1972] Ch. 286.
9 (1753), Amb. 236.
10 (1818), 2 Swanst. 181; and see *Re Geck* (1893), 69 L.T. 819, at 821, *per* LINDLEY L.J. citing Shelford, *Law of Mortmain* (1836), 260.

There are many examples of the court's refusal to direct a scheme in respect of a foreign charity. Some are cases where the charity was to operate in a country with a law of trusts;[1] others are cases where the country in question had no law of trusts, as for example Switzerland,[2] France,[3] Portugal[4] and Germany.[5]

The principle has also been stated in cases where the trust property is within the jurisdiction of the court and there is no express provision in the instrument of foundation enabling an application of the property abroad. In the Irish case of *A.-G. v. Royal Hibernian Military School*[6] a charity had failed and a question therefore arose as to the proper destination of its property which was entirely situate in Ireland and which had its origin in that country. It was held that in applying the *cy-près* doctrine the court had no alternative but to apply the property *cy-près* by means of a scheme for the carrying on of some charitable activity in Ireland. JOHNSTON J. thought that there was the "gravest doubt" whether he had jurisdiction to do anything else. A similar view has been expressed in an earlier Irish case.[7] In *Re Mirrlees' Charity*[8] a scheme sanctioned by the court for the administration of a charity provided that the income of the charity should be applied for the benefit of a particular hospital in England "or such other medical charity or charities" of any kind, school or teaching whatsoever, and partly or exclusively to one or other of such objects as the trustees might in their uncontrolled discretion from time to time determine. The trustees wished to apply the income of the charity to musical charities in Scotland. The settlor was a Scotswoman but JOYCE J. said that "the general impression" in his mind was that the income must be confined to English medical charities, and he so held. It is interesting to note that the trustees lived in Scotland and that the court had therefore at an earlier stage appointed additional trustees to supervise the administration of the scheme.

The same result has been reached in a Scottish case[9] where a testator had left a legacy to a Scottish society for the prevention of cruelty to animals "to be devoted by them specially towards the total and absolute prohibition of vivisection".[10] The society finding it impossible to administer the legacy themselves petitioned for the approval of a scheme whereby it was proposed that the trust funds should be paid over in equal shares to two anti-vivisection societies, one Scottish and one English. The Court of Session held that the English society must be excluded on the ground that the court would be unable to supervise its activities.

---

1 Scotland: *Emery* v. *Hill*, (1826) 1 Russ. 112; *Re Marr's Will Trusts*, [1936] Ch. 671; United States: *Society for the Propagation of the Gospel* v. *A.-G.* (1826), 3 Russ: 142; *New* v. *Bonaker* (1867), L.R. 4 Eq. 655; South Africa: *Re Colonial Bishoprics Fund* 1841, [1935] Ch. 148.

2 *Minet* v. *Vulliamy* (1819), cited in 1 Russ. 113, n.

3 *Martin* v. *Paxton* (1824), cited in 1 Russ. 116; *Re De Noailles* (1916), 114 L.T. 1089.

4 *A.-G.* v. *Stephens* (1834), 3 My. & K. 347.

5 *Re Robinson*, [1931] 2 Ch. 122.

6 (1928), 63 I.L.T. 86.

7 *King* v. *Long* (1918), 53 I.L.T. 60.

8 [1910] 1 Ch. 163.

9 *Glasgow Society for the Prevention of Cruelty to Animals* v. *National Anti-Vivisection Society* 1915 S.C. 757.

10 The cause of anti-vivisection was at the time thought to be charitable; see 106, *supra*.

THE APPROPRIATE ORDER

Although the general principle is quite clear, it is not always easy to predict what kind of order the court will make. For, as the cases show, the court does not always take the same course.

If the donor has nominated suitable trustees in the foreign country to whom the fund can be paid, the usual course is to direct payment to them;[1] and this applies to income as well as capital.[2] But the court will not pay over the fund if the designated trustees refuse[3] or if the person to whom it is suggested the fund should be paid over is not a person designated by the testator and there is nothing to show that he can carry the testator's intention into effect.[4]

The court, however, will not always appoint trustees to receive a legacy for charitable purposes abroad. In some cases the fund will be retained in court with payments being remitted to the persons abroad charged with distributing the fund. That was the course taken by Lord ELDON L.C. in *A.-G.* v. *Lepine*[5] where the testator had directed a moiety of his residuary personal estate to be invested and gave the income thereof to the minister and churchwardens of the parish of Dollar in Scotland for the time being, for the poor of that parish. The Lord Chancellor ordered the dividends to be paid to the minister and church officers of the parish in question for the time being.

In *A.-G.* v. *Sturge*[6] the testatrix who had established a school at Genoa by her will directed £1000 to be paid to the consular chaplain there (naming him) for its support. The chaplain had died and the legacy was ordered to be transferred to a separate account and the dividends paid to the consular chaplain for the time being, he rendering periodically an account to the judge in chambers and to the Attorney-General of its application. In *Forbes* v. *Forbes*[7] Sir JOHN ROMILLY M.R. was dealing with a bequest to executors to build a bridge in Scotland. He refused to direct a scheme and ordered that the money be lodged in court in England to await the decision of the Court of Session with regard to its ultimate destination. The court took a similar course in *Re Fraser*[8] where an English testator had bequeathed his residuary estate to his executors and to trustees to be appointed by them for the benefit of the blind in Inverness-shire. The surviving executor declined to act in the trust or even to appoint new trustees. Liberty to make an application to the Scottish court for the settlement of a scheme was granted by FRY J. to the Attorney-General rather than to the trustee. That question was simply one of convenience: as a continuing public officer the Attorney-General was a more convenient applicant than a reluctant trustee under no duties in the matter.

---

1 *Martin* v. *Paxton* (1824), cited in 1 Russ. 116; *Collyer* v. *Burnett* (1829), Tam. 79; *Lyons Corporation* v. *East India Co.* (1836), 1 Moo. P.C. 175, at 295, *per* Lord BROUGHAM; *Mitford* v. *Reynolds* (1842), 1 Ph. 97.

2 *Re Michel's Trust* (1860), 28 Beav. 39, and see *A.-G.* v. *Stephens* (1834), 3 My. & K. 347 (new trustee for charity in Lisbon).

3 *A.-G.* v. *Fraunces*, [1866] W.N. 280; *New* v. *Bonaker* (1867), L.R. 4 Eq. 655; *Re Love*, [1932] W.N. 17.

4 *Lyons Corporation* v. *East India Co.* (1836), 1 Moo. P.C. 175 (Governor-General of India); *cf. Mitford* v. *Reynolds* (1842), 1 Ph. 197 (where Government of Bengal was vested in Governor-General).

5 (1818), 2 Swanst. 181.

6 (1854), 19 Beav. 597.

7 (1854), 18 Beav. 552.   8 (1883), 22 Ch.D. 827.

The court may also direct an inquiry whether the trust can be carried into effect according to the law of the particular country.[1] On the other hand where the fund in question and the trustees are within the jurisdiction and the trusts were in fact established within the jurisdiction, albeit for charitable purposes abroad, the court has jurisdiction on a failure of the trusts to direct a scheme.[2] There is, in this context, no distinction between a cy-près scheme and a scheme which is required to supply the details of a trust.[3]

Lastly the implications of *A.-G.* v. *London Corporation*[4] should be mentioned. In that case there was a trust (contained in a scheme) for the advancement of Christianity among infidels.[5] The charity had been deprived of objects in the area where it was in fact being carried on, and the institution charged with the trusts had become subject to a foreign power.[6] The court refused to allow the institution to continue to administer the trusts which had not been territorially confined by the testator.

Settlement of schemes by the court

The court's inherent jurisdiction to regulate the administration of a charity by means of a scheme does not, however, extend to statutory charities and is very limited in respect of charities established by Royal Charter.

Because in most cases the Charity Commissioners now have equal concurrent jurisdiction with the court, the court now normally makes schemes only in contentious cases or cases which involve special complexities or difficult questions of law and fact.[7] One class of cases in which schemes are perhaps more frequently made by the court is where religious trusts have been set up by will and a scheme is required to define or delimit them.[8] Nevertheless the Charity Commissioners may if they think fit exercise their jurisdiction to order a scheme in a contentious case.[9]

The court does not have any general jurisdiction to alter the trusts of a charity founded by Royal Charter.[10] This flows from the principle that the authority of the Crown is higher than that of the court.[11] There is however a limited jurisdiction, independent of statute, to regulate and control the charity especially on financial grounds, and in that case the court is entitled to have regard to altered circumstances.[10] But the court cannot re-found or re-establish

---

1 *Thompson* v. *Thompson* (1844), 1 Coll. 381, at 393–395. See also *New* v. *Bonaker* (1867) L.R. 4 Eq. 655.

2 *Re Colonial Bishoprics Fund* 1841, [1935] Ch. 148.

3 *Ibid.*, at 177, *per* LUXMOORE J. dealing with the earlier doubt raised by MAUGHAM J. in *Re Robinson*, [1931] 2 Ch. 122.

4 (1790), 3 Bro.C.C. 171.

5 The testator had left residuary personalty for such charitable and pious uses as his executors should think fit.

6 College of William and Mary, Virginia.

7 See CA 1960, s. 18 (9).

8 See e.g. *Re Banfield*, [1968] 1 W.L.R. 846.

9 *Re Burnham National Schools* (1873), L.R. 17 Eq. 241 not following dictum of Lord ROMILLY M.R. in *Re Hackney Charities* (1865), 34 L.J. Ch. 169.

10 *Re Whitworth Art Gallery Trusts*, [1958] Ch. 461 (where many earlier cases are cited); and see *A.-G.* v. *Dedham School* (1857), 23 Beav. 356; *Re Chertsey Market* (1819), 6 Price 261; *A.-G.* v. *Browne's Hospital, Stamford* (1889), 60 L.T. 288.

11 *A.-G.* v. *Smart* (1748), 1 Ves. Sen. 72; *A.-G.* v. *Governors of Christ's Hospital*, [1896] 1 Ch. 879 at 888, *per* CHITTY J.

it, and there must not be anything in the scheme which is inconsistent with any provisions in the charter. In the absence in the charter of any express power to amend the charter the appropriate procedure for any substantial alteration is the grant and acceptance of a new charter; and, at common law, it is doubtful whether this can alter the purpose for which funds already held can be applied, at least in the case of an eleemosynary corporation.

The case of a charity whose Royal Charter of incorporation is granted after the date of the original foundation is distinguishable. In such a case the charter is merely machinery for providing an incorporated trustee, with appropriate powers to carry an already subsisting trust into effect. As a result the court can intervene.[1]

The circumstances in which the court within its inherent jurisdiction has been able to intervene and apply *cy-près* the funds of a charity founded by Royal Charter include the case where a corporation becomes extinct[2] or the income is insufficient to carry the trust into effect[3] or where a charity has lost its site by reason of a compulsory purchase order.[4]

The position so far as England and Wales are concerned has now been altered by statute. The court now has jurisdiction to make a scheme relating to a chartered charity, or to the administration of its property, notwithstanding that the scheme cannot take effect without the alteration of the charter. But the scheme must be so framed that the whole or such part of it as cannot take effect without the alteration of the charter does not purport to come into operation unless or until Her Majesty thinks fit to amend the charter in such manner as will permit the scheme or such part of it to have effect.[5] This statutory jurisdiction extends to the making of a scheme for the *cy-près* application of the property of a chartered charity.[6]

Where a scheme has been made and it appears to the Crown expedient to amend the charter, the necessary amendment may be effected, on the application of the corporation, by Order in Council.[7] Any such Order in Council may be revoked or varied in the same manner as the charter which it amends.[8]

It is thought that as a rule it will be more appropriate to apply to the Charity Commissioners who have a concurrent jurisdiction in this behalf rather than to the court.

Just as the court has no jurisdiction, apart from statute, to alter a charter, so too it has no inherent jurisdiction to alter such of the trusts of a charity as are established by or by virtue of a statute.[9] The court has no inherent jurisdiction to amend an Act of Parliament.[10] But an Act may empower the court to amend

---

1 *A.-G.* v. *Dedham School* (1856), 23 Beav. 350; and see *A.-G.* v. *Wyggeston's Hospital* (1849), 12 Beav. 113.

2 *A.-G.* v. *Hicks* (1790), Highmore, *Law of Mortmain* (2nd edn.) 336.

3 *Re Whitworth Art Gallery Trusts*, [1958] Ch. 461; *Berkhamsted School Case* (1865), L.R. 1 Eq. 102.

4 *Clephane* v. *Lord Provost of Edinburgh* (1869), 1 H.L. Sc. 417.

5 CA 1960, s. 15 (1).

6 *Ibid.*

7 CA 1960, s. 15 (2).

8 CA 1960, s. 15 (2).

9 *Re Shrewsbury Grammar School* (1849), 1 Mac. & G. 324, cf 333; *Warren* v. *Clancy*, [1898] 1 I.R. 127, C.A.; *Re Imprisoned Debtors Discharge Society's Act 1856* (1912), 28 T.L.R. 477, C.A.; *Trustees of the London Parochial Charities* v. *A.-G.*, [1955] 1 W.L.R. 42. The rule has been recognised in Australia: *A.-G.* v *Church of England Property Trust, Diocese of Sydney* (1933), 34 N.S.W. S.R. 36.

10 *A.-G.* v *Governors of Christ's Hospital*, [1896] 1 Ch. 879, at 888.

provisions contained in the statutory trusts of the charity.[1] Moreover where the relevant statute does not completely regulate the charity the inherent jurisdiction of the court extends to all matters not dealt with by the statute.[2] For example where the statute is no more than an enabling Act the court's inherent jurisdiction is not excluded.

The inherent jurisdiction of the court with regard to statutory charities has in England and Wales been affected by statute. The Charities Act 1960 provides that the court's jurisdiction over charities is not to be restricted or excluded in relation to certain classes of charities by the statutes by or under which they are established.[3] The specified classes[4] are as follows:

(1) charities established or regulated by any provision of the Seaman's Fund Winding-up Act 1851;[5]

(2) charities established or regulated by schemes under certain now repealed Acts[6] relating to endowed schools and elementary education;

(3) allotments regulated by certain provisions of the Poor Allotments Management Act 1873;[7]

(4) fuel allotments;[8]

(5) charities established or regulated under any provision of the Municipal Corporations Act 1883[9] or by any scheme under any such provision;

(6) charities regulated by schemes under the London Government Act 1899;[10]

(7) charities established or regulated by orders or regulations under certain provisions of the Regimental Charitable Funds Act 1935;[11]

(8) parochial charities regulated by the Charities Act 1960.[12]

Schemes made by or under these statutory powers may be modified as if they had been made by the court.[13] Special enabling provisions have been enacted in connection with schemes for the administration of fuel allotments. Such schemes may contain provisions for the disposal or exchange of the allotments or for their use for any purposes specified in the scheme.[14]

A scheme settled by the court for the administration of a charity can be altered by the court if the lapse of time and the change of circumstances under it for the interest of the charity that the alterations should be made.[15] It is the duty

---

1 *Re Shrewsbury Grammar School* (1849), 1 Mac. & G. 324, at 331; *Re Sutton Coldfield Grammar School* (1881), 7 App. Cas. 91; *Re Berkhamsted Grammar School*, [1908] 2 Ch. 25.

2 *Re Shrewsbury Grammar School* (1849), 1 Mac. & G. 324, at 333; *Re Motherwell's Estate*, [1910] 1 I.R. 249.

3 CA 1960, s. 15 (3).

4 The eight categories are set out in CA 1960, Sch. 4, para. 1 (a) to (h).

5 This Act was repealed by CA 1960, s. 39 (1), Sch. 5 (repealed).

6 Endowed Schools Acts 1869 to 1948 and Elementary Education Act 1870, s. 75. For the repeals, see Education Act 1973, s. 1 and CA 1960, s. 39 (1) respectively.

7 The relevant provisions of the 1873 Act are ss. 3–9.

8 Fuel allotments are " land which under any Inclosure Act or award is vested in trustees upon trust to provide poor persons with fuel directly or through rents and profits".

9 The relevant provisions were repealed by CA 1960, s. 39 (1) and Sch. 5 (repealed).

10 The relevant provisions were repealed by CA 1960, s. 39 (1), Sch. 5 (repealed).

11 The relevant provision was repealed by CA 1960, s. 48 (2), Sch. 7 (repealed).

12 As to the regulation of parochial charities, see s. 37.

13 CA 1960, s. 15 (3).

14 CA 1960, Sch. 4, para. 2 spells out the position in detail.

15 *A.-G.* v. *St. John's Hospital, Bath* (1865), 1 Ch. App. 92, at 106, *per* TURNER L.J.; *Glasgow College* v. *A.-G.* (1848), 1 H.L. Cas. 800.

M

of the Crown to protect the interests of charities, and to take the necessary proceedings for remedying any defect in them. There is no distinction between defects arising in the ordinary administration of charities and those which may arise in the administration of them under schemes settled by the court "except that in the cases in which discretion has been already exercised more care and caution ought perhaps to be exercised before alterations are made".[1] All schemes are inherently subject to future schemes.[2] The court has therefore on many occasions amended its own schemes.[3]

It has been said that the court must proceed upon application to vary its own schemes with the utmost possible caution.[4] A scheme settled by the court must not be disturbed, except upon the most substantial grounds and upon the clearest evidence, not only that the scheme does not operate beneficially but that it can by alteration be made to do so consistently with the object of the founder.[5]

Where the trusts of a scheme settled by the court are subsequently shown not to be exclusively charitable in law, the scheme may be corrected by a further scheme.[6] So too a scheme may be corrected where it is not in conformity with the original trust.[7]

The following are instances where schemes settled by the court have contained provisions which the court has at a later date seen fit to alter: a scheme making an unfair distribution among the objects of a charity,[8] a scheme imposing an unnecessary religious restriction[9] or an inappropriate restriction on the number of governors of a charity[10] or an unnecessary clause as to renewable building leases.[11]

Charities for the relief of prisoners also provide examples of schemes of the court which were varied to take account of changed circumstances.[12]

The court also enjoys special powers over certain trusts for religious education.[13]

The Attorney-General is a necessary party to any application to the court for the alteration of a scheme settled by the court, and he must either make the application himself or consent to it being made.[14] Indeed if he is satisfied that the

---

1 *A.-G. v. St. John's Hospital, Bath* (1865), 1 Ch. App. 92, at 106.

2 *Re Sutton Coldfield Grammar School* (1881), 7 App. Cas. 91 (scheme at Charity Commissioners); *Re Betton's Charity*, [1908] 1 Ch. 205.

3 *A.-G. v. London Corporation* (1790), 3 Bro.C.C. 171; *A.-G. v. Bovill* (1840), 1 Ph. 762; *A.G. v. Rochester Corporation* (1854), 5 De G.M. & G. 797; *Re Hussey's Charities* (1861), 7 Jur. N.S. 325; *A.-G. v. Hankey* (1867), L.R. 16 Eq. 149 n.

4 *A.-G. v. Bishop of Worcester* (1851), 9 Hare 328, at 361, *per* TURNER V.-C., approved by MALINS V.-C. in *A.-G. v. Stewart* (1872), L.R. 14 Eq. 17.

5 *Ibid.*; and see *Re Sekeford's Charity* (1861), 5 L.T. 488.

6 *Vernon v. I.R.Comrs.*, [1956] 1 W.L.R. 1169.

7 *A.-G. v. Buller* (1822), Jac. 407; *A.-G. v. Bovill* (1840), 1 Ph. 762.

8 *A.-G. v. Buller* (1822), Jac. 407.

9 *A.-G. v. St. John's Hospital, Bath* (1876), 2 Ch.D. 554.

10 *Re Browne's Hospital v. Stamford* (1889), 60 L.T. 288.

11 *Re Henry Smith's Charity, Hartlepool* (1882), 20 Ch.D. 516, C.A.

12 *Re Merchant Taylors' Trust* (1850), 16 L.T.O.S. 210 (relief extended): *Re Hussey's Charities* (1861), 7 Jur. N.S. 325 (gift to chaplain of one gaol extended to chaplain of new prison); *A.-G. v. Hankey* (1867), L.R. 16 Eq. 140, n. (relief extended all over England and Wales).

13 Education Act 1973, s. 2; and see CA 1960, Sch. 4, para. 1 (b) as amended by Education Act 1973, s. 2 (7).

14 *A.-G. v. Stewart* (1872), L.R. 14 Eq. 17; and see *A.-G. v. Hall* (1875), Seton, *Judgments and Orders* (7th edn.) 1259; *Re Royal Society's Charitable Trusts*, [1956] Ch. 87.

existing scheme does not operate beneficially for the charity, and thinks that he can satisfy the court that the interests of the charity can be better promoted by an altered scheme consistent with the foundation, the usage and the law, it is the duty of the Attorney-General to apply to the court for the scheme to be altered.[1]

The court will not, upon the application of one of the interested parties, alter a scheme which it has settled with the approval of the Attorney-General.[2] Equally the fact that the Attorney-General objects to a proposed alteration is a factor leading almost inevitably to the rejection by the court of the proposed alteration.[3]

Sometimes the court will not direct a scheme to deal with a particular situation but will instead take some other appropriate course. Where, for example, all that is required is an apportionment of funds that matter can be referred to the master.[4] In other cases the court retains a measure of control by giving any of the parties leave to apply if necessary. That is a course which is taken where the donor has directed a distribution of income for a limited period whether with[5] or without[6] a gift of capital; and it is a course which in such circumstances has found favour in Ireland too.[7] Alternatively the court may order the person charged with the application of a fund to account for its distribution to the court.[8] A fourth possibility is evidenced by *M'Coll* v. *Atherton*[9] where there was a bequest of consols to the minister of a particular parish on trust to apply the income for the poor of the parish at his discretion. The fund was ordered to be paid into court and the dividends were ordered to be paid to the minister.

Settlement of schemes by the Charity Commissioners

The Charity Commissioners for England and Wales have a concurrent jurisdiction with the court to establish schemes for the administration of charities.[10]

In the case of a charity, other than an exempt charity,[11] which does not have any income from property amounting to more than £50 a year the Commissioners may exercise their jurisdiction to make schemes on the application of the Attorney-General[12] or of any one or more of the charity trustees or of any person interested in the charity[13] or, if it is a local charity,[14] of any two or more inhabitants of the area of the charity.[15] Whether a charity has an income of £50 or less

---

1 *A.-G.* v. *Bishop of Worcester* (1851), 9 Hare 328, at 360.
2 *Re Sekeford's Charity* (1861), 5 L.T. 488.
3 *A.-G.* v. *Stewart* (1872), L.R. 14 Eq. 17, at 24–25.
4 *White* v. *White* (1778), 1 Bro.C.C. 12; *Re Hyde's Trusts* (1873), 22 W.R. 69.
5 *Re Lea* (1887), 34 Ch.D. 528.
6 *Waldo* v. *Caley* (1809), 16 Ves. 206; *Horde* v. *Earl of Suffolk* (1833), 2 My. & K. 59.
7 *Mahon* v. *Savage* (1803), 1 Sch. & Lef. 111; *Powerscourt* v. *Powerscourt* (1824), 1 Moll. 616.
8 *A.-G.* v. *Gleg* (1738), Amb. 584; *A.-G.* v. *Governors, etc. of Sherborne Grammar School* (1854), 18 Beav. 256.
9 (1848), 12. Jur. 1042.
10 CA 1960, s. 18 (1).
11 See at 4–6, *supra*.
12 CA 1960, s. 18 (5) (a).
13 This term is discussed at 497, *infra*.
14 Defined in CA 1960, s. 45 (1).
15 CA 1960, s. 18 (1) (b).

is to be determined by reference to its gross revenues without taking account of the yearly value of land occupied by the charity from which no income is received; and it is for the Commissioners to decide whether a charity does or does not come within this reference and their decision on the point is final.[1] In relation to any other charity, in other words to any charity with an income from property *exceeding* £50 a year, the Commissioners may not, as a rule,[2] exercise their jurisdiction to make schemes except on the application of the charity[3] or on a reference to them by the court for the purpose.[4] An application by the charity is made by all or a majority of the charity trustees and, once made, cannot effectively be withdrawn.[5]

In exercising their concurrent jurisdiction the Commissioners do not have jurisdiction to try or determine the title at law or in equity to any property as between a charity or trustee for a charity and a person holding or claiming the property or an interest in it adversely to the charity, or to try or determine any question as to the existence or extent of any charge or trust.[6]

Before the Commissioners exercise their power to make schemes they must comply with certain formalities in regard to notices. Notice must be given to the trustees and notice must be given to the public. The provisions regarding these notices are not identical.

Unless the scheme is made under a court order (where the notice would, of necessity, be otiose) the Commissioners must give notice of their intention to act to each of the *charity trustees* except (a) to any of them who cannot be found or who has no known address in the United Kingdom or (b) to the trustees who are party or privy to an application as a result of which the jurisdiction is being exercised.[7] The notice may be given by post, and if so given may be addressed to the recipient's last known address in the United Kingdom. No time is specified within which the notice is to be given.[8] Nor is there any requirement that the notice should invite representations or that any representations made must be taken into account, though the Commissioners may, of course, be expected to give proper consideration to any representations they do receive.

Before making a scheme or submitting a scheme to the court or to the Home Secretary the Commissioners must give at least one month's *public notice* of their proposals, inviting representations to be made to them within a time specified in the notice, being not less than one month from the date of the notice.[9] The notice must give such particulars of the proposals or order, or such directions for obtaining information about them and may be given in such manner as the Commissioners think sufficient and appropriate.[10] In the case of a local charity public notice is often posted outside a church school or town hall. Sometimes newspaper advertisements may be required. In all cases the trustees should ask the Commissioners for their advice on the question of notice.

In contrast to the provisions concerning notices to charity trustees, the

---

1 *Ibid.*, s. 45 (4).
2 The exception is s. 18 (6) which is discussed at 293, *infra*.
3 CA 1960, s. 18 (4) (a).
4 *Ibid.*, s. 18 (4) (b). As to such references see 512, *infra*.
5 *Re Poor's Land Charity, Bethnal Green*, [1891] 3 Ch. 400.
6 CA 1960, s. 18 (3).
7 *Ibid.*, s. 18 (8).
8 *Ibid.*
9 CA 1960, s. 21 (1).
10 *Ibid.*, s. 21 (7).

statutory provisions about public notice are mandatory in terms. The Commissioners must not make any order unless the provisions with regard to public notice have been complied with.[1] The notice must be given and must invite representations; and those representations must be taken into account. Accordingly a decision of the Commissioners to order a scheme may be challenged if there has been a failure by the Commissioners to observe any of the provisions relating to public notice or representations. On the other hand, once proper notices have been given the Commissioners may, without giving further notice, proceed with their proposals with or without modifications, even if a modification substantially alters the original proposals.[2]

Where the Commissioners make an order which is subject to appeal, the order must be published either by giving public notice of it, or by giving notice of it to all persons entitled to appeal against it, as the Commissioners think fit.[3] Furthermore where they make an order establishing a scheme for the administration of a charity, a copy of the order must be available for public inspection at all reasonable times for not less than one month after the order is published, both at the Commissioners' office and, if it relates to a local charity, at some convenient place in the area of the charity.[4]

Where the court directs a scheme for the administration of a charity to be established, it may by order refer the matter to the Commissioners for them to prepare or settle a scheme in accordance with such directions, if any, as the court sees fit to give. Any such order may provide for the scheme to be put into effect by order of the Commissioners without any further order of the court.[5] The advantage of this procedure is that it enables the expense of settling a scheme in chambers to be avoided in suitable cases.

Where the Commissioners are satisfied in regard to any charity other than an exempt charity[6] that the charity trustees ought in the interests of the charity to apply for a scheme, but have unreasonably refused or neglected to do so, the Commissioners may apply to the Home Secretary for him to refer the case to them with a view to a scheme.[7] He must give the charity trustees an opportunity to make representations to him, and if he then refers the case to the Commissioners, they may proceed without the application of the trustees. This procedure enables a scheme to be made where the trustees unreasonably fail to carry out their duty to apply for one and the interests of the charity require it. It obviates the expense of the only other available procedure: proceedings by the Attorney-General against the trustees for breach of trust. The only circumstances in which the cheaper procedure may not be invoked is where the charity is less than 40 years old and a *cy-près* scheme is desirable.[8] In the rare case where the Commissioners consider an application is desirable they may move the Attorney-General to take proceedings.[9]

In the case of other charities governed by statute the Commissioners (but not the court) have power to settle a scheme for their administration. The power

---

1 *Ibid.*, s. 21 (1).
2 *Ibid.*, s. 21 (4); see *Re Berkhamsted Grammar School*, [1908] 2 Ch. 25.
3 CA 1960, s. 21 (5).
4 *Ibid.*, s. 21 (6).
5 *Ibid.*, s. 18 (2).
6 As to exempt charities, see at 4–6, *supra*.
7 CA 1960, s. 18 (6).
8 *Ibid.*, s. 18 (6), proviso.
9 *Ibid.*, s. 28 (7).

is exercisable whenever it appears to the Commissioners on a due application[1] or on a reference by the Home Secretary[2] that it is necessary or desirable for a scheme to alter the provision made by statute or to make any other provision which goes or might go beyond the normal powers exercisable by them, or where it appears to them that it is for any reason proper for the scheme to be subject to parliamentary review.[3] An application or reference to the Commissioners is a condition precedent to the exercise of this power.[4] The scheme in such a case may be given effect by statutory instrument made by the Home Secretary, and where the scheme alters a statutory provision contained in a public general Act, the order must be approved by resolution of each House of Parliament;[5] in other cases such as those involving alteration of a private Act, the statutory instrument is subject to the negative resolution procedure and may be annulled in pursuance of a resolution of either House within 40 days after it is laid.[6]

Once a scheme has been made by statutory instrument in this way, it may be further modified or superseded by a scheme made by the court or the Commissioners as if it were a scheme brought into effect by order of the Commissioners under their concurrent jurisdiction.[7] But a scheme requiring the positive approval of Parliament may provide that the scheme shall not be modified or superseded except by the same procedure and that any modifying or superseding scheme shall be subject to the same limitation.[8]

The first scheme to be settled by the Commissioners in respect of a charity governed by statute related to an almshouse[9] which was in need of improvement but could only be improved by reducing the number of separate dwellings in the almshouse. The number of occupants of almshouses was fixed by a private Act of Parliament so that the Commissioners could not exercise their ordinary jurisdiction: their scheme therefore had to be given effect by a statutory instrument.[10] Modification of legislation provisions laid down in Private Acts of Parliament has also been carried out where a decrease in the number of church incumbents eligible for benefit and a very substantial increase in rents had resulted in an excess of income over appropriate expenditure;[11] where conditions of residence affecting trustees and beneficiaries have become burdensome and self-defeating;[12] and where a power to invest in land was required.[13] The very object of a charitable application of income in one case no longer required the income;[14] in another case certain objects were utterly obsolete and there were cumbersome and expensive administrative provisions governing the charity;[15]

---

1 *Ibid.*, s. 18 (4) or (5).   2 *Ibid.*, s. 18 (2) or (6).
3 *Ibid.*, s. 19 (1).   4 *Ibid.* s. 19 (6).
5 *Ibid.*, s. 19 (2)   6 *Ibid.*, s. 19 (3).
7 *Ibid.*, s. 19 (4).   8 *Ibid.*, s. 19 (5).
9 *St. Katherine's Hospital Ledbury Hertfordshire*, [1962] Ch. Com. Rep. 26, para. 83.
10 S.I. 1962 No. 2807.
11 *St. Martins Trust Birmingham*, [1964] Ch. Com. Rep. 39, para. 80; S.I. 1964 No. 3.
12 *The Watermen's Sunday Ferry Charity*, [1964] Ch. Com. Rep. 39–40, para. 81; S.I. 1964 No. 1054 (amalgamation with money from other sources was also permitted).
13 *King Edward's Hospital Fund for London*, [1964] Ch. Com. Rep. 39, para. 79; S.I. 1964 No. 1853.
14 *The French Protestant Episcopal Church of the Savoy Charity*, [1965] Ch. Com. Rep. 14, para. 41. The income was divided between an almshouse charity and a school both with French Protestant connections: S.I. 1965 No. 192.
15 *Society for the Discharge and Relief of Persons Imprisoned for Small Debts*, [1965] Ch. Com. Rep. 14, para. 42; S.I. 1965 No. 193.

and in another case the fall in the value of money had stultified a restriction on the share of income to which a particular church was entitled.[1] Schemes under section 19 of the Charities Act 1960 were made in all these cases, and in one of them the governors were directed to pay or apply the net income to or for such charitable institutions or charitable purposes for the benefit of objects in England and Wales as they thought fit.[2]

Radical changes in social conditions and changes in church administration may make it inappropriate for particular trustees to administer a church charity. This was the view formed by the Commissioners in the case of a charity in the parish of St. Giles, Cripplegate in the City of London, and they accordingly replaced the parish vestry[3] (the designated trustees) by the parochial church council of the newly united ecclesiastical parish of which St. Giles, Cripplegate, was now part. Opportunity was also taken to enable the income to be used for the improvement as well as the repair of St. Giles Church;[4] and the title of the charity was changed to St. Giles, Cripplegate, Church Repair Charity, London.[5]

A change of name may be desirable so as to make it plain to the public at large that the class of beneficiaries is not as restricted as the charity's name might suggest. Thus the Governesses Benevolent Institution whose beneficiaries included not only governesses but also women who had been teachers in non-maintained schools and other ladies connected with the profession of teaching changed its name to The School-mistresses and Governesses Benevolent Institution.[6]

Sometimes a scheme under section 19 has to be combined with an Order in Council under section 15, for example where a royal charter also requires amendment. This was the case with the Royal Institution of Great Britain under whose charter (as amended by an Act of Parliament of 1810 and the Royal Institution of Great Britain Charity Scheme Confirmation Act 1958) there was a prohibition *inter alia* on paying pensions to retired members of the staff who remained members of the Institution. A scheme was established providing that if and when Her Majesty should think fit to amend the charter so as to remove the payment of superannuation benefits from the prohibition on salaries, profits or emoluments to members of the Institution then the provisions of the Act of 1810 permitting the payment of salaries to professors, lecturers and officers of the Institution notwithstanding that they might be members should extend to permit also the payment of superannuation benefits to such persons. This scheme was followed by an Order in Council on 22nd February 1967 ordering that the prohibition in the charter should not apply to the payment of the super-annuation benefit in question.[7]

The Commissioners have also used their powers under section 19 to dissolve

---

1 *Church Lands Charity in the Ancient Parish of St. Pancras, London,* [1965] Ch. Com. Rep. 14–15, para. 43; S.I. 1965 No. 428.

2 Debtors' Relief Funds Charity: S.I. 1965 No. 193 (the charity was thus renamed).

3 The vicar, churchwardens and overseers of the poor and 24 other relief inhabitants of the parish: Cripplegate Vestry Act 1869.

4 City of London (Tithes) Act 1947, s. 11 only authorised repairs not improvements.

5 [1966] Ch. Com. Rep. 13–14, paras. 42–44: S.I. 1967 No. 297.

6 [1967] Ch. Com. Rep. 16–17, paras. 54–56; S.I. 1967 No. 755. An order-in-council amending the royal charter was made on 1st June 1967.

7 *The Royal Institution of Great Britain,* [1967] Ch. Com. Rep. 15–16, paras. 51–53; and see also *The School-mistresses and Governesses Benevolent Institution,* [1967] Ch. Com. Rep. 16–17, paras. 54–56 (where charter had to be amended).

an almshouse corporation, to vest its land in the Official Custodian for Charities and redefine the class from which almsmen might be drawn and various other administrative provisions.[1] In the case of the Woburn Almshouse Charity liability for repairs to the almshouses and to pay a further yearly sum for the benefit of the almspeople rested on the Duke of Bedford under the Bedford Settled Estates Act 1762 a Private Act of Parliament. These liabilities were compounded under a scheme whereby other income producing land was conveyed to the trustees, the scheme naturally containing various other provisions for the regulation of the almshouses and a wider field of potential beneficiaries.[2]

In certain cases the Commissioners are empowered to make a temporary or interim order in lieu of a scheme.[3] However before they can make such an order they must be satisfied that three conditions are fulfilled. These are (a) that in the existing circumstances the whole of the income of the charity cannot be effectively applied for the purposes of the charity; (b) that if those circumstances continue a scheme might be made for applying the surplus *cy-près*; and (c) that for any reason it is not yet desirable to make such a scheme. If these three conditions are fulfilled the Commissioners may by order authorise the trustees at their discretion (but subject to any conditions imposed by the order) to apply any accrued or accruing income for any purposes for which it might be made applicable by such a scheme.[4] Any application authorised by the order is deemed to be within the purposes of the charity.[5] The order cannot extend to more than £300 out of income accrued before the date of the order, nor to income accruing more than three years after its date, nor to more than £100 out of the income accruing in any of those three years.[6]

In cases where the conditions for a temporary order are not fulfilled it seems that income accruing during the period before the making of a *cy-près* scheme should be accumulated.[7] The statutory provisions seem to be limited to cases of partial failure since condition (a) implies that part of the income in question can still be effectively applied and condition (b) refers to the application of the surplus *cy-près*. Where there has been a total failure of the trusts there is no reason to postpone the making of a *cy-près* scheme. The power to make a temporary order is likely to be of most use where the income of the charity is for the time being more than sufficient for the carrying out of the trusts, but it is not certain that this surplus position will continue. Thus in the case of a trust to repair a church it may on the one hand seem unnecessary to accumulate the whole of the surplus income until such time as it may be needed, but on the other hand it may equally be desirable that the whole of the income arising in future years should, if necessary, be available for the purposes of the trust. In those circumstances a permanent *cy-près* scheme is inappropriate. There seems to be no reason why in such a case the Commissioners should not make a series of triennial orders in relation to the income.

In certain cases a particular statute has conferred upon the Commissioners a jurisdiction to modify schemes which the court cannot modify. Thus in *Trustees*

---

1 *The Hospital of the Holy and Blessed Trinity, Long Melford*, [1967] Ch. Com. Rep. 17–18 paras. 57–62; S.I. 1967 No. 1953.
2 [1968] Ch. Com. Rep. 5–6, paras. 8–12; S.I. 1968 No. 1694.
3 CA 1960, s. 19 (8).
4 *Ibid.*
5 *Ibid.*
6 *Ibid.*, proviso.
7 Sometimes the Commissioners have authorised *cy-près* applications of surplus income.

of the London Parochial Charities v. *A.-G.*[1] the scheme made pursuant to the City of London Parochial Charities Act 1883 conferred on the Commissioners a power to modify it in exercise of their ordinary jurisdiction but did not confer any concurrent jurisdiction on the court.

Again, any provisions with respect to allotments for recreation grounds, field gardens, or other public or parochial purposes contained in any Inclosure Act or in any award or order made in pursuance thereof, and any provision with respect to the management of any such allotments contained in any such Act, order or award, may, on the application of any district or parish council interested in any such allotment, be dealt with by a scheme of the Commissioners in the exercise of their ordinary jurisdiction, as if those provisions had been established by the founder in the case of a charity having a founder.[2]

ECCLESIASTICAL CHARITIES

The definition of "charity" in the Charities Act 1960[3] does not include the corporate property of any ecclesiastical corporation.[4] Nor does it include a trust of property which has been consecrated for the purposes of the trust.[5] But in respect of a corporation aggregate having some non-ecclesiastical purposes, the definition of "charity" does extend to its corporate property held for those purposes.[6] Nevertheless both the court and the Charity Commissioners have jurisdiction to make schemes in respect of consecrated chapels belonging to charities which are no longer needed for the purposes of the charity.[7] This jurisdiction extends to cover consecrated chapels held on charitable trusts for religious worship by the beneficiaries and staff of the charity, even though held on separate trusts from those of the charity.[8] Such a scheme may provide (1) for the demolition of the chapel and the disposal of the materials; (2) for the sale or disposal of the chapel or its site and the application of the proceeds; (3) for the appropriation of the chapel to uses specified or described in the scheme; and (4) for supplementary or incidental matters.[9] Where such a scheme is directed the bishop may if he thinks it proper to do so, by order under his seal, direct that the legal effects of consecration shall not apply to the buildings and land in question[10] or make directions as to the disposal of any human remains in or beneath the building or in the land in question.[11] Any scheme subjected to such a direction so far as it relates to the chapel shall not have effect unless and until such order is made or the bishop directs that the scheme may have effect without such an order.[12]

In relation to a charity established for ecclesiastical purposes of the Church of

---

1 [1955] 1 W.L.R. 42.
2 Commons Act 1899, s. 18.
3 CA 1960, s. 45 (1).
4 *Ibid.*, s. 45 (2) (a). "Ecclesiastical corporation" means a corporation in the Church of England established for spiritual purposes.
5 CA 1960, s. 45 (2) (b).
6 *Ibid.*, s. 45 (2) (a).
7 Pastoral Measure 1968, s. 55 (1).
8 *Ibid.* s. 55 (4).
9 *Ibid.*, s. 55 (3).
10 *Ibid.*, s. 61 (1).
11 *Ibid.* s. 65.
12 *Ibid.*, s. 55 (2).

England which is affected by a pastoral scheme or order,[1] the Charity Commissioners' powers to make schemes[2] may be exercised on the application of the diocesan board of finance for the relevant diocese, as well as on the application of the persons specified in the Charities Act 1960.[3] This power also extends to charities affected by a redundancy scheme under the Pastoral Measure 1968.[4]

The court and the Commissioners also have power to make schemes in relation to certain redundant places of public religious worship.[5] If a building, which is a place of public religious worship and is held by or in trust for a charity but is not a church subject to the provisions of the Pastoral Measure 1968,[6] is no longer required for use as a place of public religious worship and the Secretary of State for the Environment is willing to enter into an agreement for the acquisition by him under his statutory powers[7] of the building or part of it by way of gift or for less than full consideration, but the persons in whom the building is vested do not have the powers to carry out the agreement the court may establish a scheme[8] for the making and carrying out of the agreement.[9] The scheme may provide for the acquisition by the Secretary of State for the Environment of other land, held by or in trust for the charity and comprising or contiguous or adjacent to the building, and of objects ordinarily kept in the building.[9] The scheme may also provide for conferring on the Secretary of State rights of way over any land held by or in trust for the charity and rights of way hitherto enjoyed by persons attending services.[10] Further the scheme may provide for the making of an application to the Secretary of State for the restoration of the building to use as a place of public religious worship, and the Charity Commissioners may, at the Secretary of State's request, make a scheme under the Charities Act 1960[11] for the restoration of the building to such use and, if the charity has ceased to exist, for the constitution of a charity by or in trust for whom the building on its restoration is to be held.[12] With one exception[13] the provisions in the Charities Act 1960 for the making of schemes by the Commissioners[14] have effect in relation to a scheme made under the Redundant Churches and other Religious Buildings Act 1969.[15] Nothing in the latter Act prejudices any power of the court or the Charity Commissioners to establish a scheme for the administration of a charity.[16]

---

1 As to such schemes and orders see Pastoral Measure 1968, *passim.*
2 See CA 1960, s. 18.
3 Pastoral Measure 1968, Sch. 3, para. 11 (5); as to the persons specified in the Charities Act 1960: see CA 1960, s. 18.
4 Pastoral Measure 1968, s. 63 (2).
5 Redundant Churches and other Religious Buildings Act 1969, s. 4 (1) and (4); and see CA 1960, s. 18.
6 See Pastoral Measure 1968, s. 90 (1).
7 See Historic Buildings and Ancient Monuments Act 1953, s.5.
8 Under its jurisdiction over charities.
9 Redundant Churches and other Religious Buildings Act 1969, s. 4 (1); Secretary of State for the Environment Order 1970, S.I. 1970 No. 1681.
10 Redundant Churches and other Religious Buildings Act 1969, s. 4 (2).
11 See CA 1960, s. 18.
12 Redundant Churches and other Religious Buildings Act 1969, s. 4 (3).
13 CA 1960, s. 18 (6) does not apply.
14 See CA 1960, ss. 18 and 21.
15 Redundant Churches and other Religious Buildings Act 1969, s. 4 (5); Education Act 1973, s. 1 (4) (5), Sch. 2, Pt. III.
16 Redundant Churches and other Religious Buildings Act 1969, s. 7 (2).

Nothing in the New Parishes Measure 1943 enables the Church Commissioners to deal with the endowment of a charity within the meaning of the Charities Act 1960 without the consent of the Charity Commissioners.[1]

RESERVE FORCES CHARITIES

Special statutory provisions have also been made for the rearrangement of charities in England, Wales and Northern Ireland consequent upon the disbanding[2] of particular units of the reserve forces. The relevant legislation is in the Reserve Forces Act 1966, which applies to units of the naval volunteer reserve, the territorial army and the royal auxiliary air force.[3]

The main provision of the Act provides for the automatic transfer of a disbanded unit's charitable funds and property to its successor unit in the new force. Any charitable property held for the purposes of the body in question will as from the time at which the royal warrant comes into force be held for the corresponding purposes of the unit so designated.[4] The section does not apply to any property where the interest of the charity ceases on the disbandment of the unit and another person or charity has an interest contingent on that event.[5]

Owing to the division of the new reserve force into several categories, there were many cases where the automatic transfer would not have been appropriate because some of the members of the former unit would not be joining the unit designated by the royal warrant, but another unit in a different category. For this reason in suitable cases orders may be made disapplying the automatic succession. This can come about in one of two ways. First, the Commissioners may consider that the provision for automatic succession or transfer ought not to apply to all or some part of the property of the disbanded unit. If they form that view they may make an order not later than six months after the warrant comes into force.[6] The order may provide that the automatic succession shall not apply or shall cease to apply in respect of all the property affected by the warrant or only a part of it.[7]

If the charity or a trustee of or any person interested in the charity considers that the principle of automatic succession should not apply the charity, trustee or person in question can apply to the court for an order that the relevant statutory provision shall not apply to the whole or some part of the property of the disbanded unit.[8] The application to the court is hedged about by restrictions. The application to the court that the normal statutory provision shall not apply must be made not later than six months after the royal warrant comes into force.[9] The Commissioners' leave to make such an application must first be

---

1 New Parishes Measure 1943, s. 31; CA 1960, s. 48, Sch. 6.
2 This term includes amalgamation: Reserve Forces Act 1966, s. 18 (8).
3 Reserve Forces Act 1966, s. 18 (1). The necessary adaptations for Northern Ireland are in s. 18 (9) of the Act.
4 *Ibid.* A copy of the royal warrant must be delivered by post or otherwise to the Charity Commissioners and to a trustee of the charity as soon as may be after it has been made: Reserve Forces Act 1966, s. 18 (2).
5 Reserve Forces Act 1966, s. 18 (6).
6 *Ibid.*, s. 18 (2).
7 *Ibid.*
8 Reserve Forces Act 1966, s. 18 (3).
9 *Ibid.*

sought.[1] If the application for leave is refused by the Commissioners or not granted within a month (which is a deemed refusal) the application to the court can only proceed by leave of a High Court judge.[2]

Where a "disapplying" order is made, or where the Secretary of State for Defence requests the Commissioners to make provision with respect to any charitable property held for the purposes of a unit of the reserve forces which has been or will be disbanded, the Commissioners may exercise their powers under the Charities Act[3] 1960 to make schemes or to vest or transfer property without the application[4] to them which is normally required.[5]

Lastly it should be noted that where the statutory succession provision does apply to any charitable property the same jurisdiction and powers are exercisable in relation to the charity in question as would be exercisable if that provision were not statutory.[6]

APPEALS

An appeal against an order of the Charity Commissioners establishing a scheme[7] lies to the High Court.[8] Such appeals are assigned to the Chancery Division[9] to be heard and determined by a single judge.[10]

The appeal may be brought by (1) the Attorney-General,[11] (2) the charity or any of the charity trustees,[12] or (3) any person interested in the charity[13] or, in the case of a local charity, any two or more inhabitants of the area or the parish council of any parish or community comprising the area or any part of it.[14]

If the Attorney-General brings the appeal he does not require any certificate from the Commissioners that the case is a proper one for appeal.[15] Nor is he bound by the time limit on bringing an appeal which binds other appellants.[16] All other appellants, it should be stressed, require a certificate of the Commissioners or the leave of the court before they can bring an appeal.[17] Equally any appeal not brought by the Attorney-General must be brought within three months beginning with the day following that on which the order is published.[18] Publication in this context means publication of the order and not publication of the notice of the Commissioners' intention to make the order.[19]

The procedure on such an appeal is discussed elsewhere.[20]

The right of appeal against an order of the Commissioners directing a scheme

---

1 *Ibid.*

3 See CA 1960, s. 18 (1).

5 Reserve Forces Act 1966, s. 18 (5).

7 See CA 1960, s. 18 (1) (a).

9 RSC Order 108, rule 2.

11 CA 1960, s. 18 (10).

12 *Ibid.*, s. 18 (11).

13 As to this expression see 497, *infra.*

14 CA 1960, s. 18 (12).

15 *Ibid.*, s. 18 (10), *cf.* s. 18 (11).

16 CA 1960, s. 18 (10).

17 *Ibid.*, s. 18 (11) and see *Childs* v. *A.-G.* [1973] 1 W.L.R. 497. This is discussed at 515, *infra.*

18 CA 1960, s. 18 (11).

19 *Re Diptford Parish Lands*, [1934] Ch. 151.

20 See 516–518, *infra.*

2 *Ibid.*

4 See CA 1960, s. 18 (4) (a).

6 *Ibid.*, s. 18 (7).

8 *Ibid.*, s. 18 (10), (11).

10 *Ibid.*, rule 4 (1).

is not expressed to be limited to questions of law. The principles upon which the court will, on appeal, interfere with the discretion of the Commissioners were referred to by Sir GEORGE JESSEL M.R. in *Re Campden Charities*[1] when in dealing with objections raised to a scheme settled by the Commissioners: .

> "I find the scheme is in accordance with what is now the modern practice as to settling schemes and, speaking for myself, I see no objection to the details. But if I did I should not think it part of our duty to interfere. This is a scheme settled by a competent authority, the Charity Commissioners, persons not only of great but of special experience in these matters, and persons intrusted with supervision of these matters as a separate body by the legislature for that very reason. It would not be, in my opinion, sufficient for a Judge to say he thought some detail might well be different, or that if he himself had originally settled the scheme he should have put in some other arrangements than those which are specified in the scheme. He must be satisfied that the Charity Commissioners have gone wrong either by disobeying those rules of law which govern them, as well as they govern Courts of Justice, or else that there has been some slip or gross miscarriage which calls for the intervention of the court to set aside and remodel the scheme."

In *Re Burnham Schools*[2] the same learned Master of the Rolls refused to interfere with the discretion of the Charity Commissioners, on the ground that such interference could only be justified in cases of gross and palpable miscarriage,[3] or where there was an utter want of exercise of discretion.[4]

On the other hand where the Commissioners by order establish a scheme that is *ultra vires* the order will be discharged and the whole question remitted to the Commissioners for further consideration. Such a course was taken by the Court of Appeal in *Re Weir Hospital*,[5] a case which merits close attention. The testator in that case who died in 1902 had left a house at Balham and his residence, the Hawthorns at Clapham Park, upon trust to use the house at Balham as a dispensary, cottage hospital, convalescent home or other medical charity, to be called the Weir Hospital, for the benefit of the inhabitants of Streatham and the neighbourhood until a restrictive covenant which prevented the Hawthorns from being so used had expired. On expiry of the restrictive covenant the Hawthorns was to be used in conjunction or not with the Balham house for the same purpose; and the testator gave his residuary personal estate to the same trustees for the maintenance of the hospital. The trustees established a dispensary at the Balham house and maintained it in accordance with the trust of the will, accumulating the residue of the income until the expiry of the restrictive covenant binding the Hawthorns. By then the funds available for the charity amounted to £100,000. It then emerged that the Hawthorns was not suitable for a convalescent home, although it might have been used as a cottage hospital. The Charity Commissioners did not, however, consider that a cottage hospital was desirable in that particular location and, on the suggestion of the Commissioners, the trustees applied for a scheme.

---

1 (1881), 18 Ch.D, 310, at 330–331, C.A.
2 (1873), L.R. 17 Eq. 241 (selection of new trustees).
3 (1873), L.R. 17 Eq, 241, at 248.
4 *Ibid.*, at 250.
5 [1910] 2 Ch. 133, C.A.

The scheme which the Charity Commissioners approved was one whereby the dispensary was to be maintained, the Hawthorns was to be turned into a home for nurses, a very small proportion of whom were to give their services free, and the bulk of the fund was to be applied in enlarging and maintaining a general hospital, called the Bolingbroke Hospital, outside and half a mile from the boundary of the parish of Streatham. This hospital was to be renamed the Weir and Bolingbroke Hospital, and a certain number of beds were to be appropriated so as to give preference to inhabitants of Streatham. Perhaps not surprisingly the scheme was vehemently opposed by many inhabitants of Streatham and by the Wandsworth Borough Council, who had succeeded to the powers of the Streatham vestry. There was much correspondence and a public inquiry; but in the end the Commissioners made an order establishing the scheme. The Wandsworth Borough Council applied to have the order discharged and the matter remitted to the Commissioners for reconsideration.

Eve J. made no order on the application. The Court of Appeal unanimously reversed his decision. Cozens-Hardy M.R. pointed out[1] that the trustees had simply to obey the explicit directions of the testator. Of the four objects named one at least, namely a cottage hospital, was practicable. The trustees had no right to say "We do not consider a cottage hospital a good thing at Streatham, and we will not apply the charity funds for such a purpose ..." Farwell L.J. commented that it was contrary to principle that a testator's wishes should be set aside, and his bounty administered not according to his wishes, but according to the view of the Commissioners adding:[2]

> "if it is wished that testators should continue to become 'pious founders' it is eminently desirable that no doubt should be cast on the security and permanency of their bequests. One of the strongest inducements to gifts of this nature is that desire for posthumous remembrance which has inspired similar gifts for centuries."

Kennedy L.J. shared the inability of the Master of the Rolls and Farwell L.J. to find any ground of justification for the application of the *cy-près* doctrine in the circumstances of the case. The fact that, according to competent opinion, the charitable fund might have been more usefully applied in a different way was not a lawful ground for disregarding the express terms of the gift.[3]

The same Court of Appeal expressed in *Re Faraker*[4] the opinion that where there was a mere slip in a scheme ordered by the Commissioners the court could on appeal correct it.

Mention must also be made in this context of the difficult case of *Re Hanbey's Will Trusts*.[5] In that case a testator who died in 1786 had left money to the Cutlers' Company upon trust to apply the income in perpetuity to certain educational purposes of a charitable kind which were specified with great particularity. Tacked on to the gift was a proviso that in the event of trustee failing to apply the income in accordance with the precise directions given the fund should vest in Christ's Hospital London. For some considerable period of time the testator's directions had not been carried out in accordance with the

---

1 [1910] 2 Ch. 133.
2 [1910] 2 Ch. 124, at 138.
3 *Ibid.*, at 146.
4 [1912] 2 Ch. 488, C.A.
5 [1956] Ch. 264.

terms of the will. The company sought the directions of the court as to whether the gift over had or had not taken effect. DANCKWERTS J. held that he had a discretionary power to order a scheme continuing the original trusts in a different form, even though the effect of such a scheme would be to defeat the gift over. But in the exercise of that discretion he refused to direct a scheme. Accordingly he held that the gift over had taken effect. Whether in the circumstances it was even material for the learned judge to debate whether he should exercise such a discretion is open to doubt. "There is no jurisdiction to apply *cy-près* so long as any lawful charitable object of the testator's bounty is available, however inexpedient such object may appear to the court."[1] The court is not in a position to do what it pleases, but it must do that which is in accordance with the will of the testator.[2] In the exercise of that jurisdiction the court could come to only one conclusion, namely that the gift over had taken effect.

The existence of a right of appeal does not absolutely preclude the court from making an order of *certiorari* if, for example, the Commissioners exceed their jurisdiction, or there is a failure to observe the rules of natural justice in a case where they are acting in a quasi-judicial capacity. However, except in a case where the Commissioners have exceeded their jurisdiction, the court is unlikely to exercise its discretion in favour of an applicant for *certiorari*, unless he has exhausted the rights of appeal conferred by the Charities Act 1960.[3] Likewise, where the Commissioners have expressed an intention to act in a manner which exceeds their jurisdiction it will be open to the court, in a proper case, to make an order of prohibition. A proper case for prohibition or *certiorari* might arise if, for example, the Commissioners purported to determine a question of title to property as between a charity and a person claiming adversely to the charity, contrary to an express statutory provision.[4]

Lastly, it should be remembered that the Commissioners have a limited power to discharge their own orders including any orders directing a scheme or *cy-près* application. At any time within 12 months after they have made an order, the Commissioners may, if they are satisfied that it was made by mistake or on a misrepresentation or otherwise than in conformity with the Charities Act 1960, discharge the order in whole or in part, whether or not an application is made to them for the purpose.[5]

Substituted object

One important question in connection with the *cy-près* doctrine is the extent to which the court or the Commissioners may in framing a *cy-près* scheme depart from the original purpose of the trust. As the Norman-French term *cy-près* indicates the essence of the doctrine is that the new purposes should be "as near as possible" to the original purposes, and this approach has been justified on the ground that it can be assumed that the founder would wish as little deviation as possible from his expressed designs. It is also said that the spectacle of

---

1 *Re Weir Hospital*, [1910] 2 Ch. 124, at 135, *per* FARWELL L.J.
2 *Ibid.*
3 *Cf. R.* v. *Charity Commissioners for England and Wales*, [1897] 1 Q.B. 407 (*mandamus* refused because alternative remedy available).
4 CA 1960, s. 18 (3).
5 *Ibid.*, s. 40 (3).

radical alterations being made in charitable trusts would soon stem the charitable intentions of others.

The subject has been considered by the court on many occasions, with much diversity of opinion. In the leading case of *A.-G.* v. *Ironmongers' Co.*[1] Lord COTTENHAM L.C. commented:

> "There is necessarily great latitude in exercising the jurisdiction over charity funds where the direct object of the donor fails; and therefore very different opinions may be formed upon that subject in the same case."

The doctrine of *cy-près* is one of approximation.[2] The court must search out and ascertain the intention of the donor or testator and must exercise discretion in awarding the fund in question to such charitable institution which can most nearly give effect to that intention. Under no circumstances can the judgment of the court capriciously be substituted for that of the donor or testator.[3] The judge must not substitute his own conception of what would be best for what can be assumed to be the testator's intention. Thus in *Re Stanes' Will*[4] there was a gift for the poor and needy of the parish of Great Baddon, to be distributed by a trustee who had died. There were several proposals before the court. One proposal was that the fund should be distributed in bread, coals and other necessaries among the poor of the parish; the other suggestion emanating from the parishioners assembled in the vestry was that it should be applied in the education of the poor in the National Schools in the parish. Sir RICHARD KINDERSLEY V.-C. said that the intention of the testatrix was clearly to benefit the poor generally but he refused to set up a dole charity.[5] As to the other proposal he said:

> "My own inclination is especially with the wishes of this vestry, and the more so since it has the concurrence of the Attorney-General; but I must say I do not think the application of the income to the National Schools would carry out the intention of the testatrix. There are various dissenters in the parish, who though really not objecting to National Schools in themselves, yet object to many of the doctrines and much of the discipline inculcated there; and, therefore, I am bound to conclude that the National Schools do not include all the poor of the parish. Against therefore my own conception of what would be best I do not think I can accede to this petition."

In reaching this conclusion KINDERSLEY V.-C. was purporting to exercise the *cy-près* principle: having discovered the true intention of the testatrix, namely to benefit the poor generally. The case was not one where there was any failure of a purpose but rather was one where the machinery for ascertaining objects had broken down. Nevertheless the principle applied by KINDERSLEY V.-C. must be equally applicable to the true *cy-près* occasion. The court in applying the principle does not apply the fund in question to the most deserving object but to the object nearest to the original.[6]

---

1 (1841), Cr. & Ph. 208, at 227.
2 *Kensington Hospital for Women Case* (1948), 3 A.L.R. 2d 73; Shelford, *Law of Mortmain* (1836) 601.
3 *Kensington Hospital for Women Case, supra*, at 77.
4 (1853), 21 L.T.O.S. 261.
5 Dole charities were becoming progressively more unpopular.
6 *Minister of Internal Affairs and Banner* v. *Albertson*, [1941] S.R. 240.

The court will not, in the words of NAPIER L.C. in the Irish case of *Re Evans'*
Charities:[1]

"permit the benevolent intention of the testator to be defeated, but will
apply the fund to some other charitable object, selected with a careful
regard to the intention of the testator and approaching as nearly as possible
to what appears to have been his wish."

Accordingly if the donor names a particular object which is capable of taking
effect, any application *cy-près* that becomes necessary must be limited within
the confines of that object, and the mode of application must as far as possible
coincide with his wishes.[2] On the other hand if the scheme proposed substantially
gives effect to the wishes of the testator, so far as ascertainable, then the court
will not be acute, and ought not to be acute, to discover discrepancies which
certainly go to make the scheme more workable and a more desirable scheme
and do not depart from the real intention of the testator.[3] The court will therefore take into account the usefulness of the new purpose as well as its proximity
to the old one. In *Re Weir Hospital*[4] COZENS-HARDY M.R. took what one
writer[5] described as a "laxer view of the principle and one not consistent with
the authorities". What the learned Master of the Rolls said[6] in *Re Weir Hospital* was that:

"Wherever the *cy-près* doctrine has to be applied, it is competent to the
court to consider the comparative advantages of various charitable objects
and to adopt by the scheme the one which seems most beneficial."

But there is nothing in his judgment to suggest that this dictum was meant to
be an overriding statement of principle. The statement should rather be regarded
as applicable only to charitable objects equally near to the testator's intention.

The general rule then is quite clear. One charity will not be substituted for
another charity; nor will a charity intended for one purpose be applied to a
purpose altogether different; and so a gift for the relief of poverty will not be
applied for the advancement of education.[7] You may only substitute for a
particular charity which has been defined and which has failed another charity
ejusdem generis or which approaches it in nature or character. One seeming exception to this general rule was where the charity had failed by reason of the
designated purpose being illegal or against public policy. Thus, as has been
seen, gifts for the support of denominations other than the established church
were often applied to the purposes of the established church.[8]

A charity may be *cy-près* to the original object even though it seems to have
no trace of resemblance to it if no other can be found having a nearer connection.[9] This view was taken by Lord COTTENHAM L.C. in *A.-G. v. Ironmongers'*

---

1 (1858), 10 Ir. Ch. R. 271, at 283.
2 See *Re Lambeth Charities* (1853), 22 L.J. Ch. 959; *A.-G. v. Dedham School* (1857), 23
Beav. 350, at 355 (as close . . . as it can).
3 *Re De Noailles* (1916), 114 L.T. 1089, at 1094–1095.
4 [1910] 2 Ch. 124.
5 Tyssen, *Law of Charitable Bequests* (2nd edn.) 182.
6 [1910] 2 Ch. 124, at 132.
7 *Clephane v. Edinburgh Corporation* (1869), L.R. 1 Sc. & Div. 417, at 421.
8 See at 54, *supra*.
9 *A.-G. v. Ironmongers' Co.* (1841), Cr. & Ph. 208, at 227.

Co.[1] where the charitable gift was for the redemption of Christian captives in Barbary. There was a subsequent failure of the trusts because there were no longer any such captives and the gift was ultimately applied in supporting and assisting charity schools in England and Wales. In *Ex parte Magniac*[2] money had been collected for the alleviation of drought conditions but abundant rains came later and no further need arose for the use of the balance of the money. Advertisements for suggestions as to the use of the money brought no response. The chairwoman of the Anti-Drought Association (Sundays River Valley) sought an order authorising the application of the money, after payment of costs, equally to two charities in the area, the Child Welfare Society and the Women's Institute at Sundays Valley. LANSDOWN J.P. (to whom Lord COTTENHAM's dicta in *A.-G. v. Ironmongers' Co.* were cited) held that in the absence of evidence of an object cognate with the purposes of the defunct association an order would be made for the *cy-près* application of the fund as asked.[3]

So long as they are practicable, objects which are closer to the donor's intention will always be selected in preference to remoter objects.[4] That *usefulness* is also a factor to be taken into account is said to appear from *Re Prison Charities*.[5] In that case certain charitable trusts declared a century or two previously in favour of poor prisoners in the City of London had failed because of the abolition of the law of imprisonment for debt and the closing of the debtors' prisons. The Attorney-General brought in a scheme proposing that all the funds should be treated as one charity, and applied to the building, establishment and maintenance of a school for children of persons convicted of crime and undergoing sentence. Sir JAMES BACON V.-C. construed the intention of the bequests as being for the relief of poverty among adults and found no intention to relieve children or to assist education. Accordingly the proposal was not sufficiently close to the charitable intentions of the donor. In addition, however, it was suggested that the proposed scheme was (1) unnecessary as contemplating an object already partially or wholly provided for by statute; (2) inconsistent with charitable intention as tending to the relief of the public rates and taxes; (3) necessarily limited in ambit because of the costs; and (4) inexpedient as resulting in the gathering together in one establishment of children suffering from a common misfortune and thus perpetuating the memory of that misfortune. The headnote suggests that BACON V.-C. based his decision in part on three of these four additional grounds of objection, namely (1), (2) and (4). But on a careful reading of his judgment it appears that he only expressly assented to (3) and (4) as valid grounds and did not consider (3) to be sufficient on its own.

The identification of the most practicable and useful object that is nearest to the donor's original intention depends on the circumstances of the case and the evidence before the court about other available charities. To some extent also it is a question for the discretion of the judge or the Commissioners; and it is not always an easy task to forecast exactly how the particular discretion will be exercised.

An interesting case concerning competing *cy-près* schemes was recently before

---

1 (1841), Cr. & Ph. 208.

2 [1942] E.D.L. 160 (South Africa).

3 An order nisi was made enabling objections to be made before the order was made absolute.

4 *Re Bridewell Hospital* (1860), 2 L.T. 760; *Re Prison Charities* (1873), L.R. 16 Eq. 129; *A.-G. v. Duke of Northumberland* (1889), 5 T.L.R. 237; varied on appeal 5 T.L.R. 719, C.A.

5 (1873), L.R. 16 Eq. 129.

an Australian court. The testatrix in *Phillips* v. *Roberts*[1] left the residue of her estate to her trustees on trust to establish a church at a certain address and directed that the main purpose of the church should be to further the study of the Bible. There was an express statement in the will that this gift was "in pursuance of my charitable intention to benefit my fellow citizens by the improvement of Biblical Knowledge and Instruction". The trust was impracticable, but since the will plainly exhibited a general charitable intent the case for *cy-près* application was obvious. At the request of the judge both the Attorney-General and the trustees brought in schemes. The Attorney-General proposed a division of the residuary estate between six theological seminaries. The trustees proposed to make the income of the residuary estate available to a company limited by guarantee whose objects (broadly) were to carry out and publish the fruits of historical and archaeological research bearing on the authenticity, historicity, accuracy and inspiration of the Holy Scriptures. In the course of deciding which scheme was the more appropriate the judge received the evidence of a witness as to his opinion of how the testatrix would have reacted to the Attorney-General's scheme. Partly in reliance on that evidence he preferred the trustees' scheme. On appeal there was a divergence of opinion among the members of the appeal court. The majority considered that the trustees' scheme more nearly approximated to the intention of the testatrix than did that of the Attorney-General, and this conclusion was justified purely by reference to the will itself.[2] But one member of the court considered that the opinion evidence tendered was not irrelevant though the weight to be given it was a matter for the judge.[3] The dissenting appellate judge considered that evidence of the intention of the testatrix otherwise than as expressed in the will was irrelevant and that extraneous evidence was likewise unhelpful:[4] in his view neither scheme was sufficiently close to the manner of application chosen by the testatrix.

The fate of various disaster funds which show a surplus is instructive. A fund for the relief of miners suffering from a particular accident was in one case applied to the benefit of aged miners generally.[5] In another case a fund for victims of an explosion was applied for the relief of victims of storm damage or of another explosion on the footing that the original intention was to relieve distress consequent upon an unusual and grave occurrence.[6] The surplus proceeds of a flood disaster fund were applied to various other objects for the public benefit in the area, including the relief of distress caused by Act of God.[7] A fund for the victims of a forest fire was applied to establish hospitals,[8] while in another case the nearest object to relief of suffering from the consequences of a fire was held to be the relief of the financial loss suffered by the victims.[9] The disaster fund raised for the victims of a slip from a colliery tip which had engulfed a school in South Wales did not require any *cy-près* application because

---

1 (1975), 2 N.S.W.L.R. 207.
2 SAMUELS J.A. said it was unnecessary to deal with the admissibility of the evidence.
3 HUTLEY J.A. thought that the practice should approximate to that followed by the court where lack of definition is repaired by scheme.
4 MAHONEY J.A. invoked *Ironmongers' Co.* v. *A.-G.* (1844), 10 Cl. & Fin. 908, at 924.
5 *Re Hartley Colliery Accident Relief Fund* (1908), 102 L.T. 165, n.
6 *Ex parte Pretoria Explosion Victims Relief Fund*, [1954] 1 S.A. 445 (Transvaal).
7 *Re North Devon and West Somerset Relief Fund Trusts*, [1953] 1 W.L.R. 1260; see [1960] Ch. Com. Rep. 17–18, paras. 47–48.
8 *Re Northern Ontario Fire Relief Fund Trusts*, [1913] 11 D.L.R. 15.
9 *Doyle* v. *Whalen*, 31 L.R.A. 118 (Maine) (1895).

wide charitable trusts were declared at an early stage.[1] Where further suffering from a particular hazard can be foreseen a likely *cy-près* application of funds raised for a particular disaster is the relief of future disasters of the same kind.[2]

The surplus funds of a hospital for sick and wounded soldiers have been applied to relieve such sick and wounded soldiers after the hospital was sold.[3] A trust for a volunteer force which ceased to exist was applied *cy-près* to relieve persons in the defence forces of the same province.[4] In an Irish case a charity for the benefit of troops of the royal army was applied for the benefit of soldiers of the British Army.[5]

A trust for the benefit of a particular class of orphans which fails for lack of objects may be converted into a trust for a wider class of orphans.[6] A fund that is insufficient to maintain a particular institution for the relief of a particular section of the community may be applied *cy-près* for relief of that section of the community.[7] The same applies where an institution ceases to exist[8] or becomes redundant because of state-run institutions.[9]

In the field of religious charities a surplus left after maintaining the choir and choral service in a cathedral can clearly be spent on a new organ for the cathedral[10] and a surplus left after erecting a church tower can properly be applied to the erection of a new Sunday school:[11] in each case, of course, a *cy-près* order is nevertheless required.

It is no doubt a good working rule that a trust which falls squarely under one particular head of charity within Lord MACNAGHTEN's classification in the *Pemsel* case will only very exceptionally be diverted to another head. Indeed the only examples which have occurred and which therefore spring to mind are those cases where there has been a failure of a purpose under the fourth head and no purpose *ejusdem generis* can be identified. Otherwise where a trust for the relief of poverty fails the property should be and is applied to another purpose which relieves poverty, and trusts for the advancement of education and religion are replaced by other trusts for the purposes falling within the same category.[12]

Where a purpose advances religion and education at the same time it is then a matter of construction whether one purpose predominates, or whether each is equally important so that any *cy-près* application must combine both elements.

---

1 On the principle in *A.-G.* v. *Mathieson*, [1907] 2 Ch. 383, C.A. As to the Aberfan appeal and the trusts declared: see [1966] Ch. Com. Rep. 6–7, paras. 9–12.

2 *Gibson* (1900) 2 F (Ct. of Sess.) 1195 (shipwreck or other perils of the sea). The fund to rescue sea birds affected by oil from the sinking of the tanker Torrey Canyon was applied *cy-près* by the Commissioners to be used in other cases where birds had become contaminated by oil: [1971] Ch. Com. Rep. 15, para. 41.

3 *Re Welsh Hospital (Netley) Fund*, [1921] 1 Ch. 655; and see *Ex parte South African Red Cross Society*, [1929] 1 P.H., M 8.

4 *Ex parte Trustees of Transvaal Volunteers Sustentation Fund*, [1914] W.L.D. 105.

5 *Re Royal Kilmainham Hospital*, [1966] I.R. 451.

6 *Ex parte Bosman No*, [1916] T.P.D. 399 (Dutch orphans of Boer War), *cf. Ex parte Fichardt No*, [1946] O.P.D. 350 (no orphans in need: fund applied to build homes for ex-servicemen and their families).

7 *A.-G. for New South Wales* v. *Perpetual Trustee Co. Ltd.* (1940), 63 C.L.R. 209; *Parker* v. *Moseley*, [1965] V.R. 580, *Re McGwire*, [1941] I.R. 33.

8 *Dale* v. *Powell* (1897), 13 T.L.R. 466; *Spiller* v. *Maude* (1881), 32 Ch.D. 158 n., *Re Templemoyle Agricultural School* (1869), I.R. 4 Eq. 295: *Re Door of Hope* (1905), 26 N.Z.L.R. 96.

9 *A.-.G.* v. *Bullock* (1877), R.E.D. 249; *cf. Re Fitzgibbon*, [1922] 69 D.L.R. 524.

10 *Re Trusts of the Rectory of St. John in County of Cork* (1869), I.R. 3 Eq. 335.

11 *Rowe and Brown* v. *Public Trustee*, [1928] N.Z.L.R. 51.

12 *Clephane* v. *Edinburgh Corporation* (1869), 1 Sc. & Div. 417, at 421.

Part IV

Administration

Chapter 31

Charitable Corporations

A charitable corporation is, quite simply, a corporation whose corporate purpose is charitable. Thus municipal corporations do not qualify as charitable corporations: they hold their municipal property on trust for charitable purposes[1] and are *pro tanto* charitable trustees,[2] but being established partly for purposes of local administration they are not exclusively charitable. On the other hand eleemosynary corporations being constituted for the perpetual distribution of the free alms or bounty of the founder to such persons as he has directed[3] are clearly charitable corporations. It might be thought that the same could be said of ecclesiastical corporations (which exist for the furtherance of religion and perpetuating the rites of the Church[4]), but corporations which are wholly ecclesiastical are taken out of the definition of charity in the Charities Act 1960.[5]

The two main types of charitable corporation were hospitals and colleges; hospitals being created for the maintenance and relief of the poor and infirm, and colleges for the promotion of learning and the support of persons engaged in literary pursuits.[6] Colleges are institutions where the persons benefited by the charity are themselves incorporated.[7] The colleges of Oxford and Cambridge are charitable corporations[8], but, strictly speaking, the universities of Oxford and Cambridge are not.[9] On the other hand the other universities of England are eleemosynary corporations.

The term hospital is somewhat ambiguous. In its strict legal sense it means an institution for the maintenance and relief of the poor and impotent where the persons benefited by the charity are themselves incorporated.[10] Indeed, it has

---

1 Blackstone's Commentaries 459; 1 Kyd on Corporations 25; Shelford, *Law of Mortmain* (1836) 23.

2 *A.-G. v. Dublin Corporation* (1827), 1 Bli. N.S. 312, H.L.; *A.-G. v. Liverpool Corporation* (1835), 1 My. & Cr. 170, at 201; *A.-G. v. Stafford Corporation* [1878] W.N. 74.

3 Shelford, *Law of Mortmain* (1836) 23.

4 See 14 Halsbury's Laws of England (4th edn.) 691–692, paras. 1252–1256.

5 CA 1960, s. 45 (2).

6 1 Kyd on Corporations 25; *Philips v. Bury* (1694) as reported in 2 Term. Rep. 346, at 352, H.L.

7 Shelford, *Law of Mortmain* (1836) 24.

8 *R. v. Cambridge (Vice-Chancellor)* (1765), 3 Burr. 1647 at 1652, 1656; and see *Parkinson's Case* (1689), Carth. 92 at 93; *Anon.* (1698), 12 Mod. Rep. 232; *Philips v. Bury* (1694), Skin. 447, at 494, H.L. But the halls were not: see *R. v. Hertford College* (1878), 3 Q.B.D. 693, C.A., at 694.

9 *R. v. Cambridge (Vice-Chancellor)* (1765), 3 Burr. 1647; Shelford, *Law of Mortmain* 25. They are civil corporations of a very special kind.

10 Shelford, *Law of Mortmain* (1836) 27. See also *A.-G. v. Wyggeston Hospital* (1853), 16 Beav. 313; *A.-G. v. St. Cross Hospital* (1853), 17 Beav. 435: *A.-G. v. St. John's Hospital (Bedford)* (1865) 2 De G.J. & Sm. 621; *Sutton Hospital Case* (1612), 10 C. Rep. 1a at 23a, 31a; *Colchester (Lord) v. Kewney* (1866), 35 L.J. Ex. 204, at 206, affirmed, (1867) L.R. 2 Ex. 253.

been said that "if in an hospital the master and poor are incorporated, it is a college, having a common seal to act by, although it hath not the name of a college".[1] More loosely, however, the expression "hospital" has been used to denote various kinds of corporate institutions[2] for the relief of the poor or infirm; such as corporations where the estate of inheritance only is vested in the master or warden,[3] or hospital managed by an incorporated body of governors or trustee. There are many modern hospitals of this kind, while the Charterhouse and Sutton's Hospital[4] are ancient examples. The word "hospital" has also, of course, been defined in various statutes.[5]

Colleges and hospitals are not, however, the only examples of charitable corporations. There are cases of other corporations created solely to carry out charitable purposes as where charity trustees,[6] governors[7] or the schoolmaster,[8] or the schoolmaster and usher[9] have been respectively incorporated for charitable or educational objects. Charitable corporations have also in many cases been created by Act of Parliament: one may instance the Royal Patriotic Fund Corporation[10] and the Church Commissioners.[11] Even more frequently such corporations have been founded by charter, foundation by charter being thought no doubt to confer prestige. The Clergy Society[12] and most of the universities were founded by charter.

The term "foundation" as applied to the establishment of charitable corporations has two distinct meanings. It means (1) the incorporation of a body of persons and (2) the original endowment of the incorporated body.[13]

A charitable corporation may be created (1) by royal charter (2) by royal charter giving authority to the holder of an office to create corporations indefinitely[14] (3) by persons acting under royal licence[15] (4) by special Act of Parliament[16] (5) under the Companies Act 1948 to 1967[17] and by the Charity Commissioners under the Charitable Trustees Incorporation Act 1872.[18]

No particular form of words is required in the creation of a corporation

---

1 *Philips* v. *Bury* (1694), 2 Term Rep. 346, at 353, H.L.
2 *Moses* v. *Marsland*, [1901] 1 K.B. 668; and see *York* (*Dean and Chapter*) v. *Middleborough* (1828), 2 Y. & J. 196, at 216.
3 Co. Litt. 342a; Shelford, *Law of Mortmain*, 24.
4 *Sutton's Hospital Case* (1612), 10 Co. Rep. 1a.
5 See Stroud's *Judicial Dictionary* (4th edn.) under "hospital".
6 See 332–333, *infra*.
7 *Eden* v. *Foster* (1725), 2 P. Wms. 325 (grammar school).
8 *Whiston* v. *Rochester* (*Dean & Chapter*) (1849), 7 Hare 532. (cathedral school).
9 *A.-G.* v. *Price* (1744), 3 Atk. 108 at 109 (fee school); *A.-G.* v. *Magdalen College, Oxford* (1847), 10 Beav. 402 (college school); *Re Chelmsford Grammar School* (1855), 1 K. & J. 543, at 561.
10 Patriotic Fund Reorganisation Act 1903.
11 Church Commissioners Measure 1947 ss. 2, 18.
12 *Re Clergy Society* (1856), 2 K. & J. 615.
13 *Sutton Hospital Case* (1612), 10 Co. Rep. 1a at 23a, where Coke C.J. refers to the Latin terms *fundatio incipiens* and *fundatio percipiens*.
14 E.g. the Chancellor of Oxford University: 1 Blackstone's Commentaries 462.
15 *Ex parte Kirkby Ravensworth Hospital* (1808), 15 Ves. 305; *A.-G.* v. *Dulwich College* (1841), 4 Beav. 255.
16 See *Construction Industry Training Board* v. *A.-G.*, [1973] Ch. 173, C.A.
17 See *Re St. Hilda's Incorporated College, Cheltenham*, [1901] 1 Ch. 556; *Incorporated Council of Law Reporting for England and Wales* v. *A.-G.*, [1972] Ch. 73.
18 As to this Act, see 332, *infra*.

whether by Charter or by Act of Parliament: merely a clear intention to incorporate.[1]

It is competent for the Crown to establish or found a corporation which has had no previous inchoate or embryonic existence as an unincorporated body of persons, but as a matter of history and of practice this never occurs. Whether it is a charity or whether indeed it is a business corporation, there is always a prior existence; there is always some body of persons existing who can petition for the charter and submit the charter to the Crown.[2]

Charitable corporations, in so far as they are charitable, are in the words of Lord MANSFIELD L.C. "creatures of the founder".[3] The founder has of course the power to dispose, direct and regulate his own property; therefore he may make such provision as he thinks fit for the government and administration of his "creature" and the application in perpetuity of its revenues.[4] From this original power of the founder flow the rights of patronage and visitation enjoyed by the founder and his heirs.[5] The founder is not, however, at liberty to change the constitution of the corporation by increasing the number of corporations or to vary the trusts or application of the endowment or revenues[6] unless special powers in that behalf have been reserved by the charter of incorporation.[7] For this purpose a power to alter the statutes or byelaws of the corporation is not enough: such a power does not imply a power to alter the constitution or objects of the corporation.[8] If the number of corporators is not originally fixed it seems that the corporation itself may add to the number.[9]

The person providing the first gift of revenues or endowment is usually regarded as the founder of a corporation, rather than the person performing the act of incorporation.[10] If there are two or more private individuals contributing to the original endowment they together constitute the founders.[11] But the sovereign stands in a special position: if the sovereign is a party to the original endowment the sovereign alone will be founder.[12] It is otherwise if the sovereign subsequently endows a corporation originally endowed by a private individual: the private individual still remains the founder because a subsequent endowment or constitution does not constitute a new foundation.[13] *A fortiori* where a charity is established by subscriptions the original subscribers alone are the founders,

---

1 *Sutton Hospital Case* (1612), 10 Co. Rep. 1a at 23a, 28a; Shelford, *Law of Mortmain* (1836) 27.

2 *A.-G.* v. *National Hospital for the Relief and Cure of the Paralysed and Epileptic*, [1904] 2 Ch. 252, at 256.

3 *St. John's College, Cambridge* v. *Todington* (1757), 1 Burr, 158, at 200.

4 *Green* v. *Rutherforth* (1750), 1 Ves. Sen. 462, at 472; *Philips* v. *Bury* (1694), 2 Term. Rep. 346, at 352.

5 As to patronage see 193, *supra*; as to visitation see 422–433, *supra*.

6 *A.-G.* v. *Dulwich College* (1841), 4 Beav. 255; and see *Ex parte Bolton* (1789), 2 Bro. C.C. 662.

7 *R.* v. *Vice-Chancellor of Cambridge* (1765), 3 Burr. 1647, at 1656; *St. John's College, Cambridge* v. *Todington* (1757), 1 Burr. 158.

8 *Ex parte Bolton* (1789), 2 Bro. C.C. 662; *A.-G.* v. *Dulwich College* (1841), 4 Beav. 255, at 266.

9 *A.-G.* v. *Talbot* (1748), 3 Atk. 662, at 675.

10 *Sutton's Hospital Case* (1612), 10 Co. Rep. 1a, at 23a, 33a; Shelford, *Law of Mortmain* (1836) 323–324; *Anon.* (1698), 12 Mod. Rep. 232; and see *St. John's College, Cambridge* v. *Todington* (1757), 1 Burr. 158, at 200.

11 *Re St. Leonard, Shoreditch, Parochial Schools* (1884), 10 App. Cas. 304, at 308, P.C.

12 2 Co. inst. 68.

13 *Ibid.*; *A.-G.* v. *Dedham School* (1857), 23 Beav. 350.

because again the additional contributions do not constitute a new foundation.[1]
The subsequent subscribers do not found the charity; they find it existing; they
merely aid and assist it.

The legal nature of a corporate charity is not entirely clear. A particular
problem is whether such a charity holds its corporate property on trust. That
problem does not, of course, arise where the corporation holds property on
specific charitable trusts; it only arises where it holds the property as part of its
corporate funds, its objects being exclusively charitable.

Because of the rule basing the charitable jurisdiction of the court on the
existence of a trust it was generally said that a charitable corporation was necessarily a trustee of its property,[2] even though the corporation may have been
founded long before trusts were recognised by the law.[3] As regards chartered
companies the view is probably quite tenable. But a charity incorporated under
the Companies Act 1948 cannot be regarded as holding its corporate property
on any trusts. A limited company does not hold its property on trust for its
members *qua* members: the contrary proposition is "beyond the reach of sustained argument."[4]

The property of a *non-charitable* limited company is not held on trust for the
purposes set forth in the memorandum and articles.[5] If it was, the trusts would be
void.[6] It is submitted that a *charitable* company, whose objects may differ by
only a few words, is equally not a trustee of its own property. The true position
is that the company, being a legal person, holds its property absolutely for its
own benefit, but can only apply it for the purposes set out in its memorandum.
It is not *stricto sensu* a breach of trust if it applies its property for other objects:
it is rather an *ultra vires* act. The point was well put by an American court in the
case of *Brigham* v. *Peter Bent Brigham Hospital*.[7] There the testator had left the
residue of his estate to his executors to manage the same for 25 years and
accumulate the income and at the expiration of the period to form a corporation
to maintain a hospital. PUTNAM J. said:[8]

> "We should observe that the corporation contemplated by the will was
> not to hold in trust, in the technical sense of the word, the property which
> it might receive. It was to hold it for its own purposes in the usual way in
> which charitable institutions hold their assets. Such a holding is sometimes
> called a quasi-trust . . . but the holding does not constitute a true trust."

The characterisation of the corporate property of a charity corporation has
been much debated in the United States.[9] There is copious and evenly divided
authority on the point. In the end the matter may be partly one of terminology
or semantics. A charitable corporation does not hold its property absolutely or
beneficially in the same sense as an individual or non-charitable corporation

---

1 *Re St. Leonard, Shoreditch, Parochial Schools, supra.*
2 *Lydiatt* v. *Foach* (1700), 2 Vern. 410; and see *Construction Industry Training Board* v.
A.-G., [1973] Ch. 173, at 187, C.A.
3 See for example *A.-G.* v. *St. Cross Hospital* (1853), 17 Beav. 435.
4 *Bank voor Handel en Sheepvaart N.V.* v. *Slatford* [1953] 1 Q.B. 248, at 269, *per* DEVLIN J.
citing *Salomon* v. *Salomon & Co.*, [1897] A.C. 22.
5 *Bowman* v. *Secular Society, Ltd.*, [1917] A.C. 406, at 440.
6 *Re Astor's Settlement Trust*, [1952] Ch. 534; *Leahy* v. *A.-G. for New South Wales*, [1959]
A.C. 457, at 484, P.C.
7 134 Fed. 513, (1904).
8 *Ibid.* at 517.
9 See Scott, *Trusts* (3rd edn.) para. 348.1.

holds its property beneficially, since in the case of a charitable corporation the Attorney-General may move the court to restrain the diversion of charitable funds from purposes set out in the memorandum. In *Construction Industry Training Board* v. *A.-G.* BUCKLEY L.J. appears to have regarded the scheme making power of the court and the powers to intervene for the protection of charities, at the suit of the Attorney-General, as being part of its jurisdiction over charitable *trusts*. In every such case he suggests "the court would be acting upon the basis that the property affected is not in the beneficial ownership of the persons or body in whom its legal ownership is vested but is devoted to charitable purposes, that is to say held upon charitable trusts". Therefore in his view the funds from time to time in the hands of the Construction Industry Training Board were "held upon a statutory *trust* for exclusively charitable purposes". It seems that the use of the word "trust" in this context ought to be construed loosely. The company owes fiduciary duties to charity.

In *Re Manchester Royal Infirmary*[1] a corporation incorporated by special Act held funds for charitable purposes and the corporation were held to be trustees within the meaning of the Trust Investment Act 1889 and so entitled to invest property in their hands under that Act. The decision turned in part on the fact that prior to incorporation under an earlier Act the property was vested in trustees. That factor was not present in *Soldiers, Sailors and Airmen's Family Association* v. *A.-G.*[2] where a chartered company was held to be bound by the provisions of the Trustee Investments Act 1961. The Association in that case conceded that it was "in the position of a trustee with regard to its funds". Again the governors and directors of a charitable corporation though not strictly trustees themselves do occupy a position so analogous that they will not, without express authority in the instrument of foundation, receive remuneration for work done.[3]

One consequence of the analysis that the corporate property of a charitable company may not be held on trust but may constitute assets of the company applicable for the purposes of the memorandum is that members by altering the memorandum by special resolution can direct some or all of the charitable funds to purposes which are not charitable.[4] Statutory intervention has put an end to that possibility in England and Wales. The relevant provision specifies that where a charity is a company or other body corporate, and has power to alter the instruments establishing or regulating it as a body corporate no exercise of that power which has the effect of the body ceasing to be a charity is valid so as to affect the application of property previously acquired or the income of such property. The provision applies only to property acquired otherwise than for full consideration in money or money's worth, or property representing property so acquired. The effect of this provision is that where a charitable company alters its memorandum so that it ceases to be charitable, all its existing property remains applicable for its original objects, but any new property is applicable for its new objects. This is tantamount to making the company a trustee of the original property upon trusts corresponding to the

---

1 (1889), 43 Ch.D. 420.
2 [1968] 1 W.L.R. 313.
3 *Re French Protestant Hospital*, [1951] Ch. 567.
4 This possibility was noted in the Nathan Report (Cmd. 8710) para. 573. See also *I.R. Comrs.* v. *Yorkshire Agricultural Society*, [1928] 1 K.B. 611; *Baldry* v. *Feintuck*, [1972] 1 W.L.R. 552 where the position of unincorporated associations in this regard is discussed; and see also [1971] Ch. Com. Rep., paras. 26–30.

original objects, since it no longer owns the property beneficially in such a way that it is free to apply it in any way which is within its powers from time to time. Any such alteration in the memorandum must be notified to the Commissioners[1] but they have no power to prevent it being made.

The expression "charity trustees" is in the Charities Act 1960 defined to mean the persons having the general control and management of the administration of a charity.[2] In the case of a charitable company therefore the directors will for this purpose be charity trustees. They may therefore be removed by the Commissioners in any case where there has been misconduct and mismanagement in the administration of the company and new directors may be appointed.[3] Quite apart from statutory provision, the directors would be treated by the court as being in a fiduciary position and therefore unable for example to receive payment for their services unless this was authorised by the original memorandum or articles of the company.[4]

A charitable corporation may be dissolved in the same way as any other corporation. A charitable company incorporated under the Companies Act 1948 may be wound up on its own petition or on the petition of any creditor or contributory;[5] additionally it may be wound up on the petition of the Attorney-General.[6]

Once dissolved a charitable corporation is no longer in existence even though its assets are still traceable and may not be applied for any purposes other than charitable purposes.[7] A gift to a corporation which has been dissolved therefore lapses unless the charity is still being carried on albeit in a different guise.[8] At all events a charitable company which has been dissolved and struck off the register will not be restored to the register in order to take a legacy under a will of a testator dying after the date of dissolution.[9]

Lastly it should be noted that by reason of its jurisdiction over companies the Department of Trade and Industry has a limited jurisdiction over charities. The Department may grant a licence dispensing with the inclusion of the word "limited" in the name of a charitable company.[10]

---

1 CA 1960, s. 4 (6) (b).
2 *Ibid.*, s. 46 (1).
3 *Ibid*, s. 20.
4 *Re French Protestant Hospital*, [1951] Ch. 567.
5 Companies Act 1948, s. 224.
6 CA 1960, s. 30 (1).
7 *Re Stemson's Will Trusts*, [1970] Ch. 16; and see at 262–263, *supra*.
8 *Re Vernon's Will Trusts*, [1972] Ch. 300, n.
9 *Re Servers of the Blind League*, [1960] 1 W.L.R. 564.
10 Companies Act 1948, s. 19 (this is not limited to charitable companies).

Chapter 32

Appointment and Removal of Officers

This chapter discusses the appointment and removal of officers and servants of charities. By "officer" is meant a person (other than a trustee or a servant or employee) who occupies an office in the charity. In the context of religious charities vicars, chaplains, curates and non-conformist ministers and rabbis are usually officers. Fellows of university colleges and masters of endowed schools are likewise officers of the educational charities in which they discharge their teaching functions. A company secretary or treasurer is an officer; so is the master or warden of an almshouse.

Members of university colleges

Questions as to the election and removal of members of university colleges are generally decided by the visitors[1] in accordance with the statutes of the institution in question. But sometimes these matters are regulated to a certain extent by Act of Parliament.[2]

Neither the court[3] nor the visitor[4] can compel the election of any particular candidate if the college is by its statutes given absolute discretion in the matter, except where the discretion is corruptly exercised.[5]

Elections by the dean, warden, provost, master, president or other head of any college with the consent of the majority of the fellows or brethren of the corporation who have power to consent are as valid as if made by all the members of the corporation. However if the college statutes direct fellows to be elected by the head of the college *and* the majority of the fellows the concurrent vote of the head is necessary,[6] although the contrary was formerly held.[7]

Elections of fellows, scholars, officers and other persons as members of colleges, schools halls or societies, if made corruptly or for any money consideration, direct or indirect, are void.[8] Moreover any fellow, officer or scholar receiving a bribe for resigning his office or place is liable on summary conviction

---

1 As to visitors, see 422–433, *infra*.
2 See e.g. Simony Act 1588; Universities Tests Act 1871; Universities of Oxford and Cambridge Act 1877; Charities Act 1960.
3 *R. v. Hertford College* (1878), 3 Q.B.D. 693, at 705, C.A.
4 *Ex parte Wrangham* (1795), 2 Ves. 609, at 625.
5 *R. v. Hertford College, supra.*
6 *Re Catherine Hall* (1802), 5 Russ. 85, n.; *Re Queen's College Cambridge* (1828), 5 Russ. 64.
7 *Case of Clare Hall* (1788), 5 Russ. 73, n.; *Case of Gonville and Caius College* (1617), 5 Russ 76, n.
8 Simony Act 1588, s.1.

to a fine not exceeding £100[1] and the briber is disqualified for the office at the next election.[2]

The passing of an examination may be (and indeed usually is) a condition precedent to election to a fellowship. But it does not follow that coming top in the examination gives an absolute and unqualified title to be elected, unless the college statutes say so.[3]

Only one of the candidates for a close fellowship in *Re Catherine Hall*[4] fulfilled all the conditions required by the endowment, but it was held that he should none the less pass the usual fellowship examination. In such a case the standard of ability required of the candidate must be decided on general grounds without reference to the standard of ability of any particular individuals who do not satisfy the conditions of the close fellowship.[5] The wording of the relevant deed of endowment may enable intellectual pre-eminence to prevail. For example in *Re St. John's College, Cambridge*[6] the person to be elected to a fellowship was directed to be a native of a particular town "if any such shall be found *able* within the university" and this was held to enable the election of a non-native where none of the natives was of fellowship standard. In open fellowships the principle is *detur digniori*, in proprieties it is *detur, sed digno*.[7]

When the possession of real estate is a necessary qualification for certain college offices, the modern doctrines of equity are not strictly applied, and an interest in land which in equity would be considered personal estate may be sufficient.[8] When the possession of property is a disqualification for holding a fellowship, real property is in general the only property considered.[9] If possession of property of a certain amount is a qualification the qualification does not have to be shown at the election itself.[10]

The qualification that a candidate for a fellowship should be *in sacerdotio constitutus* is satisfied by a person admitted to deacon's orders.[11]

Where the qualification to be satisfied for a living to be granted to a fellow of a college was that he should not at that time "be presented, instituted or inducted into any other living" it was held that the condition was satisfied by the previous resignation of another living. It was also held that the resignation of the previous living was sufficiently effected by sending it by post to the bishop who endorsed and signed a memorandum of acceptance without any public act.[12]

The acceptance of a professorship may under college statutes cause the professor to forfeit his fellowship.[13] College statutes may also provide that for-

---

1 Simony Act 1588, s. 2; Common Informers Act 1951, s. 1 (1) (3), Schedule.
2 Simony Act 1588, s. 3.
3 *R. v. Hertford College* (1878), 3 Q.B.D. 693, at 698–699, 701, C.A.; *Downing College Case* (1837), 2 My. & Cr. 642; *Watson and Freemantle v. Warden, etc. of All Soul's College, Oxford* (1864), 11 L.T. 166.
4 (1802), 5 Russ. 85, n.
5 *Ibid.*
6 (1831), 2 Russ. & M. 603.
7 *Ibid.*, at 605. The expressions mean "let it be given to the more deserving man" and "let it be given, but to a deserving man".
8 *Case of Queen's College, Cambridge* (1821), Jac. 1, at 38.
9 *Ibid.*, at 37.
10 *Ibid.*, at 36.
11 *Re University College, Oxford* (1848), 17 L.J. Ch. 298; See also *Glasgow College v. A.-G.* (1848), 1 H.L. Cas. 800; *Re St. Catherine's Hall, Cambridge* (1849), 1 Mac. & G. 473.
12 *Heyes v. Exeter College, Oxford* (1806), 12 Ves. 336.
13 *Re Trinity College, Cambridge* (1854), 3 De G.M. & G. 742.

feiture shall take place at the expiration of one year from the time when the number of fellows in holy orders falls below that required by the statutes. The first question in *Re St. Catherine's Hall, Cambridge*[1] was whether the particular wording of the statutes which prescribed that in such an event the fellow left *recedot a collegii emolumentis* meant permanent relinquishment or a temporary or casual suspension. Lord COTTENHAM L.C. sitting as Visitor on behalf of the Queen held that it meant absolute forfeiture. He also held that the word *discedere* in college statutes as applied to a fellow vacating his fellowship was not confined to a vacancy by death.

A condition requiring a fellow to travel overseas for the second part of his tenure of the fellowship was held to be dispensed with by the acceptance of resignation due to ill health so that there was no liability to refund any part of the salary received.[2]

Vicars, chaplains and curates

PRESENTATION TO A BENEFICE

The initial right of a clerk in holy orders to hold a church and benefice is acquired by presentation, or, if the benefice is in the gift of the bishop of the diocese in which it is situate by collation.[3] Originally every church was either presentative, collative, donative, or elective.[4] However donative churches and benefices, which were filled by a donation thereof to a clerk by the patron without recourse to a bishop,[5] have since 1st January 1899 all become presentative.[6] In the case of an elective church the elected clerk is presented to the bishop.[7] The right to fill a church and benefice by presentation or collection is called an advowson or right of patronage and the owner of it is called the patron.[8]

As a general rule the right of presentation to a benefice in the established church is vested in the bishop of the relevant diocese[9] or in the patron of the particular church.[10]

Where the power of presenting to a benefice was formerly vested in the vestry of the parish, including the case where it was vested in or in trust for the parishioners the power is now in the parochial church council.[11] There is some doubt whether this is so where the advowson is vested in, or in trust for "parishioners" in a sense which is not synonymous with "the vestry". If this doubt is well founded then it is still the law that where an advowson is held in trust

---

1 (1849) 1 Mac. & G. 473.
2 *A.-G.* v. *Stephens* (1737), 1 Atk. 358.
3 Co. Litt. 119b.
4 *Ibid.*
5 Co. Litt. 344a.
6 Benefices Act 1898, s. 12.
7 *A.-G.* v. *Rutter* (1768), 2 Russ. 101, n. at 104, n. *Faulkner* v. *Elger* (1825), 4 B. & C. 449, at 450; *Edenborough* v. *Archbishop of Canterbury* (1826), 2 Russ. 93, at 104; *Carter* v. *Cropley* (1857), 8 De G.M. & G. 680, at 690.
8 Co. Litt. 119b.
9 *A.-G.* v. *Scott* (1750), 1 Ves. Sen 412.
10 *Herbert* v. *Dean and Chapter of Westminster* (1721), 1 P. Wms. 773.
11 Parochial Church Council (Powers) Measure 1956, s. 4 (1) (1); *Re Lichfield Cathedral Grant* (1929), 45 T.L.R. 583.

for the inhabitants and parishioners of a particular place the majority of the electors are entitled to *nominate* the person and the trustees must present the nominee of the majority of the electors[1] if on other grounds the election is valid.[2] Where the right of election is vested in the "inhabitants and parishioners" the electors must be persons satisfying both descriptions;[3] usage is often referred to for determining the persons entitled to vote[4] and whether they must be rate-payers.[5] Where the voters must be ratepayers, only those who have already paid may vote.[6]

The proper remedy for the case where trustees refuse to present is not *mandamus*, but an action for breach of trust.[7] The presentation of a minister who has been improperly elected may be restrained by injunction.[8] Lord ELDON was of the view that Jews but not Roman Catholics were entitled to vote at an election of a vicar by parishioners.[9] This rule still debars Roman Catholics from voting at such an election.[10]

Inhabitants and parishioners who have the right of nominating a minister may by common consent bind themselves to a particular mode of election, even though it differs from an already long established mode.[11] Lord ELDON held in one case that a ballot was not a suitable way to choose a vicar: he thought such elections should be by open poll.[12] A similar view found favour in *Faulkner* v. *Elger*[13] where the election of a curate was in issue. However a parish does have power to resolve that an election should be by ballot and to decide upon other matters touching on the mode of an election such as where and during what hours polling shall take place;[14] and the principle of the secret ballot with scrutineers is the rule nowadays. But voting by proxy is not allowed, unless authorised by the trust deed, even though proxies may sign the presentation.[15]

Irregular or even illegal conduct at a meeting to decide upon the method of election will not render the subsequent election invalid if there is no evidence of any voter having been deprived of the opportunity of voting.[16] The over-riding question is whether the election itself is substantially fair: if so it will not be disturbed.[17]

---

1 *A.-G.* v. *Parker* (1747), 3 Atk. 576; *Fearon* v. *Webb* (1802), 14 Ves. 13; *A.-G.* v. *Rutter* (1768), 2 Russ. 101, n.; *Edenborough* v. *Archbishop of Canterbury* (1826), 2 Russ. 93, at 104–105.
2 *A.-G.* v. *Cuming* (1843), 2 Y. & C. Ch. Cas. 139, at 151.
3 See 178, *supra.*
4 *Ibid.*
5 *Ibid.*
6 *Ibid.*
7 *R.* v. *Orton Vicarage Trustees* (1849), 14 Q.B. 139. A dispute between patron and bishop will be dealt with by an action of *quare impedit*: Benifices Act 1898, s. 3 (1).
8 *Carter* v. *Cropley* (1857), 26 L.J. Ch. 246, at 256; see also *A.-G.* v. *Forster* (1804), 10 Ves. 335, at 341; *A.-G.* v. *Earl of Powis* (1853), Kay 186 at 230 (master was not "fit and proper" person).
9 *Edenborough* v. *Archbishop of Canterbury* (1826), 2 Russ. 93, at 111, n.
10 Roman Catholic Relief Act 1926, s. 3.
11 *Davies* v. *Banks* (1836), 5 L.J. Ch. 274; *Shaw* v. *Thompson* (1876), 3 Ch. D. 233.
12 *Edenborough* v. *Archbishop of Canterbury* (1826), 2 Russ. 93.
13 (1825) 4 B. & C. 449.
14 *Davies* v. *Banks* (1836), 5 L.J. Ch. 274.
15 *Wilson* v. *Dennison* (1750), Amb. 82, at 87 also reported *sub. nom. A.-G.* v. *Scott* (1750), 1 Ves. Sen. 413.
16 *Shaw* v. *Thompson* (1876), 3 Ch.D. 233 (ruling of chairman contrary to resolution of meeting).
17 *Ibid.*, at 251; and see *R.* v. *Rector of Lambeth* (1838), 3 Nev. & P.K.B. 416.

If an advowson is given to trustees for the benefit of a charity[1] or if the trustees are to present a clergyman elected by the parishioners or some other class of persons[2] or a clergyman holding special opinions in the interests of a particular school of thought in the Church[3] the trust of the advowson is a charitable trust.

In the absence of any provision to the contrary all the trustees must present.[4] Yet a presentation will be upheld where one trustee dissents[5] or is incapable of consenting[6] so long as all those capable of acting have been consulted. In the case of a corporation the majority may select the presentee without using the corporate seal.[7] A power for a majority of the trustees to present may be contained in the instrument creating or regulating the trust,[8] and this of course will displace the general rule that all trustees must present. In the absence of any provision to the contrary in the trust instrument the survivors or survivor of the trustees may present.[9] The number of trustees ought, however, to be kept up.[10]

There is no "failure" on the part of trustees to appoint where there are no willing appointees.[11]

The presentation of a minister who has been improperly elected may be restrained by injunction.[12] Where, however, trustees refuse to present the proper remedy is either *quare impedit* or in equity depending on whether the right of the plaintiff is a legal or an equitable right: *mandamus* is not the proper remedy to seek and will not lie.[13]

Other religious ministers

APPOINTMENT

The appointment or election of a non-conformist minister to a particular pastorate and his tenure of that pastorate are dependent upon the terms of the trust, if any, by which the pastorate is maintained.[14] If there is no trust deed, or if the trust deed is silent on these matters regard may be had, in a proper case, to the usage of the religious body in question.[15] Where necessary an inquiry into such

---

1 *A.-G.* v. *Ward* (1829), 7 L.J.O.S. Ch. 114; *Re Shrewsbury School* (1836), 1 My . & Cr. 632.

2 *Re St. Stephen, Coleman Street, Re St. Mary Aldermanbury* (1888), 39 Ch.D. 492.

3 *Re Hunter*, [1897] 2 Ch. 105, C.A. (revsd. on other grounds *sub. nom. Hunter* v. *A.-G.*, [1899] A.C. 309, H.L.); *Re Church Patronage Trust*, [1904] 1 Ch. 41; affd., [1904] 2 Ch. 643, at 652, 654, 655, C.A.

4 *A.-G.* v. *Scott* (1750), 1 Ves. Sen. 413; and see *Seymour* v. *Bennet* (1742), 2 Atk. 482, at 483.

5 *A.-G.* v. *Cuming* (1843), 2 Y. & C. Ch. Cas. 139.

6 *A.-G.* v. *Lawson* (1866), 36 L.J. Ch. 130, especially at 134, *per* KINDERSLEY V.-C.

7 *A.-G.* v. *Davy* (1741), 2 Atk. 212. The presentation ought to be made under the common seal: Bro. Abr., Corporation (83).

8 *Foley* v. *A.-G.* (1721), 7 Bro. Parl. Cas. 249, at 254.

9 *A.-G.* v. *Bishop of Litchfield* (1801), 5 Ves. 825 (surviving trustee's heir); *A.-G.* v. *Lawson* (1866), 36 L.J. Ch. 130.

10 *A.-G.* v. *Bishop of Litchfield* (1801), 5 Ves. 825; *Davis* v. *Jenkins* (1814), 3 Ves. & B. 151, at 159.

11 *Hopper* v. *St. John's College, Cambridge* (1914), 31 T.L.R. 139.

12 *Carter* v. *Cropley* (1857), 26 L.J. Ch. 246, at 256; see also *A.-G.* v. *Forster* (1804), 10 Ves. 335, at 341; *A.-G.* v. *Earl of Powis* (1853), Kay 186, at 230.

13 *R.* v. *Orton Vicarage Trustees* (1849), 14 Q.B. 139.

14 *A.-G.* v. *Pearson* (1817), 3 Mer. 353; *Perry* v. *Shipway* (1859), 4 De G. & J. 353.

15 *A.-G.* v. *Pearson* (1817), 3 Mer. 353.

N

usage may be ordered.[1] But even then the usage is not conclusive of the matter.[2]

Where the appointment is vested in trustees an election by the majority of them[3] or by a majority of the survivors[4] is valid. On the death of the last surviving trustee the duties of the office do not devolve on his personal representatives, and if there is no provision for the creation of fresh trustees, an inquiry must be held as to the proper method of appointing them.[5]

If the pastorate is supported wholly by voluntary contributions the right of appointing a minister, where there is no provision to the contrary, is in the congregation.[6] In such a case, in true democratic tradition, the will of the majority of the congregation prevails.[7] And should there be any doubt as to what persons are entitled to participate in the election as members of the congregation, reference must be made to the facts of the particular case, including the rules (if any) of the religious body in question. Thus in *Leslie v. Birnic*[8] where a meeting house of the Church of Scotland was held in trust for the congregation it was held that persons merely occupying seats or pews, although in one sense members of the congregation, were rightly excluded from voting at the election of a minister because they were not members of the church in the sense of communicants.

The mode of election, where merely customary and not prescribed may be changed, if the change is agreed to by all the candidates and approved by a resolution passed at a public meeting of those entitled to vote.[9] Where the congregation is entitled to elect, an election of a minister is invalid if due notice of the meeting to elect is not given or if the electors are not confined to members of the congregation.[10]

The usual method for determining the validity of an election to an office of a public character is an application for an order of *mandamus*,[11] and where there are insufficient grounds to justify a *mandamus*, the court may entertain a suit to establish the right to elect.[12] Pending a decision as to the validity of his appointment a minister will generally be permitted to officiate, and is entitled to be paid his salary while continuing to do so.[13] But if he is not acting properly he will be restrained from officiating at all.[14]

---

1 *Davis v. Jenkins* (1814), 3 Ves. & B. 151; *A.-G. v. Pearson* (1817), 3 Mer. 353.

2 *A.-G. v. Pearson* (1817), 3 Mer. 353, at 403.

3 *A.-G. v. Lawson* (1866), 36 L.J. Ch. 130.

4 *Ibid.*

5 *Davis v. Jenkins* (1814), 3 Ves. & B. 151.

6 *Porter v. Clarke* (1829), 2 Sim. 520.

7 *Ibid.* Likewise where the right is expressly vested in the congregation: *Davis v. Jenkins* (1814), 3 Ves. & B. 151, at 155.

8 (1826), 2 Russ. 114.

9 See *Davies v. Banks* (1836), 5 L.J. Ch. 274. *Cf. A.-G. v. Aked* (1835), 7 Sim. 321.

10 *Perry v. Shipway* (1859), 28 L.J. Ch. 660, at 666; see also *R. v. Dagger Lane Chapel Trustees* (1804), 2 Smith K.B. 20.

11 *Davis v. Jenkins* (1814), 3 Ves. & B. 151; *cf. R. v. Barker* (1762), 1 Wm. Bl. 300 at 352. As to *mandamus*, see R.S.C. Ord. 53.

12 *Davis v. Jenkins* (1814), 3 Ves. & B. 151.

13 *Foley v. Wontner* (1820), 2 Jac. & W. 245.

14 *Perry v. Shipway* (1859), 4 De G. & J. 353; *Broom v. Summers* (1840), 11 Sim. 353; *A.-G. v. Welsh* (1844), 4 Hare 572.

QUALIFICATION AND TENURE

The eligibility of a particular condidate for a particular pastorate is determined on general principles by reference to the terms of the relevant trust deed and by his acceptance of the tenets of the sect in question.[1]

If membership of or communion with a specified religious body is a condition precedent to the holding of pastorate, one who by his opinions or actions disavows such membership or communion is absolutely disqualified.[2] An injunction to restrain trustees from electing such a person will, if necessary, be granted.[3] If a minister, who is already in office, has ceased to hold the tenets of the congregation for which the chapel was founded he will be removed.[4] And trustees who are parties to an attempt by a minister to retain his office despite his apostasy may also be removed.[5] An injunction to restrain such a minister from officiating[6] or remaining in possession of[7] the chapel or meeting house may be granted.

Unlike a beneficed minister of the Church of England who has a life interest in his office,[8] a non-conformist minister, in the absence of a special usage or agreement between the parties, holds his office at the will of the persons who appointed him.[9]

On the other hand, the minister may under the provisions of the trust deed,[10] or in the absence of express provision, according to usage,[11] be appointed for limited periods.[12] Where usage or express provisions show that the appointment is for life the appointment is nevertheless terminable on grounds of misconduct.[13] In other cases where the trust deed or usage provide no guidance, the minister's tenure of the buildings (whether chapel or minister's dwelling house) is at will and may therefore be terminated on demand;[14] in such a case the minister is not even entitled to receive notice or time in which to remove his goods, although if he returns merely to remove his goods and with no attempt to exclude the owners of the premises he would probably not be regarded as a trespasser.[15]

---

1 *Milligan* v. *Mitchell* (1833), 1 My. & K. 446.

2 *A.-G.* v. *Murdoch* (1852), 1 De G.M. & G. 86.

3 *Milligan* v. *Mitchell* (1833), 1 My. & K. 446.

4 *A.-G.* v. *Murdoch* (1852), 1 De G.M. & G. 86; *A.-G.* v. *Munro* (1848), 2 De G. & Sm.

5 *A.-G.* v. *Murdoch* (1852), 1 De G.M. & G. 86.

6 *A.-G.* v. *Welsh* (1844), 4 Hare 572.

7 *Broom* v. *Summers* (1841), 11 Sim. 353.

8 Such a life interest is dictated by public policy.

9 *A.-G.* v. *Pearson* (1817), 3 Mer. 353; *Porter* v. *Clarke* (1829), 2 Sim. 520; *Doe d. Jones* v. *Jones* (1830), 10 B. & C. 718; *Doe d. Nicholl* v. *M'Kaeg* (1830), 10 B. & C. 721; *Perry* v. *Shipway* (1859), 4 De G. & J. 353; *Cooper* v. *Gordon* (1869), L.R. 8 Eq. 249.

10 *Perry* v. *Shipway* (1859), 4 De G. & J. 353; *Dean* v. *Bennett* (1870), 6 Ch. App. 489.

11 *A.-G.* v. *Pearson* (1817), 3 Mer. 353, at 412–413, 420; *A.-G.* v. *Aked* (1835), 7 Sim. 321.

12 *A.-G.* v. *Pearson, supra*, at 413; *Porter* v. *Clarke* (1829), 2 Sim. 520; *Cooper* v. *Gordon* (1869), L.R. 8 Eq. 249, at 258–259.

13 Cru. Dig. xxv, pl. 28.

14 *Doe d. Jones* v. *Jones* (1830), 10 B. & C. 718. A resolution calling on a minister to resign may be equivalent to dismissal: *A.-G.* v. *Aked* (1835), 7 Sim. 321.

15 *Doe d. Nicholl* v. *M'Kaeg* (1830), 10 B. & C. 721.

DISMISSAL

Where the constitution of the religious body to which the pastorate is attached provides for a method of procedure in the dismissal of a minister, that procedure must be followed.[1] In the absence of any usage or agreement, it is not necessary upon dismissing a minister that any grounds should be alleged.[2] But this does not mean that the power of dismissal can be exercised unjustly or oppressively.[3] The case of *Dean* v. *Bennett*[4] is instructive.

Where a minister has been dismissed and wishes to contest the validity of his dismissal, the proper remedy is an action to recover the profits of the office.[5] A mandamus to restore him will not be granted except upon clear *prima facie* evidence of his right.[6]

Masters of endowed schools

It is beyond the scope of this work to discuss the rights and remedies of school-masters generally. This discussion which follows is concerned solely with schoolmasters of charitable foundations.

A schoolmaster of a charitable foundation may, in addition to his rights at common law, have rights and remedies in equity as an officer of a charity. In practice the relevant rules of equity governing his rights and remedies are to some extent displaced by the exercise of the statutory jurisdiction of the Charity Commissioners. But the primary rule is, of course, that the status of a school-master who is an officer of a charity depends upon the constitutional document of the charity itself. One goes to the relevant foundation or trust deed or scheme or whatever.

APPOINTMENT TO OFFICE

In appointing or selecting schoolmasters for endowed schools one should first consult the relevant instrument of foundation or scheme to see if any particular mode of appointment or selection is prescribed;[7] if so it should be followed and must result in the appointment of a person qualified under the trusts.[8] If the founder of a school makes no express provisions as to appointment or selection and does not appoint a visitor, he and his heirs, as patrons, are entitled to appoint the schoolmaster. Where trustees appoint, a majority may make the appoint-ment.

---

1 *Dr. Warren's Case* (1835), Grindrod's *Compendium* (8th edn.) 371; *cf. Long* v. *Bishop of Cape Town* (1863), 1 Moo. P.C. C.N.S. 411.
2 *Cooper* v. *Gordon* (1869), L.R. 8 Eq. 249.
3 *Dean* v. *Bennett* (1870), 6 Ch. App. 489; and see *Daugars* v. *Rivaz* (1860), 28 Beav. 233.
4 (1870), 6 Ch. App. 489.
5 *R.* v. *Jotham* (1790), 3 Term Rep. 575; *Daugars* v. *Rivaz* (1860), 28 Beav. 233.
6 *R.* v. *Jotham* (1790), 3 Term Rep. 575; and see *R.* v. *Trustees of Dagger Lane Chapel* (1804), 2 Smith 20.
7 *A.-G.* v. *Carrington* (1850), 4 De G. & Sm. 140.
8 *A.-G.* v. *Wyeliffe* (1748), 1 Ves. Sen. 80.

QUALIFICATION AND TENURE

A person to be elected schoolmaster must possess the qualifications laid down in the relevant trust document. If a master is required to be in priest's orders this requirement must be satisfied.[1] The schoolmaster of a Church of England school should be a member of that church, but this is not indispensable; the appointment of a non-conformist or a Roman Catholic would not be a breach of trust if the circumstances are sufficiently peculiar to justify it.[2]

Where the election of a schoolmaster is subject to the consent and overriding veto of a particular person, that person cannot himself hold the office and, if appointed, will be removed by the court.[3]

The tenure of a schoolmaster's office is also primarily dependent upon the constitution of the charity itself.

The schoolmaster of a charitable foundation may, according to the terms of the trust, be appointed for life. So in *Re Chipping Sodbury Grammar School*[4] it was held that the master of a free school had an estate of freehold in his office and was not removable at the pleasure of the patrons of the school. On the other hand in *R. v. Darlington School (Governors)*[5] the relevant charter of foundation empowered the governors to appoint and remove the upper master of a grammar school "according to their sound discretion" and this was held to make the master's office *ad libitum* only: he could be dismissed at pleasure. In yet another case[6] the trusts declared that the particular schoolmaster's tenure of office should last so long as he should well conduct himself and be competent in his duties. And a master may even take office subject to any future alterations to be directed by the court.[7]

REMOVAL

The right to dismiss a schoolmaster of a charitable foundation is also subject to the trusts and must be exercised in the due form (if any) prescribed by the constitution of the charity.[8]

If the master in question is appointed to hold office during pleasure the trustees may at any time remove him at their discretion so long as they do not act from corrupt or improper motives[9] and there is no need for them to give reasons for his removal.[10] But no matter how arbitrary the power of removal may be it must not be exercised oppressively or unjustly, but in a *bona fide* way, and the grounds, if stated, should be reasonable.[11]

---

1 *A.-G.* v. *Wycliffe* (1748), 1 Ves. Sen. 80.

2 *A.-G.* v. *Clifton* (1863), 32 Beav. 596, at 601. *Secus* if there is an express prohibition as for example in the Public School Act 1868.

3 *Re Risley School* (1830), 8 L.J.O.S. Ch. 129.

4 (1829) 8 L.J.O.S. 13.

5 (1844) 6 Q.B. 682.

6 *Re Phillips' Charity* (1845), 9 J.P. 741.

7 *A.-G.* v. *Louth Free School (Warden, etc.)* (1851), 14 Beav. 201.

8 *Re Alleyn's College, Dulwich* (1875), 1 App Cas. 68; *Lane* v. *Norman* (1891), 61 L.J. Ch. 149; and see *Willis* v. *Childe* (1851), 13 Beav. 117.

9 *Re Buxton School* (1847), 8 L.T.O.S. 464.

10 *Ibid.; R.* v. *Darlington School Governors* (1844), 6 Q.B. 682; *Dean* v. *Bennett* (1871), 6 Ch. 489, at 494–495.

11 *Re Fremington School* (1847), 9 L.T.O.S. 333.

Misconduct,[1] neglect of scholars,[2] neglect of prescribed duties,[3] or the holding of another office incompatible with, or involving neglect of his duties,[4] may be good grounds for dismissing a schoolmaster.

Where misconduct is put forward as a ground for removal of a schoolmaster the trustees must in the first instance reduce the charges made against him into writing and cause such charges to be communicated to him in order that he may meet them (if he is able) by evidence or otherwise.[5] An opportunity for defence must be afforded.[6] But once this has been done and the trustees have come to their conclusion upon legitimate materials which might possibly have satisfied a reasonable man intent on doing justice the court will not interfere.[7]

Everyone entitled to attend the relevant meeting should be summoned to it, notwithstanding that the decision to dismiss can be taken by a prescribed number of persons.[8] A majority of those present can dismiss subject to the views of the minority being heard.[9]

An irregularly appointed or properly dismissed schoolmaster may be retrained by injunction from intermeddling with the school or retaining possession of the schoolhouse.[10] On the other hand, if he is improperly removed the trustees may be restrained by injunction from enforcing his dismissal and ejecting him.[11] The consent and certificate of the Secretary of State is[12] not required for these proceedings.[13]

The court may also make a declaration that an appointment or a removal was void.[14] Thus in *Dummer* v. *Chippenham Corporation*[15] a schoolmaster was removed because he had voted for a particular candidate at a parliamentary election and the court declared his removal to be void.

Where a considerable time has elapsed since an invalid appointment and the schoolmaster has acted undisturbed he will only be removed if he has been guilty of misconduct.[16]

Lastly it should be remembered that where a visitatorial jurisdiction exists,[17] the court will not interfere to try the master's right to his office[18] unless there is

---

1 *Re Phillips' Charity* (1845), 9 J.P. 741.

2 *Doe d. Coyle* v. *Cole* (1834), 6 C. & P. 359.

3 *A.-G.* v. *Coopers' Co.* (1812) 19 Ves. 187. But the mere *misunderstanding* of duties is no reason for dismissal: *ibid.* at 192.

4 *A.-G.* v. *Hartley* (1820), 2 Jac. & W. 353.

5 *Re Phillips' Charity* (1845), 9 J.P. 741. The charges should be reduced to a precise form: *Fisher* v. *Jackson*, [1891] 2 Ch. 84.

6 *Doe d. Earl of Thanet* v. *Gartham* (1823), 8 Moore C.P. 368; *Lane* v. *Norman* (1891), 61 L.J. Ch. 149; *Fisher* v. *Jackson*, [1891] 2 Ch. 84.

7 *Re Fremington School* (1847), 9 L.T.O.S. 333.

8 *Fisher* v. *Jackson* [1891] 2 Ch. 84 at 101.

9 *Ibid.*, at 94.

10 *Holme* v. *Guy* (1877), 5 Ch.D. 90, C.A. Ejectment will not be until his interest therein is determined: *Doe d. Earl of Thanet* v. *Gartham* (1823), 8 Moore C.P. 368.

11 *Willis* v. *Childe* (1851), 13 Beav. 117; *Daugars* v. *Rivaz* (1860) 28 Beav. 233; *Benthall* v. *Earl of Kilmorey* (1883), 25 Ch.D. 39, C.A.; *Lane* v. *Norman* (1891), 61 L.J. Ch. 149.

12 See C.A. 1960, s. 28 replacing Charitable Trusts Act 1853, s. 17.

13 *Rendall* v. *Blair* (1890), 45 Ch.D. 139 at 156, C.A.; *Rooke* v. *Dawson*, [1895] 1 Ch. 480 (actions by master); *Holme* v. *Guy* (1877), 5 Ch.D. 90.

14 *A.-G.* v. *Carrington* (1850), 4 De G. & Sm. 140.

15 (1808), 14 Ves. 245.

16 See *A.-G.* v. *Hartley* (1820), 2 Jac. & W. 353, at 375, *per* Lord ELDON L.C.

17 Even where reserved to the Commissioners: see *R.* v. *Wilson*, [1888] W.N. 12.

18 *A.-G.* v. *Magdalen College, Oxford* (1847), 10 Beav. 402; *Whiston* v. *Dean and Chapter of Rochester* (1849), 7 Hare 532; *Willis* v. *Childe* (1851), 13 Beav. 117.

an express trust in which case the court is concerned to see that the trusts are properly executed.[1]

Headmaster and masters under the Public Schools Act 1868

Under the Public Schools Act 1868 the headmaster of each of the seven-named schools[2] is appointed by, and holds his office at the pleasure of, the respective governing body. He is liable to be dismissed without notice and without any reason being assigned.[3] In explanation of this statutory provision MALINS V.-C. in *Hayman* v. *Rugby School Governors*[4] said:

"The probable intention of the legislature in making such a provision was to avoid such contests as have so frequently occurred in the Chancery Court and the Court of Queen's Bench as to the power of trustees to remove the masters of schools. The apparent harshness of the power is mitigated by the appointment of men of high position, honour and integrity as members of the governing body, by whom it is assumed that such power, arbitrary as it is in terms, would be not harshly, unjustly, or inconsiderately exercised."

In *Hayman's* case the plaintiff, Dr. Hayman, gave up his appointment as headmaster of Bradfield College to become headmaster of Rugby. Within ten days of his appointment he received a "letter of remonstrance" signed by 20 of the 21 assistant masters and making various allegations against him. These allegations were dismissed by the trustees who had appointed him, but nevertheless it was plain that the plaintiff never had a chance of success in his post, and after three more years of misunderstanding and dissension the new governing body, constituted pursuant to the Public Schools Act 1868, dismissed him. The Vice-Chancellor held that although the plaintiff had been appointed by the old trustees in 1869, the new governing body were not bound by the rules and regulations in force prior to their appointment: their power of dismissal was conferred by the 1868 Act. Whether the headmaster should be dismissed was, according to the learned Vice-Chancellor, a decision which the legislature had left to the governing body, and with which the court should not interfere unless it was arrived at for some corrupt, improper or collateral object. The effect of the section is that[5]

"every headmaster is as much at the mercy of the governing body as a coachman is at the mercy of his master; and can be dismissed with or without reason; they are not obliged to give any reason whatever, and the court must presume that they exercise their discretion properly unless the contrary can be shown".

All other masters are appointed by and hold their offices during the pleasure of the headmaster.[6] No candidate for any mastership shall be entitled to preference by reason of his having been a scholar of or educated at the school of which he desires to be master.[7]

---

1 *Daugars* v. *Rivaz* (1859), 28 Beav. 233.
2 See at 222, footnote 6.
3 Public Schools Act 1868, s. 13.
4 (1874), L.R. 18 Eq. 28, at 68.
5 *Ibid.*, at 87.
6 Public Schools Act 1868, s. 13.
7 *Ibid.*

Other officers

The mastership or presidency of a hospital is an office the tenure of, and election to, which is governed by the instrument of foundation or, where there is no relevant statute, by usage.[1] It appears that, as a matter of principle, a mastership cannot be granted in reversion.[2] The position of pensioner within a hospital is such that the court will not scrutinise the reasons for the removal of a pensioner with the same nicety as if he was being turned out of a freehold: it is much less prejudicial to the foundation to have a pensioner turned out wrongfully than that the trustees and governors should be perpetually liable to have every action of theirs sifted and examined.[3]

A person holding the office of lecturer in a parish church is validly removed and replaced where he has got into debt and absconded abroad.[4]

The clerk to the charity does not have a freehold office but one that is tenable only at the pleasure of the trustees, and if they purport to create a freehold office for him they act in breach of their trust.[5]

Where the right of appeal in respect of a removal from office is to the visitor the complainant who has omitted to make such an appeal cannot invite the court to grant a *mandamus*.[6] The omission to set out the cause of removal in the original decree is not improper: it is permissible and may be desirable.[7]

Removal of officers under the Charities Act 1960

Two provisions of the Charities Act 1960 touch on the jurisdiction of the Commissioners to remove officers or servants of charities.

The Commissioners are empowered to exercise by order the same jurisdiction and powers as are exercisable by the High Court in charity proceedings for the purpose of removing an officer or servant of a charity.[8]

Again where the Commissioners carry out an inquiry instituted by them under section 6 of the Charities Act 1960 and are satisfied that there has been in the administration of a charity some misconduct or mismanagement and that it is necessary or desirable to act for the purpose of protecting the property of the charity of securing a proper application for the purposes of the charity of that property or of property coming to the charity, they may by order remove any officer agent of servant of the charity who has been responsible for or privy to the misconduct or mismanagement or has by his conduct contributed to it or facilitated it.[9]

---

1 *R. v. St. Bartholomew's Hospital Treasurer* (1866), 31 J.P. 277 where usage did not limit express provisions in early ordinances or a later statute.
2 *Viscount Brunker v. Atkins* (1681), T. Jo. 176.
3 *A.-G. v. Lock* (1744), 3 Atk. 164.
4 *Philips v. Walter* (1720), 2 Bro. Parl. Cas. 250.
5 *Re St. Edmund the King and Martyr* (1889), 60 L.T. 622.
6 *R. v. Dean and Chapter of Chester* (1850), 15 Q.B. 513.
7 *Ibid.*
8 CA 1960, s. 18 (1) (b).
9 *Ibid.*, s. 20 (1) (i).

Chapter 33

Capacity for Trusteeship

As a general rule any person (including in that term any corporation) who has the capacity to be trustee of a private trust may be trustee of a charitable trust. In England an infant or minor cannot be a trustee of any property[1]; and the court will on application made to it appoint a new trustee in place of a minor trustee.[2]

At one time it was thought that a corporation aggregate could not be a trustee because it had no soul and therefore no confidence could be reposed in it.[3] But the capacity of corporations to act as trustees was stated by Lord HARDWICKE L.C. to be quite clear: "undoubtedly corporations may be trustees".[4] This position is recognised in a large number of cases after the Statute of Elizabeth I where devises to corporations for a charitable use were held to be within the relief intended by that statute,[5] including devises to colleges[6] hospitals[7] and to a missionary society incorporated by charter.[8]

At common law a corporation is unable to hold property in joint tenancy and therefore is unable to act as a trustee together with another corporation or with an individual or individuals. This inconvenient inability has been dealt with by statute, which has provided that a corporation may acquire and hold any property in joint tenancy in the same manner as if it were an individual.[9]

An eleemosynary corporation is entitled to hold property in trust for its general purposes whether the members participate in the charity or not.[10] Such corporations may also accept property on special trusts connected with the objects of their foundation. Colleges, for example, may accept trusts for additional fellowships[11] or for scholarships or prizes[12] or for the maintenance of

---

1 Law of Property Act 1925, s. 20.
2 *Re Shelmerdine* (1864), 33 L.J. Ch. 474; *Re Gartside Estate* (1853), 1 W.R. 196.
3 1 *Kyd on Corporations* (1793) 72.
4 *A.-G.* v. *Landerfield* (1743), 9 Mod. Rep. 286.
5 *Flood's Case* (1616), Hob. 136; *A.-G.* v. *Tancred* (1757), 1 Eden 10, at 14; *A.-G.* v. *Brentwood School* (1833), 1 My. & K. 376, at 390; *A.-G.* v. *Liverpool Corporation* (1835), 1 My. & Cr. 171, at 201; *Incorporated Society* v. *Richards* (1841), 1 Dr. & War. 258, at 302, 303, 307, 331.
6 *Bene't (or Corpus Christi) College, Cambridge* v. *Bishop of London* (1778), 2 Wm. Bl. 1182.
7 *A.-G.* v. *Landerfield* (1743), 9 Mod. Rep. 286.
8 *Society for the Propagation of the Gospel* v. *A.-G.* (1826), 3 Russ. 142.
9 Bodies Corporate (Joint Tenancy) Act 1899; and see *Re Thompson's Settlement Trusts*, [1905] 1 Ch. 229.
10 *Lydiatt* v. *Foach* (1700), 2 Vern. 410, at 412.
11 *A.-G.* v. *Talbot* (1748), 3 Atk. 662; *A.-G.* v. *Whorwood* (1750), 1 Ves. Sen. 534, at 537; *A.-G.* v. *Flood* (1816), Hayes & Jo. Appendix xxi, xxxv; *Re Catherine Hall, Ex parte Inge* (1831), 2 Russ. & M. 590, at 596. Lord ELDON L.C. doubted whether a college could accept

schools connected with the foundation,[1] or for presentation of a living connected with the foundation.[2] It has been asserted in two works[3] that an eleemosynary corporation cannot accept a trust for purposes inconsistent with its original foundation. The authorities cited in support of this assertion[4] do not, however, seem to sustain it.

As Shelford points out some corporations have a corporate capacity for some particular purpose only; and he instanced the parson of a church who was a corporation for taking land but not goods for the benefit of the church, and churchwardens who were a corporation for taking goods but not land for the use of the church.[5] Certainly a corporation created by or under statute[6] or otherwise[7] for a particular purpose has no capacity beyond the object for which it was created and so cannot be trustee of charitable trusts except where such a function falls within its statutory authority. Local authorities may not, in the absence of special statutory powers,[8] act as trustees for an ecclesiastical charity or a charity for the relief of poverty.[9] This statutory incapacity will not necessarily frustrate gifts to local authorities for such purposes; such gifts will be applied by way of scheme unless the trusteeship of the local authority was of the essence of the gift.[10] On the other hand local authorities are at liberty to hold property on special trusts falling outside the provisions of the Local Government Act 1972 as for example on trust for the benefit of borough freemen.[11] While the statutory functions of local education authorities do not give them *ipso facto* an interest in the establishment of independent educational charities in their areas[12] a local education authority may be constituted trustee for any educational endowment or charity for purposes connected with education.[13]

In some cases a corporation sole may hold property on trust for charitable purposes. Corporations sole were originally ecclesiastical for the most part but they have never been confined to that class and today there are many examples of lay corporations sole. As has already been mentioned the Chamberlain of the

---

an addition to its foundation without the consent of the visitor: *A.-G.* v. *Catherine Hall, Cambridge* (1820), Jac. 381.

12 *A.-G.* v. *Talbot* (1748), 3 Atk. 662.

1 *A.-G.* v. *Caius College* (1837), 2 Keen 150.

2 *Green* v. *Rutherforth* (1750), 1 Ves. Sen. 462, at 473.

3 See *Tudor on Charities* (6th edn.) 401; *Grant on Corporations* 109, 124; and see 4 *Halsbury's Laws of England* (3rd edn.) 364, *cf.* 5 *Halsbury's Laws of England* (4th edn.) 442.

4 *A.-G.* v. *Whorwood* (1750), 1 Ves. Sen. 534; *A.-G.* v. *Tancred* (1757), 1 Eden 10, at 15.

5 Shelford, *Law of Mortmain* (1836) 28. As to parsons and churchwardens see 332, *infra*.

6 See *National Guaranteed Manure Co.* v. *Donald* (1859), 4 H. & N. 8, at 16; *Putney Overseers* v. *London and South Western Rail Co.*, [1891] 1 Q.B. 440, at 441.

7 See *Incorporated Society* v. *Price* (1844), 1 Jo. & Lat. 498. The Chamberlain of the City of London is by custom a corporation sole for the purpose of taking recognisances, obligations, bonds etc. for the portions of orphans: *Grant on Corporations* 629; *Fulwood's Case* (1591), 4 Co. Rep. 64b, 65a; [1558–1774] All E.R. Rep. 277, at 278; *Byrd* v. *Wilford* (1596), Cro. Eliz. 464.

8 See e.g. the Norwich Corporation Act 1933, s. 115.

9 Local Government Act 1972, s. 139 (3). As to the law prior to 1st April 1974 see *Re Armitage*, [1972] Ch. 438.

10 *Re Woolnough's Will Trusts* (1959), *Times*, 22nd Oct. As to cases where the trusteeship is of the essence, see 280, *supra*.

11 *Goodman* v. *Saltash Corporation* (1882), 7 App. Cas. 633, H.L., *Prestney* v. *Colchester Corporation and A.-G.* (1882), 21 Ch.D. 111.

12 *Re Belling*, [1967] Ch. 425.

13 Education Act 1944, s. 85.

City of London is by custom a corporation sole for certain purposes.[1] So too is the Public Trustee[2] but the Public Trustee may not accept any trust for religious or charitable purposes[3] or involving the selection of charitable objects of a settlor's bounty.[4] The Official Custodian for Charities (also a corporation sole) has been constituted by statute to hold and transfer real and personal property.[5]

Charitable gifts are frequently made to the holders of religious offices for the advancement of religions and other charitable purposes. It is therefore important to distinguish which ecclesiastical persons are corporations sole, since in the case of a corporation sole the death of the individual who is the corporation sole makes no difference to the corporation which lives in the next office-holder.

The only ecclesiastics who are corporations sole are those from the Church of England. So, in descending order of rank, an archbishop,[6] a bishop[7] a prebendary or canon,[8] some deans,[9] an archdeacon,[10] a rector (or parson)[11], a vicar[12] and a vicar choral[13] are each a corporation sole. Rectors and vicars of new benefices created by pastoral schemes[14] are also corporations sole. On the other hand, a Roman Catholic bishop is not a corporation sole even in Ireland,[15] and the same applies to a non-conformist minister.[16]

Neither the principal of a college[17] nor the mayor or bailiff of a city[18] nor the officers of a corporate body[19] or their respective successors are recognised by the law as corporations; they cannot in consequence be trustees for charitable purposes in any corporate capacity, although the particular individuals named may act as trustees[20] and may apply for registration as a corporate body.[21]

A corporation sole has always been able to hold realty upon charitable trusts, as for example where a parson holds land on charitable trusts for the poor of the parish.[22] Such realty devolves automatically on the successor of the corporator sole. But, as a general rule, a corporation sole cannot, at common law, hold leaseholds or personal property in succession. Legislation was enacted in

---

1 *Fulwood's Case* (1591), 4 Co. Rep. 64b, 65a; [1558–1774] All E.R. Rep. 277, at 278.
2 Public Trustee Act 1906, s. 1 (2).
3 *Ibid.*, s. 2 (5).
4 *Re Hampton* (1918), 88 L.J. Ch. 103.
5 CA 1960, s.3. The office of Official Custodian is discussed at 359–361, *infra*.
6 1 Roll. Abr. 512.
7 Co. Litt. 250a.
8 *Mirehouse* v. *Rennell* (1833), 1 Cl. & Fin. 527, at 538, H.L.; Cathedrals Measure 1963, s. 15 (1).
9 But not all: 1 Bl. Com. (14th edn.) 470.
10 *Tufnell* v. *Constable* (1838), 7 Ad. & El. 798.
11 *Ibid.*
12 1 Bl. Com. (14th edn.) 457; Co. Litt. 250a. Perpetual curates are now termed vicars: Pastoral Measure 1968, s. 87.
13 *Gleaves* v. *Parfitt* (1860), 7 C.B.N.S. 838.
14 Pastoral Measure 1968, s. 22 (4).
15 *A.-G.* v. *Power* (1809), 1 Ball & B. 145, at 149; *Kehoe* v. *Marquess of Lansdowne*, [1893] A.C. 451, at 457; and see *In the Goods of Lalor* (1901), 85 L.T. 643.
16 *A.-G. for Ireland* v. *Lee* (1869), I.R. 4 Eq. 84.
17 *A.-G.* v. *Gilbert* (1847), 10 Beav. 517.
18 *Ibid.*
19 *A.-G.* v. *Tancred* (1757), 1 Eden 10, at 14.
20 See the cases cited in the four preceding footnotes.
21 See Charitable Trustees Incorporation Act 1872 discussed at 332, *infra*.
22 *Banister's Case* (1600); Duke, *Law of Charitable Uses* (1676) 133; *Grant on Corporations* 648.

England to deal with this difficulty. It is provided that where either after 1925 or before 1926 any property or any interest therein has been vested in a corporation sole (including the Crown) the same, unless and until otherwise disposed of by the corporation passes and devolves to and vests in and is deemed always to have passed and devolved to or vested in the successors from time to time of such corporation. The wording of the provisions was somewhat inapposite to deal with the common law position, since leases and personalty could not be *vested* in a corporation sole *as such*.

Churchwardens do not normally constitute a corporation in the strict legal sense. In some of the early cases instances occur of churchwardens being incorporated by letters patent[1] or by charter;[2] and by the custom of the City of London the parson and churchwardens may constitute a corporation to purchase and demise land.[3] The vicar and churchwardens of St. Martin-in-the-Fields are incorporated by private Act.[4]

Those cases apart, churchwardens have what Shelford calls a corporate capacity for some particular purpose only[5] but what may perhaps more accurately be described as a quasi-corporate capacity. This quasi-corporate capacity enables churchwardens to hold personalty[6] but not realty for church purposes.[7]

A local education authority may be constituted trustees for any educational endowment or charity for purposes connected with education.[8] But their statutory functions do not give them an automatic interest in the establishment of independent educational charities in their areas.[9]

Incorporation of trustees

Charity trustees are enabled by the Charitable Trustees Incorporation Act 1872 to turn themselves into an incorporated body. The virtue of such a transformation is that it secures the perpetual succession of the trustees and saves trouble and expense, especially where there are changes in the body of trustees. The necessity of reconveying real property or transferring new securities to new names every time there is a change of trustees is avoided by the incorporation.

Legal writers have commented that the 1872 Act has been largely neglected.[10] According to the Register kept by the Commissioners under the Act[11] 97

1 *Case of St. Saviour's, Southwark* (1606), Lane 21; 1 *Kyd on Corporations* (1793) 31.
2 *Ibid.* (parishioners of Wallingford).
3 *Evelin's Case* (1639), Cro. Car. 552; see also Shelford, *Law of Mortmain* (1836) 29; *Tudor on Charities* (4th edn.) 264, note (f.); *A.-G.* v. *Leage* (1881), W.N. 167 set out in *Tudor on Charities* (4th edn.) 1041; *Fell* v. *Official Trustees of Charity Lands*, [1898] 2 Ch. 44 at 51, C.A.
4 1 Anne, Sess. 2, c. xxi (1702).
5 Shelford, *Law of Mortmain* (1836) 28.
6 Shelford, *op. cit.*, 28; *A.-G.* v. *Ruper* (1722), 2 P. Wms. 125; and see *Tufnell* v. *Constable* (1838), 7 Ad. & E.. 798.
7 Shelford; *op. cit.*, 28; *A.-G.* v. *Ruper* (1722), 2 P. Wms. 125; *Gravenor* v. *Hallum* (1767), Amb. 643 at 644; *Withnell* v. *Gartham* (1795), 6 Term. Rep. 388, at 396.
8 Education Act 1944, s. 85.
9 *Re Belling*, [1967] Ch. 425.
10 G. N. Glover (1967) 64 L.S. Gaz 431; and see *Tudor on Charities* (4th edn.) 25 and 916 ("little used"); (6th edn.) 439 ("resorted to only infrequently"). The 5th and 6th editions of *Tudor* do not reproduce the Act.
11 See Charitable Trustee Incorporation Act 1872, s.7.

charities in all have been incorporated. Taking as a convenient dividing date 1st January 1960, which of course precedes the enactment of the Charities Act 1960, the Register discloses that 55 charities were incorporated prior to 1st January 1960 and 42 since that date.[1] It is true that many of the benefits of incorporation are equally secured by a vesting of the charity property in the Official Custodian for Charities. Even more convenient perhaps is incorporation under the Companies Act 1948.[2] And doubtless these alterations explain the less frequent use of the 1872 Act procedure. But there are some types of endowed charities for which the Official Custodian is not suitable, for example some non-conformist chapels,[3] Roman Catholic monastic or conventual orders[4] and synagogues.[5] For such charities, if there is no available trust corporation, it is better that individual believers should be trustees.

Trustees of parochial and diocesan charities

Before turning to the substantive effect of the statutory provisions relating to the trustees of parochial and diocesan charities it is necessary to have in mind two important statutory definitions namely the definition of "parochial charity" and the definition of "ecclesiastical charity", a charity of the latter kind being excluded from certain provisions of the Charities Act 1960 respecting parochial charities and being subject to special provisions under the Pastoral Measure 1968.

"Parochial charity" means in relation to any parish, a charity the benefits of which are, or the separate distribution of the benefits of which is, confined to inhabitants of the parish, or of a single ancient ecclesiastical parish which included that parish or part of it, or of an area consisting of that parish with not more than four neighbouring parishes.[6]

An "ecclesiastical charity" is defined[7] by reference to a definition in the Local Government Act 1894. The term therefore includes a charity the endowment of which is held for one or more of the following purposes: (1) for any spiritual purpose which is a legal purpose; (2) for the benefit of any spiritual person or ecclesiastical officer as such; (3) for use (if a building) as a church, chapel, mission room or Sunday school or otherwise[8] by any particular church or denomination,[9] and any building which in the Charity Commissioners' opinion has been erected or provided within 40 years before 5th March 1894 mainly by or at the cost of members of any particular church or denomination; (4) for the maintenance, repair or improvement of any such building or for the maintenance of divine service in it; (5) otherwise for the benefit of any particular church or denomination, or any of its members as such.[10] Where any endowment of a charity, other than a building held for any of the above purposes,

---

1 These figures reflect the position at 1st March 1977 when the Register was inspected.
2 Companies Act 1948, s. 19.
3 I.e., with no available trust corporation.
4 Most of the incorporated Roman Catholic charities are of this type.
5 The West London Synagogue has been incorporated under the 1872 Act.
6 CA 1960, s. 45 (1).
7 *Ibid.*
8 For example a synagogue, or Talmud Torah (Jewish Sunday School).
9 *Semble* "denomination" includes non–Christian sects.
10 Local Government Act 1894, s. 75 (2).

is held in part only for some of the above purposes the charity is an ecclesiastical charity so far as that endowment is concerned.[1] Accordingly the Charity Commissioners must, on application by any person interested, make such provision for the apportionment and management of that endowment as seems to them necessary or expedient for giving effect to the part that is an ecclesiastical charity.[2] There is authority that a charity may be an "ecclesiastical charity" if its benefits are confined to members of one particular church or denomination notwithstanding that the benefits are of a temporal rather than of a religious nature.[3]

The first statutory provision falling for consideration is one dealing with parochial recreation grounds and allotments. According to this provision where trustees hold any property for the purposes of a public recreation ground, or of allotments (whether under the Inclosure Acts or otherwise) for the benefit of the inhabitants of a parish[4] having a parish council, or for other charitable purposes connected with such a rural parish, except for an ecclesiastical charity,[5] they may, with the approval of the Charity Commissioners and the consent of the parish council, transfer the property to the parish council or to persons appointed by the parish council. The council in question or their appointees will then hold the property on the same trusts and subject to the same conditions as the trustees did.[6] This provision does not, however, affect the trusteeship, control or management of any voluntary school as defined in the Education Act 1944.[7]

Where the charity trustees of a parochial charity[8] in a parish or community[9] do not include persons elected by the local government electors, ratepayers or inhabitants of the parish or appointed by the parish council or parish meeting, the parish council or parish meeting may appoint additional charity trustees, to such number as the Charity Commissioners may allow.[10] If there is a sole trustee not so elected or appointed the number of trustees may, with the approval of the Charity Commissioners be increased to three, one of the new trustees being appointed by the person holding the office of sole trustee, and the other being appointed by the parish council or the parish meeting.[10] The provisions discussed in this paragraph do not affect the trusteeship, control or management of any voluntary school as defined in the Education Act 1944.[11] Again trustees appointed under these provisions hold office for four years and are eligible for re-appointment on retiring.[12] If no previous appointment has been made under these provisions or the corresponding provision of the Local Government Act 1894 and more than one trustee is appointed, half of those appointed (or as nearly as may be) must be appointed for a term of two years only, so as to avoid the retirement of all the appointed trustees at the same time

---

1 *Ibid.*, s. 75 (2), proviso.
2 Local Government Act 1894, s. 75 (2), proviso.
3 *Re Perry Almshouses, Re Ross' Charity*, [1899] 1 Ch. 21, C.A.
4 Or, in Wales, a community: Local Government Act 1972, s. 179 (4) substitutes the words "parish" and "community" for "rural parish".
5 For ecclesiastical charity, see *supra*.
6 CA 1960, s. 37 (1).
7 *Ibid.*, s. 37 (7).
8 See 333, *supra*.
9 Local Government Act 1972, s. 179 (4).
10 CA 1960, s. 37 (2).
11 *Ibid*, s. 37 (7).
12 *Ibid.*, s. 37 (6).

and to preserve continuity.[1] Appointments to fill casual vacancies are for the remainder of the term of the previous appointment.[2] The Nathan Committee thought it important that representatives of the parish council should serve on the board of trustees of parochial charities, but was not in favour of their constituting more than one-third of the board; the hope was ventured that this principle would be honoured wherever possible.[3]

Before the passing of the Local Government Act 1894, the inhabitants of a rural parish[4] or a select vestry were sometimes entitled to appoint charity trustees for, or trustees or beneficiaries of, the charity. In such a case, assuming always that the charity is not an ecclesiastical charity, where the parish has a parish council, the appointment must now be made by the parish council, and where the parish does not have a parish council, the appointment must be made by the parish meeting.[5] The reference to "parish"[6] and "parish council" must, in relation to Wales, be read as a reference to the relevant community and community council (if any);[7] in the absence of a community council the power of appointing trustees rests with the district council.[8]

In some cases, before the passing of the Local Government Act 1894 overseers or churchwardens were *ex officio* charity trustees of or trustees for parochial charities in rural parishes, alone or jointly with others. In any such case, except where the charity is an ecclesiastical charity, the former overseer or churchwarden trustees are replaced by trustees appointed by the parish council, or if there is no parish council, by the parish meeting, to a number not greater than that of the former overseer or churchwarden trustees.[9]

Where, outside the administrative county of London,[10] overseers of a parish were immediately prior to 1st April 1927[11] charity trustees of or trustees for any charity, alone or jointly, they are replaced by trustees numbering no more than former trustees who are appointed, in the case of a rural parish, by the parish council or, if there be none, by the parish meeting.[12] In the case of an urban parish outside the administrative county of London, if before 1st April 1927 overseers of a parish as such were charity trustees of or trustees for any charity, alone or jointly, then if the existing urban parish is not comprised in a parish (within the meaning of Local Government Act 1972[13]) the power of appointing trustees rests with the district council;[14] but if it is comprised in a parish as defined in the Local Government Act 1972 the power is exercisable under the Charities Act 1960.[15]

The above provisions concerning the appointment of trustees of parochial

---

1 *Ibid.*, s. 37 (6), proviso (a).
2 *Ibid.*, s. 37 (6), proviso (b).
3 Nathan Report (Cmd. 8710) para. 600.
4 Whether or not in vestry.
5 CA 1960, s. 36 (3).
6 Substituted for rural parish, see Local Government Act 1972, s. 179 (4).
7 *Ibid.*
8 CA 1960, s. 37 (3); Local Government Act 1972, s. 210 (9) (e).
9 CA 1960, s. 37 (4), (9).
10 *Ibid.*, ss. 37 (5), 46.
11 I.e. the date on which overseers were abolished under the Rating and Valuation Act 1925 and the Overseers Order 1927, S.R. & O. 1927 No. 55: see CA 1960, s. 37 (9).
12 CA 1960, s. 37 (5).
13 Section 1.
14 CA 1960, s. 37 (5); Local Government Act 1972, s. 210 (9), (e).
15 CA 1960, s. 37 (3).

charities under subsections (3), (4) and (5) of section 37 of the Charities Act 1960 do not affect the trusteeship, control or management of any voluntary school within the meaning of the Education Act 1944[1] and do not extend to the Isles of Scilly.[2] Moreover they take effect subject to orders made under the local government legislation with respect to areas or to powers of local authorities.[3]

The Incumbents and Churchwardens (Trusts) Measure 1964[4] enables diocesan authorities by deed to vest in themselves as custodian trustees land, or personalty (if held on permanent trusts) held on charitable trusts for ecclesiastical purposes of the Church of England of which the trustees are the incumbents and churchwardens as such. The purpose of the Measure is primarily to provide a means of safeguarding the capital assets of the trusts concerned by vesting them in permanent bodies having perpetual succession. The responsibility for managing the property and applying its income remains with the incumbents and churchwardens although in some cases the diocesan authority may make other provisions for the management of the property.

The Measure applies to any interest mentioned below which is acquired or held on charitable trusts, established for ecclesiastical purposes of the Church of England and whereof (a) no present or past trustee[5] is or has been any person other than (i) an incumbent[6] or churchwardens,[6] or (ii) an ecclesiastical corporation sole acting as a joint trustee with an incumbent or churchwardens, or (b) the presently acting trustees (whether validly appointed or not) are the persons specified in (a) (i) or (ii) above, unless acting in contravention of the trust or (c) the presently acting trustee is the parochial church council not validly appointed, if the trusts have, immediately previously, been administered by the persons specified in (a) (i) or (ii) above, unless the latter were acting in contravention of the trust.[7]

The interests concerned are, as has been mentioned, estates and interests in land[6] and interests in personal property held or to be held on permanent trusts.[8] Any question as to whether personal property is held on permanent trusts is for this purpose determined by a person appointed by the bishop or, during a vacancy in a see, the guardian of the spiritualities[9] but such determination does not bind the Charity Commissioners.[9] The following are, however, excepted: any estate or interest (a) vested in an incumbent, by virtue of his office, in any church, churchyard or burial ground or in the endowments of his benefice, (b) of an incumbent in land or buildings vested in him by virtue of New Parishes Measure 1943,[10] (c) vested in the Official Custodian for Charities

---

1 *Ibid.*, s. 37 (7).

2 *Ibid.*, s. 37 (8).

3 *Ibid.*, s. 37 (8).

4 The Measure came into force on 1st January 1965; s. 6 (2). It extends to the whole of the Provinces of Canterbury and York except the Channel Islands and the Isle of Man; s. 6 (3). But an Act of Tynwald could apply it to the latter: *ibid.*

5 Other than the personal representatives of a sole surviving trustee.

6 See Incumbents and Churchwardens (Trusts) Measure 1964, s.1.

7 *Ibid.*, s. 2 (1).

8 *Ibid.*, s. 2 (2). "Permanent trusts" means any trust of property which is a permanent endowment within the Charities Act 1960, s. 45 (3).

9 Incumbents and Churchwardens (Trusts) Measure 1964, s. 2 (3). The guardian of the spiritualities, in the case of a bishopric is the archbishop of the province and in the case of an archbishopric the dean and chapter of the metropolitan church are the guardians.

10 Land and buildings acquired as sites of proposed churches, parsonage houses etc; see New Parishes Measure 1943, ss. 16 (1) (2) and 17.

(d) which is a church educational endowment (e) which is a term of years absolute for a year or from year to year on for any shorter period, (f) vested in churchwardens in the goods, ornaments and movables of the church and in an incumbent or churchwardens in any other chattel.[1]

Incumbents, churchwardens or the relevant ecclesiastical corporation are under a duty to inform the diocesan authority by notice in writing if they hold, acquire or administer an interest affected.[2]

Upon becoming aware of any property which may be affected, the diocesan authority must consider whether the Measure applies to any interest therein.[3] The diocesan authority for this purpose is the diocesan board of finance or any body appointed by the diocesan conference to act as trustees of diocesan trust property.[4] If the authority considers that the Measure does apply, notice of the proposed vesting must be given to the persons believed by the authority to have or be entitled to the general control and management of the property, to the incumbent and to the Charity Commissioners.[5] The notice should describe the property concerned and the trusts upon which it is held, state that the diocesan authority proposes to vest the property in itself as custodian trustee after a specified date which must not be less than three months after the date of the notice, and invite objections or representations before the specified date. The opportunity to object or make representations extends to the Charity Commissioners.[6] After considering all such objections, representations and advice as it may receive the authority must, when the Measure applies, make a declaration under seal vesting the interest in itself as custodian trustee.[7] Such a declaration has the operation specified in section 40 (1) (b) of the Trustee Act 1925.[8] Any other necessary persons with an interest in the property must make or concur in making the transfer.[9] The authority must also establish a scheme for the management of the charity.[10] It should be added that the jurisdiction and powers to make schemes of the High Court and Charity Commissioners are unaffected by the powers conferred by the Measure on the diocesan authority.[11]

After 1964 the acquisition of an interest in land or personal property to which the Measure applies require the consent of the diocesan authority, but an interest in personal property by gift or under a will is excepted.[12]

The managing trustee of property vested in the diocesan authority may not sell, lease, exchange, charge or take legal proceedings without the latter's consent.[13]

The practice of the Commissioners upon receiving a notice[14] is to compare the information in their records about each charity concerned with the information supplied by the diocesan authority, which the Commissioners may be able to

---

1 Incumbents and Churchwardens (Trusts) Measure 1964, s. 2 (2).
2 *Ibid.*, s. 3 (1).
3 *Ibid.*, s. 3 (2); Schedule, para. 1.
4 *Ibid.*, s. 1.
5 *Ibid.*, Schedule, para. 2 (which sets out the required contents of such a notice).
6 *Ibid.*, Schedule, paras. 2–4.
7 *Ibid.*, s. 3 (2) (5), Schedule, para. 5.
8 *Ibid.*, s. 3 (3).
9 *Ibid.*, s. 3 (4).
10 *Ibid.*, Schedule, para. 6.
12 *Ibid.*, s. 3 (6).
12 *Ibid.*, s. 4.
13 *Ibid.*, s. 5.
14 See [1967] Ch. Com. Rep., para. 84.

supplement. If, however, it appears to the Commissioners that for some reason the property specified in the notice is not one to which the Measure applies[1] then they notify the diocesan authority and enter a formal objection. This gives the Commissioners an opportunity to discuss the matter with the diocesan authority in order to ascertain whether the Measure can be validly operated. Usually, however, there is no reason for the Commissioners to make any objection or to offer any advice in respect of a notice served on them by the diocesan authority which is consequently so informed and requested to notify the Commissioners when the declaration has been executed.

The powers of the Church of England Pensions Board to act as a trustee should also be noted. The Board has power to accept a transfer of any property (whether real or personal) which is subject to existing charitable trusts for the benefit of retired clerks or church workers or the widows or dependants of deceased clerks or church workers and to administer such property as a trustee of it.[2] In this context "clerk" means any clerk in Holy Orders[3] and "church worker" means any person (other than a clerk) who is or has been employed in spiritual or temporal work in connection with the Church of England.[4] The Board determines who is a dependant having regard to all the circumstances of each case.[4]

The Board is also empowered to act as custodian trustee, or otherwise to act as trustee for limited purposes only of property held upon such trusts. In this connection subsections (1) and (2) of section 4 of the Public Trustee Act 1906 apply to the Board as they apply to the public trustee.[5] The Board is a trust corporation for the purposes of the 1925 property legislation.[6]

The problem of redundant churches within the Church of England generated legislation in the shape of the Pastoral Measure 1968. Since this Measure makes provisions for the dissolution of benefices by pastoral schemes it had to take account of ecclesiastical charities identified with the incumbent of a dissolved benefice.

Mention should also be made of the Bishops Trusts Substitution Act 1858. It was passed at a time when it frequently happened that the bishop of a diocese was trustee of real or personal property for charitable purposes or was invested with powers in relation to charities within his diocese. With the alterations in diocesan boundaries there was a clear need to make new provisions for such cases. The Act empowers the Charity Commissioners to make orders vesting charity property held upon trust by the bishop of one diocese in the bishop of another diocese, and substituting one bishop for another as trustee where the limits of the diocese have been altered and the area served by the charity is in another diocese.[7] The order made must be made on the application of the bishops concerned or one of them.[8] The order may not deal with any advowson or right of patronage or presentation (part of the possessions of a see) which

---

1 For example, because the property was vested in the Official Custodian for Charities. The Commissioners have encountered such cases: [1967] Ch. Com. Rep., para. 85.

2 Clergy Pensions Measure 1961, s. 30 (1).

3 *Ibid.*, s. 1 (1) i.e., any bishop, priest or deacon of the Church of England; s. 46 (1).

4 *Ibid.*, s. 46 (1).

5 *Ibid.*, s. 30 (2).

6 *Ibid.*, s. 31 i.e. for the purposes of LPA 1925, TA 1925, SLA 1925, AEA 1925 and the Supreme Court (Judicature) Act 1925.

7 Bishops Trusts Substitution Act 1858, s. 1.

8 *Ibid.*, s. 2.

could be dealt with by a scheme of the Church Commissioners confirmed by Her Majesty in Council.[1] Nor may it deal with any ecclesiastical patronage or power of nomination or appointment of any curate, chaplain or spiritual person under any trust without the consent of the Church Commissioners under their common seal.[1] The order may not affect trusts of a visitatorial or any other nature or character relating to the halls or colleges of Oxford and Cambridge or to Eton College, Winchester College or Westminster School.[2] The Act does not extend to endowments of an eleemosynary or any other character governed by a specific Act of Parliament.[3] Any costs necessarily incident to effecting transfers under the Act are defrayed by order of the Charity Commissioners out of the property real or personal which is the subject matter of the transfer in question as the Commissioners may direct.[4]

Suitability of trustees

It is almost too obvious to say that a trustee should be suitable for the task in hand. A candidate for trusteeship of a charity should be a person likely best to discharge the duties imposed upon him by the trust.[5] He should be knowledgeable and business-like, possess qualities of imagination and spirit, and be conscious of his commitment as a public servant.[6] Much depends, of course, on the nature of the trust. Clearly in the case of a religious trust exclusively for the benefit of members of a particular church or of a particular religious denomination or sect, only members of the church,[7] denomination or sect[8] in question should be appointed trustees. On the other hand where a charity is substantially eleemosynary in character one must not take into consideration the religious opinions of the proposed trustees or governors.[9] In the case of a charity established for purposes connected with the parish church the parson and churchwardens are natural but not essential trustees.[10] The Charity Commissioners in the case of a scheme relating to a parochial ecclesiastical charity usually insert a provision giving the parochial church council of the parish some direct representation on the governing body of the charity.[11]

Points of difference between proposed trustees even on matters of importance for the charity in question do not render them ineligible or unsuitable for

---

1 Bishops Trusts Substitution Act 1858, s. 1.
2 *Ibid.* s. 4.
3 *Ibid.*, s. 5.
4 *Ibid.*, s. 3.
5 *Baker v. Lee* (1860), 8 H.L. Cas. 495, at 513.
6 Mulreany (1966) 13 U.C.L.A. Law Review 1060.
7 *Re Norwich Charities* (1837), 2 My. & Cr. 275, at 305; *Re Scarborough Corporation* (1837), 1 Jur. 36; *Re Stafford Charities* (1857), 25 Beav. 28; *Baker v. Lee* (1860), 8 H.L. Cas. 495, at 513; *A.-G. v. Clifton* (1863), 32 Beav. 596; *Re Burnham National Schools* (1873), L.R. 17 Eq. 241, at 247.
8 *A.-G. v. St. John's Hospital, Bath* (1876), 2 Ch.D. 554; and see *Re Drogheda Charitable and Trust Estates* (1846), 2 Jo. & Lat. 422.
9 *Re Norwich Charities* (1837), 2 My. & Cr. 275; *A.-G. v. Calvert* (1857), 23 Beav. 248; *Baker v. Lee* (1860), 8 H.L. Cas. 495, at 513; *A.-G. v. Tottenham* (1870), 5 I.R. Eq. 241; *A.-G. v. St. John's Hospital, Bath* (1876), 2 Ch.D. 554.
10 *Re Donington Church Estate, Re Charitable Trusts Act 1853* (1860), 2 L.T. 10.
11 *Re Norwich Charities* (1837), 2 My. & Cr. 275; *A.-G. v. Calvert* (1857), 23 Beav. 248; *Baker v. Lee* (1860), 8 H.L. Cas. 495, at 513; *A.-G. v. Tottenham* (1870), 5 I.R. Eq. 241; *A.-G. v. St. John's Hospital, Bath* (1876), 2 Ch. D. 554.

trusteeship.[1] On the other hand past abuses of powers may properly be held against trustees whose re-appointment is sought.[2]

There is, as a general rule, no objection to trustees being related to each other.[3] But in some cases objection can be and is taken to the appointment of trustees who are related. The Charity Commissioners sometimes object in the case of charities in small parishes with but few trustees to a preponderance of members of one family if the trustees co-opt each other.

---

1 *Re Burnham National Schools* (1873), L.R. 17 Eq. 241, at 250.
2 *Re Norwich Charities* (1837), 2 My. & Cr. 275.
3 *Re Lancaster Charities, Re Charitable Trust Act 1853* (1860), 3 L.T. 582.

Chapter 34

Appointment and Removal of Trustees

First trustees

Usually a donor will expressly provide who are to be the trustees of the charitable trust constituted by his trust deed or will. But even if he has failed to provide the necessary machinery for carrying his charitable purpose into effect the charitable gift will not fail. A number of possible situations can arise. He may have given money to charity generally and indefinitely, without specifying that there is to be a trust or any precise charitable objects: in such a case the Crown as *parens patriae* is the constitutional trustee and disposes of the fund under the sign manual. On the other hand the intention to create a charitable trust may be apparent but the donor may have failed to appoint a trustee: equity will not allow the trust to fail for want of a trustee and will rectify the omission by appointing one.

Any question which arises as to who has actually been appointed must be solved by the process of construction. A problem of construction arose in *Re Lavers*[1] where property was to be vested in trustees "commonly called the Simeon Trustees (the same who have the right of presentation to the vicarage of St. Andrew in Plymouth)". The right of presentation referred to was *not* vested in the Simeon Trustees. NEVILLE J. held that the testator had obviously intended to appoint as trustees the persons in whom the right of presentation was vested: the words used indicated that the testator had a doubt whether the Simeon Trustees were the trustees he meant to designate, hence the further description.

The donor should be careful to pick as first trustees persons who have the requisite legal capacity and who are suitable.

New trustees

Inevitably vacancies will occur among the trustees of a charity. Such vacancies should be filled by persons of the requisite legal capacity who possess the qualifications (if any) specified in the instrument of foundation of the charity and who are otherwise suitable for the charity in question.

---

1 (1908), *Times*, 7th Nov.

/ SPECIFIED QUALIFICATIONS

Any new trustee proposed for appointment must possess such qualifications as may be specified in the trust instrument governing the charity.[1] So if there is an express provision that trustees must be resident in a certain locality[2] or be of a certain religious denomination[3] or not have any beneficial interest in the trust[4] persons who do not satisfy these qualifications should not be appointed. As far as residential qualifications are concerned a measure of indulgence is sometimes shown: in special circumstances the residential area may be extended[5] and in one case the requirement that trustees should be supplied from within the parish was held to be satisfied by the appointment of a trustee who worked but did not reside within the parish, albeit residing very nearby.[6] In the absence of an express provision to the contrary[7] new trustees who reside at a distance from the charitable institution may be appointed, for "it is not always desirable to intrust the management of charities to a purely local interest"[8]. Some such consideration may have been in the mind of JESSEL M.R. when he commented in *A.-G.* v. *Moises*[9] that

> the usual course in modern times in the Chancery Division is to put the management of charity estates into a body of trustees, who are ... from the neighbourhood. That is the usual course, and it has been considered and found in practice to be the best course, and the best way of managing the estates. That being so, it is clearly the proper application to make, and one which should be acceded to, unless there is some reason to the contrary."

Number of trustees

The question of how many trustees a charity should have arises both at the time the charity is constituted and where during the life of the charity vacancies occur in the trusteeship.

INITIAL CHOICE

The number of trustees chosen at the inception of a charitable trust will (or should) depend on the nature of the trust. Where the trust is limited in scope with a small corpus, for example, a trust to present a prize in a particular educa-

---

1 *A.-G.* v. *Earl of Stamford* (1843), 10 L.J. Ch. 58, at 65, 68 (trust deed); *Foord* v. *Baker* (1859), 27 Beav. 193 (scheme).
2 *A.-G.* v. *Cowper* (1785), 1 Bro. C.C. 439; *A.-G.* v. *France* (1780), *ibid.*, *A.-G.* v. *Earl of Stamford* (1843), 1 Ph. 437.
3 *Re Church Patronage Trust*, [1904] 2 Ch. 643, C.A.
4 *Foord* v. *Baker* (1859), 27 Beav. 193.
5 *Re Sekforde's Charity* (1861), 4 L.T. 321.
6 *A.-G.* v. *Earl of Stamford* (1849), 16 Sim. 453.
7 *A.-G.* v. *Earl of Devon* (1846), 16 L.J. Ch. 34, at 45 (trustees to be "near inhabiting").
8 *Re Lancaster Charities* (1860), 7 Jur. N.S. 96.
9 (1879) reported in *Tudor on Charities* (4th edn.) 1036, 1038.

tional subject, even *one* trustee may be sufficient.[1] The presence of several trustees is, however, normally desirable even in the case of small funds, so that there should be a check on possible abuses of discretion or inaction. Boards of trustees should not be too big and unwieldy. While in the case of certain chapel trusts it may be appropriate to have as many as 20 trustees, as a general rule that is too many.[2] There is, of course, no statutory limitation on the number of trustees of settlements of land in the case of land vested in trustees for charitable or public purposes, or where the net proceeds of the sale of the land are held for those purposes.[3] The Nathan Committee indicated that as a rough guide no board of trustees, however large the endowment, should consist of more than nine trustees.[4]

FILLING OF VACANCIES

In *Re Cunningham and Bradley and Wilson*[5] which was a case of a *private* trust JESSEL M.R. said that he was not aware of any rule making it compulsory on the donees of a power of appointing new trustees to keep up the full number of trustees, except in the case of a charity. Whether there is any such absolute rule in the case of charities is open to doubt, although of course it is always possible expressly to provide that the donees of the power shall not let the number of trustees drop.[6]

Certainly the *court* will not, as a rule, fill up vacancies in the trusteeship merely to reach the original number of trustees: the court requires to be satisfied that the number of existing trustees is insufficient.[7] It is not, therefore, possible to lay down any definite rule as to what number of vacancies would justify an application to the court to appoint new trustees.[8] It must all depend on the facts of the particular case. Some helpful guidance is to be got from *Re Coventry Charities*[9] which involved three charities. The first, Sir Thomas White's Charity, had originally had seven trustees of whom two were dead and two of the others had never acted. The trustees of the second, the church charity, had originally been 15 in number of whom three were dead and three had moved from the town. The general charities formed the third charity and had originally had 21 trustees of whom four were dead and four had moved. Lord LYNDHURST L.C. asked rhetorically "What is to become of charities if applications for the appointment of new trustees are to be made every seven or eight years? And he recalled that in the *Hereford* case the cost of appointing six new trustees amounted to £700. He considered that it was plundering charities to direct the appointment of new trustees, except in cases where it was demonstrably necessary. It was to be assumed that where so numerous a body of trustees as 21 was appointed, such an appointment was made with an allowance for deaths and removal. In the case of the

---

1 E.g. a headmaster.
2 See Nathan Report (Cmd. 8710) para. 571 which considered that a board of 20 trustees was too large for a county trust formed from local trusts.
3 TA 1925, s. 34 (3).
4 Nathan Report (Cmd. 8710) para. 571.
5 [1877] W.N. 258, at 259.
6 *Cf.* 4 Encyclopaedia of Forms and Precedents (4th edn.) 397. (Form 11, clause 17.)
7 *Re Worcester Charities* (1847), 2 Ph. 2845; *Re Shrewsbury Charities* (1849), 1 Mac. & G. 84; and see *Re Hereford Charities, Re Gloucester Charities* (1842), 6 Jur. 289.
8 *Re Gloucester Charities* (1853), 10 Hare App. I, iii.
9 (1845), 6 L.T.O.S. 42.

general charities 14 trustees were sufficient since on average only ten attended from the start. The average attendance of the church charity trustees was a fraction less than eight, so again no new trustees were really needed. The trustees of Sir Thomas White's Charity had very simple duties to perform: four trustees were sufficient for those duties.

A reduction from 13 to 11 trustees was held in one case insufficient to justify new appointments by the court.[1] In *Re Worcester Charities*[2] the number of trustees had decreased from 15 to ten. Lord COTTENHAM L.C. rejected the application for appointment of new trustees with the words

> "Ten are surely enough. Unless you can satisfy me on affidavit that ten is not a sufficient number and that inconvenience arises from not having more I shall not make the order."

It was not intended that the original number should be kept up. In *Re Shrewsbury Charities*[3] the requisite evidence of necessity was forthcoming and so Lord COTTENHAM made the appointment sought. Five of the original 17 trustees were dead, one resided abroad, the other was too infirm to attend, and there was a difficulty in getting a sufficient number of trustees to attend for the proper transaction of business. This last factor is important. In *Re Hereford Charities*[4] the number of trustees had fallen from 19 to 13 and this had caused the charity to require its quorum for attendance of trustees to be dropped from seven to five: this meant that effectively three persons could control the administration of the charity which the court thought plainly undesirable.

Sometimes the trust deed makes it clear that until a certain minimum is reached the power to fill up vacancies is merely discretionary.[5] Equally there may be an express provision that the number shall be made up as soon as the reduction reaches a certain point.[6]

Dissenting chapels are however treated exceptionally. Even though a majority of the trustees may be competent to act in the trusts the court will fill up the number of trustees to the original figure.[7]

Of course an application to the court necessarily occasions expense, which explains the statements of principle made by the judges. Since the Charity Commissioners now have the same powers of appointing trustees as the court[8] in practice all applications for the appointment of new trustees can be dealt with by the Commissioners. They will apply the same criteria as the courts applied, but are not of course concerned with the cost to the charity, although no doubt they are concerned not to be plagued by unnecessary applications.

Again, it is open to the court in making an order appointing new trustees,[9] or on the settlement of a scheme,[10] to give directions or provide for future

---

1 *Re Marlborough School* (1843), 13 L.J. Ch. 2; and see *Re Coates to Parsons* (1886), 34 Ch.D. 370, at 377–384.
2 (1847), 2 Ph. 284.
3 (1849), 1 Mac. & G. 84.
4 (1842), 6 Jur. 289.
5 *Re Coates to Parsons* (1886), 34 Ch.D. 370.
6 *Ibid.*, and see *Re Bedford Charity* (undated) cited in 10 Hare App. I, IV n.
7 *Davis* v. *Jenkins* (1814), 3 Ves. & B. 151, at 158–159; *A.-G.* v. *Lawson*, [1866] W.N. 343; 36 L.J.Ch. 130.
8 CA 1960, s. 18.
9 *Re East Bergholt Town Lands* (1853), 2 Eq. Rep. 90.
10 For a precedent in a draft scheme see 9 Court Forms (2nd edn.) 90, Form 64, para. 7.

appointments, and to empower the trustees to appoint others as occasion requires.[1] But usually such directions or provisions will be made by the Charity Commissioners.

Appointment of trustees out of court

APPOINTMENTS UNDER EXPRESS POWERS

The instrument governing the charity will sometimes contain an express power to appoint new trustees.[2] Whether a given power is in character a strict power or merely directory is a question of construction, which in the last resort is a matter for the court.

A strict power is one that can only be exercised in accordance with the exact circumstances prescribed by the instrument in question.[3] Thus a power to appoint a new trustee within a specified period after the death of a trustee and not after is a strict power which can only be exercised within the specified period.[4]

A directory power is one where the power conferred is general but there is an incidental direction for example that it shall be exercised at a prescribed time or within a prescribed period. In such a case the direction does not restrict the exercise of the power even if the prescribed conditions are not fulfilled. The wrongful omission of the donee to exercise the power in accordance with the direction is not fatal: the power continues to subsist nonetheless. Thus in *A.-G.* v. *Floyer*[5] there was a direction in a will that when the six trustees were reduced to three others should be appointed, and the sole surviving trustee was allowed to appoint others. In *Doe d. Dupleix* v. *Roe*[6] the opposite happened: vacancies were to be filled when the trustees were reduced to a certain number and it was held that the trustees might elect before the event occurred. A residential qualification may be merely directory;[7] and a provision that there should be a particular number of trustees may likewise be merely directory, so that an appointment in excess of the number authorised is valid.[8]

The same principles of construction apply whether the power is in a trust instrument an Act of Parliament[9] or an order of the court.[10]

In cases where it is desired to override an express provision in the power the court may assist. Thus, in *Re Barnardo*[11] the relevant trust deed prohibited the appointment of a sole trustee. An application was made to the court to appoint

---

1 *Re Puckering's Charity* (1854); Seton, *Judgments and Orders* (7th edn.) 1264.
2 For examples see 4 Encyclopaedia of Forms and Precedents (4th edn.) 401 (Form 12, clause 10) 405 (Form 13, clause 6) 411 (Form 14, clause 9) 429 (Form 18, clause 21); and 9 Court Forms (2nd edn.) 90, Form 64, para. 7 (scheme).
3 See *Foley* v. *Wontner* (1820), 2 Jac. & W. 245.
4 But an objection to a defective appointment may be barred by lapse of time: *A.-G.* v. *Cuming* (1843), 2 Y. & C. Ch. Cas. 139.
5 (1716), 2 Vern. 748; and see *Re Goosnaigh's Hospital* (1849), 13 L.T.O.S. 87; *A.-G.* v. *Cuming* (1843), 2 T. & C. Ch. Cas. 139.
6 (1794), 1 Anst. 86, at 91.
7 *A.-G.* v. *Cowper* (1785), 1 Bro.C.C. 439.
8 *Doe d.* —— v. *Stable* (1852), 16 J.P. Jo. 726.
9 *Doe d. Reed* v. *Godwin* (1822), 1 Dow. & Ry. K.B. 259.
10 *A.-G.* v. *Scott* (1750), 1 Ves. Sen. 413, at 415.
11 (1907), *Times*, 14th June.

an association registered under the Companies Acts as sole trustee in the place of retiring trustees and the court sanctioned the appointment. There are other cases where it is appropriate to obtain the sanction of the court. For example, where the court is administering a charitable trust the trustees ought not to exercise any power which they may have to appoint new trustees without the sanction of the court.[1] Nevertheless if proper persons are selected the appointment is valid.[2]

Where the trust deed or other constitutional document is lost but there have been many appointments the court presumes that the usage is well founded.[3] If necessary, for example if the trust deed is obscure on the point, an inquiry will be directed to establish who are entitled to appoint new trustees.[4]

Appointments under statutory powers

APPOINTMENT OF TRUSTEES UNDER TRUSTEE ACT 1925

In default of any express power[5] to appoint trustees in the instrument governing the charity the powers of appointment conferred by the Trustee Act 1925 are available.

The statutory power is contained in section 36 of the Trustee Act 1925, subsection (1) of which provides as follows:

"Where a trustee, either original or substituted, and whether appointed by a court or otherwise is dead,[6] or remains out of the United Kingdom[7] for more than twelve months,[8] or desires to be discharged from all or any of the trusts or powers reposed in or conferred on him, or refuses[9] or is unfit to act therein,[10] or is incapable of acting therein,[11] or is an infant, then[12] subject to the restrictions imposed by this Act on the number of trustees—

(a) the person or persons nominated[13] for the purpose of appointing new trustees by the instrument,[14] if any, creating the trust; or

---

1 *A.-G.* v. *Clack* (1839), 1 Beav. 467.

2 *A.-G.* v. *Lawson* (1866), 36 L.J. Ch. 130, at 135.

3 *A.-G.* v. *Dalton* (1851), 20 L.J. Ch. 509, at 573–574. As to usage, see *A.-G.* v. *Pearson* (1817), 3 Mer. 353, at 403; *A.-G.* v. *St. Cross Hospital* (1853), 17 Beav. 435.

4 *Davis* v. *Jenkins* (1814), 3 Ves. & B. 151, at 155 and 159.

5 The statutory power will apply unless expressly negatived or modified by any express power: *Re Wheeler and De Rochow*, [1896] 1 Ch. 315.

6 This includes a person nominated a trustee in a will but dying before the testator: TA 1925, s. 36 (8). If in an *inter vivos* trust one of the named trustees is dead *semble* the power applies: *Re Hadley* (1851), 5 De G. & Sm. 67.

7 Great Britain and Northern Ireland: TA 1925, s. 68 (20).

8 Absence must be continuous: *Re Walker*, [1901] 1 Ch. 259.

9 *Re Birchall* (1889), 40 Ch.D. 436 (disclaimer).

10 *Re Hopkins* (1881), 19 Ch.D. 61, at 69 (bankrupt).

11 Personal incapacity is meant: *Re Lemann's Trusts* (1883), 22 Ch.D. 633 (senility); *Re Blake*, [1887] W.N. 173 (mental disorder); and see *Re May* [1941] Ch. 109.

12 Family Law Reform Act 1969, s. 1 (under 18).

13 Nomination must be general: *Re Walker and Hughes' Contract* (1883), 24 Ch.D. 698; *cf. Re Wheeler and De Rochow*, [1896] 1 Ch. 315 (specified events only). Joint power does not survive death of first to die unless contrary intent appears; *Re Harding*, [1923] 1 Ch. 182.

14 Includes statute: TA 1925, s. 68 (1), (5).

(b) if there is no such person, or no such person able and willing to act,
then the surviving or continuing trustees or trustee for the time being,
or the personal representatives of the last surviving or continuing
trustee;

may, by writing, appoint one or more other persons (whether or not being
the persons exercising the power) to be a trustee or trustees in the place of the
trustee so deceased, remaining out of the United Kingdom, desiring to be
discharged, refusing, or being unfit or being incapable, or being an infant,
as aforesaid."

If the person nominated to appoint new trustees cannot be found he is deemed
to be unable or unwilling to act.[1] There is also an inability or unwillingness to
act where the existing trustees are in disagreement.[2] The expression "continuing
trustee" in relation to the exercise of the statutory power of appointment includes a refusing or retiring trustee if willing to join in the appointment.[3] But a
trustee removed against his will cannot claim to have a hand in any new appointment.[4] The executor of a sole trustee may appoint under the section[5] and so too
may the only proving executor of a surviving trustee.[6] But where all the
trustees of a will predecease the testator, the last of them to die does not come
within the meaning of the words "surviving or continuing trustee" and so
his personal representatives are not entitled to appoint.[7] Where the section
does apply, the personal representatives of a last surviving or continuing trustee
are not bound to exercise the statutory power of appointment: they may, but
they need not.[8]

Where a trustee has been removed under a power contained in the instrument creating the trust, a new trustee or new trustees may be appointed in his
place as if he were dead or, in the case of a corporation, as if the corporation
desired to be discharged from the trust.[9] If a corporate trustee is or has been
dissolved, the corporation is deemed to be and to have been from the date of
the dissolution incapable of acting in the trusts.[10]

The power of appointment given to the personal representatives of a last
surviving or continuing trustee is deemed to be exercisable by the executors
for the time being (whether original or by representation) of such surviving
or continuing trustee who have proved the will of their testator, or by the
administrators for the time being of several trustees, without the concurrence of
any executor who has renounced or has not proved.[11] But a sole or last surviving
executor intending to renounce, or all the executors where they all intend to
renounce, are deemed to have the power, at any time before renouncing
probate, to exercise the power of appointment given by the section if willing to
act for that purpose and without thereby accepting the office of executor.[12]

---

1 *Cradock* v. *Witham*, [1895] W.N. 75.
2 *Re Sheppard's Settlement Trusts*, [1888] W.N. 234 (spouses living apart).
3 TA 1925, s. 36 (8).
4 *Re Stoneham's Settlement Trusts*, [1953] Ch. 59.
5 *Re Shafto's Trusts* (1885), 29 Ch.D. 247.
6 *Re Boucherett*, [1908] 1 Ch. 180.
7 *Nicholson* v. *Field*, [1893] 2 Ch. 511.
8 *Re Knight's Will* (1883), 26 Ch.D. 82, at 89.
9 TA 1925, s. 36 (2).
10 *Ibid.*, s. 36 (3).
11 *Ibid.*, s. 36 (4).
12 *Ibid.*, s. 36 (5).

Where there is a vacancy in the trusteeship the number of trustees may legitimately be increased: the section authorises the appointment of "one or more other persons . . . to be a trustee or trustees in the place of the trustee" who has occasioned the vacancy.[1] In certain circumstances, however, the section authorises the appointment of an additional trustee or of additional trustees even where there is no vacancy in the trusteeship.[2] Prior to 1926 in the absence of an express power in that behalf such a result could only be obtained by means of an application to the court.[3] The relevant provision reads:[4]

> "Where a sole trustee, other than a trust corporation,[5] is or has been originally appointed to act in a trust, or where in the case of any trust, there are not more than three trustees (none of them being a trust corporation) either original or substituted and whether appointed by the court or otherwise, then and in any such case—
>
> (a) the person or persons nominated for the purpose of appointing new trustees by the instrument, if any, creating the trust; or
> (b) if there is no such person, or no such person able and willing to act, then the trustee or trustees for the time being;
>
> may, by writing, appoint another person or other persons to be an additional trustee or additional trustees, but it shall not be obligatory to appoint any additional trustee, unless the instrument, if any, creating the trust, or any statutory enactment provides to the contrary, nor shall the number of trustees be increased beyond four by virtue of any such appointment."

The donee of this particular power is not entitled to appoint himself[6] because the particular provision conferring the power does not say, as section 36 (1) says, "whether or not being the persons exercising the power".

The appointment must be made in writing[7] whether it is made under subsection (1) or subsection (6). Writing does not include a will.[8]

Every new trustee appointed under this statutory power has the same powers, authorities and discretions, and may in all respects act as if he had been originally appointed a trustee by the instrument, if any, creating the trust.[9]

Lastly mention should be made of the protection afforded to purchasers on the evidence contained in instruments appointing new trustees. A statement, contained in any instrument coming into operation after the commencement of the Trustee Act 1925 by which a new trustee is appointed for any purpose connected with land, to the effect that a trustee has remained out of the United Kingdom for more than 12 months or refuses or is unfit to act, or is incapable of acting, or that he is not entitled to a beneficial interest in the trust property in possession, is, in favour of a purchaser of the legal estate conclusive evidence of the matter stated.[10] In favour of such a purchaser any appointment of a new

---

1 *Ibid.*, s. 36 (1).
2 *Ibid.*, s. 36 (6).
3 *Re Gregson's Trusts* (1886), 34 Ch.D. 209.
4 TA 1925, s. 36 (6).
5 For definition of trust corporation, see *ibid.*, s. 68 (18).
6 *Re Power's Settlement Trusts*, [1951] Ch. 1074.
7 See Interpretation Act 1889, s. 20.
8 *Re Parker's Trusts*, [1894] 1 Ch. 707.
9 TA 1925, s. 36 (7).
10 *Ibid.*, s. 38 (1).

trustee depending on that statement, and any vesting declaration, express or implied, consequent on the appointment is valid.[1]

Appointments of trustees at meetings

During the latter part of the nineteenth century a simple and convenient method of appointing trustees was sanctioned by the legislature, largely at the instance of various non-conformist bodies. In particular cases trustees could be replaced at a meeting of the relevant body, the property would vest automatically in the continuing trustees, and after the expiration of six months a conclusive presumption would arise in favour of purchasers or mortgagees that the appointment was in order. The Charities Act 1960 replaced (prospectively) the provisions of the nineteenth century legislation with different provisions aimed in the same direction. But by a curious subsection the 1960 Act has given a restricted lease of life to the old law. In order therefore to understand the modern law, it is necessary to look back to what preceded it.

THE TRUSTEE APPOINTMENT ACTS

The Trustee Appointment Act 1850 (sometimes referred to as "Sir Morton Peto's Act"[2] or, more simply, as "Peto's Act") provided that where any freehold or leasehold property in England or Wales was held for certain prescribed objects by trustees for any congregation, society or body of persons associated for religious or educational purposes and no mode of appointing new trustees was prescribed in the conveyance by which the land was conveyed to the original trustees, or by any separate deed of trust, or the prescribed power had lapsed, or was not exercised within 12 months after the occurrence of a vacancy, an appointment might be made at a meeting of the congregation or society.[3] The objects for which the land was required to be held were a chapel or meeting house, a house and land for a minister, a schoolhouse with schoolmaster's house and garden or playground, a college or seminary and grounds, or rooms for meetings for the transaction of business.

The provisions of this Act were first extended to the conveyance of sites for "schools or colleges for the religious or educational training of the sons of yeomen or tradesmen or others, or for the theological training of candidates for holy orders, which are created or maintained in part by charitable aid and which in part are self-supporting ... and for the residences of schoolmasters and otherwise in connection therewith".[4] The provisions were next extended to burial grounds.[5] While it was clear that an Independent or Congregational chapel was covered by the Act[6] it was doubted whether a Wesleyan Methodist chapel held upon the trusts of the model deed for Wesleyan Methodist Chapels was within the Act, because the trusts were not for a particular congregation

---

1 *Ibid.* s. 38 (2).
2 *Bunting* v. *Sargent* (1879), 13 Ch.D. 330, at 336, *per* JESSEL M.R.
3 Trustee Appointment Act 1850, s. 1.
4 School Sites Act 1852, s. 1.
5 Trustee Appointment Act 1869, s. 1.
6 *Bunting* v. *Sargent* (1879), 13 Ch.D. 330, at 336.

but for the whole of the Wesleyan Methodist Connexion.[1] This doubt was set at rest by the Trustee Appointment Act 1890 also known as Fowler's Act.

The 1890 Act applied the provisions of the 1850 Act to land acquired by trustees in connection with any society or body of persons comprising several congregations or other sections or divisions or component parts associated together for any religious purpose when such land was held in trust for any of the following purposes: (1) a place for religious worship; (2) an endowment or provision for the maintenance of a place of religious worship or the minister thereof or provision for expenses connected therewith; (3) a burial ground; (4) a place for education and training of students, whether for the ministry or for any other purpose; (5) a school-house for a Sunday school, day school or other school; (6) a residence for a minister or schoolmaster, or for the caretaker of a place of religious worship, or of a school-house or a meeting-house, or offices or other buildings for or in connection with religious or educational purposes.[2]

The three Acts of 1850, 1869 and 1890 had to be read and construed together as one Act.[3]

Where the appointment was made at a meeting of the congregation or society the appointment had to be evidenced by deed in the statutory form set out in the Schedule to the 1850 Act or in a deed to the like effect or as near to the statutory form as circumstances allowed.[4] It was required to be under the hand and seal of the chairman for the time being of the meeting at which the choice and appointment was made, and had to be executed in the presence of that meeting and attested by two or more credible witnesses.[5] Such a memorandum was of itself sufficient and conclusive evidence that the appointment was duly made, without any evidence of the due constitution of the meeting or of the proceedings thereat.[6]

Upon any such appointment the property vested without conveyance in the new trustees jointly with the continuing trustees, if any.[7] It was not entirely clear whether trustees appointed under the 1850 Act took only the legal estate or whether the Act also enabled them to exercise the powers vested in the former trustees.

A particular advantage of appointments made under the Trustee Appointment Acts was that after the expiration of six months, unless proceedings were taken to set aside the appointment, the memorandum of the appointment became conclusive evidence in favour of a purchaser or mortgagee that the persons purporting or appearing to have been appointed trustees were the duly appointed trustees, and every conveyance or mortgage which such persons might make was as valid and effectual in favour of a purchaser or mortgagee as if made by trustees duly appointed.[8] It became settled conveyancing practice not to require proof of the deaths of the trustees who were stated to have died, although it was usual for the memorandum to state the date of death of any who had died in the intervening period. Since the procedure under the Acts

---

1 *Re Hoghton Chapel* (1854), 23 L.T.O.S. 268.
2 Trustees Appointment Act 1890, s. 2.
3 *Ibid.*, s. 1.
4 Trustee Appointment Act 1850, s. 3.
5 *Ibid.*
6 Trustees Appointment Act 1890, s. 7.
7 Trustee Appointment Act 1850, s. 1.
8 Trustees Appointment Act 1890, s. 6.

was largely used in connection with chapel trusts where there were frequently more than 20 trustees it was clearly a most convenient result not to have to investigate the deaths of persons who might very well have left the locality. The purpose of the legislation was to simplify the investigation of title and to facilitate conveyancing, and this it did.

CHARITIES ACT 1960

The Charities Act 1960 provided that the Trustee Appointment Acts 1850, 1869 and 1890 (and, so far as it applied to those Acts, the School Sites Act 1852) should be repealed as from 1st January 1961. But where on that date those Acts applied in relation to any land, their provisions continue to have effect as if they were declared as part of the trusts on which the land is held.[1] In other words the Acts died as statutes on 1st January 1961, but live on as provisions written into the instruments of foundation of charities previously subject to the Acts. Charities which were not subject to the Trustee Appointments Acts prior to 1st January 1961 are governed by the different provisions of the Charities Act 1960. Before examining the replacing provisions it is necessary to consider the terms upon which the Trustee Appointment Acts have been granted their qualified lease of life.

The position is that where any land was acquired before 1st January 1961 by any congregation, society or body of persons for the purposes mentioned in the Trustee Appointment Acts new trustees may continue to be appointed in accordance with those Acts. But the extent to which the old Acts have been fully preserved is open to doubt.

In the first place, the Trustee Appointment Acts are only to have effect as if they were contained in the conveyance or other instrument declaring the trusts on which the land is held. The conclusive presumption in favour of a purchaser or mortgagee can hardly survive enshrined in a conveyance: it would need to be in a statute to avail a purchaser or mortgagee. Accordingly if a memorandum to appointment erroneously assumes and states that a particular trustee has died the new appointment might be ineffectual: it would require express words in a statute (and not a mere provision in a deed) to enable the legal estate to pass to the new trustees without his concurrence.

Secondly, the provisions of the previous Acts relating to the vesting of the land are not expressly continued by the wording of the Charities Act 1960 although perhaps such continuance is to be implied. No assistance is to be got from the provisions of section 40 of the Trustee Act 1925 which enables a vesting declaration to be made or implied without the concurrence of the trustees from whom the legal estate is divested: those only apply where the appointment itself is made by deed, whereas a memorandum under the Trustee Appointment Acts is not itself the appointment but merely evidence of it.

In the face of these uncertainties the safer course for trustees is, perhaps, to adopt the new procedure introduced by the Charities Act 1960 instead of relying on the procedure under the Trustee Appointment Acts, unless the legal estate is vested in the Official Custodian for Charities: in that event no problem arises, as there is no question of divesting the old trustees of the legal estate.

The replacing provisions are contained in section 35 of the Charities Act

1 CA 1960, s. 35 (6).

1960. This provides that where the trusts of a charity permit the trustees to be appointed or discharged by resolution of a meeting of the charity trustees, members or new persons, a memorandum declaring a trustee to have been so appointed or discharged is sufficient evidence of the fact, if the memorandum is signed either at the meeting by the person presiding or in some other manner directed by the meeting and is attested by two persons present at the meeting.[1] Such a memorandum, if it is executed as a deed,[2] and made on or after 1st January 1961, has the like effect as a deed appointing a new trustee or discharging a retiring trustee under section 40 of the Trustee Act 1925, as if the appointment or discharge was effected by the deed.[3]

Differences between the two procedures

The provisions of section 35 of the Charities Act 1960 differ substantially from the provisions of the Trustee Appointment Acts. The main points of distinction are as follows:

(1) The replacing provisions apply to all charities[4] and not merely to the rather limited class of religious and educational charities governed by the old Acts. They also apply to institutions subject to the Literary and Scientific Institutions Act 1854.[5]

(2) The replacing provisions only apply where, under the trusts of the charity, trustees may be appointed or discharged by resolution of a meeting of charity trustees, members or other persons,[6] whereas the old Acts also applied where no mode of appointing new trustees was provided by assurance or trust instrument or if any power so provided had lapsed, and in such a case permitted the congregation, society or other body to agree upon the method of appointment.[7]

(3) The memorandum under the replacing provisions may be executed either at the meeting by the person presiding, or in some other manner directed by the meeting,[8] whereas under the old Acts the memorandum had to be executed in the presence of the meeting.[9]

(4) Under the replacing provisions the memorandum is not (as it was under the old Acts) conclusive evidence of the appointment: it is only *sufficient* evidence.[10] Accordingly if a purchaser has any reason to suspect that the facts set out in the memorandum are incorrect he is not entitled to rely on it.

(5) If the memorandum is executed under seal, it has the same operation under section 40 of the Trustee Act 1925 as if the appointment or discharge of the trustees named in it was made by the memorandum itself,[11] that is to say, it

---

1 CA 1960, s. 35 (1).
2 For a precedent: see 4 Encyclopaedia of Forms and Precedents (4th edn.), Form 46, para. 524.
3 CA 1960, s. 35 (2).
4 *Ibid.*, s. 35 (1).
5 *Ibid.*, s. 35 (5).
6 *Ibid.*, s. 35 (1).
7 Trustee Appointment Act 1850, s. 1.
8 CA 1960, s. 35 (1).
9 Trustee Appointment Act 1850, s. 3.
10 CA 1960, s. 35 (1).
11 *Ibid.*, s. 35 (2).

operates to vest in the persons who "by virtue of the deed become or are the trustees for performing the trust" all the estates, interests and rights which are capable of being so vested.[1] This implied vesting does not extend (a) to land conveyed by way of mortgage for securing money subject to the trust;[2] (b) to land held under a lease which contains any covenant, condition or agreement against assignment or disposing of the land without licence or consent, unless prior to the execution of the deed containing expressly or impliedly the vesting declaration the requisite licence or consent has been obtained, or, unless by virtue of any statute or rule of law, the vesting declaration would not operate as a breach of covenant or give rise to a forfeiture; or (c) to any share, stock, annuity or property which is only transferable in books kept by a company or other body or in manner directed by an Act of Parliament.[3] Where a trustee retires without a new trustee being appointed the memorandum has to be executed by the retiring trustee and the continuing trustees.[4] This will not happen often in practice: normally a new trustee will be appointed at the same time.[5]

(6) A memorandum which purports to have been signed and attested in accordance with section 35 (1) of the 1960 Act is on proof (whether by evidence or as a matter of presumption) of the signature presumed to have been so signed and attested unless the contrary is proved.[6] Where, therefore, a document is 20 years old it is presumed to have been duly signed, sealed and delivered according to its purport if produced from proper custody.[7] But even if the document is less than 20 years old it would normally be accepted by conveyancers at its face value unless there is ground for suspicion.

Disadvantages of replacing provisions

The extension of the memorandum procedure to all charities is plainly an improvement. But there are two signal disadvantages in the replacing provisions.

First, the limitation of the procedure to cases where the trusts of the charity expressly provide for trustees to be appointed by resolution of a meeting is unfortunate. In the past many charities relied on the Trustee Appointment Acts and did not make any express provision for the appointment of new trustees. While it is possible to make provision for the future not every charity will have the foresight to do so.

Secondly, difficulties may be caused by the provision that the memorandum is only "sufficient" evidence of the appointment or discharge.[8] If the meeting merely *appoints* new trustees, a statement in the memorandum, such as was usually contained in memoranda under the Trustee Appointment Acts, of the deaths of former trustees will not be sufficient conveyancing evidence of their death until 20 years after the execution of the memorandum. Nor will the

---

1 TA 1925, s. 40 (1).
2 *Ibid.*, s. 40 (4). Land conveyed on trust for securing debentures or debenture stock is excepted, *ibid.*
3 TA 1925, s. 40 (4).
4 *Ibid.*, s. 40 (2).
5 *Ibid.*, s. 40 (1).
6 CA 1960, s. 35 (3).
7 Evidence Act 1938, s. 4.
8 CA 1960, s. 35 (1).

o

implied vesting under section 40 of the Trustee Act 1925 operate unless it can be shown that the persons named in the memorandum are the only trustees. The difficulty can be overcome, at any rate where the trust permits the discharge of trustees by resolution at a meeting, by the meeting *discharging* all the trustees other than those intended to continue to act with the new trustees, if and so far as they have not already ceased to be trustees by reason of their death or otherwise. The memorandum will then be sufficient evidence of the discharge itself and a purchaser will not need to satisfy himself that all the old trustees have in fact died. The unfortunate result of section 35 (1) of the 1960 Act is that a purchaser, whose only concern is to get a good title, is driven to delve into questions of trusteeship which are only of concern to the charity. He also bears the cost of obtaining any death certificates not in the possession of the charity. No doubt on a future sale the purchaser can protect himself by an appropriate special condition, but the need for this could have been obviated by an appropriate statutory provision.

Appointment by the court

The High Court[1] has both an inherent jurisdiction and a statutory jurisdiction to appoint new trustees of charities.

INHERENT JURISDICTION

Equity will not allow a trust to fail for want of a trustee and that principle underlies the inherent jurisdiction which the court exercises to appoint new trustees of charities.[2] The jurisdiction may be exercised even where there is in existence a power of appointment capable of being exercised[3] although in such a case it will not usually be proper to apply to the court.[4] The jurisdiction is not limited to cases where there is a deficiency of trustees: the court may appoint additional trustees.[5] But the court has no power to appoint judicial trustees of a charity.[6]

STATUTORY JURISDICTION

Whenever it is expedient to appoint a new trustee or new trustees of any trust whether charitable or otherwise and it is found inexpedient, difficult or impracticable to do so without the court's assistance, the court may make an order for the appointment of a new trustee either in substitution for or in addition to

---

1 There is no longer a jurisdiction in the county court to appoint charitable trustees: CA 1960, s. 48; Sched. 7, Pt. I.

2 *A.-G.* v. *London Corporation* (1790), 3 Bro.C.C. 171; *A.-G.* v. *Stephens* (1834), 3 My. & K. 347.

3 *A.-G.* v. *Clack* (1839), 1 Beav. 467.

4 See *Re Gibbon's Trusts* (1882), 45 L.T. 756; *Re Higginbottom*, [1892] 3 Ch. 132 (where statutory jurisdiction was invoked).

5 *Re Burnham National Schools* (1873), L.R. 17 Eq. 241, at 246; *Re Browne's Hospital* v. *Stamford* (1889), 60 L.T. 288 (three trustees held not enough).

6 Judicial Trustees Act 1896, s. 6 (2).

any existing trustee or trustees, or although there is no existing trustee.[1] The court may additionally make an order for vesting the property in the new trustee or trustees without any conveyance.[2] Cases where it has been held to be "expedient" to appoint a trustee include[3] cases where the number of trustees has been depleted by deaths,[4] where an official person nominated as trustee no longer exists in his official character[5] and where trustees disclaim or decline to act[6] or are abroad[7] or have been removed for misconduct.[8]

The Trustee Act 1925[9] also specifically provides for the appointment by the court of a new trustee in place of one who is incapable by reason of mental disorder[10] or a bankrupt or a corporation which is in liquidation or dissolved.

An application for the appointment of a new trustee by the court must be made by originating summons, unless there are proceedings already on foot in which case the matter may be raised on a summons.[11] Before an originating summons can be issued the consent of the Charity Commissioners is necessary.[12]

Appointment by the Charity Commissioners

The Charity Commissioners have the same jurisdiction and powers as the High Court in relation to the appointment of a charity trustee or trustee for a charity[13] and as to vesting or transferring property, or requiring or entitling any person to call for or make any transfer of property or any payment.[14] This jurisdiction can, as a rule, only be exercised on the application of the charity or on an order of the court directing a scheme.[15] However in the case of a charity not having any income from property amounting to more than £50 a year, and not being an exempt charity, the Commissioners may exercise their jurisdiction in this behalf on the application of the Attorney-General, or of any one or more of the charity trustees, or of any person interested in the charity, or, in the case of a local charity, of any two or more inhabitants of the area of the charity.[16]

Before exercising their jurisdiction to appoint a new trustee, otherwise than on an order of the court, the Commissioners are required to give notice of their intention to do so to each of the charity trustees, except any that cannot be found or has no known address in the United Kingdom or who is party or privy to an application for the exercise of the jurisdiction. Any such notice may

---

1 Trustee Act 1925, s. 41 (1). The Act applies to charities: *Re Coates to Parsons* (1886), 34 Ch.D. 370 (on a statutory predecessor).
2 Trustee Act 1925, ss. 44–52, 58.
3 For other cases where it may be expedient, see the cases of private trusts; *Lewin on Trusts* (16th edn.) 425.
4 *Re Nightingale's Charity* (1844), 3 Hare. 336.
5 *A.-G. v. Stephens* (1834), 3 My. & K. 347 (office abolished by statute).
6 *Re Beverley Grammar School* (1839), 9 L.J. Ch. 91; *Re Lincoln Primitive Methodist Chapel* (1855), 1 Jur. N.S. 1011.
7 *Re Lincoln Primitive Methodist Chapel, supra.*
8 *Ex parte Greenhouse* (1815), 1 Madd. 92.
9 TA 1925, s. 41 (1).
10 See Mental Health Act 1959, s. 149 (1).
11 R.S.C. Ord. 5, r. 3.
12 See CA 1960, s. 28.
13 *Ibid.*, s. 18 (1) (b).
14 *Ibid.*, s. 18 (1) (c).
15 *Ibid.*, s. 18 (4).
16 *Ibid.*, s. 18 (5).

be given by post and, if so given, may be addressed to the recipient's last known address in the United Kingdom.[1] Again, if the matter has not been referred to the Commissioners by the court, and is a case which by reason of its contentious character, or of any special question of law or fact which it may involve, or for other reasons is considered by the Commissioners more fit to be adjudicated on by the court, the Commissioners will not have jurisdiction.[2]

An appeal against any order of the Commissioners concerning appointment of new trustees may be brought in the High Court by the Attorney-General.[3] In addition, an appeal may be brought within three months[4] of the publication of the order, by the charity or any of the charity trustees, but no such appeal may be brought except with a certificate of the Commissioners that it is a proper case for an appeal or with the leave of one of the judges of the High Court attached to the Chancery Division.[5] An application to the judge for leave to appeal against a decision of the Commissioners may be made only after the refusal of a certificate by the Commissioners and within 21 days of such refusal[6] and in the first instance the Attorney-General alone is to be joined as defendant.[7]

In appointing trustees on the settlement of a scheme, the practice of the Commissioners is to introduce a representative element, and to arrange in suitable cases that the representative element shall constitute a majority of the trustees. Sometimes they increase the number of trustees sometimes they reduce it. Provision is also often made for *ex officio* and co-optative trustees.[8]

Removal and discharge of trustees

There is an inherent jurisdiction in the court to remove existing trustees and substitute new ones in cases requiring such a remedy.[9] The jurisdiction, which is exercised in the Chancery Division, is merely ancillary to the principal duty of the court, to see that trusts are properly executed.[10] In practice, there is no need to apply to the court for the removal of a trustee as the powers of the Commissioners have been enlarged so as to enable them to exercise a concurrent jurisdiction with the court.[11] The Commissioners also have jurisdiction to remove charity trustees and other persons where it is necessary for the protection of the charity.[12] However where the Commissioners are exercising their *concurrent* jurisdiction they do so on the principles established by the court, which principles now fall to be discussed.

---

1 *Ibid.*, s. 18 (8).
2 *Ibid.*, s. 18 (9); and see *Re Burnham National Schools* (1873), L.R. 17 Eq. 241.
3 CA 1960, s. 18 (10).
4 For computing time: see *Cartwright* v. *MacCormack* [1963] 1 W.L.R. 18, C.A.
5 CA 1960, s. 18 (11).
6 R.S.C. Ord. 108, r. 3.
7 *Jones* v. *Charity Comrs.*, [1972] 1 W.L.R. 784.
8 See 9 Court Forms (2nd edn.) 90, Form 64, paras. 3 *et seq.*
9 *Letterstedt* v. *Broers* (1884), 9 App. Cas. 371, at 386, P.C. For a form of order removing a trustee, see *A.-G.* v. *Drummond* (1842), 3 Dr. & War. 162.
10 *Letterstedt* v. *Broers, supra.*
11 CA 1960, s. 18 (1) (b).
12 *Ibid.*, s. 20.

REMOVAL BY THE COURT

The most obvious case in which the court would remove a trustee was where he had been guilty of a wilful breach of trust. Some of the most wilful breaches of trust, justifying removal by the court, concern religious charities where the intentions of the founder or founders are flouted by the trustees. Thus trustees of a Presbyterian meeting house who converted it to use of Unitarians were removed.[1] A similar fate befell trustees who converted the nature of worship at their chapel from being for the benefit of "Independents" to that of "Particular Baptists".[2] Nor were the Particular Baptists free from secessionists: in *Newsome* v. *Flowers*[3] new trustees of a Particular Baptist chapel were appointed with the object of transforming the trust property to the seceding congregation but the new trustees were removed. The misapplication of rents is sufficient ground for removal,[4] while a trustee who takes a lease of part of a charity estate in wilful breach of the provisions of a scheme may be ordered to resign his office or surrender his lease.[5] These principles apply to corporations who are trustees,[6] as well as to individuals.

Where the offending trustees refused to retire voluntarily they could be ordered to pay the costs of proceedings necessary for the appointment of other trustees.[7] Such a situation could now only arise if there were an appeal from an order of the Charity Commissioners, since in almost every case the Commissioners would exercise the jurisdiction previously exercised by the court.

Where there is no *wilful* breach of trust the position is different. That is not to say that wilful breach of trust is the only ground for removal. If the continuance of the trustee would be detrimental to the trust he should, if unwilling to resign, be removed.[8]

A reason sufficient to prevent appointment does not necessarily justify removal. Thus the mere fact that a trustee does not possess a particular religious qualification is not a ground for his removal if he is otherwise unexceptionable.[9] That applies whether the trustee lacked the qualification when appointed[10] or disqualified himself at a later date.[11] Similarly the lack of a residential qualification is not of itself a sufficient ground for removing a trustee.[12] On the other

---

1 *A.-G.* v. *Pearson* (1835), 7 Sim. 290, at 309; *Shore* v. *Wilson* (1842), 9 Cl. & Fin. 355.
2 *A.-G.* v. *Aust* (1865), 13 L.T. 235.
3 (1861), 30 Beav. 461.
4 *Love* v. *Eade* (1676), Cas. temp. Finch 269; *A.-G.* v. *Dixie, Ex parte Bosworth School* (1805), 13 Ves. 519.
5 *Foord* v. *Baker* (1859), 27 Beav. 193.
6 *A.-G.* v. *Governors of Foundling Hospital* (1793), 2 Ves. 42, at 46; *Ex parte Kirkby Ravensworth Hospital* (1808), 15 Ves. 305, at 314; *A.-G.* v. *Earl of Clarendon* (1810), 17 Ves. 491, at 499; *Ex parte Greenhouse* (1815), 1 Madd. 92.
7 *A.-G.* v. *Murdoch* (1856), 2 K. & J. 571.
8 *Letterstedt* v. *Broers, supra.*
9 *Baker* v. *Lee* (1860), 8 H.L. Cas. 495, at 513; *A.-G.* v. *Clifton* (1863), 32 Beav. 596, at 601 (Church of England school: trustee a Dissenter); *A.-G.* v. *Bishop of Limerick* (1870), 18 W.R. 1192.
10 *A.-G.* v. *Clifton, supra.*
11 *A.-G.* v. *Clapham* (1853), 10 Hare 540 revsd. on other grounds (1855) 4 De G.M. & G. 591.
12 *A.-G.* v. *Earl of Stamford* (1843), 1 Ph. 737, at 747–748; *A.-G.* v. *Cowper* (1785), 1 Bro. C.C. 439.

hand removal will be justified if the trustee is at such a distance that he cannot attend to his duties.[1] A temporary absence from the United Kingdom is also no ground for removal[2] nor is an innocent breach of trust necessarily so.[3] In *A.-G.* v. *Cuming* an irregular or improper appointment was not disturbed by the court where there had been a long acquiescence and an absence of any fraud or concealment.

Bankruptcy is usually a sufficient ground for removal[4] but is not necessarily so. In *Archbold* v. *Ireland Charitable Bequest Comrs.*[5] a testamentary trustee who had a wide personal discretion together with a power to appoint a receiver of the rents of the trust estates was held not to be disqualified by his bankruptcy.

REMOVAL BY THE COMMISSIONERS

The Charity Commissioners are empowered by the Charities Act 1960 to exercise the same jurisdiction and powers as are exercisable by the High Court in charity proceedings for discharging or removing a charity trustee or trustees for a charity.[6] Such discharge or removal may be effected by scheme, but it can also be effected by order without a scheme being necessary. The jurisdiction is exercisable upon and subject to the same conditions as the jurisdiction to appoint a new trustee.[7] However when discharging or removing a trustee they need not give prior public notice if they consider it unnecessary and not in his interest to give publicity to the proposal.[8] Before making an order removing a trustee without his consent the Commissioners must give him notice inviting representations to be made to them within a time specified in the notice.[9] A removed trustee may appeal against the order removing him within three months beginning with the day following that on which the order is published.[10] But except where the removal is under section 20 of the 1960 Act following an inquiry, the certificate of the Commissioners or the leave of the court is required.[11]

Section 20 of the 1960 Act confers a power on the Commissioners to remove a trustee or charity trustee of their own motion in various situations. The first is where they have instituted an inquiry[12] and as a result of that inquiry are satisfied that there has been any misconduct or mismanagement in the administration of a charity and that it is necessary or desirable to act for the purpose of protecting the property of the charity or securing a proper application for the purposes

---

1 *A.-G.* v. *Clifton* (1863), 32 Beav. 596, at 601; and see *Doe d. Childe* v. *Willis* as reported in (1850), 15 J.P. 275; contrast *A.-G.* v. *Earl of Devon* (1846), 15 Sim. 193.

2 *Re Moravian Society* (1858), 4 Jur. N.S. 703 (proviso disqualified trustee "departing" the United Kingdom); *Archbold* v. *Ireland Charitable Bequests Comrs.* (1849), 2 H.L. Cas. 440.

3 *A.-G.* v. *Stafford Corporation* (1740), Barn. Ch. 33; *A.-G.* v. *Caius College* (1837), 2 keen 150.

4 *Bainbrigge* v. *Blair* (1839), 1 Beav. 495; *Re Roche* (1842), 1 Con. & Law. 306; *Re Barker's Trusts* (1875), 1 Ch.D. 43.

5 (1849), 2 H.L. Cas. 440.

6 CA 1960, s. 18 (1) (b).

7 See 355, *supra*.

8 CA 1960, s. 21 (2), proviso.

9 *Ibid.*, s. 21 (3); and see 355, *supra*.

10 *Ibid.*, s. 18 (11).

11 *Ibid.*, s. 18 (11), proviso.

12 Under CA 1960, s. 6.

of the charity of that property or of property coming to the charity.[1] The "inquiry" need consist of no more than an exchange of letters. The payment of excessive amounts for the remuneration of persons acting in the affairs of the charity or for other administrative purposes may amount to misconduct for this purpose,[2] and is perhaps more likely to occur in the case of a collecting charity. A technical breach of trust, such as investment outside the range of permissible investments will not necessarily entitle the Commissioners to act. But the use of the words "are satisfied" makes the Commissioners, at least if they are acting in good faith, the sole judges of whether an occasion for the exercise of their powers has arisen.[3] The power to remove a trustee in these circumstances is not available where the charity is an exempt charity.[4]

There are various other less controversial cases where the Commissioners may of their own motion remove trustees or charity trustees. They are as follows:

(1) Where the trustee is a bankrupt[5] or a corporation in liquidation[6] or is incapable of acting by reason of mental disorder[7] within the meaning of the Mental Health Act 1959;

(2) Where the trustee has not acted, and will not declare his willingness or unwillingness to act;

(3) Where the trustee is outside England and Wales or cannot be found or does not act, and his absence or failure to act impedes the proper administration of the charity.[8]

The Official Custodian for Charities

INTRODUCTION

Until 1961 there were two distinct corporations, under the control of the Charity Commissioners, whose function was to act as bare trustees to preserve charity property. They were the Official Trustee of Charity Lands and the Official Trustees of Charitable Funds. Their functions are now amalgamated in the Official Custodian for Charities who is treated for all purposes as their successor. Accordingly, all property vested in the Official Trustees of Charitable Funds and the Official Trustee of Charity Lands is now vested in the Official Custodian for Charities.[9] So too references to the Official Trustees of Charitable Funds and to the Official Trustee of Charity Lands in any Act, scheme, deed or other document now takes effect, so far as the context permits, as if the official Custodian for Charities had been mentioned instead.[10]

---

1 *Ibid.*, s. 20 (1).
2 *Ibid.*, s. 20 (2).
3 See 443, *infra.*
4 CA 1960, s. 20 (12).
5 As to the principles guiding the court in the exercise of its discretion where a trustee becomes bankrupt: *Re Barker's Trusts* (1875), 1 Ch.D. 43; *cf. Re Adams' Trust* (1879), 12 Ch.D. 634.
6 Once dissolved the corporation cannot act as trustee: TA 1925, s. 36 (3).
7 For definition of mental disorder: see Mental Health Act 1959, s. 4 (1). Whether a trustee is mentally disordered is primarily a question of fact for the Commissioners.
8 CA 1960, s. 20 (3).
9 *Ibid.*, s. 48 (6).
10 *Ibid.*

APPOINTMENT AND GENERAL FUNCTIONS

The Official Custodian for Charities is an officer of the Charity Commissioners. He is chosen by them[1] and is required to perform his duties in accordance with such general or special directions as they give him.[2] His expenses (except those reimbursed to him or recovered by him as trustee for any charity) must be defrayed by them.[3] He has no specific term of office under the Act: the Charity Commissioners have power to designate an Official Custodian "from time to time".

The legal status of the Official Custodian is that of a corporation sole having perpetual succession and using an official seal which is officially and judicially noticed.[4]

Like his predecessors he does not in general exercise any powers of management over the property vested in him. However the Act has placed him in a different legal position from them by declaring, in section 17 (1), that as trustee of any property vested in him he shall have the same powers duties and liabilities and be entitled to the same rights and immunities as a corporation appointed a custodian trustee under section 4 of the Public Trustee Act 1906 except that he has no power to charge fees.[5] This change and the provision in section 16 (2) of the Charities Act 1960, that personal property held in trust for a charity may be transferred to him with his agreement has had the important result that he can conduct routine business relating to stocks, shares and other securities without having to refer each case of transfer to or from his account to the Commissioners for an order, the procedure that the Official Trustees of Charitable Funds were required to follow.

The sole exception to the general rule that the Official Custodian may not exercise powers of management is that the Official Custodian may be appointed to manage a common investment fund. But he has not, in fact, been appointed as a trustee of the Charities Official Investment Fund. His position under the scheme establishing the Charities Official Investment Fund is analogous to that of a company registrar. He is also strictly the only contributor to the Fund since all assets must be vested in his name before contribution which he carries out on the instructions of the trustees of participating charities. He keeps the register of shares and distributes the dividends declared.[6]

He is not liable as trustee for any loss or misapplication of any charity property unless it is occasioned by or through his wilful neglect or default or that of any person acting for him,[7] in which case the Consolidated Fund is liable to compensate the charity for the loss suffered.[8] The expression "wilful default" has, of course, been defined in the context of the liability of trustees under the Trustee Act 1925.[9]

---

1 *Ibid.*, s. 3 (2).
2 *Ibid.*, s. 3 (3).
3 *Ibid.*
4 *Ibid.*, s. 3 (1).
5 These remain solely the responsibility of the charity trustees.
6 [1962] Ch. Com. Rep. 14, para. 42.
7 CA 1960, s. 3 (5).
8 *Ibid.*
9 See *Re Vickery*, [1931] 1 Ch. 572; *Re Lucking's Will Trusts*, [1968] 1 W.L.R. 866; *Re City Equitable Fire Co., Ltd.*, [1925] 1 Ch. 407.

The books of account and records of the Official Custodian are kept under the directions of the Treasury.[1] The Treasury will specify what books of account and records are to be kept and the manner in which accounts are to be prepared. The accounts so prepared are examined and certified by the Comptroller and Auditor General[2] and the annual report[3] of the Charity Commissioners to the Home Secretary must include a copy of the accounts so prepared for any period ending in or with the year, and of the certificate and report of the Comptroller and Auditor General with respect to those accounts.

VESTING OF PROPERTY IN THE OFFICIAL CUSTODIAN

Any property real or personal held by or in trust for a charity may be vested in the Official Custodian for Charities. Such property may be vested in him by an order of the court[4] or of the Charity Commissioners.[5] Where appropriate the order will authorise or require the person in whom such property is vested to transfer it to the Official Custodian, or may appoint any person to transfer it to him.

Personal property held by or in trust for a charity, or comprised in any testamentary gift to a charity may with the agreement of the Official Custodian be transferred to him; and his receipt for any such property comprised in a testamentary gift is a complete discharge of the personal representatives.[6] In this context personal property extends to any real security, but does not extend to any interest in land other than by way of security.[7] Accordingly a lease held beneficially by or in trust for a charity, although personal property, could not be assigned to the Official Custodian under this provision, but only under an order of the court.

Where any land or interest in land is vested in the Official Custodian in trust for a charity, the charity trustees[8] may in his name and on his behalf execute and do all assurances and things which they could properly require him to execute or do to carry out any transaction affecting the land or interest which is authorised by order of the court or of the Commissioners, or to grant any lease for a term ending not more than 22 years after it is granted, not being a lease granted wholly or partly in consideration of a fine, or to accept the surrender of a lease.[9] Similarly the charity trustees have the same power to make obligations entered into by them binding on the land or interest as if it were vested in them; and any covenant, agreement or condition which is enforceable by or against the custodian by reason of the land being vested in him is enforceable by or against the charity trustees as if the land or interest were vested in them.[10] It should be noted that where any land is vested in the Official Custodian in trust

---

1 CA 1960, s. 3 (6).
2 *Ibid.*, s. 3 (7).
3 As to the annual report, see CA 1960, s.1 (5).
4 CA 1960, s. 16 (1).
5 *Ibid.*, s. 18 (1) (c). But this is subject to the conditions contained in s. 18 (4) and (5).
6 CA 1960, s. 16 (2).
7 *Ibid.*
8 Or the body corporate of the Charity; CA 1960, s. 17 (4).
9 CA 1960, s. 17 (2).
10 CA 1960, s. 17 (3).

for a charity, the trustees of the charity and not the custodian are deemed to be the "landlord" for the purposes of the Landlord and Tenant Act 1927.[1] The provisions enabling the charity trustees to act in the name of the Official Custodian and on his behalf[2] do not authorise them to impose any personal liability on him.[3]

Where the Official Custodian is entitled as trustee for a charity to the custody of securities or documents of title relating to the trust property, he may permit them to be in the possession or under the control of the charity trustees, without thereby incurring any liability.[4]

The court[5] may by order discharge the Official Custodian from his trusteeship as regards all or any property vested in him in trust for a charity.[6] Where he is discharged from his trusteeship of any property, or the trusts on which he holds any property come to an end the court may make and give all necessary and expedient vesting orders and directions.[7] No person acting in conformity with such an order or any order vesting property in the Official Custodian, or giving effect to it, is liable for any loss occasioned thereby, and no person is excused from acting in conformity with such an order by reason of the order having been in any way improperly obtained.[8] The vesting or transfer of any property in accordance with such an order does not operate as a breach of any covenant or condition against alienation or give rise to a forfeiture.[8]

The Official Custodian may act as custodian trustee in relation to shared church buildings.[9]

On the incorporation of charity trustees under the Charitable Trustees Incorporation Act 1872 (which is still in force[10]) all property held by any person in trust for the charity automatically vests in the incorporated trustees. But the granting of a certificate of registration of the trustees does not affect the vesting of the property previously vested in the Official Custodian.[11]

---

1 Landlord and Tenant Act 1927, s. 24 (4).
2 I.e. CA 1960, s. 17 (2), (3).
3 *Ibid.*, s. 17 (9).
4 *Ibid.*, s. 17 (6).
5 And accordingly the Charity Commissioners; see CA 1960, s. 18 (1) (b).
6 *Ibid.*, s. 16 (3).
7 *Ibid.*, s. 16 (4).
8 *Ibid.*, s. 16 (5).
9 Sharing of Church Buildings Act 1969, s. 2 (4).
10 Discussed at 332–333, *supra*.
11 CA 1960, s. 48 and Sch. 6.

Chapter 35

Powers, Duties and Liabilities of Trustees

Powers

The powers of charity trustees are derived from the instrument, if any, creating the trust, from the general law and from statute.

EXERCISE OF POWERS

The question who is entitled to exercise a power to prescribe the particular mode in which a charitable intention shall be carried out is a question of construction.[1] Where a power is exercisable at the discretion of a particular person, another cannot exercise it.[2] But in *In the Goods of M'Auliffe*[3] where there was a gift of residue to one of the executors "to be disposed of as she shall think fit at her discretion for the benefit of" a Roman Catholic convent and both the executors predeceased the testatrix, the court made a grant of administration with the will annexed to the superioress of the convent on proof of the permanence of the convent and of the fitness of the superioress of the convent having regard to her powers to receive and apply the legacy. The rationale of the decision was that payment over to the superioress would have been a fair exercise of the discretion by the deceased executrix and that if the court was of the opinion that the funds would be safe in the hands of the superioress, it would be justified in doing the same.[4]

A power given to executors is exercisable by continuing[5] or surviving executors[6] but not by one who renounces[7] or by persons subsequently appointed trustees.[8] Powers given to trustees, even to a testator's "said trustees" are *prima facie* given them *ex officio* as an incident of their office and are therefore exercisable by the trustees for the time being. The mere fact that the power is one requiring the exercise of a very wide personal discretion is not enough to exclude the *prima facie* presumption and the testator's reliance on the individuals to the exclusion of the holders of the office for the time being must be expressed in clear and apt language.[9] In a suitable case the court itself may appoint new trustees to hold the charity's funds while leaving the original trustees nominated by the founder to select the objects of the charity.[10]

---

1 *Re Mainwaring*, [1891] 2 Ch. 261, C.A., at 267–268.
2 *In the Goods of M'Auliffe*, [1895] P. 290.   3 *Ibid.*, at 290.
4 *Ibid.*, at 292, following *Walsh* v. *Gladstone* (1843), 1 Ph. 290.
5 *Re Mainwaring*, [1891] 2 Ch. 261, C.A.   6 *A.-G.* v. *Gleg* (1738), Amb. 584.
7 *A.-G.* v. *Fletcher* (1835), 5 L.J. Ch. 75.   8 *Hibbard* v. *Lamb* (1756), Amb. 309.
9 *Re Smith*, [1904] 1 Ch. 139 (non-charity case).
10 *Re Taylor's Charity, Ex parte Blackburn* (1820), 1 Jac. & W. 297.

Where a power of selection is given to a trustee with general or particular objects pointed out, and the trustee fails to execute the trust, the power of disposition is carried out by the court.[1]

Trustees upon whom discretionary powers have been conferred are not bound to state reasons for any conclusion at which they may arrive in fulfilling their duties. But their discretion must be exercised with an absence of indirect motives, honestly and with a fair consideration of the subject.[2] On the other hand if the trustees think it fit to state a reason, and the reason is one which does not justify their conclusions, then the court may say that they have acted by mistake or in error and will correct their decision.[3] The court will likewise interfere if they have acted corruptly[4] or improperly.[5]

Charity trustees may borrow money,[6] but they will be personally liable to repay the loan, although entitled to be repaid out of the property of the charity if it is available and sufficient for that purpose. They may also insure the charity property[7] compromise questions relating to the interests of the charity[8] and, with the authority of the court or the Attorney-General, may make *ex gratia* payments in order to discharge moral obligations.[9]

They also have the power to act without unanimity, for the general rule is that a majority of trustees of a charitable trust acting within the limits of the instrument of foundation[10] bind the minority.[11]

POWERS OF DISPOSITION

The powers of charity trustees to dispose of charity property whether by way of sale, lease, exchange, mortgage or otherwise are derived both from the general law and from statute, as well as from any express provision in the instrument creating the charity. The importance of these powers is such that analysis in this chapter would make the chapter disproportionately long. Accordingly the powers of disposition are dealt with elsewhere.

POWERS UNDER TRUSTEE ACT 1925

All the provisions of the Trustee Act 1925 apply to charity trustees in the same way as to ordinary trustees, with two express exceptions. The two exceptions

---

1 *Moggridge* v. *Thackwell* (1792), 1 Ves. 464, at 474; affd. (1803) 7 Ves. 36, at 86.

2 *Re Wilkes's (Beloved) Charity* (1851), 3 Mac. & G. 440.

3 *Ibid.*, at 448. In *A.-G.* v. *Mosely* (1848), 2 Dep.G. & Sm. 398, at 403. KNIGHT BRUCE V.-C. assumed that the withholding of a discretionary consent for an insubstantial reason could not be impeached, *sed quaere*.

4 *A.-G.* v. *Harrow School (Governors)* (1754), 2 Ves. Sen. 551; and see also *A.-G.* v. *Gleg* (1738), Amb. 584; *Waldo* v. *Caley* (1809), 16 Ves. 206, at 212.

5 *A.-G.* v. *Boucherett* (1858), 25 Beav. 116.

6 As to their powers to charge the charity property to secure a loan, see CA 1960, s. 29, discussed at 389 *infra*.

7 TA 1925, s. 19. The Charity Commissioners have stated that in their view it is clearly the duty of charity trustees to insure the charity property for its *full* value and keep it so insured: [1972] Ch. Com. Rep. 28, paras 82–84.

8 See *Andrew* v. *Merchant Taylors' Co.* (1802), 7 Ves. 223.

9 *Re Snowden*, [1970] Ch. 700.

10 *Ward* v. *Hipwell* (1862), 3 Giff. 547.

11 *Re Whiteley*, [1910] 1 Ch. 600.

are that the power for trustees to raise money by sale or mortgage of any part of the trust property for the purpose of applying capital money for any purpose authorised by the trust instrument does not apply to trustees of property held for charitable purposes,[1] and, secondly, that the number of trustees holding land on charitable trusts may exceed four.[2]

Consequently charity trustees have the same powers of investment[3] of compounding liabilities,[4] of insuring,[5] of employing agents,[6] of delegating trusts during their absence abroad[7] of appointing new trustees[8] and of retiring from their trusteeship[9] as are enjoyed by trustees of a private trust.

POWERS UNDER CHARITIES ACT 1960

Co-operation between charity trustees and local authorities or other charities is encouraged by a statutory power conferred on charity trustees enabling them to co-operate with other charities and local authorities.[10]

Charity trustees also enjoy a statutory power to delegate the execution of documents. Subject to the trusts of the charity, charity trustees may confer on not less than two of their number a general authority or an authority limited in such way as the trustees think fit to execute in the names and on behalf of the trustees assurances or other deeds or instruments for giving effect to transactions to which the trustees are a party.[11] This power is in addition to and not in derogation of any other power available to the trustees[12] such as the general power to act by a majority[13] or to delegate authority in the administration of trusts.[14]

An authority to execute any deed or instrument is sufficient if given in writing signed by the trustees or by resolution of a meeting of the trustees, notwithstanding the want of any formality which would otherwise be required.[15] Thus authority for two trustees to execute a deed may be given without the formality of the authority being itself executed under seal, contrary to the general law. The authority may be given so that the powers conferred are exercisable by any of the trustees or may be restricted to named persons or in any other way.[16]

Subject to any restriction expressed in it, once given the authority continues until revoked, notwithstanding any change in the charity trustees or in the persons who from time to time constitute any class of persons authorised to execute instruments.[17] Accordingly if an authority is given in general terms for

---

1 TA 1925, s. 16.
2 *Ibid.*, s. 34 (3).
3 *Ibid.*, ss. 1–11; and see 400, *infra*.
4 *Ibid.*, s. 15.
5 *Ibid.*, s. 19.
6 *Ibid.*, s. 23.
7 *Ibid.*, s. 25.
8 *Ibid.*, ss. 35–38.
9 *Ibid.*, s. 39.
10 CA 1960, s. 12, discussed at 456, *infra*.
11 *Ibid.*, s. 34 (1).
12 *Ibid.*, s. 34 (5).
13 See *Re Whiteley*, [1910] 1 Ch. 600.
14 TA 1925, ss. 23, 25; Powers of Attorney Act 1971, s. 9.
15 CA 1960, s. 34 (2) (a).
16 *Ibid.*, s. 34 (2) (b).
17 *Ibid.*, s. 34 (2) (c).

any two trustees to execute instruments, it may continue indefinitely.[1] A deed or instrument executed in pursuance of such an authority has the same effect as if executed by all the trustees.[2] Such an authority will also implicitly authorise the persons named or referred to in it to execute instruments in the name and on behalf of the Official Custodian for Charities, in any case in which the trustees as a whole would have power to do so, unless a contrary intention appears in the authority.[3]

Where a deed or instrument purports to be executed in pursuance of such an authority, then in favour of a person who then or afterwards in good faith acquires for money or money's worth an interest in or charge on property or the benefit of any covenant or agreement expressed to be entered into by the charity trustees, it will be conclusively presumed to have been duly executed under proper authority.[4] "Good faith" means or involves a belief that all is being regularly and properly done;[5] so that if the purchaser has no reason to suspect that the statutory provisions have not been complied with, he is fully protected provided that he receives a conveyance or other document which purports to be executed under proper authority and he does not need to ask for any further guidance of the authority. It is still necessary for a purchaser to satisfy himself that the persons named in the conveyance are in fact the trustees for the time being of the charity; the statutory provisions only remove the necessity of proving that the persons who actually execute the conveyance have been duly authorised to do so by the trustees.

Duties

The duties of charity trustees are for the most part the same as those of ordinary trustees. The divergencies flow from the fact that in the case of ordinary trusts there are beneficiaries, while in the case of a charitable trust there is a purpose to be fulfilled and that statute has imposed special duties on charity trustees.

DUTIES ON ACCEPTANCE OF TRUST

A person accepting the office of trustee of a charity must, like any other trustee, acquaint himself with the terms of the trust. He must, therefore, inspect the relevant instruments: the trust deed or charter or will or scheme or Act of Parliament which regulates the terms of the charity and of his office. Equally he must see to it that all the property subject to the charitable trusts is vested in the joint names of himself and his co-trustee and that all the title deeds are subjected to their joint control. Where the person accepting the office of trustee is a new trustee of an existing charity he must investigate any suspicious circumstances tending to suggest that there has been a prior breach of trust, and if it emerges that any such breach of trust has been committed he must take the appropriate action to secure its remedy. He must check that any money in-

---

1 *Ibid.*, s. 34 (2).
2 *Ibid.*, s. 34 (1).
3 *Ibid.*, s. 34 (3); as to the power of charity trustees to execute instruments in the name of and on behalf of the Official Custodian, see *ibid.*, s. 17 (2), (3).
4 *Ibid.*, s. 34 (4).
5 *Mogridge* v. *Clapp*, [1892] 3 Ch. 382, at 401, *per* KAY L.J.

vested on behalf of the charity is so invested in accordance with any investment powers expressly conferred on the trustees or conferred on them by statute.

DUTY TO OBSERVE THE TRUST

These initial duties performed, the overriding duty of the trustees is to carry out the charitable trust in accordance with the relevant instrument setting out the trust, and not to deviate from its terms.[1] If it appears to them that the main purpose of the trust cannot be efficiently accomplished without departing from the terms of the trust, their proper course is to apply for a scheme.[2]

A few examples will serve to show the approach of the courts to the duty of observance. An obvious breach of trust occurs when a trustee diverts a fund intended for one charitable object to another, for example for the poor of a parish other than that designated by the donor,[3] or for the repair of a different church from that named by the donor.[4] Money given for the benefit of the poor is misappropriated if applied in building a conduit.[5] Money given for repairing a church, mending the highways, and relieving the poor is misemployed if spent in finding a preacher to officiate in the parish.[6] Equally a trustee of one charity should not mix its funds with those of another charity of which he is trustee and then apply the funds indiscriminately.[7] It is otherwise if one fund is given for several charities.[8]

Trustees have no power to vary the specific mode of application directed by the founder, unless the trust deed so provides.[9] No matter how desirable a change in application would be;[10] no matter that the change is approved by the original subscribers or (where the trust is for the benefit of a particular locality) that the inhabitants or parishioners support the change;[11] the trustees must abide by the terms of their trust.[12] Accordingly, a gift for the benefit of decayed householders cannot be applied for the benefit of the poor of the parish generally.[13] A fund to provide a preacher should not be applied in aid of the poor[14]; property devised to discharge a tax should not be diverted to the use of certain poor people.[15] A gift of a capital sum intended for investment must not be applied as income;[16] and where capital has been applied for income purposes it should be replaced out of future income where this is possible.[17]

---

1 Duke, *Law of Charitable Uses* (1676) 116.
2 *Andrews* v. *M'Guffog* (1886), 11 App. Cas. 313, at 329, H.L.
3 *A.-G.* v. *Brandreth* (1842), 1 Y. & C. Ch. Cas. 200.
4 *Re St. John the Evangelist, D'Aungre's Charity* (1888), 59 L.T. 617; and see *Re Church Estate Charity, Wandsworth* (1871), 6 Ch. App. 296.
5 *Wivelescom Case* (1629), Duke, *Law of Charitable Uses* (1676) 94.
6 *Man* v. *Ballet* (1682), 1 Vern. 43.
7 *A.-G.* v. *Newbury Corporation* (1838), Coop. Pr. Cas. 72, at 77; *Andrews* v. *M'Guffog* (1886), 11 App. Cas. 313, H.L.
8 *A.-G.* v. *Geary* (1817), 3 Mer. 513.
9 See 189, *supra*.
10 *Re Campden Charities* (1881), 18 Ch.D. 310, at 328–329.
11 *A.-G.* v. *Kell* (1840), 2 Beav. 575; *A.-G.* v. *Bovill* (1840), 1 Ph. 762.
12 *A.-G.* v. *Coopers Co.* (1812), 19 Ves. 187; *A.-G.* v. *Vivian* (1826), 1 Russ. 226, at 237; *A.-G.* v. *Bushby* (1857), 24 Beav. 299; *Ward* v. *Hipwell* (1862), 3 Giff. 547.
13 *Ex parte Fowlser* (1819), 1 Jac. & W. 70.
14 Duke, *Law of Charitable Uses* (1676) 116.
15 *A.-G.* v. *Bushby* (1857), 24 Beav. 299.
16 *A.-G.* v. *Belgrave Hospital*, [1910] 1 Ch. 73.
17 *Andrews* v. *M'Guffog* (1886), 11 App. Cas. 313, at 330, H.L.

Where the benefits of a charity are intended exclusively for members of one religion or sect, it is a breach of trust to extend the benefit of the charity to outsiders. In *Shore v. Wilson*[1] the intended beneficiaries of two charities set up by Lady Hewley were Protestant Dissenters,[2] and it was held to be a misapplication where the trustees had applied income of the charities for the benefit of Unitarians. A similar conclusion was reached in *Drummond v. A.-G. for Ireland*[3] where it was held that Unitarians were not entitled to participate in a charity founded in 1710 for the benefit of Protestant Dissenters. If a founder has directed that only persons conforming to the Church of England shall be the recipients of his bounty his will must be followed.[4] But clear and unequivocal words are needed to exclude persons of a particular religious belief from the benefits of a purely eleemosynary nature.[5]

In deciding whether there has been a breach of some denominational trust the court has often been faced with nice doctrinal questions. The preliminary question is to establish the nature of trust. If land or money has been given for maintaining "the worship of God"[6] or the promotion of "Godly learning and knowledge"[7] and nothing more is said the court construes (and will execute) the trust in favour of the established form of religion; and dissenters cannot be appointed trustees.[8] But though the trustees of a Church of England school must be members of the Established Church, it does not follow that the children of dissenters are not to be admitted into the school, or even that the master may not be a dissenter, though the latter appointment could only be justified by peculiar circumstances.[9] Once the court has discovered the doctrines intended to be promoted by a particular religious trust it will then inquire to see whether those doctrines are being observed.[10]

A chapel established for a particular form of worship or doctrinal teaching must not be converted by the trustees to some other form[11] even with the consent of the congregation,[12] and *a fortiori* if there are dissentients.[13] Problems of this kind do not arise in connection with the Church of England (which is established by law) nor with the Roman Catholic Church whose beliefs and form of worship do not fluctuate. They only occur in connection with "free" churches whose

---

1 (1842), 9 Cl. & Fin. 355, H.L.
2 This was established by extrinsic evidence: *ibid.*, at 499–578.
3 (1849), 2 H.L. Cas. 837.
4 *A.-G. v. Calvert* (1857), 23 Beav. 248, at 255.
5 *A.-G. v. Calvert* (1857), 23 Beav. 248, at 257–258.
6 *A.-G. v. Pearson* (1817), 3 Mer. 353, at 409.
7 *Re Ilminster School* (1858), 2 De G. & J. 535; affd. by an equally divided court *sub nom.* *Baker v. Lee* (1860), 8 H.L. Cas. 495.
8 *Baker v. Lee* (1860), 8 H.L. Cas. 495; *Re Stafford Charities* (1857), 25 Beav. 28; *A.-G. v. Clifton* (1863), 32 Beav. 596.
9 *A.-G. v. Clifton* (1863), 32 Beav. 596; and see *A.-G. v. Calvert* (1857), 23 Beav. 248, at 261; *Re Perry Almshouses*, [1899] 1 Ch. 21, C.A.
10 *A.-G. v. Murdoch* (1852), 1 De G.M. & G. 86; *A.-G. v. Anderson* (1888), 58 L.T. 726.
11 *Craigdallie v. Aikman* (1813), 1 Dow. 1; *A.-G. v. Pearson* (1817), 3 Mer. 353, at 400, 418, 419; *Foley v. Wontner* (1820), 2 Jac. & W. 245, at 247; *Dill v. Watson* (1836), 2 Jo. Ex. Ir. 48; *Milligan v. Mitchell* (1837), 3 My. & Cr. 72; *A.-G. v. Munro* (1848), 2 De G. & Sm. 122; *A.-G. v. Wilson* (1848), 16 Sim. 210; *General Assembly, of the Free Church of Scotland v. Lord Overtoun*, [1904] A.C. 515, at 613 *et seq.*, H.L. But see *Westwood v. McKie* (1869), 21 L.T. 165 (differences only in discipline).
12 *Broom v. Summers* (1840), 11 Sim. 353; *A.-G. v. Welsh* (1844), 4 Hare 572; *A.-G. v. Murdoch* (1852), 1 De G.M. & G. 86; *A.-G. v. Rochester Corporation* (1854), 5 De G.M. & G. 797; *Ward v. Hipwell* (1862), 3 Giff. 547; *A.-G. v. Aust* (1865), 13 L.T. 235.
13 *A.-G. v. Anderson* (1888), 58 L.T. 726.

existence, in the ultimate, depends upon an association founded in contract. The contract between the adherents is to abide by the doctrine and form of worship contemplated by the founders. For that reason it was held in *Craigdallie* v. *Aikman*[1] that a chapel established for the doctrines of the Established Church of Scotland could not be converted to the use of members of the Free Church. This decision, which was a decision of the House of Lords on appeal from a Scottish court, was followed by Lord ELDON L.C. in *A.-G.* v. *Pearson*[2] who considered the case of an institution established for the express purpose of such form of religious worship, or the teaching of such particular doctrines as the founder thought most conformable to the principles of the Christian religion, and commented:[3]

"I do not apprehend that it is in the power of individuals, having the management of that institution, at any time to alter the purpose for which it was founded, or to say to the remaining members 'We have changed our opinions—and you who assemble in this place for the purpose of hearing the doctrines and joining in the worship, prescribed by the founder, shall no longer enjoy the benefit he intended for you unless you conform to the alteration which has taken place in our opinions'."

The principles laid down in *Craigdallie* v. *Aikman*[4] were reviewed by the House of Lords in *General Assembly of Free Church of Scotland* v. *Lord Overtoun*[5] which arose out of the union in 1900 of two Presbyterian churches in Scotland, namely the Free Church of Scotland and the United Presbyterian Church. The united body was known as the United Free Church of Scotland. In the Free Church of Scotland the union was approved by a very large majority; in the United Presbyterian Church the union was agreed to unanimously. A small number of minorities and a larger number of laymen in the Free Church of Scotland disapproved of the union. This dissentient minority claimed declaratory relief in respect of the property of the Free Church of Scotland that had been vested in the trustees of the new united body. The House of Lords held[6] that the Free Church had no power, where property was concerned, to alter or vary the doctrine of the Church, or to unite with another church which did not profess the same doctrines. The case was therefore remitted to the Court of Session with a direction to give the declaratory relief sought. Lord ALVERSTONE C.J. observed that the law applicable to funds which have been given for the purpose of a voluntary association such as the Free Church was well settled. Such funds, in the absence of express provision,[7] must be applied for the benefit of those who adhere to the original principles of the founders.[8] On the other hand if a congregation unites with another body and those who disagree with the union do not object promptly they may find themselves out of court by the operation of the doctrine of estoppel or acquiescence.[9] A further refinement is that congregations of the same sect may differ

---

1 (1813), 1 Dow. 1.
2 (1817), 3 Mer. 353.
3 *Ibid.*, at 400.
4 (1813), 1 Dow. 1.
5 [1904] A.C. 515.
6 Lords MACNAGHTEN and LINDLEY dissenting.
7 E.g. providing for schism.
8 [1904] A.C. 515, at 704.
9 *Cairncross* v. *Lorimer* (1860), 3 Macq. 827, H.L. (three year delay) following *Pickard* v. *Sears* (1837), 6 Ad. & El. 469.

upon non-fundamental doctrines and still be proper objects of the same charity. What is or is not a fundamental doctrine for this purpose is a question for the court[1] and not the trustees. Among Particular Baptists the doctrines of strict and open admission to the Lord's Supper were admitted. Accordingly it was held in two cases that a congregation could legitimately change its practice in relation to the admission of persons to the Lord's Supper, whenever it pleased.[2] Likewise a congregation is at liberty to make new regulations in matters not involving any contravention of the trusts by which it is governed.[3]

A liberal construction is, where possible, placed on charitable trusts. Expenditure may therefore be allowed though not within a narrow reading of the words declaring the trust.[4] Thus in *Anderson* v. *Wrights of Glasgow*[5] where a charity was established for the benefit of a guild and its poor brethren it was held that the trustees had not committed any breach of trust by subscribing out of the trust fund towards the erection of a school in return for a right to have a number of boys educated there free.

A trustee of charity property who inadvertently pays more than the income of the property to the charity is not entitled to claim against the charity for reimbursement.[6]

DUTY TO PROTECT TRUST PROPERTY

A trustee of a charity is under a duty, as is an ordinary trustee, to protect the trust property.[7] In this connection he must, as we have seen,[8] reduce the property into possession and see that it is properly invested in authorised investments. He must moreover keep the property safe. In performing this duty of safe custody he is not bound to look with more prudence to the affairs of the charity than to the management of his own affairs.[9] But this assertion requires a gloss. Much more is in fact expected from trustees acting for a permanent charity, than can be expected from the ordinary prudence of a man in dealings between himself and other persons. A man acting for himself may indulge his own caprices, and consider what is convenient or agreeable to himself, as well as what is strictly prudent, and his prudent motives cannot afterwards be separated from the others which may have governed him. Trustees of a charity, within the limits of their authority, whatever they may be, should be guided only by a desire to promote the lasting interest of the charity.[10]

On any footing, it is a plain (and indeed gross) breach of trust for trustees to occasion the destruction of the trust property.[11]

---

1 *Newsome* v. *Flowers* (1861), 10 W.R. 26.

2 *A.-G.* v. *Gould* (1860), 28 Beav. 485; *A.-G.* v. *Etheridge* (1862), 32 L.J. Ch. 161.

3 *Milligan* v. *Mitchell* (1837), 2 My. & Cr. 72; *A.-G.* v. *Murdoch* (1852), 1 De G.M. & G. 86; *A.-G.* v. *Anderson* (1888), 57 L.J. Ch. 543, at 549.

4 *A.-G.* v. *Stamford Corporation* (1747), 2 Swan 591; *Wilkinson* v. *Malin* (1832), 2 Tyr. 544, at 570; *A.-G.* v. *Foyster* (1794), 1 Aust. 116, at 122.

5 (1865), 12 L.T. 805, H.L.

6 *A.-G.* v. *Gibbs* (1847), 1 De G. & Sm. 156, at 160; affd. 2 Ph. 327.

7 Duke, *Law of Charitable Uses* (1676) 116.

8 See 366, *supra*.

9 *A.-G.* v. *Dixie, Ex parte Bosworth School* (1805), 13 Ves. 519, at 534; *Learoyd* v. *Whiteley* (1887), 12 App. Cas. 727, at 733.

10 *A.-G.* v. *Kerr* (1840), 2 Beav. 420, at 428, *per* Lord LANGDALE M.R.

11 *Ex parte Greenhouse* (1815), 1 Madd. 92, at 108; reversed on technical grounds; (1827), 1 Bli. N.S. 17.

DUTY TO APPLY FOR A SCHEME

In *National Anti-Vivisection Society* v. *I.R.Comrs.*[1] LORD SIMONDS stated that where social habits and needs have changed or the law has changed so that an established charity becomes superfluous or even illegal trustees were under a duty to apply to the Commissioners or the court for a *cy-près* scheme. This duty is now enshrined in statutory language declaring that trustees are under a duty, where the case permits and requires the property to be applied *cy-près*, to secure its effective use for charity by taking steps to enable it to be so applied.[2] Likewise, if there is some difficulty in administering the charity, the trustees should apply to the Charity Commissioners or to the court for directions.[3] Trustees cannot, however, apply the trust property *cy-près* of their own motion.

DUTY OF LOYALTY

A *private* trustee must be loyal to the interests of the beneficiaries. The charity trustee owes his duty of loyalty to the public. The content of this duty is well established. As Lord HERSCHELL observed in *Bray* v. *Ford*:[4]

> "It is an inflexible rule of a Court of Equity that a person in a fiduciary position is not, unless otherwise expressly provided, entitled to make a profit; he is not allowed to put himself in a position where his interest and duty conflict."

The duty of loyalty, then, is a duty not to let interest conflict with duty. The duty, it is to be observed, applies not merely to trustees but to all persons in a fiduciary position. Thus it applies to members of advisory committees of charities[5] and co-directors of a corporate trustee.[6] Moreover, it is not necessary to show that a conflict of interest and duty is inevitable; the possibility of conflict or of influencing a decision is enough.[7]

There are two aspects of the trustee's duty of loyalty. First, he must, in general, act gratuitously. Secondly he must not otherwise profit from his trust.

Duty to act gratuitously

Ever since the case of *Robinson* v. *Pett*[8] in 1734 it has been "an established rule that a trustee . . . shall have no allowance for his care and trouble: the reason of which seems to be, for that on these pretences, if allowed, the trust estate

---

1 [1948] A.C. 31, H.L.

2 CA 1960, s. 13 (5). The usual procedure is to apply to the Charity Commissioners under s. 18 or 19. In rare cases it may be proper to apply to the court, but only with the leave of the Charity Commissioners.

3 *Ibid.*, ss. 18 and 19.

4 [1896] A.C. 44.

5 *Re Barber* (1886), 34 Ch.D. 77.

6 *Re French Protestant Hospital*, [1951] Ch. 567.

7 *Aberdeen Railway Co.* v. *Blaikie Brothers* (1854), 1 Macq. 461, *Re Brooke Bond & Co., Ltd.'s Trust Deed*, [1963] Ch. 357.

8 (1734), 3 P. Wms. 249, at 251.

might be loaded, and rendered of little value". So strict is the application of this rule that even if a trustee has spent a very great deal of time and trouble on managing a business to the great advantage of the trust, yet he will not be allowed anything by way of remuneration.[1] This rule is a rule of equity. There is statutory provision in England enabling a trustee to reimburse himself or pay or discharge out of the trust premises all expenses incurred in or about the execution of the trusts or powers.[2] In such circumstances, of course, there is no question of the trustee *profiting* from his trust: he merely breaks even.

The equitable rule may be overriden by express provision in the relevant instrument of foundation. For example the settlor himself may have included in the trust deed a charging clause.[3] Where that is the case, the charging clause is construed strictly.[4] On the other hand, it has long been the practice of the Charity Commissioners to include in their schemes a clause providing that no trustee shall receive remuneration or be interested in the supply of goods or services at the cost of the charity. Such a clause is in most cases appropriate. But the Commissioners have recognised that in country districts particularly in small villages such provisions may be too restrictive. They have, therefore, in some cases adopted an alternative form of clause which, while providing reasonable safeguards, will permit the appointment of suitable persons as trustees without preventing them from supplying work or goods to a charity. This alternative clause provides that a trustee shall absent himself from any meeting of the trustees at which they are discussing any transaction in which he is interested in the supply of services, work or goods at the cost of the charity and, further, that the other trustees must be satisfied that any transaction arising out of their deliberations is advantageous to the charity.[5]

A further exception to the general rule is the rule in *Cradock* v. *Piper*.[6] This rule has been described as one which is "exceptional and anomalous and not to be extended".[7] But it is well established. The rule is directed to cases where a solicitor-trustee or his firm is concerned on behalf of the trust in court proceedings.[8] It enables such a trustee or his firm to claim profit costs, provided that the trustee or his firm is acting for the trustees as a body and that those costs do not exceed what would have been charged if the trustee or his firm had been acting for the co-trustees alone. The rule is limited to the costs incurred in litigation.[9]

The court also has an inherent jurisdiction to authorise the payment of remuneration to a trustee either prospectively or retrospectively,[10] and whether the trustee is appointed by the court or out of court.[11] This inherent jurisdiction it has been said "should be exercised only sparingly and in exceptional cases".[12] Apart from its inherent jurisdiction the court has also been clothed by statute

---

1 *Brocksopp* v. *Barnes* (1820), 5 Madd. 90; *Barrett* v. *Hartley* (1866), L.R. 2 Eq. 789.
2 TA 1925, s. 30 (2).
3 *Willis* v. *Kibble* (1839), 1 Beav. 559.
4 *Re Gee*, [1948] Ch. 284; *Re Chalinder and Herrington*, [1907] 1 Ch. 58, at 61.
5 See [1970] Ch. Com. Rep. 33, paras. 92 and 93.
6 (1850), 1 Mac. & G. 664.
7 *Per* UPJOHN J. in *Re Worthington*, [1954] 1 All E.R. 677, at 679.
8 *Re Barber* (1886), 34 Ch.D. 77; *Re Corsellis* (1887), 34 Ch.D. 675, C.A.
9 *Re Barber*, *supra*.
10 *Boardman* v. *Phipps*, [1967] 2 A.C. 46, H.L.
11 *Re Freeman's Settlement Trusts* (1887), 37 Ch.D. 148; *Re Masters*, [1953] 1 W.L.R. 81.
12 *Re Worthington*, [1954] 1 All E.R. 677, at 679; *Re Barbour's Settlement*, [1974] 1 W.L.R. 1198.

with a qualified statutory power to authorise remuneration. It is provided by section 42 of the Trustee Act 1925 that—

> "where the court appoints a corporation, other than the Public Trustee, to be a trustee either solely or jointly with another person, the court may authorise the corporation to charge such remuneration for its services as trustee as the court may think fit.

In Canada the ambit of the statutory jurisdiction is considerably wider.[1]

Although the Public Trustee cannot act as a custodian trustee in relation to a trust exclusively for religious or charitable purposes[2] and the Official Custodian for charities has no power to charge fees,[3] any banking or insurance company or other body corporate entitled under the rules made under section 14 of the Public Trustee Act 1906 to act as custodian trustee may charge and retain and pay out of the trust property fees not exceeding the fees chargeable by the Public Trustee as custodian trustee.[4] These fees are laid down by orders made under section 9 of the Public Trustee Act 1906.

Lastly it is to be noted that a common investment scheme may make provision for remunerating persons appointed trustees, even a trustee of a participating charity.[5]

Duty not to profit from the trust

In the context of charitable trusts as in the case of a private trust, the purchase of the trust property by a trustee is a breach of the duty not to profit from the trust. Such "self-dealing" is prohibited.[6] Likewise a trustee must not sell or loan his own assets to the trust.[7] Moreover he will be obliged to account as a constructive trustee for profits received by virtue of his position as a trustee, including any gains acquired through the exploitation of some opportunity arising out of the trust office. Thus a charity trustee who uses his position as trustee to secure himself a directorship must disgorge his salary or fees.[8] A charity trustee who renews a lease in his own name will be held a constructive trustee of his acquisition.[9]

If instead of renewing the lease he purchases the reversion in his own name the trustee will only be a constructive trustee of the reversion if there has been fraud,[10] or where the lease was removable by custom or agreement[11] or where he acquired the reversion by virtue of his position as leaseholder.[12]

---

1 See Waters, *Law of Trusts in Canada* (1974) 624–625 and 804 *et seq.*
2 Public Trustee Act 1906, s. 2 (5).
3 CA 1960, s. 17 (1).
4 Public Trustee Act 1906, s. 4 (3).
5 CA 1960, s. 22 (4) (a).
6 The transaction is voidable at the instance of the Attorney-General: *A.-G.* v. *Earl of Clarendon* (1810), 17 Ves. 491, at 500 (lease); and see *Holder* v. *Holder*, [1968] Ch. 353, C.A. (private trust).
7 *Gilbert* v. *McLeod Infirmary*, 64 S.E. (2d) 524 (1951).
8 *Re Francis* (1905), 92 L.T. 77; *Re Macadam*, [1946] Ch. 73; *cf. Re Dover Coalfield Extension, Ltd.*, [1908] 1 Ch. 65, C.A.; *Re Gee*, [1948] Ch. 284.
9 *Keech* v. *Sandford* (1726), Sel. Cas. Ch. 61 (renewal).
10 See *Bevan* v. *Webb*, [1905] 1 Ch. 620.
11 *Phillips* v. *Phillips* (1885), 29 Ch.D. 673.
12 *Griffith* v. *Owen*, [1907] 1 Ch. 195, at 204.

DUTY TO REGISTER AND PROVIDE INFORMATION

Duties in regard to the registration of charities are also imposed on charity trustees. Thus, it is the duty of the charity trustees of any charity which is not registered nor excepted from registration[1] to apply for it to be registered, and to supply the document and information required in connection therewith;[2] and of the charity trustees (or last charity trustees) of any institution which is for the time being registered to notify the Commissioners if it ceases to exist, or if there is any change in its trusts, or in the particulars of it entered in the register, and to supply to the Commissioners particulars of any such change and copies of any new trusts or alterations of the trusts; and any person who makes default in carrying out any of the duties imposed regarding registration may be required by order of the Commissioners to make good that default.[3]

Charity trustees are also under a duty to furnish information and give evidence at any inquiry relating to the charity which the Charity Commissioners may order.[4] This duty does not, however, extend to trustees of existing charities.

DUTY TO KEEP ACCOUNTS

All charity trustees are under an obligation to keep proper books of account with respect to the affairs of the charity; and charity trustees not required by or under the authority of any other statute to prepare periodical statements of account must prepare consecutive statements of account consisting on each occasion of an income and expenditure account relating to a period of not more than 15 months and a balance sheet relating to the end of that period.[5] The trustees must preserve the books of account and the statements of account for at least seven years unless the charity ceases to exist and the Commissioners permit them to be destroyed or otherwise disposed of.[6]

Statements of account relating to a parochial charity,[7] other than an ecclesiastical charity[8] in a rural parish must be sent annually to the parish council or to the chairman of the parish meeting and must be presented at the next parish meeting.[9]

DUTY TO TRANSMIT ACCOUNTS

The trustees of charities other than exempt charities are also under a duty to transmit statements of account giving the prescribed information about the affairs of the charity to the Commissioners on request.[10] In the case of a charity

---

1 As to exception from registration, see 447–448, *infra*.
2 The documents and information required are referred to in CA 1960, s. 4 (5).
3 CA, s. 4 (6).
4 *Ibid.*, s. 6.
5 *Ibid.*, s. 32 (1).
6 *Ibid.*, s. 32 (2).
7 For the meaning of "parochial charity," see 333, *supra*.
8 For the meaning of "ecclesiastical charity", see 333–334, *supra*.
9 CA 1960, s. 32 (3).
10 *Ibid.*, s. 8 (1).

having a permanent endowment there is an obligation on the trustees to transmit yearly statements without any request, unless the charity is excepted by order or regulations.[1] The yearly statements of account need only refer to the permanent endowment of the charity and not to other assets of the charity. Exempt charities are not under any obligation to transmit statements of accounts whether on request or automatically.[2]

A charity can only be excepted by order or regulations from the obligation to transmit *annual* accounts. It should be noted that exception from the duty to transmit such accounts is not coterminous with the duty to register. A charity excepted by order or regulations from the obligation to register will not necessarily be excepted from the obligation to transmit annual accounts.

The charities which have been excepted by regulations include charities administered by Regional Hospital Boards, Boards of Governors of teaching hospitals and Hospital Management Committees,[3] certain religious trusts conditional upon the upkeep of graves,[4] certain religious charities accounting to the Methodist Conference or to a committee or department established by the Methodist Conference, charities for the advancement of religion of which certain named Baptist Congregational and other denominational Trust Corporations are charity or custodian trustees,[5] or of which specified Diocesan Trust Corporations of the Church of England are charity or custodian trustees.[6] Charities wholly or mainly concerned with the promotion of the efficiency of any of the armed forces of the Crown are also excepted from the duty to send annual accounts provided that they are not charities holding land for any estate or interest greater than a tenancy from year to year or charities benefiting persons other than serving members of the armed forces or charities for the exhibition or preservation of articles of historical interest.[7]

Any statement of account which is transmitted to the Commissioners may be kept by them for such period as they think fit and during that period it is open to public inspection at all reasonable times[8] and copies or extracts may be obtained on payment of a reasonable fee.[9]

The Commissioners declared policy regarding situations in which they will request accounts is that a request will be made where it is necessary to examine the accounts in connection with some proposal about which a charity is seeking their assistance, where a question has arisen about the way in which a charity is being administered or where a new charity has been established with trusts in very general terms which do not make it clear precisely what kind of activities it is proposed to undertake.[10] A request does not of course imply the existence of mismanagement, but clearly where there is reason to suppose that there has been mismanagement the power to request accounts will be used.[11]

The Commissioners have by regulations[12] prescribed the information to be

---

1 *Ibid.*
2 *Ibid.*, s. 8 (7).
3 S.I. 1963 No. 210.
4 S.I. 1963 No. 2074, reg. 2.
5 S.I. 1963 No. 2074, reg. 3.
6 S.I. 1964 No. 1825.
7 S.I. 1965 No. 1056.
8 CA 1960, s. 8 (2).
9 *Ibid.*, s. 9 (2).
10]1967] Ch. Com. Rep. 26, para. 94.
11 [1967] Ch. Com. Rep. 26, para. 94.
12 Charities (Statements of Account) Regulations 1960, S.I. 1960 No. 2425.

included in a statement of account transmitted to them. The information to be included consists of:

(1) Particulars of the assets, and the persons in whom they are vested, on the day of the year to which the charity's accounts are made up, distinguishing between assets forming part of the permanent endowment and other assets.

(2) The approximate amount of the liabilities on that day.

(3) The amount of the receipts in the year ending on that day, classified according to the nature of the receipt and distinguishing between receipts forming part of the permanent endowment and other receipts.

(4) The amount of the payments made during that year, classified according to the nature of the payment and distinguishing between payments made out of the permanent endowment and other payments.

In general, charity trustees are not obliged to have their accounts profession-ally audited. However the terms of their trust may require it, and trustees of a war charity or a charity for the disabled are under a special statutory obligation to have their accounts professionally audited.[1] Moreover, the Commissioners are empowered under the Charities Act 1960 to require by order that the condition and accounts of a charity (other than an exempt charity[2]) for such period as they think fit shall be investigated and audited by an auditor appointed by them.[3] An auditor acting under these provisions must belong to one of the professional bodies listed in the Act and has a right of access to all books, accounts and documents relating to the charity which are in the possession of the charity trustees or to which they have access.[4] He is entitled to require from any trustee, officer or servant of the charity, past or present, such information and explanation as he thinks necessary for the performance of his duties.[5] Any person who fails to afford to an auditor any facility to which he is entitled may be ordered by the Commissioners to make good his default,[6] and disobedience to such an order may, on the application of the Commissioners to the High Court, be punished in the same way as a contempt of court.[7] At the end or during the progress of the audit the auditor must make such reports to the Commissioners about the audit or about the accounts or affairs of the charity as he thinks the case requires, and he must send a copy of any such report to the trustees of the charity.[8] The expenses of any audit under these provisions, in-cluding the remuneration of the auditor, will be paid by the Commissioners[9] out of monies provided by Parliament.[10]

An auditor appointed under the Act must be a member of one of the follow-ing bodies: the Institute of Chartered Accountants in England and Wales, the Society of Incorporated Accountants, the Institute of Chartered Accountants of Scotland, the Association of Certified and Corporate Accountants, the Institute of Chartered Accountants in Ireland and any other body of accountants estab-lished in the United Kingdom and for the time being recognised for the pur-

1 See 465, *infra*.
2 CA 1960, s. 8 (7).
3 *Ibid.*, s. 8 (3).
4 *Ibid.*, s. 8 (4) (a).
5 *Ibid.*, s. 8 (4) (b).
6 *Ibid.*, s. 8 (6).
7 *Ibid.*, s. 41.
8 *Ibid.*, s. 8 (4) (c).
9 *Ibid.*, s. 8 (5).
10 *Ibid.*, s. 44 (1) (b).

poses of the Companies Act 1948, section 161 (1) (a) by the Department of Trade and Industry.[1]

Even where there is no legal requirement that the accounts of a particular charity should be audited the Commissioners have indicated that it would be prudent of trustees, for their own protection, to invite some independent person to audit the accounts. Where the funds are adequate the trustees would be justified in employing an accountant to audit the accounts.[2]

Liabilities

There is a rebuttable presumption that trustees have faithfully discharged their duty.[3] But where charity trustees have misapplied trust property they are strictly liable to make good any deficiency or loss.[4] The worst form of misapplication is where the trustee improperly retains for his own benefit trust money such as an increase in the rent of charity[5] land or some officer's salary or annuity.[6] Other examples of misapplication are where trustees use trust money for purposes not sanctioned by the trust[7] or occasion the destruction of the trust property[8] or improperly alienate it[9] or negligently allow others to misappropriate it.[10]

A threatened diversion of charitable funds to a non-charitable purpose or to unauthorised charitable purposes may be restrained by injunction. In *Baldry v. Feintuck*[11] the Sussex University students union was threatening to apply union funds to charitable purposes not authorised by its constitution and to political purposes. BRIGHTMAN J. granted an injunction to restrain such application of the funds which would have been in breach of trust.

The rule as to the personal liabilities of charitable trustees was expressed by Lord ELDON L.C. in *A.-G.* v. *Exeter Corporation*[12] in the following terms:

> "With respect to the general principle on which the Court deals with the trustees of a charity, though it holds a strict hand on them when there is wilful misapplication, it will not press severely upon them when it sees nothing but mistake. It often happens from the nature of the instrument creating the trust that there is great difficulty in determining how the funds of a charity ought to be administered. If the administration of the funds, though mistaken, has been honest and unconnected with any corrupt

---

1 *Ibid.*, s. 8 (3). The Faculty of Auditors, for example, is not so recognised.

2 [1966] Ch. Com. Rep. 26.

3 *A.-G.* v. *Earl of Stamford* (1843), 1 Ph. 737, at 747.

4 *Haberdashers' Co.* v. *A.-G.* (1702), 2 Bro. Parl. Cas. 370, H.L.

5 *Kennington Hastings Case* (1612), Duke, *Law of Charitable Uses* (1676) 71.

6 *A.-G.* v. *Bedford Corporation* (1754), 2 Ves. Sen. 505 (usher's salary); *A.-G.* v. *Bolton* (1796), 3 Anst. 820 (preacher's annuity).

7 *A.-G.* v. *Brewer's Co.* (1816), 1 Mer. 495; *A.-G.* v. *Cambridge Corporation* (1836), 5 L.J. Ch. 357.

8 *Ex parte Greenhouse* (1815), 1 Madd. 92, at 109 (chapel).

9 *A.-G.* v. *East Retford Corporation* (1838), 3 My. & Cr. 484; *A.-G.* v. *Wisbeach Corporation* (1842), 11 L.J. Ch. 412.

10 *A.-G.* v. *Leicester Corporation* (1844), 7 Beav. 176.

11 [1972] 1 W.L.R. 552.

12 (1826), 2 Russ. 45, at 54 followed in *Andrews* v. *M'Guffog* (1886), 11 App. Cas. 313, at 324, H.L. (*bona fide* intermixing of trust funds).

purpose, the Court, while it directs for the future refuses to visit with punishment what has been done in the past. To act on any other principle would be to deter all prudent persons from becoming trustees of charities."

Accordingly, slight irregularities will not attract severe censure where there is no corrupt motive.[1] Nor will trustees be made to account for money paid out to officers of the charity under a mistaken interpretation of the trust instrument.[2] It has even been suggested that trustees would not be made to account for property bought from rents mistakenly thought to belong to the trustees.[3] Some cases indicate that the court tends to be more lenient to a corporate trustee than to an individual.[4] The promptness of the defaulting trustee to assist in setting the matter right is an important element to be considered in the exercise of the discretion of the court to overlook mistaken breaches of trust.[5]

Quite apart from its equitable discretion the court has a jurisdiction to relieve against breeches of trust under the Trustee Act 1925. If it appears to the court that a trustee is or may be personally liable for any breach of trust but has acted honestly and reasonably and ought partly to be excused for the breach and for omitting to obtain the court's directions in the matter in which he committed the breach, the court may relieve him wholly or partly from that personal liability.[6] The burden of proving that he acted honestly and reasonably lies on the trustee[7] who has an uphill task if he is a paid trustee.[8] But each case will turn on its own facts.[9]

The Charity Commissioners, it should be noted, have said that if trustees have departed from their trusts in the honest belief that what they were doing was better for the community they serve, they need have no fear of approaching the Commissioners to ask them for a scheme to alter the purposes of their charities. Failure to keep within the trusts, the Commissioners acknowledge, may often be evidence of the need to alter the purposes of the charity rather than a dereliction of duty on the part of the trustees.[10]

Where a trustee of a charity has misapplied funds belonging to the charity he is accountable in respect of the misapplied funds and interest thereon. Two questions arise in connection with this accountability. First, how far back will accounts be carried? Secondly for what rate of interest will a defaulting trustee be accountable?

DATE FROM WHICH ACCOUNTS RUN

In determining the date from which accounts against trustees of a charitable trust shall run, the court is guided by the particular facts of the particular case.

---

1 *A.-G.* v. *Joliffe* (1822), 2 Coop. *temp.* Cott. 229.
2 *A.-G.* v. *Dean and Canons of Christ Church* (1826), 2 Russ. 321.
3 *A.-G.* v. *Master Wardens, etc. of Wax Chandlers' Co.* (1873), L.R. 6 H.L.1.
4 *A.-G.* v. *Baliol College, Oxford* (1744), 9 Mod. Rep. 407, at 409–410; *A.-G.* v. *East Retford Corporation* (1833), 2 My. & K. 35, at 37–38; *A.-G.* v. *Newbury Corporation* (1834), 3 My. & K. 647, at 651; *A.-G.* v. *Caius College* (1837), 2 Keen 150, at 169.
5 *A.-G.* v. *Pretyman* (1841), 4 Beav. 462, at 466, *per* Lord LANGDALE M.R.
6 TA 1925, s. 61; see also Snell, *Principles of Equity* (27th edn.) 279.
7 *Re Stuart*, [1897] 2 Ch. 583.
8 *National Trustees Co. of Australasia* v. *General Finance Co. of Australasia*, [1905] A.C. 373, P.C.
9 *Re Kay*, [1897] 2 Ch. 518, at 524.
10 [1970] Ch. Com. Rep. 16, para. 44.

Because each case is decided on its own merits the dates to which accounts against charity trustees are carried back differ considerably.[1] The court may even conclude that the prosecution of accounts and inquiries would not be beneficial but prejudicial to the interests of charity, in which case they will be refused. That is an appropriate course where the litigation would be expensive and the benefit to charity trifling because of the sum involved.[2] Where there has been a *wilful* misapplication of funds accounts are usually ordered to be taken against the trustees from the date at which the misapplication started.[3] On the other hand, where the misapplication has been *innocent*, accounts are normally directed to run from the commencement of the action.[4] That, however, is a general rule which yields where the circumstances so require. Thus in some cases accounts have been ordered to be carried back to the date at which notice was given to the trustees questioning the propriety of the application.[5] In other cases the accounts have run from the date of the decree declaring the application improper,[6] or from the date of the last appointment of a new trustee.[7]

LIABILITY FOR INTEREST OR PROFITS

Where an ordinary (i.e. private) trustee is required to compensate the trust estate for the loss it has sustained, he is normally liable in addition to pay interest at four per cent.[8] The liability of a charity trustee is in this and other respects the same. In certain circumstances however a charity trustee may be liable for a higher rate. First, if he has in fact received more, he will be liable for what he has in fact received.[9] Secondly, if he should have received more, he will be liable for what he should have received, as, for example, where he calls in a mortgage carrying a higher rate of interest.[10] Thirdly, if it can fairly be presumed that he received more, as where he has used the trust money for his own purpose or for trading he will either be charged five per cent.[11] or else will be accountable

---

1 *A.-G.* v. *Davey* (1854), 19 Beav. 521, at 527.

2 *A.-G.* v. *Shearman* (1839), 2 Beav. 107.

3 *A.-G.* v. *Cashel Corporation* (1842), 3 Dr. & War. 294; *A.-G.* v. *Davey* (1854), 19 Beav. 521, at 527.

4 *A.-G.* v. *Joliffe* (1822), 1 L.J.O.S. Ch. 43; *A.-G.* v. *Winchester Corporation* (1824), 3 L.J.O.S. Ch. 64; *A.-G.* v. *Stationers' Co.* (1831), 9 L.J.O.S. Ch. 229; *A.-G.* v. *Caius College* (1837), 2 Keen 150, at 166; *A.-G.* v. *Harper* (1838), 8 L.J. Ch. 12; *A.-G.* v. *Drapers' Co.*, *Kendricks Charity* (1841), 4 Beav. 67; (1847), 10 Beav. 558; *A.G.* v. *Christ's Hospital* (1841), 4 Beav. 73; *A.-G.* v. *Hall* (1853), 16 Beav. 388, at 395; *A.-G.* v. *Davey* (1854), 19 Beav. 521; *A.-G.* v. *Masters Wardens, etc. of the Wax Chandlers' Co.* (1873), L.R. 6 H.L. 1, at 15.

5 *A.-G.* v. *Berwick-upon-Tweed Corporation* (1829), Taml. 239; *A.-G.* v. *East Retford Corporation* (1833), 2 My. & K. 35, at 37; *A.-G.* v. *Cambridge Corporation* (1836), 5 L.J. Ch. 357.

6 *A.-G.* v. *Tufnell* (1849), 12 Beav. 35.

7 *A.-G.* v. *Newbury Corporation* (1834), 3 My. & K. 647.

8 *Imperial Mercantile Credit Association* v. *Coleman* (1873), L.R. 6 H.L. 189; *Re Hulkes* (1886), 33 Ch.D. 552. Certainly three per cent is no longer an appropriate rate: *Re Davy*, [1908] 1 Ch. 61. And it is arguable that Bank of England minimum lending rate should be used as a base: see *Wallersteiner* v. *Moir (No.* 2), [1975] 2 W.L.R. 389 (breach of fiduciary duty).

9 *Re Emmet's Estate* (1881), 17 Ch.D. 142.

10 See *Jones* v. *Foxall* (1852), 15 Beav. 388.

11 *A.-G.* v. *Solly* (1829), 2 Sim. 518; *A.-G.* v. *Cambridge Corporation* (1836), 5 L.J. Ch. 357. Perhaps one per cent. above Bank of England minimum lending rate is now appropriate: see *Wallersteiner* v. *Moir (No.* 2), [1975] Q.B. 373; [1975] 1 All E.R. 849.

for the profits actually made[1] or if he has mixed his own money with the trust money a proportionate share of the profits.[2] The court will not however order an account of profits for part of the time and interest for the remainder: it must be one or the other.[3] Whether the interest is simple or compound is in the discretion of the court. In relation to private trusts the present practice is to charge compound interest where trust funds have been employed in trade[4] and this practice is likely to apply to a charity trustee who uses the trust property for trading purposes.[5] In one case a trustee who set up a title adverse to the charity was charged compound interest.[6]

The circumstances in which an agent acting for a charity trustee can be made accountable other than to his principal are necessarily out of the ordinary. An agent is liable to account only to his principal and the case of a charity generally forms no exception to the rule.[7] If the rule were otherwise, very serious inconvenience would follow. The moment that one could trace the money of a charity into the hands of any person in whatever capacity he would be a necessary party to proceedings. On the other hand an agent may put himself into the position of a constructive trustee or quasi-trustee by interfering and assisting in a breach of trust knowingly.[8] Thus where committee men connived in a breach by corporation trustees the committee men were held personally liable.[9] In *A.-G.* v. *Wilson*[10] a corporation was trustee of a charity and members of the governing body were, on the principle just cited, held liable for injury to the charity caused by their default. So too a town clerk who retained trust funds for his own benefit with the consent of a municipal corporation and with full awareness that such retention was in breach of trust was, in another case, held jointly liable with the corporation for the breach of trust.[11]

Where the court makes a declaration that a corporation is liable to make good the loss occasioned by breach of a charitable trust, the court will not specifically charge the loss on the general corporate property but will leave the plaintiff to enforce his remedy by the usual process (which is sequestration) against the corporation.[12] A person injured by a breach of trust committed by the trustees of a charity cannot be indemnified out of the charity property: the law in this respect is the same in England and Scotland.[13]

---

1 *Re Davis*, [1902] 2 Ch. 314; *Gordon* v. *Gonda*, [1955] 1 W.L.R. 885, C.A.
2 *Docker* v. *Somes* (1834), 2 My. & K. 655.
3 *Vyse* v. *Foster* (1872), 8 Ch. App. 309, at 334.
4 *Jones* v. *Foxall* (1852), 15 Beav. 388; *Wallersteiner* v. *Moir* (*No. 2*) [1975] Q.B. 373; [1975] 1 All E.R. 849, *cf. Burdick* v. *Garrick* (1870), 5 Ch. App. 233 (simple).
5 *A.-G.* v. *Cambridge Corporation* (836), 5 L.J. Ch. 357 *cf. A.-G.* v. *Solly* (1829), 2 Sim. 518 (simple).
6 *Incorporated Society* v. *Richards* (1841), 1 Dr. & War. 258.
7 *A.-G.* v. *Earl of Chesterfield* (1854), 18 Beav. 596.
8 *Ibid.*
9 *Charitable Corporation* v. *Sutton* (1742), 2 Atk. 400, at 405.
10 (1840) Cr. & Ph. 1.
11 *A.-G.* v. *Leicester Corporation* (1844), 7 Beav. 176.
12 *A.-G.* v. *East Retford Corporation* (1838), 3 My. & Cr. 484.
13 *Heriot's Hospital (Feoffees)* v. *Ross* (1846), 12 Cl. & Fin. 507, H.L.

Limitation of actions

Prior to the passing of the Real Property Limitation Act 1833 charities were not bound by any statute of limitation.[1] Charities were not in fact expressly mentioned in the 1833 Act, but it was soon established that its provisions extended to charities.[2] The governing statute of limitation in England is the Limitation Act 1939. The 1939 Act makes no express mention of charities or charitable trustees but it is quite clear that both actions by charities against strangers and actions brought by or on behalf of the objects against the charitable trustees stand for limitation purposes on the same footing as similar actions with no element of charity. Wherever the word person occurs in the 1939 Act[3] it includes any body of persons corporate or unincorporate.[4] And since the words "trust and "trustee" in the 1939 Act have the same meanings as in the Trustee Act 1925[5] they plainly include charitable trust and charitable trustee.[6]

When a charity trustee commits a breach of trust he is entitled to take any limitation point open to a private trustee. An action by a beneficiary under a trust to recover trust property, whether real or personal, from the trustee or to sue in respect of any breach of trust will normally be barred after the expiration of six years from the date on which the cause of action accrued.[7] The words "action by a beneficiary under a trust" are not very apt to describe an action by the Attorney-General on behalf of charity; but no-one doubts that section 19 of the Limitation Act 1939 does apply to such an action.[8] In three types of case, however, no lapse of time will operate as a bar to proceedings. The "excepted" cases are proceedings by a beneficiary (*a*) in respect of any fraud[9] or fraudulent breach of trust to which the trustee was a party or privy[10] (*b*) to recover from the trustee trust property[11] or the proceeds thereof in the possession of the trustee or (*c*) to recover from the trustee trust property or the proceeds thereof previously received by the trustee and converted to his use.

Time runs from the date when the right of action accrued or from the date of the breach of trust. But accrual may be postponed or the running of time delayed by reason of fraud or mistake.

Charity trustees may acquire a valid title to land by possession under a void

---

1 *A.-G.* v. *Coventry Corporation* (1702), 2 Vern. 396, at 399; *A.-G.* v. *Exeter Corporation* (1826), Jac. 443, at 448; *A.-G.* v. *Christ's Hospital* (1834), 3 My. & K. 344.

2 *Incorporated Society* v. *Richards* (1841), 1 Dr. & War. 258; *Charitable Donations and Bequests Comrs.* v. *Wybrants* (1845), 2 Jo. & Lat. 182; *St. Mary Magdalen College* v. *A.-G.* (1857), 6 H.L. Cas. 189.

3 See Limitation Act 1939, ss. 3, 4 (3), 12.

4 Interpretation Act 1889, s. 19.

5 Limitation Act 1939, s. 31 (1).

6 See TA 1925, s. 68 (17).

7 Limitation Act 1939, s. 19 (2).

8 *President of St. Mary Magdalen College, Oxford* v. *A.-G.* (1857), 6 H.L. Cas. 189 (on different statutory wording).

9 Probably "fraud" here connotes some measure of dishonesty: *Collings* v. *Wade*, [1896] 1 I.R. 340 *cf. Re Sale Hotel* (1897), 77 L.T. 681 revsd. on another point (1898) 78 L.T. 368; and see Frank, *Limitation of Actions* 74–75.

10 See *Thorne* v. *Heard*, [1894] 1 Ch. 599, at 608; affd., [1895] A.C. 495.

11 Including rents and profits notionally assumed to have been received: *Re Howlett*, [1949] Ch. 767.

lease provided they pay no rent while their possession continues,[1] or they may acquire title by adverse possession under a void conveyance.[2] Equally they may acquire title by adverse possession where they retain possession after their title has determined. While they hold adversely to the true owner they hold the property on the charitable trusts which the ineffective instrument purported to establish or which were validly existing before their title determined.[3]

Where there is a tenancy at will the limitation period runs from the end of one year after the commencement of the tenancy or from its earlier determination.[4] But where there is a tenancy from year to year or other period with out a lease in writing the limitation period starts to run from the end of the first year or other period[5] or from the last payment of rent.[6]

The other side of the coin is demonstrated where the Attorney-General acting in the interests of charity seeks to have a voidable disposition of the trustees set aside. Time will run against the charity from the moment of the disposition.[7]

Claims adverse to a charity such as may arise on a gift over from one charity to another[8] or on a reverter to the settlor[9] may be barred by lapse of time. Where that occurs the charity trustees hold under the trusts of the charity and not for their own personal benefit.[10] If a person obtains possession of charity land by fraud time will not run in his favour so long as the fraud is concealed but it will start to run from the date of its discovery or the date when with reasonable diligence it could have been discovered.[11]

---

1 *President and Governors Magdalen Hospital* v. *Knotts* (1879), 4 App. Cas. 324, H.L.; *Bunting* v. *Sargent* (1879), 13 Ch.D. 330; *Webster* v. *Southey* (1887), 36 Ch.D. 9, at 19 (mortmain); *cf. Bishop of Bangor* v. *Parry*, [1891] 2 Q.B. 277.

2 *Churcher* v. *Martin* (1889), 42 Ch.D. 312 (mortmain).

3 *Re Lacy*, [1899] 2 Ch. 149; *Re Ingleton Charity*, [1956] Ch. 585.

4 Limitation Act 1939, s. 9 (1).

5 *Ibid.*, s. 9 (2).

6 *Ibid.*, s. 9 (2); see *Bunting* v. *Sargent* (1879), 13 Ch.D. 330; *Webster* v. *Southey* (1887), 36 Ch.D. 9; see also *President and Governors Magdalen Hospital* v. *Knotts* (1879), 4 App. Cas. 324, at 335, H.L.

7 *A.-G.* v. *Davey* (1859), 4 De G. & J. 136; *A.-G.* v. *Payne* (1859), 27 Beav. 168.

8 See *Re Orchard Street Schools Trustees*, [1878] W.N. 211; *Christ's Hospital* v. *Grainger* (1849), 1 Mac. & G. 460.

9 *Re Ingleton Charity*, [1956] Ch. 585.

10 *Ibid.*

11 Limitation Act 1939, s. 26; *Hovenden* v. *Lord Annesley* (1806), 2 Sch. & Lef. 607, at 634.

Chapter 36

Dealings in Charity Property

Introduction

Even before the legislature stepped in, the Court of Chancery had placed various restrictions on dealings in charity property. Some of these restrictions were lifted by the Charitable Trusts Act 1853 and the Charitable Trusts Act 1860: other restrictions were confirmed and consolidated in the Charitable Trusts Amendment Act 1855. The Nathan Committee examined all these provisions and concluded that they were, on the whole, justifiable;[1] and accordingly, on the repeal of the old legislation, the bulk of the restrictions and enabling provisions were re-enacted in the Charities Act 1960.

The aim of the various provisions which are to be discussed in this chapter is to preserve and husband the endowment so that it may continue to benefit the community.

To that end, section 29 of the Charities Act 1960 in particular imposes restrictions on the powers of charity trustees (i) to mortgage, sell, lease or otherwise dispose of charity land or (ii) to mortgage other property without an order of the court or of the Commissioners. Trustees of charitable endowments in Scotland do not labour under the burden of these restrictions,[2] nor indeed do trustees of private trusts. Why then are they necessary in the case of charitable trusts? The Nathan Committee answered this point in the following way:[3]

> "In the case of a private trust the beneficiaries are usually in a position to keep some watch on the activities of the trustees. This is conspicuously not the case with the great majority of charitable trusts where the beneficiaries or potential beneficiaries may well be a group of individuals not capable either of acting in concert or of obtaining skilled advice nor even with any clear knowledge of what provisions the trust instrument contains. They may even be unaware that they are potential beneficiaries. Moreover, what is a more important consideration, the great mass of charitable trusts are relatively small and in the hands of laymen of vicars, churchwardens, and others who might not, if this control were removed, think it necessary to employ skilled advice, as their counterparts in private trusts commonly think it prudent to do."

It is however still necessary to consider whether in the first place the trustees have the power to effect the transaction in question. This is quite independent of

---

1 Nathan Report (Cmd. 8710) paras. 244–250.
2 The 1960 Act does not apply to Scotland.
3 Nathan Report (Cmd. 8710) para. 246.

the question as to whether the consent of the Charity Commissioners is required
to a proposed transaction.

Trustees' powers of disposition

The trustees' powers to deal with charity property may arise either under the
general law, or under the instrument or statute of foundation, or under the
Settled Land Act 1925 or under section 23 of the Charities Act 1960.

GENERAL POWERS

There is no positive rule of law absolutely prohibiting the sale of charity lands,
but such a sale is rarely justifiable, the presumption being that persons who give
lands to a charity intend that they should be devoted to that purpose in perpetuity.[1] Nevertheless trustees have a general power at law to sell charity estates
upon their own initiative, whether expressly authorised by the instrument of
foundation[2] or not[3] if such sale is beneficial to the charity.[4] This general power
is not confined to charity lands: it extends, *a fortiori*, to other property held by
charity trustees.

Transactions of this kind are dangerous both for the trustees and for the
purchaser.[5] The trustees on the one hand must show that they have not been guilty
of a breach of trust,[6] the purchaser on the other hand must show that the sale
was beneficial to the charity and justified by the circumstances.[7] Where,
however, the origin of a charity does not appear, and a sale has taken place at
a very distant date, and has since been acquiesced in, those facts may afford
ground to presume that there was originally power to sell, and such presumption
will be made in favour of long enjoyment.[8]

Likewise, trustees of charity lands have a general power to lease,[9] exchange[10] or

---

1 *President etc of St. Mary Magdalen College, Oxford v. A.-G.* (1857), 6 H.L. Cas. 189, at
205. See also Shelford, *Law of Mortmain* (1836) 687; *Newcastle Corporation v. A.-G.* (1845),
12 Cl. & Fin. 402, H.L.

2 *Re Mason's Orphanage and London and North Western Rail. Co.*, [1896] 1 Ch. 596, C.A.
at 604.

3 *Ibid.*, and see *Re Howard Street Congregational Chapel, Sheffield*, [1913] 2 Ch. 690, at 695,
per ASTBURY J. See also *Re Manchester New College* (1853), 160 Beav. 610, at 628–629.

4 *A.-G. v. Hungerford* (1834), 2 Cl. & Fin. 357, at 374–375; *A.-G. v. South Sea Co.* (1841),
4 Beav. 453; *A.-G. v. Warren* (1818), 2 Swan. 291, at 303; *A.-G. v. Pilgrim* (1849), 12 Beav.
57, at 60; on appeal (1850) 2 H. & Tw. 186; *A.-G. v. Davey* (1854), 19 Beav. 521, at 525.

5 Sugden, *Law of Property*, 535; *A.-G. v. Newark-upon-Trent Corporation* (1842), 1
Hare 395.

6 *A.-G. v. South Sea Co.* (1841), 4 Beav. 453, at 458–459. See *A.-G. v. Kell* (1840), 2 Beav.
575 *A.-G. v. Bishop of Manchester* (1867), L.R. 3 Eq. 436.

7 *A.-G. v. South Sea Co.* (1841), 4 Beav. 453; *Re Clergy Orphan Corporation* [1894] 3 Ch.
145, C.A., at 154; *A.-G. v. Brettingham* (1840), 3 Beav. 91, at 95; *Re Manchester New College*
(1853), 16 Beav. 610.

8 *St. Mary Magdalen College, Oxford v. A.-G.* (1857), 6 H.L. Cas. 189, at 205, *per* Lord
CRANWORTH L.C. See also *A.-G. v. Cross* (1817), 3 Mer. 524; *A.-G. v. Warren* (1818), 2
Swan. 291, at 306.

9 *A.-G. v. Warren* (1818), 2 Swan. 291.

10 The court may, of course, authorise a beneficial exchange: *Mildmay v. Lord Methuen*
(1851), 14 Beav. 121 n. See also *Re Newton's Charity* (1848), 12 Jur. 1011.

mortgage them. It is the duty of trustees to administer the trust estate in a provident way and so dispositions which are consistent with provident administration may be valid whether or not the trustees have express powers to make them.

A power to exchange does not authorise a demise in consideration of another demise.[1]

A doubt has been raised as to whether the statutory provisions relating to the disposal of charity land supplanted the common law powers.[2] The basis for this doubt is not sufficiently indicated; but, having regard to the fact that such a doubt has been adumbrated in a treatise of authority it is obviously unsafe for trustees to rely on the general powers implied by the law.

EXPRESS POWERS

The statute, charter, trust instrument or memorandum of association governing the charity may confer express powers of dealing with charity property and, of course, these powers may have been given subject to the following of certain procedures or the obtaining of certain consents. Such powers are not cut down by the Settled Land Act 1925. Nor do they have to be exercised in accordance with the provisions of that Act, as if they were additional powers comprised in a settlement.

STATUTORY POWERS: SETTLED LAND ACT 1925

Trustees holding land on charitable trusts have in reference to such land all the powers which are conferred by the Settled Land Act 1925 on the tenant for life of settled land and on the trustees of a settlement.[3] These powers are in addition to any express powers. Section 29 (1) of the Settled Land Act 1925 provides as follows:

> "For the purposes of this section all land vested or to be vested in trustees on or for charitable, ecclesiastical or public trusts or purposes shall be deemed to be settled land, and the trustees shall without constituting them statutory owners, have in reference to the land all the powers which are by this Act conferred on a tenant for life and on trustees of a settlement.

There is some argument about the precise scope of this section. One view is that trustees of charity land held for the very purpose of advancing the particular charitable object have no power to sell the land under section 29 (1) of the Settled Land Act 1925. Thus it is said that chapel trustees who hold land expressly for use as a chapel can only sell it if the Commissioners empower them to do so by means of a scheme. As against this it is to be noted that section 29 (1) does say that *"all* land vested . . . in trustees . . . on or for charitable . . . trusts or purposes" shall be deemed to be settled land.

---

1 *President and Governors Magdalen Hospital* v. *Knotts* (1877), 26 W.R. 141; on appeal without taking this point (1878), 26 W.R. 640, C.A.; (1879), 4 App. Cas. 324, H.L.; *Re Female Orphan Asylum* (1867), 15 W.R. 1056.

2 5 Halsbury's Laws of England (4th edn.) 479, para. 808.

3 SLA 1925, s. 29 (1).

P

The power to sell under the Settled Land Act 1925 is a power to sell any part of it or any easement, right or privilege of any kind over or in relation to the land.[1] Such a sale must be made for the best consideration in money that can reasonably be obtained,[2] which may be in the form of a perpetual or terminable rent.[3]

The Settled Land Act powers include not only a power to sell but also a power to exchange land for other land or rights over or in relation to land, with or without the payment of money for equality of exchange.[4] Such exchanges must be made for the best consideration in land or in land and money that can reasonably be obtained.[5]

The leasing powers under the same statute enable trustees to grant leases of charity land, any part of it or right over or in relation to it, for any purpose for a term not exceeding 999 years in the case of a building or forestry lease, 100 years in the case of a mining lease or 50 years in the case of any other lease.[6] The lease must be made by deed, except in the case of a term of not more than three years, and must take effect in possession within one year or in reversion after a current term with seven years or less outstanding.[7] It must reserve the best rent reasonably obtainable, having regard to any fine[8] taken and to the circumstances generally[9] and there must be a covenant[10] by the lessee to pay the rent and a condition of re-entry on non-payment.[11] The lessee must execute a counterpart and deliver it to the trustees.[12]

The Settled Land Act powers also include powers of mortgaging for specified purposes, all of which relate to the well-being of the land, either by authorised improvements or by discharging incumbrances or other liabilities.[13] But trustees of property held for charitable purposes do not have the power, enjoyed by other trustees under section 16 of the Trustee Act 1925, to raise capital money for other purposes even though under the express trusts of the charity capital money may be applied for those purposes.

Under the Settled Land Act there is a power to grant options over the land, any part of it or any right over or in relation to it, at a price which must be fixed at the granting of the option[14] and must be the best reasonably obtainable in all the circumstances[15] to be exercisable within an agreed number of years not exceeding ten.[16]

Naturally where the trusts of the charity authorise the trustees to carry out any proposed transaction the trustees do not need to rely on the Settled Land Act powers.[17] But if the trustees want to exercise Settled Land Act powers they

---

1 SLA 1925, s. 38 (i).
2 *Ibid.*, s. 39 (1); and see s. 39 (5).
3 *Ibid.*, s. 39 (2)–(4).
4 *Ibid.*, s. 38 (iii).
5 *Ibid.*, s. 40 (1).
6 *Ibid.*, s. 41.
7 *Ibid.*, s. 42 (1) (i), (5) (ii).
8 Any fine will be capital money; *ibid.*, s. 42 (4).
9 *ibid.*, s. 42 (1) (ii).
10 In the case of a short lease in writing for "covenant" read agreement: *ibid.*, s. 42 (5) (ii).
11 *Ibid.*, s. 42 (1) (iii).
12 *Ibid.*, s. 42 (2).
13 *Ibid.*, s. 71.
14 *Ibid.*, s. 51 (1).
15 *Ibid.*, s. 51 (3).
16 *Ibid.*, s. 51 (2).
17 *Re Booth and Southend-on-Sea Estate's Co.'s Contract*, [1927] 1 Ch. 579.

must still obtain any consents or orders expressly required by the trust instrument.[1] And, in either case, where the purchaser has notice that the land is held on charitable trusts he must see that any consents or orders requisite for authorising the transaction have been obtained.[2]

MISCELLANEOUS SPECIAL STATUTORY POWERS

Trustees holding land for charitable purposes may grant up to one acre of land for the purposes of the School Sites Act 1841.[3] They may also with the consent of the Charity Commissioners grant up to one acre of land as a site for a literary or scientific institution.[4]

Charity trustees are expressly empowered under the Landlord and Tenant Act 1927 to grant a lease relieving them from any liability as landlords to pay compensation for improvements.[5]

The powers of local authorities to dispose of land under the Local Government Act 1972 must also be mentioned. County, district, London borough, parish and community councils, the Greater London Council, and the parish trustees of a parish acting with the consent of the parish meeting, may dispose of land held by them including land held for charitable purposes in any manner they wish.[6] Unless the disposal is by way of short tenancy[7] the Secretary of State's consent[8] is required if the disposal is for a consideration less than the best that could be reasonably obtained.[9] Moreover this statutory power of disposal does not authorise local authorities to dispose of land in breach of any trust, covenant or agreement binding on them,[10] or to dispose of charitable land forming part of a permanent endowment or used for functional purposes without an order of the court or the Charity Commissioners.[11] Indeed it is expressly provided that the powers conferred by the Act are not to be treated as statutory authority under section 29 (3) of the Charities Act 1960 enabling charitable property to be disposed of without an order.[12] Capital money received in consideration of the disposal of charity land must be applied in accordance with any directions given under the Charities Act 1960.[13]

Charity trustees have been given an express statutory power to sell by agreement land which is subject to a compulsory purchase order. The power is probably superfluous because of the wide power of sale conferred by the Settled Land Act 1925.

---

1 SLA 1925, s. 29 (2).
2 *Ibid.*, s. 29 (1).
3 School Sites Act 1841, s. 6.
4 Literary and Scientific Institutions Act 1854, s. 6.
5 Landlord and Tenant Act 1927, s. 14.
6 Local Government Act 1972, ss. 123 (1), 127 (1) 270 (1).
7 A term or residue of a term not exceeding seven years: Local Government Act 1972, ss. 123 (7), 127 (5).
8 See *ibid.*, s. 128.
9 *Ibid.*, ss. 123 (2), 127 (2).
10 *Ibid.*, s. 131 (1) (a).
11 CA 1960, s. 29; Local Government Act 1972, s. 131 (3).
12 Local Government Act 1972, s. 131 (3).
13 *Ibid.*, ss. 123 (6) and 127 (4).

STATUTORY POWERS: CHARITIES ACT 1960

Whether or not a transaction is within the powers exercisable by charity trustees under the trust instrument or under the Settled Land Act, the Commissioners may sanction it by order under section 23 of the Charities Act 1960. Such an order may either authorise a particular transaction or give a more general authority.[1] In the latter event the order will probably make it clear whether any further consent under section 29 is required for specific dealings.

Dealings where consent is required

DISPOSITIONS OF LAND

Subject to certain exceptions,[2] and notwithstanding anything expressed in the trusts of the charity[3] no land in England or Wales which forms part of the *permanent endowment* of a charity or, alternatively, which is held by or in trust for a charity and is or has at any time been occupied for the purposes of the charity, may be mortgaged or charged by way of security for the repayment of money borrowed,[4] or sold, leased, or otherwise disposed of without an order[5] of the court[6] or of the Charity Commissioners.[7]

Two categories of charity land are thus subject to restrictions on dealing, namely (1) land forming part of a *permanent endowment*, and (2) land which is or has at any time been *occupied for the purposes of a charity*. Land of the latter kind is generally termed "functional land" and includes not only buildings in which the administration of the charity is carried on, but also land such as playing fields vested in charity trustees, village halls, almshouses, and in the case of a charity which provides houses for its beneficiaries or officers, any house so provided. Land forming part of the permanent endowment of a charity is land bought with funds that could not be spent freely without distinction between capital and income.[8]

In practice, charity land often falls into both categories, as functional land is frequently bought with funds forming part of the permanent endowment.

But what is the position if the land has been bought purely as an investment, with money which could be spent without distinction between capital and income? The answer is that no order is required for any disposition of land in this third category: the disposition will merely be governed by the ordinary principles of trust law.

---

1 See CA 1960, s. 23 (2). Some acts cannot be authorised: *ibid.*, s. 23 (5), (6).
2 For the exceptions, see CA 1960, s. 29 (3), (4).
3 CA 1960, s. 29 (3).
4 The restrictions on mortgages and charges apply to property other than land.
5 Any such order must be formal and under seal: *B.I.U. Estates, Ltd.* v. *Chichester Diocesan Fund and Board of Finance Incorporated* (1963), 186 Estates Gazette 261.
6 For the meaning of "court", see CA 1960, s. 46.
7 CA 1960, s. 29 (1) and (2).
8 CA 1960, ss. 45 (3) and 46.

MORTGAGES OF PROPERTY

The restrictions surrounding dispositions of charity land extend in the case of mortgages and charges to all property forming part of the permanent endowment of a charity. No such property may without an order[1] of the court or of the Charity Commissioners be mortgaged or charged by way of security for the repayment of money borrowed. It is to be noted that this provision applies to "property" a term which is given no further definition and which must include property of any kind, whether land, securities or any other kind of personal property. Property forming part of the endowment of a charity is property bought with funds that could not be spent freely without distinction between capital and income.[2]

Effect of non-compliance with statutory restrictions

PERMANENT ENDOWMENT LAND

In the case of any dealing with land forming part of the permanent endowment the requirement of an order is absolute. Accordingly any transaction entered into in respect of such an endowment without the required order is wholly *void* and not merely voidable.[3] Indeed it has been held that a contract for such a dealing is also void unless the relevant order is obtained before the date of the contract[4] or unless the sale was made subject to the consent of the Commissioners.[5] In *Milner* v. *Staffordshire Congregational Union (Inc.) Trustees*[6] a purchaser who had entered into a contract to purchase charity land before the vendor had obtained the necessary consent was held not to be bound by the contract and to be entitled to recover his deposit. Where, therefore, no consent has been obtained, the purchaser, lessee or mortgagee ought to satisfy himself that the trusts on which the land is held enable the charity to apply the proceeds of the disposition without distinction between capital and income. A purchaser of land held on charitable trusts who has notice that the land is so held is also bound to see that any consents or orders requisite for authorising the transaction have been obtained, and, for this purpose, he should investigate the deed or other instrument declaring the trusts. In any case of doubt or difficulty the purchaser will be protected if the trustees obtain an opinion from the Commissioners under section 24 stating that no order is required.

---

1 Any such order must be formal and under seal: *B.I.U. Estates, Ltd.,* v. *Chichester Diocesan Fund and Board of Finance Incorporated* (1963), 186 Estates Gazette 261.
2 CA 1960, ss. 45 (3) and 46.
3 *Bishop of Bangor* v. *Parry,* [1891] 2 Q.B. 277.
4 *Milner* v. *Staffordshire Congregational Union (Inc.) Trustees* [1956] Ch. 275; [1956] 1 All E.R. 494.
5 *Michael Richards' Properties, Ltd.* v. *Corporation of Wardens of St. Saviour's Parish Southwark,* [1975] 3 All E.R. 416.
6 [1956] Ch. 275.

PURELY FUNCTIONAL LAND

In the case of functional land which does *not* form part of the permanent endowment, a transaction entered into without the requisite consent will be valid in favour of a person who (then or afterwards) in good faith acquires an interest in, or charge on, the land for money or money's worth. Nevertheless, this provision does not, it is submitted, absolve the purchaser from his obligation under section 29 of the Settled Land Act 1925 to see that all necessary consents and orders are obtained; and, for this purpose, the purchaser may if he wishes require a statutory declaration (at his own expense) verifying that the land has not at any time been occupied for the purposes of the charity. But a purchaser must still satisfy himself that the trusts on which the land is held enable the charity to use the proceeds of sale without distinction between capital and income. Only if the land does not in fact form part of the permanent endowment and if the purchaser's inquiries have led him to believe that it has never been occupied for the purposes of the charity does the provision protect him against misinformation on the past occupation of the land.

Dealings where consent is not required

The restrictions contained in section 29 of the Charities Act 1960 are not of universal application. Certain transactions are exempted; and so are certain charities.

EXEMPTED TRANSACTIONS

In the following cases the sanction of an order is not required.

(i) No order is required for any transaction for which general or special authority is expressly given (without the authority being made subject to the sanction of an order) by any statutory provisions contained in or having effect under an Act of Parliament or by any scheme legally established.[1] An example of statutory authority is to be found in sections 6 to 8 of the Land Clauses Consolidation Act 1845 under which lands may be purchased from charity trustees compulsorily or by agreement; sales under this Act do not require the sanction of the Commissioners,[2] but in practice sales originally intended to be carried out compulsorily are often carried out under the authority of an order of the Commissioners thus avoiding the inconvenience of the purchase money being paid into court under section 69 of that Act. The expression "a scheme legally established" means a scheme established by the court or the Commissioners or the Secretary of State,[3] but it does not include the original trust founding the charity (unless such foundation was by statute) nor does it include a royal charter incorporating the charity.[4]

---

1 CA 1960, s. 29 (3) (a).

2 *St. Thomas's Hospital (Governors)* v. *Charing Cross Rail. Co.* (1861), 1 John. & H. 400, at 406.

3 *Re Mason's Orphanage and London and North Western Rail. Co.,* [1896] 1 Ch. 596.

4 *A.-G.* v. *National Hospital for Relief and Cure of the Paralysed and Epileptic,* [1904] 2 Ch. 252.

(ii) No order is required for the granting of a lease for a term ending not more than 22 years after it is granted, not being a lease granted wholly or partly in consideration of a fine or premium.[1] A lease for a longer period than that authorised by this provision is absolutely void, but if the lessee enters and pays rent on a yearly basis he may become a tenant from year to year on such terms of the lease as are applicable to a yearly tenancy. If any fine or premium is taken on the grant of a lease (however short the term) the Commissioners' consent is required, because the fine or premium is capital money.[2] Consent is also required where a lease is granted for less than the best rent reasonably obtainable, whatever the length of the term, because such a lease requires the same order as a sale.[3]

(iii) No order is required for any disposition of an advowson.

EXEMPT AND EXCEPTED CHARITIES

The restrictions contained in section 29 of the Charities Act 1960 do not apply to exempt charities or to any charity excepted by order or regulations. Exempt charities are dealt with elsewhere in this work. Exception from the requirements of section 29 should be distinguished from exceptions from the requirement of registration or from the requirement to furnish accounts and the three types of exception do not necessarily apply to the same charities.

Five sets of regulations have so far been made under section 29.

(1) The Charities (Methodist Church) Regulations 1961[4] which came into operation on 20th February 1961 except from the provisions of section 29 any mortgage, charge, sale, lease or other disposal of land which is held upon trusts and with and subject to powers and provisions which are the same as those of, and are declared or adopted by reference to one of the five model deeds of the Methodist church particularised in the schedule to the regulations.[5]

(2) The Charities (Baptist Congregationalist and Unitarian Churches and Presbyterian Church of England) Regulations 1961[6] except from control any mortgage, charge, sale, lease or other disposal of land if (*a*) the land is held by a body named in the Schedule to the Regulations (whether alone or jointly with another person or persons) as a duly constituted trustee or custodian trustee of the land; and (*b*) during the period of three years immediately preceding the transaction, or where the land was acquired during that period, since the land was acquired by or for the charity, the land has not been used otherwise than as one or more of the following: a place of worship, a burial ground, a Sunday school, a church hall, a residence for a minister of religion, a residence for a caretaker of one of the foregoing places or the curtilage of one of the foregoing places.

(3) The Charities (Religious Premises) Regulations 1962[7] exempt from control

---

1 CA 1960, s. 29 (3) (b).
2 See SLA 1925, s. 42 (4).
3 SLA 1925, s. 29 (2).
4 S.I. 1961 No. 225.
5 Printed at 699, *infra*.
6 S.I. 1961, No. 1282. *Semble* the land does not have actually to have been used for any of these purposes: it is sufficient if it has been used for no other purpose. A purchaser is entitled (at his own expense) to a statutory declaration as to prior use.
7 S.I. 1962 No. 1421. Printed at 702, *infra*.

any *sale*[1] of land if (*a*) the land is held by or for a charity for the advancement of religion, and (*b*) during the period of three years immediately preceding the sale, or where the land was acquired during that period, since the land was acquired by or for the charity, the land has not been used otherwise than for certain purposes (which are the same as those listed in the Charities (Baptist, Congregational and Unitarian Churches and Presbyterian Church of England) Regulations considered above) and (*c*) it is certified on behalf of the charity at the time of the sale that the proceeds of sale are to be applied in or towards the provision of other land or premises. "A charity for the advancement of religion" is not confined to the Christian religion, and the reference in these Regulations to a Sunday school or church hall is to be construed, in the case of a charity for the advancement of a religion other than Christianity, as a reference to a school or hall of a similar kind.

(4) The Charities (Society of Friends, Fellowship of Independent Evangelical Churches and Presbyterian Church of Wales) Regulations 1962[2] except from control a charity for the advancement of religion as regards any mortgage, charge, sale, lease or other disposal of land if (*a*) the land is held whether alone or jointly with another person by the Friends Trust Ltd., the Fellowship of Independent Evangelical Churches or the Properties Board of the Calvinistic Methodist Church of Wales or Presbyterian Church of Wales, as a duly constituted trustee or custodian trustee of the land and (*b*) during the period of three years immediately preceding the transaction or, where the land was acquired during that period, since the land was acquired by or for the charity, the land has not been used otherwise than for certain purposes (which are the same as those listed in the Charities (Baptist, Congregational and Unitarian Churches and Presbyterian Church of England) Regulations 1961 considered above).

(5) The Charities (Church of England) Regulations 1963[3], except certain diocesan trust corporations listed in the schedule thereto[4] from the provisions of section 29 of the Charities Act 1960 as regards any mortgage, charge, sale, lease or other disposal of land if during the period of three years preceding the transaction or since the land was acquired (if it was acquired during that period) the land has not been used otherwise than for one or more of certain specified purposes. The purposes specified are a place of worship, a burial ground, a Sunday school, a church hall, a residence for a minister of religion, a residence for a caretaker of such a place or places, or the curtilage of such a place or places. The land must be held by the particular diocesan trust corporation either alone or jointly with another person or persons, as a duly constituted trustee or custodian trustee of the land and not for its own purposes.

Excepting *orders* have also been made either in relation to a particular transaction, or generally but for a limited period.

---

1 *Cf.* the wider exemption in the first two mentioned Regulations including the repayment of money borrowed for that purpose.
2 S.I. 1962 No. 1815. Printed at 703, *infra.*
3 S.I. 1963 No. 1062.
4 Printed at 704–705, *infra.*

Duties of trustees on sale: practice notes issued by Commissioners

The Charity Commissioners have issued notes intended to give general guidance to charity trustees who are contemplating a sale of any of the land belonging to their charity. It is on these official notes that much of what follows is based.

Trustees are bound in any dealing with charity property to give primary consideration to the interests of the charity. For example, land should seldom be sold at all if it is needed for occupation for the purposes of the charity, unless better premises are to be provided elsewhere. Nor should any land be sold if, in the long run, it will be to the financial benefit of the charity to keep it, unless there is such a pressing need for liquid funds as to outweigh this consideration.

If trustees decide to sell, they are under a legal obligation to secure the most advantageous terms for the charity; this normally means that they must take reasonable steps to obtain the highest possible price. They have no right to sell for less either for the sake of a prospective purchaser to whom they feel under a moral obligation or in order to prevent the property being put to a use of which they do not personally approve. If trustees sell for less than the best price that they could reasonably have obtained, they may render themselves personally liable, in proceedings for breach of trust, to make good the loss to the charity. Trustees might well be held liable in this way, and would certainly expose themselves to criticism if they sold the land to a speculator on terms that enabled him to resell shortly afterwards at a profit.

Where there is a proposal to sell charity land surveyors should be instructed by the trustees of the charity to inspect the property in question and to make a valuation and report of the information of the Charity Commissioners.[1] The official notes issued by the Commissioners require that the report should deal with such of the following points as are relevant:

(1) In every report the surveyor should state clearly whether in his opinion a sale is the best course to adopt in the interests of the charity rather than that the property should be dealt with in some other way.

(2) A general description of the property (including the name of the borough, urban district or civil parish in which it is situated), its area, the Ordnance Survey Map number and edition and if agricultural, the mode of cultivation. A plan of the property showing its abuttals and approaches should be supplied.

(3) The tenancy and present rental of the property, the condition of any buildings, and the amount and incidence of any fixed outgoings.

(4) The present letting value, and the amount of outlay required to maintain a full rent or to secure an improved rent.

(5) The estimated selling value in an open market both subject to the tenancy, if any, and with vacant possession. In the case of a tenancy the surveyor should state what are the prospects of obtaining vacant possession in the near future.

(6) Where it is proposed to sell a property subject to an existing lease:

(i) The estimated value of the property subject to the lease

(ii) The estimated value of the property freed from the lease and with vacant possession.

---

1 See the Official Leaflet of the Charity Commissioners, S.A. 3 (S).

(7) Whether the property could be more advantageously sold by private contract or by public auction and, if it is recommended that the property be offered for sale by public auction in more than one lot, the description, area and separate value of each lot.

(8) The effect of a sale of the property proposed to be sold upon any property to be retained by the trustees and what covenants, if any, should be imposed on a sale for the benefit of any property retained.

(9) The future use or development of the land to be gathered from the development plan prepared by the local planning authority under the Town and Country Planning Acts, bye-laws and subsisting covenants restrictive of the user of the land.

(10) Whether the surveyor recommends that the trustees should seek planning permission and what bearing will this have on the value of the land.

Registered land

A number of problems arise in connection with charity land under the system of registered conveyancing introduced by the Land Registration Act 1925. One set of problems concerns the first registration of a charity's title to particular land: the other relates to dealings with land already registered in which a charity is involved.

FIRST REGISTRATION

In some areas of England and Wales registration of title to land is, in given circumstances, compulsory,[1] while in other areas it is voluntary.[2]

If a charity acquires freehold land by conveyance on sale or is granted a lease for a term of years absolute not being less than 40 years from the date of the delivery of the grant or takes an assignment on sale of leasehold land held for a term of years absolute having not less than 40 years to run from the date of delivery of the assignment and the land is situated in an area where registration is compulsory on sale, an application must be made on behalf of the charity for the registration of its title to the land within two months of the relevant disposition, or, if extension of this period is granted, within such extended period. If this is not done the disposition will become void so far as it conveys or grants a legal estate.[3]

In all other cases application may be made voluntarily by or on behalf of a charity for the registration of its title to any estate or interest capable of registration.[4]

The procedure on applications for registration and the effect of registration are the same in the case of charity land as in the case of other land, subject to certain special provisions that are applicable to charity lands.

---

1 For an up-to-date list of areas of compulsory registration, see the lists in 17 Encyclopaedia of Forms and Precedents (4th edn.) 257–262, para. 230 and cumulative Noter Up (1976).

2 Voluntary registration has been suspended, except in certain classes of cases: LRA 1966, s. 1 (2); and see 17 Encyclopaedia of Forms and Precedents (4th edn.) 186–188.

3 Land Registration Act 1925, s. 123.

4 But only when the suspension of voluntary registration ends.

No special form is prescribed for the application for the first registration of charity land. The application should be made on whichever of the printed forms of application is appropriate. The form applicable will depend on the circumstances of the case as for example, whether the land is freehold or leasehold, whether the applicant is or is not a corporate body or whether or not the land has been recently purchased. Persons in a fiduciary capacity, such as the trustees of a charity, are expressly empowered to apply for first registration.[1] The application form should disclose the fact that they are trustees of the particular charity and the applicant should normally produce the trust deed or relevant scheme containing the trust provisions, or a verified copy of it.

On an application for first registration made by a corporation or a body of trustees in whom property from time to time vests such evidence should be produced to the Registrar as he may direct of incorporation or of the provisions under which the property vests together with evidence of the applicant's power to deal with the land.[2] And if there are any restrictions on the applicant's powers of alienation, the Registrar is, in every case, bound to enter an appropriate restriction on the register.[3]

In the case of land belonging to a charity which cannot be sold without the consent of the Charity Commissioners[4] the following provisions set out in rule 60 of the Land Registration Rules 1925 as amended apply:

"A. Where there are managing trustees[5] whether or not the land is vested in them, they shall be the persons to apply for the first registration under the sections 4 and 8 of the Act[6] of one of the following person or persons as proprietor thereof.

(1) Where the land is vested in the [official Custodian for Charities][7] he shall be registered as proprietor thereof[8] subject to the production of either

(a) (i) a conveyance to him together with the original or an office copy of the order of the court or the Commissioners authorising him to accept such conveyance; or (ii) an official copy of the order, scheme, or other instrument vesting the land in him; and in either case the conveyance or other dispotition (if any) of the land for the benefit of the charity; or

(b) evidence that the land has become vested in him under the provisions of a statute.

(2) Where the land is vested in a corporation (not being [the Official Custodian for Charities]) on trust to deal with the same in accordance with the directions of the managing trustees of the charity the corporation shall be registered as proprietors.

---

1 LRA 1925, s. 93.

2 LRR 1925, r. 259.

3 *Ibid.*, rr. 39, 60–32. As to the appropriate restriction or restrictions, see 4 Encyclopaedia of Forms and Precedents (4th edn.) 534–538.

4 As to land which cannot be sold without such consent see 388, *supra*.

5 The expression "managing trustees" for the purposes of this rule includes a committee of management: LRR 1925, r. 60D.

6 I.e. the Land Registration Act, 1925 (LRA 1925): see LRR 1925, r. 1 (1).

7 The words in square brackets were substituted by CA 1960, s. 48 (6).

8 See LRA 1925, s. 98 (as amended by CA 1960, s. 48 (1), Sch. 6).

(3) In any other case the managing trustees shall be registered as proprietors, and shall be entered on the register as the managing trustees for the time being of the charity.[1]

B. Where there are no managing trustees and the land is vested in a corporation, the corporation may upon their own application be registered as proprietors.

C. In every case in which land is registered under this rule a restriction in Form 12 shall be entered in the register.

D. In this rule the expression 'managing trustees' includes a committee of management."

Although the above provisions are stated to apply to land belonging to a charity which cannot be sold without the consent of the Commissioners they would appear to be equally applicable to the first registration of all charity land.

Exempt charities[2] and charities excepted by order or regulations[3] can sell their land without the consent of the Charity Commissioners. But in other cases where on an application for registration of any land it is in the opinion of the Registrar doubtful whether the land can be sold without the consent of the Charity Commissioners the registration must not be completed until either (*a*) there has been produced to the Registrar a certificate granted by the Commissioners under rule 62 of the Land Registration Rules 1925 or (*b*) notice of the proposal to register the title without the entry of the prescribed form of restriction requiring such consent has been served by the Registrar on the Attorney-General.[4] In the event of the Attorney-General after receipt of such notice entering an objection to the registration of the title without this restriction, the Registrar is required to refer the case for the opinion of the High Court.[5]

By rule 62 it is provided that if the Charity Commissioners certify by an order under seal[6] that any land may be sold without their consent, or may be sold without their consent so long as a particular condition is satisfied, the Registrar may accept such certificate as conclusive evidence that the prescribed restriction[7] need not be entered against the title or that a conditioned restriction only need be entered, or that if the prescribed restriction is already entered it may be removed or suitably modified.

DEALINGS WITH LAND ALREADY REGISTERED

Where an application is made to register a transfer of registered land in favour of a charity which is a corporate body, evidence of incorporation and of the applicant's power to deal with the land must be produced.[8] The transfer is required to be in Form 35 in the Schedule to the Land Registration Rules 1925.[9] If the statute, memorandum and articles or other instrument constituting the

---

1 As to when trustees are registered collectively, see 332, *supra.*
2 As to exempt charities, see 4–6, *supra.*
3 As to the making of such regulations and orders, see 391–392, *supra.*
4 LRR 1925, r. 61.
5 *Ibid.*
6 No fee is charged for issuing such an order.
7 See 4 Encyclopaedia of Forms and Precedents (4th edn.). Form 55A, 534.
8 LRR 1925, r. 259.
9 *Ibid.*, r. 121 (1).

charity contains any limit on the extent of the land that may be held or any provisions as to the purposes for which if may be used, the transfer must contain a statement that such limit has not been exceeded or showing that purposes for which the land is to be used.[1] A transfer of registered land to trustees on charitable trusts must be in the prescribed form.[2] Unless the trusts of the charity are declared by or appear from the transfer itself the transfer must refer to the trust deed, will, statute or other instrument under which the trusts arise and a certified copy of that deed or instrument must be supplied to the Land Registry.[3] And in this case, too, if a transfer is made under a statute or other authority which contains any limit as to the extent of land which may be acquired, the transfer must contain a statement showing that such limit has not been exceeded.[4] The Registrar must be satisfied that the transfer is in accordance with the law relating to charitable uses.[5]

When the Registrar is satisfied that the land cannot be sold without the consent of the Charity Commissioners the Land Registration Rules 1925 provide that he must enter the prescribed form of restriction[6] with any such modifications as the case may require and he thinks fit.[7] Where he is doubtful whether or not the land can be sold without such consent, the procedure is the same as when doubt arises on an application for first registration.[8] And where it appears to him that a right of pre-emption or reverter or restrictive condition or any other like right or restriction exists or may arise, he must enter notice of the right or condition, or a restriction or inhibition protecting the right or condition in such manner or form as he thinks fit.[9]

Where a charitable trust of land which is already registered is declared by the proprietor he must forthwith and before executing any transfer, charge or other disposition of the land, or dealing with the land in any way, produce the land certificate and the original or a certified copy of the deed or other declaration of trust to the Registrar, who must cause the appropriate prescribed[10] restriction to be entered on the register if the circumstances so require.[11]

The Official Custodian for Charities may be registered as proprietor on behalf of any charity or foundation in the following cases:

(1) Where the managing trustees of the charity or foundation are registered as proprietors of the land on production of an official copy of an order by a competent authority vesting the land in him;

(2) Where they are not so registered, on production of a transfer to them and of an official copy of an order by a competent authority vesting the land in him;

(3) Where the land is vested in the Official Custodian under a statute on production of such evidence that it is so vested as the Registrar may require.[12]

---

1 *Ibid.*, r. 121 (2), (3).
2 *Ibid.*, r. 122 (1), Schedule, Form 36.
3 *Ibid.*, r. 122 (1).
4 LRR 1925, r. 122 (1).
5 *Ibid.*, r. 123 (1). Until the abolition of the law of mortmain in the 1960 Act he was also concerned to see that the mortmain laws had been complied with.
6 LRR 1925, Schedule, Form 12.
7 *Ibid.*, r. 123 (2).
8 *Ibid.*, r. 123 (3).
9 *Ibid.*, r. 123 (4).
10 I.e. by LRR 1925, r. 123.
11 *Ibid.*, r. 124.
12 LRR 1925, r. 128 (1).

Where the Official Custodian is registered under (2) above the title acquired under the transfer to the managing trustees of the charity or foundation is for the purposes of those provisions of the Land Registration Act 1925 relating to the effect of registration of dispositions[1] and to implied covenants in charges[2] deemed to have been registered and the Official Custodian is deemed to be the transferee; but for the purposes of the provision[3] which relates to implied covenants on transfer of leaseholds, the managing trustees are deemed to be the transferees.[4]

Where the Official Custodian for Charities is registered as proprietor of land on behalf of any charity or foundation, the managing trustees for the time being of the charity or foundation may register an address for service of notices and all notices which under the Land Registration Rules are required to be sent to the proprietor, must then be sent to the managing trustees at the registered address instead of the proprietor.[5] The registered address may be changed as occasion may require.[6]

Where any reference is made in the register to the managing trustees for the time being of a charity or foundation, the Registrar may, if he thinks fit, accept a certificate under the seal of the Charity Commissioners certifying the names of such trustees as conclusive evidence that the persons so named are the trustees at the date of the certificate.[7]

The Charity Commissioners have issued two leaflets setting out their views on the form of transfer suitable for use on sale of registered land vested in the Official Custodian for Charities[8] and the form of transfer of registered land suitable for use where the legal estate is not vested in the Official Custodian but in the trustees.[9]

Where registered land is vested in the Official Custodian for Charities, and the transfer is made to carry out a sale authorised by the Charity Commissioners, the following points should be noted. The Official Custodian for Charities will not execute the transfer because, when the transaction which the transfer is to carry out has been authorised by the Commissioners, the charity trustees have power[10] to execute and transfer in the name and on behalf of the Official Custodian. The transfer should be executed by all the trustees or by two or more of them authorised to do so in pursuance of section 34 of the Charities Act 1960. A declaration should be made in the transfer that it is executed pursuant to whichever statutory provision or provisions were invoked[11] and this declaration will be accepted by the Land Registry as sufficient evidence that the transfer has been executed accordingly. In view of the provisions of section 17 (5) of the Charities Act 1960 the charity trustees cannot impose any personal liability on the Official Custodian and the transfer should not purport to do so. He should not be a party to any declaration of value that may required. The Land Registry

---

1 See LRA 1925, ss. 20 and 23.
2 See *ibid.*, s. 28.
3 See *ibid.*, s. 24.
4 See LRR 1925, r. 128 (2).
5 *Ibid.*, r. 129 (1).
6 *Ibid.*, r. 129 (2).
7 *Ibid.*, r. 130.
8 Official Leaflet of the Charity Commissioners, SA 12.
9 Official Leaflet of the Charity Commissioners, SA 13.
10 See CA 1960, s. 17.
11 I.e. under CA 1960, s. 17 or ss. 17 and 34.

will require a list of the trustees certified as being the present trustees by the clerk or solicitor to the charity. This will normally be contained in a letter from the clerk or solicitor to the charity. The official leaflet contains a form of transfer in conformity with the views set out in the leaflet. But the Commissioners point out that the form of the transfer is primarily a matter for the purchaser to decide. If the form of transfer submitted by the purchaser does not provide for execution by the Official Custodian, does not purport to impose any personal liability on him or make him a party to any declaration of value that may be required and is not open to objection in other respects, it may properly be accepted by the trustees although it is not in accordance with the views expressed in the leaflet. In any event the draft of the transfer should not be submitted to the Commissioners or to the Official Custodian for approval.

On the sale of registered land which is registered in the names of the trustees of a charity, and not in the name of the Official Custodian for Charities, the transfer should be executed by all the trustees or by two or more of them author-ised to do so in pursuance of section 34 of the Charities Act 1960.[1] Where the transfer is executed pursuant to the last-mentioned provision it should contain a declaration that it is so executed; this declaration will be accepted by the Land Registry as sufficient evidence of execution by virtue of the section.[2] Unless the transferors are the persons named in the register as the trustees of the charity, the Land Registry will require a list of the trustees certified as being the present trustees by the clerk or solicitor to the charity.[3] The draft leaflet dealing with such sales sets out a form of transfer, but again the Commissioners recognise that the form of the transfer is primarily a matter for the purchaser to decide; and so long as the solicitor to the charity is satisfied that it is not open to objec-tion it may properly be accepted by the trustees even if it is not in accordance with the views expressed in the official leaflet. Here again the draft of the transfer should not be submitted to the Commissioners for approval.

Where, under the trusts of a charity, trustees of property held for the purposes of the charity may be appointed or discharged by resolution of a meeting of the charity trustees, members or other persons, the trustees may, if they wish, be registered collectively as "the trustees of the [X charity]" instead of in their individual names.[4] The advantage of this method of registration is that it avoids the necessity for recording on the register deaths, transmissions and new appoint-ments. If an application is subsequently made to register a transfer by the trustees and there have been changes in them since the date of registration, certified copies of the relevant memoranda of appointment or discharge should be lodged in appropriate cases with the application. A letter from the clerk or solicitor of the charity certifying that the persons so named as trustees are the present trustees of the charity will, however, also be accepted as sufficient alternative evidence.

---

1 See Official Leaflet of the Charity Commissioners, SA 13.
2 *Ibid.*
3 *Ibid.*
4 CA 1960, s. 35 (1). As to the form of restriction entered on the register, see 4 Encyclo-paedia of Forms and Precedents (4th edn.) 538, Form 55G.

Chapter 37

Investment of Trust Funds

Introduction

The powers and duties of charity trustees in regard to the investment of funds belonging to the charity are, like those of private trustees in relation to private trusts, governed by any special provisions of the trust instrument[1] extending or limiting their statutory powers.

The statutory investment powers are contained principally in the Trustee Investments Act 1961. Until this Act was passed the range of securities in which trustees whether of a charity or a private trust were authorised to invest, in the absence of special provisions, was defined in the Trustee Act 1925 and was limited to government stocks and certain other first class securities producing a fixed income and normally with a fixed redemption value and date. The policy of the law founded on the assumption that the real value of money would remain stable was designed to avoid the risk of loss to trust capital or income. But chronic inflation sabotaged this underlying assumption and the limited investment powers under the Trustee Act 1925 became a burden. The Nathan Committee[2] recommended that subject to certain safeguards charity trustees should be empowered to invest up to one-half of their trust funds in debentures, stocks and shares (including equity stocks and shares) of companies whose shares were quoted on the London Stock Exchange. The Committee's recommendations were accepted in general by the Government and the result was the Trustee Investments Act 1961 which empowered all trustees (whether of charities or of private trusts) in the absence of a contrary intention, to invest up to one-half of their trust funds in a wide range of investments, including ordinary stocks and shares in substantial public companies, and, in addition, imposed a duty on trustees to have regard to the need for diversification of investments of the trust, in so far as is appropriate to the circumstances of the trust.[3] The Act also requires trustees to take proper advice from a person experienced in financial matters before investing under the new statutory powers in any investment other than Defence Bonds, Savings Certificates and certain bank deposits,[4] and to take similar advice at intervals so long as they retain any investment made under those powers.[5] The powers and duties of charity trustees

---

1 See e.g. *Soldiers', Sailors' and Airmen's Family Association* v. *A.-G.*, [1968] 1 All E.R. 448, n. [1967] 1 W.L.R. 127.
2 Nathan Report (Cmd. 8710) paras. 289–296.
3 TIA 1961, s. 6 (1).
4 *Ibid.*, s. 6 (2).
5 *Ibid.*, s. 6 (3).

under the Act of 1961 are set out in a Charity Commission leaflet,[1] procurable on application, which also explains the purpose of common investment funds set up under the Charities Act and their special advantages for small charities.

Replacement of capital: practice of Commissioners

Capital money may with the sanction of the Charity Commissioners be used in the repair improvement or modernisation of buildings owned by charities, or for rebuilding, or in other circumstances where a charity has an urgent need for ready money. In these circumstances the Commissioners are prepared to consider the proposed expenditure, and, if satisfied that the project is in the best interests of the charity, to sanction the resort to capital, provided that the capital will be replaced out of future income.[2]

It has always been the practice of the Commissioners following that of the courts before the Commission was first established, to require that any capital monies of a charity, which with their authority are expended for any purpose other than the purchase of investments or land should be replaced. The rare exceptions to this requirement have occurred in most unusual circumstances. Of course this imposes on charitable trusts a more stringent requirement than obtains in private trusts where, for instance, the rules in the Third Schedule to the Settled Land Act 1925 permit certain expenses to be met out of capital. But the view is taken that this stringency is essential to preserve the capital of charities which, unlike private settlements, are intended to last for ever.[3]

The power of the Commissioners to direct the replacement of capital is derived from the statutory authority in section 23 (4) of the Charities Act 1960 which provides that the directions which may be given under an order made under that section include "directions . . . for requiring expenditure charged to capital to be recouped out of income within a specified period".

Recognising that trustees who are administering charities, part of whose capital is being replaced usually need to know the date on which the replacement will be completed and the income that has been diverted to the accumulation account will again become available for the current purposes of the charity, the directions given by the Charity Commissioners follow the words of section 23 (4) of the Charities Act 1960 by requiring recoupment "within a specified period".

The period within which recoupment will in a particular case be required must depend both on the nature of the transaction and the financial circumstances of the charity. Until the repeal of section 30 of the Charitable Trusts Amendment Act 1855, which required that all money borrowed on mortgage should be repaid within 30 years, the Commissioners felt obliged by analogy with this statutory provision to require the replacement of capital within at least 30 years; but since the repeal of that section by the Charities Act 1960, the period of 30 years is no longer regarded as a maximum. Generally speaking, a period such as 20 years may be regarded as normal for the replacement of the expense of minor repairs or the erection of buildings with a short life, whereas 30 years

---

1 Leaflet T.P. 1 see Appendix 4, 731–736, *infra*; and see also *Lewin on Trusts* (16th edn.) 323–351; *Underhill on Trusts* (12th edn.) 381–420.
2 [1963] Ch. Com. Rep. 20 (paras. 55–56).
3 *Ibid.*, para. 57.

is considered reasonable for thorough improvements or the provision of reasonably good agricultural buildings. Where the expense has been incurred in the provision of new buildings intended to have a long life, longer periods such as 40, 50 or even 60 years can be approved. But the Commissioners are always prepared to agree to a shorter period where the trustees wish it and the financial condition of the charity permits, and are also ready to consider making the period longer than would otherwise have seemed reasonable if there is a pressing need for immediate income.[1] The normal practice is that the period during which the recoupment account shall last is settled at an early stage in the discussions with the trustees.

The actual amount of capital to be set aside in the account will depend both on the length of the term and on the amount spent. The policy of the Commissioners is to provide for the setting aside of enough capital to effect a cash replacement according to the ordinary tables for sinking funds taken at an estimated rate of interest likely to be obtained throughout the period of recoupment. The rate taken as the basis at present is $4\frac{1}{2}$ per cent. These figures can from the $4\frac{1}{2}$ per cent. compound interest tables be expressed with adequate accuracy as a series of simple fractions. Thus, if the accumulation account is to last 20 years, then capital having a value of three-quarters of the amount spent will have to be set aside; but if the period is 30 years, then only one-third need be set aside. In this way trustees can at an early stage in planning the financing of the work estimate the reduction in their available income which will result from it.[2]

The direction given by the Commissioners when the cost of the work is known is that capital of a certain cash value must be transferred to a special account to be accumulated for a fixed period, and that at the end of that period, whatever may be the outcome of the account, the funds in it are to be returned to the general capital of the charity. Trustees are not deprived, even when an order is made under section 23, of their discretion to choose the particular security in which the recoupment account is to be invested, but the Commissioners do try to see that the trustees have received advice including the advantages of accumulation in a common investment fund.[3] It is not feasible to include in the calculation of a recoupment account an estimate of the effect of growth and it has, therefore, to be based on a pound to pound replacement. By taking up accumulation shares in a common investment fund, however, trustees can expect that the charity will receive, in addition, the element of capital growth which would have accrued over the duration of the account.[4]

Recovery and redemption of rentcharges

Rentcharges created for charitable purposes and rentcharges issuing out of charity land are subject to the same incidents and recoverable by the same procedure as other rentcharges.[5] The Charity Commissioners have, however,

---

1 *Ibid.*, 22, para. 62.
2 *Ibid.*, para. 63.
3 E.g. The Charities Official Investment Fund or (in the case of an almshouse charity) the National Association of Almhouses Common Investment Fund.
4 [1963] Ch. Com. Rep. 23 (para. 64).
5 See 32 Halsbury's Laws of England (3rd edn.) 532.

certain special powers under the Charities Act 1960 with respect to the compulsory redemption of rentcharges and for taking proceedings for their recovery.[1]

Actions to recover rentcharges which appear to belong to charities may be brought by the Attorney-General.[2]

RECOVERY

Prior to the Charities Act 1960 the Commissioners had power, with the sanction of the Attorney-General, to institute proceedings in their own name on behalf of a charity for the recovery of any property belonging to the charity, the annual income of which did not in the opinion of the Commissioners exceed £20.[3] The main advantage of proceedings under the now repealed Charitable Trusts (Recovery) Act 1891 was that the risk of costs, which might otherwise absorb the whole of the charity's property, was borne by the Commissioners in the same way as if proceedings had been instituted by the Attorney-General[4] in a charity matter.

The 1960 Act is both wider and narrower. It is wider in that the relevant section[5] empowers the Commissioners to take legal proceedings on behalf of the charity for recovery of a rentcharge issuing out of any land, or out of the rents, profits or other income of any land, or any periodical payment other than rent reserved on a lease or for compelling payment thereof whatever the amount of the rentcharge or payment[6] and without obtaining the consent of the Attorney-General.[6] It is narrower in that the new power extends only to rentcharges and other periodical payments, though the Commissioners have a similar power to take proceedings for the recovery of the redemption price where a charity rentcharge is redeemed.[7]

Proceedings may be instituted in the name of the Charity Commissioners for England and Wales and will not abate or be affected by any change in the persons who are the Commissioners notwithstanding that the Commissioners are not incorporated.[8]

In any proceedings to recover or compel payment of any rentcharge or other periodical payment claimed by or on behalf of a charity out of land or the rents, profits or other income of land (other than rent reserved on a lease) whether the proceedings are brought by the Commissioners or by the charity itself there is a statutory presumption that if the rentcharge is shown to be paid at any time for 12 consecutive years to or for the benefit of the charity, it is perpetual and no proof of its origin is necessary.[9] The presumption is rebuttable, and the defendant may be able to show that the payments were made under a rentcharge or trust of limited duration. But the statutory presumption removes any possible difficulty in proving the origin of ancient charitable rentcharges.

---

1 CA 1960, s. 27.
2 *Re Herbage Rents*, [1896] 2 Ch. 811, citing earlier cases.
3 Charitable Trusts (Recovery) Act 1891, s. 3.
4 As to proceedings by the Attorney-General, see *Re Herbage Rents*, [1896] 2 Ch. 811.
5 CA 1960, s. 27 (1).
6 *Cf.* Charitable Trusts (Recovery) Act 1891, s. 3.
7 CA 1960, s. 27 (5); see 405, *infra*.
8 *Ibid.*, Sch. 1, para. 4.
9 *Ibid.*, s. 36 (1).

Under the old law[1] a corresponding presumption could only be relied upon in proceedings instituted by the Commissioners, though a presumption might arise under the general law from long continued payment.[2]

Proceedings brought in the High Court by the Commissioners are assigned to the Chancery Division and are started by originating summons.[3] Any documents required or authorised to be served on the Commissioners in such proceedings must be served on the Treasury Solicitor.[4]

REDEMPTION

The Commissioners are empowered by statute[5] to require the redemption of charity rentcharges, or any other periodical payments except rent reserved on a lease.[6] The procedure for compulsory redemption is for the Commissioners to give to the estate owner in respect of the fee simple in the land a notice to treat with the charity trustees for the redemption of the rentcharge.[7] Where the rentcharge is payable in respect of a term of years, the notice to treat is given to the estate owner of that estate rather than to the fee simple owner.[8] In the case of settled land the "estate owner" will be the tenant for life or the statutory owners, as the case may be. And where an estate owner of land liable to a rentcharge pays it through an agent, a notice to treat, if given to the agent on behalf of the estate owner is deemed to be given to the estate owner, notwithstanding that the accepting of the notice is not within the scope of the agent's authority.[9]

The estate owners and the charity trustees have a period of ten years from the time of the service of the notice within which to negotiate the amount to be paid for the redemption of the rentcharge. If, at the end of that time, the rentcharge is still subsisting the estate owner of the relevant estate in the land is liable to pay the redemption price to the charity or to the person entitled as trustee to receive it for the charity; on payment or tender of the redemption notice the estate owner is entitled to a proper and effective release of the rentcharge, or, at his request, a proper and effective transfer of it to a person nominated by him.[10] The redemption price under this procedure is determined in accordance with regulations made by the Treasury,[11] and those regulations provide that the redemption price is the gross annual amount of the rentcharge multiplied by the number of years' purchase obtained by dividing into 100 the mean current gross yield per cent. of certain specified government securities.[12] The release will be executed by the charity or the trustees for the charity, and since these

---

1 Charitable Trusts (Recovery) Act 1891, s. 5.
2 *A.-G.* v. *West* (1858), 27 L.J. Ch. 789 (30 years).
3 R.S.C. Ord. 108, r. 2.
4 *Ibid.*, r. 6.
5 CA 1960, s. 27.
6 *Ibid.*, s. 27 (9).
7 *Ibid.*, s. 27 (8).
8 *Ibid.*
9 *Ibid.*
10 *Ibid.*, s. 27 (3).
11 *Ibid.*, s. 27 (4).
12 See Charities (Redemption of Rentcharges) Regulations 1962, S.I. 1962 No. 2376, printed in 4 Halsbury's Statutory Instruments (1st Reissue) 58.

provisions, in effect, enable a compulsory sale of the rent to be made,[1] it will still require the authority of an order of the Commissioners[2] although once the notice to treat has been given the Commissioners have no discretion to refuse to make such an order. The Commissioners may take proceedings on behalf of a charity for recovery of sums due for the redemption of a rentcharge.[3]

Where a charity rentcharge affecting settled land is redeemed the redemption price is payable out of capital.[4]

Where the estate owner of land liable to a rentcharge has by law or by contract any right of indemnity or contribution in respect of the rentcharge against any person or property, then on his redeeming the rentcharge under the compulsory provisions of the Act he will have the like right of indemnity or contribution in respect of the redemption price.[5]

For the purposes of the Land Charges Act 1925 and the Land Registration Act 1925 a notice to treat under section 27 of the Charities Act 1960 is treated as a land charge, and those Acts apply to it as they apply to an estate contract.[6] Consequently a purchaser of the land subject to the rentcharges will not be bound by the notice to treat unless, in the case of unregistered land, it is registered as a Class C (iv) land charge, or in the case of registered land, a notice or caution is entered on the register, before completion of the purchase.[7] Presumably the charity bears the expenses of registration.[8]

The provisions of section 27 enabling the Commissioners to compel the redemption of charity rentcharges do not affect the statutory provisions of the Law of Property Act 1925[9] under which the owner of the land liable to a rentcharge or any person interested therein can also obtain compulsory redemption. It might therefore pay an estate owner to consider his chances under the alternative procedures: he will at any rate have ten years to make up his mind after receipt of the notice to treat from the Commissioners. A rentcharge may also be discharged by the court on a sale or exchange of the land which is subject to it,[10] though this method of redemption would probably be more expensive than either of the others.

No powers of apportionment of rentcharges are given to the Commissioners under the provisions of the Charities Act 1960 although, if an agreement were reached between the owner of an estate liable to a rentcharge, and the charity entitled to the rentcharge, the Commissioners could approve it under their general powers[11] if they considered it expedient in the interest of the charity. In simple cases the *owner* of the land may obtain an apportionment under the Law of Property Act 1925.[12] But many charitable rentcharges are charged on areas of land in fragmented ownership and the only way for the charity to obtain redemption of such rentcharges will be by agreement with the person who

---

1 *Cf. Re Carr's Settlement*, [1933] Ch. 928, at 933 (a case on LPA 1925, s. 191).
2 Under CA 1960, s. 29 (1).
3 *Ibid.*, s. 27 (5).
4 SLA 1925, s. 73 (1) (ii).
5 CA 1960, s. 27 (6).
6 *Ibid.*, s. 27 (8).
7 Land Charges Act 1925, ss. 10 (1), 13 (1); Land Registration Act 1925, s. 59 (2), (6).
8 See Land Charges Act 1925, s. 12 (2).
9 LPA, 1925, s. 191.
10 *Ibid.*, s. 50.
11 I.e. under CA 1960, s. 23.
12 LPA 1925, s. 191 (7).

actually pays them, such agreement being sanctioned by the Commissioners under section 23 of the Charities Act 1960.

Compulsory redemption is usually expensive for the charity concerned, involving the trustees in the expense of employing a solicitor and possibly of supplying a map of the land subject to the rentcharges. The Commissioners therefore have decided that the power should only be exercised in those cases where the charity trustees have considerable difficulty in collecting the rent-charge and, except in special circumstances, where the amount of the yearly payment is not less than £5. A normal upper limit for compulsory redemp-tion of £20 a year has also been set on the footing that this sum seems the maximum which can be so redeemed without being unduly onerous; at 15 years' purchase this figure means a demand for a capital sum of £300.[1]

The usual practice of the Commissioners is to require charity trustees to invest the net redemption moneys in the name of the Official Custodian for Charities, except where the charity's investments are held in the name of another corporate trustee. The redemption price calculated in accordance with the formula contained in regulations made by the Treasury[2] is such that the redemption money can be invested in undated government stocks to produce a yearly income for the charity approximately equal to the amount of the rent-charge. Investment in this way means, however, that there is little possibility of obtaining any increase in the yearly income, while the real value of both capital and income may continue to fall. The Commissioners therefore encourage charity trustees to choose an investment which can reasonably be expected to produce a growing income over the long term even though the income obtain-able from it initially may be less than the amount of the rentcharge. They consider the Charities Official Investment Fund[3] as very suitable for this purpose especially when the sums available for investment are comparatively small.[4]

With larger rentcharges the owner of the land charged may be willing to redeem the rentcharge but unable to find the capital sum required and may sug-gest payment of the redemption price by instalments over a period of years. If the proposals are acceptable to the charity trustees and are, on the face of them, reasonable they will be considered sympathetically. Redemption by instalments would almost certainly involve the trustees in higher costs and the estate owner is expected to pay these, since the arrangement would be for his benefit.[5]

Sometimes where land out of which a rentcharge issues is being acquired by a body having compulsory powers of acquisition (usually a local authority), the acquiring authority has been known to issue to the trustees a notice to treat for the release of the rentcharge under the threat of compulsory extinguishment if agreement is not reached. If the amount of the consideration money offered is less than the minimum price for the rentcharge calculated under the Treasury regulations, the Commissioners are not prepared to authorise the trustees to release the rentcharge, and if the acquiring authority refuses to increase its offer in respect of the rentcharge to the minimum price thus calculated it will have to proceed strictly in accordance with the statutory provisions affecting the

1 [1967] Ch. Com. Rep. 14, para. 45.
2 Charities (Redemption of Rentcharges) Regulations 1962, S.I. 1962 No. 2376, printed in 4 Halsbury's Statutory Instruments (1st Reissue) 58.
3 See 409 *infra*.
4 [1967] Ch. Com. Rep. 14–15, para. 46.
5 *Ibid.* 15, para. 47.

extinguishment of rentcharges. The Commissioners take the view that in laying down formulae for calculating the redemption price of a rentcharge in section 191 of the Law of Property Act 1925[1] and by means of Treasury regulations,[2] Parliament intended the redemption price to be such as could on investment produce an income approximating to the amount of the rentcharge. They therefore deprecate the practice of some acquiring authorities of offering sums equal to about eight or nine years' purchase of the rentcharge, amounts which are obviously disadvantageous to the charities concerned.[3]

Where boundaries are confused, or it is not known out of what land the rentcharge issues,[4] or the legal title to the land is not clear or is defective,[5] a legal rentcharge may be enforced in equity in favour of a charity where the right could not be enforced at law. This is in accordance with the well-established principle that equity will aid defective assurances in favour of charities.[6]

A charitable rentcharge may be barred under the Limitation Act 1939.[7] But where there is no person to represent the charity so as to make a claim the time does not run under the statute. In *A.-G.* v. *Persse*[8] a testator devised a rentcharge as a salary for a schoolmaster, to be appointed by the owner for the time being of the estate on which the rent was charged. A schoolmaster was never appointed. Twenty-seven years later proceedings to enforce the trust were started, and it was held that no schoolmaster having been appointed, the Statute of Limitations could not run against the demand of a non-existent person.

Common investment funds

GENERAL

Common investment funds were not unknown before the passing of the Charities Act 1960. Common investment schemes had been made in a number of cases, particularly where a number of charities were administered by the same trustee[9] or were otherwise closely connected. The Universities and Colleges (Trusts) Act 1943 empowered the Universities of Oxford and Cambridge and their constituent colleges, and also Winchester College, to make schemes providing for trusts for purposes connected with the respective university or college to be administered as a single fund, such schemes to be approved by Order-in-Council.[10] Other universities had obtained private Acts establishing

---

1 See at 405, *supra*.

2 Charities (Redemption of Rentcharges) Regulations 1962, S.I. 1962 No. 2376.

3 [1967] Ch. Com. Rep. 15, para. 48.

4 *A.-G.* v. *Wilkins* (1853), 22 L.J. Ch. 830, at 832; 17 Beav. 285, at 291.

5 *Re Herbage Rents, Greenwich*, [1896] 2 Ch. 811, at 825 per Stirling, J.; *Foley's Charity Trustees* v. *Dudley Corporation*, [1910] 1 K.B. 317, C.A., and see *Woodford Parish* v. *Parkhurst* (1639), Duke, *Law at Charitable Uses* (ed. Bridgeman) 378.

6 Shelford, *Law of Mortmain* (1836) 514; and see Gareth Jones, *History of the Law of Charity 1532–1827* (1969) 60 ff. and 135 ff. for a discussion of this principle.

7 *A.-G.* v. *Wilkins* (1853), 17 Beav. 285, at 293; *A.-G.* v. *Stephens* (1855), 6 De G.M. & G. 111, at 146; *President, etc., of St. Mary Magdalen College Oxford* v. *A.-G.* (1857), 6 H.L. Cas. 189.

8 (1842), 2 Dr. & War. 67; see also *Incorporated Society* v. *Richards* (1841), 1 Dr. & War. 258, at 288.

9 Such a scheme was and is known as a pooling scheme: see 408, *infra*.

10 Universities and Colleges (Trusts) Act 1943, ss. 2 and 3.

common investment funds.[1] Moreover it was open to the Court and the Commissioners and the Secretary of State to make what was called a pooling scheme authorising a single body of trustees holding the investments of a number of charitable trusts to treat those investments for investment purposes as a single whole.[2] However, separate bodies of trustees could not combine their holdings for such a purpose since this would have involved them in delegating their powers of investment.

The Charities Act 1960 overcame the difficulty caused by the non-delegability of investment powers by authorising delegation to trustees appointed to manage a common investment fund. Section 22 went further than the qualified recommendations of the Nathan Committee[3] and conferred on the court, the Commissioners and the Secretary of State a general power to make schemes for the establishment of common investment funds. The essential features of these schemes are that (*a*) the property transferred to the fund by or on behalf of a charity participating in the scheme is to be invested under the control of trustees appointed to manage the fund, and that (*b*) the participating charities are to be entitled to a proportionate share of the capital and income of the fund, the shares to be determined by reference to the amount or value[4] of the property transferred to the fund by or on behalf of each of them, and to the value[4] of the fund at the time of the transfers.[5]

Any two or more charities may now apply to the Court or the Commissioners to make a common investment scheme.[6] Where a single body of trustees administer a number of charities they may now apply under section 22 for a pooling scheme.[7]

It still remains the case that a pooling scheme can only be made when there is a single body of trustees administering a number of charities: it is basic to the concept of a pooling scheme that there is no difference of trusteeship among the constituent charities. What such a scheme does is to empower the trustees to "pool" the endowments of the different charities: then each charity is regarded as interested in an appropriate undivided aliquot proportion of the total pool of all the investments. Following the practice of the Court the Commissioners, in their schemes, now commonly authorise the trustees to bring into the pool other charities which they administer (or may in future administer) although they are not named in the scheme.[8] Until 1963 pooling schemes were made by the Courts under their inherent jurisdiction to make schemes for charities;[9] and the Commissioners followed them in their practice. However part of the decision of WILBERFORCE J. in *Re London University's Charitable Trusts*[10] is based on the assumption that a pooling scheme is also a common investment fund scheme for the purposes of section 22 of the Charities Act 1960. Apparently, therefore, a pooling scheme can be made either under the inherent jurisdiction, or under section 22 or both. However the Commissioners expressly draft their pooling

---

1 See, for example, Liverpool University Act 1931; Birmingham University Act 1948.
2 *Re Royal Society's Charitable Trusts*, [1956] Ch. 87.
3 As to which see Nathan Report (Cmd. 8710) para. 556.
4 Market value not par value.
5 CA 1960, s. 22 (1).
6 *Ibid.*, s. 22 (2).
7 *Re London University's Charitable Trusts*, [1964] Ch. 282.
8 [1963] Ch. Com. Rep. 16–17, para. 45.
9 *Re Royal Society's Charitable Trusts*, [1956] Ch. 87.
10 [1964] Ch. 282.

schemes under section 22 to avoid any doubt as to their nature. They are ready to establish such schemes whenever they are shown to be useful.[1]

If two or more bodies of trustees wish to unite in pooling the endowments of the charities which they administer, then the requisite scheme is a common investment scheme. In this case an entirely distinct body of trustees has to be appointed to manage the pooled endowments. The scheme will contain carefully considered provisions for equality of treatment between the charities belonging to the different bodies of trustees. Their rights to bring in further endowments, to withdraw endowments to receive dividends and to make representations about the management of the fund will also be regulated by the scheme. Thus, a scheme of this nature is necessarily far more complicated than a simple pooling scheme. The Commissioners have indeed anticipated the need for such a scheme by the establishment of the Charities Official Investment Fund which by its size offers greater opportunities for the diversification of investments than a more modest common investment fund. The Commissioners recognise, however, that there may be occasions when a group of trustees may prefer that a common investment fund should be set up to meet their own particular needs. The Commissioners have stated that in such cases they would not refuse to embark on the establishment of a new common investment fund, provided that the amount of the funds available was large enough to give the managers of the new fund an ample opportunity for satisfactory investment. They require, however, that there should be some nexus between the charities which are expressed to be eligible to participate in the fund; such nexus might be geographical instead of being functional. To date, the Commissioners have not, since the launching of the Charities Official Investment Fund, had the occasion to undertake the establishment of a new common investment fund. Clearly a great deal of preparatory work would have to be carried out by the applicant trustees in order to assemble both suitably qualified persons and the means for securing the proper management of the new common investment fund.[2]

CONTENTS OF COMMON INVESTMENT SCHEMES

A common investment scheme may make provision for all matters connected with the establishment, investment, management and winding up of a common investment fund, and the Charities Act 1960 specifies various provisions which may be included in such a scheme. These include provisions for the remuneration of trustees holding or managing the fund; for restricting the size of the fund or regulating, as to time, amount or otherwise, the right to transfer property or withdraw from the fund, and enabling sums to be advanced from the fund on loan to a participating charity pending the withdrawal of the property from the fund by the charity; for enabling income to be withheld from distribution with a view to avoiding fluctuations in the amounts distributed, and generally for regulating distributions of income; for enabling money to be borrowed temporarily for the purpose of enabling payments to be made out of the fund; for enabling questions arising under the scheme as to the right of a charity to participate or as to the rights of participating charities

---

1 [1963] Ch. Com. Rep. 17–18, para. 47.
2 *Ibid.*, 17, para. 46.

or as to any other matter to be conclusively determined by the decision of the trustees managing the fund or in any other manner; for regulating the accounts and information to be supplied to participating charities.[1] The Charities Act 1960 does not expressly confer on the managing trustees powers greater than those conferred by the Trustee Investments Act 1961. However, in *Re London University Charitable Trusts*[2] WILBERFORCE J. held that an extension to the range of investments authorised by the Trustee Investments Act 1961 should be allowed in the case of investments of trusts being consolidated with an existing combined investment pool over which the trustees already enjoyed an extended power of investment. The convenience of administration and saving of expense which would be achieved by permitting the extended range of investment was a special circumstance which satisfied the accepted principle that extensions beyond the 1961 statutory range of investments should only be permitted in special circumstances.

A common investment scheme set up under the 1960 Act may include a provision for enabling sums to be deposited by or on behalf of a charity on the basis that (subject to the provisions of the scheme) the charity shall be entitled to repayment of the sums deposited and interest thereon at a rate determined by or under the scheme. When sums are deposited in this way pursuant to a scheme, the shares of the charities participating in the scheme otherwise than by way of deposit must be calculated after excluding such amounts as are from time to time reasonably required for repayment of deposits and interest on deposits, including amounts required by way of reserve.[3] Nevertheless any capital appreciation of the investments representing the deposits will accrue wholly to the charities participating otherwise than by way of deposit.

A common investment scheme may provide for the assets of the common investment fund or any of them to be vested in the Official Custodian for Charities, and if made by the Commissioners or if they consent may also appoint him or authorise him to be appointed to manage the fund or any part of it. If he is appointed managing trustee the Official Custodian will have, subject to the provisions relating to the office of Official Custodian, the same powers, duties and liabilities as other managing trustees. Does this mean that he is entitled to charge fees in his capacity as managing trustee? The Act does not expressly say so. As a general rule the Official Custodian has no powers of management and no power to charge fees, but section 17 (1) of the Charities Act 1960 which specifically denies him the power to charge fees is expressed to be subject to the provisions of the Act. Section 22 gives him the same powers as other managing trustees when he is acting as such and this must surely give him the power to charge fees for his administrative work just as they can.

Where a common investment scheme does provide for the Official Custodian for Charities to exercise any discretion with respect to the investment of the fund it must make provision for him to be advised by a committee of persons who have special experience of investment and finance or of the administration of trusts, or who represent or are nominated by bodies having that experience.[4]

---

1 CA 1960, s. 22 (4).
2 [1964] Ch. 282.
3 CA 1960, s. 22 (5).
4 *Ibid.*, s. 22 (6).

MISCELLANEOUS PROVISIONS

Section 22 of the Charities Act 1960 sets out various other provisions relating to common investment funds.

Except in so far as a common investment scheme provides to the contrary, the rights under it of a participating charity are not capable of being assigned or charged, nor is any trustee, or other person concerned in the management of the common investment fund, required or entitled to take account of any trust or other equity affecting a participating charity or its property or rights.[1]

Every charity has power to participate in common investment schemes, unless the power is excluded by a provision specifically referring to common investment schemes in the trusts of the charity.[2]

A common investment fund is deemed for all purposes to be a charity,[3] and the assets of the fund are treated for the purposes of the Charities Act 1960 as a permanent endowment,[4] in other words as subject to a restriction on their being expended between income and capital.[5] Accordingly in the case of a common investment fund statements of account have to be transmitted annually to the Commissioners,[6] the assets cannot be mortgaged or charged by way of security for the repayment of money borrowed without an order of the court or of the Commissioners; nor if they consist of land in England or Wales be sold, leased or otherwise disposed of without such an order;[7] and no part of the capital of the fund can be paid out to the participating charities in the form of income. Exceptionally, however, if the scheme establishing the fund admits to participation only charities not having permanent endowments, the fund as a whole is treated as a charity not having a permanent endowment; and similarly if the scheme admits only exempt charities, the fund itself is an exempt charity for the purposes of the Act.[8]

The persons managing a common investment fund are not treated for the purposes of the Prevention of Fraud (Investments) Act 1958 as carrying on the business of dealing within the meaning of that Act,[9] and the same applies to similar funds established under statutory powers for the exclusive benefit of charities.[10]

Ex gratia payments

Prior to 1969 the Charity Commissioners were frequently asked by trustees of charities to allow them to make voluntary payments out of their funds to meet what seemed to them to be a valid moral obligation even though it had no

---

1 *Ibid.*, s. 22 (7).
2 *Ibid.*, s. 22 (8).
3 CA 1960, s. 22 (9). Accordingly it is registrable but its charitable nature is nevertheless not open to challenge.
4 CA 1960, s. 22 (9).
5 *Ibid.*, s. 45 (3).
6 *Ibid.*, s. 8 (1).
7 *Ibid.*, s. 29 (1).
8 *Ibid.*, s. 22 (9).
9 *Ibid.*, s. 22 (10).
10 *Ibid.*, s. 22 (11).

legal basis. A typical case was where the intentions of a testator had been frustrated by the operation of some facet of the law of wills, with the result that the charity received a large legacy at the expense of some person who had lost his claim to a legacy obviously intended for him. The Commissioners took the view that not only did trustees have no power under their trusts to make an ex gratia payment, but also there was no way in which the Commissioners could provide authority for trustees to do so. Similarly, for a very long time it was the settled practice adopted by the junior counsel advising the Attorney-General in charity matters to say that no authority could be given to charities to make these voluntary payments. There was, however, no reported case in which the court had laid down this rule and the practice had come to be questioned.[1]

While it was felt that a change of practice might be desirable it was considered that a new practice ought not to be adopted without the authority of the court. Two cases in which the Attorney-General encouraged the plaintiffs to submit the facts to the court so that they could be treated as test cases were eventually heard together in the Chancery Division in 1969. These were the cases of *Re Snowden*[2] and *Re Henderson*.[3]

In *Re Snowden*[4] the testator gave all the shares he might hold at the date of his death in three named companies in certain proportions to three persons who were his nearest relations and in whose welfare he always took a great interest. He then gave pecuniary legacies (mostly to charities) and directed that the pecuniary legatees should receive his residuary estate "in the similar proportions as they received legacies". By the date of his death the testator had disposed of his holdings in the three companies, and the proceeds of sale were represented in his estate by cash. The result was that nothing passed under the gift to the relations but the residue was of course greatly increased as was the benefit to each pecuniary legatee who shared in the residue. Most, but not all, of the charities considered that they were under a moral obligation to make a payment out of the residuary legacies to go some way towards achieving the obvious intention of the testator and expressed to wish to give up the whole or part of their respective shares. Accordingly the surviving executors took out a summons to ascertain whether effect could be given to their wish.

The facts in *Re Henderson*[5] were somewhat different because there were no specific named charities which benefited and which could consider whether or not an ex gratia payment should be made. The testatrix by her holograph will gave several pecuniary legacies and among them £3000 each to her nephew and niece and left "Anything over to Charitys". At some unidentified date she added in red ink "or ½ each of my shares" to the right of the names of her nephew and niece. Letters of administration with the will annexed were granted to her husband but without including the red ink additions. He considering it probable that the testatrix intended the two legatees to share the amount by which the sum of their legacies was exceeded by the value of the shares took out a summons asking for directions that, on the Attorney-General signifying that he would acquiesce in the payment, the administrator might be allowed to make

---

1 [1969] Ch. Com. Rep., para. 26.
2 *Re Snowden*, [1970] Ch. 700.
3 *Re Henderson*, [1970] Ch. 700.
4 [1970] Ch. 700.
5 [1970] Ch. 700.

some reasonable payment to provide increased legacies for the nephew and niece.

In both cases, then, the question was whether the court or the Attorney-General could authorise charity trustees who wish to do so to make an ex gratia payment out of charity funds pursuant to some apprehended moral obligation. Counsel were unable to find any authority denying the existence of such a power. The only argument against the existence of such a power which commended itself to the learned judge was that to admit it would be to open the door to numbers of applications to charity trustees by persons who might say with greater or less plausibility that their reasonable expectations would be defeated if the charity retained the money in question and that some ex gratia payment ought to be made. Although that argument was a weighty one it seemed to CROSS J. that it would be very hard to justify the denial of the existence of the power referred to.[1] He advanced four reasons for his belief that the court and the Attorney-General had the power to authorise ex gratia payments. First, it would be odd if charities which depend for their continued existence on the recognition by members of the public of a moral obligation to give to them could not themselves give effect to moral obligations. Secondly, such a rule would deny to the court or the Attorney-General in the case of charities a power which existed in other cases—those of mental defectives[2] and children[3]—that might be said to be somewhat analogous. Thirdly, in sanctioning compromises by charities, the courts have taken into account the moral merits of claims made against charities. Lastly, there are some old cases from which it appears that trustees of charities who have committed breaches of trust over a long period of years might properly be asked to make good a sum less than that which was strictly due.[4] If, as appeared from those cases, the court acting on the advice of the Attorney-General had power to relieve charity trustees from the obligation to make good in full breaches of trust for which they had been shown to be answerable, and so in effect to retain money which belonged to the charity, it would be extraordinary that there should be no power in the court or the Attorney-General to allow charity trustees to apply charitable funds in discharge of a moral obligation of the charity.[5]

Having concluded that the power existed, CROSS J. said that the power was not one to be exercised lightly or on slender grounds but was a power to be exercised only where it could be fairly said that, if the charity were an individual, it would be morally wrong for him to refuse to make the payment. A distinction should be drawn between cases like *Re Snowden* and *Re Henderson* in which the testator or testatrix never intended the charity to receive so large a gift as it did receive and other cases where the testator's relations considered that he was not morally justified in leaving his money to a charity rather than to them. In the latter case there would as a rule be no moral obligation resting upon the charity and no authority should be given for it to make a payment.[6] There might be cases in which an ex gratia payment out of charity funds would be justified; for example the testator in making the gift to the charity might have been breaking

---

1 [1970] Ch. 700, at 709.
2 See Mental Health Act 1959, s. 102 (1) (c).
3 *Re Clore's Settlement Trusts*, [1966] 1 W.L.R. 955; *Re C.L.* [1969] 1 Ch. 587, at 599.
4 See e.g. *A.-G.* v. *Exeter Corporation* (1827), 2 Russ. 362; *A.-G.* v. *Brettingham* (1840), 3 Beav. 91; *A.-G.* v. *Pretyman* (1841), 4 Beav. 462.
5 [1970] Ch. 700, at 710.
6 *National Provincial Bank* v. *Moore* (1967), 111 Sol. Jo. 357.

a solemn, though not legally enforceable, promise to leave it to someone else. However, the learned judge was of the view that the instances in which an ex gratia payment would be justified would be rarer in the cases where the testator clearly intended to leave the money to charity and not to the claimant, than in those in which the testator's obvious intention to benefit the claimant had been frustrated through some oversight or legal technicality.[1]

CROSS J. also discussed the practice that should be followed. In cases like the *Snowden* case in which individual charities are concerned it is in the first place for the charity trustees to decide whether or not they wish to make an ex gratia payment having regard to the strength of any supposed moral obligation. If they decide to do so they then apply to the Charity Commissioners. The approach to the Commissioners should not be made by the claimant asking for the payment who must put his case to the charity concerned. The Commissioners consider the facts submitted to them and may perhaps ask for more information. They then make a report to the Attorney-General who will decide whether or not the trustees are to be given authority to make a payment. If the case put up seems to the Commissioners to be ill-founded, they will usually explain to the trustees why it is considered that the Attorney-General should not be troubled with it. In those cases where no individual charity is concerned, but, as in the *Henderson* case, there is a legacy to charity generally the approach should be made normally on behalf of the executors to the Treasury Solicitor who will report to the Attorney-General.[2]

---

1 [1970] Ch. 700, at 711.
2 [1969] Ch. Com. Rep., para. 30.

Part V

Jurisdiction

Chapter 38

The Crown and the Court

The Crown

PROTECTIVE ROLE OF THE CROWN

The character of *parens patriae* which formerly made the Crown the protector of wards[1] and lunatics[2] makes it the protector of charity in general.[3] Thus it is said that the Crown as *parens patriae* has a superintending power over all charities apart from and antecedent to the Statute of Charitable Uses 1601 which power has been delegated to the courts.[4] Accordingly where persons who are named as trustees of charities fail in the performance of their duties either by death or by a disability or refusal to act, the constitution has provided a trustee in the person of the Sovereign. Blackstone observed that[5] "the king as *parens patriae* has the general superintendance of all charities which he now exercises by the keeper of his conscience the chancellor; and, therefore, whenever it is necessary the Attorney-General, at the relation of some informant who is actually called the relator, files ex officio an information[6] in the Court of Chancery, to have the charity properly established". It is the duty of the Crown, as *parens patriae* to protect property devoted to charitable uses, and that duty is executed by the officer who represents the Crown for all forensic purposes; and on that foundation rested the right of the Attorney-General in such cases to obtain by information[6] the interposition of a court of equity.[7] Lord REDESDALE said in *Ludlow Corporation* v. *Greenhouse*:[8]

> "that the ground stated in all the books is this, that the King is to be considered as the *parens patriae*; that he is the protector of every part of his

---

1 *Eyre* v. *Countess of Shaftsbury* (1724), 2 P. Wms. 102.

2 *Viscount Falkland* v. *Bertie* (1696), 2 Vern. at 342. The statutory jurisdiction under the Mental Health Act 1959 has in effect superseded the exercise of the royal prerogative over lunatics: see Heywood and Massey, *Court of Protection Practice* (9th edn.) 5–10.

3 *A.-G.* v. *Brown* (1818), 1 Swan 265, at 291; originally the bishop or ordinary was the protector of charities: Gareth Jones, *History of the Law of Charities* (1532–1827) (1969) 4–9.

4 But prior to 1597 there was no adequate procedure enabling the Crown to enforce a charitable use or gift: Jones, *op. cit.*, 21–22.

5 3 Bl. Com. 427. But if there is a charter with proper powers, there is no ground for the controlling interposition of the court: *A.-G.* v. *Middleton* (1751), 2 Ves. Sen. 327.

6 The information has been superseded by the writ of summons: see 488, *infra*.

7 *Wellbeloved* v. *Jones* (1822), 1 Sim. & St. 40, at 43.

8 (1827), 1 Bli. N.S. 17, at 48.

Q

subjects; and that, therefore, it is the duty of his officer, the Attorney-General, to see that justice is done to every part of those subjects."

Certain charitable corporations are subject to the visitatorial jurisdiction of the Crown.[1] The jurisdiction is exercised by the Lord Chancellor acting on behalf of the Crown.[2]

PREROGATIVE POWER OF THE CROWN

It was held as early as 1675 that where there is a general gift to charity with no trust interposed the disposition of the gift was in the Crown.[3] In *A.-G. v. Peacock*[4] a testator had given the residue of his estate "to charitable uses for the good of the poor forever". FINCH L.K. held that the doctrine of prerogative *cy-près*, which until then had only applied where the gift was to illegal charitable objects, applied to gifts to indefinite charitable objects. In the event the *cy-près* application directed by the Crown was for the benefit of teaching poor boys at Christ's Hospital arithmetic and the art of navigation. In *Clifford v. Francis*[5] a testator devised the surplus of his estate after the debts should be paid to his executors to be disposed of by them for pious uses: this was a general gift to charity and it was held that the King was the disposer of the charity. Lord NORTH L.K. reached a similar decision in *A.-G. v. Syderfen*[6] where a testator had declared that money should be applied for such charitable uses as he had formally directed in writing and no writing could be found. Likewise a gift "to be applied to charitable and pious uses generally",[7] a testamentary direction that "if there is any money left unemployed I desire it may be given in charity"[8] and a bequest of money "all to be given for charitable purposes"[9] all fell to be disposed by the Crown under the sign manual, and not by the court. Other cases in which the gift has been held to be disposable by the Crown and not the court include a case where there was a bequest of stock to the Government in exoneration of the National Debt[10] and a case where there was a gift "unto my country England"[11] and also cases where there was a gift to a non-existent charity with no trust interposed[12] or to an institution dissolved after the testator's death but before payment again with no trust interposed.[13] Whether in these

---

1 See 424, *infra*.

2 See 424, *infra*.

3 *A.-G. v. Peacock* (1676), Cas. temp. Finch 245. At one time the Crown also exercised its prerogative in the case of gifts to superstitious uses which were also charitable: see Gareth Jones, *History of the Law of Charities (1532–1827)* (1969) 76–87, 151–153; Sheridan and Delany, *The Cy-près Doctrine* 71–73.

4 (1675), Cas. temp. Finch 245; 2 Lev. 167; and see Jones, *op. cit.*, 88–90 for a full account of the case.

5 (1679), Freem. Ch. 330.

6 (1683), 1 Vern. 224.

7 *A.-G. v. Herrick* (1772), Amb. 712.

8 *Legge v. Asgill* (1815), Turn. & R. 265, n.

9 *Kane v. Cosgrave* (1873), I.R. 10 Eq. 211.

10 *Newland v. A.-G.* (1809), 3 Mer. 684.

11 *Re Smith* [1932] 1 Ch. 153, C.A.

12 *Re Bennett* [1960] Ch. 18 where the earlier inconsistent cases are all cited; *cf. Re Conroy* (1973), 35 D.L.R. (3d) 752 where with the approval of the Attorney-General the judge directed a scheme.

13 *Re Slevin*, [1891] 2 Ch. 236, C.A. *cf. Hayter v. Trego* (1830), 5 Russ. 113; *Re Soley* (1900), 17 T.L.R. 118.

days there is any virtue in preserving the distinction between judicial and prerogative *cy-près* is open to doubt.[1]

Where the disposition falls to be dealt with by the Crown the court having declared that the gift is a valid charitable gift makes an order that the Attorney-General be at liberty to take such steps as he may be advised to ascertain the Sovereign's pleasure as to the disposal of the gift.[2] The Attorney-General then applies to the Sovereign for a warrant under the sign manual disposing of the property.[3] A form of letter or warrant under the sign manual is to be found in the Irish case of *Kane* v. *Cosgrave*.[4]

The court

From the earliest times the Court of Chancery exercised an inherent jurisdiction over the execution of charitable trusts[5] and that jurisdiction is now vested in the Chancery Division of the High Court of Justice.[6] It is said in the books that the jurisdiction depends, indeed depends exclusively,[7] on the existence of a *trust*. But this statement requires qualification or, at any rate, a loose construction of the word "trust". Companies and other corporate bodies established for charitable purposes are subject to the jurisdiction of the court even though they may not be trustees, in the conventional or strict sense, of their property.

The court exercises both a non-appellate and an appellate jurisdiction over charitable trusts. The *non-appellate* jurisdiction of the court in relation to charities is dealt with under three headings, namely (1) proceedings concerning the validity of dispositions to charity (2) matters arising in the course of administration of charitable trusts and (3) its inherent jurisdiction amplified by statute to make schemes.

APPELLATE JURISDICTION

The *appellate* jurisdiction is exercised (1) where there is an appeal against any decision of the Charity Commissioners to enter or not to enter an institution in the register of charity or to remove or not to remove an institution from the register (2) where there is an appeal against an order of the Charity Commissioners establishing a scheme for the administration of a charity or regulating the charity. It is sometimes said that there is a right of appeal against the Charity Commissioners' refusal to authorise charity proceedings. But an application to the court for leave to take such proceedings is not strictly an appeal.[8]

In addition the court has in certain circumstances power to exercise control over the conduct of visitors.[9]

---

1 See [1974] A.S.C.L. 508, at 514 (J. Hackney).
2 For a form of order see 9 Court Forms (2nd edn.) 85–86.
3 *Da Costa* v. *De Pas* (1754), Amb. 228; *A.-G.* v. *Herrick* (1772), Amb. 712.
4 (1873), I.R. 10 Eq. 211, at 214–215.
5 See *Wakeryng* v. *Bayle* (circa 1422–70) 1 Calendar of Proceedings in Chancery lvii; *Lyon* v. *Hewe* (circa 1465–83) 2 Calendar of Proceedings in Chancery xliv; *Payne's Case* (temp Eliz) Duke, *Law of Charitable Uses* (ed. Bridgman) 154.
6 Supreme Court of Judicature (Consolidation) Act 1925, s. 56.
7 *Tudor on Charities* (6th edn.) 302; but see *Re Bennett*, [1960] Ch. 18, at 26, *per* VAISEY J.
8 See 514, *infra*.
9 See 431, *infra*.

NON-APPELLATE JURISDICTION

Validity of charitable dispositions

Many of the cases in the books, and particularly those concerned with the definition of charity, turn on the validity of particular dispositions. Sometimes the question is whether a gift (testamentary or *inter vivos*) is, on the true construction of the relevant will or deed, a gift for a charitable purpose or charitable purposes, or whether an existing body to whom a gift has been made is, in fact, charitable. Sometimes a donor misdescribes the object of his bounty and it becomes necessary for the court to decide on the evidence which of several competing claimants is entitled. Again a question of construction may arise where a gift fails, as for example because it has been made to a non-existent institution or is initially impossible. It then becomes material to discover whether the donor had a general charitable intention. Or the point at issue may be whether a gift offends the rule against perpetuities.

In all of the above-mentioned cases the court as part of its inherent jurisdiction to construe and interpret instruments has jurisdiction to determine the point in question. And in certain cases the courts exercise a statutory jurisdiction.

ADMINISTRATION OF CHARITABLE TRUSTS

Much of the jurisdiction in relation to the administration of charitable trusts has now in practice been transferred to the Charity Commissioners. As a general rule such questions now only come before the court with the consent of the Charity Commissioners. The position is that all "charity proceedings" as defined by the Charities Act 1960 must be authorised by an order of the Charity Commissioners, unless the charity proceedings relate to an exempt charity. In the latter case no authorising order is required.

Charity proceedings

"Charity proceedings" are defined as proceedings in any court in England or Wales brought under the court's jurisdiction with respect to charities or the administration of a trust for charitable purposes.[1]

The ancestor of the modern provision that charity proceedings must be authorised by the order of the Commissioners was the requirement that the Commissioners' consent be obtained before any proceedings for obtaining any relief, order or direction concerning or relating to any charity or its estate, funds, property or income were commenced by any person, which was said to relate exclusively to matters of administration.[2]

Despite the substantial differences in wording between these two provisions, the modern provision was apparently intended to consolidate the existing law as to charity proceedings. Accordingly cases decided under the old law are

---

1 CA 1960, s. 28 (8).
2 See Charitable Trusts Act 1853, s. 17 (repealed).

still, it is thought, relevant, though in the last resort difficult or borderline cases must be decided by reference to the wording of the modern provision and in particular to the definition of charity proceedings.

The definition of "charity proceedings" points a contrast between the court's jurisdiction with respect to *charities* in the first limb and the court's jurisdiction with respect to the *administration* of a trust for charitable purposes in the second limb. The latter jurisdiction covers the power of the court to appoint and remove trustees, to sanction dealings with the trust property, to enforce the performance of trusts and redress breaches of trust. The inherent power of the court to alter or modify trusts to a greater or lesser degree by schemes is not truly a question of administration and it is thought that the first limb of the definition of charity proceedings refers (and can only refer) to the jurisdiction to make schemes.

The following are examples of charity proceedings:

(1) an action for the administration by the court of a charitable trust;

(2) any application for a scheme in the course of the administration of a charitable trust;

(3) an application seeking the appointment discharge or removal of a charity trustee or trustee for a charity;

(4) an application for the vesting or transfer of charity property;

(5) any application to approve a proposed transaction involving trust property;

(6) an application to authorise the mortgage, charging, sale, lease or other disposal of charity property.

The following categories of proceedings are not for this purpose "charity proceedings" either because they fall outside the definition of charity proceedings or because the statutory provision with regard to legal proceedings expressly excludes them:

(1) applications involving the administration of an exempt charity;

(2) proceedings brought in a pending cause or matter;

(3) the bringing of any appeal;

(4) where proceedings are taken by the Attorney-General, with or without a relator;

(5) where proceedings are brought to determine whether a trust is charitable or not;

(6) actions whether legal or equitable to enforce individual rights not relating to the administration of a charitable trust;

(7) proceedings in which any property is claimed or relief sought adversely to a charity;

(8) proceedings which arise in the course of the administration of a charitable trust but which raise a question of construction only.

Chapter 39

The Visitor

Definition and origins

Some charities are subject to the jurisdiction of a visitor.[1] The office of a visitor is a peculiar one and the term "visitor" can only be defined by reference to the functions of a visitor. Thus, one writer defines visitors as "persons having a private or domestic judicial authority over eleemosynary, lay and ecclesiastical corporations for the correction of the life and conduct of the members and the adjudication of disputes between them".[2] A more succinct definition is to be found in the dictionary: a visitor "is one who visits officially for the purpose of inspection or supervision, in order to prevent or remove abuses or irregularities".[3] These descriptive definitions naturally require exposition.

In origin, the visitor is a creature of the canon law. This ecclesiastical origin was acknowledged by the court in the leading case of *Philips* v. *Bury*.[4] It was in the Church that the need for a visiting arbitrator or umpire was first felt. Both at diocesan and at parochial levels the visitor was a convenient supervisor of government and corrector of abuses. During the sixteenth and seventeenth centuries the law became well established: ecclesiastical corporations were liable to visitation by the bishop, and, subject to any other appointment by the founder, lay corporations of an eleemosynary type were subject to the visitation of the founder and his heirs.[5]

The various kinds of charitable corporations are discussed elsewhere.[6] It is sufficient for present purposes to note that an ecclesiastical corporation is one which exists for the furtherance of religion and perpetuating the rites of the Church,[7] and that eleemosynary corporations are such as are constituted for the perpetual distribution of the free alms or bounty of the founder of them to such persons as he had directed.[8] The latter are generally hospitals[9] or colleges[10] but

---

1 Mitcheson, *Opinion on the Visitation of Charities* (1887); and see especially, J. W. Bridge (1970) 86 L.Q.R. 531–551.
2 Mitcheson, *op. cit.*, 1.
3 Shorter Oxford English Dictionary (3rd edn.).
4 (1694), 1 Ld. Raym. 5, at 7 and 8.
5 Holdsworth, *A History of English Law*, Vol. IX, 58.
6 See 311–312, *supra*.
7 1 Blackstone's Commentaries 470; *A.-G.* v. *St. Cross Hospital* (1853), 17 Beav. 435, at 465.
8 1 Blackstone's Commentaries 470. The term "eleemosynary charity" is not a term of art like a judicially established definition: *Re Armitage*, [1972] Ch. 438, at 444.
9 In the old sense of an institution for the needy infirm or aged: see *Philips* v. *Bury* (1694), 2 Term Rep. 346, at 352, 353; *Dilworth* v. *Stamps Comr.*, [1899] A.C. 197.
10 *Philips* v. *Bury* (1694), 2 Term Rep. 346, at 352, 353.

at any rate for the purposes of visitation corporate schools[1] may be classified as eleemosynary charities and likewise modern universities.[2]

Nature of visitatorial jurisdiction

The visitatorial power vested in the visitor enables him to settle disputes between the members of the corporation of which he is visitor, to inspect and regulate their actions and behaviour, and generally to correct all abuses and irregularities in the administration of the charity.[3] Although, as Shelford points out, the visitatorial power may in the past often have been abused or allowed to remain dormant when active interference was required,[4] it is a convenient jurisdiction for settling private disputes. In addition it has the advantage of being less expensive than legal proceedings.

The theoretical justification of the visitatorial jurisdiction is that "the founder of a charity is the legislator with respect to the statutes or the code of law prescribed for the regulation of his foundation" and that "a visitor appointed by the founder is a proper judge of [such] laws".[5]

The source of the jurisdiction is "the property of the donor, and the power everyone has to dispose, direct and regulate his own property; like the case of patronage; . . . the nature of his power is *forum domesticum*, the private jurisdiction of the founder".[6] And this domestic forum of the visitor is peculiarly well adapted for determining all disputes which arise between the members of learned societies.[7] It has therefore been suggested that the visitor may have an important role to play in the modern universities.[8]

Lastly it is to be observed that a visitor's decision on matters within his jurisdiction is final, and not open to review by the court.[9] It has even been said that the visitor himself cannot relieve against his own sentence.[10] On the other hand an action for damages will lie against him for exceeding his jurisdiction.[11]

Constitution of the visitor

GENERAL PRINCIPLES

Civil corporations are subject to the jurisdiction of the Queen's Bench Division: the Crown's prerogative to visit such corporations is exercised by the judges, administering the common law of England.[12]

---

1 *Eden* v. *Foster* (1725), 2 P. Wms. 325; *A.-G.* v. *Price* (1744), 3 Atk. 108.
2 See (1970), 86 L.Q.R. 531, at 533–534.
3 1 Blackstone's Commentaries 467; *Philips* v. *Bury* (1694), Skin. 447, at 484, H.L.
4 Shelford, *Law of Mortmain* (1836) 330.
5 Shelford, *op. cit.*, 360.
6 *Green* v. *Rutherforth* (1750), 1 Ves. Sen 462, at 472.
7 Shelford, *Law of Mortmain* (1836) 330.
8 (1970) 84 L.Q.R. 531 *et seq.*, especially at 550–551.
9 *A.-G.* v. *Lock* (1744), 3 Atk. 164, at 165; *A.-G.* v. *Talbot* (1748), 3 Atk. 662, at 674; *A.-G.* v. *Catherine Hall, Cambridge* (1820), Jac. 381, at 392; *A.-G.* v. *Dedham School* (1857), 23 Beav. 350.
10 *Philips* v. *Bury* (1694), as reported in Show. Parl. Cas. 35 at 52, H.L. *Sed quaere.*
11 *Green* v. *Rutherforth* (1750), 1 Ves. Sen. 462, at 470.
12 See Shelford, *Law of Mortmain* (1836), 324–325. *Quaere* whether the court acts in the capacity of visitor.

Ecclesiastical corporations are, as a rule, visitable by the ordinary.[1] This was formerly the case with most spiritual hospitals, abbeys and priories. But royal foundations, free chapels, and donatives are exempt from visitation of the ordinary and are subject to that of the patron, whether that patron be the Queen or a subject;[2] and the Queen visits either by the Lord Chancellor, or by commissioners or in person.[3] Some spiritual hospitals were specially exempted from the visitation of the ordinary and subject only to that of the Pope. When the jurisdiction of the Pope was abolished the exemption was continued and the visitation ordered to be by commission from the sovereign under the great seal.[4] Some of the Oxford colleges are subject to the visitation of the Bishop of Lincoln in whose diocese Oxford formerly was: the jurisdiction of the bishop points to the ecclesiastical origins of the colleges in question.[5]

Where an eleemosynary corporation was founded by a private person the old rule was that in default of directions by the founder as to visitation,[6] the founder and his heirs were the visitors.[7] If the founder's heirs failed[8] or could not be found[9] or were lunatic,[10] the visitatorial power devolved upon the Crown and was exercised by the great seal. Descent to the heir was, of course, abolished by statute[11] and the question has been raised how far this affects visitatorial rights. The answer is surely that the jurisdiction vests in the Crown: the heirs have "failed".

The visitation of universities deserves separate mention. The Universities of Oxford and Cambridge being civil corporations do not have a visitor: they are subject to the control of the courts.[12] Hence the Court of Common Pleas was able to intervene in *Dr. Bentley's* case.[13] The colleges at Oxford and Cambridge are however eleemosynary corporations and so visitable. The modern universities are also eleemosynary corporations and so have or are entitled to have a visitor. They are established for the promotion of learning in the same way as the component colleges of the two ancient universities. The distinction in nature between the two ancient universities and the modern universities is to be ascribed rather to history than to logic.

As has been said, the founder may delegate his power of visitation; and this he may do either generally or specially. A person appointed in general terms is a

---

1 *Philips* v. *Bury* (1694), Skin. 447, H.L.; *Birmingham School Case* (1725), Gilb. Ch. 178, at 180; *A.-G.* v. *Archbishop of York* (1831), 2 Russ. & M. 461, at 466; *Re Hartshill Endowment* (1861), 30 Beav. 130. See also The Cathedral's Measure 1963, s. 6.

2 Co Litt 344a; *Anon.* (1698), 12 Mod. Rep. 232; *Farchild* v. *Gayre* (1604), Cro. Jac. 63.

3 Co Litt 96a; and 344a.

4 25 Hen. 8 c. 21, s. 20.

5 See 1 Blackstone's Commentaries 470.

6 E.g. specifying that another person and his heirs should be visitor.

7 *Eden* v. *Foster* (1725), 2 P. Wms. 325; *Philips* v. *Bury* (1694), Skin 447, at 483, H.L. The heir's prediction could be excluded: *St. John's College, Cambridge* v. *Todington* (1757), 1 Burr. 158, at 200.

8 *R.* v. *Master and Fellows of St. Catherine's Hall* (1791), 4 Term. Rep. 233. The earlier view of Lord MANSFIELD was overruled: *ibid.*, at 240 n. See also *Ex parte Wrangham* (1795), 2 Ves. 609.

9 *A.-G.* v. *Black* (1805), 11 Ves. 191.

10 *A.-G.* v. *Dixie* (1805), 13 Ves. 519, at 533.

11 AEA 1925, s. 45.

12 1 Blackstone's Commentaries 491; *R.* v. *Vice-Chancellor of Cambridge* (1765), 3 Burr. 1647.

13 *R.* v. *Cambridge University* (1723), 1 Stra. 557.

general visitor with the same jurisdiction as the founder,[1] unless there is an express derogation from his powers.[2] A special visitor[3] is one whose powers are specially limited. Whether a given visitor is special or general depends on the terms of his appointment. It "must be collected from the whole purview of the statutes" of the corporation "considered together what power the founder meant to give the Visitor".[4] Thus where the visitor of a modern university "may inspect the University, its buildings, laboratories, and general work, equipment, and also the examination, teaching and other activities of the University"[5] the powers conferred on the visitor are so general and wide-ranging that they constitute general visitatorial powers. Indeed (as has been indicated) the courts tend to regard a visitor's powers as general unless they are expressly restricted.[6]

In some cases a general visitor may also have jurisdiction as a special visitor and may, in appropriate circumstances, proceed in either character.[7] Alternatively a founder may designate a general visitor and appoint a special visitor for a particular purpose: the jurisdiction of the general visitor will then be excluded in cases falling within the power of the special visitor.[8] Another possibility is that the founder prescribes a particular procedure, without recourse to the visitor in the first instance.[9] The functions of a visitor may even be divided among a number of special visitors, each appointed for special purposes and subjected to the control of a superior visitor who has power to remove them.[10] If a visitatorial power is *prima facie* general, express words are needed to abridge it in any respect.[11]

CONSTRUCTION OF APPOINTMENTS

No technical words or precise form of words are necessary for the appointment of a general or special visitor. It is enough if the intention to appoint is apparent.[12] And this, invariably, is a question of construction. A visitor may even be appointed by implication. Thus in *A.-G. v. Talbot*[13] the Chancellor of Cambridge University was held to be the general visitor of Clare Hall without express words of appointment, it being implied from various branches of the visitatorial power being expressly given to him; from his having the interpretation of

---

1 *A.-G. v. Talbot* (1748), 1 Ves. Sen. 78; *St. John's College, Cambridge v. Todington* (1757), 1 Burr. 158.

2 *R. v. Bishop of Worcester* (1815), 4 M. & S. 415 at 420 *per* Lord ELLENBOROUGH C.J., and 421 per DAMPIER, J.

3 The term was also applied to a visitor other than the Crown: Mitcheson, *Opinion on the Visitation of Charities* (1887) 5.

4 *St. John's College, Cambridge v. Todington* (1757), 1 Burr. 158, at 201; *Bishop of Ely v. Bentley* (1732), 2 Bro. Parl. Cas. 220, H.L.

5 University of Exeter, Charter, Art. 6. For similar provisions in other Charters, see (1970) 84 L.Q.R. 532, 535.

6 See footnote 2, *supra*.

7 *Bishop of Ely v. Bentley* (1732), 2 Bro. Parl. Cas. 220, H.L.

8 *St. John's College, Cambridge v. Todington* (1757), 1 Burr. 158.

9 *R. v. Bishop of Ely* (1788), 2 Term Rep. 290, at 335.

10 *A.-G. v. Middleton* (1751), 2 Ves. Sen. 327, at 329.

11 *R. v. Bishop of Worcester* (1815), 4 M. & S. 415.

12 *A.-G. v. Talbot* (1748), 1 Ves. Sen. 78; *A.-G. v. Middleton* (1751), 2 Ves. Sen. 327; *St. John's College, Cambridge v. Todington* (1757), 1 Burr. 158.

13 (1748) 1 Ves. Sen. 78.

the statutes; and from an express exclusion of the founder's heir. Likewise Lord ELDON in *Ex parte Kirkby Ravensworth Hospital*[1] considered that the power of determining disputes arising on the statutes might be construed as giving a visitatorial power, though the power of construing statutes did not of itself constitute a person a general visitor if other visitatorial functions were exercisable by other persons.

A visitatorial power is not to be implied merely from the use of the word "governor".[2] But the statutes of the foundation in question may make it clear that the governors are to be visitors, by providing, for example, that the governors should have powers to visit and of a motion.[3] A leading case on this point is *Eden* v. *Foster*[4] which concerned King Edward VI Grammar School in Birmingham and which is also referred to as the *Birmingham School Case*.[5] The school was founded by King Edward VI who endowed the school and by his letters patent appointed perpetual governors thereof who were thereby empowered to make laws and ordinances for the better government of the school. The letters patent did not, however, appoint any express visitor. The legal estate of the endowment was vested in the governors and they were entrusted with the receipt of rents and profits. It was held that the governors were not visitors and that a commission to visit the governors and call them to account was well issued. The receipt of rents and profits clearly excluded the governors from exercising any visitatorial jurisdiction: there would in modern terminology be a conflict of interest and duty if the governors were visitors. On the other hand the bare possession of the legal estate on its own would not prevent governors from exercising a visitatorial jurisdiction.[6] A beneficial interest in a charity prevents a person becoming a visitor of that charity:[7] a man cannot visit himself.

A general visitatorial power may cease and revive: during any period of suspension the jurisdiction will, in default of any provision in that behalf, be exercised by the courts.[8] An illustration is to be found in *R.* v. *Bishop of Chester* where a *mandamus* was issued to the Bishop of Chester to admit a chaplain of the collegiate church of Manchester. The bishop objected that it was a royal foundation and set out the constitution. It emerged that the bishop had become warden of the college in question and as he could not visit himself his visitatorial power was suspended. Because no visitatorial power was in force it was held that the court had jurisdiction and a peremptory *mandamus* was ordered. A special statute was later passed to vest the visitatory jurisdiction in the Crown while the wardenship was held with the bishopric.[10]

---

1 (1808), 15 Ves. 305, at 315.
2 *Eden* v. *Foster* (1725), 2 P. Wms. 325; *A.-G.* v. *Governors of Harrow School* (1754), 2 Ves. Sen. 551.
3 *A.-G.* v. *Lock* (1744), 3 Atk. 164; *Sutton's Hospital Case* (1612), 10 Co. Rep. 1a at 23a, 31a.
4 (1726), 2 P. Wms. 325.
5 (1726), Gilb. Ch. 178.
6 *A.-G.* v. *Middleton* (1751), 2 Ves. Sen. 327, at 329.
7 *R.* v. *Bishop of Chester* (1728), 5 Stra. 797; *R.* v. *Dean of Rochester* (1851), 17 Q.B. 1.
8 See *R.* v. *Bishop of Ely* (1788), 2 Term Rep. 290; *Green* v. *Rutherforth* (1750), 1 Ves. Sen. 462, at 471.
9 (1728), 2 Stra. 797.
10 2 Geo. 2 c. 29 discussed in Shelford, *Law of Mortmain* (1836) 368.

VISITATORIAL FUNCTIONS

There are two leading divisions of the visitatorial functions which are utterly distinct one from the other. The visitor has in all cases first an original or spontaneous jurisdiction; secondly, one founded on application made to him by some person or persons possessed of a good *locus standi* in the visitatorial forum.

In exercising the first of these two functions the visitor acts by way of what is called a *general* visitation. The visitor physically visits the corporation of which he is the visitor and does so of his own accord. Such visitations are extremely rare and at any rate at Oxford were virtually obsolete by the middle of the last century.[1] Since they are of purely historical interest they require no extended treatment in this work.

A visitation (which is necessarily general) must be distinguished from a particular act of visitatorial authority. The right of general visitation was frequently limited so as to be exercisable only at specified periodic intervals; where that was the case a purported general visitation at any other time was a nullity.[2] No such result can occur when general visitation is expressly permitted at the will of the visitor.[3] But as regards his other function it is well established that "a visitor has a standing, constant authority at all times to hear the complaints and redress the grievances of the particular members".[4] The power of adjudicating and giving relief upon complaints is incident to the office of general visitor[5] and may be exercised between visitations[6] or where there has been no visitation within living memory.[7] The visitor may also provide a solution to any difficulty which may be referred to him by the members in a friendly application, without the complaint of any party who could be said to be aggrieved.

Since "whatever relates to the internal arrangements and dealings with regard to the government and management of the house, of the domus, of the institution, is properly within the jurisdiction of the Visitor"[8] the questions which may come before a visitor are multifarious. His duty is to judge according to the statutes of the foundation and this naturally empowers him to interpret the relevant statutes. Many of the old cases concern colleges at the ancient universities and relate to the election and removal (called "amotion") of corporators such as the master[9] or fellows.[10] The election of the master of a hospital[11] and the

---

1 Mitcheson, *Opinion on the Visitation of Charities* (1887) 11, note 23.

2 *Philips* v. *Bury* (1694), 2 Term Rep. 346.

3 As at All Souls College, Oxford and the University of Bristol.

4 *Philips* v. *Bury* (1694) 2 Term Rep. 346, at 348 *per* HOLT C.J., [1558–1774] All E.R. Rep. 53, at 554.

5 *St. John's College, Cambridge* v. *Todington* (1757), 1 Burr. 158, at 202, *per* Lord MANSFIELD.

6 *A.-G.* v. *Price* (1744), 3 Atk. 108, at 109.

7 *Cf. Re University of Sydney, Ex parte King* (1944), 44 S.R. N.S.W. 19, at 43, *per* HALSE ROGERS J.

8 *Thomson* v. *University of London* (1864), 33 L.J. Ch. at 634.

9 *R.* v. *Patrick* (1667), 2 Keb. 164; 1 Lev. 65; *Bishop of Ely* v. *Bentley* (1732), 2 Bro. Parl. Cas. 220, H.L. (expulsion of Dr. Richard Bentley).

10 *A.-G.* v. *Talbot* (1748), 3 Atk. 662, at 675; *Ex parte Wrangham* (1795), 2 Ves. 609; *Re Catherine Hall* (1831), 2 Russ. & M. 590; *Ex parte Buller* (1855), 25 L.T.O.S. 102.

11 *A.-G.* v. *Archbishop of York* (1831), 2 Russ. & M. 461, at 468.

election or removal of members of a corporation such as governors[1] or school-masters[2] or pensioners[3] or the sister of a hospital[4] all fall within the province of the visitor. A more contemporary illustration of the ambit of the visitor's jurisdiction in educational institutions is to be found in the case of *Herring* v. *Templeman*[5] which concerned the dismissal of a student at a teachers' training college of which the Archbishop of Canterbury was the visitor. At first instance[6] BRIGHTMAN J. struck out the plaintiff's statement of claim on the basis that the matters raised therein came within the exclusive jurisdiction of the visitor. The plaintiff claimed that the resolution of the governing body to accept the academic board's recommendation to dismiss him was in breach of natural justice. The learned judge held that the complaints about the procedure adopted by the academic board and the governing body were matters which touched the internal affairs or government of the college and were therefore confined to the exclusive province of the visitor. RUSSELL L.J. delivering the judgment of the Court of Appeal[7] affirmed the decision on different grounds. The plaintiff was not a *member* of the college and the jurisdiction of the visitor to adjudicate on a dispute involving an alleged breach of contract between the governing body and a non-member was doubted by the Court of Appeal who refused to strike out the statement of claim on the grounds which found favour below. Nevertheless the claim was misconceived[8] and there had not, in fact, been any breach of natural justice.

The distribution and application of college revenues is a matter for the visitor:[9] it is a question of internal management. For that reason the Lord Chancellor representing the Queen as visitor of Christ Church, Oxford, sanctioned the appropriation of part of the revenues of the college to augment the stipend of the Regius Professorship of Greek which was on the same foundation as the college.[10] Further questions of internal management are whether a fellow of a college has a right to let his chambers,[11] whether a master of a hospital is bound to reside in the master's house[12] or perform divine service,[13] whether a travelling fellow must be a member of the college[14] and how a university should conduct its examinations.[15] Abuses of management in an institution falling short

---

1 *A.-G.* v. *Dixie, Ex parte Bosworth School* (1805), 13 Ves. 519; *A.-G.* v. *Earl of Clarendon* (1810), 17 Ves. 491, at 498.

2 *Whiston* v. *Dean and Chapter of Rochester* (1849), 7 Hare 532; *R.* v. *Dean and Chapter of Rochester* (1851), 17 Q.B. 1.

3 *Philips* v. *Bury* (1694), 2 Term Rep. 352, at 353 and 357.

4 *R.* v. *Wheeler* (1674), 3 Keb. 360.

5 [1973] 2 All E.R. 581; affd. [1973] 3 All E.R. 569.

6 [1973] 2 All E.R. 581.

7 [1973] 3 All E.R. 569.

8 *Ibid.*, at 588.

9 *A.-G.* v. *Dulwich College* (1841), 4 Beav. 255; and see *A.-G.* v. *Talbot* (1748), 1 Ves. Sen. 78.

10 *Re Christ Church* (1866), 1 Ch. App. 526.

11 *A.-G.* v. *Stephens* (1737), 1 Atk. at 360.

12 *A.-G.* v. *Smythies* (1836), 2 My. & Cr. 135, at 142. Normally he should reside at the master's house but he may be exempted by ill health; *Re St. Mary Magdalen Hospital, Colchester* (1843), 12 L.J. Ch. 375.

13 *A.-G.* v. *Crook* (1836), 1 Keen 121.

14 *A.-G.* v. *Stephens, supra.*

15 *Thomson* v. *University of London* (1864) 33 L.J. Ch. 625 (LL.D. degree); *Thorne* v. *University of London,* [1966] 2 Q.B. 237, C.A. (LL.B. degree). The plaintiff already held a Ph.D. and seems to have been no mean advocate: see *Herring* v. *Templeman,* [1973] 2 All E.R. 581, at 590, *per* BRIGHTMAN, J.

of breach of trust are matters for the visitor and not the court.[1] Again it is clear that an alleged breach of the statutes of an institution is a proper matter for the visitor of that institution to consider. In *R.* v. *Dunsheath*[2] an officer of London University was alleged to have refused to perform a duty placed upon him by the statutes of the university: it was said that he should have convened a meeting of convocation to consider a motion alleging political discrimination within the university. Lord GODDARD C.J. said that in his view the officer's refusal was essentially a matter for the visitor because it was a domestic question. He continued:[3]

> "The officer objects to calling this meeting on the ground that the matter sought to be discussed is not a matter relating to the university. Whether it is such a matter is essentially a question for the Visitor who is also presumed to understand the statutes generally relating to the university."

Procedure of visitors

Except in the rare case where there is a general visitation, any question for the visitor should be put before him on appeal.[4]

The forms prescribed by the statutes must be observed.[5] An application to the Crown as visitor is by petition[6] and that is an appropriate form for appeals to other visitors.[7]

The procedure on the appeal is a matter for the visitor who is not bound to proceed according to the rules of common law.[8] At the ancient universities because the visitors of particular colleges were often bishops or archbishops it is not surprising that procedures closely resembling the procedure of the ecclesiastical courts were adopted. Indeed Mitcheson puts the matter more generally:[9]

> "... visitors have in England generally adopted as closely as possible the procedure of the ecclesiastical courts; for if they are to give to the parties interested a fair hearing they can hardly adopt a more simple procedure".

An example of a visitor who was a layman adopting ecclesiastical procedure is to be found in *Hopkins* v. *Jones*[10] where Lord HARDWICKE L.C., acting as Visitor of Jesus College, Oxford, during the minority of the official visitor held that proceedings in the appeal before him should be conducted in accordance with the rules of the civil law. Some ecclesiastical procedures are more elaborate than others. In *Burton* v. *St. John's College, Cambridge and Pegge*[11] the proceedings

---

1 *A.-G.* v. *Magdalen College, Oxford* (1847), 10 Beav. 402. See the Report at (1847), 7 Hare 564, n. for particulars of abuses.

2 [1951] 1 K.B. 127.

3 [1951] 1 K.B. 127, at 134.

4 *R.* v. *Bishop of Ely* (1788), 2 Term Rep. 290, at 338, *per* BULLER J.

5 Comyn's Digest Visitor C.

6 *Ex parte Wrangham* (1795), 2 Ves. 609; *A.-G.* v. *Black* (1805), 11 Ves. 191; *Re Catherine Hall, Ex parte Inge* (1831), 2 Russ. & M. 590; *Re Queen's College, Cambridge* (1825), 5 Russ. 64; *Re University College, Oxford* (1848), 2 Ph. 521; *Re Christ Church* (1866), 1 Ch. App. 526.

7 See e.g. Squibb, *Founders' Kin*, 201 (Appeal Documents); *Spencer* v. *All Souls College* (1762), Wilm. 163.

8 *R.* v. *Bishop of Ely*, *supra*, at 338, *per* BULLER J.

9 *Opinion on the Visitation of Charities* (1887) 13–14.

10 (1750), unreported cited in Squibb, *Founders' Kin* 53–54.

11 (1727), cited in Squibb, *op. cit.*, 54.

were started by a petition to the Bishop of Ely as Visitor who issued a citation which was served on the college by fixing it on the chapel door during the time of divine service and on the respondent Pegge (who had been preferred to the petitioner) personally. Each of the respondents lodged a set of allegations signed by their counsel. After the hearing the sentence was pronounced followed by a monition served by the apparitor on the President of the College. The final formality was the certificate of obedience to the monition by the College.

Comparatively simple appeals would be dealt with by a summary procedure under which the appeal would be referred to two commissaries for report[1] or heard by the visitor with assessors[2] and then the matter would be concluded by an interlocutory act having the force of a definitive sentence.[3] It is submitted that this was the simple summary procedure described in Comyn's Digest[4] as *de plano, sine strepitu, et figura judicii*.[5]

The system of adopting ecclesiastical forms has been spoken of with approval in the American courts.[6] The summary procedure of ecclesiastical courts embodies the universal and most elementary principles of judicial process and is as little technical as possible. It is these universal principles of judicial process alone which visitors are required to follow.

If an appeal is exhibited to the visitor he must take it,[7] unless it is of a frivolous nature.[8] If there are any proceedings pending against the appellant they should be stayed by the visitor pending the appeal: if the appeal is by an expelled member he should be restored pending the appeal.[9] The visitor ought to require all parties interested in the appeal to appear before him: he does this by citing them.[10] For that reason, no proceedings ought to be taken against an absent party until he has been cited.[11]

The evidence adduced before a visitor may be written or oral[12] on oath or otherwise[13] as the visitor may require. In hearing an appeal a visitor is engaged in a judicial act and so like a judge he cannot determine the appeal without hearing the parties concerned or at least giving them an opportunity to be heard.[14] The rule *audi alteram partem* is a principle of natural justice that applies to the visitatorial function as much as to the judicial function. The only difference is that in the visitatorial form the word "hearing" is to be more liberally interpreted. The visitor does not have to hear the parties personally or even

---

1 *Hickman v. Brasenose College* (1760), and *Love v. All Souls College* (1770), cited in Squibb, *op. cit.*, 54.
2 *Master v. All Souls College* (1792), *ibid.; Spencer v. All Souls College* (1762), Wilm. 163.
3 For a precedent see Squibb, *op. cit.*, 205.
4 Comyn's Digest Visitor C.
5 An ecclesiastical procedure: see H. Conset, *The Practice of the Spiritual or Ecclesiastical Courts* (3rd edn., 1708) 178.
6 *Murdock v. Phillips Academy* (1833), 12 Pick. 262, at 264–265 (Massachusetts).
7 Comyn's Digest Visitor C.
8 Shelford, *Law of Mortmain (1836)* 379.
9 *Ibid.*
10 *R. v. Cambridge University* (1723), 8 Mod. Rep. 148, at 163; see also *Watson and Freemantle v. Warden, etc. of All Souls College, Oxford* (1864), 11 L.T. 166.
11 Comyn's Digest Visitor C.
12 *R. v. Bishop of Ely* (1794), 5 Term Rep. 475.
13 Shelford, *Law of Mortmain* (1836) 379; and see *Green v. Rutherforth* (1750), 1 Ves. Sen. 462, at 473.
14 *R. v. Bishop of Ely* (1788), 2 Term Rep. 290, at 336; *R. v. Cambridge University* (1723), 8 Mod. Rep. 148; see also *R. v. Gaskin* (1799) 8 Term. Rep. 209; *Doe d. Earl of Thanet v. Gartham* (1823), 8 Moore C.P. 368, at 371.

receive oral evidence: it is enough if he reaches his decision after receiving the grounds of appeal and the answer to it in writing.[1] He can administer an oath and require an answer on oath but he must give a convenient time for an answer and also for the examination of witnesses.[2]

The visitatorial jurisdiction of the Crown is exercised by the Lord Chancellor,[3] but the Crown may also visit by special commissioners.[4] The application to the Crown as visitor is by petition.[5] The Lord Chancellor when exercising this visitatorial jurisdiction is not bound to follow any particular forms of procedure,[6] but he must, before hearing the petition, satisfy himself that the Crown is in fact the visitor.[7]

Control over visitors

The jurisdiction of the visitor is exclusive and, as a rule, his determinations are final and conclusive. No appeal lies from a decision of the visitor. But the court does have a limited judicial control over visitors' decisions. In certain circumstances prohibition or a *mandamus* will lie against a visitor. But a visitor is not subject to *certiorari*: in this respect a visitor may be compared to an ecclesiastical court against which prohibition may issue but which is not subject to *certiorari*. The reason why *certiorari* is not available in respect of a visitatorial decision is that the system of law administered by the visitor differs from that administered by the courts. The courts apply the common law and statute law: the visitor applies the law contained in the charter or statutes of the corporation. No such difficulty arises in connection with prohibition. For prohibition is a prerogative writ designed to prevent any inferior court from exceeding its jurisdiction.

If a visitor acts without jurisdiction[8] or in excess of his jurisdiction[9] a prohibition lies against him. So too a prohibition will be granted where a visitor proceeds contrary to his citation or inflicts penalties not warranted by the statutes of the charity. That was what happened in *Bentley* v. *Bishop of Ely*[10] where the visitor in question could only expel the Master of Trinity College, Cambridge (who was Dr. Richard Bentley) for some prescribed offence if the Master had twice been formally admonished: the Master had not been so admonished and a prohibition to restrain his expulsion issued. Submission to a visitor's jurisdiction is not a bar to prohibition where the visitor acts without jurisdiction or in excess of it: the visitor cannot be clothed with an authority which he has

---

1 *R.* v. *Bishop of Ely* (1794), 5 Term Rep. 475, at 477.
2 Shelford, *op. cit.*, 379.
3 Co. Litt. 96a; *R.* v. *St. Catherine's Hall* (*Master and Fellows*) (1791), 4 Term Rep. 233, at 244; *A.-G.* v. *Dixie* (1805), 13 Ves. 519; *A.-G.* v. *Clarendon* (*Earl*) (1810), 17 Ves. 491, at 498; *Re Christ Church* (1866), 1 Ch. App. 526.
4 Comyn's Digest Visitor A; *Eden* v. *Foster* (1725), 2 P. Wms. 325, at 326; Shelford, *Law of Mortmain* (1836) 333.
5 *Re Christ Church* (1866), 1 Ch. App. 526.
6 *Queen's College, Cambridge Case* (1821), Jac. 1, at 19.
7 *Re Garstang Church Town School* (1829), 7 L.J.O.S. Ch. 169, at 172.
8 *R.* v. *Bishop of Chester* (1748), 1 Wm. Bl. 22, at 25; *Whiston* v. *Dean and Chapter of Rochester* (1849), 7 Hare 532, at 558.
9 *Bishop of Chichester* v. *Harward and Webber* (1787), 1 Term Rep. 650 (no power to fill up vacancy in cathedral stalls).
10 (1729), 1 Barn. 192.

not got by any appearance, answer or pleading of any party.[1] Moreover his want of jurisdiction may be called in question at any time, indeed even after sentence and even by the person who invoked his purported jurisdiction in the first place.[2]

But given that a visitor has the requisite jurisdiction, some informality or irregularity in his acts will not ground a prohibition. A case in point is *Bishop of Ely* v. *Bentley*[3] where the visitor in his capacity as special visitor cited the master of a college to appear before him: he should have cited him in his capacity of general visitor, but the point was held immaterial since he had both capacities and accordingly prohibition did not lie.

An interesting question can arise where the visitatorial power is alleged to be in someone other than the office holder who by long usage has exercised it. A prohibition will not be issued in such a case on the motion of a single member of a corporation who suggests that the power is in another.[4] But if there are several claimants to the office of visitor or several corporators who contend that the usage is contrary to the statutes of the corporation, the issue would be tried.[5]

Whether the procedure which a visitor adopts in exercising his jurisdiction can be made the grounds of a prohibition (or indeed a *mandamus*) was at one time a vexed question. Judges have sometimes spoken as if under no circumstances would they inquire into the way in which a visitatorial jurisdiction had been exercised, so long as they were clear that the visitor had jurisdiction.[6] It is true that an English court will never re-hear, on the *merits*, a case which the visitor has decided. But there is force in Mitcheson's view[7] that where a visitor's procedure offends against express directions in the statutes of the corporation, or against certain rules of judicial process which every visitor is bound to follow, in other words where in fact the visitor is not acting in his capacity of visitor, but in some other arbitrary and self-assumed position, he is in reality exceeding his jurisdiction and should be restrained by the courts.[8]

In certain cases there is a qualified check on the conduct of visitors in the shape of proceedings for *mandamus*.

Mandamus lies to secure the performance of a public duty, in the performance of which the applicant has a sufficient legal interest: it is, therefore, frequently used as a device for securing the performance by inferior courts and tribunals of that duty to exercise their jurisdiction. So far as visitors are concerned the purpose of *mandamus* is, as Lord BROUGHAM pointed out, merely to put the visitatorial power into motion, not to interfere with the visitor's exercise of his power.[9] If he acts in good faith within his jurisdiction his act cannot be reviewed by the court.[10]

Visitatorial inactivity was one of the vices to which the Brougham Commis-

---

1 *Green* v. *Rutherforth* (1750), 1 Ves. Sen. 462, at 470–471.
2 *Ibid.*
3 (1732), 2 Bro. Parl. Cas. 220, H.L.
4 *Martyn* v. *Archbishop of Canterbury* (1738), Andr. 258.
5 *Ibid.*
6 *Philips* v. *Bury* (1694), 2 Term Rep. 346; *St. John's College, Cambridge* v. *Todington* (1757), 1 Burr. 158; *R.* v. *Bishop of Ely* (1750), 1 Wils. 266.
7 *Opinion on the Visitation of Charities* (1887) 5.
8 *R.* v. *Bishop of Ely* (1788), 2 Term Rep. 290, at 336; *R.* v. *Gaskin* (1799), 8 Term Rep. 209; *R.* v. *Cambridge University* (1723), 8 Mod. Rep. 148.
9 *A.-G.* v. *Archbishop of York* (1831), 2 R. & M. 461, at 468–469.
10 *R.* v. *Bishop of Ely* (1794), 5 Term Rep. 475, at 477.

sions drew attention.[1] If a person is clearly entitled to act as visitor but does not act or declines to act he can be compelled by *mandamus* to act.[2] At one time there was some doubt whether if a visitor refused to receive and hear an appeal the court would compel him by *mandamus* to do so. In *Usher's* case[3] the doubt was raised but not resolved because the court wished to satisfy itself whether the persons in question were in fact the visitors before considering the propriety of *mandamus* to compel the hearing of an appeal; what happened to the case after that is not known. Lord HARDWICKE also voiced doubts in *Dr. Walker's Case*[4] where he is reported to have said that "he did not know of any instance of the court having granted a mandamus to a visitor to execute his power, though at the same time he did not know but the court might do so". These doubts were composed in *R. v. Bishop of Lincoln*[5] in which one Dr. Halifax complained of the undue election to the office of rector of Lincoln College, Oxford. The Bishop, who was the visitor, refused to hear the appeal of Dr. Halifax who prayed a *mandamus*. It was held that where by the statutes of a college a visitor is appointed to interpret those statutes and an appeal is lodged with him the court will compel him to hear the parties and form some judgment though they will not oblige him to go into the merits if he decides that the appeal has come before him too late.

The court will not grant a *mandamus* to compel any person to exercise a jurisdiction to which he was not most clearly appointed. There is a simple reason for this: if a *mandamus* is granted against the supposed visitor and the supposition proves false and the Crown is found to be the visitor, the Attorney-General might come for a prohibition. In that event the court would be acting most absurdly by commanding and prohibiting a man to exercise one and the same jurisdiction.[6]

If the statutes of a corporation require a particular officer to carry out the sentence of the visitor a *mandamus* will not issue against that officer because that would be to interfere with the privileges of the visitor.[7] On the other hand where corporations are in breach of the law of the land and are removable under statue a *mandamus* may issue to the governing body to remove them.[8]

Although in accordance with the principles of natural justice an appellant has a right to be heard by the visitor,[9] and that right may be enforced by *mandamus*,[10] once the visitor has heard an appeal on a matter within his jurisdiction and made his decision it is not open to appeal, unless (of course) the statutes of the corporation expressly so provide. The court will not therefore issue a *mandamus* to restore a fellow or member of a college,[11] or a chaplain of a college,[12] or a sister of a hospital, Charterhouse boys, Bluecoat or other almsmen.[13]

---

1 See Fearon, *Endowed Charities* (1855) 12.
2 *R. v. Dunsheath*, [1951] 1 K.B. 127, at 134. 3 (1699), 5 Mod. Rep. 452.
4 (1736), Lee temp. Hard. 212. 5 (1785), 2 Term Rep. 338, n.
6 *R. v. Bishop of Ely* (1750), 1 Wm. Bl. 52, at 58 citing *Brideoak's Case*.
7 *R. v. Bishop of Ely* (1738), Andr. 176.
8 *R. v. St. John's College, Cambridge* (1693), 4 Mod. Rep. 233; but see *R. v. Gower* (1694), 3 Salk. 230.
9 See 430, *supra.*
10 *R. v. Bishop of Ely* (1788), 2 Term Rep. 290.
11 *Dr. Widdrington's Case* (1662), 1 Lev. 23; *Appleford's Case* (1672), 1 Mod. Rep. 82; *R. v. Warden of All Souls College, Oxford* (1681), T. Jo. 174; *Parkinson's Case* (1689), 3 Mod. Rep. 265; *A.-G. v. Governors of Atherstone Free School* (1834), 3 My. & K. 544, at 550; *R. v. Hertford College* (1878), 3 Q.B.D. 693, C.A.
12 *Prohurst's Case*, (1691), Carth. 168. 13 *R. v. Wheeler* (1674), 3 Keb. 360.

Chapter 40

The Charity Commissioners

Introduction

Until 1973 there were two Central Authorities concerned with the administration of charity law, namely the Charity Commissioners and the Secretary of State for Education and Science.

The Charity Commissioners for England and Wales were first appointed under the Charitable Trusts Act 1853,[1] but their constitution is now governed by the Charities Act 1960. However, their powers with regard to wholly educational endowments were (with limited exceptions) transferred to the Board of Education in 1900;[2] and the Minister of Education subsequently succeeded to these powers until 1st January 1961. The powers of the Commissioners in respect of other endowments held on trusts which were partly educational or related to education were likewise transferred to the Minister of Education in 1949.[3] Then, under the Charities Act 1960, the jurisdiction of the Minister of Education was confirmed.[4] On 1st April 1964 the Ministry of Education was re-named and thereafter all the powers of the Minister were enjoyed by the Secretary of State for Education and Science.[5] The Charities Act 1960 preceded this change in nomenclature.

Constitution

The constitution of the Charity Commissioners is set out in the First Schedule to the Charities Act 1960. This provides for a Chief Charity Commissioner and two other commissioners. Of these three, at least two must be barristers or solicitors[6]; but it is not necessary that the Chief Commissioner himself should be legally qualified, so long as the other two are. In addition, the Home Secretary may, if he thinks fit (and with the approval of the Treasury), appoint not more than two additional commissioners who need not be legally qualified.

---

1 See Charitable Trusts Act 1853, ss. 1–8.

2 Board of Education (Powers) Orders in Council 1900 (S.R. & O. 1900 No. 600) 1901 (S.R. & O. 1901 No. 587); 1902 (S.R. & O. 1902 No. 647) continued by the Education Act 1944, s. 121 and the Education (Miscellaneous Provisions) Act 1948, s. 1 (5).

3 Education (Miscellaneous Provisions) Act 1948, s. 1; and S.I. 1949 No. 1845, S.I. 1950 No. 520.

4 And the orders and statutory instruments referred to in the last two notes were repealed. See Charities Act 1960, s. 48 (2) and Sch. 7, Pt. I.

5 S.I. 1964 No. 490. The jurisdiction ended on 1st February 1974: Education Act 1973 s.1. (1) (a) and (5); S.I. 1973 No. 1661.

6 CA 1960, Sch. 1, para. 1 (1), (2).

Commissioners are appointed by the Home Secretary and are deemed for all purposes to be civil servants.[1] They can therefore be transferred from one department of the civil service to another to the advantage both of the public and of the civil servants concerned.[2] Again, they will be subject to removal in the same way as other civil servants.[3] And, as civil servants they are of course disqualified from membership of the House of Commons.[4] The salaries and allowances of the Commissioners are fixed by the Home Secretary subject to Treasury approval.[5]

The Home Secretary has power with Treasury approval to appoint not more than two additional Commissioners (bringing the total up to five) who need not be legally qualified.[6]

The Chief Commissioner may with the approval of the Treasury as to number and conditions of service appoint such assistant commissioners and other officers and such servants as he thinks necessary for the proper discharge of the functions of the Commissioners and of the Official Custodian for Charities.[7] These officers and servants will be paid such salaries or remuneration as the Treasury may determine.[8]

Where the Commissioners act as a board the quorum is two: in the case of an equality of votes the Chief Commissioner or in his absence the Commissioner presiding has the second or casting vote.[9]

The Commissioners have power to regulate their own procedure and subject to any such regulations and to any directions of the Chief Commissioner, any one commissioner or any assistant commissioner may act for and in the name of the Commissioners.[10] The Commissioners are also empowered to act despite any vacancy in their number.[11]

Legal proceedings may be instituted by or against the Commissioners in the name of the Charity Commissioners for England and Wales and will not be affected by any change in the persons who are the Commissioners.[12] For the purpose of authenticating documents (whether for use in legal proceedings or otherwise) the Commissioners are empowered to use an official seal which will be officially and judicially noticed.[13]

Relations with the Home Secretary

The Nathan Report suggested that there should be a Minister for the Charity Commission with strictly limited powers to approve any rules or regulations

---

1 *Ibid.*, Sch. 1, para. 1 (3).
2 H. of C. Official Report of Standing Committee A (24th May 1960) cols. 10, 26–27 (Mr. David Renton, Joint Under-Secretary of State for the Home Department).
3 An amendment to permit them to hold office during good behaviour was repealed; H. of C. Official Standing Committee A (26th May 1960) cols. 50–74.
4 House of Commons Disqualification Act 1957, s. 1 (1) (b).
5 CA 1960, Sch. 1, para. 1 (4).
6 *Ibid.*, Sch. 1, para. 1 (5).
7 *Ibid.*, Sch. 1, para. 2 (1).
8 *Ibid.*, Sch. 1, para. 2 (2).
9 *Ibid.*, Sch. 1, para. 3 (4).
10 *Ibid.*, Sch. 1, para. 3 (3).
11 *Ibid.*, Sch. 1, para. 3 (5).
12 *Ibid.*, Sch. 1, para. 4.
13 *Ibid.*, Sch. 1, para. 3 (1).

made by the Commissioners and to give guidance of a general character only but with no control over, or responsibility for, the day to day administration of the Commissioners or their decisions in particular cases. The Committee felt some hesitation in suggesting to which Minister these functions might appropriately be entrusted but plumped for a non-departmental Minister such as the Lord President of the Council or the Lord Chancellor, with the Home Secretary as second preference. The Government in fact preferred the Home Secretary. Yet there is no express power in the Charities Act 1960 for the Home Secretary to give general guidance, although as responsible Minister he would not, perhaps, require an express power. And there is no obligation binding the Commissioners to accept such guidance. It seems clear that the Nathan Committee itself did not propose that the Minister should be empowered to give directions which the Commissioners would be bound to carry out. After mooting the possibility of a system where directions of a general nature might be given by the Minister, the Committee reported:[1]

> "We propose that the Minister to represent the views of the Commissioners in Parliament and in the Government should be empowered to approve rules and regulations and to give the Commissioners general guidance only—*not directions.*"

The Act appears to carry out this proposal, although only by implication. Generally, a civil servant must obey the Minister who appoints him and who is answerable to Parliament for him. But there is an exception where a statutory power gives that civil servant independence. Two subsections in the Act do just that. It is provided by section 1 (3) that the Commissioners shall have the general function of promoting the effective use of charitable resources, by encouraging the development of better methods of administration, by giving charity trustees information or advice on any matter affecting the charity, and by investigating and checking abuses. Again, section 1 (4) requires the Commissioners so to act in the case of any charity as best to promote and make effective the work of the charity in meeting the needs designated by its trusts. Moreover section 1 (4) also provides that the Commissioners shall not themselves have power to act in the administration of a charity.

Direct interference by the Home Secretary in the administration of charitable funds can be met by two arguments. First, the duty of the Commissioners is to act in the best interests of charity, and secondly the trustees remain independently responsible for the administration of their particular charity and the Commissioners can only exercise compulsory powers where the trustees have been guilty of some abuse.

Inquisitorial powers

INQUIRIES

Very wide powers of inquiry are vested in the Commissioners. The Commissioners may institute inquiries with regard to charities, or a particular charity or class of charities, either generally or for particular purposes. But there is one qualification. Their powers of scrutiny do not extend to exempt charities.[2]

---

1 Nathan Report (Cmd. 8710) para. 374.   2 CA 1960, s. 6 (1).

The inquiry may be public or private and may be conducted either by the Commissioners themselves or by some person appointed by them to conduct it and make a report to them.[1] For the purposes of the inquiry any person may be required by order or by precept to furnish accounts and statements in writing relating to the subject matter of the inquiry if the matter is one on which he has or can reasonably obtain information, to return answers in writing to any questions or inquiries addressed to him on any such matter, and to verify any such accounts, statements or answers by statutory declaration, or to attend at a specified time and place to give oral evidence or to produce documents in his custody or control.[2] However a person claiming to hold any property adversely to a charity or freed or discharged from any charitable trust or charge, will not be required to furnish any information or produce any document relating to that property or any trust or charge alleged to affect it.[3] Such a claim would have to be decided in proceedings between the charity trustees and that person instituted in the ordinary courts. And the mere setting up of an adverse claim will not be sufficient to oust the Commissioners' jurisdiction. It is for the court to decide whether such a claim is well-founded.[4]

For the purposes of any inquiry under section 6 of the Charities Act 1960 evidence may be taken on oath, and the person conducting the inquiry may for that purpose administer oaths, or may instead of administering an oath require the person examined to make and subscribe a declaration of the truth of the matters about which he is examined.[5]

Where the evidence is given on oath a person wilfully giving false evidence will be guilty of perjury.[6] A person who refuses to comply with an order or precept requiring him to furnish information or attend at a hearing may, on the application of the Commissioners to the High Court, be dealt with as for contempt of court.[7] In addition any person who wilfully alters, suppresses, conceals or destroys any document which he may be required to produce for an inquiry is guilty of an offence punishable on summary conviction by a fine not exceeding £100 or imprisonment for a term not exceeding up to six months, or both.[8]

POWER TO CALL FOR DOCUMENTS

By section 7 of the Charities Act 1960 power is conferred on the Commissioners to order any person having in his possession or control any documents relating to a charity to furnish them with copies of or extracts from any of those documents, or, unless the document forms part of the records of a court or a public or local authority to transmit the document itself to them for their inspection.[9] The Commissioners are entitled without payment to keep any copy or extract so furnished to them; and where a document so transmitted to them relates

---

1 *Ibid.*, s. 6 (2).
2 *Ibid.*, s. 6 (3).
3 *Ibid.*, s. 6 (6).
4 *Re Sir Robert Peel's School at Tamworth* (1868) 3 Ch. App. 543, at 550, C.A.
5 CA 1960, s. 6 (4).
6 Perjury Act 1911, s. 1.
7 CA 1960, s. 41 (1).
8 *Ibid.*, s. 6 (9).
9 *Ibid.*, s. 7 (1).

only to one or more charities, they may keep it or may deliver it to the charity trustees or to any other person who may be so entitled.[1] Where a document is kept by the Commissioners under this section, evidence of its contents may be given by means of a copy certified by any officer of the Commissioners authorised by them to act for this purpose,[2] in the same way as if the documents had been deposited with them voluntarily for safe keeping under section 25,[3] and regulations may be made providing for the destruction or disposal of such document after such period or in such circumstances as may be prescribed.[4] The section does not apply to persons claiming to hold property adversely to a charity[5] if their claim is well-founded;[6] nor does it apply to persons properly having the custody of documents relating only to an exempt charity.[7] A person guilty of disobedience to an order of the Commissioners under section 7 is, on the application of the Commissioners to the High Court, punishable as a contempt of court.[8]

The Commissioners may, instead of making an order under section 7, authorise any of their officers to inspect and take copies of or extracts from the records or other documents of a court or of any public registry or office of records for any purpose connected with the discharge of the functions of the Commissioners or of the Official Custodian for Charities.[9]

Administrative powers

INTRODUCTION

The administrative powers of the Commissioners include power to authorise dealings with charity property and generally to authorise transactions beneficial to a charity, power to advise charity trustees power to take steps for the preservation of charity documents, power to order taxation of a solicitor's bill of costs for business done for a charity, and powers for the recovery or redemption of rentcharges. The need for the consent of the court or the Commissioners to transactions involving the disposition of charity land or the mortgaging or charging of property forming part of a charity's permanent endowment is dealt with elsewhere[10] as is the recovery and redemption of rentcharges.[11]

POWER TO ADVISE CHARITY TRUSTEES

On the written application of any charity trustee the Commissioners may give him their opinion or advice on any matter affecting the performance of his

---

1 *Ibid.*, s. 7 (3).
2 See *ibid.*, s. 25 (3)
3 *Ibid.*, s. 25 (5).
4 *Ibid.*, s. 25 (4).
5 *Ibid.*, s. 7 (4).
6 The genuineness of the claim may be investigated by the court: see *Re Sir Robert Peel's School at Tamworth* (1868), 3 Ch. App. 543, at 550.
7 CA 1960, s. 7 (5).
8 *Ibid.*, s. 41.
9 *Ibid.*, s. 7 (2).
10 See 388–389, *supra*.
11 See 402–407, *supra*.

duties as such.[1] Such advice may be given orally or by letter, and need not be embodied in a formal order.[2] Trustees are sometimes reluctant to embark on correspondence with the Commissioners for fear that they may not be able to explain the point on which they need guidance or may attract censure for some mistake. But the business of the Charity Commissioners, as one Annual Report observes,[3] is to be helpful and in particular where trustees have made mistakes in good faith, to help them to put their affairs in order for their own protection.

A trustee acting in accordance with the most up-to-date opinion or advice of the Commissioners given to him under section 24 of the Charities Act 1960 is deemed to have acted in accordance with his trust, unless when he does so either he knows or has reasonable cause to suspect that the advice was given in ignorance of material facts or the decision of the court has been obtained on the matter, or proceedings are pending to obtain one.

An application for advice may be made by any trustee, and if there is a dispute between several trustees the minority may obtain protection by asking the advice of the Commissioners. Should the Commissioners in such a case consider the majority to be right they may tactfully ask the trustees as a whole to submit the point for their advice and so avoid some of the difficulties arising out of such a dispute. Advice given pursuant to an application under this section costs nothing and gives absolute protection to the trustee who acts on it. Not unnaturally solicitors and Chancery counsel find themselves consulted on points of charity administration less frequently than was the case before the 1960 Act.

POWERS FOR PRESERVATION OF CHARITY DOCUMENTS

Powers for the Commissioners to preserve charity documents are the subject of statutory provision. They may either enrol any deed, will or other document relating to a charity in books provided by them,[4] or accept for safe keeping any document of, or relating to, a charity (including one which has ceased to exist) unless the document is required by some other document to be kept elsewhere.[5]

A document enrolled by or for the time being deposited with the Commissioners need not be produced in legal proceedings if instead, evidence of its content may be given by means of a copy certified by any officer of the Commissioners generally or specially authorised by them to act for this purpose; and a document purporting to be such a copy will be received in evidence without proof of the official position authority or handwriting of the person certifying it.[6] The Home Secretary is empowered to make regulations under which documents deposited with the Commissioners may be destroyed or otherwise disposed of after such period or in such circumstances as may be prescribed.[7] Neither has so far availed himself of the power of making such regulations.

The provisions relating to the proof of the contents of documents and their

---

1 CA 1960, s. 24 (1).
2 *Cf.* Charitable Trusts Act 1853, s. 16 (repealed) where a formal order was required.
3 [1963] Ch. Com. Rep. 40, para. 111.
4 CA 1960, s. 25 (1).
5 *Ibid.*, s. 25 (2).
6 *Ibid.*, s. 25 (3).
7 *Ibid.*, s. 25 (4).

destruction extend also to any documents kept by the Commissioners under section 7 (3) of the Act[1] and to any documents enrolled by or deposited with them under the old legislation.[2]

POWER TO ORDER TAXATION OF SOLICITOR'S BILL

The Commissioners have power to order taxation of a solicitor's bill of costs.[3]

Judicial powers

INTRODUCTION

The Commissioners have jurisdiction which is generally speaking concurrent with that of the High Court to establish schemes, to appoint, discharge or remove trustees, to remove officers or servants, and to vest or transfer property. They also enjoy further powers concurrently with the High Court to make schemes for the administration of charities governed by Royal Charter or by statute without cost to the charities concerned. In certain circumstances the Commissioners may act of their own motion for the protection of charities. All these powers are in their nature *judicial* powers: they are the sort of powers which the court exercises.

CONCURRENT JURISDICTION WITH THE HIGH COURT

Subject to the provisions of the Charities Act 1960 the Commissioners may by order exercise the same jurisdiction and powers as are exercisable by the High Court in charity proceedings for the following purposes:

(a) establishing a scheme for the administration of a charity;
(b) appointing, discharging or removing a charity trustee or trustee for a charity, or removing an officer or servant;
(c) vesting or transferring property, or requiring or entitling any person to call for or make any transfer of property or any payment.[4]

The circumstances where the court will order a scheme (whether *cy-près* or otherwise) are dealt with elsewhere.[5] All that need be said here is that the Commissioners have no jurisdiction to determine the title to any property as between a charity and a person holding or claiming the property or an interest in it adversely to the charity, or to determine any question as to the existence of any charge or trust.[6] These are matters for the court alone: the Commissioners can only act where the trusts are clearly charitable.

The Commissioners are empowered on the application of any charity trustee

---

1 *Ibid.*, s. 25 (5).
2 *Ibid.*, s. 48 (3).
3 See 532, *infra.*
4 CA, 1960, s. 18 (1).
5 See Chapters 24–31.
6 CA 1960, s. 18 (3).

or trustee for a charity to exercise their concurrent jurisdiction for the purpose of discharging him from his trusteeship.[1] This procedure is much less costly than the exercising of an express power of appointment and is, in addition, useful where a sole trustee or one of two trustees wishes to retire, because in such circumstances the power to retire conferred by section 39 of the Trustee Act 1925 is not available. As a last resort a sole trustee who wishes to retire but cannot find any other person willing to take on the trusteeship may pay the trust fund into court under section 63 of the Trustee Act 1925 and obtain a discharge in this way; but this course should not be followed unless there are reasonable grounds for it,[2] and so the trustee should first apply to the Commissioners for an order discharging him.

EXERCISE OF THE CONCURRENT JURISDICTION

The Commissioners cannot exercise their concurrent jurisdiction of their own motion, but only where an application has been made to them. There are several ways in which a matter may come before the Commissioners.

First, where the court directs a scheme for the administration of a charity to be established, the court may by order refer the matter to the Commissioners for them to prepare or settle a scheme in accordance with such directions (if any) as the court sees fit to give.[3] Any such order may provide for the scheme to be put into effect by order of the Commissioners without any further order of the court.[4]

Secondly, the Commissioners can in every case exercise their jurisdiction on the application of the charity concerned[5] even if the charity is an exempt charity.[6] Charity trustees may act by a majority,[7] so that a majority of the trustees may apply for the removal of a minority, though their application will not necessarily be granted. A minority cannot apply on behalf of the charity, but any trustee can ask the Commissioners for advice.[8]

Thirdly, in the case of a charity not having any income from property amounting to more than £50 a year,[9] and not being an exempt charity,[10] the Commissioners may exercise their concurrent jurisdiction on the application of the Attorney-General, or of any one or more of the charity trustees, or of any person interested in the charity, or of any two or more inhabitants of the area of the charity, if it is a local charity.[11] A "local charity" is a charity established for purposes which are by their nature or by the trusts of the charity directed wholly or mainly to the benefit of a particular area.[12]

---

1 *Ibid.*, s. 18 (7).
2 *Re Giles* (1886), 34 W.R. 712.
3 CA 1960, s. 18 (2).
4 *Ibid.*
5 *Ibid.*, s. 18 (4). Charity includes charitable trustees as well as a corporate charity; see ss. 45 (1) and 46.
6 As to exempt charities, see 4–6, *supra*.
7 *Re Whiteley*, [1910] 1 Ch. 600.
8 CA 1960, s. 24.
9 As to how the income of a charity is computed for this purpose, see CA 1960, s. 45 (4).
10 As to exempt charities, see 4–6, *supra*.
11 CA 1960, s. 18 (5).
12 *Ibid.*, s. 45 (1).

Lastly, where in the case of a charity, other than an exempt charity, the Commissioners are satisfied that the charity trustee ought in the interests of the charity to apply for a scheme, and have been unreasonable in refusing or neglecting to do so, the Commissioners may apply to the Home Secretary[1] for him to refer the case to them with a view to a scheme, and if, after giving to the charity trustees an opportunity of making representations to him, the Home Secretary does so refer the case, the Commissioners may proceed accordingly without any such application as has been mentioned[2] being made to them.[3] The Commissioners cannot in such a case alter the purposes of a charity, unless 40 years have elapsed since the date of its foundation.[4]

Once the jurisdiction of the Commissioners has been invoked it cannot be terminated by withdrawal of the application before an order is made.[5] But it is expressly provided that the Commissioners must not exercise their concurrent jurisdiction in any case (other than one referred to them by order of the court) which by reason of its contentious character or of any special question of law or of fact which it may invoke, or for other reasons the Commissioners may consider more fit to be adjudicated upon by the court.[6] This provision does not deprive the Commissioners of jurisdiction over contentious cases: it merely enables them to exercise their discretion in the matter.[7]

FURTHER SCHEME MAKING POWERS

It has already been seen that the powers of the court to make schemes in relation to charities governed by Royal Charter or by certain general statutes derive from the Charities Act 1960. These powers are also enjoyed by the Commissioners by virtue of their concurrent jurisdiction. Statute has also conferred on the Commissioners (but not on the court) power to settle schemes for the administration of charities governed by statute, not being a statute falling within Schedule 4 to the Charities Act 1960. Again, in certain circumstances the Commissioners (but not the court) are empowered to make orders authorising the temporary application *cy-près* of a limited amount of the income of a charity.

Powers to act for the protection of charities

The Commissioners are empowered by statute to act of their own motion for the protection of charities. Their powers so to do fall into two categories. First, they have wide powers to act where there has been misconduct or mismanage-

---

1 The particular provision refers to "the Secretary of State". By the Intrepretation Act 1889, s. 12 (3) "Secretary of State" means one of Her Majesty's Principal Secretaries of State for the time being. In practice the jurisdiction here referred to is exercised by the Home Secretary.

2 I.e. under CA 1960, s. 18 (4) or (5).

3 *Ibid.*, s. 18 (6).

4 *Ibid.*, s. 18 (6), proviso.

5 *Re Poor Lands Charity, Bethnal Green*, [1891] 3 Ch. 400.

6 CA 1960, s. 18 (9).

7 *Re Burnham National Schools* (1873), L.R. 17 Eq. 241 (a case on the provision's statutory precursor).

ment in the administration of a charity.[1] These powers are an extension of similar powers which were first introduced in relation to a limited class of charities by section 5 of the War Charities Act 1940.[2] Secondly, they have powers to remove trustees and appoint new trustees where it is expedient to do so.[3] These latter powers broadly correspond to the powers given to the court by the Trustee Act 1925.[4]

POWER TO PROTECT CHARITIES FROM MISMANAGEMENT

Where the Commissioners are satisfied as the result of an inquiry instituted by them[5] that there has been misconduct or mismanagement in the administration of a charity, other than an exempt charity, and that it is necessary or desirable to act for the purpose of protecting the property of the charity or securing a proper application for the purposes of the charity of that property or of property coming to the charity, they may of their own motion take one or more specified courses of action. It is necessary to analyse the conditions which must be fulfilled before these powers become exercisable. First, the Commissioners must have instituted an inquiry under section 6 of the Charities Act 1960.[6] Next, as a result of that inquiry they must be satisfied[7] that there has been misconduct or mismanagement in the administration of the charity: payment of excessive amounts for the remuneration of persons acting in the affairs of the charity, or for other administrative purposes may amount to misconduct for this purpose.[8] Thirdly, the Commissioners must also be satisfied that it is necessary or desirable to act for the purpose of protecting the property of the charity or securing a proper application for the purposes of the charity of that property, or of property coming to the charity. Obviously in some cases action is neither necessary nor desirable. For example, a technical breach of trust by competent trustees, such as an investment outside the authorised range of investments, will not necessarily entitle the Commissioners to act.

The requirement that the Commissioners shall be "satisfied" should be noted. The use of the words "are satisfied" makes the Commissioners, at least if acting in good faith, the sole judges of whether an occasion for the exercise of their powers has arisen.[9] Where they are so satisfied, they have power to do for that purpose and of their own motion all or any of the following things:[10]

(1) They may by order remove any trustee, charity trustee, officer, agent or servant of the charity who has been responsible for or privy to the misconduct or mismanagement, or has by his conduct contributed to it or facilitated it,[11] or

---

1 CA 1960, s. 20 (1).
2 Discussed at 468, *infra*.
3 CA 1960, s. 20 (3) and (4).
4 TA 1925, s. 41.
5 Under CA 1960, s. 6.
6 *Semble* an exchange of letters may be a sufficient inquiry: see CA 1960, s. 6 (3) (a).
7 The meaning of "satisfied" is considered at 453, *infra*.
8 CA 1960, s. 20 (2).
9 See, for example, *Re City of Plymouth (City Centre) Declaratory Order, 1946*, [1947] K.B. 702; *Re Beck and Pollitzer's Application*, [1948] 2 K.B. 339; *cf. Ross-Clunis* v. *Papadopoulls*, [1958] 1 W.L.R. 546, P.C.
10 CA 1960, s. 20 (1).
11 *Ibid.*, s. 20 (1) (i).

suspend him from the exercise of his office or employment for a period not longer than three months pending the consideration of his removal;[1] in the case of suspension they may make provision for matters arising out of it, and in particular for enabling other persons to execute instruments in his name or otherwise act for him;[2] in the case of the suspension of a charity trustee they may adjust the rules governing the proceedings of the charity trustees to take account of the reduction in the number capable of acting during the period of suspension.[3]

(2) They may make orders relating to the vesting of property held by or in trust for the charity in the Official Custodian for Charities, or authorising or requiring the persons in whom any such property is vested to transfer it to him;[4] disobedience to such an order is punishable as a contempt of court.[5]

(3) They may order any bank or other person who holds money or securities on behalf of the charity, or of any trustee for it, not to part with the money or securities without the Commissioners' approval.[6] Contravention of such an order is an offence punishable on summary conviction with a fine of up to £100, or imprisonment for a term not exceeding six months, or both; but proceedings for such an offence may only be instituted by or with the consent of the Commissioners.[7]

(4) They may, notwithstanding anything in the trusts of the charity, by order restrict the transactions which may be entered into, or the nature or amount of the payments which may be made, in the administration of the charity without their approval.[8] No penalty is laid down for contravention of such an order, but contravention would no doubt constitute a breach of trust.

ADDITIONAL POWERS TO REMOVE AND APPOINT TRUSTEES

The Commissioners may also of their own motion remove and appoint trustees (but not any other officer or servant of a charity) in less controversial cases. These cases are discussed elsewhere.[9]

---

1 *Ibid.*, s. 20 (8).
2 *Ibid.*
3 *Ibid.*
4 *Ibid.*, s. 20 (1) (ii).
5 *Ibid.*, s. 41.
6 *Ibid.*, s. 20 (1) (iii).
7 *Ibid.*, s. 20 (10).
8 *Ibid.*, s. 20 (1) (iv).
9 See 358, *supra.*

Chapter 41

Registration of Charities

The register

Since 1961 there has been a central register of charities. This central register was set up by the Charities Act 1960 following the recommendations of the Nathan Committee. In fact, the registration of charities had been made compulsory by the Charitable Donations Registration Act 1812[1] which required the trustees of all charitable trusts then in existence or founded thereafter to register certain particulars with the local clerk of the peace; he in turn was required to forward a copy to the enrolment office of the Court of Chancery. But the Act of 1812 was more honoured in the breach than in the observance. At the time of the Nathan Report it was a dead letter: and the committee noted that it had only been half-heartedly observed even at the time it was passed.[2]

The advantages of a properly maintained central register are obvious. Such a register enables information to be collected and made available to the public, and in particular social workers, so that charities capable of meeting a particular social need can be more easily discovered. And so it is with the central register. But there are at least two other subsidiary advantages in the registration provisions of the Charities Act 1960. First, the register enables the Charity Commissioners themselves, if they are minded to exercise their powers of changing the objects of obsolescent charitable trusts, to take into account the resources already available and to put the funds with which they are dealing to the use which seems best in the interests of the community. Secondly, various fiscal benefits accrue to registered charities; for, so long as an institution is on the register, it is conclusively presumed to be a charity and so is automatically entitled to such fiscal and rating reliefs as are available, subject of course to the fulfilment of the other conditions necessary to obtaining those reliefs.

A properly maintained register should obviously be as comprehensive as possible. Accordingly, registration is, subject to the exceptions from registration set out below, compulsory.

Provision is made in the 1960 Act for the establishment and maintenance by the Commissioners of a register of charities.[3] It is the duty of the Commissioners to maintain the register.

The register is kept on a card index system, the particulars of each charity being entered on a separate card.

The register is open to public inspection and is intended to be used. It has a

---

1 Repealed by CA 1960, s. 48 and Sch. 7.
2 See Nathan Report (Cmd. 8710) para. 147.
3 CA 1960, s. 4 (1).

classified index so that inquirers can look up charities under their purposes, their titles and the areas they benefit.

With every application for the registration of a charity there must be supplied to the Commissioners copies of its trusts (or, if they are not set out in any extant document, particulars of them) and such other documents or information as may be prescribed or as the Commissioners may require.[1] If the trusts are in fact contained in a scheme made by the Commissioners or if the Commissioners already have a copy of the trusts there is no need for anyone to supply a copy of the trusts.[2] Nor is there any need to notify the Commissioners of any change made with respect to a registered charity by such a scheme.

When a charity applies for registration the Commissioners send a printed application form[3] together with notes to assist the applicant in filling it up[4] and a form specifying those charities which are exempt from registration.[5] Religious charities are sent a special leaflet.[6] None of these forms is on general sale but they are obtainable from most local authority offices, Councils of Social Service, Rural Community Councils and Citizens' Advice Bureaux.

The register contains essential information about the purposes for which charities exist, how to get in touch with them and, if known, the approximate income available. This information is reproduced in classified form in three indexes, one containing index slips filed on a geographical basis, another slips filed alphabetically and the third slips filed in accordance with the purposes of the charity. Local authorities are also supplied with copies of the slips for charities operating in their areas, to be kept in the local index of charities, and copies of slips for national charities to be kept at ten regional centres.[7] So far as possible there is recorded on the index slip of each charity the income bracket within which the charity falls, though some charities have been unable to specify a regular annual income.[8]

Charities excepted from compulsory registration

All charities are required to be registered except (1) exempt charities, (2) charities excepted by order or regulations from registration, and (3) charities having neither any permanent endowment nor any income from property amounting to more than £15 a year nor the use and occupation of any land. In addition no charity is required to be registered in respect of any registered place of worship.

EXEMPT CHARITIES

Exempt charities, that is to say charities within the Second Schedule of the Charities Act 1960,[9] are not required to be registered, though they may register

---

1 *Ibid.*, s. 4 (5).
2 *Ibid.*, s. 4 (8).
3 RE. 1.
4 RE. 3.
5 RE. 4.
6 RE. 4 R.
7 [1970] Ch. Com. Rep., para. 17; reproduced in Maudsley and Burn, *Trusts and Trustees: Cases and Materials* (1972) 399.
8 *Ibid.*, para. 20; reproduced in Maudsley and Burn, *op. cit.* 399.
9 CA 1960, s. 4 (4) (a).

voluntarily if they so wish. Since exempt charities are discussed elsewhere in this book[1] no further elaboration is necessary here.

CHARITIES EXCEPTED BY ORDER OR REGULATIONS

Some charities have been individually excepted by order, as for example charities vested in diocesan trustees of the Roman Catholic Church and the Church in Wales.

To date five categories of charity have been excepted from the requirement of registration by regulations.

(i) Certain voluntary schools

All voluntary schools within the meaning of the Education Acts 1944 to 1967 which are charitable and have no permanent endowment other than the premises of or connected with the school have been excepted.[3]

(ii) Certain Boy Scout and Girl Guide charities

An exception has been made for *funds* not representing permanent endowments belonging to units or trustees for units of the Boy Scouts Association or the Girl Guides Association which are being accumulated for the purposes of the unit and which produced an income of more than £15 a year.[4] But *land* such as scout huts belonging to local units must be registered.

(iii) Certain charities for the advancement of religion

Almost all funds and institutions for the advancement of religion are charities in the eyes of the law and therefore have to be registered in the central register, unless they fall into one of the excepted classes explained below. Charities for social welfare purposes, such as relief of the sick or poor, education, moral welfare, convalescent homes, even though managed by and confined to members of a particular denomination or place of worship are not of course principally concerned with the advancement of religion and so must be registered. The exceptions from registration can conveniently be divided into those which apply to all denominations and those which apply to particular denominations.

There are two exceptions which apply to all denominations. First, there is no need to register any property (other than land) held and applicable for the general purposes of parochial church councils and church trustees and other bodies established wholly or mainly to make provision for public religious worship (including Sunday school worship and the like) whether or not of the Christian religion, provided in every case that the income from such property does not amount to more than £100 a year.[5] Nor, in the second place, is it necessary to register a charity for the advancement of religion where the application of its income in a particular manner is conditional upon a grave, tomb or personal monument being kept in good order provided in every case

---

1 See at 4–6, *supra*.   2 [1963] Ch. Com. Rep. 10, para. 24.
3 Charities (Exception of Voluntary Schools from Registration) Regulations 1960, S.I. 1960 No. 2366.
4 Charities (Exception of Certain Charities for Boy Scouts and Girl Guides from Registration) Regulations 1961, S.I. 1961 No. 1044.
5 Charities (Exception from Registration and Accounts) Regulations 1963, S.I. 1963 No. 2074, and see CA 1960, s. 4 (4) (places of worship).

that the income of the charity does not amount to more than £50 a year.[1] Here again the exception applies only where the present purpose of the charity is one for the advancement of religion. If the present purpose is to provide some social welfare benefit, it must be registered. Where the trusts provide that if the grave or monument is not kept in good order, the funds instead of being applied for religious purposes are to go to some social welfare purpose, no steps need be taken to register the charity unless and until the funds become applicable for the social welfare purpose.[2]

Also exempt from registration are charities accounting to the Methodist conference or synods, the Baptist trust corporations and various other non-conformist bodies.[3] Church of England diocesan trust corporations are exempted[4] but charities vested in diocesan trustees of the Roman Catholic Church and the Church in Wales are dealt with by individual orders.[5]

(iv) Certain charities for the promotion of the efficiency of the armed forces

An exception from registration (as well as from transmitting accounts to the Commissioners otherwise than on request) has been made in the case of any charity wholly or mainly concerned with the promotion of the efficiency of any of the armed forces of the Crown, not being (*a*) a charity having any land in England or Wales for any estate or interest greater than a tenancy from year to year; or (*b*) a charity whose objects extend to the relief or assistance of any person not being a *serving* member of those forces; or (*c*) a charity for the exhibition or preservation of articles of historical interest.[6]

(v) All universities which are not exempt charities[7]

Lastly, every university which is not an exempt charity is nevertheless excepted from registration. Thus the University of Buckingham which is not an exempt charity at the date of writing is excepted from the duty to register.[8]

Duty of trustees to register

At first, not all trustees of charities were under a duty to register their charities. Apart from trustees of charities exempt or excepted from liability to register it was only trustees of new charities (i.e. charities taking effect after the commencement of the 1960 Act) who were placed under an immediate duty to register.[8] The intention was, so far as existing charities were concerned, to impose the liability to register in stages, county by county;[9] this was in fact done by a

---

1 Charities (Exception from Registration and Accounts) Regulations 1963, printed at 706, *infra*.
2 *Ibid.*
3 *Ibid.*
4 Charities (Exception from Registration and Accounts) Regulations 1964, S.I. 1964 No. 1825.
5 [1963] Ch. Com. Rep. 10, para. 24.
6 Charities (Exception from Registration and Accounts) Regulations 1965, S.I. 1965 No. 1056.
7 S.I. 1966 No. 965.
8 CA 1960, s. 4 (2) and (10).
9 *Ibid.*, s. 4 (10) (repealed).

series of statutory instruments,[1] and now all but exempt and excepted charities must be registered.

No time limit within which charities must register is prescribed; nor, in the first place, are there any penalties for failure to register. Nevertheless it is expressly provided that charity trustees of any charity which is not registered nor excepted for registration must apply for it to be registered and must supply the documents and information required by the Commissioners.[2] There is no obligation, however, to supply copies of schemes made otherwise than by the court, or copies of documents already in the Commissioners' possession.[3] Any person who fails to carry out this duty may be required by order of the Commissioners to make good his default.[4] If the trustees refuse to carry out such an order, the Commissioners may apply to the High Court which may deal with the recusants as for contempt of court.[5] The application will take the form of a motion to commit, and if the court is of the opinion that the order was lawful, it may either commit the trustees, or make a declaration that there has been a contempt and order the trustees to pay the costs of the motion.[6] It is clear from the applications for registration which the Commissioners continue to receive that there are still a considerable number of charities, particularly small parochial charities, which ought to have applied for registration but have not done so and these include charities known to the Commissioners from previous dealings with them which have not responded to the reminders sent to them about their duty to register. But most of the charities known to the Commissioners which have failed to register are small local ones and to date no case has occurred in which the Commissioners consider that it would have been appropriate to resort to the somewhat heavy-handed procedure of committal proceedings for dealing with recalcitrant trustees. Instead they have tried to bring pressure to bear on such trustees in other ways, for instance through councils of social service and organisers of local reviews of charities.[7]

Once the charity is registered there is a continuing duty on the trustees to supply information to the Commissioners. The charity trustees (or last charity trustees) of any institution for the time being registered must notify the Commissioners if it ceases to exist, or if there is any change in its trusts or in the particulars of it entered in the register and must supply particulars of any such change and copies of any new or altered trusts.[8] But statutory equity requires nothing in vain; and there is no obligation to notify changes made by, or to supply copies of, schemes made otherwise than by the court; nor when reference is made to them need copies of documents already in the possession of the Commissioners be supplied.[9] Any person failing to perform these continuing duties may be required by order to make good the default.[10]

---

1 See S.I. 1961 Nos. 987, 1867; S.I. 1962 Nos. 698, 2166.
2 See CA 1960, s. 4 (6) (a).
3 *Ibid.*, s. 4 (8).
4 *Ibid.*, s. 4 (6).
5 *Ibid.*, s. 41.
6 For form of order, see *Re Gilchrist Educational Trust* [1895] 1 Ch. 367, at 373.
7 [1970] Ch. Com. Rep., para. 22; reproduced in Maudsley and Burn, *Trusts and Trustees: Cases and Materials* (1972) 400.
8 CA 1960, s. 4 (6) (b).
9 *Ibid.*, s. 4 (8).
10 *Ibid.*, s. 4 (6).

R

Voluntary registration

Any institution which is a charity within the meaning of the Charities Act 1960, but which is not subject to compulsory registration, may apply for voluntary registration, but the Commissioners have a discretion whether or not to enter it in the register. On applying, the trustees must furnish such particulars as the regulations relating to registration require. Trustees of a voluntarily registered charity must still notify the Commissioners if it ceases to exist or if there is any change in its trusts or in the particulars entered in the register. Where a charity excepted from registration has voluntarily registered it may still at any time be removed from the register and must be removed at the request of the charity.

Criteria applied by the Charity Commissioners

In determining whether or not a particular trust or corporation is charitable the Commissioners apply the principles adopted by the court.[1] In doing so they believe that they are entitled and expected to follow the court in extending the field of charity by analogy from cases already decided. Just as the court has treated the concept of charity flexibly and has been ready to extend the meaning of charitable purposes to meet changed circumstances so too the Commissioners conceive themselves charged to display a flexible attitude.[2] The Commissioners keep in mind the approach adopted by the Chief Inspector of Taxes and the Special Commissioners of Inland Revenue towards novel claimants to charitable status especially where an institution has long enjoyed relief from income tax.[3] The Commissioners also take account of their previous decisions on charitable status, mirroring the courts' acceptance of the principle of *stare decisis*.[4] Where there are no written trusts the decision on charitable status will be based on evidence of the activities carried on by the applicant for charitable status:[5] the absence of a written constitution does not of itself automatically lead to a refusal to register, but there has to be some evidence that the institution is subject to charitable trusts.[6]

Certain devices in drafting have attracted unfavourable comment and opposition from the Charity Commissioners. One such device is the use of the word "education" to describe activities which are, in fact, propagandist: it is important to note that a purpose which is not charitable cannot be made charitable merely by representing it to be a form of education.[7] The second device to which exception is taken is the use of very wide general terms: this is particularly undesirable where the proposed charity has a more limited purpose, particularly if the charity is intending to appeal to the public.[8] A third ploy is that of listing a number of objects, some perhaps charitable and others less obviously so, and then declaring that the institution concerned is to be confined to carrying out such of the listed objects as are charitable or that such objects

---

1 [1966] Ch. Com. Rep. 10, para. 29. See at 718, *infra*.
2 *Ibid.*
3 [1966] Ch. Com. Rep. 11, para. 30.
4 [1966] Ch. Com. Rep. 12, para. 33.
5 *Caldey Abbey*, [1969] Ch. Com. Rep. 9, para. 19.
6 *The Barmouth Sailors' Institute*, [1966] Ch. Com. Rep. 31, App. A.6.
7 [1966] Ch. Com. Rep. 13, para. 38.
8 *Ibid.*, para. 39.

shall be carried out by charitable means only. In cases where such a question-begging formula is used the Commissioners consider themselves entitled to inquire what are the intended activities in order to see whether those activities can be authorised in terms of clearly defined charitable objects.[1]

Removal from the register

As has been said the Commissioners have a *power* to remove a charity from the register when it is an excepted charity, and a *duty* to remove an excepted charity from the register on the request of its trustees. They also have a duty to remove from the register (1) any institution which no longer appears to them to be a charity (2) any charity which ceases to exist or (3) any charity which ceases to operate.[2]

INSTITUTION WHICH NO LONGER APPEARS TO BE A CHARITY

There are some authorities in the books which might suggest that the use of the words "appears" in section 4 (3) of the Charities Act 1960 makes the Commissioners, if *bona fide*, sole arbiters of the matter in question.[3] But whether an institution is a charity or not is a pure question of law and provision is made for an appeal to the High Court against any decision of the Commissioners to remove an institution from the register.[4] On such an appeal the court does not pay any attention to any view of the Commissioners on the issue: the question is decided by the court.

It is not, of course, possible to draw up an exhaustive list of cases in which an institution which is charitable ceases to be so. But the following three cases are the most obvious instances.

First, a charitable trust may be set up by an instrument reserving a power of revocation. So long as the power is not exercised the charity will remain secure on the register but if the power of revocation is exercised and new non-charitable trusts are declared the trust will cease to be charitable and will have to be removed from the register.

Secondly, a charity company may alter its objects in such a way that it becomes a non-charitable institution.[5] Here again removal from the register must follow.

Thirdly, an institution may, when registered, have been considered charitable according to the law as then understood. But a subsequent legal decision may show that understanding to be wrong, or a statute could specifically provide that a particular purpose should no longer be deemed charitable, or again a subsequent legal decision could hold that purposes which were charitable at the date of registration were no longer so.[6] The case of the anti-vivisection societies

---

1 *Ibid.*, para. 40; and see [1964] Ch. Com. Rep. 11–12, para. 25.
2 CA 1960, s. 4 (3).
3 See 443, *supra.*
4 CA 1960, s. 5 (3).
5 See also at 315–316, *supra.* As to the difficulties which may ensue where the changed objects are to be charitable, see [1971] Ch. Com. Rep., paras. 26–30.
6 In the two latter cases the trustees would be under a duty, after removal from the register, to seek a *cy-près* scheme: CA 1960, s. 13 (1) (2).

is in point. In *Re Foveaux*[1] decided in 1895 the cause of anti-vivisection was held
to be a charitable purpose; but this case was overruled by the House of Lords in
1947 in *National Anti-Vivisection Society* v. *I.R.Comrs.*[2] which held that in truth
anti-vivisection never had been charitable. This was not a case of a change in the
law but of a clarification in the law, disposing of a misunderstanding.

CHARITY CEASING TO EXIST

A charity may cease to exist when all its funds have been exhausted or if it is
created by an instrument which reserves a power of revocation and the power is
exercised. A charitable company may cease to exist when it is wound up and
struck off the register.

CHARITY DOES NOT OPERATE

It is not clear when a charity can be said not to operate. Presumably it does not
cover the case where the trustees fail to act, for in such a case a much less drastic
remedy than removal from the register is available; the trustees can be compelled
to act or can be replaced. Perhaps one example of a charity which "does not
operate" is a defunct charitable company i.e. a charitable company which is
dead for all practical purposes with no funds but still on the Companies Register.
Such a company has not lost its charitable nature, nor has it ceased to exist but
it may be removable from the central register on the ground that it does not
operate.

PROCEDURE ON REMOVAL

No provision is made in the Charities Act 1960 for the service of any notice of
an intention to remove a charity from the register.[3] However the procedure
adopted by the Commissioners in the case of *The Scott Bader Commonwealth Ltd.*[4]
is likely to be adopted on future occasions. Re-examination of the objects of a
registered charity resulted in the Commissioners forming the view that the
company should not have been registered as a charity. The company was
accordingly told that it was proposed to remove it from the register of charities
and was given the opportunity to submit a memorandum setting out legal
arguments in support of its claim to be a charity, an offer which it accepted but
to no avail.

Claims and objections to registration

Any person who is or may be affected by the registration of an institution as a
charity may, on the ground that it is not a charity, object to its being *entered by*

---

1 [1895] 2 Ch. 501.
2 [1948] A.C. 31.
3 *Cf.* the power of the Registrar of Companies to strike off a company when it "is not
carrying on business or in operation" under Companies Act 1948, s. 353 (three *separate*
notices required).
4 See [1967] Ch. Com. Rep. 48 (Appendix D, Part II).

the Commissioners in the register.[1] Likewise, in respect of an institution which is already registered, any person who is or may be affected by the registration may, on the ground that the institution in question is not a charity, apply to the Commissioners to *remove* that institution from the register.[2] The Charities Act 1960 specified that provision might be made by regulations as to the way in which any such objection or application should be made, prosecuted or dealt with;[3] but to date no such regulations have been made.

Objection to entry on the register cannot, under these provisions, be raised by trustees of the charity who claim that they are excepted from the obligation to register: the only ground for objection under these provisions is that the institution in question is not a charity.

Objections and applications are (and are likely to be) made in the main by the Revenue or by the rating authorities, or by persons who would benefit under a will, trust instrument or resulting trust, if the institution was held not to be charitable. In a sense, any ordinary taxpayer, or ratepayer in the area in which the relevant institution operates, is or may be affected by the registration of that institution, because the tax or rate burden is increased by such registration. But it is open to doubt whether such a fiscal interest is sufficient to give the ordinary taxpayer or ratepayer a *locus standi* to object to a particular proposed or actual registration.

An appeal may be brought in the High Court against any decision of the Commissioners to enter or not to enter an institution in the register, or to remove or not to remove an institution from the register. The appeal may be brought by the Attorney-General, or by the persons who are or who claim to be the charity trustees of the institution, or by any person who has duly[4] objected to registration or applied for removal from the register and whose objection or application has been disallowed.[5]

If the Commissioners decide to enter an institution in the register, or not to remove an institution from the register and there is an appeal to the High Court against that decision, then pending the final outcome of the appeal the entry in the register will be maintained but will be marked "in suspense".[6] While the entry is thus in suspense the institution is deemed not to be on the register for the purpose of the conclusive presumption as to charitable status which follows from the fact of registration.[7] The exact statutory wording provides that the entry is to be in suspense "until the Commissioners are satisfied whether the decision of the Commissioners is or is not to stand". If the words "are satisfied" are given their normal construction it would mean that the Commissioners, at least if acting in good faith, are to be the sole judges of the matter in question.[8] But it seems that the words are not used here in their usual sense, and that the Commissioners really have no discretion but are bound to abide by the final

---

1 CA 1960, s. 5 (2).
2 *Ibid.*
3 *Ibid.*
4 *Ibid.*
5 *Ibid.*, s. 5 (3). For the procedure, see at 517, *infra.*
6 *Ibid.*, s. 5 (4).
7 CA 1960, s. 5 (4).
8 See e.g. *Re City of Plymouth (City Centre) Declaratory Order, 1946*, [1947] K.B. 702, C.A.; *Re Beck and Pollitzer's Application*, [1948] 2 K.B. 339; and see also *Thorneloe and Clarkson, Ltd.* v. *Board of Trade*, [1950] 2 All E.R. 245; *Smith* v. *East Elloe Rural District Council*, [1956] A.C. 736, H.L.; *cf. Ross-Clunis* v. *Papadopoullos*, [1958] 1 W.L.R. 546.

outcome of the appeal. The effect is merely to allow the Commissioners to keep the entry in suspense until the matter is finally disposed of. Thus on the one hand they are not bound to give effect to an order of the High Court which is subject to appeal to the Court of Appeal or the House of Lords. But equally, on the other hand, they may end the suspension as soon as they know that the appeal is not going to be proceeded with, even though it may not have been actually dismissed for want of prosecution. The conclusive nature of the register accounts for the special marking "in suspense". For if an institution is restored to the register even temporarily before an appeal is finally disposed of, it would be entitled to income tax and rating relief during the period of its restoration. On the other hand, the fact that the institution is deemed not to be on the register does not mean that it is not charitable, so that if at the end of the day it succeeds in establishing its charitable status it will still be entitled to income tax and rating relief for the period when it was, so to speak, in limbo.

Any question affecting the registration or removal from the register of an institution may, notwithstanding that it has been determined by a decision on appeal to the High Court, be considered afresh by the Commissioners, and shall not be concluded by that decision.[1] In other words, the decision of the High Court does not make the question *res judicata* so as to prevent it from being re-opened. The Commissioners may reconsider any such question "if it appears to the Commissioners that there has been a change of circumstances or that the decision is inconsistent with a later decision, whether given on such appeal or not". The phrase "appears to the Commissioners" in this context means no more than that the Commissioners may take the initiative to re-open a particular decision: it does not preclude the Revenue or the trustees from challenging the view of the Commissioners that there has been no change of circumstances or no later inconsistent decision.

Effect of registration

An institution is, for all purposes other than rectification of the register, conclusively presumed to be or to have been a charity at any time when it is or was on the register of charities.[2] There is, however, no presumption (conclusive or otherwise) the other way. In other words, the fact that an institution is not registered or that its application for registration has been refused by the Commissioners is no evidence that it is not a charity.[3]

As between the charity and the fiscal or rating authorities the operation of the conclusive presumption is simple enough. No tax or rates[4] are exigible in respect of any period during which the institution is on the register. If the institution is not registered the question of its liability to income tax or to rating will be decided, if necessary, by the courts.

---

1 CA 1960, s. 5 (5).
2 CA 1960, s. 5 (1).
3 *Re Murawaki's Will Trusts*, [1971] 1 W.L.R. 707.
4 *Wynn* v. *Skegness Urban District Council*, [1967] 1 W.L.R. 52; *Finch* v. *Poplar Borough Council* (1967), 66 L.G.R. 324.

Chapter 42

Local Authorities

Index of local charities

A council has power to maintain an index of local charities[1] or of any class of local charities in the council's area, and to publish information contained in the index or summaries or extracts taken from it.[2] By "council" is meant a county district or London borough council[3] and for this purpose (and certain others)[4] the Greater London Council and the Inner London Education Authority have the status of county councils and Greater London and the Inner London Education Area have the status of counties.[5] The City of London has the status of a London borough and the Common Council of the City of London has the status of a London borough council.[6]

The Commissioners must, on request, supply free of charge copies of such entries in the register of charities as are relevant to the council's index, with particulars of any changes in entries of which copies have been supplied before; and the Commissioners may arrange that they will without further request supply a council with particulars of any such changes.[7] The council's index, like the central register, must be open to public inspection at all reasonable times.[8]

A council may, if it wishes, employ a voluntary organisation as its agent to maintain its index, on such terms and within such limits and in such cases as they may agree.[9] "Voluntary organisation" for this purpose means any non-profit-making organisation other than a public or local authority.[10]

Where any of a council's functions are discharged by a joint board, the joint board will have the same powers under section 10 as the council concerned as respects local charities in that council's area which are established for purposes similar or complementary to any services provided by the board.[11]

---

1 Defined by s. 45 (1) in relation to any area as "a charity established for purposes which are by nature or by the trusts of the charity directed wholly or mainly to the benefit of that area or part of it".
2 CA 1960, s. 10 (1).
3 Ibid.; Local Government Act 1972, s. 210 (9) (a) (b).
4 I.e. for purposes of CA 1960, ss. 6 and 10–12.
5 London Government Act 1963, s. 81 (9) (a).
6 Ibid., s. 81 (9) (b).
7 CA 1960, s. 10 (2).
8 Ibid., s. 10 (3).
9 Ibid., s. 10 (4).
10 Ibid.
11 Ibid., s. 10 (5).

Review of local charities

A council has power, with the consent of the charity trustees, to initiate and carry out in co-operation with the trustees a review of the working of any group of local charities with the same or similar purposes in the council's area.[1] After consultation with the trustees, the local authority may make a report on the review to the Commissioners and such recommendations arising from it as the authority thinks fit.[2] It may also co-operate with other persons in a review of the working of local charities in its area, with or without other charities, or join with other persons in initiating and carrying out such a review.[3] No review initiated by a council under these provisions can extend to any charity without the consent of the charity trustees, nor to any ecclesiastical charity.[4] Reviews initiated by a district or London borough council may not extend to the working in any county of a local charity established for purposes similar or complementary to any services provided by county councils, unless the county council consents to the review being so extended.[5] A council may employ a voluntary organisation as their agent to carry out a review and in certain circumstances a joint board may act.[6]

Co-operation with and between charities

Any local council[7] and any joint board discharging the functions of such a council may make arrangements with any charity established for purposes similar or complementary to services provided by the council or board for co-ordinating the activities of the council or board with those of the charity in the interests of persons who may benefit from those services or from charity.[8] Whether or not such arrangements have been made with such a charity, it may also disclose to the charity in the interests of those persons, information obtained in connection with the services provided by the council or board.[9]

In this context local council means (1) the council of a county London borough, district or rural parish (2) the Common Council of the City of London, the Greater London Council and the Inner London Education Authority; and (3) the Council of the Isles of Scilly.[10]

Notwithstanding anything in the trusts of a charity, charity trustees[11] may, where it appears to them likely to promote or make more effective the work of the charity, co-operate in any review (whether or not initiated under section 11 of the Charities Act 1960) of the working of charities or any class of charities,[12]

---

1 *Ibid.*, s. 11 (1); Local Government Act 1972, s. 210 (9) (b).
2 *Ibid.*
3 CA 1960, s. 11 (2).
4 *Ibid.*, s. 11 (3).
5 CA 1960, s. 11 (4); Local Government Act 1972, s. 210 (9) (b).
6 *Ibid.*, s. 11 (5) applies s. 10 (4) (5) to the review provisions in s. 11.
7 See footnote 10, *infra*.
8 CA 1960, s. 12 (1).
9 *Ibid.*
10 *Ibid.* London Government Act 1963, s. 81 (9) (a); Local Government Act 1972, ss. 179 (3) 210 (9) (c), 272, Sch. 30.
11 For definition of charity trustees: see CA 1960, s.46.
12 *Ibid.*, s. 12 (2) (a).

or make arrangements with a local authority or with another charity for co-ordinating their activities with those of the authority or of the other charity[1] or publish information of other charities with a view to bringing them to the notice of those for whose benefit they are intended.[2] They may also defray the expense of doing any of those things out of any income or money applicable as income of the charity.[3]

Common good funds

The Nathan Report was strongly in favour of establishing common good funds both national and local, for the general benefit of the community.

The term "common good" comes from Scotland. The Royal Burghs of Scotland at one time possessed, and most of them still possess a Common Good, that is a fund consisting of investments and other types of property held by the Town Council "in trust for behoof of the community". It corresponds fairly closely to the "Borough Fund" of the English municipal borough which, until its abolition comparatively recently, could be used "for the public benefit of the inhabitants and improvements of the borough", or, in other words, for useful public purposes outside the scope of the Council's statutory services.[4]

In the United States the term used for the same idea is "Community Trust" and a substantial number of community trusts exist in the large and middle-sized cities. They appear to owe their origin in part at least to the common practice of founders of charitable trusts in the United States appointing local bankers as the holding and investment trustees of their benefactions. The initiative in forming the trusts usually comes from the banks themselves. The principal objects of these trusts appear to be two-fold: (1) by combining a number of separate endowments and donations in a single pool, to secure the benefit of a single unified financial administration and more particularly of a single investment policy under skilled control; (2) to distinguish between the management of the investments and other property in the pool, on the one hand, and the disbursal of the net income to the beneficiaries of the trust on the other, and to place the former in the hands of a committee of bankers and other financial experts and the latter in the hands of lay trustees, including leading citizens and public men such as the Mayor, the Judge of the Probate Court, the President of a local university and so forth. The community trust has been described by the National Committee on Foundations and Trusts for Community Welfare as follows:[5]

> "A Community Trust is a local charitable foundation consisting of capital gifts and bequests usually from local sources and, subject to the terms of any such gifts or bequest, distributing its current income currently and portions of principal as available or as directed by the donor or testator primarily for the benefit of the people of its locality. It is free from partisan, sectarian or commercial control, preferably not limited in its trust relations to any one bank nor in its benefits to any one institution or any one type

---

1 *Ibid.*, s. 12 (2) (b).
2 *Ibid.*, s. 12 (2) (c).
3 *Ibid.*, s. 12 (2).
4 Nathan Report (Cmd. 8710) para. 605.
5 *Ibid.*, para. 606.

of service. Except for necessary and reasonable administrative expense it makes its distributions ordinarily through other agencies and broadly for the promotion of health, social welfare, education, culture and character of the people of its locality".

These community trusts are in no sense official but they have been accepted so widely as responsible and valuable bodies that in practice the state courts in dealing with obsolete or defective trusts are often prepared to regard the handing over of the endowment to the care of the Community Trust as the best method of giving effect to the founders' intentions.[1]

The Nathan Committee considered that a local trust of this type could do much, by itself or in concert with local councils of social services and other bodies, to keep under continuous review all the voluntary agencies—not just charitable trusts—for social welfare in its area and to relate their activities to the needs of the area and to the services being provided by public authorities; and generally to stimulate and support experimental work and to encourage the best use of the charitable resources available. The Committee thought, however, that local common good trusts should be spontaneous in origin and unofficial in character, and that the State should be content to play the part of recognising them if certain conditions were fulfilled, and of granting them certain privileges, notably the privilege, subject to safeguards, of permitting the Commissioners to transfer to them endowments which are no longer serving a useful purpose, or funds held on trusts which have failed or been held to be invalid, where the persons entitled cannot be found.[2] The Committee also favoured the setting up by statute of national common good trusts for England and Wales, with trustees appointed by the Queen in Council, and recommended that the Government should transfer *bona vacantia* to them.[3]

The Government rejected the idea of national common good funds but agreed that it would be advantageous if local common good funds were established more widely. Accordingly with a view to encouraging the formation of such funds section 31 of the Charities Act 1960 contains provisions protecting the expression "common good" which will have the effect of ensuring that it is only used by charities which are approved by the Commissioners. The section has two branches: it prohibits the use of the words "common good" in the name of any institution in England or Wales, other than a body corporate established by Royal Charter, unless the consent of the Commissioners has been obtained;[4] and it forbids the invitation of gifts in money or in kind to the funds of, or to any fund managed by, an institution which has the words "common good" in its name (other than a body corporate established by Royal Charter) or to any fund described in or in connection with the invitation by a name which includes the words "common good" (otherwise than as part of the name of such a body corporate) unless the like consent has been obtained.[5] Any person contravening these provisions is liable on summary conviction to a fine not exceeding £50.[6]

The purpose of forbidding appeals for funds without the Commissioners'

---

1 *Ibid.*, para. 607.
2 *Ibid.*, para. 610.
3 *Ibid.*, paras. 615–619.
4 CA 1960, s. 31 (2).
5 *Ibid.*, s. 31 (1).
6 *Ibid.*, s. 31 (3).

consent seems to be to allay the fears of voluntary societies lest a common good trust should become a powerful competitor in the field of voluntary finance. The section does not prevent the trust from making its existence and objects known to the public, and the American experience has been that the existence of a community trust has led to gifts of sums, considered too small to form the endowment of an independent trust, which would not in other circumstances find their way into charitable channels.

Applications under section 31 of the Charities Act 1960 to use the words "common good" have in fact been very few and the Commissioners have approved the use of the words for only four funds, two of which were established since the Act was passed. The large foundations whose use of the name has been approved are:

The Yorkshire Common Good Fund
The City of Manchester Common Good Fund[1]
The County Borough of Huddersfield Common Good Fund
The Birmingham Common Good Fund.

The last mentioned common good fund was in existence prior to the 1960 Act and the Nathan Committee noted[2] that it has done particularly valuable work in purchasing land in and around Birmingham as it came on to the market and subsequently disposing of it to the Birmingham Corporation for public purposes at the original purchase price, a price much below that which the corporation themselves would have had to pay if they had resorted to compulsory purchase. Other activities included grants for boys' and girls' clubs, for the establishment of community centres, for encouraging gardening on the corporation housing estates, and for many other useful objects. The City of Manchester Common Good Fund was established by the Lord Mayor of Manchester. Its declaration of trust directs the trustee to "hold the capital and income of any money or other property received for the trust upon trust to be used for any charitable purposes directed wholly or mainly to the benefit of the City of Manchester (whatever its area for the time being) or of the immediate neighbourhood or any part of the said city as the trustees shall from time to time in their discretion determine".[3]

The Commissioners have expressed the view that the title "Common Good" should be reserved "for large funds having wide objects covering all charitable purposes for the benefit of the inhabitants of a substantial area . . . in addition . . . any charity using this title should have a substantial permanent endowment and should not be susceptible of possible limited duration".[4] Elsewhere their practice is declared to be to give consent only where the charity's features comprise a sizeable permanent endowment, a wide range of charitable benefits over a considerable sector of the population and some authoritative and representative council or board of trustees for its direction.[5] The residents of the Frecheville Estate numbering some 1500 were too small a sector of the population to justify a trust for their benefit being allowed to call itself the Frecheville Common Good Trust.[6] No approval was given to the title "Borough of

---

1 See (1962) 106 Sol. Jo. 466.
2 Nathan Report (Cmd. 8710) para. 609.
3 (1962), 106 Sol. Jo. 466.
4 [1964] Ch. Com. Rep. 42, para. 86.
5 *Ibid.*, [1970] Ch. Com. Rep. 22, para. 61.
6 [1964] Ch. Com. Rep. 41, para. 85.

Eastleigh Common Good Fund" because there was no intention to form a *permanent* endowment and the promoters stated that the annual income would be dependent on the subscription of the public.[1]

War charities and charities for the disabled

Certain charities have been subject to registration since well before the Charities Act 1960.

During the First World War the authorities expressed considerable alarm about the exploitation of public benevolence by unscrupulous persons. A committee was therefore set up to report on this question and the result of the report was the enactment of the War Charities Act 1916[2] which was designed to stop such exploitation and to prevent waste, overlapping and a great deal of bad administration. The War Charities Act 1916 was confined to war charities of the 1914–18 war but its provisions were made applicable to charities for the blind by the Blind Persons Act 1920.[3]

At the start of the Second World War similar concern was felt about possible abuses and the War Charities Act 1940[4] replaced the 1916 Act except with regard to charities for the blind. However the Blind Persons Act 1920 was repealed by the National Insurance Act 1948[5] and the provisions of the War Charities Act 1940 (hereinafter called the Act) now extend, with certain modifications,[6] to every fund, institution, association and undertaking having for its sole or principal object or among its principal objects the promotion of the welfare of persons disabled by blindness,[7] deafness, dumbness, or other persons substantially and permanently handicapped by illness, injury or congenital deformity or such other disability as may be prescribed by the Secretary of State.[8]

By a "war charity" is meant any fund, institution, association or undertaking whether established before or after the passing of the Act, having for its sole or principal object or among its principal objects the relief of suffering or distress, or the supply of needs or comforts to persons affected by the 1914–18 War, the 1939–1945 War or any past or future war to which the Act is applied by Order-in-Council, and any other charitable object connected with any such war or act of aggression.[9] Taken on its own, this definition might be thought to suggest that a war charity need not have exclusively charitable objects, in other words need not be a charity. The Act, however, uses the terms "war charity" and "charity" interchangeably when dealing with war charities.[10] And it is specifically provided that whether a *charity* is a war charity or a charity for the disabled is to be finally determined by the Charity Commissioners.[11] The persons who may

---

1 [1964] Ch. Com. Rep. 42, para. 87.
2 6 & 7 Geo. 5 c. 43.
3 10 & 11 Geo. 5 c. 49.
4 3 & 4 Geo. 6 c. 31, printed at 603, *infra.*
5 9 & 10 Geo. 6 c. 81.
6 See National Assistance Act 1948, s. 41 (2).
7 A blind person is one so blind as to be unable to perform any work for which eyesight is essential; National Assistance Act 1948, s. 64.
8 National Assistance Act 1948, s. 41.
9 War Charities Act 1940, s. 11 (1). No Order-in-Council has been made under the Act.
10 See War Charities Act 1940, ss. 1–3.
11 *Ibid.*, s. 11 (2); Charities for Disabled Persons Regulations, reg. 6.

apply to the Commissioners for such a determination, and the relevant procedure, are specified in regulations made under the Act.[1] It is not lawful to make
an appeal to the public for donations or subscriptions in money or in kind to
any war charity or charity for disabled persons, or to raise or attempt to raise
money for any such charity by promoting or assisting to promote any bazaar,
sale, entertainment or exhibition or by any similar means, unless the charity is
registered or exempted from registration under the Act, and written approval[2]
has been given by the management committee or person responsible for the
administration of the charity or a duly authorised officer of the charity.[3]
Contravention of this provision is an offence[4] punishable by imprisonment for
a period not exceeding six months or a fine not exceeding £100, or both.[5]
But proceedings for such an offence can be instituted only by or with the consent
of the Charity Commissioners.[6] And collections at divine service in a place of
worship[7] are outside the provisions dealing with appeals to the public.[8]

All posters, bills, circulars, advertisements and notices relating to such appeals
must state the name of the charity and carry the words "Registered under the
War Charities Act 1940."[9]

Where the Act is made applicable to some new war or act of aggression by
Order-in-Council[10] the provisions of section 1 (1) of the Act do not apply as
respects registration and exemption until two months after the making of the
Order-in-Council, unless within that period registration is refused nor do they
apply pending a decision on any application for registration or exemption made
within that period.[11]

When selling or soliciting orders for goods, a war charity or charity for
disabled persons may, provided it is duly registered, represent that blind or
disabled persons are employed in producing, preparing or packing the goods,
or benefit from the sale, without having to register under the Trading Representations (Disabled Persons) Act 1958.[12]

Registration

The registration authorities for the purposes of the War Charities Act 1940 are:
(1) the London borough councils and the councils of non-metropolitan counties
and metropolitan districts (2) the Common Council of the City of London,
which may act through a committee comprising persons who are not council

---

1 War Charities Regulations 1940, reg. 30, Sch. 7; Charities for Disabled Persons
Regulations, reg. 6.
2 As to conditions on which approval is given, see War Charities Regulations, 1940,
reg. 26.
3 War Charities Act 1940, s. 1 (1).
4 *Ibid.*
5 *Ibid.*, s. 9 (2).
6 *Ibid.*, s. 9 (3).
7 A Scientologist chapel is not a place of worship: see *R.* v. *Registrar-General, Ex parte
Segerdal*, [1970] 2 Q.B. 697; and for "place of public worship" see 563, *infra*.
8 War Charities Act 1940, s. 1 (1) proviso.
9 War Charities Regulations 1940, reg. 27.
10 *Ibid.*, s. 11 (1) (c).
11 *Ibid.*, ss. 1 (3) and 11 (1) (ii).
12 Trading Representations (Disabled Persons) Act 1958, s. 1 (1), (2) (b).

members and (3) the council of the Isles of Scilly.[1] In the case of charities for disabled persons not falling within the definition of war charities the registration authorities are: the councils of non-metropolitan counties and metropolitan boroughs and the councils of London boroughs and the Common Council of the City of London.[2]

An application for registration has to be in the prescribed form,[3] signed by some person or persons duly authorised on behalf of the charity. The application must be sent, together with a registration fee (returnable in the event of registration being refused), to the registration authority for the area in which the administrative centre of the charity is situate.[4] Any question as to where the administrative centre of the charity is situate is finally determined by the Charity Commissioners.[5] At least one week before the application is made there must be inserted in at least two newspapers circulating in the area a statement in the prescribed form of the intention to make an application and the time limit and place for making objections.[6] The present form of statement[7] specifies that any objections to the proposed registration should be sent in writing to the relevant authority within 14 days from the date of the statement.[8] The registration authority may allow a further period of up to 14 days from the expiration of the period specified in the statement, for the production of evidence in support of objections.[9]

Subject to certain particular provisions[10] the registration authority must, after considering duly notified objections, accede to an application duly made in accordance with the Act and furnish a certificate of registration.[11] There is a prescribed[12] form of certificate. Changes in the particulars must be notified to the authority which must make the necessary alterations.[13]

A registration authority may exempt from registration under the Act any war charity or charity for disabled persons if satisfied that it is established in good faith, and is of so limited a character as respects the area of its actual or prospective activities or as respects its duration or objects, or as respects the value of the money and property likely to be obtained that registration in the interests of the public is not necessary; and the authority may exempt the charity for an indefinite or a limited period.[14] An application for exemption must be in the prescribed form,[15] signed by some person or persons duly

1 War Charities Act 1940, s. 10 (1), (2); Local Government Act 1972, s. 210 (8).

2 National Assistance Act 1940, ss. 37 (2), 41 (2) (a); Local Authorities Social Services Act 1970, s. 1; Local Government Act 1972, s. 195 (1) (6), Sch. 23 para. 2, (8), (9).

3 War Charities Act 1940, s. 2 (1). The form is prescribed by the War Charities Regulations 1940, S.R. & O. 1940 No. 1533, reg. 3, Sch. I.

4 *Ibid.*, s. 2 (1).   5 *Ibid.*, s. 2 (9).

6 War Charities Act 1940, s. 2 (1).

7 Prescribed by War Charities Regulations 1940, reg. 4, Sch. 3; and the Charities for Disabled Persons Regulations 1948, S.I. 1948 No. 1455, reg. 4.

8 War Charities Regulations 1940, reg. 4.

9 *Ibid.*, reg. 5.   10 See discussion of refusal of registration, 463, *infra.*

11 War Charities Act 1940, s. 2 (1).

12 *Ibid.*, reg. 6, Sch. 4; Charities for Disabled Persons Regulations 1948, reg. 3.

13 War Charities Regulations 1940, regs. 15 and 16.

14 *Ibid.*, s. 1 (2); National Assistance Act 1948, s. 41 (1). A war charity exempted under the War Charities Act 1916 (repealed) is not necessarily exempted under the 1940 Act: see War Charities Regulations 1940, reg. 14.

15 See War Charities Regulations 1940, reg. 3 and Sch. 2. Changes in particulars must be notified to the registration authority who must make the necessary alterations; regs. 15 and 16.

authorised on behalf of the charity. There is no fee; but the application must be sent to the registration authority for the area in which the administrative centre of the charity is situate.[1] On exempting a charity the registration authority must furnish a certificate of exemption, specifying the period of exemption if the exemption is for a limited period.[2]

It is an offence, punishable with a fine of up to £100 or imprisonment of up to six months or both,[3] to make a false statement or false representation in applying for registration or exemption under the Act or in notifying any change requiring alterations in the particulars entered in any register or list kept under the Act;[4] it is also an offence (punishable with like penalties) for a person falsely to represent himself to be an officer or agent of a war charity.[5] But proceedings in respect of any of these offences can only be instituted by or with the consent of the Charity Commissioners.[6]

A registration authority *must* refuse to register a charity unless it is satisfied that a management committee consisting of at least three persons has been appointed to administer it.[7] A registration authority *may* also refuse to register a charity if it is satisfied that (1) the charity is not established, or is not being carried on, in good faith; (2) the charity is not being or is not likely to be properly administered; (3) the total value of the money and property likely to be applied towards the objects of the charity (including any money or property already so applied) is inadequate in proportion to the total value of the money and property likely to be obtained and already obtained for those objects; (4) remuneration or reward which is excessive in relation to the total value of the money and property likely to be applied towards the objects is likely to be, or has been, retained or received by any person out of the money and property obtained for those objects; (5) the authority has not been furnished with information reasonably required by them for the purpose of informing itself as to any of the matters specified in (1) to (4).[8]

The authority *may* also refuse to register a charity for disabled persons not coming within the definition of a war charity if it objects are adequately attained by a registered charity.[9]

In any other case the authority *must*, after considering any objections,[10] grant any application duly made and must furnish a certificate of registration[11] the form of which is prescribed.[12]

There is a set procedure to be followed when an authority refuses to register a charity. The authority is required to notify its decision to refuse registration to the committee of the charity and this must be done forthwith[13] and must include

---

1 As to questions on such situation: see War Charities Act 1940, s. 9 (2).
2 War Charities Act 1940, s. 1 (2). For prescribed forms, see War Charities Regulations 1940, reg. 6, Sch. 5; *cf.* the Charities for Disabled Persons Regulations 1948, reg. 3.
3 War Charities Act 1940, s. 9 (2).
4 *Ibid.*, s. 8 (a).
5 *Ibid.*, s. 8 (b).
6 *Ibid.*, s. 9 (3).
7 *Ibid.*, s. 2 (2).
8 *Ibid.*, s. 2 (2).
9 National Assistance Act 1948, s. 41 (2) (c).
10 Which in the event are capable of being rejected.
11 War Charities Act 1940, s. 2 (1).
12 War Charities Regulations 1940, reg. 6, Sch. 4; Charities for Disabled Persons Regulations 1948, reg. 3.
13 War Charities Regulations 1940, reg. 19.

statements showing upon which of the grounds specified in the Act the decision has been taken.[1]

An appeal against a refusal to register lies to the Commissioners, and, if they allow the appeal, the registration authority must register the charity.[2] Any such appeal must be made to the Commissioners in writing within 14 days from the date of the intimation of the refusal or within such further time as may be allowed by the Commissioners; and the appeal must be accompanied by a statement giving the reasons for the appeal.[3] At the same time the appellants must give notice of the appeal to the registration authority and the latter must forthwith communicate to the Commissioners full particulars of the reasons for their decision.[4] Any such appeal may be determined by the Commissioners, if both the appellants and the registration authority concur, on an agreed statement of facts submitted to them in writing and without the attendance before them of the appellants or the registration authority in person or by their representatives. In default of such agreement the appellants and the registration authority have to supply to the Commissioners summaries of the evidence which they respectively desire to adduce and upon being informed of the day, time and place appointed by the Commissioners for hearing the appeal the appellants and the registration authority or some person or persons representing them respectively must attend and adduce evidence as may be required for determination of the questions arising on the appeal.[5]

Every registration authority is obliged to keep a register containing particulars of all charities registered by it, and lists containing particulars of all charities refused registration or exempted from registration by it.[6] The particulars required in the case of registered charities are: (a) the name of the charity; (b) the date of establishment; (c) the precise objects; (d) the address of the administrative centre; (e) the full names, address and occupation or description of the Secretary; (f) like particulars in respect of the Treasurer; (g) like particulars in respect of the Chairman and two other members of the Committee; (h) the name and address of the bank or banks at which the account of the charity is kept; (i) the name, address and qualification or other description of the auditor; (j) the date of application for registration; (k) the date of registration; and (if a charity be removed from the register) the date of removal.[7]

The lists of charities refused registration and the lists of charities exempted from registration are required to contain the following particulars in respect of every charity so refused registration or exempted from registration: (a) the name of the charity; (b) the date of establishment; (c) the precise objects; (d) the address of the administrative centre; (e) the full names, address and occupation or description of each person applying on behalf of the charity for registration or exemption; (f) the name and address of the bank or banks at which the account of the charity is kept; (g) the considerations which have led the authority to refuse registration or to exempt the charity from registration; and (h) the date of refusal or exemption.[8]

---

1 *Ibid.*, reg. 21.
2 *Ibid.*, s. 2 (3).
3 *Ibid.*, reg. 22.
4 *Ibid.*, reg. 23.
5 *Ibid.*, reg. 24.
6 War Charities Act 1940, s. 2 (5).
7 War Charities Regulations 1940, reg. 7.
8 *Ibid.*, reg. 12.

The register and lists are, at all reasonable times, open to the inspection of all persons interested free of charge, and such persons may on payment of a fee of 1p make copies of or extracts from any entry in the register or lists relating to a specific charity. Copies of or extracts from any such entry in the register or lists are supplied to any interested person on payment of a fee at the rate of 2p per folio of 72 words for each copy or extract. Copies or extracts so supplied are certified by the signature of the clerk to the registration authority or of some person authorised to act on his behalf when the copies or extracts are obtained from the authority, and by the signature of the Secretary to the Commissioners or some person authorised on his behalf if the copies or extracts are obtained from the Commissioners.[1]

If a charity's administrative centre is transferred from the area of one registration authority to that of another, the first authority, after giving notice in writing in the prescribed form[2] to the management committee of the charity and to the second authority and affording a reasonable opportunity for raising any question as to the situation of the administrative centre,[3] must transmit the particulars of registration of the charity to the second authority, which in turn must enter the particulars on its register; the charity will then be deemed to have been registered by the second authority.[4] If at the time of the transfer the first authority is engaged in an investigation of the affairs of the charity, the authority may postpone the transmission of the registration particulars until the investigation is completed.[5]

Every registration authority must send forthwith to the Commissioners a copy of all particulars entered in its register and lists and notify any changes that occur in the register or lists;[6] and the Commissioners must keep a combined register of all registered charities and a combined list of all charities whose applications for registration have been refused and a combined list of all charities exempted from registration.[7] The entries relating to registered charities are sent by the registration authority on a separate register sheet.[8]

Once a charity is registered as a war charity it is still required to observe various conditions. It must, in the first place, continue to be administered by a management committee consisting of not less than three persons; and minutes must be kept of the committee's meetings in which the names of members present are recorded.[9] Proper books of accounts must be kept, containing such particulars as may be prescribed from time to time (including details of property acquired other than money). The accounts must be audited, either annually or more frequently as the registration authority with the Commissioners' consent may require, by an *independent*[10] person who is a member of an association or

---

1 *Ibid.*, reg. 18; as affected by the Decimal Currency Act 1969, s. 10 (1).
2 The form is prescribed by War Charities Regulations 1940, reg. 17, Sch. 6.
3 This is determined by the Commissioners (War Charities Act 1940, s. 2 (9)) and any representation or reference to them must be in writing supported by a statement giving reasons and any facts relied on in support thereof; War Charities Regulations, 1940, reg. 29.
4 War Charities Act 1940, s. 2 (6).
5 *Ibid.*, s. 2 (6), proviso.
6 *Ibid.*, s. 2 (7).
7 *Ibid.*, s. 2 (8).
8 War Charities Regulations 1940, reg. 10.
9 War Charities Act 1940, s. 3 (a).
10 I.e. not related or associated in business with any member of the committee or other officer of the charity: War Charities Regulations 1940, reg. 9.

society of accountants incorporated before 1940 or accepted by the registration authority as competent,[1] and copies of the audited accounts must be sent to the authority.[2] Duly audited accounts must be sent at least once in every period of 12 months but the registration authority (with the consent of the Commissioners) or the Commissioners themselves may call for such accounts at any time. Such accounts must include particulars of receipts and expenditure of money only, although every registered charity must also keep a sufficient record of all dealings with articles in kind of whatever nature.[3]

All moneys received on account of the charity must be paid into a separate account in the registered name of the charity at such bank or banks as are specified in the register.[4] The committee must furnish the registration authority and the Commissioners with any particulars which they may at any time require[5] with regard to the accounts and other records; and the books of account and other records of the charity and all documents relating to them must be open to inspection at any time by any person duly authorised by the registration authority or the Commissioners.[6]

Every member of the committee of a war charity is responsible for securing compliance with the statutory conditions and the various regulations prescribed from time to time, but this duty may be delegated in writing to some officer of the charity (being the Secretary Treasurer or other responsible officer), who is solely responsible for securing compliance with the conditions and regulations if he has accepted the delegation in writing and notice of the delegation has been given to the appropriate registration authority.[7] Failure to observe the statutory conditions may lead to the removal of a charity from the register;[8] and a person responsible for securing compliance with the statutory conditions or the regulations who fails to do so is guilty of an offence[9] for which there is a summary penalty of £5.[10]

A registration authority may remove a war charity or a charity for disabled persons from the register on the same grounds as those on which registration may be refused[11] or in the event of non-compliance with the conditions as to administration and accounts set out in section 3 of the Act.[12] On the decision of a registration authority to remove a charity from the register the authority must forthwith notify their decision to the committee of the charity and must forthwith furnish to the Commissioners full particulars of the reasons for such removal and all information in their possession as to the funds and securities of the charity and the persons holding them.[13] The notification to the committee of the charity must include statements showing upon which of the grounds

---

1 War Charities Regulations 1940, reg. 9.
2 War Charities Act 1940, s. 3 (b).
3 War Charities Regulations 1940, reg. 25.
4 War Charities Act 1940, s. 3 (c); War Charities Regulations 1940, reg. 8.
5 A registration authority requires the Commissioners' consent to call for accounts at any time: War Charities Regulations 1940, reg. 25.
6 War Charities Act 1940, s. 3 (d).
7 War Charities Regulations 1940, reg. 28.
8 War Charities Act 1940, s. 2 (2) (b).
9 *Ibid.*, s. 4 (2).
10 *Ibid.*, s. 9 (1).
11 I.e. those set out in War Charities Act 1940, s. 2 (2); applied to charities for disabled persons by National Assistance Act 1948, s. 41 (1).
12 War Charities Act 1940, s. 2 (2) (b).
13 War Charities Regulations 1940, reg. 19.

specified in section 2 (2) of the Act the decision has been taken.[1] Within 14 days of receipt of the notification of the decision the committee of the charity must surrender the certificate of registration to the registration authority.[2] After a charity has been removed from the register and the appeal (if any) against removal has been dismissed, or the time for appeal has expired, the registration authority must give notice of removal in at least two newspapers circulating in the area.[3] An appeal against removal from the register lies to the Commissioners, and must be made in writing within 14 days from the date of the intimation of the decision or within such further time as may be allowed by the Commissioners, and must be accompanied by a statement giving the reasons for the appeal.[4] The appellants must at the same time give notice of the appeal to the registration authority.[5] The procedure on the appeal itself is the same as that on an appeal against refusal to register.[6] It the appeal is allowed the registration authority must forthwith restore the charity to the register.[7]

A registration authority may also withdraw an exemption from registration which it has granted. This it may do if it is no longer satisfied that the original grounds for exemption still apply.[8] The authority must notify the decision to the committee of the charity and must furnish the Commissioners with full particulars of the reasons for the withdrawal and all information in the authority's possession as to the funds and securities of the charity and the persons holding them.[9] Within 14 days after the receipt of notification of the decision to withdraw the exemption of a charity from registration the committee must surrender the certificate of exemption to the registration authority.[10] A committee must also make such a surrender as soon as the period for a limited certificate of exemption has expired.[11] On representations being made to them, and after hearing the registration authority and the persons responsible for the administration of the charity the Commissioners may direct the registration authority to withdraw the exemption.[12]

If representations are made to the Commissioners as respects any registered or exempted war charity or charity for disabled persons, that grounds exist justifying removal from the register or withdrawal of exemption by the registration authority, as the case may be, and the Commissioners, after giving the registration authority and the management committee or other person responsible for the administration of the charity a full opportunity of making representations,[13] are satisfied that the grounds exist, they may direct the authority to remove the charity from the register, or as the case may be, to withdraw the exemption. In either case the authority must comply with the directions, and, in the case of removal from the register must in addition forthwith give notice of removal in two newspapers circulating in the area.[14] Additional powers are conferred on the Commissioners where (*a*) a charity is

1 *Ibid.*, reg. 21. 2 *Ibid.*, reg. 20.
3 War Charities Act 1940, s. 2 (4).
4 War Charities Regulations 1940, reg. 22.
5 *Ibid.*, reg. 23. 6 See 464, *supra*.
7 War Charities Regulations 1940, reg. 20.
8 War Charities Act 1940, s. 1 (2) which sets out those grounds.
9 War Charities Regulations 1940, reg. 19.
10 *Ibid.*, reg. 20. 11 *Ibid.*, reg. 20.
12 War Charities Act 1940, s. 5 (1).
13 These must be in writing supported by a statement giving reasons and details of supporting facts: War Charities Regulations 1940, reg. 29.
14 War Charities Act 1940, s. 5 (1); National Assistance Act 1948, s. 41 (1).

removed from the register or (*b*) registration of it is refused or (*c*) the Commissioners are satisfied that there would be grounds for refusing an application for the registration or exemption of a charity not already registered or exempted or (*d*) the Commissioners are satisfied that the objects of any charity have failed altogether or have become obsolete or useless.

By virtue of these additional powers the Commissioners may (1) order any bank or other person who holds money or securities on behalf of the charity not to part with such money or securities without the Commissioners' authority;[1] (2) order that any such money or securities be paid or transferred to the Official Custodian for Charities as in a case falling within subsection (1) of section 20 of the Charities Act 1960 and make any appropriate vesting order;[2] or (3) establish a scheme for the regulation of the charity as in a case falling within section 18 of the Charities Act 1960, but without the necessity of any application or reference being made to them for the purpose.[3] Non-compliance with an order not to part with money or securities without the Commissioners' authority or to pay or transfer money or securities to the Official Custodian for Charities is an offence[4] punishable with a fine not exceeding £100 or a term of imprisonment not exceeding six months or both;[5] but proceedings in connection with these offences cannot be instituted except by or with the consent of the Commissioners.[6] In the case of removal of a charity from the register, or refusal of its registration, the Commissioners may exercise their powers of controlling and making vesting orders despite a pending appeal against the removal or refusal. But the making of a scheme must await the determination of a pending appeal;[7] and in those cases where the Commissioners are satisfied that there would be grounds for refusing an application for the registration or exemption of the charity or that the objects of the charity have failed a scheme should not be established without first giving the management committee or person responsible for the administration of the charity a full opportunity for making representations in writing supported by a statement giving reasons and setting out the supporting facts.[8]

The Commissioners have for the purposes of their functions under section 5 of the Act and for the purposes of any appeal to them under the Act all such powers with respect to requiring accounts, statements, written answers to inquiries, the attendance of persons for examination on oath or otherwise, the production of documents, the furnishing of copies and extracts from documents, the examination of registers and records, and the transmission of documents for examination, as are exercisable by them in relation to charities under the Charities Act 1960 and the latter Act accordingly applies.[9] They also have powers subject to the approval of the Home Secretary to make regulations for carrying the Act into effect.[10]

On any inquiry under the War Charities Act 1940 the Charity Commissioners must state the reasons for their decision if they are requested to do so.[11]

---

1 War Charities Act 1940, s. 5 (2) (i).
2 *Ibid.*, s. 5 (2) (ii).   3 *Ibid.*, s. 5 (2) (iii).
4 *Ibid.*, s. 5 (3).   5 *Ibid.*, s. 9 (2).
6 *Ibid.*, s. 9 (3).   7 *Ibid.*, s. 5 (4) (a).
8 *Ibid.*, s. 5 (4) (b).   9 *Ibid.*, s. 5 (5); CA 1960, s. 48 (1), Sch. 6.
10 War Charities Act 1940, s. 4; see War Charities Regulations 1940, S.R. & O. 1940 No. 1533; Charities for Disabled Persons Regulations 1948, S.I. 1948 No. 1455.
11 Tribunals and Inquiries Act 1971, s. 12 (1) (a); Tribunals and Inquiries (Discretionary Inquiries) Order 1967, S.I. 1967 No. 451, at 3; Schedule, para. 14.

Chapter 43

Restrictions on Fund Raising

Charities depend on voluntary contributions. Some of these contributions are made without soliciting on their part. A testator will remember a particular charity in his will because he approves of its activities, and may well have subscribed to the charity in his lifetime. Charities advertise in newspapers and magazines making direct appeals to the public and to testators' legal advisers. But there are other ways of raising money. Collections can be made in the streets or from house to house or money can be raised by means of raffles and lotteries and the like. There are, however, various statutory regulations affecting these last mentioned methods of raising money.

Street collections

Certain authorities are empowered to make regulations with respect to the places where and the conditions under which persons may be permitted in any street or public place, within the police area, to collect money or sell articles for the benefit of charitable or other purposes and a person who acts in contravention of any such regulation is liable to a fine.[1] Regulations made under this provision do not come into operation until they have been confirmed by the Secretary of State, and published for such time and in such manner as he may direct.[2] Such regulations do not apply to the selling of articles in any street or public place where the articles are sold in the ordinary course of trade, and for the purpose of earning a livelihood, and no representation is made by or on behalf of the seller that any part of the proceeds of sale will be devoted to any charitable purpose.[3] The authorities who are empowered to make such regulations are: (a) the Common Council of the City of London, (b) the police authority for the Metropolitan Police District and (c) the council of each district, but any regulations made by a district council cannot have effect with respect to any street or public place which is within the Metropolitan Police District as well as within the district.[4]

The expression "street" in this context "includes any highway and any

---

1 Police Factories &c. (Miscellaneous Provisions) Act 1916, s. 5; Local Government Act 1972, s. 251 (2), Sch. 19, para. 22. The fine is £2 for the first offence; £5 for each and every subsequent offence.

2 Police Factories etc. (Miscellaneous Provisions) Act 1916, s. 5 (1), proviso (a).

3 Police Factories etc. (Miscellaneous Provisions) Act 1916, s. 5 (1), proviso (b).

4 *Ibid.*, s. 5 (1A). This subsection was added by Local Government Act 1972, s. 251 (2), Sch. 19, para. 22.

public bridge, road, lane, footway, square, court, alley or passage, whether a thoroughfare or not".

The intending organiser of a "flag day" must therefore consult the authority in the relevant area to ascertain the contents of the relevant regulations. Formerly these were, with one exception, not contained in any statutory rules and orders or statutory instrument: the exception being the Metropolitan Police District.[1] However the Charitable Collections (Transitional Provisions) Order 1974[2] contains model street collection regulations which a district council is authorised to adopt by resolution without the need for the regulations to be confirmed by the Secretary of State.

House to house collections

DEFINITIONS

Charities not infrequently raise money by means of house to house collections. This fact is the justification for discussing the statutory restrictions on house to house collecting[3] even though those restrictions also apply to house to house collections for purposes which are not in the strict sense charitable.

The House to House Collections Act 1939[4] which, together with regulations made thereunder,[5] constitutes the code on this subject is entitled "an Act to provide for the regulation of house to house collections for *charitable* purposes; and for matters connected therewith". But section 11 (1) of the Act makes it clear that "charitable purpose" is used in a wide and special sense: it includes "any charitable, benevolent or philanthropic purpose, whether or not the purpose is charitable within the meaning of any rule of law". In the ensuing discussion the word "charitable" is used in this wide and *special* sense, and "the Act" means the House to House Collections Act 1939.

The Act provides that no collection for a "charitable" purpose may be made unless the requirements of the Act as to a licence for promotion of the collection are satisfied.[6]

A house to house collection means an appeal to the public, made by means of visits from house to house (including business premises) to give for consideration[7] or not, money or other property.[8] A collection is deemed to be made for a particular purpose where the appeal is made in association with a representation that the money or other property appealed for, or part of it will be applied for that purpose.[9]

---

1 See S.R. & O. 1926 No. 848, as amended by S.I. 1963 No. 685.
2 S.I. 1974 No. 140.
3 Statutory restrictions on *street* collections vary with the police authority concerned. As far as the metropolitan district is concerned: see S.R. & O. 1926 No. 848 as amended by S.I. 1963 No. 685.
4 Printed at 596, *infra*.
5 The House to House Collections Regulations 1947 (S.R. & O. No. 2662) as amended by the House to House Collections Regulations 1963 (S.I. 1963 No. 684) printed at 684, *infra*.
6 House to House Collections Act, 1939, s. 1 (1).
7 So a sale of goods is included: *Carasu, Ltd.* v. *Smith,* [1968] 2 Q.B. 383, D.C.
8 House to House Collections Act 1939, s. 11 (1).
9 *Ibid.,* s. 11 (2).

REQUIREMENT OF A LICENCE

The general rule is that the promoter of a house to house collection must have a licence, although exemptions are granted in certain cases. A "promoter" is a person who causes others to act, whether for remuneration or otherwise, as collectors for the purpose of the collection; a "collector" is a person who makes an appeal in the course of house to house visits.[1]

If a person promotes a collection for a charitable purpose without a licence authorising him, or another under whose authority he acts, to do so, and a collection for that purpose is made in any locality pursuant to his promotion, he is guilty of an offence[2] and liable on summary conviction to a penalty not exceeding six months' imprisonment or a fine of £100 or both.[3]

A "collection" means an appeal to the public made by means of visits from house to house, to give whether for consideration or not money or other property.[4] In *Carasu, Ltd.* v. *Smith*[5] it was held that an activity was a "collection" for this purpose if a person was induced to purchase an article on the representation that part of the proceeds would go to a charitable purpose. In coming to this decision the Divisional Court bore in mind the provision that a collection is deemed to be made for a particular purpose where the appeal is made in association with a representation that the money or other property appealed for, or part of it, will be applied for that purpose.[6] The term "house" in the expression house to house is not to be restrictively construed to mean only a dwelling-house: it includes a place of business,[7] and so a public house is a house.[8] In order for there to be a collection it must be shown either that the person charged was seen to go from one house to another or that there is evidence to show that that is what he was about to do when he was found to be collecting in one house.[9] A bogus charity collector may well be just as much a nuisance in a public house as he would be moving from door to door down the street but the mischief aimed at by the House to House Collections Act 1939 is limited to a collection which is conducted by visits from house to house.[10] The Act does not apply to house to house collections made by a registered pool promoter who holds a licence under the Pool Competitions Act 1971 permitting house to house collection of entry money and so forth.[11]

A collector who acts in any locality for the purpose of a collection for a charitable purpose without there being in force a licence authorising a promoter under whose authority he acts, or authorising the collector himself, to promote a collection in that locality for that purpose is guilty of an offence.[12] The penalty for that offence on a first conviction is a fine not exceeding £5 and

---

1 *Ibid.*, s. 11 (1).
2 *Ibid.*, s. 1 (2).
3 *Ibid.*, s. 8 (1).
4 *Ibid.*, s. 11 (1).
5 [1968] 2 Q.B. 383, D.C.
6 House to House Collections Act 1939, s. 11 (2).
7 *Ibid.*, s. 11 (1).
8 *Hankinson* v. *Dowland*, [1974] 1 W.L.R. 1327.
9 *Ibid.*
10 *Ibid.*, at 1331, *per* Lord WIDGERY C.J.
11 Pool Competitions Act 1971, s. 3 (5).
12 House to House Collections Act 1939, s. 1 (3); *Carasu, Ltd.* v. *Smith*, [1968] 2 Q.B. 383, D.C.

for every subsequent conviction is not more than three months' imprisonment or a fine not exceeding £25 or both.[1]

Exemption from the provisions of the 1939 Act may be granted in respect of a particular collection in a locality or over a wider area.

If the chief officer of police[2] for the police area[2] comprising a locality in which a collection for a charitable purpose is being, or is proposed to be, made is satisfied that the purpose is local in character and that the collection is likely to be completed within a short period of time, he may grant to the person who appears to him to be principally concerned in the promotion a certificate exempting the grantee, or any person authorised by him to act as promoter or collector in relation to that collection, from the provisions of the 1939 Act[3] (other than those relating to the unauthorised use of badges[4] and the requirements of collectors' names[5]). The functions conferred on a chief officer of police by the 1939 Act or regulations made under it may be delegated by him to any police officer not below the rank of inspector.[6] The Commissioner of Police for the metropolitan police district may not, however, delegate his licensing functions.[7] A local exemption certificate of this kind gives the name of each promoter and specifies the purpose of the collection, the locality to which it is to be confined and the dates within which it is to be carried out. It also recites the fact that only the provisions relating to the unauthorised use of badges and the obligation to give one's name to a police constable on demand apply to the collection and that these statutory provisions are set out on the back of the certificate.[8] Where such a certificate is granted none of the otherwise applicable regulations made under the Act apply to a collection made in accordance with this certificate.[9]

The chief officer may grant a similar certificate where he is satisfied that the collection is on behalf of a war charity exempted from registration under the War Charities Act 1940[10] or of a charity for disabled persons so exempted.[11]

Exemption from the 1939 Act may also be granted by the Secretary of State (i.e. the Home Secretary) over wide areas. Where the Secretary of State is satisfied that a person pursues a charitable purpose throughout the whole of England[12] or a substantial part of it and is desirous of promoting collections for that purpose, he may by order direct that such person shall be exempt from the necessity of having a licence as respects all collections for that purpose in the localities described in the order.[13] Whilst such an order is in force, as respects collections in any locality, the provisions of the 1939 Act have effect in relation to the person exempted, to a promoter of a collection in that locality for that purpose acting under the authority of the person exempted, and to a collector

---

1 House to House Collections Act 1939, s. 8 (2).
2 These phrases are defined in Police Act 1964, s. 62 (a), (b), Sch. 8.
3 House to House Collections Act 1939, s. 1 (4).
4 See *ibid.*, ss. 5, 8 (4).
5 See *ibid.*, s. 6 (obligation to give name to police constable on demand) and s. 8.
6 House to House Collections Act 1939, s. 7 (2).
7 *Ibid.*, s. 9 (2); Local Government Act 1972, s. 251 (2), Sch. 29, para. 23 (5).
8 House to House Regulations 1947, reg. 3 (1) and Sch. 1.
9 *Ibid.*, reg. 3 (2).
10 See the War Charities Act 1940, s. 7 (2); and see the discussion at 460, *supra*.
11 National Assistance Act 1948, s. 41 (1).
12 This includes Wales and Berwick upon Tweed; Wales and Berwick Act 1746, s. 3.
13 House to House Collections Act 1939, s. 3 (1).

for that purpose as if a licence authorising the exempted person to promote a collection in that locality for that purpose were in force.[1] An application for an exemption order must be made not later than the first day of the month preceding that in which it is proposed to commence the collection, but the Secretary of State may grant an application made out of time if satisfied there are special reasons.[2] Any exemption order made by the Secretary of State may be revoked or varied by a subsequent order.[3]

APPLICATIONS FOR LICENCES AND THEIR REFUSAL OR REVOCATION

Application for a licence is made by the person promoting or proposing to promote a collection in a locality to the licensing authority for the area comprising that locality. The licensing authority in the City of London is the Common Council, in the metropolitan police district the Commissioner of Police and elsewhere the district council of the locality.[4] The Commissioner of Police may not delegate his licensing powers.[5] The application must be made in the prescribed manner[6] not later than the first day of the month preceding that in which it is proposed to commence collection although the licensing authority can waive this requirement if satisfied that there are special reasons for so doing.[7] The application must specify the purpose and locality of the collection. If it is in order then, subject to the provisions following, the authority must grant him a licence to promote a collection within that locality for that purpose. Where the application is successful a licence will be granted for such period not exceeding 12 months as may be specified in the application and will, unless previously revoked, remain in force for the period specified. However the authority may grant a licence for a shorter or longer period (but not for a period exceeding 18 months) if this appears to them to be expedient to provide for simultaneous expiration of licences to be granted in respect of collections which in their opinion are likely to be proposed annually or continuously over a long period.[8]

The licensing authority may refuse to grant a licence, or revoke a grant already granted if it appears to it that—[9]

(1) the total amount likely to be applied for charitable purposes as the result of the collection, including any amount already so applied, is inadequate in proportion to the value of the proceeds[10] likely to be received (including any proceeds already received);

(2) remuneration which is excessive in relation to such total amount is likely

---

1 *Ibid.*, s. 3 (1).
2 House to House Collections Regulations 1947, reg. 4 (2).
3 House to House Collections Act 1939, s. 3 (2).
4 House to House Collections Act 1939, s. 2 (1A); Local Government Act 1972, s. 251 (2), Sch. 29, para. 23 (2).
5 House to House Collections Act 1939, s. 9 (2).
6 The application must be in the form specified in the House to House Collections Regulations 1947, Sch. 2 (see reg. 4 (1)).
7 House to House Collections Regulations 1947, reg. 4 (2).
8 House to House Collections Act 1939, s. 2 (2).
9 House to House Collections, Act 1939, s. 2 (3); Local Government Act 1972, s. 251 (2), Sch. 29, para. 23 (3).
10 I.e. "all money and other property given, whether for consideration or not, in response to the appeal": House to House Collections Act 1939, s. 11 (1).

to be, or has been, retained out of the proceeds of the collection by any person;

(3) the grant would facilitate on offence of begging,[1] or that such an offence has been committed in connection with the collection;

(4) the applicant or holder of the licence is not a fit and proper person to hold a licence by reason of conviction in the United Kingdom of certain offences[2] or conviction in any part of the Queen's dominions of any offence involving a finding of fraud or dishonesty of a kind likely to be facilitated by the grant of a licence;

(5) the applicant or holder of the licence, in promoting a collection in respect of which a licence has been granted to him, has failed to exercise due diligence to secure that persons authorised by him to act as collectors were fit and proper persons, to secure compliance by such persons with the provisions of regulations made under the Act, or to prevent prescribed badges or prescribed certificates of authority being obtained by unauthorised persons.

(6) the applicant or holder of the licence has refused or neglected to furnish the authority with such information as it has reasonably required for informing itself as to matters specified in (1) to (5) above.[3]

The authority may also refuse to grant a licence if satisfied that the collection is for a war charity (including a charity for disabled persons) which is not for the time being registered or exempted from registration under the War Charities Act 1940.[4]

If the authority refuses to grant a licence, or revokes a licence which has been granted, it must forthwith give written notice to the applicant or former licence holder stating the ground or grounds upon which the licence has been refused or revoked and informing him of his right of appeal to the Secretary of State whose decision is final.[5] Any such appeal must be brought within 14 days from which the notice is given.[6] If the appeal is allowed the authority must forthwith issue a licence or cancel the revocation as the case may be.[7]

CONDUCT OF COLLECTIONS

The manner in which house to house collections may be carried out and the conduct of promoters and collectors in relation to such collections is governed by regulations made by the Secretary of State.[8] The regulations in force are the House to House Collections Regulations 1947 as amended by statutory instrument:[9] they are subject to annulment by resolution of either House of Parlia-

---

1 The offence referred to is an offence under the Vagrancy Act 1824, s. 3.

2 The offences not specified in the Schedule to House to House Collections Act 1939. They are: assault concerning bodily harm or common assault (Offences against the Person Act 1861, s. 47); Child-stealing (*ibid.*, s. 56); offences relating to street collections (Police Factories etc. (Miscellaneous Provisions) Act 1916, s. 5; Local Government Act 1972, s. 251 (2), Sch. 29 para. 22); rape, indecent assault or abduction (Sexual Offences Act 1956, ss. 1, 14, 17, 20); robbery, burglary, and blackmail (House to House Collections Act 1939, s. 2 (3) (d), schedule; Theft Act 1968, s. 33 (2), Sch. 2, Pt. III).

3 House to House Collections Act 1939, s. 2 (3) (a)–(f) inclusive.

4 War Charities Act 1940, s. 7 (1). See discussion at 462, *supra*.

5 House to House Collections Act 1939, s. 2 (4).

6 *Ibid.*, s. 2 (5).

7 *Ibid.*, s. 2 (6).

8 House to House Collections Act 1939, s. 4 (1) (2).

9 The regulations are printed as amended by House to House Collections Regulations 1963 (S.I. 1963 No. 684) at 684, *infra*.

ment.[1] Any person who contravenes or fails to comply with the provisions of any such regulations is guilty of an offence[2] and liable, on summary conviction, to a fine not exceeding £5.[3]

Street collections for charities, as distinct from house to house collections, are subject to a separate code of statutory provisions and regulations.[4]

A promoter must ensure that every collector has issued to him a certificate of authority in the prescribed form and duly completed (except as regards the signature of the collector) and signed by or on behalf of the chief promoter of the collection.[5] Similarly the promoter must provide the collector with a prescribed badge and, if money is to be collected a collecting, box or receipt book.[6] He must also exercise all due diligence to secure that all certificates of authority and prescribed badges obtained for the purposes of a collection are destroyed when no longer required.[7]

A person who, in connection with any appeal made by him to the public in association with a representation that the appeal is for a charitable purpose displays or uses (1) a prescribed badge or prescribed certificate of authority not being a badge or certificate for the time being held by him for the purposes of an appeal, or (2) any badge or device, or any certificate or other document so nearly resembling a prescribed badge or, as the case may be, a prescribed certificate of authority as to be calculated to deceive, is guilty of an offence.[8] The penalty on summary conviction is not more than six months' imprisonment or a fine of not more than £100 or both.[9] In *R. v. Davison*[10] it was held by the Court of Appeal that the words "any appeal" were not restricted to appeals by house to house collections: "any appeal" means what it says and covers any appeal made to the public in association with a representation that it is for a charitable purpose. The Court of Appeal also considered the meaning of the words "calculated to deceive" and said they meant "likely to deceive or intended to deceive".[11] In other words the crucial test in the matter is objective not subjective.

Every promoter of a collection must exercise all due diligence to ensure that persons authorised to act as collectors are fit and proper persons and to secure their compliance with the provisions of the regulations.[12] To exercise due diligence to prevent something being done is to take all reasonable steps to prevent it.[13]

---

1 House to House Collections Act 1939, s. 4 (4).
2 *Ibid.*, s. 4 (3).   3 *Ibid.*, s. 8 (3).
4 See the Police, Factories etc. (Miscellaneous Provisions) Act 1916, s. 5; Local Government Act 1972, s. 251 (2), Sch. 29, para. 22 and the regulations made thereunder.
5 House to House Collections Regulations 1947, reg. 6 (1) (a).
6 *Ibid.*, reg. 6 (1) (b) and (c). Badges are obtainable from H.M. Stationery Office and the form is prescribed in Sch. 4 to the regulations.
7 House to House Collections Regulations 1947, reg. 17.
8 House to House Collections Act 1939, s. 5.
9 *Ibid.*, s. 8 (4).
10 [1972] 1 W.L.R. 1540.
11 A very careful direction on the part of the judge is therefore called for: see [1972] 1 W.L.R. 1540, at 1544.
12 House to House Collections Regulations 1947, reg. 5.
13 *Tesco Supermarkets, Ltd.* v. *Nattrass*, [1972] A.C. 153, at 203 *per* Lord DIPLOCK; and see *Riverstone Meat Co. Pty.* v. *Lancashire Shipping Co., Ltd.*, [1960] 1 Q.B. 536, at 581, *per* WILLMER L.J. ("an obligation to exercise reasonable care"). The latter case was reversed in the House of Lords without affecting the dictum of WILLMER, L.J.: see [1961] A.C. 807, H.L.

No person under the age of sixteen years may act or be authorised to act as a collector of money.[1]

Every collector must sign the certificate of authority and badge, produce the certificate on demand,[2] wear the badge prominently during collecting, and return both to the promoter when the collection is completed or on the demand of the promoter.[3] A police constable may require any person whom he believes to be acting as a collector for the purpose of a collection for a charitable purpose to declare to him immediately his name and address and to sign his name; failure to comply with this requirement is an offence for which the penalty on summary conviction is a fine not exceeding £5.[4]

Where a collector is collecting money by means of a collecting box he may only accept contributions which are placed in the box; if he is collecting money by any other means he must give a signed receipt.[5] In a case where a promoter has been granted an order of exemption he may with the Secretary of State's permission arrange an envelope collection.[6] Collecting boxes with seals unbroken must be returned to the promoter when they are full, or the collection is completed or the collector does not wish to act any longer. When a receipt book is exhausted it must also be returned and so too if the collection is completed or the collector no longer wishes to act. Collecting boxes must be opened in the presence of the promoter and another responsible person, or where it is delivered unopened to a bank by a responsible bank official. Receipt books and contributions received therewith must be examined by the promoter and another responsible person. The amount in cash box or book must be listed with the distinguishing number of the box or book.[7]

No collector may importune any person to the annoyance[8] of such person, or remain in, or at the door of, any house if requested by any occupant of the house to leave.[9]

The chief promoter of a collection for which a licence has been granted must furnish an account to the authority granting the licence within one month of the expiry of the licence.[10] Where an order of exemption has been made the chief promoter must furnish the account annually to the Secretary of State.[11] In either case the time for furnishing the account may be extended if the authority or the Secretary of State is satisfied that there are special reasons for so doing.[12] In appropriate cases the account for house to house collections may be combined with that required for street collections.[13] The accounts must be in the prescribed form and duly certified[14] and vouched.[15]

A person who in furnishing any information for the purposes of the House

---

1 House to House Collections Regulations 1947, Reg. 8 (amended by S.I. 1963 reg. 684).
2 Whether of a police constable or an occupant of a house.
3 House to House Collections Regulations 1947, reg. 7.
4 House to House Collections Act 1939, s. 6.
5 House to House Collections Regulations 1947, reg. 10.
6 *Ibid.*, reg. 13 where the provisions for envelope collections are detailed.
7 *Ibid.*, reg. 12.
8 See *Tod-Heatly* v. *Benham* (1880), 40 Ch.D. 80; *Downie* v. *Taylor*, [1954] V.L.R. 603.
9 House to House Collections Regulations 1947, reg. 9.
10 *Ibid.*, reg. 14 (1).
11 *Ibid.*, reg. 14 (2).
12 *Ibid.*, reg. 14 (3).
13 *Ibid.*, reg. 14 (4).
14 *Ibid.*, reg. 15, Schs. 5–7.
15 *Ibid.*, reg. 16.

to House Collections Act 1939, knowingly or recklessly makes a statement false in a material particular is guilty of an offence, and is liable on summary conviction to imprisonment for a term not exceeding six months or to a fine not exceeding £100 or to both.[1]

Where an offence under the House to House Collections Act 1939 committed by a corporation is proved to have been committed with the consent or connivance of, or to be attributable to any culpable neglect of duty on the part of any director, manager, secretary, or other officer[2] of the corporation, he, as well as the corporation, is deemed to be guilty of an offence and is liable to be proceeded against and punished accordingly.[3]

Lotteries, raffles and competitions

Since some charities raise funds by means of lotteries and prize competitions a summary of those statutory provisions which particularly affect charities or the kind of lotteries which they might wish to promote is appropriate.

Subject to the provisions of the Lotteries and Amusements Act 1976,[4] all lotteries in Great Britain which do not constitute gaming are unlawful.[5] It is therefore of prime importance to establish what constitutes a lottery, before considering the conditions under which certain lotteries may lawfully be promoted. Competitions and amusements will also be considered, including charity pool competitions.

DEFINITION OF A LOTTERY

There is no statutory definition of a lottery but there is abundant case law on the point. In *Taylor* v. *Smetten*[6] the Divisional Court approved the definition in Webster's dictionary "a distribution of prizes by lot or chance". There are three essentials of a lottery: (1) consideration, (2) a prize and (3) chance.[7] The simplest form of lottery incorporating all these elements is where the adventurers contribute to a fund which they agree among themselves shall be unequally divided between them upon the happening of an agreed event. This is the form of the ordinary sweepstake which is a lottery.[8] Whether the organiser is to derive a profit from the scheme is irrelevant,[9] but the participant must stand the risk of losing.[10]

---

1 House to House Collections Act 1939, s. 8 (6).
2 As to who are officers of companies, see the cases cited in Stroud, *Judicial Dictionary* (4th edn.) 1833.
3 House to House Collections Act 1939, s. 8 (7).
4 The Act was passed on 22nd July 1976 and comes into force immediately after the coming into force of the last of the provisions of the Lotteries Act 1975: see Lotteries and Amusements Act 1976, s. 25 (9). See Preface.
5 Lotteries and Amusements Act 1976, s. 1.
6 (1883), 11 Q.B.D. 207, D.C.; *Barclay* v. *Pearson*, [1893] 2 Ch. 154; *Director of Public Prosecutions* v. *Bradfute and Associates, Ltd.*, [1967] 2 Q.B. 291, at 295, per Lord PARKER C.J.
7 *R.* v. *Moose Jaw Recreational and Cultural Development Soc* (1969), 68 W.W.R. 681 (debentures redeemable by lot: lottery).
8 *R.* v. *Hobbs*, [1898] 2 Q.B. 647, C.C.R.; *Hardwick* v. *Lane*, [1904] 1 K.B. 204, D.C.
9 *Allport* v. *Nutt* (1845), 1 C.B. 974; *Hardwick* v. *Lane, supra.*
10 *Wallingford* v. *Mutual Society* (1880), 5 App. Cas. 685.

Contribution

The first of the three essentials mentioned above, namely consideration is usually referred to in terms of contributions by the participants. Thus in *Barnes* v. *Strathern*[1] Lord CLYDE said of a lottery that it:

> —"usually, if not always, takes the form of the creation of a fund by the participants in the lottery, who buy tickets or pay subscriptions in consideration of an offer by the promoters to award them a prize on some contingency the happening whereof depends on chance".

Lord SANDS thought that the definition might perhaps seem to be incomplete and that it might be said that there must be super-added an element of allurement and contribution.[2]

More recently it has been said by Lord PARKER C.J. in *Whitbread & Co., Ltd.* v. *Bell*[3] that in a lottery there "must be some payment or contribution if not towards the prizes themselves at any rate towards funds i.e. profits out of which prizes are provided". However this statement may need qualification in view of the decision of the Divisional Court in *Willis* v. *Young and Stembridge*[4] which Lord PARKER C.J. classified as a case which depends entirely on its special facts. The proprietors of a weekly newspaper cause medals to be distributed gratuitously among members of the public, each medal bearing a distinctive number with the words "Keep this, it may be worth £100. See the 'Weekly Telegraph' today". The winning numbers which were arbitrarily selected by the newspaper proprietors and were unknown to the distributors were published weekly in the newspaper. There was in fact no need to buy the paper to find out who had won, but it was proved in evidence that a great number of participants did buy the paper, not to read it, but to find out the winning numbers. As a result the paper's circulation increased by some 20 per cent. during the course of the scheme. It was held that although it was possible for an individual holder of a medal to obtain a prize without paying anything for his chance, the medal holders as a body collectively contributed sums of money to the fund out of which the money came for the prizes and the scheme was an unlawful lottery. Whether the *Willis* case is one from which many general principles can safely be drawn is open to doubt. Counsel for the defendants in the *Whitbread*[5] case specifically kept open whether the *Willis* case had been correctly decided and Lord HODSON in *M'Collom* v. *Wrightson*[6] found it "unnecessary to consider whether the case was rightly decided".

Prize

The requirement that there should be a prize does not mean that there must be an identifiable prize fund. It is sufficient if the scheme has the overall object of the distribution of money by chance.[7] For that reason a chain letter scheme may be a lottery.[8]

---

1 1929, S.C. (J.) 41, at 46.   2 *Ibid.*, at 48.
3 [1970] 2 Q.B. 547, at 555. This qualifies earlier wider dicta (cited with approval) in *Douglas* v. *Valente* 1968 S.L.T. 85, at 87: see [1970] 2 Q.B. 547, at 557.
4 [1907] 1 K.B. 448.   5 [1970] 2 Q.B. 547, at 557.
6 [1968] A.C. 522, at 528.
7 *Atkinson* v. *Murrell*, [1973] A.C. 289.   8 *Ibid.*

The fact that no part of the money which is paid for lottery tickets goes to the purchase of the prize because, for example, the prize is presented is not a material factor.[1] The fact that every participant in the scheme gets something of value or even full value for his or her contribution does not prevent the scheme from being a lottery. The purchaser of a newspaper[2] or a packet of sweets[3] or tea[4] or a theatre seat[5] may get full value for the money paid, but if in addition the purchaser had the chance of getting something of value by way of a prize, there is a lottery. Nothing in these cases was added to the price for the chance; but the chance by offering an inducement to others to purchase so increases sales that it becomes possible to provide the prizes out of the profits.

On the other hand a theatre which for each evening of a particular week selected the names of two persons from the telephone directory to whom complimentary tickets were presented were not conducting a "scheme by which prizes ... are gained ... by ... mode of chance" in other words a lottery, since though the distribution of seats was by chance the complimentary tickets received under the scheme were not "prizes" and the word "gained" imported some notion of conscious striving on the part of the person who gains, and the recipients of the tickets had occupied a merely passive role.[6] Indeed there was no contribution to the scheme by the donees of the tickets at all.

The opportunity to win a prize by skill may itself be a prize, so that if that opportunity is distributed by lot or chance the distribution is a lottery.[7]

Chance

Chance is the very kernel of a lottery. Indeed the cases establish that distribution in a lottery must depend *wholly* upon chance. The leading authority is the decision of the Court of Appeal in *Hall* v. *Cox*[8] a case in which the defendant published a newspaper called "The Rocket" containing an offer of a money prize for a correct prediction of the number of births and deaths in London during a specified week ending four weeks later. Competitors were not limited to one prediction but each prediction had to be put on a separate coupon and there was only one coupon in each newspaper. The offer by the newspaper armed competitors with statistics about births and deaths in the corresponding week of the previous year. A. L. SMITH L.J. with whom RIGBY and COLLINS L.J. concurred held that the competition was not a lottery, saying:[9]

> "The result, no doubt, depends largely on chance, but not entirely, and the cases shew that to constitute a lottery it must be a matter depending entirely upon chance."

---

1 *Bartlett* v. *Parker*, [1912] 2 K.B. 497 (bicycle raffled at dance).
2 *Hall* v. *McWilliam* (1901), 85 L.T. 239, D.C.; *Willis* v. *Young and Stembridge*, [1907] 1 K.B. 448, D.C.
3 *Hunt* v. *Williams* (1888), 52 J.P. 821, D.C.
4 *Taylor* v. *Smetten* (1883), 11 Q.B.D. 207; *Howgate* v. *Ralph* (1929), 141 L.T. 512.
5 *Morris* v. *Blackman* (1864), 2 H. & C. 912; *Minty* v. *Sylvester* (1915), 114 L.T. 164.
6 *Metropolitan Theatre Co., Ltd.* v. *Police*, [1956] N.Z.L.R. 55.
7 *Director of Public Prosecutions* v. *Bradfute and Associates Ltd.*, [1967] 2 Q.B. 291; *cf. R.* v. *Young* (1957), 24 W.W.R. 83.
8 [1899] 1 Q.B. 198, C.A.
9 [1899] 1 Q.B. 198, at 200; followed in *Hobbs* v. *Ward* (1929), 45 T.L.R. 373, at 374, *per* Lord HEWART C.J.

He held that there was an element of skill in the inquiry in the case before him dependent on the investigation of the returns for previous years and the consideration of the increase of population the death rate and suchlike statistical investigations. The case was comparable to those cases[1] where it had been held that the offer of a prize for forecasting the result of a horse race was not a lottery, because the skilled knowledge of the competitor was an ingredient in the matter. Lord HAILSHAM L.C. summarising the effect of these authorities said in *News of the World, Ltd.* v. *Friend*[2] that "a lottery being a distribution of prizes by lot or chance it came to be held that, even if a quite modest degree of skill entered into the decisive test the competition escaped". Another case where the court discovered the requisite "modest degree of skill" was *Scott* v. *Director of Public Prosecutions*[3] where the terms of the competition were that each competitor had to select one of a number of given words and compose a short sentence which defined or illustrated the word selected, the initial letter of each word in the sentence to be a letter occurring in the selected word; that all the sentences reaching the editor of the newspaper would receive careful consideration and that the decision of the editor as to the prize winners would be final. The Divisional Court held that as the competition was one involving some degree of skill on the part of the competitors and as there was no evidence that the number of competitors was so large as to make it impossible for the sentences to be considered on their merits,[4] the competition was not one the result of which depended entirely on chance and that it was not therefore a lottery. LUSH J. said that he could not see how the presence or absence of a "standard" could convert an adjudication into a lottery or not a lottery according as the merit was of a low or high order;[5] and he expressed the view that a decision according to honest taste or fancy was not a decision by chance and nothing else, however justly one might belittle the class or degree of merit.[6] ATKIN J. added:[7]

> "any kind of skill or dexterity whether bodily or mental, in which persons can compete would prevent a scheme from being a lottery if the result partly depended upon such skill or dexterity."

The correct answer to a picture puzzle in another case depended on the exercise of considerable skill or even a great deal of skill:[8] obviously in such a case there is no lottery at all. That is also true of many literary competitions[9] or competitions involving wit and originality.[10] A competition in which competitors had to estimate the number of buttons in a glass jar has been held to depend on skill, as the approximation of the number of buttons depended on the exercise of judgment, observation and mental effort.[11]

---

1 *Caminada* v. *Hulton* (1891), 64 L.T. 572; *Stoddart* v. *Sagar*, [1895] 2 Q.B. 474.
2 [1973] 1 W.L.R. 248, at 25.
3 [1914] 2 K.B. 868, D.C.
4 *Cf. Blyth* v. *Hulton & Co., Ltd.* (1908), 24 T.L.R. 719, C.A. (where there was evidence to that effect).
5 [1914] 2 K.B. 868, at 876.
6 *Ibid.*, at 877.
7 *Ibid.*, at 880.
8 *Witty* v. *World Service Ltd.*, [1936] Ch. 303. The case turned on the statutory precursor of the Lotteries and Amusements Act 1976, s. 14 (1) (b).
9 *Sobye* v. *Levy* (1909), 9 C.L.R. 496 (limerick competition involving skill).
10 *R.* v. *Bertram Davies* (1915), T.P.D. 155 (picture title competition).
11 *R.* v. *Jamieson* (1884), 7 O.R. 149; and see *R.* v. *Dodds* (1884), 4 O.R. 390; *Dunham* v. *St. Croix Soap Manufacturing Co.* (1897), 34 N.B.R. 243.

Although it has been said that if merit or skill plays *any* part in determining the distribution there has been no lottery and there is no offence,[1] a gloss was added by HUMPHREYS J. in *Moore v. Elphick*:[2]

> "The merit or skill must be real skill which has some effect. It must be something more than a scintilla of skill so that it can fairly be said that the distribution of the prize, the allocation of the prize, in the particular case, was due to two causes, not one cause with possibly a scintilla of some other cause added to it, but two separate causes, one being skill the other being chance."

This dictum goes no further than saying that the law pays no attention to an insignificant element of skill: *de minimis non curat lex*. A refinement of this principle is that where only an insignificant proportion of the participants in fact exercise skill, the remainder being content to accept an entry provided by the promoter, the scheme is a lottery.[3] But the dictum of CASSELS J. in *Moore v. Elphick*[4] that the test is whether "chance predominates and is the one outstanding feature" is not presaged or echoed in any of the decided cases.

There have, of course, been many cases of competitions, the final result of which was determined by chance: such competitions have been held to be lotteries and, therefore, illegal, even though a degree of skill was required to winnow out all but the final competitiors. Thus, a competition to determine the order of merit of the roles of Ellen Terry, to be decided by the votes of the competitors themselves was a lottery,[5] and so was a competition, similarly decided, in which the prizes were offered for the "correct" order of merit of 13 named commodities, all dog foods.[6] The same rule caught the missing word competition in *Barclay v. Pearson*[7] because the word to which success was attached was selected arbitrarily from a number of more or less appropriate solutions. It would apparently have been different if the competitors had been asked to supply the most appropriate word.[8] The competitors in the crossword competition in *Coles v. Odhams Press, Ltd.*[9] were likewise not required to submit the most appropriate solutions to clues which admitted of alternative solutions. The competition editor had prepared beforehand a test solution of the puzzle and the prize was to be awarded to the competitor whose solution happened to correspond most closely to that of the competition editor, although if all the solutions sent in were examined and compared on their merits, the solution of that competitor might not be found to be intrinsically the best. In other words, as Lord HEWART C.J. aptly put it:[10]

> "the competitors [were] invited to pay a certain number of pence to have the opportunity of taking blind shots at a hidden target".

---

1 *Scott v. Director of Public Prosecutions*, [1914] 2 K.B. 868, at 874.
2 [1945] 2 All E.R. 155, at 156.
3 *Singette, Ltd., v. Martin*, [1971] A.C. 407, H.L.; see also *Barker v. Mumby*, [1939] 1 All E.R. 611, D.C.
4 [1945] 2 All E.R. 155, at 162.
5 *Challis v. Warrender* (1930), 144 L.T. 437, D.C.
6 *Hobbs v. Ward* (1929), 45 T.L.R. 373, D.C.
7 [1893] 2 Ch. 154; and see *R. v. Jones* (1923), E.D.L. 97.
8 [1893] 2 Ch. 154, at 165, *per* STIRLING J.; and see *Scott v. Director of Public Prosecutions*, [1914] 2 K.B. 868, at 878.
9 [1936] 1 K.B. 416, D.C.
10 [1936] 1 K.B. 416, at 426.

s

In two other cases where on the facts it was found that prizes for completing a limerick depended on the arbitrary will of the editor and not on any objective standard, the competition was held to be an illegal lottery.[1]

A competition in which a prize is offered for forecasting the number of goals scored by a number of football teams on the same day has been held to be a lottery[2] and so has a weather forecasting competition.[3]

It must however be borne in mind that a competition which does not constitute a lottery may yet be a prize competition made unlawful by the Lotteries and Amusements Act 1976.[4]

LAWFUL LOTTERIES

Society's Lottery

A society which is established and conducted wholly or mainly for charitable purposes may have what is called a "society's lottery" promoted on its behalf on certain conditions.[5] Such a lottery is not unlawful if (1) it is promoted in Great Britain; and (2) the society is for the time being registered under the Lotteries and Amusements Act 1976 and (3) it is promoted in accordance with a scheme approved by the society and (4) *either* the total value of the tickets or chances to be sold is £5000 or less *or* the scheme is registered with the Gaming Board before any tickets or chances are sold.[6] In this context the term "society" includes an institution, organisation or association of persons by whatever name called, and any separate branch or section thereof.[7]

An application for the registration of a charitable society for the purposes of the provisions relating to societies' lotteries is made to the registration authority[8] in whose area the office or head office of the society is situated.[9] The relevant registration authorities in England are the Common Council of the City of London, the London borough councils, the district councils and the Council of the Isles of Scilly. In Wales they are the district councils.[10] The application must specify the purposes for which the society is established and conducted,[11] and upon the application being duly made and on payment of a fee of £10 the registration must, except in the circumstances stated below, register the society in a register kept for that purpose and notify the society in writing that it has

---

1 *Blyth* v. *Hulton & Co. Ltd.* (1908), 24 T.L.R. 719, C.A.; *Smith's Advertising Agency* v. *Leeds Laboratory Co.* (1910), 26 T.L.R. 335, C.A.; *cf. Sobye* v. *Levy* (1909), 9 C.L.R. 496 (where in making the award the judge considered the appropriateness of the line, the metre and the rhyme; held no lottery).

2 *Boucher* v. *Rowsell*, [1947] 1 All E.R. 870; *Turner* v. *Chief Constable of Liverpool* (1965), 115 L.Jo. 711.

3 *R.* v. *Pearson* (1893), 37 Sol. Jo. 749; *cf. R.* v. *Regina Agricultural and Industrial Exhibition Association Ltd.*, [1932] 2 W.W.R. 131 (estimates of future average temperatures of seven named cities on certain days from statistical data supplied to competitors not a lottery).

4 Lotteries and Amusements Act 1976, s. 14; discussed at 488, *infra*.

5 *Ibid.*, s. 5 (1).

6 *Ibid.*, s. 5 (3) (a)–(d).

7 *Ibid.*, s. 23 (1).

8 *Ibid.*, Sch. 1, para. 1 (1).

9 *Ibid.*, Sch. 1, para. 1 (2).

10 *Ibid.*

11 *Ibid.*, Sch. 1, para. 2.

done so.[1] Thereafter the registered society must pay to the registration authority on 1st January in each year while it is registered a fee of £5, and any such fee which remains unpaid after the date on which it becomes payable may be recovered by the authority as a debt.[2] It should be added that registration of any society under the provisions of the Betting, Gaming and Lotteries Act 1963[3] has effect as a registration under the relevant provisions of the 1976 Act.[4]

Registration of a society may, however, be refused or revoked if, after giving the society concerned an opportunity to be heard it appears to the authority that any person has been convicted of any one of several specified offences committed in connection with a lottery promoted or proposed to be promoted on behalf of the society, or that the society is not or has ceased to be a society established and constituted wholly or mainly for charitable purposes.[5]

The specified offences[6] are: those itemised in section 2 of the 1976 Act,[7] contravention of any requirement of any regulation made under the Act in respect of a society's lottery,[8] failure to send in a return or giving or certifying a return known to contain false or misleading information,[9] any offence under section 42 or 45 of the Betting, Gaming and Lotteries Act 1963[10] and any offence involving fraud or dishonesty.

Where registration is refused or revoked the registration authority must forthwith notify the society of the refusal or revocation and the society may appeal within 21 days to the Crown Court by giving notice to the appropriate court officer and to the registration authority.[11] In the case of a revocation of a registration until the time for giving notice of appeal has expired, and if such notice is duly given, until the appeal is determined or abandoned, the registration is deemed to continue in force and if the court confirms the revocation it may order the registration to continue in force for a further period of up to two months from the date of the order.[12] A society may at any time apply to the registration authority for cancellation of registration and in such a case the authority must cancel the registration accordingly.[13]

Except where a society's lottery is promoted in accordance with a scheme registered with the Gaming Board[14] the promoter of a society's lottery must, not later than the end of the third month after the date of the lottery send to the registration authority a return certified by two other members of the society, being persons of full age appointed in writing by the governing body of the society.[15] The return must show: (1) a copy of the scheme under which the

---

1 *Ibid.*, Sch. 1, para. 3.
2 *Ibid.*, Sch. 1, para. 9.
3 Betting, Gaming and Lotteries Act 1963, Sch. 7 (repealed).
4 Lotteries and Amusements Act 1976, Sch. 1, para. 10.
5 *Ibid.*, Sch. 1, para. 4 and s. 5 (1).
6 See *ibid.*, Sch. 1, para. 4 (2).
7 These are general lottery offences previously contained in Betting, Gaming and Lotteries Act 1963, s. 42.
8 Lotteries and Amusements Act 1976, s. 13.
9 Whether under Lotteries and Amusements Act 1976, Sch. 1, para. 14 or its statutory predecessor Betting, Gaming and Lotteries Act 1963, Sch. 7, para. 12.
10 These are general lottery offences and offences relating to small lotteries (now societies' lotteries).
11 Lotteries and Amusements Act 1976, Sch. 1, para. 5.
12 *Ibid.*, Sch. 1, para. 7.
13 *Ibid.*, Sch. 1, para. 8.
14 Which is exempted: *ibid.*, Sch. 1, para. 12.
15 *Ibid.*, Sch. 1, para. 11.

lottery was promoted; (2) the whole proceeds of the lottery; (3) the sums appropriated out of those proceeds on account of expenses and of prizes respectively; (4) the particular purpose or purposes to which proceeds of the lottery were applied[1] and the amount applied for that purpose, or for each of those purposes, as the case may be; and (5) the date of the lottery.[2] The registration authority must keep the return for at least 18 months, deposited at their office, and allow anyone to inspect it during office hours free of charge.[3] Failure to send a return or giving or certifying a return known to contain false or misleading information is an offence.[4]

The requirement that a society's lottery must be promoted in accordance with a scheme approved by the society has already been noted.[5] The 1976 Act requires a society to submit to the Gaming Board any such scheme if the total value of the tickets or chances to be sold in any lottery promoted in accordance with that scheme exceeds £5000.[6] The Gaming Board must register any scheme so submitted to them unless (1) the society is not registered with the registration authority or (2) the scheme is contrary to law or (3) except where the Secretary of State otherwise directs, the Gaming Board is not satisfied either that all lotteries promoted by or on behalf of the applicant within the last five years have been properly conducted, or that all fees payable under the Act have been paid, or that all requirements of the Gaming Board concerning the provision of accounts or other information have been complied with[7] or (4) except where the Secretary of State otherwise directs it appears to the Gaming Board that an unsuitable person[8] will be employed for reward in connection with the promotion of a lottery under the scheme.[9]

The Gaming Board may revoke the registration of any scheme on the same grounds as would have required it to refuse registration[10] and also where it appears to them that an unsuitable person[11] has been employed for reward in connection with the promotion of any lottery under that scheme.[12] Revocation of registration of any scheme in these circumstances will not affect any lottery in respect of which any tickets of chances have already been sold at the date of revocation.[13]

The Secretary of State can direct the Gaming Board to restore any registration which the Gaming Board have revoked on any of the grounds contained in (3) and (4) above[14] or on the ground that an unsuitable person has been employed for reward in connection with the promotion of a lottery,[15] and the

---

1 Pursuant to *ibid.*, s. 5 (4).
2 *Ibid.*, Sch. 1, para. 11.
3 *Ibid.*, Sch. 1, para. 13.
4 *Ibid.*, Sch. 1, para. 14.
5 See 482 and 483, *supra*. Lotteries and Amusements Act 1976, s. 5 (3) (c).
6 *Ibid.*, Sch. 2, para. 2.
7 As to these requirements, see *ibid.*, Sch. 2, para. 6.
8 An unsuitable person is one who has been convicted of one of the specified offences: Lotteries and Amusements Act 1976, Sch. 2, para. 3 (2). The offences specified in this sub-paragraph are the same as those in Sch. 1, para. 4 (2) discussed at 483, *supra*.
9 Lotteries and Amusements Act 1976, Sch. 2, para. 3 (1).
10 See the preceding paragraph.
11 See footnote 8, *supra*.
12 Lotteries and Amusements Act 1976, Sch. 2, para. 4 (2).
13 *Ibid.*, Sch. 2, para. 4 (3).
14 I.e. under *ibid.*, Sch. 2, para. 3 (1) (c) and (d).
15 I.e. under *ibid.*, Sch. 2, para. 4 (2).

Gaming Board is bound to give effect to any such direction.[1] The restoration will take effect from the date of revocation or whatever later date is specified in the direction.[2]

The Gaming Board has power to require the provision of accounts in relation to any lottery promoted under a scheme registered by them, and any other information which they may need in respect of any lottery promoted or to be promoted under a scheme registered by them or submitted to them for registration.[3]

On an application for the registration of a scheme a prescribed fee is payable to the Gaming Board and where more than one lottery is to be promoted under a scheme registered by the Gaming Board a further prescribed fee is payable for each lottery promoted under that scheme.[4]

A society may not hold more than 52 society's lotteries in any period of 12 months. However, when the date of two or more society's lotteries promoted on behalf of one society is the same and the total value of the tickets or chances to be sold in those lotteries does not exceed £10 000, all those lotteries will be treated as one.[5] The date of any lottery promoted on behalf of a society must generally not be less than seven days after the date of any previous lottery promoted on behalf of that society.[6] But, exceptionally, the date of a lottery promoted for the purpose of selling tickets or chances wholly or mainly to persons attending a particular athletic or sporting event may be less than seven days after the date of a previous lottery promoted on behalf of the society.[7]

Various detailed rules are also laid down for a society's lottery. The promoter of the lottery must be a member of the society authorised in writing by the governing body of the society to act as the promoter; and every ticket and every notice or advertisement of the lottery lawfully exhibited distributed or published must specify the name of the society, the name and address of the promoter and the date of the lottery.[8] The price of every ticket or chance has to be the same[9] and must not exceed 25p;[10] and the price of any ticket must be stated on the ticket.[11] No person should be admitted to participate in a society lottery in respect of a ticket or chance except after payment to the society of the whole price of the ticket or chance; and in no circumstances should any money received for or on account of a ticket or chance be returned.[12]

A distinction is drawn in respect of the permissible amount or value of a prize between a society lottery where the total value of the tickets or chances to be sold is £5000 or less and a lottery pursuant to a scheme registered with the Gaming Board before any tickets or chances are sold. In the case of the former no prize must exceed £1000 in amount or value.[13] In the case of the latter, no

---

1 *Ibid.*, Sch. 2, para. 5 (1).
2 *Ibid.*, Sch. 2, para. 5 (2).
3 *Ibid.*, Sch. 2, para. 6. It is an offence knowingly or recklessly to give to the Board any information which is false in a material particular: *ibid.*, Sch. 2, para. 8.
4 *Ibid.*, Sch. 2, para. 7 (1).
5 *Ibid.*, s. 10 (1) (a).
6 *Ibid.*, s. 10 (2).
7 *Ibid.*
8 *Ibid.*, s. 11 (1).
9 *Ibid.*, s. 11 (3).
10 *Ibid.*, s. 11 (2).
11 *Ibid.*, s. 11 (3).
12 *Ibid.*, s. 11 (4).
13 *Ibid.*, s. 11 (5).

prize must exceed in value or amount £1000 for a short term lottery[1] £1500 for a medium term lottery[2] and £2000 for any other lottery;[3] and the total value of the tickets or chances sold must not exceed £10 000 for a short term lottery,[1] £20 000 for a medium term lottery[2] and £40 000 for any other lottery.[4]

The amount of the proceeds of a society's lottery appropriated for the provision of prizes must not exceed half the whole proceeds of the lottery.[5] The amount of the proceeds of a society's lottery appropriated on account of expenses (exclusive of prizes) must not exceed whichever is the less of (1) the expenses actually incurred and (2) where the whole proceeds of the lottery do not exceed £5000 25 per cent. of those proceeds of (if the whole proceeds exceed £5000) 15 per cent. of those proceeds or such larger percentage not exceeding 25 per cent. as the Gaming Board may authorise in the case of a particular lottery.[6]

The Secretary of State is also empowered by the statute to make regulations regarding societies' lotteries.[7]

If any requirement of the Lotteries and Amusements Act 1976 or of any regulation made under it in respect of a society's lottery is contravened[8] the promoter of that lottery and any other person who is party to the contravention is guilty of an offence.[9] There are however several defences which the statute expressly recognises. First, it is a defence for a person charged with any such offence only by reason of his being the promoter of that lottery to prove that the contravention occurred without his consent or connivance and that he exercised all due diligence to prevent it.[10] Secondly it is a defence for any person charged with an offence in respect of an appropriation made in contravention of the provisions relating to the amount of the proceeds of a society's lottery that may be appropriated to prizes or to expenses (exclusive of prizes[11]) to prove (1) that the proceeds of the lottery fell short of the sum reasonably estimated; and (2) that the appropriation was made in order to fulfil an unconditional undertaking as to prizes given in connection with the sale of the relevant tickets or chances or in respect of expenses actually incurred; and (3) that the total amounts appropriated in respect of prizes or expenses did not exceed the amounts which could lawfully have been appropriated out of the proceeds of the lottery under the relevant provisions[12] if the proceeds had amounted to the sum reasonably estimated.[13] Lastly it is a defence for any person charged with an offence in respect of a contravention of the provision relating to frequency of

---

1 A lottery is "short term" if less than one month has passed between the date of that lottery and the date of a previous lottery promoted on behalf of the same society: *ibid.*, s. 11 (10) (a).

2 A lottery is "medium term" if less than three months but not more than one month has passed between the date of that lottery and the date of a previous lottery promoted on behalf of the same society: *ibid.*, s. 11 (10) (b).

3 *Ibid.*, s. 11 (7).

4 *Ibid.*, s. 11 (8), (9).

5 *Ibid.*, s. 11 (11).

6 *Ibid.*, s. 11 (12), (13).

7 *Ibid.*, s. 12. No regulations have yet been promulgated.

8 "Contravention" in relation to any requirement, includes a failure to comply with that requirement, and cognate expressions are construed accordingly: *ibid.*, s. 23 (1).

9 *Ibid.*, s. 13 (1).

10 *Ibid.*, s. 13 (2).

11 See *ibid.*, s. 11 (11), (12), and (13).

12 *Ibid.*

13 *Ibid.*, s. 13 (3).

societies' lotteries[1] or of the provisions relating the size of the prize or the value
of the tickets or chances sold where the lottery is promoted under a scheme
registered with the Gaming Board[2] to prove that the date of a lottery was later
than he had expected for reasons which he could not foresee.[3]

Private lottery

Little more than a passing mention need be made of private lotteries. Such
lotteries are not unlawful, but since they are confined to members of a society
and persons who work and reside on the same premises,[4] the attraction of such
a lottery for a charity appeal organiser must be small. Various conditions have
to be observed in the promotion and conduct of a private lottery, notably a
condition that the whole of the proceeds (after deducting expenses) must be
devoted to prizes, or in the case of such a lottery promoted by a society, to
prizes or the purposes of that society.[5] There are restrictions on the notices or
advertisements allowed in connection with such a lottery.[6] The price of each
ticket or chance has to be the same and the price must be stated on the ticket[7]
which must also carry on the face of it other specified information.[8] Tickets
have to be allotted by way of sale and upon receipt of the full price[9] and must
not be sent through the post.[10]

Small incidental lotteries conducted at bazaars, dances etc.

Small lotteries which are incidental to certain entertainments are, subject to
certain conditions, permitted as lawful lotteries. The entertainments or events
involved in this statutory dispensation fall within the description of "exempt
entertainment" and this term means "a bazaar, sale of work, fete, dinner,
dance, sporting or athletic event or other entertainment of a similar character,
whether limited to one day or extending over two or more days".[11] A lottery
promoted as an incident of an exempt entertainment is not unlawful if certain
conditions are observed in connection with its promotion and conduct.[12] The
relevant conditions are that (1) the whole proceeds of the entertainment and of
the lottery, after certain deductions for expenses have been made,[13] must be

---

1 See *ibid.*, s. 10.
2 See *ibid.*, s. 5 (3) (d) (ii).
3 *Ibid.*, s. 13 (4).
4 *Ibid.*, s. 4 (1).
5 *Ibid.*, s. 4 (3) (a).
6 *Ibid.*, s. 4 (3) (b).
7 *Ibid.*, s. 4 (3) (c).
8 *Ibid.*, s. 4 (3) (d).
9 *Ibid.*, s. 4 (3) (e). No part of the price can be returned.
10 *Ibid.*, s. 4 (3) (f).
11 *Ibid.*, s. 3 (1).
12 *Ibid.*, s. 2 (2).
13 There may be deducted the expenses of the entertainment excluding expenses incurred
in connection with the lottery, expenses in printing lottery tickets, and a sum not exceeding
£50 (or such other sum as may be specified in an order of the Secretary of State) as the
promoters of the lottery think fit to appropriate on account of any expense incurred by
them in purchasing prizes: *ibid.*, s. 3 (3) (a).

devoted to purposes other than private gain,[1] a condition which is easily satisfied in the case of a lottery for the purposes of charity; (2) no prize in the lottery is to be a money prize;[2] (3) the tickets or chances in the lottery must not be sold or issued, nor its result declared, except on the premises where the entertainment takes place and during the progress of the entertainment;[3] and (4) the facilities for participating in lotteries, or those facilities together with any other facilities for participating in lotteries or gaming must not be the only, or the only substantial, inducement to persons to attend the entertainment.[4] If any of these provisions is contravened[5] every person concerned in the promotion or conduct of the lottery is guilty of an offence unless he proves that the contravention occurred without his consent or connivance and that he exercised all due diligence to prevent it.[6] The lottery does not, however, become an illegal lottery because of a breach of any of the conditions.[7]

COMPETITIONS AND AMUSEMENTS

It is unlawful to conduct in or through any newspaper,[8] or in connection with any trade or business or the sale of any article to the public any competition in which prizes are offered for the forecasts of the result either of a future event or of a past event the result of which is not yet ascertained or not yet generally known or any other competition success in which does not depend in a substantial degree on the exercise of skill.[9] However nothing in this provision with respect to the conducting of competitions in connection with a trade or business applies to sponsored pool betting.[10] The words "in connection with any trade or business" were held to mean that there must be some nexus between the carrying on of the competition and the trade or business in respect of which it is said to have been carried on in some connection.[11] The term "competition" does not necessarily involve the idea of several persons pitting their skill against one another[12] so that if a newspaper were to offer a prize for any successful forecast of a given future event, that would be a competition. Football pools conducted through newspapers are competitions in which prizes are offered for forecasts of the results of a future event and so are unlawful competitions in accordance with this provision.[13]

---

1 *Ibid.*, s. 3 (3).

2 *Ibid.*, s. 3 (3) (b). "Money" includes a cheque, banknote, postal order or money order: *ibid.*, s. 23 (1).

3 *Ibid.*, s. 3 (3) (c).   4 *Ibid.*, s. 3 (3) (d).

5 "Contravention" in relation to any requirement includes a failure to comply therewith; and cognate expressions are to be construed accordingly; s. 23 (1).

6 *Ibid.*, s. 3 (2). For penalties: see *ibid.*, s. 20 (1).

7 See *Stacey* v. *Wilkins*, [1946] K.B. 271, D.C. (a case on *private* lotteries).

8 "Newspaper" includes any journal, magazine or other periodical publication: Lotteries and Amusements Act 1976, s. 23 (1).

9 *Ibid.*, s. 14 (1). For the legal context in which the predecessor of this provision came to be enacted, see *News of the World, Ltd.* v. *Friend*, [1973] 1 W.L.R. 248, H.L., at 251.

10 Lotteries and Amusements Act 1976, s. 14 (2).

11 *I.T.P. (London), Ltd.* v. *Winstanley*, [1947] K.B. 422, at 426, *per* Lord GODDARD C.J.

12 *Elderton* v. *United Kingdom Totalisator Co., Ltd.*, [1946] Ch. 57, at 64, C.A. *per* Lord GREENE M.R.; *Whitbread & Co.* v. *Bell*, [1970] 2 Q.B. 547, D.C. at 557–558.

13 *Bretherton* v. *United Kingdom Totalisator Co., Ltd.*, [1945] K.B. 555, *Elderton* v. *United Kingdom Totalisator Co., Ltd.*, supra. The latter case was criticised in *Zeidman* v. *Owen*, [1950] 1 K.B. 593, D.C. but not its *ratio decidendi*.

The words "forecast", "event" and "result" must be given their ordinary and natural meaning.[1] What is aimed at is the kind of competition depending on a correct forecast of the result of a race[2] or a correct prediction of the number of births and deaths in London during a named week.[3] Accordingly it was held in *News of the World, Ltd.* v. *Friend*[4] that entries in a spot-the-ball competition to be judged by a panel of experts do not constitute "forecasts" of the result of an "event".

Any person contravening the provisions with regard to competitions promoted through newspapers or in connection with businesses is guilty of an offence without prejudice to any liability of the offender to be proceeded against under the provisions relating to lotteries.[5]

Subject to the observance of certain conditions, it is lawful to provide at an exempt entertainment[6] amusement with prizes which in fact constitutes a lottery or gaming or both.[7] However such amusement must not constitute gaming to which Part II of the Gaming Act 1968 applies[8] nor must it be gaming by means of a machine to which Part III of that Act applies.[9] The conditions are (1) that the whole proceeds of the entertainment (including the proceeds of any such amusements) after deducting the expenses of the entertainment, including the expenses incurred in connection with any such amusements and the provision of prizes and any other amounts authorised to be deducted, are devoted to purposes other than those of private gain; and (2) that the opportunity to win prizes at such amusements or that opportunity together with facilities offered for participating in lotteries or gaming (whether by machine or not) is not the only, or only substantial, inducement to persons to attend the entertainment.[10] If either of these provisions is contravened,[11] every person concerned in the provision or conduct of the amusement is guilty of an offence unless he proves that the contravention occurred without his consent or connivance and that he exercised all due diligence to prevent it.[12]

A gaming machine can only be used at an exempt entertainment if the whole of the proceeds of the entertainment including the proceeds of the use of the machine and of any lottery provided as an incident of the entertainment, are devoted to purposes other than private gain. The term "private gain" is to be construed[13] by reference to the definition of private gain in section 51A of the Gaming Act 1968 which is the same as the definition found in the Lotteries and

---

1 *News of the World, Ltd.* v. *Friend*, [1973] 1 W.L.R. 248, H.L.

2 See e.g. *Stoddart* v. *Sagar*, [1895] 2 Q.B. 474.

3 See *Hall* v. *Cox*, [1899] 1 Q.B. 198.

4 [1973] 1 W.L.R. 248, H.L. (marking the position of a football on a photograph).

5 Lotteries and Amusements Act 1976, s. 14 (3). In *Whitbread & Co., Ltd.* v. *Bell*, [1970] 2 Q.B. 547 proceedings were taken under the provisions dealing with lotteries as well as those dealing with newspaper competitions.

6 Exempt entertainment is defined in Lotteries and Amusements Act 1976, s. 3 (1), discussed at 487, *supra*.

7 *Ibid.*, s. 15.

8 I.e. gaming on premises licensed or registered under Part II (ss. 9–25) of that Act.

9 Lotteries and Amusements Act 1976, s. 15 (1) (2). Machines within Part III of the Gaming Act 1968 include fruit machines, and slot machines which do not merely afford the player a free game on winning.

10 Lotteries and Amusements Act 1976, s. 15 (4).

11 For the meaning of "contravention" and cognate terms, see *Ibid.*, s. 23 (1) and footnote 5, at 488, *supra*.

12 Gaming Act 1968, s. 33 (1) and (2).

13 *Ibid.*, s. 51A added by Lotteries and Amusements Act 1976, Sch. 4, para. 5.

Amusements Act 1976.[1] Certain expenses may be deducted namely (1) expenses of the entertainment including those incurred in connection with the use of the machine but excluding the expenses of any lottery promoted as an incident of the entertainment (2) the expenses incurred in printing tickets in any such lottery and (3) not more than £10 appropriated for the purpose of purchasing prizes for any such lottery.[2] The opportunity to win prizes by means of the machine or that opportunity together with facilities for participation in lotteries or permitted gaming must not be the only, or the only substantial, inducement to persons to attend the entertainment.[3] The Secretary of State has power to impose additional restrictions on the use of gaming machines at such entertainments by means of regulations.[4]

CHARITY POOL COMPETITIONS

Some charities derive substantial income from pool betting. The present law on this form of fund-raising is contained in the Pool Competitions Act 1971 which has been extended by order until 26th July 1977. The background to the Pool Competitions Act 1971 is that in 1969 a pool promotor, registered under the provisions of the Betting, Gaming and Lotteries Act 1963 who promoted competitions analogous to football pools partly for the benefit of medical research was convicted of offences under the lotteries law. These convictions were upheld in *Singette, Ltd.* v. *Martin,*[5] which held that competitions in which the large majority of competitors did not make forecasts of their own but relied on luck were an unlawful lottery and not pool betting. It was apparent that this judgment would affect not merely the medical research which was supported by this competition but also charitable organisations such as the Spastics Society, and sports organisations who derived substantial income from such competitions. The Pool Competitions Act 1971 was therefore introduced by the Government of the day as a short term measure to safeguard the interests of the charities and sporting clubs concerned.

If a registered pool promoter[6] satisfies the Gaming Board for Great Britain that in the 12 months ending with 24th November 1970, he held at least nine competitions for prizes depending on sporting events for the financial benefit[7] of a society[8] established and conducted wholly or mainly, *inter alia* for charitable purposes, and that each of the nine or more competitions would have constituted lawful pool betting business[9] the Gaming Board must grant the promoter

---

1 Lotteries and Amusements Act 1976, s. 22.

2 Gaming Act 1968, s. 33 (3).

3 *Ibid.*, s. 33 (4).

4 *Ibid.*, s. 33 (5). No regulations have yet been made.

5 [1971] A.C. 407, H.L.

6 A person registered for the purpose of pool betting: see Betting, Gaming and Lotteries Act 1963, s. 4 (2) incorporated by Pool Competitions Act 1971, s. 7 (1).

7 See Pool Competitions Act 1971, s. 7 (4), discussed at 491 *infra,* for what has to be taken into account.

8 "Society" includes an institution, organisation or association of persons, by whatever name called, and any separate branch thereof: Pool Competitions Act 1971, s. 7 (1).

9 In other words pool betting business conducted in accordance with the statutory requirements on the assumption that the entries and entry money were bets and stakes, that all competitors had made forecasts as to the outcome of the relevant sporting events, and the prizes had been for making such forecasts: Pool Competitions Act 1971, s. 1 (2) (b). As to the statutory requirements, see Betting, Gaming and Lotteries Act 1963, Sch. 2, para. 13.

a certificate under the Pool Competitions Act 1971.[1] A "competition for prizes" in this context means a competition where the allocation of prizes depends upon the outcome of sporting events of which each competitor has the right to forecast the outcome, and prizes can be won both where a competitor forecasts the outcome and where he does not.[2] "Competition" includes any scheme or arrangement for the distribution of prizes among persons who have paid to participate.[3] In considering whether and to what extent financial benefit is derived from a competition, account must be taken of all receipts, however calculated and whether or not derived from entry moneys, and of any expenses incurred or outgoings borne by the society as part of the arrangements under which it obtains the financial benefit.[4]

A registered pool promoter succeeding to a pool betting business or a substantial part of such a business, whose predecessor was a registered pool promoter who would have been entitled to a certificate, may also apply, but in his case the Gaming Board has a discretion to refuse the certificate.[5] The certificate must name or identify the societies which have benefited from competitions held in the qualifying period[6] and, if granted to the successor to a qualifying pool betting business, must name or identify the previous promoter.[7] An application for a certificate must be in writing in such form and accompanied by such information as the Gaming Board may require.[8]

A registered pool promoter who holds a certificate under the Pool Competitions Act 1971 may obtain from the Gaming Board a licence authorising him to hold competitions for prizes.[9] The Gaming Board must so far as practicable[10] exercise their powers so as to secure that each of the societies named or identified in the certificate will derive financial benefit from the authorised competitions; and it may attach to the licence such terms and conditions as are in their opinion needed for this purpose, having regard to the yearly financial benefit which any relevant society is likely to derive from authorised competitions, and the amount which such society actually derived from competitions held in the 12 months ending with 24th November 1970.[11] The Gaming Board must also attach to the licence such terms and conditions as it thinks appropriate for safeguarding the interests of the competitors and for giving them full information about the rules of the competitions and any related schemes or arrangements, the disposal and application of money collected, and the identities of the relevant society and the licence holder.[12] It may also attach to the licence such terms and conditions as to (1) the number or kind of competitions authorised by the licence and (2) the entry and other money to be collected and the manner in which it may be collected.[13]

---

1 Pool Competitions Act 1971, ss. 1 (1), (2), 7 (1).
2 *Ibid.*, s. 7 (2).
3 *Ibid.*   4 *Ibid.*, s. 7 (4).
5 *Ibid.*, s. 1 (3).
6 Namely the 12 months ending with 24th November 1970: *ibid.*, s. 7 (1).
7 *Ibid.*, s. 1 (4).
8 *Ibid.*, s. 1 (5).   9 *Ibid.*, s. 2 (1).
10 "Practicable" is not the same as "reasonably practicable", *Marshall* v. *Gotham, Ltd.*, [1954] A.C. 360, at 373, *per* Lord REID.
11 Pool Competitions Act 1971, s. 2 (3).
12 *Ibid.*, s. 2 (4).
13 *Ibid.*, s. 3 (1). If the licence provides that the money may be collected by house to house collectors, the House to House Collections Act 1939 does not apply: Pool Competitions Act 1971, s. 3 (5). As to the House to House Collections Act 1939, see at 470, *supra.*

The Gaming Board may cancel a licence at any time, and any term or condition may be imposed or varied or withdrawn at any time.[1] They have a complete discretion as to whether to grant or refuse an application for a licence, whether to cancel a licence at any time and whether to impose or vary or withdraw any terms or conditions as respects a licence, either on the granting of the licence or at any subsequent time; and they have a complete discretion to decide the nature of the terms or conditions as respects the licence.[2] In one situation however the Gaming Board must cancel the licence: that is where the Commissioners of Customs and Excise certify to the Gaming Board that pool betting duty payable by the licence holder remains unpaid.[3] The period for which the licence is valid must be stated in the licence and will be a period of 12 months or such shorter period as may be requested by the applicant.[4] Licences, once granted, may be renewed.[5]

The Gaming Board may require the holder of, or the applicant for, a licence to supply it with such information as it may specify with regard to any business of his which involves the holding of competitions, lotteries or pool betting.[6] They may also require the licence holder or applicant to allow them to inspect and copy his books, records and other documents, and to afford it such other facilities in relation to that business as they may from time to time specify.[7] A licence holder must also make such periodical returns as the Gaming Board may from time to time require.[8] The Gaming Board may also require the accountant appointed[9] in respect of the business of a licence holder or applicant to supply information as to that business and to allow the Gaming Board to inspect and copy books, records and documents held by him.[10]

Any person who fails to comply with any term or condition attached to a licence or who knowingly[11] or recklessly[12] provides information false[13] in a material particular to the Gaming Board is guilty of an offence and liable on summary conviction to a fine of not more than £400, or on conviction on indictment to a fine of unlimited amount.[14] In the case of a body corporate, any director, manager, secretary or similar officer, or person purporting to act as such, with whose consent or connivance the offence was committed, or to whose neglect it was attributable, may also be prosecuted.[15] A competition[16] is not to be

---

1 *Ibid.*, s. 3 (2).
2 *Ibid.*, s. 3 (6).
3 *Ibid.*, s. 3 (3).
4 *Ibid.*, s. 3 (4).
5 *Ibid.*, s. 3 (4), proviso.
6 *Ibid.*, s. 4 (1) (a)–(c), (2).
7 *Ibid.*
8 *Ibid.*, s. 4 (1) (d).
9 I.e. appointed under the Betting, Gaming and Lotteries Act 1963, Sch. 2, para. 12.
10 Pool Competitions Act 1971, s. 4 (3).
11 As to what is tantamount to knowledge: see *Taylor's Central Garages (Exeter), Ltd.* v. *Roper* (1951), 115 J.P. 445; and see *Mallon* v. *Allon*, [1963] 3 All E.R. 843, at 847 and *Wallworth* v. *Balmer*, [1966] 1 W.L.R.16.
12 On the meaning of this expression see, especially, *Derry* v. *Peek* (1889), 14 App. Cas. 337: *R.* v. *Grunwald*, [1963] 1 Q.B. 935.
13 What is literally true may be false because of some important omission: *R.* v. *Lord Kylsant*, [1932] 1 K.B. 442; and *cf. Curtis* v. *Chemical Cleaning and Dyeing Co., Ltd.*, [1951] 1 K.B. 805, at 809, C.A. *per* DENNING L.J.
14 *Pool Competitions Act* 1971, ss. 3 (8) and 4 (4).
15 *Ibid.*, s. 7 (5). The body corporate will be liable too.
16 For the meaning of "competition", see 491, *supra.*

treated as authorised by a licence if the licence is not in force at the time of the sporting event on which the allocation of prizes depends, or if there has been a failure to comply with any term or condition of the licence before that time.[1] If an applicant for a licence fails to comply with any requirement as to the provision of information documents or other facilities his application may be refused.[2]

A registered pool promoter who has promoted competitions for prizes[3] without a licence, but who has since applied for, or been granted, a licence, cannot be prosecuted in respect of his earlier competitions without the consent of the Director of Public Prosecutions.[4]

The fees payable in respect of the grant of a certificate under the Pool Competitions Act 1971 in such amount not exceeding £100 as the Gaming Board may determine,[5] and for the grant of a licence under that Act (other than by way of renewal) the fee is such amount between £100 and £3000 as the Gaming Board may determine.[6] On renewal the fee is such amount between £50 and £2500 as the Gaming Board may determine.[7]

---

1 Pool Competitions Act 1971, s. 7 (3).
2 *Ibid.*, s. 4 (5).
3 For the meaning of "competition for prizes", see *ibid.*, s. 7 (2), summarised at 491, *supra*.
4 *Ibid.*, s. 6 (1), (2).
5 Pool Competitions Act 1971, s. 5 (1) (b), (2); Pool Competitions (Fee for Certificate) Order 1971, S.I. 1971 No. 1613.
6 Pool Competitions Act 1971, s. 5 (1) (c), (2); Pool Competitions (Licence Fees) Order 1971, S.I. 1971 No. 2167, art. 2 (a). On an application for variation or withdrawal of a term or condition of a licence, a fee of not more than £10 may be charged, and if the application is granted, a further fee of not more than £100 is payable: art. 2 (b), (c).
7 Pool Competitions (Fee for Renewal of Licence) Order 1973, S.I. 1973 No. 1076.

Part VI

Court Proceedings

Chapter 44

Actions and Other Proceedings

Definition of charity proceedings

Charity proceedings are statutorily defined[1] as "proceedings in any court in England or Wales brought under the court's jurisdiction with respect to charities,[2] or brought under the court's jurisdiction with respect to trusts in relation to the administration of a trust for charitable purposes".

The jurisdiction of the court in these matters has already been discussed.[3] It is in effect a jurisdiction over the administration of charities and charitable trusts. Accordingly, charity proceedings must be confined to proceedings of an administrative nature. An application to determine whether a trust or bequest is charitable or not does not fall within the definition of charity proceedings[4] nor does an application claiming any property or relief adversely to a charity.[5] Actions brought by charities to enforce common law rights or individual equitable rights not relating to the administration of a charitable trust are likewise not charity proceedings.

Who may take charity proceedings

Charity proceedings may be taken with reference to a charity either by the charity or by any of the charity trustees, or by any person interested in the charity, or by any two or more inhabitants of the area of the charity, if it is a local charity, but not by any other person.

The charity itself will take proceedings only if it is incorporated: otherwise proceedings will have to be taken by one or more of its trustees acting on behalf of the charity. More troublesome perhaps is the reference to "any person interested in the charity". This rather vague expression would seem to include a recipient of the charity's benefits and it is thought that it might be wide enough to include other persons *connected* with the charity, such as an officer or servant, regardless of financial or material interest. A mere altruistic interest

---

1 CA 1960, s. 28 (8).

2 This phrase was considered in *Construction Industry Training Board* v. *A.-G.*, [1973] Ch. 173, C.A.

3 See 420–421, *supra*.

4 *Re St. Giles and St. George Bloomsbury Volunteer Corps.* (1858), 25 Beav. 313, at 316; *Re Strum's Trusts* (1904), 91 L.T. 192; *Re Belling*, [1967] Ch. 425; *Hauxwell* v. *Barton-upon-Humber Urban District Council*, [1974] Ch. 432.

5 *Brittain* v. *Overton* (1877), 25 Ch.D. 41 n.; *Benthall* v. *Earl of Kilmorey* (1883), 25 Ch.D. 39, 44–45.

would not, however, be enough: otherwise it would not have been necessary to make a special reference to "inhabitants of the locality" in the case of local charities.

Authorisation of proceedings

No "charity proceedings" relating to any charity *other than an exempt charity* can be entertained or proceeded with in any court unless the taking of the proceedings is authorised by order of the Commissioners. That was also the position under the old law. But the 1960 Act further provides that the Commissioners shall not, without special reasons, authorise the taking of charity proceedings where in their opinion the case can be dealt with by them under the powers of the Act. Under section 18 of the Act, it will be remembered, the Commissioners enjoy a concurrent jurisdiction with the High Court for certain purposes. Nevertheless the Commissioners are directed by section 18 (9) not to exercise their jurisdiction under that section in any case which, by reason of its contentious character, or of any special question of law or fact which it may involve, or for other reasons, they may consider more fit to be adjudicated on by the Court. In such cases they will of course give the requisite authorisation more readily.

Originating process

Charity proceedings and proceedings brought in the High Court by virtue of the Charities Act 1960 are assigned to the Chancery Division and, subject to what follows, must be begun by originating summons.[1] In this context "charity proceedings" means proceedings in the High Court brought under the Court's jurisdiction with respect to charities or brought under the Court's jurisdiction with respect to trusts in relation to the administration of a trust for charitable purposes.[2] Examples of "proceedings brought in the High Court by virtue of the Charities Act 1960 are appeals against registration and non-registration[3] and appeals from the Charity Commissioners[4].

Where the question before the court is as to the validity of a charitable gift an originating summons is clearly appropriate.[5] Where the question arises during administration proceedings the wide definition of charity proceedings contained in section 28 (3) of the Charities Act 1960 will in most cases prevent the use of a writ. Subject to this, however, any case where there is likely to be a substantial issue of fact[6] or which includes allegations of misconduct should be begun by writ.[7] So claims against trustees of, for example, a religious charity charging them with breach of trust or default in the performance of their duties, while properly constituted if commenced either by writ or originating summons should normally be begun by writ. If an action alleging breach of trust or

---

1 R.S.C. Ord. 108, r. 2.   2 *Ibid.*, r. 10.
3 See CA 1960, s. 5 (3).   4 See *ibid.*, ss. 18 (10), 28 (5).
5 See 9 Court Forms (2nd edn.) 31–36.
6 R.S.C. Ord. 5, r. 4 (2) (b).
7 *Re Sir Lindsay Parkinson & Co., Ltd.'s Settlement Trusts*, [1965] 1 All E.R. 609, n.; [1965] 1 W.L.R. 372. The old procedure was by way of information: see Gareth Jones, *History of the Law of Charity 1532–1827* (1969), 21, 34–37, 54–56.

misconduct is started by originating summons the court has power to grant relief nonetheless, but this is without prejudice to its power[1] to order the proceedings to continue as if they had been begun by writ.[2]

An application to the Lord Chancellor as visitor on behalf of the Crown is by petition. In cases where the visitor is someone other than the Crown then, subject to any express provision in the statutes of the charity, no particular form of application is prescribed, although Mitcheson notes that ecclesiastical forms are followed and this practice has been spoken of with approval in American courts.[3] A petition is really the most appropriate form.

Parties

The choice of parties to proceedings involving charity is governed by much the same considerations as apply in the case of proceedings involving private trusts. As a general rule, therefore, the parties will include all the personal representatives who have proved or all the trustees either as plaintiffs or as defendants,[4] and such of the persons who have or may have an interest in the subject matter of the proceedings (whether as actual or possible beneficiaries) are necessary parties.[5] However these general rules are subject to two qualifications. In the first place only certain specified persons may take "charity proceedings". Secondly the Attorney-General is usually a necessary party.

Where the question before the court is whether a particular gift is charitable or whether the *cy-près* doctrine applies the actual or possible beneficiaries and therefore proper parties to the proceedings will generally be numerous persons or bodies having the same interest whether as beneficiaries under the trust instrument, next of kin under a partial intestacy or beneficiaries under a resulting trust. In certain cases the Treasury Solicitor may be concerned to argue that the funds in question are *bona vacantia*.

THE ATTORNEY-GENERAL

As a general rule the Attorney-General is a necessary party to all actions relating to charities.[6] He represents the Crown, the protector of all persons interested in charity funds.[7] But he also represents the beneficial interest, in other words the objects of the charity.[8] So, when it is necessary for the beneficial interest to be represented in court the Attorney-General should be made party to the proceedings,[9] whether as the representative of charity in general or of the objects of an identified charity. When he has been made a party for that purpose all beneficiaries are bound;[10] and conversely where beneficiaries bring proceedings

---

1 Under R.S.C. Ord. 28, r. 8.   2 R.S.C. Ord. 85, r. 4.
3 *Murdock* v. *Phillips Academy* (1833), 12 Pick. 262, at 264–265; and see at 429, *supra*.
4 R.S.C. Ord. 85, r. 3 (1).
5 R.S.C. Ord. 85, r. 3 (2).
6 *Wellbeloved* v. *Jones* (1822), 1 Sim. & St. 40; *A.-G.* v. *Brodie* (1846), 6 Moo. P.C.C. 12, P.C.
7 *Re Sekeford's Charity* (1861), 5 L.T. 488.
8 See *Ware* v. *Cumberlege* (1855), 20 Beav. 503, at 511; *Re King* [1917] 2 Ch. 420.
9 See *Strickland* v. *Weldon* (1885), 28 Ch.D. 426, at 430.
10 *Vince* v. *Walsh* (1855), 3 W.R. 7; *Saunders* v. *Howes* (1857); *Tudor on Charities* (4th edn.) 1043; *Re Sekeford's Charity* (1861), 5 L.T. 488.

to which the Attorney-General should have been made a party he is not bound by any order made if he has not been joined as a party.[1] Indeed the Attorney-General may be allowed[2] to appeal against a decision in proceedings to which he was not a party in the court of first instance.[3] On the other hand if the Attorney-General was joined but did not oppose the making of a particular order he should not re-open the discussion by an appeal, although the court will not dismiss the appeal on that ground alone.[4]

Putting aside, for convenience, the principles applicable in administration proceedings, the following are cases where it has been held that the Attorney-General is a necessary party: where there is a question whether a gift is a valid or invalid charitable gift[5] or where it is necessary to determine whether a claim to the benefit of a charity is properly founded,[6] or to enforce the execution of a charitable purpose, or to remedy an abuse or misapplication of charity funds, or to administer a charity.[7]

The principles affecting the joinder of the Attorney-General in administration proceedings were discussed in *Ware* v. *Cumberlege*[8] by Sir JOHN ROMILLY M.R. who, in a much cited passage, said:[9]

"The Attorney-General represents all absent charities, and it is sufficient to have him here to represent all absent charities. But absent charities may obviously be of two different characters: they may either be under gifts to specified individual charities, or to charity generally. In case the gift is for charity generally, no one can represent it but the Attorney-General, and he must be here to represent such general charities.[10] Where there are specified individual charities, then the Attorney-General's presence is not universally necessary; but it is required by the court on various occasions, as, for instance, where any rules are required for the regulation of the internal conduct of the charity itself, such as the establishment of a scheme and the like; there the Attorney-General is necessary for the purpose of aiding and assisting the court in directing and sanctioning the general system and principle that ought to govern charities of those descriptions. But there are other cases where there is no question as to the conduct or management of the charities, but only whether the charity is entitled to a particular legacy or not. In those cases, the Attorney-General is rather in the nature of a trustee for those charities, and the court prefers having before it the charities beneficially interested, for the purpose of putting their interests before the court in the light which they consider most favourable to them. In those cases I think it preferable that the charity itself should appear, rather than that the Attorney-General should represent it. There may be mixed cases in which it is impossible to lay down a rule beforehand, and in

---

1 *A.-G.* v. *Leage* (1881), cited in *Tudor on Charities* (4th edn.) 1041, at 1044, *per* KAY J. discussing *Saunders* v. *Howes* (1857), cited in *Tudor on Charities* (4th edn.) 1043.
2 Upon special leave granted by the Court of Appeal.
3 *Re Faraker*, [1912] 2 Ch. 488, C.A.
4 *Christ's Hospital* v. *Grainger* (1849), 19 L.J. Ch. 33, at 36.
5 *Cook* v. *Duckenfield* (1743), 2 Atk. 563; *Kirkbank* v. *Hudson* (1819), 7 Price 212; and see *Re Love*, [1932] W.N. 17. For forms see 9 Court Forms (2nd edn.) 31–48, Forms 1–18.
6 *Re Magdalen Land Charity, Hastings* (1852), 9 Hare, 624.
7 *Ware* v. *Cumberlege* (1855), 20 Beav. 503.
8 (1855), 20 Beav. 503.   9 *Ibid.*, at 511.
10 See *A.-G.* v. *Bowyer* (1798), 3 Ves. 714, at 726; *Boughey* v. *Minor*, [1893] P. 181; *Re Pyne*, [1903] 1 Ch. 83; and see, also, *Practice Note*, [1945] W.N. 38.

which the court must act on the matter before it in such manner as, according to the best exercise of its discretion and judgment, it may think best calculated to promote justice."

The Attorney-General is not a necessary party in administration proceedings where there is a legacy to the treasurer or other officer of an established charitable institution as part of its general funds[1] or to named trustees and there is a question as to the validity of the trusts of which they are trustees.[2] Nor is he a necessary party where there is a gift of either a capital sum[3] or recurrent sums[4] to be distributed to charity immediately or periodically by specified trustees; or where the action is for an account in respect of a legacy given to a charity.[5] In all such cases the charity itself must be a party.

The Attorney-General is generally a necessary party when the question is whether a particular bequest is charitable[6] or is applicable *cy-près*[7] or where there is a gift to an established charitable institution to be held on trusts which differ from the trusts upon which the general funds of the institution are held.[8]

The Attorney-General is not a necessary party where the trust in question is not charitable.[9] Accordingly the inhabitants of Clapham were wrong to bring proceedings in the name of the Attorney-General where the school in dispute was not a charity school.[10] In some old cases it was held that advowsons held on trust for parishioners were not charity property and that therefore proceedings by the Attorney-General were not maintainable with regard to such trusts.[11] But these decision cannot now be supported on that point: a trust of an advowson for parishioners is charitable.[12]

In an anonymous case[13] decided by Lord HARDWICKE it was held that the Attorney-General was not a necessary party to proceedings concerning a private charity. The body in question was a voluntary society constituted to provide by weekly subscriptions for such of the members as should become necessitous and their widows. Lord HARDWICKE said:[14]

> "This is not such a society as makes it necessary for the Attorney-General in behalf of the Crown to be a party in order to see to the right application of the money, but is in the nature only of a private charity."

---

1 *Wellbeloved* v. *Jones* (1822), 1 Sim. & St. 40; *In the Goods of M'Auliffe*, [1895] P. 290.

2 See *Practice Note*, [1945] W.N. 38; in such cases there is no universal rule that the Attorney-General must be a party.

3 *Re Barnett* (1860), 29 L.J. Ch. 871. But see *Re Lea* (1887), 34 Ch.D. 528.

4 *Waldo* v. *Caley* (1809), 16 Ves. 206; *M'Coll* v. *Atherton* (1848), 12 L.T.O.S. 25; and see *Horde* v. *Earl of Suffolk* (1833), 2 My. & K. 59 (where Attorney-General claimed legacy as *bona vacantia*).

5 *Chitty* v. *Parker* (1792), 4 Bro.C.C. 38.

6 See cases cited in footnote 5 at 500, *supra*.

7 *Re Taylor* (1888), 58 L.T. 538; *Re Unite* (1906), 75 L.J. Ch. 163. For forms, see 9 Court Forms (2nd edn.) 49, 63, Forms 19 and 34.

8 *Wellbeloved* v. *Jones* (1822), 1 Sim. & St. 40; *Sons of the Clergy Corporation* v. *Mose* (1839) 9 Sim. 610; and see *A.-G.* v. *Warren* (1818), 2 Swan. 291.

9 *A.-G.* v. *Whorwood* (1750), 1 Ves. Sen. 534, at 536 (devise to a college held not to be a trust for charity); *A.-G.* v. *Brereton* (1752), 2 Ves. Sen. 425, at 426; *A.-G.* v. *Newcombe* (1807), 14 Ves. 1, at 7; *Prestney* v. *Colchester Corporation* (1882), 21 Ch.D. 111.

10 *A.-G.* v. *Hewer* (1700), 2 Vern. 387 (dispute over mastership).

11 See *A.-G.* v. *Parker* (1747), 1 Ves. Sen. 43; *A.-G.* v. *Forster* (1804), 10 Ves. 335; *A.-G.* v. *Newcombe* (1807), 14 Ves. 1.

12 *Re St. Stephen, Coleman Street* (1888), 39 Ch.D. 492; *Hunter* v. *A.-G.*, [1899] A.C. 309, at 315, H.L.

13 *Anon.* (1745), 3 Atk. 277.   14 *Ibid.*

In substance the decision that the society was a private charity was a decision that it was no charity at all. On this score the case would now in all probability be differently decided, because a trust for poor members of a club or association is charitable.[1] Certainly in at least two cases involving friendly societies the Attorney-General was present.[2]

Where, whether the trust is charitable or not, the parties taking the proceedings are clothed with the necessary powers to sue by statutory provision, the Attorney-General is not a necessary party.[3] Nor is the Attorney-General a necessary party to an action by third persons against charity trustees for specific performance of an agreement[4] or to an application for the appointment of a new trustee.[5]

THE RELATOR

The relator in an action is a person who is aggrieved in a matter of public interest and who satisfies the Attorney-General that the subject-matter of the action is such as to justify the use of that officer's name. His name describes his function, for one meaning of the word "relator" is: informer.

The introduction of a relator in actions relating to charities is now almost outmoded. But a word about relator actions is still, perhaps, appropriate. Briefly, in actions where some public interest is involved, for example where it is sought to enforce a public duty, restrain interference with a public right, abate a public nuisance or obtain an injunction where criminal sanctions have proved unavailing, the person wishing to sue may not bring an action in his own name, but must bring it as a relator in the name of the Attorney-General.[6] Accordingly in a relator action the Attorney-General is the *nominal* plaintiff for the relator, who conducts the case and who will be liable to pay any costs.

Any private individual who is not under any disability and who thinks that a charity has been abused may act as relator[7] and there is no objection to there being more than one relator.[8] Any or all of the trustees of the charity may be relators:[9] so may corporations,[10] companies,[11] district councils,[12] local education authorities[13] and ratepayers.[14] However where a corporate body does act as

---

1 See *Re Young's Will Trusts*, [1955] 1 W.L.R. 1269: *cf. Re Hobourn Aero Components, Ltd.'s Air Raid Distress Fund*, [1946] Ch. 194, C.A.

2 *Spiller* v. *Maude* (1881), 32 Ch.D. 158 n; *Pease* v. *Pattinson* (1886), 32 Ch.D. 154.

3 *Prestney* v. *Colchester Corporation* (1882), 21 Ch.D. 111 where the power was contained in Municipal Corporations Act 1835, s. 2 (repealed); *cf. Re Christ Church Inclosure Act* (1888), 38 Ch.D. 520, C.A.; affd. *sub nom. A.-G.* v. *Meyrick*, [1893] A.C. 1, H.L. (no such provision).

4 *A.-G.* v. *Warren* (1818), 2 Swan. 291, at 311; *Neville Estates, Ltd.* v. *Madden*, [1962] Ch. 832.

5 *A.-G.* v. *Cooper* (1861), 8 Jur. N.S. 50.

6 For a recent discussion: see *Gouriet* v. *Union of Post Office Workers*, [1977] 2 W.L.R. 310, C.A.

7 Shelford, *Laws of Mortmain* (1836) 424.

8 *A.-G.* v. *Earl of Clarendon* (1810), 17 Ves. 491 (several inhabitants).

9 *A.-G.* v. *Griffith* (1807), 13 Ves. 565, at 571, citing *A.-G.* v. *Talbot* (unreported).

10 *A.-G.* v. *Logan*, [1891] 2 Q.B. 100, at 104; *A.-G.* v. *Ashborne Recreation Ground Co.*, [1903] 1 Ch. 101.

11 *A.-G.* v. *Merthyr Tydfil Union* [1900] 1 Ch. 516, C.A.

12 *A.-G.* v. *Wimbledon House Estate Co., Ltd.*, [1904] 2 Ch. 34.

13 *A.-G.* v. *Price* (1908), 72 J.P. 208.

14 *London County Council* v. *A.-G.*, [1902] A.C. 165, H.L.

relator and by so doing exceeds its statutory authority there is a risk that the Attorney-General will be left to bear the costs.[1]

In *A.-G.* v. *Bucknall*[2] the question was whether there was a gift of both the principal and interest of a particular fund for the benefit of the donor's poor relations. An information was brought at the relation of one of the donor's poor relations. Lord HARDWICKE L.C. said:

"it is not absolutely necessary that relators, in an information for a charity, should be the persons *principally*[3] interested for the court will take care at the hearing to decree in such a manner as will best answer the purposes of the charity; and therefore any persons though the most remote in the contemplation of the charity may be relators in these cases".

Lord GIFFORD M.R. in *A.-G.* v. *Vivian*[4] went further when he said:

"I do not apprehend that it ever has been required of a relator to show that he has *any* interest in the relief sought".

After citing the opinion of Lord REDESDALE he concluded that the character of relator "does not seem to require the least particle of private interest in the due administration of [a] charity".[5] In *Southmolton Corporation* v. *A.-G.*[6] Lord CRANWORTH appears to have frowned upon the relator because he was "an entire stranger, having no connection with the town of Southmolton", but did not dismiss the information on that ground. At any rate, it is not irrelevant in a statement of claim to indicate the relator's interest.[7]

A relator must *not* be a person in indigent circumstances:[8] this is because a relator is liable for costs.

The real plaintiff is not usually the relator[9] but the Crown acting through the Attorney-General.[10] However where the relator is personally interested he may be a co-plaintiff in his personal capacity.[11] Under the old practice where the relator was joined as a co-plaintiff because of a personal interest the proceeding was called an information and bill.[12]

A relator's action is the action of the Attorney-General: the Attorney-General and not the relator is the party prosecuting the cause and the court will not, therefore, allow counsel for the relator to be heard in any other character than as counsel for the Attorney-General.[13] The consequence of this is that if the Attorney-General has permitted the relator to select and instruct counsel he

---

1 *A.-G.* v. *Logan*, [1891] 2 Q.B. 100, at 104.
2 (1741), 2 Atk. 328.
3 This word was stressed by Lord GIFFORD M.R. in *A.-G.* v. *Vivian* (1826), 1 Russ. 226, at 236.
4 (1826), 1 Russ. 226, at 236.
5 (1826), 1 Russ. 226, at 236.
6 (1854), 5 H.L. Cas. 1, at 27.
7 *A.-G.* v. *Rickards* (1843), 6 Beav. 444; affd. (1844), 1 Ph. 383; and (1845), 12 Cl. & Fin. 30, H.L.
8 *Fellows* v. *Barrett* (1836), 1 Keen 119, at 120.
9 *A.-G.* v. *Logan*, [1891] 2 Q.B. 100, at 106.
10 *Ibid.* But the relator is "the life of the suit": see *Calvert on Parties* (2nd Edn.) 398.
11 *A.-G.* v. *Heelis* (1824), 2 Sim. & St. 67; *A.-G.* v. *Vivian* (1826), 1 Russ. 226, at 236; *Lang* v. *Purves* (1862), 15 Moo. P.C.C. 389, P.C.
12 S. A. de Smith, *Judicial Review of Administrative Action* (3rd Edn.) 401.
13 *A.-G.* v. *Ironmongers' Co.* (1840), 2 Beav. 313, at 328.

cannot subsequently argue against the views being put forward in his name.[1] There is however one case in which the Attorney-General was allowed to appear as counsel for the defendant to an information filed by relators in his name.[2]

A relator who is also plaintiff cannot be heard in person. He cannot appear on behalf of the Attorney-General; and the fact that the relator is a plaintiff in his own right by virtue of some personal interest does not enable him to be heard in person, for the court will not separate the proceeding in which he is plaintiff from that in which he is relator.[3]

The Attorney-General may appear either in person or by counsel[4] or he may authorise the relator to conduct the case and instruct counsel on his behalf. If the Attorney-General takes the last-mentioned course he cannot then appear independently:[5] counsel for the relator represents the Attorney-General. But this rule yields to exception since the court may, if it thinks fit, direct that the Attorney-General shall be at liberty to attend any proceedings relating to a scheme separately from the relator.[6]

Before the name of any person is used in any action as a relator, that person must give a written authorisation so to use his name to his solicitor[7] and the authorisation must be filed in the central office, or, if the writ or originating summons is to issue out of a district registry, in that registry.[8] In the case of a corporate body acting as a relator the authority must be under seal.

Before a writ or originating summons is issued in a relator action the Attorney-General's consent must be obtained by taking or sending to the Law Officers' Department at the Royal Courts of Justice.[9]

1. Two copies of the proposed writ and statement of claim, or originating summons;

2. A certificate by counsel[10] that the action is a proper one to be begun by the Attorney-General, that the originating process and pleadings are proper for his consent, and that without the Attorney-General's approval the relator will be unable to obtain complete relief;

3. A certificate by the relator's solicitor that the relator is a proper person so to act and that, if ordered to do so, he is competent to pay the costs of the action;[11]

4. A statement of facts, and copies of any relevant correspondence with the proposed defendant, and a copy of any other document necessary to explain the application.

---

1 *A.-G.* v. *Sherborne Grammar School Governors, etc.* (1854), 18 Beav. 256, at 264.

2 *Shore* v. *Wilson* (1842), 9 Cl. & Fin. 355, at 475, H.L.

3 *A.-G.* v. *Barker* (1838), 4 My. & Cr. 262.

4 *A.-G.* v. *Green* (1820), 1 Jac. & W. 303, at 305; *Ludlow Corporation* v. *Greenhouse* (1827), 1 Bli. N.S. 17, at 65, H.L.

5 *A.-G.* v. *Sherborne Grammar School Governors, etc.* (1854), 18 Beav. 256, at 264; see also *A.-G.* v. *Dove* (1823), Turn. & R. 328; *A.-G.* v. *Barker* (1838), 4 My. & Cr. 262; *A.-G.* v. *Ironmongers' Co.* (1840), 2 Beav. 313.

6 For such a direction see Seton, *Judgments and Orders* (7th edn.) 1246.

7 The relator must act by a solicitor: *A.-G. (Humphreys)* v. *Erasmus Smith's Schools (Governors)*, [1910] I.R. 325.

8 R.S.C. Ord. 15, r. 11.

9 For a letter applying for the Attorney-General's fiat see 30 Court Forms (2nd edn.) 57, Form 30.

10 See *ibid.*, Form 31.

11 See 30 Court Forms (2nd edn.) 58, Form 32.

If the Attorney-General consents (and he has a discretion in the matter)[1] he will sign one copy of the writ and statement of claim, or originating summons, in the margin, and the writ or summons so signed becomes the original.[2] Each copy of the writ and statement of claim, or originating summons, must have the Attorney-General's name written on it. It is not the practice of the Attorney-General to consent unless and until he is satisfied that all appropriate steps have been taken to resolve the dispute, and that no other remedy is available.

When one of several relators dies the proceedings are not affected at all. But if all the relators die, or if a sole relator dies[3] or becomes mentally disordered,[4] the court will stay proceedings until a new relator is appointed. This is to ensure that some person may be made answerable for the costs.[5] Before a new relator can be appointed the Attorney-General's consent must be obtained,[6] unless of course the Attorney-General himself applies to the court.[7] Assuming however that the consent of the Attorney-General is required it should be applied for by letter[8] enclosing the relevant documents, including the original writ or originating summons previously signed by the Attorney-General, on which he will indorse his consent to the new relator. Naturally the new relator must give an authorisation for his name to be used,[9] and application must be made to the court for leave to make the requisite amendments.[10]

Before any amendment can be made in the writ, statement of claim or originating summons two copies of the document containing the proposed amendments must be left with the Attorney-General together with counsel's certificate that the amendment is proper for the Attorney-General's consent.[11] If he consents he signs one copy[12] and returns it to the relator's solicitor for service.

Where an action is begun in the ordinary way and it is subsequently appreciated that it should have been begun as a relator action, the existing plaintiff should apply to the Attorney-General by letter[13] enclosing the necessary papers[14] for his fiat and having obtained that fiat must then apply to the court[15] for an order that the Attorney-General be added as plaintiff.

Where a relator who is also a plaintiff dies and his interest does not pass to a co-plaintiff, an order to carry on the proceedings is required.[16]

---

1 *London County Council* v. *A.-G.*, [1902] A.C. 165, H.L.
2 See Practice Masters' Rules, c. 5.
3 *A.-G.* v. *Powel* (1763), Dick. 355; *A.-G.* v. *Haberdashers' Co.* (1852), 15 Beav. 397, at 404.
4 *A.-G.* v. *Tyler* (1764), 2 Eden 230.
5 *A.-G.* v. *Smart* (1748), 1 Ves. Sen. 72.
6 *Anon.* (1726), Cas. temp. King 69.
7 *A.-G.* v. *Plumptree* (1820), 5 Madd. 452. For a summons, see 30 Court Forms (2nd edn.) 60, Form 38.
8 See 30 Court Forms (2nd edn.) 59, Form 36.
9 R.S.C. Ord. 15, r. 11; and see 30 Court Forms (2nd edn.) 60, Form 37.
10 For a summons and supporting affidavits see 30 Court Forms (2nd edn.) 60, Forms 38 and 30.
11 See 30 Court Forms (2nd edn.) 61, Forms 40 and 41.
12 Practice Masters' Rules, r. 5.
13 See 30 Court Forms (2nd edn.) 61, Form 42.
14 These are the same as are required to initiate relator actions: see 504, *supra*.
15 See 30 Court Forms (2nd edn.) 62–63, Forms 43–45.
16 See R.S.C. Ord. 15, r. 7.

OTHER PERSONS AS PARTIES

Apart from the statutory restriction on who may bring charity proceedings,[1] the general rule is that all persons interested in the subject matter of the action and within the jurisdiction of the court ought to be parties.[2]

Persons who merely conceive themselves to be interested in establishing the validity of the trust are not persons interested for this purpose.[3] Thus local inhabitants have no *locus standi* to bring proceedings to establish that particular property is held upon charitable trusts.[4] On the other hand persons (not being the general objects of the charity) who have a beneficial or possible beneficial interest in the subject matter of the action must be parties. Accordingly under the old law the heir-at-law was a necessary party where the proceedings were to determine whether surplus funds belonged to him or to a charity,[5] or whether there was a resulting trust for his benefit[6] or where he was by implication visitor of a charity and an action was instituted for the execution of the trusts.[7] Descent to the heir has been abolished; but whenever there is a possibility of a resulting trust, the persons interested under the resulting trust are necessary parties. Likewise a schoolmaster was held a necessary party to an action to have surplus charity funds applied for his benefit.[8] The identification of the necessary parties is dictated by the content of the action. Where land subject to a charge in favour of charity was alleged to have been improperly sold the purchaser is a proper party.[9] In an action to set aside a lease lessees, underlessees and assignees should be joined[10] and a lessee even when not made a party may be given leave to attend.[11]

Where a legacy charged on land was given to a charity and an action to ascertain the profits of the land was instituted it was held that the executors should be parties.[12] But in an action to establish a charity rentcharge it is not necessary to join all the persons whose estates may be liable; the court will decide whether the rentcharge in question is charged on the estate of the person actually before the court and will direct an inquiry as to who are the other persons alleged to be liable.[13] In this respect the court treats charity rentcharges exceptionally: in the case of an action to establish a non-charitable rentcharge all the persons whose estates are liable must be parties.[14]

---

1 See CA 1960, s. 28, discussed at 497, *supra.*

2 Shelford, *Law of Mortmain* (1836) 430.

3 *Practice Note,* [1945] W.N. 38; *cf. Re Belling,* [1967] Ch. 425.

4 *Hauxwell* v. *Barton-upon-Humber Urban District Council,* [1974] Ch. 432.

5 *A.-G.* v. *Haberdashers' Co.* (1792), 4 Bro. C.C. 103, at 106; *Ludlow Corporation* v. *Greenhouse* (1827), 1 Bli. N.S. 17, at 55, H.L.

6 *A.-G.* v. *Green* (1789), 2 Bro. C.C. 492.

7 *A.-G.* v. *Gaunt* (1790), 3 Swan. 148, n. The devolution of the visitatorial power since descent to the heir was established is discussed at 424, *supra.*

8 *A.-G.* v. *Smart* (1748), 1 Ves. Sen. 72.

9 *Southmolton Corporation* v. *A.-G.* (1854), 5 H.L. Cas. 1.

10 *A.-G.* v. *Backhouse* (1810), 17 Ves. 283, at 285; *Ludlow Corporation* v. *Greenhouse* (1827), 1 Bli. N.S. 17, at 73; *A.-G.* v. *Greenhill* (1863), 33 Beav. 193.

11 *A.-G.* v. *Pretyman* (1845), 8 Beav. 316.

12 *A.-G.* v. *Twisden* (1678), Cas. temp. Finch 336.

13 *A.-G.* v. *Jackson* (1805), 11 Ves. 365, at 367, 372; *A.-G.* v. *Naylor* (1863), 1 Hem. & M. 809; *cf. Re Herbage Rents,* [1896] 2 Ch. 811 (tenant for years not liable).

14 *A.-G.* v. *Jackson* (1805), 11 Ves. 365, at 367.

The master of a school was held a necessary party to proceedings which sought to have surplus funds applied for his benefit.[1] At the other end of the scale on an inquiry to determine whether it was beneficial to a charity that almshouses should be sold and rebuilt on other land certain parishioners applied on behalf of themselves and others to be served with notice of all proceedings and for liberty to attend the inquiry, and it was held that their application should be refused because their interest was already sufficiently represented by the Attorney-General.[2]

Where the Attorney-General appears on behalf of a charity the trustees of that charity may at the court's discretion be heard in support of the Attorney-General;[3] and the court will also hear trustees who in good faith differ from relators.[4]

Whether persons with a contingent interest in a charitable fund should be made parties to any proceedings concerning that fund depends on the circumstances of the case. Thus trustees of a college who were contingently entitled to a legacy the income of which had for many years been paid to a minister were held not to be necessary parties to an action to establish the charity.[5] On the other hand in proceedings seeking accounts and reference to the master to direct schemes the proceedings were held to be defective for want of parties because the Archbishop of York who was entitled to appoint the schoolmaster of a charitable school in default of his being appointed within two months by other persons was not a party.[6]

Mere strangers to a charitable trust are not proper parties to any legal proceeding relating to it. Thus members of an ecclesiastical synod who were not members of the congregation on whose behalf they purported to sue had no title to sue for the removal of the minister and trustees of the congregation.[7] Usually the original subscribers to a charitable fund are not necessary parties to proceedings in connection with such a fund, because they have no interest in it.[8] But if they retain an interest they should be joined.[9]

Persons who have not been joined as parties but who can show a *prima facie* right to intervene may be allowed by the court to attend.[10] Again if any necessary parties are omitted, or unnecessary parties are inserted the court upon application will usually allow the proper alterations to be made.[11]

Where a charity is a necessary party to any proceedings it is important to see whether it is incorporated or unincorporated. An incorporated charity is properly sued in its own name, but service is effected by serving the president or other chief officer or the secretary, treasurer or other similar officer.[12] An

---

1 *A.-G.* v. *Smart* (1747), 1 Ves. Sen. 72.

2 *Ironmongers' Co.* v. *Roberts* (1909), *Times*, 24th June.

3 *Solicitor-General* v. *Bath Corporation* (1849), 18 L.J. Ch. 275, at 276; *Whicker* v. *Hume* (1851), 14 Beav. 509, at 528; affd. (1858) 7 H.L. Cas. 124.

4 *Solicitor-General* v. *Bath Corporation* (1849), 18 L.J. Ch. 275, at 277.

5 *A.-G.* v. *Goddard* (1823), Turn. & R. 348.

6 *A.-G.* v. *St. John's College* (1835), 7 Sim. 241.

7 *Lang* v. *Purves* (1862), 15 Moo. P.C.C. 389, P.C.

8 *A.-G.* v. *Gardner* (1848), 2 De G. & Sm. 102; *A.-G.* v. *Munro* (1848), 2 De G. & Sm. 122, at 161, 162.

9 *Minn* v. *Stant* (1851), 15 Beav. 49.

10 *A.-G.* v. *Shore* (1836), 1 My. & Cr. 394; *A.-G.* v. *Pretyman* (1845), 8 Beav. 316; *Re Shrewsbury Grammar School* (1849), 1 Mac. & G. 324.

11 Shelford, *Law of Mortmain* (1836) 431; R.S.C. Ord. 15, r. 6.

12 See R.S.C. Ord. 65, r. 3.

unincorporated charity is (subject to any provision made in the rules) properly sued by suing its treasurer, secretary or other responsible officer "on behalf of" the charity, which must be named, and service is effected by serving him.[1] It is incorrect to sue an unincorporated charity simply by its name,[2] or to join a body of persons who do not form a corporation as parties under a corporate name[3] but if this incorrect course is taken the responsible officer should enter an appearance on behalf of the charity.[4]

Where proceedings are taken against the trustees of a charity all of them must be joined and not only the acting trustees.[5] But in an action to remedy a breach of trust not every person participating in the breach is a necessary party.[6]

A trustee who is abroad and not amenable to process was in an old case held not to be a necessary party.[7]

An agent employed by the trustees to manage the affairs of a charity and who receives charity money in his capacity as agent is not a proper party to proceedings against the trustees for accounts and a scheme.[8] But if he wrongfully retained charity property he would certainly be a proper defendant for the trustees to sue. An action by some agents against others to recover trust property is improperly constituted.[9]

Where new trustees are appointed *pendente lite* but are not made parties to proceedings for the administration of a charity, they are not so bound by a decree made in such proceedings as to be absolutely precluded from defending.[10]

Compromise

Questions relating to charities may be compromised and the terms of the compromise may be confirmed by the court. This may happen, for example, in cases where it is doubtful whether a bequest or devise to charity is valid and a compromise is reached by dividing the property between the charity and the other claimants such as the heir-at-law, next of kin and residuary legatee.[11]

Trustees for charities have power to compromise claims under the Trustee Act 1925[12] and the Charity Commissioners may by order sanction a compromise of claims on behalf of a charity or against a charity either without taking or without continuing proceedings.[13]

---

1 *Re Pritt* (1915), 85 L.J. Ch. 166; [1915] W.N. 134.

2 *Bloom* v. *National Federation of Discharged and Demobilised Sailors and Soldiers* (1918), 35 T.L.R. 50, C.A. (claim against war charity in its registered name struck out).

3 *A.-G.* v. *Chester Corporation* (1849), 1 H. & Tw. 46.

4 *Re Pritt* (1915), 85 L.J. Ch. 166; *cf. Bloom* v. *National Federation of Discharged and Demobilised Sailors and Soldiers* (1918), 35 T.L.R. 50, C.A.

5 *Re Chertsey Market, Ex parte Walthew* (1819), 6 Price 261.

6 *A.-G.* v. *Leicester Corporation* (1844), 7 Beav. 176. See R.S.C. Ord. 15, r. 12.

7 *Monill* v. *Lawson* (1719), 2 Eq. Cas. Abr. 167 pl. 13.

8 *A.-G.* v. *Chesterfield* (1854), 18 Beav. 596.

9 *Strickland* v. *Weldon* (1885), 28 Ch.D. 426.

10 *A.-G.* v. *Foster* (1842), 2 Hare 81.

11 *A.-G.* v. *Launderfield (or Landerfield)* (1743), 9 Mod. Rep. 286; *Re Simpson's Will* (circa 1786) cited in 5 Ves. 304; *A.-G.* v. *Bishop of Oxford* (1786), cited in 4 Ves. 431; *Andrew* v. *Masters and Wardens of the Merchant Taylors' Co.* (1802), 7 Ves. 223; *Andrew* v. *Trinity Hall, Cambridge* (1804), 9 Ves. 525, at 532, 533; *A.-G.* v. *Trevelyan* (1847), 16 L.J. Ch. 521.

12 TA 1925, s. 15.

13 See CA 1960, s. 23 (2).

It is sometimes said, at any rate in relation to orders by way of scheme, that where the Attorney-General is in agreement with the course taken he is recited to be "not objecting" instead of "consenting".[1] The proposition that "the Attorney-General does not consent"[2] is hardly borne out by what is said in the cases. Thus in *Andrew* v. *Masters and Wardens of the Merchant Taylors' Co.*[3] a compromise applying part of a fund to the establishment of certain scholarships and exhibitions at St. John's College, Oxford (with which the Merchant Taylors' Company were connected) and giving the rest to the next of kin was, the Attorney-General consenting, established by decree. The fund in question had been left to Trinity Hall, Cambridge, after various life interests and the college had refused to accept the gift after the death of the tenants for life. The Master was directed to receive a proposal in order to have it determined whether the trusts could be executed *cy-près*.[4] The decree of Lord LOUGHBOROUGH L.C. was affirmed on appeal by the House of Lords in 1800 and the compromise was reached before Sir WILLIAM GRANT M.R. just over two years later.[5] Counsel who appeared for the Attorney-General consented on his behalf and Sir WILLIAM GRANT M.R. said "I wish the Attorney-General's consent to appear".[6] The question in *Re King*[7] was whether a charity which was cited in a probate action but did not appear was bound by a compromise assented to by the Attorney-General. YOUNGER J. held that the Attorney-General had compromised the proceedings on behalf of all the charities: the compromise had been notified to all and none had objected. The compromise was signed by the Attorney-General and other counsel and the terms of compromise were filed and made a rule of the court.[8] Clearly, therefore, YOUNGER J. was correct to refer (as he did) to the Attorney-General's *consent*.[9]

Function of the Attorney-General

The Attorney-General acts in charity matters either *ex officio*[10] or *ex relatione*. He acts *ex officio* as the officer of the Crown and, as such, the protector of charities: it is the duty of officers of the Crown to protect and not to attack charities.[11] For that reason where the Attorney-General is a proper party and the Attorney-General's office is vacant or he is ill[12] or concerned in the case in

---

1 See 9 Court Forms (2nd edn.) 45; and see *Re Snowden*, [1970] Ch. 700 where the order recited that the Attorney-General did not object.

2 *Ibid.*

3 (1802), 7 Ves. 223.

4 *A.-G.* v. *Andrew* (1798), 3 Ves. 633.

5 *Andrew* v. *Masters and Wardens of the Merchant Taylors' Co.* (1802), 7 Ves. 223.

6 *Andrew* v. *Masters and Wardens of the Merchant Taylors' Co.* (1802), 7 Ves. 223, at 224–225; and see the sequel to the case: *Andrew* v. *Trinity Hall, Cambridge* (1804), 9 Ves. 525, especially at 532–533 (compromise decreed with consent of Attorney-General binding on next of kin).

7 [1917] 2 Ch. 420.

8 [1917] 2 Ch. 420, at 422.

9 [1917] 2 Ch. 420, at 429.

10 *Re Bedford Charity* (1819), 2 Swan 520; *A.-G.* v. *Dublin Corporation* (1827), 1 Bli. N.S. 312, at 351; *Mucklow* v. *A.-G.* (1816), 4 Dow. 1, at 15.

11 *Wallis* v. *Solicitor-General for New Zealand*, [1903] A.C. 173, at 182, P.C.

12 Shelford, *Law of Mortmain* (1836) 399; *R.* v. *Wilkes* (1770), 4 Burr. 2527 at 2554, H.L.; *Ludlow Corporation* v. *Greenhouse* (1827), 1 Bli. N.S. 51.

another capacity, the Solicitor-General is the proper person to take his place.[1] The Attorney-General also acts *ex relatione* at the request of a person called a relator who thinks that the charity is being or has been abused.[2] When the Attorney-General acts at the request of a relator he must sign the original writ.[3] Except for the purposes of costs there is no practical difference between proceedings started by the Attorney-General in his own right and proceedings started by him in which there is a relator.

The statutory restrictions on the institution of "charity proceedings" do not affect the right of the Attorney-General to commence charity proceedings with or without a relator.[4] The Attorney-General may, of course, start and carry on proceedings of his own motion. But he may do so on a reference by the Charity Commissioners. If the Commissioners think it desirable that proceedings be taken by the Attorney-General with reference to a charity (other than an exempt charity)[5] or its property or affairs they must so inform him and send him such statements and particulars as they think necessary to explain the matter.[6]

Where the Attorney-General sues *ex officio* he controls the proceedings as a matter of course.[7] But he also has entire control of the proceedings where they have been instituted at the request of a relator[8] even where he does not act personally.[9] No amendment can be made[10] or notice of motion given[11] without the consent of the Attorney-General. At any time he can stay the proceedings. Again a matter may only be referred to arbitration with the prior consent of the Attorney-General[12] and his consent is also necessary before any award can be acted upon.[13]

The court does not consider it the duty of the Attorney-General to contend for his strict rights in charity cases; in cases of hardship it sanctions acting with forbearance towards the parties, and will postpone its decision, to give the parties an opportunity of entering into an arrangement with the Attorney-General. If, however, the Attorney-General insists on his strict legal rights the court will enforce them.[14]

---

1 *A.-G.* v. *Bristol Corporation* (1820), 2 Jac. & W. 294; *A.-G.* v. *Ironmongers' Co.* (1834), 2 My. & K. 576.

2 *A.-G.* v. *Logan*, [1891] 2 Q.B. 100, at 103; and see *A.-G.* v. *Cockermouth Local Board* (1874), L.R. 18 Eq. 172 pt 176.

3 Supreme Court Practice 1976, para. 15/11/2.

4 CA 1960, s. 28 (6).

5 As to exempt charities, see 4–6, *supra*.

6 CA 1960, s. 28 (7).

7 *A.-G.* v. *Haberdashers' Co.* (1852), 15 Beav. 397.

8 *Andrew* v. *Master and Wardens of the Merchant Taylors' Co.* (1802), 7 Ves. 223; *Ludlow Corporation* v. *Greenhouse* (1827), 1 Bli. N.S. 17, at 65, H.L.; *A.-G.* v. *Ironmongers' Co.* (1840), 2 Beav. 313, at 328–329.

9 Shelford, *Law of Mortmain* (1836) 400; *A.-G.* v. *Hewitt* (1804), 9 Ves. 232.

10 Shelford, *op. cit.* 403; *A.-G.* v. *Fellows* (1820), 1 Jac. & W. 254 (pleading amended without consent taken off file). The Attorney-General may amend as of right: *A.-G.* v. *Ray* (1843), 11 M. & W. 464.

11 *A.-G.* v. *Wright* (1841), 3 Beav. 447.

12 *A.-G.* v. *Hewitt* (1804), 9 Ves. 232; *A.-G.* v. *Fea* (1819), 4 Madd. 274; and see *Prior* v. *Hembrow* (1841), 8 M. & W. 873.

13 *A.-G.* v. *Hewitt* (1803), 9 Ves. 232; and see *A.-G.* v. *Clements* (1822), Turn. & R. 58.

14 *A.-G.* v. *Brettingham* (1840), 3 Beav. 91; and see *Re Snowden*, [1970] Ch. 700 (*ex gratia* payments); discussed at 412–414, *supra*.

Procedure relating to schemes

In many non-contentious cases the Charity Commissioners may settle the scheme, either on an application to them for the purpose[1] or on a reference by the court.[2] In other cases the court retains control over the scheme which it directs.

There are various ways in which the court may make provision for a scheme.

In simple cases where the fund is small[3] or the provisions required are short and uncomplicated the court's directions may be embodied in the order made by the judge at chambers or in open court without any direction for a scheme to be settled.[4] The order will simply recite that it is made "by way of scheme."[5] The court has taken this course where it was only necessary to decide a question of construction[6] or to give a slight supplemental direction[7] or to make some small modification or variation to existing trusts.[8]

Sometimes a reference to the master is directed to apportion a fund among specified charities without settling a scheme.[9] In *Re Lousada*[10] where there was a gift of £50 to "the London poor" and no charity of that name could be identified, CHITTY J. himself directed the executors to distribute the money among poor boxes at certain Metropolitan police courts: the fund was too small to justify the delegation of choice to a Chancery master.

If, however, a scheme is required the court will direct a scheme to be settled.[11] The scheme will contain all the machinery needed to regulate the administration of the charity. The drafting of the scheme by the designated party or parties is not the "settling" of the scheme. The scheme is actually "settled" by being approved and ordered to be carried into effect. The direction given will usually be in general terms "that a scheme be settled by the Judge". The judge who directs the scheme to be settled will usually direct who is to "bring in" the scheme: this is normally the trustees,[12] but occasionally the Attorney-General.[13] The persons thus indicated in the order will then draft the scheme. Where the draft is not prepared by the Attorney-General it must be submitted to the Treasury Solicitor for approval by the Attorney-General.[14] When ready the scheme is taken into chambers to obtain the approval of the judge.[15] The matter

---

1 CA 1960, s. 18 (1). For a form of application, see 9 Court Forms (2nd edn.) 80 Form 52; and for a scheme see *ibid.*, 104, Form 73.

2 CA 1960, s. 18 (2). For a form of order see 9 Court Forms (2nd edn.) 83, Form 57.

3 *Re Lousada* (1887), 82 L.T. Jo. 358.

4 *A.-G.* v. *Brandeth* (1842), 1 Y. & C. Ch. Cas. 200; *Clum Hospital Warden and Bretherton* v. *Lord Powys* (1842), 6 Jur. 252; *Re Delmar Charitable Trust*, [1897] 2 Ch. 163, at 168.

5 For an example, see 9 Court Forms (2nd edn.) 80 Form 53.

6 See *Re Randell* (1888), 38 Ch.D. 213.

7 *Gillan* v. *Gillan* (1878), 1 L.R. Ir. 114.

8 *Re Richardson* (1888), 58 L.T. 45.

9 *White* v. *White* (1778), 1 Bro. C.C. 12, at 15; *Re Hyde's Trusts* (1873), 22 W.R.69.

10 (1887), 82 L.T. Jo. 358.

11 For forms of order directing schemes to be settled, see 9 Court Forms (2nd edn.) 80–82, Forms 53–56. For a form referring the matter to the Charity Commissioners, see *ibid.*, 83, Form 57.

12 *A.-G.* v. *Stepney* (1804), 10 Ves. 22, at 29; *Jemmit* v. *Verril* (1826), Amb. 585, n.; and *cf. Re Lea* (1887), 34 Ch.D. 528, at 533.

13 *Smith* v. *Kerr (No. 2)* (1905), 74 L.J. Ch. 763, at 767.

14 *Re Wyersdale School* (1853), 10 Hare, App. II, lxxiv.

15 *Ibid.*

is taken into chambers either on a summons issued for that express purpose or, if the scheme is the only matter to be dealt with, on a summons to proceed.[1] The summons should, in any event, be served on the Attorney-General.[2] Sir JOHN LEACH V.-C. apparently introduced a regulation requiring the Attorney-General to attend before the master in every case of reference for the settlement of a scheme. But his *practice* was not to require the attendance of the Attorney-General except when it was absolutely necessary. For that reason in *A.-G. v. Haberdashers' Co.*[3] Sir CHARLES PEPYS M.R. did not require such attendance where the fund did not much exceed £1100 and was appropriated to the relief of poverty.

The summons is first returnable before a Chancery master. Except in cases that are purely formal the summons will then be adjourned to be heard by the judge in chambers[4] on a Monday morning when a Chancery judge in each group hears chambers summonses. If any points are objected to, the summons may be adjourned into open court.[5] Once the scheme has been sanctioned it is scheduled to the order approving it.[6]

Alternatively, the court may by order refer the matter to the Commissioners for them to prepare or settle a scheme in accordance with such directions (if any) as the court sees fit to give.[7] Any such order may provide for the scheme to be put into effect by order of the Commissioners (as if prepared by them in the exercise of their power to establish a scheme for the administration of a charity)[8] and without any further order of the court.[9] An order referring the matter to the Commissioners has obvious attractions both in terms of convenience and the saving of costs. But although in practice such orders are frequently made they are not invariably appropriate. A scheme relating to a religious charity or one likely to give rise to legal discussion should remain before the judge.

Usually a scheme will provide only a general framework of administration leaving details to the discretion of trustees. A frequent practice, which has the approval of the Charity Commissioners is to confer on the trustees power to regulate the day-to-day administration of the charity by rules.[10] In this connection it is as well to bear in mind that if hard and fast directions are contained in a scheme they can only be modified by means of a scheme. It should be stressed that any relevant rules must be clear, since otherwise it may be necessary to apply to the court to construe the rules.[11]

As a general rule the Attorney-General must be present at the settlement of a

---

1 See 9 Court Forms (2nd edn.) 86, Form 61; and see, generally, R.S.C. Ord. 44, r. 14 (3).

2 *Re Hanson's Trust* (1852), 9 Hare, App. I, liv.

3 (1835), 2 My. & K. 817.

4 See 9 Court Forms (2nd edn.) 87, Form 62.

5 See *ibid.*, 88, Form 63.

6 See *ibid.*, 92–101, Forms 65–72; and see Seton, *Judgments and Orders* (7th edn.) 1248. Formerly the practice was to file the scheme signed by the judge or certified by the Master as having been approved by the judge, in the Central Office; see Daniell, *Chancery Practice* (8th edn.) 1735 and Seton, *op. cit.*, 1248.

7 CA 1960, s. 18 (2).

8 That is, under CA 1960, s. 18 (1) (a).

9 CA 1960, s. 18 (2).

10 See e.g. the scheme established by the Commissioners under the title of the *Winchester Rural District Welfare Trust*, in [1964] Ch. Com. Rep. 75, at 79.

11 For an adaptable precedent for such an application: see 9 Court Forms (2nd edn.) 70, Form 42.

scheme and so must be served with a summons to attend. When he attends he may raise objections to the scheme or particular provisions. He attends the settlement of a scheme of a charity to protect the interests of all and for that reason the court may refuse to allow the attendance of interested persons even at their own expense.[1] Examples are to be found in the books of cases where persons have been allowed to attend on the settlement of a scheme at their own expense.[2] In *Re Shrewsbury Grammar School*[3] there was a surplus of charity funds and the trustees of the school prepared a scheme to deal with the surplus which also contained certain alterations in the general management of the school but in no way inconsistent with the school's original constitution. The scheme was prepared with a view to submitting the same to the consideration of the Master upon obtaining the sanction of the court to a reference for that purpose. Lord COTTENHAM L.C. directed a reference to the Master to consider the scheme. Counsel for St. John's College, Cambridge, which had a right of patronage in appointing the headmaster and which was entitled to be furnished with accounts of expenditure quarterly asked for liberty to attend before the Master. Lord COTTENHAM L.C. held that where the charity was not likely to derive benefit from the attendance and where the parties seeking to attend had no individual interest they might attend, but at their own expense.[4] The headmaster on the other hand was personally interested in at any rate some of the points arising in the scheme. Lord COTTENHAM said:[5]

> "I think much will depend upon what is done in the Master's office, for if the headmaster's attendance arises out of matters in which he is personally interested, he is entitled to his costs; but if he is not so interested, he ought not to go before the Master at all. The court cannot, therefore, very well decide by anticipation that he ought to attend on all matters."

The headmaster was therefore given liberty to attend but the question of his costs was reserved. In *A.-G. v. Shore*[6] Lord COTTENHAM allowed two distinct sets of petitioners each sharing a *prima facie* right to intervene in proceedings before the Master for the settlement of a scheme. But he reserved consideration of the question of costs until the Master should have made his report and indicated that only one bill of costs would be allowed.[7] In other cases, according to Sir JOHN ROMILLY M.R.[8] he repeatedly refused to allow parties to attend, even at their own expense, because their attendance would increase the costs of the other parties.

---

1 *A.-G. v. St. Cross Hospital* (1854), 18 Beav. 475; *A.-G. v. Wimborne School* (1847), 10 Beav. 209 (Ecclesiastical Commissioners); *Re Sekeford's Charity* (1661), 5 L.T. 488.
2 See, for example, *A.-G. v. Ironmongers' Co.* noted in *A.-G. v. Shore* (1836) at 1 My. & Cr. 394, at 398–399.
3 (1849), 1 Mac. & G. 324.
4 *Ibid.*, at 335.
5 *Ibid.*, at 334.
6 (1836), 1 My. & Cr. 394.
7 *Ibid.*, at 400–401.
8 *A.-G. v. St. Cross Hospital* (1854), 18 Beav. 475.

T

Applications for leave of the court

In certain cases it is necessary to apply to one of the judges of the Chancery Division for leave to take charity proceedings or for leave to appeal against an order of the Charity Commissioners. In order to take charity proceedings in respect of a charity which is not an exempt charity, persons other than the Attorney-General require the authority of the Charity Commissioners; and the requisite authority is given in the shape of an order.[1] Where the necessary authority is refused the disappointed applicant may apply instead to one of the judges of the High Court attached to the Chancery Division for leave to take the proceedings in question.[2] Likewise, in most cases where it is desired to appeal against an order of the Charity Commissioners made under section 18 or section 20 of the Charities Act 1960 the appellant must in the first instance obtain a certificate that it is a proper case for appeal.[3] If the certificate is refused, the appellant may apply to a Chancery judge for leave to appeal.[4]

APPLICATION FOR LEAVE TO TAKE PROCEEDINGS

An application for leave to take "charity proceedings" must be made within 21 days of the refusal of the Commissioners to give the necessary authority.[5] The first step is to obtain a provisional assignment to a group of Chancery judges.[6] The application must be made by lodging in the Chancery Registrar's Office a statement showing:

    (1) the name, address and description of the applicant;
    (2) particulars of the proceedings which it is desired to take;
    (3) the date of the Commissioners' refusal to grant the order;
    (4) the grounds on which the applicant alleges that it is a proper case for taking proceedings[7]; and
    (5) if it be the case, that any party to the proposed proceedings consents to the application.[8]

The application may be made *ex parte* in the first instance.[9] If the judge on considering the application so directs, the Commissioners must furnish him with a written statement of their reasons for refusing the order, and a copy of that statement must be sent from the Chancery Registrar's Office to the applicant.[10] The judge may decide to grant the leave sought without a hearing[11] in which

---

1 CA 1960, s. 28 (2).
2 *Ibid.*, s. 28 (5).
3 *Ibid.*, ss. 18 (11) proviso, and 20 (7); R.S.C. Ord. 18, r. 3 (1). For the exceptions see 515, *infra*.
4 CA 1960, s. 18 (11), proviso.
5 R.S.C. Ord. 108, r. 3 (2).
6 CA 1960, s. 28 (5).
7 R.S.C. Ord. 108, r. 3 (3).
8 R.S.C. Ord. 108, r. 3 (4).
9 *Ibid.*
10 R.S.C. Ord 108, r. 3 (5).
11 R.S.C. Ord. 108, r. 3 (6).

case a copy of the judge's order must be sent from the Chancery Registrar's Office to the applicant and the Commissioners.[1] Otherwise the application must be set down for hearing (in chambers if the judge so directs),[2] and notice of the day and time fixed for the hearing must be sent from the Chancery Registrar's Office to the applicant.[3]

APPLICATIONS FOR LEAVE TO APPEAL

Leave to appeal against an order of the Charity Commissioners is only required where there is a right of appeal[4] and the Charity Commissioners have refused to certify that the case is a proper case for appeal. Not all appeals require such a certificate. Thus an appeal against a decision of the Charity Commissioners to enter or not to enter an institution in the register of charities or to remove or not to remove an institution from the register does not require any certificate:[5] the right to appeal is absolute and so no question of leave to appeal can arise. Nor does the Attorney-General require any certificate from the Charity Commissioners to enable him to appeal from any order of the Commissioners under sections 18 or 20 of the Charities Act 1960.[6] In one other exceptional case under section 20 an appeal may be brought without any certificate of the Commissioners or leave of the court.[7]

Where an order has been made by the Commissioners under section 18 of the Charities Act 1960 and the right of appeal is not barred[8] a certificate of the Charity Commissioners that the case is a proper one for appeal is required,[9] unless the appellant is the Attorney-General. Accordingly if a certificate is refused the appeal can only be prosecuted by obtaining first the leave of the court. It will be remembered that section 18 gives to the Commissioners the same powers as the court has to make orders establishing a scheme for the administration of the charity, for appointing, discharging or removing a charity trustee or trustee for a charity or removing an officer or servant of the charity, and for vesting or transferring property or requiring or entitling any person to call for or make any transfer of any property or any payment.[10]

As has been said the Commissioners have statutory powers to make, of their own motion, various orders for the protection of charities.[11] These powers are contained in section 20 of the Charities Act 1960 and relate mainly to the appointment and removal of trustees and the removal of officers and servants of a charity in given cases, and to the protection of the property of a charity.

---

1 R.S.C. Ord. 108, r. 3 (7).

2 R.S.C. Ord. 108, r. 3 (6).

3 R.S.C. Ord. 108, r. 3 (7).

4 A right of appeal is conferred in respect of orders concerning registration: CA 1960, s. 5 (3). So too schemes or orders made under ss. 18 and 20 are appealable.

5 See CA 1960, s. 5 (3).

6 *Ibid.*, s. 18 (10) and (11), and s. 20 (7).

7 *Ibid.*, s. 20 (7).

8 A trustee, officer or servant removed by the Commissioners with the concurrence of the charity trustees or the approval of the special visitor (if any) of the charity has no right of appeal: CA 1960, s. 18 (11) parenthesis. But if such a person is removed pursuant to s. 20 (1) the right of appeal is absolute: s. 20 (7).

9 CA 1960, s. 18 (11), proviso.

10 *Ibid.*, s. 18 (1).

11 See 442, *supra*.

Orders made under section 20 are appealable.[1] But, with one exception, the appeal can only be prosecuted if the Commissioners have certified that it is a proper case for an appeal or a Chancery judge has given leave to appeal after the Commissioners have refused a certificate. The exception is where the Commissioners have by order, after an inquiry instituted under section 6 of the Charities Act 1960, removed a trustee, charity trustee, officer, agent or servant of a charity under the power contained in section 20 (1). In such a case the person so removed has an absolute right to appeal, subject to observing the time limits and no certificate or leave is required.[2]

The procedure on seeking leave to appeal where a certificate has been refused is the same as that which obtains where the Commissioners refuse to authorise the taking of charity proceedings. First, it is necessary to obtain from the Central Office a provisional assignment to a group of Chancery judges. Then an application must be made, *ex parte* in the first instance, to a Chancery judge within 21 days of the refusal of the certificate.[3] The application is made by lodging in the Chancery Registrar's Office a copy of the proposed originating summons and a statement showing:

(1) the applicant's name, address and description;
(2) particulars of the order against which it is desired to appeal;
(3) the date of the Commissioners' refusal to grant the certificate;
(4) the grounds on which the applicant alleges that it is a proper case for an appeal;[4] and
(5) if it be the case, that any other party to the proposed appeal consents to the application.[5]

If the judge on considering the application so directs, the Commissioners must furnish him with a written statement of their reasons for refusing a certificate and a copy of that statement must be sent from the Chancery Registrar's Office to the applicant.[6] The judge may decide to grant the leave sought without a hearing,[7] in which case a copy of the judge's order must be sent from the Chancery Registrar's Office to the applicant and the Commissioners.[8] Otherwise the application must be set down for hearing (in chambers, if the judge so directs)[9] and notice of the day and time fixed for the hearing must be sent from the Chancery Registrar's Office to the applicant.[10]

Appeals

The cases in which an appeal may lie to the High Court against orders or decisions of the Charity Commissioners have already been mentioned. Decisions

---

1 CA 1960, s. 20 (7).
2 *Ibid.*, s. 20 (7); and see s. 18 (11).
3 *Ibid.*, s. 18 (11), proviso; R.S.C. Ord. 108, r. 3 (2) and (4).
4 R.S.C. Ord. 108, r. 3 (3).
5 R.S.C. Ord. 108, r. 3 (4).
6 R.S.C. Ord. 108, r. 3 (5).
7 R.S.C. Ord. 108, r. 3 (6).
8 R.S.C. Ord. 108, r. 3 (7).
9 R.S.C. Ord. 108, r. 3 (6).
10 R.S.C. Ord. 108, r. 3 (7).

of the Commissioners concerning registration are appealable.[1] An appeal also lies to the High Court against an order of the Commissioners establishing a scheme for the administration of a charity[2] or an order regulating a charity.[3]

DECISIONS ABOUT REGISTRATION

The Charity Commissioners can decide to enter or not enter an institution on the register of charities or to remove or not to remove an institution from that register. An appeal against such a decision may be brought in the High Court[4] by the Attorney-General, by the persons who are or claim to be the charity trustees[5] of the institution, or by any person whose objection to the registration of an institution as a charity or whose application for its removal from the register has been disallowed.[6]

An appeal against a decision of the Commissioners relating to entries on the register of charities must be brought by originating summons[7] taken out in the Chancery Division[8] and is heard and determined by a single judge.[9] The Attorney-General (unless he is the appellant) is a necessary defendant in addition to any other person who is a proper defendant.[10] The originating summon must state the grounds of the appeal, and except with the leave of the judges hearing the appeal, the appellant is not entitled to rely on any ground not so stated.[11]

The originating summons must be served on the Treasury Solicitor (on behalf of the Charity Commissioners)[12] and on every party within 28 days after the date on which notice of the Commissioners' decision was given to the appellant.[13]

No special rules govern the form and content of evidence to be provided in support of the appeal. The usual rules will presumably apply and affidavit evidence will be sworn and filed in support.

ORDERS MAKING SCHEMES OR REGULATING CHARITY

An appeal against an order of the Charity Commissioners establishing a scheme for the administration of the charity[14] or regulating the charity[15] lies to the High

---

1 CA 1960, s. 5 (3).
2 *Ibid.*, s. 18 (1) (a).
3 *Ibid.*, ss. 18 (1) (b), (c), 20.
4 *Ibid.*, s. 5 (3).
5 "Charity trustees": see *ibid.*, s. 46.
6 *Ibid.*, s. 5 (3). As to objections to registration and applications for removal: see s. 5 (2).
7 See 9 Court Forms (2nd edn.) 105, Form 74.
8 R.S.C. Ord. 108, rr. 2 and 5 (2).
9 R.S.C. Ord. 108, r. 5 (1).
10 R.S.C. Ord. 108, r. 5 (2).
11 R.S.C. Ord. 108, r. 5 (3).
12 R.S.C. Ord. 108, r. 6.
13 R.S.C. Ord. 55, r. 4 (1) (b), (2) (4) which applies by virtue of Ord. 55, r. 1 (1), (4).
14 See CA 1960, s. 18 (1) (a).
15 See *ibid.*, ss. 18 (1) (b), (c), 20.

Court.[1] Such appeals are assigned to the Chancery Division[2] to be heard and determined by a single judge.[3]

The appeal may be brought by (1) the Attorney-General,[4] (2) the charity or any of the charity trustees,[5] (3) any person removed from any office or employment by the order, unless he is removed with the concurrence of the charity trustees or with the approval of the special visitor (if any) of the charity,[6] (4) where the order establishes a scheme: any person interested in the charity or, in the case of a local charity, any two or more inhabitants of the area or (with the consent of the parish meeting) the parish council of any rural parish comprising the area or any part of it.[7]

If the Attorney-General brings the appeal he does not require any certificate from the Commissioners that the case is a proper one for appeal.[8] Nor is he bound by the time limit on bringing an appeal which binds other appellants.[9] All other appellants require a certificate of the Commissioners or the leave of the court before they can bring an appeal,[10] unless the case is one where the appellant is a person removed by the order appealed against from the office of trustee, charity trustee, officer agent or servant of the charity after an inquiry by the Commissioners.[11] Equally any appeal not brought by the Attorney-General must be brought within three months beginning with the day following that on which the order is published.[12] "Publication" in this context means publication of the order and not publication of the notice of the Commissioners' intention to make the order.[13]

---

1 See *ibid.*, ss. 18 (10)–(12), 20 (7).
2 R.S.C. Ord. 108, r. 2.
3 R.S.C. Ord. 108, r. 4 (1).
4 CA 1960, s. 18 (10)
5 *Ibid.*, ss. 18 (11), 20 (7).
6 *Ibid.*
7 *Ibid.*, s. 18 (12). As to local charity see at 455, *supra.*
8 *Ibid.*, ss. 18 (10), 20 (7).
9 *Ibid.*, s. 18 (10), (11).
10 See discussion at 514, *supra.*
11 CA 1960, s. 20 (7); and see s. 18 (11).
12 *Ibid.*, s. 18 (11).
13 *Re Deptford Parish Lands*, [1934] Ch. 151.

Chapter 45

Costs

The Attorney-General

LIABILITY FOR COSTS

In charity proceedings[1] and indeed whenever he is suing in discharge of his public duty[2] the Attorney-General never pays costs, even when he loses his case. The statutory provisions enabling an order of costs to be made against the Crown[3] do not apply in such cases.

Similarly where the Attorney-General appears with the sanction of the court, he cannot be liable for costs to any other party.[4]

RIGHT TO COSTS

In charity cases the Attorney-General is entitled to receive costs which would have been awarded to him as a private litigant;[5] equally as Lord COTTENHAM once said "the Attorney-General never receives costs in a contest in which he could have been called upon to pay them had he been a private individual".[6]

In administration actions where the Attorney-General is joined to represent the interests of charity he is usually given his costs on a common fund basis out of the estate,[7] even if the proceedings are unsuccessful so far as charity is concerned.[8] In *Hunter* v. *A.-G.*[9] where the Attorney-General tried unsuccessfully to support a judgment of the Court of Appeal in his favour, the House of Lords

---

1 *Cf. A.-G.* v. *Dean and Canons of Windsor* (1860), 8 H.L. Cas. 369, at 459.

2 Shelford, *Law of Mortmain* (1836) 474; *A.-G.* v. *Earl of Ashburnham* (1823), 1 Sim. & St. 394, at 397; *A.-G.* v. *Dublin Corporation* (1827), 1 Bli. N.S. 312, at 351, 352, H.L.; *Ludlow Corporation* v. *Greenhouse* (1827), 1 Bli. N.S. 17, at 48, H.L.; *A.-G.* v. *Chester Corporation* (1851), 14 Beav. 338; *Re Macduff*, [1896] 2 Ch. 451, at 475, C.A.

3 Administration of Justice (Miscellaneous Provisions) Act 1933, s. 7 (1) replacing the Crown Suits Act 1855. It was held that the 1855 Act did not apply to informations or actions in the nature of informations: *A.-G.* v. *Dean and Canons of Windsor* (1860), 8 H.L. Cas. 369, at 459.

4 *Re Bedford Charity* (1857), 26 L.J. Ch. 613.

5 *A.-G.* v. *Earl of Ashburnham* (1823), 1 Sim. & St. 394; *Re Cardwell*, [1912] 1 Ch. 779.

6 *A.-G.* v. *London Corporation* (1850), 2 Mac. & G. 247, at 269.

7 See e.g. *Mills* v. *Farmer* (1815), 19 Ves. 483, at 490; *Re Preston's Estate*, [1951] Ch. 878, at 881; *Re Amory*, [1951] 2 All E.R. 947, n.

8 *Moggridge* v. *Thackwell* (1803), 7 Ves. 36, at 88; *A.-G.* v. *Earl of Ashburnham* (1823), 1 Sim. & St. 394, at 396.

9 [1899] A.C. 309.

allowed him his costs out of the estate but intimated that if the estate had not been large he would not necessarily have received his costs.

Where the court sanctions an application to Parliament to effect certain changes in the constitution of a charity the Attorney-General is entitled to his costs out of the estate even if the application does not succeed.[1] He may also receive his costs in interlocutory applications made independently of the relator.[2]

Where the Attorney-General is entitled to his costs and an order is made against a particular defendant to pay those costs and that defendant becomes insolvent the costs may be ordered to be paid out of the charity estate.[3]

In cases where the Attorney-General's right to costs is established he is held entitled to costs on a common fund basis.[4]

WHAT COSTS ARE ALLOWED

In addition to his costs on a common fund basis,[5] the Attorney-General may receive charges and expenses properly incurred by him in relation to the matter but which do not strictly constitute costs in the matter. In such a case a statement must be submitted to the court giving the ground of the claim: if the claim is challenged the statement must be in the form of an affidavit, but the actual bill of costs need not be submitted to the court at this stage.[6] As Sir JOHN ROMILLY M.R, pointed out:[7] "the province of the taxing master is to determine whether the costs incurred are properly charged in particular matters, which are specified; but it is not his province to determine whether the trustees or the Attorney-General properly embarked in certain proceedings; that is the province of the court; and when the court has determined that they properly did so embark, then the taxing master is to determine whether the costs charged for that purpose are proper".

Where in the course of an *ex officio* action the Attorney-General takes particular proceedings which he later abandons the costs of those proceedings may be excepted from the general costs of the action[8]. But, as has already been said, the mere failure of an application by the Attorney-General does not preclude him from entitlement to costs.[9]

Several cases touch on the position of the Attorney-General as regards costs when he appears separately from relators. If he attends separately from the relator, by his own solicitor and without an order of the court, he is not allowed his own separate costs.[10] It is otherwise where collusion is suspected between

---

1 *Re Bedford Charity* (1857), 26 L.J. Ch. 613.

2 Shelford, *Law of Mortmain* (1836) 474; *A.-G.* v. *Earl of Ashburnham* (1823), 1 Sim. & St. 394. But see footnote 10, *infra.*

3 *A.-G.* v. *Lewis* (1845), 8 Beav. 179.

4 *Moggridge* v. *Thackwell* (1792), 1 Ves. 464, at 475; affd. (1803), 7 Ves. 69, at 88; (1807), 13 Ves. 416; *Miles* v. *Farmer* (1815), 19 Ves. 483, at 490; *A.-G.* v. *Stewart* (1872), L.R. 14 Eq. 16, at 25; *Re Cardwell*, [1912] 1 Ch. 779.

5 See footnote 7, at 519, *supra.*

6 *Re Dulwich College* (1873), L.R. 15 Eq. 294.

7 *Ibid.*, at 296.

8 *A.-G.* v. *Ward* (1848), 11 Beav. 203, at 208.

9 See cases cited in footnotes 8 and 9 at 519, *supra.*

10 *A.-G.* v. *Dove* (1823), Turn. & R. 328 following *A.-G.* v. *Huntingdon Corporation* (1821), Turn. & R. 329 n.

the defendants and the relators: in such a case the Attorney-General may receive his costs of appearing separately provided he has first applied to the court.[1]

Where a brief is delivered to the Attorney-General but he does not personally appear the costs of his brief may still be allowed:[2] this is because the Attorney-General's duty is distinct from the mere duty and responsibility of counsel attending at the hearing to argue the case.

Relator

The circumstances in which a relator's action may be brought and the manner in which such an action should be conducted have already been discussed.[3] Since the relator is answerable for the costs of a relator's action he should be a person of adequate means.[4] The court may direct him to give security for costs[5] but will not do so where he has the dual role of plaintiff and relator.[6]

The appropriate order for costs in a relator's action will naturally differ with each case. There are three possibilities: (i) the relator may be called upon to pay the costs (ii) the relator will be discharged without costs and (iii) the relator will be entitled to costs. Each of these will be dealt with in turn.

LIABILITY FOR COSTS

There are certain cases where the court will mark its disapproval of a relator's conduct in starting proceedings, by ordering him to pay the costs. So where proceedings are manifestly unnecessary, because they are in contradiction to the rights of the charity as established by its charter[7] the relators must pay the costs "as nothing" in the words of Lord HARDWICKE . . . is to be more discouraged than the bringing information conversely for the benefit of the charity, but contrary to the real charity.[8] So if relators seek to enforce an improper agreement[9] the court may order the relators to pay the costs. In *A.-G.* v. *Hartley*[10] proceedings were started involving very expensive inquiries and containing gross imputations on the conduct of individuals and other unproven allegations, upon which no relief was or could be given; it was held that the relator should pay the costs sustained by the defendants by reason of the allegations of misconduct. In *A.-G.* v. *Earl of Mansfield* where *inter alia* various charges of misconduct were

---

1 *A.-G.* v. *Wyggeston Hospital* (1855), Seton, *Judgments and Orders* (6th edn.) 1290; and see *A.-G.* v. *Dove* (1823), Turn. & R. 328.

2 *A.-G.* v. *Drapers' Co.* (1841), 4 Beav. 305; and see *Cockburn* v. *Raphael* (1843), 12 L.J. Ch. 263.

3 See at 502, *supra*.

4 *A.-G.* v. *Knight* (1837), 3 My. & Cr. 154. And his solicitor should give a certificate to that effect: see 30 Court Forms (2nd edn.) 58, Form 32; Daniell, *Chancery Forms* (7th edn.) 26.

5 *A.-G.* v. *Rochester Corporation* (1680), Shelford, *Law of Mortmain* (1836) 425.

6 *A.-G.* v. *Knight* (1837), 3 My. & Cr. 154.

7 *A.-G.* v. *Parker* (1747), 3 Atk. 576; *A.-G.* v. *Smart* (1748), 1 Ves. Sen. 72.

8 *A.-G.* v. *Smart* (1748), 1 Ves. Sen. 72. As to informations, see 498, *supra*.

9 *A.-G.* v. *Gleg* (1738), 1 Atk. 356 (agreement by three charity trustees to carve up the funds).

10 (1820), 2 Jac. & W. 353, at 370.

made against the wardens and governors of a grammar school the proceedings were dismissed but the relators only had to pay the costs of the proceedings relating to the removal and replacement of the officers: all the other costs down to the hearing were directed to be paid and retained out of the funds of the charity as between solicitor and client.[1] Again where a person is unjustifiably made a party to relator proceedings they will be dismissed as against him with costs to be paid by the relators.[2] Proceedings instituted from a private matter of revenge nursed by the relator will likewise incur the punishment of an order for costs against the relator.[3] So will vexatious conduct.[4]

DISALLOWANCE OF COSTS

A relator who totally fails to make out his case cannot be given costs: the most he can claim is to have no order for costs against him.[5] Thus in *A.-G. v. Braithwaite*[6] relators who made a *bona fide* but unsuccessful application to the court to divert charitable funds to purposes obviously not contemplated by the trust were not allowed their costs. A similar result should ensue when a relator acts *bona fide* but in error in order to protect a charity,[7] though in at least one such case the court allowed the relator his costs.[8] Even where his application is successful in part, the relator may not get his costs where the proceedings have been conducted with unnecessary expense.[9]

RIGHT TO COSTS

Lord LANGDALE M.R. laid down the rule that the relator in a charity action "where there is nothing to impeach the propriety of the suit and no special circumstances to justify a special order, is, upon obtaining a decree for the charity, entitled to have his costs as between solicitor and client, and to be paid the difference between the amount of such costs and the amount of the costs which he may recover from the defendants out of the charity fund".[10] There are some cases where he may also be given his charges and expenses, but such cases depend upon their peculiar circumstances.[11] On the other hand, a relator may be allowed

---

1 (1827), 2 Russ. 501, at 538; see also *Southmolton Corporation v. A.-G.* (1854), 5 H.L. Cas. 1, at 39.

2 *A.-G. v. Berry* (1846), 11 Jur. 114.

3 *A.-G. v. Middleton* (1751), 2 Ves. Sen. 327, at 330; *A.-G. v. Bosanquet* (1841), 11 L.J. Ch. 43.

4 *Aylet v. Dodd* (1741), 2 Atk. 238.

5 *A.-G. v. Oglander* (1790), 1 Ves. 246.

6 (1885), 2 T.L.R. 56, C.A.

7 *A.-G. v. Bolton* (1796), 3 Anst. 820. *Aliter* if he acts *mala fide.*

8 *A.-G. v. Bosanquet* (1841), 11 L.J. Ch. 43; and see *Hauxwell v. Barton-upon-Humber Urban District Council*, [1974] Ch. 432.

9 *A.-G. v. Cullum* (1836), 1 Keen 104; and see *A.-G. v. Holland* (1837), 2 Y. & C. Ex. 683; *A.G. v. Berry* (1847), 11 Jur. 114.

10 *A.-G. v. Kerr* (1841), 4 Beav. 297, at 303; and see *A.-G. v. Berwick-upon-Tweed Corporation* (1829), Taml. 239.

11 *A.-G. v. Kerr* (1841), 4 Beav. 297, at 303 *per* Lord LANGDALE M.R.; *A.-G. v. Taylor* (1802), cited in 7 Ves. 424 (costs allowed beyond those taxed); *A.-G. v. Skinners' Co.* (1821), Jac. 629, at 630; *A.-G. v. Winchester Corporation* (1824), 3 L.J.O.S. Ch. 64.

only costs as between party and party and no extra costs out of the charity fund as, for example, where the action though partially successful, does not substantially benefit the charity.[1] Or, again, though costs may be denied him, he may be allowed money actually spent by him, though without the consent of the master, if at the end of the day the expenditure has been of use to the charity.[2]

Costs may be given to a relator who is changed before the hearing of the action[3] or to a relator who acts mistakenly but with *bona fide* interests at heart of benefiting charity.[4] In the days of the old forms of proceedings a relator who chose the wrong form but with the consent of the Attorney-General was allowed his costs.[5] But he was not always able to claim his costs where he failed to get such consent first.[6] These principles presumably apply to the case where relief is sought by action which might have been obtained by originating summons.

A curious situation arose in *A.-G. v. Shore*.[7] Due to their peculiar character and position[8] the relators were incapable of adequately representing and protecting the interests of all the objects of a charity. Persons not parties to the proceedings each showing a *prima facie* claim to intervene before the master applied for leave to do so, which was granted on terms that only one bill of costs would be allowed against the charity estate. This principle is still applicable.

Where proceedings are started by plaintiffs who have no *locus standi*, and the Attorney-General takes over the proceedings, the court may in its discretion reserve the costs of interlocutory matters until trial, on the footing that if the proceedings turn out to have been of benefit to charity the unsuccessful plaintiffs should get their costs.[9]

Charity trustees

The rules applicable to the costs of charity trustees are in general the same as those which apply to the costs of private trustees.[10] In some ways, however, as SUGDEN L.C. prointed out in *A.-G. v. Drummond*[11] charity trustees are better off than ordinary trustees.

RIGHT TO COSTS

Charity trustees are normally entitled to be paid out of the trust funds all costs, charges and expenses properly incurred by them in the execution of or in

---

1 *A.-G. v. Fishmongers' Co.* (1837), 1 Keen 492, at 501. See *A.-G. v. Drummond* (1842), 3 Dr. & War. 162, at 165.
2 *A.-G. v. Ironmongers' Co.* (1847), 10 Beav. 194.
3 *A.-G. v. Tyler* (1838), Coop. Pr. Cas. 358.
4 *A.-G. v. Bosanquet* (1841), 11 L.J. Ch. 43.
5 *A.-G. v. Biddulph* (1853), 22 L.T.O.S. 114.
6 *A.-G. v. Holland* (1837), 2 Y. & C. Ex. 683.
7 (1836), 1 My. & Cr. 394.
8 The case was a contest between Presbyterians and Unitarians.
9 *Hauxwell* v. *Barton-upon-Humber Urban District Council* [1974] Ch. 432; and see *A.-G. v. Brewers' Co.* (1717), 1 P. Wms. 376.
10 Shelford, *Law of Mortmain* (1886) 467 *et seq.*; *Man* v. *Ballet* (1682), 1 Ves. 43.
11 (1842), 3 Dr. & War. 162, at 163–164.

connection with the trust.[1] If the parties in an action who are ordered to pay the trustees' costs are unable to do so, the trustees may recoup themselves out of the charity funds or estate;[2] and if they recover only party and party costs from an opponent, they are entitled to reimburse themselves out of the trust funds the difference between party and party and solicitor and client costs. Moreover, the right of trustees to costs as between themselves and their *cestui qui trust* is based upon contract, and is not within the discretion of the court. Trustees, therefore, who have not been guilty of culpable neglect of their duty under the contract cannot be deprived of their costs.[3]

LIABILITY FOR COSTS

Where a succession of charity trustees has for a long period acted wrongly but *innocently* in the administration of the trust, the present trustees may, at the discretion of the court, be allowed their costs out of the charity funds. Thus in *A.-G.* v. *Drummond*[4] where the trustees had in error allowed Unitarians to participate in a trust property confined to another body Sir EDWARD SUGDEN L.C. said:[5]

> "No doubt the general rule is, as it has been stated to be, that a trustee who acts wrongly and against whom there has been a decision is not entitled to costs. But it can hardly be said that the rule applies to a case of this nature, where for more than a century the funds have been applied in a manner in which the parties are now found fault with for having so applied them. I should treat the present trustees with great hardship if I were now to decide that they were not entitled to their costs when all their predecessors have escaped. The case is different from that of private trustees, where each must suffer for the consequences of his own mistake. Here there has been a succession of trustees and were I to refuse the present trustees their costs, it would be, in fact, to visit upon them individually the error of their predecessors."

Likewise in *A.-G.* v. *Caius College*[6] where charity funds had been misapplied by generations of trustees over two centuries but with no corrupt or improper motive and large amounts had, through care and economy, been accumulated for the benefit of the foundation, the trustees were allowed their costs. But the court, in its discretion, may disallow the trustees their costs. Thus in *Shore* v. *Wilson*[7] the trustees, who were all Unitarians, applied charity rents for the benefit of Unitarians when they should have applied them for Protestant Dissenters only. They appealed unsuccessfully against the judgment of the Vice-Chancellor ordering their removal and Lord LYNDHURST thought they should certainly not get their costs out of the charity fund. On appeal to the House of Lords they were ordered to pay the respondent's costs.

---

1 *A.-G.* v. *Norwich Corporation* (1837), 2 My. & Cr. 406, at 424.
2 *A.-G.* v. *Lewis* (1845), 8 Beav. 179.
3 See *Cotterell* v. *Stratton* (1872), 8 Ch. App. 295, at 302; *Turner* v. *Hancock* (1882), 20 Ch.D. 303, C.A.
4 (1842), 3 Dr. & War. 162.
5 At 163–164.
6 (1837), 2 Keen 150.
7 (1842), 9 Cl. & Fin. 355, H.L.

On the other hand trustees who take prompt steps to remedy an innocent and accidental breach of trust will not be made to pay the costs.[1] Nor will charity trustees be visited with costs just because the Charity Commissioners have misinterpreted an Act of Parliament.[2]

In the days when it required an Act of Parliament to regulate certain charities[3] trustees could be at risk as to the costs of an *unsuccessful* application if they did not get the prior consent of the court.[4] But if they made a *successful* application it did not matter if they had not got prior sanction from the court: they got their costs.[5]

In *Daugars* v. *Rivaz*[6] charity trustees were ordered to pay the costs of an action brought by a wrongly removed pastor of the French Protestant church. They did not do so but charged the costs of £2876 to the charity's funds. At the suit of the Attorney-General they were ordered by Sir JOHN ROMILLY M.R. to refund the amount taken from the charity with interest at four per cent.[7] Equally if the court does not allow trustees their costs they are not entitled to raid the charity's funds for their costs; and, if they do, they will be ordered to repay the amount taken.[8]

The position of charity trustees who have committed a breach of trust that is beneficial to the charity is not entirely settled. In *A.-G.* v. *Caius College*[9] the trustees of the Perse Foundation who were the master and fellows of Caius College, Cambridge, misapplied the funds over a very long period of time but without any corrupt intention. When proceedings were launched without warning against them they had already started to redress the breaches of trust into which they had been inquiring; and the breaches had resulted in very substantial financial benefits for the foundation. In these circumstances after very much hesitation Lord LANGDALE M.R. allowed the trustees their costs out of the charity's funds. A different course was taken in *Solicitor-General* v. *Bath Corporation*[10] where claims were made by the Solicitor-General on behalf of the Bath Free Grammar School against the defendant corporation as trustee of the charity. The claims were that the trustee had mixed up certain lands with its own property and granted building leases with, incidentally, great benefit to the charity. The claims of the charity only partly succeeded and no fraud was imputable to the trustee corporation. A scheme was also prayed in respect of the charity. WIGRAM V.-C. to avoid the expense and difficulty of apportioning and setting off the costs gave none to the trustee corporation and ordered those of the other defendants and of the relators to be paid out of charitable funds.[11] In another case trustees who had greatly exceeded the estimate for building authorised by the court were disallowed the costs of an inquiry whether the expenditure was for the benefit of the charity.[12]

---

1 *A.-G.* v. *Drapers' Co.* (1841), 4 Beav. 67.

2 *Moore* v. *Clench* (1875), 1 Ch.D. 447, at 450–451.

3 This is no longer necessary: CA 1960, s. 19.

4 *Re Bedford Charity* (1857), 26 L.J. Ch. 613.

5 *A.-G.* v. *Vigor* (1805), cited in 2 Russ., at 519. *Aliter* if the application was unsuccessful: *A.-G.* v. *Earl of Mansfield* (1827), 2 Russ. 501, at 519.

6 (1860), 28 Beav. 233.   7 *A.-G.* v. *Daugars* (1863), 33 Beav. 621.

8 *A.-G.* v. *Mercers' Co.* (1870), 18 W.R. 448 (the sum was £4000).

9 (1837), 2 Keen 150.

10 (1849), 18 L.J. Ch. 275. The office of Attorney-General was vacant when proceedings were started.

11 See at 278 ("the right course, and one not unfrequently adopted by the Court").

12 *A.-G.* v. *Armitstead* (1854), 19 Beav. 584.

Different considerations obviously apply where trustees have been guilty of culpable breach of trust. If an action is made necessary by any particular instance of misconduct on the part of the trustees whether the misconduct be negligence[1] the appointment of officials contrary to the terms of the trust[2] or some other dereliction of duty[3] they must pay the costs occasioned by their improper behaviour, though not, it seems, the costs of a subsequent reference to the master to settle a scheme.[4] Trustees may, therefore, be fixed with the costs of the action where they have claimed unsuccessfully to be entitled beneficially to property belonging to a charity,[5] though in one case where the trustees had disregarded the opinion of their own counsel that the property in question was charitable the Attorney-General did not press for costs against them personally.[6] Likewise trustees will be liable for costs where they have committed a breach of trust and acted in a spirit of animosity[7] or have wilfully suppressed evidence thereby obstructing the course of justice[8] or have negligently professed ignorance of matters which they might have ascertained from an examination of their documents.[9] In *A.-G.* v. *Clack*[10] where, pending proceedings instituted for the purpose of having new trustees appointed, the surviving trustees themselves appointed new trustees out of court and the appointment was subsequently set aside, they were ordered personally to pay all the extra cost occasioned by their act. So, too, it has been said that charity trustees removed from office for misconduct may be ordered to pay the costs of vesting the trust property in the new trustees.[11] Again, where trustees of a religious congregation adopt religious views which disqualify them from their trusteeship and dig their heels in and do not retire they answer in costs for the consequences.[12] But if a trustee voluntarily retires from such a trust because of a difference of opinion he pays no costs; whether he will receive costs is a question for the discretion of the court and may depend on the circumstances of his retirement.[13]

When the Charity Commissioners have to bring proceedings to enforce compliance with an order properly made by them the trustees will have to pay the cost of those proceedings.[14]

Trustees who pay the trust fund into court and thereby discharge themselves from the office of trustee should simply serve the Attorney-General with notice of their payment into court leaving him to take the necessary steps for the

---

1 *Haberdashers' Co.* v. *A.-G.* (1702), 2 Bro. Parl. Cas. 370, H.L.

2 *Salop Town* v. *A.-G.* (1726), 2 Bro. Parl. Cas. 402, H.L.; *A.-G.* v. *Lord Carrington* (1850), 4 De G. & Sm. 140.

3 *A.-G.* v. *Mercers' Co.* (1833), 2 My. & K. 654 (misapplication of legacies).

4 *A.-G.* v. *Mercers' Co.* (1833), 2 My. & K. 654.

5 *A.-G.* v. *Drapers' Co., Kendrick's Charity* (1841), 4 Beav. 67; *A.-G.* v. *Christ's Hospital* (1841), 4 Beav. 73; *Re St. Stephen, Coleman Street* (1888), 39 Ch.D. 492.

6 *A.-G.* v. *Webster* (1875), L.R. 20 Eq. 483, at 492.

7 *A.-G.* v. *Stroud* (1868), 19 L.T. 545.

8 *Hertford Corporation* v. *Hertford Poor* (1713), 2 Bro. Parl. Cas. 377, H.L.

9 *A.-G.* v. *East Retford Corporation* (1833), 2 My. & K. 35; reversed without affecting this point (1838), 3 My. & Cr. 484; and see *Solicitor-General* v. *Bath Corporation* (1849), 18 L.J. Ch. 275, at 277.

10 (1839), 1 Beav. 467.

11 *Coventry Corporation* v. *A.-G.* (1720), 7 Bro. Parl. Cas. 235, H.L., at 237-238; *Ex parte Greenhouse* (1815), 1 Madd. 92, at 109.

12 *A.-G.* v. *Murdoch* (1856), 2 K. & J. 571.

13 *Ibid.*, at 573, *per* PAGE-WOOD V.-C.

14 *Re Gilchrist Educational Trust*, [1895] 1 Ch. 367 (motion to commit); and see *Re St. Brides, Fleet Street* (1877), 35 Ch.D. 147, n.; affd., [1877] W.N. 149, C.A.

administration of the fund. If they then take the improper course of applying to the court for a scheme they will not be allowed their costs of the necessarily abortive application.[1]

Trustees who fail to render accounts are liable for the costs of proceedings to compel an account whether at the suit of the Attorney-General[2] or of the Charity Commissioners.[3] But if the accounts show that the trustees are not indebted to the trust, no subsequent costs on either side will be given.[4]

A trustee or member of a corporation who severs his defence and supports a successful action by the plaintiff will be allowed his costs on the common fund basis out of the trust property, the costs to be recovered over against the other trustees or corporations as between party and party.[5]

Trustees who are made plaintiffs to an action without their consent are allowed their costs of an application to have their names struck out.[6] Where unjustifiable proceedings are taken against charity trustees the plaintiff may be ordered to pay the trustees' costs on the common fund basis so that the charity fund may be kept intact.[7]

When the Official Custodian is made a party to legal proceedings he must be indemnified against costs: accordingly if there is no fund out of which to pay his costs the plaintiff will be ordered to pay them.[8]

When part of charity property is forfeited by breach of some condition by charity trustees and the trustees appeal from the decision and fail, the only fund out of which costs would be payable is, *ex hypothesi*, no longer in their possession. The trustees are not entitled to their costs out of other charity property.

Costs relating to charitable gifts by will

As a rule the costs of proceedings rendered necessary by obscurity in a will, for example, to determine the validity of a particular charitable bequest[9] are payable out of the testator's residuary personal estate.[10] But there is no absolute right to costs out of the estate and the causing of unnecessary expense is discouraged by withholding costs where appropriate.[11] Costs may also be disallowed where they are incurred in prosecuting hopeless claims.[12] And charities having the same interest are not allowed the costs of separate appearance.[13]

---

1 *Re Poplar and Blackwall Free School* (1878), 8 Ch.D. 543.
2 *A.-G.* v. *Gibbs* (1847), 2 Ph. 327.
3 *Re Gilchrist Educational Trust*, [1895] 1 Ch. 367.
4 *A.-G.* v. *Gibbs* (1847), 2 Ph. 327.
5 *A.-G.* v. *Chester Corporation* (1851), 14 Beav. 338; *A.-G.* v. *Mercers' Co., Re St. Paul's School* (1870), 18 W.R. 448.
6 *A.-G.* v. *Maryatt* (1838), 2 Jur. 1060.
7 *Edenborough* v. *Archbishop of Canterbury* (1826), 2 Russ. 93, at 112; *A.-G.* v. *Cuming* (1843), 2 Y. & C. Ch. Cas. 139, at 155; *Andrews* v. *Barnes* (1888), 39 Ch.D. 133, C.A.
8 *Re Church Patronage Trust*, [1904] 1 Ch. 41, at 51.
9 *Kirkbank* v. *Hudson* (1819), 7 Price 212, at 222; *A.-G.* v. *Hinxman* (1820), 2 Jac. & W. 270, at 278; *Giblett* v. *Hobson* (1833), 5 Sim. 651, at 662; affd. (1834), 3 My. & K. 517; *Daly* v. *A.-G.* (1860), 11 I.Ch.R. 41.
10 *Philpott* v. *President and Governors of St. George's Hospital* (1857), 6 H.L. Cas. 338, at 374; *Wilson* v. *Squire* (1842), 13 Sim. 212; *Daly* v. *A.-G.* (1860), 11 I.Ch.R. 41, at 49.
11 *Re Amory*, [1951] 2 All E.R. 947, n. (costs withheld); *cf. Re Daysh* (1951), 1 T.L.R. 257 (costs allowed).
12 See 528, *infra*.   13 *Foxen* v. *Foxen* (1864), 13 W.R. 33.

Where, as is frequently the case, a will contains a direction about the payment of "testamentary expenses" that expression is construed as covering the costs of an administration action.[1]

If a dispute arises between persons claiming a charitable legacy and those interested in residue as to whether the legacy is or is not payable, the costs of the ensuing litigation are payable out of the estate.[2] An executor cannot by paying a disputed charitable legacy into court under section 63 of the Trustee Act 1925 exonerate the residue from its proper burden.[3]

Where, on the other hand, executors admit a legacy to be payable and sever it from the estate the costs of any ensuing litigation are borne by the legacy and not by the estate.[4] Thus where executors have set aside a sum to meet a charitable legacy and have administered the estate by dividing the residue, the costs of proceedings to secure the legacy must be paid out of the severed legacy.[5] But if the contest is between persons claiming the legacy and those interested in the general estate, the costs are borne by the estate;[6] there can be no severance until it has been decided that the legacy is payable. The mere fact that the executors have set apart a sum to answer the legacy, if payable, does not amount to a severance.[7]

An admission by an executor of assets for the payment of a charitable legacy extends to an admission of assets for the payment of costs to secure payment of the legacy, if the court thinks fit to direct them.[8]

Where the source of difficulty is the testator's misdescription of a charitable institution which he intended should receive a legacy, and more than one institution claims the legacy, the costs even of unsuccessful claimants, as between solicitor and client, notwithstanding the opposition of the residuary legatees are often directed to be paid out of the estate; but where in the opinion of the court a claim is hopeless and not made *bona fide* the unsuccessful claimant may be ordered to pay his own costs, and in some cases may be ordered to pay the costs of other parties.[9] FARWELL J. in one case stated that a society which appeared in court to support a claim which was not admitted must not expect as of right to be paid its costs out of the estate and might in certain events have to pay costs.[10] In *Re Preston's Estate*[11] the costs of particular claimants were not allowed beyond a point in the proceedings where it had become plain that the claims were hopeless. In *Re Vernon's Will Trust*[12] the second defendants the Coventry and District Cripples' Guild were not allowed their costs out of the estate because "they had absolutely no possibility of any interest because they did not exist at the time the will was made".[13]

---

1 *Penny* v. *Penny* (1879), 11 Ch.D. 440.
2 *A.-G.* v. *Lawes* (1849), 8 Hare 32, at 43.
3 *Re Birkett* (1878), 9 Ch.D. 576, at 581 (payment under Trustee Relief Act 1847).
4 *A.-G.* v. *Lawes* (1849), 8 Hare 32, at 43; *Re Lycett* (1897), 13 T.L.R. 373.
5 *Governesses' Benevolent Institution* v. *Rusbridger* (1854), 18 Beav. 467.
6 *A.-G.* v. *Lawes* (1849), 8 Hare 32, at 43.
7 *Ibid.*
8 *Philanthropic Society* v. *Hobson* (1833), 2 My. & K. 357.
9 *Re Clarke* (1907), 97 L.T. 707; *cf. Re Lycett* (1897), 13 T.L.R. 373 (costs payable out of severed *legacy*).
10 *Re Millington* (1932), *Times*, 14th Jan. 4; and *Re Clara Jones* (1949), cited in *Re Preston's Estate*, [1951] Ch. 878.
11 [1951] Ch. 878.   12 [1972] Ch. 300, n.
13 This fact does not appear from the report. The quotation is from the transcript of the shorthand notes of Mr. C. H. Norman.

In cases where the next of kin are made parties to an administration action relating to a charity, and no improper point is raised on their behalf, they are as a rule[1] allowed their costs on a common fund basis.[2] Next of kin are not, however, entitled to such costs as of right.[3] Accordingly such costs have been refused to next of kin who unsuccessfully contested a charitable bequest.[4] The heir-at-law was in the same position,[5] and if he brought an unnecessary suit the court would direct the costs to be paid out of the real estate.[6] Sometimes the heir-at-law was allowed charges and expenses in addition to costs,[7] and the next of kin would appeal to be similarly placed. On the other hand if next of kin take proceedings against residuary devisees alleging that there is a secret void trust for charitable purposes but not supporting such allegation with evidence, they will be liable for the costs.[8]

Formerly there was a rule that the costs of an administration action were to be paid out of residue generally, and not primarily out of a lapsed share and this rule applied when a share was given to charity and lapsed.[9] The modern rule is that as regards solvent estates, property of the deceased undisposed of by will becomes primarily liable, subject to the retention of a fund to meet pecuniary legacies and for testamentary and administration expenses, and subject to any contrary provision in the will.[10]

Payment and apportionment of costs payable out of charity funds

The costs of proceedings relating to a charity are, in some cases, ordered to be raised by mortgage.[11] Such a mortgage might relate to the whole[12] or only a part of the charity estate.[13] In raising costs out of charity property by a mortage the court is anxious to provide for its extinction by a sinking fund.[14]

The court has a general power to direct the sale of a charity estate[15] but will exercise such power only in exceptional circumstances.[16] It is therefore open to the court to authorise the sale of part of charity estates in order to provide for

---

1 Even where this claim does not succeed: *Gaffney v. Hevey* (1837), 1 Dr. & War. 12 at 25; *Carter v. Green* (1857), 3 K. & J. 591 at 608; *Lewis v. Allenby* (1870), L.R. 10 Eq. 668·
2 Previously solicitor and client costs were allowable.
3 *Whicker v. Hume* (1851), 14 Beav. 509, at 528 (heir got only party and party costs); *Aria v. Emanuel* (1861), 9 W.R. 366; *Wilkinson v. Barber* (1872), L.R. 14 Eq. 96, at 99.
4 *Wilkinson v. Barber* (1872), L.R. 14 Eq. 96; *Practice Direction (Costs)* [1960] 1 W.L.R. 114.
5 *A.-G. v. Haberdashers' Co.* (1792), 4 Bro.C.C. 178; *Currie v. Pye* (1811), 17 Ves. 462; *A.-G. v. Kerr* (1841), 4 Beav. 297, at 299; *James v. James* (1849), 11 Beav. 397.
6 *Leacroft v. Maynard* (1791), 1 Ves. 279.
7 *A.-G. v. Haberdashers' Co.* (1793), 4 Bro.C.C. 178; *A.-G. v. Kerr* (1841), 4 Beav. 297.
8 *Paine v. Hall* (1812), 18 Ves. 475.
9 *Blann v. Bell* (1877), 7 Ch.D. 382; *contra, Taylor v. Mogg* (1858), 27 L.J. Ch. 816; and see *Linley v. Taylor* (1859), 1 Giff. 67.
10 AEA 1925, s. 34 (3), Sch. 1, Pt. II, para. 1.
11 Shelford, *Law of Mortmain* (1836) 477.
12 *A.-G. v. Bishop of St. David's* (1849), Seton, *Judgments and Orders* (7th edn.) 1269; *Re Lambeth Charities* (1850), Seton, *op. cit.* (7th edn.) 1247; *A.-G. v. Archbishop of York* (1853), 17 Beav. 495; *A.-G. v. Murdoch* (1856), 2 K. & J. 571.
13 *A.-G. v. Atherton (Atherstone) School Governors* (1833), Shelford, *op. cit.*, 477.
14 *A.-G. v. Archbishop of York* (1853), 17 Beav. 495.
15 *A.-G. v. Nethercoat* (1840), cited in 1 Hare 400.
16 *A.-G. v. Newark-upon-Trent Corporation* (1842), 1 Hare 395.

the payment of costs. Again the payment of costs may be directed out of the income of a charity fund.[1] Thus in *A.-G.* v. *Smythies*[2] the costs of an application by a new master of a hospital in Colchester for payment of the income of a fund in court were held by Sir JOHN ROMILLY M.R. to be payable out of the income.

In another case[3] a relator who had obtained on order for payment of his costs by a charitable corporation was held entitled to charge them on a fund standing to the credit of the corporation at the Bank of England, the fund representing the proceeds of sale of an advowson.

Where proceedings are taken to recover a particular fund or estate belonging to a charity the costs should in the first instance fall on the property which is the subject matter of the proceedings. But the costs will be paid out of the general funds of the charity derived from different estates if justice to the relator or the interests of the charity so require.[4]

The circumstances in which an *apportionment* of costs takes place should be mentioned. The costs of settling one scheme for a number of charities will be apportioned suitably according to their annual incomes[5] and an application for the payment out of the funds of one of them will be refused.[6] If the costs are in fact paid out of an existing available fund not belonging to all the charities concerned, the costs will nevertheless ultimately be borne ratably by all.[7] On the other hand where a charity includes two classes of estates both of which are the subject of proceedings while the costs of the proceedings are borne proportionately the costs of establishing a scheme for one of the two estates must be borne by that estate alone.[8]

Again where several distinct charities created by a testator are vested in the same trustees the costs of proceedings relating to one charity alone are not payable out of the funds of the others but must be borne entirely by the relevant charity.[9]

In non-charity cases a defendant may be ordered to pay costs to a co-defendant.[10] Where the Attorney-General takes proceedings on behalf of a charity and there are two sets of defendants namely two trustees of the charity and another party who in the court is held liable to pay the costs, the court may direct the defendant so liable to pay the costs of the trustees directly instead of ordering the trustees' costs to be paid out of the charity fund and afterwards to be repaid by that defendant.[11]

The costs of making an unsuccessful application to the court in a charity matter may be given out of the charity funds if there are *bona fide* substantial grounds for the application.[12] This is so even if the application is based on a

---

1 *Re Saffron Walden Charity* (1857), Seton, *Judgments and Orders* (7th edn.) 1250.
2 (1853), 16 Beav. 385.   3 *A.-G.* v. *Thetford Corporation* (1860), 2 L.T. 370.
4 *A.-G.* v. *Kerr* (1841), 4 Beav. 297, at 303, *per* Lord LANGDALE.
5 *Re Saffron Walden Charity* (1857), Seton, *Judgments and Orders* (7th edn.) 1250. For a form of order: see *ibid.*
6 *Re Hertford Charity* (1852), 19 Beav. 518, n. (appointment of trustees).
7 *Re Stafford Charities* (1858), 26 Beav. 567.
8 *A.-G.* v. *Skinners' Co.* (1827), 2 Russ. 407, at 446.
9 *A.-G.* v. *Grainger* (1859), 7 W.R. 684.
10 *Rudow* v. *Great Britain Mutual Life Assurance Society* (1881), 17 Ch.D. 600, at 608, C.A., *per* JESSEL M.R.; *Sanderson* v. *Blyth Theatre Co.*, [1903] 2 K.B. 533.
11 *A.-G.* v. *Chester Corporation* (1851), 14 Beav. 338, at 341; *A.-G.* v. *Mercers' Co., Re St. Paul's School* (1870), 18 W.R. 448, at 450.
12 *Re Storie's University Gift* (1860), 2 De G.F. & J. 529.

misconception of law so long as the application is in good faith.[1] But the costs of vexatious proceedings[2] or of proceedings under an inappropriate procedure[3] are not allowed out of the charity funds. In some cases the court will dismiss an application without any order as to costs.[4]

Where an unnecessary party, by setting up a claim, is in consequence made a party to proceedings, he will be left to bear his own costs and will not be able to recover them out of the charity funds.[5] A person who attends proceedings before the master in regard to matters in which he is not interested will not be given his costs out of the charity fund[6] unless he can show that the charity is likely to benefit from his attendance.[7] But any party to proceedings under an order who has not been directed to attend may apply to the court for leave to attend any part of the proceedings at the cost of the fund and to have the conduct of those proceedings either in addition to or in substitution for any other party.[8]

Compulsory acquisition of charity land

On the compulsory acquisition of charity land pursuant to the provisions of the Compulsory Purchase Act 1965 and where the compensation is paid into court under those provisions[9] the High Court may order[10] the acquiring authority to pay the costs (including reasonable charges and expenses) of and incurred in consequence of the purchase of land,[11] the investment of the compensation paid into court or of its re-investment in the purchase of other land[12] and of all proceedings relating to orders for those matters except such as are occasioned by litigation between adverse claimants.[13] The costs of only one application for re-investment are allowed, except where it appears to the High Court that it is for the benefit of the parties interested in the compensation that it should be invested in the purchase of land in different sums and at different times.[14]

Where the legal estate in the land is vested in the Official Custodian for Charities and the compensation has been fixed, the Official Custodian is not bound to receive the compensation so as to relieve the acquiring authority from the cost of payment into court and investment.[15]

Where the charity trustees apply for the transfer of a fund in court to the account of the Official Custodian for Charities for the purpose of re-investment the application is treated as an application for the payment of money out of

---

1 *Re Betton's Charity* (1907), 77 L.J. Ch. 195, at 197.
2 *Re Chertsey Market, Ex parte Walthew* (1819), 6 Price 261.
3 *Re Phillipot's Charity* (1837), 8 Sim. 381, at 392.
4 *Giblett v. Hobson* (1833), 5 Sim. 651, at 662; *A.-G. v. Stewart* (1872), L.R. 14 Eq. 17, at 25.
5 *Re Shrewsbury School* (1849), 1 Mac. & G. 85.
6 *Re Shrewsbury Grammar School* (1849), 1 Mac. & G. 324, at 334.
7 *Ibid.*, at 335.
8 R.S.C. Ord. 44, r. 7.
9 Compulsory Purchase Act 1965, s. 2, Sch. 1, para. 6 (2).
10 But not whose payment into court was necessitated by wilful refusal to accept the money or convey the property, or wilful neglect to make a good title: Compulsory Purchase Act 1965, s. 26 (1).
11 *Ibid.*, s. 26 (2) (a), (3).
12 *Ibid.*, s. 26 (2) (b), (3).
13 *Ibid.*, s. 26 (3) (d).
14 *Ibid.*, s. 26 (4).
15 *Re Leeds Grammar School*, [1901] 1 Ch. 228.

court and the acquiring authority is liable for the costs of the application.[1]
But the costs of the subsequent re-investment by the Official Custodian are not
payable by the acquiring authority.[2]

The form of the order for the payment of dividends arising from a fund in
court to the trustees is important. The order should be for the payment of the
dividends to the trustees *for the time being*. In *Re Audenshaw School*[3] the dividends
arising from a fund in court had been ordered to be paid to the *existing* trustees
of a charity. The appointment of new trustees necessitated an application to the
court for variation of the order and the costs of the application were not payable
by the compulsory purchaser.

Miscellaneous provisions as to costs

TAXATION ON ORDER OF CHARITY COMMISSIONERS

The Charity Commissioners may order that a solicitor's bill of costs for business
done for a charity or for charity trustees[4] or trustees for a charity be taxed by
the appropriate taxing officer.[5] On any such order the taxation proceeds as if
the taxation had been ordered by the court in which the costs are taxed and the
costs are borne in the same way as if an order for taxation had been obtained
at the instance of the charity or trustees liable to pay the bill;[6] that is to say, if
one-sixth of the amount of the bill is taxed off the solicitor must pay the costs of
the taxation, but otherwise they must be borne by the charity.[7] The taxing
officer may, however, certify any special circumstances, and upon circumstances
so certified the court may make such order respecting payment of the costs as
it may think fit, as by depriving the solicitor of the costs of the taxation although
less than one-sixth is taxed off, or allowing him the costs though one-sixth or
more has been taxed off.

If the bill has been paid, the Commissioners may only order it to be taxed if
they are of opinion that it contains exorbitant charges; and they have no power
to order taxation of a solicitor's costs where they have been the subject of an
agreement, or where 12 months have elapsed since the bill has paid, since the
court itself could not order taxation in those cases.[8]

It appears that the Commissioners may make an order for taxation of a
solicitor's bill of their own motion, and they may wish to do so as a result of
scrutinising the accounts of a charity and making inquiries of the trustees. If the
trustees themselves did not wish to challenge the bill, the conduct of a taxation
ordered by the Commissioners of their own motion would present some

---

1 *Re Bristol Free Grammar School Estates* (1878), 47 L.J. Ch. 317; *Re Bishop Monk's Horfield
Trust* (1881), 43 L.T. 793; *Re Rector and Churchwardens of St. Alban's, Wood Street* (1891),
66 L.T. 51. If the Attorney-General has to be a party to the application, his costs must be
paid by the acquiring authority. *Re London Brighton and South Coast Rail Co.* (1854), 18
Beav. 608.
2 *Re Bishop Monk's Horfield Trust* (1881), 43 L.T. 793.
3 (1863), 1 New Rep. 255.
4 For the meaning of "charity" and "charity trustee", see CA 1960, ss. 45 and 46.
5 CA 1960, s. 26 (1).
6 *Ibid.*, s. 26 (2).
7 Solicitors Act 1957, s. 69 (5) and proviso (ii) thereto.
8 CA 1960, s. 26 (3).

difficulty, since it seems that the Commissioners cannot themselves take any part in it, but in the absence of the party chargeable with the bill the taxation can still proceed *ex parte*.

The charity trustees as the persons chargeable with the bill, may under the general law apply to the court for a bill to be taxed, and such an application would not require the leave of the Commissioners since the proceedings would not be "charity proceedings" as defined.[1] However in the ordinary case the trustees should apply in any case of doubt to the Commissioners, thus obtaining full protection for themselves and a saving of costs for the charity.

SCALE OF COSTS

In matters of equitable jurisdiction the court has the power to order an unsuccessful litigant to pay the costs of the action on a common fund basis (formerly called solicitor and client basis).[2] Costs of all parties have in many cases been allowed out of a charity fund on this basis[3] but there is no general rule to that effect.[4] In *Martin* v. *Maugham*[5] where the court directed a scheme to carry out the undefined charitable intention of a testator it was said that in the case of a settlement of a scheme by the court it was not customary to give costs on the common fund basis except by consent.

If the court thinks that the proceedings were not instituted for the benefit of charity or have been conducted with unnecessary expenditure, the successful plaintiff may be awarded only party and party costs,[6] or even no costs at all.[7]

INTEREST ON COSTS

Interest is recoverable on the costs which one party is ordered to pay another.[8] But it is not so recoverable on costs directed to be raised out of a charity estate or fund,[9] unless the court in the exercise of its discretion as to costs so directs.[10] The appropriate rate of interest is probably ten per cent. which is the rate applicable under the Judgment Debts (Rates of Interest) Order 1977.[11]

---

1 See *ibid.*, s. 28 discussed at 420–421, *supra*.

2 *Andrews* v. *Barnes* (1888), 39 Ch.D. 133; and see *Edenborough* v. *Archbishop of Canterbury* (1826), 2 Russ. 93; *A.-G.* v. *Cuming* (1843), 2 Y. & C. Ch. Cas. 139.

3 *A.-G.* v. *Carte* (1746), 1 Dick 113, *Moggridge* v. *Thackwell* (1803), 7 Ves. 36, at 69, 88; *Bishop of Hereford* v. *Adams* (1802), 7 Ves. 324, at 332; *Mills* v. *Farmer* (1815), 1 Mer. 55; *Gaffney* v. *Hevey* (1837), 1 Dr. & War. 12, at 25; *Wickham* v. *Marquis of Bath* (1865), L.R. 1 Eq. 17, at 25 *cf. A.-G.* v. *Stewart* (1872), L.R. 14 Eq. 17.

4 *Aria* v. *Emanuel* (1861), 9 W.R. 366; *Wilkinson* v. *Barber* (1872), L.R. 14 Eq. 96, at 99.

5 (1844), 13 L.J. Ch. 392, at 394.

6 *A.-G.* v. *Fishmongers' Co.* (1837), 1 Keen 492, at 501.

7 *A.-G.* v. *Cullum* (1837), 1 Keen 104.

8 See the Judgments Act 1838, ss. 17 and 18; Administration of Justice Act 1970, s. 44; Judgment Debts (Rate of Interest) Order 1977, S.I. 1977 No. 141.

9 *A.-G.* v. *Nethercote* (1841), 11 Sim. 529.

10 *A.-G.* v. *Bishop of St. David's* (1849), Seton, *Judgments and Orders* (7th edn.) 1269 (and see Seton, *op. cit.* (6th edn.) 1290, for form of order), where four per cent. was given.

11 S.I. 1977 No. 141.

PROCEEDINGS BEFORE ATTORNEY-GENERAL

The costs of proceedings before the Attorney-General to obtain his fiat to such proceedings as require it, as for example a relator action and the costs of proceedings before him with reference to the withdrawal of his fiat pending an appeal may be made costs in the action.[1] But the court has no jurisdiction to order payment of costs incurred in proceedings before the Attorney-General which were not taken with the direction or sanction of the court.[2]

COSTS OF APPEALS

There must be a substantial ground for an appeal by defendants in a charity suit if they are to avoid liability for costs should the appeal be unsuccessful.[3] As a general rule in the case of appeals the costs of all parties should not be allowed out of the charity funds, "because" in the words of Lord CRANWORTH "such allowance rather encourages appeals where they are known and felt to be desperate".[4]

---

1 *A.-G.* v. *Halifax Corporation* (1871), L.R. 12 Eq. 262.
2 *A.-G.* v. *Harper* (1838), 8 L.J. Ch. 12 (application by way of memorial).
3 *A.-G.* v. *Rochester Corporation* (1854), 5 De G.M. & G. 797.
4 *Bruce* v. *Deer Presbytery* (1867), L.R. 1 Sc. & Div. 96, at 98, H.L.

Part VII

Taxation and Rating

Chapter 46

Fiscal Advantages

Introduction

Charities enjoy a number of fiscal advantages or privileges both as regards taxes and rates. The purpose of this chapter is, primarily, to discuss the scope of these advantages which have assumed a leading importance for organisations claiming charitable status.

Relief from income tax has been granted to charities ever since Pitt introduced income tax. The Income Tax Act 1799 exempted from the tax the income of any "corporation, fraternity or society established for charitable purposes". Between 1816 and 1842 there was no income tax in England, but on its re-introduction the exemption for charities was revived. The exemption only came under serious attack[1] once during the nineteenth century in 1863, but the view that the exemption "is not a privilege – it is a right"[2] prevailed. The Inland Revenue did, however, challenge the *scope* of the exemption in *Income Tax Special Purposes Comrs.* v. *Pemsel*,[3] contending that the exemption did not apply to trusts other than for the relief of poverty. The result of the decision in the House of Lords in that case was that charitable status automatically entailed exemption, provided the other conditions of exemption were observed. All charities benefited: no distinction could be drawn between one type or category of charitable purpose and another. This consequence has had its critics ever since, and raises the question of the rationale of the special treatment accorded to charities.

To some extent, of course, it is true that fiscal exemption was (and is) justified because charities perform functions which otherwise it would fall for government or local authorities to discharge. But this is not universally true. The advancement of religion and the prevention of cruelty to, or suffering by, animals provide two obvious examples of charitable objects which have never been directly subsidised by the state or by local authorities.

There are in fact two analyses of these privileges. The first is that such fiscal benefits represent a form of subsidy by the State. This view was accepted by the Report of the Radcliffe Commission which said:[4]

---

1 By Gladstone when he was Chancellor of the Exchequer; see Owen, *English Philanthropy 1660–1960*, 331–332 for a summary of the attack and its repulse.
2 The words were those of Benjamin Disraeli: Owen, *op. cit.*, 332.
3 [1891] A.C. 531.
4 Final Report of the Royal Commission on the Taxation of Profits and Income (Cmd. 9474, 1955) para. 175; and see Geoffrey Cross Q.C. (1956) 72 L.Q.R. 187, at 204.

"accepting the view that all parts of the national income are prima facie subject to a tax on income, the system does amount in effect to a grant of public moneys towards the furtherance of such causes to come within the legal category of charity without Parliamentary control of their individual purposes or of their administration . . ."

The other view has been forthrightly put in a memorandum submitted by the Independent Schools Joint Committee to a recent Parliamentary committee:[1]

"The income of individuals and corporate bodies belongs to those to whom it accrues. It is for Parliament to decide how much shall be removed in the form of taxation. Freedom from taxation is not a form of subsidy"

Another writer[2] has written that,

". . . the income of charity property is relieved of income tax, since otherwise the Crown would be taking part of the income and applying it to public purposes chosen by itself instead of by the donor".

It will however be seen in the discussion which follows that there has been a gradual and (some would say) insidious[3] erosion of the traditional fiscal privileges, despite the payment of lip service to the principles of the unity of charity and its equal partnership with Government.

In 1920 the Royal Commission on the Income Tax recommended that for the purposes of income tax "charities" should be specifically redefined.[4] A more restrictive definition of charity for tax purposes was also proposed by the Radcliffe Commission in its final report in 1955. They suggested that a statutory definition which would correspond more closely with accepted ideas of what is a charity would be: the relief of poverty, the prevention or relief of distress, the advancement of education, learning and research and the advancement of religion.[5] In other words what was, in effect, proposed was an enlargement of the first three classes in *Pemsel's*[6] case, with the omission of the fourth heterogeneous class referred to by Lord MACNAGHTEN.[7]

Not long after the Report of the Radcliffe Commission, one writer suggested that much confusion in the law of charities could be avoided if the question of what is a charity for the purposes of the law of trusts were separated from the question of what is a charity for the purpose of fiscal advantages.[8] At that time, and indeed even now, a judge who decides that a particular purpose or institution is charitable is deciding a question of fiscal exemption as well as of status. The same writer pointed out that the decision may be made in a "Chancery" case or in a "Revenue" case. In the former the contest is between charity on the one

---

1 See 10th Report from the Expenditure Committee Session 1974–75, Charity Commissioners and their Accountability, Vol. II, 250.

2 C. P. Hill, late Chief Charity Commissioner, quoted in 10th Report from the Expenditure Committee Session 1974–75, Charity Commissioners and their Accountability, Vol. II, 252; and see C. P. Hill, *A Guide for Charity Trustees* (2nd edn.) 100–101.

3 See e.g. Memorandum of J. D. Livingston Booth, Director of Charities Aid Foundation: 10th Report from the Expenditure Committee Session 1974–75, Charity Commissioners and their Accountability, Vol. II, 290.

4 Royal Commission on the Income Tax (1920, Cmd. 615) paras. 305–309.

5 Final Report of the Royal Commission on the Taxation of Profits and Income (1955, Cmd. 9474) paras. 168–175.

6 *Income Tax Special Purposes Comrs.* v. *Pemsel*, [1891] A.C. 531.

7 Unless the prevention or relief of distress falls under the fourth head.

8 Geoffrey Cross Q.C. (1956), 72 L.Q.R. 187, at 204.

hand and the next of kin or residuary legatees on the other; and the claims of charity tend to be favoured and are seldom challenged beyond the court of first instance. The result is that there are many border-line decisions in favour of charity at first instance. In Revenue cases there is no leaning in favour of charity and the cases are often argued through the appellate courts.

No legislation along the lines favoured by the Radcliffe Commission has been introduced. This was, apparently, because although such legislation would have cut out the "undeserving" cases it would also have cut out "a lot of cases which would generally be regarded as deserving—for example trusts for the provision of recreation grounds, the repair and preservation of historical monuments, the preservation of the natural beauty of the countryside and the organisation of welfare institutions such as village halls and women's institutes."[1] But there is no particular magic in the list of objects considered "deserving" by the Radcliffe Commission. A statutory definition of objects to be granted fiscal exemption could, no doubt, expand the list favoured by the Radcliffe Commission.

What has been said so far with regard to exemption from income tax applies *mutatis mutandis* to exemption from other fiscal burdens. The terms of these exemptions adopt, as will be seen, the definition of charity given in the income tax legislation.

Income tax and corporation tax

INCOME TAX

Contrary to a widespread popular belief, charities do not enjoy any general exemption from tax on their income. Particular exemptions have been granted in respect of tax under different Schedules and to these must be added various extra-statutory and other concessions allowed in practice.

The exemptions can conveniently be classified under three heads: (1) exemptions for income from ownership and occupation of land; (2) exemptions for income chargeable under Schedules C, D and F; and (3) exemptions for income from profits of a trade. On the other hand it should be noted that there are no exemptions for income from abroad chargeable under Cases IV and V of Schedule D. Nor is income chargeable under Case VI exempt, unless it is income arising from land. Again, income chargeable under Schedule E is not exempt, save in respect of expenses of directors or employees earning more than £2000 per annum: the statutory provisions by virtue of which expense allowances paid to directors by bodies corporate or unincorporate or to certain employees by their employers are treated as income of the recepients do not apply in relation to bodies established for charitable purposes only.

---

1 10th Report from the Expenditure Committee Session 1974–75, Charity Commissioners and their Accountability, Vol. II, 87 (memorandum submitted by the Board of Inland Revenue).

Exemptions for income from ownership or occupation of land

The first exemption from tax under this head is provided by section 360 (1) (a) of the Income and Corporation Taxes Act 1970. This provides for:

"exemption from tax under Schedules A and D in respect of the rents and profits of any lands, tenements, hereditaments or heritages belonging to a hospital, public school or almshouse, or vested in trustees for charitable purposes, so far as the same are applied to charitable purposes only."

The concluding words should be noted: the exemption in respect of rents and profits from land, tenements, hereditaments or heritages belonging to the defined institutions only applies *so far as the same are applied to charitable purposes only.*

Hospital

There are many judicial definitions of the word "hospital"[1] which is a word of a chameleon-like quality. In *Needham* v. *Bowers*[2] CHARLES J. held that the language of the Income Tax Acts in conferring exemption on hospitals "must be restricted to hospitals supported wholly or in part by charity" and did not, therefore, apply to a hospital which was self-supporting. The decision in *Needham* v. *Bowers* was expressly approved, though distinguished, in *Cawse* v. *Nottingham Lunatic Hospital*[3] where a lunatic hospital with a substantial charitable endowment and taking paying patients at varying prices was held to be a "hospital" within the meaning of the income tax exemption. As POLLOCK J. pointed out, the fact that there were paying patients did not affect the "original eleemosynary character of the institution". A hospital wholly maintained by the payments of patients on the other hand could not be entitled to exemption. This was the point made by ROWLATT J. in *Royal Antediluvian Order of Buffaloes* v. *Owens*.[4]

"Now there is one limitation which appears established by authority and that is that there must be some charitable, and I prefer to use the word eleemosynary, element about the maintenance of a hospital to make it a hospital within the meaning of the Act. If it is a hospital which is, as a whole, maintained by the payments of the patients, whether some pay less than their cost and others more, or however it is, if it is maintained by the payments of the patients, it is not a hospital within the meaning of the exemption".

Public school

The term "public school" is not a term of art. FRY L.J. in *Blake* v. *London Corporation*[5] itemised the following characteristics of such a school:

"a perpetual foundation; a portion of its income is derived from charity; it is managed by a public body; no private person has any interest in the

---

1 See 2 Stroud, *Judicial Dictionary* (4th edn.) 1256–1258.
2 (1888), 21 Q.B.D. 436.
3 [1891] 1 Q.B. 585.
4 (1928), 13 T.C. 176, at 182.
5 (1887), 19 Q.B.D. 79.

school; no profit was or is in the contemplation of its founders or managers; and lastly the object of the school is the benefit of a large class of persons." [1]

The question in *Girls Public Day School Trust, Ltd.* v. *Ereaut*[2] was whether Wimbledon High School, a girls' day school, was a public school within the exemption. It was held by the House of Lords that the question whether a particular institution was a public school within the exemption had to be decided by reference to the common understanding of the term and that this was a question of fact for the Commissioners. Viscount HAILSHAM considered the effect of the decision in *Blake* v. *London Corporation*,[3] and rejected the argument that the criteria stated in the judgment of FRY L.J. were conclusive or exhaustive. FRY L.J. had expressly disclaimed any attempt to lay down a definition of what would or would not be a public school in all cases; but he was indicating some characteristics which enabled him to say that the school in question in *Blake's* case, the City of London School, was a public school. This is not in the least the same thing as saying that no school which does not possess all these characteristics can come within the expression. The House of Lords found ample evidence[4] to support the Commissioners' finding of fact in respect of Wimbledon High School and refused to review that finding.

One of the cases referred to in the speech of Viscount HAILSHAM was the decision of ROWLATT J. in *Birkenhead School, Ltd.* v. *Dring*.[5] In that case a limited company carried on a high class secondary school under the Articles which provided that no bonus dividend or profit was to be paid, allotted or divided to or amongst the members. Practically the whole of the receipts of the company arose from fees paid by the pupils. ROWLATT J. upheld the Commissioners' finding that the school was not a public school saying:[6]

> "The school has not really any permanent . . . character about it . . . I certainly think that the element of permanency, without using it in its technical sense, which is connoted by the word 'foundation' something of that sort is part of the essentials of a public school."

The correctness of the decision has not been impugned.[7] But in so far as the dicta cited above imply that it is of the essence of a public school that there must be something in the nature of a foundation which renders it necessary that it should be permanently carried on as such, they go too far. The existence of a perpetual foundation is one of the factors which require consideration, but it is not by itself conclusive.[8]

The fact that a school is denominational does not prevent it being a public school[9] but an exclusive Quaker school was outside the definition because it did not "follow the lines which the ordinary public follow in the matter of schools".[10]

---

1 *Ibid.*, at 82.
2 [1931] A.C. 12.
3 (1886), 18 Q.B.D. 437; (1887), 19 Q.B.D. 79.
4 See [1931] A.C. 12, at 25–26.
5 (1926), 11 T.C. 273.
6 *Ibid.*, at 277.
7 Viscount HAILSHAM thought the decision correct: [1931] A.C. 12 at 25.
8 *Girls' Public Day School Trust, Ltd.* v. *Ereaut*, [1931] A.C. 12, at 25.
9 *Cardinal Vaughan Memorial School Trustees* v. *Ryall* (1920), 36 T.L.R. 694 (Roman Catholic school).
10 *Ackworth School General Committee* v. *Betts* (1916), 84 L.J.K.B. 2112.

The age and academic qualifications of the students as well as the content of the education would appear to be relevant. Accordingly a divinity hall intended for the training of graduates for the ministry of the Free Church of Scotland is not a public school,[1] nor is a technical college for young people above the ordinary school age and entering on the threshold of industrial life.[2]

Almshouse

An almshouse is according to one leading dictionary "a house founded by private charity especially for the aged poor".[3] It has been said judicially to be "equivalent to a 'house provided for the reception of poor persons'".[4] But "it is not necessary that the inmates should be entirely destitute, or that it should supply all their wants".[5] It is sufficient that the people who become inmates go there as a matter of charity.[6]

Lands etc., vested in trustees for charitable purposes

The meaning of the expression "charitable purposes" has already been amply considered.[7] In most cases the question whether any land, tenements, heredita-ments or heritages are vested in trustees for charitable purposes is answered by reference to the register of charities: an institution is for all purposes other than rectification of the register conclusively presumed to be or to have been a charity at any time when it is or was on the register of charities.[8]

The fact that the section mentions the words "hospital, public school or almshouse" does not cut down the meaning of "trustees for charitable purposes", so that for example a university[9] or a technical college[10] may claim exemption under section 360 (1) (a) of the Income and Corporation Taxes Act 1970.

The second exemption under this head is contained in section 260 (1) (b) of the 1970 Act which provides that exemption shall be granted "from tax under Schedule B in respect of any lands occupied by a charity". A "charity" for this purpose means "any body of persons or trust established for charitable purposes only";[11] and a "body of persons" means "any body politic, corporate or collegiate, and any company, fraternity, fellowship and society of persons whether corporate or not corporate".[12] Whether land is "occupied" by a charity is a question which has been considered frequently in relation to relief from rates[13] and decisions on the meaning of "occupation" in rating law are applicable to income tax.[14]

---

1 *Bain v. Free Church of Scotland* (1897), 3 T.C. 537.
2 *Scottish Woollen Technical College Galashiels v. I.R.Comrs.* (1926), 11 T.C. 139, Ct. of Session (Lord BLACKBURN dissenting). But it may be a charity within the section: *ibid.*
3 *Shorter Oxford English Dictionary* (3rd edn.).
4 *Mary Clark Home Trustees v. Anderson*, [1904] 2 K.B. 645, at 651, *per* CHANNELL J.
5 *Ibid.*, at 657.
6 *Ibid.*, at 656.
7 See 7–119, *supra*.
8 CA 1960, s. 5 (1).
9 *R. v. Income Tax Comrs., Ex parte University College of North Wales* (1909), 5 T.C. 408.
10 *Scottish Woollen Technical College Galashiels v. I.R.Comrs.* (1926), 11 T.C. 139.
11 TA 1970, s. 360 (3).
12 *Ibid.*, s. 526 (5).
13 See the discussion at 556–558, *infra*.
14 *Mitcham Golf Course Trustees v. Ereaut*, [1937] 3 All E.R. 450, at 452D.

Exemptions for income chargeable under Schedules C, D and F

Charities enjoy exemption by virtue of section 360 (1) (c) of the Income and Corporation Taxes Act 1970:

    (i) from tax under Schedule C in respect of any interest,[1] annuities,[2] dividends[3] and shares of annuities,

    (ii) from tax under Schedule D in respect of any yearly interest[4] or other annual payment,[5] and

    (iii) from tax under Schedule F in respect of any distribution[6]

where the income in question forms part of the income of a charity, or is, according to the rules or regulations established by Act of Parliament charter, decree, deed of trust or will applicable to charitable purposes only, and so far as it is applied to charitable purposes only.

This exemption has been extended by extra-statutory concession to bank interest, whether yearly or not, received by charities and to discounts on Treasury Bills held by charities.[7]

Profits or gains arising from the carrying on of a trade by a charity are not exempt from tax under section 360 (1) (c) and are therefore assessable under Schedule D.[8] But trading profits made by trustees and handed over by them to a charity under the terms of their trust are annual payments and are therefore exempt under section 360 (1) (c).[9]

In order that the exemptions under this head may apply, three conditions must be satisfied:

    (1) the receipt by the charity must be income

    (2) the income must form part of the income of a body of persons or trust established for charitable purposes only, or must according to the rules established by the relevant instrument be applicable for charitable purposes only

    (3) the income must be applied for charitable purposes only.

By the first of these requirements is meant that the income should have the quality and nature of income in the hands of the charity.[10] The covenantor must not be entitled to receive appreciable amenities and benefits from the charity in

---

1 See *Bennett v. Ogston* (1930), 15 T.C. 374, at 379; *Westminster Bank, Ltd. v. Riches* (1947), 28 T.C. 159, at 189.

2 See *Scoble v. Secretary of State in Council for India*, [1903] 1 K.B. 494; affd. *Secretary of State in Council of India v. Scoble*, [1903] A.C. 299; *cf. I.R.Comrs. v. Land Securities Investment Trust, Ltd.*, [1969] 1 W.L.R. 604; and see *Morant Settlement Trustees v. I.R. Comrs.*, [1948] 1 All E.R. 732.

3 See *George Drexler Ofrex Foundation Trustees v. I.R.Comrs.*, [1966] Ch. 675.

4 *Corinthian Securities, Ltd. v. Cato*, [1970] 1 Q.B. 77, C.A.; *cf. Garston Overseers v. Carlisle*, [1915] 3 K.B. 381.

5 See *I.R.Comrs. v. Whitworth Park Coal Co., Ltd.*, [1958] Ch. 792, at 815 *et seq.*

6 See TA 1970, s. 233 as amended by FA 1972, s. 106, Sch. 22, paras. 1–4.

7 Extra-Statutory Concession B9; see Revenue booklet "Extra-Statutory Concessions in operation at August 1 1970" (IR 1).

8 *Brighton College v. Marriott*, [1926] A.C. 192.

9 *R. v. Income Tax Special Comrs., Ex parte Shaftesbury Home and Arethusa Training Ship*, [1923] 1 K.B. 393.

10 *Campbell v. I.R.Comrs.*, [1970] A.C. 77.

return for his covenanted gift.[1] In deciding whether the second of the three requirements is satisfied, the sensible course is first to consult the central register of charities. Non-entry in that register of the body of persons or trust is not decisive; but it will then become necessary, by reference to the principles already discussed, to see that the institution if any is exclusively charitable or that an exclusively charitable destination is prescribed by the relevant instrument. If a trust deed provides for charitable purposes and non-charitable purposes, and the provision for non-charitable purposes is void for perpetuity with the result that the whole fund is subject to a trust for charitable purposes, the trust is *established* for charitable purposes only nevertheless.[2] On the other hand if some income is to be applied to non-charitable purposes and the balance (if any) is to go to specified charitable purposes the income is not "*applicable* for charitable purposes only".[3] The third requirement that the income must be actually applied to charitable purposes only was discussed in *I.R.Comrs. v. Educational Grants Association.*[4] The respondent association was founded and managed by Metal Box, Ltd. It was clearly established for charitable purposes namely to advance education. But in so far as the trustees had applied income for the benefit of children of the employees of Metal Box, Ltd. the income had not been applied for charitable purposes only.

A further exemption is to be found in Section 360 (1) (d) of the Income and Corporation Taxes Act 1970 which provides that specific exemption shall be granted "from tax under Schedule C in respect of any interest, annuities, dividends or shares of annuities which are in the names of trustees and are applicable solely towards the repairs[5] of any cathedral, college, church or chapel, or any building used solely for the purpose of divine worship[6] so far as the same are applied to those purposes".

Lastly, mention must be made under this head of the provision that dividends on stocks, securities or annuities standing in the name of the Official Custodian for Charities, or in other names certified by the Charity Commissioners to the Bank of England *to* be exempt from income tax, must be paid free of tax.[7] This provision enables charities to receive dividends without deduction of tax so that they are not put to the trouble of making repayment claims.

Exemption for profits of trading

A highly important, but circumscribed, exemption is enjoyed by charities in respect of trading income. A charity is entitled to exemption from Schedule D "in respect of the profits of any trade carried on by the charity if the profits are applied solely to the purposes of the charity and either: (i) the trade is exercised in the course of the actual carrying out of a primary purpose of the charity, or

---

1 *I.R.Comrs.* v. *National Book League*, [1957] Ch. 488, C.A., *Taw and Torridge Festival Society* v. *I.R.Comrs.* (1959), 38 T.C. 603.

2 *George Drexler Ofrex Foundation Trustees* v. *I.R.Comrs.* [1966] Ch. 675.

3 *Lawrence* v. *I.R.Comrs.* (1940), 23 T.C. 333.

4 [1967] Ch. 993.

5 As to the meaning of the word "repairs", see Stroud, *Judicial Dictionary*, (4th Edn.) 2338.

6 As to what is meant by worship see *R.* v. *Registrar-General Ex parte Segerdal*, [1970] 2 Q.B. 697.

7 TA 1970, Sch. 5, Pt. I, para. 4.

(ii) the work in connection with the trade is mainly carried out by beneficiaries of the charity".[1]

"Trade" in this context includes every trade, manufacture, adventure or concern in the nature of trade.[2] Activities which fall within the meaning of the word "trade" and which have been carried on by charities include: letting out rooms for entertainment[3], running a restaurant open to outsiders,[4] bookselling,[5] carrying on a public school,[6] promoting a music festival to which the public were on payment admitted.[7]

Apart from the effect of the statutory exemptions when a trade is carried on by a charity, tax is chargeable on the profits of the trade notwithstanding that the profits are, and can only be, applied to the purposes of the charity.[8]

Income under deeds of covenant

One of the most important areas in which the exemption contained in section 360 (1) (c) of the Income and Corporation Taxes Act 1970 operates is in relation to covenanted gifts of income. Any income[9] which, by virtue or in consequence of any disposition made, directly or indirectly, by any person (other than a disposition made for valuable and sufficient consideration) is payable to or applicable for the benefit of any other person for a period which cannot exceed six years[10] is deemed for purposes of taxation to be the income of the person, if living, by whom the disposition was made, and not to be the income of any other person.[11] In this context "disposition" includes any trust, covenant, agreement or arrangement.[12] The consequence of this provision is that if a person executes a deed of covenant to pay income to a charity for a period which can exceed six years that income becomes the income of the charity and any "annual payment" which is part of the income of a charity applicable to charitable purposes only and which is applied to charitable purposes only is exempt from income tax.

Another feature of the seven year deed of covenant is that a charity is able to claim *repayment* of tax deduction from certain annual payments made to the charity under such a deed. Up to 1972–73 charities were able to recover standard rate income tax at 38·75 per cent. on their income from deeds of covenant where the income had already suffered from deduction of tax, and the sum payable under the deed was expressed to be such a sum as after deduction of income tax at the standard rate should amount to a certain net figure. From 1973–74 the words "standard rate" are read as referring to the basic rate.[13] The

---

1 *Ibid.*, s. 360 (1) (e).

2 *Ibid.*, s. 526 (5).

3 *Coman* v. *Rotunda Hospital Dublin (Governors)*, [1921] 1 A.C. 1.

4 *Grove* v. *Young Men's Christian Association* (1903), 88 L.T. 696.

5 *Religious Tract and Book Society of Scotland* v. *Forbes* (1896), 3 T.C. 415.

6 *Brighton College* v. *Marriott*, [1926] A.C. 192.

7 *I.R.Comrs.* v. *Glasgow Musical Festival Association* (1926), 11 T.C. 154.

8 *St. Andrew's Hospital, Northampton* v. *Sheersmith* (1887), 19 Q.B.D. 624; *Psalms and Hymns Trustees* v. *Whitwell* (1890), 3 T.C. 7; *Davis* v. *Mater Misericordiae Hospital Dublin Superioress*, [1933] I.R. 480; and see the cases cited in footnotes 3 to 7, *supra*.

9 The income must be income which could be income for United Kingdom tax purposes: *Becker* v. *Wright*, [1966] 1 W.L.R. 215.

10 Calendar years: *I.R.Comrs.* v. *St. Luke's Hostel Trustees* (1930), 15 T.C. 682.

11 TA 1970, s. 434.

12 *Ibid.*, s. 434 (2).

13 FA 1971, Sch. 7, para. 2.

result of the introduction of a basic rate of 30 per cent. was that charities in whose favour covenants had been made which provided for payment of a stated net amount after deduction of tax would recover less tax than before. For that reason transitional relief was introduced for charities for the years 1973–77. Subject to certain conditions they can claim the tax at the basic rate plus a proportion of the difference between the basic rate and 38·75 per cent. The relevant basic rates and proportions are:

1973–74	30 per cent. plus the entire difference
1974–75	33 per cent. plus three-quarters of the difference
1975–76	35 per cent. plus half the difference
1976–77	35 per cent. plus a quarter of the difference.

The conditions are (1) that the charity was entitled to repayment of tax in 1971–72 in respect of a payment recovered by it under a net covenant and (2) that the charity is entitled to repayment in 1973–74, 1974–75, 1975–76, 1976–77 in respect of a payment received by it under *any* net covenant made before 6th March 1973.[1]

By extra-statutory concession,[2] tax is not charged on profits of bazaars, jumble sales, gymkhanas, carnivals, fireworks displays and similar activities arranged by voluntary organisations for the purpose of raising funds for charity provided certain conditions are satisfied. Tax is not charged on such profits if (1) the organisation is not regularly trading (2) the trading is not in competition with other traders (3) the activities are supported substantially because the public are aware that any profits will be devoted to charity, and (4) the profits are transferred to charities or are otherwise applied for charitable purposes.

CORPORATION TAX

Exemption in respect of income

Charitable corporations enjoy the same tax exemptions as are enjoyed by trustees of charities in relation to the income of the charity. This is because "any provision of the Income Tax Acts which confers an exemption from income tax . . . shall have the like effect for purposes of corporation tax."[3]

Exemption in respect of capital gains

A charitable corporation is exempted from corporation tax on gains accruing to it which are applicable and applied for charitable purposes: such gains are not chargeable gains.[4]

---

1 FA 1973, s. 52.
2 Concession C5 in the IR Booklet, Extra-statutory Concessions in operation at 1st August 1970.
3 TA 1970, s. 250 (4).
4 *Ibid.*, s. 265 (2).

Capital gains tax

A charity is exempted from capital gains tax on gains accruing to it which are applicable and applied for charitable purposes: such gains are not chargeable gains.[1]

If property held on charitable trusts ceases to be subject to charitable trusts the trustees are treated as if they had disposed of, and immediately re-acquired, the property for its then market value,[2] and are liable to capital gains tax on any chargable gain resulting from that disposal.[3] Any gain on the disposal is treated as not accruing to the charity.[4] Subject to a time limit, the trustees are also liable to tax on any gains from disposal of assets made while the property was held on charitable trusts (and therefore exempted) if and so far as any of the property ceasing to be subject to charitable trusts represents, directly or indirectly, the consideration for those disposals.[5] Any gain on the disposal is treated as not accruing to the charity.[6] The time limit referred to is in respect of the assessment. An assessment to capital gains tax under the last-mentioned provision may not be made more than three years after the end of the year of assessment in which the property ceases to be subject to charitable trusts.[7]

Where there is a disposal of an asset to a charity or one of certain specified bodies[8] otherwise than by way of bargain at arm's length the general rule deeming the consideration to be equal to market value[9] does not apply. But if the disposal is by way of gift (including gifts in settlement)[10] or for a consideration not exceeding the expenditure allowable for capital gains tax purposes,[11] the disposal and acquisition is treated[12] as being made for such consideration as will secure that neither a gain nor a loss accrues on the disposal.[13] For the purpose of any subsequent disposal by the charity or body in question the acquisition by the person making the disposal is treated as the acquisition of that charity or body.[14] The exemption on disposals applies also to deemed disposals e.g. on the termination of a life interest.[15]

---

1 FA 1965, s. 35 (1).
2 As to the meaning of "market value", see *ibid.*, s. 44.
3 *Ibid.*, s. 35 (2) (a).
4 *Ibid.*
5 *Ibid.*, s. 35 (2) (b).
6 *Ibid.*
7 *Ibid.*, s. 35 (2); TA 1970, s. 538 (1), Sch. 16.
8 The specified bodies are listed in FA 1975, Sch. 6 para. 12: see FA 1972, s. 119 (1) (b), as amended by FA 1975, s. 53.
9 I.e. FA 1965, s. 22 (4).
10 FA 1972, s. 119 (2).
11 I.e. for a consideration not exceeding the sums allowable as a deduction under the FA 1965, s. 22 (a), Sch. 6, Pt. I, para. 4.
12 I.e. for the purposes of the capital gains tax provisions of FA 1965, Pt. III (ss. 19–45) but not for the purposes of FA 1971, s. 57 (exemptions and reliefs for small disposals).
13 FA 1972, s. 119 (1) (2) (a).
14 *Ibid.*, s. 119 (2) (b).
15 *Ibid.*, s. 119 (3).

Capital transfer tax

Capital transfer tax, as its name indicates, is a tax on transfers of capital. These include not merely gifts *inter vivos* and by will, but also devolution on intestacy and distributions from, and certain other events in relation to, trusts. The tax has replaced estate duty but goes much further than estate duty in taxing *inter vivos* transfers of capital. Gifts to charity,[1] and charitable trusts[2] in relation to their settled property and distributions are both accorded favourable treatment.

GIFTS TO CHARITY

Gifts to charity if made more than one year before the death of the transferor are entirely exempt from the tax, no matter how large the gift. A gift made within one year of the transferor's death or made on his death will be totally exempt from the tax if less than £100,000.[3] In addition there is an unlimited exemption where property is given to a charity by a distribution payment.[4]

The exemption in relation to gifts to charity does not apply if the testamentary or other disposition by which the property is given takes effect on the termination after the transfer of any interest or period (e.g. to A for life and then to charity).[5] Secondly the exemption does not apply in relation to any property if the testamentary or other disposition by which the property is given depends on a condition which is not satisfied within 12 months after the transfer.[6] Thirdly, the gift will not be exempt if (*a*) the testamentary or other disposition by which the property is given is defeasible, or (*b*) the property is an interest in other property and that interest is less than the donor's or the property is given subject to an interest reserved or created by the donor or is given for a limited period or (*c*) the property or any part of it may become applicable for purposes other than charitable purposes.[7]

When an individual has made transfers to a charity or charities exceeding £100,000 in value in the year preceding his death, the excess is chargeable to tax on his death. Earlier transfers will be exempt before later transfers; where the value transferred by more than one chargeable transfer made by the same person on the same day depends on the order in which the transfers are made, they shall be treated as made in the order which results in the lowest value chargeable.[8] Transfers which are in excess of the £100,000 limit are chargeable as gifts at the higher rate scale, but only the charity or charities will be liable for the tax[9] so there will be no question of grossing up.

---

1 "Charity" has the same meaning as in the Income Tax Acts: FA 1975, s. 51 (1). So it means a charity established by United Kingdom law.
2 Charitable has the same meaning as in the Income Tax Acts: FA 1975, s. 51 (1).
3 *Ibid.*, Sch. 6, para. 10 (1).
4 *Ibid.*, Sch. 6, para. 10 (2). As to distribution payments see *ibid.*, Sch. 5, para. 6.
5 *Ibid.*, Sch. 6, para. 15 (1).
6 *Ibid.*, Sch. 6, para. 15 (2).
7 *Ibid.*, Sch. 6, para. 15 (3) which is further elaborated in para. 15 (4).
8 *Ibid.*, s. 43 (2).
9 *Ibid.*, s. 26 (3).

CHARITABLE TRUSTS

The charges to capital transfer tax on distributions and deemed distributions, and the periodic charge do not apply to property held upon trust for charitable purposes only.[1]

Stamp duty

Prior to 1963 a lower rate of stamp duty applied where a conveyance or transfer was made to a body of persons established for charitable purposes only, or to the trustees of a trust for such purposes.[2] When broadly one rate of stamp duty was introduced in 1963, no special treatment was needed for charities.[3] But the wheel turned a full circle in 1974 when the rate of duty was doubled again.[4] Relief was then re-introduced in respect of instruments executed on or after 1st August 1974.[5] The position now is that in the case of a conveyance or transfer made to a body of persons established for charitable purposes only, or to the trustees of a trust so established, the duty remains the same as before the Finance Act 1974, approximately 50p per £50 or part of £50. But adjudication is necessary. Conveyances or transfers to charities are equally subject to the relief for "small conveyances", where the appropriate certificate is given; in such cases adjudication is not required.[6]

Value added tax

Value added tax was introduced by the Finance Act 1972 and replaced with effect from 1st April 1973 purchase tax[7] and selective employment tax.[8] The tax is levied on all goods and services supplied in the United Kingdom in the course of a business (which includes a trade profession or vocation). Certain supplies are "zero-rated" and certain supplies are "exempt". There is no special treatment meted out to charities as a class, but, in general, charities do not pay value added tax for the simple reason that they are not supplying goods and services in any commercial sense. In technical terms most charities are "exempt" in that they will not be liable for tax on the goods and services which they supply free of charge or at reduced cost; but they are unable to reclaim "input tax", that is the value added tax charged on goods and services supplied to them.

Nevertheless value added tax is chargeable on the supply of goods and services by a charity, when the supply is in the course of a business carried on by the

---

1 *Ibid.*, Sch. 5, para. 20.
2 FA 1958, s. 34 (6).
3 FA 1963, Sch. 14, Pt. IV.
4 FA 1974, s. 49 and Sch. 11. The changes took effect in Great Britain on 1st May 1974 and in Northern Ireland on 1st August 1974.
5 *Ibid.*, s. 49 (2).
6 See *ibid.*, Sch. 11, paras. 3–4.
7 For relief from purchase tax in certain cases, see Purchase Tax Act 1963, s. 20 (repealed).
8 For refunds of selective employment tax paid by charities, see Selective Employment Payments Act 1966, s. 5 (1) (repealed).

charity.[1] Consequently a charity which has taxable outputs of goods or services e.g. the sale of greetings cards or fancy goods or the provision of catering facilities is required to be registered as a taxable person unless entitled to exemption as a small trader. But a charity which does not make any taxable supplies of goods or services (for example one which provides nothing except free services) is neither required nor allowed to register.[2] A charity which supplies an exempt service e.g. education within the terms of Exemption Group 6 in Schedule 4 to the Finance Act 1972 is not required to register in respect of this exempt service (though it would still be required to register in respect of any taxable supplies of goods or services if these exceeded the limits of taxable turnover, namely £5000).[3]

Where a charity supplies goods or services for the relief of distress to distressed persons at substantially less than cost, e.g. by using donations and gifts to its charitable funds, or grants from central or local government sources, the supply is considered not to be in the course of a business within the meaning of the value added tax legislation: such a supply is therefore outside the scope of the tax.[4] In this context a grant must be a general payment in aid of charitable funds (sometimes called a "block" grant) and not a consideration for specific services such as a capitation fee.

The supply of certain goods by charities is zero-rated in some circumstances.[5] The effect of such zero-rating is that no tax is charged on the supply.[6]

The supply to the Royal National Institute for the Blind, the National Listening Library or other similar charities of magnetic tapes specially adapted for the recording and reproduction of speech for the blind or severely handicapped or of tape recorders designed for the reproduction of sound from such tape or parts and accessories for such tapes and tape recorders is zero-rated.[7] So too is the supply to a charity of wireless receiving sets solely for gratuitous loan to the blind.[8] Also zero-rated is the supply of medical and scientific equipment where it is purchased with funds provided by a charity or from voluntary contributions and is being donated to a designated non-profit-making hospital or research institution solely for use in medical research.[9] The supply to and repair or maintenance for the Royal National Life-boat Institution of any lifeboat is also zero-rated.[10] The zero-rating applies whatever the tonnage and includes rubber dinghies as well as conventional lifeboats.[11]

Where a charity is registered for VAT purposes by reason of the fact that it has ordinary business activities resulting in a gross turnover exceeding £5000 a year zero-rating applies to the supply of any goods donated by a charity established primarily for the relief of distress. The "relief of distress" in this context means the relief of poverty, or the making of provision for the cure or

---

1 FA 1972, s. 2 (2).   2 Customs and Excise Notice No. 701, para. 42 (a).
3 *Ibid.*, No. 700, paras. 12 and 13.
4 See the discussion at 549, *infra.*
5 FA 1972, s. 12 (2). Zero-rated goods and supplies are listed in Sch. 4: *ibid.*
6 *Ibid.*, s. 12 (1).
7 *Ibid.*, Sch. 4, Group 4, Item 1 (as amended by the Value Added Tax (Consolidation) Order 1976 S.I. 1976 No. 128.
8 *Ibid.*, Item 2 (as amended by the Value Added Tax (Consolidation) Order 1976 S.I. 1976 No. 128.
9 FA 1972, Sch. 4, Group 16, Item 3 (as amended by the Value Added Tax (Consolidation) Order 1974 S.I. 1976 No. 128.
10 FA 1972, Sch. 4, Group 10, Item 3.
11 H.M. Customs and Excise Notice No. 701, 47.

mitigation or prevention of, or for the care of persons suffering from or subject to, any disease or infirmity or disability affecting human beings (including the care of women before, during and after child birth). Zero-rating under this item applies to the sale by a charity established primarily for the relief of distress in a charity gift shop or at a fete, bazaar or jumble sale, of new or used goods donated to it, except where they are donated from the stock of a taxable person and their total cost to that person exceeded £10.[1] It does not apply, however, where goods are sold on behalf of their owner by a charity for a commission: in such a case, if the charity is a taxable person the tax applies at the standard rate on the commission charged to the owner for selling his goods.[2]

All goods exported by charities which are registered for VAT purposes are zero-rated and input tax related to them may be reclaimed subject to the usual rules.[3]

Subject to certain conditions, the supply of medical or scientific equipment is zero-rated. The equipment must have been purchased with funds supplied by a charity, or with voluntarily subscribed funds; *and* the equipment must be for donation to a designated non-profit-making hospital or research institution solely for use in medical research, diagnosis or treatment.[4] The relief does not apply to purchases of equipment by hospitals or research institutions for their own use, or to supplies where the hospital or research institution receiving the equipment has contributed wholly or partly towards the purchase funds; and the relief does not extend to consumable or other goods, for example, films, inks, stationery, spare parts and so forth, which are not in themselves identifiable as medical or scientific equipment (even though they may be required for use with or in the repair of equipment properly purchased on a zero-rated basis). The hospital or institution to whom the equipment is to be given must be named in the purchase order, which should be signed by a responsible person in the charitable organisation, and retained by the registered supplier as his authority for zero-rating the transaction. A charitable organisation wishing to import medical or scientific equipment under this provision should make application to the local Customs and Excise VAT office well in advance of importation, giving full particulars, including the proposed date and place of importation.[5]

The provision by a youth club of the facilities available to its members is exempt from value added tax.[6] Similarly educational charities are exempt from accounting for tax on their educational supplies.[7]

In addition to these reliefs the Department of Customs and Excise treats supplies of goods or services to distressed persons[8] at substantially below cost for the relief of their distress as not being made "in the course of business". Such supplies are thus (as has already been said) outside the scope of the tax. "Substantially below cost" in this context means that the charity must charge the distressed person no more than 80% of the actual monetary cost to the charity making the supply. In determining its actual costs incurred in making supplies

---

1 *Ibid.*, 59; and see FA 1972, Sch. 3, para. 6.
2 H.M. Customs and Excise Notice No. 701, 59.
3 FA 1972, Sch. 4, Group 16, Item 2.
4 FA 1972, Sch. 4, Group 16, Item 3.
5 H.M. Customs and Excise Notice No. 701, 59–60.
6 FA 1972, Sch. 5, Group 6, Item 4.
7 FA 1972, Sch. 5, Group 6, Items 1 to 3.
8 For example, meals on wheels.

for the relief of distress the charity is |entitled to take only out-of-pocket expenses into account. Capital expenditure on buildings, notional charges for the depreciation of capital assets, the creation of financial reserves for repairs and maintenance (as opposed to *actual* repair or maintenance costs incurred during the year in question) and the notional cost of any unpaid labour provided by voluntary helpers should all be ignored in making the calculation.[1] The meaning of the expression "relief of distress" has already been discussed.[2] Supplies (including the provision of subsidised holidays) by charities to persons aged 65 years or more, to physically or mentally handicapped persons, to the chronically sick and to the poor, all fall within the definition of "relief of distress". It has been agreed that where charities make free loans of or hire out aids for the disabled at a nominal charge, such supplies will be considered to be "business" supplies. Charities which are registered for VAT purposes and which make such supplies may reclaim tax charged to them on wheelchairs and similar aids purchased on or after 7th April 1976, if the related supplies made by them qualify for zero-rating under items 2 and 3 of Zero-rating Group 14.[3]

Supplies of food and drink (other than alcoholic liquor) made by charities from hospital trolleys, canteens or shops to "in-patients" or "out-patients" in hospitals or other institutions are exempt as to the provision of care.[4] Supplies of stationery, toilet articles or other goods which are neither food nor drink are excluded from the exemption. This exemption does not extend to supplies made to the staff or to visitors, nor does it include supplies made by charities running residential homes or day clubs unless such homes and clubs are themselves approved licensed, registered or exempted from registration by any Minister or other authority. Examples of institutions to which this exemption applies are: old persons' homes and homes for disabled persons, nursing homes, residential homes for mentally disordered persons, homes for children, day nurseries and play groups, Christian Science Houses (i.e. sanatoria).[5]

Mention should also be made of an administrative relief relating to the position of branches of charities. If a charity has branches which enjoy only limited autonomy in managing their financial and other affairs, that charity and its branches constitute a single "legal person" for VAT registration purposes. If, however, the branches of a charity are truly autonomous in that they have complete control over their financial and other affairs, the branches will be treated as separate entities for VAT purposes and a branch will be required to register only if it has a taxable turnover above the exemption limits. If a charity is in any doubt as to the position of its branches for VAT registration purposes, it should consult its local VAT office.[6]

Finally several concessions allowed in connection with charities and the importation of certain goods should be noted:[7]

(1) VAT is waived on imported articles (other than tobacco and alcoholic liquor) given or lent to charitable institutions. The waiver does not apply to articles intended for sale.

---

1 Leaflet No VLD/9/76 available at Customs and Excise VAT offices.
2 See at 548–549, *supra*.
3 FA 1972, Sch. 4, Group 14.
4 FA 1972, Sch. 5, Group 7, Item 4.
5 For the relevant legislation, see H.M. Customs and Excise Notice No. 701, at 79.
6 Leaflet No. VLD/9/76 obtainable at Customs and Excise VAT offices.
7 These concessions are not published officially, but see Goodman Report (1976) 63–64.

(2) The British Red Cross Society is allowed to receive by gift supplies of tobacco free of VAT for distribution to sick or wounded servicemen and disabled ex-servicemen.

(3) VAT is waived on Christmas trees sent as gifts to non-profit-making organisations for public exhibition at Christmas time in connection with charitable activities.

(4) Relief is also given from VAT on gifts of used clothing and medical supplies imported by certain charities for sorting repacking and re-exportation for free distribution abroad.

(5) Units of United States Air Force and Navy stationed in the United Kingdom are allowed to make gifts to charitable organisations (such as old people's homes and orphanages) from stocks of articles, new or used which have been imported into or obtained in the United Kingdom without payment of VAT. The gifts must be of a kind which will be used or consumed by the beneficiaries of the organisation and are not to be sold or used in any way to raise funds. However, liquor and tobacco products are again excluded from this concession.

Payment of VAT is not required on goods imported solely for the purpose of being demonstrated at a meeting or exhibition which is primarily organised for a charitable purpose.[1]

Development land tax

Development land tax is a tax which arises on a disposal of an interest in land situated in the United Kingdom and made on or after 1st August 1976.[2] The tax is payable on the realisation of the development value of the land. A person becomes liable to the tax on the realised development value which accrues on the disposal of the relevant interest in the land, irrespective of that person's residence.[3]

Originally charities were not intended to be exempt in any respect from the tax. However, following the publication of the original White Paper[4] on the Community Land Scheme there was considerable lobbying by charities in general and the churches in particular to secure exemption for charities. Certain concessions were ultimately made, in particular in respect of land held by charities on 12th September 1974, sometimes called pre-White Paper day land, which, subject to certain conditions, is exempt. But the notion that post-White Paper land will bear tax marks the end of a tradition of exempting charities from taxation and sets a precedent that in the eyes of some[5] is unfortunate.

The primary exemption from development land tax relates to interests in land held on 12th September 1974.[6] For this purpose, it should be noted, an interest in land must be treated as held by a charity[7] on that date if, under the

---

1 Value Added Tax (Imported Goods) Relief (No. 1) Order 1973, S.I. 1973 No 327.
2 Development Land Tax Act 1976, s. 1 (1).
3 *Ibid.*, s. 1 (2).
4 White Paper on "Land" (Cmnd. 5730) 12th September 1974.
5 E.g. The National Council of Social Service: see 907 H. of C. Official Report 940, at 965 (15th March 1976) (Mr. Timothy Raison).
6 Development Land Tax Act 1976, s. 24 (1).
7 "Charity" has the same meaning as in TA 1970, s. 360: Development Land Tax Act 1976, s. 47 (1).

will of a person who died before that date, the charity would at that date have been absolutely entitled to that interest if the administration of the deceased's estate had been completed.[1] Again, an interest in land acquired by a charity under a conditional contract entered into on or before 12th September 1974 is treated as held by the charity on that date.[2] The rule laid down is that development land tax is not chargeable on any realised development value accruing to a charity on the disposal of an interest in land which: (*a*) was held by the charity on 12th September 1974; or (*b*) was held by another charity on that date and has at no time between that date and the time of the disposal been held otherwise than by a charity; or (*c*) is the retained interest or the granted interest in relation to a previous disposal of an interest in land which, immediately before that disposal, fell within (*a*) or (*b*) or indeed (*c*) itself and which has at no time between the time of its acquisition and the time at which it is disposed of been held otherwise than by a charity.[3] The situations envisaged by (*a*) and (*b*) are readily comprehensible: the former is the situation where the interest disposed of by the charity was held by that *same* charity on 12th September 1974, while the latter situation is where the interest disposed of by a charity was held by a *different* charity on 12th September 1974 and at all material times in the interim was vested in charity. The wording of (*c*) is lacking in lucidity. It deals in fact with two kinds of interest which are defined elsewhere in the legislation. Both interests arise on a part disposal[4] of an interest in land. The "retained interest" on the part disposed of an interest in land is that interest which by virtue of the chargeable person's previous ownership of the interest disposed of, he has immediately after the disposal.[5] The "granted interest" refers to the interest granted on a part disposal of an interest in land where the owner of that interest grants a lease or other interest out of, or by virtue of his ownership of, his interest or where the owner of that interest grants to another his interest in some but not all of the land in which that interest subsisted before the grant.[6] Accordingly the exemption envisaged by (*c*) applies where there is realised development value accruing to a charity on the disposal of a retained interest (such as a reversion) or a granted interest (such as a leasehold interest) and such interest before it was severed was either (1) on or before 12th September 1974 part and parcel of the interest of the *same* charity as is disposing of it or (2) on 12th September 1974 was part and parcel of the interest of a *different* charity so long as the interest had throughout been vested in charity, or (3) itself a retained or granted interest. An illustration may lighten the darkness. If a charity owned a freehold on 12th September 1974 and later granted a lease to another charity, then provided that either the freehold or the leasehold remain in the ownership of some charity (including, of course, the original charity), when those interests are eventually disposed of by the charity which ultimately holds them they will be exempt from tax.

Where a lease was held by a charity on 12th September 1974 and subsequently became merged in another interest without its ever having been held

---

1 *Ibid.*
2 *Ibid.*, s. 24 (8).
3 Development Land Tax Act 1976, s. 24 (1).
4 "Part disposal" is defined in s. 3 of the Development Land Tax Act 1976 and includes not merely disposal of some portion of the land or some interest (such as a leasehold) in it but also deemed part disposals.
5 Development Land Tax Act 1976, s. 3 (5) (a).
6 *Ibid.*, s. 3 (5) (b).

otherwise than by a charity and then after the merger the combined or "greater" interest is acquired by another charity again without its ever having been held otherwise than by a charity the exemption for the original lease is preserved. The merged interest is deemed to continue as a separate entity for the purpose of the exemption regarding interests in land held by charity on 12th September 1974.[1] A calculation is made apportioning the consideration to the interest entitled to the exemption in order to ascertain the amount of exemption due to the charity.[2] However, after the date when the lease would have come to an end by effluxion of time the exemption ceases to operate:[3] the exemption does not survive the notional death of the notional lease.

There is a parallel provision[4] covering the case of an option held on 12th September 1974 which is subsequently exercised without its ever having been held otherwise than by a charity, and the interest acquired by virtue of the exercise of the option is subsequently acquired by *another* charity without that interest ever having been held otherwise than by a charity. The exemption for the original option is preserved despite its merger in the interest under the option.[4]

The exemption in respect of interests in land held by charities on 12th September 1974 is not a final and absolute exemption: it is, so to speak, an exemption *nisi*, because if the charity ceases at any time after an exempt disposal to be a charity it will then become liable to the tax on the disposal.[5] Immediately after the charity ceases to be a charity the amount of realised development value treated as accruing is the amount of the exemption which was obtained on the original disposal. But such amount of realised development value is limited to the market value of the property (if any) held by the body immediately before it ceases to be a charity and which is not immediately after that time held for charitable purposes by another body.[6] Consequently if a charity is wound up but its assets are applied *cy-près* there is no charge to the tax as there would be no property which does not remain impressed with trusts in favour of charitable purposes. In other cases where a charity ceases to be a charity, its liability to development land tax remains, but the realised development value is limited to the value[7] of any property[8] held.

Where a charity begins a project of material development,[9] the beginning of

---

1 *Ibid.*, s. 24 (2).   2 *Ibid.*, Sch. 2, para. 8.
3 *Ibid.*, s. 24 (3).
4 *Ibid.*, s. 24 (4).
5 *Ibid.*, s. 24 (6).
6 *Ibid.*, s. 24 (7).
7 I.e. the open market value: Land Development Tax Act 1976, s. 7 (1).
8 This refers to all property not just land.
9 "Material development" means any development other than: (a) development for which planning permission is granted by a general development order for the time being in force, or would be so granted, but for a direction given under the order, or a condition imposed in any planning permission granted or deemed to be granted otherwise than by such an order, and which is carried out so as to comply with any condition or limitation subject to which planning permission is or would be so granted; and (b) development which is excluded from being material development by Sch. 4, Pt. II: Development Land Tax Act 1976, s. 7 (7). "Development" means the carrying out of building, engineering, mining or other operations in, on, over or under land, or the making of any material change in the use of any buildings or other land, subject to the further provisions of the Town and Country Planning Act 1971: *ibid.*, s. 47 (1). "Project of material development" is any project or scheme in pursuance of which any material development is, or is to be carried out: *ibid.*, Sch. 1, para. 1.

which is the occasion of a deemed disposal,[1] and which relates to a building or to other land to be used in whole or in part for the purposes of the charity, and the land was *not* held by a charity on 12th September 1974, there is a qualified exemption from the tax. In such circumstances, the realised development value properly attributable to such property is deferred until the first subsequent disposal which is neither a deemed disposal nor, if the relevent interest is a lease, a surrender of a lease in exchange for another lease back of the same land or substantially the same land.[2] A building or other land is treated as used by a charity if and to the extent that it is occupied solely by the charity for its own use, or is otherwise used solely for carrying out the charitable purposes of that charity.[3] Unless it appears to the Board or, on an appeal, to the Commissioners that a project of material development relates exclusively to property to be used by charity in this way, the proportion properly attributable to the property to be used by the charity and the method of apportionment adopted shall be such as appears to the Board or, on appeal, to the Commissioners concerned to be just and reasonable.[4] If there is a partial exemption in respect of a merged lease or option which was held on 12th September 1974[5] the value of the exemption is deducted first from the realised development value, and it is a proportion of the remainder that is taken as deferred.[6]

If subsequently the whole, or any part of a building or other land for which deferment is granted ceases to constitute property used by a charity and either ceases to be held by a charity, or a non-qualifying use is established, then the deferment ends and a liability for development land tax arises.[7] A non-qualifying use is established when the building, or other land, or part thereof, is used in such circumstances that it does not constitute property used by a charity for at least half of any continuous period of 24 months.[8] Accordingly the non-qualifying use will be taken to be established at the expiry of the 365th day in the period of the non-qualifying use.[9]

A lease is not treated as a disposal which brings into play a charge to deferred development land tax if it is made on such terms as to secure that the land is used for the charitable purposes of the charity.[10] Where an interest for which there is development land tax deferment is part of an assembly of land or interests in land, the disposal of that assembly is treated as a disposal of that part and so brings into play the charge to development land tax.[11]

---

1 See *ibid.*, s. 2 (1).
2 *Ibid.*, s. 25 (1).
3 *Ibid.*, s. 25 (2).
4 *Ibid.*, s. 25 (3).
5 See *ibid.*, s. 24 (1), (2) and (4).
6 *Ibid.*, s. 25 (4).
7 *Ibid.*, s. 25 (6).
8 *Ibid.*, s. 25 (7).
9 *Ibid.*
10 *Ibid.*, s. 25 (8).
11 *Ibid.*, s. 25 (9).

Chapter 47

Rating

Introduction

HISTORY

It is desirable, and indeed necessary to a proper understanding of the decided cases, to say a little about the history of charities under the rating law.[1] After earlier uncertainty it was established as a result of the decision of the House of Lords in *Mersey Docks and Harbour Board* v. *Cameron*[2] that hereditaments, other than places of public religious worship, belonging to charitable (including ecclesiastical) organisations and held or used for their charitable purposes did not possess any immunity in law from liability to rates unless under or in accordance with the provisions of statute. A number of local Acts made such provision, as did some public and general Acts, notably the Scientific Societies Act 1843 (which gave rise to a considerable body of case law), the Sunday and Ragged Schools (Exemption from Rating) Act 1869 and the Voluntary Schools Act 1897.

From 1865 onwards some local authorities did as a matter of practice accord a measure of relief to charities not possessing statutory rights of immunity. This was done by a variety of administrative measures, some of doubtful validity (for example, by omitting hereditaments from the rating list or rating them only on a nominal valuation), and, after 1925, by the exercise of a statutory power to remit or reduce rates. There was, however, no discernible pattern still less uniformity, in these practices.

In 1955 Parliament provided, for the first time, statutory relief from rates as a general principle applicable to all charities and, speaking generally, confirmed some of the various reliefs which had been given extra-statutorily by rating authorities since about 1865.[3] The provision was only a stop gap. A committee was set up under Sir Fred Pritchard in 1958 and its Report[4] ("the Pritchard Report") published in 1959 was followed by the enactment of section 11 of the Rating and Valuation Act 1961 which gave effect to a majority of the Pritchard

---

1 For a fuller survey, see Report of the Committee on the Rating of Charities and Kindred Bodies (1959, Cmnd, 831); Owen, *English Philanthropy 1660–1690* (1964) 340–345.

2 (1865), 11 H.L.C. 443.

3 Rating and Valuation (Miscellaneous Provisions) Act 1955, s. 8; repealed by the General Rate Act 1967, s. 117 (1) and Sch. 14. For criticisms of the 1955 Act: see Waters, "The Rating of Charitable and Similar Organisations" (1959) Current Legal Problems 115.

4 Report of the Committee on the Rating of Charities and Kindred Bodies (1959, Cmnd. 831); discussed by Waters (1960) 23 M.L.R. 68–72.

Committee's recommendations.[1] Section 11 of the 1961 Act was, in due course, replaced by section 40 of the General Rates Act 1967—a consolidating Act. It is this provision which, in the main, contains the law relating to the rating of charities, although the section immediately preceding it is also relevant since it relieves places of religious worship from rates.

SCHEME OF THE LEGISLATION

The scheme of the legislation now in force in England[2] is to provide for three classes of rating relief in respect of charities and complete rating relief in respect of places of public worship, church halls and certain other buildings ancillary to places of public worship. The categories of rating relief afforded to charities comprise: (1) mandatory relief for most charities to the extent of one-half of the rates for which they would otherwise be chargeable; (2) discretionary relief for most charities in excess of that mandatory relief; (3) discretionary relief only for certain specified charities. Mandatory rating relief from the whole of the rates is granted in respect of the "religious" buildings already mentioned.

Mandatory relief for charities

Mandatory relief may be claimed in respect of any hereditament occupied by, or by trustees for, a charity and wholly or mainly used for charitable purposes (whether of that charity or of that and other charities).

The word "hereditament" in this context means property which is or may become liable to a rate being a unit of such property which is, or would fall to be, shown as a separate item in the valuation list.[3] "Charity" means an institution or other organisation established for charitable purposes only; "organisation" includes any persons administering a trust.[4] But a charitable institution falling within Schedule 8 to the General Rate Act 1967 is not eligible for mandatory rating relief.[5]

Two substantive questions arise. First, are the premises in question occupied by a charity? Secondly, are the premises wholly or mainly used for charitable purposes? Only if both questions are answered affirmatively is mandatory relief available.

OCCUPATION BY A CHARITY

In some cases it is clear that the charity or trustees of the charity are in occupation of the relevant hereditament. But more difficult questions arise where the charity has provided a house for servants or staff. The leading case on this problem is

---

1 For the discussion see Maurice, "Rating Relief for Charities" (1964) 28 Conv. N.S. 20.

2 For commentaries on the Irish legislation, see Delany, "Rating Exemption on the ground of Charitable or Public Use" (1960) 13 N.I.L.Q. 316; Carswell, "Rating Exemption and Charitable Purposes" (1965) 16 N.I.L.Q. 88; Lowry, "Some Reflections on Ratings" (1966) 17 N.I.L.Q. 256; Brady, "Charitable Purposes and Ratings Exemption in Ireland" (1968) 3 Ir. Jur. (N.S.) 114; Brady, "House of Lords, Charities and Rating Relief in Northern Ireland" (1973) 24 N.I.L.Q. 106.

3 General Rate Act 1967, s. 115 (1).

4 *Ibid.*, s. 40 (9).

5 *Ibid.*, s. 40 (2).

the decision of the House of Lords in *Glasgow Corporation* v. *Johnstone*.[1] The congregational board of a church claimed rating relief in respect of a house occupied rent-free as a residence by the church officer whom they employed on a whole-time basis at a weekly wage. The house formed part of the same building as the church and indeed the only access to the house was through the church. It was a condition of his employment that while his employment lasted he should occupy the house with his wife and that he should vacate it on termination of that employment. He was required to attend the services, check the collections and keep the church premises clean and tidy; part of his duties were those of a caretaker. However if he had resided near the church he could still have carried out his duties, though with some loss of efficiency. It was held that the house was occupied by the charity since the church officer's residence was directed to the more efficient performance of his duties. Lord GUEST made it clear that the fact that a servant or officer is required as a term of his employment to reside in a particular house is not *per se* sufficient: the requirement must be with a view to the more efficient performance of his duties.

The authorities on vicarious occupation were helpfully summarised by Lord UPJOHN in *Valuation Comr. for Northern Ireland* v. *Fermanagh Protestant Board of Education*:[2]

"First, if it is essential to the performance of the duties of the occupying servant that he should occupy the particular house, or it may be a house within a closely defined perimeter, then it being established that this is the mutual understanding of the master and the servant, the occupation for rating and other ancillary purposes is that of the master and not of the servant. . . . Secondly, there is the case where it is not essential for the servant to occupy a particular house or to live within a particular perimeter, but by so doing he can better perform his duties as servant to a material degree; then, in such case, if there is an express term in the contract between master and servant that he shall so reside, the occupation for rating and ancillary purposes is treated as the occupation of the master and not of the servant."

The claims for rating relief in the case of *Northern Ireland Valuation Comr.* v. *Fermanagh Protestant Board of Education*[3] related to six dwelling-houses within the precincts of a school which were used as residences for assistant masters and the house of the school's vice-principal, also within the precincts. A distinction was drawn. Although there was no express term requiring either masters or the vice-principal to reside in their respective houses, an obligation so to reside could be implied in the case of the vice-principal from the nature of the duties he had to perform; no such implications arose in the case of the assistant masters whose residence in a particular house was a convenience rather than a necessity. Accordingly only in the case of the vice-principal's house was the charity in occupation. Lord PEARSON said that more weight should be ascribed to the practical realities than to the conveyancing:[4]

"Of course the contractual arrangements are important factors to be taken into account in deciding what is the dominant character and purpose

---

1 [1965] A.C. 609.   2 [1969] 1 W.L.R. 1708, at 1722.
3 [1969] 1 W.L.R. 1708; and see *Windsor University* v. *City of Windsor Assessment Comr.*, [1965] 51 D.L.R. (2d) 112 (President's on-campus house).
4 [1969] 1 W.L.R. 1708, at 1725.

of the occupation, but they could be artificially devised for securing advantages in respect of taxation or rating, and therefore should not be taken as affording the sole test or necessarily in all cases the decisive test for the identification of the rateable occupier".

This dictum echoes what was said in *Glasgow Corporation* v. *Johnstone*[1] about a capricious (express) requirement that a servant should live in a particular house, and casts doubt on contracts in which an express obligation to reside is included but in which the better performance of the employee's duties is not substantially furthered by the residence. Such contracts will not ground a successful claim for rating relief.

On the other hand a house provided for a groundsman and caretaker at a school was held to be occupied by the school in *Hirst* v. *Sergent*.[2] The house backed on to the school sports ground and the employee was able to prevent vandalism. There was no written agreement of employment or of tenancy but it was clear that the groundsman's work as a caretaker required him to live there and the absence of an express contractual provision to that effect was irrelevant. The same applies to a house occupied by the warden at a bird reserve[3] or a warden of National Trust property whose contracted duties and residence are of material assistance to the carrying out of the trust's activities.[4]

WHOLLY OR MAINLY USED FOR CHARITABLE PURPOSES

In addition to requiring that premises shall be "occupied by . . . a charity" the provision laying down the conditions for mandatory relief requires that the premises shall be "wholly or mainly used for charitable purposes (whether of that charity or of that and other charities)". The distinction between the two conditions is not always very clear. But the latter requirement in respect of the user of the premises for charitable purposes was considered by the House of Lords in *Glasgow Corporation* v. *Johnstone*. There, it will be remembered, the church board were held to be occupiers and so their use of the house occupied by the church officer fell to be considered. The appellants contended that it was used as a residence and for no other purpose. The church board used the house to have a servant on the spot to assist them in the more efficient performance of their charitable activities. Lord REID said:

> "I think that it is much too narrow a view simply to see whether any charitable activity is carried on in the house. . . . If the use which the charity makes of the premises is directly to facilitate the carrying out of its main charitable purposes, that is, in my view, sufficient to satisfy the requirement that the premises are used for charitable purposes."

Lord HODSON agreed with the view that once the conclusion is reached that the charity is the occupier the viewpoint of the occupier and not of the resident must be taken. Occupation by trustees must as a rule be notional and if the use to which the house were put were the test it would be seldom that a dwelling-

---

1 [1965] A.C. 609, at 629, *per* Lord GUEST.
2 (1966), 111 Sol. Jo. 54.
3 *Royal Society for the Protection of Birds* v. *Hornsea Urban District Council*, [1975] R.A. 26.
4 *National Trust for Places of Historic Interest or Natural Beauty* v. *Comr. of Valuation*, [1975] R.A. 121.

house would qualify. The use to which the premises were being put by the occupiers in *Glasgow Corporation* v. *Johnstone* was to house a resident church officer for the proper and more efficient carrying out of those church affairs which were the responsibility of that officer. Lord EVERSHED delivered a concurring speech and Lord WILBERFORCE agreed with Lord REID while Lord GUEST dissented on this.

Rating relief can be claimed by a charity in respect of premises which it occupies if the use which it makes of them to quote Lord REID,[1] is "wholly ancillary to" or "directly facilitates" the carrying out of its main charitable purpose. The ambit of these expressions was explored by the House of Lords in the later case of *Oxfam* v. *Birmingham City District Council*[2]. Obviously, an office where the necessary clerical and administrative work of a charity is done is being used directly to facilitate the main object of the charity, and that point was conceded by the rating authority in the *Oxfam* case. Again, the letting of property to lodgers so that the rent can be applied to the purposes of the charity is not a user of the premises wholly ancillary to or directly facilitating the main purpose of the charity.[3] It is otherwise where the property is let in fulfilment of a charitable purpose as in *Soldiers', Sailors' and Airmen's Families Association* v. *Merton Corporation*[4] where suites were provided for the widows and unmarried daughters of officers on "a very unusual kind of tenancy" which gave the association a very tight control of the suites and put the association in paramount occupation of the suites. It is also directly facilitating the purposes of a holiday centre for miners and their families to admit outsiders whose payments would help the charity to meet its overheads and be run economically. In the case of *Oxfam* v. *Birmingham City District Council*[5] itself Oxfam claimed relief from rates in respect of its gift shops. These shops which were staffed by voluntary helpers were used for the sale of articles (mostly clothing) donated to Oxfam, the profit from the sales being applied to the objects of Oxfam. Lord CROSS OF CHELSEA who delivered the leading speech drew the line:[6]

> "so as to exclude from relief user for the purpose of getting in, raising or earning money for the charity, as opposed to user for purposes directly related to the achievement of the objects of the charity".

The distinction drawn in *Aldous* v. *Southwark London Borough Council*[7] between using premises for the getting in of money by managing charity property and using them to raise fresh money was not supportable. The charity gift shops could not be said to be directly facilitating the main object of the charity and so there could be no relief in respect of them. But a shop selling nothing but goods manufactured by the blind would be entitled to relief: the sale of such goods would directly facilitate the charitable object of providing employment for the blind.

In the words of one Government spokesman in the House of Lords the *Oxfam* decision "put an unfortunate revenue cat among the charitable pigeons".[7]

---

1 [1965] A.C. 609, at 622.
2 [1976] A.C. 126.
3 *Polish Historical Institution* v. *Hove Corporation* (1963), 61 L.G.R. 438.
4 [1967] 1 W.L.R. 127.
5 [1976] A.C. 126.
6 *Ibid.*, at 146.
7 [1968] 1 W.L.R. 1671.
8 House of Lords Official Report, Vol. 371, col. 85 (Baroness Birk).

Remedial legislation to extend mandatory and discretionary relief to charity gift shops is contained in the Rating (Charity Shops) Act 1976. In future, a hereditament will be treated as used wholly or mainly for charitable purposes if it is used wholly or mainly for the sale of goods donated to a charity and the proceeds of sale are applied for the purposes of the charity.

The distinction drawn in the *Oxfam* case between user for the purpose of getting in, raising or earning money for the charity as opposed to user for purposes directly related to the achievement of the objects of the charity still remains, qualified only in the particular case of charity gift shops.

It remains only to consider the authority of *Aldous* v. *Southwark London Borough Council*[1] in the light of the critical dicta of Lord CROSS OF CHELSEA in the *Oxfam* case. The *Aldous* case concerned the rating of certain hereditaments owned and occupied by the estate governors of Dulwich College. The estate governors held and managed the property of the trust other than that held by the college governors which administered Dulwich College and Alleyn's School. The Court of Appeal held that four hereditaments occupied by the estate governors were entitled to relief, namely (1) the estate offices from which the estate and funds vested in the governors were managed (2) the estate work-shops and stores used in connection with the maintenance and repair of the houses on the estate, (3) a house used as a residence by the estate bailiff or fore-man, and (4) a cottage used as a residence by the wood keeper. Counsel on both sides in the *Oxfam* case rejected the distinction drawn by Lord DENNING M.R. and WINN L.J. in the *Aldous* case between using premises for the getting in of money by managing charity property and using them to raise fresh money and the distinction was rejected by Lord CROSS OF CHELSEA. Dealing with the actual decision Lord CROSS OF CHELSEA said:[2]

> "The truth is that the running of the Dulwich Estate was analogous to the carrying on of a business and that all the hereditaments in question—including the Estate Offices—were being used for activities which had as little to do with the furtherance of education as the running of the boarding houses in Hove had to do with research into modern Polish history."

Nevertheless he did not go so far as to say that the decision in the *Aldous* case was wrong on the facts: it could possibly be justified on the basis that there was a trust for the management and exploitation of the charity property which had to be regarded as itself a separate trust. But if that was so, the case was a very special one which affords no general guidance on the interpretation of the section.

Mandatory rating relief may also be claimed in respect of any hereditament held upon trust for use as an almshouse.[3] The meaning of the word "almshouse" has already been discussed in relation to the tax exemption for income from the ownership or occupation of land.[4]

Discretionary relief in excess of mandatory relief

Rating authorities have the power, i.e. discretion, to reduce or remit the payment of rates in respect of any hereditament qualifying for mandatory relief.

---

1 [1968] 1 W.L.R. 1671.   2 [1976] A.C. 126, at 146.
3 General Rate Act 1967, s. 40 (1) (b).   4 See 540, *supra*.

Hereditaments occupied by charities or held on trust as almshouses and qualifying for mandatory rating relief may get further relief and the combined effect of the mandatory relief and the discretionary relief may be that factual exemption is achieved.

Discretionary relief only

Certain charities are expressly excluded from mandatory relief although their occupation of the relevant hereditaments *prima facie* falls within the wording of section 40 (1) (a) of the 1967 Act. They are not however excluded from the possibility of getting discretionary relief. The charities in question are those institutions listed in Schedule 8 to the 1967 Act. The Minister of Housing and Local Government has power by order to amend the list. The list is now as follows:

1. The universities of Birmingham, Bristol, Cambridge, Durham, East Anglia, Essex, Exeter, Hull, Keele, Kent at Canterbury, Lancaster, Leeds, Leicester, Liverpool, London, Manchester, Newcastle-upon-Tyne, Nottingham, Oxford, Reading, Sheffield, Southampton, Sussex, Wales, Warwick and York, the Loughborough University of Technology, the University of Aston in Birmingham, the City University, Brunel University, the University of Surrey, the University of Bradford, the Bath University of Technology, the University of Salford and the Open University, but exclusive in the case of the University of London of the institution of that university known as Goldsmith's College.

2. The colleges, institutions and schools of the universities of Durham, London and Wales, with the exception of—

(a) the following colleges of the University of Durham, that is to say, the College of the Venerable Bede, St. Chad's College and St. John's College; and

(b) the following colleges and institute of the University of London, that is to say, New College, Richmond College, the Neological department of King's College, London as defined in the King's College London (Transfer) Act 1908, the Lister Institute of Preventive Medicine and Heythrop College.

3. The Federated Institutes of the British Postgraduate Medical Federation, with the exception of the Institute of Cancer Research.

4. The University of Manchester Institute of Science and Technology.

5. The London Graduate School of Business Studies.

6. The colleges and halls in the universities of Oxford and Cambridge.

Procedure for obtaining relief

APPLICATION FOR RELIEF

Mandatory relief in respect of hereditaments occupied by charities or held upon trust for use as an almshouse must be claimed by giving notice in writing to the rating authority,[1] but no special form is required. If the hereditament in question

---

1 General Rate Act 1967, s. 40 (1).

is qualified for relief, then the amount of rates chargeable in respect of the hereditament for any period during which it is so qualified, being a period beginning
not earlier than the rate period[1] in which the notice is given, is not to exceed
one-half of the amount which would otherwise be chargeable.[2] The relief then
continues while the hereditament is qualified but if the hereditament ceases
to be qualified for a time the relief must be claimed again.[3]

So far as *discretionary* relief is concerned there is, of course, no room for any
claim: the relief is entirely *ex gratia* and cannot be insisted on as of right. There
is therefore no set procedure for soliciting discretionary relief.

REMEDIES FOR ENFORCEMENT OF RELIEF

The right to *mandatory* relief in respect of hereditaments occupied by charities or
held upon trust for use as an almshouse may be enforced by seeking a declaration
in the High Court,[4] by an appeal against the rate to the Crown Court,[5] or by
refusing to pay the rate demand and contesting the subsequent application by
the rating authority to the magistrates for the issue of a distress warrant.[6] In the
last mentioned case the magistrates may not have jurisdiction if the facts are
complicated and disputed.[7]

A rating appeal to the Crown Court must be commenced by giving notice
to the appropriate officer of the Crown Court within 21 days from the date of
publication of the rate, or the act or thing done by the rating authority, or the
giving of notice to the rating authority as to the neglect or omission concerned,
whichever is the latest.[8]

In relation to *discretionary* relief the only circumstances in which legal
proceedings might be contemplated would be where a rating authority wished
to grant relief but feared that the institution in question was one which did not
fall within the relevant provisions as to qualification[9]. In such a case amicable
proceedings to obtain a declaration are possible.

Mandatory relief for places of religious worship and ancillary premises

Mandatory rating relief in the form of total exemption from rates is available
in respect of places of public religious worship and various buildings ancillary
thereto. No hereditament falling within the relevant statutory definitions of
"places of public religious worship" or the various specified ancillary buildings
thereto is liable to be rated for any period.

---

1 Rate period means "a year or part of a year, being a year or part for which a rate is
made": see *ibid.*, s. 115 (1).
2 *Ibid.*, s. 40 (1).
3 *Ibid.*, s. 40 (1), proviso.
4 E.g. *Soldiers', Sailors' and Airmen's Families Association* v. *Merton Corporation* [1967]
1 W.L.R. 127, C.A.; *Wynn* v. *Skegness Urban District Council*, [1967] 1 W.L.R. 52.
5 See General Rate Act 1967, s. 7; Courts Act 1971, s. 8, Schs. 1 and 9.
6 E.g. *Hirst* v. *Sargent* (1966), 12 R.R.C. 234; *Evans* v. *Brook*, [1959] 2 All E.R. 399;
Wellesley Nautical School v. *Blyth Borough Council* (1960), 6 R.R.C. 152.
7 See *Evans* v. *Brook*, [1959] 2 All E.R. 399, at 402, *per* Lord PARKER C.J.
8 General Rate Act 1967, s. 7 (1); S.I. 1971 No. 1292.
9 *Ibid.*, s. 40 (5).

Disputes as to whether particular premises are exempt are heard first by the local valuation court which decides how the hereditament should be entered in the valuation list. Any person who appeared before a local valuation court on the hearing of an appeal and is aggrieved by its decision may appeal within the prescribed period to the Lands Tribunal. The prescribed period is currently 28 days from the date of the decision of the local valuation court.[1] From the Lands Tribunal an appeal lies to the Court of Appeal.

PLACES OF PUBLIC RELIGIOUS WORSHIP

The places of public religious worship which enjoy exemption from rates comprise places of public religious worship which belong to the Church of England or to the Church in Wales or which are for the time being certified as required by law as places of religious worship.[2] No great difficulty should be occasioned by the question whether a particular public worshipping place belongs[3] to the Church of England or the Church in Wales. It is a question of fact whether premises used by Protestant dissenters, Roman Catholics, Jews or any other religious denomination are *certified* as places of religious worship as required by the Places of Worship Registration Act 1855. Certification under the 1855 Act applies only to the premises of religious bodies other than the Church of England and the Church in Wales. Moreover certification does not confer automatic exemption from rates. The registration may be challenged by the rating authority[4].

First, in order to qualify for exemption from rates the premises must form a *separate* hereditament. Accordingly a school chapel may be a place of public religious worship,[5] but it will not be exempt if it forms part of the hereditament comprising the school.[6]

Secondly, the hereditament must be a place of "religious worship". These words were considered recently by the Court of Appeal in *R. v. Registrar General, Ex parte Segerdal*,[7] where the Church of Scientology applied unsuccessfully for an order of *mandamus* directing registration of its chapel at East Grinstead under the Places of Worship Registration Act 1855. Lord DENNING M.R. said that:[8]

> " 'place of meeting for religious worship'. . . connotes . . . a place of which the principal use is as a place where people come together as a congregation or assembly to do reverence to God. It need not be the God which the Christians worship. It may be another God, or an unknown God, but it

---

1 The period prescribed by rules under Lands Tribunal Act 1949, s. 3: see General Rate Act 1967, s. 77; and see Lands Tribunal Rules 1975 (S.I. 1975 No. 299) r. 9 (1).

2 General Rate Act 1967, s. 39 (1) (a).

3 The word is to be understood in its everyday sense: *cf. Re Miller, ex parte Official Receiver*, [1893] 1 Q.B. 327.

4 *Church of Jesus Christ of Latter-Day Saints* v. *Henning*, [1964] A.C. 420.

5 *Shrewsbury Schools* v. *Shrewsbury Borough Council and Plumpton (Valuation Officer)* (1960), 7 R.R.C. 313 (Lands Tribunal).

6 *Shrewsbury School (Governors)* v. *Hudd (Valuation Officer)* (1966), 13 R.R.C., 21 (Lands Tribunal).

7 [1970] 2 Q.B. 697.

8 *Ibid.*, at 707.

must be reverence to a deity. There may be exceptions. For instance, Buddhist temples are properly described as places of meeting for religious worship. But apart from exceptional cases of that kind, . . . the governing idea behind the words 'place of meeting for religious worship' is that it should be a place for the worship of God."

BUCKLEY L.J. said,[1] "Worship I take to be something which must have some at least of the following characteristics: submission to the object worshipped, veneration of that object, praise, thanksgiving, prayer or intercession . . . I do not say that you would need to find every element in every act which could properly be described as worship, but when you find an act which contains none of those elements, in my judgment it cannot answer to the description of an act of worship." The Church of Scientology failed in its claim because its creed appeared "to be more a *philosophy* of the existence of man or of life, rather than a religion".[2] There was "nothing in it of reverence for God or a deity, but simply instruction in a philosophy".[3]

The showing of religious films to an audience as part of a service can constitute public religious worship.[4] But a performance of the trial scene from *The Merchant of Venice* is obviously not an act of worship.[5] Presumably a performance of a nativity play or miracle play is capable of being an act of worship, though much, no doubt, would depend on the circumstances of the performance.

Thirdly, the religious worship must be *public*. The words "public religious worship" had their genesis in the Poor Rate Exemption Act 1833, and bear the same meaning as they did in that Act. This was made clear by Lord PEARCE in *Church of Jesus Christ of Latter-Day Saints*[6] v. *Henning* which concerned a claim that the Mormon Temple at Godstone should be exempt from rates as a place of public religious worship. The Temple was not open to the public at large, but only to a selected class of the Mormon sect known as "Mormons of good standing" who were in possession of a form of certificate known as "a recommend". The House of Lords refused rating exemption to the Temple. Lord PEARCE pointed out that the Poor Rate Exemption Act 1833, from which the words "public religious worship" were derived, was passed with the intention of extending the privileges of exemption enjoyed by the Anglican churches to similar places of worship belonging to other denominations. Since the Church of England worshipped with open doors and its worship was in that sense public, it was unlikely that the legislators intended by the word "public" some more subjective meaning which would embrace in the phrase "public religious worship" any congregational worship observed behind doors closed to the public. Lord PEARCE found it impossible therefore to hold that the words "places of public religious worship" included places which, though from the worshippers' point of view they were public as opposed to domestic, yet in the more

---

1 *Ibid.*, at 709.

2 *Ibid.*, at 707, *per* Lord DENNING M.R.

3 *Ibid.*

4 *British Advent Missions, Ltd.* v. *Cane and Westminster City Council* (1954), 48 R. & I.T. 60 (Lands Tribunal).

5 *Walton-le-Dale Urban District Council* v. *Greenwood* (1911), 105 L.T. 547 (such a performance prevented premises from being *exclusively* appropriated to public religious worship).

6 [1964] A.C. 420.

ordinary sense were not public since the public was excluded.[1] Lord REID, Lord MORRIS OF BORTH-Y-GEST and Lord DEVLIN agreed with Lord PEARCE.[2] Lord MORRIS OF BORTH-Y-GEST said:[3]

> "The conception of public religious worship involves the coming together for corporate worship of a congregation or meeting or assembly of people; it further involves that the worship is in a place which is open to all properly disposed persons who wish to be present."

Mention should perhaps also be made of the Australian Case of *Association of the Franciscan Order of Friars Minor* v. *City of Kew*[4] where in considering a statutory exemption for "land used exclusively for public worship" LOWE J. held, *inter alia*, that the chapel of an Enclosed Order of Carmelite Nuns was not exempted. He said that "worship to be public must . . . be open without discrimination to the relevant public". By the word "relevant" he left open the question of how universal and undiscriminating must be the admission of the public. The question, as Lord PEARCE pointed out in *Henning*,[5] is one of fact and difficult questions might arise whether some discrimination is insufficient to deprive the worship of its public character. The fact that in an ordinary parish church there is a legal right in the incumbent to exclude people who are not parishioners[6] does not render the worship at the parish church other than public, because in point of practice the parish churches of England are open to everyone and anyone who chooses to come and is ready to be well behaved.[7]

There is no requirement, as there was under the Act of 1833, that the hereditament for which exemption is claimed must be *exclusively* used for public religious worship. In deciding whether a hereditament is a place of public religious worship the matter must be looked at broadly, and a hereditament is not disqualified from exemption because it contains accommodation not strictly ancillary to public religious worship. This is amply demonstrated by the decision of the Lands Tribunal in *Board of Directors of Ninth Church of Christ Scientist* v. *Westminster City Council and Cane*[8] which concerned premises in Marsham Street, Westminster, known as the Ninth Church of Christ Scientist. The premises comprised an auditorium used as a Christian Science Church, a Sunday School and seven smaller rooms. These seven smaller rooms were entered in the valuation list as the rateable portion of the church and the appellant board claimed exemption in respect of them as a place of public religious worship. The seven rooms were: a members' room containing notices, correspondence and other matters of interest to members and open to daily use by them; a sales literature room, used for committee meetings and also on one day a week for the sale and lending to the public of Christian Science literature; a committee room; a board room; a clerk's room; a treasurer's room and a crèche in which small children could be cared for while their parents attended

---

1 [1964] A.C. 420, at 440.
2 Lord EVERSHED felt considerable doubt but did not disagree: see *ibid.*, at 434.
3 *Ibid.*, at 435.
4 [1944] 3 V.L.R. 199.
5 [1964] A.C. 420, at 440.
6 See *Cole* v. *Police Constable 443A*, [1937] 1 K.B. 316.
7 See *per* Lord DENNING M.R. in *Henning* v. *Church of Jesus Christ of Latter-Day Saints*, [1962] 1 W.L.R. 1091, at 1097.
8 [1958], 3 R.R.C. 35 (Lands Tribunal); distinguishing *Springfield Synagogue* v. *Gladwin* (1957), 2 R.R.C. 338 (Lands Tribunal); and see *Saskatoon Episcopal Corporation* v. *Saskatoon City* [1936] 2 W.W.R. 91.

service. Sir William Fitzgerald held that the wording of the statute indicated that the matter should be viewed broadly and that the church as a whole, including the seven rooms, was a place of public religious worship within the meaning of the statute and was therefore wholly exempt from rates.

Premises are used for the purposes of public religious worship none the less because some of the minor or less important parts of those premises are not used for public worship.[1] But any parts which are not ancillary must be minor or less important parts, so that premises used for the business purposes of a religious organisation are not rendered exempt because of the presence on the premises of a chapel used for public religious worship.[2]

ANCILLARY PREMISES

Certain buildings ancillary to places of public religious worship are also exempt from rating. They comprise: "any church hall, chapel hall or similar building used in connection with any such place of public religious worship and so used for the purposes of the organisation responsible for the conduct of public religious worship in that place".[3] These hereditaments are exempt whether they form a separate hereditament or merely constitute part of one hereditament with the place of religious worship in connection with which they are used. There is no requirement that the hereditament for which exemption is claimed must be *exclusively* used for the specified purpose, though doubtless the specified purpose should be the main or at least a substantial use.[4]

The meaning of the words "church hall, chapel hall or similar building" was discussed in *West London Methodist Mission Trustees* v. *Holborn Borough Council*[5] by the Divisional Court. The hereditament with which the court was concerned consisted of Kingsway Hall, which was for all practical purposes a Methodist church or chapel and a building called Wesley House which adjoined it. The latter building was used for the purposes of a youth club, small religious meetings, sales of work, church socials, a luncheon club, mission offices, mission committee meetings, living accommodation for resident staff, a Sunday school, a crèche and a roof playground. Lord GODDARD C.J. thought it quite obvious that it was a building akin to a church hall or chapel hall and so within the statutory wording: it was a building in which a great number of activities of, and in connection with, the Methodist church were conducted. He refused to apply a structural criterion in judging what was a "similar building", saying:[6]

> "Architecturally, I dare say, it is not what one thinks of as a church hall, but I am quite certain that this section is not to be tested by some architectural test."

An extensive and most helpful discussion of the phrase "any church hall, chapel hall or similar building" is to be found in the Northern Ireland case of *Mageean*

---

1 *Stradling* v. *Higgins*, [1932] 1 Ch. 143, at 152, *per* MAUGHAM J. The case was on a provision in the Places of Worship (Enfranchisement) Act 1920 but is relevant to the 1967 Act: *Rogers* v. *Lewisham Borough Council*, [1951] 2 K.B. 768, at 776, *per* BIRKETT L.J.
2 *Morley* v. *Society for the Promotion of Christian Knowledge* (1960), 53 R. & I.T. 326 (Lands Tribunal).
3 General Rate Act 1967, s. 39 (2) (b).
4 *Westminster Roman Catholic Diocese* v. *Hampshire*, [1975] R.A. 1 (Lands Tribunal).
5 (1958), 3 R.R.C. 86.
6 *Ibid.*, at 91.

v. *Valuation Comr.*[1] The relevant statute in Northern Ireland provides exemption for any hereditament consisting of "a church hall, chapel hall or similar building held by a religious body, so long as that hall or building is used mainly or exclusively for purposes connected with that body". The requirement in the English statute that the halls to which it refers must be "used in connection with" a place of public worship finds no echo in the Northern Ireland statute. This is because it "is not unfamiliar in Northern Ireland to find halls bearing all the indicia of church halls and belonging to a particular religious denomination yet not attached to or used in connection with a particular church or other place of worship". The hereditament in question in *Mageean's* case adjoined Queen's University, Belfast, and was known as the Catholic Chaplaincy. The building comprised an assembly room, lecture and committee rooms, a library and a canteen, and there was also certain residential accommodation occupied by the Roman Catholic Dean of Residences at the University. The Chaplaincy was open daily and was used for social and recreational purposes by Roman Catholic graduates and undergraduates of the University, and meetings of certain Roman Catholic religious societies connected with the University were held there. The building also contained a chapel and sacristy in which religious services were held regularly on weekdays but not on Sundays. The chapel and sacristy had been distinguished as exempt in the valuation lists but the appellent trustees contended that the remainder of the building was also entitled to exemption. It was held by the Northern Ireland Court of Appeal, CURRAN L.J. dissenting, that the hereditament was a "church hall, chapel hall or similar building" and so entitled to exemption. A church or chapel hall was according to Lord MacDERMOTT C.J. a hall used to further the work or meet the needs of a group or community of worshippers associated for the purpose of their religion. The group or community may be a congregation or a more loosely knit body such as members of a university or a garrison having a common religious faith. If a building is so used it is immaterial that the activities carried on in it are merely ancillary to the advancement of religion.[2] BLACK L.J. gave a description of the typical activities of a church or chapel hall and after reviewing some of the earlier cases said:[3]

> "I am of opinion that a hereditament will not necessarily cease to be a church hall merely because in addition to being used for religious meetings it is also used for social and recreational purposes designed to further the work of the religious body by which it is held and to hold together the members and adherents of that body."

The expression "similar building" was construed both by Lord MacDERMOTT C.J. and by BLACK L.J. as meaning a building fulfilling purposes similar to those of a church or chapel hall.

A Christian Science reading room, committee room and librarian's room have been treated as a "similar building", i.e. a building similar to a church or chapel hall;[4] but a building used as diocesan offices, although containing a chapel, did not fall within the description, because it was not connected with a place of

1 [1960] N.I. 141.
2 [1960] N.I. 141, at 152–153.
3 *Ibid.*, at 157.
4 *Board of Directors of Ninth Church of Christ Scientist* v. *Westminster City Council and Cane* (1958), 3 R.R.C. 35 (Lands Tribunal).

public religious worship and because the activities carried on there were not associated with a church hall.[1]

EFFECT OF LETTING EXEMPT PREMISES FOR OTHER PURPOSES

The letting[2] of a hereditament, or part of a hereditament, which is exempt as a place of public religious worship or as premises ancillary thereto, for a use other than the specified purpose does not necessarily, but may, defeat exemption.[3] No gross value for rating purposes is to be ascribed to such a hereditament unless the annual amount of the payments accruing due, as consideration for lettings of the hereditament, or parts thereof, exceeded the average amount of the expenses attributable to those lettings.[4] Where a gross value does fall to be ascribed to the hereditament it is to be assessed by reference only to the amount of the excess of payments over expenses.[5] A tenant's share must be allowed in arriving at the gross value.[6]

The exemption is lost, to the extent thus calculated, in the rating year following that in which any payments in consideration of a letting of the hereditament or part thereof accrued due.[7]

---

1 *Church House Trustees* v. *Dimmick* (1959), 5 R.R.C. 185 (Lands Tribunal); *cf. Morley* v. *Society for the Promotion of Christian Knowledge* (1960), 53 R. & I.T. 326 (Lands Tribunal).
2 By way of tenancy *or licence:* General Rate Act 1967, s. 39 (3).
3 *Ibid.,* s. 39 (3).
4 *Ibid.,* s. 39 (3) (b).
5 *Ibid.,* s. 39 (3) (c).
6 See *Williamson* v. *Hayes and Hauber's Executors and Trustees of Roman Catholic Diocese of Southwark* (1959), 5 R.R.C. 119 (Lands Tribunal); *Church House Trustees* v. *Dimmick* (1959), 5 R.R.C. 185 (Lands Tribunal).
7 General Rate Act 1967, s. 39 (3) (a).

Part VIII

Miscellany

Chapter 48

Other Legislation Affecting Charities

This chapter deals with residual matters. It has been seen that special provision has been made in fiscal legislation for charities. In the heterogeneous collection of statutes discussed in the following papers are to be found other examples of privileged treatment being meted out to charities for varying reasons, as well as provisions which tidy up the interrelation of charitable and social security benefits.

Legislation against discrimination

In two fields of human and social relations statute has intervened to prevent what is considered to be unfair discrimination, namely discrimination against persons on account of their race or sex. Charities have been accorded some exemption under the statutes relating to racial discrimination[1] and to sex discrimination.

The Race Relations Act 1968[2] was enacted in order to make unlawful discrimination on the grounds of colour, race or ethnic or national origins in any of the following: (a) the provision of goods facilities and services,[3] (b) employment,[4] (c) trade unions, employers' and trade associations[5] or (d) the disposal of housing accommodation, business premises or other land.[6] For the purposes of the Act a person discriminates against another if on the ground of colour, race or ethnic or national origins he treats that other in any of the situations outlined in (a), (b), (c) and (d) above less favourably than he treats or would treat other persons and the word discrimination is to be read accordingly.[7]

There were prior to the passing of the Race Relations Act 1968 many charitable trusts which restricted the dispositions which could be made under them to beneficiaries of a particular category, whether by reference to residence, nationality or country of origin. In such cases trustees complying with the terms of the trust by refusing applications from persons who did not fall within the specified category might, unless exempted from the operation of the Act, find themselves falling foul of its provisions.

Accordingly it was provided that nothing in Part I of the Race Relations Act

1 For the American cases and literature on racially discriminatory trusts, see Sheridan, "Cy-près in Spate", (1972) A.A.L.R. 101, at 105–107.
2 The Race Relations Act 1976, enacted on 22nd November 1976, comes into operation on a day or days to be appointed. On 1st March 1977 no day had been appointed. For a note on the Act, see Appendix 5.
3 Race Relations Act 1968, s. 2.   4 *Ibid.*, s. 3.
5 *Ibid.*, s. 4.   6 *Ibid.*, s. 5.
7 *Ibid.*, s. 1 (1). The Race Relations Act 1976 widens the concept: see Appendix 5.

1968 is to (*a*) be construed as affecting a provision which is contained in a future charitable instrument and confers benefits on persons of a particular race, particular descent or particular ethnic or national origins; or (*b*) render unlawful any act which is done in order to comply with any such provision or with provisions[1] of any existing charitable instrument of any description. "Charitable instrument" in this context means an enactment passed or instrument made for purposes which are exclusively charitable according to the law of England and Wales. A future instrument is one taking effect after the commencement of the Race Relations Act 1968 and an existing instrument means an instrument taking effect before the commencement of that Act.[2] Thus both existing and future charitable trust instruments enjoy the benefit of the exemption.

A trust instrument may discriminate in favour of persons of a particular race, descent, or ethnic or national origin,[3] but not against such persons. Accordingly schools for the education of Pakistanis or Frenchmen and trusts in favour of future immigrants from Pakistan may lawfully be confined to persons falling within those descriptions. But a provision *excepting* persons on racial grounds would fall foul of the Act. The provision limiting residence in the hostel to "dominion students of European origin" which was circumvented by the operation of the *cy-près* doctrine in *Re Dominion Hall Students' Trust*[4] would, for example, contravene the Act.

Another field in which it is alleged that unfair discrimination takes place is that of sex discrimination and discrimination on the ground of marriage. The purpose of the Sex Discrimination Act 1975 was to make discrimination on the grounds of sex unlawful in the fields of employment and training (where discrimination against married persons is also made unlawful) in education, in the provision of goods, facilities and services, and in the disposal and management of premises.

Where a charitable instrument contains a provision for conferring benefits on persons of one sex only (disregarding any benefits to persons of the opposite sex which are exceptional or are relatively insignificant)[5] anything done by the charity trustees to give effect to that provision is not made unlawful by the Act.[6] For this purpose "charitable instrument" means an enactment or other instrument passed or made for charitable purposes, or an enactment or other instrument so far as it relates to charitable purposes. This exemption safeguards the position of the large number of what may be called "single-sex" charities. Some of these are well known national organisations like the YMCA, the YWCA and the Boy Scouts and Girl Guides. But the vast majority consist of the hundreds of small parochial charities whose benefits are restricted to elderly spinsters, poor widows, retired schoolmasters and so on. The exception applies to advertisements indicating that the benefits of the charity are available to persons of one sex only: such advertisements would be "done by the charity trustees to give effect to" the provision for conferring benefits on persons of one sex only.[7]

---

1 *Ibid.*, s. 9 (1).

2 *Ibid.*, s. 9 (2).

3 The position of Jews, i.e. persons of Jewish faith, under the Act is unclear: see Race Relations Board, 1st Annual Report, 13. It is questionable whether they fall within any of the enumerated categories.

4 [1947] Ch. 183.

5 Sex Discrimination Act 1975, s. 43 (2).

6 *Ibid.*, s. 43 (1) (b).   7 *Ibid.*

The exemption, it should be noted, does not apply to all the activities of a charity only to activities done to give effect to the "single sex" restriction of benefit. Advertising for and selecting paid staff is not such an activity and in the sphere of employment of paid staff charities are bound by the relevant provisions of the Act.

There are special provisions for educational charities.[1] These provisions enable the trustees of a single-sex educational charity in England and Wales to apply to the Secretary of State for a modification of the trust to benefit both sexes. They apply to any trust deed or other instrument which concerns property applicable for or in connection with the provision of education in any establishment falling within a specified group, and which in any way restricts the benefits available under the instrument to persons of one sex.[2] The specified group comprises:[3] (1) educational establishments maintained by a local education authority, (2) independent schools which are not special schools, (3) special schools which are not maintained by a local education authority, (4) universities and (5) establishments not falling within the previous categories providing full-time or part-time education and designated by the Secretary of State under section 24 of the Act.[4] An application for the removal or modification of a restriction of benefits to one sex may be made by the trustees or the body in charge of the relevant educational establishment,[5] referred to in the Act as the responsible body.[6] If on such an application the Secretary of State is satisfied that the removal or modification of the restriction would conduce to the advancement of education without sex discrimination, he may by order make such modifications of the instrument as appear to him expedient for removing or modifying the restriction, and for any supplemental or incidental purposes.[7] If the trust was created by gift or bequest, no order may be made until 25 years after the date on which the gift or bequest took effect, unless the donor or his personal representatives or the personal representatives of the testator, have consented in writing to the making of the application for the order.[8] The applicants or applicant will be required by the Secretary of State to publish a notice[9] containing particulars of the proposed order and stating that representations may be made to the Secretary of State within a period[10] specified in the notice.[11] The Secretary of State is under a statutory duty to require the applicants to publish such a notice.[12] The applicants must publish the notice in whatever manner is specified by the Secretary of State, and the cost of any publication of the notice may be met out of the trust property.[13] Naturally before making any order the Secretary of State must take into account any

---

1 *Ibid.*, s. 78.
2 *Ibid.*, s. 78 (1).
3 *Ibid.*, s. 22, table paragraphs 1–5.
4 For the establishments designated see Sex Discrimination (Designated Educational Establishments) Order 1975, S.I. 1975 No. 1902 and the Sex Discrimination (Designated Educational Establishments) (Wales) Order 1975, S.I. 1975 No. 2113.
5 Sex Discrimination Act 1975, s. 78 (2).
6 *Ibid.*, s. 22. The table to s. 22 indicates in each case which is the "responsible body".
7 *Ibid.*, s. 78 (2).
8 *Ibid.*, s. 78 (3).
9 "Notice" means notice in writing: *ibid.*, s. 82 (1).
10 The period must be not less than one month from the date of the notice: *ibid.*, s. 78 (5).
11 *Ibid.*, s. 78 (4).
12 *Ibid.*
13 *Ibid.*, s. 78 (5).

representations duly made in accordance with the notice and the Act requires him to take such representations into account.[1]

Consumer credit

The Consumer Credit Act 1974 which is based on the recommendations made in the Crowther Committee's Report on Consumer Credit[2] establishes for the protection of consumers a new system[3] of licensing and other control of persons concerned with the provision of credit or the supply of goods on hire or hire purchase.

Certain types of consumer credit agreement where the creditor is a charity which is specified in an order of the Secretary of State for Prices and Consumer Protection are exempt from the provisions regulating consumer credit agreements.[4] Broadly the exemption is designed to cover the case where the agreement involves the debtor in a mortgage of land and the credit does not exceed £5000. More particularly the exemption only applies (1) where the agreement is a debtor–creditor–supplier agreement[5] financing the purchase of land or the provision of dwellings on any land, secured in either case by a land mortgage on that land, or (2) where the agreeement is a debtor–creditor[6] agreement secured by any land mortgage, or (3) where the agreement is a debtor-creditor-supplier agreement financing a transaction which is a linked transaction in relation to an agreement falling under head (1) or an agreement falling under head (2) financing the purchase of any land or the provision of dwellings on any land and secured by a land mortgage on the relevant land.[7]

It has been provided that in the case of charities in England and Wales the Secretary of State shall not make, vary or revoke any exempting order without consulting the Charity Commissioners.[8] The Charity Commissioners have agreed to advise the Department of Prices and Consumer Protection, in respect of any application they receive from an institution claiming to be a charity established in England and Wales, whether the institution is a registered or exempt charity, whether its name is correctly stated, and whether they know of any reason why the applicant should not be granted the exemption.[9]

---

1 *Ibid.*, s. 78 (7).
2 March 1971, Cmnd. 4596.
3 Administered by the Director-General of Fair Trading.
4 Consumer Credit Act 1974, s. 16. A consumer credit agreement is a personal credit agreement by which the creditor provides the debtor with credit exceeding £5000: *ibid.*, s. 8.
5 Broadly, such an agreement is one where the supplier is either the same person as the creditor or a party to arrangements (actual or anticipated) between himself and the creditor. For definition, see Consumer Credit Act 1974, s. 12.
6 In such an agreement a supplier either does not figure at all, or figures without any arrangement between himself and the creditor. For a more precise definition, see Consumer Credit Act 1974, s. 13.
7 *Ibid.*, s. 16 (2).
8 *Ibid.*, s. 16 (3).
9 [1975] Ch. Com. Rep. 9, para. 17.

Community land

The Community Land Act 1975 has two main objectives. The first is to enable the community to control the development of land in accordance with its needs and priorities. The second is to restore to the community the increase in the value of land arising from development being allowed to take place.[1] These objections will be affected in part by the Act and in part by the introduction of development land tax.[2] So far as the Act is concerned two stages are envisaged. As from the 6th April 1976[3] the authorities specified in the Act[4] have power to acquire by agreement or compulsorily all outstanding material interests in any land which they consider suitable for development, other than exempt development.[5] They will not be under any duty to acquire any such outstanding interests. At the start of the second period, namely on the "relevant date" which will be fixed by the Secretary of State,[6] the power of the authorities to acquire such interests will be replaced by a duty to acquire all such outstanding material interests needed within ten years for "relevant development".[7]

The Act contains a number of special provisions relating to charities.

First, a material interest[8] in land held by a charity[9] on 12th September 1974 is not treated as an outstanding material interest.[10] Consequently charities will be able to carry out development (if planning permission is obtained) on land which they owned on 12th September 1974. A charity is treated as the owner of a material interest at a particular time if at that time it has or had entered into a binding contract for its acquisition, or subject only to completion of the administration of a deceased person's esate, is or was entitled to it under the terms of the deceased person's will.[11]

In the second place, the valuation basis for land which since 12th September 1974 has always been owned by a charity (but not necessarily the same charity throughout) will continue to be market value for 11 years, or until the second appointed day, whichever period ends later.[12] The second appointed day, when the compensation for all land compulsorily acquired will be based on current use value, cannot be brought into force until all relevant development has been designated by orders[13] for all areas of Great Britain.[14]

---

1 See White Paper, Land (1974, Cmnd. 5730), para. 16; a note on the Act: see H. W. Wilkinson (1976), 39 M.L.R. 311–317.

2 Development Land Tax was introduced by the Development Land Tax Act 1976, discussed at 551, *supra*.

3 The first appointed day for the purposes of the Act: see Community Land Act 1975, s. 7 (1).

4 *Ibid.*, s. 1 (1).

5 *Ibid.*, s. 15 (1).

6 *Ibid.*, ss. 7 and 18 (6).

7 *Ibid.*, s. 18 (5).

8 This means the freehold or a lease the unexpired term of which at the relevant time is not less than six years: *ibid.*, s. 6 (1).

9 "Charity" has the same meaning as in TA 1970, s. 360: Community Land Act 1975, s. 6 (1). So it means "any body of persons or trust established for charitable purposes only". For the meaning of body of persons see TA 1970, s. 526 (5).

10 Community Land Act 1975, s. 4 (1) (b).

11 *Ibid.*, s. 4 (2).

12 *Ibid.*, s. 25 (6).

13 Under Community Land Act 1975, s. 18.

14 *Ibid.*, s. 7 (3) (a).

Thirdly, after the period just referred to has elapsed compensation for land which for a period of seven years before the date of assessment has been owned by a charity (but not necessarily the same charity throughout) and has been used "wholly or mainly for charitable purposes"[1] will be based on "prevailing use value". In other words for the purposes of assessing the compensation it must be assumed that planning permission would be granted for any development by virtue of which the use of the land would be made to correspond with the use which prevails in the case of contiguous or adjacent land.[2] The Charity Commissioners have pointed out that this provision will be of particular value in cases where the current use value of the property is comparatively low; as for example in the case of a disused chapel in a residential or shopping area.[3]

For the purposes of the two preceding paragraphs the charity is treated as owning the land if it has a binding contract for its acquisition or is entitled to the interest under the law of succession.[4]

Housing rents and subsidies

Under the provisions of the Housing Finance Act 1972 housing authorities are required to operate rent rebate and rent allowance schemes for the benefit of tenants living in their areas. Occupants of almshouses who occupied their accommodation as licensees (albeit making weekly contributions) could only recover the full amount of their weekly contribution from the Supplementary Benefits Commission. The Housing Rents and Subsidies Act 1975 provided that the local authority had to treat almspeople as though they were private tenants.[5] This concession was brought into operation with effect from 17th November 1975.[6] Almspeople now have the option of claiming either an allowance under the new provisions or supplementary benefit, whichever is the more advantageous.

Social security benefits

The maximum amount of any weekly pension or allowance made by a charity to any person which may be disregarded by the Supplementary Benefits Commission in assessing that person's entitlement to benefit is at present £4.[7] The disregard of £4 a week, which includes other sources of income as well as charity allowances, is the maximum disregard possible and charity trustees cannot assume that a weekly allowance of £4 to each and every beneficiary will be disregarded. Indeed if a beneficiary has income from other sources to

---

1 For the meaning of "wholly or mainly used for charitable purposes": see *Oxfam* v. *Birmingham City Council*, [1976] A.C. 126, H.L. and the rating cases discussed at 558, *supra*.

2 Community Land Act 1975, s. 25 (5).

3 [1975] Ch. Com. Rep. 8, para. 15.

4 Community Land Act 1975, s. 25 (7).

5 Housing Rents and Subsidies Act 1975, s. 12, adding s. 19A to Housing Finance Act 1972.

6 Allowances for Almspeople (Appointed Day) Order 1975, S.I. 1975 No. 1565; Almshouse Contributions (Allowances) (England and Wales) Regulations 1975, S.I. 1975 No. 1564.

7 Social Security Benefits Act 1975, s. 11, Sch. 3, para. 5; Social Security Benefits Act 1975 (Commencement No. 2) Order 1975, S.I. 1975 No. 1336.

which the disregard provisions apply, the whole or part of any allowance from charitable funds may simply relieve public funds by reducing the recipient's entitlement to supplementary benefit. For this reason the Department of Health and Social Security suggest that before granting any weekly allowance charity trustees should check with the Department's local office in each case to see whether the person concerned is in receipt of any other income all or part of which is being disregarded.[1]

It should be noted that in calculating a person's resources for the purposes of supplementary benefit a notional income of 25p must be assumed for each complete £50 of capital in excess of £1200.[2]

---

1 [1975] Ch. Com. Rep. 11–12, para. 29.
2 Social Security Benefits Act 1975, s. 11, Sch. 3, para. 3.

Chapter 49

Conflict of Laws

This chapter is concerned with the problem of deciding what law governs a charitable trust when one or more of its elements are to be found in another jurisdiction. In England the topic has attracted very little discussion,[1] whether in the decided cases or in legal literature. However there is now a growing interest in the wider subject of trusts in the conflict of laws, an interest which is reflected in separate treatment of the subject in textbooks on the conflict of laws[2] and on trusts.[3] Not surprisingly, considering the number of state jurisdictions, the American experience in this field is very much greater; and it is to that experience that reference may profitably be made for appropriate solutions of particular problems,[4] where English guidance is lacking.

In the first place it is important to characterise the issue requiring the selection of a particular governing law. Distinctions must be drawn between formal validity, capacity and essential validity, and between questions of construction and questions of administration.[5] In relation to formal validity and capacity there is nothing to distinguish charitable trusts from private trusts.

Whether a trust for a particular purpose is a valid charitable trust is a question of essential validity. The question whether a testator has exhibited a paramount charitable intent is one of construction. And the question whether a scheme should be directed because of a supervening failure is a question of administration. Finally, issues involving fiscal privileges are in a category of their own.

A number of traditional distinctions must first be drawn.

Testamentary trusts and *inter vivos* trusts are not always subject to the same rules.

There is also the distinction between trusts of movables and trusts of immovables. This is not the place for a comprehensive discussion of what property is classified as movable or immovable,[6] a question which in any event falls to be answered by the *lex situs* of the property in question.[7] But certainly all estates, interests and charges in or over English land are immovables.[8] Thus freehold and

---

1 But see V. T. H. Delany (1961) 10 I.C.L.Q. 385–400.

2 Dicey and Morris, *Conflict of Laws* (9th edn.) 651–664; Morris, *Conflict of Laws* (1971) 401–411; Graveson, *Conflict of Laws* (7th edn.) 528–542.

3 Keeton and Sheridan, *Law of Trusts* (10th edn.) 413–426; and see Waters, *Law of Trusts in Canada* (1974) Ch. 29.

4 See Land, *Trusts in the Conflict of Laws* (1940); Scott, *Trusts* (3rd edn.) 3766–4159, paras. 553–664.

5 As to the appropriate law to govern formal validity and capacity, see Dicey and Morris, *Conflict of Laws* (9th edn.) 592–600.

6 For such a discussion, see Dicey and Morris, *Conflict of Laws* (9th edn.) 500–506.

7 See e.g. *Re Berchtold*, [1923] 1 Ch. 192.

8 See *Re Hoyles*, [1911] 1 Ch. 179, at 183, 186, C.A.

leasehold land constitute immovables:[1] so do freehold land subject to a trust for sale (if unsold)[2] rentcharges[3] mineral rights[4] and the interest of a mortgagee.[5] The sale proceeds of land in England are normally movables.[5] Chattels (other than chattels real)[6] stocks and shares and cash are movables.

Validity

MOVABLES

Although the essential validity of a testamentary *gift* of movables is governed by the law of the domicile at the date of his death, in other words by the *lex domicilii*, it has been suggested that the essential validity of a testamentary *trust* of movables should be governed by the proper law of the trust.[7]

Certainly in the case of a charitable trust there is much to recommend such a rule. Take for example a case where a testator leaves investments to trustees who are domiciled abroad to hold upon trust for a purpose which by the law of the place where the trust is to be administered is charitable but which in English law is not so. It is an unattractive proposition that such a trust fails. But there are authorities which suggest that a trust for a purpose which is not valid in this country must fail notwithstanding that it is to be executed abroad.

In *Habershon* v. *Vardon*[8] one Nadir Baxter by his will left £1000 to aid the political restoration of the Jews to Jerusalem. KNIGHT-BRUCE V.-C. held the bequest void because it would not be charitable according to the law of England. "If it could be understood to mean anything" he said, "it was to create a revolution in a friendly country."[9] It was on the same reasoning that the gift in *Re Moore*[10] of £10 000 to the Pope "to use and apply at his sole and absolute discretion in the carrying out of the sacred office" failed. Such a gift could consistently with the terms thereof be applied to promoting the temporal power of the Pope, which would be a political purpose contrary to public policy. POWELL J. said that it was "plain that where, as in this case, the objects of the trusts are stated in indefinite terms not capable of being controlled and if necessary executed by the court, the gift not being necessarily applicable to charitable purposes as legally defined, and being applicable to purposes not only not charitable, but possibly illegal according to the laws of this country, is void". [11] In both *Habershon* v. *Vardon*[12] and *Re Moore*[13] the effectuation of the

---

1 *Freke* v. *Lord Carbery* (1873), L.R. 16 Eq. 461.
2 *Re Berchtold*, [1923] 1 Ch. 192.
3 *Chatfield* v. *Berchtold* (1872), 7 Ch. App. 192.
4 *Re Trepca Mines, Ltd.*, [1960] 1 W.L.R. 1273, C.A.
5 *Re Hoyles*, [1911] 1 Ch. 179, C.A.; but see *Haque* v. *Haque* (No. 2) (1965), 114 C.L.R. 98 (High Ct. of Australia).
6 I.e. leaseholds.
7 Morris, *Conflict of Laws* (1971) 402–403; Graveson, *Conflict of Laws* (7th edn.) 536–537.
8 (1851), 4 De G. & Sm. 467.
9 *Ibid.*, at 468. The trust was political and "not consistent with our amicable relations with the Sublime Porte".
10 [1919] 1 I.R. 316.
11 [1919] 1 I.R. 316, at 357.
12 (1851), 4 De G. & Sm. 467.
13 [1919] 1 I.R. 316.

purpose abroad was in fact contrary to English public policy. Would the same result ensue if there was nothing contrary to public policy in the trust that was intended to operate abroad? Such a case, it is conceived, is analogous to that of a trust intended to operate abroad which infringes the English rule against perpetuities but is valid in the country of administration. In *Fordyce* v. *Bridges*[1] an English testator left the residue of his personal estate to trustees upon trust to convert it into money and invest it in the purchase of land in England or Scotland, such land if in England to be held according to the limitations in his will affecting the testator land in England but if in Scotland in accordance with a Scottish entail. An objection was made that the bequest of a sum to be invested in a regular Scottish entail was void as a perpetuity according to English law. Lord COTTENHAM L.C. dealt with this argument quite shortly:[2]

> "The rules acted upon by the Courts in this country with respect to testamentary dispositions tending to perpetuities relate to this country only ... the fund [*sc.* in question] being to be administered in a foreign country is payable here, though the purpose to which it is to be applied would have been illegal if the administration of the fund had to take place in this country.

This principle was exemplified by the well-established rule in cases of bequests within the statutes of mortmain. A charity legacy void in this country under the old, now repealed, mortmain law is good and payable in England if for a charity in Scotland. The decision in *Fordyce* v. *Bridges*[3] was followed in the Australian case of *Re Mitchner*[4] where a bequest to trustees resident in Germany to be applied on trusts in Germany which infringed the Queensland rule against perpetuities was held not *ipso facto* invalid: an inquiry was ordered to determine whether the gift could be effectuated under German law. And the same position has been reached by the American courts. Thus it has been said that it is no part of the policy of the State of New York to interdict perpetuities or gifts in mortmain in Pennsylvania or California.[5] The only recent case to discuss the conflict between the law of the testator's domicile and the law of the place of intended administration in relation to charitable trusts is the unsatisfactory case of *Jewish National Fund* v. *Royal Trust Co.*[6] decided by the Supreme Court of Canada on appeal from the British Columbia Court of Appeal. The testator who was domiciled in British Columbia left his residuary estate (which was to converted into money) to his executor and trustee to pay it to the Jewish National Fund (Keren Kayemeth Le-Israel) Inc. of New York[7] to be used by the trustees of that body as a continuing and separate trust for the purchase of tracts of land in Palestine the United States or any British Dominion for the

---

1 (1848), 2 Ph. 497.
2 (1848), 2 Ph. 497, at 515.
3 (1848), 2 Ph. 497.
4 [1922] St.R.Qd. 252.
5 *Chamberlain* v. *Chamberlain* 43 N.Y. 424, at 434 (1871); *Robb* v. *Washington and Jefferson College*, 103 App. Div. 327 (1905) (N.Y.); *Re Grant's Will*, 101 N.Y.S. 2d 423 (1905); *Re Chappell's Estate*, 213 P. 684 (1923); *Amerige* v. *A.-G.*, 88 N.E. 2d 126 (1949); and see Gray, *The Rule Against Perpetuities* (4th edn.) 288, para. 263.3.
6 (1965), 53 D.L.R. (2d) 577), discussed in Waters, *Law of Trusts in Canada*, 964–965.
7 The agent of the New York fund in Israel, Keren Kayemeth Le-Israel is recognised as a charitable organisation by the State of Israel: (1965), 53 D.L.R. (2d) 577, at 585. But the English counterpart of the New York fund is not charitable: *Keren Kayemeth Le Jisroel, Ltd.* v. *I.R.Comrs.*, [1932] A.C. 650.

establishment therein of Jewish colonies. Each colony was to be known as the Frank Schechter Colony. The receipt of the money by Jewish National Fund to the executor and trustee was to release it from any further responsibility. Some of the next of kin queried the validity of the residuary bequest and the executor accordingly applied to the court to have the matter determined. In the courts below[1] the next of kin contended that the residuary clause was void for uncertainty or alternatively that it created a perpetual trust which was not charitable, and therefore void. The Jewish National Fund argued that the bequest constituted an absolute gift to it, alternatively that it was not void for uncertainty and created a good charitable trust. No argument was addressed to the inferior courts on the conflict of laws. However in the Supreme Court of Canada the appellant deployed a further argument namely (1) that in the law of British Columbia the rule against perpetuities was one based on considerations of internal policy and did not apply to invalidate a trust of movables created by a testator domiciled in British Columbia if the trust was to be administered outside that Province; (2) that the trust created by the residuary bequest was to be administered in the State of New York (3) that the validity of the gift according fell to be determined according to the law of that State and (4) that by that law the trust was valid and charitable.[2]

In the Supreme Court of Canada there was a division of opinion. The majority agreed with the decision in the appellate court that the gift was not an absolute gift but one impressed into a trust. The majority further held that if the law of British Columbia was the relevant law to apply, the conclusion of the appellate court that the trust was not charitable was correct. However CARTWRIGHT J., who delivered the majority judgment, then went on to consider the applicability of the law of New York State. He said that for the purposes of the appeal he was prepared to assume, without finally deciding, that if the testator had directed that his residuary estate be paid to the appellant to be used by its trustees for the purchase of land in New York State to be held for the purposes set out in the residuary bequest the validity of the clause should be determined by the law of New York State. But that was not what had been provided. The trustees had a choice as to where to purchase land, and in some of the specified countries the trusts would or might be void.[3] CARTWRIGHT J. said that it seemed to him

"that a trust of movables void under the law of the testator's domicile and under that of many other countries in which the trustees are authorised to carry it out cannot be rendered valid by the circumstances that the trustees are permitted, but not required, to carry it out in a country in which it could be regarded as valid".

The minority judgment was delivered by JUDSON J.,[4] who referred to several statements in the textbooks and in decided cases to the effect that the question was governed by the law of the place in which the trust was to be administered.

---

1 *Re Schechter* (1963), 37 D.L.R. (2d) 433 (WOOTTON J.); on appeal, *sub nom, Royal Trust Co. and Jewish National Fund* v. *Richter* (1964), 43 D.L.R. (2d) 417 (British Columbia C.A.).
2 Evidence was given that a gift to the particular corporation was a valid charitable gift under the law of New York: (1965), 53 D.L.R. (2d) 577, at 585.
3 Unless the contrary was alleged and proved the presumption, said the judge, was that the law of all the other relevant countries was the same as that of British Columbia: see [1965] 53 D.L.R. (2d) 577, at 582.
4 SPENCE J. concurred with him.

After rehearsing the argument of the next of kin: that the law of the State of New York had nothing to do with the administration of the trust; that the law of the *situs* of the purchase of land would govern and that the will permitted the trust to be administered in a multitude of places; and that the trust failed if it would be non-charitable in any of them, JUDSON J. stated that he thought the argument failed *in limine*:[1]

> "The British Columbia executorship has ended. The residue is to be turned over to New York trustees upon clearly defined trusts which are recognised as valid by the law of that state. At that moment it becomes a New York trust to be administered there according to the law of that state. What difficulties of administration, if any, may be encountered outside the boundaries of that state are of no further concern to the Court of the domicile."

The minority view seems preferable to that of the majority. It is difficult to perceive the relevance of potential *leges situs*, particularly since it is hardly likely that trustees in the place of administration would choose to purchase land in a jurisdiction which repudiates the validity of the trust.

An *inter vivos* trust of movables for a charitable purpose is, as to its essential validity, governed by its proper law.[2] That proper law is the system of law with which it has its closest and most real connection. But a settlor constituting a charitable trust during his lifetime may, it is submitted, designate the law which is to govern the essential validity of the trust, provided that the designated law has some substantial connection with the trust in question. The possibility of an express selection of a proper law in the case of a *private* trust was certainly contemplated by COZENS-HARDY L.J. in the case of *Re Fitzgerald*.[3] In addition there are numerous American authorities relating to private trusts which support the proposition that such a selection is effective[4] provided that (1) the law selected does indeed have some substantial connection[5] with the trust[6] and (2) the trust does not infringe some strong principle of public policy in the place whose law would otherwise govern the settlement. There appears to be no good reason to confine this principle to private trusts, denying it to charitable trusts.

In default of any express designation of the law to govern the validity of the trust, the appropriate governing law is the proper law. The isolation of the proper law in any given case is not necessarily an easy task.[7] But in some cases the proper law is obvious. This is certainly the case where the settlor has fixed the administration of the trust in a particular jurisdiction: if that jurisdiction would uphold the trust, so too will the court of the domicile of the settlor. This

---

1 (1965), 53 D.L.R. (2d) 577, at 588–589.

2 *Iveagh* v. *I.R.Comrs.*, [1954] Ch. 364; *Revenue Comrs.* v. *Pelly*, [1940] I.R. 122; *Lindsay* v. *Miller*, [1949] V.L.R. 13.

3 *Re Fitzgerald*, [1904] 1 Ch. 573, at 587; and see *A.-G.* v. *Jewish Colonisation Association*, [1901] 1 K.B. 123; *Trustees Executors and Agency Co., Ltd.* v. *Margottini*, [1960] V.R. 417, at 419; *Augustus* v. *Permanent Trustee Co. (Canberra), Ltd.*, [1971] A.L.R. 661.

4 *Shannon* v. *Irving Trust Co.*, 9 N.E. 2d 792 (1937); *Re Pratt*, 168 N.E. 2d 709 (1960); *City Bank Farmers Trust Co.* v. *Meyn*, 34 N.Y.S. 2d 373 (1942).

5 For example that it is the law of the place where the trust is to be administered, or the domicile of the settlor or the *lex situs* of the property.

6 *City Bank Farmers Trust Co.* v. *Cheek*, 93 N.Y.L.J. 2941, 7th June 1935.

7 See Scott, *Trusts* (3rd edn.) 3919–3931, paras. 599–601.

will be so even if the domestic law of that domicile would not uphold the trust.[1]

IMMOVABLES

In the context of *testamentary* trusts for charitable purposes, where the subject matter of the trust is an immovable, such as land, two particular questions of essential validity may arise.

First, the land may be situated in a country where a devise or bequest for charitable purposes is invalid if the will is executed within a certain designated short period, such as a month or a year prior to his death.[2] In such a case the *lex situs* will apply even though there is no such restriction on testamentary disposition in the law of the testator's domicile.[3] Thus in *Curtis* v. *Hutton*[4] the testator who died domiciled in Scotland devised lands which were situated in England for charitable purposes in Scotland. Sir WILLIAM GRANT M.R. held the devise failed because the will had been executed less than 12 months previously and English law, which invalidated gifts in those circumstances, applied:[5]

"The validity of every description of real estate must depend upon the law of the country in which that estate is situated".

On the other hand where a gift of money in England was directed to be applied in the purchase of land in Scotland for charitable purposes, Scottish law, which did not forbid such gifts, was held applicable.[6]

The second question relates to the validity of trust provisions contained in the will.

The essential validity of a testamentary trust of an immovable (such as land) situate abroad and intended to be retained in trust is governed by the law of the country in which the immovable is situate (*lex situs*).[7] The *lex situs* in this context means whatever law the foreign court would apply in the circumstances, which might be the law of some other country, and not its domestic law.[8] Accordingly that law determines whether any gifts to charities or trusts for charitable purposes are valid.[9] Thus if a testator dies domiciled in England leaving freehold property in California upon trust to be used as a centre to promote peace and world understanding the trust being valid by Californian law[10] should be upheld by the English court, although under English law the purposes are not charitable.[11]

---

1 *Robb* v. *Washington and Jefferson College*, 78 N.E. 359 (1906) (charitable trust invalid by law of New York but valid under law of Pennsylvania).

2 Prior to the enactment of the Mortmain and Charitable Uses Act 1891, a devise for charitable purposes in a will executed within 12 months of the testator's death was void: see Mortmain Act 1736. For similar statutory provisions in the United States: see Scott, *Trusts* (3rd edn.) 2821–2828, para. 362.4.

3 See *Sinnott* v. *Moore*, 39 S.E. 415 (1901) (Georgia); *cf. Parkhurst* v. *Roy* (1882), 7 A.R. 614 where the *lex situs* was also the *lex domicilii* and the devise contravened the mortmain statutes.

4 (1808), 14 Ves. 537; and see *Duncan* v. *Lawson* (1889), 41 Ch.D. 395.

5 (1808), 14 Ves. 537, at 541.

6 *Mackintosh* v. *Townsend* (1809), 16 Ves. 330.

7 *Earl Nelson* v. *Lord Bridport* (1846), 8 Beav. 547; *Re Miller*, [1914] 1 Ch. 511; *Freke* v. *Lord Carbery* (1873), L.R. 16 Eq. 461.

8 *Re Ross*, [1930] 1 Ch. 377; *Re Duke of Wellington*, [1947] Ch. 506.

9 *Duncan* v. *Lawson* (1889), 41 Ch.D. 394; *Re Hoyles*, [1911] 1 Ch. 179.

10 *Estate of Peck*, 335 P 2d 185 (1959). It is assumed there is no mortmain objection.

11 See at 113–114, *supra*.

Equally if the testamentary trusts are invalid under the *lex situs* the English court should not uphold the trust even though it would be valid under English domestic law. There is no English authority precisely in point: the authorities cited above deal either with private trusts or with invalidity under mortmain provisions. But on principle the *lex situs* ought to prevail, and there are cases in the United States which confirm such prevalence.[1] It is difficult to conceive of a trust charitable according to English law but not valid in a country which recognises charitable trusts. An example could occur of a gift in remainder which is an imperfect trust provision within the ambit of the Charitable Trusts Validation Act 1954, but which relates to land in a jurisdiction which has no statutory salvage provisions.[2] Were a testator domiciled in England to devise land in Sri Lanka for the purposes of serving as a dispensary for sick animals,[3] the gift might fail as being for a purpose which is not charitable according to the *lex situs*.[4] A like doom would probably await a gift by a testator domiciled in England of land in the Republic of South Africa for the sort of multi-racial establishment that London House[5] has now become, unless the law of South Africa would rescue the gift by applying it *cy-près*.

In the United States different considerations have been held to be applicable where the land devised on charitable trusts is directed to be sold and the proceeds of sale remitted to be administered in another jurisdiction. Here it is said that the governing law is the law of the place where the trust is to be administered, unless that law conflicts with some strong policy of the law of the *situs*.[6] There is an English decision at first instance, not (it is true) relating to charities, which suggests that an English court would come to a similar conclusion.[7]

The substantial or essential validity of an *inter vivos* trust for charitable purposes of land or other immovables should, if the land is to be retained in the trust, be governed by the *lex situs*. That is certainly the law in the United States[8] and it is submitted the same principle would apply in England. There should be no distinction between testamentary and *inter vivos* trusts in this respect. Similarly, if there is a direction that the land be sold and the proceeds remitted to a country where the trust would be valid, the latter law should, as in the case of testamentary trusts, generally be the governing law. Only if to apply that law would conflict with some strong principle of public policy in the *lex situs*, should the *lex situs* govern the case.[9] What has been said so far relates to an *inter vivos* trust consisting *solely* of immovables: such a trust is governed by the *lex situs*. But a query has been raised as to the reasonableness of such a governing principle where the *inter vivos* trust comprehends both immovables and movables. The

---

1 See *Succession of Meadors*, 135 So. 2d 679 (1962) (land in Louisiana); *cf. Butler v. Green* 19 N.Y. Supp. 890 (1892).

2 E.g. Queensland, South Australia, Tasmania. As to statutory provisions in Canada, see Waters, *Law of Trusts in Canada* (1974) 510–511.

3 According to English law such a trust, if altruistic, would be charitable; see *London University v. Yarrow* (1857) 1 De G. & J. 72.

4 See Cooray, *Reception in Ceylon of the English Trust* (1971) 170.

5 As to which see *Re Dominion Students' Hall Trust* [1947] Ch. 183.

6 *Chamberlain v. Chamberlain*, 43 N.Y. 424 (1871); *Hope v. Brewer*, 32 N.E. 558 (1892); *Re Merritt*, 75 N.Y.S. 2d 828 (1947); *In re Milks' Will*, 102 N.Y.S. 2d 52 (1951); and see Scott, *Trusts* (3rd edn.) para. 651, at 4117–4119.

7 *Re Piercy*, [1895] 1 Ch. 83. The case has been approved in the House of Lords: *Philipson-Stow v. I.R.Comrs.* [1961] A.C. 727, at 744–745, *per* Lord SIMONDS.

8 *Peabody v. Kent*, 138 N.Y. Supp. 32 (1912); affd. 107 N.E. 51 (1914).

9 See footnotes 6 and 7, *supra*.

argument is that a trust should be treated as one unit and governed therefore by one law,[1] namely the proper law of the trust. Nevertheless the English courts have constantly applied the *lex situs* to the essential validity of trusts of immovables.

Construction

The law which governs the construction of a trust of movables is the law intended by the testator or settlor.[2] The testator or settlor may have designated a particular law to govern the question of construction: if so the court may, it is submitted, give effect to his choice of law whether or not it has any connection with the creation or the administration of the trust.[3] If on the other hand no law has been designated the applicable law will be presumed to be, in the case of a testamentary trust, the law of the testator's domicile of the date of executing the will[4] and in the case of an *inter vivos* trust the proper law of the trust.[5]

So far as testamentary trusts of immovables are concerned, the applicable law for questions of construction will again be that intended by the testator as in the case of movables.[6] One leading work on the conflict of laws states the law thus:[7]

> "A will of immovables must be construed according to the system of law intended by the testator. This is presumed to be the law of his domicil at the time when the will is made, but the presumption will be rebutted if evidence is adduced from the language of the will proving that he made his dispositions with reference to some other legal system. If, however, the interest that arises from such construction is not permitted or not recognised by the lex situs the latter law must prevail."

Support for the proposition that in the case of a will devising immovables[8] questions of construction are *prima facie* governed by the law of the domicile of the testator at the time of his executing the will is to be found in *Philipson-Stow* v. *I.R.Comrs.*[9] where Lord DENNING after stating that the proper law regulating the disposition of immovables by will is the law of the situs, said:

> "There is, perhaps, again an exception in regard to the *construction* of his will: for if a question should arise as to the interpretation of the will it will normally fall to be construed according to the law of his domicile at the time when he made his will."[10]

---

1 See Dicey and Morris, *Conflict of Laws* (9th edn.) 658.
2 *Philipson-Stow* v. *I.R.Comrs.*, [1961] A.C. 727, at 761 (will).
3 See the American cases: *Re Cheney's Estate*, 109 N.Y.S. 2d 704 (1952); *Re Nichol's Trust*, 148 N.Y.S. 2d 854 (1956); *Application of City Bank Farmers Trust Co.*, 166 N.Y.S. 2d 772 (1957).
4 *Philipson-Stow* v. *I.R.Comrs.*, [1961] A.C. 727, at 761; Wills Act 1963, s. 4; *Re Wilkinson*, [1934] 1 D.L.R. 544.
5 *Perpetual Executors and Trustees Association of Australia, Ltd.* v. *Roberts*, [1970] V.R. 732.
6 *Re McMorran*, [1958] Ch. 624, at 634.
7 Cheshire, *Private International Law* (9th edn.) 517.
8 The principle is well established as regards movables: *Anstruther* v. *Chalmer* (1826), 2 Sim. 1; *Re Fergusson's Will*, [1902] 1 Ch. 483; *Re Cunnington*, [1924] 1 Ch. 68.
9 [1961] A.C. 726.
10 *Ibid.*, at 761.

Lord DENNING then went on to consider the effect of a change of domicile between the date of execution of the will and the date of the death of the testator and said:

> "If a question arises as to the interpretation of a will and it should appear that the testator has changed his domicile between making his will and his death, his will may fall to be construed according to the law of his domicile at the time he made it."[1]

Elsewhere are to be found decisions that, unless a contrary intention appears in the will, the system of law presumed to be intended by a testator to govern questions of construction relating to immovables is that of his domicile at the date of executing the will.[2] However if the interest created by the will is not permitted or not recognised by the law of the situs, the law of the situs will constitute the governing law.[3]

A distinction must be drawn between questions which relate to the administration of the trust and those which relate to the disposition of the trust property itself. Where the constructional problem relates to a matter of administration it is in most cases appropriate to turn to the *lex situs* because the trust will normally be administered where the immovable is situated. Accordingly the local law of the situs should govern the question whether charitable trustees have any and if so what powers of disposition over the property in question.[4] But if the relevant will directs or authorises a sale of the trust property and the transmission of the proceeds of such sale to another jurisdiction, presumably the law of the latter jurisdiction will be applied in construing any administrative powers relating to the trust.

On the other hand, if the question of construction goes to the destination of the property under the devise or testamentary trust there is a division of opinion in the American cases as to the applicable law.[5] Some cases support the application of the *lex situs*. But many others have referred to the law of the testator's domicile, which is certainly the applicable law so far as movables are concerned. For example in *Houghton* v. *Hughes*[6] the court said:

> "The general rule, both as to wills of personalty and realty, seems to be that a will is to be interpreted according to the laws of the country or state of the domicile of the testator, since he is supposed to have been conversant with those laws."

The testator who is domiciled in England and makes his will with professional assistance is indeed more likely to have intended the law of his domicile to govern such a question of construction; and the choice of that law as the governing law for that purpose achieves a neat result: equal treatment for movables and immovables.

Lastly, what law governs the interpretation of an *inter vivos* trust of

---

1 *Ibid.*; and see Wills Act 1963, s. 4 which statutorily confirms the principle enunciated by Lord DENNING.

2 *Trotter* v. *Trotter* (1828), 4 Bli. N.S. 502; *Studd* v. *Cook* (1883), 8 App. Cas. 577; *Macleay* v. *Treadwell*, [1937] A.C. 626.

3 *Re Miller*, [1914] 1 Ch. 511. On the distinction between this case and *Studd* v. *Cook* (1883), 8 App. Cas. 577, see Cheshire, *Private International Law* (9th edn.) 518.

4 *Re Moses*, [1908] 2 Ch. 235 (private trust); *McLoughlin* v. *Shaw*, 111 Atl. 62 (1920) (private trust).

5 See Scott, *Trusts* (3rd edn.) paras. 648, 4096–4098.

6 79 Atl. 909 (1911).

immovables? Such a trust is likely to be set up by a deed in which the land (taking the commonest type of immovable) is the only subject matter of the trust. Whether the settlor declares himself trustee of the land or conveys it to trustees in the appropriate jurisdiction it is submitted that questions of construction of the settlement would be governed by the *lex situs*.

Administration

The administration of a charity encompasses a variety of matters. The question who may appoint or be appointed a new trustee, the powers and duties of trustees, the distinction between income and capital, the range of permissible investments, the right of trustees to remuneration, the liability of trustees for breach of trust and their rights to contribution: all these are matters of administration which relate both to private and to charitable trusts. But there are two matters of administration which are peculiar to charities, namely the power of the court to frame a scheme for the administration of a charity and the power of the court to direct an application of charitable trust funds *cy-près*.

In relation to *private* trusts the general rule, it would appear, is that matters of administration are governed by the law of the place where the trust is administered.[1] The English and Commonwealth authorities in point are few and far between.

The place of administration is the country where the trustees carry on the work of the trust[2] and this usually is in the country in which the trustees reside or carry on business.[3] If under a testamentary trust the testator has expressly designated another country as that in which the trust is to be administered the law of that country will be applied to the administration of the trust. A testator may impliedly designate the place of administration, for it is reasonable to infer that the testator expects the trustee to administer the trust at his or its domicil or place of business. In the case of an *inter vivos* trust of movables the position is the same.[4]

So far as charitable trusts are concerned, the same rules are applied as in the case of private trusts. However most questions of administration are solved by the use of a scheme. Here, as has already been shown,[5] the general rule is that the court will refuse to direct a scheme in respect of a foreign charity i.e. a charity administered abroad. If the trustees are within the jurisdiction both the courts[6] and the Charity Commissioners[7] have the necessary control to direct a scheme and may do so. The place of administration in such a case is the place of the residence or the place of business of the trustees.

In *Re Vagliano*[8] the testamentary directions of the testator made it clear that

---

1 See Dicey and Morris, *Conflict of Laws* (9th edn.) 860.

2 *Re Cigala's Settlement Trusts* (1878), 7 Ch.D. 351; *Re Smyth*, [1898] 1 Ch. 89.

3 *Re Pollak's Estate*, [1937] T.P.D. 91 (trustee was bank in London); *Perpetual Executors and Trustees Association of Australia, Ltd.* v. *Roberts*, [1970] V.R. 732.

4 *Cf. Re Hewitt's Settlement*, [1915] 1 Ch. 228; see also Delany (1961), 10 I.C.L.Q. 385, at 389–390.

5 See at 284–287, *supra*.

6 *A.-G.* v. *Gibson* (1835), 2 Beav. 317, n.; *Ironmongers' Co.* v. *A.-G.* (1844), 10 Cl. & Fin. 908.

7 *Re Duncan* (1867), 2 Ch. App. 386.

8 (1905), 75 L.J. Ch. 119.

the trust fund whose income was to be paid to certain trustees "for charitable objects in the Island of Cephalouda was to remain in a bank in England. The trustees were, with one exception, persons residing in England. BUCKLEY J. in these circumstances held that the court could direct a scheme to be settled and brought into chambers.

The same principles apply where there is a failure of objects such as would in England constitute a *cy-près* occasion. If the trust fund and the trustees (or the majority of them) are in England and the foreign objects fail, the English court can direct a *cy-près* application.[1]

The position where the trust is being (or is to be) administered abroad gives rise to distinctions.

Where a testator has provided for a charitable object to be carried out abroad and the accomplishment of that object is impossible or impracticable from the outset the first question which arises is as to the intention of the testator. This is a question of interpretation of the will and falls to be determined by the law of his domicile.[2] If that court discovers a paramount charitable intent the court may still decline to order any scheme on the basis that it is for the court of place where the trust is to be administered to frame a *cy-près* scheme.[3] Of course in deciding what is as near as possible to the testator's intention the latter court will be involved in the task of intrepretation; but this function is subordinate to the administrative function: it is an incidental question[4] falling to be determined by the law of the place of administration.

The case of supervening failure of a testamentary charitable trust to be executed abroad is different. In such a case the question whether the trust has indeed failed, and if so whether and how the property should be applied *cy-près*, ought to be determined by the law of the country or state in which the trust is being administered rather than by the *lex domicilii* of the testator. Certainly there are American decisions which expressly[5] or impliedly[6] proceeded on this assumption, and it is hardly open to doubt that an English court would disregard a foreign testator's domiciliary law if a trust administered in England were to fail.

Taxation

Whatever other indulgence may be shown to a "foreign" charitable trust one particular indulgence is not granted. Exemption from income tax in England and Wales is confined to a body of persons or trust established in the United Kingdom for charitable purposes only.[7] A body or trust established elsewhere

---

1 *Re Colonial Bishoprics Fund*, [1935] Ch. 148; and see *A.-G.* v. *Fraunces*, [1866] W.N. 280 (where the trust fund was in court in England and the courts of Virginia had no *cy-près* powers).

2 *Howard Savings Institution* v. *Peep*, 34 N.J. 494, (1961). See *supra*.

3 *Re Joseph's Will Trust* (1907), 26 N.Z.L.R. 504; *Kytherian Association of Queensland* v. *Sklavos* (1958), 101 C.L.R. 56; *Re Masoud* (1961), 28 D.L.R. 2d 646.

4 As to the incidental question: see Dicey and Morris, *Conflict of Laws* (9th edn.) 34-38; Cheshire, *Private International Law* (9th edn.) 54-58.

5 *Franklin Foundation* v. *A.-G.*, 163 N.E. (2d) 662 (1960) where the court commented that the contrary had not been argued.

6 *Exeter* v. *Robinson Heirs*, 55 A. 2d 622 (1947); and see *Anna Jaques Hospital* v. *A.-G.*, 167 N.E. 2d 875 (1960) where the law of the place of administration was the same as the *lex domicilii*.

7 TA 1970, s. 360.

is excluded from the ambit of exemption. This position was established by the decision of the House of Lords in *Camille and Henry Dreyfus Foundation Inc. v. I.R.Comrs.*[1] where the foundation in question was a corporation incorporated under the laws of the State of New York primarily "to advance the science of chemistry, chemical engineering and related sciences as a means of improving human relations and circumstances throughout the world". The question for decision was whether royalties received by the foundation were exempt from income tax under the statutory precursor[2] of the present exemption. The relevant provision gave exemption "from tax . . . under Schedule D in respect of any yearly interest or other annual payments, forming part of the income of any body of persons or trust established for charitable purposes only". Lord NORMAND accepted the statement of JENKINS L.J. in the Court of Appeal that " 'trust'. . . must be taken as referring to trusts taking effect and enforceable under the law of the United Kingdom".[3] But Lord NORMAND was careful to emphasise that this meaning of the word "trust" depended on the context of the particular statutory provision and not on the connotation of the word "trust" alone.[4]

This interpretation of the words "trust established for charitable purposes only" must presumably apply equally in those other statutory provisions granting fiscal exemptions to such trusts. The expression "trust established for charitable purposes only" or a close equivalent is adopted by or incorporated by reference into the legislation relating to capital gains tax,[5] capital transfer tax,[6] stamp duty[7], development land tax[8] and rating.[9]

---

1 [1956] A.C. 39.
2 Income Tax Act 1918, s. 37 (1) (b).
3 *Camille and Henry Dreyfus Foundation Inc. v. I.R.Comrs.*, [1954] Ch. 672, at 706.
4 See [1956] A.C. 39, at 48, H.L.
5 FA 1965, s. 35 (1).
6 FA 1975, s. 51 (1).
7 FA 1974, s. 49 (2).
8 Development Land Tax Act 1976, s. 47 (1).
9 General Rate Act 1967, s. 40 (9).

Appendix 1

Statutes

Contents

The Charitable Trustees Incorporation Act 1872

(35 & 36 Vict. c. 24)

An Act to facilitate the Incorporation of Trustees of Charities for Religious, Educational, Literary, Scientific, and Public Charitable Purposes, and the Enrolment of certain Charitable Trust Deeds [27th June 1872]

1. Upon application of trustees of any charity, Commissioners may grant certificate of registration as a corporate body

. . . It shall be lawful for the trustees or trustee for the time being of any charity for religious, educational, literary, scientific, or public charitable purposes, to apply, in manner herein-after mentioned, to the Charity Commissioners for a certificate of registration of the trustees of any such charity as a corporate body; and if the Commissioners, having regard to the extent, nature, and objects and other circumstances of the charity, shall consider such incorporation expedient, they may grant such certificate accordingly, subject to such conditions or directions as they shall think fit to insert in their certificate relating to the qualifications and number of the trustees, their tenure or avoidance of office, and the mode of appointing new trustees, and the custody and use of the common seal; and the trustees of such charity shall thereupon become a body corporate by the name described in the certificate, and shall have perpetual succession and a common seal, of which the device shall be approved by the Commissioners, and power to sue and be sued in their corporate name, and to hold and acquire, . . . and by instruments under their common seal to convey, assign, and demise, any present or future property, real or personal, belonging to, or held for the benefit of, such charity, in such and the like manner, and subject to such restrictions and provisions, as such trustees might, without such incorporation, hold or acquire, convey, assign, or demise the same for the purposes of such charity. . . .

Section 1 partly repealed by the S.L.R. (No. 2) Act 1893 and CA 1960, s. 48 (2), Sch. 7, Pt. II.

2. Estate to vest in body corporate

The certificate of incorporation shall vest in such body corporate all real and personal estate, of what nature or tenure soever, belonging to or held by any person or persons in trust for such charity, and thereupon any person or persons in whose name or names any stocks, funds, or securities shall be standing in trust for the charity, shall transfer the same into the name of such body corporate, [except that the foregoing provisions shall not apply to property vested in the official custodian for charities]; and all covenants and conditions relating to any such real estate enforceable by or against the trustees thereof before their incorporation shall be enforceable to the same extent and by the same means by or against them after their incorporation. . . .

Section 2 amended by the substitution of the words in square brackets, and partly repealed, by CA 1960, s. 48 (1), Sch. 6 and s. 48 (2), Sch. 7 respectively.

3. Particulars respecting application

Every application to the Commissioners for a certificate under this Act shall be in writing, signed by the person or persons making the same, and shall contain the several particulars specified in the schedule hereto, or such of them as shall be applicable to the case. The said Commissioners may require such declaration or other evidence in verification of the statements and particulars in the application, and such other particulars, information, and evidence, if any, as they may think necessary or proper.

4. Nomination of trustees, and filling up vacancies

Before a certificate of incorporation shall be granted, trustees of the charity shall have been effectually appointed to the satisfaction of the Commissioners; and where a certificate of incorporation shall have been granted vacancies in the number of the trustees of such charity shall from time to time be filled up so far as shall be required by the constitution or settlement of the charity, or by any such conditions or directions as aforesaid, by such legal means as would have been available for the appointment of new trustees of the charity if no certificate of incorporation had been granted, or otherwise as shall be required by such conditions or directions as aforesaid; and the appointment of every new trustee shall be certified by or by the direction of the trustees to the Commissioners, either upon the completion of such appointment or when the next return of the yearly income and expenditure of the charity shall or ought to be made to the Commissioners under the general law, with which the certificate of such appointment shall be sent; and within one month after the expiration of each period of five years after the grant of a certificate of incorporation, or whenever required by the Commissioners, a return shall be made to the said Commissioners by the then trustees of the names of the trustees at the expiration of each such period with their residences and additions.

5. Liability of trustees and others, notwithstanding incorporation

After a certificate of incorporation has been granted under the provisions of this Act all trustees of the charity, notwithstanding their incorporation, shall be chargeable for such property as shall come into their hands, and shall be answerable and accountable for their own acts, receipts, neglects, and defaults, and for the due administration of the charity and its property, in the same manner and to the same extent as if no such incorporation had been effected; and nothing herein contained shall diminish or impair any control or authority exerciseable by the Commissioners over the trustees who shall be so incorporated, but they shall remain subject jointly and separately to such control and authority as if they were not incorporated.

6. Certificate to be evidence of compliance with requisitions

A certificate of incorporation so granted shall be conclusive evidence that all the preliminary requisitions herein contained and required in respect of such incorporation have been complied with, and the date of incorporation mentioned in such certificate shall be deemed to be the date at which incorporation has taken place.

7. Commissioners to keep record of applications for certificates, etc., and charge fees for inspection

The said Commissioners shall keep a record of all such applications for and certificates of incorporation, and shall preserve all documents sent to them under the provisions of this Act; and any person may inspect such documents, under the direction of the Commissioners, and any person may require a copy or extract of any such document to be certified under the hand of the secretary or chief clerk of the said Commissioners; and there shall be paid for such certified copy or extract a fee; to be fixed by the Commissioners, not exceeding fourpence for each folio of such copy or extract.

8. Enforcement of orders and directions of Commissioners

All conditions and directions inserted in any certificate of incorporation shall be binding upon and performed or observed by the trustees as trusts of the charity, and shall also be enforceable by the same means or in the same manner as any orders made by the Commissioners under their ordinary jurisdiction may now be enforced.

9. (*Rep. by the Finance Act* 1949, *s.* 52 (10) *and Sch.* 11, *Part V.*)

10. Gifts to charity before incorporation to have same effect afterwards

After the incorporation of the trustees of any charity pursuant to this Act every donation, gift, and disposition of property, real or personal, theretofore lawfully made (but not having actually taken effect), or thereafter lawfully made by deed, will, or otherwise to or in favour of such charity, or the trustees thereof, or otherwise for the purposes thereof, shall take effect as if the same had been made to or in favour of the incorporated body or otherwise for the like purposes.

11. (*Rep. by the Corporate Bodies' Contracts Act* 1960, *s.* 4 (2) *and Schedule; see now s.* 1 *of that Act.*)

12. Payments on transfers in reliance on corporate seal protected

Any company or person who shall make or permit to be made any transfer or payment bona fide, in reliance on any instruments to which the common seal of any body corporate created under this Act is affixed, shall be indemnified and protected in respect of such transfer or payment, notwithstanding any defect or circumstance affecting the execution of the instrument.

13. (*Rep. by the Mortmain and Charitable Uses Act* 1888, *s.* 13 *and Schedule.*)

14. Definition of terms "public charitable purposes," "trustees"

The words "public charitable purposes" shall mean all such charitable purposes as come within the meaning, purview, or interpretation of the statute of the forty-third year of Queen Elizabeth, chapter four, or as to which, or the administration of the revenues or property applicable to which, the Court of Chancery has or may exercise jurisdiction; and the word "trustees" shall include the governors, managers, or other persons having the conduct or management of any charity.

15. Short title

This Act may be cited for all purposes as "The Charitable Trustees Incorporation Act 1872."

SCHEDULE
Section 3

The objects of the charity and the rules and regulations of the same, together with the date of and parties to every deed, will, or other instrument, if any, creating, constituting, or regulating the same.

A statement and short description of the property, real and personal, which at the date of the application is possessed by or belonging to or held on behalf of such charity.

The names, residences, and additions of the trustees of such charity.

The proposed title of the corporation, of which title the words "Trustees" or "Governors" . . . shall form part.

The proposed device of the common seal, which shall in all cases bear the name of incorporation.

The regulations for the custody and use of the common seal.

Schedule partly repealed by CA 1960, s. 48 (1), (2), Sch. 6 and Sch. 7, Pt. I.

The House to House Collections Act 1939

(2 & 3 Geo. 6 c. 44)

An Act to provide for the regulation of house to house collections for charitable purposes; and for matters connected therewith [28th July 1939]

1. Charitable collections from house to house to be licensed

(1) Subject to the provisions of this Act, no collection for a charitable purpose shall be made unless the requirements of this Act as to a licence for the promotion thereof are satisfied.

(2) If a person promotes a collection for a charitable purpose, and a collection for that purpose is made in any locality pursuant to his promotion, then, unless there is in force, throughout the period during which the collection is made in that locality, a licence authorising him, or authorising another under whose authority he acts, to promote a collection therein for that purpose, he shall be guilty of an offence.

(3) If a person acts as a collector in any locality for the purposes of a collection for a charitable purpose, then, unless there is in force, at all times when he so acts, a licence authorising a promoter under whose authority he acts, or authorising the collector himself, to promote a collection therein for that purpose, he shall be guilty of an offence.

(4) If the chief officer of police for the police area comprising a locality in which a collection for a charitable purpose is being, or is proposed to be, made is satisfied that that purpose is local in character and that the collection is likely to be completed within a short period of time, he may grant to the person who appears to him to be principally concerned in the promotion of the collection a certificate in the prescribed form, and, where a certificate is so granted, the provisions of this Act, except the provisions of sections five and six thereof and the provisions of section eight thereof in so far as they relate to those sections, shall not apply, in relation to a collection made for that purpose within such locality and within such period as may be specified in the certificate, to the person to whom the certificate is granted or to any person authorised by him to promote the collection or to act as a collector for the purposes thereof.

2. Licences

(1) Where a person who is promoting, or proposes to promote, a collection in any locality for a charitable purpose makes to the [licensing] authority for the . . . area comprising that locality an application in the prescribed manner specifying the purpose of the collection and the locality (whether being the whole of the area of the authority or a part thereof) within which the collection is to be made, and furnishes them with the prescribed information, the authority shall, subject to the following provisions of this section, grant to him a licence authorising him to promote a collection within that locality for that purpose.

(A) In this section "licensing authority" means—

(a) in relation to the City of London, the Common Council;
(b) in relation to the Metropolitan Police District, the Commissioner of Police for the Metropolis; and
(c) in relation to a district exclusive of any part thereof within the Metropolitan Police District, the district council.

(2) A licence shall be granted for such period, not being longer than twelv months, as may be specified in the application, and shall, unless it is previously revoked, remain in force for the period so specified:

Provided that, if it appears to a [licensing] authority to be expedient to provide for the simultaneous expiration of licences to be granted by them in respect of collections which in their opinion are likely to be proposed to be made annually or continuously over a long period, they may, on the grant of such a licence, grant it for a period shorter or longer than that specified in the application therefor, or for a period longer than twelve months (but not exceeding eighteen months), as may be requisite for that purpose.

(3) A [licensing] authority may refuse to grant a licence, or, where a licence has been granted, may revoke it, if it appears to the authority—

(a) that the total amount likely to be applied for charitable purposes as the result of the collection (including any amount already so applied) is inadequate in proportion to the value of the proceeds likely to be received (including any proceeds already received);

(b) that remuneration which is excessive in relation to the total amount aforesaid is likely to be, or has been, retained or received out of the proceeds of the collection by any person;

(c) that the grant of a licence would be likely to facilitate the commission of an offence under section three of the Vagrancy Act 1824, or that an offence under that section has been committed in connection with the collection;

(d) that the applicant or the holder of the licence is not a fit and proper person to hold a licence by reason of the fact that he has been convicted in the United Kingdom of any of the offences specified in the Schedule to this Act, or has been convicted in any part of His Majesty's dominions of any offence conviction for which necessarily involved a finding that he acted fraudulently or dishonestly, or of an offence of a kind the commission of which would be likely to be facilitated by the grant of a licence;

(e) that the applicant or the holder of the licence, in promoting a collection in respect of which a licence has been granted to him, has failed to exercise due diligence to secure that persons authorised by him to act as collectors for the purposes of the collection were fit and proper persons, to secure compliance on the part of persons so authorised with the provisions of regulations made under this Act, or to prevent prescribed badges or prescribed certificates of authority being obtained by persons other than persons so authorised; or

(f) that the applicant or holder of the licence has refused or neglected to furnish to the authority such information as they may have reasonably required for the purpose of informing themselves as to any of the matters specified in the foregoing paragraphs.

(4) When a [licensing] authority refuse to grant a licence or revoke a licence which has been granted, they shall forthwith give written notice to the applicant or holder of the licence stating upon which one or more of the grounds set out in subsection (3) of this section the licence has been refused or revoked and informing him of the right of appeal given by this section, and the applicant or holder of the licence may thereupon appeal to the Secretary of State against the refusal or revocation of the licence as the case may be and the decision of the Secretary of State shall be final.

(5) The time within which any such appeal may be brought shall be fourteen days from the date on which notice is given under subsection (4) of this section.

(6) If the Secretary of State decides that the appeal shall be allowed, the [licensing] authority shall forthwith issue a licence or cancel the revocation as the case may be in accordance with the decision of the Secretary of State.

Subsection (1A) was inserted, sub-ss. (1), (2) proviso, (3), (4) and (6) were amended by the substitution of the words in square brackets, and sub-s. (1) was partly repealed by the Local Government Act 1972, ss. 251, 272 (1), Sch. 29, para. 23 and Sch. 3.

3. Exemptions in the case of collections over wide areas

(1) Where the Secretary of State is satisfied that a person pursues a charitable purpose throughout the whole of England or a substantial part thereof and is

desirous of promoting collections for that purpose, the Secretary of State may by order direct that he shall be exempt from the provisions of subsection (2) of section one of this Act as respects all collections for that purpose in such localities as may be prescribed in the order, and whilst an order so made in the case of any person is in force as respects collections in any locality, the provisions of this Act shall have effect in relation to the person exempted, to a promoter of a collection in that locality for that purpose who acts under the authority of the person exempted, and to a person who so acts as a collector for the purposes of any such collection, as if a licence authorising the person exempted to promote a collection in that locality for that purpose had been in force.

(2) Any order made under this section may be revoked or varied by a subsequent order made by the Secretary of State.

4. Regulations

(1) The Secretary of State may make regulations for prescribing anything which by this Act is required to be prescribed, and for regulating the manner in which collections, in respect of which licences have been granted or orders have been made under the last foregoing section, may be carried out and the conduct of promoters and collectors in relation to such collections.

(2) Without prejudice to the generality of the powers conferred by the foregoing subsection, regulations made thereunder may make provision for all or any of the following matters, that is to say:—

(a) for requiring and regulating the use by collectors, of prescribed badges and prescribed certificates of authority, and the issue, custody, production and return thereof, and, in particular, for requiring collectors on demand by a police constable or by any occupant of a house visited to produce their certificates of authority;

(b) in the case of collections in respect of which licences have been granted, for requiring that the prescribed certificates of authority of the collectors shall be authenticated in a manner approved by the chief officer of police for the area in respect of which the licence was granted, and that their prescribed badges shall have inserted therein or annexed thereto in a manner and form so approved a general indication of the purpose of the collection;

(c) for prohibiting persons below a prescribed age from acting, and others from causing them to act, as collectors;

(d) for preventing annoyance to the occupants of houses visited by collectors;

(e) for requiring the prescribed information with respect to the expenses, proceeds and application of the proceeds of collections to be furnished, in the case of collections in respect of which licences have been granted, by the person to whom the licence was granted to the . . . authority by whom it was granted, and, in the case of collections in respect of which an order has been made, by the person thereby exempted from the provisions of subsection (2) of section one of this Act to the Secretary of State, and for requiring the information furnished to be vouched and authenticated in such manner as may be prescribed.

(3) Any person who contravenes or fails to comply with the provisions of a regulation made under this Act shall be guilty of an offence.

(4) Any regulations made under this Act shall be laid before Parliament as soon as may be after they are made, and if either House of Parliament, within the period of forty days beginning with the date on which the regulations are laid before it, resolves that the regulations be annulled, the regulations shall thereupon become void, without prejudice, however, to anything previously done thereunder or to the making of new regulations.

In reckoning any such period of forty days as aforesaid, no account shall be taken of any time during which Parliament is dissolved or prorogued or during which both Houses are adjourned for more than four days.

Subsection (2) (*e*) was partly repealed by the Local Government Act 1972, ss. 251, 272 (1), Sch. 29, para. 23 (4), Sch. 30.

5. Unauthorised use of badges, etc.

If any person, in connection with any appeal made by him to the public in association with a representation that the appeal is for a charitable purpose, displays or uses—

(a) a prescribed badge, or a prescribed certificate of authority, not being a badge or certificate for the time being held by him for the purposes of the appeal pursuant to regulations made under this Act, or

(b) any badge or device, or any certificate or other document, so nearly resembling a prescribed badge or, as the case may be, a prescribed certificate of authority as to be calculated to deceive,

he shall be guilty of an offence.

6. Collector to give name, etc., to police on demand

A police constable may require any person whom he believes to be acting as a collector for the purposes of a collection for a charitable purpose to declare to him immediately his name and address and to sign his name, and if any person fails to comply with a requirement duly made to him under this section, he shall be guilty of an offence.

7. Delegation of functions

(1) ...

(2) The functions conferred on a chief officer of police by this Act or regulations made thereunder may be delegated by him to any police officer not below the rank of inspector.

Subsection (1) was repealed by the Local Government Act 1972, s. 272 (1), Sch. 30.

8. Penalties

(1) Any promoter guilty of an offence under subsection (2) of section one of this Act shall be liable, on summary conviction, to imprisonment for a term not exceeding six months or to a fine not exceeding one hundred pounds, or to both such imprisonment and such fine.

(2) Any collector guilty of an offence under subsection (3) of section one of this Act shall be liable, on summary conviction, in the case of a first conviction,

to a fine not exceeding five pounds, or in the case of a second or subsequent conviction, to imprisonment for a term not exceeding three months or to a fine not exceeding twenty-five pounds, or to both such imprisonment and such fine.

(3) Any person guilty of an offence under subsection (3) of section four of this Act shall be liable, on summary conviction, to a fine not exceeding five pounds.

(4) Any person guilty of an offence under section five of this Act shall be liable, on summary conviction, to imprisonment for a term not exceeding six months or to a fine not exceeding one hundred pounds, or to both such imprisonment and such fine.

(5) Any person guilty of an offence under section six of this Act shall be liable, on summary conviction, to a fine not exceeding five pounds.

(6) If any person in furnishing any information for the purposes of this Act knowingly or recklessly makes a statement false in a material particular, he shall be guilty of an offence, and shall be liable, on summary conviction, to imprisonment for a term not exceeding six months or to a fine not exceeding one hundred pounds, or to both such imprisonment and such fine.

(7) Where an offence under this Act committed by a corporation is proved to have been committed with the consent or connivance of, or to be attributable to any culpable neglect of duty on the part of, any director, manager, secretary, or other officer of the corporation, he, as well as the corporation, shall be deemed to be guilty of that offence and shall be liable to be proceeded against and punished accordingly.

9. Application to metropolitan police district

(1) . . .

(2) The functions which may be delegated by a chief officer of police by virtue of subsection (2) of section seven of this Act shall not include any functions conferred on the [Commissioner of Police for the Metropolis by virtue of his being a licensing authority within the meaning of section 2 of this Act].

Subsection (1) was repealed, and sub-s. (2) was amended by the substitution of the words in square brackets, by the Local Government Act 1972, ss. 251, 272 (1), Sch. 29, para. 23 (5), Sch. 30.

10. (*Applies to Scotland.*)

11. Interpretation

(1) In this Act the following expressions have the meanings hereby respectively assigned to them, that is to say:—

"charitable purpose" means any charitable, benevolent or philanthropic purpose, whether or not the purpose is charitable within the meaning of any rule of law;

"collection" means an appeal to the public, made by means of visits from house to house, to give, whether for consideration or not, money or other property; and "collector" means, in relation to a collection, a person who makes the appeal in the course of such visits as aforesaid;

"house" includes a place of business;
"licence" means a licence under this Act;

. . .

"prescribed" means prescribed by regulations made under this Act;
"proceeds" means, in relation to a collection, all money and all other property given, whether for consideration or not, in response to the appeal made;
"promoter" means, in relation to a collection, a person who causes others to act, whether for remuneration or otherwise, as collectors for the purposes of the collection; and "promote" and "promotion" have corresponding meanings.

(2) For the purposes of this Act, a collection shall be deemed to be made for a particular purpose where the appeal is made in association with a representation that the money or other property appealed for, or part thereof, will be applied for that purpose.

Section 11 was partly repealed by the Police Act 1964, s. 64 (3), Sch. 10, Pt. I.

12. Short title, commencement, interpretation and extent

(1) This Act may be cited as the House to House Collections Act, 1939.

(2) (*Rep. by the S.L.R. Act* 1950.)

(3) References in this Act to any enactment shall be construed as references to that enactment as amended by any subsequent enactment.

(4) This Act shall not extend to Northern Ireland.

SCHEDULE
Section 2

Offences to which paragraph (*d*) of subsection (3) of section two applies

Offences under sections forty-seven to fifty-six of the Offences against the Person Act 1861.

Offences under sections thirteen, fourteen, and twenty-five to thirty of the Larceny Act 1916.

Offences in Scotland involving personal violence or lewd, indecent, or libidinous conduct, or dishonest appropriation of property.

Offences under the Street Collections Regulation (Scotland) Act 1915.

Offences under section five of the Police, Factories, etc. (Miscellaneous Provisions) Act 1916.

The War Charities Act 1940

(3 & 4 Geo. 6 c. 31)

An Act to provide for the registration and control of war charities, and for the extension
of the objects of certain war charities; and for purposes connected with the matters
aforesaid [27th June 1940]

1. Prohibition against appeals for war charities unless registered or exempted

(1) It shall not be lawful to make any appeal to the public for donations or subscriptions in money or in kind to any war charity, or to raise or attempt to raise money for any such charity by promoting or assisting to promote any bazaar, sale, entertainment or exhibition, or by any similar means, unless—

(a) the charity is registered or exempted from registration under this Act; and

(b) approval in writing has been given by the management committee or person responsible for the administration of the charity, or a duly authorised officer of the charity;

and if any person contravenes the provisions of this subsection, he shall be guilty of an offence:

Provided that this subsection shall not apply to any collection at divine service in a place of public worship.

(2) A registration authority may exempt from registration under this Act any war charity if they are satisfied that the charity is established in good faith, and is of so limited a character as respects the area in which the activities of the charity are or will be carried on, or as respects the duration or the objects of the charity, or as respects the value of the money and property likely to be obtained, that it is unnecessary in the interests of the public that the charity should be registered; and the registration authority may exempt the charity for an indefinite or a limited period, and may, if they are no longer satisfied as to the matters aforesaid, withdraw the exemption.

The registration authority, on exempting a charity, shall furnish a certificate of exemption which shall, if the exemption is for a limited period, specify that period.

(3) Subsection (1) of this section, so far as it requires the war charity concerned to be registered or exempted from registration under this Act shall not apply to any war charity until the expiration of two months after the passing of this Act, unless the registration authority within that period refuses to register the charity, nor to any war charity pending the decision of the registration authority on an application for the registration or exemption of the charity made within that period.

2. Registration of war charities

(1) Application for registration or exemption from registration under this Act shall be in the prescribed form and shall be sent to the registration authority for the area in which the administrative centre of the charity is situate, and at least one week before sending an application for registration there shall be

inserted in not less than two newspapers circulating in the said area a statement in the prescribed form of the intention to make such an application and of the time within which, and the place at which, objections to the application may be made; and, subject to the following provisions of this section, the authority shall, after considering any such objections, grant any such application duly made in accordance with this Act and furnish a certificate of registration.

(2) No charity shall be registered under this Act unless the registration authority are satisfied that a responsible committee or other body (in this Act referred to as a "management committee"), consisting of not less than three persons, has been appointed to administer the charity, and a registration authority may refuse to register any charity, or may remove any charity from the register kept by them, if they are satisfied—

(a) that the charity is not established, or is not being carried on, in good faith;

(b) that the charity is not being or is not likely to be properly administered or, in the case of removal from the register, that the conditions specified in the next following section of this Act have not been complied with;

(c) that the total value of the money and property likely to be applied towards the objects of the charity (including any money and property already so applied) is inadequate in proportion to the total value of the money and property likely to be obtained for those objects (including any money and property already so obtained);

(d) that remuneration or reward which is excessive in relation to the total value of the money and property likely to be applied towards the objects of the charity is likely to be, or has been, retained or received by any person out of the money and property obtained for those objects;

(e) that the authority have not been furnished with information reasonably required by them for the purpose of informing themselves as to any of the matters specified in the foregoing provisions of this subsection.

(3) An appeal from a refusal by a registration authority to register any charity, or from the decision of a registration authority to remove any charity from the register, shall lie to the Charity Commissioners and, if as a result of the appeal the Charity Commissioners decide that the application for registration ought not to be refused or, as the case may be, that the charity ought not to be removed from the register, the registration authority shall register the charity or, as the case may be, restore the charity to the register.

(4) Where a war charity has been removed by the registration authority from the register, and either an appeal to the Charity Commissioners has been dismissed or no such appeal has been made and the time for making such an appeal has expired, the registration authority shall give notice of the removal of the charity in at least two newspapers circulating in their area.

(5) Every registration authority shall keep a register, containing such particulars as may be prescribed, of all the charities registered by them under this Act, and lists, containing such particulars as may be prescribed, of all charities the registration of which has been refused by them under this Act and of all charities which have been exempted by them from registration.

(6) Where the administrative centre of any registered war charity is transferred from the area of the registration authority by whom the charity is for the time being registered to another area, the authority shall, after giving notice in writing in the prescribed form to the management committee of the charity and to the registration authority for the area to which the administrative centre has been transferred and affording a reasonable opportunity for raising any question as to the situation of the administrative centre, transmit to the last named authority the particulars of registration of that charity, and that authority shall enter the particulars on the register kept by them and the charity shall thereafter be deemed to have been registered by them:

Provided that, if at the time of the transfer the registration authority from whose area the administrative centre of the war charity is transferred is engaged in an investigation of the affairs of the charity, the authority may postpone the transmission of the particulars of registration of the charity until the completion of the investigation.

(7) Every registration authority shall forthwith send to the Charity Commissioners a copy of all particulars entered in the register and lists kept by them under this section, and shall forthwith notify the Charity Commissioners of any changes in the register or lists.

(8) The Charity Commissioners shall keep a combined register of all charities registered under this Act, and a combined list of all charities in respect of which applications for registration under this Act have been refused, and a combined list of all charities which have been exempted from registration under this Act.

(9) Any question as to where the administrative centre of any charity is situate shall be finally determined by the Charity Commissioners.

3. Conditions to be complied with by registered charities

Charities registered under this Act shall comply with the following conditions:—

(a) the charity shall be administered by a management committee consisting of not less than three persons, and minutes shall be kept of the meetings of the management committee in which shall be recorded the names of the members of the committee attending the meetings;

(b) proper books of account shall be kept, containing such particulars (including particulars of property acquired other than money), as may be prescribed, and the accounts shall be audited, either annually or at such more frequent intervals as the registration authority with the consent of the Charity Commissioners may require, by an independent person who possesses the prescribed qualifications or is on other grounds accepted by the registration authority as competent for the purpose, and copies of the accounts so audited shall be sent to the registration authority;

(c) all money received by the charity shall be paid into a separate account kept in the name of the charity at such bank or banks as may be specified in the particulars of the charity entered in the register;

(d) such particulars with regard to accounts and other records as the registration authority or the Charity Commissioners may require shall be furnished to the registration authority or the Charity Commissioners, and the books of account and other records of the charity and all documents relating thereto shall be open to inspection at any time by any person duly authorised by the registration authority or by the Charity Commissioners.

4. Regulations

(1) The Charity Commissioners may, subject to the approval of the Secretary of State, make regulations—

(a) providing for the inspection of registers and lists kept under this Act, and the making and the furnishing and certification of copies thereof and extracts therefrom;

(b) prescribing the fee (not exceeding ten shillings) to be paid on registration, and the fees for making or obtaining copies of, and extracts from, registers and lists;

(c) requiring notification to the registration authority of any changes requiring alterations in the particulars entered in the register or any such list;

(d) requiring, on the withdrawal of the exemption or removal from the register of any war charity, the surrender of the certificate of exemption or registration, as the case may be;

(e) requiring appeals and advertisements made or issued by or on behalf of any war charity to state that the charity is registered under this Act;

(f) prescribing, in relation to any of the conditions specified in the last foregoing section of this Act, or any of the requirements of the regulations, the persons who are to be responsible for securing compliance therewith;

(g) prescribing the procedure for making appeals or representations or referring questions to the Charity Commissioners under this Act, and limiting the time within which such appeals may be made;

(h) generally for carrying this Act into effect;

and in this Act the expression "prescribed" means prescribed by the regulations.

(2) If any person who under the regulations is responsible for securing compliance with any regulation or with any condition specified in the last foregoing section of this Act fails to do so, he shall be guilty of an offence.

5. Powers of Charity Commissioners

(1) If—

(a) representations are made to the Charity Commissioners, as respects any war charity registered or exempted from registration under this Act, that grounds exist which would under the provisions of this Act justify the registration authority in removing the charity from the register or, as the case may be, in withdrawing the exemption; and

(b) the Commissioners, after giving the registration authority and the management committee or person responsible for the administration of the charity a full opportunity of making representations, are satisfied that grounds exist as aforesaid;

the Commissioners may direct the registration authority to remove the charity from the register or, as the case may be, withdraw the exemption, and the registration authority shall comply with the direction and, in the case of a removal, forthwith give the notice required by subsection (4) of section two of this Act.

(2) Subject to the provisions of this section, where—

(a) any war charity is removed from the register;
(b) an application for the registration of any war charity is refused;
(c) the Charity Commissioners are satisfied, as respects any war charity which is not for the time being registered or exempted from registration under this Act, that if an application for the registration of the charity were made, there would be grounds for refusing the application; or
(d) the Charity Commissioners are satisfied that the objects of any war charity have failed altogether or have become obsolete or useless;

the Charity Commissioners may—

(i) order any bank or other person who holds money or securities on behalf of the charity not to part with the money or securities without the authority of the Commissioners;
(ii) order any money or securities held on behalf of the charity to be paid or transferred to the official custodian for charities as in a case falling within subsection (1) of section twenty of the Charities Act, 1960;
(iii) establish a scheme for the regulation of the charity as in a case falling within section eighteen of that Act, but without the necessity of any application or reference being made to them for the purpose.

(3) If any person fails to comply with any such order as is mentioned in paragraph (i) or paragraph (ii) of the last foregoing subsection, he shall be guilty of an offence.

(4) The Charity Commissioners may exercise their powers under subsection (2) of this section in the cases mentioned in paragraphs (a) and (b) thereof, notwithstanding that an appeal is pending, but shall not exercise their power of establishing such a scheme as aforesaid—

(a) in a case where an appeal is pending, until the appeal has been determined; or
(b) in the cases mentioned in paragraphs (c) and (d) of the said subsection, without giving the management committee or person responsible for the administration of the charity a full opportunity for making representations.

(5) The Charity Commissioners shall, for the purposes of their functions under this section and for the purposes of any appeal to them under this Act, have in relation to war charities all such powers with respect to requiring accounts, statements, written answers to inquiries, the attendance of persons for examination on oath or otherwise, the production of documents, the furnishing of copies and extracts from documents, the examination of registers and records, and the transmission of documents for examination as are exercisable by them [in relation to charities under the Charities Act 1960, and that Act shall apply accordingly.]

Subsections (2) and (5) were amended by the substitution of the words in square brackets by CA 1960, s. 48 (1), Sch. 6.

6. Extension of objects of war charity within the meaning of War Charities Act 1916

The objects of any war charity within the meaning of the War Charities Act 1916, may, with the consent of the Charity Commissioners, be extended so as to include any charitable object referred to in the definition in this Act of "war charity", being an object similar to the original objects of the charity, and the funds of the charity may be applied to any object so included in like manner as to the original objects of the charity.

7. Amendment of House to House Collections Act 1939, in relation to war charities

(1) A police authority may refuse to grant a licence authorising a person to promote a collection as defined by the House to House Collections Act 1939, if the authority is satisfied that the collection is for a war charity which is not for the time being registered or exempted from registration under this Act.

(2) If the chief officer of police for the police area comprising a locality in which any such collection is being or is proposed to be made, is satisfied that it is on behalf of a war charity for the time being exempted from registration under this Act, he may grant to the person who appears to him to be principally concerned in the promotion of the collection a certificate to that effect, and any such certificate shall have the like effect as a certificate granted under subsection (4) of section one of the House to House Collections Act 1939.

8. False statements

If any person—

    (a) in any application for registration or exemption from registration under this Act, or in any notification of any change requiring alterations in the particulars entered in any register or list kept under this Act, makes any false statement or false representation;

    (b) falsely represents himself to be an officer or agent of a war charity;

he shall be guilty of an offence.

9. Penalties for offences

(1) Any person guilty of an offence under section four of this Act shall be liable on summary conviction to a fine not exceeding five pounds.

(2) Any person guilty of any other offence under this Act shall be liable on summary conviction to a fine not exceeding one hundred pounds or to imprisonment for a term not exceeding six months, or to both such fine and such imprisonment.

(3) No proceedings for an offence to which the last foregoing subsection applies shall be instituted except by or with the consent of the Charity Commissioners.

10. Registration authorities

(1) For the purposes of this Act, the registration authority shall—

    (a) as respects the City of London, be the Common Council of the City of London;

(b) as respects any borough, the council of the borough;
(c) as respects the Isles of Scilly, be the council of the Isles of Scilly;
(d) elsewhere, be the council of the county.

(2) The Common Council of the City of London may act through a committee of the council, which may, if the council think fit, comprise persons who are not members of the council.

(3) Regulations made under section four of this Act shall—

(a) provide that, subject to such conditions (other than a condition requiring the payment of any fee for registration) as may be prescribed, any war charity registered at the passing of this Act under the War Charities Act 1916, shall be deemed to be registered under this Act by the registration authority for that charity;

(b) provide for the transfer of registers and other records kept under the War Charities Act 1916, by authorities who are not registration authorities under this Act to the appropriate registration authorities under this Act;

(c) provide for such consequential and incidental matters as may be necessary.

Subsection (1) (b) substituted by the Local Government Act 1972, s. 210 (8).

11. Definition of war charity

(1) In this Act the expression "war charity" means any fund, institution, association or undertaking, whether established before or after the passing of this Act, having for its sole or principal object or among its principal objects the relief of suffering or distress caused, or the supply of needs or comforts to persons affected, by—

(a) any war in which His Majesty was engaged during the years nineteen hundred and fourteen to nineteen hundred and eighteen;

(b) any war in which His Majesty is engaged at the passing of this Act; and

(c) any war or act of aggression, whether occurring before or after the passing of this Act, to which His Majesty by Order in Council declares this Act to be applicable;

and any other charitable object connected with any such war or act of aggression:
Provided that—

(i) the said expression does not include any charity for the blind within the meaning of section three of the Blind Persons Act 1920;

(ii) in relation to any charity which becomes a war charity by virtue of an Order in Council made under paragraph (c) hereof, subsection (3) of section one of this Act shall have effect as if for the reference to the passing of this Act there were substituted a reference to the date of the Order.

(2) Any question whether a charity is a war charity shall be finally determined by the Charity Commissioners.

(3) The provisions of this Act, except in so far as they provide for the extension of the objects of certain war charities and make it an offence for any person—

(a) to make an appeal or raise or attempt to raise money for any war charity, without the approval in writing of the management

Y

committee or person responsible for the administration of the charity, or a duly authorised officer of the charity;

(b) falsely to represent himself to be an officer or agent of a war charity;

shall not apply to the Royal Patriotic Fund Corporation or to any war charity administered by a government department.

12. (*Applies to Scotland.*)

13. (*Rep. by the Northern Ireland Constitution Act 1973 s. 41 (1) and Sch. 6, Part I.*)

14. Short title, extent and repeal

(1) This Act may be cited as the War Charities Act 1940.

(2) This Act . . . shall not extend to Northern Ireland.

(3) The War Charities Act 1916, and the War Charities (Scotland) Act 1919, are hereby repealed:

Provided that—

(a) (*rep. by the National Assistance Act 1948, s. 62 (3) and Sch. 7*);

(b) without prejudice to any provision of the Interpretation Act 1889, this repeal shall not affect the validity of any orders or schemes made under either of the said repealed Acts and in force at the passing of this Act, and in so far as any such orders or schemes could have been made under this Act, they shall be deemed to have been so made and this Act shall have effect accordingly.

Subsection (2) amended by the Northern Ireland Constitution Act 1973, s. 41 (1), Sch. 6, Pt. I.

The National Assistance Act 1948

(11 & 12 Geo. 6 c. 29)

41. Registration of charities for disabled persons

(1) The War Charities Act 1940, shall, subject to the provisions of this section, have effect as if throughout that Act references to a war charity included references to any charity for disabled persons, that is to say, any fund, institution, association or undertaking, whether established before or after the passing of this Act, having for its sole or principal object or among its principal objects the promotion of the welfare of persons to whom section twenty-nine of this Act applies, [not being persons to whom that section applies by virtue of the amendment thereto made by the Mental Health Act 1959, or the Mental Health (Scotland) Act 1960].

[(1A) (*Applies to Scotland.*)]

(2) In the application of the said Act of 1940 to charities for disabled persons, the provisions of that Act shall have effect subject to the following provisions of this subsection:—

(a) the registration authorities shall be the councils [which are registration authorities for the purposes of section 37 of this Act;]

(b) in relation to charities not being war charities as defined in the said

Act of 1940 as originally enacted, subsection (3) of section one of that Act shall be amended by the substitution for the reference to the passing of that Act of a reference to the coming into operation of this section;

(c) notwithstanding anything in subsection (1) of section two of the said Act of 1940, the registration authority may refuse to register a charity if they are satisfied that its objects are adequately attained by a charity registered in accordance with this section;

(d) regulations made by the Charity Commissioners under section four of the said Act of 1940 shall be subject to the approval of the Minister of Health instead of the Secretary of State;

(e) paragraph (e) of subsection (1) of the said section four (under which regulations may require appeals and advertisements to state that a charity is registered under the said Act of 1940) shall have effect as if for the words "under this Act" there were substituted the words "in accordance with the National Assistance Act 1948".

(3) Regulations made under section four of the said Act of 1940 shall provide, in the case of a charity for disabled persons which immediately before the coming into operation of this section was registered under the Blind Persons Act 1920, or the War Charities Act 1940, for the registration to have effect as registration in accordance with this section, and shall make such consequential provisions as may be necessary for that purpose.

(4) ...

Subsection (1) amended by the insertion of the words in square brackets by the Mental Health (Scotland) Act 1960, ss. 113 (1), 114, Sch. 4.

Subsection (1A) inserted by the Social Work (Scotland) Act 1968, s. 95 (1), Sch. 8, para. 15.

Subsection (2) (*a*) amended by the insertion of the words in square brackets by the Local Government Act 1972, s. 195, Sch. 23, para. 2.

Subsection (4) repealed by the Purchase Tax Act 1963, s. 41 (1), Sch. 4, Pt. I.

The Charitable Trusts (Validation) Act 1954

(2 & 3 Eliz. 2 c. 58)

An Act to validate under the law of England and Wales, and restrict to charitable objects, certain instruments taking effect before the sixteenth day of December, nineteen hundred and fifty-two, and providing for property to be held or applied for objects partly but not exclusively charitable, and to enable corresponding provision to be made by the Parliament of Northern Ireland

[30th July 1954]

1. Validation and modification of imperfect trust instruments

(1) In this Act, "imperfect trust provision" means any provision declaring the objects for which property is to held or applied, and so describing those objects that, consistently with the terms of the provision, the property could be used exclusively for charitable purposes, but could nevertheless be used for purposes which are not charitable.

(2) Subject to the following provisions of this Act, any imperfect trust provision contained in an instrument taking effect before the sixteenth day

of December, nineteen hundred and fifty-two, shall have, and be deemed to have had, effect in relation to any disposition or covenant to which this Act applies—

(a) as respects the period before the commencement of this Act, as if the whole of the declared objects were charitable; and

(b) as respects the period after that commencement as if the provision had required the property to be held or applied for the declared objects in so far only as they authorise use for charitable purposes.

(3) A document inviting gifts of property to be held or applied for objects declared by the document shall be treated for the purposes of this section as an instrument taking effect when it is first issued.

(4) In this Act, "covenant" includes any agreement, whether under seal or not, and "covenantor" is to be construed accordingly.

2. Dispositions and covenants to which the Act applies

(1) Subject to the next following subsection, this Act applies to any disposition of property to be held or applied for objects declared by an imperfect trust provision, and to any covenant to make such a disposition, where apart from this Act the disposition or covenant is invalid under the law of England and Wales, but would be valid if the objects were exclusively charitable.

(2) This Act does not apply to a disposition if before the sixteenth day of December, nineteen hundred and fifty-two, property comprised in, or representing that comprised in, the disposition in question or another disposition made for the objects declared by the same imperfect trust provision, or income arising from any such property, had been paid or conveyed to, or applied for the benefit of, the persons entitled by reason of the invalidity of the disposition in question or of such other disposition as aforesaid, as the case may be.

(3) A disposition in settlement or other disposition creating more than one interest in the same property shall be treated for the purposes of this Act as a separate disposition in relation to each of the interests created.

3. Savings for adverse claims, etc.

(1) Subject to the next following subsection, where a disposition to which this Act applies was made before, and is not confirmed after, the commencement of this Act, the foregoing sections shall not prejudice a person's right, by reason of the invalidity of the disposition, to property comprised in, or representing that comprised in, the disposition as against the persons administering the imperfect trust provision or the persons on whose behalf they do so, unless the right accrued to him or some person through whom he claims more than six years before the sixteenth day of December, nineteen hundred and fifty-two; but the persons administering the imperfect trust provision, and any trustee for them or for the persons on whose behalf they do so, shall be entitled, as against a person whose right to the property is saved by this subsection, to deal with the property as if this subsection had not been passed, unless they have express notice of a claim by him to enforce his right to the property.

(2) No proceedings shall be begun by any person to enforce his right to any property by virtue of the foregoing subsection after the expiration of one year beginning with the date of the passing of this Act or the date when the

right first accrues to him or to some person through whom he claims, whichever is the later, unless the right (before or after its accrual) either—

(a) has been concealed by the fraud of some person administering the imperfect trust provision or his agent; or

(b) has been acknowledged by some such person or his agent by means of a written acknowledgment given to the person having the right or his agent and signed by the person making it, or by means of a payment or transfer of property in respect of the right;

and if the period prescribed by this subsection for any person to bring proceedings to recover any property expires without his having recovered the property or begun proceedings to do so, his title to the property shall be extinguished.

This subsection shall not be taken as extending the time for bringing any proceedings beyond the period of limitation prescribed by any other enactment.

(3) For the purposes of the foregoing subsections, a right by reason of the invalidity of a disposition to property comprised in, or representing that comprised in, the disposition shall not be deemed to accrue to anyone so long as he is under a disability or has a future interest only, or so long as the disposition is subject to another disposition made by the same person, and the whole of the property or the income arising from it is held or applied for the purposes of that other disposition.

(4) Subsections (2) to (4) of section thirty-one of the Limitation Act 1939 (which define the circumstances in which, for the purposes of that Act, a person is to be deemed to be under a disability or to claim through another person), shall apply for the purposes of the foregoing subsections as they apply for the purposes of that Act.

(5) Where subsection (1) of this section applies to save a person's right to property comprised in, or representing that comprised in, a disposition, or would have so applied but for some dealing with the property by persons administering the imperfect trust provision, or by any trustee for them or for the persons on whose behalf they do so, the foregoing sections shall not prejudice the first-mentioned person's right by virtue of his interest in the property to damages or other relief in respect of any dealing with the property by any person administering the imperfect trust provision or by any such trustee as aforesaid, if the person dealing with the property had at the time express notice of a claim by him to enforce his right to the property.

(6) A covenant entered into before the commencement of this Act shall not be enforceable by virtue of this Act unless confirmed by the covenantor after that commencement, but a disposition made in accordance with such a covenant shall be treated for the purposes of this Act as confirming the covenant and any previous disposition made in accordance with it.

4. Provisions as to pending proceedings and past decisions and tax payments

(1) Subject to the next following subsection, effect shall be given to the provisions of this Act in legal proceedings begun before its commencement, as well as in those begun afterwards.

(2) This Act shall not affect any order or judgment made or given before its commencement in legal proceedings begun before the sixteenth day of

December, nineteen hundred and fifty-two, or any appeal or other proceedings consequent on any such order or judgment.

(3) Where in legal proceedings begun on or after the said sixteenth day of December, any order or judgment has been made or given before the commencement of this Act which would not have been made or given after that commencement, the court by which the order or judgment was made or given shall, on the application of any person aggrieved thereby, set it aside in whole or in part and make such further order as the court thinks equitable with a view to placing those concerned as nearly as may be in the position they ought to be in having regard to this Act:

Provided that proceedings to have an order or judgment set aside under this subsection shall not be instituted more than six months after the commencement of this Act.

(4) This Act shall not, by its operation on any instrument as respects the period before the commencement of the Act, impose or increase any liability to tax nor entitle any person to reclaim any tax paid or borne before that commencement, nor (save as respects taxation) require the objects declared by the instrument to be treated for the purposes of any enactment as having been charitable so as to invalidate anything done or any determination given before that commencement.

5. (*Rep. by the Northern Ireland Constitution Act* 1973, *s.* 41 (1), *Sch.* 6, *Part I.*)

6. Application to Crown

This Act, and (except in so far as the contrary intention appears) any enactment of the Parliament of Northern Ireland passed for purposes similar to the purposes of this Act, shall bind the Crown.

7. Short title

This Act may be cited as the Charitable Trusts (Validation) Act 1954.

The Recreational Charities Act 1958

(6 & 7 Eliz. 2 c. 17)

An Act to declare charitable under the law of England and Wales the provision in the interests of social welfare of facilities for recreation or other leisure-time occupation, to make similar provision as to certain trusts heretofore established for carrying out social welfare activities within the meaning of the Miners' Welfare Act 1952, to enable laws for corresponding purposes to be passed by the Parliament of Northern Ireland, and for purposes connected therewith [13th March 1958]

1. General provision as to recreational and similar trusts, etc.

(1) Subject to the provisions of this Act, it shall be and be deemed always to have been charitable to provide, or assist in the provision of, facilities for recreation or other leisure-time occupation, if the facilities are provided in the interests of social welfare:

Provided that nothing in this section shall be taken to derogate from the principle that a trust or institution to be charitable must be for the public benefit.

(2) The requirement of the foregoing subsection that the facilities are provided in the interests of social welfare shall not be treated as satisfied unless—

(a) the facilities are provided with the object of improving the conditions of life for the persons for whom the facilities are primarily intended; and

(b) either—

(i) those persons have need of such facilities as aforesaid by reason of their youth, age, infirmity or disablement, poverty or social and economic circumstances; or

(ii) the facilities are to be available to the members or female members of the public at large.

(3) Subject to the said requirement, subsection (1) of this section applies in particular to the provision of facilities at village halls, community centres and women's institutes, and to the provision and maintenance of grounds and buildings to be used for purposes of recreation or leisure-time occupation, and extends to the provision of facilities for those purposes by the organising of any activity.

2. Miners' welfare trusts

(1) Where trusts declared before the seventeenth day of December, nineteen hundred and fifty-seven, required or purported to require property to be held for the purpose of activities which are social welfare activities within the meaning of the Miners' Welfare Act 1952, and at that date the whole or part of the property held on those trusts or of any property held with that property represented an application of moneys standing to the credit of the miners' welfare fund or moneys provided by the Coal Industry Social Welfare Organisation, those trusts shall be treated as if they were and always had been charitable.

(2) For the purposes of this section property held on the same trusts as other property shall be deemed to be held with it, though vested in different trustees.

3. Savings and other provisions as to past transactions

(1) Nothing in this Act shall be taken to restrict the purposes which are to be regarded as charitable independently of this Act.

(2) Nothing in this Act—

(a) shall apply to make charitable any trust, or validate any disposition, of property if before the seventeenth day of December, nineteen hundred and fifty-seven, that property or any property representing or forming part of it, or any income arising from any such property, has been paid or conveyed to, or applied for the benefit of, the persons entitled by reason of the invalidity of the trust or disposition; or

(b) shall affect any order or judgment made or given (whether before or after the passing of this Act) in legal proceedings begun before that day; or

(c) shall require anything properly done before that day, or anything done or to be done in pursuance of a contract entered into before that day, to be treated for any purpose as wrongful or ineffectual.

(3) Except as provided by subsections (4) and (5) of this section, nothing in this Act shall require anything to be treated for the purposes of any enactment as having been charitable at a time before the date of the passing of this Act, so as to invalidate anything done or any determination given before that date.

(4) For the purposes of income tax, this Act shall not require anything to be treated as having been charitable at a time before the date of the passing of this Act unless it would have been so treated in accordance with the practice applied by the Commissioners of Inland Revenue immediately before the eighteenth day of December, nineteen hundred and fifty-two; but, subject to that and to paragraphs (a) and (b) of subsection (2) of this section, there shall be made all such adjustments, whether by way of repayment of tax, additional assessment or otherwise, as are made necessary in relation to income tax by the retrospective operation of sections one and two of this Act, and nothing in the Income Tax Act 1952, shall preclude the repayment by virtue of this Act of tax for the year 1946–47 or a subsequent year of assessment if a claim is made in that behalf to the Commissioners of Inland Revenue within two years from the date of the passing of this Act.

(5) As respects stamp duty on any instrument executed before the date of the passing of this Act, this Act shall not require anything to be treated as having been charitable for the purposes of subsection (1) of section fifty-four of the Finance Act 1947 (which excepted instruments in favour of charities from certain increases of stamp duty under that Act), unless it would have been so treated in accordance with the practice applied by the Commissioners of Inland Revenue immediately before the eighteenth day of December, nineteen hundred and fifty-two; but subject to that and to paragraphs (a) and (b) of subsection (2) of this section, where more stamp duty has been paid on an instrument executed on or after the said eighteenth day of December and before the date of the passing of this Act than ought to have been paid having regard to sections one and two of this Act, the provisions of sections ten and eleven of the Stamp Duties Management Act 1891, shall apply as if a stamp of greater value than was necessary had been inadvertently used for the instrument, and relief may be given accordingly, and may be so given notwithstanding that, in accordance with the provisions of section twelve of the Stamp Act 1891, the instrument had been stamped before the passing of this Act with a particular stamp denoting that it was duly stamped.

An application for relief under the said section ten as applied by this subsection may be made at any time within two years from the date of the passing of this Act, notwithstanding that it is made outside the time limited by that section.

4. (*Rep. by Northern Ireland Constitution Act 1973 s. 41 (1), Sch. 6, Part I.*)

5. Application to Crown
This Act, and (except in so far as the contrary intention appears) any enactment of the Parliament of Northern Ireland passed for purposes similar to section one of this Act, shall bind the Crown.

6. Short title and extent
(1) This Act may be cited as the Recreational Charities Act 1958.

(2) Sections one and two of this Act shall affect the law of Scotland and Northern Ireland only in so far as they affect the operation of the Income Tax Acts or of other enactments in which references to charity are to be construed in accordance with the law of England and Wales [or, without prejudice to the foregoing generality, of the Local Government (Financial Provisions etc.) (Scotland) Act 1962.]

Subsection (2) was amended by the substitution of the words in square brackets by the Local Government (Financial Provisions, etc.) (Scotland) Act 1962, s. 12 (1) and Sch. 2.

The Charities Act 1960

(8 & 9 Eliz. 2 c. 58)

An Act to replace with new provisions the Charitable Trusts Act 1853 to 1939, and other enactments relating to charities, to repeal the mortmain Acts, to make further provision as to the powers exercisable by or with respect to charities or with respect to charities or with respect to gifts to charity, and for purposes connected therewith
[29th July 1960]

PART I

THE CENTRAL AUTHORITIES

1. The Charity Commissioners

(1) There shall continue to be a body of Charity Commissioners for England and Wales, and they shall have such functions as are conferred on them by this Act in addition to any functions under any other enactment not repealed by this Act.

(2) The provisions of the First Schedule to this Act shall have effect with respect to the constitution and proceedings of the Commissioners and other matters relating to the Commissioners and their officers and servants.

(3) The Commissioners shall (without prejudice to their specific powers and duties under other enactments) have the general function of promoting the effective use of charitable resources by encouraging the development of better methods of administration, by giving charity trustees information or advice on any matter affecting the charity and by investigating and checking abuses.

(4) It shall be the general object of the Commissioners so to act in the case of any charity (unless it is a matter of altering its purposes) as best to promote and make effective the work of the charity in meeting the needs designated by its trusts; but the Commissioners shall not themselves have power to act in the administration of a charity.

(5) The Commissioners shall, as soon as possible after the end of every year, make to the Secretary of State a report on their operations during that year, and he shall lay a copy of the report before each House of Parliament.

2. (*Rep., with savings to sub-ss.* (1)–(3) *and* (5), *by the Education Act 1973, s.* 1 (1) (*a*), (3)–(5), *Sch.* 1, *para.* 1 (2)–(7), *Sch.* 2, *Parts II and III.*

3. The official custodian for charities

(1) There shall be an "official custodian for charities", whose function it shall be to act as trustee for charities in the cases provided for by this Act; and the official custodian for charities shall be by that name a corporation sole having perpetual succession and using an official seal, which shall be officially and iudicially noticed.

(2) Such officer of the Commissioners as they may from time to time designate shall be the official custodian for charities.

(3) The official custodian for charities shall perform his duties in accordance with such general or special directions as may be given him by the Commissioners, and his expenses (except those reimbursed to him or recovered by him as trustee for any charity) shall be defrayed by the Commissioners.

(4) Anything which is required to or may be done by, to or before the official custodian for charities may be done by, to or before any officer of the Commissioners generally or specially authorised by them to act for him during a vacancy in his office or otherwise.

(5) The official custodian for charities shall not be liable as trustee for any charity in respect of any loss or of the misapplication of any property, unless it is occasioned by or through the wilful neglect or default of the custodian or person acting for him; but the Consolidated Fund shall be liable to make good to a charity any sums for which the custodian may be liable by reason of any such neglect or default.

(6) The official custodian for charities shall keep such books of account and such records in relation thereto as may be directed by the Treasury, and shall prepare accounts in such form, in such manner and at such times as may be so directed.

(7) The accounts so prepared shall be examined and certified by the Comptroller and Auditor General, and the report to be made by the Commissioners to the Secretary of State for any year shall include a copy of the accounts so prepared for any period ending in or with the year, and of the certificate and report of the Comptroller and Auditor General with respect to those accounts.

(8) (*Rep. by the Education Act* 1973, *s.* 1 (4), (5), *Sch.* 2, *Part III.*)

PART II

PROVISIONS FOR INQUIRING INTO, MAKING KNOWN AND CO-ORDINATING CHARITABLE ACTIVITIES

Registration of charities

4. Register of charities

(1) There shall be a register of charities which shall be established and maintained by the Commissioners and in which there shall be entered such particulars as the Commissioners may from time to time determine of any charity there registered.

(2) There shall be entered in the register every charity not excepted by subsection (4) below; and a charity so excepted may be entered in the register at the request of the charity, but (whether or not it was excepted at the time

of registration) may at any time, and shall at the request of the charity, be removed from the register.

(3) Any institution which no longer appears to the Commissioners to be a charity shall be removed from the register, with effect, where the removal is due to any change in its purposes or trusts, from the date of that change; and there shall also be removed from the register any charity which ceases to exist or does not operate.

(4) The following charities are not required to be registered, that is to say,—

(a) any charity comprised in the Second Schedule to this Act (in this Act referred to as an "exempt charity");

(b) any charity which is excepted by order or regulations;

(c) any charity having neither any permanent endowment, nor any income from property amounting to more than fifteen pounds a year, nor the use and occupation of any land;

and no charity is required to be registered in respect of any registered place of worship.

(5) With any application for a charity to be registered there shall be supplied to the Commissioners copies of its trusts (or, if they are not set out in any extant document, particulars of them), and such other documents or information as may be prescribed or as the Commissioners may require for the purpose of the application.

(6) It shall be the duty—

(a) of the charity trustees of any charity which is not registered nor excepted from registration to apply for it to be registered, and to supply the documents and information required by subsection (5) above; and

(b) of the charity trustees (or last charity trustees) of any institution which is for the time being registered to notify the Commissioners if it ceases to exist, or if there is any change in its trusts, or in the particulars of it entered in the register, and to supply to the Commissioners particulars of any such change and copies of any new trusts or alterations of the trusts;

and any person who makes default in carrying out any of the duties imposed by this subsection may be required by order of the Commissioners to make good that default.

(7) The register (including the entries cancelled when institutions are removed from the register) shall be open to public inspection at all reasonable times; and copies (or particulars) of the trusts of any registered charity as supplied to the Commissioners under this section shall, so long as it remains on the register, be kept by them and be open to public inspection at all reasonable times, except in so far as regulations otherwise provide.

(8) Nothing in the foregoing subsections shall require any person to supply the Commissioners with copies of schemes for the administration of a charity made otherwise than by the court, or to notify the Commissioners of any change made with respect to a registered charity by such a scheme, or require a person, if he refers the Commissioners to a document or copy already in the possession of the Commissioners . . . to supply a further copy of the document; but where by virtue of this subsection a copy of any document need not be supplied to the

Commissioners, a copy of it, if it relates to a registered charity, shall be open to inspection under subsection (7) above as if supplied to the Commissioners under this section.

(9) In this section "registered place of worship" means any land or building falling within section nine of the Places of Worship Registration Act, 1855, as amended by this Act (that is to say, the land and buildings which, if this Act had not been passed, would by virtue of that section as amended by subsequent enactments be partially exempted from the operation of the Charitable Trusts Act, 1853), and for the purposes of this subsection "building" includes part of a building.

(10) . . .

Subsections (8) and (10) partly repealed and replaced by the Education Act 1973, s. 1 [Crown Copyright, reproduced by permission of the Controller, H.M.S.O.]

5. Effect of, and claims and objections to, registration

(1) An institution shall for all purposes other than rectification of the register be conclusively presumed to be or have been a charity at any time when it is or was on the register of charities.

(2) Any person who is or may be affected by the registration of an institution as a charity may, on the ground that it is not a charity, object to its being entered by the Commissioners in the register, or apply to them for it to be removed from the register; and provision may be made by regulations as to the manner in which any such objection or application is to be made, prosecuted or dealt with.

(3) An appeal against any decision of the Commissioners to enter or not to enter an institution in the register of charities, or to remove or not to remove an institution from the register, may be brought in the High Court by the Attorney General, or by the persons who are or claim to be the charity trustees of the institution, or by any person whose objection or application under subsection (2) above is disallowed by the decision.

(4) If there is an appeal to the High Court against any decision of the Commissioners to enter an institution in the register, or not to remove an institution from the register, then until the Commissioners are satisfied whether the decision of the Commissioners is or is not to stand, the entry in the register shall be maintained, but shall be in suspense and marked to indicate that it is in suspense; and for the purposes of subsection (1) above an institution shall be deemed not to be on the register during any period when the entry relating to it is in suspense under this subsection.

(5) Any question affecting the registration or removal from the register of an institution may, notwithstanding that it has been determined by a decision on appeal under subsection (3) above, be considered afresh by the Commissioners and shall not be concluded by that decision, if it appears to the Commissioners that there has been a change of circumstances or that the decision is inconsistent with a later judicial decision, whether given on such an appeal or not.

Powers of Commissioners and Minister to obtain information, etc.

6. General power to institute inquiries

(1) The Commissioners may from time to time institute inquiries with regard to charities or a particular charity or class of charities, either generally or for particular purposes:

Provided that no such inquiry shall extend to any exempt charity.

(2) The Commissioners may either conduct such an inquiry themselves or appoint a person to conduct it and make a report to them.

(3) For the purposes of any such inquiry the Commissioners may by order, and a person appointed by them to conduct the inquiry may by precept, require any person (subject to the provisions of this section)—

(a) to furnish accounts and statements in writing with respect to any matter in question at the inquiry, being a matter on which he has or can reasonably obtain information, or to return answers in writing to any questions or inquiries addressed to him on any such matter, and to verify any such accounts, statements or answers by statutory declaration;

(b) to attend at a specified time and place and give evidence or produce documents in his custody or control which relate to any matter in question at the inquiry.

(4) For the purposes of any such inquiry evidence may be taken on oath, and the person conducting the inquiry may for that purpose administer oaths, or may instead of administering an oath require the person examined to make and subscribe a declaration of the truth of the matters about which he is examined.

(5) The Commissioners may pay to any person the necessary expenses of his attendance to give evidence or produce documents for the purpose of an inquiry under this section, and a person shall not be required in obedience to an order or precept under paragraph (b) of subsection (3) above to go more than ten miles from his place of residence unless those expenses are paid or tendered to him.

(6) No person claiming to hold any property adversely to a charity, or freed or discharged from any charitable trust or charge, shall be required under this section to furnish any information or produce any document relating to that property or any trust or charge to affect it.

(7) Where the Commissioners propose to take any action in consequence of an inquiry under this section, they may publish the report of the person conducting the inquiry, or such other statement of the results of the inquiry as they think fit, in any manner calculated in their opinion to bring it to the attention of persons who may wish to make representations to them about the action to be taken.

(8) The council of a county, . . . county district . . ., the Common Council of the City of London and the council of a . . . borough may contribute to the expenses of the Commissioners in connection with inquiries under this section into local charities in the council's area.

(9) If any person wilfully alters, suppresses, conceals or destroys any document which he may be required to produce under this section, he shall be liable on

summary conviction to a fine not exceeding one hundred pounds, or to imprisonment for a term not exceeding six months, or to both.

Subsection (8) partly repealed by the London Government Act 1963, s. 93 (1), Sch. 18, Pt. II, and the Local Government Act 1972, s. 272 (1), Sch. 30.

7. Power to call for documents, and search records

(1) The Commissioners may by order require any person having in his possession or control any books, records, deeds or papers relating to a charity to furnish them with copies of or extracts from any of those documents or, unless the document forms part of the records or other documents of a court or of a public or local authority, require him to transmit the document itself to them for their inspection.

(2) Any officer of the Commissioners, if so authorised by them, shall be entitled without payment to inspect and take copies of or extracts from the records or other documents of any court, or of any public registry or office of records, for any purpose connected with the discharge of the functions of the Commissioners or of the official custodian for charities.

(3) The Commissioners shall be entitled without payment to keep any copy or extract furnished to them under subsection (1) above; and where a document transmitted to them under that subsection for their inspection relates only to one or more charities and is not held by any person entitled as trustee or otherwise to the custody of it, the Commissioners may keep it or may deliver it to the charity trustees or to any other person who may be so entitled.

(4) No person claiming to hold any property adversely to a charity, or freed or discharged from any charitable trust or charge, shall be required under subsection (1) above to transmit to the Commissioners any document relating to that property or any trust or charge alleged to affect it, or to furnish any copy of or extract from any such document.

(5) No person properly having the custody of documents relating only to an exempt charity shall be required under subsection (1) above to transmit to the Commissioners any of those documents, or to furnish any copy of or extract from any of them.

8. Receipt and audit of accounts of charities

(1) Statements of account giving the prescribed information about the affairs of a charity shall be transmitted to the Commissioners by the charity trustees on request; and, in the case of a charity having a permanent endowment, such a statement relating to the permanent endowment shall be transmitted yearly without any request, unless the charity is excepted by order or regulations.

(2) Any statement of account transmitted to the Commissioners in pursuance of subsection (1) above shall be kept by them for such period as they think fit; and during that period it shall be open to public inspection at all reasonable times.

(3) The Commissioners may by order require that the condition and accounts of a charity for such period as they think fit shall be investigated and audited by an auditor appointed by them, being a member of one of the following bodies:—

The Institute of Chartered Accountants in England and Wales;

The Society of Incorporated Accountants;

The Institute of Chartered Accountants of Scotland;

The Association of Certified and Corporate Accountants;

The Institute of Chartered Accountants in Ireland;

Any other body of accountants established in the United Kingdom and for the time being recognised for the purposes of paragraph (a) of subsection (1) of section one hundred and sixty-one of the Companies Act, 1948, by the Board of Trade.

(4) An auditor acting under subsection (3) above—

(a) shall have a right of access to all books, accounts and documents relating to the charity which are in the possession or control of the charity trustees or to which the charity trustees have access;

(b) shall be entitled to require from any charity trustee, past or present, and from any past or present officer or servant of the charity such information and explanation as he thinks necessary for the performance of his duties;

(c) shall at the conclusion or during the progress of the audit make such reports to the Commissioners about the audit or about the accounts or affairs of the charity as he thinks the case requires, and shall send a copy of any such report to the charity trustees.

(5) The expenses of any audit under subsection (3) above, including the remuneration of the auditor, shall be paid by the Commissioners.

(6) If any person—

(a) fails to transmit to the Commissioners any statement of account required by subsection (1) above; or

(b) fails to afford an auditor any facility to which he is entitled under subsection (4) above;

the Commissioners may by order give to that person or to the charity trustees for the time being such directions as the Commissioners think appropriate for securing that the default is made good.

(7) This section shall not apply to an exempt charity.

9 Exchange of information, etc.

(1) The Commissioners may furnish the Commissioners of Inland Revenue and other government departments and local authorities, and the Commissioners of Inland Revenue and other government departments and local authorities may furnish the Commissioners, with the names and addresses of institutions which have for any purpose been treated by the person furnishing the information as established for charitable purposes or, in order to give or obtain assistance in determining whether an institution ought to be treated as so established, with information as to the purposes of the institution and the trusts under which it is established or regulated.

(2) The Commissioners shall supply any person, on payment of such fee as they think reasonable, with copies of or extracts from any document in their possession which is for the time being open to public inspection under this Act.

Powers of local authorities and of charity trustees

10. Local authority's index of local charities

(1) The council of a county or of a [district or London borough] may maintain an index of local charities or of any class of local charities in the council's area, and may publish information contained in the index, or summaries or extracts taken from it.

(2) A council proposing to establish or maintaining under this section an index of local charities or of any class of local charities shall, on request, be supplied by the Commissioners free of charge with copies of such entries in the register of charities as are relevant to the index or with particulars of any changes in the entries of which copies have been supplied before; and the Commissioners may arrange that they will without further request supply a council with particulars of any such changes.

(3) An index maintained under this section shall be open to public inspection at all reasonable times.

(4) A council may employ any voluntary organisation, . . . as their agent for the purposes of this section, on such terms and within such limits (if any) or in such cases as they may agree; and for this purpose "voluntary organisation" means any body of which the activities are carried on otherwise than for profit, not being a public or local authority.

(5) A joint board discharging any of a council's functions shall have the same powers under this section as the council as respects local charities in the council's area which are established for purposes similar or complementary to any services provided by the board.

(6) . . .

(7) . . .

Subsection (1) amended by the substitution of the words in square brackets, sub-s. (4) partly repealed, sub-ss. (6) and (7) repealed by the Local Government Act 1972, ss. 210 (9), (10), 272 (1), Sch. 30.

11. Reviews of local charities by local authority

(1) The council of a county or of a [district or London borough] may, subject to the following provisions of this section, initiate, and carry out in co-operation with the charity trustees, a review of the working of any group of local charities with the same or similar purposes in the council's area, and may make to the Commissioners such report on the review and such recommendations arising from it as the council after consultation with the trustees think fit.

(2) A council having power to initiate reviews under this section may co-operate with other persons in any review by them of the working of local charities in the council's area (with or without other charities), or may join with other persons in initiating and carrying out such a review.

(3) No review initiated by a council under this section shall extend to any charity without the consent of the charity trustees, nor to any ecclesiastical charity.

(4) No review initiated under this section by the council of a [district or

London borough] shall extend to the working in any county of a local charity established for purposes similar or complementary to any services provided by county councils, unless the review so extends with the consent of the council of that county . . .

(5) Subsections (4) [and (5)] of the last foregoing section shall apply for the purposes of this section as they apply for the purposes of that.

Subsections (1), (4) and (5) amended by the substitution of the words in square brackets, and sub-s. (4) partly repealed by the Local Government Act 1972, ss. 210 (9) (b), (10), 272 (1), Sch. 30.

12. Co-operation between charities, and between charities and local authorities

(1) Any local council and any joint board discharging any functions of such a council may make, with any charity established for purposes similar or complementary to services provided by the council or board, arrangements for co-ordinating the activities of the council or board and those of the charity in the interests of persons who may benefit from those services or from the charity, and shall be at liberty to disclose to any such charity in the interests of those persons any information obtained in connection with the services provided by the council or board, whether or not arrangements have been made with the charity under this subsection.

In this subsection "local council" means the council of a county, of a [London borough], of a county district, . . . or of a rural parish, and includes also the Common Council of the City of London and the Council of the Isles of Scilly.

(2) Charity trustees shall, notwithstanding anything in the trusts of the charity, have power by virtue of this subsection to do all or any of the following things, where it appears to them likely to promote or make more effective the work of the charity, and may defray the expense of so doing out of any income or moneys applicable as income of the charity, that is to say,—

(a) they may co-operate in any review undertaken under the last foregoing section or otherwise of the working of charities or any class of charities;

(b) they may make arrangements with an authority acting under subsection (1) above or with another charity for co-ordinating their activities and those of the authority or of the other charity;

(c) they may publish information of other charities with a view to bringing them to the notice of those for whose benefit they are intended.

Subsection (1) amended by the substitution of the words in square brackets, and partly repealed, by the Local Government Act 1972, s. 210 (9) (c), (10) and s. 272 (1), Sch. 30, respectively.

Part III

Application of property cy-près, and assistance and supervision of charities by court and central authorities

Extended powers of court, and variation of charters

13. Occasions for applying property cy-près

(1) Subject to subsection (2) below, the circumstances in which the original purposes of a charitable gift can be altered to allow the property given or part of it to be applied cy-près shall be as follows:—

(a) where the original purposes, in whole or in part,—

    (i) have been as far as may be fulfilled; or

    (ii) cannot be carried out, or not according to the directions given and to the spirit of the gift; or

(b) where the original purposes provide a use for part only of the property available by virtue of the gift; or

(c) where the property available by virtue of the gift and other property applicable for similar purposes can be more effectively used in conjunction, and to that end can suitably, regard being had to the spirit of the gift, be made applicable to common purposes; or

(d) where the original purposes were laid down by reference to an area which then was but has since ceased to be a unit for some other purpose, or by reference to a class of persons or to an area which has for any reason since ceased to be suitable, regard being had to the spirit of the gift, or to be practical in administering the gift; or

(e) where the original purposes, in whole or in part, have, since they were laid down,—

    (i) been adequately provided for by other means; or

    (ii) ceased, as being useless or harmful to the community or for other reasons, to be in law charitable; or

    (iii) ceased in any other way to provide a suitable and effective method of using the property available by virtue of the gift, regard being had to the spirit of the gift.

(2) Subsection (1) above shall not affect the conditions which must be satisfied in order that property given for charitable purposes may be applied cy-près, except in so far as those conditions require a failure of the original purposes.

(3) References in the foregoing subsections to the original purposes of a gift shall be construed, where the application of the property given has been altered or regulated by a scheme or otherwise, as referring to the purposes for which the property is for the time being applicable.

(4) Without prejudice to the power to make schemes in circumstances falling within subsection (1) above, the court may by scheme made under the court's jurisdiction with respect to charities, in any case where the purposes for which the property is held are laid down by reference to any such area as is mentioned in the first column in the Third Schedule to this Act, provide for enlarging the area to any such area as is mentioned in the second column in the same entry in that Schedule.

(5) It is hereby declared that a trust for charitable purposes places a trustee under a duty, where the case permits and requires the property or some part of it to be applied cy-près, to secure its effective use for charity by taking steps to enable it to be so applied.

14. Application cy-près of gifts of donors unknown or disclaiming

(1) Property given for specific charitable purposes which fail shall be applicable cy-près as if given for charitable purposes generally, where it belongs—

  (a) to a donor who, after such advertisements and inquiries as are reasonable, cannot be identified or cannot be found; or

  (b) to a donor who has executed a written disclaimer of his right to have the property returned.

(2) For the purposes of this section property shall be conclusively presumed (without any advertisement or inquiry) to belong to donors who cannot be identified, in so far as it consists—

  (a) of the proceeds of cash collections made by means of collecting boxes or by other means not adapted for distinguishing one gift from another; or

  (b) of the proceeds of any lottery, competition, entertainment, sale or similar money-raising activity, after allowing for property given to provide prizes or articles for sale or otherwise to enable the activity to be undertaken.

(3) The court may by order direct that property not falling within subsection (2) above shall for the purposes of this section be treated (without any advertisement or inquiry) as belonging to donors who cannot be identified, where it appears to the court either—

  (a) that it would be unreasonable, having regard to the amounts likely to be returned to the donors, to incur expense with a view to returning the property; or

  (b) that it would be unreasonable, having regard to the nature, circumstances and amount of the gifts, and to the lapse of time since the gifts were made, for the donors to expect the property to be returned.

(4) Where property is applied cy-près by virtue of this section, the donor shall be deemed to have parted with all his interest at the time when the gift was made; but where property is so applied as belonging to donors who cannot be identified or cannot be found, and is not so applied by virtue of subsection (2) or (3) above,—

  (a) the scheme shall specify the total amount of that property; and

  (b) the donor of any part of that amount shall be entitled, if he makes a claim not later than twelve months after the date on which the scheme is made, to recover from the charity for which the property is applied a sum equal to that part, less any expenses properly incurred by the charity trustees after that date in connection with claims relating to his gift; and

  (c) the scheme may include directions as to the provision to be made for meeting any such claim.

(5) For the purposes of this section, charitable purposes shall be deemed to "fail" where any difficulty in applying property to those purposes makes

that property or the part not applicable cy-près available to be returned to the donors.

(6) In this section, except in so far as the context otherwise requires, references to a donor include persons claiming through or under the original donor, and references to property given include the property for the time being representing the property originally given or property derived from it.

(7) This section shall apply to property given for charitable purposes, notwithstanding that it was so given before the commencement of this Act.

15. Charities governed by charter, or by or under statute

(1) Where a Royal charter establishing or regulating a body corporate is amendable by the grant and acceptance of a further charter, a scheme relating to the body corporate or to the administration of property held by the body (including a scheme for the cy-près application of any such property) may be made by the court under the court's jurisdiction with respect to charities notwithstanding that the scheme cannot take effect without the alteration of the charter, but shall be so framed that the scheme, or such part of it as cannot take effect without the alteration of the charter, does not purport to come into operation unless or until Her Majesty thinks fit to amend the charter in such manner as will permit the scheme or that part of it to have effect.

(2) Where under the court's jurisdiction with respect to charities or the corresponding jurisdiction of a court in Northern Ireland, or under powers conferred by this Act or by any enactment relating to charities of the Parliament of Northern Ireland, a scheme is made with respect to a body corporate, and it appears to Her Majesty expedient, having regard to the scheme, to amend any Royal charter relating to that body, Her Majesty may, on the application of that body, amend the charter accordingly by Order in Council in any way in which the charter could be amended by the grant and acceptance of a further charter; and any such Order in Council may be revoked or varied in like manner as the charter it amends.

(3) The jurisdiction of the court with respect to charities shall not be excluded or restricted in the case of a charity of any description mentioned in the Fourth Schedule to this Act by the operation of the enactments or instruments there mentioned in relation to that description, and a scheme established for any such charity may modify or supersede in relation to it the provision made by any such enactment or instrument as if made by a scheme of the court, and may also make any such provision as is authorised by that Schedule.

Property vested in official custodian

16. Entrusting charity property to official custodian, and termination of trust

(1) The court may by order vest any property held by or in trust for a charity in the official custodian for charities, or authorise or require the persons in whom any such property is vested to transfer it to him, or appoint any person to transfer any such property to him.

(2) Where any personal property is held by or in trust for a charity, or is comprised in any testamentary gift to a charity, the property may with the agreement of the official custodian for charities be transferred to him; and his

receipt for any such property comprised in a testamentary gift to a charity shall be a complete discharge of the personal representative.

In this subsection, the expression "personal property" shall extend to any real security, but shall not include any interest in land otherwise than by way of security only.

(3) Where property is vested in the official custodian for charities in trust for a charity, the court may make an order discharging him from the trusteeship as respects all or any of that property.

(4) Where the official custodian for charities is discharged from his trusteeship of any property, or the trusts on which he holds any property come to an end, the court may make such vesting orders and give such directions as may seem to the court to be necessary or expedient in consequence.

(5) No person shall be liable for any loss occasioned by his acting in conformity with an order under this section or by his giving effect to anything done in pursuance of such an order, or be excused from so doing by reason of the order having been in any respect improperly obtained; and no vesting or transfer of any property in pursuance of this section shall operate as a breach of a covenant or condition against alienation or give rise to a forfeiture.

17. Supplementary provisions as to property vested in official custodian

(1) Subject to the provisions of this Act, where property is vested in the official custodian for charities in trust for a charity, he shall not exercise any powers of management, but he shall as trustee of any property have all the same powers, duties and liabilities, and be entitled to the same rights and immunities, and be subject to the control and orders of the court, as a corporation appointed custodian trustee under section four of the Public Trustee Act 1906, except that he shall have no power to charge fees.

(2) Where any land or interest in land is vested in the official custodian for charities in trust for a charity, the charity trustees shall have power in his name and on his behalf to execute and do all assurances and things which they could properly require him to execute or do—

    (a) for carrying out any transaction affecting the land or interest which is authorised by order of the court or of the Commissioners; or

    (b) for granting any lease for a term ending not more than twenty-two years after it is granted, not being a lease granted wholly or partly in consideration of a fine, or for accepting the surrender of a lease.

(3) Where any land or interest in land is vested in the official custodian for charities in trust for a charity, the charity trustees shall have the like power to make obligations entered into by them binding on the land or interest as if it were vested in them; and any covenant, agreement or condition which is enforceable by or against the custodian by reason of the land or interest being vested in him shall be enforceable by or against the charity trustees as if the land or interest were vested in them.

(4) In relation to a corporate charity, subsections (2) and (3) above shall apply with the substitution of references to the charity for references to the charity trustees.

(5) Subsections (2) and (3) above shall not authorise any charity trustees or charity to impose any personal liability on the official custodian for charities.

(6) Where the official custodian for charities is entitled as trustee for a charity to the custody of securities or documents of title relating to the trust property, he may permit them to be in the possession or under the control of the charity trustees, without thereby incurring any liability.

Powers of Commissioners and Minister to make schemes, etc.

18. Concurrent jurisdiction with High Court for certain purposes

(1) Subject to the provisions of this Act, the Commissioners may by order exercise the same jurisdiction and powers as are exercisable by the High Court in charity proceedings for the following purposes, that is to say:—

(a) establishing a scheme for the administration of a charity;
(b) appointing, discharging or removing a charity trustee or trustee for a charity, or removing an officer or servant;
(c) vesting or transferring property, or requiring or entitling any person to call for or make any transfer of property or any payment.

(2) Where the court directs a scheme for the administration of a charity to be established, the court may by order refer the matter to the Commissioners for them to prepare or settle a scheme in accordance with such directions (if any) as the court sees fit to give, and any such order may provide for the scheme to be put into effect by order of the Commissioners as if prepared under subsection (1) above and without any further order of the court.

(3) The Commissioners shall not have jurisdiction under this section to try or determine the title at law or in equity to any property as between a charity or trustee for a charity and a person holding or claiming the property or an interest in it adversely to the charity, or to try or determine any question as to the existence or extent of any charge or trust.

(4) Subject to the following subsections, the Commissioners shall not exercise their jurisdiction under this section as respects any charity, except—

(a) on the application of the charity; or
(b) on an order of the court under subsection (2) above.

(5) In the case of a charity not having any income from property amounting to more than fifty pounds a year, and not being an exempt charity, the Commissioners may exercise their jurisdiction under this section on the application—

(a) of the Attorney General; or
(b) of any one or more of the charity trustees, or of any person interested in the charity, or of any two or more inhabitants of the area of the charity, if it is a local charity.

(6) Where in the case of a charity, other than an exempt charity, the Commissioners are satisfied that the charity trustees ought in the interests of the charity to apply for a scheme, but have unreasonably refused or neglected to do so, the Commissioners may apply to the Secretary of State for him to refer the case to them with a view to a scheme, and if, after giving the charity trustees an opportunity to make representations to him, the Secretary of State does so, the Commissioners may proceed accordingly without the application required by subsection (4) or (5) above:

Provided that the Commissioners shall not have power in a case where they act by virtue of this subsection to alter the purposes of a charity, unless forty years have elapsed from the date of its foundation.

(7) The Commissioners may on the application of any charity trustee or trustee for a charity exercise their jurisdiction under this section for the purpose of discharging him from his trusteeship.

(8) Before exercising any jurisdiction under this section otherwise than on an order of the court, the Commissioners shall give notice of their intention to do so to each of the charity trustees, except any that cannot be found or has no known address in the United Kingdom or who is party or privy to an application for the exercise of the jurisdiction; and any such notice may be given by post and, if given by post, may be addressed to the recipient's last known address in the United Kingdom.

(9) The Commissioners shall not exercise their jurisdiction under this section in any case (not referred to them by order of the court) which, by reason of its contentious character, or of any special question of law or of fact which it may involve, or for other reasons, the Commissioners may consider more fit to be adjudicated on by the court.

(10) An appeal against any order of the Commissioners under this section may be brought in the High Court by the Attorney General.

(11) An appeal against any order of the Commissioners under this section may also, at any time within the three months beginning with the day following that on which the order is published, be brought in the High Court by the charity or any of the charity trustees, or by any person removed from any office or employment by the order (unless he is removed with the concurrence of the charity trustees or with the approval of the special visitor, if any, of the charity):

Provided that no appeal shall be brought under this subsection except with a certificate of the Commissioners that it is a proper case for an appeal or with the leave of one of the judges of the High Court attached to the Chancery Division.

(12) Where an order of the Commissioners under this section establishes a scheme for the administration of a charity, any person interested in the charity shall have the like right of appeal under subsection (11) above as a charity trustee, and so also, in the case of a charity which is a local charity in any area, shall any two or more inhabitants of the area and the parish council of any rural parish comprising the area or any part of it; . . .

(13) . . .

Subsection (12) partly repealed by the Local Government Act 1972, s. 210 (9) (d) (10) and s. 272 (1), Sch. 30. Subsection (13) repealed by the Education Act 1973, s. 1 (4), (5), Sch. 2. Pt. III.

19. Further powers to make schemes or alter application of charitable property

(1) Where it appears to the Commissioners that a scheme should be established for the administration of a charity, but also that it is necessary or desirable for the scheme to alter the provision made by an Act of Parliament establishing or regulating the charity or to make any other provision which goes or might go beyond the powers exercisable by them apart from this section, or that it is for any reason proper for the scheme to be subject to parliamentary review, then (subject to subsection (6) below) the Commissioners may settle a scheme accordingly with a view to its being given effect under this section.

(2) A scheme settled by the Commissioners under this section may be given effect by order of the Secretary of State made by statutory instrument, and a draft of the statutory instrument shall be laid before Parliament.

(3) Without prejudice to the operation of section six of the Statutory Instruments Act, 1946, in other cases, in the case of a scheme which goes beyond the powers exercisable apart from this section in altering a statutory provision contained in or having effect under any public general Act of Parliament, the order shall not be made unless the draft has been approved by resolution of each House of Parliament.

(4) Subject to subsection (5) below, any provision of a scheme brought into effect under this section may be modified or superseded by the court or the Commissioners as if it were a scheme brought into effect by order of the Commissioners under section eighteen of this Act.

(5) Where subsection (3) above applies to a scheme, the order giving effect to it may direct that the scheme shall not be modified or superseded by a scheme brought into effect otherwise than under this section, and may also direct that that subsection shall apply to any scheme modifying or superseding the scheme to which the order gives effect.

(6) The Commissioners shall not proceed under this section without the like application or the like reference from the Secretary of State, and the like notice to the charity trustees, as would be required if they were proceeding (without an order of the court) under section eighteen of this Act; but on any application or reference made with a view to a scheme, the Commissioners may proceed under this section or that as appears to them appropriate.

(7) Notwithstanding anything in the trusts of a charity, no expenditure incurred in preparing or promoting a Bill in Parliament shall without the consent of the court or the Commissioners be defrayed out of any moneys applicable for the purposes of a charity:
Provided that this subsection shall not apply in the case of an exempt charity.

(8) Where the Commissioners are satisfied—

(a) that the whole of the income of a charity cannot in existing circumstances be effectively applied for the purposes of the charity; and
(b) that, if those circumstances continue, a scheme might be made for applying the surplus cy-près; and
(c) that it is for any reason not yet desirable to make such a scheme;

then the Commissioners may by order authorise the charity trustees at their discretion (but subject to any conditions imposed by the order) to apply any accrued or accruing income for any purposes for which it might be made applicable by such a scheme, and any application authorised by the order shall be deemed to be within the purposes of the charity:
Provided that the order shall not extend to more than three hundred pounds out of income accrued before the date of the order, nor to income accruing more than three years after that date, nor to more than one hundred pounds out of the income accruing in any of those three years.

(9) . . .

Subsection (9) repealed by the Education Act 1973, s. 1 (4), (5), Sch. 2, Pt. III.

20. Power to act for protection of charities

(1) Where the Commissioners are satisfied as the result of an inquiry instituted by them under section six of this Act—

(a) that there has been in the administration of a charity any misconduct or mismanagement; and

(b) that it is necessary or desirable to act for the purpose of protecting the property of the charity or securing a proper application for the purposes of the charity of that property or of property coming to the charity;

then for that purpose the Commissioners may of their own motion do all or any of the following things:—

(i) they may by order remove any trustee, charity trustee, officer, agent or servant of the charity who has been responsible for or privy to the misconduct or mismanagement or has by his conduct contributed to it or facilitated it;

(ii) they may make any such order as is authorised by subsection (1) of section sixteen of this Act with respect to the vesting in or transfer to the official custodian for charities of property held by or in trust for the charity;

(iii) they may order any bank or other person who holds money or securities on behalf of the charity or of any trustee for it not to part with the money or securities without the approval of the Commissioners;

(iv) they may, notwithstanding anything in the trusts of the charity, by order restrict the transactions which may be entered into, or the nature or amount of the payments which may be made, in the administration of the charity without the approval of the Commissioners.

(2) The references in subsection (1) above to misconduct or mismanagement shall (notwithstanding anything in the trusts of the charity) extend to the employment for the remuneration or reward of persons acting in the affairs of the charity, or for other administrative purposes, of sums which are excessive in relation to the property which is or is likely to be applied or applicable for the purposes of the charity.

(3) The Commissioners may also remove a charity trustee by order made of their own motion—

(a) where the trustee . . . is a bankrupt or a corporation in liquidation, or is incapable of acting by reason of mental disorder within the meaning of the Mental Health Act 1959;

(b) where the trustee has not acted, and will not declare his willingness or unwillingness to act;

(c) where the trustee is outside England and Wales or cannot be found or does not act, and his absence or failure to act impedes the proper administration of the charity.

(4) The Commissioners may by order made of their own motion appoint a person to be a charity trustee—

(a) in place of a charity trustee removed by them under this section or otherwise;

(b) where there are no charity trustees, or where by reason of vacancies in their number or the absence or incapacity of any of their number the charity cannot apply for the appointment;

(c) where there is a single charity trustee, not being a corporation aggregate, and the Commissioners are of opinion that it is necessary to increase the number for the proper administration of the charity;

(d) where the Commissioners are of opinion that it is necessary for the proper administration of the charity to have an an additional charity trustee, because one of the existing charity trustees who ought nevertheless to remain a charity trustee either cannot be found or does not act or is outside England and Wales.

(5) The powers of the Commissioners under this section to remove or appoint charity trustees of their own motion shall include power to make any such order with respect to the vesting in or transfer to the charity trustees of any property as the Commissioners could make on the removal or appointment of a charity trustee by them under section eighteen of this Act.

(6) Any order under this section for the removal or appointment of a charity trustee or trustee for a charity, or for the vesting or transfer of any property, shall be of the like effect as an order made under section eighteen of this Act.

(7) Subsections (10) and (11) of section eighteen of this Act shall apply to orders under this section as they apply to orders under that, save that where the Commissioners have by order removed a trustee, charity trustee, officer, agent, or servant of a charity under the power conferred by subsection (1) of this section, an appeal against such an order may be brought by any person so removed without a certificate of the Commissioners and without the leave of one of the judges of the High Court attached to the Chancery Division.

(8) The power of the Commissioners under subsection (1) above to remove a trustee, charity trustee, officer, agent or servant of a charity shall include power to suspend him from the exercise of his office or employment pending the consideration of his removal (but not for a period longer than three months), and to make provision as respects the period of the suspension for matters arising out of it, and in particular for enabling any person to execute any instrument in his name or otherwise act for him and, in the case of a charity trustee, for adjusting any rules governing the proceedings of the charity trustees to take account of the reduction in the number capable of acting.

(9) Before exercising any jurisdiction under this section, the Commissioners shall give notice of their intention to do so to each of the charity trustees, except any that cannot be found or has no known address in the United Kingdom; and any such notice may be given by post and, if given by post, may be addressed to the recipient's last known address in the United Kingdom.

(10) If any person contravenes an order under paragraph (iii) of subsection (1) above, he shall be liable on summary conviction to a fine not exceeding one hundred pounds, or to imprisonment for a term not exceeding six months, or to both; but no proceedings for an offence punishable under this subsection shall be instituted except by or with the consent of the Commissioners.

(11) . . .

(12) This section shall not apply to an exempt charity.

Subsection (3) partly repealed by the Criminal Law Act 1967, s. 10 (2), Sch. 3, Pt. III.

21. Publicity for proceedings under ss. 18 to 20

(1) The Commissioners shall not make any order under this Act to establish a scheme for the administration of a charity, or submit such a scheme to the court or the Secretary of State for an order giving it effect, unless not less than one month previously there has been given public notice of their proposals, inviting representations to be made to them within a time specified in the notice, being not less than one month from the date of such notice, and, in the case of a scheme relating to a local charity in a rural parish (other than an ecclesiastical charity), a draft of the scheme has been communicated to the parish council or, in the case of a parish not having a parish council, to the chairman of the parish meeting.

(2) The Commissioners shall not make any order under this Act to appoint, discharge or remove a charity trustee or trustee for a charity (other than the official custodian for charities), unless not less than one month previously there has been given the like public notice as is required by subsection (1) above for an order establishing a scheme:

Provided that this subsection shall not apply in the case of an order discharging or removing a trustee if the Commissioners are of opinion that it is unnecessary and not in his interest to give publicity to the proposal to discharge or remove him.

(3) Before the Commissioners make an order under this Act to remove without his consent a charity trustee or trustee for a charity, or an officer, agent or servant of a charity, the Commissioners shall, unless he cannot be found or has no known address in the United Kingdom, give him not less than one month's notice of their proposal, inviting representations to be made to them within a time specified in the notice.

(4) Where notice is given of any proposals as required by subsections (1) to (3) above, the Commissioners shall take into consideration any representations made to them about the proposals within the time specified in the notice, and may (without further notice) proceed with the proposals either without modification or with such modifications as appear to them to be desirable.

(5) Where the Commissioners make an order which is subject to appeal under subsection (11) of section eighteen of this Act, the order shall be published either by giving public notice of it or by giving notice of it to all persons entitled to appeal against it under that subsection, as the Commissioners think fit.

(6) Where the Commissioners make an order under this Act to establish a scheme for the administration of a charity, a copy of the order shall, for not less than one month after the order is published, be available for public inspection at all reasonable times at the Commissioners' office and also at some convenient place in the area of the charity, if it is a local charity.

(7) Any notice to be given under this section of any proposals or order shall give such particulars of the proposals or order, or such directions for obtaining information about them, as the Commissioners think sufficient and appropriate, and any public notice shall be given in such manner as they think sufficient and appropriate.

(8) Any notice to be given under this section, other than a public notice, may be given by post and, if given by post, may be addressed to the recipient's last known address in the United Kingdom.

Establishment of common investment funds

22. Schemes to establish common investment funds

(1) The court or the Commissioners may by order make and bring into effect schemes (in this section referred to as "common investment schemes") for the establishment of common investment funds under trusts which provide—

(a) for property transferred to the fund by or on behalf of a charity participating in the scheme to be invested under the control of trustees appointed to manage the fund; and

(b) for the participating charities to be entitled (subject to the provisions of the scheme) to the capital and income of the fund in shares determined by reference to the amount or value of the property transferred to it by or on behalf of each of them and to the value of the fund at the time of the transfers.

(2) The court or the Commissioners may make a common investment scheme on the application of any two or more charities.

(3) A common investment scheme may be made in terms admitting any charity to participate, or the scheme may restrict the right to participate in any manner.

(4) A common investment scheme may make provision for, and for all matters connected with, the establishment, investment, management and winding up of the common investment fund, and may in particular include provision—

(a) for remunerating persons appointed trustees to hold or manage the fund or any part of it, with or without provision authorising a person to receive the remuneration notwithstanding that he is also a charity trustee of or trustee for a participating charity;

(b) for restricting the size of the fund, and for regulating as to time, amount or otherwise the right to transfer property to or withdraw it from the fund, and for enabling sums to be advanced out of the fund by way of loan to a participating charity pending the withdrawal of property from the fund by the charity;

(c) for enabling income to be withheld from distribution with a view to avoiding fluctuations in the amounts distributed, and generally for regulating distributions of income;

(d) for enabling moneys to be borrowed temporarily for the purpose of meeting payments to be made out of the fund;

(e) for enabling questions arising under the scheme as to the right of a charity to participate, or as to the rights of participating charities, or as to any other matter, to be conclusively determined by the decision of the trustees managing the fund or in any other manner;

(f) for regulating the accounts and information to be supplied to participating charities.

(5) A common investment scheme, in addition to the provision for property to be transferred to the fund on the basis that the charity shall be entitled to a share in the capital and income of the fund, may include provision for enabling sums to be deposited by or on behalf of a charity on the basis that (subject to the provisions of the scheme) the charity shall be entitled to repayment of the sums deposited and to interest thereon at a rate determined by or under the

scheme; and where a scheme makes any such provision it shall also provide for excluding from the amount of capital and income to be shared between charities participating otherwise than by way of deposit such amounts (not exceeding the amounts properly attributable to the making of deposits) as are from time to time reasonably required in respect of the liabilities of the fund for the repayment of deposits and for the interest on deposits, including amounts required by way of reserve.

(6) A common investment scheme may provide for the assets of the common investment fund or any of them to be vested in the official custodian for charities, and, if made by the Commissioners or if they consent, may also appoint him or authorise him to be appointed trustee to manage the fund or any part of it, and as managing trustee he shall, subject to section three of this Act, have the same powers, duties and liabilities as other managing trustees; but where a common investment scheme provides for the official custodian for charities to exercise any discretion with respect to the investment of the fund it shall make provision for him to be advised by a committee of persons who have special experience of investment and finance or of the administration of trusts, or who represent or are nominated by bodies having that experience.

(7) Except in so far as a common investment scheme provides to the contrary, the rights under it of a participating charity shall not be capable of being assigned or charged, nor shall any trustee or other person concerned in the management of the common investment fund be required or entitled to take account of any trust or other equity affecting a participating charity or its property or rights.

(8) The powers of investment of every charity shall include power to participate in common investment schemes, unless the power is excluded by a provision specifically referring to common investment schemes in the trusts of the charity.

(9) A common investment fund shall be deemed for all purposes to be a charity, and the assets of the fund shall be treated for the purposes of this Act as a permanent endowment, except that if the scheme establishing the fund admits to participation only charities not having a permanent endowment, the fund shall be treated as a charity not having a permanent endowment; and if the scheme admits only exempt charities, the fund shall be an exempt charity for the purposes of this Act.

(10) The persons managing a common investment fund shall not be treated for the purposes of the Prevention of Fraud (Investments) Act 1958, as carrying on the business of dealing in securities within the meaning of that Act, nor shall subsection (1) of section fourteen of that Act (which restricts the distribution of circulars relating to investments) prohibit the distribution or possession of any document by reason only that it contains an invitation or information relating to a common investment fund.

(11) Subsections (9) and (10) above shall apply not only to common investment funds established under the powers of this section, but also to any similar fund established for the exclusive benefit of charities by or under any enactment relating to any particular charities or class of charity.

(12) . . .

Subsection (12) repealed by the Education Act 1973, s. 1 (4), (5), Sch. 2, Pt. III.

Miscellaneous powers of Commissioners and Minister

23. **Power to authorise dealings with charity property, etc.**

(1) Subject to the provisions of this section, where it appears to the Commissioners that any action proposed or contemplated in the administration of a charity is expedient in the interests of the charity, they may by order sanction that action, whether or not it would otherwise be within the powers exercisable by the charity trustees in the administration of the charity; and anything done under the authority of such an order shall be deemed to be properly done in the exercise of those powers.

(2) An order under this section may be made so as to authorise a particular transaction, compromise or the like, or a particular application of property, or so as to give a more general authority, and (without prejudice to the generality of subsection (1) above) may authorise a charity to use common premises, or employ a common staff, or otherwise combine for any purpose of administration, with any other charity.

(3) An order under this section may give directions as to the manner in which any expenditure is to be borne and as to other matters connected with or arising out of the action thereby authorised; and where anything is done in pursuance of an authority given by any such order, any directions given in connection therewith shall be binding on the charity trustees for the time being as if contained in the trusts of the charity:

Provided that any such directions may on the application of the charity be modified or superseded by a further order.

(4) Without prejudice to the generality of subsection (3) above, the directions which may be given by an order under this section shall in particular include directions for meeting any expenditure out of a specified fund, for charging any expenditure to capital or to income, for requiring expenditure charged to capital to be recouped out of income within a specified period, for restricting the costs to be incurred at the expense of the charity, or for the investment of moneys arising from any transaction.

(5) An order under this section may authorise any act, notwithstanding that it is prohibited by any of the disabling Acts mentioned in subsection (6) below, or that the trusts of the charity provide for the act to be done by or under the authority of the court; but no such order shall authorise the doing of any act expressly prohibited by Act of Parliament other than the disabling Acts or by the trusts of the charity, or confer any authority in relation to a disused church as defined in that subsection, or shall extend or alter the purposes of the charity.

(6) The Acts referred to in subsection (5) above as the disabling Acts are the Ecclesiastical Leases Act 1571, the Ecclesiastical Leases Act 1572, the Ecclesiastical Leases Act 1575, and the Ecclesiastical Leases Act 1836; and in that subsection "disused church" means a building which has been consecrated and of which the use or disposal is regulated, and can be further regulated, by a scheme having effect under the Union of Benefices Measures, 1923 to 1952, or the Reorganisation Areas Measures, 1944 and 1954, and extends to any land which under such a scheme is to be used or disposed of with a disused church, and for this purpose "building" includes part of a building.

24. Power to advise charity trustees

(1) The Commissioners may on the written application of any charity trustee give him their opinion or advice on any matter affecting the performance of his duties as such.

(2) A charity trustee or trustee for a charity acting in accordance with the opinion or advice of the Commissioners given under this section with respect to the charity shall be deemed, as regards his responsibility for so acting, to have acted in accordance with his trust, unless, when he does so, either—

(a) he knows or has reasonable cause to suspect that the opinion or advice was given in ignorance of material facts; or

(b) the decision of the court has been obtained on the matter or proceedings are pending to obtain one.

25. Powers for preservation of charity documents

(1) The Commissioners may provide books in which any deed, will or other document relating to a charity may be enrolled.

(2) The Commissioners may accept for safe keeping any document of or relating to a charity, and the charity trustees or other persons having the custody of documents of or relating to a charity (including a charity which has ceased to exist) may with the consent of the Commissioners deposit them with the Commissioners for safe keeping, except in the case of documents required by some other enactment to be kept elsewhere.

(3) Where a document is enrolled by the Commissioners or is for the time being deposited with them under this section, evidence of its contents may be given by means of a copy certified by any officer of the Commissioners generally or specially authorised by them to act for this purpose; and a document purporting to be such a copy shall be received in evidence without proof of the official position, authority or handwriting of the person certifying it or of the original document being enrolled or deposited as aforesaid.

(4) Regulations may make provision for such documents deposited with the Commissioners under this section as may be prescribed to be destroyed or otherwise disposed of after such period or in such circumstances as may be prescribed.

(5) Subsections (3) and (4) above shall apply to any document transmitted to the Commissioners under section seven of this Act and kept by them under subsection (3) of that section, as if the document had been deposited with them for safe keeping under this section.

26. Power to order taxation of solicitor's bill

(1) The Commissioners may order that a solicitor's bill of costs for business done for a charity, or for charity trustees or trustees for a charity, shall be taxed, together with the costs of the taxation, by a taxing officer in such division of the High Court as may be specified in the order, or by the taxing officer of any other court having jurisdiction to order the taxation of the bill.

(2) On any order under this section for the taxation of a solicitor's bill the taxation shall proceed, and the taxing officer shall have the same powers and duties, and the costs of the taxation shall be borne, as if the order had been made,

on the application of the person chargeable with the bill, by the court in which the costs are taxed.

(3) No order under this section for the taxation of a solicitor's bill shall be made after payment of the bill, unless the Commissioners are of opinion that it contains exorbitant charges; and no such order shall in any case be made where the solicitor's costs are not subject to taxation on an order of the High Court by reason either of an agreement as to his remuneration or of the lapse of time since payment of the bill.

27. Powers for recovery or redemption of charity rentcharges

(1) Where it appears to the Commissioners that a charity is entitled to receive a rentcharge issuing out of any land, or out of the rents, profits or other income of any land, they may take legal proceedings on behalf of the charity for recovering the rentcharge or compelling payment.

(2) Where a charity is entitled to receive a rentcharge issuing out of any land, the Commissioners may give to the estate owner in respect of the fee simple in the land (or, if the rentcharge is payable in respect of an estate for a term of years, then to the estate owner in respect of that estate) a notice to treat with the charity trustees for the redemption of the rentcharge.

(3) Where a notice to treat is given under subsection (2) above in respect of any land, and the rentcharge is still subsisting at the expiration of ten years from the date on which the notice is given, then (subject to the provisions of this section) the person who is then the estate owner in respect of the relevant estate in the land shall be liable to pay the redemption price to the charity or to the person entitled to receive it as trustee for the charity, and on payment or tender of the redemption price shall be entitled to a proper and effective release of the rentcharge (or, if he has so requested, a proper and effective transfer of it to a person nominated by him).

(4) For the purposes of subsection (3) above the redemption price for a rentcharge shall be such as may be determined in accordance with regulations made by the Treasury.

(5) Proceedings for the recovery of sums due under subsection (3) above may be taken by the Commissioners on behalf of the charity.

(6) Where an estate owner of land liable to a rentcharge has by law or by contract any right of indemnity or contribution in respect of the rentcharge against any person or property, then on his redeeming the rentcharge in accordance with subsection (3) above he shall have the like right of indemnity or contribution in respect of the redemption price.

(7) For the purposes of the Land Charges Act 1925, and of the Land Registration Act 1925, a notice to treat under this section shall be treated as a land charge affecting the estate of the estate owner to whom it is given, and those Acts shall apply to the notice to treat as they apply to an estate contract.

(8) Where an estate owner of land liable to a rentcharge pays it through an agent, a notice to treat under this section, if given to the agent on behalf of the estate owner, shall for the purposes of this section be deemed to be given to the estate owner, notwithstanding that the agent's authority from the estate owner does not extend to accepting the notice on his behalf.

(9) This section shall apply to any periodical payment other than rent incident to a reversion as it applies to a rentcharge.

Miscellaneous

28. Taking of legal proceedings

(1) Charity proceedings may be taken with reference to a charity either by the charity, or by any of the charity trustees, or by any person interested in the charity, or by any two or more inhabitants of the area of the charity, if it is a local charity, but not by any other person.

(2) Subject to the following provisions of this section, no charity proceedings relating to a charity (other than an exempt charity) shall be entertained or proceeded with in any court unless the taking of the proceedings is authorised by orders of the Commissioners.

(3) The Commissioners shall not, without special reasons, authorise the taking of charity proceedings where in their opinion the case can be dealt with by them under the powers of this Act.

(4) This section shall not require any order for the taking of proceedings in a pending cause or matter or for the bringing of any appeal.

(5) Where the foregoing provisions of this section require the taking of charity proceedings to be authorised by an order of the Commissioners, the proceedings may nevertheless be entertained or proceeded with after the order had been applied for and refused leave to take the proceedings was obtained from one of the judges of the High Court attached to the Chancery Division.

(6) Nothing in the foregoing subsections shall apply to the taking of proceedings by the Attorney General, with or without a relator.

(7) Where it appears to the Commissioners, on an application for an order under this section or otherwise, that it is desirable for legal proceedings to be taken with reference to any charity (other than an exempt charity) or its property or affairs, and for the proceedings to be taken by the Attorney General, the Commissioners shall so inform the Attorney General, and send him such statements and particulars as they think necessary to explain the matter.

(8) In this section "charity proceedings" means proceedings in any court in England and Wales brought under the court's jurisdiction with respect to charities, or brought under the court's jurisdiction with respect to trusts in relation to the administration of a trust for charitable purposes.

(9) The Charities Procedure Act 1812, and so much of any local or private Act establishing or regulating a charity as relates to the persons by whom or the manner or form in which any charity proceedings may be brought shall cease to have effect.

29. Restrictions on dealing with charity property

(1) Subject to the exceptions provided for by this section, no property forming part of the permanent endowment of a charity shall, without an order of the court or of the Commissioners, be mortgaged or charged by way of security for the repayment of money borrowed, nor, in the case of land in England or Wales, be sold, leased or otherwise disposed of.

z

(2) Subsection (1) above shall apply to any land which is held by or in trust for a charity and is or has at any time been occupied for the purposes of the charity, as it applies to land forming part of the permanent endowment of a charity; but a transaction for which the sanction of an order under subsection (1) above is required by virtue only of this subsection shall, notwithstanding that it is entered into without such an order, be valid in favour of a person who (then or afterwards) in good faith acquires an interest in or charge on the land for money or money's worth.

(3) This section shall apply notwithstanding anything in the trusts of a charity, but shall not require the sanction of an order—

> (a) for any transaction for which general or special authority is expressly given (without the authority being made subject to the sanction of an order) by any statutory provision contained in or having effect under an Act of Parliament or by any scheme legally established; or
>
> (b) for the granting of a lease for a term ending not more than twenty-two years after it is granted, not being a lease granted wholly or partly in consideration of a fine; or
>
> (c) for any disposition of an advowson.

(4) This section shall not apply to an exempt charity, nor to any charity which is excepted by order or regulations.

The operation of this section has been—

a. Modified by the Housing Act 1974, s. 2 (3), and

b. Excluded by the Sharing of Church Buildings Act 1969, s. 8 (3) and by the Fire Precautions (Loans) Act 1973, s. 1 (7).

30. Charitable companies

(1) Where a charity may be wound up by the High Court under the Companies Act 1948, a petition for it to be wound up under that Act by any court in England or Wales having jurisdiction may be presented by the Attorney General, as well as by any person authorised by that Act.

(2) Where a charity is a company or other body corporate, and has power to alter the instruments establishing or regulating it as a body corporate, no exercise of that power which has the effect of the body ceasing to be a charity shall be valid so as to affect the application of any property acquired under any disposition or agreement previously made otherwise than for full consideration in money or money's worth, or of any property representing property so acquired, or of any property representing income which has accrued before the alteration is made, or of the income from any such property as aforesaid.

31. Protection of expression "common good"

(1) It shall not be lawful, without the consent of the Commissioners, to invite gifts in money or in kind to the funds of, or to any fund managed by, an institution which has the words "common good" in its name, other than a body corporate established by Royal charter, or to any fund described in or in connection with the invitation by a name which includes the words "common good" otherwise than as part of the name of such a body corporate.

(2) The words "common good" shall not, without the consent of the Commissioners, be used in the name of any institution established in England or Wales, other than a body corporate established by Royal charter.

(3) Any person contravening subsection (1) or (2) of this section shall be guilty of an offence and liable on summary conviction to a fine not exceeding fifty pounds.

Part IV

Miscellaneous provisions as to charities and their affairs

32. General obligation to keep accounts

(1) Charity trustees shall keep proper books of account with respect to the affairs of the charity, and charity trustees not required by or under the authority of any other Act to prepare periodical statements of account shall prepare consecutive statements of account consisting on each occasion of an income and expenditure account relating to a period of not more than fifteen months and a balance sheet relating to the end of that period.

(2) The books of account and statements of account relating to any charity shall be preserved for a period of seven years at least, unless the charity ceases to exist and the Commissioners permit them to be destroyed or otherwise disposed of.

(3) The statements of account relating to a parochial charity in a rural parish, other than an ecclesiastical charity, shall be sent annually to the parish council or, if there is no parish council, to the chairman of the parish meeting, and shall be presented by the council or chairman at the next parish meeting.
. . .

Subsection (3) partly repealed by the Local Government Act 1972, s. 272 (1), Sch. 30.

33. Manner of giving notice of charity meetings, etc.

(1) All notices which are required or authorised by the trusts of a charity to be given to a charity trustee, member or subscriber may be sent by post, and, if sent by post, may be addressed to any address given as his in the list of charity trustees, members or subscribers for the time being in use at the office or principal office of the charity.

(2) Where any such notice required to be given as aforesaid is given by post, it shall be deemed to have been given by the time at which the letter containing it would be delivered in the ordinary course of post.

(3) No notice required to be given as aforesaid of any meeting or election need be given to any charity trustee, member or subscriber, if in the list above mentioned he has no address in the United Kingdom.

34. Manner of executing instruments

(1) Charity trustees may, subject to the trusts of the charity, confer on any of their body (not being less than two in number) a general authority, or an authority limited in such manner as the trustees think fit, to execute in the names and on behalf of the trustees assurances or other deeds or instruments for giving effect to transactions to which the trustees are a party; and any deed or instrument executed in pursuance of an authority so given shall be of the same effect as if executed by the whole body.

(2) An authority under subsection (1) above—

    (a) shall suffice for any deed or instrument if it is given in writing or by resolution of a meeting of the trustees, notwithstanding the want of any formality that would be required in giving an authority apart from that subsection;

    (b) may be given so as to make the powers conferred exercisable by any of the trustees, or may be restricted to named persons or in any other way;

    (c) subject to any such restriction, and until it is revoked, shall, notwithstanding any change in the charity trustees, have effect as a continuing authority given by and to the persons who from time to time are of their body.

(3) In any authority under this section to execute a deed or instrument in the names and on behalf of charity trustees there shall, unless the contrary intention appears, be implied authority also to execute it from them in the name and on behalf of the official custodian for charities or of any other person, in any case in which the charity trustees could do so.

(4) Where a deed or instrument purports to be executed in pursuance of this section, then in favour of a person who (then or afterwards) in good faith acquires for money or money's worth an interest in or charge on property or the benefit of any covenant or agreement expressed to be entered into by the charity trustees, it shall be conclusively presumed to have been duly executed by virtue of this section.

(5) The powers conferred by this section shall be in addition to and not in derogation of any other powers.

35. Transfer and evidence of title to property vested in trustees

(1) Where, under the trusts of a charity, trustees of property held for the purposes of the charity may be appointed or discharged by resolution of a meeting of the charity trustees, members or other persons, a memorandum declaring a trustee to have been so appointed or discharged shall be sufficient evidence of that fact, if the memorandum is signed either at the meeting by the person presiding or in some other manner directed by the meeting, and is attested by two persons present at the meeting.

(2) A memorandum evidencing the appointment or discharge of a trustee under subsection (1) above, if executed as a deed, shall have the like operation under section forty of the Trustee Act 1925 (which relates to vesting declarations as respects trust property in deeds appointing or discharging trustees), as if the appointment or discharge were effected by the deed.

(3) For the purposes of this section, where a document purports to have been signed and attested as mentioned in subsection (1) above, then on proof (whether by evidence or as a matter of presumption) of the signature the document shall be presumed to have been so signed and attested, unless the contrary is shown.

(4) This section shall apply to a memorandum made at any time, except that subsection (2) shall apply only to those made after the commencement of this Act.

(5) This section shall apply in relation to any institution to which the Literary

and Scientific Institutions Act 1854, applies, as it applies in relation to a charity.

(6) The Trustee Appointment Act 1850, the Trustee Appointment Act 1869, the Trustees Appointment Act 1890, and in so far as it applies any of those Acts the School Sites Act 1852, shall cease to have effect; but where, at the commencement of this Act the provisions of those Acts providing for the appointment of trustees apply in relation to any land, those provisions shall have effect as if contained in the conveyance or other instrument declaring the trusts on which the land is then held.

36. Miscellaneous provisions as to evidence

(1) Where, in any proceedings to recover or compel payment of any rentcharge or other periodical payment claimed by or on behalf of a charity out of land or of the rent, profits or other income of land, otherwise than as rent incident to a reversion, it is shown that the rentcharge or other periodical payment has at any time been paid for twelve consecutive years to or for the benefit of the charity, that shall be prima facie evidence of the perpetual liability to it of the land or income, and no proof of its origin shall be necessary.

(2) In any proceedings, the following documents, that is to say—

    (a) the printed copies of the reports of the Commissioners for enquiring concerning charities, 1818 to 1837, who were appointed under the Act 58 Geo. 3 c. 91 and subsequent Acts; and

    (b) the printed copies of the reports which were made for various counties and county boroughs to the Charity Commissioners by their assistant commissioners and presented to the House of Commons as returns to orders of various dates beginning with the eighth day of December, eighteen hundred and ninety, and ending with the ninth day of September, nineteen hundred and nine;

shall be admissible as evidence of the documents and facts stated in them.

(3) Evidence of any order, certificate or other document issued by the Commissioners may be given by means of a copy retained by them, or taken from a copy so retained, and certified to be a true copy by any officer of the Commissioners generally or specially authorised by them to act for this purpose; and a document purporting to be such a copy shall be received in evidence without proof of the official position, authority or handwriting of the person certifying it.

37. Parochial charities

(1) Where trustees hold any property for the purposes of a public recreation ground, or of allotments (whether under inclosure Acts or otherwise), for the benefit of inhabitants of a rural parish having a parish council, or for other charitable purposes connected with such a rural parish, except for an ecclesiastical charity, they may with the approval of the Commissioners and with the consent of the parish council transfer the property to the parish council or to persons appointed by the parish council; and the council or their appointees shall hold the property on the same trusts and subject to the same conditions as the trustees did.

This subsection shall apply to property held for any public purposes as it applies to property held for charitable purposes, . . .

(2) Where the charity trustees of a parochial charity in a rural parish, not being an ecclesiastical charity nor a charity founded within the preceding forty years, do not include persons elected by the local government electors, ratepayers or inhabitants of the parish or appointed by the parish council or parish meeting, the parish council or parish meeting may appoint additional charity trustees, to such number as the Commissioners may allow; and if there is a sole charity trustee not elected or appointed as aforesaid of any such charity, the number of the charity trustees may, with the approval of the Commissioners, be increased to three of whom one may be nominated by the person holding the office of the sole trustee and one by the parish council or parish meeting.

. . .

(3) Where, under the trusts of a charity other than an ecclesiastical charity, the inhabitants of a rural parish (whether in vestry or not) or a select vestry were formerly (in 1894) entitled to appoint charity trustees for, or trustees or beneficiaries of, the charity, then—

    (a) in a parish having a parish council, the appointment shall be made by the parish council or, in the case of beneficiaries, by persons appointed by the parish council; . . .

(4) Where overseers as such or, except in the case of an ecclesiastical charity, churchwardens as such were formerly (in 1894) charity trustees of or trustees for a parochial charity in a rural parish, either alone or jointly with other persons, then instead of the former overseer or churchwarden trustees there shall be trustees (to a number not greater than that of the former overseer, or churchwarden trustees) appointed by the parish council or, if there is no parish council, by the parish meeting.

(5) Where, outside the county of London, overseers of a parish as such were formerly (in 1927) charity trustees of or trustees for any charity, either alone or jointly with other persons, then instead of the former overseer trustees there shall be trustees (to a number not greater than that of the former overseer trustees) appointed—

    (a) where the parish is a rural parish, by the parish council or, if there is no parish council, by the parish meeting; and

    (b) where the parish is an urban parish, but is comprised in a borough included in a rural district, by the borough council; and

    (c) where the parish is an urban parish not so comprised, by the rating authority;

but, if in the case of an urban parish the area of the council making the appointment comprises other parishes also and is divided into wards for the election of councillors, the appointment shall be made on the nomination of the councillors for the ward or wards comprising the parish.

(6) Any appointment of a charity trustee or trustee for a charity which is made by virtue of this section shall be for a term of four years, but a retiring trustee shall be eligible for re-appointment:

Provided that—

    (a) on an appointment under subsection (2), where no previous appointments have been made by virtue of that subsection or of the corresponding provision of the Local Government Act 1894, and more than one trustee is appointed, half of those appointed (or as nearly as may be) shall be appointed for a term of two years; and

(b) an appointment made to fill a casual vacancy shall be for the remainder of the term of the previous appointment.

(7) This section shall not affect the trusteeship, control or management of any voluntary school within the meaning of the Education Act 1944.

(8) The provisions of this section shall not extend to the Isles of Scilly, and shall have effect subject to any order (including any future order) made under any enactment relating to local government with respect to local government areas or the powers of local authorities.

(9) In this section the expression "formerly (in 1894)" relates to the period immediately before the passing of the Local Government Act 1894, and the expression "formerly (in 1927)" to the period immediately before the first day of April, nineteen hundred and twenty-seven; and the word "former" shall be construed accordingly.

Subsections (1), (2), (3) partly repealed by the Local Government Act 1972, s. 272 (1). Sch. 20. Subsections (3)–(5) modified by the Local Government Act 1972, s. 210 (9) (10),

38. Repeal of law of mortmain

(1) . . .

(2) . . .

(3) The repeal by this Act of the Mortmain and Charitable Uses Act 1891, shall have effect in relation to the wills of persons dying before the passing of this Act so as to abrogate any requirement to sell land then unsold, but not so as to enable effect to be given to a direction to lay out personal estate in land without an order under section eight of that Act or so as to affect the power to make such an order.

(4) Any reference in any enactment or document to a charity within the meaning, purview and interpretation of the Charitable Uses Act 1601, or of the preamble to it, shall be construed as a reference to a charity within the meaning which the word bears as a legal term according to the law of England and Wales.

(5) No repeal made by this Act shall affect any power to hold land in Northern Ireland without licence in mortmain; . . .

Subsections (1) and (2) repealed by the Education Act 1973, s. 1 (4), Sch. 2, Pt. I. Subsection (5) partly repealed by the Northern Ireland Constitution Act 1973, s. 41 (1), Sch. 6, Pt. I.

39. Repeal of obsolete enactments

(1) . . .

(2) Where the trusts of a charity are at the commencement of this Act wholly or partly comprised in an enactment specified in the Fifth Schedule to this Act, or in an instrument having effect under such an enactment, the operation of those trusts shall not be affected by the repeal of that enactment by this Act.

Subsection (1) repealed by the Education Act 1973, s. 1 (4), Sch. 2, Pt. I.

PART V

SUPPLEMENTARY

40. Miscellaneous provisions as to orders of Commissioners or Minister

(1) Any order made by the Commissioners under this Act may include such incidental or supplementary provisions as the Commissioners think expedient for carrying into effect the objects of the order, and where the Commissioners exercise any jurisdiction to make such an order on an application or reference to them, they may insert any such provisions in the order notwithstanding that the application or reference does not propose their insertion.

(2) Where the Commissioners make an order under this Act, then (without prejudice to the requirements of this Act where the order is subject to appeal) they may themselves give such public notice as they think fit of the making or contents of the order, or may require it to be given by any person on whose application the order is made or by any charity affected by the order.

(3) The Commissioners at any time within twelve months after they have made an order under this Act, if they are satisfied that the order was made by mistake or on misrepresentation or otherwise than in conformity with this Act, may with or without any application or reference to them discharge the order in whole or in part, and subject or not to any savings or other transitional provisions.

(4) Except for the purposes of subsection (3) above or of an appeal under this Act, an order made by the Commissioners under this Act shall be deemed to have been duly and formally made and not be called in question on the ground only of irregularity or informality, but (subject to any further order) have effect according to its tenor.

(5) This section shall apply to orders made under any Act amended by this Act, if made by virtue of that amendment, as it applies to orders made under this Act.

41. Enforcement of orders of Commissioners or Minister

A person guilty of disobedience—

(a) to an order of the Commissioners under subsection (3) of section six or under section seven of this Act, or to a precept under that sub-section; or

(b) to an order of the Commissioners under section eighteen or twenty of this Act requiring a transfer of property or payment to be called for or made; or

(c) to an order of the Commissioners requiring a default under this Act to be made good;

may on the application of the Commissioners to the High Court be dealt with as for disobedience to an order of the High Court.

42. Appeals from Commissioners or Minister

(1) Provision shall be made by rules of court for regulating appeals to the High Court under this Act against orders or decisions of the Commissioners.

(2) On such an appeal the Attorney General shall be entitled to appear and be heard, and such other persons as the rules allow or as the court may direct.

(3) Subsection (1) of section sixty-three of the Supreme Court of Judicature (Consolidation) Act, 1925, shall not apply to such an appeal in so far as it requires an appeal from any person to the High Court to be heard and determined by a divisional court.

43. Regulations

(1) Save as otherwise provided by this Act, any power to make regulations which is conferred by this Act shall be exercisable by the Secretary of State.

(2) Regulations may be made for prescribing anything which is required or authorised by this Act to be prescribed.

(3) Any power of the Treasury [or Secretary of State] to make regulations under this Act shall be exercisable by statutory instrument, which shall be subject to annulment in pursuance of a resolution of either House of Parliament.

Subsection (1) substituted, and sub-s. (3) as originally enacted amended by the substitution of the words in square brackets, by the Education Act 1973, s. 1 (3), Sch. 1, para. 1 (1), (7).

44. Expenses

(1) There shall be defrayed out of monies provided by Parliament—

    (a) the remuneration and allowances payable under this Act to the Commissioners and to their officers and servants . . . ; and

    (b) any administrative expenses incurred for the purposes of this Act by the Secretary of State, . . . or the Commissioners.

(2) Any fees received . . . by the Commissioners under this Act shall be paid into the Exchequer.

(3) There shall also be defrayed out of monies provided by Parliament any increase in the sums payable out of monies so provided by way of rate-deficiency grant or exchequer equalisation grant under the enactments relating to local government in England and Wales or in Scotland, being an increase attributable to the expenditure under this Act of any council or joint board—

    (a) in contributing to the expenses of inquiries instituted under this Act by the Commissioners or the Minister of Education in relation to charities; or

    (b) in or in connection with the establishment or maintenance of an index of local charities; or

    (c) in carrying out or co-operating in a review of local charities.

(4) . . .

Subsection (1) (a) partly repealed by the Superannuation Act 1972, s. 29 (4), Sch. 8. Subsections (1) (b) and (2) partly repealed, and sub-s. (3) repealed, by the Education Act 1973, s. 1 (4), (5), Sch. 2, Pts. I and III. Subsection (4) repealed by the Local Government Act 1972, s. 272 (1), Sch. 30.

45. Construction of references to a "charity" or to particular classes of charity

(1) In this Act, except in so far as the context otherwise requires,—

    "charity" means any institution, corporate or not, which is established for charitable purposes and is subject to the control of the High Court in the exercise of the court's jurisdiction with respect to charities;

"ecclesiastical charity" has the same meaning as in the Local Government Act 1894;

"exempt charity" means (subject to subsection (9) of section twenty-two of this Act) a charity comprised in the Second Schedule to this Act;

"local charity" means, in relation to any area, a charity established for purposes which are by their nature or by the trusts of the charity directed wholly or mainly to the benefit of that area or of part of it;

"parochial charity" means, in relation to any parish, a charity the benefits of which are, or the separate distribution of the benefits of which is, confined to inhabitants of the parish, or of a single ancient ecclesiastical parish which included that parish or part of it, or of an area consisting of that parish with not more than four neighbouring parishes.

(2) The expression "charity" is not in this Act applicable—

(a) to any ecclesiastical corporation (that is to say, any corporation in the Church of England, whether sole or aggregate, which is established for spiritual purposes) in respect of the corporate property of the corporation, except to a corporation aggregate having some purposes which are not ecclesiastical in respect of its corporate property held for those purposes; or

(b) to any trust of property for purposes for which the property has been consecrated.

(3) Subject to subsection (9) of section twenty-two of this Act, a charity shall be deemed for the purposes of this Act to have a permanent endowment unless all property held for the purposes of the charity may be expended for those purposes without distinction between capital and income, and in this Act "permanent endowment" means, in relation to any charity, property held subject to a restriction on its being so expended.

(4) References in this Act to a charity not having income from property to a specified amount shall be construed by reference to the gross revenues of the charity, but without bringing into account anything for the yearly value of land occupied by the charity apart from the pecuniary income (if any) received from that land; and any question as to the application of any such reference to a charity shall be determined by the Commissioners, whose decision shall be final.

(5) The Commissioners may direct that for all or any of the purposes of this Act an institution established for any special purposes of or in connection with a charity (being charitable purposes) shall be treated as forming part of that charity or as forming a distinct charity.

(6) Any reference in this Act to a charity which is excepted by order or regulations shall be construed as referring to a charity which is for the time being permanently or temporarily excepted by order of the Commissioners, or is of a description permanently or temporarily excepted by regulations, and which complies with any conditions of the exception; and any order or regulation made for this purpose may limit any exception so that a charity may be excepted in respect of some matters and not in respect of others.

46. Other definitions

In this Act, except in so far as the context otherwise requires,—

. . .

"charitable purposes" means purposes which are exclusively charitable according to the law of England and Wales;

"charity trustees" means the persons having the general control and management of the administration of a charity;

"the Commissioners" means the Charity Commissioners for England and Wales;

"the county of London" means the administrative county of London;

"the court" means the High Court and, within the limits of its jurisdiction, any other court in England or Wales having a jurisdiction in respect of charities concurrent (within any limit of area or amount) with that of the High Court, and includes any judge or officer of the court exercising the jurisdiction of the court;

"institution" includes any trust or undertaking;

"permanent endowment" shall, subject to subsection (9) of section twenty-two of this Act, be construed in accordance with subsection (3) of the last foregoing section;

"trusts", in relation to a charity, means the provisions establishing it as a charity and regulating its purposes and administration, whether those provisions take effect by way of trust or not, and in relation to other institutions has a corresponding meaning.

Definition of "Attorney General" repealed by the Courts Act 1971, s. 56 (4), Sch. 11, Pt. II.

47. (*Rep. by the Northern Ireland Constitution Act 1973, s. 41 (1), Sch. 6, Part I.*)

48. Consequential amendments, general repeal and transitional provisions

(1) The enactments mentioned in the first column of the Sixth Schedule to this Act shall be amended as provided in the second column of that Schedule.

(2) . . .

(3) The Commissioners may take the like action under this Act in consequence of any application or enquiry under the Charitable Trusts Acts 1853 to 1939, as if the application or enquiry had been made for the corresponding purpose under this Act; and subsections (3) to (5) of section twenty-five of this Act shall extend (with any necessary adaptations) to documents enrolled by the Commissioners or deposited with them under those Acts.

(4) The repeal by this Act of the Charitable Trusts Acts 1853 to 1939, shall not invalidate any scheme, order, certificate or other document issued under or for the purposes of those Acts, so far as the document is capable after the commencement of this Act of having effect either for its original purpose or for any corresponding purpose of this Act; but any such documents shall continue to have effect for any such purpose (except in so far as they are modified or superseded under the powers of this Act), and shall in the case of an order be appealable, enforceable and liable to be discharged as if this Act had not been passed; and any such document, and any document under the seal of the

official trustees of charitable funds, may be proved as if this Act had not been passed.

(5) The repeal by this Act of any enactment which authorises the taking of legal proceedings, or regulates any legal proceedings, shall not affect the operation of that enactment in relation to proceedings begun before the commencement of this Act, nor shall section twenty-eight of this Act apply to any proceedings so begun.

(6) The official custodian for charities shall be treated as the successor for all purposes both of the official trustee of charity lands and of the official trustees of charitable funds, as if the functions of the said trustee or trustees had been functions of the official custodian, and as if any such trustee or trustees had been, and had discharged his or their functions as, holder of the office of the official custodian; and accordingly (but without prejudice to the generality of the foregoing provision, and subject to any express amendment or repeal made by this Act) as from the commencement of this Act—

(a) all property vested in the said trustee or trustees shall vest in the official custodian, and shall be held by him as if vested in him under section sixteen of this Act for the purposes for which it was held by the said trustee or trustees; and

(b) any Act, scheme, deed or other document referring or relating to the said trustee or trustees shall, in so far as the context permits, have effect as if the official custodian had been mentioned instead.

(7) The specific provisions of this Act as to the effect of any repeal shall not be taken to exclude the general provisions contained in section thirty-eight of the Interpretation Act 1889, except in so far as those general provisions are inconsistent with the specific provisions in this Act.

Subsection (2) repealed by the Education Act 1973, s. 1 (4), Sch. 2, Pt. I.

49. Short title, extent and commencement

(1) This Act may be cited as the Charities Act, 1960.

(2) This Act shall extend—

(a) . . .

(b) to Scotland in so far as Part II of the Seventh Schedule repeals any enactment having any application in Scotland; and

(c) to Northern Ireland in so far as it relates to the amendment of Royal Charters;

but, subject to that, this Act shall not extend to Scotland or Northern Ireland.

(3) The following provisions of this Act shall come into force on the date it is passed, that is to say, section one with the First Schedule, section thirty-eight with the repeals in Part II of the Seventh Schedule, and section forty-seven; but, save as aforesaid, this Act shall not come into force until the beginning of the year nineteen hundred and sixty-one.

In sub-s. (2) (a), reference to the powers of the Parliament of Northern Ireland were repealed by the Northern Ireland Constitution Act 1973, s. 4 (1), Sch. 6, Pt. I, and reference to the House of Commons Disqualification Act 1957 was repealed by the House of Commons Disqualification Act 1975, s. 10 (2), Sch. 3. It is submitted that the remaining unqualified reference to Scotland and Northern Ireland should have been repealed also.

SCHEDULES

FIRST SCHEDULE Section 1

CONSTITUTION, ETC., OF CHARITY COMMISSIONERS

1.—(1) There shall be a Chief Charity Commissioner, and two other commissioners.

(2) Two at least of the commissioners shall be barristers or solicitors.

(3) Subject to sub-paragraph (6) below, the chief commissioner and the other commissioners shall be appointed by the Secretary of State, and shall be deemed for all purposes to be employed in the civil service of the Crown.

(4) There may be paid to each of the commissioners such salary and allowances as the Secretary of State may with the approval of the Treasury determine.

(5) If at any time it appears to the Secretary of State that there should be more than three commissioners, he may with the approval of the Treasury appoint not more than two additional commissioners.

(6) . . .

2.—(1) The chief commissioner may, with the approval of the Treasury as to number and conditions of service, appoint such assistant commissioners and other officers and such servants as he thinks necessary for the proper discharge of the functions of the Commissioners and of the official custodian for charities.

(2) There may be paid to officers and servants so appointed such salaries or remuneration as the Treasury may determine.

(3) . . .

3.—(1) The Commissioners may use an official seal for the authentication of documents, and their seal shall be officially and judicially noticed.

(2) The Documentary Evidence Act 1868, as amended by the Documentary Evidence Act 1882, shall have effect as if in the Schedule to the Act of 1868 the Commissioners were included in the first column and any commissioner or assistant commissioner and any officer authorised to act on behalf of the Commissioners were mentioned in the second column.

(3) The Commissioners shall have power to regulate their own procedure and, subject to any such regulations and to any directions of the chief commissioner, any one commissioner or any assistant commissioner may act for and in the name of the Commissioners.

(4) Where the Commissioners act as a board, two shall be a quorum; and in the case of an equality of votes the chief commissioner or in his absence the commissioner presiding shall have a second or casting vote.

(5) The Commissioners shall have power to act notwithstanding any vacancy in their number.

4. Legal proceedings may be instituted by or against the Commissioners by the name of the Charity Commissioners for England and Wales, and shall not abate or be affected by any change in the persons who are the commissioners.

Paragraphs 1 (6) and 2 (3) repealed by the Education Act 1973, s. 1 (4), Sch. 2, Pt. I.

Sections 4 and 45   SECOND SCHEDULE

                                        EXEMPT CHARITIES

The following institutions, so far as they are charities, are exempt charities
within the meaning of this Act, that is to say—

(a) any institution which, if this Act had not been passed, would be
    exempted from the powers and jurisdiction under the Charitable
    Trusts Acts 1853 to 1939, of the Commissioners or Minister of Educa-
    tion (apart from any power of the Commissioners or Minister to
    apply those Acts in whole or in part to charities otherwise exempt) by
    the terms of any enactment not contained in those Acts other than
    section nine of the Places of Worship Registration Act 1855;

(b) the universities of Oxford, Cambridge, London and Durham, the
    colleges and halls in the universities of Oxford, Cambridge and Dur-
    ham and the colleges of Winchester and Eton;

(c) any university, university college, or institution connected with a uni-
    versity or university college, which Her Majesty declares by Order in
    Council to be an exempt charity for the purposes of this Act;

(d) the British Museum;

(e) any institution which is administered by or on behalf of an institution
    included above and is established for the general purposes of, or for
    any special purpose of or in connection with, the last-mentioned
    institution;

(f) the Church Commissioners and any institution which is administered
    by them;

(g) any registered society within the meaning of the Industrial and Provi-
    dent Societies Act 1893, and any registered society or branch within
    the meaning of the Friendly Societies Act 1896.

[(h) the Board of Governors of the Museum of London.]

[(i) the British Library Board.]

Paragraph (h) inserted by the Museum of London Act 1965, s. 11. Paragraph (i) inserted
by the British Library Act 1973, s. 4 (2).

Section 13   THIRD SCHEDULE

                        ENLARGEMENT OF AREAS OF LOCAL CHARITIES

Existing area	Permissible enlargement
1. The county of London ..	Any area comprising the county of London.
2. Any area in the county of London and not in, or partly in, the city of London.	(i) Any area in the county of London and not in, or partly in, the city of London;
	(ii) the area of the county of London, exclusive of the city of London;
	(iii) any area comprising the area of the county of London, exclusive of the city of London;

Existing area	Permissible enlargement
2. Any area in the county of London and not in, or partly in, the city of London.	(iv) any area partly in the county of London and partly in any adjacent parish or parishes (civil or ecclesiastical), and not partly in the city of London.
3. A [district]	Any area comprising the [district].
4. Any area in a [district] ..	(i) Any area in the [district] (ii) the [district] (iii) any area comprising the [district] (iv) any area partly in the [district] and partly in any adjacent [district].
5. A parish (civil or ecclesiastical), or two or more parishes, or an area in a parish, or partly in each of two or more parishes.	Any area not extending beyond the parish or parishes comprising or adjacent to the area in column 1.

Paragraphs 3 and 4 amended by the substitution of the words in square brackets by the Local Government Act 1972, s. 210 (9), (10).

FOURTH SCHEDULE   Section 15

Court's Jurisdiction over Certain Charities Governed by or under Statute

1. The court may by virtue of subsection (3) of section fifteen of this Act exercise its jurisdiction with respect to charities—

(a) in relation to charities established or regulated by any provision of the Seamen's Fund Winding-up Act 1851, which is repealed by this Act;

(b) in relation to charities established or regulated by schemes under the Endowed Schools Acts 1869 to 1948, or section seventy-five of the Elementary Education Act 1870 [see below];

(c) in relation to allotments regulated by sections three to nine of the Poor Allotments Management Act 1873;

(d) in relation to fuel allotments, that is to say, land which, by any enactment relating to inclosure or any instrument having effect under such an enactment, is vested in trustees upon trust that the land or the rents and profits of the land shall be used for the purpose of providing poor persons with fuel;

(e) in relation to charities established or regulated by any provision of the Municipal Corporations Act 1883, which is repealed by this Act, or by any scheme having effect under any such provision;

(f) in relation to charities regulated by schemes under the London Government Act 1899;

(g) in relation to charities established or regulated by orders or regulations under section two of the Regimental Charitable Funds Act 1935;

(h) in relation to charities regulated by section thirty-seven of this Act, or by any such order as is mentioned in that section.

2. Notwithstanding anything in section nineteen of the Commons Act 1876, a scheme for the administration of a fuel allotment (within the meaning of the foregoing paragraph) may provide—

(a) for the sale or letting of the allotment or any part thereof, for the discharge of the land sold or let from any restrictions as to the use thereof imposed by or under any enactment relating to inclosure and for the application of the sums payable to the trustees of the allotment in respect of the sale or lease; or

(b) for the exchange of the allotment or any part thereof for other land, for the discharge as aforesaid of the land given in exchange by the said trustees, and for the application of any money payable to the said trustees for equality of exchange; or

(c) for the use of the allotment or any part thereof for any purposes specified in the scheme.

Paragraph 1 (b) is modified in relation to s. 15 (3) of this Act by the Education Act 1973, s. 2 (7), (9) for the purposes of which s. 15 (3) is deemed to have effect as if at the end of para 9 (b) there were added the words "or by schemes given effect under section 2 of the Education Act 1973".

Section 39   FIFTH SCHEDULE

(*Rep. by the Education Act 1973, s. 1 (4), Sch. 2, Pt. I.*)

SIXTH SCHEDULE

(*The schedule subsequentially amends the Places of Worship Registration Act 1855, s. 9; the Charitable Trustees Incorporation Act 1872, s. 2 and Schedule; the National Debt (Conversion) Act 1888, s. 28 (2); the Copyhold Act 1894, ss. 76 and 77 (the amendments applying to the sections as applied by the Law of Property Act 1922, s. 138 (4) or 139 (2)); the Open Spaces Act 1906, s. 4 (1); the Land Registration Act 1925, s. 98; the Landlord and Tenant Act 1927, s. 24 (4); the Administration of Justice Act 1928, s. 15 (1); the Local Government Act 1933, ss. 169, 170; the War Charities Act 1940, s. 5 (2) (ii), (iii), (5); the Income Tax Act 1952, Sch. 8, Part I, para. 8; the Housing Repairs and Rent Act 1954, s. 33 (1), (d); the Administration of Justice Act 1956, s. 52 (1); the New Parishes Measure 1943 (No. 1), ss. 14 (1) (b), 31; and the Re-organisation Areas Measure 1944, s. 48.*

The schedule is partly repealed by the Education Act 1973, s. 1 (4), (5), Sch. 2, Pts. I, III, in relation to the Re-organisation Areas Measure 1944 and the New Parishes Measure 1943.)

SEVENTH SCHEDULE

Section 48

(Rep. by the Education Act 1973, s. 1 (4), Sch. 2, Pt. I.)

The Reserve Forces Act 1966

(1966 c. 30)

18. Rearrangement of charities in England and Wales and Northern Ireland on disbanding of units

(1) Subject to the provisions of this section, where by warrant of Her Majesty—

(a) a unit of the volunteer reserve or the army reserve is designated as the successor of a body of either of those reserves which has been or is to be disbanded; or

(b) a unit of the royal auxiliary air force is designated as the successor of a body of that force which has been or is to be disbanded,

any charitable property held for the purposes of the body in question shall, as from the time at which the warrant comes into force, be held for the corresponding purposes of the unit so designated.

(2) The Secretary of State shall, as soon as may be after it is made, deliver a copy of any such warrant by post or otherwise to the Charity Commissioners and to a trustee of the charity in question; and if the Commissioners consider that the foregoing subsection should not apply to all or part of the property affected by the warrant they may, at any time within the period beginning with the date on which the warrant is made and ending with the expiration of six months beginning with the date on which the warrant comes into force, make an order providing that that subsection shall not apply or shall cease to apply to the property or part.

(3) If a charity affected by such a warrant as is mentioned in subsection (1) of this section or any trustee of or person interested in such a charity considers that subsection (1) of this section should not apply to all or part of any property which belongs to the charity and is affected by the warrant, then, subject to subsections (2) to (5) of section 28 of the Charities Act 1960 (which provide that charity proceedings may not be begun without the consent of the Charity Commissioners or leave of a judge of the High Court), the charity, trustee or person interested as the case may be may, at any time within the period of six months beginning with the date on which the warrant comes into force, apply to the court for an order providing that subsection (1) of this section shall cease to apply to the property or part; and for the purposes of the said subsection (5), in its application to proceedings under this subsection, an application for an order of the Charity Commissioners authorising such proceedings shall be deemed to be refused if it is not granted during the period of one month beginning with the day on which the application is received by the Commissioners.

(4) No such warrant or order as aforesaid shall affect the validity of anything done or omitted with respect to any property affected by the warrant or order before a copy of it is served on a trustee of the charity in question.

(5) In any case where—

(a) an order is made under the foregoing provisions of this section; or
(b) the Secretary of State requests the Commissioners to make provision with respect to any charitable property held for the purposes of a body of the volunteer reserve, the army reserve or the royal auxiliary air force which has been or is to be disbanded,

the Commissioners may, notwithstanding anything in subsection (4) of section 18 of the Charities Act 1960, exercise their jurisdiction under that section with respect to the property to which the order or request relates.

(6) The foregoing provisions of this section shall not apply to any charitable property held for the purposes of such a body as is mentioned in subsection (1) of this section if, under the terms on which the property is so held, any interest of the charity in question in the property is determined on the disbanding of that body and any person or charity other than the charity aforesaid has an interest in the property contingent upon the determination of the said charity's interest.

(7) Where subsection (1) of this section applies to any charitable property, the same jurisdiction and powers shall be exercisable in relation to the charity in question as would be exercisable if that subsection were not a provision of an Act of Parliament regulating the charity.

(8) Subject to the next following subsection, in this section "charitable property" means property belonging to a charity, and "the court" and "charity" have the same meanings as in the Charities Act 1960; and references to disbandment of a body include references to its amalgamation with another body.

(9) The foregoing provisions of this section shall have effect in their application to Northern Ireland as if—

(a) for any reference to the Charity Commissioners there were substituted a reference to the Ministry of Finance for Northern Ireland;
(b) in subsection (3) for the words from "subject to" to "High Court" there were substituted the words "subject to section 29 (3) of the Charities Act (Northern Ireland) 1964 (under which an application for an order of the court in connection with the administration of a charity may not be made without the consent of the Attorney General for Northern Ireland)" and the words from "and for the purposes" onwards were omitted;
(c) in subsection (5) for the words "subsection (4) of section 18 of the Charities Act 1960" there were substituted the words "subsection (1) of section 13 of the Charities Act (Northern Ireland) 1964 and irrespective of the value of the property in question"; and
(d) in subsection (8) for the reference to the Charities Act 1960 there were substituted a reference to the said Act of 1964;

. . .

Subsection (9) partly repealed the Northern Ireland Constitution Act 1973, s. 41 (1), Sch. 6, Pt. I.

The General Rate Act 1967

(1967 c. 9)

Miscellaneous exemptions and reliefs

39. Relief for places of religious worship

(1) Subject to the provisions of this section, and without prejudice to any exemption from, or privilege in respect of, rates under any enactment other than this section, no hereditament to which this section applies shall, in the case of any rating area, be liable to be rated for any rate period.

(2) This section applies to the following hereditaments, that is to say—

(a) places of public religious worship which belong to the Church of England or to the Church in Wales (within the meaning of the Welsh Church Act 1914), or which are for the time being certified as required by law as places of religious worship; and

(b) any church hall, chapel hall or similar building used in connection with any such place of public religious worship, and so used for the purposes of the organisation responsible for the conduct of public religious worship in that place,

and also applies to any hereditament consisting of such a place of public religious worship as is mentioned in paragraph (a) of this subsection together with one or more church halls, chapel halls or other buildings such as are mentioned in paragraph (b) thereof.

(3) Where a hereditament to which this section applies, or any part of such a hereditament, is or has been let (whether by way of a tenancy or of a licence) for use otherwise than as a place of public religious worship, or, as the case may be, for use otherwise than as mentioned in subsection (2) (b) of this section—

(a) the hereditament shall not be exempted by virtue of subsection (1) of this section from being rated for any rate period if any payment in consideration of such a letting of the hereditament or part thereof accrued due in the last year before the beginning of that rate period; but

(b) no gross value for rating purposes shall be ascribed to the hereditament unless the average annual amount of the payments accruing due, as consideration for such lettings of the hereditament or parts thereof, exceeds the average annual amount of the expenses attributable to those lettings; and

(c) if such a gross value falls to be ascribed to the hereditament, by reason that the average annual amount of those payments exceeds the average annual amount of those expenses, the gross value shall be assessed by reference only to the amount of the excess.

40. Relief for charitable and other organisations

(1) If notice in writing is given to the rating authority that—

(a) any hereditament occupied by, or by trustees for, a charity and wholly or mainly used for charitable purposes (whether of that charity or of that and other charities); or

(b) any other hereditament, being a hereditament held upon trust for use as an almshouse,

is one falling within this subsection, then, subject to the provisions of this section, the amount of any rates chargeable in respect of the hereditament for any period during which the hereditament is one falling within either paragraph (a) or paragraph (b) of this subsection, being a period beginning not earlier than the rate period in which the notice is given, shall not exceed one-half of the amount which would be chargeable apart from the provisions of this subsection:

Provided that where a hereditament ceases to be one falling within the said paragraphs (a) and (b), a previous notice given for the purposes of this subsection shall not have effect as respects any subsequent period during which the hereditament falls within either of those paragraphs.

(2) No relief under the foregoing subsection shall be given in the case of a hereditament falling within paragraph (a) thereof for any period during which the hereditament is occupied by an institution specified in Schedule 8 to this Act.

(3) The Minister may by order amend the provisions of Schedule 8 to this Act by adding any institution which in his opinion ought to be classified with the institutions mentioned in that Schedule or omitting any institution or altering the description of any institution.

(4) An order under subsection (3) of this section may be made so as to have effect from any date not earlier than the beginning of the rate period in which it is made, and shall be subject to annulment in pursuance of a resolution of either House of Parliament.

(5) Without prejudice to the powers conferred by section 53 of this Act, a rating authority shall have power to reduce or remit the payment of rates chargeable in respect of—

(a) any hereditament falling within subsection (1) (a) or (b) of this section;
(b) any other hereditament which is occupied for the purposes of one or more institutions or other organisations which are not established or conducted for profit and whose main objects are charitable or are otherwise philanthropic or religious or concerned with education, social welfare, science, literature or the fine arts;
(c) any other hereditament which is occupied for the purposes of a club, society or other organisation not established or conducted for profit and is wholly or mainly used for purposes of recreation,

for any such period as is mentioned in subsection (6) of this section:

Provided that any such reduction or remission shall cease to have effect on a change in the occupation of the hereditament in respect of which it was granted.

(6) Any reduction or remission of rates determined under subsection (5) of this section may at the discretion of the rating authority be granted—

(a) for the year in which, or the year next following that in which, the determination to grant it is made; or
(b) for a specified term of years, not exceeding five, beginning not earlier than the year in which the determination was made nor more than twenty-four months after the date of the determination; or
(c) for an indefinite period beginning not earlier than the last-mentioned year, subject, however, to the exercise by the rating authority of their powers under subsection (7) of this section.

(7) Where any such reduction or remission is granted for an indefinite period the rating authority may, by not less than twelve months' notice in writing given to the occupiers of the hereditament, terminate or modify the reduction or remission as from the end of a year specified in the notice.

(8) The foregoing provisions of this section shall not apply to any hereditament to which section 39 of this Act applies or to any hereditament occupied (otherwise than as trustee) by any authority having, within the meaning of the Local Loans Act 1875, power to levy a rate.

(9) In this section "charity" means an institution or other organisation established for charitable purposes only, and "organisation" includes any persons administering a trust; and a hereditament an interest in which belongs to a charity or any ecclesiastical corporation and in which (in right of that interest)—

(a) the persons from time to time holding any full-time office as clergyman or minister of any religious denomination, or

(b) any particular person holding such an office,

have or has a residence from which to perform the duties of the office, or in which (in right of the said interest) accommodation is being held available to provide such a residence for such a person, shall be treated for the purposes of this section as occupied by a charity and wholly or mainly used for charitable purposes, whether or not it would be so treated apart from this provision.

(10) The Minister may, on the application of any rating authority appearing to him to be concerned, by order repeal or amend any local enactment which confers an exemption from or abatement of, or a power to reduce or remit a payment of, rates in respect of any particular hereditament or of hereditaments of any class if it appears to him that a right to relief arises in respect of that hereditament or hereditaments of that class under subsection (1), or that a reduction or remission may be granted in respect thereof under subsection (5), of this section, and may by that order make such other amendments of any other local enactments as appear to him to be necessary in consequence of the repeal or amendment and such transitional provision as appears to him to be necessary or expedient in connection with the matter; and in this subsection, the expression "local enactment" means a provision of any local and personal Act or private Act or of any order or other instrument in the nature of any such Act.

SCHEDULE 8   Section 40

Charities Excluded from Mandatory Relief

1. The universities of Birmingham, Bristol, Cambridge, Durham, East Anglia, Exeter, Hull, Keele, Kent at Canterbury, Lancaster, Leeds, Leicester, Liverpool, London, Manchester, Newcastle upon Tyne, Nottingham, Oxford, Reading, Sheffield, Southampton, Sussex, Wales, Warwick and York, but exclusive in the case of the University of London of the institution of that university known as Goldsmiths' College [the Loughborough University of Technology] [the University of Aston in Birmingham] [The City University] [Brunel University] [the University of Surrey] [the University of Bradford] [the Bath University of Technology] [the University of Salford] [the Open University].

2. The colleges, institutions and schools of the universities of Durham, London and Wales, with the exception of—

(a) the following colleges of the University of Durham, that is to say, the College of the Venerable Bede, St. Chad's College and St. John's College; and

(b) the following colleges and institute of the University of London, that is to say, New College, Richmond College, the theological department of King's College London as defined in the King's College (Transfer) Act 1908, and the Lister Institute of Preventive Medicine [Heythrop College].

3. The Federated Institutes of the British Postgraduate Medical Federation, with the exception of the Institute of Cancer Research.

4. [The University of Manchester Institute of Science and Technology].

5. . . . [the London Graduate School of Business Studies].

6. The colleges and halls in the universities of Oxford and Cambridge.

By the Rating (Charitable Institutions) (No. 1) to (No. 7) Orders 1967, S.I. 1967 Nos. 406–412, the entries printed between the first seven pairs of square brackets in para. 1 were added and the institutions replaced by those universities were deleted from para. 5, by the Rating (Charitable Institutions) (No. 8) Order 1967, S.I. 1967 No. 413; para. 4 was substituted and the Chelsea College of Science and Technology was deleted from para. 5; by the Rating (Charitable Institutions) (No. 9) Order 1967, S.I. 1967 No. 1336 the entry printed between the last but one pair of square brackets in para. 1 was added and the institution replaced by that university was deleted from para. 5; and by the Rating (Charitable Institutions) Order 1970, S.I. 1970 No. 490, the entry printed between the last pair of square brackets in para. 1 was added and the entry printed between the pair of square brackets in para. 5 was substituted and an entry was deleted from that paragraph.

By Rating (Charitable Institutions) Order 1971, S.I. 1971 No. 2007, Heythrop College was added to para. 2 (b).

The Income and Corporation Taxes Act 1970

(1970 c. 10)

PART XIII

SPECIAL EXEMPTIONS

360. Charities

(1) The following exemptions shall be granted on a claim in that behalf to the Board—

(a) exemptions from tax under Schedules A and D in respect of the rents and profits of any lands, tenements, hereditaments or heritages belonging to a hospital, public school or almshouse, or vested in trustees for charitable purposes, so far as the same are applied to charitable purposes only,

(b) exemption from tax under Schedule B in respect of any lands occupied by a charity,

(c) exemption—

      (i) from tax under Schedule C in respect of any interest, annuities, dividends or shares of annuities,

(ii) from tax under Schedule D in respect of any yearly interest or other annual payment, and

(iii) from tax under Schedule F in respect of any distribution,

where the income in question forms part of the income of a charity, or is, according to rules or regulations established by Act of Parliament, charter, decree, deed of trust or will, applicable to charitable purposes only, and so far as it is applied to charitable purposes only,

(d) exemption from tax under Schedule C in respect of any interest, annuities, dividends or shares of annuities which are in the names of trustees and are applicable solely towards the repairs of any cathedral, college, church or chapel, or of any building used solely for the purpose of divine worship, so far as the same are applied to those purposes,

(e) exemption from tax under Schedule D in respect of the profits or any trade carried on by a charity, if the profits are applied solely to the purposes of the charity and either—

(i) the trade is exercised in the course of the actual carrying out of a primary purpose of the charity, or

(ii) the work in connection with the trade is mainly carried out by beneficiaries of the charity.

(2) . . .

(3) In this section "charity" means any body of persons or trust established for charitable purposes only.

Subsection (2) repealed by the Finance Act 1971, s. 56 (3), Sch. 14, Pt. IV.

The Education Act 1973

(1973 c. 16)

Educational trusts

1. General provisions as to educational trusts

(1) There shall cease to have effect—

(a) section 2 of the Charities Act 1960 (by which, as originally enacted, the powers of the Charity Commissioners were made exercisable concurrently by the Minister of Education); and

(b) the Endowed Schools Acts 1869 to 1948 (which made provision for the modernisation of educational trusts by schemes settled and approved in accordance with those Acts).

(2) The Secretary of State may by order—

(a) make such modifications of any trust deed or other instrument relating to a school as, after consultation with the managers, governors or other proprietor of the school, appear to him to be requisite in consequence of any proposals approved or order made by him under section 13 or 16 of the Education Act 1944 (which relate to the establishment of and changes affecting schools); and

(b) make such modifications of any trust deed or other instrument relating to a school as, after consultation with the governors or other proprietor of the school, appear to him to be requisite to enable the governors or proprietor to meet any requirement imposed by regulations under section 33 of the Education Act 1944 (which relates in particular to the approval of schools as special schools); and

(c) make such modifications of any trust deed or other instrument relating to or regulating any institution that provides or is concerned in the provision of educational services, or is concerned in educational research, as, after consultation with the persons responsible for the management of the institution, appear to him to be requisite to enable them to fulfil any condition or meet any requirement imposed by regulations under section 100 of the Education Act 1944 (which authorises the making of grants in aid of educational services or research);

and any modification made by an order under this subsection may be made to have permanent effect or to have effect for such period as may be specified in the order.

This subsection shall be construed, and the Education Acts 1944 to 1971 shall have effect, as if this subsection were contained in the Education Act 1944.

(3) In connection with the operation of this section there shall have effect the transitional and other consequential or supplementary provisions contained in Schedule 1 to this Act.

(4) The enactments mentioned in Schedule 2 to this Act (which includes in Part I certain enactments already spent or otherwise no longer required apart from the foregoing provisions of this section) are hereby repealed to the extent specified in column 3 of the Schedule.

(5) Subsection (1) (a) above and Part III of Schedule 2 to this Act shall not come into force until such date as may be appointed by order made by statutory instrument by the Secretary of State.

2. Special powers as to certain trusts for religious education

(1) Where the premises of a voluntary school have ceased (before or after the coming into force of this section) to be used for a voluntary school, or in the opinion of the Secretary of State it is likely they will cease to be so used, then subject to subsections (2) to (4) below he may by order made by statutory instrument make new provision as to the use of any endowment shown to his satisfaction to be or have been held wholly or partly for or in connection with the provision at the school of religious education in accordance with the tenets of a particular religious denomination; and for purposes of this section "endowment" includes property not subject to any restriction on the expenditure of capital.

(2) No order shall be made under subsection (1) above except on the application of the persons appearing to the Secretary of State to be the appropriate authority of the denomination cornerned; and the Secretary of State shall, not less than one month before making an order under that subsection, give notice of the proposed order and of the right of persons interested to make representations on it, and shall take into account any representations that may be made to him by any person interested therein before the order is made; and the notice shall be given—

(a) by giving to any persons appearing to the Secretary of State to be trustees of an endowment affected by the proposed order a notice of the proposal to make it, together with a draft or summary of the provisions proposed to be included; and

(b) by publishing in such manner as the Secretary of State thinks sufficient for informing any other persons interested a notice of the proposal to make the order and of the place where any person interested may (during a period of not less than a month) inspect such a draft or summary, and by keeping a draft or summary available for inspection in accordance with the notice.

(3) An order under subsection (1) above may require or authorise the disposal by sale or otherwise of any land or other property forming part of an endowment affected by the order, including the premises of the school and any teacher's dwelling-house; and in the case of land liable to revert under the third proviso to section 2 of the School Sites Act 1841 the Secretary of State may by order exclude the operation of that proviso, if he is satisfied either—

(a) that the person to whom the land would revert in accordance with the proviso cannot after due enquiry be found; or

(b) that, if that person can be found, he has consented to relinquish his rights in relation to the land under the proviso and that, if he has consented so to do in consideration of the payment of a sum of money to him, adequate provision can be made for the payment to him of that sum out of the proceeds of disposal of the land.

(4) Subject to subsection (3) above and to any provision affecting the endowments of any public general Act of Parliament, an order under subsection (1) above shall establish and give effect, with a view to enabling the denomination concerned to participate more effectively in the administration of the statutory system of public education, to a scheme or schemes for the endowments dealt with by the order to be used for appropriate educational purposes, either in connection with voluntary schools or partly in connection with voluntary schools and partly in other ways related to the locality served or formerly served by the voluntary school at the premises that have gone or are to go out of use for such a school; and for this purpose "use for appropriate educational purposes" means use for educational purposes in connection with the provision of religious education in accordance with the tenets of the denomination concerned.

(5) A scheme given effect under this section may provide for the retention of the capital of any endowment and application of the accruing income or may authorise the application or expenditure of capital to such extent and subject to such conditions as may be determined by or in accordance with the scheme; and any such scheme may provide for the endowments thereby dealt with or any part of them to be added to any existing endowment applicable for any such purpose as is authorised for the scheme by subsection (4) above.

(6) An order under subsection (1) above may include any such incidental or supplementary provisions as appear to the Secretary of State to be necessary or expedient either for the bringing into force or for the operation of any scheme thereby established, including in particular provisions for the appointment and powers of trustees of the property comprised in the scheme or, if the property is not all applicable for the same purposes, of any part of that property, and for the property or any part of it to vest by virtue of the scheme in the first trustees under the scheme or trustees of any endowment to which it is to be added or, if not so vested, to be transferred to them.

(7) Any order under this section shall have effect notwithstanding any Act of Parliament (not being a public general Act), letters patent or other instrument relating to, or trust affecting, the endowments dealt with by the order; but section 15 (3) of the Charities Act 1960 (by virtue of which the court and the Charity Commissioners may exercise their jurisdiction in relation to charities mentioned in Schedule 4 to the Act notwithstanding that the charities are governed by the Acts or statutory schemes there mentioned) shall have effect as if at the end of paragraph 1 (b) of Schedule 4 to the Act there were added the words "or by schemes given effect under section 2 of the Education Act 1973".

(8) This section shall apply where the premises of a non-provided public elementary school ceased before 1st April 1945 to be used for such a school as it applies where the premises of a voluntary school have ceased to be used for a voluntary school.

(9) This section shall be construed, and the Education Acts 1944 to 1971 shall have effect, as if this section were contained in the Education Act 1944.

SCHEDULES

SCHEDULE 1

Transitional and Supplementary Provisions as to Charities etc.

1.—(1) In section 43 of the Charities Act 1960, in its application to regulations made on or after the appointed day, there shall be substituted for subsection (1)—

> "(1) Save as otherwise provided by this Act, any power to make regulations which is conferred by this Act shall be exercisable by the Secretary of State";

and in subsection (3) for the words (as originally enacted) "the Secretary of State or the Minister of Education" there shall be substituted the words "or the Secretary of State".

(2) Section 210 (3) of the Local Government Act 1972 (which makes special provision for certain charitable property to vest in local education authorities, if it is held for purposes of a charity registered in a part of the charities register maintained by the Secretary of State by virtue of section 2 of the Charities Act 1960) shall have effect, unless the appointed day is later than the end of March 1974, as if the reference to a charity registered in a part of the register which is maintained by the Secretary of State were a reference to a charity so registered immediately before the appointed day.

(3) Any register, books and documents which on the appointed day are in the possession or custody of the Secretary of State for Education and Science, or of the Secretary of State for Wales, and which in his opinion he requires no longer by reason of the repeal of section 2 (1) of the Charities Act 1960, shall be transferred to the Charity Commissioners.

(4) The repeal by this Act of section 2 (1) of the Charities Act 1960 shall not affect the operation of section 2 (1)—

> (a) in conferring on the Charity Commissioners functions belonging at the passing of that Act to the Minister of Education; or

(b) in extending to the Charity Commissioners references to the Secretary of State for Education and Science or the Secretary of State for Wales (or references having effect as if either of them were mentioned) so as to enable the Commissioners to discharge any such functions as aforesaid or to act under or for the purposes of the trusts of a charity;

but on the appointed day any functions so conferred and any reference so extended shall, subject to sub-paragraph (5) below, cease to be functions of or to extend to either Secretary of State.

(5) Where it appears to the Secretary of State for Education and Science or the Secretary of State for Wales that any reference which, in accordance with sub-paragraph (4) above would on the appointed day cease to extend to him, is not related (or not wholly related) to the functions ceasing to belong to him by the repeal of section 2 (1) of the Charities Act 1960, he may by order made at any time, whether before the appointed day or not, exclude the operation of that sub-paragraph in relation to the reference and make such modifications of the relevant instrument as appear to him appropriate in the circumstances.

(6) The repeal of section 2 (1) of the Charities Act 1960 shall not affect the validity of anything done (or having effect as if done) before the appointed day by or in relation to the Secretary of State for Education and Science or the Secretary of State for Wales, and anything so done (or having effect as if so done) in so far as it could by virtue of section 2 (1) have been done by or in relation to the Charity Commissioners shall thereafter have effect as if done by or in relation to them.

(7) In this paragraph "appointed day" means the day appointed under section 1 (5) of this Act.

2.—(1) Where before the passing of this Act a scheme under the Endowed Schools Acts 1869 to 1948 has been published as required by section 13 of the Endowed Schools Act 1873, the scheme may be proceeded with as if section 1 of this Act had not been passed.

(2) Where before the passing of this Act a draft scheme under the Endowed Schools Acts 1869 to 1948 has been prepared in a case in which effect might be given to the scheme by order under section 2 of this Act, and the draft scheme has been published as required by section 33 of the Endowed Schools Act 1869, the scheme may be proceeded with in pursuance of section 2 of this Act as if section 2 (2) (a) and (b) had been complied with on the date this Act is passed.

3. The repeals made by this Act in sections 17 and 100 of the Education Act 1944 shall not affect any order made by virtue of the provisions repealed, or the operation in relation to any such order of section 111 of that Act (which relates to the revocation and variation of orders).

SCHEDULE 2

Repeals

Part I

Repeals or Spent etc. Enactments

Chapter	Short Title	Extent of Repeal
8 & 9 Geo. 5 c. 39	The Education Act 1918.	Section 14.
		In section 47, the words from "except" to "direct" and the words from "and the Board" onwards.
		Section 52 (1) from the first "and" onwards.
7 & 8 Geo. 6 c. 31	The Education Act 1944.	Section 119.
		Section 121, except proviso (a).
		Schedule 9.
1 & 2 Eliz. 2 c. 33	The Education (Miscellaneous Provisions) Act 1953.	Section 14.
		Section 17 (2).
		Schedule 2.
2 & 3 Eliz. 2 c. 70	The Mines and Quarries Act 1954.	In section 166 the words "section 14 of the Education Act 1918", and the words "the said section 14".
		In Schedule 4 the entry relating to the Education Act 1918.
8 & 9 Eliz. 2 c. 58	The Charities Act 1960.	Section 4 (10).
		Section 38 (1) and (2).
		Section 39 (1).
		Section 44 (3).
		Section 48 (2).
		Section 49 (3).
		In Schedule 1, paragraph 1 (6) and paragraph 2 (3).
		Schedule 5.
		In Schedule 6 the entry for the Reorganisation Areas Measure 1944.
		Schedule 7.
9 & 10 Eliz. 2 c. 34	The Factories Act 1961.	In section 167 the words "section 14 of the Education Act 1918".
1963 c. 33	The London Government Act 1963.	In section 81, subsections (1) to (8) (but not so as to alter the charity trustees of any charity) and subsection (10).

Part II

General

Chapter	Short Title	Extent of Repeal
32 & 33 Vict. c. 56	The Endowed Schools Act 1869.	The whole Act.
36 & 37 Vict. c. 86	The Endowed Schools Act 1873.	The whole Act.
12 & 13 Geo. 5 c. 50	The Expiring Laws Continuance Act 1922.	In Schedule 1, the entry for the Endowed Schools Act 1869.
7 & 8 Geo. 6 c. 31	The Education Act 1944.	In section 17 (6) (as added by the Education Act 1968) the words from "or such modifications" to "trust deed". Section 86. Section 100 (4).
11 & 12 Geo. 6 c. 40	The Education (Miscellaneous Provisions) Act 1948.	Section 2. In section 11 (1) the words from the first "and" to the following "Schedule". In section 14, in subsection (2) the words from "(except" to the following "1908)" and the words from "and the said" onwards, and in subsection (3) the words from "(other" to the following "provisions)" and the words from "and the said" onwards. In Schedule 1, Part II.
8 & 9 Eliz. 2 c. 58	The Charities Act 1960.	Section 2 (4).
1968 c. 17	The Education Act 1968.	In Schedule 1, in paragraph 2, the words from "or such modifications" to "trust deed".
	Church Assembly Measure	
1967 No. 2	The Extra-Parochial Ministry Measure 1967.	In section 2 (5), the words "and section 53 of the Endowed Schools Act 1869" and the words "and endowed".

Part III

Repeals Relating to Charities

Chapter	Short Title	Extent of Repeal
10 & 11 Geo. 6 c. 44	The Crown Proceedings Act 1947.	Section 23 (3) (e).
8 & 9 Eliz. 2 c. 58	The Charities Act 1960.	Section 2 (1), (2), (3) and (5). Section 3 (8). In section 4 (8) the words "or of the Minister of Education". In section 10 (6) the words "and to the Minister of Education". Section 18 (13). Section 19 (9). Section 20 (11). Section 22 (12). In section 44, in subsection (1) (b) the words "the Minister of Education" and in subsection (2) the words "by the Minister of Education or". In Schedule 6, in the entry relating to section 31 of the New Parishes Measure 1943 the words "or Minister of Education".
1969 c. 22	The Redundant Churches and other Religious Buildings Act 1969.	In section 4, in subsection (3) the words "and the Secretary of State for Education and Science" and in subsection (4) the words "and (13)".
	Church Assembly Measures	
6 & 7 Geo. 6 No. 1	The New Parishes Measure 1943.	In section 31 the words "or of the Board of Education" and the words "or Minister of Education" inserted by the Charities Act 1960.
1968 No. 1	The Pastoral Measure 1968.	Section 90 (3).

Appendix 2

Statutory Instruments Etc.

Contents

The War Charities Regulations 1940

S.R. & O. 1940 No. 1533

1. (1) These Regulations may be cited as the War Charities Regulations 1940, and shall come into force on the date on which they are approved by the Secretary of State.

(2) These Regulations shall not extend to Scotland.

2. In these Regulations, unless the contrary intention appears:—

(a) the expression "the Commissioners" means the Charity Commissioners for England and Wales;

(b) the expression "the Act" means the War Charities Act 1940, and the expression "the Act of 1916" means the War Charities Act 1916;

(c) the expressions "the Register" and "the Lists" mean respectively the Register and the Lists kept by a Registration Authority under the Act;

(d) the expression "Committee" means the Committee or other body or person responsible for the administration of a War Charity;

(e) the expression "the appropriate Registration Authority" in relation to any particular War Charity or Charity registered under the Act of 1916 means the Registration Authority for the area in which the administrative centre of that Charity is situate.

3. Every application to a Registration Authority for registration or exemption under the Act of a War Charity shall be made in the forms set forth in the First and Second Schedules respectively to these Regulations and shall be signed by some person or persons duly authorised on behalf of the Charity. If the application is for registration a fee of 5s. shall be paid to the Registration Authority when the application is made, such fee to be returned in the event of the application for registration being refused.[1]

4. Before any application is made for registration a statement in the form set forth in the Third Schedule to these Regulations shall be published by the Committee in not less than two newspapers circulating in the area in which the administrative centre of the Charity is situate giving notice of the intention to

---

1 The reference to 5s. is now to be construed as a reference to 25p: Decimal Currency Act 1969, s. 10 (1).

apply for registration. Every such statement shall be published not less than one week before the application for registration is made and shall specify that any objections to the proposed application shall be sent in writing to the Registration Authority within 14 days from the date of the statement. A copy of the newspapers containing the statement shall be supplied to the Registration Authority when the application for registration is made.

5. The Registration Authority before deciding whether or not the application for registration shall be granted, may allow a further period (not exceeding fourteen days from the expiration of the period required to be specified in the published notice) for the production of evidence in support of any objections.

6. The Certificate of registration or exemption to be furnished by the Registration Authority shall be issued to the Committee in the forms respectively set forth in the Fourth and Fifth Schedules to these Regulations.

7. The Register shall contain the following particulars in respect of every Charity registered under the Act:—
- (a) the name of the Charity;
- (b) the date of establishment;
- (c) the precise objects;
- (d) the address of the administrative centre;
- (e) the full names, address and occupation or description of the Secretary;
- (f) the full names, address, and occupation or description of the Treasurer;
- (g) the full names, addresses, and occupations or descriptions of the Chairman and two other members of the Committee;
- (h) the name and address of the bank or banks at which the account of the Charity is kept;
- (i) the name, address and qualification or other description of the Auditor;
- (j) the date of application for registration;
- (k) the date of registration; and
- (l) (if a Charity be removed from the Register) the date of removal.

8. Every account at a Bank of a Charity registered under the Act shall be kept in the registered name of the Charity.

9. The Auditor shall be an independent person who is a member of an association or society of accountants incorporated at the date on which these Regulations come into force or is on other grounds accepted by the Registration Authority as competent for the purpose. No person shall be deemed to be independent if he is related to or associated in business with any member of the Committee or other officer of the Charity.

10. A duplicate of the entries relating to each Charity registered under the Act shall be entered by the Registration Authority on a separate Register Sheet and such Sheet shall forthwith be sent to the Commissioners.

11. Subject to the following conditions any War Charity registered at the passing of the Act under the Act of 1916 shall be deemed to be registered under the Act by the appropriate Registration Authority:—
- (1) If the Registration Authority under the Act of 1916 are the appropriate Registration Authority they shall transcribe into the Register the

existing particulars of registration amended so far as may be required and shall send a fresh duplicate Register Sheet to the Commissioners. They shall at the same time enter a note in the Register kept by them under the Act of 1916 recording that the Charity has been so registered by them under the Act and send a notification thereof to the Commissioners.

(2) If the Registration Authority under the Act of 1916 are not the appropriate Registration Authority they shall give notice to the appropriate Registration Authority and the Committee in the form set forth in the Sixth Schedule to these Regulations and after the expiration of the period specified in the notice and the settlement of any question raised within that period as to the situation of the administrative centre they shall transmit to the appropriate Registration Authority the existing particulars of registration of the Charity and shall enter a note accordingly in the Register kept by them under the Act of 1916 and send a notification thereof to the Commissioners. The appropriate Registration Authority shall enter the particulars on the Register together with such amendments thereof as may be required and shall send a fresh duplicate Register Sheet to the Commissioners and shall at the same time inform the Registration Authority under the Act of 1916 that the Charity has been so registered by them under the Act.

(3) Upon the registration of the Charity under the Act and this Regulation

(a) the appropriate Registration Authority shall issue to the Committee a Certificate of Registration and no fee in respect of such registration or Certificate shall be payable;

(b) if the Registration Authority under the Act of 1916 are not the appropriate Registration Authority they shall forthwith deliver to the appropriate Registration Authority all books papers accounts and other records in their possession relating exclusively to the Charity, and shall enter a note accordingly in the Register kept by them under the Act of 1916.

12. The Lists of Charities refused registration and the Lists of Charities exempted from registration shall contain the following particulars in respect of every Charity so refused registration or exempted from registration:—

(a) the name of the Charity;
(b) the date of establishment;
(c) the precise objects;
(d) the address of the administrative centre;
(e) the full names, address and occupation or description of each person applying on behalf of the Charity for registration or exemption;
(f) the name and address of the bank or banks at which the account of the Charity is kept;
(g) the considerations which have led the Authority to refuse registration or to exempt the Charity from registration; and
(h) the date of refusal or exemption.

13. A duplicate of the entries relating to each Charity refused registration or exempted from registration shall be entered by the Registration Authority on a separate List Sheet and such Sheet shall forthwith be sent to the Commissioners.

14. A War Charity exempted at the passing of the Act from registration under the Act of 1916, shall not be deemed to be exempted from registration under the Act and shall not be exempt unless and until exemption has been granted by the appropriate Registration Authority in the manner provided in these Regulations.

15. Any changes occurring from time to time in the particulars required to be entered in the Register or any List in relation to any particular Charity shall be communicated by the Committee forthwith to the Registration Authority who shall make the necessary alteration in the Register or such List and shall forthwith notify the same to the Commissioners.

16. In the event of a change being made in the name of a Charity which has been registered or exempted from registration under the Act the Committee shall forthwith produce to the Registration Authority the Certificate of Registration or the Certificate of Exemption as the case may be together with a certified extract from the minutes of the Committee or other evidence that the change has been duly authorised, and the Registration Authority shall insert therein the new name of the Charity and return the Certificate to the Committee.

17. In the event of a change in the Administrative Centre of a Charity registered under the Act making necessary a transfer from one Registration Authority to another under subsection 6 of section 2 of the Act notice shall be given to the Committee and to the appropriate Registration Authority by the Registration Authority by whom the Charity is for the time being registered in the form set forth in the Sixth Schedule of these Regulations and upon the expiration of the period specified in the Notice the transfer shall be carried out and paragraphs (2) and (3) (b) of Regulation 11 of these Regulations shall apply *mutatis mutandis* as if the Registration Authority making such transfer were a Registration Authority under the Act of 1916; Provided that if the Registration Authority by whom the Charity is for the time being registered are engaged in an investigation of the affairs of the Charity the transmission of the particulars of registration may be postponed as provided in the above-mentioned subsection.

18. The Register and Lists shall at all reasonable times be open to the inspection of all persons interested free of charge, and such persons may on payment of a fee of 3d. make copies of or extracts from any entry in the Register or Lists relating to a specific Charity.[1] Copies of or extracts from any such entry in the Register or Lists shall be supplied to any such person on payment of a fee at the rate of 4d. per folio of 72 words for each copy or extract.[2] Such last-mentioned copies or extracts shall be certified by the signature of the Clerk to the Registration Authority or of some person authorised to act on his behalf when the copies or extracts are obtained from the Authority, and by the signature of the Secretary to the Commissioners or some person authorised on his behalf if the copies or extracts are obtained from the Commissioners.

---

1 The reference to 3d. is now to be construed as a reference to 1p by virtue of s. 10 (1) of the Decimal Currency Act 1969.

2 The reference to 4d. is now to be construed as a reference to 2p: Decimal Currency Act 1969, s. 10 (1).

19. Upon the decision of a Registration Authority to refuse to register a Charity or to remove a Charity from the Register or to refuse or withdraw exemption of a Charity from registration, the Registration Authority shall forthwith notify such decision to the Committee of the Charity and in the case of removal from the Register or withdrawal of exemption the Registration Authority shall forthwith furnish to the Commissioners full particulars of the reasons for such removal or withdrawal and all information in their possession as to the funds and securities of the Charity and the persons holding them.

20. Within fourteen days after the receipt of notification of the decision of a Registration Authority to remove a Charity from the Register or to withdraw the exemption of a Charity from registration the Committee shall surrender to the Registration Authority the Certificate of Registration or Certificate of Exemption as the case may be. Where exemption from registration has been granted for a limited period the Committee shall surrender in like manner the Certificate of Exemption forthwith after the expiration of the period for which such exemption was granted. If as the result of an appeal to the Commissioners a Charity is restored to the Register the Registration Authority shall forthwith return the Certificate of Registration to the Committee.

21. The notification of the decision of a Registration Authority to refuse to register a Charity or to remove a Charity from the Register shall include statements showing upon which of the grounds specified in subsection (2) of section 2 of the Act the decision has been taken.

22. Any appeal from the refusal of a Registration Authority to register a Charity or from the decision of a Registration Authority to remove a Charity from the Register shall be made to the Commissioners in writing within fourteen days from the date of the intimation of the refusal or decision or within such further time as may be allowed by the Commissioners, and shall be accompanied by a statement giving the reasons for the appeal.

23. The appellants shall at the same time give notice of the appeal to the Registration Authority and in the case of refusal to register the Authority shall forthwith communicate to the Commissioners full particulars of the reasons for their decision.

24. Any such appeal may be determined by the Commissioners if both the appellants and the Registration Authority concur, on an agreed statement of facts submitted to them in writing and without the attendance before them of the appellants or the Registration Authority in person or by their representatives. In default of such agreement the appellants and the Registration Authority shall supply to the Commissioners summaries of the evidence which they respectively desire to adduce and upon being informed of the day, time and place appointed by the Commissioners for hearing the appeal the appellants and the Registration Authority or some person or persons representing them respectively shall attend and adduce evidence as may be required for determination of the questions arising on the appeal.

25. Duly audited accounts of every War Charity registered under the Act shall be sent to the Registration Authority at least once in every period of twelve months; but the Registration Authority with the consent of the Commissioners or the Commissioners may call for such accounts at any time. Such accounts shall include particulars of receipts and expenditure of money only, but with a view to meeting the requirements of section 3 (b) of the Act every registered Charity shall keep a sufficient record of all dealings with articles in kind of whatever nature.

26. If any bazaar, sale, entertainment or exhibition is promoted to raise money for a War Charity registered under the Act, the approval required by section 1 of the Act shall not be given save on condition that an account of all receipts and expenditure in connexion with the bazaar, sale, entertainment or exhibition shall be rendered to the Committee.

27. Where any appeal is made to the public for donations or subscriptions in money or in kind to any War Charity registered under the Act or any attempt is made to raise money for any such Charity by promoting any bazaar, sale, entertainment or exhibition, or by any similar means, the name of the Charity as appearing in the Certificate of Registration shall be stated in full in all posters, bills, circulars, advertisements and notices relating to such appeal or attempt to raise money with the addition of the words "Registered under the War Charities Act 1940".

28. Every person who is for the time being a member of the Committee of a War Charity registered under the Act shall be responsible in respect of that Charity for securing compliance with the conditions specified in section 3 of the Act and the requirements of these Regulations: Provided that if and so long as the Committee have delegated in writing the duty of securing compliance with any such condition or requirement to some officer of the Charity, being the Secretary, Treasurer or other responsible officer of the Charity and the delegation has been accepted in writing by such officer and notice of such delegation and of its acceptance has been given to the appropriate Registration Authority such officer alone shall be responsible for securing compliance therewith.

29. Any representation or reference of a question to the Commissioners under sections 2 (6) and (9) and 5 (1) (2) and (4) of the Act shall be made to them in writing and shall include or be accompanied by a statement giving the reasons for such representation or reference and any facts relied upon in support thereof.

30. Any application to the Commissioners under section 11 (2) of the Act to determine the question whether a Charity is a War Charity within the meaning of the Act may be made to them by or on behalf of any Registration Authority concerned or any Police Authority or the Commissioner of Police of the Metropolis or the Committee of the Charity and shall be made in the form set forth in the Seventh Schedule to these Regulations and shall be signed by some person or persons duly authorised on behalf of the Authority or Charity and shall be accompanied by full information as to the objects and constitution of the Charity.

F.1.

FIRST SCHEDULE

FORM OF APPLICATION FOR REGISTRATION

WAR CHARITIES ACT 1940

Application for Registration

(I) (We) the undersigned being (a person) (persons) duly authorised on behalf of the Charity called

Insert name
of Charity.

hereby apply to have the said Charity registered under the above-mentioned Act.

The following are particulars of the Charity:—

(1) The date of establishment.
(2) The precise objects.
(3) The address of the Administrative Centre.
(4) The full names, address and occupation or description of the Secretary.
(5) The full names, address and occupation or description of the Treasurer.
(6) The full names, addresses and occupations or descriptions of the Chairman and two members of the Committee.
(7) The name and address of the Bank or Banks at which the account of the Charity is kept.
(8) The name, address and qualification or other description of the Auditor of the accounts.

(I) (We) hereby declare that the above particulars are correct in every respect and that the Auditor is not related to or associated in business with any member of the Committee or other officer of the Charity.

Signature ....

Address ....

Signature ....

Address ....

Signature ....

Address ....

Date ....

NOTE.—(1) The foregoing particulars are required by the Regulations made by the Charity Commissioners under the Act, and it is an offence against the Act to make any false statement in an application for registration.

NOTE.—(2) This application should be sent to the Registration Authority for the area in which the Administrative Centre of the Charity is situate and should be accompanied by the prescribed registration fee of 5s. and copies of the newspapers containing the published notice required under s. 2 (1) of the Act and Regulation 3 of the said Regulations.

F.2.

SECOND SCHEDULE

FORM OF APPLICATION FOR EXEMPTION

WAR CHARITIES ACT 1940

Application for Exemption

(I) (We) the undersigned being (a person) (persons) duly authorised on behalf of the Charity called

Insert name
of Charity.

hereby apply to have the said Charity exempted from registration under the above-mentioned Act.

The following are particulars of the Charity:—

(1) The date of establishment.
(2) The precise objects.
(3) The address of the Administrative Centre.
(4) The full names, address and occupation or description of the Secretary.
(5) The full names, address and occupation or description of the Treasurer.
(6) The area within which and the period of time during which appeals for subscriptions are or will be made.
(7) An approximate estimate of the maximum amount expected to be raised by such appeals.
(8) The reasons for claiming that the Charity should be exempted as desired.

(I) (We) hereby declare that the above particulars are correct in every respect.

Signature ....

Address ....

Signature ....

Address ....

Signature ....

Address ....

Date ....

NOTE.—(1) The foregoing particulars are required by the Regulations made by the Charity Commissioners under the Act, and it is an offence against the Act to make any false statement in an application for exemption.

NOTE.—(2) By s. 1 (2) of the Act it is provided that a Charity can be exempted from registration under the Act if the Registration Authority are satisfied (*a*) that the Charity is established in good faith and (*b*) that it is of so limited a character as respects the area in which its activities are or will be carried on or as respects its duration or objects or as respects the value of the money and property likely to be obtained that it is unnecessary in the interests of the public that the Charity should be registered. A Charity may be exempted for an indefinite or a limited period and exemption may be subsequently withdrawn.

NOTE.—(3) This application should be sent to the Registration Authority for the area in which the Administrative Centre of the Charity is situate.

F.3.

THIRD SCHEDULE

FORM OF STATEMENT TO BE INSERTED IN NEWSPAPERS OF INTENTION TO APPLY FOR REGISTRATION

War Charities Act 1940

Notice is hereby given that it is proposed to apply to the
Council for the registration under the above-mentioned Act of
the objects of which are shortly as follows:—

Insert Name of Council.

Insert Name of Charity.

Insert short description of objects.

and the administrative centre of which is situate at

Insert address.

Any objections to the proposed registration should be sent in writing to the above-named Council within 14 days from the date of this notice.

Dated   19   .

NOTE.—This Notice is required by s. 2 (1) of the Act to be inserted at least one week before the application for registration is made in not less than two newspapers circulating in the area in which the administrative centre of the Charity is situate.

This date should be as nearly as possible the date on which this notice is first published in a newspaper.

F.4.

FOURTH SCHEDULE

FORM OF CERTIFICATE OF REGISTRATION

War Charities Act 1940

IT IS HEREBY CERTIFIED that the Charity called

was on the   day of   19   REGISTERED by the
Council under the above-mentioned Act.

Signed ....

for and on behalf of the above-
named Council.

F.5.

FIFTH SCHEDULE

FORM OF CERTIFICATE OF EXEMPTION

War Charities Act 1940

IT IS HEREBY CERTIFIED that the Charity called

Delete if not
required.

was on the   day of   19   EXEMPTED by the
                Council from registration under the above-mentioned
Act [until the   day of   19   .]
                Signed ....
                            for and on behalf of the above-
                                    named Council.

F.6.

SIXTH SCHEDULE

FORM OF NOTICE ON A TRANSFER OF REGISTERS AND OTHER RECORDS BY ONE
REGISTRATION AUTHORITY TO ANOTHER

War Charities Act 1940

Insert name
of Charity.

Insert name
of new
Registration
Authority.

Insert name
of Charity.

Delete which-
ever is not
required.

Insert name
of existing
Registration
Authority.

Insert name
of new
Registration
Authority.

Insert name
of Clerk and
name of existing
Registration
Authority.

Delete which-
ever is not
required.

To the Committee of
To the Clerk of the   Council.

    Notice is hereby given that the Administrative Centre of the
[being situate at   ]
(having been removed on the   from
                            to
) the   Council
propose at the expiration of 14 days from this date to transmit to the
            Council the particulars of registration of the said Charity
and all books, papers, accounts and other records relating exclusively thereto.
                Signed ....
                        for and on behalf of the above-
                                named Council.

    This notice is given pursuant to [s. 10 (2)] (s. 2 (6)) of the above-mentioned
Act.

F.7.

SEVENTH SCHEDULE

APPLICATION FOR DECISION WHETHER A CHARITY IS A WAR CHARITY

To the Charity Commissioners for England and Wales

In the Matter of the War Charities Act 1940

(I being a person duly authorised on behalf of the   )

((I) (We) the undersigned being (a person) (persons) duly authorised on behalf of the Charity) hereby apply to the Charity Commissioners for England and Wales to determine the question whether the   is a War Charity within the meaning of the above-mentioned Act.

Insert name of
Authority and
delete whichever
is not required

The following are particulars of the Charity:—

   (1) The date of establishment.
   (2) The precise objects.
   (3) The address of the Administrative Centre.
   (4) The Charity affords relief in connection with War or acts of aggression in the manner and to the extent set out below:—

Insert name
of Charity

(I) (We) hereby declare that the above particulars are correct in every respect.

Signature ....

Address ....

Signature ....

Address ....

Signature ....

Address ....

Date ....

NOTE.—(1) These particulars are required by the Regulations made by the Charity Commissioners under the Act.

NOTE.—(2) Under s. 11 of the Act the expression "War Charity" means any fund, institution, association or undertaking, whether established before or after the passing of the Act, having for its sole or principal object or among its principal objects the relief of suffering or distress caused, or the supply of needs or comforts to persons affected, by

   (a) Any War in which His Majesty was engaged during the years 1914 to 1918,

   (b) Any War in which His Majesty was engaged at the passing of the Act, and

(c) Any War or act of aggression, whether occurring before or after the passing of the Act, to which His Majesty by Order in Council has declared the Act to be applicable,

and any other charitable object connected with any such War or act of aggression. The expression does not, however, include any Charity for the blind within the meaning of s. 3 of the Blind Persons Act 1920.

The House to House Collections Regulations 1947

S.R. & O. 1947 No. 2662

These regulations were modified by the Local Authorities etc. (Miscellaneous Provisions) (No. 2) Order 1974, S.I. 1974 No. 595, reg. 4 (2) to the effect that for any reference to a police authority there would be substituted a reference to a licensing authority within the meaning of s. 2 of the House to House Collections Act 1939 as amended by Sch. 29 to the Local Government Act 1972, and any reference to a police area to be construed accordingly.

1. Title and extent

(1) These regulations may be cited as the House to House Collections Regulations 1947, and shall come into operation on the twenty-ninth day of December 1947.

(2) These regulations shall not extend to Scotland.

2. Interpretation

(1) In these regulations, unless the context otherwise requires,—

"The Act" means the House to House Collections Act 1939;

"chief promoter", in relation to a collection, means a person to whom a licence has been granted authorising him to promote that collection or in respect of whom an order has been made directing that he shall be exempt from the provisions of subsection (2) of section 1 of the Act as respects that collection;

"collecting box" means a box or other receptacle for monetary contributions, securely closed and sealed in such a way that it cannot be opened without breaking the seal;

"licence" means a licence granted by a police authority under section 2 of the Act;

"order" means an order made by the Secretary of State under section 3 of the Act;

"prescribed badge" means a badge in the form set out in the Fourth Schedule to these regulations;

"prescribed certificate of authority" means a certificate in the form set out in the Third Schedule to these regulations;

"receipt book" means a book of detachable forms of receipt consecutively numbered with counterfoils or duplicates correspondingly numbered;

"street collection" means a collection or sale to which regulations made under section 5 of the Police, Factories, etc. (Miscellaneous Provisions) Act 1916, apply.

(2) A mark shall for the purposes of these regulations be deemed to have been made on a collecting box if it is made on a wrapper securely gummed to the collecting box.

(3) The Interpretation Act 1889 applies to the interpretation of these regulations as it applies to the interpretation of an Act of Parliament.

3. Local collections of a transitory nature

(1) Every certificate granted under subsection (4) of section 1 of the Act shall be in the form set out in the First Schedule to these regulations, and sections 5 and 6 and subsections (4) and (5) of section 8 of the Act shall be set forth on the back of every such certificate.

(2) Where such a certificate is granted as aforesaid, the provisions of these regulations shall not apply, in relation to a collection made for the purpose specified on the certificate, within the locality and within the period so specified, to the person to whom the certificate is granted or to any person authorised by him to act as a collector for the purposes of that collection.

4. Applications for licences and orders

(1) An application for a licence shall be in the form set out in the Second Schedule to these regulations, and shall give the particulars there specified.

(2) An application for a licence or for an order shall be made not later than the first day of the month preceding that in which it is proposed to commence the collection:

Provided that the police authority or, as the case may be, the Secretary of State may grant the application notwithstanding that it was not made within the time required by this paragraph if satisfied that there are special reasons for so doing.

5. Responsibility of promoters as respects collectors.—Every promoter of a collection shall exercise all due diligence—

(a) to secure that persons authorised to act as collectors for the purposes of the collection are fit and proper persons; and

(b) to secure compliance on the part of persons so authorised with the provisions of these regulations.

6. Certificates of authority, badges, collecting boxes and receipt books

(1) No promoter of a collection shall permit any person to act as a collector, unless he has issued or caused to be issued to that person—

(a) a prescribed certificate of authority duly completed (except as regards the signature of the collector) and signed by or on behalf of the chief promoter of the collection;

(b) a prescribed badge, having inserted therein or annexed thereto a general indication of the purpose of the collection; and

(c) if money is to be collected, a collecting box or receipt book marked with a clear indication of the purpose of the collection and a distinguishing number, which indication and number shall, in the case of a receipt book, also be marked on every receipt contained therein in addition to the consecutive number of the receipt.

(2) Every promoter of a collection shall exercise all due diligence to secure—

(a) that no prescribed certificate of authority, prescribed badge, collecting box or receipt book is issued, unless the name and address of the collector to whom it is issued have been entered on a list showing in respect of any collecting box or receipt book the distinguishing number thereof; and

(b) that every prescribed certificate of authority, prescribed badge, collecting box or receipt book issued by him or on his behalf is returned when the collection is completed or when for any other reason a collector ceases to act as such.

(3) In the case of a collection in respect of which a licence has been granted—

(a) every prescribed certificate of authority shall be given on a form obtained from His Majesty's Stationery Office, and every prescribed badge shall be so obtained; and

(b) every prescribed certificate of authority shall be authenticated, and the general indication on every prescribed badge of the purpose of the collection shall be inserted therein or annexed thereto, in a manner approved by the chief officer of police for the area in respect of which the licence was granted.

7. Duties of collectors in relation to certificates and badges.—Every collector shall—

(a) sign his name on the prescribed certificate of authority issued to him and produce it on the demand of any police constable or of any occupant of a house visited by him for the purpose of collection;

(b) sign his name on the prescribed badge issued to him and wear the badge prominently whenever he is engaged in collecting; and

(c) keep such certificate and badge in his possession and return them to a promoter of the collection on replacement thereof or when the collection is completed or at any other time on the demand of a promoter of the collection.

[**8. Age limit.**—No person under the age of 16 years shall act or be authorised to act as a collector of money.]

9. Importuning.—No collector shall importune any person to the annoyance of such person, or remain in, or at the door of, any house if requested to leave by any occupant thereof.

10. Collection of money

(1) Where a collector is collecting money by means of a collecting box, he shall not receive any contribution save by permitting the person from whom it it received to place it in a collecting box issued to him by a promoter of the collection.

(2) Where a collector is collecting money by other means than a collecting box, he shall, upon receiving a contribution from any person, forthwith and in the presence of such a person enter on a form of receipt in a receipt book issued to him by a promoter of the collection and on the corresponding counterfoil or duplicate the date, the name of the contributor and the amount contributed, and shall sign the form of receipt, the entries and signature being in ink or indelible pencil, and shall hand the form of receipt to the person from whom he received the contribution.

11. Duty of collectors to return boxes and books.—Every collector, to whom a collecting box or receipt book has been issued, shall—
- (a) when the collecting box is full or the receipt book is exhausted, or
- (b) upon the demand of a promoter of the collection, or
- (c) when he does not desire to act as a collector, or
- (d) upon the completion of the collection,

return to a promoter of the collection that collecting box with the seal unbroken or that receipt book with a sum equal to the total amount of the contributions (if any) entered therein.

12. Examination of boxes and books

(1) Subject as provided in paragraph (2) of this regulation, a collecting box when returned shall be examined by, and, if it contains money, be opened in the presence of, a promoter of the collection and another responsible person.

(2) Where a collecting box is delivered unopened to a bank, it may be examined and opened by an official of the bank in the absence of a promoter of the collection.

(3) As soon as a collecting box has been opened, the contents shall be counted and the amount shall be entered with the distinguishing number of the collecting box on a list, which shall be certified by the persons making the examination.

(4) Every receipt book when returned and all sums received therewith shall be examined by a promoter of the collection and another responsible person, and the amount of the contributions entered in the receipt book shall be checked with the money and entered with the distinguishing number of the receipt book on a list, which shall be certified by the persons making the examination.

13. Provision for envelope collections

(1) Where the promoter of a collection to whom an order has been granted informs the Secretary of State that he desires to promote an envelope collection, and the Secretary of State is of opinion that the collection is for a charitable purpose of major importance and is suitably administered, the Secretary of State may, if he thinks fit, give permission for the promotion of an envelope collection.

(2) Where an envelope collection is made in accordance with this regulation—
- (a) every envelope used shall have a gummed flap by means of which it can be securely closed;
- (b) no collector shall receive a contribution except in an envelope which has been so closed; and
- (c) these regulations shall have effect subject to the following modifications:—
  - (i) sub-paragraph (c) of paragraph (1) of regulation 6 shall not apply;
  - (ii) regulation 10 shall not apply;
  - (iii) regulations 11 and 12 shall have effect as if each envelope in which a contribution is received were a collecting box;
  - (iv) in regulation 11 for the words "with the seal unbroken" there shall be substituted the word "unopened";

(v) in paragraph (3) of regulation 12 for the words "As soon as a collecting box has been opened" there shall be substituted the words "As soon as the envelope has been opened" and the words "with the distinguishing number of the collecting box" shall be omitted.

(3) In this regulation "envelope collection" means a collection made by persons going from house to house leaving envelopes in which money may be placed and which are subsequently called for.

14. Promoters to furnish accounts

(1) The chief promoter of a collection in respect of which a licence has been granted shall furnish an account of the collection to the police authority by which the licence was granted within one month of the expiry of the licence:

Provided that if licences are granted to the same person for collections to be made for the same purpose in more than one police area, a combined account of the collections made in all or any of those police areas may, by agreement between the chief promoter and the respective police authorities, be made only to such of the respective police authorities as may be so agreed.

(2) The chief promoter of a collection in respect of which an order has been made shall furnish an account annually to the Secretary of State so long as the order remains in force, and if the order is revoked a final account shall be furnished within three months of the date of the revocation of the order.

(3) The police authority or the Secretary of State may extend the period within which an account is required to be furnished to the authority or to him, as the case may be, if satisfied that there are special reasons for so doing.

(4) The chief promoter of a collection which is made in connection in whole or in part with a street collection of which an account is required to be furnished to a police authority by regulations made under section 5 of the Police, Factories, etc. (Miscellaneous Provisions) Act 1916, may, if the said police authority agrees, combine the accounts of the house to house collection, in so far as it is made in connection with the street collection, with the accounts of the street collection, and the amount so included in the combined account shall not be required to form part of the account required to be furnished under paragraph (1) or, as the case may be, paragraph (2) of this regulation, so, however, that in the case of an account furnished under the said paragraph (2) the account shall show, in addition to an account in respect of moneys received from house to house collections not made in connection with a street collection, a statement showing the total proceeds of all combined collections, the total expenses and the balance applied to charitable purposes.

15. Form and certification of accounts.—The account required by the preceding regulation—

(a) where money has been collected, shall be furnished in the form set out in the Fifth Schedule to these regulations and, where property has been collected and sold, shall be furnished in the form set out in the Sixth Schedule to these regulations, and in either case shall be certified by the chief promoter of the collection and by an independent responsible person as auditor; and

(b) where property (other than money) has been collected and given away or used, shall be furnished in the form set out in the Seventh Schedule to these regulations and shall be certified by the chief promoter and by every person responsible for the disposal of the property collected.

16. Vouching of accounts

(1) Every account furnished under paragraph (a) of regulation 15 of these regulations shall be accompanied by vouchers for each item of the expenses and application of the proceeds and, in the case of a collection of money, by every receipt book used for the purposes of the collection and by the list referred to in paragraph (2) of regulation 6 of these regulations and the list referred to in regulation 12 of these regulations.

(2) Paragraph (1) of this regulation shall not apply to an account certified by an auditor who is a member of an association or society of accountants incorporated at the date of these regulations or is on other grounds accepted as competent by the authority to which the account is submitted, but where in such a case the vouchers, receipt books and lists mentioned in the said paragraph (1) are not submitted with an account, the chief promoter shall ensure that they are available for three months after the account is submitted and shall, if the authority to which the account was submitted so requires at any time within that period, submit them to that authority.

17. Disposal of disused certificates of authority, etc.—The chief promoter of a collection shall exercise all due diligence to secure that all forms of prescribed certificates of authority and prescribed badges obtained by him for the purposes of the collection are destroyed when no longer required in connection with that collection or in conne)tion with a further collection which he has been authorised to promote for the same purpose.

FIRST SCHEDULE *Regulation 3.*

FORM OF CERTIFICATE OF EXEMPTION OF A LOCAL COLLECTION OF A TRANSITORY NATURE

In pursuance of section 1 (4) of the House to House Collections Act 1939, I hereby certify that I am satisfied that the collection, of which particulars are given below, is for a charitable purpose which is local in character, and is likely to be completed within a short period of time.

Accordingly the provisions of that Act (other than those set forth over-leaf ✱) will not apply, in relation to a collection made for the purpose and within the locality and period indicated below, to the promoter(s) named below or to any person authorised by $\frac{him}{them}$ to act as a collector for the purposes of the collection.

(Signed)..

PARTICULARS OF COLLECTION

Name(s) of promoter(s).
Purpose of collection.

Locality to which collection is to be
confined.
Date of commencement of collection.
Date beyond which collection must
not continue.

Sections 5, 6, 8 (4) and 8 (5) of the Act are to be set forth on the back of the certificate.

Regulation 4   SECOND SCHEDULE

Form of Application for Licence

To the Police Authority for (*here insert name of police area*).

In pursuance of section 2 of the House to House Collections Act 1939, I hereby apply for a licence authorising me to promote the collection, of which particulars are given below.

Date..............................   (*Signed*)..................................

Particulars of Collection

1. Surname of applicant (*in block letters*).
   Other names.
2. Address of applicant.
3. Particulars of charitable purposes to which proceeds of collection are to be applied. (Full particulars should be given and, where possible, the most recent account of any charity which is to benefit should be enclosed.)
4. Over what parts of the police area is it proposed that the collection should extend?
5. During what period of the year is it proposed that the collection should be made?
6. Is it proposed to collect money?
7. Is it proposed to collect other property? If so, of what nature? and is it proposed to sell such property or to give it away or to use it?
8. Approximately how many persons is it proposed to authorise to act as collectors in the area of the police authority to which the application is addressed?

9. Is it proposed that remuneration should be paid out of the proceeds of the collection—
    (a) to the collectors?
    (b) to other persons?
    If so, at what rates and to what classes of persons?

10. Is application being made for licences for collections for the same purpose in other police areas?
    If so, to what police authorities?
    And, approximately, how many persons in all is it proposed to authorise to act as collectors?

11. Has the applicant, or to the knowledge of the applicant, anyone associated with the promotion of the collection, been refused a licence or order under the Act, or had a licence or order revoked?
    If so, give particulars.

12. Is it proposed to promote this collection in conjunction with a street collection? If so, is it desired that the accounts of this collection should be combined wholly or in part with the account of the street collection?

13. If the collection is for a War Charity, state if such charity has been registered or exempted from registration under the War Charities Act 1940, and give name of registration authority and date of registration or exemption.

Regulations 2 and 6.   THIRD SCHEDULE

FORM OF PRESCRIBED CERTIFICATE OF AUTHORITY

HOUSE TO HOUSE COLLECTIONS ACT

COLLECTOR'S CERTIFICATE OF AUTHORITY

(Here insert name of collector in block letters)

of *(here insert address of collector)*

is hereby authorised to collect for

(here insert the purpose of the collection)

in *(here insert the area within which the collector is authorised to collect, being an area within which the collection has been authorised)*

*during the period *(here insert the period during which the collector is author-

ised to collect, being a period during which the collection has been authorised)*

Signature of collector—	*Signed—*

---

* This entry may be omitted in the case of a collection in respect of which an order has been made.

Regulation 7 is to be set forth on the back of the certificate.

FOURTH SCHEDULE *Regulations 2 and 6.*

FORM OF PRESCRIBED BADGE

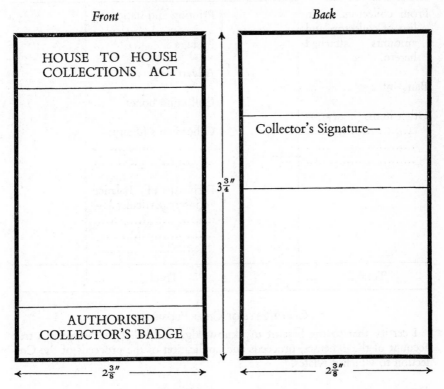

Front   Back

HOUSE TO HOUSE COLLECTIONS ACT

AUTHORISED COLLECTOR'S BADGE

Collector's Signature—

$3\frac{3}{4}''$

$2\frac{3}{8}''$ $2\frac{3}{8}''$

FIFTH SCHEDULE *Regulation 15.*

FORM OF ACCOUNT OF EXPENSES, PROCEEDS AND APPLICATION OF PROCEEDS OF COLLECTION OF MONEY

(a) Surname of chief promoter (*in block letters*).
(b) Other names (*in block letters*).
Address of chief promoter.
Purpose of collection.
Area to which account relates.
Period to which account relates.

All amounts to be entered *gross*.

PROCEEDS OF COLLECTION		EXPENSES AND APPLICATION OF PROCEEDS	
	£ s. d.		£ s. d.
From collectors, as in lists of collectors and amounts attached hereto.		Printing and stationery	
		Postage	
		Advertising	
Bank Interest		Collecting boxes ...	
Other items (if any):—		Other items (if any:—	
		Disposal of Balance (insert particulars):—	
Total		Total	

CERTIFICATE OF CHIEF PROMOTER

I certify that to the best of my knowledge and belief the above is a true account of the expenses, proceeds and application of the proceeds of the Collection to which it relates.

Date................................   (*Signed*)................................

CERTIFICATE OF AUDITOR

I certify that I have obtained all the information and explanations required by me as auditor and that the above is in my opinion a true account of the expenses, proceeds and application of the proceeds of the collection to which it relates.

Date................................   (*Signed*)................................

Qualifications................................

Regulation 15.   SIXTH SCHEDULE

FORM OF ACCOUNT OF EXPENSES, PROCEEDS AND APPLICATION OF PROCEEDS OF COLLECTION OF PROPERTY SOLD OR COLLECTED FOR SALE

(a) Surname of chief promoter (*in block letters*).
(b) Other names (*in block letters*).
Address of chief promoter.

Purpose of collection.
Area to which account relates.
Period to which account relates.

CASH ACCOUNT

All amounts to be entered *gross*.

MONETARY RECEIPTS	£ s. d.	EXPENSES AND APPLICATION OF MONETARY RECEIPTS	£ s. d.	£ s. d.
Amount obtained during period of account by sales of property collected. Bank Interest ... ... Other items (if any):—		Items of expense incurred during period of account, *other than* expenses incurred for the purpose of converting property collected into cash, viz.:—		£
		Items of expense incurred during period of account for the purpose of converting property collected into cash, viz.:—		£
		Disposal of Balance insert particulars):—		£
Total		Total ...	......	

VALUATION OF PROPERTY COLLECTED

Estimated value of property collected during period of
    account   ...   .

If the estimated value is not equal to the difference between the "amount
obtained by sales of property collected" and the total of the "items of expense
incurred during period of account for the purpose of converting property collected into cash", as stated in the cash account, an explanation should be given.

CERTIFICATE OF CHIEF PROMOTER

I certify that to the best of my knowledge and belief the above is a true
account of the expenses and the value and application of the proceeds of
the collection to which it relates, and that none of the property to which it
relates has been disposed of otherwise than by sale, unless found useless and
destroyed or otherwise disposed of as rubbish.

Date................................   (*Signed*)....................................

CERTIFICATE OF AUDITOR

I certify that I have obtained all the information and explanations required
by me as auditor and that the above is in my opinion a true account of the
monetary receipts and expenses and application of the monetary receipts of the
collection to which it relates.

Date................................   (*Signed*)....................................

Regulation 25.   SEVENTH SCHEDULE

FORM OF ACCOUNT OF COLLECTION OF PROPERTY (OTHER THAN MONEY) GIVEN
AWAY, USED OR COLLECTED FOR GIVING AWAY

(a) Surname of chief promoter (*in block letters*).
(b) Other names (*in block letters*).
Address of chief promoter.
Purpose of collection.
Area to which account relates.
Period to which account relates.

I certify that to the best of my knowledge and belief all property collected
in the collection of which particulars are given above (unless found useless and
destroyed or otherwise disposed of as rubbish) has been given away or used for
charitable purposes as follows:—

(Here insert particulars of disposal of property collected.)

(Signed) .... Chief promoter.

....

....

....

Date ....

I further certify that the above certificate has been signed by every person responsible for the disposal of the property collected.

Date...............................   *(Signed)*...................................

Chief promoter.

The Charities for Disabled Persons Regulations 1948

S.I. 1948 No. 1455

1. Subject as hereinafter provided the War Charities Regulations 1940 (which are hereinafter referred to as the 1940 Regulations) shall have effect as if throughout those regulations references to a war charity included references to a charity for disabled persons as defined in section 41 (1) of the National Assistance Act 1948, and as if in respect of a charity for disabled persons the expression "registration authority" meant the registration authority laid down in section 41 (2) (a) of the said Act of 1948 (who are hereinafter referred to as the appropriate authority).

2. Any charity for disabled persons registered at the passing of the said Act of 1948 under the Blind Persons Act 1920, or the War Charities Act 1940, shall be deemed to be registered in accordance with the said Act of 1948 by the appropriate authority and the arrangements set forth below shall be carried out:

(i) If the registration authority under the said Acts of 1920 or 1940 are the appropriate authority, they shall transcribe into the register kept by them under the said Act of 1940 the existing particulars of registration and mark the register sheet "Charity for Disabled Persons" or, if the said particulars are already entered in the said register, mark the existing register sheet "Charity for Disabled Persons". In either case the appropriate authority shall send to the Charity Commissioners a duplicate register sheet similarly marked.

(ii) If the registration authority under the said Acts of 1920 or 1940 are not the appropriate authority, they shall transmit to the appropriate authority the existing particulars of registration of the charity and shall enter a note accordingly in the register kept by them under the said Act of 1920 or the said Act of 1940 as the case may be. The appropriate authority shall enter the particulars in the register kept by them under the said Act of 1940, mark the register sheet "Charity for Disabled Persons" and send to the Charity Commissioners a duplicate register sheet similarly marked. The appropriate authority shall notify that the charity has been registered to the registration authority under the said Acts of 1920 or 1940 who shall then deliver to the appropriate authority all books, papers, accounts and other records in their possession relating exclusively to the charity.

(iii) The appropriate authority shall issue to the committee of the charity a fresh certificate of registration in the form prescribed in number 3 of these regulations for which no fee shall be payable. The committee shall surrender to the appropriate authority the original certificate of registration.

3. Certificates of registration of charities for disabled persons shall be in the form set forth in the fourth schedule to the 1940 Regulations, save that after the heading "War Charities Act 1940" shall be added the heading "National Assistance Act 1948" and save that for the words "Registered under the above-mentioned Act" shall be substituted the words "Registered in accordance with the National Assistance Act 1948".

4. When application is made for the registration of a charity for disabled persons the statement of intention to apply for registration required to be inserted in newspapers shall be in the form set forth in the third schedule to the 1940 Regulations, save that after the heading "War Charities Act 1940" shall be added the heading "National Assistance Act 1948" and save that for the words "registration under the above-mentioned Act" shall be substituted the words "registration in accordance with the National Assistance Act 1948".

5. When an appeal is made to the public or an attempt is made to raise money for a charity for the disabled number 27 of the 1940 Regulations shall have effect, save that for the words "Registered under the War Charities Act 1940" shall be substituted the words "Registered in accordance with the National Assistance Act 1948".

6. Application may be made to the Charity Commissioners to determine whether a fund, institution, association or undertaking is a charity for disabled persons by anyone mentioned in number 30 of the 1940 Regulations.

7. These regulations may be cited as the Charities for Disabled Persons Regulations 1948, and shall come into force on the 5th July 1948.

8. These regulations shall not extend to Scotland.

The Charities (Exception of Voluntary Schools from Registration) Regulations 1960

S.I. 1960 No. 2366

1. These regulations may be cited as the Charities (Exception of Voluntary Schools from Registration) Regulations 1960, and shall come into operation on the first day of January 1961.

2. All voluntary schools, within the meaning of the Education Acts 1944 to 1959, being charities and having no permanent endowment other than the premises of, or connected with, the school, are hereby excepted from the duty to be registered under subsection (2) of section 4 of the Charities Act 1960.

The Charities (Methodist Church) Regulations 1961

S.I. 1961 No. 225

1. A charity shall be excepted from the provisions of section twenty-nine of the Charities Act 1960, as regards any mortgage, charge, sale, lease or other disposal of land which is held upon trusts and with and subject to powers and provisions which are the same as those of, and are declared or adopted by reference to, a deed mentioned in the Schedule to these Regulations.

2. The Interpretation Act 1889, shall apply to the interpretation of these Regulations as it applies to the interpretation of an Act of Parliament.

3. These Regulations may be cited as the Charities (Methodist Church) Regulations 1961, and shall come into operation on the twentieth day of February 1961.

SCHEDULE

MODEL DEEDS OF THE METHODIST CHURCH

Date	Parties	Name by which commonly known
3rd July 1832	John Sutcliffe and others	Wesleyan Methodist Chapel Model Deed.
24th March 1864 ..	Rev. Richard Davies and others.	Model Chapel Trust Deed of the Primitive Methodist Connexion.
11th December 1903 ..	Rev. Albert Clayton and others.	Wesleyan Methodist Secondary Schools' Trust Deed.
22nd April 1908 ..	Henry Arthur Clowes and others.	Model Deed of the United Methodist Church.
15th December 1932 ..	His late Majesty King George V and others.	Model Deed of the Methodist Church.

The Charities (Exception of Certain Charities for Boy Scouts and Girl Guides from Registration) Regulations 1961

S.I. 1961 No. 1044

1. These regulations may be cited as the Charities (Exception of Certain Charities for Boy Scouts and Girl Guides from Registration) Regulations 1961, and shall come into operation on the 22nd day of June 1961.

2. Charities comprising funds, not being permanent endowments, belonging to units, or to trustees for units, of the Boy Scouts Association or the Girl Guides Association, which are being accumulated for the purposes of the unit and which produce an income of more than £15 a year, are hereby excepted from the duty to be registered under subsection (2) of section 4 of the Charities Act 1960.

The Charities (Baptist, Congregational and Unitarian Churches and Presbyterian Church of England) Regulations 1961

S.I. 1961 No. 1282

1. A charity for the advancement of religion shall be excepted from the provisions of section twenty-nine of the Charities Act 1960 as regards any mortgage, charge, sale, lease or other disposal of land, if—

    (a) the land is held by a body named in the Schedule to these Regulations (whether alone or jointly with another person or persons) as a duly constituted trustee or custodian trustee of the land; and

    (b) during the period of three years immediately preceding the transaction, or, where the land was acquired during that period, since the land was acquired by or for the charity, the land has not been used otherwise than as one or more of the following:—

        (i) a place of worship;

        (ii) a burial ground;

        (iii) a Sunday school;

        (iv) a church hall;

        (v) a residence for a minister of religion;

        (vi) a residence for a caretaker of a place or places listed above;

        (vii) the curtilage of a place or places listed above.

2. The Interpretation Act 1889 shall apply to the interpretation of these Regulations as it applies to the interpretation of an Act of Parliament.

3. These Regulations may be cited as the Charities (Baptist, Congregational and Unitarian Churches and Presbyterian Church of England) Regulations 1961, and shall come into operation on the seventeenth day of July 1961.

SCHEDULE

PART I

BAPTIST TRUST CORPORATIONS

The Association of Strict Baptist Churches Limited.
The Baptist Union Corporation Limited.
The Bristol and District Association of Baptist Churches (Incorporated).
The Cardiff and District Baptist Board (Incorporated).
The D. F. and M. Welsh Baptist Corporation.

The Devon Baptist Association Corporation Limited.
The East Midlands Association of Strict Baptist Churches Limited.
The East Midland Baptist Association (Incorporated).
The Lancashire and Cheshire Association of Baptist Churches (Incorporated).
The Leicester Association of Baptist and Union Churches (Incorporated).
The London Baptist Property Board Limited.
The Strict and Particular Baptist Trust Corporation.
The Suffolk and Norfolk Association of Strict Baptist Churches Limited.
The Welsh Baptist Union Corporation Limited.
The West Midland Baptist (Trust) Association (Incorporated).
The Wilts and East Somerset Baptist Association (Incorporated).
The Yorkshire Association of Baptist Churches and Home Mission or Itinerant Society (Incorporated).

PART II
CONGREGATIONAL TRUST CORPORATIONS

The Congregational Union of England and Wales (Incorporated).
The Berks South Oxon and South Bucks Congregational Union (Incorporated).
The Cambridgeshire and Huntingdonshire Congregational Union (Incorporated).
The Cheshire Congregational Union (Incorporated).
The Devon Congregational Union (Incorporated).
The Dorset Congregational Association (Incorporated).
The Durham and Northumberland Congregational Union (Incorporated).
The Essex Incorporated Congregational Union.
The Congregational Union of Gloucestershire and Herefordshire (Incorporated).
The Hampshire Congregational Union (Incorporated).
The Hertfordshire Congregational Union (Incorporated).
The Kent Congregational Association (Incorporated).
The Lancashire Congregational Union (Incorporated).
The Leicestershire and Rutland Congregational Union (Incorporated).
The Lincolnshire Congregational Union (Incorporated).
The London Congregational Union (Incorporated).
The Monmouthshire Congregational Union (Incorporated).
The Norfolk Congregational Union (Incorporated).
The Northamptonshire Association of Congregational Churches (Incorporated).
The Nottinghamshire Congregational Union (Incorporated).
The Shropshire Congregational Union (Incorporated).
The Somerset Incorporated Congregational Union.
The Staffordshire Congregational Union (Incorporated).
The Suffolk Congregational Union (Incorporated).
The Surrey Congregational Union (Incorporated).
The Sussex Congregational Union (Incorporated).
The Warwickshire Congregational Union (Incorporated).
The Wilts and East Somerset Congregational Union (Incorporated).
The Yorkshire Congregational Union and Home Missionary Society (Incorporated).
The English Congregational Union of North Wales (Incorporated).
The South Wales English Congregational Union (Incorporated).
The Union of Welsh Independents (Incorporated).

PART III

UNITARIAN TRUST CORPORATIONS

The British and Foreign Unitarian Association Incorporated.

PART IV

PRESBYTERIAN CHURCH OF ENGLAND CORPORATIONS

The Presbyterian Church of England Trust.

The Charities (Religious Premises) Regulations 1962

S.I. 1962 No. 1421

1. A charity for the advancement of religion shall be excepted from the provisions of section 29 of the Charities Act 1960 as regards any sale of the charity's land, being land to which these Regulations apply, if it is certified on behalf of the charity at the time of the sale that the proceeds of the sale are to be applied in or towards the provision of other land or premises to be used in place of the land sold.

The reference in this Regulation to the provision of other land or premises shall be construed as including a reference to the repayment of money borrowed for that purpose.

2. These Regulations shall apply to land which has not been used during the period of three years immediately preceding the sale (or, where the land was acquired during that period, since the land was acquired by or for the charity) otherwise than as one or more of the following:—

    (a) a place of worship;
    (b) a burial ground;
    (c) a Sunday school;
    (d) a church hall;
    (e) a residence for a minister of religion;
    (f) a residence for a caretaker of a place or places listed above;
    (g) the curtilage of a place or places listed above.

A reference in this Regulation to a Sunday school or church hall shall be construed, in the case of a charity for the advancement of a religion other than Christianity, as a reference to a school or hall of a similar kind.

3. The Interpretation Act 1889 shall apply to the interpretation of these Regulations as it applies to the interpretation of an Act of Parliament.

4. These Regulations may be cited as the Charities (Religious Premises) Regulations 1962 and shall come into operation on 1st August 1962.

The Charities (Society of Friends, Fellowship of Independent Evangelical Churches and Presbyterian Church of Wales) Regulations 1962

S.I. 1962 No. 1815

1. A charity for the advancement of religion shall be excepted from the provisions of section 29 of the Charities Act 1960 as regards any mortgage, charge, sale, lease or other disposal of land, if—

    (a) the land is held by a body named in the Schedule to these Regulations (whether alone or jointly with another person or persons) as a duly constituted trustee or custodian trustee of the land; and

    (b) during the period of three years immediately preceding the transaction, or, where the land was acquired during that period, since the land was acquired by or for the charity, the land has not been used otherwise than as one or more of the following:—

        (i) a place of worship;
        (ii) a burial ground;
        (iii) a Sunday school;
        (iv) a church hall;
        (v) a residence for a minister of religion;
        (vi) a residence for a caretaker of a place or places listed above;
        (vii) the curtilage of a place or places listed above.

2. The Interpretation Act 1889 shall apply to the interpretation of these Regulations as it applies to the interpretation of an Act of Parliament.

3. These Regulations may be cited as the Charities (Society of Friends, Fellowship of Independent Evangelical Churches and Presbyterian Church of Wales) Regulations 1962 and shall come into operation on 1st September 1962.

SCHEDULE

TRUST CORPORATIONS

Friends Trusts Limited.

The Fellowship of Independent Evangelical Churches.

The Properties Board of the Calvinistic Methodist Church of Wales or Presbyterian Church of Wales.

The Charities (Excepted Accounts) Regulations 1963

S.I. 1963 No. 210

1. A charity administered by a Regional Hospital Board, Board of Governors of a teaching hospital or Hospital Management Committee within the meaning of the National Health Service Act 1946 shall be an excepted charity for the purposes of section 8 (1) of the Charities Act 1960.

2. These Regulations may be cited as the Charities (Excepted Accounts) Regulations 1963 and shall come into operation on 14th February 1963.

The Charities (Church of England) Regulations 1963

S.I. 1963 No. 1062

1. A charity for the advancement of religion shall be excepted from the provisions of section 29 of the Charities Act 1960 as regards any mortgage, charge, sale, lease or other disposal of land, if—

(a) the land is held by a body named in the Schedule to these Regulations (whether alone or jointly with another person or persons) either as a duly constituted trustee or custodian trustee of the land or by virtue of the land having been vested in that body in pursuance of section 5 of the Parochial Church Councils (Powers) Measure 1921 or section 6 (2) of the Parochial Church Councils (Powers) Measure 1956; and

(b) during the period of three years immediately preceding the transaction, or, where the land was acquired during that period, since the land was acquired by or for the charity, the land has not been used otherwise than as one or more of the following:—

   (i) a place of worship;
   (ii) a burial ground;
   (iii) a Sunday school;
   (iv) a church hall;
   (v) a residence for a minister of religion;
   (vi) a residence for a caretaker of a place or places listed above;
   (vii) the curtilage of a place or places listed above.

2. The Interpretation Act 1889 shall apply to the interpretation of these Regulations as it applies to the interpretation of an Act of Parliament.

3. These Regulations may be cited as the Charities (Church of England) Regulations 1963 and shall come into operation on 24th June 1963.

SCHEDULE

DIOCESAN TRUST CORPORATIONS

The Canterbury Diocesan Board of Finance.
The York Diocesan Board of Finance.

———

The London Diocesan Fund.
The London Diocesan Board of Finance.
The Trustees of the Bishop of London's Fund Registered.
The Durham Diocesan Board of Finance.
The Winchester Diocesan Board of Finance.

———

The Bath and Wells Diocesan Board of Finance.
Birmingham Diocesan Trustees Registered.
The Birmingham Diocesan Board of Finance.
Blackburn Diocesan Board of Finance.
The Bradford Diocesan Board of Finance.
The Bristol Diocesan Board of Finance.
The Bristol Diocesan Trust.
The Carlisle Diocesan Board of Finance.
The Chelmsford Diocesan Board of Finance.
The St. Albans and Chelmsford Church Trust.
The Chester Diocesan Board of Finance.
The Chichester Diocesan Fund and Board of Finance (Incorporated).
Coventry Diocesan Trustees Registered.
The Coventry Diocesan Board of Finance.
The Derby Diocesan Board of Finance.
The Ely Diocesan Board of Finance.
The Exeter Diocesan Board of Finance.
The Exeter Diocesan Trust.
The Gloucester Diocesan Trust Limited.
The Guildford Diocesan Board of Finance.
The Hereford Diocesan Board of Finance.
The Leicester Diocesan Board of Finance.
The Lichfield Diocesan Trust.
The Lincoln Diocesan Trust and Board of Finance.
The Liverpool Diocesan Board of Finance.
Manchester Diocesan Board of Finance.
The Newcastle Diocesan Society.
The Newcastle Diocesan Board of Finance.
The Norwich Diocesan Board of Finance.
The Oxford Diocesan Board of Finance.
The Peterborough Diocesan Board of Finance.
Portsmouth Diocesan Board of Finance.
The Ripon Diocesan Board of Finance.
The Rochester Diocesan Society and Board of Finance.
The St Albans Diocesan Board of Finance.
The St. Edmundsbury and Ipswich Diocesan Board of Finance.
The Salisbury Diocesan Board of Finance.
The Sheffield Diocesan Trust and Board of Finance.
The Rochester and Southwark Diocesan Church Trust.
The Southwell Diocesan Board of Finance.
The Board of Finance of the Diocese of Truro.
The Wakefield Diocesan Church Organization Society.
The Worcester Diocesan Board of Finance.
Worcester Diocesan Trust Registered.

The Charities (Exception from Registration and Accounts) Regulations 1963

S.I. 1963 No. 2074

General funds of religious bodies

1. Parochial church councils and church trustees and other bodies established wholly or mainly to make provision for public religious worship (including Sunday school worship and the like), whether or not of the Christian religion, are hereby excepted from the duty to be registered under section 4 (2) of the Act in respect of any property (other than land) held and applicable for their general purposes:

Provided that this Regulation shall not apply in any case where the income from such property amounts to more than one hundred pounds a year.

Trusts conditional upon the upkeep of graves

2.—(1) A charity to which this Regulation applies is hereby excepted from the duty to be registered under section 4 (2) of the Act, and it shall be an excepted charity for the purposes of section 8 (1) thereof.

(2) This Regulation shall apply to a charity for the advancement of religion where the application of its income in a particular manner is conditional upon a grave, tomb or personal monument being kept in good order:

Provided that this Regulation shall not apply in any case where the income of the charity amounts to more than fifty pounds a year.

Charities otherwise notified to the Commissioners

3.—(1) A charity to which this Regulation applies is hereby excepted from the duty to be registered under section 4 (2) of the Act, and it shall be an excepted charity for the purposes of section 8 (1) thereof.

(2) The exceptions provided by this Regulation in relation to a charity are conditional upon the Charity Commissioners being notified, from time to time as the case may require, of the following:—

    (a) the name of the charity;

    (b) a brief summary of its purposes and its area of benefit;

    (c) the postal address of any land in England and Wales occupied for its purposes; and

    (d) brief particulars of any other property of the charity or, alternatively, the approximate amount of its annual income from property, indicating in either case whether the property or income forms part of or, as the case may be, is derived from a permanent andowment.

(3) This Regulation applies to a charity wholly or mainly concerned with the advancement of religion, being a charity—

    (a) in respect of which accounts are sent annually to the Methodist Conference, a Methodist Synod or any connexional or other committee or department appointed or established by the Methodist Conference; or

    (b) of which a body named in the Schedule to these Regulations is a charity trustee or custodian trustee.

Church of England charities

4. Without prejudice to Regulations 1 and 2 of these Regulations, a charity connected with the Church of England and wholly or mainly concerned with the advancement of religion is hereby excepted until 1st January 1965 from the duty to be registered under section 4 (2) of the Act.

Interpretation

5.—(1) In these Regulations the expression—

"advancement of religion" includes the relief of ministers and former ministers of religion and their families;

"the Act" means the Charities Act 1960.

(2) The Interpretation Act 1889 shall apply for the interpretation of these Regulations as it applies for the interpretation of an Act of Parliament.

Revocations

6. The Charities (Exception of Religious Charities from Registration) Regulations 1961 and the Charities (Exception of Religious Charities from Registration) Regulations 1962 are hereby revoked.

Citation and commencement

7. These Rules may be cited as the Charities (Exception from Registration and Accounts) Regulations 1963 and shall come into operation on 1st January 1964.

Regulation 3 (3)

SCHEDULE

PART I

BAPTIST TRUST CORPORATIONS

The Association of Strict Baptist Churches Limited.
The Baptist Union Corporation Limited.
The Bristol and District Association of Baptist Churches (Incorporated).
The Cardiff and District Baptist Board (Incorporated).
The D. F. and M. Welsh Baptist Corporation.
The Devon Baptist Association Corporation Limited.
The East Midlands Association of Strict Baptist Churches Limited.
The East Midland Baptist Association (Incorporated).
The Lancashire and Cheshire Association of Baptist Churches (Incorporated).
The Leicester Association of Baptist and Union Churches (Incorporated).
The London Baptist Property Board Limited.
The Strict and Particular Baptist Trust Corporation.
The Suffolk and Norfolk Association of Strict Baptist Churches Limited.
The Welsh Baptist Union Corporation Limited.
The West Midland Baptist (Trust) Association (Incorporated).
The Wilts and East Somerset Baptist Association (Incorporated).
The Yorkshire Association of Baptist Churches and Home Mission or Itinerant Society (Incorporated).

PART II

CONGREGATIONAL TRUST CORPORATIONS

The Congregational Union of England and Wales (Incorporated).
The Berks South Oxon and South Bucks Congregational Union (Incorporated).
The Cambridgeshire and Huntingdonshire Congregational Union (Incorporated).
The Cheshire Congregational Union (Incorporated).
The Devon Congregational Union (Incorporated).
The Dorset Congregational Association (Incorporated).
The Durham and Northumberland Congregational Union (Incorporated).
The Essex Incorporated Congregational Union.
The Congregational Union of Gloucestershire and Herefordshire (Incorporated).
The Hampshire Congregational Union (Incorporated).
The Hertfordshire Congregational Union (Incorporated).
The Kent Congregational Association (Incorporated).
The Lancashire Congregational Union (Incorporated).
The Leicestershire and Rutland Congregational Union (Incorporated).
The Lincolnshire Congregational Union (Incorporated).
The London Congregational Union (Incorporated).
The Monmouthshire Congregational Union (Incorporated).
The Norfolk Congregational Union (Incorporated).
The Northamptonshire Association of Congregational Churches (Incorporated).
The Nottinghamshire Congregational Union (Incorporated).
The Shropshire Congregational Union (Incorporated).
The Somerset Incorporated Congregational Union.
The Staffordshire Congregational Union (Incorporated).
The Suffolk Congregational Union (Incorporated).
The Surrey Congregational Union (Incorporated).
The Sussex Congregational Union (Incorporated).
The Warwickshire Congregational Union (Incorporated).
The Wilts and East Somerset Congregational Union (Incorporated).
The Yorkshire Congregational Union and Home Missionary Society (Incorporated).
The English Congregational Union of North Wales (Incorporated).
The South Wales English Congregational Union (Incorporated).
The Union of Welsh Independents (Incorporated).

PART III

OTHER TRUST CORPORATIONS

Friends Trusts Limited.
The British and Foreign Unitarian Association Incorporated.
The Fellowship of Independent Evangelical Churches.
The Presbyterian Church of England Trust.
The Properties Board of the Calvinistic Methodist Church of Wales or Presbyterian Church of Wales.

The Charities (Exception from Registration and Accounts) Regulations 1964

S.I. 1964 No. 1825

1.—(1) A charity wholly or mainly concerned with the advancement of religion shall, in respect of any property or income to which this Regulation applies, be—

(a) excepted from the duty to be registered under section 4 (2) of the Act; and

(b) an excepted charity for the purposes of section 8 (1) of the Act.

(2) This Regulation applies to property for the time being held by a body named in the Schedule to these Regulations (whether alone or jointly with another person or persons) either as a duly constituted trustee or custodian trustee thereof or by virtue of the property having been vested in that body by or in pursuance of any Measure passed by the National Assembly of the Church of England, and to any income from property so held.

2. The exceptions provided by Regulation 1 of these Regulations in relation to a charity are conditional upon the Charity Commissioners being notified, from time to time as the case may require, of the following:—

(a) the name of the charity;

(b) a brief summary of its purposes and its area of benefit;

(c) the postal address of any land in England and Wales occupied for its purposes and held as mentioned in Regulation 1 (2) of these Regulations; and

(d) brief particulars of any other property of the charity so held or, alternatively, the approximate amount of the annual income from that property, indicating in either case whether the property or income forms part of or, as the case may be, is derived from a permanent endowment.

3.—(1) In these Regulations the expression—

"advancement of religion" includes the relief of ministers and former ministers of religion and their families;

"the Act" means the Charities Act 1960.

(2) The Interpretation Act 1889 shall apply for the interpretation of these Regulations as it applies for the interpretation of an Act of Parliament.

4. These Regulations may be cited as the Charities (Exception from Registration and Accounts) Regulations 1964 and shall come into operation on 1st January 1965.

Regulation 1 (2)

SCHEDULE

Church of England

Diocesan Trust Corporations

The Canterbury Diocesan Board of Finance.
The York Diocesan Board of Finance.

The London Diocesan Fund.
The London Diocesan Board of Finance.
The Trustees of the Bishop of London's Fund Registered.
The Durham Diocesan Board of Finance.
The Winchester Diocesan Board of Finance.

The Bath and Wells Diocesan Board of Finance.
Birmingham Diocesan Trustees Registered.
The Birmingham Diocesan Board of Finance.
Blackburn Diocesan Board of Finance.
The Bradford Diocesan Board of Finance.
The Bristol Diocesan Board of Finance.
The Bristol Diocesan Trust.
The Carlisle Diocesan Board of Finance.
The Chelmsford Diocesan Board of Finance.
The St. Albans and Chelmsford Church Trust.
The Chester Diocesan Board of Finance.
The Chichester Diocesan Fund and Board of Finance (Incorporated).
Coventry Diocesan Trustees Registered.
The Coventry Diocesan Board of Finance.
The Derby Diocesan Board of Finance.
The Ely Diocesan Board of Finance.
The Exeter Diocesan Board of Finance.
The Exeter Diocesan Trust.
The Gloucester Diocesan Trust Limited.
The Guildford Diocesan Board of Finance.
The Hereford Diocesan Board of Finance.
The Leicester Diocesan Board of Finance.
The Lichfield Diocesan Trust.
The Lincoln Diocesan Trust and Board of Finance.
The Liverpool Diocesan Board of Finance.
Manchester Diocesan Board of Finance.
The Newcastle Diocesan Society.
The Newcastle Diocesan Board of Finance.
The Norwich Diocesan Board of Finance.
The Oxford Diocesan Board of Finance.
The Peterborough Diocesan Board of Finance.

Portsmouth Diocesan Board of Finance.
The Ripon Diocesan Board of Finance.
The Rochester Diocesan Society and Board of Finance.
The St. Albans Diocesan Board of Finance.
The St. Edmundsbury and Ipswich Diocesan Board of Finance.
The Salisbury Diocesan Board of Finance.
The Sheffield Diocesan Trust and Board of Finance.
The Rochester and Southwark Diocesan Church Trust.
The Southwell Diocesan Board of Finance.
The Board of Finance of the Diocese of Truro.
The Wakefield Diocesan Church Organization Society.
The Worcester Diocesan Board of Finance.
Worcester Diocesan Trust Registered.

The Charities (Exception from Registration and Accounts) Regulations 1965

S.I. 1965 No. 1056

1. A charity to which these Regulations apply is hereby excepted from the duty to be registered under section 4 (2) of the Charities Act 1960, and it shall be an excepted charity for the purposes of section 8 (1) of that Act.

2. These Regulations shall apply to a charity wholly or mainly concerned with the promotion of the efficiency of any of the armed forces of the Crown, not being—

    (a) a charity having any land in England and Wales for any estate or interest greater than a tenancy from year to year;

    (b) a charity whose objects extend to the relief or assistance of any person not being a serving member of those forces; or

    (c) a charity for the exhibition or preservation of articles of historical interest.

3. The Interpretation Act 1889 shall apply for the interpretation of these Regulations as it applies for the interpretation of an Act of Parliament.

4. These Regulations may be cited as the Charities (Exception from Registration and Accounts) Regulations 1965 and shall come into operation on 15th May 1965.

Rules of the Supreme Court
Order 108

(R.S.C. 1965)

PROCEEDINGS RELATING TO CHARITIES: THE CHARITIES ACT
1960

Interpretation (O. 108, r. 1).

1.—(1) In this Order—

"the Act" means the Charities Act 1960;

"certificate" means a certificate that a case is a proper one for an appeal;

"charity proceedings" means proceedings in the High Court brought under the Court's jurisdiction with respect to charities or brought under the Court's jurisdiction with respect to trusts in relation to the administration of a trust for charitable purposes;

"the Commissioners" means the Charity Commissioners for England and Wales.

(2) References in this Order to the Commissioners shall, in relation to any matter in which the Minister of Education has acted under or by virtue of the Act, be construed as references to that Minister.

Assignment to Chancery Division (O. 108, r. 2).

2. Charity proceedings and proceedings brought in the High Court by virtue of the Act shall be assigned to the Chancery Division and, subject to rules 3 and 4, be begun by originating summons.

Amended by RSC (Amendment) 1972, S.I. 1972 No. 813.

Application for leave to appeal or to take charity proceedings (O. 108, r. 3).

3.—(1) An application shall not be made under section 18 (11) of the Act for leave to appeal against an order of the Commissioners unless the applicant has requested the Commissioners to grant a certificate and they have refused to do so.

(2) An application under the said section 18 (11) or under section 28 (5) of the Act for leave to take charity proceedings must be made within 21 days after the refusal by the Commissioners of a certificate or, as the case may be, of an order authorising the taking of proceedings.

(3) The application must be made by lodging in the Chancery Registrar's Office a statement showing—

   (a) the name, address and description of the applicant;

   (b) particulars of the order against which it is desired to appeal or of the proceedings which it is desired to take;

   (c) the date of the Commissioners' refusal to grant a certificate or an order authorising the taking of proceedings;

   (d) the grounds on which the applicant alleges that it is a proper case for an appeal or for taking proceedings.

(4) The application may be made *ex parte* in the first instance and if it is made with the consent of any other party to the proposed appeal or proposed proceedings that fact shall be mentioned in the statement.

(5) If the judge on considering the application so directs, the Commissioners shall furnish him with a written statement of their reasons for refusing a certificate or, as the case may be, an order authorising the taking of proceedings, and a copy of any such statement shall be sent from the Chancery Registrar's Office to the applicant.

(6) Unless, after considering the applicant's statement and the statement (if any) of the Commissioners, the judge decides to grant the leave applied for without a hearing, the application shall be set down for hearing, and the hearing may be in chambers if the judge so directs.

(7) Where the application is determined without a hearing, a copy of the judge's order shall be sent from the Chancery Registrar's Office to the applicant and the Commissioners; and where the application is to be set down for hearing, notice of the day and time fixed for the hearing shall be sent from the Office to the applicant.

Application for enforcement of order of Commissioners (O. 108, r. 4).
4.—Order 52, rule 1 (4), shall apply in relation to an application under section 41 of the Act as if for the reference in that rule to a single judge of the Queen's Bench Division there was substituted a reference to a single judge of the Chancery Division.

Appeal against order, etc., of Commissioners (O. 108, r. 5).
5.—(1) An appeal against an order or decision of the Commissioners shall be heard and determined by a single judge.

(2) Such an appeal must be brought by originating summons to which the Attorney-General, unless he is the appellant, shall be made a defendant in addition to any other person who is a proper defendant thereto.

(3) An originating summons under this rule must state the grounds of the appeal and, except with the leave of the judge hearing the appeal, the appellant shall not be entitled to rely on any ground not so stated.

Service on Commissioners (O. 108, r. 6).
6. Any document required or authorised to be served on the Commissioners in proceedings to which this Order relates must be served on the Treasury Solicitor in accordance with Order 77, rule 4 (2).

The Charities (Exceptions of Universities from Registration) Regulations 1966

S.I. 1966 No. 965

Citation and commencement
1. These regulations may be cited as the Charities (Exception of Universities from Registration) Regulations 1966 and shall come into operation on 11th August 1966.

Exception of Universities from Registration
2. Every university which is not an exempt charity within the meaning of the Charities Act 1960 shall be excepted from registration under the Act.

Appendix 3

Extracts from the Charity Commissioners' Reports

Contents

Report of the Charity Commissioners for England and Wales for the year 1966

THE COMMISSIONERS' DECISIONS ON CHARITABLE PURPOSES

27. Now that the registration of charities has been in progress for nearly six years, it seems opportune to consider some of the problems that have emerged and to give a brief explanation of our practice. By the end of 1966 we had registered 63,500 charities and had rejected 800 applications for registration,[1] but during this period there has been no appeal to the High Court under section 5 (3) of the Charities Act against our decisions either to register or to reject[2]. It is not suggested that the lack of any appeal against us implies that everyone has been happy with our decisions: appeals to the High Court cost money. It appears that those, such as rating authorities, who might have an interest to deny that an institution is a charity feel that there are no cases in which the point at issue is of sufficient importance to warrant the spending of money in challenging our decision. On the other hand, the institution whose claim to be a charity has been rejected has often made representations to the effect that it cannot afford to go to the court and is also afraid of damaging publicity: it prefers to put forward proposed amendments to its objects in the hope of satisfying us that words have been found which are charitable in law.

28. Section 5 (1) of the Charities Act provides that an institution which is on the register shall be conclusively presumed to be a charity and this has given us power in effect to decide that an institution is a charity, subject only to an appeal to the High Court. We have no similar power to decide that an institution is not a charity, because no conclusive presumptions are to be drawn from its absence from the register, but experience has shown that a decision not to register an institution is likely to result in its losing many of the advantages enjoyed by charities. Thus in the absence of appeals to the court, it has, over the past six years, fallen to us or to the Secretary of State for Education and Science[3]

---

1 The total number registered up to 31st December 1976 was 122,715. The number of applications rejected in 1976 was 38; and 760 charities had at that time been removed from the register since its reception.

2 For reported appeals since 1966 see *Incorporated Council of Law Reporting for England and Wales* v. *A.-G.*, [1972] Ch. 73, C.A.; *Construction Industry Training Board* v. *A.-G.*, [1973] Ch. 173, C.A.

3 All charities are now subject to the jurisdiction of the Charity Commissioners.

to decide whether an existing institution is a charity. Cases not involving existing institutions continue to come before the courts, usually on the construction of a will, in which a decision is reached affecting the law of charitable purposes.

29. It has long been recognised that the court has treated the concept of charity flexibly and has been ready to extend the meaning of "charitable purposes" to meet changed circumstances. It is our belief that when Parliament entrusted us with the duty of registering charities and thereby of determining the charitable status of applicant institutions it expected us to bring to this task the flexibility which the court had already shown. Since Parliament has provided that appeal from our decision lies to the High Court, it is clear that we must reach our decision on charitable status as a matter of law, applying the principles adopted by the court. In doing so, however, we believe that we are entitled and expected to follow the court in extending the field of charity by analogy from cases already decided. It would surely have been a serious and unintended result of the passing of the Charities Act if the field of charity had become fixed and limited by the decisions already reached in the courts and consequently capable of enlargement only on the few occasions when one of the class of cases mentioned at the end of the last paragraph or an appeal against a decision of ours comes before the court.

30. Many cases have already come before us in which new voluntary and non-profit-making bodies have been founded to meet new problems thrown up by changing social needs. Acting on analogy with court decisions in broadly similar cases we have felt it right to regard the field of charity as extending to some of these bodies. We have had as an example the practice of the Chief Inspector of Taxes (Claims Division) in allowing relief from tax to organisations whose claims to be charities did not fall into a category originally recognised as charitable although analogous to a case in some such category. In this the Chief Inspector of Taxes has doubtless been guided by the confidential decisions of the Special Commissioners of Inland Revenue. There have been many instances in which it would have been unreasonable for us not to have followed the line already adopted by these authorities especially where an institution had long enjoyed relief from income tax.

31. The problem whether a newly formed society is a charity when its purposes are unlike any which the court has already considered can on occasion prove extremely difficult. As the judges themselves have admitted charity law is not always governed by logic nor are the decisions entirely consistent. For instance, it has more than once been stated in judgments that if a purpose is to be regarded as charitable it must fall within the spirit and intendment of the preamble to the Elizabethan Statute of Charitable Uses of 1601 (see, for example, Lord Simonds in *Williams' Trustees* v. *Inland Revenue Commissioners*, [1947] A.C. 447, at page 455); nor can it be argued that this doctrine is affected by the fact that the Charities Act, in repealing the Mortmain and Charitable Uses Act 1888, has removed the express preservation of this preamble to which Lord Simonds drew attention. It does appear, however, that almost all the cases in which this doctrine has been mentioned have been cases in which the court decided that the institution before it was not a charity. There are many other cases in which the court, when deciding that some society was a charity, did not pause to trace its connection with the Elizabethan preamble. We believe, that, although we must never lose sight of the list of charitable instances in the

preamble, we are entitled to enter in the register organisations whose connection with any of them may seem tenuous, provided that the court has given us a lead in a decision about a comparable organisation.

32. Another doctrine in charity law which causes many problems is expressed in the statement that although a charity must be for the benefit of the community, not all purposes that are for the benefit of the community are necessarily charitable: if an institution is to be charitable its purposes must be for the benefit of the community in a way which the law recognises as charitable. This can, however, be interpreted indifferently either as restricting the field of charity within the limits of previous decisions or as permitting an almost unrestricted flexibility. We do not believe that either of these extremes is right; and it is our hope that by constant attention to previous court decisions, we shall succeed in developing from them, with the approval of the court if there is an appeal, such a concept of the field of charity as may meet the needs of the community.

33. We think it important to mention these matters not only by way of explaining how we interpret our duties in deciding whether or not to register organisations as charities, but also because it is clear that in the absence of any regular flow of appeals from our decisions we shall inevitably move further and further away from cases decided by the court. In considering future applications we must necessarily take account of what, acting as a Board of Commissioners, we have previously decided, as the court takes account of its previous decisions, and this cannot but gradually extend the field of charity. Such continual development appears to us to be inevitable as attempts are made within the concept of charity progressively to meet the needs of a society which is not itself static.

34. It may be useful to mention one or two other matters that arise in connexion with our consideration of charitable purposes. We consider that we are bound by the decisions of the courts to base our decision whether an institution is a charity upon the words used in its constitution or other instrument of government, particularly where the words appear in a deed or in the memorandum of association of a company. Words to define a charitable purpose must be clear and certain. Many organisations have applied to us to register objects expressed in terms so obscure and containing so much that is merely emotive that the objects were uncertain or unenforceable.

35. There have been a few cases in which it has become apparent that an institution's activities are in conflict with the words used and are in no sense charitable; in such cases we have preferred, whenever possible, to put a construction on the words which will permit the known activities, even though this has inevitably involved our rejecting the application for registration as a charity. But there have been times when the words have been so free from doubt that we have had no option but to register the institution with the caution that in future its objects must be strictly observed.

36. Some of our non-legal correspondents have questioned the justification for the importance which the law attaches to the words used rather than to the institution's activities. It is felt by such correspondents that it should be enough to examine the activities of the institution to decide whether it is a charity and that two organisations both doing the same things should be equally qualified for registration. But this fails to take account of the fact that the law must be concerned principally with the obligation imposed on the institution to pursue

certain objects. It is this obligation which establishes it as a charity; and so long as an institution is free to pursue any activities it wishes it cannot be treated as an established charity, however much its current activities may resemble those of other recognised charities.

37. The problem of interpreting words presents a somewhat different aspect when we are asked to consider draft documents intended to set up proposed charities. It is not unusual to find an attempt to dress up the purposes of the proposed institution in words which it is hoped will be accepted as charitable even though the purposes, so phrased, are quite remote from the true intentions of the promoters. We are convinced that this is a highly unsatisfactory course and that the governing instrument of every institution should show unequivocally what the institution really sets out to achieve. Three particular devices call for comment.

38. The first is the over-working of the word "education". Ingenious draftsmen have found it possible to embrace within this word a vast variety of activities, mainly propagandist, which do not come within the meaning of the "advancement of education" as it is used in charity law. A purpose which is not charitable cannot be made charitable merely by representing it to be a form of education.

39. The second device is the use of very wide general terms. It is of course true that there are some founders of charities, particularly those who are settling part of their own personal fortune, who genuinely expect to apply the settled property for all manner of charitable purposes; in such a case the general words are not intended to conceal a more limited true purpose. But, nonetheless, they may be difficult to interpret and it is undesirable that they should be used in any case where the proposed charity has a more limited purpose, particularly if the charity is intending to appeal to the public and not be merely the vehicle for the founder's own benevolence.

40. The third device is that of enumerating a number of objects, some perhaps charitable and others less obviously so, and then declaring that the institution is to be confined to carrying out such of the listed objects as are charitable. We have already commented on this device in paragraph 25 of our report for 1964. This approach begs the question, prevents the real purpose of the institution from being readily recognised and quite unnecessarily introduces difficulty in construing and acting upon the documents in which it is used. If a proposed charity shows us a draft instrument incorporating such a phrase we consider ourselves entitled to enquire what are intended to be its activities, with a view to seeing whether those activities can be authorised in terms of clearly fidened charitable purposes.

41. As in our reports for the last two years we give a list, in Appendix A, of the cases in which decisions on or affecting charitable status have been reached by us, sitting as a Board. As was to be expected, there were fewer cases considered last year at this level than in previous years, and this reflects both a reduction in the number of institutions applying for registration and the fact that a great deal more work is now done in advising on draft documents. We find that advice given by our staff on a document still in draft is usually readily accepted by those concerned with the foundation of the charity. No problem then arises when the institution applies for registration.

Report of the Charity Commissioners for England and Wales for the year 1967, paras. 17-21 and Appendix B

CHARITIES FOR THE RELIEF OF POVERTY

17. The plight of the poorest section of the community has been progressively relieved by the statutory welfare services which have come into being during the past few decades. One consequence of this is that trustees of charities for the relief of the poor sometimes find themselves faced with the problem of how to apply the income of their charity in accordance with the trusts and at the same time avoid repeating or abating the financial benefits provided by the statutory services. Nevertheless there is still considerable scope for the assistance which can be given by trustees of charities for the poor and it is now especially important that they should ask themselves how far they are achieving the real object of their charity and consider how effective their efforts are today.

18. To meet present day needs we have prepared a new common-form clause to be used in our schemes providing for the relief of those in need. The new clause is very simple and much shorter than the form previously in use but we append to schemes in which it is used a note giving some general advice regarding the application of the income and containing examples of ways in which the trustees of these charities may be able to render worthwhile assistance to those in need. A copy of the new clause and note is reproduced in Appendix B. A shortened form of the new clause is used, without the note, where the income available is less than £25 a year.

19. A charity's funds can of course be applied only in accordance with its trusts. If those trusts are unduly restrictive or if trustees are in doubt whether the trusts of their charity allow them to use their funds in the way they would like, they should write to us. In appropriate cases, it may be possible for us to establish a scheme to change the trusts. It seems likely, however, that in the majority of cases the existing trusts will allow the trustees to use their funds for the relief of the poor in a variety of ways other than those which have been usual in the past. The term "poor" should not be regarded as confined to the destitute but taken as referring to any persons who are in genuine need.

20. It is a recognised rule that the income of a charity for the relief of the poor must not be used in such a way as directly to relieve rates, taxes or other public funds. To make sure that they comply with this rule we recommend the trustees of such charities to keep in touch with the local officers of the Ministry of Social Security[1] and of the welfare departments of their local authorities regarding the help that can be given in general out of public funds to persons in need and the effect upon such help of grants from charitable sources. We also suggest that the trustees consult local welfare officers about particular cases. Such contacts may also enable trustees to find out about people in the area served by their charity who have needs which cannot be met in full by the statutory services.

21. For the benefit of charity trustees who do not need a new scheme for their charities we are preparing a leaflet covering these points and reproducing the list of examples which is included in the note mentioned above.

---

1 Now the Department of Health and Social Security.

APPENDIX B, PARAGRAPH 18—RELIEF IN NEED

Relief in need.—(1) The object of the Charit   shall be to relieve either generally or individually persons resident in the Parish of who are in conditions of need, hardship or distress.

(2) The Trustees shall apply the income of the Charit   for that object by making grants of money or providing or paying for items, services or facilities calculated to reduce the need, hardship or distress or such persons.

(3) The Trustees may pay for such items, services or facilities by way of donations or subscriptions to institutions or organisations which provide or which undertake in return to provide such items, services or facilities for such persons.

Restrictions.—In applying the income of the Charit   the Trustees shall observe the following restrictions:

(1) They shall not apply any part of the income directly in relief of rates, taxes or other public funds but may apply income in supplementing relief or assistance provided out of public funds.

(2) They shall not commit themselves to repeat or renew the relief granted on any occasion in any case.

Note

This note has no legal force as part of the scheme but shows the kind of relief that the charity can properly give.

Relief in Need

Charities for relief in need operate in the same field as statutory services; trustees who administer such charities should be careful to avoid repeating or abating those services. Charity trustees should accordingly acquaint themselves with the system of social benefits, the effect upon them of grants from charitable sources and the gaps left by them which can be filled by charitable services or facilities to relieve those in need.

By consulting local officers of the Ministry of Social Security[1] and those in the welfare and other departments of the local authority concerned with persons in need, the trustees may learn what assistance and services these authorities can give in particular circumstances, whether by way of special grants or otherwise, and may also be able to find out about people living within the charity's area of benefit who have needs which the statutory services are unable to relieve completely. In this way the trustees may ensure that a regular allowance from the charity or the provision of some item or facility will not affect supplementary benefits available from the Ministry of Social Security in a given case.

Charity trustees should not regard themselves as being confined to giving relief in those cases of need which are also eligible for supplementary benefits or as being limited to providing those items which have been allowed for in calculating the amount of supplementary payments.

---

1 Now the Department of Health and Social Security.

The provisions of the scheme give the trustees a wide choice in the sort of relief that they can give out of the income of the charity so long as the need is clear. Whatever relief they give must be given only to assist the kind of persons mentioned, must be related to the needs of each case, and must be reasonable in the circumstances, taking into account what relief is available from other sources. Some examples follow and others may occur to trustees:

1. Grants of money to or for the benefit of such persons in the form of—
   (a) weekly allowances for a limited period to meet a particular need or
   (b) special payments to relieve sudden distress, sickness, or infirmity, or
   (c) payment of travelling expenses for such persons entering or leaving hospitals, convalescent homes or similar institutions, or for relatives visiting such persons in such institutions particularly where more frequent visits are desirable than payments from public funds will allow, or
   (d) subscriptions to secure the admission of such persons (or to benefit such persons when admitted) to almshouses, or to homes or hostels for the residence or care of old, infirm or homeless persons.

2. The provision of items for such persons which may well be—
   (a) gifts of furniture, bedding, clothing, food, fuel, heating appliances, or
   (b) loans of expensive apparatus (which may be more appropriate than outright gifts) such as radio or television sets for widows with large families.

3. The provision of facilities for such persons such as—
   (a) the supply of tools or books or payment of fees for instruction or examination or travelling expenses so as to help them to earn their living, or
   (b) arrangements for a recuperative holiday or change of air for those long deprived of this.

Further examples follow of the sort of help that can be given in particular when such persons are also old, sick, convalescent, disabled, handicapped or infirm, whether mentally or physically:

4. The provision of items either outright or, if expensive and appropriate, on loan, such as—
   (a) special food, medical or other aids, nursing requisites or comforts;
   (b) television or radio sets for the lonely, bedridden or housebound;
   (c) television or radio licences;
   (d) washing machines suitable for soiled clothing and bed linen.

5. The provision of services such as bathing, escort services, exchange of library books, foot care, gardening, hair washing, shaving, help in the home, house decorating and repairs, laundering, meals on wheels, nursing aid, outings and entertainments, physiotherapy in the home, reading, shopping, sitting-in, tape-recording for the housebound, travelling companions.

6. The provision of facilities such as transportation, or arrangements for a period of rest, recuperation or change of air in or through any convalescent home or other institution or organisation or for temporary relief for those

having the care of the person concerned or arrangements for close relatives to visit or care for patients.

The trustees may either pay directly for such items, services or facilities, or advance money to beneficiaries so that they can do so.

Report of the Charity Commissioners for England and Wales for the year 1969, paras. 8-16 (reprinted as Appendix A to the Report for the year 1973)

POLITICAL ACTIVITIES BY CHARITIES

7. We have remarked from time to time in our previous reports on the difficulties which face us, particularly in the discharge of our quasi-judicial functions, in applying the law of charity to new activities which grow out of the constantly changing needs of society. In a world in which the pace of social change seems ever to be increasing we shall inevitably continue to be faced with new or extended activities, the charitable nature of which has never been the subject of consideration by the courts. We are, however, often bound to consider how far such activities may properly be regarded as consonant with charitable purposes both in connexion with our responsibility for registering charities and with our function of giving advice to charity trustees.

8. One contemporary development which has given us some concern has been the increasing desire of voluntary organisations for "involvement" in the causes with which their work is connected. Many organisations now feel that it is not sufficient simply to alleviate distress arising from particular social conditions or even to go further and collect and disseminate information about the problems they encounter. They feel compelled also to draw attention as forcibly as possible to the needs which they think are not being met, to rouse the conscience of the public to demand action and to press for effective official provision to be made to meet those needs. As a result "pressure groups", "action groups" or "lobbies" come into being. But when a voluntary organisation which is a charity seeks to develop such activities it nearly always runs into difficulties through going beyond its declared purposes and powers. No charity should, of course, undertake any activity unless it is reasonably directed to achieving its purposes and is within the powers conferred by the charity's governing instrument.

9. This development has resulted in our having to consider in a number of different contexts the extent to which individual charities may properly engage in activities which may be described generally as of a political nature, and further whether it is possible for us to indicate in a general way what in our view are the pitfalls for which charities must be on the lookout. We endeavour in the following paragraphs to give some guidance on this matter, but we would emphasise that the law is based on a limited number of decided cases and there is some danger in trying to stretch them . . . to cover the whole of the ground. In the last resort any particular case must be judged on all the circumstances pertaining to it, and what we say below must be regarded as guidance of only the most general kind which may well need to be modified when applied to individual cases. We are always ready to give our opinion on any particular case where the

trustees are in doubt, although many charities likely to come into contact with this problem will have their own legal advisers to whom they should turn for advice in the first instance.

10. It is a well-established principle of charity law that a trust for the attainment of a political object is not a valid charitable trust and that any purpose with the object of influencing the legislature is a political purpose. Thus no organisation can be a charity and at the same time include among its purposes the object of bringing influence to bear directly or indirectly on Parliament to change the general law of the land. If the governing instrument of an organisation were to give it power, other than in a way merely ancillary to some charitable purpose, to play a part in bringing political pressure to bear, that by itself would throw serious doubt on the organisation's claim to be a charity. Thus it is very unlikely that it will lie within any charity's purposes and powers to sponsor action groups or bring pressure to bear on the government to adopt or alter a particular line of action. In the past it was recognised that such activity lay well outside the true field of charity although, as will be mentioned below, there are other more traditional approaches to Parliament and to the government that have long been accepted as perfectly proper for a charity. Today, however, it seems that the limitations on action of this kind are not always recognised by those responsible for running charities.

11. Those trustees who feel that their charity should become involved in the political field frequently seek to justify such action as coming within the field of "education". In our report for 1966 we mentioned the misuse of this word in the governing instruments of some organisations applying for registration as charities. Increasingly we are confronted by attempts to represent as educational a variety of activities which are primarily of a propagandist nature and which accordingly cannot be accepted as coming within the meaning of the "advancement of education" as it is used in charity law. There is a similar tendency for those registered charities which have as a subsidiary object the education of the public in the particular aspect of charity with which the organisation is concerned (for instance the need for the relief of poverty in under-developed countries) to overstep the boundary of what might properly be described as education and pass outside their declared purposes into the field of propaganda. There is obvious difficulty in determining exactly where this boundary lies but if a charity with general objects, such as the relief of poverty or distress, issues literature urging the government to take a particular course or organises sympathisers to apply pressure for that purpose to their elected representatives, we think it is clear that the boundary has been overstepped.

12. We would emphasise that it is not for us to judge whether the object of a propagandist or political activity is morally or socially right or wrong although we can appreciate the reasons why some charities feel a moral obligation to attempt to influence policies. We are concerned simply with the law of charity and with seeking to ensure that funds which are impressed with charitable trusts are used for the purposes of those trusts and not for other purposes which could not be recognised as charitable. However small the proportion of the income of a charity which may be used in this way, we believe that the charity will be led into difficulties if it appears to be giving its support to any objects that are not strictly within its charitable purposes.

13. We have, where it has seemed to us to be necessary, brought these considerations to the notice of individual charities. We are aware, however, that there

may be other charities, which have perhaps not yet discussed their problems with us, and which are hesitating about promoting their objects by activities which might perhaps be considered to be political activities. We believe that it might help charities to realise what they have power to do if we point the contrast by giving some examples of such activities which we believe can justifiably be regarded as being proper for a charity. These examples fall into three classes, the first and third of which present little difficulty. The first class comprises those examples in which it is the government itself which is investigating or has propounded proposals for changes in the law. Government officials frequently seek advice and information from those who are responsible for running charities and the charities quite properly respond. Similarly by publishing a green or white paper the government may impliedly invite comments from the public generally and a charity may justifiably avail itself of such an invitation to make any comments which may appear to be useful. Again when a parliamentary bill has been published a charity will be justified in supplying relevant information to a member of either House and such arguments to be used in debate as it believes will assist the furtherance of its purposes. So also there can be other cases, not involving legislation, in which a charity is entitled to persuade a Member to support its cause in Parliament, for instance, where the question arises whether a government grant is to be made or continued to a particular charity.

14. The second class of examples, which includes those in which the charity itself or with others wishes to put forward proposals for changes in the law, can be more difficult to justify. It is probably unobjectionable for a charity to present to a government department a reasoned memorandum advocating changes in the law provided that in doing so the charity is acting in furtherance of its purposes. On the other hand, a charity can only spend its funds on the promotion of public general legislation if in doing so it is exercising a power that is merely ancillary to its charitable purposes. But here again difficulty arises in defining the boundary between what is merely ancillary and what amounts to adopting a new purpose in itself. A charity would be well advised to seek advice either from its legal advisers or from us before undertaking any such activities.

15. Finally, the third class of examples comprises cases where, although Parliament is involved, it appears to us that the reason for approaching it is not to be regarded as political. This, for instance, includes legislation that is only intended to confer enabling powers, such as the Sharing of Church Buildings Act which is mentioned in paragraphs 36 to 39 of this report. By supporting the passage of this Act the various charities involved were seeking to obtain wider powers to carry out their purposes. Similarly, virtually all private bills are free from taint of political activities. A private bill is in the nature of litigation as much as of legislation and the action of supporting or opposing such a bill resembles a court action and nearly always has no political tinge. We feel, therefore, that the principle laid down by the courts that a political object is not a charitable purpose should not be extended in such a way as to deny to a charity that right to promote or oppose private legislation which is enjoyed by public and private bodies in general. Thus in every session some charities, with our consent under section 19 (7) of the Charities Act, promote private bills which may set out to alter the constitution of the charity or to give it powers which only Parliament can confer. An example of such a bill in the present session is the National Trust Bill. The case mentioned in paragraphs 23 and 24 of this

report provides an example of a charity which in order to realise its charitable purposes played a part in opposing a private bill.

16. There are two general points which we should like to mention in concluding this section of our report. First, if the trustees of a charity do stray into the field of political activity their action will be in breach of trust and those responsible for the action could be called on at law to recoup to the charity any of its funds which have been spent outside its purposes. Moreover a charity is not entitled to tax relief on income which is not applied to charitable purposes. But the fact that political action had been taken in the name of the charity would not affect its status as a charity nor constitute a reason for removing it from the register of charities. If, however, doubt had been cast on the correctness of the original registration removal might be considered by us or by the High Court on an appeal by any other body interested. Secondly we think it should also be borne in mind that if charities step outside the sphere of activities to which the law confines them they may not only prejudice the support they receive from some people, who could resent the new activities, but they may also eventually endanger the privileged position which charities as a whole have been accorded by the state. The attempts now being made in the United States to curtail the privileges enjoyed by charitable foundations there result in part from allegations that some of those foundations have been using their funds for purposes which are essentially political.

Report of the Charity Commissioners for England and Wales for the year 1970, paras. 42-44, 46

42. The relaxation of the rule relating to failure has enabled us over the last 10 years to assist many charities which wish to serve the local community in more modern and effective ways. As we have indicated above, this process had started 100 years before the Charities Act; but many of the schemes which our predecessors made during that time have in their turn grown out of date. The process of modifying the objects of charities, whether local or national, is an ever-continuing process. Thus the original terms of a charitable gift of the 18th century or earlier may have required the trustees to distribute to poor persons loaves of bread, candles or particular kinds of clothing. Even by the end of the 19th century many such trusts had failed, but the schemes which we then made prescribed in narrow terms the amounts of income which could be given in direct grants, or the particular institutions (e.g. a hospital or a clothing club) to which subscriptions might be granted, or the particular purposes (e.g. the cost of an outfit on entering a trade or the provision of passage money to aid emigration) to which contributions might be made. The amount of money which might be granted by way of temporary relief in cases of unexpected loss or sudden destitution was always most carefully limited as our predecessors were concerned less the indiscriminate distribution of gifts by a charity might have the effect of pauperizing the beneficiaries. Only too often neither the terms of the original gift nor the terms of the subsequent scheme appear to us to be achieving the basic intention of the donor, which was usually to make a real contribution towards relieving distress. In such cases we substitute more general provisions allowing the trustees to use the charity's resources in ways which will relieve need in whatever form it may still be found to exist. It is therefore our

practice to make the provisions of the scheme as wide as possible, but we also add an explanatory note, which is strictly not part of the scheme, to draw the trustees' attention to those ways which we know of at present in which the income may be usefully applied.

43. We have made good use of the power contained in section 13 (1) (*e*) (i) which makes it clear that a cy-près scheme can be made where the original purposes in whole or in part have, since they have been laid down, been adequately provided for by other means. For example, we have made schemes for a number of charities established for the repair of roads and bridges, substituting for those purposes other general purposes for the benefit of local inhabitants which could include, for instance, the promotion of the arts, the provision of seats or shelters, the preservation of old buildings, or the improvement of local amenities.

44. Although we have been able to do much in these ways to help charities to reorientate themselves in modern conditions, much undoubtedly still remains to be done. There can be no doubt that the publicity given to the Charities Act and the need to register charities has made many trustees aware also of our readiness to help them; and the actual process of supplying the information on registration has drawn the attention of some trustees to the extent to which the trusts they should be following are now out of date. The local reviews of charities, to which we have already referred, are also performing a useful function in helping to stimulate trustees to make the applications for schemes without which we cannot normally move. But even where reviews are being undertaken there are always some trustees who, despite the obvious need for the trusts of their charities to be modernised, are not willing to make application to us. It may be that trustees sometimes hesitate to approach us for fear that they will be penalised for not having followed their trusts to the letter. If, however, trustees have departed from their trusts in the honest belief that what they were doing was better for the community they serve, they need have no fear of approaching us to ask for a scheme to alter the purposes of their charities. Failure to keep within the trusts may often be evidence of the need to alter the purposes of the charity rather than of dereliction of duty on the part of the trustees.

46. Section 14 of the Act was designed to overcome the difficulties which previously arose when money was collected for a particular charitable purpose and that purpose then turned out to be unattainable. Mention was made in the debates on this provision in Committee in the House of Commons of a fund which was raised to provide a new hospital, but when the project had to be abandoned it was held that the money should be returned to the subscribers, who had to be regarded as having a particular, as distinct from a general, charitable intention in making their gifts. Section 14 provides that if the donors of funds for a purpose which is no longer practical cannot be identified or found or, if they can be found, they execute a disclaimer of their right to have the property returned, they can be deemed to have had a general charitable intention so that the money they contributed can be applied cy-près. We have been able to make a number of schemes under this provision enabling money to be used for other charitable purposes which previously could not have been used.

Appendix 4

Leaflets Issued by the Charity Commissioners

Contents

[Crown Copyright, reproduced by permission of the Controller, H.M.S.O.]

Trustee Investments Act 1961, T.P. 1

1. These notes are intended as a guide for charity trustees to the main provisions in the Act which affect their powers of investment and to assist them in the investment of trust funds. They are not to be taken as an authoritative interpretation or as a substitute for the Act itself. Copies of the Act can be obtained from H.M. Stationery Office or through any bookseller.

2. These general notes cannot deal with the particular circumstances of individual trusts; and if charity trustees have any problem on which they would like advice, the Charity Commissioners will be glad to assist them if they can. They cannot, however, undertake to provide specific advice on investments unless the trustees have vested the property in the Official Custodian for Charities. Other trustees should consult their usual advisers or some qualified person. The methods by which securities are bought and sold are generally familiar, and there is no reason to change arrangements whereby trustees do business through a broker or banker. Any trustees who wish to make use of a broker for investment or advice may obtain a list of member firms which are willing to take on such business from the Secretary, Stock Exchange, London, E.C.2. If the investments are already held by the Official Custodian for Charities, enquiries and requests for advice should be addressed to him at Wellington House, Buckingham Gate, London, S.W.1.

SUMMARY OF PROVISIONS

3. The Act permits trustees to invest trust funds in a wider range of investments than was previously authorised. Before the Act, unless trustees had express powers under the trust instrument, they could invest only in the securities prescribed by the Trustee Act 1925 (commonly known as the Trustee List). The First Schedule to the new Act divides the schedule of investments permitted to trustees into three parts, attaching different conditions to investment in each. The investments in Parts I and II are called "narrower-range" investments (referred to in these notes as NR) and the investments in Part III are called "wider-range" investments (here referred to as WR). Part I of the First Schedule consists mainly of small savings securities encashable at any time and subject to an upper limit on holdings. Part II comprises well secured investments bearing fixed interest which correspond roughly to the previous Trustee List but also includes debentures, quoted on a recognized Stock Exchange, of United

Kingdom companies with a share capital of not less than £1,000,000 that have paid a dividend on their shares in each of the last five years. The WR investments in Part III include equity stocks and shares of similar companies, which are also quoted. A summary of the schedule of authorized investments is given at the end of these notes.

4. Trustees may invest at any time in Part I investments; before investing in Part II investments they must take advice; and before investing in Part III (WR securities) they must not only take advice but also divide the trust fund into two equal parts, only one of which may include WR investments.

DUTIES OF TRUSTEES IN CHOOSING AND RETAINING INVESTMENTS

5. The Act imposes obligations on trustees whether or not they propose to go outside the old Trustee List. When exercising their powers of investment, it is their duty (section 6 (1)) to have regard to the need to diversify their investments and to suit their investments to the requirements of the charity (e.g. for high income or for a capital sum at a future date). The advice which they must obtain and consider before investing in any but Part I investments should have regard to these factors (section 6 (2)). The advice is to come from a person whom the trustees reasonably believe to be qualified by reason of his ability and practical experience of financial matters to give it (section 6 (4)). The advice must be given in writing or be subsequently confirmed in writing (section 6 (5)). The adviser may be one of the trustees or one of their officers or employees.

6. The obligation to obtain and consider advice also applies to the retention of investments made under the powers in the Act in Part II and Part III investments. Trustees should review their investments and take such advice at such intervals as appear appropriate, having regard to the circumstances of the charity and nature of the investments (section 6 (3)).

DIVISION OF TRUST FUNDS

7. If, after taking advice, the trustees decide to use the power to invest in WR investments, the trust fund will have to be divided into two parts of equal value at the time the division is made (section 2 (1)). One is called the narrower-range part and the other the wider-range part. Once this division is made, it is permanent and no subsequent division is permitted. Each part may be invested and re-invested independently of the other. The narrower-range part of the fund must be invested only in NR investments; the other may be invested in either NR or WR investments. If any of the property attributed to the narrower-range part consists at any time of WR investments they must either be transferred to the wider-range part of the fund, with a compensating transfer to the narrower-range part, or re-invested in NR investments as soon as may be. Although on the initial division the value of the two parts is equal, their relative values will subsequently fluctuate, for instance, as a result of the changing values of the securities or of a bonus issue or a withdrawal of capital.

8. It is open to trustees if they wish to obtain a valuation of the property for the purpose of dividing the fund. Such valuation should be made in writing by a

person whom the trustees reasonably believe to be qualified to make it and this would protect the trustees (section 5).

ACCRUALS TO AND WITHDRAWALS FROM THE TRUST FUND AFTER DIVISION

9. The Act lays down rules for deciding to which part of the fund any new property which may accrue shall be allocated. There are two possibilities:

(a) the new property may have accrued as the direct result of the ownership of an investment in one part of the fund, in which case the new property is to be treated as belonging to that part. But if this would involve attributing a WR security to the NR part, then the new property must be transferred to the WR part and a compensating transfer of equal value made to the NR part in return (section 2 (3) (a)).

(b) if the new property does not result from the property already held (for instance, a fresh gift) then it must be divided equally between the two parts or, if it is not convenient to divide it, other property must be transferred from the part that it is added to, so as to ensure that the value of each part is increased equally (section 2 (3) (b)).

10. A "rights" issue (i.e. where the trustees have to pay any money to obtain new shares, even though they pay less than the shares are worth) is not to be regarded as an accrual in this sense, but must be treated as an investment (section 2 (3)). Therefore, if the rights issue when accepted would be a WR security, the consideration money must come from the WR part of the fund; the question of which part of the fund held the property in respect of which the rights arose is irrelevant.

11. If the trustees need to withdraw investments from the trust fund (for instance, to sell them and apply the proceeds for the purposes of the charity) they may withdraw them from either or both parts of the fund as they think appropriate (section 2 (4)). But this freedom does not relieve them from the ordinary duty of trustees to act prudently.

SPECIAL POWERS AND PROVISIONS IN TRUST INSTRUMENTS

(i) *Restrictions on investment*

12. No restriction on trustees' powers of investment contained in a trust instrument (other than an Act of Parliament or an instrument made under an Act of Parliament) will limit the trustees' authority to use all the powers of investment conferred by the Act, provided that the instrument was made before the date of the Act (3rd August 1961) (section 1 (3)).

(ii) *Wider powers of investment*

13. Nothing in the Act reduces the powers of investment given to the trustees by their trust instrument (section 3 (1)) or by the Charities Act. If those powers are already very wide the trustees may be able to ignore the powers given by the

Act. But they have a continuing duty which is underlined by the Act to have
regard to the need to diversify the investments and to suit them to the requirements of the trust; and this aspect must be considered in deciding whether or
not to use the powers given in the Act in addition to the powers arising under
the trust instrument.

14. Where the trust instrument requires that the trust fund or part of it shall
be invested in any investment for the time being authorized by law for investment of trust property (or similar words), this now means that the fund or that
part of it may be invested in the ways authorized by and subject to the conditions
prescribed by the Act (section 3 (2)).

(iii) *Special powers of investment*

15. The rules in the Act governing the use of the powers in the Act to invest in
WR investments at the same time as special powers conferred by trust instruments, depend on the nature and date of the instrument (section 3 (3) and (4)):

(a) **ordinary trust instruments**

Powers to invest outside the NR list conferred by ordinary trust
instruments (i.e. other than the exceptional ones listed at (b) below),
and this includes nearly all powers held by charity trustees to invest in
land, are to be preserved by carrying all investments made under those
powers to a separate part of the fund, called the special-range property.
The remaining NR investments can then be divided equally into the
NR part and the WR part; the latter part can then be invested in WR
investments not authorized by the trust instrument. If special-range
property has to be realized (e.g. if land is sold) and the proceeds are not
re-invested in other special-range property, it must be divided equally
between the NR and WR parts of the fund (Second Schedule).

(b) **exceptional instruments**

Other rules apply if the powers are conferred by either (i) a Court
Order made within 10 years before the passing of the Act (3rd August
1961) or (ii) an Act of Parliament or an instrument made under an Act
(including a scheme of the Commissioners) made within the same
period and relating specifically to the trust in question or (iii) a local
Act passed at any time during the 1960–61 Session of Parliament. In
these cases the special powers are not separately preserved and there are
no provisions for special-range property. If, after taking advice, the
trustees decide to use the powers in the Act to invest in WR investments, the whole trust fund must be divided equally; and if this cannot
be done without attributing investments other than NR investments
to the NR part, then those investments must be sold and converted into
NR investments before there is authority under the Act for the making
or retention of any WR investment (Third Schedule).

COMMON INVESTMENTS FUNDS UNDER SECTION 22 OF THE CHARITIES ACT 1960

16. The funds of many charities are too small to obtain the full benefit of the Trustee Investments Act and section 22 of the Charities Act 1960 empowers the Commissioners, on the application of two or more charities, to make schemes for the establishment of common investment funds in which a number of charities can pool their property for investment and management by trustees appointed for the purpose.

17. The powers of investment of every charity include the power to participate in common investment funds, except in the very rare instance of this power being expressly excluded by the trusts of the charity (section 22 (8) Charities Act). Subject to any restrictions in the terms of a common investment fund, the trustees of any charity, large or small, may contribute the whole or a part of the charity property to it. If they contribute a part only, and wish to invest some other part of the remainder in WR investments, they must make the division of that remainder into the two equal parts; the shares in the common investment fund are to be regarded as special-range property.

18. To meet a widespread demand for a common investment fund which would give small charities an opportunity to enjoy the advantages of diversification of their investments, the Charity Commissioners have established the Charities Official Investment Fund which came into operation on the 8th January 1963. This Fund is under the general control and direction of independent trustees appointed by the Commissioners and advised by a panel of three investment experts. The trustees of the Fund have unrestricted powers of investment.

19. The Charities Official Investment Fund is open to all charities whose securities are vested in the Official Custodian for Charities. Any charity wishing to participate, whether or not its investments are already vested in the Official Custodian, should write to him at Wellington House, Buckingham Gate, London, S.W.1, for further information and application forms.

SUMMARY OF THE SCHEDULE OF AUTHORIZED INVESTMENTS

Narrower-range investments

Part I (not requiring advice)

1. Defence Bonds, National Savings Certificates, National Development Bonds (including Ulster) and British Savings Bonds.

2. Deposits in the Post Office Savings Bank, and Trustee Savings Banks.

Part II (requiring advice)

1. Fixed-interest securities issued by the British Government (including Northern Ireland), Treasury Bills or Tax Reserve Certificates.

2. Securities guaranteed by the British Government (including Northern Ireland).

3. Fixed-interest securities issued by a public authority or nationalised industry in the United Kingdom.

4. Fixed-interest securities issued and registered in the United Kingdom by the Government of or a public authority in any Commonwealth territory.

5. Fixed-interest securities issued and registered in the United Kingdom by the International Bank for Reconstruction.

6. Debentures issued by a company incorporated in the United Kingdom, with a share capital of not less than £1,000,000 which has paid a dividend on all its share capital in each of the five preceding years.

7. Stock of the Bank of Ireland.

8. Debentures of the Agricultural Mortgage Corporation Ltd. (or its Scottish equivalent).

9. Loans to local authorities and other authorities in the United Kingdom which satisfy certain conditions.

10. Debentures, preference or guaranteed stock of statutory water undertakings.

11. Deposits by way of special investment in a trustee savings bank.

12. Deposits in a designated building society.

13. Mortgages of freehold or leasehold property with an unexpired term of not less than 60 years.

14. Perpetual rentcharges on land.

Wider-range investments

Part III

1. Any quoted securities issued by a company incorporated in the United Kingdom with a share capital of not less than £1,000,000 which has paid a dividend on all its share capital in each of the five preceding years.
2. Shares in a designated building society.
3. Units in a unit trust authorized by the Board of Trade.

Note: Only those securities that are fully paid up and are repayable in sterling are included in the Schedule.

Homes for Old People, T.P. 5

A REPRINT OF PARAGRAPHS 22 TO 29 OF THE REPORT OF THE CHARITY COMMISSIONERS FOR ENGLAND AND WALES FOR THE YEAR 1967

22. The National Corporation for the Care of Old People have drawn our attention to a small inquiry which they conducted during the year into the extent to which charities providing homes for old people impose limits on the income and capital which a qualified applicant for admission may possess. The phrase "homes for old people" is used in this and subsequent paragraphs to mean

residential homes in which old people, who by reason of their age are in need of care and attention, are lodged, boarded and looked after. The Corporation have indicated that they believe that there is a wide misunderstanding of the extent to which such charities may, without jeopardising their charitable status, admit old people who are not also poor. There is also doubt how far such charities are entitled to make a reasonable charge to cover all the services they provide. It may well be that the doubt felt by trustees on this score is restraining them from making their charities as useful to old people as they would wish. We therefore feel that we should give an explanation of the position as it appears to us.

23. The relief of aged persons is a charitable purpose of itself, whether or not poverty is relieved at the same time (see *In re Robinson* [1951] Ch. 198, [1950] 2 All E.R. 1148 and the cases reported in the note on page 1150 of the latter report; *In re Lewis* [1955] Ch. 104). This means that if a society exists solely to provide a service which will relieve the disabilities of old age its purposes will be charitable. Voluntary homes for old people offer an obvious example of this principle, because these institutions provide a service of care and attention needed by old people who can no longer look after themselves in their own homes.

24. Since homes for old people can be charitable without having to be for the relief of poverty, they are not subject to the same financial considerations as charities that provide nothing more than housing for the aged poor. The two particular financial aspects with which we are here concerned are: (a) the fact that charges may be made to meet the whole cost of running the home and (b) the fact that no limit need be imposed on the income or capital belonging to candidates for admission.

25. It is now settled law that a charitable home for old people may make such charges as may be necessary to meet the cost of running the home. (See *In re Adams* [1968] Ch. 80 and the judgment of the Privy Council in *Re Resch's Will Trusts*, [1969] 1 A.C. 514, [1967] 3 All E.R. 915. These cases concerned hospitals but the arguments apply equally to a home for old people; see *The Abbeyfield (Harpenden) Society Limited* v. *Woods* [1968] 1 W.L.R. 374, C.A.). The charging of such fees will not necessarily result in the exclusion of old people who are poor, since most of them are able to obtain financial help in appropriate instances from other sources such as professional or trade benevolent funds, local or national charities or local welfare authorities, which will enable them to pay full fees. When the charges which a home needs to make are higher than the poorer old people can afford, it is better that they should be provided for in this way rather than by a graduation in the charges, because the harmony of a home can be lost if the occupants do not all pay much the same amount for similar accommodation.

26. Unless there is an adequate endowment fund those who are running a home for old people must be ready to set the charges at a figure high enough to cover all the expenses that will be incurred. The home, if it is to be a success, must be properly staffed and the staff properly paid and accommodated. In addition to this and other ordinary running costs, the scale of charges should allow for vacancies in the home and for the building up of reserve funds to meet expenses such as heavy repairs and the redecoration of the building.

27. We have been told that an old person with some money of his own may well find himself excluded from voluntary homes but still not have enough money to pay the fees of many private homes run for profit. There

CC

is therefore a need for homes for old people able to accommodate those who have money of their own. At present old people in this category are often denied admission into a voluntary home because its management committee have laid down an arbitrary means test which excludes them. It is only where the trusts of the charity confine the benefit of the home to old people who are poor that there is any need for the management committee to seek its candidates for admission only among the poor; and therefore in other cases there is no good reason for the committee to refuse admission to old people merely because their income or capital exceeds some arbitrary level. Doubtless the committee will wish to enquire about a candidate's means in order to decide whether or not the full fees can be paid; but in other respects the financial condition of the applicant for admission should usually play only a small part in deciding whether or not that applicant is the one most in need of the services which the charity offers.

28. It appears that societies and associations are still being formed to establish homes for old people with trusts which confine their benefits to the aged poor or those with severely restricted amounts of income or capital. This limitation is regrettable if it has no better basis than a fear that the trust might otherwise not be charitable or results from the unthinking use of an unsuitable precedent of a deed or set of rules intended to constitute a charity for housing the aged poor. Sometimes the limitation to the poor, or even an express upper limit on applicants' income or capital, appears in a scheme that has been established by us or our predecessors. It is possible that such a scheme was made at a time when this aspect of charity law was not as clear as it now is and the limitation to poverty may have been introduced as a precaution. Where that is so the provisions of the scheme could now be reconsidered. On the other hand some existing homes for old people derive from old donations which were expressly confined to the poor; and where it can be shown that from its origins a charity had an unambiguous limitation to the poor then there can be no justification for that charity serving a category of old people who cannot be reasonably described as poor. Even in this context, however, it is to be remembered that the term "poor" is flexible and any old person who is prevented by his financial circumstances from obtaining in the area in which he lives that care and attention which his age makes necessary may be regarded to that extent as poor.

29. To sum up, the charitable status of a society or institution which provides a home for old people, or some other service calculated to alleviate the special needs of old people, cannot be called into question merely because the benefits of that home or institution are not confined to old people who are poor or because that home or institution makes charges on a scale reasonably calculated to meet all its outgoings but not to produce a profit. Furthermore, there is a need today for homes able to accommodate old people who have some money of their own and if new homes of this sort are to be founded they will probably not be able to carry on and maintain a good standard without making quite high charges.

Charity Commission for England and Wales
Charities for the Relief of Sickness

1. The Charity Commissioners are conscious that the development of the National Health Service and other statutory services has overtaken many of the

traditional objects of charities for the relief of sickness, or the benefit of the sick poor, so that trustees have found it difficult to know how best to apply their income. There are, however, still many ways in which the trustees of such charities can usefully supplement the actual benefits provided by the statutory services. Trustees will often find it useful to keep in touch with officers of the local authority concerned with health and welfare about the best ways of giving assistance to the sick. The appendix below sets out examples of the sort of assistance which the Department of Health and Social Security has suggested might be given by voluntary bodies, without overlapping the statutory services.

2. These examples are intended as suggestions only and not as an exhaustive list. Ways of extending the list will no doubt occur to trustees of these kinds of charity, who should direct their efforts towards providing or paying for items, services or facilities which are calculated to alleviate the suffering or assist the recovery of sick, convalescent, disabled, handicapped or infirmed persons resident in the area which the charity serves provided that such benefits are not readily available from other sources. Trustees, in deciding what action to take, should be satisfied that there is a clear need and that the benefits they provide are related to the needs of each case and are reasonable in the circumstances.

3. Trustees may either pay directly for the benefits they provide, or may advance money to beneficiaries to pay for benefits or may make arrangements for the benefits to be provided by other organisations in return for subscriptions or donations.

4. Trustees are, however, bound by the trusts of their charity and will be unable to adopt any of the examples that conflict with those trusts. In particular, if the trusts are for the benefit of the sick poor, the funds should be used to provide benefits only for sick people who are financially unable to provide those benefits for themselves. If trustees are in doubt they should consult the Charity Commissioners. If the trusts do not permit them to use the charity income to meet some real need, it is hoped that a suitable opportunity to consider a revision of the trusts will occur when a local review of charities of this class is held in the area. If, however, the trustees consider that a modification of the trusts is urgently required they should apply to the Commissioners, without waiting for a local review.

5. In the trusts of a charity for the relief of sickness or the benefit of the sick poor the words "sickness" and "sick" can usually be interpreted as including mental sickness and mentally sick.

APPENDIX

Items that could be provided, either outright or on loan, preferably the latter in the case of expensive apparatus, include bedding, clothing, food (including special food), fuel, heating appliances, medical or other aids, nursing requisites or comforts, television or radio sets or licences, washing machines (suitable for soiled clothing and bed linen).

Services that could be provided include bathing, escort services, exchange of library books, foot care, gardening, hair washing, shaving, help in the home, house decorating and repairs, laundering, meals on wheels, nursing aid, outings and entertainments, physiotherapy in the home, reading, shopping, sitting-in, tape-recording for the housebound, travelling companions.

Facilities that could be provided include arrangements for a period of rest or change of air or to secure the benefits of any convalescent home or other institution or organisation or to provide temporary relief for those having the care of the sick or handicapped person: help for close relatives to visit or care for patients: transport facilities.

Appendix 5

Race Relations Act 1976

Race Relations Act 1976

(1976 c. 74)

34. Charities

(1) A provision which is contained in a charitable instrument (whenever that instrument took or takes effect) and which provides for conferring benefits on persons of a class defined by reference to colour shall have effect for all purposes as if it provided for conferring the like benefits—

(a) on persons of the class which results if the restriction by reference to colour is disregarded; or

(b) where the original class is defined by reference to colour only, on persons generally;

but nothing in this subsection shall be taken to alter the effect of any provision as regards any time before the coming into operation of this subsection.

(2) Nothing in Parts II to IV shall—

(a) be construed as affecting a provision to which this subsection applies; or

(b) render unlawful an act which is done in order to give effect to such a provision.

(3) Subsection (2) applies to any provision which is contained in a charitable instrument (whenever that instrument took or takes effect) and which provides for conferring benefits on persons of a class defined otherwise than by reference to colour (including a class resulting from the operation of subsection (1)).

(4) In this section "charitable instrument" means an enactment or other instrument passed or made for charitable purposes, or an enactment or other instrument so far as it relates to charitable purposes, and in Scotland includes the governing instrument of an endowment or of an educational endowment as those expressions are defined in section 135 (1) of the Education (Scotland) Act 1962.

In the application of this section to England and Wales, "charitable purposes" means purposes which are exclusively charitable according to the law of England and Wales.

Commentary

The Race Relations Act 1976 consolidates and amends the previous law on race relations. It was enacted on 22nd November 1976. The Act comes into operation on such day as the Secretary of State may appoint and different days may be so appointed for different provisions and different purposes.[1] No day has yet been appointed. Part I of the Act contains definitions. "Racial discrimination" is re-defined so as to include indirect or latent discrimination.[2] Overt discrimination takes place where one person on racial grounds[3] treats another person less favourably than he treats or would treat other persons in any circumstances relevant for the purposes of the Act.[4] But it is now classed an act of discrimination where in any circumstances relevant for the purposes of the Act a person applies to another person a requirement or condition which he applies or would apply equally to persons not of the same racial group[5] as that other but (i) which is such that the proportion of persons of the same racial group as that other person who can comply with it is considerably smaller than the proportion of persons not of that racial group who can comply with it; (ii) which he cannot show to be justifiable irrespective of the colour, race, nationality or ethnic or national origins of the other person to whom it is applied; and (iii) which is to the detriment of the other person because he cannot comply with it.[6] Less favourable treatment of a person after he or she has brought proceedings or given evidence or information under the Act or done anything under or by reference to the Act or alleged a breach of the Act is classified as "discrimination by victimisation".[7] Such discrimination also occurs if the discriminator treats the other person less favourably by reason of the fact that the discriminator knows that the other person intends to do any of those things[8] or suspects that the person victimised has done, or intends to do, any of them.[9] Discrimination by victimisation does not occur where the treatment complained of is meted out to a person on account of an allegation made by that person which was false and not made in good faith.[10] In other words he who bears false witness under the Act is not protected.

Charities are not, in general, exempt from the restrictions imposed by the Race Relations Act 1976. Thus charitable trustees and the officers of a charitable institution must not discriminate on racial grounds in the field of employment against applicants or employees.[11] Equally they must not on racial grounds discriminate against anyone in the provision of goods, facilities or services.[12]

---

1 Race Relations Act 1976, s. 79 (2).
2 *Ibid.*, s. 1.
3 "Racial grounds" means any of the following grounds, namely colour, race, nationality or ethnic or national origins: *ibid.*, s. 3 (1).
4 *Ibid.*, s. 1 (1) (a). Segregating a person from other persons on racial grounds is treating him less favourably than they are treated: *ibid.*, s. 1 (2).
5 "A group of persons defined by reference to colour, race, nationality or ethnic or national origins": *ibid.*, s. 3 (1).
6 *Ibid.*, s. 1 (1) (b).
7 *Ibid.*, s. 2.
8 I.e., bringing proceedings, giving evidence or information under the Act, and so forth.
9 Race Relations Act 1976, s. 2.
10 *Ibid.*, s. 2 (2).
11 *Ibid.*, s. 4 (1).
12 *Ibid.*, s. 20.

A body in charge of a charitable educational establishment[1] must not discriminate against a person on racial grounds in the terms on which it offers to admit him to the establishment as a pupil or by refusing or deliberately omitting to accept an application for his admission to the establishment as a pupil.[2] In relation to one who is already a pupil of the establishment in question the responsible body must not, on racial grounds, discriminate against that pupil in the way it affords him access to any benefits, facilities or services, or by refusing or deliberately omitting to afford him access to them, or by excluding him from the establishment or subjecting him to any other detriment.[3]

Again in the disposal or management of premises, the general rule is that discrimination on racial grounds is unlawful.[4] Only if the discrimination results from the benefits of the charity being confined to a class of persons defined otherwise than by reference to colour and the provision of the premises constitute a charitable benefit will the discrimination be lawful.[5] Except in certain narrowly circumscribed situations it is also unlawful for charities acting as landlords to discriminate in the matter of consents for assignment or subletting.[6]

Trustees or officers of charities must not apply discriminatory practices[7] nor publish or cause to be published discriminatory advertisements[8] nor issue instructions to discriminate or apply any discriminatory practices.[9] Nor must they induce or attempt to induce anyone to discriminate against another on racial grounds in a relevant field.[10] Aiding unlawful acts under the Act is itself an unlawful act.[11]

Under the Race Relations Act 1968, as has been seen,[12] a trust instrument was permitted to discriminate in favour of (but not against) persons of a particular race, descent, or ethnic or national origin. Under the 1976 Act a provision contained in any charitable instrument[13] and which provides for conferring benefits on persons of a class defined by reference to *colour* is subjected to special treatment. Such a provision takes effect for all purposes as if it provided for conferring like benefits on persons of the class which results if the restriction by reference to colour is disregarded.[14] Where the original class is defined by reference to colour only the trust will be treated as one for persons generally.[15]

In relation to a provision contained in a charitable instrument which provides for conferring benefits on persons of a class defined otherwise than by reference to colour nothing contained in Parts II, III and IV of the Act (which deal with discrimination in the employment field, discrimination in other fields and other unlawful acts) is to be construed as affecting such a provision or will render unlawful an act done in order to give effect to such a provision.[16]

---

1 E.g. a university or a public or other school registered as a charity.
2 Race Relations Act 1976, s. 17 (a) and (b).
3 *Ibid.*, s. 17 (c).
4 *Ibid.*, s. 21.
5 *Ibid.*, s. 34.
6 *Ibid.*, s. 24.
7 *Ibid.*, s. 28.   8 *Ibid.*, s. 29.
9 *Ibid.*, s. 30.
10 *Ibid.*, s. 31.
11 *Ibid.*, s. 33.
12 See at 572, *supra.*
13 An enactment or other instrument passed or made for charitable purposes: Race Relations Act 1976, s. 34 (4).
14 *Ibid.*, s. 34 (1) (a).
15 *Ibid.*, s. 34 (1) (b).   16 *Ibid.*, s. 34 (2).

Appendix 6

Abbreviations

Abbreviations

Statutes, Orders and Rules

AEA 1925	Administration of Estates Act 1925
CA 1960	Charities Act 1960
CLPCA 1883	City of London Parochial Charities Act 1883
CTA 1914	Charitable Trusts Act 1914
CTVA 1954	Charitable Trusts Validation Act 1954
FA	Finance Act
LPA 1925	Law of Property Act 1925
LRA 1925	Land Registration Act 1925
LRR 1925	Land Registration Rules 1925
PSA 1868	Public Schools Act 1868
RCA 1958	Recreational Charities Act 1958
R.S.C.	Rules of the Supreme Court 1965
S.I.	Statutory Instrument
SLA 1925	Settled Land Act 1925
TA 1925	Trustee Act 1925
TA 1970	Income and Corporation Taxes Act 1970
TIA 1961	Trustee Investments Act 1961

Reports

Nathan Report (1952) Cmd. 8710	Report of the Committee on the Law and Practice relating to Charitable Trusts (1952)
Goodman Report (1976)	Charity Law and Voluntary Organisations Report of the Goodman Committee

Legal Periodicals

A.-A.L.R.	Anglo American Law Review
A.S.C.L.	Annual Survey of Commonwealth Law
Can. Bar Rev.	Canadian Bar Review
C.L.J.	Cambridge Law Review
Conv. N.S.	Conveyancer and Property Lawyer New Series
Ch. Com. Rep.	Report of Charity Commissioners for England and Wales
L.Q.R.	Law Quarterly Review
M.L.R.	Modern Law Review
Sol. Jo.	Solicitors' Journal

Books

Bl. Com.	Blackstone's Commentaries
Bro. Abr.	Sir R. Brooke's Abridgement
Cru. Dig.	Cruise's Digest of the Law of Real Property, 7 vols.

Index